GERMAN IMMIGRANTS

Lists of Passengers Bound from Bremen to New York, 1863–1867

GERMAN IMMIGRANTS

Lists of Passengers Bound from Bremen to New York, 1863-1867

With Places of Origin

Compiled by
Gary J. Zimmerman &
Marion Wolfert

CLEARFIELD

Reprinted for
Clearfield Company, Inc. by
Genealogical Publishing Co., Inc.
Baltimore, Maryland
2006

Library of Congress Catalogue Card Number 88-81476
International Standard Book Number 0-8063-1225-4
Made in the United States of America

Explanation of the Text

The destruction of the Bremen passenger lists has been a great hindrance to the historical and demographic study of German immigration to America. In many cases the Bremen lists were the sole source of information concerning the place of origin of an immigrant family. The importance of Bremen as a port of departure makes this loss even more lamentable.

As far as can be ascertained by German archivists, lists of emigrants sailing from Bremen were kept beginning in 1832. These lists were used to compile statistical reports for the government and port authorities. Owing to a lack of space, the lists from 1832 to 1872 were destroyed in 1874. Thereafter the lists were shredded every two years. From 1907 the original lists were again kept on a permanent basis, but with the destruction of the Statistical Land Office on October 6, 1944, all remaining lists perished. Transcripts of some twentieth-century lists (1907, 1908, 1913, 1914) were recently discovered at the German State Archives in Koblenz—the product of a college study—but no nineteenth-century transcripts have as yet been uncovered.

This partial reconstruction of Bremen passenger lists, 1863-1867, is based on American sources, specifically, *Passenger Lists of Vessels Arriving at New York* (National Archives Microfilm Publication M237), and is a continuation of two earlier volumes covering 1847–1854 and 1855–1862. Not all Bremen passengers of the 1863–1867 period are included in this work, however; only those for whom a specific place of origin in Germany is given. Of the total number of passenger arrival records, roughly 21% provide such information; the other 79% give only "Germany" as the place of origin. The benefit of having these 35,000 passenger arrivals indexed is that it provides immediate access to place of origin information, which the voluminous nature of the New York arrival lists heretofore prevented. Future volumes in this series will cover later years of arrival, and eventually Bremen arrivals at other major U.S. ports.

Imperfections and peculiarities in the original lists, as well as difficulties encountered in the computerization process, make it imperative that all entries found herein be compared against the original manifests. It is apparent from the lists themselves that the information had been supplied verbally by the passengers, since obvious name and place-name misspellings occur frequently. Therefore, all possible spelling variations must be searched for. A good example is the surname MEYER, which is found in the lists under eight different spellings: Meyer, Meier, Mayer, Meir, Mayr, Myar, Myer and even Mjar. The majority of spellings may vary only slightly, but because of the alphabetical arrangement of this work these variants are often separated.

In the original lists many given names and surnames were partially or completely anglicized. More often than not given names were carried over into their English equivalents; and on rare occasions a surname was translated. The name SCHMIDT, for example, might be listed as SMITH; BRAUN as BROWN, etc. When this occurs, as with other questionable spellings, an entry is added under what is assumed to be the original German spelling, to facilitate the researcher.

Misspelled place names have been corrected on a limited basis. Place names with spellings grossly in error were examined, and an accurate spelling sought. Sometimes a correct spelling could not be established, and the spelling as found in the original was retained. The corrected spellings sometimes represent the compilers' opinion of the way the original should read; but since there is the risk that an incorrect judgment was made, all entries should be compared with the original.

Some names may be difficult to locate because of peculiarities in the German language. German surnames that carry an "umlaut," i.e. a modified vowel (Ä, Ö, Ü), have been changed to their English equivalents; thus Ä = AE, Ö = OE, Ü = UE, and are so indexed. Some surnames that should have had modified vowels were left unmodified in the originals. The name MÜLLER is found as both MUELLER and MULLER in the text, as well as the anglicized form MILLER. Surnames composed of two or more distinct words have been alphabetized under the final word. Thus von WEGNER is found as WEGNER, v.; de GREVE as GREVE, de; and AUF DEM KAMP as KAMP, auf dem. French names like D'ARTENAY are not separated.

The majority of the records contain abbreviations that vary from list to list. Many are standard German abbreviations, but some given-name abbreviations are odd, and are therefore difficult to recognize. A table of the most frequently used abbreviations is included in this work. Names that have been abbreviated often make it difficult to tell the sex of the passenger. In many cases, therefore, the sex of the passenger is noted in parenthesis. Several lists were composed entirely of initials, and several others employed the use of German nicknames, which may be unfamiliar to researchers. Some of the more commonly used nicknames and their equivalents are listed below:

Bernhard = Bernd	Johann = Hans
Catharina = Trina	Magdalena = Lena
Elisabeth = Beta, Louise, Elise	Margaretha = Greta
Friedrich = Fritz	Matthias = Theiss
Friederike = Rika	Valentin = Veit
Georg = Joerg	Wilhelmine = Minna
Helena = Lena	

German regional dialects account for a great deal of inconsistency in surname and place name spellings. Certain consonants can be pronounced alike, allowing for a variety of spelling possibilities. The following table of equivalent consonants will assist in determining alternative spellings:

B = P	as Ebstein = Epstein	TZ = Z	as Dietz = Diez = Tietz
F = V	as Focke = Vocke	C = K = G	as Cunkel = Kunkel
D = T	as Dentel = Tendel		= Gungel
S = Z	as Seidler = Zeidler	I = J = Y	as Ide = Jede = Yde

German dipthongs also allow for a great deal of variety in spelling. Some combinations of vowels produce exactly the same sound, which make them interchangeable. Some examples of these are:

AE = E = EE as Faendrich = Fendrich = Feendrich
AI = AY = EI = EY as Kaiser = Kayser = Keiser = Keyser
OI = EU = AU = AEU as Broihahn = Breuhahn = Bräuhahn
= Braeuhahn
I = IE = IH as Bilke = Bielke = Bihlke = Biehlke
E = EE = EH as Frese = Freese = Frehse
Also sometimes I = UE as Gingerich = Guengerich = Juengerich

Use of the German unasperated "H" occurs frequently in these manifests. Not having a sound, this letter can be placed in several locations without affecting the pronunciation. The process of alphabetization will make such spellings widely separate, however, such as WOLLEBEN = WOHLLEBEN, WALTER = WALTHER, OELSNER = OEHLSNER. The doubling of letters is also frequently found, as in the names HERMANN = HERRMANN and ULMANN = ULLMANN. All possibilities should be sought, although duplicate entries have been added under the more common spellings of some surnames.

The computerization process has necessitated the abbreviating of place names. Most of these are suffixes and prefixes, and have been abbreviated as follows:

Unt.	= Unter	---fd.	= ---feld
Ob.	= Ober	--hsn.	= --hausen
Gr.	= Gross	--bch.	= ---bach
Kl.	= Klein	---bg.	= ---berg or ---burg
Ndr.	= Nieder	---df.	= ---dorf

Increasing numbers of Poles and Czechs appear in the manifests, many of whose names are grossly misspelled. The ships' captains who made these lists often transposed these names into German phonetic spellings, such as KUTSCHERA for KUČERA, NÜRSCHAN for NÝŘANY, etc. Additional problems were encountered in trying to read the captains' handwriting. Easily mistaken were the letters "u" for "n", "o" for "a", "t" for "f" and "l". A good example of this is the name HAUSCHILDT, which was several times mistaken for HANSCHILDT. With the more common names these problems were corrected, but undoubtedly some errors are still to be found. With any questionable spelling, great care has been taken to preserve the manifest's original version.

When more than one person of a particular surname travelled together (as in a family), they have been grouped under the name of the first family member appearing on the list. Thus the wife and children of a passenger will follow on the line just below that of the head of household. The integrity of the family was in this way retained, but it is necessary to scan all entries of a particular surname in case the individual sought is listed under another family member.

The reference numbers are composed of two parts. The first part is the year of arrival, the second the number of the passenger list for that year. Within each year all the lists are numbered. The table of references included in this volume provides the name of the arriving vessel, the date of its arrival in New York, and the call number of the National Archives' microfilm (series 237). A sample entry follows:

BEIERLEIB, Johann 60 Lustberg 61-1640

This entry states that the 60-year-old Johann Beierleib arrived in New York in 1861 (61 = 1861) and appears on list 1640 for that year. The table of references, under 61-1640, gives

Norma 10 Nov 1861 107

This indicates that Johann Beierleib was on the ship *Norma* which arrived in New York on November 10, 1861. The original list can be found on microfilm roll 107.

Questions regarding the transcription of the names and places which appear in this volume can be directed to the German Immigration Archive, P.O. Box 11391, Salt Lake City, Utah 84147. This archive retains the original transcriptions and can attempt to identify places for which correct spellings were not available.

Gary J. Zimmerman
Marion Wolfert

Table of Abbreviations

Places

A., Aus.	Austria
B., Ba.	Baden, Bavaria
Bad., Bd.	Baden
Bav., Bv.	Bavaria
Br.	Braunschweig
C.H., Curh.	Kurhessen
H.	Hessen, Hannover
Ha., Hann.	Hannover
He., Hess.	Hessen
KH., KHe., Kurh.	Kurhessen
Na., Nass.	Nassau
N.Y.	New York
O., Old.	Oldenburg
Oest.	Austria
P., Pr., Prss.	Prussia
S., Sa., Sachs., Sax.	Saxony
W.	Wuerttemberg, Waldeck
Wa., Wald.	Waldeck
Wu., Wue., Wuert., Wrt.	Wuerttemberg

Ages (infants)

bob	born on board ship
by	baby
d	days old
m	months old
w	weeks old

Given Names

A.	Anna
Ad.	Adam, Adolph, Adalbert
Alb.	Albert, Albin, Albrecht
Andr.	Andreas

Ant.	Anton
Aug.	August, Augusta
Balt.	Balthasar
Bar., Barb.	Barbara
Bern., Bernh.	Bernhard
Carol., Carole.	Caroline
Cas., Casp.	Caspar
Cat., Cath.	Catharine
Charl.	Charles, Charlotte
Chr., Christ.	Christian, Christoph
Chr'tne	Christine, Christiane
Clem.	Clement, Clementine
Con., Conr.	Conrad
Dan.	Daniel
Diedr.	Diedrich
Dom.	Dominicus
Dor.	Dorothea, Dorette, Doris
Eberh.	Eberhard
Ed., Edw.	Eduard
El., Els.	Elisabeth
Em.	Emil, Emanuel, Emma, Emilie
Eman.	Emanuel
Eng.	Engel
Ern.	Ernst, Ernestine
Ferd.	Ferdinand
Fr.	Friedrich, Franz
Fr'd, Friedr.	Friedrich
Fr'ke	Friederike
Fr'z	Franz
Geo.	Georg
Gert.	Gertrude
Gottfr.	Gottfried
Gotth.	Gotthard
Gottl.	Gottlieb
Gust.	Gustav
Heinr., Hr., Hch.	Heinrich
Hen., Henr., Hen'tte	Henriette
Her., Herm.	Hermann, Hermine
Ign.	Ignatz
J.	Johann
Jac.	Jacob
Jas.	James
Joh., Johs.	Johannes
Jos.	Joseph
Jul., Juls.	Julius, Julie
Kath.	Katharine

Lor., Lor'z	Lorenz
Lud., Ludw.	Ludwig, Ludolph
M., Mar.	Maria
Magd.	Magdalena
Marg.	Margaretha
Mart.	Martin
Matth.	Matthias, Mathilde
Max.	Maximilian
Mic., Mich.	Michael
Nic., Nicol.	Nicolaus
Pet.	Peter
Ph., Phil.	Philipp
Reg.	Regina
Rob.	Robert
Ros.	Rosine, Rosalie
Rud.	Rudolph
Sal., Sol.	Salomon
Seb.	Sebastian
Sim.	Simon
Soph.	Sophia
Th.	Theodor, Thomas, Theophilus
Theo., Theod.	Theodor, Theophilus
Ther.	Therese
Traug.	Traugott
Val., Valen.	Valentine
Vic., Vict.	Victor, Victoria
Vin., Vinc.	Vincent
Wilh., Wm.	Wilhelm, Wilhelmine
Wilh'mne	Wilhelmine
Wolfg.	Wolfgang

TABLE OF REFERENCES

YR–LIST	SHIP	DATE OF ARRIVAL			FILM #
63-6	Herzog v. Brabant	3	Jan	1863	225
63-13		6	Jan	1863	225
63-15	New York	7	Jan	1863	225
63-53		23	Jan	1863	225
63-97	Hansa	9	Feb	1863	225
63-168	New York	5	Mar	1863	226
63-244	Hansa	1	Apr	1863	226
63-296	Bremen	15	Apr	1863	227
63-350	New York	29	Apr	1863	227
63-398	Herzog v. Brabant	11	May	1863	228
63-482	Hansa	26	May	1863	229
63-551	America	8	Jun	1863	229
63-614	Adler	22	Jun	1863	230
63-693	New York	8	Jul	1863	230
63-752	Hansa	20	Jul	1863	231
63-821	America	3	Aug	1863	232
63-822	Charlotte	3	Aug	1863	232
63-862	Bremen	18	Aug	1863	232
63-908	Geestemuende	1	Sep	1863	232
63-917	New York	2	Sep	1863	232
63-953	Hansa	15	Sep	1863	233
63-990	America	28	Sep	1863	233
63-1003	Friedrich	3	Oct	1863	233
63-1010	Washington	5	Oct	1863	234
63-1038	Bremen	14	Oct	1863	234
63-1069	America	23	Oct	1863	234
63-1085	New York	28	Oct	1863	235
63-1136	Hansa	14	Nov	1863	235
63-1178	America	23	Nov	1863	235
63-1218	Bremen	11	Dec	1863	236
64-23	New York	13	Jan	1864	237

YR–LIST	SHIP	DATE OF ARRIVAL			FILM #
64-73	America	3	Feb	1864	237
64-138	Bremen	1	Mar	1864	238
64-170	Hansa	15	Mar	1864	238
64-199	Herzog v. Brabant	22	Mar	1864	238
64-214	America	28	Mar	1864	238
64-331	Bremen	28	Apr	1864	239
64-343	Nord Amerika	3	May	1864	239
64-363	Hansa	10	May	1864	240
64-427	America	23	May	1864	240
64-432	Adler	24	May	1864	240
64-433	Gutenberg	24	May	1864	240
64-456	Jupiter	28	May	1864	241
64-495	Bremen	3	Jun	1864	241
64-593	Hansa	24	Jun	1864	242
64-639	New York	30	Jul	1864	242
64-665	Ferdinand	12	Jul	1864	242
64-687	America	18	Jul	1864	243
64-739	Herzog v. Brabant	28	Jul	1864	243
64-782	Bremen	5	Aug	1864	243
64-840	Hansa	16	Aug	1864	244
64-885	Joh. Lange	29	Aug	1864	244
64-886	New York	29	Aug	1864	244
64-904	Nord Amerika	5	Sep	1864	245
64-920	Maryland	8	Sep	1864	245
64-938	America	13	Sep	1864	245
64-992	Bremen	30	Sep	1864	245
64-1022	Hansa	10	Oct	1864	246
64-1053	New York	25	Oct	1864	246
64-1108	America	7	Nov	1864	247
64-1161	Bremen	25	Nov	1864	247
64-1206	Hansa	9	Dec	1864	248
65-4	New York	3	Jan	1865	248
65-7	Hermann	4	Jan	1865	248
65-38	Amaranth	18	Jan	1865	248
65-55	America	30	Jan	1865	248
65-116	New York	1	Mar	1865	249
65-151	Hansa	14	Mar	1865	249
65-189	America	27	Mar	1865	249
65-243	New York	13	Apr	1865	250
65-402	Hansa	22	May	1865	251
65-594	America	3	Jul	1865	253
65-713	F. Reck	1	Aug	1865	254

YR–LIST	SHIP	DATE OF ARRIVAL			FILM #
65-770	Herzog v. Brabant	15	Aug	1865	255
65-856	Alamo	6	Sep	1865	255
65-865	Ferdinand	8	Sep	1865	256
65-898	Emilie	16	Sep	1865	256
65-948	Geestemuende	2	Oct	1865	257
65-950	Jupiter	2	Oct	1865	257
65-974	Bremen	10	Oct	1865	257
65-1024	Hansa	27	Oct	1865	257
65-1030	Joh. Kepler	28	Oct	1865	258
*65-1030A	Fides	28	Oct	1865	258
65-1031	Wieland	28	Oct	1865	258
65-1088	America	9	Nov	1865	258
65-1095	Iris	11	Nov	1865	258
65-1140	Matador	20	Nov	1865	259
65-1189	Bremen	8	Dec	1865	259
66-72	Helene	22	Jan	1866	261
66-83	Herzog v. Brabant	25	Jan	1866	261
66-109	New York	1	Feb	1866	261
66-147	Bremen	15	Feb	1866	261
66-221	New York	15	Mar	1866	262
66-346	Johann	17	Apr	1866	263
66-349	Reinhard	18	Apr	1866	263
66-412	Marco Polo	8	May	1866	264
66-413	Shakespere	8	May	1866	264
66-469	Johanna	16	May	1866	265
66-576	Hermann	4	Jun	1866	266
66-577	Charlotte	4	Jun	1866	266
66-578	Hermann	4	Jun	1866	266
66-623	Herzog v. Brabant	9	Jun	1866	267
66-650	Dora	13	Jun	1866	267
66-666	Energie	16	Jun	1866	267
66-668	Asia	16	Jun	1866	267
66-679	Hansa	18	Jun	1866	267
66-704	New York	25	Jun	1866	268
66-734	Bremen	2	Jul	1866	268
66-837	Gazelle	21	Jul	1866	269
66-907	Joseph Haydn	6	Aug	1866	270
66-934	New York	14	Aug	1866	270
66-984	America	27	Aug	1866	270

*In the text, passengers arriving on ship 1030A are listed under 1030, as there was not enough space to accomodate an extra character.

YR–LIST	SHIP	DATE OF ARRIVAL			FILM #
66-1031	Hermann	10	Sep	1866	271
66-1093	Hansa	27	Sep	1866	271
66-1127	New York	5	Oct	1866	272
66-1128	Marco Polo	5	Oct	1866	272
66-1131	Bremen	9	Oct	1866	272
66-1155	America	15	Oct	1866	272
66-1203	Deutschland	29	Oct	1866	273
66-1243	Mozart	8	Nov	1866	273
66-1248	Asia	9	Nov	1866	273
66-1313	Gabain	28	Nov	1866	274
66-1327	America	3	Dec	1866	274
66-1373	Deutschland	20	Dec	1866	274
67-7	Hansa	2	Jan	1867	275
67-353	Kosmos	2	May	1867	278
67-599	Tuiska	17	Jun	1867	281
67-600	Amaranth	17	Jun	1867	281
67-795	Arristides	29	Jul	1867	283
67-806	Olbers	30	Jul	1867	283
67-954	Anna	9	Sep	1867	285
67-992	Admiral	18	Sep	1867	286
67-1005	Helene	23	Sep	1867	286

GERMAN IMMIGRANTS

Lists of Passengers Bound from
Bremen to New York,
1863–1867

NAME	AGE	RESIDENCE	YR-LIST
AAGARD, Rasmus	26	Copenhagen	66-0666
AARR, Julius	16	Bahlingen	65-0243
ABAROWSKY, Thilo	30	Magdeburg	65-1030
Marie 29			
ABBE, Bruno	28	Dresden	65-0950
ABEL, Anna	31	Wachenheim	66-0147
Heinrich 4			
ABEL, August	42	Muehlhausen	66-0109
Marie 43, Carl 13			
ABEL, Barbara	2	Foerst	66-0147
ABEL, Emilie	30	Obernkirchen	65-0004
Bertha 6			
ABEL, Georg	35	Hottendorbach	63-1010
ABEL, Heinr.	27	Luederstreit	64-0214
ABEL, Henry	28	New York	63-0244
ABEL, Johann F.	56	Kleinau	65-0770
Elisabeth 46, Friederike 24, Louise 12			
Christian 10, Gustav 8, Bertha 6			
Alwine 4			
ABEL, Louis	40	New York	63-0398
ABELE, T.(m)	33	Joehlingen	64-0495
ABELIS, Josepha	17	Neumettel	64-0886
Rosalia 18			
ABENDROTH, Doroth.	58	Jastrop	65-0713
Henriette 26, Barbara 21, Emilie 15			
ABENSETH, Joh. Ant	42	New York	63-0693
Helene Wilh. 29			
ABERLE, Cath.	26	Pflegeldorf	63-0482
ABERLE, Emil	24	Mannheim	66-1127
ABERLE, Martin	32	Pflegenberg	64-0687
Caroline 25			
ABHAU, Ernst	20	Babra	63-0990
ABICH, Ernst	21	Hannover	64-0739
ABILES, Ferd.	24	Paris	63-0990
ABKING, Wilhelmine	22	Rusbend	66-0934
Ernestine 20			
ABLER, Heinrich	38	Evansville	66-0412
ABRAHAM, A.	28	Heubach	64-0782
ABRAHAM, August	24	Preussen	63-0862
ABRAHAM, Bertha	32	Lispenhausen	66-0984
ABRAHAM, Caroline	47	Coeln	64-0427
A. (f) 16, Joh. (f) 15, H. (f) 12			
W. (m) 7, Eva 6, Otto 4, Pauline 5			
ABRAHAM, Em.	59	Coeln	63-0917
ABRAHAM, Jos.	17	Posen	65-0594
ABRAHAM, Lazarus	16	Darmstadt	66-1155
ABRAHAM, Michael	26	Liszkowke	66-0469
Wilhelmine 24, Gustav 3, Augusta 3m			
ABT, Edward	18	Stuttgart	64-0170
ABT, Paul Hr.	19	Esslingen	64-0886
ABTS, H.J.	33	Ostfriesland	64-0495
Hilke 29, Gretje 7, Boele 4, Albert 10m			
ACHEBOELLER, Wilh.	22	Verswald	66-1128
ACHELIS, Fr.	20	New York	64-0427
ACHELPOHL, Albrect	19	Linen	64-0885
ACHILIS, Friedrich		Bemen	66-1031
ACHILIS, Thomas	22	New York	63-0244
ACHILLES, Fr'drke.	25	Braunschweig	63-1178
August 3, baby 3m			
ACHMANN, Friedr.	44	Rastenburg	64-0687
Doroth. 41, Carl Aug. 19, Henriette 17			
ACHTELSTAETTER, A.	43	Handberg	66-0412
Anna Maria 39, Peter 7, Conrad 5, Georg 3			
ACKENHAUSEN, Hugo	7	Hammerscheid	65-0189
ACKER, C.	37	Gomardingen	64-0992
ACKER, Cath.	19	Steinfurt	64-0992
Dorothea 18			
ACKER, Otto	22	Dissen	64-1053
ACKERHAUS, Louise	52	Kirchhof	64-0739
ACKERMANN, Alex'dr	21	Dessau	63-0752
ACKERMANN, Anton	34	Offenbach	63-0953
ACKERMANN, Chr.	23	America	64-0495
ACKERMANN, Eilert	45	Strahholt	66-0412
Ette 50, Jann 23, Hiske 19, Fokke 16			
Eilert 5, Reinder 7			
ACKERMANN, Friedr.	25	Syke	66-0221
ACKERMANN, Georg	29	Umstadt	65-0189
Wilhelmine 22			

NAME	AGE	RESIDENCE	YR-LIST
ACKERMANN, Gerd.	23	Kl.Ahlendorf	65-0243
ACKERMANN, Heinr.	26	Diemerode	66-1155
Martha 27, baby 10m, Martha 27, baby 10m			
ACKERMANN, James	25	Riniken	63-0482
ACKERMANN, Joh.	27	Elfershausen	65-0713
ACKERMANN, Kaetche	34	Offenbach	63-1136
Anna 9			
ACKERMANN, Ludwig	30	Carmkow	66-1203
ACKERMANN, Marg.	22	Neustadt	65-1189
ADAM, C.(m)	26	Preussen	64-0363
ADAM, H.	22	Lippe Detmold	66-0413
ADAM, Herrmann	22	Naseband	66-0469
ADAM, S.B.	19	Alzey	63-1136
ADAMED, Anna	23	Kuttenberg	66-1203
Zenka 11m			
ADAMS, Heike Volke	39	Rhaude	64-0739
ADAMS, Julius	18	Lohrt/Pr.	64-0920
ADAMUTZ, Joseph	32	Boehmen	66-0349
ADDINGER, J.G.	20	Zuerich	64-0363
ADELBERGER, Adam	23	Seckman	63-0862
ADELER, Elise	22	Setsch	66-0623
ADELER, Hermann	20	Shlum	66-0623
ADELMANN, Friedr.	28	Emreuth	64-0433
ADELRICH, Ernst	17	Bennersdorf	67-0599
ADEN, Gerhard M.	17	Aurich	66-1128
ADEN, Jan.	15	Holtrup	66-1128
Nanke 18			
ADERS, Ernst L.	16	Neuenkirchen	64-0363
ADICK, Joh. F.	24	Spike	63-1218
ADICKES, Ernst	37	Dorumer Atten	64-0885
Anna 36, Friederike 8, Heinrich 5			
Elise 9m			
ADLER, A.(m)	19	Coeln	64-0495
ADLER, Adelheid	21	Oberdorf	64-1022
Bertha 19			
ADLER, Adolph	20	Epperier	63-0953
ADLER, Aron	18	Oberwiesse	65-1024
ADLER, Fanny	14	Neudorf	66-0650
ADLER, Heinrich	23	Genzheim/Hess	65-0038
ADLER, Hirsch	29	Storndorf	65-0594
Caroline 26, A.M. 55			
ADLER, Isaac	24	Hahnstadt	65-1024
ADLER, Jette	22	Laupheim	64-1161
Philipp 24			
ADLER, Josef	23	Krotzenberg	66-0147
ADLER, Louis	40	Baltimore	63-0482
ADLER, Moses	16	Oberseemen	66-0984
ADLER, Siegmund	26	Tolkern	66-0934
Joseph 18			
ADLER, Wilhelmine	19	Hochheim	64-1108
ADOLPH, Augusta	16	Borgholzhsn.	66-1031
ADOLPHI, Gg. Aug.	19	Schwedt	63-0482
ADRIAN, Gabriel	17	Oberensingen	66-0734
ADRIAN, Ge.	17	Westhofen	65-1189
AELLEN, F.(m)	26	Switz.	64-0170
AESCHBACH, Friedr.	22	Argau	65-0948
AFFELBACH, Johann	24	Hessia	66-0412
AGGEN, Agge R.	40	Ostfriesland	63-0752
Trietje 30, Joachim 9, Siemen 6, Stinns 4			
Antje 10m			
AGNETT, Albert	30	Berlin	66-0083
AGROLI, Giolio	24	Italy	63-1136
AGSTER, Heinrich	20	Alsfeld	66-1327
AHAUS, Franz	25	Schiipsen	65-0402
AHBE, Chr.	22	Marktuhl	65-0007
AHDERS, Wilhelm	19	Neuenkirchen	63-0482
AHE, Dora	24	Winnigstedt	63-0752
AHE, v.d. Chris.	17	Rhaden	66-1031
AHE, v.d. Fr.	20	Minde	66-0577
AHLBORN, Laura	24	Schneiden	66-1127
AHLBRAND, Peter	29	Langenheim	65-0189
AHLEFELD, Adolph	19	Hagen	64-0343
AHLEFELD, Victor	15	Hannover	66-0576
AHLERS, Carl	19	Vechta	64-0920
AHLERS, Gerd.	24	Iprump	65-0402
AHLERS, Henriette	40	Lingen	63-1010
Friedr. 16, Minna 14, Carl 9, Cathrine 5			
AHLERS, Johann	25	Wildeshausen	66-1093

NAME	AGE	RESIDENCE	YR-LIST
AHLERS, Marg.	26	Haard	65-1030
AHLERT, Anna F.	17	Grevenwiesen	63-0917
AHLERT, Friedr.	17	Dissen	65-0950
AHLHAUSEN, Johanna	42	Weil	64-1108
Anna 5			
AHLRICHS, Heinr.	16	Neuhaus	64-0073
AHLSHEIMER, H.(m)	48	New Orleans	64-0427
Cath. 62, Joh. G. 33, Wilhelmine 22			
Caroline 13, J.G. 3, J.A. 2, B.(f) 34			
S.(f) 19, Carl 17, Daniel 7, Daniel 6			
AHNE, Franz	26	Goinsterdorf	63-0398
AHNEMANN, Friedr.	18	Astendorf	66-1243
AHNEN, v. Wm.	23	Otterndorf	64-0432
AHNTE, L.	27	Prussia	63-1003
M. 20			
AHRENBECK, Margret	31	Warendorf	66-1373
AHREND, Joh.	39	Lutterberg	65-1024
Marie 35, Anna 11, Wilhelm 8, Louise 11			
Carl 3m			
AHRENDS, Gustav	19	Cassel	66-0221
AHRENDT, Herrmann	26	Preussen	63-1069
AHRENDTS, Henry	20	Cassel	63-1178
AHRENHOLZ, Ludw.	30	Walsrode	65-0402
AHRENS, Aug.	38	Bremen	65-0402
Elise 7			
AHRENS, Christ.	25	New York	63-0350
AHRENS, E.T.(m)	20	Midlum	64-0331
AHRENS, Elisab.	26	Loeningen/Old	64-0920
AHRENS, Geerd	35	Norden	64-0170
Geertje 60			
AHRENS, H.J.	32	Mulmshorn	64-0992
AHRENS, Heinr.	24	Diepholz	66-1373
AHRENS, Heinrich	18	Bremervoerde	66-1093
AHRENS, Herm H.	30	Dielingen	64-0920
Maria Elis. 32, Anna Louise 6			
Louise Eng. 3, Friedr. Hr. 57			
AHRENS, Hermann	21	Seebergen	66-0734
AHRENS, Hermann	16	Drangstedt	66-0666
AHRENS, Jan	28	Esens	66-0668
Gerd 33			
AHRENS, Joh.	19	Stadthagen	64-0432
AHRENS, Julius	26	Delmenhorst	63-1038
AHRENS, Marie	23	Geestemuende	65-0243
Marie 9m			
AHRENS, Meta	16	Beverstedt	65-1095
AHRENS, Rebecca	14	Heestedt	63-0350
AHRENS, Rebecca	18	Hannover	66-1093
AHRENS, Theodor	36	Stadtlohn	65-0948
AHRENS, Wilhelm	16	Northum	66-1031
AHRENSFELD, Diedr.	27	Bramstedt	66-1128
AHRING, Friedrich	17	Barthausen	66-1031
AICH, Adolph	23	Ehningen	66-0469
Rudolph 21			
AICHELE, Christian	36	Unt.Weissbach	66-0576
AICHELMANN, Cath.	24	Harthausen	64-0214
AICHER, Christ.	20	Mickelbach	64-0427
AICHER, Emerenzia	50	Mahlstetten	66-0679
AIGN, Ma.(f)	56	Bayern	64-0495
AITSCHUL, Sara	47	Landau	63-1038
Rosa 20, Emilie 9, Clementine 7, Elise 5			
AITTS, Peter	44	Loga	64-0739
AKERMANN, Fr.	25	Entliburg	65-0898
ALAUN, Peter	40	St. Gallen	63-0350
ALBACK, Andreas	32	Oppershofen	66-1155
Eva 28, Franciska 6, Heinrich 2, baby 4m			
ALBAND, Aug.	32	New York	63-0752
ALBENESINS, E.	22	Andelfingen	65-1189
Paul 19			
ALBER, Charles Fr.	20	Esslingen	63-0296
ALBERG, Cath.	26	Quint	63-1136
ALBERG, Francis	37	Gerolstein	63-1136
Marie Anna 34, Cath. 8, Charles 3			
John 10m			
ALBERG, Henry	32	Chicago	63-1136
Maria 33, Cath. 11m			
ALBERLE, Albertine	20	Gernsbach	64-0840
ALBERS, A.	23	Bokah	65-1024
ALBERS, Carl	20	Waldeck	64-0938

NAME	AGE	RESIDENCE	YR-LIST
ALBERS, Ernst	21	Barop	66-0934
ALBERS, F. Ger.	16	Wittmund	65-0856
ALBERS, Franziska	24	Hoexter	65-1088
ALBERS, Gg.	19	Wittmund	65-0856
ALBERS, Heinr.	12	Hemelingen	65-0402
ALBERS, Heinr.	17	Hannover	64-0427
ALBERS, Heinrich	25	Hannover	66-0577
ALBERS, Henry	38	New York	63-1136
ALBERS, J.G.	32	Oldenburg	64-0495
ALBERS, Joh. Henr.	22	Buhlerweit	66-0984
ALBERS, Mina	27	Holtrup	66-1128
ALBERS, Theodor	29	Aldorf	65-1030
ALBERS, Wiecher	32	Upleward	64-1022
ALBERS, William	25	Bremen	63-1038
ALBERT, Anton	29	Oldenburg	66-1093
ALBERT, Emmerich	16	Gr. Mustadt	66-0576
ALBERT, Francis	11	Belgien	63-0168
Mary 9			
ALBERT, Heinr.	17	Dissen	65-0950
Ernst 15			
ALBERT, Johann	30	Elberfeld	66-0346
ALBERT, Jos.	23	Gamberg	65-1189
ALBERT, Michel	27	Hoefen	64-0593
ALBERT, William	25	New York	63-0917
Eugenea 20			
ALBERTUS, Carl Fr.	34	Naumburg	64-0739
Wilhelmine 39, Marie 12, Caroline 6			
Emilie 4, Amalia 7m			
ALBERTUS, Johannes	24	Philadelphia	66-0837
ALBRAND, Conr.	35	Lichtenau	64-1053
Anna 30			
ALBRECH, Wend.	44	New York	66-0221
ALBRECHT, A.	30	St. Louis	63-0296
ALBRECHT, A.	19	Bremen	63-1003
ALBRECHT, Anna G.	21	Rhoda	65-1031
Elisabeth 20			
ALBRECHT, Chr.	58	Halle	63-0482
Wilhelm 15			
ALBRECHT, Christ.	16	Coburg	64-0593
ALBRECHT, Christ.	30	Weinsberg	65-0116
ALBRECHT, Elis.	22	Weinheim	63-1136
ALBRECHT, Franz	28	Baden	66-0576
ALBRECHT, Franz	25	Birkendorf	66-1155
ALBRECHT, Frdr.	26	Dielsdorf	65-0243
ALBRECHT, Georg	16	Hildesheim	63-0917
ALBRECHT, Hermann	31	Gollantsch	66-0679
ALBRECHT, Jeanne C	22	Bremen	62-0244
ALBRECHT, Joh.	36	Cassabrueck	66-1243
Anna 22, Joh. 5, Philipp 6m			
ALBRECHT, Johann	30	Bremen	64-0456
ALBRECHT, Johann	20	Schrecksbach	65-1030
Anna Gela 31			
ALBRECHT, Johanna	20	Claushagen	64-0886
ALBRECHT, Jos.	24	Bueren	66-0576
ALBRECHT, Maria	27	Goettingen	64-0363
ALBRECHT, Wilhelm	33	Bremen	65-0189
ALBRING, Henry	32	Schweiz	63-1136
ALDERS, Alrich	29	Papenburg	64-0938
ALET, Nicolaus	12	Fischbach	67-0007
ALEXANDER, Heinr.	32	Wuerttemberg	66-0576
ALEXANDER, Henry	29	New York	63-0482
Tiene 26, Venne 6			
ALEXANDER, S.	36	New York	64-0170
Ottitie 25, Cornelia 18			
ALEXANDER, Samuel	19	Wolfshagen	66-1093
Rosa 21			
ALFERMAN, Anton	34	Paderborn	65-1095
ALFERS, Bernhard	22	Buhlerweit	66-0984
Johann 30			
ALFERS, Charlotte	50	Hannover	64-0427
Maria 29, Anna M. 7, Ursula 6, Lena 5			
Sus. 3, M.(f) 6m, Wilhelm 5			
ALGE, Anton	22	Sauldorf	65-0243
ALHEIT, Adam	14	Ndr.Vorschutz	63-1069
ALLARD, Hermann	27	Muenster	66-0576
ALLDACH, Juergen	18	Lichtenpelz	66-0623
ALLE, Jacob	17	Grafenberg	66-0221
ALLEMEYER, Wilh.	18	Hilter	66-1031

NAME	AGE	RESIDENCE	YR-LIST
ALLENDORF, Wilh.	37	New York	66-0221
ALLERS, Chr.	27	New York	64-0432
ALLERS, Friederike	19	Zerbst	66-1155
ALLERS, L.N.(m)	19	Geestendorf	64-0023
ALLES, Elisab.	47	Baltersweiler	65-0402
Clara 21, Anton 58, Peter 15, Wilhelm 12			
ALLEWOOD, Henry	47	Geneva	63-0551
ALLMERS, Heinrich	20	Wittlage	66-1093
ALLMUTT, Henry	22	London	66-0576
ALLROGGE, Friedr.	18	Himbsen	66-1031
ALLRUTH, W.	33		63-0917
ALLSTAEDT, Joh. H.	27	Duttleben	65-0948
ALMANDINGER, Al.	37	Muehlhausen	66-1155
ALMANDINGER, David	20	Jebenhausen	64-0214
ALPERS, Anna	23	Langenhausen	67-0600
ALRICHS, B.D.	25	Lande	64-0331
ALRUTH, Sophie	24	Hessen	66-0734
ALSBACH, Emil	25	Buffalo	63-0917
ALSBACHER, Jette	27	Unsleben	64-0886
ALSCHEID, Weinand	19	Alscheid	66-0704
ALSHEIM, Lorenz	22	Windheim	66-0704
ALSHOFF, Joh. Hch.	44	Muenster	64-0886
Gertrude 41, Heinr. 17, Herm. 5			
ALSTADT, Joh.	24	Creuznach	65-1024
ALSTADT, Johannes	18	Schlotzen	66-1155
ALSTER, Reinhard	24	Oberkaufungen	66-0934
ALSWEDE, Sophia	30	Elze	63-1178
Charles 5, Conrad 11m			
ALT, Anna Eva	20	Berglicht	64-0331
ALT, Peter	24	Gambach	63-0862
ALT, Wolfgang	24	Schemersdorf	63-0551
ALT, v. Casp.	25	Eichelheim	65-0950
ALTDOERFER, Gottl.	24	Kirchheim	67-0007
ALTEBOCKWINKEL, St	29	Westenhof	66-1155
ALTECKEN, Alfred	18	Prussia	64-0138
ALTEN, Christ.	39	Holtensen	65-0898
Sophie 34, Sophie 9, August 6, Wilhelm 1			
ALTEN, George	27	Bremen	63-0296
ALTEN, v. J.	30	Bremen	64-0427
ALTENBERG, Cht.(m)	17	Pfalz	64-0170
ALTENBERND, Friedr	27	Lingen	65-0865
Heinrich 26, Anna 29			
ALTENBURG, F.E.(m)	43	Gotha	64-0023
ALTENBURG, Johann	29	Neudorf-Abau	65-1095
ALTENHEINER, James	40	Katzeweschbch	63-0296
Louise 16			
ALTENHOF, C.	20	Bremervoerde	66-0413
ALTENKRAEMER, Gg.	26	Huernbach	64-1022
ALTHAUS, Aug.	35	Rinteln	64-0170
Heinr. 29			
ALTHOEFER, Herm.	23	Osnabrueck	66-1203
ALTHOF, Friederike	55	Steinrundorf	63-1010
Friederike 24, August 15, Heinrich 8			
ALTHOFF, Franz	32	Osnabrueck	66-1128
Wilhelmine 30, Franz 5, Heinrich 6m			
ALTHOFF, Heinr.	19	Dissen	65-0950
Heinr. 3			
ALTHOFF, Heinrich	26	Osnabrueck	66-1128
Wilhelm 27			
ALTHOLZ, Ludwig	57	Niedercappeln	67-0007
ALTING, Anna	70	Aurich	65-1030
ALTONA, Magdalene	19	Dingen	63-1178
ALTSCHUL, Nathan	54	Landau	63-0821
Rudolph 14, Lina 22, Celestine 20			
ALTVATER, Heinr.	15	Hunibach	65-0243
ALTVATER, Jacob	37	Rabenhausen	65-0594
Berthold 20			
ALTWOBNER, J.H.	28	Salzbergen	64-0331
AMAN, Dorothea	22	Colberg	64-0427
AMAND, Henry	23	Ulrichstein	64-0593
AMANN, Franz	21	Baden	66-0469
AMANN, Franz	28	Herdwangen	66-0349
AMANN, Frz. Josef	36	Boehmen	66-0349
AMANNE, Marie	27	Oldenburg	64-0886
AMBACH, Wilhelm	49	Greiz	66-1373
Paul 7			
AMBACHER, Christ.	26	Neidlingen	66-0083
AMBORN, Christian	21	Monsheim	66-0679

NAME	AGE	RESIDENCE	YR-LIST
Elisabeth 19			
AMBROS, C.G.	26	Pennsylvania	66-0934
AMEIS, Christine	17	Colberg	64-0427
AMELGIS, Aug.	23	Hoerste	65-0898
AMELSBERG, Cord	25	Leer	64-0593
AMELSBERG, Frank	31	Ihrhove	65-0243
Falke 24			
AMELUNG, Theodor	20	Belm	66-1093
AMEND, Carl	25	Callel	66-1327
Reinhard 20			
AMEND, Johann	30	Krumbach	66-0734
Margarethe 59, Elise 25			
AMENDE, Carl	34	Bebra	64-1206
Helene 61, Caroline 18			
AMENDE, Hrch.	29	Peningsehl	65-0974
Maria 25			
AMGERER, A.	22	Fuerth	64-0782
AMIEL, Andre	40	France	64-0170
Mrs. 38, child 14			
AMLING, Christian	27	Ohrdruf	66-0576
AMMANN, Clara	22	Krumbach	65-0243
Wilhelmine 24			
AMMANN, Louise	20	Gratz	66-0221
AMMANN, Th.	32	Prussia	64-0427
Gertrude 26, Catharina 3, Joseph 2			
baby 6m			
AMMENHAUSEN, Gottf	20	Harburg	67-0007
AMMENT, Phil.	18	Forchheim	64-0073
AMMERHEIM, Georg	22	Aschaffenburg	67-0007
AMMERMANN, H.D.	36	Bundersee	64-0331
Johanna 21			
AMON, Jacob	21	Didelsheim	65-0713
AMSBACHER, S.	18	Achim	65-0974
Doris 6, F. 14			
ANCHIER, (m)	30	Paris	65-0055
ANDENRIETH, C.F(f)	27	Rommelshausen	64-0331
ANDER, Johann Paul	22	Buchen	66-1373
ANDERKEN, S.	19	Colenfeldt	65-1189
ANDERLE, Ign.	36	Boehmen	63-0917
Agathe 23, Jos. 3, Anna 1			
ANDERMANN, Heinr.	18	Hemsen	65-0898
Dorothea 16			
ANDERSECK, Marie	33	Bremerhaven	65-0055
Mathilde 6, baby 1			
ANDERSEN, Bent.	40	Copenhagen	66-0666
Anna 32, Olef 4, Anna Louise , Sophia 6m			
ANDERSEN, Niels	37	Gottenburg	66-0666
ANDERSEN, Peter	20	Copenhagen	66-0666
ANDERSON, John	48	England	64-0170
ANDERWIESER, Cath.	45	Augsburg	65-1088
Johann 6			
ANDING, Conrad	50	Schmalkalden	66-1313
Barbara 32, Anna 10			
ANDRE, Carl	17	Philadelphia	66-0704
ANDRE, Christian	34	Hannover	63-0822
ANDRE, Daniel	54	Herzberg	64-0456
Wilhelmine 47, Augusta 22, Minna 8			
ANDRE, Georg	23	Osnabrueck	65-0594
ANDREAS, Christian	34	Ndr.Dunzebach	64-0170
Anna Martha 32, Cath. 9, Joh. Peter 5			
Heinr. 3, Otto 6m			
ANDREAS, Friedr.	48	Gr. Bisdorf	64-0593
Marie 49, Marie 21, Friedr. 18, John 16			
Friederike 14, Christine 9			
ANDREAS, Peter	36	Ormesweiler	66-1373
ANDREES, Nicolaus	28	Braetz	64-1053
ANDRES, Angela	50	Muenster	63-0551
ANDRES, Magd.	19	Oppenau	64-1022
ANDRO, Carl	18	Oversleben	65-1095
Pauline 21			
ANGELBECK, August	29	Nellinghof	63-1038
Catharine 23, Gerhard 9m			
ANGERMANN, Alwin	19	Hof	66-0109
ANGERMANN, Johanna	47	Luetzelbach	64-0639
Friedr. 15, Elisabeth 12, Anna 7			
Margaretha 58, Johanna 30, Johann 7			
Emilie 5			
ANGERMUELLS, Cath.	59	Coburg	63-0244

NAME	AGE	RESIDENCE	YR-LIST
Friedrike 26, Fernanda 14			
ANGERSBACH, Minna	24	Offenbach	66-0734
ANGERSTEIN, Louise	22	Carlsruhe	67-0007
ANIS, Max	19	Pforzheim	64-0639
ANISHANSEL, Carl	31	Germany	63-0953
ANKELE, Mathias	20	Oeschingen	66-1373
ANKERBRAND, Margar	26	Syetzlos	66-0576
Anton 8			
ANNABERG, Louise	15	Frankenberg	64-0782
ANNBACHER, B.(m)	18	Neidlingen	64-0331
ANNSBACH, C.	17	Menzingen	66-0413
ANPEL, Heinr.	28	Hannover	66-1373
ANSBACHER, Sophie	22	Fuerth	64-1022
ANSCHUETZ, Johann	40	Vegesack	65-1024
ANSTEDT, Jacob	36	Donseider	66-0221
Eva 28, Jacob 9m, Margareth 28			
ANSTEMANN, Lisette	20	Bevergen	66-1373
ANTE, Philipp		Hallenberg	66-1203
ANTEMANN, Therese	26	Bevergen	66-1373
Josephine 22			
ANTEMEYER, Jos.	22	Osnabrueck	65-0974
ANTHE, Bernh.	49	Preussen	64-0214
Joseph 20			
ANTL, John	20	Gudamsberg	65-0151
ANTON, Georg	16	Ellerstadt	65-0007
ANTON, Heinrich	29	Altmitlau	63-0015
ANTON, Heinrich	17	Bueckeburg	66-1127
ANTONIA, Karrel	28	Pilsen	66-1093
APANIER, Math.	47	Illinois	64-0495
APEL, B.	16	Meutershausen	65-1189
APEL, Chris.	31	Blankenhein	63-0482
APEL, Lisette	24	Culmbach	64-0886
APEL, Martha	60	Nentershausen	66-1327
Wilhelmine 21, Christine 19			
APFELBAUM, Emil	37	Vermont	66-0109
APFINK, F.(m)	40	United States	64-0593
APP, Caroline	18	Zeisenhausen	66-0679
APP, Conrad	30	Rothen	66-1131
APP, Philippina	29	Darmstadt	64-1053
APPEL, (m)	37	Witzenhausen	64-0170
J.J.(f) 9, Mathilde 5			
APPEL, Caroline	16	Kammerborn	66-0413
APPEL, Cath	19	Homborn	63-1085
APPEL, Christ.	27	Veilsdorf	66-0576
APPEL, Christoph	22	Lorsch	65-0151
Barbara 24			
APPEL, George	42	Olmen	64-0593
Anna 40			
APPEL, Heinr.	61	Oberlaub	64-0687
Marie 61, Christian 23, Caroline 17			
APPEL, Helmar	25	Giessen	66-0221
APPEL, Henriette	24	Heidingfeld	63-0097
Anna 1			
APPEL, Johannes	29	Schutten	66-0412
APPELBAUM, Bab.	19	Furth	64-0782
APPENZELLER, Gottl	18	Zeffenhausen	64-0170
APPENZELLER, Wm.	26	Carlsruhe	64-0782
APPOLANT, Rosa	27	New York	64-0427
Louise 29, Heinr. 18, Wm. 16, Carl 7			
Louise 6, baby 9m, Christina 20, Leon 4			
Julie 3, Francisca 2			
ARB, Joh.	47	Westofen	65-0594
Sybilla 40, Catharina 19, Marg. 17			
Joh. 9, Elise 7			
ARBIN, Daniel	16	Wetter	66-0704
ARBIN, Sly	39	Baltimore	66-0704
ARBURG, Hch.	17	Greussen	64-0363
AREND, Christine	25	Hessen	66-0469
AREND, Pierre	25	Belgien	63-0350
ARENDES, Marie	17	Borgentreich	67-0795
ARENDS, Alfred	25	Clausthal	65-0004
ARENDS, B.	28	Ohne	64-1161
ARENDS, Menno	14	Jennelt	64-1022
ARENDT, B.	40	Bremen	65-0974
Dorette 37, Johanne 7			
ARENDT, Carl	17	Rothenburg	65-1088
ARENHORSTERBAUMR,G	46	Almersloh	66-1031
Gerhard 46			
ARENS, F.	17	Bremen	66-0413
ARENS, Gretje	25	Ost Friesland	66-0577
ARENS, Johann	56	Harstedt	66-1248
Wilhelmine 33, Caroline 10			
ARENSTEIN, Wilh.	40	Boehmen	66-0704
ARENT, Elise	17	Neustadt	66-0837
ARENT, Jacob	21	Asloch	66-0837
ARETZ, Nath.	34	Neuss	64-0138
AREULBRING, Wilh.	22	Muenchhausen	67-0007
ARFMANN, Betti	26	Vegesack	64-0840
ARFMANN, Eimer	17	Meienburg	66-1031
ARFMANN, H.	36	New York	63-1136
ARKEBAUER, Theen	24	Firrel	66-1248
Ricke 18, Arda 20, Hiske 23			
ARKENBERG, Agnes	32	Oldenburg	66-0221
Marie 24			
ARKOSZEWSKI, John	27	Wiskittno	66-0578
ARKULARIUS, Bertha	19	Marburg	66-1155
ARLETH, Friedr.	37	Vaihingen	64-1022
ARMBRUESTER, Elise	23	Rosenthal	65-1030
ARMBRUESTER, Jos.	38	New Orleans	63-1085
Ernst 17, Johanna 24, Wilhelmine 40			
ARMBRUST, Daniel	21	Aachen	65-0116
ARMBRUSTER, Elisa	20	Wallfach	63-1085
Anna 38, Anton 19, Francis 9, Joseph 2			
ARMBRUSTER, Friedr	29	Chicago	63-1178
ARMBRUSTER, H.	44	Sindelfingen	63-1003
H. 17, F. 16, R. 15			
ARMBRUSTER, Heinr	24	Lauterecken	64-0363
ARNAU, Elisabeth	29	Selz	66-1203
ARNDT, E.(m)	23	Bremen	64-0495
ARNDT, Michael	32	Ludwigsdorf	65-0770
ARNHEITER, Helene	23	Darmstadt	66-1127
ARNING, Aug.	19	Talle	64-0214
ARNING, Gottlieb	54	Quincy	63-1010
ARNOLD, (m)	35	Prussia	63-1218
ARNOLD, August	37	Nordhausen	66-0147
ARNOLD, Barbara	42	Schittach	65-0007
ARNOLD, Ch.	41	Thalheim	64-0331
Johanna 21			
ARNOLD, Christ.	31	Dreyhaken	63-1010
ARNOLD, Christine	23	Heidelberg	66-0704
ARNOLD, Conrad	17	Magdeburg	66-1127
ARNOLD, Ferdinand	26	Sundheim	65-0948
ARNOLD, Friederike	22	Bretzfeld	65-0116
ARNOLD, Friedr.	47	Glogau	66-1128
Johanna S. 40			
ARNOLD, Joh.	44	Rothenburg	64-1206
Anna Marie 14, Jacob 7, Christiane 4			
Catharina 3, Dorothea 2, Johannes 6m			
ARNOLD, Johann	20	Ob.Sichringl	67-0007
ARNOLD, Wilhelm	25	Wallduern	66-0147
ARNOLD, Wilhelm	22	Stollberg	66-1093
ARNOLD, Wilhelmine	54	Oelsnitz	65-0898
ARNOLDI, Albert	28	Paderborn	66-1093
ARNOLDI, Fritz	18	Hannover	66-0412
ARNSTEIN, Therese	24	Koenigswart	64-0427
ARONSCHILD, Roesla	58	Fuerth	66-1203
ARONSTEIN, Moritz	20	Minden	66-0109
ARP, Anna Marg.	19	Osterbruch	64-0432
ARPEN, Heinrich	17	Lohne	66-0679
ARTH, Gustav	16	Brockhausen	66-1248
ARTKOETTER, Gertr.	25	Heppenheim	66-0734
ARTOT, Jahn	18	Heersfeld	66-1243
ARTZ, Joseph	29	Trier	64-0938
Wolfgang 62, Anna Maria 53, Anna 8			
ARZT, Carl	17	Bredenkopf	65-0402
ARZT, Christ.	40	Hof	63-0398
ASCHE, Friedrich	28	Schneeren	65-0948
ASCHE, Wilhelm	25	Schneeren	65-0948
Dorothea 22, Wilhelmine 9m			
ASCHEBERG, Carl	20	Oldenburg	64-1022
ASCHEIMER, Barb.	23	Oting/Bayern	66-0346
ASCHENBACH, Joh.	26	Schweine	66-1248
ASCHENBACH, Joh.	15	Oberndorf	66-1313
ASCHENBERGER, Elis	21	Bern	63-1069
ASCHENDORF, Heinr.	19	Raab	67-0007
ASCHENMOOR, Carl	35	Cincinnati	64-0023

NAME	AGE	RESIDENCE	YR-LIST
Johanna 21			
ASCHER, Friederike	24	Loebau	66-1203
ASCHMANN, Carl	33	Ludenscheit	65-0948
ASENDORF, Hermann	25	Riede	66-1031
ASHORN, Johanna	27	Essen	66-0668
ASING, Emelie	29	Pottendorf	66-1243
ASMANN, Louis	29	Bauenstein	64-0170
Math. 40			
ASMUS, Carl	40	Schoeningen	66-0837
ASMUS, Caroline	59	Woellmarshaus	63-1038
ASMUS, Friederike	28	Schorningen	66-1373
Maria 2, Robert 11m			
ASMUS, Johannes	20	Falkenberg	66-0412
ASMUS, Louis	16	Bremervoerde	66-0984
ASPELMEIER, Louise	18	Westphalen	66-1031
ASSEL, Jacob	27	Hohscheit	65-0243
ASSENMACHER, M.(m)	33	Bohndorf	64-0023
ASSMANN, Eleonore	35	Eisfeld	64-1053
ASSMANN, Georg	39	Nenterhausen	66-0349
Augusta 46			
ASSMANN, Heinrich	11	Nenterhausen	66-0349
An. Marth. 7, Friedrich 2			
ASSMANN, Ludwig	26	Wuertemberg	66-0221
ASSMUSS, Martha	18	Ellenberg	63-0990
AST, Heinrich	49	Altheim	66-0221
AST, Phil.	58	Schweiz	66-0704
Juliane 56, Theresia 24			
ASTHOLZ, Adolph	20	Grohnde	66-0934
Anna Helene 9			
ASWOLD, P. August	38	Thifurt	66-0666
ATZ, Jac. Ferd.	19	Gronau	66-0221
ATZBACH, Marie	24	Hausen	64-0138
AUB, Albert	22	Bayreuth	64-0782
AUB, Max	30	Frankfurt	65-0007
AUBERT, Pierre	30	Havre	64-1053
AUCHMANN, Hermann	26	Bersenbrueck	66-1093
AUCKMANN, Friedr.	27	Bersenbrueck	66-1093
AUD, Catharina	37	Raterbach	66-0349
Eva 15			
AUE, Conrad	24	Bernbach	67-0007
AUE, Minna	26	Rheda	63-0350
Friedrich 11m			
AUE, Wilhelm	26	Rheda	65-0865
Anna 24			
AUER, Anna	55	Gailingen/Boh	65-0243
Caroline 30, Augusta 23, Maria 19			
August 8, Louise 3, Robert 9m, Mathilde 5			
Minna 10m			
AUER, Conr.	23	Schaffhausen	65-0898
AUER, Georg	15	Dinkelsbuehl	66-0668
AUER, Hermann	23	Zuerich	65-1024
AUER, J.	18	Ohnenheim	63-1003
AUER, Johanna	24	Wicherau	65-0402
Max 1			
AUER, Pet.	25	Unterhalau	65-0898
AUER, Senas	58	Gailingen	65-0243
Ludw. 32			
AUERBACH, C.(f)	38	Stuttgart	65-0189
AUERSWALD, Christ.	33	Sachsen	64-0739
AUFERMANN, G.(m)	28	Paris	64-0023
AUFFINGER, Joseph	27	Buchau	65-0594
AUGSBURG, Henning	29	New York	66-0109
AUGSTENBERGER, Jos	26	Neuler	66-1203
AUGUSTIN, S.(m)	20	Osnabrueck	64-0331
AUGUSTIN, Valentin	25	Eiderhagen	66-0412
AUKAMP, Friedr.	25	Wagenfeld	63-0482
Friedr. 14			
AUKELE, Mathias	20	Oeschingen	66-1373
AULBERT, Friedr.	18	Vehrte	66-1031
AULBERT, Johann	29	Melle	66-0984
AULMANN, Philipp	38	New York	63-1178
Elisabeth 42, Henry 9			
AULT, Louis	45	New York	63-0917
AUMANN, Friedr.	27	Pollhagen	64-0214
AUMUELLER, Babette	23	Proevelsdorf	66-1203
Anna 14			
AUMUELLER, Kunig.	19	Hirboldhausen	63-1136
AURICH, Friedrich	23	Glauchau	66-1373

NAME	AGE	RESIDENCE	YR-LIST
AURSTETER, J.	24	Dennitz	66-0413
AUST, L.	31	Posen	64-0992
AUSTERMANN, Friedr	36	Detmold	66-1031
Helene 31, Emilie 7, Friedrich 5			
August 3			
AUSTERMANN, Henry	51	Detmold	66-1327
AUTENWIETH, Gottl.	22	Rommelshausen	64-1053
AVERBECK, Franz	17	Deintrup	64-0938
Berahardine 22			
AVET, Delphine	33	Montgeroult	63-0551
child 7, child 5, child 3			
AVRIL, Jacob	37	Neustadt	63-0551
AXEN, Joh.	37	Jever	64-0665
Margaretha 40, Wilhelmine 14			
AXT, Ferdinand	33	Messkirch	65-0243
AXT, Joseph	42	Wien	66-0576
AYERS, Joseph	32	New York	66-0109
BAADE, Friedr.	17	Melle	66-0984
BAADEN, Carl	17	Remingen	66-1327
BAADTE, Anton	20	Neuleringen	66-1373
BAAK, Sidona	21	Sauldorf	63-0296
Anna Maria 9m			
BAAS, Joh.	28	Bechtheim	65-0116
BAASCH, Albert	30	Marienwerder	63-0015
BABAR, Johann	40	Uplodt	63-0614
Anna 36, Christian 11, Anna 7, Edmund 2			
BABEL, A.	34	Heidersdorf	23-0865
BABEL, Anna M.	25	Spierheim	66-0221
BABILLE, Aug.	58	West Bend	64-0138
BABIN, H.	34	Bremen	63-0752
wife 28, son 3, daughter 5			
BABKA, Maria	23	Tyrol	66-0623
BACH, August	23	Schmoeller	66-0668
BACH, August	19	Ebersbach	66-1327
BACH, Carl	19	Coeln	64-1161
BACH, Chris.	16	Eckhardtsbonn	63-0482
BACH, David	16	Monsheim	63-1038
BACH, Friederike	26	New York	66-0734
BACH, Heinrich	16	Nambach	66-0984
BACH, Heinrich	27	Lingen	66-1031
BACH, Isaac	69	Heppenheim	64-0427
Marg. 2, Friedr. 28, Eva 23			
BACH, Isac	18	Muehringen	66-0704
BACH, Isidor	38	Essen	66-0221
BACH, Jacob	18	Bartenheim	66-0147
BACH, Jette	22	Binswangen	64-0427
BACH, Joh.	25	Niederstein	64-0782
BACH, Johann	24	Lingen	64-0456
BACH, Leopold	19	Bienswangen	63-0953
BACH, Mich.	36	Roth	64-1108
BACH, Paulus	18	Eisenach	64-0885
BACH, S.J.	27	New York	63-1136
wife 22			
BACH, Wilhelm	18	Darmstadt	66-0221
BACH, Wilhelmine	26	Schmalkalden	63-1069
BACHARACH, K.	20	Neuenkirchen	64-0639
BACHARACH, Sally	17	Paderborn	66-1127
Moritz 20			
BACHEL, Marie	22	Baiern	66-0704
Marie 9m			
BACHENHEIMER, Gust	18	Breddenau	66-0984
BACHER, August	18	Zellerfeld	64-1022
BACHERT, Max	20	Baden	66-0109
BACHMANN, Adam	40	Heringa	64-0433
Maria 42, Anna Elise 17, Elisabeth 14			
Anna Magd. 8, Jacob 7			
BACHMANN, Aug.	24	Constanz	64-0363
BACHMANN, David	28	Schweiz	66-0147
BACHMANN, Emil	14	Ilmenau	63-0990
BACHMANN, Ester	50	Kriegstabe	64-0992
Carl 16, Cacilie 19			
BACHMANN, F.A.	25	New York	63-0693
BACHMANN, Franz	38	Haibach	64-0840
BACHMANN, Friede.	48	Ochsenbach	66-0679
Friederike 18, Wilhelmine 15			
Christiane 14, Moritz 10, Louise 9			
Christian 7, Marie 2			
BACHMANN, J.H.	26	Chicago	64-0170

NAME	AGE	RESIDENCE	YR-LIST
BACHMANN, Louis	45	Milwaukee	64-0687
BACHMANN, Louise	28	Reckershausen	63-0953
BACHMANN, Ludwig	18	Heinebach	66-1203
BACHMANN, Rich.	19	Leipzig	65-0007
BACHMEYR, Marie	28	Oehringen	66-1155
BACHNER, Maria	20	Gandersheim	64-0363
BACHRACH, Moritz	18	Paderborn	65-0402
BACHRACH, Salomon	17	Grebenau	65-0594
BACHSMEYER, Wilh.	25	Rahden	65-1088
BACHSTUHL, Conrad	40	Torgau	66-1373
BACHUR, Ad.	20	Breslau	65-0038
BACION, Catharina	16	Luccimin	64-0433
BACK, Augusta	29	Hessen	66-0734
BACK, Sidona	21	Sauldorf	63-0296
Anna Maria 9m			
BACK, Wm.	49	Dornassenheim	64-0886
Friedr. 19, Regina 15, Wilhelmine 7			
Adam 5			
BACKEBRANDT, M.(m)	25	Eisebeck	64-0214
BACKHAUS, August	27	Lohningen	65-0865
BACKHAUS, David	58	Wolchow	65-0402
BACKHAUS, Frz.Hch.	26	Erkel	65-0950
BACKHAUS, H.	31	Borstel	65-1031
Louise 29, Heinrich 5, Wilhelmine 3			
Wilhelm 6m			
BACKHAUS, Heinrich	25	Esdorf	66-1155
BACKHAUS, Hinr.	16	New Orleans	64-0432
BACKHOFER, Marg.	14	Nuernberg	64-0023
Andreas 24			
BACKMANN, Clemens	25	Oldenburg	64-0920
Maria 20			
BACKNER, Johannes	28	Niederafleidn	64-0214
BACKOFER, Agnes	61	Buffalo	64-0687
BACKOOF, Joh.	28	Buffalo	63-1178
BACKS, Ferd.	19	Herstelle	64-0593
BACKS, Wilhelm	16	Westphalen	66-0469
BADCKE, Herm.	28	Brensin/Pr.	65-0038
BADE, Carl	18	Carmen	64-0840
BADE, Heinr.	28	Heiligstadt	64-0170
Martha 26, Elise 6m			
BADE, Mathias	27	Wuerthe	67-0007
BADENHOP, John H.	28	New York	63-1085
BADER, Cathar.	26	Durmersheim	66-0704
BADER, Franz	16	Muenster	66-0576
BADER, Johann	41	Muenster	66-0576
Anna 36, Catharine 7, Gertraude 6			
Therese 25			
BADER, Julius	27	Dresden	64-0363
BADER, Ludw.	23	Sindelfingen	65-0189
BADER, Michael	43	Wien	66-0934
Marie 35, Rosa 4, Gustav 2, Johann 6m			
BADER, Philip	19	Grafenberg	66-0147
BADER, Thomas	29	Oberhausen	65-1095
BADERS, Martin	42	Emden	66-0837
Ehje W. 42, Albertine 20			
BADETT, Johanna	25	Buchwald	66-0412
Joh. Dorothe 29			
BAECHE, John	22	Southhampton	66-0109
BAECK, Theodor	19	Aurich	66-0576
Augusta 24			
BAECKER, A.	23	Wolthusen	66-0413
BAECKER, Carl	19	Bavaria	66-0679
BAECKER, Georg	27	Harheim	66-1248
BAECKER, Gottfried	22	Harheim	66-1248
Philippine 23, baby (f) 1			
BAEHLER, Regina	26	Grafenlueder	66-1031
BAEHR, Anna	22	Jever	65-1088
Lina 18			
BAEHR, Catharine	38	Lahr	65-0055
Marie 7, Mathilde 3			
BAEHR, Conrad	32	Aulendiebach	64-0427
BAEHR, Friedr.	25	Riesslage	64-0687
BAEHRING, Albert	17	Volkstadt	65-0974
BAEHRING, Theodor	34	Altenstein	63-1178
BAEHRINGER, J.Jac.	51	Durnau	63-0917
BAEHRLE, Reinhard	33	Benchen	66-0109
BAELZER, Heinr.	24	Reiskirchen	64-0593
BAEME, Christian H	27	Gesmold	63-1069

NAME	AGE	RESIDENCE	YR-LIST
BAEMROTH, Peter	27	Emmerstaedt	66-0576
BAER, Adolph	18	Stuttgart	63-1069
BAER, Anna	19	Northeim	66-1127
BAER, E.	24	Padusch	65-1189
BAER, Elisabeth	16	Gauersheim	65-0948
BAER, Gottfried	25	Landshut	63-1069
BAER, Isidor	19	Bromberg	65-0950
BAER, Joh.	32	Bingen	64-1206
BAER, Martin	20	Baden	66-0576
BAER, Samuel	26	New York	64-0073
BAER, Siemon	36	Neustadt	66-0984
Marie 30			
BAER, William	23	Detroit	63-0551
BAERNER, Mary	20	Bremen	63-0917
BAETGER, H.(m)	36	Harrisburg	64-0023
BAETJER, Anna	17	Bremen	67-0806
BAETZ, Christ.	28	Varenholz	64-0639
BAETZ, Elise	36	Hersfeld	66-1093
Anna 7, Elise 9, Antonia 6, Amalie 3			
BAETZ, Ludw.	18	Undingen	66-1313
BAEUERLE, Eva Mar.	20	Enzthal	64-0214
BAEUERLE, John	25	Goettelfingen	63-0296
BAEUME, Johann	20	Unterlakowitz	66-1373
BAEUMLER, Baldw.	19	Lobichau	63-0953
BAFFERT, Paul	25	Naila	64-0138
BAGELMEYER, Fritz	19	Bielefeld	65-1088
BAGEMANN, Carl Aug	51	Rheda	64-0920
Aug. 19, Minna 16, Wilhelm 10, Gustav 6			
BAGGER, Jacob	28	Goettelfingen	66-0147
BAGINSKY, Vinces	38	Bromberg	64-0456
Antonia 34, Magdalena 9, Cecilie 5			
Wladislawa 3, Bronislawa 10m			
BAGOWSKY, Simon	18	Schneidemuhl	64-0170
BAGUS, Johannes	16	Hauswolz	65-1030
Appolonia 25			
BAHLE, Ed.	28	Elberfeld	65-0007
BAHLMANN, Clement.	19	Warendorf	63-0551
Hermann 15			
BAHMANN, Jacob	17	Westhausen	66-1373
BAHMEIER, Friedr.	18	Westphalia	66-0469
BAHMERT, Marg.	52	Obernburg	63-1136
Apollon 9, Elisabeth 4			
BAHN, Friedr.	23	Althaningen	65-0007
BAHNKE, J.G.	58	Poblotz	63-1003
BAHNMEIER, Ad.	28	New York	63-0990
BAHR, Hermann	40	Guedenhagen	66-0469
Friederike 36, Wilhelm 10, Caroline 8			
Bertha 3			
BAHRENBORG, Joh.	15	Fischerhude	64-0593
BAHRENBURG, Adelh.	20	Fischerhude	66-1031
BAHSEL, Heinr.	15	Kammerborn	65-0038
Jette 22, Henriette 51			
BAI, Eva Cathar.	19	Alfdorf	66-1155
BAIE, Andreas	54	Wenjen	66-0650
Justine 53, August 17, Caroline 15			
Carl 9			
BAIER, August	22	Michalineske	66-0578
BAIER, Conrad	19	Fangenberg	66-0623
BAIER, Edmund	33	Huenfeld	65-1030
Caspar 39			
BAIER, Joseph	30	Gelchsheim	66-1203
BAIER, Peter	20	Leimbach	66-1327
BAIER, Valentin	24	Oberzell	63-0551
BAIER, Victor	19	Gutenberg	63-1038
BAIERLIM, Johanna	31	Bamberg	66-0668
BAIERLOTZEN, Barb.	28	Steinwiesen	66-0934
BAIERLOTZER, Andr.	36	Steinwiesen	66-0934
BAIERMANN, Wilhelm	19	Otterndorf	66-1248
BAIL, Nicolas	23	New York	64-0214
BAILER, Henry	30	Trochtelfinge	63-1136
Friedr. 23, Ida 11m			
BAIME, Anna M.	32	Gesmold	63-1069
BAISS, Leonhard	29	Ebelsbach	66-1203
BAITHER, Carl	45	Breitenstein	64-1022
Cath. 48			
BAKENHUS, Henry	34	Germany	63-0821
Amalie 21			
BAKER, Hilbert	19	Wulthusen	66-0469

NAME	AGE	RESIDENCE	YR-LIST
BAKER, Samuel	45	Rhode Island	63-0097
BAKES, Anton	31	Boehmen	63-1218
Emanuel 5			
BAKESCH, Josephine	34	Kuttenberg	64-0214
Anna M. 23, Alois 9m			
BAKKER, Arend	26	Nithhuizen	66-0734
BAKKER, Wiebe	29	Zand	65-1095
BALDE, Regine	27	Umstadt	66-0576
BALE, Friedrich	19	Dorum	66-0734
BALENBERG, Anna	25	New York	66-0984
BALKEMEIER, Anna	26	Sundhatten	64-0593
BALL, Cath.	19	Krehwinkel	64-0331
BALL, Catharine	28	Wuerttemberg	66-0109
BALL, Xaver	23	Hochnoessingn	66-1155
BALLAUF, Wilhelm	16	Muenden	66-1127
BALLDAUF, Joseph	22	Altenstadt	66-1327
BALLEFELD, Conrad	26	Viermuenden	66-0623
BALLER, Franz	26	Grosszimmern	64-0138
BALLERUFF, Ludvica	20	Warburg	65-0151
BALLIN, Jac.	17	Frankfurt	64-1108
BALLMANN, John	33	Arsten	63-0350
BALLMER, Isaac	26	Winterbach	64-0138
BALLMER, Michael	28	Vollnog	66-0576
Anton 26			
BALMY, V.	34	Paris	64-0593
W. 14			
BALSER, Augusta	24	Giessen	63-0917
BALSER, H.	42	Hattenrod	65-0402
Anna 38, Elisab. 19, Carl 16, Philipp 13			
Conrad 8			
BALSER, Wilh.	26	Buedingen	65-0243
BALTHASAR, E.(f)	29	Barmen	64-0427
Anna 35, Anna 7, Maria 6, Cath. 4			
Luehr 9m, Ewald 9m			
BALTHASAR, Ewald	29	Barmen	63-0917
BALTZER, John	23	Stockheim	63-1218
Maria 9m			
BALZER, Caspar	59	Marburg	63-0752
BALZER, Christine	21	Thalitter	67-0795
BALZER, Johann	20	Welf	66-0623
BALZER, Magda.	20	Buchen	64-0427
BAMBACH, Johann	36	New York	66-0147
Barbara 28, Johannes 15, Marie 9			
Louise 7, Christian 4, Johann 11m			
BAMBERGER, Abrah.	20	Burgkundstadt	63-0862
BAMBERGER, Abraham	14	Gr. Hessen	66-0704
BAMBERGER, Carl	21	Burgkunstadt	65-0243
BAMBERGER, G.	22	Brooklyn	63-0990
BAMBERGER, Herm.	25	Burgkundstadt	63-0862
BAMBERGER, Joh.	24	Friedensdorf	65-0594
Elisab. 24, Hannchen 30, Jettchen 7			
Poli 6			
BAMBERGER, Joseph	17	Neidenstein	64-0687
BAMBERGER, Louise	30	Fuerth	64-0938
BAMBOR, Joseph	17	Warburg	65-1088
Bertha 20			
BAMELLI, Pierre	36	Italy	63-1136
BAMINGER, Joseph	38	Hohenstadt	66-1373
Margaretha 39, Wendelin 14, Mariane 8			
Joseph 6			
BAMMANN, Martin	17	Rotenburg	64-0739
BANDER, Emilie	21	Berlin	65-1024
BANDER, Heinrich	21	Osnabrueck	64-0639
BANDER, Julius	29	Stuttgart	65-1024
BANDHAGEN, H.(m)	25	Uelze	64-0427
BANDROEJ, Friedr.	68	France	63-0350
BANDURA, Stanislas	31	Soessnowd	66-0469
Johanna 35, Franz 2, Casimir 3m			
BANE, Andreas	36	Wuertemberg	66-0679
BANEB, Friedr.	29	Neustadt	64-0639
BANFELS, H.	34	Hustedt	64-0782
BANFF, A.B.(f)	21	Ernsthausen	64-0214
BANG, Philipp	21	Hildburghsn.	64-0433
BANGEL, Nicolas	37	New York	63-0917
Victoria 36			
BANGERS, Peter	24	Weiher	66-1093
BANGERT, Christ.	49	Thalitter	67-0795
Carl 20, Hch. 18, Wilhelmine 16			
Louise 12, Marie 10			
BANISCH, Andreas	39	Wolferstaedt	64-0433
BANK, Johann	45	Saltern	64-0170
Elisab. 41, Amalia 41, Lydia 9, Anna 4			
Theodor 2			
BANK, Johann	36	Neuenhausen	66-0576
BANK, v.d. H.	29	Aachen	64-0593
BANKE, Robert	36	Aachen	65-0243
BANKE, Wm.	21	Ristedt	64-0495
BANKEN, Margarethe	18	Ottenstein	65-1095
BANN, Daniel	26	Wetter	66-1128
BANN, Ester	20	Nordheim	66-0704
Henriette 19			
BANN, Martin	47	Wuerttenberg	66-0221
Marie 52, Chrs. 18, Louise 16, Marie 14			
Catharine 7			
BANN, Rose Pauline	25	Bohlheim	65-0770
BANNAT, Daniel	38	Zweibruecken	66-1203
Magdalene 30			
BANNE, Carl	21	Neuenheim	66-1131
BANNER, Joh.	19	Rothenburg	65-0007
BANNMANN, Sophie	54	Gross-Sottrum	63-0551
Cath. 18, Margarethe 15			
BANNSHOF, Joh.Ludw	24	Thalheim	63-0244
John Cas. 10			
BANSE, Friedr.	29	Magdeburg	63-0398
Wilhelmine 24, Anna 8m, Charlotte 59			
BANSE, Otto	24	Magdeburg	63-0296
BANSSEN, Lina	26	Eisenach	64-0214
BANSTEDTER, Henry	23	Weissenburg	65-0243
Caroline 23			
BANTLE, Anton	32	Eppendorf	66-1093
BANTLE, Marie	19	Herren Zimmer	63-0097
BANTLIN, Charles	22	Ulm	63-0168
BANZER, Hugo	27	Osnabrueck	65-1140
BANZHAF, William	37	Philadelphia	63-0551
BAPST, Friedr.	47	Giessen	63-0953
BARANDON, Ernst	23	Verden	63-0614
BARB, Anna	57	Oberkachen	66-0668
BARBARASCK, Anna	11m	Malaus	64-0639
BARBES, Wm.	18	Goslar	65-0038
BARBEY, A.	56	Paris	63-0168
BARCKE, Joh.	36	Birsitz/Pr.	65-0038
BARDENHAGEN, Elisa	17	Ertzen	65-1031
BARDENWERPER, Rob.	24	Braunschweig	63-0953
BAREIS, Caroline	28	Rohrdorf	66-1327
BARENBURG, Fr.	23	Bremen	64-0214
BARETAR, Johann	26	Kehlberen	66-0679
BARFF, (m)	25	Washington	63-1038
BARFKUSCHT, Christ	38	Preussen	63-0917
Caroline 40, Ernst 21, August 11			
Albert 9, Augusta 7, Wilhelmine 5			
Pauline 11m			
BARFUSS, Emil	19	Berlin	63-0953
BARG, Ludwig W.	23	Essern	66-0083
BARGER, G.L.	45	Weida	63-0917
BARGULT, John	30	Michelburg	63-1218
BARHORST, Ferd.	38	Oldenburg	66-0984
Heinr. 27			
BARHORST, Joseph	22	Fhorst	66-0984
Henr. 19			
BARINGER, Johanna	16	Burg	66-0679
BARK, Heinz	29	Syke	63-0015
BARK, Jacob	62	Caupueckels	66-0083
Anna Marie 58, Wilhelm 21, Elisabeth 19			
Anna Maria 16, Franz 14			
BARKARDT, Wm.	22	Riegeln	64-0023
BARKAU, Herm.	25	Meierhofen	63-1085
BARKE, August	20	Friedrichshor	66-0578
BARKHAUSEN, C.H.	46	Bueckeburg	64-0495
Ernestine 34, Wilhelmine 5, baby 6m			
BARLAG, Joseph	19	Hollage	64-1022
BARLAGE, Joh. H.	26	Accum	66-0704
baby 1			
BARMANN, Ludw.	33	Pr. Friedland	66-0704
Albertine 25, Franziska 6m			
BARMANN, William	32	Hasbergen	63-0693
BARMER, Theod.	27	Stiessen	65-1030

NAME	AGE	RESIDENCE	YR-LIST
BARMET, Magdalena	6	Kasshofen	66-1203
Jacob 3, Daniel 9m			
BARNER, C.	24	Wagenfeld	63-1085
BARQUET, Chr.	26	Muhlberg	64-0495
BARRABAS, Heinrich	20	Dorum	66-1128
BARRE, Heinr.	19	Paderborn	66-1327
BARRIE, Conrad	26	Friedrichstal	65-0243
BARSCHLER, Louise	52	Diedelsheim	64-1022
BARSTE, Theodor	28	Drensteinfurt	63-0693
Elisabeth 17			
BARTA, Jan	42	Boehmen	63-0862
BARTASCH, Adolph	35	America	63-0917
Amalie 40, Ad. 9, Rudolph 6			
BARTE, Joseph	32	Boehmen	63-0614
BARTEL, Maria	27	Boehmen	63-1218
Wenzel 2			
BARTEL, Regina	18	Ingolstadt	64-0363
BARTEL, Robert	25	Buchholz	67-0600
BARTELNER, Ferdin.	21	Sontheim	66-0650
BARTELS, Adelheid	20	Oberneuland	64-1161
BARTELS, Caroline	20	Luethorst	66-0221
BARTELS, Charlotte	20	Lutzenberg	66-0109
BARTELS, Christian	25	Kreutznach	65-0151
BARTELS, Christine	20	Bergfreiheit	64-1108
BARTELS, Elise	32	Braunschweig	66-1093
Johanna , Elise 5, Christian 3			
BARTELS, Fritz	15	Hannover	63-0822
BARTELS, Hermann	24	Ebersdorf	67-0007
BARTELS, Joh.	23	Fuchsendorf	65-0116
BARTELS, Sophie	28	Oberneuland	63-1218
BARTELT, Hulda	18	Preussen	63-0990
BARTENSTEIN, Salom	27	Roedelheim	65-0055
BARTH, Alfr.	21	Barmen	65-0898
BARTH, Anton	20	Westhausen	66-1327
BARTH, Carl Georg	43	Reuss-Greitz	66-1243
BARTH, Gregor	33	Preussen	66-0083
Josephine 30, Fransiska 4, Malwine 1			
BARTH, Heinr.	37	Dietendorf	64-0840
Caroline 31, August 7, Lina 5, Louise 4			
Friedr. 3			
BARTH, Jakob	21	Wuertemberg	63-1069
BARTH, Jest	43	Linkershausen	64-0495
Georg 34, Cath. 43, C.(f) 15, Peter 13			
Elisab. 5, Marg. 7, Jest 6, Johs. 3			
BARTH, Johann Geo.	28	Hafenprepach	66-0623
Dorothea 65			
BARTH, John	24	Sinkershausen	65-0055
Peter 38			
BARTH, Julius	59	Brostdorf	63-1085
BARTH, Louis	20	Camstadt	63-1136
BARTH, Nicolaus	30	Oberringelhm.	66-1327
BARTH, Rudolf	19	Marburg	65-1095
BARTH, Samuel	31	Baltimore	63-0862
BARTHE, Clement	35	France	63-1038
BARTHEL, Carl	24	Hildburghsn.	66-1155
BARTHELS, Christof	19	Horsten	65-1095
BARTHMER, Daniel	38	Willen	64-0885
BARTHOLD, Georg	29	Katus	63-0990
BARTHOLD, Louis	19	Dolgen	66-0679
BARTHOLD, Philipp	20	Gernsheim	66-0147
BARTHOLOMAE, Fritz	26	Bentheim	64-0904
Philippine 19, Christine 2			
BARTHOLOMAUS, Crln	20	Gettenbach	65-0948
BARTIG, Aug.	25		66-0650
Ernstine 21			
BARTIZAL, Adalbert	51	Budweiss	66-0837
Maria 37, Maria 10, Therese 6, Cath. 2			
BARTKOWSKY, Aug.	30	Posen	64-0432
Johanna 39, Joachim 5, Magdalena 15			
Caroline 3			
BARTLING, H.H.	17	Eggeberg	65-1189
BARTLING, Hermann	26	Hannover	66-1155
BARTLING, Johann	27	Wesselhoevede	65-0713
BARTMANN, George	25	Missouri	66-0984
BARTMANN, Simon	24	St. Louis	66-0934
BARTOLOME, Philipp	30	Chicago	66-0984
Sophia 20			
BARTOSCH, John	21	Boehmen	63-0752
BARTOSCH, Jos.	29	Bohemia	64-0782
Anna 26, Josefa 5, Margaretha 4, baby			
BARTSCHEER, Marie	19	Wellen	64-0331
Johanna 21			
BARZ, Carl Friedr.	24	Berlin	66-0837
BASCH, Pauline	30	Berlin	65-0402
BASCHDORFF, Alex	29	Schwerin	64-1206
BASQUE, Joseph	40	Muehlheim	63-0990
Adelaide 33, Alphous 9, Arthur 8, Minna 7			
BASSE, August	52	Crincy	64-0886
BASSE, Johann Ant.	19	Graubuenden	63-0693
BASSE, Sophie	22	Dielingen	64-0920
BASSE, Theodor	25	Hannort	65-0004
BASSEY, John	35	Indianapolis	63-0917
BASSIN, Otto	23	Weissenbrunn	63-1178
BASSINER, Bertha	19	Frauensee	63-0917
BASSLER, Albert	21	Waldkirch	64-0170
BAST, Nicolaus	34	Mengersheim	65-0151
BASTIAN, Louise	22	Bischoffen	65-0974
BASTIAN, W.(m)	26	Oldenburg	64-0331
BASTIN, Louis	18	Eberbach	64-1053
BATA, Joh.	36	Neusedel	66-0704
Anna 27, Joseph 5, Anna 8, Catharina 3			
Franziska 17			
BATA, Josepha	60	Marokote	66-0704
BATENHOP, Herm.	25	Strasburg	64-0170
BATER, Gertrude	21	Witzenhausen	66-0704
BATH, Ulrich	30	Torgau	66-1373
Rudolph 20			
BATHMANN, Cathar.	16	Lintig	66-0934
BATHMANN, Gesche	23	Fischerhude	66-0734
BATHMANN, Johs.	16	Bremen	64-0840
BATHMEYER, Engelh.	22	Stoermen	65-1030
BATRUNK, Carl Rob.	22	Leipzig	63-0053
BATSCHANG, Carl	23	Gochsheim	66-1155
BATT, Joh.	14	Calmbach	64-0214
BATTERMANN, Ed.	18	Bueckeburg	64-0495
BATTERMANN, Sophie	20	Prussia	64-0138
BATTMEYER, Anton	19	Leer	66-0083
BATZ, Adolf	20	Oberkaufungen	65-0950
BATZ, Elisabeth	24	Kaufungen	66-0934
BAUCH, Erdmann	29	Waldsachsen	64-0593
BAUDERMANN, Marg.	26	Coblenz	66-0734
BAUEN, F. (f)	53	Ziesar	64-0427
Marie 21			
BAUER, (m)	26	Benrath	63-1085
BAUER, A.G.(m)	15	Kirchheim	64-0331
Johanna 21			
BAUER, Abrah.	17	Schotten	63-0350
BAUER, Amalie	22	Wien	66-1031
BAUER, And.	35	Ambach	64-0992
Marie 47, Carl 7			
BAUER, Anna Maria	32	Schorndorf	65-0950
BAUER, Arnold C.	17	Affoltenbach	64-0886
BAUER, August	38	Gellersen	66-0934
Wilhelmine 33, August 9, Friedrich 4			
Wilhelm 9m			
BAUER, B.(m)	21	Zerbst	64-0023
BAUER, B.C.	23	Adelsberg	65-1088
BAUER, Balh.	20	Sungingen	63-1136
BAUER, Bapt.	23	Muenchen	65-0402
BAUER, Barbara	16	Hessberg	64-0214
BAUER, Benedict	74	Bavaria	66-0679
BAUER, C.	26	Kleinsbach	64-1161
BAUER, Carl	50	Harford	66-0704
BAUER, Carl	23	Mainz	66-1243
BAUER, Carl	21	Siefenheim	66-1131
BAUER, Carl	35	Gefill	65-0948
Johanne 36, Ernst 9, Robert 5, Fritz 5m			
Pauline 18, Minna 16			
BAUER, Carl	32	New York	64-0214
BAUER, Caroline	25	Schatten	63-0693
BAUER, Caspar	29	Steppach	64-0363
Peter 37			
BAUER, Catharina	24	Worms	66-0704
G. 2, Carl 16			
BAUER, Charles	43	Naumburg	66-1248
BAUER, Christ. A.	37	Goettingen	63-0822

NAME	AGE	RESIDENCE	YR-LIST
BAUER, Christian	5	Laufen	63-1069
BAUER, Conrad	28	Heiligenstadt	64-0170
BAUER, Eduard	19	Reichenbach	63-0097
BAUER, Emma	19	Hildburghsn.	65-0974
BAUER, F.(m)	23	Harthausen	64-0331
BAUER, Fanny	17	Eschelberg	64-0331
BAUER, Fr.	26	Braunschweig	63-1085
BAUER, Franciska	28	Heidingsfeld	65-0950
BAUER, Franz	26	Hausen	66-0578
BAUER, Friedercke	60	Louisville	66-0734
BAUER, Georg	32	Hannover	66-0221
BAUER, Georg	25	Wien	66-0576
BAUER, Georg	29	Zeisenhaus	64-0992
BAUER, Georg	18	Rothenburg	66-1327
BAUER, Gottf.	21	Oberkind	64-0992
BAUER, Heinr.	27	Chicago	64-0170
BAUER, Heinrich	29	Orb	64-0433
BAUER, Heinrich	37	Haselbach	65-1189
BAUER, Henriette	22	Lehe	65-1024
BAUER, Hyronimus	18	Ottenhofen	66-1155
BAUER, Jacob	19	Hofernwailer	66-1243
BAUER, Jettchen	20	Schotten	63-1136
BAUER, Joh.	21	Wuerttemberg	66-0576
BAUER, Joh. Jan	33	Oberwalden	64-1053
Sophie 26, Elise 9m, Anna 59			
Joh. Gottl. 40			
BAUER, Joh. Ulrich	26	Osweil	66-1127
BAUER, Johann	23	Altendiez	66-0576
BAUER, Johann	25	Egglofstein	64-1022
BAUER, Johanna	22	Sax.-Meiningn	64-0432
BAUER, Joseph	8	Kirchheimbol.	66-0109
BAUER, Joseph	24	Hanau	63-1085
BAUER, Julius	15	Naila	64-0938
BAUER, Loeb.	22	Schotten	64-0840
BAUER, Louise	23	Giessen	66-1127
Louise 3m			
BAUER, Ludwig	61	Gellersen	66-0934
Melsine 60, Wilhelm 26			
BAUER, Maria	26	Brunsbach	66-1131
BAUER, Mart.	20	Gerlachsheim	63-0350
BAUER, Mathilde	22	Ulm	66-0704
BAUER, Mathilde	17	Zellerfeld	66-0704
BAUER, Max	35	Wien	65-0007
Cath. 34			
BAUER, Moritz	18	Lehe	63-0822
BAUER, Pauline	25	Mechenhard	65-1030
BAUER, Peter	24	Dahlenfeld	65-0243
BAUER, Rudolph	24	Goeppingen	66-1031
Elise 22			
BAUER, Sophie	18	Holzmaden	66-0221
Gottl. 18			
BAUER, Susanne	26	Philadelphia	64-0073
baby 9m			
BAUER, Ulricke	26	New York	63-0917
Hermine 8m			
BAUER, Valentin	25	Gemmersdorf	67-0007
BAUER, Wilhelm	25	Stuttgart	66-0837
BAUERFELD, Friedr.	23	Wundersleben	64-0593
William 17			
BAUERLE, Friedr.	33	Baden	66-0576
BAUERSACHS, Frdr.	30	Sonneberg	64-0495
BAUERSCHMIDT, Anna	23	Wambach	64-1022
BAUERSCHMIDT, Joh.	18	Graefenberg	64-0687
BAUERSCHMIDT, Joh.	26	Wandbock	64-1022
BAUGHARD, Leopold	16	Seckingen	64-0343
BAUHAUS, Anton	40	Rhede	66-0704
Christine 26, Johannes 5, Bernhard 2			
Franciska 6m			
BAUHOLZER, Joh.	16	Feckenhausen	64-0687
BAUK, Margarethe		Heimersberg	66-1327
BAULE, Heinrich	27	Soehre	67-0007
BAULE, Johannes	24	Sillium	67-0007
BAUM, Anton	59	Punderich	63-1038
BAUM, Catharina	18	Osnabrueck	66-1127
BAUM, Christine	21	Biedesheim	63-1136
BAUM, Isaac	25	Nonweiler	64-1022
BAUM, Jacob	60	Biedesheim	65-0007
BAUM, Joh. Gg.	23	Auggen	63-1038
BAUM, Maier	30	Ossau	64-0782
BAUM, Mathias	35	Kattendorf	66-0221
BAUM, Sophie	22	Nordheim	65-0770
BAUM, Wilhelm	19	Iba	66-0576
BAUMANN, A.W.	40	Moordorf	63-1069
BAUMANN, Adam	27	Unterschental	64-0992
BAUMANN, Aug.	30	New Zell	66-0413
BAUMANN, August	23	Wuerehowa	66-0469
Henriette 52, Hermann 22			
BAUMANN, Barbara	38	Bavaria	63-0822
BAUMANN, Carl	17	Frendelberg	66-0934
BAUMANN, Caroline	28	Hasselfelde	63-0482
BAUMANN, Christian	16	Grossasbach	63-0482
BAUMANN, Christine	24	Carlsfeld	64-0593
BAUMANN, Eilert	24	Firrel	66-1248
BAUMANN, Fr.	34	New Orleans	63-0953
BAUMANN, G.	27	Rosenbeck	65-0974
BAUMANN, Heinr.	18	Heinade	65-0243
BAUMANN, Henriette	24	Waldstetten	64-0739
BAUMANN, Jac.	24	Cassel	64-0992
Regina 23			
BAUMANN, Joh Alb.	23	Ockum	65-0189
BAUMANN, Leonhard	26	Gelnhausen	64-0938
BAUMANN, Ludw.	20	Heibronn	63-1010
BAUMANN, Ludwig	28	New York	66-0934
BAUMANN, Margareth	21	Selsryk	65-1031
BAUMANN, Maria	23	Lottheim	66-0666
BAUMANN, Minna	20	Kirchhardt	64-0331
BAUMANN, Minna	20	Dissen	66-1128
BAUMANN, P.	18	Steisslingen	64-0782
BAUMANN, Robert	18	Frankfurt a/m	66-1248
BAUMANN, Rod.	23	Juersch	63-0821
BAUMANN, Walpur	44	Staufen/Pr.	65-0116
BAUMANN, Wm.	29	Schwiesheim	64-1053
Anna 28			
BAUMBACH, Johann	30	Beyreuth	66-0109
BAUMBERGER, Felix	27	Riesbach	63-0296
BAUMEISTER, E.	20	Balingen	63-1003
BAUMEISTER, Georg	58	Bahlingen	65-0243
BAUMEISTER, Paulin	20	Wuertemberg	66-0984
BAUMER, Franziska	50	Hoboken	65-1088
BAUMER, Kauwald	30	Germany	63-0953
BAUMEYER, Franz A.	24	Ob.Schaffhsn.	63-0551
BAUMGAERTNER, A.	46	Baltimore	63-1038
BAUMGAERTNER, Cath	21	Langenbruecke	65-0116
BAUMGAERTNER, Frz.	43	Buocht	63-0551
Josepha 36			
BAUMGAERTNER, Hch.	28	Staudenbuehl	66-0469
BAUMGAERTNER, Sam.	23	Niederwyl	64-0840
BAUMGAERTNER, Wilh	26	Oberkirchen	67-0007
BAUMGARDT, Anna C.	46	Curhessen	63-0822
Johannes 18			
BAUMGARDT, Oscar H	21	Cassel	63-1178
BAUMGART, Amalie	22	Naumburg	66-0349
BAUMGART, Augusta	19	Voelkershsn.	66-1031
BAUMGART, Lotte	18	Lohrwitz	64-0782
L. 16			
BAUMGART, Wm.	25	Darmen	64-0782
BAUMGARTEN, Franz	21	Wisconsin	66-0734
BAUMGARTEN, Henr't	24	Eisenberg	66-1373
BAUMGARTEN, Nic.	35	Bobendorf	66-0346
Maria 24, Anna 2			
BAUMGARTEN, Plato	33	Mackenzell	66-0349
BAUMGARTEN, Steph.	36	Boehmen	66-0221
Therese 31, Anton 3, Stephan 2, Joseph 2m			
BAUMGARTNER, Carol	26	Sachsenhein	64-0433
BAUMGARTNER, Rose	21	Hersfolingen	63-1085
BAUMGARTNER, Xaver	13	Martlingen	64-1108
BAUMHOEFER, Wilh.	19	Merberg	66-0734
BAUMKOETTER, Clem.	31	New York	66-0679
BAUMRUCKA, Johann	22	Staab	66-1373
BAUMSTARK, Bernhd.	15	Rothenfels	66-0704
BAUMUELLER, Ferd.	21	Zedlitz	66-0668
BAURMEISTER, Wilh.	22	Obermehle	64-0363
BAUSCHULTE, Christ	22	Ledde	65-0948
BAUSENER, Franz	20	Mainz	64-1022
BAUSMANN, Philpine	23	Neustadt	64-1206
BAUSS, Marg. Elis.	26	Regenhausen	66-0650

NAME	AGE	RESIDENCE	YR-LIST
Christine 20, Melchior 26, Tobias 25			
BAUSSANCOURT, Adam	16	Muehlhofen	65-0402
BAUSSANCOURT, Nath	64	Ingelnheim	64-0639
Elisab. 57, Eva 20			
BAUTE, Ludwig	21	Oldendorf	66-1031
BAUTH, Elisabeth	24	Memshardt	67-0007
Franz 17			
BAUTHE, Ernst Hr.	25	Minden	65-1031
Johanna 21, Heinrich 1			
BAUTLE, Elisabeth	22	Strassberg	63-0917
BAUTLER, Louis	24	Mariendorf	66-1248
BAVERUNGEN, Friedr	35	Luechtringen	63-0296
BAY, Caroline	23	Spatzenhof	64-0427
Christine 15, Louise 18			
BAY, Erdmann	52	Wuepau	64-0840
BAYER, Anna Cath.	18	Frankenberg	64-0456
BAYER, Caspar	23	Schnedheim	64-0886
BAYER, Engelbert	24	Geismar	66-1243
BAYER, Friedr.	36	St. Louis	66-0984
Eduard 34, Helene 22			
BAYER, G.A.	25	Remlingen	66-0221
BAYERMANN, Elisab.	19	Bavaria	66-0679
BAYFELD, J.	17	Lubrance	64-0639
BAYHA, Minna	25	Stuttgart	63-0551
BAYR, Conrad	57	Berlin	64-0593
Maria 55			
BAYTA, Catharina	26	Mittelstadt	66-0934
BEAR, Bernhard	29	New York	64-0427
Christian 30, Bertha 18			
BEAUPAIN, Johannes	34	Frankenberg	66-0577
Peter 17, Johannes 9			
BEAURON, Sag.	60	Switz	63-0015
BEAUZY, Barbara	23	Hessen	66-0109
Sybilla 5, Barbara 3			
BECCARD, Fr.	23	Waldau	65-0402
BECHE, auf der Wh.	27	Osnabrueck	65-0770
BECHER, Wilhelm	23	Meininghausen	64-0886
BECHLE, Caroline	32	Greiz	66-1093
Joseph 5, Anna 3, Ernestine 9			
BECHLER, Georg	23	Schwiesheim	64-1053
BECHLINGER, Conrad		Bieber	63-1218
Catharine , Andreas , Catharine			
Catharine , Ludwig , Conrad			
Elisabeth 5, Christian 3, Louise inf			
BECHSOLDT, Georg	25	Schotten	64-0840
BECHSTEIN, Paul	18	Ludwigsburg	64-0214
BECHT, Johann	30	Pern	66-1031
BECHT, Peter	43	New Orleans	63-1038
BECHTE, Christian	20	Wildbad	67-0007
BECHTEL, Augusta	22	France	63-1038
BECHTEL, Joseph	16	Niederhulz	66-1031
BECHTHOLD, Anna	19	Rainrod	64-0363
BECHTHOLD, Caspar	21	Neusig	65-0594
BECHTHOLD, John	22	Merkenfritz	63-0482
John 9			
BECHTHOLD, Louis	31	New York	66-0679
BECHTHOLD, Peter	43	Emsdorf	64-0739
Freube 18, Christine 16, Lina 13			
Carsten 18, Fockea 15, Woeckea 7			
Swantje 3			
BECHTHOLD, Reinh.	21	Schotten	66-1127
BECHTLE, John Geo.	35	Philadelphia	63-1178
BECHTLER, Friedr.	30	Buedingen	63-0953
BECHTOLD, Wilh'mne	27	Stornfels	64-0593
BECHTOLL, Heinrich	46	Dutenhafen	65-1024
Cathar. 34, Louise 8, Heinrich 5			
Catharine 3, August 2m			
BECK, Carl	33	Baldrechten	64-0023
BECK, Carl	20	Nuertingen	64-1053
BECK, Cathrine		Dettingen	63-1218
Pauline 15			
BECK, Chr.	23	Raaber	67-0600
BECK, Deog.	49	Muenchen	64-1161
BECK, Diedr.	39	New York	63-0862
BECK, Elisabeth	46	Gmuenden	66-1128
BECK, Eustachius	18	Grosselfingen	66-1313
BECK, Franz	47	New York	63-0398
BECK, Friederike	36	Springfield	66-0109

NAME	AGE	RESIDENCE	YR-LIST
Waldama 9			
BECK, Friedr	32	Osweil	65-0594
Anna 24, Wilhelm 10m, Cath 28, Friedr. 6			
Jac. 4, Wilhelmine 10m			
BECK, Gerh.	72	Jever	64-0687
BECK, Heinr.	30	California	64-0687
BECK, Heinr.	28	Friesmerberg	65-0243
BECK, Heinrich	40	Gruenenplan	63-0097
BECK, Heinrich	22	Metzingen	65-1088
BECK, Henry	28	New York	64-0363
BECK, J.G.(m)	53	Meisenheim	64-0363
BECK, Jacob	44	Lixfeld	66-0578
Catharine 42, Catharine 9, Jacob 7			
Margarethe 5			
BECK, James	31	Muehlberg	63-1085
BECK, Joh. Georg	21	Bitz	66-1373
BECK, John	23	United States	63-0953
BECK, Josefa	55	Ruolfingen	65-0594
BECK, Katlin	25	Carlstadt	64-0938
BECK, Ludwig	28	Altdorf/Bad.	65-0950
BECK, Marie	18	Obermerle	64-0840
BECK, Pauline	22	Bitz	65-1024
Adolph 16			
BECK, Rudolph	30	Kenzingen	66-0109
BECK, Wilhelm	24	Ravensburg	65-0151
BECKARDT, Anton	25	Neuenkirchen	63-0015
BECKAY, Theodor	35	Emden	65-1095
BECKEL, Louis	25	Stuttgart	65-0594
BECKEMEIER, Louise	59	Luebbecke	64-0432
Caroline 21, Wilhelm 17			
BECKEN, Georg C.	46	Wittmund	66-0623
BECKER, Marie	31	Ruethersdorf	66-0934
BECKER, Adam	24	Simmern	63-1136
BECKER, Alexander	17	Altenstadt	66-0984
BECKER, Amadeus	20	Freiss	66-1128
BECKER, Anton	17	Oppershofen	66-1155
BECKER, Aug.	24	Wolfenhausen	65-0594
Mathilda 19, Mathilda 1, Henriette 23			
BECKER, August	27	Grossalmerode	64-0433
BECKER, Barbara	24	Oberlimbach	66-1248
BECKER, Bertha	9	Hesse Homburg	63-0015
BECKER, Carl	29	Ostheim	66-0650
BECKER, Carl	14	Obergleen	64-1053
BECKER, Caspar	33	Wolfenbuettel	64-0938
Helene 26, Heinr. 2, Elise 11m			
BECKER, Cath.	57	Hanau	65-1189
Franz 18, Adolph 7, Manchen 5			
BECKER, Charles	33	Philadelphia	66-0221
BECKER, Charlotte	23	Dehme	65-0007
BECKER, Chr. Jos.	29	Hildesheim	67-0599
Sophie 29			
BECKER, Christian	28	Zwingenberg	63-0614
Christiane 27, Peter 2			
BECKER, Christina	19	Reimenroh	66-0578
BECKER, Christine	42	Liedolsheim	64-0363
Ludwig 14, Wilhelm 9, Sophie 17			
BECKER, Claus	41	Jever	66-0147
BECKER, Clemens	24	Seidewitz	64-0363
BECKER, Diedr.	18	Neuenhuelsted	64-0593
BECKER, Diedrich	20	Bahlum	66-1031
BECKER, Eduard	25	Cassel	64-0214
BECKER, Elis.	20	Gontershausen	64-0214
BECKER, Elisab.	28	Kurhessen	64-0432
BECKER, Elise	24	Rheinpfalz	66-0576
Anna 17			
BECKER, Elise	18	Eschbach	64-0214
BECKER, Ernst	27	Darmstadt	63-0097
BECKER, Francis	30	Alsenborn	63-0244
BECKER, Friedrich	33	Waidenhausen	66-1203
BECKER, Georg	29	Cincinnati	64-0073
BECKER, Georg	23	Eimsheim	63-1218
BECKER, Georg	42	Cassel	66-0704
Elisabeth 58			
BECKER, Georg	24	Lippstadt	66-1155
BECKER, Gerh. Hch.	21	Haste	63-1010
BECKER, Heinrich	21	Bremervoerde	64-0840
BECKER, Helene	20	Meyesack	64-0138
BECKER, Henry	32	New York	63-0551

NAME	AGE	RESIDENCE	YR-LIST
BECKER, Herm.	23	Voerden	64-1022
BECKER, Herm.	18	Haseluene	66-1203
BECKER, Hermann	31	Aerzen	63-0482
BECKER, J.	23	Dehren	65-1189
BECKER, Jacob	29	Basel	64-0495
BECKER, Jacob	39	Raunheim	65-0151
BECKER, Joh.	24	Ruppertsberg	65-0594
BECKER, Johann H.	19	Elberfeld	66-0412
BECKER, Johanna	21	Nienbergen	65-0974
BECKER, Johanna	24	Oldenburg	64-0363
BECKER, Johannes	23	Hessloh	65-0770
Elisabeth 25			
BECKER, Johannes	22	Oberafleiden	64-0363
BECKER, John	25	Frohnhausen	66-1155
BECKER, Josephine	22	Gich	66-0704
BECKER, Josephine	21	Fritzlar	64-0593
BECKER, Jost	20	Dildershaus	64-0593
Anna 23			
BECKER, Justus	17	Altenbusch	66-1373
BECKER, Lisette	24	Lienen	65-1189
BECKER, Louise	23	Westphalen	66-0469
BECKER, Ludwig	70	Amelith	63-1069
Louise 61, Sophie 33			
BECKER, Maria	42	Oldendorf	64-0840
BECKER, Marie	26		66-0734
BECKER, Nannchen	22	Himbach	66-1327
BECKER, Nic.	23	Bischofsthron	65-0007
BECKER, O.L.(m)	21	Braunschweig	63-0097
BECKER, Pauline	30	Osterode	66-1127
BECKER, Peter	30	Quebec	64-0138
BECKER, Peter	39	Pfungstadt	66-0734
BECKER, Rosa	19	Altenstadt	65-0055
BECKER, Simon	38	Friesenheim	65-1088
Sophia 36, Leonhard 2			
BECKER, Sophie	28	Waldshut	66-1203
BECKER, Theodor	32	Hilckenbach	63-0244
BECKER, Theodor	30	Zuechlichau	66-0668
BECKER, Therese	50	Washington	63-0862
Georg 7			
BECKER, W.	38	Lissa	64-0782
BECKER, Wilhelm	31	Westphalen	63-0398
BECKER, Ziborah	39	Doernbach	64-1108
Lion 74, Caroline 11, Jacob 9, Heinrich 5			
Bertha 4, Marie 3, Rosamunde 1m			
BECKERMANN, J.	54	Verden	63-1218
BECKERT, Regina	27	Friedrichshaf	65-1088
BECKES, Johannes	27	Oberafleiden	64-0214
BECKMANN, A.M.	19	Cappeln/Hann	65-0038
BECKMANN, Alex.	24	Seesem	65-0243
Pauline 22, Marie 2m, Maria 59			
BECKMANN, Anna	23	Oeren	66-0578
BECKMANN, Anton	20	Legden	66-0623
BECKMANN, August	18	Tecklenborg	67-0007
BECKMANN, Bernhard	52	Verden	65-0950
Anna maria 50, Bernhard 25, Anna Cath. 23			
Anna 10, Agnes 20			
BECKMANN, Carl	25	Otterndorf	66-0576
BECKMANN, Carol.	20	Versmold	63-0953
BECKMANN, Caroline	21	Hummerten	66-0576
BECKMANN, Christ.	35	Itzehoe	64-1022
Heinr. 14, Wm. 24, Marie 19			
BECKMANN, Diedrich	50	Estorf	66-1031
Sophie 22, Minna 18, Diedrich 13			
BECKMANN, Diedrich	26	Freiburg	66-1128
BECKMANN, Franz	36	St. Paul	66-0934
Marie 22			
BECKMANN, Gottlieb	22	Oberneuland	66-0668
BECKMANN, Heinrich	19	Exter	66-0576
BECKMANN, Heinrich	26	Rahden	65-1088
BECKMANN, Henry W.	23	Drecke	63-1178
BECKMANN, Herrmann	23	Waltrup	65-0770
BECKMANN, Joh.	23	Prussia	64-0170
BECKMANN, Jos.	24	Mettigen	63-1010
BECKMANN, Lina	24	Bremervoerde	66-0578
BECKMANN, Marie	26	Tilsen	63-0953
Joh. Fr. 17, John Herm. 9			
BECKMANN, Wilh.	25	Eschershausen	66-0650
BECKMANN, Wm.	21	Harrishausen	64-0427

NAME	AGE	RESIDENCE	YR-LIST
BECKMEIER, Carl	43	Huellhorst	65-0189
Sophie 17, Ludwig 7			
BECKONET, Heinrich	25	Emsdetten	66-0576
BECKORT, August	16	Wolbeck	66-1031
Wilhelm 15			
BECKSOLDT, Cath.	59	Scholten	64-0840
BECKSTEIN, Georg	30	Oberngeis	66-0668
Anna 30, Elisabeth 18, Anna 17, Conrad 14			
Heinrich 7, Marie 9, Caroline 5			
BECKUM, Henriette	23	Essen	64-1206
BEDCKE, Carl	26	Treptow/Pr.	65-0038
Hanna 22, Hermann 11m			
BEEDMANN, B.E.	31	Boston	64-0023
BEEKER, Johannes	25	Eschwege	66-1093
BEENKE, Margarethe	23	Intschede	66-0704
BEER, Abrah.	23	Buchau	66-0576
BEER, Louis	25	New York	66-0147
BEER, Marc	15	Koschnitz	64-0992
Hirsch 17			
BEER, Minna	39	Soest	66-1127
Lisette 8			
BEER, Salomon	18	Baden	67-0007
BEER. Jette	16	Frankfurt	66-0469
BEERGER, Wilh.	28	Seggensen	66-0349
BEERMANN, Bernhard	32	Berlin	63-0990
BEERMINK, Berend	24	Hesepe	65-1024
BEEZ, Chr.	35	Eisfeld	65-0974
Robert 19			
BEGEMANN, Elle(m)	27	Aurich	64-0456
BEGERMANN, Lucas	38	Hannover	63-0821
BEGERS, Anna	22	Bremen	64-0363
BEGSTERMANN, Bernh	28	Osnabrueck	66-1093
Heinrich 25, Friedrich 19			
BEHLE, H.	16	Vasbeck	65-1189
BEHLING, Gustav	32	Quebec	63-0482
BEHLING, Heinrich	18	Helmarshausen	66-0934
BEHLING, Joh.	50	Kalberg	66-0577
Louise 47, Bertha 17, August 13			
Wilhelmine 10			
BEHM, Louis	26	New York	63-0097
Heinr. 29			
BEHMANN, Henry	23	Petershagen	63-0296
BEHME, Louise	29	Haevern	63-0821
BEHMER, Henry	36	St. Louis	63-0244
BEHNE, Joh. H.	25	Spaan	63-0482
Margar. 22			
BEHNEMANN, Heinr.	24	Bremerhafen	66-0623
BEHNKE, Peter W.	18	Ostervanna	63-1010
BEHNKEN, Hch.	27	New York	64-0363
Hedwig 15			
BEHNKEN, Johann	19	N. Buelstedt	66-1127
BEHNKEN, Johanna	22	Bremen	64-0363
BEHNKEN, Marie	14	Hannover	65-1024
BEHR, C.	40	Hannover	63-1178
BEHR, Christian	51	Loebenstein	66-0734
Louise 44, Louise 22, Marie 19			
Heinrich 13, Ida 9, Anton 6, Bertha 4			
BEHR, Christian	21	Loebenstein	66-0734
BEHR, Franz	25	Curhessen	66-0934
BEHR, Wm. Heinr. E	24	Osnabrueck	66-0704
BEHRE, Carl	23	Dolhausen	66-1313
BEHREN, v. Christ.	59	Westphalen	66-1031
Anna 57, Christian 35, Caroline 34			
Heinrich 3, Christian 9			
BEHREND, Berend A.	32	Wiesens	66-1128
Trintje 25, Anna 2, Albert 6m			
BEHREND, Dora	35	Berlin	64-0687
Lina 26			
BEHREND, Wilhelm	31	Sautin	67-0599
BEHRENDER, Carl	27	Ekenhausen	65-1030
BEHRENDS, Fritz	20	Oberneuland	65-0594
BEHRENDT, Marie	37	Stralsund	66-0704
Louise 13			
BEHRENS, Anton	26	Alverdissen	65-1088
Elise 28			
BEHRENS, Claus	21	Sudweyhe	64-0214
H.(m) 17			
BEHRENS, Diedr.	30	Bremen	67-0007

NAME	AGE	RESIDENCE	YR-LIST
BEHRENS, Diedrich	22	Zeven	66-0623
Johann 18			
BEHRENS, Fr. W.	28	Vollbuettel	63-1178
BEHRENS, Friedrich	21	Alverdissen	66-0984
BEHRENS, Fritz	25	Muenster	67-0600
BEHRENS, G.W.	30	Hohenkirchen	66-0413
Altine 30, Johanna 8, Anna 6			
Friederike 4, Margarethe 2, Marie 25			
BEHRENS, Gesche	18	Fischerhude	66-1031
BEHRENS, H.	21	Stuckenbostel	64-1161
BEHRENS, Heinr.	22	Kloppenburg	64-0432
BEHRENS, Heinr.	19	Rotenburg	64-0739
Friedr. 14			
BEHRENS, Heinrich	72	Padingbuettel	66-0934
BEHRENS, Heinrich	19	Oldendorf	66-1128
BEHRENS, Henry	30	Duesseldorf	63-1136
Josepha 25			
BEHRENS, Ilse	22	Peine	63-0990
BEHRENS, Joh.	17	Oldenburg	66-0469
BEHRENS, John	21	Langen	63-0752
BEHRENS, Le.(f)	21	Braunschweig	64-0331
BEHRENS, Marie	20	Ippensen	66-1155
BEHRENS, Martin	26	Bremen	64-0456
BEHRENS, Meta	18	Hannover	65-1189
BEHRENS, Peter	21	Bodenstedt	64-0992
BEHRENS, Wilhelm	30	Wolfenbuettel	64-0639
BEHRENTZ, Wilhelm	27	Erfurt	66-0412
BEHRINGER, Theodor	18	Stuttgart	66-1127
BEHRLE, Fr.	22	Offenburg	64-0427
BEHRMANN, Heinr.	28	Fuerstenau	64-0214
BEHRMANN, Louise	18	Hannover	66-1373
BEHRYE, Sophie	19	Westerstede	66-0704
BEICHTER, Carl Wm.	20	Solingen	63-0822
BEIER, Jacob	40	Wittjenborn	64-0456
Marg. 35, Marg. 10, Cunigunda 7			
Ferdinand 1			
BEIERMANN, Bernh.		Fuersteuberg	66-1093
BEIL, Catharine	21	Schusterthal	65-0055
BEILEN, Emil	26	Berlin	64-0363
BEILING, Margar.	20	Eichloch	66-0412
BEILING, Maria	24	Woerstadt	65-0116
BEINHAUER, Christ.	24	Melsungen	67-0806
BEINHAUER, Elisab.	20	Melsungen	65-0713
BEINING, F.	25	Solingen	66-0413
BEINKE, Clara	18	Minden	65-1031
BEISER, Leonhard	14	Neckarstein	67-0007
BEISHEIM, Peter	31	Curhessen	63-0822
BEISHEIN, Henrich	37	Heringa	64-0433
Catharina 41			
BEISNER, Friedr.	19	Holtensen	66-1203
BEISSEL, Henry	28	Schweiz	63-0953
BEISTERBERG, Heinr	21	Schwarme	66-1248
BEITZ, Carl	23	Huttingen	65-0004
BEJACH, Floro	17	Zempelburg	66-1127
BEKER, Barbara	23	Grosenlueder	66-0469
BELASCHAUT, Jos. W	35	Boehmen	66-0349
Joseph 19			
BELINA, Franz	42	Boehmen	63-0917
Pauline 44, Pauline 17, Anna 7, Josepha 9			
Rosalie 2m			
BELING, G.A.	45	Bremen	64-0593
BELING, Heinrich	22	Brenken	66-0576
BELKER, Jacob	17	Brumstadt	66-1327
BELLENGER, M.(m)	35	Mexico	64-0073
BELLER, John Anton	24	Moehringen	66-1155
BELLERSTEIN, Bernh	25	Arnsberg	66-0679
BELLING, Friedrich	28	Urasch	66-1093
BELLM, Carl	23	Langenbrueken	66-1327
BELLMANN, Helene	24	Debbern	64-1053
BELLMANN, Louis	22	Raumland	66-0734
BELMOND, Leopold	27	Baden	64-1053
BELTZ, Catharina	18	Mainz	66-1031
Francisca 15			
BELY, Wenzel	25	Boehmen	64-0023
BELZ, Ant.	29	Philippsburg	66-1243
BELZ, Maria	19	Dexbach	66-0221
BELZ, Marie	20	Berghofen	66-1155
BELZEUER, Johann	7	Leivinstadt	64-0840

NAME	AGE	RESIDENCE	YR-LIST
BEMBOHN, Marie	18	Lingen	65-0865
BEMGER, G.	27	Lemfoerde	63-1085
Tiene 26, Venne 6			
BEMIG, Fr.	79	Baiern	63-1178
BENCKE, Otto	17	Holtrup	66-0679
BENDA, Jacob	39	Boehmen	66-0221
BENDEL, Bernh.	17	Oldenburg	64-0073
BENDER, Catharina		Marburg	66-1373
BENDER, Conrad	29	Kallstadt	64-1022
BENDER, Elisabeth	23	Erbach	65-1030
BENDER, Elise	24	Frankenthal	63-0551
BENDER, Georg	30	Hungen	66-0934
BENDER, Georg Jos.	24	Vallendar	63-0482
BENDER, Helene	36	Wiesbaden	66-1373
Louischen 8			
BENDER, Ludw.	36	Bahlingen	66-1313
BENDER, Margareth	29	Bechtolsheim	63-1218
BENDER, Mich.	18	Wachbach	65-0974
BENDER, P.	41	Rockelshausen	64-0782
Adolphina 40, Jacob 7, Anton 6, Wilhelm 5			
Anna 4m			
BENDER, Wilhelm	21	Nordhausen	64-0840
Robert 19			
BENDER, Wilhelmine	20	Oldenburg	64-0170
BENDERT, Louise	30	Wuerth	65-1030
BENDHEIM, D.	15	Darmstadt	63-1178
BENDL, Andr.	37	Boehmen	63-0821
Anna 40, Wenzislaus 9, Joseph 4, Maria 6			
Anton 8, John 11			
BENECKER, Heinrich	15	Bremerlehe	66-0577
BENEDICT, Emil	28	New York	66-0221
BENEDICT, Friedr.	30	Kella	66-0679
BENEDICT, Friedr.	24	New York	66-0679
Pauline 20			
BENEDICT, Loew	58	Carlsbad	65-0594
Phil. 7			
BENEKE, Diedrich	31	Braunschweig	66-1248
BENEKER, Caroline	16	Lehe	66-0837
BENENCKEN, Diedr.	24	New York	64-0432
BENESCH, Franz	17	Neusedel	66-0704
Joseph 19, Franz 51, Maria 51			
BENFER, Elisabeth	18	Bernburg	66-0577
BENG, Severin	16	Offenburg	64-0687
BENGERT, Fr.	24	Vasbeck	65-1189
Elisabeth 18			
BENICKENDORF, Jul.	30	Berlin	66-0109
BENIER, George	18	Paris	63-0917
BENISCH, Augusta	41	Pressburg	66-0934
Laura 21, Johann			
BENISCH, Joh.	42	Pressburg	65-0243
Joseph 17, Elisabeth 14, Maria 34, Joh. 5			
Franz 4, Maria 10m			
BENJAMIN, Freerk	38	Loquard	66-0349
Hauk 31, Simon 3			
BENJAMIN, Johanna	17	Bleckede	65-0402
BENJAMIN, Moritz	34	Vienna	66-0679
Catharina 24, Victor 10m			
BENJUS, Sophia	18	Reinheim	63-1136
BENKE, Joh.	32	Berlin	65-0243
BENKEN, Joh.	21	Hannover	64-0427
BENKER, Johann	22	Asch	66-0734
BENNDORF, H.	18	Hohenkirchen	65-0116
BENNER, Edw.	23	Hespenthal	64-0023
BENNER, Johann	39	Gilgelsdorf	66-0346
Rosalie 29, Johann 5, Maria 1			
BENNER, Otto	21	Reddighausen	66-0668
Reinh. 17			
BENNER, Waldburg	24	Wahlwies	67-0007
Constantina 19			
BENNESCH, Joseph	40	Boehmen	66-0221
Elisabeth 39, Anna 18, Joseph 7, Maria 5			
BENNING, Joh.	19	Fehlen	66-0349
BENNING, Magd.	13	Osthofen	63-0953
BENNINGSEN, G(m)	37	New York	64-0023
BENROTH, Heinr.	22	Oppenhiem	64-0427
BENS, Johann H.	58	Muehlheim	66-0623
Catharine 40, Lisette 20, Catharine 18			
Joseph 17, Wilhelm 13, Johann 2			

NAME	AGE	RESIDENCE	YR-LIST
BENSE, Minna	24	Hoexter	65-0402
BENSEL, Adam	51	New Orleans	63-0990
Elisabeth 47, John 22, Georg 9			
Barbara 36, Catharina 8, Margaretha 33			
Henry 14, Catharine 9, Mary 7			
Catharine 20			
BENSEN, Adelheid	19	Lintig	66-0934
BENSEN, Conrad	17	Hitzeln	66-1373
BENSER, Christian	19	Untertuerkhm.	67-0007
BENSER, Elisabeth	18	Bernburg	66-0577
BENSHAUSEN, Friedr	18	Hagen	66-0734
BENSING, Maria	28	Melle	66-0984
BENSSIN, Peter	31	Grosspeistar	65-0713
Anna 32			
BENSTEDT, Rosalie	30	Gernrode	65-0950
BENSTEIN, Joseph	42	Milwaukee	63-1085
BENTE, Fr.	38	Bremen	65-0189
Gustav 4			
BENTE, Henry	32	New York	63-0917
BENTE, N.	27	Bremen	63-1003
M. 26, C. 4, E. 2			
BENTHEIM, Aug.	30	Schweiz	63-1136
BENTHEIM, Metje	29	Hannover	66-0577
BENTSCHE, Joseph	68	Carlsruhe	64-0886
BENZ, Chas.	30	United States	63-1038
BENZ, Na.	22	Reutlingen	66-1155
BENZEL, Albert	38	Moschitz	66-0578
Hermann 12			
BENZEL, R.	22	Holzmaden	65-0974
BENZIGER, J.	43	Heiden	64-0782
Elsbeth 33			
BEPPLER, Georg	36	Allendorf	65-0594
BEPPLER, Joh. Mart	24	Deilingen	66-1313
BERAN, John	38	Boehmen	63-0482
Clara 37, Clara 7, Ottilie 5			
BERBERT, Georg	19	Darmstadt	63-0614
BERCK, John	33	Erzhausen	63-1136
BERCKHOF, G.H.	30	Leer	63-0693
BERDING, Wilhelm	23	Vechta	64-0920
BERENBERG, Bertha	29	Meinershagen	66-1327
BEREND, Carl	26	Oberbenbach	66-1327
BERENDS, Claas C.	35	Ostfriesland	64-0214
Juergendina 35, Berends 9, Geerds 8			
Bernhard 6, Aje 2			
BERENDS, Gerriet	20	Wiesens	66-1128
Anna 53, Aaltje 24, Albertina 6m			
BERENDS, Hermann	26	Hannover	66-0679
BERENSMEYER, J.H.	32	Quincy	63-1010
Pauline 9m			
BERES, Joh. Christ	26	Nassau	65-0007
BERG, Aug.(m)	23	Buxtehude	64-0331
BERG, August	44	Kl. Freden	63-0244
E. 50			
BERG, Elsb.	19	Broeckelsbach	64-0782
Eva 22			
BERG, Franz	28	Mildenen	64-0992
BERG, Gustav	35	Offenbach	64-0992
Sarah 34, Caroline 7, Emil 11m			
BERG, Heinrich	24	Rademin	63-0614
BERG, Jacob	24	Langendiebach	66-1327
BERG, Johanna	10	Obrigneim	64-0495
BERG, Moritz	16	Burgebach	66-1327
BERG, Nathan	26	Offenberg	63-0953
BERG, Nickolaus	47	Weschnitz	63-1069
BERG, Nicol.	55	Butzbach	65-0402
Sophie 49			
BERG, Seligmann	27	Weddenheim	64-0782
Hannchen 23, Elise 2, Heinrich 3m			
BERG, Wihlem	26	Bitburg	65-0151
BERG, v. Edmund	19	Werterstede	66-0221
BERGEN, Gottl.	64	Schlieben	65-1030
BERGENRISCH, Minna	22	Quakenbrueck	65-1024
BERGENTHAL, James	34	Duesseldorf	63-0551
BERGER, Brigitte	26	Altleiningen	64-0170
BERGER, Carl	17	Muenster	66-0576
Jacob 15			
BERGER, Chr.	22	Holzminden	63-0482
BERGER, Ed.	28	Minden	64-1108
BERGER, Elise	18	Strasburg	65-0116
BERGER, Emilie	21	Ronau	66-0650
BERGER, Friedrich	25	Hannover	66-0412
BERGER, Gustav	25	Baden	66-0221
Catharine 28			
BERGER, Heinrich	24	Leavenworth	66-0934
BERGER, Henry	15	Oberbawitz	63-0990
BERGER, Joh. W.	26	Leichlingen	65-0038
BERGER, Johann	22	Baden	66-0576
BERGER, Julius	19	Mutterstadt	65-0189
BERGER, Maria	40	Oschaty	63-0482
BERGER, Otto	19	Nenndorf	66-1031
BERGER, P. August	33	London	66-1127
Anna 29, Emilie 4, Ellen 1, Gertrude 6m			
BERGER, Philip	45	Preston	66-0679
BERGER, Samuel	23	Radolin	66-0650
Rosine 56			
BERGER, Sophie	21	Frankfurt	65-1088
BERGER, Th.	27	Hohenstaat	66-1313
BERGER, Wilh. Jos.	25	Grenzhausen	66-1373
BERGER, Wilhelm	28	Loerrach	66-1155
Marie 25, Wilhelm 2			
BERGER, Wm.	29	Barnau	63-1003
BERGERHAUSEN, Joh.	42	Haerde	63-0614
Lisette 26			
BERGERT, Jacob	25	Villmar	67-0007
BERGFT, Johanna C.	69	Burgstadt	64-0938
BERGHAMER, J.	20	Baden	63-1085
BERGHANS, Joseph	27	Cassel	66-1127
BERGHAUS, Jacob	29	Assler	66-0221
BERGHEIM, Lina	25	Carlshaven	64-0938
BERGHOEFER, Elisab	36	Darmstadt	66-0679
BERGHORN, Louise	29	Neudorf	67-0806
Wilhelm 25, Wilhelmine 15			
BERGK, Conrad	23	Langgoens	64-1108
Anna Elisa 23			
BERGKAMP, Gerhard	42	Wegemuehle	66-0984
Marianne 35, Mariane 7, Minna 3			
Henrich 5, Bernhard 9m			
BERGKAMP, H.H.	35	Aukum	63-0862
BERGMANN, Adolph	22	Braunschweig	66-0469
BERGMANN, Adolph	31	Busnang	65-0116
BERGMANN, Charltt.	23	Rheda	65-0243
BERGMANN, Chr'tine	21	Stemmen	65-1024
BERGMANN, Ferdin'd	18	Atsah	66-0679
Wilhelm 16			
BERGMANN, Fr.	35	Hagen	65-0898
Sophie 32, Fritz 8, Heinr. 4			
BERGMANN, Heinr.	30	Schlusselburg	63-0398
BERGMANN, Heinr.	22	Bohmle	65-0898
Fritz 20, Wilhelm 16, Christoph 14			
Charlotte 8, Hermann 6, Anna Marie 44			
BERGMANN, Heinr.	19	Schlusselburg	65-0950
BERGMANN, Heinrich	25	Zellerfeld	66-0704
BERGMANN, Joh.Geo.	22	Althausen	64-0427
BERGMANN, Johann	31	Cincinnati	66-0984
BERGMANN, Ludw.	20	Segelhorst	66-1243
BERGMANN, Wilhelm	31	Luechtingen	64-0593
BERGMANN, William	18	New York	63-0917
BERGMEIER, P.(f)	21	Rauenberg	64-1161
BERGMEYER, Anne M.	17	Westerwiede	66-0934
BERGNER, Walter	25	Gera	64-0138
BERGOLD, Emil	19	Hohenstein	67-0007
Richard 18			
BERGOLD, Ferdinand	45	Hohenstein	64-0433
BERGOLTEN, Carol.	26	Braunschweig	65-0974
Heinrich 4, Juste 40, Heinrich 3			
BERGR, Marie C.	20	Crefeld	63-0822
Anna Margret 17			
BERGSCHNEIDER, Hh.	26	Ledde	65-0948
Heinrich Frd 26, Wilhelmine 28			
Friedr. Wilh 1			
BERGSIKER, Flor.	21	Cassenborn	63-1010
BERGWEILER, Johann	23	Mayen	65-1030
BERINGER, Leopold	41	Pointen	65-0055
BERKE, Louis	29	Schoningen	66-0469
BERKER, Wilh.	40	Wenkbach	66-1313
Lisbeth 18, Wilhelm 9m			

NAME	AGE	RESIDENCE	YR-LIST
BERKLING, C.J.(m)	19	Bremen	64-0363
BERKMEYER, Josepha	20	Garbeck	65-1088
BERLA, Elise	24	Burgsteinfurt	67-0795
BERLA, Sara	39	New York	66-0934
BERLAGE, Agnes	24	Recke	66-1093
BERLAGE, Anna	24	Borghorst	66-0623
BERLAGE, Ludw.	25	Lengerich	64-0343
BERLE, Caroline	17	Breisach	64-0023
BERLE, Regine	25	Darmstadt	66-0576
BERLINER, Salomon	24	Ndr.Staedten	66-0734
Feist 18			
BERLING, Johann	18	Alfhausen	66-1093
BERMANN, August	18	Pyrmont	66-1155
Magnus 23			
BERMANN, Simon	27	Funen	67-0353
Wilhelmine 24			
BERMER, Dorothea	40	Neudiedendorf	63-0953
Henrike 9			
BERMETTLER, Jams.A		Buocht	63-0551
BERMGARN, Johann	39	Leer	66-1203
Gretje 39, Johannes 11, Friedrich 3			
Johanna 1			
BERMINGER, Franz	24	Burgkunstadt	64-0427
BERMUTH, Charles	28	New York	66-0109
BERN, Emma	42	Cannstadt	66-1031
BERNANSLO, Albert	22	Merzig	66-1327
BERNARD, Mich Th.	24	Mainz	63-0097
BERNART, Dan.	19	Philadelphia	63-0862
BERNAU, Jac.	59	Almersleben	65-1024
Anna 57, C.Fr. 27			
BERNBROCKE, Franz	38	Crincy	64-0886
BERNDS, Nicolaus	36	Werlte	64-0433
BERNDT, Christ.	35	Schoenfeld	66-1248
Dorothea 28, Ernestine 3, Augusta 9m			
BERNDT, Gottlieb	36	Schoenberg	64-0938
BERNDT, Leonhdt.	22	Neusatz	64-0023
BERNECKE, H.(m)	28	Bremen	64-0331
BERNEISER, Georg	35	Elz	64-0495
BERNER, F.	59	Grunbach	64-0782
Catharine 59, Friederike 20, Friedrich 29			
Jacob 19			
BERNER, Wilhelm	20	Steinheim	67-0007
BERNGES, Johannes	28	Fischborn	64-0639
BERNHARD, Elisa	21	Berglicht	64-0331
BERNHARD, Engel	22	Rusbend	66-0934
BERNHARD, Ernst	19	Minsen	66-0934
BERNHARD, John	40	Friedensdorf	63-1218
BERNHARD, M.	19	Immgenhaide	66-0413
BERNHARD, Nicolaus	35	Medart	63-1038
BERNHARD, Wilhelm	19	Berlin	67-0600
BERNHARDT, Chr'tne	19	Darmstadt	66-0679
BERNHARDT, Isidor	21	Berlin	63-0862
BERNHARDT, Marie	60	Darmstadt	66-0679
BERNHEIM, B.	21	Laupheim	64-1161
BERNHEIM, S.	21	Rottweil	65-1189
BERNHEIM, Sam.	23	Buchau	64-0495
BERNHEIMER, Anna	21	Ringsheim	63-0862
BERNHEIMER, Leopld	26	Wuerttemberg	63-0551
BERNING, Hch.	27	Heppen	64-1022
Marie 22, August 6m			
BERNING, Joseph	27	Coesfeld	65-1030
Anna 21			
BERNING, Philipp	15	Iberau	66-0623
BERNING, Rudolf	18	Steinfurth	66-0734
BERNINK, Dina	30	Delden	65-1095
BERNS, Charles	38	New York	63-0097
Emilie 38			
BERNSTEIN, Albert	27	Berringen	66-0469
BERNUTH, v. C. (m)	38	Havre	64-0331
BEROLSHEIMER, Wm.	18	Fuerth	63-1218
BEROTH, Michael	19	Eschach	66-1313
BERRESHEIM, Georg	41	Montreal	64-0138
Marie 24			
BERSCH, Georg	28	Bolkhausen	66-0221
BERSCH, W.	22	Germany	63-0862
BERSCH, Wilh.	24	Hanau	66-1127
BERTHOLD, Arnold	26	Detmond	66-1127
BERTHOLD, Gottlieb	22	Detmold	64-0840

NAME	AGE	RESIDENCE	YR-LIST
BERTHOLD, Johanna	20	Detmold	64-0427
BERTIG, Carl	23	Heilbronn	66-1155
BERTINO, Louis	40	France	64-0073
BERTLING, G.	22	Spelle	64-0782
BERTNIG, Elisa	44	Dinklage	66-0984
Henr. 6			
BERTRAM, Alb.	24	Bremen	65-0007
BERTRAM, Anna	20	Aurich	66-1327
BERTRAM, Carl	21	Biedenkopf	64-0687
Elise 23			
BERTRAM, Carl	18	Esens	66-1327
BERTRAM, Caroline	22	Oxhausen	65-0950
BERTRAM, Ernst	16	Germany	66-0666
Minna 20, Louise 19			
BERTRAM, Louis	36	Darmstadt	64-0687
Elise 34			
BERTSCH, Andreas	28	Wuerttemberg	66-0109
BERTSCH, Louis	24	Metzingen	64-0687
BERTSCH, Pauline	19	Heilbronn	66-1093
BERTSCHE, Pius	17	Deisslingen	65-0402
BERTSCHINGER, Joh.	30	Ryken	66-1203
BERTZ, Jacob	27	Meerfelden	65-0004
BERWANGER, James	17	Grosseichholz	63-1218
BERWANGER, Leopold	17	Holzheim	66-0679
BESEL, James	15	Gandersheim	63-1038
BESSEL, Joseph	31	Friedland	65-0856
BESSIER, Johann	48	Andam/Pruss.	66-0469
BESSING, Ernst Lud	27	Heilbronn	64-1053
BESSLER, Jacob	23	Reichmannsdrf	66-0147
BEST, Jacob	24	Koengernheim	65-0243
BESTE, Henry	23	New York	64-0073
BESTEL, Carl	39	New York	66-0704
George 9			
BESUSCH, Anna	23	Hemska	66-1155
BETHE, Herm.	23	Bremerhaven	63-1010
BETHGE, Gust.	28	Peoria	64-0782
BETHMANN, Marcus	16	Geissa	64-0214
BETKE, Carl	18	Bielefeld	66-0679
BETKE, Emilie	23	Pr. Friedland	66-0704
BETKE, Theodor	14	Zempelburg	66-0704
BETSCHI, Carl	17	Heidenheim	66-0576
BETT, Ernestine	23	Wuertemberg	66-0704
BETTCHER, Wilhelm	31	Wollenberg	66-0578
Johanna 34			
BETTEN, V.(f)	52	Bremerhaven	63-0551
Friedrich 21, Elise 15			
BETTING, Simon	28	Denkingen	64-0138
BETTMANN, Mathilde	23	Altenkunstadt	64-0840
BETZ, Caroline	21	Muddelsbach	64-0214
BETZ, Cath.	20	Pfordt	64-0782
BETZ, Jacob	35	Birkbach	66-0221
Magdalena 25			
BETZ, Mich.	36	Magstadt	63-0350
Elisabeth 24			
BETZ, Sophie	13	Heibronn	63-1010
BETZEL, Ba.	24	Hohefeldt	65-1189
BETZER, Joh.	14	Neustadt	65-0189
BETZLER, Jul.	35	Oberdorf	64-0495
BETZOLD, Michael	35	Wuertenberg	66-0221
BEUDER, C.(f)	20	Newark	64-0495
Julie 6			
BEUER, Wilhelm	22	Staffelstein	65-0770
Caroline 18			
BEUERMANN, Friedr.	17	Sattenhausen	66-1031
BEURMANN, Ferd.	20	Gimse	63-0862
BEUSE, Minna	24	Hoexter	65-0402
BEUSS, Ferd.	20	Giessen	66-0221
Lina 16			
BEUSSER, H.J.	27	Stuttgart	65-0116
BEUST, v. Tuisko		Schleiz	63-0821
BEUTELSBACHER, Gl.	18	Stuttgart	63-1069
BEUTELSBACHER, M.	17	Manbach	64-0782
BEUTELSCHIESS, C	22	Brucke	64-0331
Johanna 21			
BEUTELSPACHER, C.	33	Wuertemberg	66-0984
BEUTENMUELLER, Cat	28	Uhingen	63-1178
Eduard 7			
BEUTLER, Anton	30	Paderborn	64-0214

NAME	AGE	RESIDENCE	YR-LIST
BEUTLER, Elisabeth	26	Paderborn	64-0886
BEUTNER, H.(f)	50	Breslau	64-0687
BEUTZLER, Adolph	19	Hannover	66-1155
BEVERFORDEN, Carl	18	Bramsche	65-0948
BEVERMANN, Friedr.	19	Oberfranken	66-1131
BEVERUNGEN, Will.	39	New Orleans	63-0482
BEXEROTH, Adam	33	Maryland	63-1136
Louise 32			
BEXEROTH, John	24	Pferdedorf	63-1136
BEXTER, Heinr.	31	Orincy	64-0782
BEYER, Adam	23	Neudorf	65-0770
BEYER, Anna	26	Scharmbeck	64-0782
BEYER, Anna	25	Rengshausen	64-0739
BEYER, Aug.	23	Michalinka	66-0413
BEYER, Carl	21	Albertsthal	67-0007
BEYER, Cath.	22	Epplingen	64-0840
BEYER, Christ.	16	Sulz	64-0687
BEYER, Christian	28	Wenjen	66-0650
BEYER, Christian	25	Noerdlingen	66-1093
BEYER, Chs. G.	21	Meissen	64-0593
BEYER, Emilie	23	Ronnenberg	65-0770
BEYER, Ernst	25	Weissen	66-1248
BEYER, Friederike	20	Oberohr	66-0704
BEYER, Heinrich	25	Muensterberg	66-1093
BEYER, Jacob	32	New York	63-0398
Rosalie 25, Carl 7, Johanna 4, Willy 1			
BEYER, Johanna	28	Geismar	66-0349
BEYER, Julius	23	Krimke	66-0413
Wilhelmine 27, Ottilie 1			
BEYER, Leopold	19	Frankenberg	64-0214
BEYER, Lorenz	30	Wendelsheim	64-0782
BEYERLE, Aloys	43	Bollmershofen	67-0007
Ursula 34			
BEYERSDORF, John C	20	Coburg	63-0244
BEZEL, Valentin	22	Dettelbach	66-0083
BIBO, Simon	21	Brakel	65-0007
BICK, Carl	20	Herbsen	64-1206
BICK, Friedrich	19	Waldeck	66-1248
BICK, Johann	27	Varensell	66-1203
BICKEL, G.A.	25	Eichenrode	63-1085
BICKENBERG, Jean	34	Switz.	64-0170
Emma 26			
BICKER, Anton	18	Ohmes	66-1127
BICKERT, Maria	24	Grosenlueder	66-0469
BICKERT, Wilh'mine	23	Meyerndorf	66-0837
BICKHOFFER, John	36	Punninghausen	63-0917
BICKLER, Ph.	17	Ettenschiess	64-1161
BICKROEGER, Herman	26	Walle	67-0007
BIDDKER, Elisabeth	50	Brilon	65-0974
Albert 22, Franz 16, Joseph 14			
Gertrude 18, Maria 7, Richard 5m			
BIDDKER, Hrch.	30	Brilon	65-0974
Therese 25, Catharine 2, Johann 6m			
BIDE, Theodor	36	Frankenhausen	66-1155
Augusta 36, Amalie 7, baby 10m			
BIDLINGMAIER, Chr.	16	Plochingen	66-0576
Wilhelmine 19			
BIDLINGMEIER, Anna	19	Wellingen	66-0147
BIDLINGMEIER, Lou.	19	Plochingen	66-0576
BIEBER, Andreas	36	Kschentz	66-1093
BIEBER, Bernh.	45	St. Louis	63-0168
BIEBER, Marianne	19	Langenschwanz	63-0917
BIEBERBACH, Eva	24	Sax.-Meiningn	64-0432
Louise 18			
BIECKER, August	35	Crefeld	63-0917
Sophie 24, August 9, Albert 8			
Clothilde 2, baby 4m			
BIEDENBACH, Albert	17	Kirchhasel	66-1155
Moritz 19			
BIEDERBECK, Elise	24	Dinklage	64-0363
BIEG, Catharine	39	Ndr.Alfingen	66-1093
Crescentia 15			
BIEGE, C.	17	Breslen	63-0013
BIEGG, Alois	20	Oldheim	65-0594
BIEK, James	21	Hohfeld	63-1038
BIEK, John	40	Hohfeld	63-1038
BIELEFELD, Carl	28	Welda	64-1022
Marie 24			

NAME	AGE	RESIDENCE	YR-LIST
BIELEFELD, Henry	25	Madison	66-1313
Minna 24, Otto 4, Johanna 2, Henry 9m			
BIELER, Carl	25	Frankfurt	66-0109
Amalie 20			
BIELERSEN, Heinr.	17	Wietzen	65-1088
Wilhelmine 26			
BIEN, Amalie	40	Wiesbaden	66-0704
BIEN, Casp.	29	Wienhausen	63-0013
BIENEMANN, Levy	19	Anroechte	64-0170
BIENEMANN, Louis	20	Anruechte	65-1088
BIENEN, Joh. Bernh	22	Spahn	64-0938
BIERBAUM, Chr. Hr.	18	Ledenburg	64-0687
BIERBAUM, Louise	21	Osnabrueck	66-1093
BIERBAUM, Martin	58	Ledenberg	66-0679
Marie 59, Johann 17			
BIERDAMPFER, D.	17	Ingelfingen	64-0992
BIERE, Fr.	33	Harbeist	65-1088
BIEREN, Conrad	26	Frohnhausen	65-0974
Catharine 22			
BIERHATTER, Marian	22	Loebingen	63-0953
BIERMAAS, J.		Holzheim	63-1003
BIERMANN, Arnold	25	Varensell	66-1203
BIERMANN, Betty	26	Hoyer	66-1127
BIERMANN, Heinr.	20	Hasbergen	63-0398
BIERMANN, Louise	20	Wittlage	66-1155
BIERMANN, Ludw.	19	Hannover	64-1053
BIERMANN, Moritz	45	Boehmen	63-1136
Nanette 34, Anna 9, Lena 7, Victoria 4			
Daniel 4, Peppi 7m			
BIERMANN, Rud.	50	Drakenburg	63-0752
Marg. 51, Marie 18, Elise 14, Doris 9			
BIERSACK, Peter	29	Worms	64-0363
BIERWIRTH, S.	24	Hertzberg	66-0413
BIERWITZ, Marg.	24	Vegesack	64-0170
Herm. 9m			
BIES, John Jac.	17	Unterhausen	66-1155
BIESBECK, Johann	22	Keiterzell	63-0953
BIETZE, Wm.	32	Ummeln	64-0687
BIEVER, Angela	22	Zewe	63-0990
BILDERMANN, Wilh.	21	Buende	65-1095
BILEG, Mathias	52	Boehmen	64-0432
Anna 40			
BILGER, Egmont	28	Frankfurt/M	63-1136
BILIMEK, Carl	31	Weisskirchen	64-0073
BILING, Anna	44	Bremen	64-0739
Ernst 7			
BILL, Johannes	24	Nauenheim	63-0006
BILLANT, (m)	47	New Orleans	63-1218
wife 45, Wm. Andre 10, Paul Andre 1			
L.B. 10m, Martha 35, Caroline 11			
BILLER, Ignatz	42	Wien	66-0109
BILLERBECK, August	32	Laudon	67-0007
BILLHARZ, A.	28	Sigmaringen	65-0116
BILLING, Paul	34	Wuerzburg	65-0151
BILMS, Ferdinand	15	Walsrode	63-0614
BILSING, Carl Frdr	42	Boston	66-0221
BIMMER, Ferd.	33	Scheidnitz	64-0938
Louise 25, Louise 9m			
BIMS, Simon	18	Huffelsheim	66-1155
BINDBUETEL, Christ	57	Hundelshausen	66-0668
Margarethe 22			
BINDER, Friedr.	17	Andeer	64-0427
BINDER, Fritz	21	Sottruw	66-1248
BINDER, Johann	28	Mannheim	66-0668
BINDER, Juliana	19	Guntersblume	65-1095
BINDER, Wilhelm	33	Crefeld	66-0412
BINDER, Wilhelm	43	Walderdingen	64-1206
BINDERMANN, Franz	22	Mulhwand	65-0007
BINDERMANN, Hans	56	Velgau	64-0665
Karl 20, Joachin 30, Dorothea 34, Marie 5			
Louise 6m			
BINDING, Theodor	34	Frankfurt	66-1327
BINDT, Ignatz	46	Treffelstein	63-0551
Cath. 44, Michael 21, Barbara 18			
Margarethe 13, Catharine 9, Justine 7			
James 3, baby 6m			
BING, Herz	18	Linden	66-0221
BINGEL, Adam	28	Reibrectenbch	64-0170

NAME	AGE	RESIDENCE	YR-LIST
Friederike 25			
BINGER, Andreas	31	Veilsdorf	66-1131
Peter 25			
BINGER, Franz	38	Lippstadt	66-0577
BINGER, Paul	30	Strasburg	65-0116
BIRGEL, Heinr.	35	Williamsburg	63-0990
BIRK, Barbara	42	Trottingen	65-0402
Anna 15, Martin 12, Ursula 4, Christine 1			
Mathias 19			
BIRK, Cav.	44	Trostingen	64-0495
Mart. 42			
BIRK, Jacob	48	Kolschhausen	66-0576
Peter 18, Wilhelm 16			
BIRK, Joh. M.	25	Vihringen	66-1243
BIRKEMAYER, Wm.	24	Culmbach	64-0840
BIRKEMEYER, Wm.	38	Zevenitz	65-0007
Elise 34			
BIRKENFELD, Bernh.	29	Ankum	66-0679
Jenni 24			
BIRKENSTOCK, Heinr	37	Schlotten	66-1243
Marie 26			
BIRKENSTOCK, Louis	19	Frankfurt	66-0109
BIRKERT, Barbara	28	Oberstetten	66-1373
Anton 11m			
BIRKLE, Agathe	18	Altdorf/Bad.	65-0950
BIRKMAIER, A.	26	Hannover	63-1178
BIRMELL, Christ.	26	Ilaningen	64-0593
BIRNBAUM, W.L.	23	Fuerth	64-0593
BIRRESCH, Jos.	27	Boehmen	64-0495
Ma. 28, Jos. 5, Elsb. 3, Cath 10m			
BIRSCH, Georg	41	Ingenhain	66-0147
BIRTNER, A.(m)	30	New York	63-0097
BISCHING, C.	32	Stolzenau	64-1161
BISCHITZ, (f)	21	Prag	66-0147
BISCHKOP, Sophie	42	Liebenau	63-1178
Henry			
BISCHOF, Hinr.	33	Charlesburg	63-0350
Anna 32, Meta 9, Anton 7, Catarina 5			
John 2, baby (m) 6m			
BISCHOFF, Carl	20	Dietlingen	64-0214
BISCHOFF, Casp.	33	Urrhausen	64-0023
Johanna 21			
BISCHOFF, Christ	35	Naila	64-0938
Susanne 35			
BISCHOFF, Conrad	26	Aschendorf	63-0953
BISCHOFF, D.H.	19	Bremen	63-0296
BISCHOFF, Franz	18	Dissen	66-0984
BISCHOFF, Frz.	29	Glandorf	65-0151
BISCHOFF, Gath.(m)	19	Besenfeld	64-0170
BISCHOFF, Gustav	23	Coburg	66-1373
BISCHOFF, H.(m)	28	New York	64-0363
BISCHOFF, Heinrich	21	Hannover	66-1243
BISCHOFF, Herm	31	Loeningen	63-0953
BISCHOFF, Kunigund	21	Leutbold	63-1085
BISCHOFF, Louise	48	Bockenem	64-0331
BISCHOFF, Marie	32	Hildburghsn.	64-1108
Elisab. 7, Marg. 4			
BISCHOFFBERGER, J.	36	Oberegg	64-0331
BISCHOFFSBERGER, J	30	Berwerk	63-0482
Anna 28			
BISCHOFFSBERGER, U	17	St Antonien	63-0482
BISCHOFWERDER, Max	17	Lissa	65-0402
BISPING, Friedrich	24	Steinfurth	66-0623
BISSINGER, Ph.(m)	29	New York	64-0073
BISSOIRE, Elise	25	Winzingen	64-0427
BITT, Christine	20	Buchenau	66-0934
BITT, Gust.	22	Freiburg	63-0244
Caroline 51, Cath. 25, Christine 25			
William 11			
BITTEL, Johann	26	Darmstadt	65-0865
BITTEL, S.	21	Darmstadt	65-1189
BITTER, Friedr.	20	Bremen	63-0752
BITTER, Joh. Jost	19	Bremen	64-0023
BITTER, Wilhelm	15	Weddewarden	64-0456
BITTLER, Elisabeth	16	Darmstadt	66-0576
BLACKRING, H.	19	Isselburg	65-0974
BLAESER, Anna	30	Herbstein	65-1024
BLAESING, Louise	16	Preussen	63-0990
BLAETTERLEIN, J.F.	25	Oberhasslau	63-0953
BLAHA, Helene	26	Bohemen	64-0782
BLAHA, John	28	Caslau	64-0593
Antonia 23, Anton 3, Francisca 2			
BLANCKE, J.	29	Paderborn	66-0413
BLANCKE, Maria	23	Borghorst	66-0623
BLANK, Andreas	25	Balgholz	65-0243
BLANK, Meta	22	Bremen	63-0614
Louise 15			
BLANK, Peter	22	Niederheim	64-0938
BLANKE, Heinrich	22	Gleustedt	64-0456
BLANKENBURG, Carl	19	Erfurt	64-0639
BLANKENBURG, Rudlf	22	Basel	65-0116
Marie 29			
BLANKENBURG, v.Max	24	Russow	63-0821
BLANKENFELS, David	26	Bichowe	66-0413
Rosine 52			
BLANKENHEIM, James	35	St. Louis	63-1178
Lechem 13			
BLANKENHORN, Elise	17	Frankenthal	63-0862
BLANKENHORN, Jane	23	Kirchheim	63-0097
BLASS, A.M.(f)	18	Rissingen	64-0331
BLASS, Marie	26	Hannover	63-1038
BLASSE, Mina	23	Westphalen	66-0734
Carl 5, Julius 2			
BLATHE, Heinr.	14	Dresden	67-0599
BLATT, E.	25	Hattenbach	64-0782
Sara 20, Amalie 18			
BLATTNER, Georg Fr	18	Weil	66-1373
BLAU, Theresia	24	Waldurn	66-1203
BLAUE, Wilh.	23	Landau	66-0734
BLAUFUSS, Hedwig	19	Marburg	66-0984
BLAUM, Maria	39	Worms	66-1203
Catharina 9			
BLAUME, Wilhelm	25	Warber	66-0734
BLECH, Carl A.H.	15	Neuhaus	64-0427
BLECHER, Georg	26	Russbach	66-1243
Caroline 25			
BLECHER, Heinrich	26	Rehburg	65-1095
BLECHER, Maria	30	Hildesheim	65-0402
BLECHSCHMIDT, Lou.	20	Goldisthal	66-1248
BLECK, Claus	24	Neuhaus	66-0623
BLECKENSTEIN, G.W.	44	Schwarzenbach	63-0097
BLECKER, Georg	42	Hildburghsn.	65-0189
BLEECK, Claus H.	22	Hannover	64-0432
BLEI, Adam	19	Eisenach	64-0885
BLEI, Helene	33	Fuerth	63-0006
BLEICHER, Jos.	58	Ebnat	64-0938
BLEIER, Magdalene	24	Bubendorf	66-1031
BLEINZIG, F.	18	Haller	65-1189
BLELL, Otto	17	Marienwerder	66-0623
BLENDERMANN, Annet	42	Vegesack	64-0138
Johann 7, Marie 2			
BLENKER, Marianne	57	Preussen	63-0990
BLENNER, Wilhelm	17	Marburg	65-1088
BLER, B.	17	Kralowitz	66-0413
BLESCH, Augusta	28	New York	64-0739
BLESCH, Heinr.	19	Hatzbach	64-0739
Elisab. 43, Elisab. 7, Georg 14			
Catharine 16, Gertrude 18			
BLESKE, Carl	35	Rutlitz	66-0668
Sophie 58			
BLESS, Nicolaus	22	Heppenheim	63-1010
BLESSING, Carl	53	Boll	66-0221
Susanna 47, Cathar. 25, Eva 7, Chrs. 5			
BLESSING, David	30	Ruhlbronn	63-0350
BLESSING, Jacob	15	Lehneberg	66-0221
BLESSMANN, Friedr.	43	Goettingen	66-0577
Charlotte 43, Rosine 18, Heinrich 16			
Wilhelm 14, Louise 11, Carl 6, August 3			
BLETZER, de Eduard	25	Trier	64-1053
BLEY, Ferdinand	30	Bremen	66-0349
BLEY, Gerhard	18	Cloppenburg	63-0752
BLEY, J.H.(m)	25	Jeverland	64-0214
BLEY, Valentin	46	Empertshausen	65-0770
Anna Elisab. 50, Wilhelm 15			
BLEZ, Wilhelm	25	Baden	66-0147
BLICKLE, Friedr.	20	Boblingen	66-1203

NAME	AGE	RESIDENCE	YR-LIST
BLIDEL, Emma	19	Muenden	64-0840
BLIND, Wilhelm	17	Nueztingen	64-0593
BLOCH, Christoffer	18	Veilsheim	65-1031
BLOCH, Edmund	18	Floss	66-1155
BLOCH, Emanuel	19	Likswitz	66-0734
BLOCH, Henry	30	Switz.	64-0170
Sophie 25			
BLOCH, Ignatz	16	Ganaritz	66-0679
BLOCH, Rosa	24	Muhlhausen	64-0992
BLOCHER, Joh.	17	Frohnhausen	65-0974
BLOCK, Anna	20	Ernsthausen	64-0938
BLOCK, Anna	22	Leeste	66-1127
BLOCK, Bertha	16	Hohenems	64-0992
BLOCK, C.(m)	26	Husum	64-0495
M.(f) 20			
BLOCK, Carl	32	Braunschweig	63-0006
BLOCK, Caspar	37	Wohnfeld	64-0782
Marie 37, Elisabeth 7, Heinrich 6			
BLOCK, F.	21	Bavaria	64-0593
BLOCK, Georg L.	45	Carlsruhe	64-0687
Josephine 36, Frieda 11m			
BLOCK, George	40	Bernstadt	64-0782
BLOCK, Ignatz	26	Wirrchucin	66-0578
BLOCK, James	18	Piseck	63-0482
Theresa 15			
BLOCK, Jeanette	18	Muehrengen	64-0687
BLOCK, Johann	19	Leeste	66-1127
BLOCK, Misses	24	New York	63-1136
sister 18			
BLOCK, Rosa	15	Muehlo	65-1024
BLOCKBERGER, Bernh	26	Germany	66-0666
Hermann 20			
BLOCKHAUS, Marie	20	Zeven	64-0739
BLOECHER, Joh.	23	Biedenkopf	64-0687
BLOECKER, Wm.	16	Herzhausen	64-0782
BLOEDEL, Jacob	28	Oppenheim	66-0109
BLOEM, Gu.	30	Vollenerkonig	66-1031
BLOESER, Louis	24	Bremen	65-0151
BLOESSNER, Antonia	44	Wackenzell	66-1131
BLOETH, Joseph	30	Lichtenberg	66-0147
BLOHM, J.	28	Duanfelde	64-0782
BLOHM, Joh. Wm.	24	Langwarden	64-0456
BLOHM, Johann	14	Fischerhude	64-0363
BLOHM, Nicolaus	21	Neuenkirchen	63-0482
BLOHORN, (f)	23	Lahr	63-1038
BLOME, C.	17	Bielefeld	66-0413
BLOME, Heinrich	16	Bremen	64-0199
BLOME, Hermann	46	Bremen	65-1088
Catharine 25, Margarethe 13, Hermann 8			
Anna 6			
BLOME, John	26	Blandern	64-1161
BLOMKER, Wilh.	28	Lengerich	64-0214
Lisette 24, Wilh. 2			
BLONDEL, Joseph	40	Liebentig	66-0576
BLOOM, M.	33	Louisville	63-1136
BLOS, John	23	Saalfeld	66-1131
BLOSSBERG, Chrs.	24	Elberfeld	66-0221
BLUDON, August	26	Einbeck	65-0770
BLUECHER, Theodor	28	Dresden	63-0990
BLUEM, Anton	16	Worms	63-0953
BLUEM, Johanette	21	Worms	65-0402
Rosa 19, Eleonore 7, Ferd. 22			
BLUEMKE, Juliane	26	Czarnikau	66-1327
Anna 35			
BLUETH, Suerchen	27	Lengsfeld	65-1030
BLUETHNER, Adolph.	32	Loga	64-0739
Dinette 14, Valket 7, Cardine 6			
Sopie 11m, Adolphine 19			
BLUHM, Ed.	24	Wehlau	64-0992
BLUHM, R.	22	Leipzig	64-0495
BLULST, Aug.	18	Rottweil	64-0782
BLUM, Albert	19	Sul	66-1131
BLUM, Anselm	64	New York	64-0214
Clara 59			
BLUM, August	24	Oldenburg	65-0116
BLUM, Carl	34	Hagelloch	66-1131
BLUM, Emanuel	18	Nassau	66-0679
BLUM, Hermann	17	Inscheck	67-0007

NAME	AGE	RESIDENCE	YR-LIST
BLUM, Isidor	21	Weiler	66-0734
BLUM, Jac.	53	Eichelsachsen	64-0331
BLUM, Johann H.		Roedenau	66-0623
BLUM, John	27	Rosenfeld	63-0482
BLUM, Juliane	20	Eichelsachsen	63-0244
BLUM, Kasper	22	Grewenau	66-0578
BLUM, Margarethe	15	Nentershausen	63-0006
BLUM, Nicolas	18	Oberkalbach	64-0427
BLUM, Otto	19	Gr. Busek	63-1038
BLUM, Philip	24	Meyyaren	66-0679
BLUM, Rosalie	28	Frankfurt	64-0992
BLUME, August	19	Thedinghausen	66-0469
BLUME, Friedrich	12	Bremen	66-0576
Hermann 9			
BLUMELING, Bertha	22	New York	66-0576
Bertha 11			
BLUMENFELD, Moritz	20	Homberg	65-1031
Hannchen 18			
BLUMENHARDT, Fr.	29	Neckariems	65-0594
Sophie 23, Gobke 27			
BLUMENSCHEIN, Mary	25	Breusbach	65-0189
BLUMENSTEIN, A.Cat	18	Quindel	66-0412
BLUMENTHAL, E.	23	Altenur	64-0639
BLUMENTHAL, G.	15	Neuenkirchen	65-0974
BLUMENTHON, Julius	17	Battenfeld	66-1155
BLUMENTRITT, Joh.	37	Roda	65-0189
BLUMER, Ferdinand	47	Birkenwerda	66-0623
Emilie 47			
BLUMMERS, Peter	28	Niederaulheim	63-1178
BLURN, Peter	56	Clerensenter	64-0639
BLUST, Stephan	32	Fautenbach	63-0482
BLUST, Theresia	23	Rottweil	63-1038
BOBRINK, Henrich	23	Hessia	66-0412
BOCHER, Georg	23	Flensungen	64-0687
BOCHMANN, Christ.	54	Muelsen	66-1327
Christine 62, Hugo 3			
BOCK, Anna Barb.	19	Wehrhausen	66-1127
BOCK, Aug.	20	Zerwig	64-0840
Wm. 16			
BOCK, Carl Julius	25	Vizig	66-0650
BOCK, Caroline	18	Fuerth	66-1031
BOCK, Cathar.	21	Elberfeld	66-0221
BOCK, Christine	42	Zerwich	65-0898
Friederike 19, Marie 15, Wilhelmine 9			
BOCK, Friederike	16	Hoff	65-1024
BOCK, Fritz	24	Gruenenplan	63-1038
BOCK, H.(m)	21	Herlau	64-0495
BOCK, Helene	24	Milwaukee	64-0363
BOCK, Hermine	31	Kleinbismark	66-0650
BOCK, Johann	23	Lohne	66-0934
Hermann 23			
BOCK, Joseph	29	Lengenfeld	64-0639
John 24			
BOCK, Joseph	29	Rinik	65-1031
BOCK, M.E.	35	Grossentaft	63-1003
P.. 12			
BOCKE, H.W.	20	Minden	64-1108
BOCKEL, Th.	40	Baltimore	64-0782
BOCKELMANN, Georg	30	Ahlfeld	66-1128
BOCKEN, Carl	18	Bremen	66-1093
BOCKER, Anna C.	18	Niederufflen	64-0639
BOCKER, Jacob	28	Worms	64-1022
BOCKER, Marie C.	23	Voerden	63-1085
BOCKER, Wm.	17	Suelbeck	64-0782
BOCKHAUS, Johann	28	Worms	66-1093
BOCKHOFF, Adelh. F	42	Leer	64-0886
H. Albrecht 14, Gerh.Andreas 12			
Adelheid 7, Ludw. Friedr 5, Alfred Wm. 4			
Peter Diedr. 2			
BOCKHORST, Cath.	24	Badbergen	64-0073
BOCKLAGE, Joh.	26	Grothe	66-0576
BOCKLAHN, John B.	24	Gehrte	63-0350
BOCKLING, Martin	30	St Juergen	63-1136
BOCKMANN, Joh.	25	Gr. Munnelage	66-0984
Anna 33, Anna 1, Hermann 65, Catharine 65			
BOCKSTRUCK, Heinr.	18	Weglighausen	65-0189
BODDE, Theodor	57	Norskirchen	66-1327
Theodor 23			

NAME	AGE	RESIDENCE	YR-LIST
BODE, August	38	Nordheim	65-0004
BODE, Carl	19	Hein	63-1010
BODE, Eduard	34	Elten	65-0151
BODE, Ernst	30	Dorum	65-0151
BODE, Friedrich	23	Hagen	66-0109
BODE, Fritz	19	Dorum	66-0704
BODE, Heinr.	38	Verden	66-0934
Mathilde 32, Heinrich 7, baby 2m			
BODE, Heinrich	26	Goettingen	63-0822
BODE, Joh.	18	Hannover	66-0576
BODE, Sophie	23	Bassum	66-1128
BODEMANN, Wm.	13	Quackenbrueck	63-1038
BODEN, Geo.	25	Varel	64-1022
Meta 23			
BODEN, v. Sophie	24	Bremen	64-0840
BODENBENDER, Henry	25	Hassenhausen	63-0990
BODENBURG, Carl	16	Leesen	64-0886
BODENHAUS, Friedr.	35	Helminghausen	66-0984
Carolus 21, Augusta 8m			
BODENHAUSEN, Joh.	55	Bavaria	63-0822
Louise Cath. 52, Magdalene 27, Johann 17			
Catharine 1			
BODENHEIMER, Wm.	24	Runkerod	67-0007
BODENSCHATZ, Heinr	27	Gesell	65-0770
BODENSTAB, G.A.	50	Mimee	64-0138
BODMER, Louise	25	Switz	66-0679
BODMER, Rudolph	21	Zuerich	63-0752
BODSON, (f)	45	Rouen	63-0350
Harry 12, Felicie 15, Jean 7, Ferdine 4			
BOECK, Anton	25	Hintersingen	66-0576
BOECK, Chares	32	Vienna	63-0015
Gabriela 24, Louise 4			
BOECKEMEYER, Bernh	18	Lubbecke	65-0594
Creszencia 35, Ludw. 15, Wilh. 15			
BOECKER, Carl	43	Prss. Muenden	65-1095
BOECKER, Catharina	22	Vildern	66-1248
BOECKER, H.	19	Bremen	64-0665
BOECKER, Johann	20	Burkhards	66-1248
BOECKER, Wilhelm	16	Hannover	66-1373
BOECKING, Ad.	30	Bonn	63-1136
BOECKLER, Lisette	25	Neustadt a/H	64-0138
BOECKLIN, Eduard	37	Esslingen	64-1022
BOECKMANN, Diedr.	15	Voerden	64-1022
BOECKMANN, Joseph	19	Palmzohl	63-1038
BOEDECKER, Christ.	20	Bremen	63-1085
John H. 38, Maruy 24, John H. 9m			
BOEDECKER, Gusto	52	Cincinnati	65-0116
BOEDEKER, Elisbeth	50	Brilon	65-0974
Albert 22, Franz 16, Joseph 14			
Gertrude 18, Maria 7, Richard 5m			
BOEDEKER, Friedr.	17	Borchel	64-0739
BOEDEKER, H.	15	Nienburg	66-0413
BOEDEKER, Hrch.	30	Brilon	65-0974
Therese 25, Catharine 2, Johann 6m			
BOEDEKER, Johanna	27	Hannover	66-0984
BOEDEKER, Wilh.	30	Dinklage	66-0984
BOEGER, Caroline	26	Detmold	66-1031
Caroline 3m			
BOEGER, Conr.	28	Buke	65-0402
BOEGER, Elise	21	Drakenburg	66-0704
BOEGER, Friederike	25	Drakenburg	66-0704
BOEHLE, Bernhard	29	Bueren	66-0576
BOEHLE, Martha	27	Breitenbach	66-1313
BOEHLING, Otto	19	Runthal	66-1031
BOEHM, Adolph	23	New York	66-0984
BOEHM, Arnold	27	Woerrstadt	66-0147
BOEHM, August	19	Neuenstein	65-1024
BOEHM, Babette	40	Frankfurt	66-1155
BOEHM, Benedict	22	Pilsen	66-1031
Jacob 21			
BOEHM, Christoph	35	Torsgruen	66-0666
BOEHM, Clara	22	Guentersdorf	67-0599
BOEHM, Creszencia	26	Heilbach	66-0679
Gertrud 2, Helena 9m			
BOEHM, Emmerich	24	Heilbach	66-0679
Kilian Traug 4, Jacob 6, Barbara 33			
BOEHM, Friederike	25	Einoedhausen	66-1031
BOEHM, Friedrich	40	Kurnick	65-1030

NAME	AGE	RESIDENCE	YR-LIST
BOEHM, Hirsch	62	Hernighausen	66-0984
Sara 56, Moses 7, Jettchen 6			
BOEHM, Joseph	45	Davern	67-0599
Anna 34, Anna 8, August 2			
BOEHM, Lorenz	25	Bellheim	67-0007
BOEHM, Rosalia	46	Boehmen	66-0349
BOEHMANN, Herm.	44	Cincinnati	63-0953
BOEHME, Cathr.	47	Gieboldshsn.	65-1088
Anton 8			
BOEHMER, August	37	Sieboldhausen	64-0433
BOEHMER, August	21	Celle	66-1031
BOEHMER, Casper	49	Schoenebeck	63-0917
BOEHMER, Christ.	21	Behren	66-1203
BOEHMER, Ferd.	25	Herdorf	65-0948
Justine 30, Christ. 11m			
BOEHMER, Franz	26	Benninghausen	63-0917
Elisabeth 32, Maria 2			
BOEHMER, Friedr.	24	Minden	65-1031
Marie 24, Wilhelm 1			
BOEHMER, Margareth	27	Bavaria	63-0822
BOEHNE, (m)	30	Hannover	65-0189
BOEHNE, Anna	19	Heeste	64-0639
BOEHNE, Carl	62	Fuerstenberg	64-0639
Henriette 19, August 15			
BOEHNE, Heinr.	48	Hockhorst	66-0734
Caroline 46, Wilhelmine 18, Carl 15			
BOEHNE, Heinr.	21	Rehden	64-0886
BOEHNER, John	43	Newark	64-1161
BOEHNING, A.	24	Huhnfeld	65-0898
BOEHNING, Heinr.	44	Rieste	66-1373
Lisette 25			
BOEHNINGEN, Marg.	60	Wichmansdorf	66-1127
BOEHNLEIN, Ba.	24	Wiesentheil	65-0402
BOEHR, Chr.	53	Frankenthal	63-0551
Margarethe 47, Christ. 14, Catherina 8			
BOEHRINGER, Friedr	26	Geurrigheim	65-0055
BOEKE, Fritz	23	Hohenhausen	64-0456
BOEKER, Charlotte	23	Norderney	64-0593
Heinr. 7			
BOEKER, Heinr.	52	Warpsen	63-1038
Dorette 53			
BOEKER, Wilhelmine	15	Wulferdingshs	65-1095
BOEKERS, Ellenbein	22	Engert	65-0950
BOEKLE, Joh. G.	25	Herrenberg	65-0038
BOELJES, Joh. Fr.	50	Aurich	65-1030
Dina 50, Ludwig 24, Anna 21, Wilhelm 16			
Friedrich 14			
BOELKER, A.	20	Brake	63-0482
BOELKER, Friedrich	42	Albertinhof	66-1248
Bertha 38			
BOELL, Philippine	20	New York	66-0679
BOELSEN, Heiko	48	Aurich	64-0432
Engeline 15			
BOELTER, Christoph	56	Moorschuetz	66-0412
Anna Susanne 51, Christoph 7			
BOEME, Chr.	22	Altenweddingn	63-1003
K. 19, E. 46, M. 23, M. 12, F. 8, A. 8			
C. 1			
BOEMER, Wm.	36	Illinois	63-0752
BOENDERS, Johann	16	Norden	64-1022
BOENECKE, Christ.	45	Nordenbeck	65-0948
Caroline 45, friedrich 19, Marie 15			
Heinrich 7, Paull 2			
BOENECKE, Hermann	25	Barnstorf	66-1373
BOENIG, Louis	26	Lennep	63-1178
BOENING, Augusta	17	Schoenfeld	67-0599
Fritz 8			
BOENING, C.Fr.G.	18	Lashorst	65-0898
BOENKER, Catharina	49	Hahlen	66-0349
Friedrich 9			
BOENNER, Friedrich	21	Arnsberg	63-0614
Gustav 19, Maria 17, Wilhelm 15			
BOERGER, Anna Cath	26	Talge	63-0482
BOERGER, Franz	36	Damme	65-0055
BOERGER, Maria	26	Essniger	66-1093
BOERKIRCHEN, Joh.	33	Affalterbach	64-1022
BOERMANN, Ignaz	40	Holitz	67-0007
BOERNER, Emil	29	Clebon	66-0734

NAME	AGE	RESIDENCE	YR-LIST
BOERNER, Ernst	18	Sachs.-Weimar	66-0349
Sophie 15			
BOERNER, Heinr.	26	Hilgenbach	65-0004
BOERNER, W.	27	Frankenhausen	65-0974
Friederike 19			
BOERNER, Wm.	20	Heiligenbach	65-0116
BOERNGER, Heinr.	26	Langenbuba	66-0576
BOERRIES, Carl	19	Loeningen	64-0938
BOERS, Bernh.	63	Drensteinfurt	64-0687
Anna 63, Bernh. 27, Anna 24			
BOERSE, Joh.	32	Recklinghsn.	65-0402
BOES, Georg	29	Kurhessen	66-0469
BOESCH, Anna	29	Ahlsen	66-0668
BOESCH, Carl	29	Bettelbrunn	65-0038
BOESCH, Franziska	23	Bruchsal	66-1203
BOESCH, Gottlieb	19	Ebersdorf	64-0885
BOESCH, H.A.	37	Lehe	64-1053
BOESCH, Jacob	19	Grossenhein	64-0456
BOESCHE, Hermann	27	Klingena	64-0199
BOESCHEN, Cathar.	22	Jever	65-0770
BOESCHEN, Claus	21	Hassendorf	64-0992
BOESCHEN, Diedr.	22	Sievern	65-0189
BOESCHER, Daniel	31	Rheinpfalz	66-0221
Cathar. 31, Elisabeth 4, Caroline 2			
Daniel 9m			
BOESCHER, Hinrich	19	Kuhstedt	63-0614
BOESE, Carl	27	Westrup	66-1373
BOESE, Heinr.	18	Bremen	63-0398
BOESE, Heinrich	22	Ecksteven	64-0456
BOESE, Heinrich	21	Riede	66-1373
BOESE, Juliane	46	Neuhaus	66-0413
Henriette 29, Friedrike 15			
BOESE, Louise	60	Guedenhagen	66-0469
BOESE, Wilh.	30	Braunschweig	63-0821
BOESENFELL, Lina	18	Nuernberg	66-1155
BOESING, Hr.	36	Tehlen	66-0349
BOESKE, Aug.	27	Bromberg	64-0432
Henriette 24, Wm. 4, Aug. 9m			
BOESSEL, G. Aug.	29	Lengerich	63-1085
BOESSER, Caspar	30	Gehaus	63-1038
Elisabeth 20			
BOESSER, Cath. E.	59	Fischbart	63-1038
BOETJER, Johann	18	Achim	66-0666
Anna 23			
BOETTCHER, Adam	47	Gemkt	64-0665
Anna 50, Philipp 22, Anna 26, Justus 17			
BOETTCHER, Catrine	21	Achim	65-1030
BOETTCHER, Dietr.	23	Leipzig	65-1030
Victoria 19			
BOETTCHER, Gustav	46	Quakertown	66-0934
BOETTCHER, Heinr.	24	Bremen	64-0885
BOETTCHER, Heinr.	50	Scharmbeck	66-1313
Marie 18, Anna 16			
BOETTCHER, J.Henry	34	New York	63-0917
BOETTCHER, Johanna	31	Hannover	66-0147
Louise 26			
BOETTCHER, Marie	27	Romansliest	66-0934
BOETTCHER, Mina	17	Loxstedt	65-1030
BOETTCHER, Ph.	19	Wagenfeld	66-1243
BOETTCHER, Wilhelm	27	Schneidemuehl	66-0934
baby 6m			
BOETTGER, Georg	34	Fernbreitenbh	63-1178
BOETTGER, Heinrich	31	Eisleben	64-0456
BOETTGER, M. Engel	23	Oster Cappeln	65-0950
BOETTICKER, Theod.	27	Duesseldorf	64-0639
BOETTIGER, Jacob	24	Biebesheim	64-1053
BOETTJER, John	24	Bremen	63-1136
BOGASCH, Carl	58	Kempen	65-1088
Ottilie 53, Salmar 9			
BOGEHOLZ, August	20	Fahlhausen	66-1243
BOGEL, William	30	Hannover	63-1136
D.L. 30, Stella 9			
BOGENER, Cathar.	25	Bogen	64-1022
BOGGENKAMP, Barth	19	Oeren	66-0578
BOGNER, Anton	22	Bayern	64-0432
BOHAGE, Adam	17	Butzbach	63-1218
BOHE, Anna	19	Harpenfeld	66-0221
BOHIN, Wilhelm	19	Osnabrueck	66-0704

NAME	AGE	RESIDENCE	YR-LIST
BOHL, Jacques	21	France	63-0350
BOHLANDER, Joh.	18	Hohensalza	64-0170
BOHLE, Hermann	19	Umbeck	63-0917
BOHLEN, Anna	18	Sandstedt	63-0398
BOHLEN, Ludwig	34	Oberndorf	65-0151
BOHLENDER, Elisab.	59	Pfeddelsheim	64-0170
BOHLEYER, Joh.Mich	23	Lauffen	63-1038
BOHLING, Joh.	19	Hannover	64-0427
BOHLING, Luetge	18	Neuenhuelsted	64-0593
BOHLMAN, Augusta	19	Sophienburg	66-0650
August 29, Albertine 22, Bertha 3			
Friedr. Aug. 6m			
BOHLMANN, Anna	26	Blendern	66-0578
BOHLMANN, Carl	35	Colberg	66-0577
BOHLMANN, Ernestin	23	Kottenhammer	66-0734
Friedrich A. 3, Emma 10m			
BOHLMANN, Heinr.	24	Gr. Starensch	67-0007
Angeline 50, Hermann 19, Heinrich 15			
Marie 24, Anne 12, Catharina 7			
BOHLMANN, Marg.	22	Bremen	63-0953
BOHLMANN, Math.	22	Bremen	63-0482
BOHLMANN, Meta	48	Bremen	64-0363
Johanna 18			
BOHLSEN, Johann	36	Oldenburg	66-0984
Albert 18			
BOHM, Barbara	26	Philadelphia	63-0551
BOHM, Franz	24	Prussia	64-0363
BOHM, Jacob	20	Imshausen	64-0665
BOHME, Caroline	24	Borich/Wald.	66-0469
BOHME, W.	30	Oberpiera	64-0886
BOHMER, Franz	43	Wetzlar	64-0138
BOHMER, Heinr.	26	Zell	64-0170
BOHMER, L.	24	Ostercappeln	65-0974
BOHN, C.(m)	19	Osnabrueck	64-0214
BOHN, Carl	21	Loewenstein	66-0576
BOHN, Christine	19	Wetzheim	63-1085
BOHN, Louise	18	Lengsfeld	66-1128
BOHNDORF, Johanna	40	Nordhausen	64-0938
BOHNE, Berno	17	Charlottenbrg	63-1218
BOHNE, Carl	42	Eisleben	23-0865
BOHNE, Eduard	32	Leipzig	64-0214
Anna 34			
BOHNE, William	35	New York	63-0862
BOHNENBERGEN, Cath	22	Engelsbrand	66-0412
BOHNER, Rosine	27	New York	63-0953
BOHNHARDT, Sophie	21	Eisenach	64-0170
BOHNMANN, Otto	26	Neuhof	66-0734
BOHNSACK, Christ.	46	Riebau	63-0614
Anna Elisab. 37, Wilhelm 9			
BOHR, Heirich	26	Osterwick	65-1030
BOHR, Johann	20	Lehe	63-1069
BOHRER, Charles	24	New Orleans	63-0953
BOHRER, Ph.	18	Oberstein	65-1189
BOHRMANN, Marie A.	24	Ibbenbueren	64-0886
BOISSARD, Cath.	30	Paris	65-0007
baby 6m			
BOITLSEN, Theodor	36	Neuscharrel	66-0984
Margarethe 24			
BOKEMANN, August	25	Boesingfeld	66-0984
BOLD, Francis	18	Hambach	63-1218
BOLD, Friedrich	27	Hermersberg	63-0296
BOLESLAWSKY, Gust.	33	Wien	63-0917
Leopoldine 29			
BOLICKLE, Martin	17	Bitz	64-0433
BOLIN, Andreas	49	Gottenburg	66-0666
BOLL, F.(m)	35	Husterford	64-0331
BOLL, Ferdinand	26	Baden	66-0109
BOLL, Heinrich	29	Philadelphia	66-0668
BOLL, Joseph	31	Stadtlohn	66-1127
BOLL, Marie	28	Krauchenowis	64-0495
Johanna 22, Magd. 4, Mart. 2, baby 6m			
BOLLAKER, Carl	17	Westphalen	66-0469
BOLLE, Augusta	23	Thiede	67-0007
BOLLER, Jacob	24	Bettingen	66-0221
BOLLERSCHEN, Joh.	25	Pluinbusch	64-0170
BOLLERT, Louis	40	Hildesheim	64-0495
Ca.(f) 22, Marie 1m, Carl 50, Marie 27			
L.(f) 5			

NAME	AGE	RESIDENCE	YR-LIST
BOLLING, Heinr.	33	Rotenburg	64-0073
Julius 14			
BOLLINGER, Andreas	23	Wulfershausen	66-1327
BOLLINGER, G.F.	25	Rothenburg	65-0151
BOLLMANN, Anna	28	Ahrssen	64-1053
BOLLMANN, Bernh.	19	Cloppenburg	64-0427
BOLLMANN, Conrad	27	Braunschweig	66-1031
BOLLMANN, H.	27	Ostercappeln	64-0782
BOLLWEG, Joh. Jos.	15	Baden	63-0822
BOLLWINKEL, Clemen	24	Mittelsbueren	66-1373
BOLNAD, Louis	22	Osterholz	63-1010
BOLSHER, Burgh.	29	California	63-1085
BOLTE, Aug.	30	Warendorf	65-0189
BOLTE, Dorothea	30	Stolzenau	66-0577
BOLTE, E.	18	Neu Morschen	64-0665
BOLTE, F.	23	Rinden	66-1313
BOLTE, F.	25	Delmenhorst	64-1161
BOLTE, Franz	25	Bremen	63-0822
Johanna 28			
BOLTE, Fz.	30	Holzminden	64-1206
BOLTE, H.	38	Elberfeld	64-1161
BOLTE, M. Ferd.	28	Gesmold	63-1038
BOLTER, August	22	Dissen	65-0950
BOLTER, Friedr.	39	Dissen	65-0950
Wilhelmine 41, Wilhelmine 18, Heinrich 16			
Fritz 14, August 9, Wilhelm 7			
Henriette 4, Marie 10m			
BOLZ, Anna Cath.	50	Hessen	64-0432
BOMMERSHEIM, Julia	15	Hessen	63-0822
BOMMOES, Cath.	20	Bingenhaim	64-0073
BONACKER, Therese	17	Cassel	66-0412
BONDE, Herm.	23	Orbeta	64-0023
BONDSTADT, Charltt	23	Hannover	63-1136
BONER, Albert	18	Hovestadt	63-0752
BONGER, Fd.	20	Ruhrbach	64-0593
BONHACK, C. Fr.	21	Mainz	63-1010
BONIGK, Chris.	19	Breslau	63-0015
BONK, Johannes	21	Leer	65-1088
Joh. Heinr. 21			
BONKY, Moritz	7	Boehmen	64-0687
BONMUELLER, Rich.	26	Frankfurt	64-0885
BONN, C.P.	23	Himmighofen	63-1003
BONN, Johann Chr.		Walden	66-1155
BONNFELDT, Conrad	21	Beckum	63-0482
BONRAU, Peter	43	Eitorf	63-1136
BOODE, Heinrich	32	Meppen	66-0346
BOOK, Fritz	17	Geestendorf	64-0739
BOOM, v.d. Aug.	18	Stadtlohn	66-1127
Cathar. 20			
BOOR, Henriette	50	Peine	67-0600
BOORIG, M.	58	Dunsenhausen	66-0413
Rosine 52			
BOOS, Cath.	21	Bahlingen	63-1136
BOOS, Heinrich	43	Bulstein	66-0934
Wilhelmine 32, August 9, Ludwig 7			
Heinrich 5, Emil 3, baby 9m			
BOPART, Heinrich	27	Opkan	66-0679
BOPP, Carl	15	Laibach	66-1131
BOPPERT, Franzizka	30	Straubenzel	63-1010
BORCHACHT, Eduard	23	Petershagen	65-1095
BORCHARDT, Martin	47	Grielow	66-0668
BORCHELT, Hinrich	23	Verden	64-0739
BORCHER, Cath.	20	Koehlen	64-0840
Anna 16			
BORCHER, Louise	27	Winnenberg	65-1024
Apollonia 9, baby 9m			
BORCHERDING, C.(m)	55	New York	64-0363
BORCHERDING, H.	23	Balkum	65-1024
BORCHERDING, Heinr	20	Suedhaemmern	66-0469
BORCHERDING, Soph.	20	Huttbergen	66-0934
BORCHERDING, Soph.	1	Schlesinghsn.	64-0992
BORCHERS, Caroline	20	Ringstedt	66-1093
BORCHERS, Fr.	27	Linden	64-0495
L.(f) 28			
BORCHERS, Herm.	58	Bunde	64-0170
Ankea 58, Albert 17			
BORCHERT, Albertin	18	Erbsen	65-1030
BORCHERT, Ernst	20	Verden	66-1373

NAME	AGE	RESIDENCE	YR-LIST
BORCHES, Carl	41	Muenster	66-1243
BORCHIO, Maria	43	Italia	63-0015
BORDA, Johann	37	Prag	66-0083
Catharine 31, Wenzel 6, Johann 2			
BORDEMANN, Anna	26	Wardenburg	66-0734
BORDMEYER, H.(m)	28	Salzbergen	64-0331
Johanna 21			
BORDORF, Cathre.	35	Bremen	63-0821
BORENS, Mathias	29	Euren	63-0990
BORG, Wilhelm	23	Hannover	64-1022
BORGEHOLZ, Carl	33	Dettmold	66-1243
BORGERS, Elise	40	Sandstedt	63-0350
Gustav 9, Adelheid 8, John 7			
BORGETT, Joseph	26	Glaue	66-0984
BORGGREVE, F.(m)	26	Bevergern	64-0331
BORGMANN, A.	23	Versmold	65-0974
BORGMANN, Aug.	30	Zeestendorf	64-0138
BORGMANN, Heinr.	18	Damme	64-0170
BORGMEYER, A.	20	Lar	66-0934
BORGSTEDE, J.H.	17	Drehle	65-1024
BORJES, Louise	32	Faehr	65-1088
Diedrich 5, Johannes 9m			
BORK, Jacob	65	Bronnshausen	67-0954
Anna 49, Elisabeth 18, Philipp 10			
Georg 8			
BORK, Johanna	23	Preussen	64-0363
BORKHOLZ, Charles	34	Preussen	63-1136
Regine 31, William 7, Wilhelmine 4			
Augusta 9m			
BORLE, Friedrich	19	Dorum	66-0734
BORMANN, A.	28	Schoeningen	65-0007
Caroline 25, Toni (f) 4			
BORMANN, Carl	21	Rabber	65-1031
BORMANN, Caroline	1	Pr. Friedland	66-0704
BORMANN, Ernst	17	Minsen	66-0934
BORMANN, Heinrich	43	Odenstedt	66-0734
Dorothea 42, Caroline 11, Johanna 9			
Heinrich 2, Carl 10m, Amalie 17			
BORMANN, Louise	23	Frohnhausen	66-1155
BORMANN, Sophie	15	Hasbergen	63-0398
BORN, Anna	30	Lobernheim	66-1093
Ernst 9, Catharina 4, Johann 3, Anna 7m			
BORN, Anton	32	Prussia	64-0427
Rosalia 25, baby 9m			
BORN, Elise	23	Wallenberg	66-0734
Augusta 21			
BORN, Gustav	33	Breslau	65-1030
BORN, Philip	18	Darmstadt	66-1127
BORN, Philipp	18	Brambach	67-0007
BORNEMANN, August	23	Wetben	66-1373
BORNEMANN, C.W.	36	Kirchberg	64-0495
BORNEMANN, Wilhelm	19	Bremen	66-1327
BORNHOLTZ, A.(m)	31	Bremerhofen	64-0138
Frand.(f) 26, Lina 8			
BORNSCHEIN, Aug. F	48	New York	64-0199
BORNSCHIER, Elisb.	23	Weissenboesel	64-0886
BOROWEK, Anton	58	Crauder	66-1155
Anna 55, Aloisa 29			
BORRUS, Aug.	21	Bunnen	63-1038
BORSCH, Leonhard	20	Fuerth	65-0713
BORSCHACH, Jos.	28	Switzerland	64-0138
BORSDORFF, (m)	33	New York	63-0990
BORST, Amalie	18	Geislingen	63-1069
BORSTEL, Marie C.	33	Bremen	67-1005
Helene 9			
BORTFELDT, Ma.(m)	17	Luedingworth	64-0363
BOSCH, Carl	28	Scheveningen	66-0083
Elisabeth 58, Caroline 8			
BOSCH, Chr.	26	Alsen	65-0898
Catharine 54, Sophie 19, Louise 13			
BOSCH, Emma	22	Wesselwald	66-1248
BOSCH, Gustav	17	Ringsheim	67-0353
Pauline 16			
BOSCH, Joh.	19	Appeln	65-1024
BOSCH, Johann	28	Hartefeld	66-1128
Catharine 23, baby bob			
BOSCH, Lisette	27	Brooklyn	63-1038
BOSCH, Xaver	27	Wuerttemberg	66-0934

NAME	AGE	RESIDENCE	YR-LIST
BOSCHE, Fanny	25	Peru	66-0984
BOSCHEN, Conrad	24	Groeplingen	63-0097
BOSCHENMEYER, J.	37	Quakenbrueck	64-0992
Louise 36, Johanna 39, Heinrich 7, Meta 5			
Diedrich 4, Wilhelm 3, August 11m			
BOSCHMANN, Christ.	58	Muelsen	66-1373
BOSE, Bernh.	24	Westrup	63-1136
Henriette 23, Louise 3, Henry 11m			
BOSER, Maria Elise	24	Kappeln	63-1069
BOSHAR, Philipp	30	Ruebelberg	66-0576
BOSMA, Sander	20	Weenermoor	66-0668
BOSS, Carl	18	Geisburg	65-0865
BOSS, Chr.	21	Switz.	63-0350
BOSSARD, Henry	29	New York	64-0432
BOSSE, Bernhard	26	Lehen	64-1053
BOSSE, Ernst	32	Rehburg	66-0576
Lisette 26, Johanna 4, Ernst 9m			
BOSSE, Franz	9	Borgloh	63-1038
BOSSE, Franz	14	Leer	66-1131
BOSSE, Heinr.	36	Magdeburg	63-0398
BOSSE, Louis	21	Hannover	67-0007
BOSSER, Nicolaus	21	Sudenweyhe	64-0885
BOSSERT, Georg	23	Rothweil	66-0221
BOSSERT, James	34	Carlsruhe	63-1218
BOSSMANN, Johannes	68	Freisa	65-1024
BOTAMINO, Jacob	16	Muehlbach	65-0948
BOTELSMANN, Minna	15	Hamburg	64-0886
BOTH, Ele.(f)	26	Burweiler	64-0782
BOTH, J.G.	31	Schorndorf	66-0413
BOTH, Sophie	23	Hindheim	64-0639
BOTSCH, Magdalena	28	Wildbach	66-0934
baby 3m			
BOTT, Babette	23	Bruchsal	63-1085
BOTT, John	37	Warsau	63-0862
BOTTIGES, Joh. Hr.	40	Zanne	66-1248
Rebecca 38, Doris 7, Lina 5, Wilhelm 7			
BOTTMER, Louise	31	Rheda	66-1128
Helene 4, Adolph 6m			
BOTTMER, v. Chr.	45	Hungaria	63-0244
BOTZOW, Wilhelm	24	Berlin	65-0770
BOUGILOT, Therese	23	New York	64-0073
BOURAUEL, Peter	43	Preussen	63-0398
BOURNAUF, Ernestin	21	France	63-0350
Alexandrine 30, Maria 19			
BOUSSIER, Alex'dr.	27	Matanzas	66-0934
BOVEN, Heinrich	32	Meppen	65-1088
Anna 22, Helene 10m			
BOWE, Chr.	29	Wannsfeld	65-0007
BOWE, Heinrich	16	Backum	66-1127
BOWENSKY, Joseph	46	Cestone	67-0007
Cathrine 46, Marie 21, Johann 20			
Joseph 17			
BOY, Chs.	28	Lodersleben	64-0593
BOYAR, Magdalene	32	New York	63-0244
BOYD, Sara	52	Stuttgart	64-0639
Minna 24			
BOYNEBURGH, v. W.	42	Gotha	64-0170
BRAASCHE, Fr.	20	Wolfenbuettel	63-1010
BRACHHOLD, Jacob	20	Wildbad	66-0984
BRACHMANN, Ludw.	38	Sax.-Meiningn	64-0432
BRACHT, Carl	18	Paderborn	64-1161
BRACHT, Heinrich	26	Ellenhausen	66-1248
Christian 30, Friedrich 19			
BRACKHAHN, Aug.	55	Kemmnade/Br.	65-0038
Caroline 17			
BRACKMANN, August	25	Billerbeck	66-1031
BRAECK, Carl	37	Klein Bislau	66-0469
Susanna 30, Wilhelm 6m			
BRAENDLIN, Johann	24	Istein	66-0668
BRAERKL, Christian	51	Markgroningen	66-0576
Ernestine 19, Christian 2			
BRAEUER, Marie	28	Esen	67-0992
BRAEUTIGAM, Eduard	19	Pflazdorf	66-0623
Marie 16			
BRAGER, M.	39	Fortsheim	66-0413
BRAIVOGEL, Johann	27	Preussen	66-0221
BRAKE, Maria	23	Esterwegen	66-1131
Marie 23			

NAME	AGE	RESIDENCE	YR-LIST
BRAKE, Ollig	45	Esterwegen	66-1131
Heinrich 4, Lina 35, Ollig 2, Wilhelm 22			
BRAKEBUSH, A.	30	Wohlenhausen	64-0992
Heinrich 27			
BRAKELKEN, Elise	18	Drifsethe	66-0934
BRAKENHOFF, E. (m)	27	Nordgeorgfehn	64-0331
BRAM, V.W.	30	Chemnitz	65-1189
BRAMBECK, August	20	Neckargartach	66-0934
BRAMER, Johann	26	Berlin	66-0679
BRAMKAMP, Johanna	21	Bramkampf	66-0704
BRAMKE, William	17	Bernhausen	66-1131
BRAMM, Conrad		Lauterbach	63-0614
BRAMSTEDT, Diedr.	25	Neuenkirchen	66-1093
BRAMSTEDT, Hermann	19	Wiesenstedt	66-1093
BRANCH, Sophie	19	Gerabronn	66-0704
BRAND, (f)	48	Geestendorf	65-0974
Heinrich 7, Herrmann 9m			
BRAND, Adolph	20	Breslau	65-1031
BRAND, Anna	24	Essen	64-0938
BRAND, Carl	23	Staken	67-0007
BRAND, Wilh.	20	Bevera	66-0984
BRAND, William	27	Burgstall	63-1038
BRANDAU, A.	29	Heiligenstadt	64-0665
BRANDAU, Andreas	20	Wabern	66-0734
BRANDAU, Dorothea	29	Piefe	66-0934
BRANDAU, Elise	25	Hilter	65-0007
BRANDAU, H.O.	34	Hamburg	64-0331
BRANDAU, Hch.Ludw.	21	Hilte	63-1069
BRANDEIS, Jacob	43	Boehmen	63-0990
BRANDEIS, Joseph	24	Boehmen	63-0990
BRANDENBURGER, A.	21	Weissenberg	65-1189
* BRANDENBURGER, Joh	22	Weissenberg	64-0593
BRANDENSTEIN, H.	23	Huemmel	64-0593
Emma 15			
BRANDES, Chrs.	8	Grohnde	66-0934
BRANDES, Friedrich	29	Peine	65-1030
Caroline 22, Hermann 1			
BRANDES, H.F.	20	California	63-0917
BRANDES, Heinr.	30	Brunkensen/Br	65-0038
BRANDES, Ludwig	30	Bremke	65-1030
Regine 35, Catharine 9m			
BRANDHORST, C.F.	43	Duesseldorf	65-0038
BRANDHORST, Heinr.	15	Hille	64-0214
BRANDIS, L.(m)	21	Hannover	64-0427
BRANDSTAEDTER, Joh	20	Altenrieth	64-0593
BRANDSTETTER, Magd	66	Benchen	66-0109
BRANDT, August		Dissen	66-1031
BRANDT, Carl	34	Clausthal	65-0151
BRANDT, Carl	30	Stadthagen	65-0770
Marie 28, Wilhelm 4, Pauline 2, Marie 3m			
BRANDT, Carl Fr.	28	Eilenburg	66-1313
BRANDT, Charlotte	17	Zeckwerder/Pr	65-0038
David 16			
BRANDT, Friedrich	23	Geiselheim	66-0576
BRANDT, Georg	28	Abafleth	66-1128
BRANDT, Gottlieb	49	Pommern	66-0469
Wilhelmine 46, Hermann 18, Carl 13			
Ernestine 10, August 2, Wilhelmine 16			
BRANDT, H.	16	Delmenhorst	66-0934
BRANDT, H.	25	Hulshagen	65-0402
BRANDT, Hermann	20	Meinberg	64-1053
BRANDT, Johann	38	Rehme	65-1095
Anna M. 24, Friedr.Louis 13, Simon 9			
Friedrich 7, Maria Louise 3, Karoline 1			
BRANDT, Johanna	21	Preussen	63-0990
BRANDT, Joseph	24	Steinfeld	65-0948
BRANDT, Luitjen	35	Kl.Ahlendorf	65-0243
Gretje 30, Harm L. 7, Jan W. 5, Wilh. 2			
BRANDT, Maria	18	Hommetshausen	65-0402
BRANDT, Marie	23	Estel	65-0189
BRANDT, Mathilde	16	Meinsen	66-0984
BRANDT, Mina	17	Reckendorf	66-0704
BRANDT, Sophie	23	Walsrode	64-0739
BRANGER, Philipp	47	Mineralpoint	66-0984
BRANHOFF, Georg	20	Alsfeld	64-0885
BRANING, Pantalon	40	Illinois	66-0984
Anna 19			
BRANKMANN, Heinr.	38	Hildesheim	65-0865

NAME	AGE	RESIDENCE	YR-LIST
BRANKMUELLER, Hch.	41	Hannover	66-0679
Caroline 40, Caroline 18, Louise 9			
Christine 8, Johanna 4, Dorette 2			
BRANSCHEIDT, Fr.	29	New York	64-0023
BRANZ, Carl Aug.	21	Mosbach	67-0007
BRASCH, Benjamin	26	Tempelberg	64-0214
BRASE, Heinr.	30	Bolschle	64-0992
Caroline 28, Wilhelmine 7, Louise 6m			
BRASS, Caspar	32	Lippstadt	66-0577
BRASSE, Chr.	17	Pr. Minden	63-0398
BRASSE, Elise	24	Dissen	63-0917
BRASSEL, Adolph	22	Memphis	63-0693
BRATFISCH, Marie	31	Friedmansdorf	66-0576
Marie 8, Selma 6, Franzisca 2			
Heinrich 10m			
BRATIE, Henry	10	New York	63-0917
BRATRSOWSKY, Franz	38	Boehmen	64-0427
Josepha 37, Anna 14, Maria 7			
BRAUCH, Catharina	28	Gerabron	66-0704
BRAUCH, Wm.	36	Kreuznach	64-0023
BRAUDER, Appolonia	58	Rippoldsen	66-0734
BRAUER, C.L.	27	Bremen	63-1085
BRAUER, Christian	23	Peoria	66-1127
Marie 23			
BRAUER, F. (m)	31	Stettin	64-0331
BRAUER, Marcus	25	Bockel	64-0427
BRAUN, Abraham	28	Brake	66-0147
BRAUN, Adam	16	Hattenbach	66-0623
BRAUN, Albertine	26	Spaidringen	63-0990
BRAUN, Andreas	18	Kilidostetten	63-1038
BRAUN, Anna Marie	26	Holzhausen	64-1053
BRAUN, Anton	22	Neuenheim	63-0244
BRAUN, Aug.	18	Steinbach	63-1136
BRAUN, August	46	Barmen	63-1069
BRAUN, Blasius	18	Tittlingen	64-0331
BRAUN, Caroline	17	Baumbach	64-0782
BRAUN, Catharine	19	Stockhausen	65-1031
BRAUN, Elisa	28	Baltimore	64-0427
BRAUN, Engelbert	23	Neudingen	64-1022
BRAUN, Fanny	27	New York	66-0576
BRAUN, Friedr.	24	New York	64-0170
BRAUN, Friedrich	55	Neustettin	66-0837
Augusta 24			
BRAUN, G.	22	Derending	64-0639
BRAUN, Gottlieb	26	Wilkowa	66-0469
BRAUN, Heinrich	18	Eiderhagen	66-0412
Anna Elisab. 17			
BRAUN, Heinrich	23	Giessen	66-1327
BRAUN, Jacob	16	Waldorf	66-0147
BRAUN, Jacob	49	Muelsen	66-1373
BRAUN, Jacob	20	Weilheim	64-0363
BRAUN, Joh.	32	Uslede	64-1108
Lina 22			
BRAUN, Joh. H.	21	Mossbach/Weim	65-0038
BRAUN, Johann	24	Allendorf	66-0349
BRAUN, Johann	36	Egenstein	66-0083
Susanne 26			
BRAUN, Johann	22	Schwabach	66-0083
BRAUN, John	33	Gr. Bisdorf	64-0593
Caroline 34, Clara 9m			
BRAUN, John Chr.	29	Bruchsal	63-0551
Ernestine 27, Chr. 11m			
BRAUN, Joseph	25	Dietingen	66-1155
BRAUN, Joseph	25	Kreuznach	66-1373
BRAUN, Louise	57	Landau	64-0427
Marie 20			
BRAUN, Mathilde	22	Oberlahn	63-0006
BRAUN, Michael	31	Wien	66-0934
Margarethe 32, Marie 9m			
BRAUN, Nicolaus	28	Cassel	66-1373
BRAUN, Pauline	23	Waldheim	63-0990
BRAUN, Theodor	30	Lich	66-1093
BRAUN, W.	36	Baden	64-0593
Sophie 15, Lisa 14, Peter 7			
BRAUN, Wilhelm	23	Hechtheim	66-0576
BRAUN, Wm.	22	Oppenau	64-0138
BRAUN, v. Adolph	20	Oehringen	66-1203
BRAUNAGER, Julius	20	Wuertemberg	66-0984

NAME	AGE	RESIDENCE	YR-LIST
BRAUNBECK, W. G.	46	Gr. Aschbach	63-0482
BRAUNE, August	24	Roennebeck	66-0668
BRAUNERT, Joseph	43	Ratibor	66-0083
BRAUNINGER, Christ	18	Stettin	64-0170
BRAUWEIDEN, Geo'in	40	New York	64-0687
BREBBERMANN, Soph.	33	Uchte	65-0948
August 5, Wilhelm 3			
BRECHNITZ, V.(m)	19	Manburg	64-0495
BRECHT, Anna	20	Michelfeld	66-1203
BRECHT, Ernst	32	Fischbach	66-1155
BRECHT, J.	22	Mickelfeld	64-1161
BRECHT, Marg.	26	Auenstein	65-0189
BRECKERBAUM, Wilh.	20	Uslar	64-0687
Christine 17			
BRECKLE, Rosine	20	Osweil	65-0151
BRECKMANN, Clara	23	Bremen	66-0577
BRECKSCHEVE, Wlmne	22	Helle	66-0623
Sophie 17			
BREDE, Johann	23	Landwursten	67-0007
BREDEHOEF, Luetje	22	Nenndorf	67-0599
BREDEHOFF, Joseph	24	Coeln	64-0886
Marie 25			
BREDEHORST, D.	21	Bremen	64-1108
BREDEMEYER, Ch.	31	Melle	63-0551
BREDEMEYER, Joh.	40	Nienburg	64-0687
BREDEMEYER, Wm.	27	Pr. Minden	63-1038
BREDEN, Anna	36	Driftsethe	66-1127
Sophie 1			
BREDEN, Hermann	25	Wiste	66-1093
BREDHORST, v. Sixt	28	Hannover	66-0577
BREDIG, Ernestine	28	Posen	66-0221
BREEN, Franz	19	Breitenthal	67-0007
BREFELDT, Gerhard	24	Gronau	64-0840
Adelheid 60, Angela 28, Catharina 21			
Maria Anna 19, Gertrude 16			
BREHM, Carl	26	Osnabrueck	64-0363
BREHM, Ernst	46	Eisfeld	64-0665
Amalie 41, Hugo 13			
BREHM, Heinrich	41	New York	66-0934
Anna 23, Louise 18, August 19, Wilhelm 9			
BREHMAIER, Carl	36	Erzen	66-1243
George 34			
BREHMER, Carl	31	Preussen	66-0469
BREIDENBACH, Math.	29	Hofgeismar	66-0679
BREIDING, Augusta	20	Homberg	65-1030
Elisabeth 17			
BREIHAN, Heinrich	26	Gitter	66-0221
BREINGEN, Friedr.	25	Brackennag	63-0482
BREINING, Eduard	19	Plieningen	64-1206
BREININGER, Fr'dke	35	Backnang	64-0138
BREIT, Leopold	48	Wien	64-0456
Maria 33			
BREITACKER, D.(m)	30	Dottingen	64-0073
BREITENBACH, Ph.	36	Sievershausen	66-0413
Caroline 33			
BREITENBURGER, Jul	24	Minden	65-1031
BREITSCHNEIDER, A.	23	Ehrenfriedr.	63-0482
BREITSPUCKER, Hch.	42	Pommern	66-0469
Friederike 35, Friedr. 12, Albert 3			
BREITUNG, Martha	42	Gr. Almerode	65-0004
BREITWIESER, Ph.	34	Gruenstadt	64-0495
BREKE, Anna Marie	24	Bissendorf	65-0948
BREKEL, Friederike	30	Salmbach	66-0704
BRELLIE, Heinr.	30	Hartem	66-0704
BREM, Johannes	27	Augum	65-0243
BREMANN, G.F.	34	Bremen	64-0331
Johanna 21			
BREMEN, Elisabeth	53	Lienen	66-0679
Ernst 21			
BREMEN, J.(m)	27	New York	64-0331
BREMENNEN, Elis.	55	Atsberg	64-0427
BREMER, Anna	19	Weidenhausen	64-1108
BREMER, Fr.	37	Holte	64-0739
Johanna 37, Hinrica 3, Johann 11m			
BREMER, Friederike	21	Dorum	66-0704
BREMER, Friedrich	24	Prussia	63-1218
BREMER, Hermann H.	18	Wittorf	66-0934
BREMER, Joachim	32	Strolph	66-1327

NAME	AGE	RESIDENCE	YR-LIST
Maria 40, Louise 6, Maria 5			
BREMER, Joh.	30	Martfeld	65-0055
BREMER, Johann G.	24	Egenhausen	66-1327
BREMER, Minna	21	Eschershausen	63-0482
BREMKE, Joseph	32	New York	63-0168
BREMS, Anna	28	Hoenteln	65-1030
BREMS, Joh. H.	21	Schwarme	64-1206
Carsten 32			
BREMSER, Gustav	19	Magdeburg	65-0865
BREND, E.(m)	7	Elberfeld	64-0495
BRENER, Gottfried	39	Bergheim	66-1031
Margarethe 22, Sigismund 4			
BRENNECKE, Carl	18	Polle	66-1373
BRENNECKE, Chr.	28	Barnsen	64-0639
BRENNECKE, Georg	21	Bremen	63-0693
BRENNECKE, Heinr	28	Eschede	64-0214
BRENNECKE, Heinr.	54	Hannover	64-0432
Marie 52, Heinr. 11, Minna 9			
BRENNEL, Emil	20	Leibis	66-0934
BRENNER, Fr. Ferd.	19	Osterfeld	63-0821
BRENNER, Friedr.	20	Harzberg	64-0363
BRENNER, L.	48	Wiesbaden	64-0992
BRENNER, Marie	55	Osnabrueck	67-0600
BRENNINGER, Cath.	19	Forchtenberg	66-1203
BRENNSTIEL, Friedr	21	Osnabrueck	63-1069
BRENZEL, Catharina	25	Curhessen	63-0822
BRENZING, Marie	15	Wichmansdorf	66-1127
BRENZMANN, August	23	Groning	66-0469
Wilhelmine 23			
BRESCH, Me. (f)	42	Schutter	64-0363
Caspar 15			
BRESLAND, Rose	18	Philadelphia	63-0482
BRETHAUER, Ludw.	36	Eschenstrudt	65-0038
Cath. Elis 31			
BRETSCHNEIDER, Fr.	25	Ehrenfriedhof	65-0594
BRETSCHNEIDER, Hch	32	Jueseheld	66-0623
BRETZGER, Chr'tne.	14	Wuertemberg	63-0822
BRETZGER, Margaret	25	Wuerttemberg	63-0822
BREUER, Gottfried	39	Bergheim	66-1031
Margarethe 22, Sigismund 4			
BREUER, Gust.	23	Althofen	63-1085
BREUER, Jos.	26	Mackesdorf	64-0331
Johanna 21			
BREUER, Meta	23	Holzel	64-1206
BREUN, L.	40	Halle	63-0168
BREUSEL, Conr.	24	Hersfeld	65-0898
BREUSING, Adolph	30	Osnabrueck	64-0782
BREYER, Andreas	50	New York	63-0821
BREYER, Clara	47	Boehmen	63-1038
BREYER, Hugo	30	Breslau	65-1088
Pauline 23			
BREZOWSKY, Mar. An	33	Oberliebig/A.	63-0822
BRIAN, Aug.	27	St Antonia	66-0679
BRICHHAUSEN, Otto	18	Horn	66-0704
BRICKMANN, H.	51	Braamsche	66-0679
Margarethe 20			
BRICKMANN, Juergen	34	Worms	66-0679
Noll 21			
BRICKWEDEL, G.Hen.	39	Drangstedt	66-0221
BRIEDE, Philipp	21	Marburg	66-1128
BRIEGEL, Joh.	27	Marzenheim	64-0782
Christine 27, Philipp 2, George 3m			
BRIEGGEMANN, Soph.	24	Petershagen	66-0734
Sophie 3m			
BRIEL, Johann	34	Berlin	64-1053
BRIEN, G.W.	15	Bremen	63-1085
BRILE, Heinrich	15	Steppach	66-0679
BRILL, Andr.	35	Rodenberg	64-0214
BRILL, Anna Cath.	56	Landefeld	66-0412
Johann Jacob 16			
BRILL, August	19	Friedrichshor	66-0578
BRILL, Caroline	29	Koenigsdorf	65-0038
BRILL, Lud. Christ	29	Kurhessen	66-0349
BRILLE, Cathre.	23	Braunau	63-0990
Friedrich 11m, Elise			
BRILLE, Maria	28	Braunau	63-0990
Emma 11m			
BRILLENSTEIN, Joh.	32	Markt Erlbach	64-0214

NAME	AGE	RESIDENCE	YR-LIST
Joh. 32, Cath 32, Margar. 8, Friedr. 5			
BRINCKMANN, Louise	15	Westphalen	66-0469
BRINGMANN, Cath. M	21	Hildburghsn.	64-0886
BRINGMANN, Georg	43	Hausroeder	65-1088
Charlotte 32, Minna 5, Carl 9			
BRINGMANN, H.A.	31	Osnabrueck	64-0593
BRINGMANN, Joh.	57	Wendershausen	63-0398
Christine 29, Peter 17			
BRINK, Friedrich	18	Unterluebbe	64-0433
BRINK, Marie	59	Mettlingen	65-0189
Elise 22, Josephine 19, Hugo 18			
BRINKEN, T.W.(m)	31	Hadersleben	64-0023
BRINKHOFF, Louise	24	Dortmund	65-1088
BRINKMANN, Anna	28	Lemgo	66-1093
BRINKMANN, Anna	25	Erdinghausen	64-1108
BRINKMANN, Antion.	28	Ankum	66-0679
BRINKMANN, August	25	Kreiensen	65-0004
Heinrich 19			
BRINKMANN, E.	49	Lippe Detmold	66-0413
Wilhelmine 36, Fritz 15, Ernst 9, Minna 6			
Caroline 4, Simon 10m			
BRINKMANN, Eduard	24	Boystenburg	65-0151
BRINKMANN, Friedr.	22	Melle	67-0007
BRINKMANN, Friedr.	40	Wietgen	64-0739
Sophie 48			
BRINKMANN, H.	35	Newport	64-0687
BRINKMANN, Heinr.	34	Dinklage	65-0948
BRINKMANN, J.C.	21	Delmenhorst	64-0427
BRINKMANN, Joh. C.	22	Buschhausen	64-0885
BRINKMANN, Karl	18	Eichhorst	64-0665
BRINKMANN, Lisette	20	Oldenburg	66-0221
BRINKMANN, Ludw.	31	Lippoldsberg	66-0650
BRINKMANN, Ludwig	17	Wulferdingen	64-0433
Ernst 22			
BRINKMANN, Marie	19	Husede	66-0668
BRINKMANN, Math.	28	Magdeburg	64-0214
wife 22, baby 9m			
BRINKMANN, Wilhelm	35	Coburg	66-1327
BRINKMEIER, Lewis	16	Pr. Minden	63-0244
BRINKMEYER, C.(m)	55	Minden	64-0495
H.(f) 43			
BRINKOETTER, Henrt	25	Beckhorst	65-0950
BRINKSCHULTE, Anna	66	Almersloh	66-1031
BRIOR, John	25	Ellerbeck	63-1218
BRITTEN, Anna	56	Irsch	65-0007
Elise 29, Cath. 22, Magd. 9			
BROC, Charles	26	Frankenthal	63-0693
BROCH, Carl	35	Huelsen	66-0109
BROCH, Julie	19	Wald	63-0990
BROCHMANN, Anna M.	50	Wanna	64-0456
Marg. 26, Rebecca 16			
BROCHMANN, Minna	21	Sievern	67-0795
BROCK, Julius	30	Berlin	63-1085
BROCKE, Caroline	21	Einbeck	66-1131
BROCKELMANN, Fr'dr	17	Visselhoevede	66-1031
BROCKER, Carl	47	Retzen	63-1010
BROCKER, Ludwig	23	Hullhorst	65-0898
BROCKHAGEN, Joh.	58	Garbeck	64-0938
Cath. 58, Florentine 19			
BROCKHAUS, Anastas	38	Muehlheim	64-0170
BROCKHAUS, Emilie	21	Stadtlohn	66-1127
BROCKHAUS, Fritz	40	New York	63-0822
BROCKHAUSEN, Carl	20	Horn	63-1178
BROCKHAUSEN, Hch.	26	Hoexter	64-0840
BROCKHOFF, Bernard	36	Lohne	64-0433
BROCKLING, Josefin	28	Dellbruch	66-1248
BROCKLINGER, Anna	29	Philadelphia	64-0331
BROCKMANN, Carolne	20	Krukam	64-0433
BROCKMANN, Conrad	48	Haustenbeck	65-1088
Elisabeth 41, Henriette 15, Wilhelm 13			
Friedrich 12, Conrad 3			
BROCKMANN, Franz	26	Haseluene	66-1373
BROCKMANN, Joh. Ch	33	Otterndorf	63-0990
Johanna 25, Henry 2			
BROCKMANN, Joh. H.	64	Fladerlohhaus	66-0984
Adelheid 56, Joh. Heinr. 33, Catharina 34			
Anna 7, Johann 10m			
BROCKMANN, John	24	Bucken	63-0953

NAME	AGE	RESIDENCE	YR-LIST
BROCKMEYER, Cat. F	31	Westbarthsn.	63-0917
Hermann 4			
BROCKMEYER, Friedr	28	Dohren	64-0138
Ernst 15			
BROCKMEYER, Wlh'mn	23	Prussia	64-0432
BROCKSCHMIDT, Hch.	34	Osnabruck	64-0427
BROCKSTEDT, Joseph	27	Hamburg	65-0713
BRODBAECKER, Wm.	18	Darmstadt	66-0837
BRODT, Jacob	25	Strueth	65-0402
BROECKER, Mary	21	Sutthausen	64-0343
BROEDER, Tobias	42	Gumbach	65-0594
Magdalena 35, Cath. 7, baby 10m, Lina 20			
BROEGE, Peter	20	Twistringen	65-0151
BROEKELMANN, Georg	18	Manil/Pr.	64-1053
Cath 25			
BROELL, E.L.	26	Durlach	64-0138
BROENLAGE, Lisette	21	Suttrup	66-1127
BROENLICH, Joseph	17	Truban	66-1203
BROENNER, Amalia	21	Poppenheim	64-0639
BROENSTRUP, Minna	23	Ledde	65-0898
BROERING, Heinr.	18	Dinklage	66-0984
BROERMANN, L.J.	25	Wersen	64-0639
BROERMANN, Wilh.	18	Ostercappeln	65-0898
BROHE, Jos.	28	Bonn	64-0170
BROHNSACK, Christ.	46	Riebau	63-0614
Anna Elisa. 37, Wilhelm 9			
BROICH, Carl Ed.	24	Solingen	63-0822
Friedr.Aug. 18			
BROKAMP, Heinrich	24	Oldenburg	66-0221
BROKHASKER, E.	17	Schwartz Kost	66-0413
BROM, Franz	32	Bingen	65-0770
BROMANN, Joseph	28	Hoeppnigen	64-0840
BROMM, Anna	48	Kurhessen	63-0398
Theresia 18			
BRONK, v. Philipp	33	Polen	66-0666
Antonia 23, Anna 9m			
BROOK, Heinrich	40	Kr.Salzwedel	67-0599
Dorothea 24, Friederike 9m			
Joh. Joachim 55, Dorothea El. 50			
BROSANG, Julie	30	Bremen	64-0427
BROSANG, William	29	Gross.Bruckw.	63-0752
BROSCH, Carl	54	Wald	63-0398
Julie 52, Kuno 17, Clara 13, Anna 9			
BROSCHART, Seb.	58	Waldfischbach	65-0950
BROSKSHUS, H.(m)	16	Hurrel	64-0170
BROSSE, F.W.	16	Rheine	66-0221
BROSSIN, Maria	26	Viegrehen	65-0116
BROUER, Jan	39	Veenhusen	64-0363
Bratje 42, baby 6m, Harmke 15, Eitje 13			
Henderje 10, Greetje 8, Bredje 5, Coene 2			
BROZECK, Johann	27	Schneidemuehl	66-0679
Augusta 29			
BRUCH, Christoph	50	Bromberg	64-0432
Wilhelmine 49, Ernestine 21			
Wilhelmine 17, Anna Wilh. 13, Aug. 5			
BRUCHHEIMER, Chrs.	20	Ottenhausen	66-0221
BRUCK, Theod.	28	New York	64-0495
BRUCKCHEN, Cath.	20	Hochwiese	65-0770
BRUCKHARDT, Isaac	26	Hermanstein	64-0782
BRUCKHOFF, Wilhelm	20	Putzbach	65-1031
BRUCKMANN, Ernstin	41	Bremervoerde	66-0679
BRUCKMANN, Heinr.W	23	Wanna	64-0456
BRUCKNER, Carl	17	Coblenz	66-0984
BRUDER, Anton	21	Offenburg	64-0214
BRUDER, Jean Bapt.	31	Suisse	63-0822
BRUDER, Othmar	16	Mederschopfhm	64-0073
Julie 18			
BRUECHER, Carl	44	Gr. Mustadt	66-0576
Eva 48, Cath. 15, Marie 9, Carl 5			
BRUECHNER, Adam	31	Steinfeld	67-0795
BRUECK, Alex	30	Zuerich	65-0974
BRUECK, Dan.	28	Bechenheim	64-0687
BRUECK, Johs.	28	Hermanstein	64-0782
Elisab. 23			
BRUECK, Justus	22	Altenbusch	64-0840
Wilhelm 25			
BRUECK, L.	28	Hoboken	66-1155
Louis 6			

NAME	AGE	RESIDENCE	YR-LIST
BRUECK, Philipp	23	Hermannstein	66-0576
BRUECKER, Agnes	52	Neustadt	65-1088
Caroline 26, Carl 24, Marie 14, Regine 12			
Bertha 6			
BRUECKMANN, Carl	26	Oberkaufen	66-0083
BRUECKMANN, Heinr.	17	Kaufungen	66-0934
BRUECKNER, Eduard	20	Sonnenberg	66-1327
BRUECKNER, H.	26	Sachsen	63-1003
K. 48			
BRUECKNER, Marg.	29	Coburg	64-0170
Fritz 4			
BRUECKNER, Sophie	33	Herford	66-0734
BRUEGE, Theodor	28	Erlbach	66-1203
BRUEGEL, Dorothea	21	Lauf	66-0704
BRUEGEMANN, Wilh.	23	Buehr	63-0953
BRUEGER, Carl Gott	50	New York	66-0109
BRUEGGE, Meta	20	Stolp	66-0934
BRUEGGE, v.d. C.	42	Versmold	65-0950
Herm. Heinr. 12, Heinr. Wilh. 7			
Heinr. Carl 4, Friedr. Wilh 10			
Charlotte 42			
BRUEGGEMANN, A.(m)	27	Osnabrueck	64-0331
BRUEGGEMANN, Claus	17	Bassum	66-0679
Wilhelm 20, Johann 18			
BRUEGGEMANN, Heinr	45	Hannover	66-1131
BRUEGGEMANN, T.	26	Lehden	66-0413
BRUEGGEMANN, Wilh.	31	Stadtlohn	66-1127
BRUEGGEMENN, Heinr	29	Verden	65-0243
Bertha 30, Lina 7, Marie 11m, Bertha 1m			
BRUEGGER, Joh. Hn.	43	Wirsum	65-1030
Maria Cath. 36, Anna 4m			
BRUEHL, Kunigunda	26	Long Island	63-0990
BRUEHM, Caroline	18	Waldeck	65-0007
BRUEHNER, Elise	20	Baiersdorf	66-1203
BRUEHNING, Heinr.	40	Wappen	64-0363
BRUEN, W.L.	36	Assmannshsn.	64-0427
BRUEND, Kunigunde	18	Ringstedt	66-1031
BRUENGER, Heinrich	24	Laar	66-0679
BRUENGER, Rudolph	17	Dissen	66-1128
BRUENING, Adolph	24	Linsen	23-0865
BRUENING, Beta	57	Bremen	63-0953
Henriette 26			
BRUENING, Bruen	20	Bassum	66-1127
BRUENING, Eduard	23	Bremen	66-0984
BRUENING, H.	30	Columbus	63-0953
BRUENING, Hch.Ludw	19	Minden/Pr.	63-0822
BRUENING, Joh.	27	Verden	65-0950
BRUENING, Johann	7	New York	66-0984
BRUENINGS, H.	16	Lehe	63-0821
BRUENINGS, Herm.	30	San Francisco	66-0984
Johanna 22, Johann 11m			
BRUENJES, Anna	21	Hambergen	64-1206
BRUENNA, John	41	Washington	66-0934
BRUENNEL, Franzska	19	Prag	66-0147
BRUENNER, Franz	19	Hohenberg	66-1093
BRUENNING, Heinr.N	15	Wanna	64-0456
BRUENR, Conr.	27	Sand	65-0189
BRUER, Friedr.	32	Hildesheim	66-0577
Dorothea 36			
BRUESSEL, Hulda	10	Stettin	67-0954
BRUETTING, Mariann	28	Bucherreuth	66-0412
BRUGGEMANN, Minna	20	Emstetten	66-1031
BRUK, Jacob	37	Gladenbach	66-1373
BRUKE, Wilhelm	25	Estwege	66-1373
BRUKHEIM, Sara	27	Bures	65-0402
BRUMEIS, Hyronimus	21	Veilsdorf	66-1131
BRUMHOP, D.(m)	23	Bremen	64-0331
BRUMLOOP, Diedrich	24	Bremen	65-0948
BRUMM, Christian	15	Rauschenberg	66-0412
BRUMM, Conrad	17	Rauschenberg	66-0668
BRUMMER, A.	40	Austria	64-0992
BRUMMER, Heinrich	43	Waldeck	66-0577
Caroline 35, Heinrich 14, Johannes 11			
Elisabeth 9			
BRUMMER, J.	29	Giessen	64-0687
BRUMMER, Rosine	31	Baus	65-1088
Maria 41			
BRUMMUND, Frdr.	30	Obenstroh	65-0116

NAME	AGE	RESIDENCE	YR-LIST
BRUMMUND, Gerh.	25	Obenstrohe	64-0214
BRUMSIEK, Aug.	58	Koenigslutter	63-0990
Henry 17			
BRUN, Jacq.	18	Switzerland	63-0990
BRUNCKAU, Sophia	55	Klarenhorst	66-0837
Lisette 21, Chr. Sophie 17, Konrad 15			
Heinrich 10			
BRUND, Friederike	23	Wildbach	66-0984
BRUNE, Cath.	20	Borgholzhsn	64-0170
BRUNE, Chr.	21	Preussen	64-0331
BRUNE, Friedr.	26	Wester Cappel	66-0469
Christian 21			
BRUNE, Friedr.	29	Hessen	66-0734
BRUNE, Friedr.	60	Mettingen	64-0840
BRUNE, Heinrich	25	Bockhorst	65-0974
BRUNE, wilhelm	19	Osnabrueck	67-0599
BRUNERS, Heinrich	19	Bremen	63-0053
BRUNERT, Angda	24	Rebbeke	64-0433
BRUNGER, Brone	32	Bakemoor	63-0006
BRUNING, Anna	23	Hannover	64-0739
Charlotte 16			
BRUNING, Rudolph	24	Muenster	63-0006
BRUNK, Friedrich	44	Preussen	63-1136
Anna 38, John 15, Augusta 13, William 8			
Julius 7, Christian 5, Emilie 9m			
BRUNKE, Christian	24	Wannbuettel	64-0904
BRUNKE, Wilhelm	32	Jerze	67-0007
BRUNKEN, T.M.(m)	29	Norden	64-0170
BRUNKER, A.(m)	25	Wien	64-0331
BRUNKHARDT, Johann	34	Ruedesheim	66-0679
Anna 31, baby (f) 3m			
BRUNKHORST, Johann	58	Harderstedt	66-1128
Catharine 45, Johann 26, Heinrich 22			
Elisabeth 19, Caspar 15, Jacob 7			
BRUNKHORST, Marg.	24	Ahrenswalde	66-0984
BRUNNER, Za.(f)	14	Furstenau	64-0782
BRUNNS, Cath.	21	Riesch	64-0782
BRUNNWASSER, Moriz	24	Tapolz	63-1218
Rosa 24			
BRUNO, Carl	40	New York	66-0109
BRUNO, Gottlieb	46	Pommern	66-0469
Friederike 48, Carl 18, Wilhelmine 16			
August 10, Louise 22			
BRUNS, Ahlert	26	Edewecht	65-0594
BRUNS, Amalie	23	Braunschweig	65-0974
BRUNS, Annchen	30	New York	64-0687
BRUNS, Antje	25	Ost Friesland	66-0577
BRUNS, Ar.(m)	21	Oyth	64-0331
BRUNS, Aug.	16	Braunschweig	65-0974
BRUNS, August	22	Goslar	66-0679
BRUNS, Carl Adolph	23	Hellmstedt	66-0577
BRUNS, Cathre.	30	Bremen	63-0821
Heinr. 9, Johanna 7, Conrad 4, baby 9m			
BRUNS, Diedrich	36	Bremen	64-0886
Marie 41			
BRUNS, Eduard	21	Wanna	63-0482
BRUNS, Ernst	20	Polle	67-0007
Marie 24			
BRUNS, F.(m)	18	Detmold	64-0331
BRUNS, Friedr. Hr.	39	Nenndorf	67-0599
BRUNS, Friedrich	25	Germany	66-0666
BRUNS, Friedrich	27	Hedneeg	67-0007
BRUNS, Fritz	24	Drieburg	64-0214
BRUNS, Geike R.	35	Ostfriesland	64-0214
Taadje 26, Berend 4, Rieke 4			
BRUNS, Gerh.	21	Cloppenburg	64-0427
BRUNS, H.	25	Bueckeburg	65-1189
BRUNS, H.(m)	18	Bremen	64-0214
BRUNS, Henry	16	Bremen	64-0363
Anna 19			
BRUNS, Joh.	16	Hannover	64-0073
BRUNS, Joh. E.	16	Boehmerwald	65-0243
BRUNS, Johanne	30	Like	63-0821
Christian 9, Mary Ann 4, Nicolaus 11m			
BRUNS, Jost	26	Bremen/Hann.	65-0038
BRUNS, Ludwig	32	Berenbostel	66-1155
BRUNS, Marie	24	Bremen	66-0704
BRUNS, Nicolaus	16	Bremen	63-0482
Joh. Conr. 29			
BRUNS, Rudolph	29	Harem	64-0214
BRUNS, Ulfertus	29	Imgun Faehr	66-1031
Catharine 26, Ankelina 5, Antje 3			
Eberhard 11m			
BRUNS, Wilhelm	29	Langel	64-0199
BRUNZEL, Jenny	30	New York	66-0704
Eugen 8, Max 4, Gertrude 1			
BRUNZL, Caroline	20	Prag	66-0147
BRUSELER, Caroline	21	Beinrode	66-1203
BRUST, Peter	20	Schwarzerden	65-0243
BRUSTJE, Pauline	22	Leuchtkirch	66-1155
BUB, Mathias	23	Eppenheim	65-0770
BUBECK, F.	26	Rommelshausen	64-0782
BUBER, Christoph	23	Alsfeld	66-1327
BUBLITZ, August	33	Hagenow	66-0668
Caroline 33, Albert 7, Hermann 6			
Emilie 2			
BUBLITZ, Joh.Heinr	35	Taasde	66-0578
Henriette 37, Augusta 8, Bertha 3			
Wilhelm 2			
BUBOLTZ, Heinrich	27	Goestein	66-0578
Henriette 27, Wilhelm 2, Wilhelmine 5			
BUCH, August	23	Pittsburg	63-0953
BUCH, Friedr.	24	Stadeln	63-0482
BUCHAR, Joseph	28	Boehmen	63-0614
BUCHDRUCKER, Soph.	20	Reckendorf	63-0482
BUCHENROTH, Carl	27	Markgroningen	65-0713
BUCHHABERLE, Chrlt	30	Durlach	66-1131
BUCHHEIT, Joh.	33	Hohmuelbach	66-0147
BUCHHEIT, Louise	16	Hohmuelbach	66-0147
BUCHHOLZ, Christ.	53	Schoenfeld	65-0004
Wilhelmine 47, Christ. 26, Augusta 14			
August 9, Julius 7, Mathilde 6, Pauline 5			
Ottilie 2			
BUCHHOLZ, Emil	21	Pommern	63-0752
BUCHHOLZ, Heinrich	39	Stolzenau	65-1031
Dorothea 38, Fritz 15, Heinrich 9			
Diedrich 7, Wilhelm 5, Sophie 1			
BUCHHOLZ, Johann	26	Vernigirsch'd	65-0948
BUCHHOLZ, W.	23	Windhorst	66-0413
M. 28			
BUCHHOLZ, Wilhelm	24	Groning	66-0469
BUCHHOLZ, Wilhelm	24	Groning	66-0469
BUCHING, Johann W.	21	Marburg	65-0770
BUCHLER, Adolph	26	Schweiz	64-0138
Emil 23			
BUCHMANN, Chr.	57	Dippack	67-0795
Matheus 15			
BUCHMANN, Heinrich	25	Hohmuelbach	66-0147
Charlotte 23			
BUCHMEYER, Wilhelm	25	Deckbergen	66-0934
BUCHMUELLER, Joh.	39	Mussbach	65-0055
BUCHMUELLER, Wilh.	34	Durmersheim	66-0704
BUCHMUELLER, Wm.	26	Muehlheim	63-0990
BUCHNER, Charles	28	Bach	63-1178
Caroline 22, Sophie 2, William 9m			
BUCHNER, Fr'derike	47	Kirchheim	65-0007
BUCHNER, Ludwig	17	Bach	65-0713
Caroline 23, Wilhelmine 20			
BUCHROEDER, H.	25	Hannover	64-0593
BUCHSENSCHUETZ, H.	18	Lottheim	66-0666
BUCHSPIES, Elias	51	Heidersbach	63-0398
Augusta 41, Ernestine 15, Gottlieb 13			
Ernst 4			
BUCHTENKIRCH, Dor.	32	Stadelerwald	66-1031
Dora 6, Fanny 2			
BUCHTER, Carl Wilh	20	Solingen	63-0822
BUCHTMANN, Herm. H	55	Barnstorf	63-1178
BUCHTRUCKER, Barb.	19	Reckendorf	66-0704
BUCK, Barbara	59	Elsingen	64-0782
Christine 26			
BUCK, Franz	26	Almerssau	66-1327
BUCK, Franz	24	Altheim	66-1373
BUCK, Friedrich	20	Muflingen	66-0679
BUCK, Herman	31	Wiste	66-1093
Meta 31, Marie 8, Catharine 6			
BUCK, Johann	17	Oeren	66-0578

NAME	AGE	RESIDENCE	YR-LIST
Sophie 21			
BUCK, Johann	20	Wiste	66-1093
BUCKARD, Anna	22	Boehmen	64-0023
Johanna 21			
BUCKER, H.	25	Stuhrop	65-1088
Anton 28			
BUCKERT, August	25	Brunkesen	66-1248
BUCKHOFF, P.	17	Graet-Siel	66-0413
BUCKING, W.(f)	27	Pr. Minden	64-0331
BUCKMANN, Franz	19	Braamsche	66-0679
BUCKMUELLER, A.E.	23	Havre	64-0331
BUCKSCHARDT, Georg	19	Hoexter	63-0862
BUDDE, Friedr.	47	Haustenbeck	65-1088
Sophie 49, Friedrich 15, Heinrich 10			
Wilhelm 6			
BUDDE, H.	44	Newport	64-0687
Elise 17			
BUDDE, Hermann	31	Minden	66-0837
BUDDE, Maria	18	Wellendorf	64-0938
BUDDECKE, Dan.F.	24	Wellingen	64-0427
BUDDELMANN, Anna	19	Harsefeld	66-0984
BUDDELMANN, John	29	Bremen	63-0821
BUDDEMEYER, Carl	43	Schuettorf	65-0243
Gesina 37, Liena 7, Gesina 5, Frdr. 5			
Henni 10m			
BUDECKER, Joh.Her.	29	Holsten	63-1038
BUDELMANN, Arend	22	Brinkum	63-1178
BUDEMEYER, H.	19	Lohe	66-1313
BUDICKE, Pauline	24	Bromberg	64-0456
BUDKE, Stephan	28	Hollage	66-1128
Maria Agnes 21			
BUDLOWSKY, Pauline	21	Boehmen	66-0147
BUDNICK, Albert Wm	22	Poblotz	63-0614
BUDNICK, Martin	42	Poblotz	63-0614
Constanza 53, Hermann 17, Johanne 14			
Albert 11			
BUECHEL, Maria	26	Mauern	63-0482
BUECHER, Maria El.	24	Markendorf	64-0920
BUECHER, Marie	30	Kirchheim	67-0992
BUECHLER, Martin	23	Michelstadt	64-0593
BUECHLER, Wm.	34	New York	64-0427
BUECHNER, Joh. Aug	30	Oldorf	64-0214
BUECHNER, Johann	33	Hameln	66-1203
BUECHNER, Maria	28	Oldorf	64-0214
Anna 6, Louise 3, baby 1			
BUECHNER, Wilhelm	22	Darmstadt	66-0576
BUECK, Sophie	23	Hall	66-1327
BUECKER, Heinrich	31	Hannover	66-1127
Catharina 32, Sophie 9, Caroline 6			
Margarethe 3, Rudolph 9m			
BUECKERT, Louise	17	Connweiler	66-1093
BUECKERT, Sophie	34	Neubilgen	66-1093
Wilhelm 4, baby 2m			
BUECKING, Friedr.	25	Hanover	64-0138
BUECKING, Joh.	28	Rethosen	66-0679
BUECKLER, Peter	44	Milwaukee	63-0990
Barbara 15, James 13			
BUEDEFELD, Carl	46	Braunschweig	64-1022
Carl 7, Paul 5			
BUEHHEIM, Wolff	17	Wahra	64-0593
BUEHL, Marie	18	Wuertenberg	66-0221
BUEHLER, Adelbert	19	Messkirch	65-0243
Frieda 17			
BUEHLER, Johann	20	Adelmannsfeld	66-0349
Therese 30, Joseph 3			
BUEHLER, John	19	Wildbach	66-0934
BUEHLER, Louise	53	Calw	66-1093
Salome 48			
BUEHLER, Rudolph	21	Urasch	66-1093
BUEHLER, Wilhelm	19	Koenig	66-1203
BUEHLMEYER, J.Geo.	27	Frankfurt	65-0055
BUEHNER, Georg	28	Empertshausen	65-0770
BUEHRER, Christine	19	Niedereinmend	66-0704
BUEHRER, Christine	21	Urach	65-0974
BUEHRLE, Euphrosin	56	Altdorf/Bad.	65-0950
BUEHRMANN, Aug.	41	Uslar	65-1024
Charlotte 29, Louis 7, Anna 4			
BUEKELMEYER, Louis	26	Limberg/Pr.	64-0920

NAME	AGE	RESIDENCE	YR-LIST
BUELLER, Gordian	23	Kalkbrim	63-1085
BUENGENER, Lisette	17	Hoexter	63-0953
BUENGER, Fr.	30	Brockum	65-1024
Gesine 26, Frd. 9, Wme. 21, Herm. 3			
BUENO, Elijio	20	Bremen	63-0097
BUENTING, Joh.	21	Leer	65-0898
BUER, H.(m)	24	Worms	64-0331
BUERCKNER, Julius	28	Berlin	66-1155
BUERGER, Alexander	17	Detmold	64-0073
BUERGER, Babette	40	Fuerth	65-1189
Carl 9			
BUERGER, Ferdinand	44	Romansart	63-0614
Henriette 38			
BUERGER, Susanne	29	Lieser	63-1178
BUERING, Margar.	29	Meppen	65-0898
BUERK, Ludwig	33	Friedrichsfld	63-0990
Wilhelmine 33, Ludwig 3, Frieda 6m			
BUERK, Theod.	20	Oberwisheim	65-0151
BUERKER, Chrs.	28	Bettingen	66-0221
Marie 22			
BUERKLE, Barbara	42	Betzenriede	66-0412
Margarethe 14, Maria Barba. 9			
Elisabeth 7, August 3, Jacob 9m			
BUERKLE, Joseph	27	Schoenenbach	66-0083
BUERKLE, Rosina	20	Sigmaringen	66-0221
BUERMANN, Fr.	24	France	63-0862
BUERMANN, Heinrich	43	Westkirchen	66-1093
Marie 44			
BUEROSSE, Ernst	25	Nordstemmen	64-0138
Caroline 22			
BUERS, Herm.	28	Naurode	65-0189
BUERSCHNER, Caspar	57	Meiningen	66-0704
Marie 53, Valentin 14, Martin 26, Anna 26			
Oswald 5, Christoph 3, Oswald 1			
BUESCHE, Wilhelm	29	Heinsen	66-0934
BUESER, Catharina	29	Manil	64-1053
BUESING, Anna	22	Aumund	64-0427
BUESING, Herm.	26	Ostfriesland	63-0822
Anna 23, Santje 11m			
BUESS, R.(m)	35	Mardau	64-0331
BUETE, Wilhelm	21	Lemgo	66-1203
BUETTEMEYER, Chr.	21	Isenstedt	66-1031
BUETTER, Justus	35	New York	63-1038
BUETTERICH, Sabine	39	Eger	66-1031
Anna 5, Sabine 10m			
BUETTNER, Bernhard	33	Mainz	63-0822
BUETTNER, Bernhard	30	Dresden	65-0770
Anna Florent 22			
BUETTNER, Joh. C.	36	Varel	66-0577
BUETTNER, Marg.	28	Cincinatti	63-1038
BUETTNER, Therese	25	Basbeck	63-0693
BUEXTER, Philipp	17	Heppelsbach	66-1203
BUGERT, Jacob	25	Villmar	67-0007
BUGTELLA, Cathrina	42	Bohemia	66-0469
Anna 19, Rosalia 8			
BUHA, Frd.	48	Klueckhof	64-0992
Henriette 44, Friedrich 16, Amalie 6			
Wilhelmine 11m			
BUHL, Hermann	26	Claussen	65-1024
BUHLER, (f)	42	Newark	63-0990
G. (m) 54, baby 10m			
BUHLERT, Friedrike	54	Walsrode	64-0593
BUHMANN, Martha	26	Leer	64-0992
BUHR, Charles E.	43	Frankfurt a/M	63-0917
Theresia 25, Caroline 3m			
BUHR, de Joh. H.	30	Folmhusen	65-0243
BUHRMANN, Dorette	21	Gittelte	66-0734
BUISKER, Fidde	29	Rorichum	64-0495
Joh. 35			
BUISSINGER, Cath.	18	Kitzingen	63-1136
BUKAREL, Kaspar	29	Hayengen	65-1095
Joseph 33, Nicolaus 10, Otto 7, Xaver 5			
BUKER, Tina	24	Dollhausen	66-1128
BULDNA, Marie	26	Boehmen	64-0023
Johanna 21			
BULDRA, Franz	24	Boehmen	63-0614
Joseph 26			
BULINGER, Pauline	27	Christgarten	64-0170

NAME	AGE	RESIDENCE	YR-LIST
BULLERICH, Mathen	40	Eger	66-0704
BULLHUSEN, Gesine	20	Hannover	64-1108
Meta 18			
BULLMUELLER, Bernh	59	Gemmern	66-0984
BULLWINKEL, H.	30	Oldenburg	65-1024
BULLWINKEL, Heinr.	27	Hambergen	64-1206
BULLWINKEL, Johann	20	Bremervoerde	66-0934
BULLWINKEL, Johann	16	Hannover	65-0038
BULTMANN, Sophie	20	Vegesack	64-0687
BUMANN, Alois	46	Rust	65-0007
Ursula 44, Eduard 23, Emma 19			
BUMGARN, Johann	39	Leer	66-1203
Gretje 39, Johannes 11, Friedrich 3			
Johanna 1			
BUMMOULD, G.	24	Friedrichsbrg	66-0413
BUNDE, Carl	36	Korlein	67-0353
BUNDE, Christian	36	Helminghausen	66-0984
Wilhelmine 36, Heinrich 17, Wilhelm 15			
Johannette 7, Wilhelmine 5, Caroline 2			
BUNDENDAHL, Friedr	28	Warmbeck	66-0072
Wilhelmine 29			
BUNDORFF, C.(f)	16	Osnabrueck	64-0495
BUNDSCHUH, Ludw.	30	Hardheim	63-0752
BUNERT, Paul	26	Charlottenbrg	64-0495
BUNGER, Luise	18	Loebenstein	66-0734
BUNGERTS, Heinr.	23	Prussia	64-0427
BUNGSTORF, Aug.	28	Hardegsen	64-0363
BUNGUIER, Joseph	60	France	63-0350
Marie 46			
BUNK, Fr.	19	Brakenheim	65-0116
BUNK, Johann	28	Intschede	66-0704
BUNK, Lina	27	Dorum	67-0806
BUNKE, Margarethe	23	Intschede	66-0704
BUNN, Anna M.	22	Friesenheim	63-0006
Catharina 19, Elisabeth 15, baby			
BUNSE, Heinr.	25	Preussen	64-0214
BUNSELMEIER, Minna	18	Iburg	66-1128
BUNSELMEYER, Aug.	21	Cleve	66-0837
BUNTE, Anna	9	Drehle	66-1093
BUNTE, Diedrich	33	Deckbergen	66-0934
Philippine 25			
BUNTE, Emilie	21	Lemgo	65-1088
BUNTE, Fr. Wm.	31	Westfalen	64-0432
BUNTE, Gustav	14	Lemgo	66-0704
BUNTE, Johann	29	Wierup	66-0984
BUNTE, Maria	17	Leer	66-1131
BUNTROCK, Caroline	24	Hagenow	66-0668
BUNZING, Joh. G.	23	Thueningen	64-0886
BUOL, Christian	49	Oberurbach	63-0990
Maria 44, Barbara 20, Christian 19			
John 16			
BUOL, Rosine	12	Oberurbach	63-0990
Friederike 10, Henry 9			
BUR, Barbara	29	Sulzdorf	64-0992
BURADE, Fritz	34	Brake	63-1178
BURBACH, Diedrich	35	New York	66-0679
Catharine 30, Theodor 6			
BURBOTT, Friedrich	37	Poblotz	63-0614
Charlotte 27, Albert 3, Auguste 2			
BURCH, F.G.	24	Dunsenhausen	66-0413
BURCHARD, Babette	23	Tuchersfeld	63-0862
BURCHARD, Emilie	31	Aachen	63-1218
BURCHARD, Martin	24	Hessen	66-0734
BURCHARDS, Nichael	44	Sacho	67-0353
Amalie 40, Wilhelm 9, Friedrich 7			
Augusta 6, Ernestine 4, Ferdinand 5m			
Carl 51			
BURCKARD, Alex	18	Steinbach	65-0007
BURCKARDT, Fr.(m)	20	Fisibach	64-0023
BURCKHARD, Bertold	35	Kommatau	63-0053
BURCKHARDT, James	28	Philadelphia	63-1136
BURDORF, Johann	14	Osnabrueck	65-1030
BURECHBACHER, Mart	23	Trostingen	63-0990
BURES, Joseph	48	Boehmen	63-0953
BURF, Johann	54	Balingen	66-1203
BURG, Rudolf	24	Obernsennerhf	66-0576
BURGDORF, Carl	48	Gotha	64-0456
Ernestine 33, Maria 10			
BURGDORF, Ernestin	33	Gotha	64-0456
Marie 10			
BURGEN, G.(m)	20	Haltingen	64-0331
BURGER, Albert	25	Lemberg	64-0687
BURGER, Anna	20	Schwabach	66-0576
BURGER, Chr.	18	Oberhessenbch	63-0482
BURGER, Clemens	26	Kattenwestern	65-0116
BURGER, Joseph	56	Welldingen	63-0990
BURGER, Joseph	24	Nagy Ida	65-0007
Jette 21, Jacob 9			
BURGER, Peter	23	Ohmbach	64-0495
BURGGRAF, Ann	8	Wiesbaden	66-0934
Johann 6			
BURGHARD, Louis	21	Hannover	64-1108
Gustav 16			
BURGHARDT, A.M.	24	Giessen	63-0350
BURGHARDT, Aug.	20	Messingen	64-0214
BURGHARDT, G.M.	21	Unt.Reichenbh	64-0639
BURGHARDT, Marie	24	Heiligenstadt	64-0665
BURGHOF, Carl	21	Eschenhausen	66-1131
BURGHOLZ, Theodor	34	Freckenhorst	63-0482
BURGISLAUS, J.	25	Schleswig	65-1189
BURGMANN, Carl	42	Asch	66-1203
Anna 37, Leopold 9, Lisette 6, Anna 1			
BURGMANN, Georg	32	Sachsen-Mein.	66-0349
BURGMANN, Wilhelm	17	Dissen	66-1128
BURHEN, Otto	19	Neugesterode	66-1203
BURHENNE, Cathrine	24	Instrode	66-1248
BURHENNE, Gustav	29	New York	63-0244
Elisabeth 23, Emilie 5, John 3			
BURI, Frd.	18	Donaueschingn	64-0363
BURI, Ulrich	26	Switz	64-0170
BURICKA, Alois	46	Caslau	64-0593
Carl 15			
BURJATA, Josepha	35	Boehmen	64-0023
Johanna 21			
BURK, Georg	35	Frohenhausen	65-0948
BURK, Rich.	23	Warmbrunn	63-0168
BURKART, Chris.	22	New York	63-1218
BURKART, Julius	19	Rottweil	66-0734
BURKEN, Magd.	23	Seimliete	64-0639
BURKENHAUSER, Hen.	22	Hessen	66-0109
BURKERT, Margareth	20	Oberstetten	66-1155
BURKERT, Xaver	56	Rottweil	66-1155
Marie 42			
BURKET, Wenzel	36	Boehmen	64-0427
Marie 33, Alois 4, Wenzel 9m			
BURKHARD, Gustav	22	Hagenbach	66-0576
BURKHARDT, A.(m)	21	Neidlingen	64-0363
BURKHARDT, Adolph	40	Berlin	63-0917
BURKHARDT, August	50	Merseburg	66-1093
Friederike 46, Friederike 23, Louise 20			
Minna 15, Emma 12			
BURKHARDT, Carl	31	Ernstweiler	65-0007
BURKHARDT, Eduard	27	Eichenberg	64-0363
BURKHARDT, J.F.	21	Aartrupp	65-0189
BURKHARDT, Johann	23	Breitenberg	66-1203
BURKHARDT, John J.	34	Tuebingen	63-0168
BURKHARDT, Valent.	32	Baden	66-0679
BURKHART, Hermann	8	Posen	63-0752
Emma 9			
BURKMANN, August	31	Ritterode	66-1155
BURKNER, Chr.	24	Berlin	63-0350
BURKNER, Lina	17	Kissingen	66-1093
BURLACH, J.(m)	25	Amsterdam	64-0331
BURLAGE, Margareth	25	Esterwegen	66-1131
Wilhelm 23, Elisabeth 23			
BURLAGE, Marie	14	Nordkirchen	66-1093
Josephine 18			
BURLE, Victoria	22	Durlach	64-0687
BURMEISTER, Chr.	17	Hille	65-1088
BURMEISTER, Friede	23	Uthlede	64-0456
BURMESTER, Aug.	18	Uthlede	65-0950
BURMESTER, Carl Hr	16	Pr. Minden	67-0599
BURMESTER, Heinr.	29	San Francisco	63-0990
BURMTIECK, Anna	21	Koenigslutter	63-0990
BURNS, Christine	28	France	63-0350
BURODE, Theo.	31	Ober Brake	63-0168

NAME	AGE	RESIDENCE	YR-LIST
BURR, Michaelis	28	Bodenheim	65-0004
BURR, Rob.	25	New York	63-1136
BURRICHTER, Henry	30	Issenbach	63-0862
Friedrich 27, Friederike 17			
BURSCHALL, Cath.	23	Laudenbach	65-0055
Heinr. 45			
BURTEL, Carl	24	Winnweder	64-0363
BURWITZ, Eduard	24	Kottbus	63-0006
BUS, Caroline	26	Hasslach	66-0704
BUSBACHER, Friede.	18	Kersenhain	66-0679
BUSCH, Albert	24	Leeste	65-0974
BUSCH, Andreas	18	Koengernheim	65-0243
BUSCH, Aug.	27	Hoertheim	64-0593
BUSCH, Carl	17	New York	63-0752
BUSCH, Carsten	23	Eintinghausen	65-0189
BUSCH, Catharine	24	Muenchhausen	63-0398
BUSCH, Elisabeth	19	Luderscheim	66-1248
BUSCH, Elise	20	Hilter	66-0837
Gertrude 22			
BUSCH, Emilie	26	Gera	66-1093
BUSCH, F.H.	23	Crefeld	64-0687
BUSCH, Friedr.	25	Stolzenau	66-0577
BUSCH, Gertrud	60	Belm	63-1010
Margarethe 21			
BUSCH, Gustav	20	Stuttgart	65-0116
BUSCH, J.G.(m)	22	Neidlingen	64-0331
BUSCH, J.G.(m)	12	Salzbergen	64-0331
BUSCH, Johanna	27	Lichtenborn	65-0974
BUSCH, Karl	18	Neuenkirchen	66-0837
BUSCH, Marie	32	Elberfeld	65-1024
BUSCH, Theresia	25	Boehmen	64-0687
BUSCH, Wilhelm	24	Groeppendorf	67-0007
BUSCHE, Caspar	25	Oldenburg	66-1093
BUSCHE, Heinr.	37	Mansbach	65-0898
BUSCHEMEYER, H.	32	Borstel	64-0782
Wilhelmine 17, Lena 21			
BUSCHER, Sebastian	30	Altstaedten	63-1085
BUSCHHEIM, Wolf	27	New York	66-0734
BUSCHHORN, Friedr.	24	Barenborstel	66-1373
BUSCHMANN, Elisab.	22	Brinkum	64-0456
BUSCHMANN, H.	29	Dover	66-0413
BUSCHMANN, W.	18	Rahden	65-1088
BUSCHMEYER, Wilh.	41	Westphalen	66-0469
Marie 43, Caroline 14, Marie 9, Louise 8			
Friederike 2			
BUSCHOW, Gust.	20	Preussen	64-0432
BUSCHPLER, Alphons	21	Dresden	63-0350
BUSCHTA, Ab.	39	Boehmen	64-0495
El.(f) 37, Frz. 16, Joh. 13			
BUSCHTA, Joh.	7	Boehmen	64-0495
J.(m) 6, Joh.(m) 5, Ma.(f) 4, Martin 11m			
Aron 29			
BUSDICKER, J.P.	20	Buhre	65-1030
BUSE, Diedr. Heinr	26	Bremen	64-0456
BUSE, E.	22	Hoya	63-1003
BUSE, Ferdinand	56	Kolberg/Pr.	63-0822
Elisabeth 53			
BUSE, Joh. G.	25	Muehlberg	65-1024
BUSH, Heinrich	17	Eisenach	66-1373
BUSING, Dorette	27	Luttorf	64-0495
N.(f)			
BUSING, H.	39	Nopke	64-0495
L. 37, Heinrich 12, Sophie 7			
Wilhelmine 6, Marien 3, Alwine 1m			
BUSKE, Friedrich	26	Preussen	63-1136
BUSKING, Carl	36	America	64-0138
BUSKUEHL, H.	18	Huedenhausen	63-0953
BUSMANN, Louis	21	Luebbeke	66-1313
BUSO, Adolph	22	Belle	66-1373
BUSS, Anna	26	Emden	65-1088
Bernhard 8m			
BUSS, Conrad	21	Eberstadt	66-1373
BUSS, Fan.	26	Leer	66-0984
BUSS, Johann	28	Schwitz/Wuert	66-0469
Wilhelm 23			
BUSSARA, M.	25	Diesslingen	64-0782
BUSSE, Aug.	20	Hannover	63-1136
BUSSE, Augusta	21	Magdeburg	64-0593
BUSSE, Caroline	28	Westphalia	66-0469
BUSSE, Gottlieb	32	Kopaschin	66-0650
BUSSE, Heinrich	17	Drehle	66-1127
BUSSE, Herm.	28	Magdeburg	64-0170
BUSSMANN, Ernst	38	Wellingen	64-0427
Anna M. 32, Marie 2			
BUSSMANN, Philpine	15	Bremen	67-0007
BUSSWOLTER, Bernh.	20	Nienburg	65-1030
BUTH, H.G.	23	Friedberg	65-0856
BUTJAR, Thomas	40	Nemish	66-1327
Barbara 35			
BUTKE, J.	21	Haste	64-0782
BUTKER, Marie	23	Kirchdorf	66-0650
BUTSCH, Gottfr.	65	Cincinnati	66-0984
BUTSCH, Heinrich	24	Fraukirsch	66-1093
BUTSCHER, Joseph	27	Daugendorf	66-1373
BUTSCHROF, Friedr.	17	Beverstedt	67-0599
BUTT, Margarethe	22	Niendorf	65-1095
BUTTEL, Nicol.	17	Baden	66-0734
BUTTER, Leopold	31	Hannover	66-0221
Theresia 29			
BUTTERBAUM, Carol	22	Hann. Stroehm	64-0593
BUTTERBROD, Aug.	34	Kazemierzelso	63-0821
BUTZ, Conr.	51	Grauenwiesbch	65-0594
BUTZ, Michael	25	Uhingen	66-1203
BUTZKE, Wilhelm	30	Prussia	64-0363
BUVER, Angela	22	Zewe	63-0990
BUWIG, Amalie	27	Berlin	64-0073
Wilhelm 13			
BUXBAUM, Lisette	22	Marburg	66-0934
Johanna 20			
BUXTEN, Robert	14	Ahmsen	65-1088
BUZIN, Theodor	31	Zackenzin/Prs	66-0072
Emilie 33			
CAEMMERLOHR, Henry	32	Sulzbach	63-0482
CAERNER, Charlotte	19	Hueffe	64-0433
CAESAR, Carl	34	New York	63-1085
CAESAR, G.A.	28	Bremen	63-0097
CAESAR, Mathias	33	Krain	67-0007
CAFFENBERGER, Conr	16	Luetzelbach	65-1088
CAGELMEYER, Herm.	30	Eisenach	66-0984
CAHEN, Emily	24	Canada	63-0693
Julian Max 1			
CAHN, D.	40	New York	63-0482
Helene 35, Renni 11m			
CAHN, Fanny	29	Hochheim	66-1093
CAHN, Joseph		Allsfeld	63-0917
CAHRS, Gesche	59	Neuenhuelsted	64-0593
CALDER, Max	20	Mannheim	64-0495
CALDEROR, Juan	40	New Granada	63-0693
CALL, Tomas	40	Schwarzburg	66-0679
CALLENIUS, Theodor	25	Dorum	65-0189
CALLMEYER, Gustav	21	Bremen	63-0097
CAMBEIS, Carl			64-0073
CAMLADE, Joh.	15	Quakenbrueck	64-0992
CAMMANN, heinrich	30	Mainburg	64-1022
Meta 25			
CAMMER, zur F.R.	30	Hoehenmoor	66-0704
CAMMERER, Gustav	16	Honhardt	66-1031
CAMMERT, Frd.	37	Bremen	64-0023
CAMMERT, Meta	30	Orlebshausen	65-0007
CAMP, Henry B.	20	New York	66-0934
CAMPBETT, J.	47	New York	63-0917
Mary 23			
CAMPE, v. Aug.	28	Stadtoldendrf	63-1178
CAMPSEN, Anna	63	Rechtenfleth	65-1024
CAMUS, J.C.	25	Lingen	64-0495
CANAALE, Samuel	30	Paris	64-1053
CANISIUS, F.	34	Wien	63-0821
CANTELO, Charlotte	30	Illinois	64-0363
John 9, Jenny 5			
CANTELO, M.	40	New York	64-0593
CARET, A.D.	36	Paris	63-0821
CARL, Andr.	36	Gerstingen	64-0639
Emilie 26, Gustav 7			
CARL, Caspar	28	Lauterbach	65-1030
CARL, Emil	22	Hoya	65-0594
CARL, Franz	19	Bueckeburg	66-1127

NAME	AGE	RESIDENCE	YR-LIST
CARL, Friederike	66	Pommern	66-0578
CARL, Friedr.	11	Gedern	63-1010
CARL, Otto	20	Harau	66-0934
CARL, P.	24	Frankenhausen	65-1189
CARL, Phillipp	42	Friedelshsn.	65-0948
CARLES, Sophie	59	Wimmen	63-1085
CARLI, Christoph	53	New York	63-0990
CARLS, L.(m)	29	Berlin	64-0214
wife 21			
CARLSEN, Aug.	32	Bremen	64-0214
CARME, Catherina	35	Bern	63-0168
CARO, Catharine	23	Hoergenau	65-0950
CARO, Therese	50	Cuestrin	63-0752
Flora 23, Minna 19, Henriette 14			
CAROLI, Friedr.	26	Dietendorf	64-0840
CAROS, Charl.	24	Ritterhude	65-0950
CARSTEN, Heinrich	48	New Orleans	66-0679
CARSTENS, August	22	Midlum	66-0578
CARSTENS, Becka	21	Wertenwisch	63-1136
CARSTENS, Betti	32	Bremen	66-0679
Doris 42			
CARSTENS, Dorothea	23	Nordholz	65-0402
CARSTENS, Emil	28	Lingen	66-1203
CARSTENS, H.	19	Hemelingen	64-0639
CARZILIUS, Peter	31	Isenburg	64-1053
CASPAR, Anton	24	Boehmen	63-0990
Theresia 23, Anton 9m			
CASPAR, Franz	19	Herstelle	64-0593
Richard 19			
CASSEBOHM, C.	43	Schoeningen	65-0007
Marie 29, Caroline			
CASSEL, Lina	21	Mainz	64-0992
CASSELBACH, E.H.	18	Oedenburg	66-0934
CASSENFLUG, A.	56	Neustadt/R.	64-0992
CASSENS, Anna	28	Syke	66-1093
Dorothea 25, Marie 22			
CASSENS, Marie	43	Henzing	67-0599
CASSENS, Wilke	40	Oldenburg	64-0363
Antje 30			
CASSIAN, Chris.	15	Milwaukee	63-0350
CASTENDYK, J.D.	22	Bremen	65-0402
CASTRETIUS, R.L.	25	Darmstadt	63-0953
CASTRI, (m)	57	London	63-1085
(f) 18			
CEJKA, Franz	36	Dowaritz	66-1131
Rosalia 35, Anna 8, Wenzel 4			
CELLARIUS, H.	31	New York	63-0168
CERMARK, Franz	33	Boehmen	63-0398
CERNAK, Cas. Marie	21	Boehmen	66-0349
CERNAUSCHEK, Paul	20	Boehmen	66-0349
CERWENY, Mathias	19	Unterlakowitz	66-1373
CHADIN, Wenzel	36	Malin	64-0433
CHALANDA, Wenzel	40	Strakowitz	65-0594
CHAPPIUS, v. Ant.	28	Preussen	66-0147
Marie 26, Alexandra 24, Helene 22			
CHART, Pauline	34	Schweiz	66-0934
Louise 18, Elise 14, Anna 7			
CHARWAT, Jos.	32	Bohemia	64-0363
CHATELOT, Joseph	37	France	63-0015
Marie 60			
CHATLAIN, Heinr.	30	Rouen	65-0004
CHAVEREOT, Leonh.	60	New York	64-0023
CHEIM, Christ.	18	Kreilsheim	66-0934
CHEIN, L.	50	Eperjes	63-1218
Fanny 44, Cathar. 17, Elias 9, Sali 7			
Mali 5			
CHEPLENSKY, J.	31	Wolonsch	66-0413
Maria 34, Albert 2, Joseph 8m			
CHERMACK, Emma	27	Gang	67-0007
CHEVALIER, Christ.	42	Aich	63-0953
CHLODIUS, H.			63-1003
CHODIMA, Nathan	50	Boehmen	66-0221
Elise 44, Joseph 14, Wenz. 7, Nathan 5			
CHORENGEL, Carl	18	Bilshausen	64-0433
CHORENGEL, G.F.	40	Bremerlehe	64-0432
Helene 25, Johann 14, Wm. 13, Heinr. 8			
Johanna 6			
CHRISSELIUS, Th.	25	Friedeburg	65-1024

NAME	AGE	RESIDENCE	YR-LIST
CHRIST, Anna	28	Mastershausen	64-0331
CHRIST, Friedrich	25	Simmersfeld	66-0147
CHRIST, Heinr.	17	Schlichtum	66-0837
CHRIST, Heinrich	22	Butzbach	66-1093
CHRIST, Herm.	16	Haigerloch	64-0170
CHRIST, Joh.	42	Bayern	63-0398
CHRIST, Katharina	31	Baiern	63-1069
Michael 7, Maria 6, Theresa 4, Johann 2			
CHRIST, Ludwig	24	Rohrbach	64-0992
CHRIST, Nicolaus	37	Hambach	63-1136
Philipp 27			
CHRISTENSEN, Hans	30	Copenhagen	66-0666
CHRISTENSEN, Lars	31	Copenhagen	66-0666
CHRISTIANS, Harm	29	Ost Friesland	66-0577
CHRISTMANN, Adam	24	Weissenburg	65-0243
CHRISTMANN, Ernest	17	New York	66-0576
CHRISTMANN, Joh.	42	Trenten	66-0704
CHRISTMANN, Valent	35	Pittsburg	64-0687
CHRISTMANN, Valent	32	Hannover	65-0243
CHRISTOFFERS, Joh.	35	Bremen	65-1030
CHRISTOPH, J.H.(m)	20	Kleinhegersdf	64-0023
CHRISTOPHERS, Frdr	30	Hannover	66-1127
Franke 30, Marie 2			
CHRLER, Catharine	66	Bartenstein	64-0886
CHUNTE, Anton	31	Fillinghausen	64-0840
CIESKI, Vincent	26	Stooden	66-0578
Anna 52			
CISELE, Xaver	23	Eberstadt	66-1327
CITRON, Herz	37	Trymeszno	66-0679
Caspar 7, Emil 5			
CITRON, Nanny	27	Trzemesno	66-0679
Ernestine 9, Rosalie 8, baby 6m			
CLAAS, Heinr.	27	Muenster	25-0950
Auguste 29, Johanna 9, Bernhard 3			
Christian 10m			
CLAINGNE, Joseph	21	France	63-0015
CLANLOT, Therese	13	Dillingen	64-1022
CLARIUS, Minna	17	Windecken	66-0679
CLARUS, Paul Just.	31	Leipzig	64-0886
CLAS, Margaretha	20	Gontershausen	64-0214
CLASEN, W.(m)	17	New Orleans	64-0214
CLASING, Carl	22	Frille	64-0214
Carl 9, Friedr. 15			
CLASS, Georg	22	Zainingen	67-0007
Wilhelm 14			
CLASSEN, Meta	15	Bremen	66-1093
CLASSON, Anton	28	Esens	66-1128
Elisabeth 23, Gerd 3			
CLAU, Heinr.	33	Coblenz	64-0938
CLAUS, Adine	24	Eppenheim	65-0770
CLAUS, August	23	Dollach	66-0679
CLAUS, Carl	22	Doebeln	65-0243
CLAUS, Clemens	34	Wasbeck	64-0427
CLAUS, Conrad	54	Waltinghausen	67-0795
Dorothea 54, Engelmann 25			
Maria Sophie 16, Dorothea 8, Engel 15			
Conrad 9, Christoph 7			
CLAUS, Jacob	28	Neustadt	65-1024
CLAUS, Peter	24	Iba	64-0456
CLAUS, Theodor	29	Giffhorn	65-0713
Wilhelmine 19, Heinrich 15			
CLAUSING, Heinr.	19	Vehrte	66-1031
CLAUSING, Joh.	21	Bremen	65-0594
CLAUSMEYER, Aug.	22	Bittendorf	64-1108
CLAUSMEYER, Wlhmne	26	Minden	65-1031
CLAUSS, Ludwig	30	Beverstadt	65-0594
CLAUSSEN, J.C.	35	Bremen	65-0402
CLAUSSEN, M.J.	48	New York	63-1218
CLAVIUS, Philipp	36	Windecken	64-0170
CLEEFF, Ch. Wilmne	31	Solingen	65-0038
Sophia 9, Friedr. Wm. 8, Ernst B. 11m			
CLEMENS, Joseph	36	New York	63-0990
Anna 9			
CLEMENS, Julius	36	Magdeburg	67-0599
CLEMENT, Joh.	35	Schloth	64-0687
CLIEN, Ernestine	48	Liegnitz	64-0886
CLINAR, Johann	13	Truban	66-1203
CLISINO, Ludwig	16	Suelzfeld	66-1243

NAME	AGE	RESIDENCE	YR-LIST
CLOCKE, C.(m)	23	Westfalen	64-0495
CLOID, Conrad	26	Preussen	66-0221
CLOID, Joseph	25	Preussen	66-0221
Louise 25			
CLOPPENBURG, John	35	Frisoythe	63-0482
John H. 38, Maruy 24, John H. 9m			
CLOSTER, Bernh.	28	Westphalen	66-0734
COBER, Ma.(f)	55	Boehmen	64-0495
COBERG, Salomon	37	Dankelshausen	66-1203
COBLENZ, J.J.	30	New York	64-0593
COBLENZER, Simon	32	Hillentrup	65-0116
COELLEN, Alexander		Osburne	66-1373
COELLMANN, Hirsch	27	Kehrtopf	66-0083
COELMER, Cathre.	19	Dornholz	63-0821
COENEN, Victor H.	25	Aachen	66-0109
COERS, Fritz	25	Bremen	66-1203
COERSSY, Gisela	26	Wien	65-1189
COHEN, Sarah	32	New York	64-0495
COHN, A.	27	Jechenich	64-0782
COHN, Abraham	23	Ibbenbuehren	66-0083
Janette 49, Hanchen 21, Bertha 15			
COHN, Ad.	16	Bremen	63-1085
COHN, C.	17	Hannover	63-1085
COHN, Ernst	30	Bremen	66-0221
COHN, F.	29	Kralowitz	66-0413
Adalbert 19			
COHN, Hedwig	26	Dresden	63-0482
COHN, Johanna	60	Nakel	65-0594
Eva 24			
COHN, Joseph		Allsfeld	63-0917
COHN, Julius	23	Berlin	65-0856
COHN, Louis	36	Breslau	64-0495
COHN, Lucie	19	Berlin	65-0004
Siegfried 3m			
COHN, Roeschen	23	Berlin	66-1155
COHN, Wilh.	18	Soden	65-0402
COHNS, Fanny	22	Wollstein	65-0974
COIGNE, Bernard	34	Paris	63-0917
COLAMUS, C.H.	26	Hanau	63-0482
COLLAGE, Franz	20	Neuenkirchen	64-0433
COLLIN, Catharine	55	Mainz	66-1203
COLLIN, Margarethe	21	Holzhausen	66-0734
COLLMANN, Fr.	35	Bremen	64-0331
Johanna 21			
COLLMANN, Gideon	36	Philadeophia	66-0576
Anna 26, Sophie 2			
COLLMANN, Hiska	30	Virrel	64-1053
COLLMANN, Magd.	17	Hainbach	64-0170
Anna C. 22			
CONERT, Mathias	40	Billerbeck	64-1206
Bernard 33			
CONFELDT, August	16	Guetersloh	63-0917
CONIS, Augusta	26	Weida	64-0938
Pauline 7, Laura 5, Richard 3			
CONO, Adolph	23	Mannheim	63-1085
CONRAD, Carl	30	Erlingen	66-1155
CONRAD, Friedrich	24	Oberecken	66-0147
CONRAD, G.	24	Hoffenstadt	64-0992
CONRAD, Gustav	33	Wittenburg	64-0433
CONRAD, Heinr.	37	Osthergen	65-0189
CONRAD, James	41	Osthofen	63-0821
Anna Mary 34, Anna Mary 9, Elizabeth 8			
John Georg 6, Ignatz 3, Gustav 9m			
CONRAD, Johannes	21	Schotten	66-1031
CONRAD, Louise	15	Rainrod	64-0593
CONRAD, Ottilie	27	Gelighaim	66-1243
CONRAD, Wilhelmine	55	Damitz	64-0665
Wilhelmine 20			
CONRADI, Aug.	15	Celle	64-0593
CONRADI, Wilhelm	33	Hannover	64-0886
CONRADS, F.	20	Coburg	65-0007
CONRADS, Louis	29	Danzig	67-0007
CONRADT, Charles W	21	Castel	63-0917
CONRADY, Sophie	17	Windheim	66-0650
Wilhelmine 20			
CONRATH, Anna M.	25	Lion	64-1108
CONRATH, Phil.	29	Jocksgrimm	65-0007
Regina 21			

NAME	AGE	RESIDENCE	YR-LIST
CONSTANTIN, An Cth	26	Hessen	64-0432
CONSTAPEL, Taatje	25	Norden	64-1022
CONZ, Gottlob	16	Giglingen	65-0713
CONZE, Florentin	57	Beverungen	64-0593
Antonia 25			
CONZER, J.	32	Onstilledingn	66-0413
COOK, Heinr.	34	Alsfeld	64-0687
COPERSKI, Rosalie	28	Polajewa	66-0650
Jacob 30, Andreas 6m			
COPPEL, Agatha	30	Scheveningen	66-0083
CORBIS, Herm.	24	Westerrode	66-1373
CORDEAU, Edmund	24	Paris	64-0363
CORDES, Becka	16	Achim	65-0594
CORDES, Bernhard	58	Westfalen	64-0432
Bernhardine 38			
CORDES, Carsten	24	Drifseln	64-0495
CORDES, Catharina	23	Driftseth	64-0456
CORDES, Catharina	21	Theesdorf	65-0116
CORDES, Chr.	21	Etelsen	64-0427
CORDES, D.(m)	28	Bothel	64-0331
CORDES, Diedr.	15	Grossflotum	66-0984
CORDES, Diedr.	17	Thedinghausen	65-0189
CORDES, Emilie	16	Baltimore	63-0990
CORDES, Herm. Died	31	Bremen	66-0221
CORDES, Hermann	16	Stemmen	66-1031
Christian 19			
CORDES, Hermann	9	Elze	66-1127
CORDES, Johann	18	Iddingen	66-0668
CORDES, Johann	35	Hannover	66-1031
CORDES, Joseph	18	Osterbruch	66-1127
CORDES, Louise	15	Lovesloh/Hann	64-0920
CORDES, Margaretha	17	Osterburg	64-0593
CORDES, Minna	14	Bremen	64-0639
CORDES, Wilhelm	26	Glandorf	66-1127
CORDING, W.	23	Suhlingen	65-1031
CORDTS, Rebecca	25	Altenwalde	66-1327
COREUFLO, Juliane	52	Friedrichstal	65-0243
Edw. 27, Pauline 19, Philippine 16			
Leonhard 7			
CORMANN, Johann	21	Loeningen	66-0984
CORNBACH, Clara	26	Berlin	64-0992
CORNELIUS, Dorette	17	Dorum	64-1022
CORNELIUS, Joh.	51	Elsfleth	65-0402
CORNELIUS, Wilhe.	48	Otterndorf	66-0576
Wilhelmine 20, Friedrich 32, Sophie 9			
CORNELSEN, G.(m)	21	Osterberg	64-0331
CORNET, Lucas	33	Wietmarschen	64-0214
CORREA, Anna	25	Hamburg	63-1085
CORSSEN, C.T.	20	Bremen	64-0495
CORSSEN, Marg.	28	New York	64-0427
CORTUM, Adelheid	20	Bremen	66-1248
CORWAN, Josefa	24	Boehmen	66-0349
COSQUINO, Cathrine	59	Rheda	66-0734
Lottche 19			
COSQUINO, Louise	24	Pella	66-0734
COSSELMANN, An.Cat	22	Grossalmerode	64-0433
COSTE, Francois	44	Marseille	63-0990
COTTGE, F.	28	Frommingen	66-0413
COTTIER, Visse	26	Bern	63-0244
COURTENAY, Mr.	35	Belfothe	64-0073
COVALLICK, Felix	23	Rosenberg	66-0837
COVERN, v. Anna	24	Bremen	66-0578
CRAB, Barbara	48	Boll	64-0363
CRAEMER, W.	27	Rawolesko	66-0413
Gustav 7m, P. 25, Bertha 3			
CRAFTS, Walther	24	West Newton	63-0862
CRAMER, C.J.	27	Ostfriesland	64-0495
CRAMER, Caspar	23	Wildeshausen	64-0343
CRAMER, D.	35	New York	64-0687
CRAMER, Friedr.	28	Wadeloh	64-1053
CRAMER, Georg	28	Vechold	64-0170
Heinr. 22			
CRAMER, Gottlieb	25	New York	63-0821
CRAMER, Gustav	25	Delmenhorst	66-0679
CRAMERT, Franz	34	Bremen	64-0840
CRANHOLD, Carl	35	Schoenberg	64-0170
Lina 32, Sophie 11m			
CRASS, Elise	18	Hanau	66-0704

NAME	AGE	RESIDENCE	YR-LIST
CRAWIG, Wensel	35	Preussen	66-0083
Catharine 28, Fransiska 9m			
CREDNER, Herm.	23	Hannover	65-0116
CREERY, James	27	Baltimore	63-0821
servant (f) 16			
CRESSMEYER, Wm.	24	Volmardingsen	64-1053
CROCOL, James	32	Buffalo	63-0296
CROEHLING, Casp.	20	Rossdorf	66-1243
CRONEMEYER, G.	30	Detmold	64-0886
CRUSIUS, J.N.	22	Lehr	63-0350
CUBA, Joh.	37	Boehmen	64-0427
CULLMANN, Ph. (m)	19	Fischbach	64-0214
CULLMANN, Phil.	41	New York	64-0687
CULMANN, E.	36	Lauran	65-0594
(f) 20, Julius 3			
CURDT, Conradt		Steinhude	66-1373
CURDTS, Louis	19	Wolfenbuettel	63-1218
CURDTS, Louis	38	Glatten	63-1218
Ellen 29, Eduard 8, Emma 6, Louis 2			
Charles 3m			
CYRA, Johann	32	Preussen	63-0398
Magdalena 37, Marie inf, Anton 6			
CZENZEC, Alex	18	Wien	64-0023
CZERMACK, Anna	53	Kuttenberg	66-1373
CZERNY, Cath.	37	Bohemia	64-0363
CZIKALLA, J.	40	Kross	63-0350
Susanne 36, Apollonia 9, Juliane 8			
Frances 5, Anton 3, Rosalie 3m			
CZISKE, Franz	30	Staren	66-0578
Justina 27, Martha 9m			
CZISKE, Joseph	30	Staren	66-0578
Rosine 36			
DAAB, Eva E.	16	Gr. Bieberau	64-0886
Catherine 21			
DAAKE, Friedrich	29	Bruchhaus	66-0679
DACHLER, Beata	27	Appenzell	64-0023
DACHLER, Frdr.	22	St.Gallen	65-0243
DACHTELMUELLER, B.	25	Oelbersheim	64-0992
DADE, Morris	16	Mobile	63-0168
DAEBBEN, Heinr.	21	Haseluenne	67-0007
DAEGELE, Hermann	24	Baden	66-0109
Eleonora 20			
DAEHN, Johanna	21	Schwarza	66-0668
DAELL, Carl Christ	18	Laubach	65-0865
DAELLER, Ludwig	36	Coellin	65-0713
DAEMON, Jacob	16	Bockenberg	63-1038
DAENECKE, Fd.	50	Smolary	64-0593
DAENZER, C.	42	St. Louis	63-0482
Caroline 40, Caroline 4			
DAEUMMER, Joh.Aug.	48	Kahle	65-1030
Gottl. Heinr 46			
DAHL, Regina	20	Geestendorf	63-0917
DAHLE, Johann	24	Eistrup	67-0007
DAHLEN, v. C.	36	Bashausen/Hes	63-1010
Heinrich 16			
DAHLER, Georg	18	Ahlen	66-0413
DAHLER, Louise	25	Rheda	63-0350
Gustav 11m			
DAHLHOFF, Cath.	24	Borghorst	66-1313
DAHLMANN, Carl	40	Turnow	66-1248
Johanna 43, Bertha 20, Wilhelmine 16			
Augusta 12			
DAHM, J.A.	52	Paterson	64-0138
DAHNKE, A.A.	24	Kirchweyhe	64-0495
DAHNKEN, Carsten	14	Balben	65-0055
DAHNKEN, Meta	51	Bremen	65-0243
DAISS, Ch.	18	Lippoldsweilr	64-0782
DAISS, Chris.	34	Oberurbach	65-0116
DAKERMANN, Anna	23	Brechtheim	66-1203
DALACOUS, Louis	25	Germany	66-0666
Louise 22			
DALFUES, Carl	26	Oeddsheim	66-0734
DALHOFF, Maria	49	Lingen	65-0950
Minna 22, Friederike 9, Ernst 4			
Elisabeth 16			
DALLMANN, Albert	26	Annaberg	66-0577
Ferdinand 23, Wilhelmine 23, Friedr. 20			
DALLMEYER, Friedr.	40	Landesbergen	66-1131

NAME	AGE	RESIDENCE	YR-LIST
DAMBERT, Elise	16	Oberlaub	64-0687
DAMCKE, Friedrich	25	Servea	63-0614
DAMM, Heinr.	22	Oberbenbach	66-1327
DAMM, Joh. Chr.	33	Langensalza	65-1030
DAMM, Johannes	30	Erxdorf	64-0639
DAMM, Leopold	19	Damm	65-0594
DAMMANN, Elisa	24	Peine	64-0840
Elisa 9m			
DAMMANN, Marie	28	Bremerhafen	63-0614
DAMMENS, Otto	24	St. Louis	64-0639
DAMMER, Hugo	20	Koenigsberg	64-0992
DAMMER, Joh.	30	Vehs	66-0576
Marie 31			
DAMMERER, Fr. Wm.	31	Ovenstedt	64-0938
DAMMERMANN, Louise	24	St. Louis	63-0953
Caroline 16			
DAMMERMUTH, Johann	28	Villmar	67-0007
DAMMEYER, Friedr.	18	Eldagsen	66-0934
DAMON, Phillip	54	Hochwiesel	63-0006
Johannes 16, Adeline 20, Elise 10			
DANBERT, Joh. Conr	39	Braunschweig	63-1178
Anna 21			
DANCK, Johann	76	Verona	66-1155
Theresia 38, Anna 16, Johann 13, Joseph 7			
DANDANT, (f)	40	France	63-1038
Amalie 6, Mary 8, Mathilda 10			
DANDT, Chs.	18	Giessen	63-0862
DANECKER, Anna B.	13	Leidrinen	63-1038
DANELSKI, M.	34	Exyn	66-0413
Marie 25, C. 1			
DANES, August	22	Coppenbruegge	66-0679
DANGBERG, Aug.	31	Nevada	64-0073
DANGEL, Ursula	21	Altheim	66-1373
DANGNELE, Georg	67	Badbergen	64-0992
Augusta 26			
DANHAM, Elisabeth	32	Arzberg	67-0806
DANHOF, Claus H.	40	Wuethausen	64-0456
Saartje 36, Hindrick 8, Albert 6			
Jantje 4, Laurens 2			
DANIEL, Franz	30	Chosien	66-0650
Antonia 19, Paul 1			
DANIELS, J.D.(m)	23	Loquard	64-0331
Johanna 21			
DANIELS, Peter	43	Niederau/Pr.	65-0038
DANKER, Sophie	23	Sievern	65-0007
DANKERS, Marg.	17	Bremervoerde	65-0974
DANNECKER, Chr'tne	50	Oberurbach	63-0350
DANNEKER, Johann	26	Geichingen	65-0243
DANNEMANN, Georg	24	Grabow	67-0007
DANNENBAUM, Nadam	24	Hansbach	63-0693
Caroline 25, Abraham 6m			
DANNER, Carl	25	Bahlingen	64-0593
Elis. 23, Ludw. 2, Emma 3m, Georg J. 23			
DANNERMANN, Ernest	33	Pr. Minden	64-0432
Marie 37, Louise 13			
DANNHAEUSER, Emil	19	Buchau	66-0576
DANSING, August	26		66-0984
Emilie 24			
DANTE, Franz	21	Prussia	64-0363
DANZ, A.E.	22		63-1010
DANZ, Elisabeth	57	Pittsburg	66-0704
DANZ, Giovanni	22	New York	63-1136
DANZEISEN, Cathar.	30	Tauchersreuth	66-0576
Catnarine 8			
DANZEISEN, R.	38	Eichstetten	65-0055
DANZIG, Hermann	17	Selters	66-1031
DANZIGER, Charltt.	36	Berlin	64-1161
Moritz 14, Friedrich 7, Gustav 5, Hugo 4			
Rosa			
DANZIGER, Max	27	Thorn	66-0147
DAPPING, Wilhelm	20	Hoexter	64-0363
DARLICH, Caroline	20	Browenau	66-0413
DARMS, Leonh.	40	Illand	63-0821
DARMSTAEDTER, Gabr	49	Pfeddersheim	64-0593
Susanne 42, Wilhelmine 7, Phil 5, Anton 5			
Anna 4, Cath. 2, Jacob 3m			
DARP v. Aug.	32	Solingen	64-0782
DARZOW, Marie	20	Hagenow	66-0668

NAME	AGE	RESIDENCE	YR-LIST
Caroline 25			
DASBECK, Caroline	25	Hessen	66-0984
DASCHEL, Renate	25	Sophienburg	66-0650
DASMANN, Wilhelm	16	Brochterbeck	64-0199
DASSAU, Max	23	Marienberg	66-0578
DASSEL, Conrad	42	Braunschweig	63-0053
Sophie 44, Sophie 18, Louise 16			
Dorothea 14, Mina 12, Marie 10, Carl 6			
DASSEL, Georg	31	Braunschweig	63-0053
DASSOW, Friedr.	26	Stolzenberg	65-1140
DAUB, Eva E.	16	Gr. Bieberau	64-0886
Catherine 21			
DAUB, Julius	24	Bonn	66-1373
DAUB, Ludwig	40	Obergleen	64-1053
Elisab. 40, Heinr. 15, Elise 13			
Catharina 7, Carl 5, August 4, Jacob 2			
DAUBACH, H.	36	Coblenz	66-0413
Amalie 39, Wilhelm 10, Karl 7, Fritz 5			
Clementine 3, Amalie 2, Anna 10m			
DAUBE, Henry	32	Philadelphia	63-0097
DAUBER, Georg	18	Curhessen	66-0577
DAUBERT, Elisa	18	Gauersheim	66-1248
DAUBERT, Henr.	16	Bremervoerde	66-0984
DAUBERT, Wilhelm	36	Erbsen	65-1030
Wilhelmine 36, Wilhelm 7, Louis 2			
Ridgen 2m			
DAUDENHEIMER, Jac.	22	Underheim	66-0221
DAUDT, Chr.	23	Kirschbronbch	64-0593
DAUDT, Christoph	18	Pfungstadt	66-0734
Ferd. 16			
DAUE, Wilh.	24	Rinteln	66-0221
DAUER, Catharine	25	Wiesbaden	65-0055
DAUER, Heinr.	20	Wiesbaden	65-0402
DAUM, Peter	27	Mannheim	64-0739
DAUN, Peter	15	Gemuenden	65-0151
DAUNKER, Christ	22	Oberurbach	65-0116
Louise 25			
DAUNN, Otto	54	Cumberland	65-0974
Margarethe 20, Heinrich 9, Wilhelm 9			
Emilie 8, Marie 7			
DAUNTH, Emanuel	17	Limbach	63-0917
DAUSCHA, Josephine	30	Marbach	65-0007
Marie 9, Carl 10			
DAUT, Marie	22	Wuerttemberg	66-0221
DAVID, Jeanette	21	Elmhausen	64-0687
DAVID, Nathan	28	Kreffelbach	66-1131
DAVID, Neumann	15	Kachau/Hung.	64-0920
DAVIDS, J.	24	Luedenscheid	65-1189
DAVIDSOHN, J.	13	Helmarshausen	66-0984
Rosalie 14			
DAVITS, W.	27	Westerinmarsh	66-0413
DAWISON, Bogumil	48	Dresden	66-0984
Constanza 38			
DEBAUNUY, (f)	30	Rouen	63-0350
Victoria 4, Antoinette 2			
DEBBE, J. Friedr.	18	Dissen	65-0950
DEBENDER, Caroline	22	Hessen	66-0734
DEBRING, Henry	24	Baltimore	66-0704
DEBUS, Johannes	33	Schierloch	66-0221
DECAZES, Ed.	24	Paris	64-0214
DECKE, Johann	30	Nuernberg	67-0007
Rudolph 7			
DECKELBACH, Johann	30	Mittelsemen	65-0865
Margarethe 28, Casper 7, Johannes 6			
Elisabeth 3, Margarethe 1			
DECKEM. Hr.	24	Cloppenberg	64-0938
Anna 20			
DECKER, Anje	40	Groningen	65-0007
DECKER, Heinrich	30	Bochum	65-0770
DECKER, Henry	17	Bremerhafen	64-0343
DECKER, Johann	19	Bocke	64-1022
DECKER, John	24	Buehren	66-0576
DECKER, Susanna	33	New York	63-0917
Carl 9, Julie 7, Jean 4			
DECKER, Wm.	43	Oldendorf	64-0840
DECKERT, Franz	16	Mergentheim	66-1155
DECKERT, Gust. A.	19	Leopoldshafen	65-0038
DECKERT, Jean	19	Cassel	66-0679

NAME	AGE	RESIDENCE	YR-LIST
DEEGEN, Adolph	25	Bamberg	63-1038
DEEKEN, Conr. A.	30	Schmertheim	64-0427
DEERING, Carl	39	New York	66-0704
Carl 9			
DEES, Gottlieb	24	Bruch	64-0427
DEETJEN, Helene	23	Bremen	63-1136
DEETJEN, Johanna	22	Sandstedt	63-0398
DEETJEN, Louis	38	Matanzas	63-1136
DEFFNER, Adam	23	Heimlichenbch	63-0296
DEFORT, Caroline	23	Frommertheim	66-1031
DEGELMANN, Joh.Ad.	33	Haula	64-0739
DEGEN, Albert	34	Sondershausen	66-0221
DEGEN, Marg.	18	Maineck	63-0990
DEGENHARDT, Christ	20	Duderstadt	66-1128
DEGENHARDT, Elisab	33	Wannfried	66-1373
August 6m			
DEGERING, (m)	34	Chicago	64-0427
Barb 36, Gottlieb 7, A.(m) 5, Regina 1			
wife 30, Emilie 6			
DEGERING, Christ.	30	Schmadenstedt	66-1373
DEGERINK, Ludw.	31	Braunschweig	65-1189
DEGLEN, v.d. Joh.		Visselhoevede	66-1203
DEGLER, Jacobin	54	Lienzingen	65-1189
Johanna 23, J. 15, G. 13			
DEHLE, Lena	19	Stadthagen	66-1127
DEHLEF, Valt.	25	Kirchhasel	64-0214
DEHLENBECK, Johann	16	Bremen	66-1093
DEHLES, Andreas	34	Kirchhassel	65-0243
DEHLS, Herm.	73	Vegesack	64-0343
DEHM, Eva	29	Soehlingen	64-0433
DEHM, Maria	24	Maikam	65-1095
DEHM, Rosine	46	Unt.Weissbach	65-0151
Friederike 7			
DEHN, Anna	18	Hainbach	64-0170
DEHNBOSTEL, Chr.	26	Neuenkirchen	64-0343
DEHRMANN, Johanna	55	Bremen	66-0413
DEHRS, Margaretha	17	Flonheim	66-1327
DEIBIG, Jacob	36	Chicago	64-1053
DEICHMAN, Charles	25	Hofgeismar	63-0296
Christiane 16			
DEICHMANN, August	20	Daverden	66-0984
DEICHMANN, Gottl.	28	Petershagen	65-1095
DEICHMANN, Minna	17	Hofgeismar	66-1093
DEIDL, Victus	40	Nussdorf	63-0482
DEIGER, Caroline	20	Freiburg	66-0934
DEIHRER, Paulus	25	Aschenhausen	65-1030
DEIKE, Diedr.	31	New York	63-0953
DEINLEIN, Pankratz	29	Paulendorf	66-1373
Marie 30, Georg 2			
DEINSKEMPER, B.	20	Asgerberg	66-0413
DEISCH, Joh. Gg.	36	Augsburg	67-0795
DEISSINGER, Ludwig	23	Tripstadt	63-0990
DEISSLER, Peter	33	Kesselborn	65-0151
DEIST, Gottfrey	46	Cassel	63-0015
DEISTER, Heinrich	17	Hildesheim	65-1140
DEISTER, Kunig.	20	Gandgesheim	65-0007
DEISTERBERG, Carol	24	Zowen	66-0469
Carl 15			
DEISTEROTH, Conrad	27	Friedewald	66-0576
DEITEL, Elisabeth	20	Baden	66-0469
DEITERS, Chr.	38	Holzminden	66-0577
DEITERS, Johann	29	Berenbostel	66-1155
DELEUS, Ludwig	28	Goennern	66-0221
DELISHAUER, Eduard	18	Frankfurt a/m	66-1248
DELLE, Otto	19	Aldingen	66-1313
DELLEN, v. W.	33	New Orleans	63-1085
DELOES, Johann	36	St. Juergen	66-1203
DELVENTHAL, Herm.	19	Hannover	66-1203
DEMANN, Ludwig	38	Brunswick	63-0822
DEMAR, Joseph	36	Steinbach	63-0398
DEMCKE, F.	27	Magdeburg	65-1189
DEMECKE, Robert	24	Braunfels	64-0170
DEMKE, August	29	Sophienburg	64-0214
DEMMLER, Francis	19	Hohneck	63-1218
DEMMLER, Marie	25	Stuttgart	65-0189
DEMPEL, Joh.	22	Seibelsdorf	67-0795
DEMUTH, Agnes	23	Dresden	66-0934
DEMUTH, Catharine	45	Baden	66-0576

NAME	AGE	RESIDENCE	YR-LIST
Caroline 14			
DEMUTH, Joh. P.	19	Herfingen	65-0243
DEMUTH, Moses	22	Rimbach	65-1024
Lina 18			
DENCKAS, Rob.	28	Weenermoor	64-0331
Johanna 21			
DENCKER, Meta	25	Hornknop	66-1313
DENECKE, Heinr.	22	Hannover	65-0770
DENGEL, Christine	24	Schwabsburg	66-0734
DENICKE, Julius	23	Hannover	63-0822
DENJERLE, J.G.	27	Wildberg	64-0593
DENKER, Tr.(f)	24	Thedinghausen	64-0495
DENKS, Dorothea	37	Palve	65-0594
DENKS, Heinr.	54	Paloe	65-0594
DENNELEIN, J.(m)	30	Dovingstadt	64-0331
DENNEMANN, H.	53	Wien	65-0055
DENNEWITZ, Wilhelm	23	Coellede	66-1373
DENNING, Heinrich	30	Quincy	66-0349
DENTGES, S.	19	Crefeld	64-0639
DENTINGER, G.(f)	21	Irslingen	64-0495
DENZLER, Louise	19	Schweiz	66-0147
Johanna 26			
DEPENBRAK, Regina	23	Rieste	66-0734
Margarethe 20, Lisette 17			
DEPENBROCK, Bernh.	20	Rieste	64-0687
DEPENDINER, Marie	25	Mettingen	63-1010
DEPKE, Maria Elis.	22	Rodinghausen	64-0920
DEPKEN, G.	20	Bremen	64-0593
DEPKEN, John	24	Hastedt	63-0168
DEPNER, Mar.(f)	20	Seelenfeld	64-0427
DEPPE, August	25	New York	63-0917
DEPPE, Louise	24	Frohnhausen	63-0551
DEPPELMANN, Otilia	34	Waldeck	67-0007
Hermine 29			
DEPPER, Joseph	38	Hopsen	64-0687
Anna 58, Theresa 18			
DEPPING, L.	20	Bremen	66-0413
DEPPMANN, Anna	36	Muenster	64-0639
DEPPNER, Math.(f)	20	Eisenach	64-0170
DEPPOLD, G.F.	23	Eggenreuth	64-0331
DERA, Gertrude	21	Obermannsdorf	66-0704
DERBER, Jos.	23	Weiberg	66-1243
DERDING, Carl	27	Bovensen	66-0679
DERKHEIM, Franz	41	Bremen	64-0593
Wife 20			
DERKHIEM, Agnes	40	Bremen	63-0821
DERLETH, Veit	33	Eisleben	63-0398
DERN, Balthasar	22	Giessen	64-0456
DERN, Georg	22	Watzenborn	63-0168
DERR, Joh. A.	27	Oberballbach	64-0840
DERSCH, Theresia	27	Sarbeck	66-1127
DERSCHAIL, Michael	19	Dragsweinsdor	65-0948
DERSTORFF, Rosine	21	Winkel	66-0349
DESCH, Chrs.	36	New Jersey	66-0221
DESCHNER, H.	32	New York	63-0752
DESCHNER, Marg.	35	Zella	65-1024
DESENBERG, Bernh.	30	Kalamackzan	63-0917
DESENBERG, Mariann	33	Lipsringe	64-1022
Benno 7, Rosa 5, Julius 3, Emilie 2			
Sigmund 9m			
DESSAU, Ph.(f)	28	New York	64-0495
G.(m) 6, H.(f) 4			
DESSNER, Gottlieb	17	Stadthagen	64-0214
Heinr. 22, Caroline 21			
DETERING, Wilh'mne	18	Stroehen	65-1031
DETERMANN, August	40	Becke	67-0007
DETERS, Catharine	50	Schale	66-0679
Friederike 12			
DETERS, Charlotte	43	Luebbecke	64-1206
DETERS, Elise	22	Stolp	66-0934
Henrich 20			
DETERS, Gerh.	24	Schale	64-1022
DETERS, Joh	42	Schabe	64-0687
Anna 40, Joh. Gerh. 11, Joh. Friedr. 7			
Joh. Heinr. 5, Caroline 1			
DETERS, Lambert	17	Schale	64-0363
DETERS, Luebbe	18	Oldenburg	66-0984
Heinrich 28			

NAME	AGE	RESIDENCE	YR-LIST
DETJEN, Anton	29	New York	66-0109
DETJEN, Mathilde	28	St.Petersburg	66-0109
DETMERS, Henry	24	Oldenburg	65-0770
DETSCH, Joh.	33	Haig	65-1030
DETTE, Krdr.	23	Liebenburg	65-0116
DETTLING, Martin	21	Nordstetten	64-0331
DETTMER, Henry	30	New York	66-0679
DETTMER, Herm. Chr	21	Hessel	65-0243
DETTMER, Sophie	22	Hoexter	64-0886
DETTMER, Wilhelm	19	Hannover	66-1373
DETTMEYER, Gottl.	48	Illinois	66-0704
DEUBEL, Js.	51	Budinghain	64-0782
DEUBEL, W.H.	39	New York	63-0821
DEUBER, Jac.	28	Greuth	64-0593
DEUDATO, Milinoric	46	Morigns	64-0331
DEUERLICH, Albert	48	Goettingen	64-1206
DEUERLING, Andreas	25	Northeim	66-0623
DEUERLING, Paul	25	Washington	66-0623
Catharine 21, Margarethe 9m			
DEUSCHLE, Cathrine	20	Oberensingen	66-0734
DEUSSMANN, Johann	17	Rheine	66-1131
DEUSTELMANN, J.	28	Vernich	64-0782
DEUTSCH, Isaac	42	Bromberg	66-0083
DEUTSCH, Rud.	25	Mussbach	64-0214
DEUTSCHER, Jac.	27	Krakau	63-0821
DEUTSCHMANN, Const	19	Hertzberg	64-0023
DEUZLER, Wm.	26	Nordheim	66-0734
DEVEL, Christ	20	Hilbe	64-1108
DEVELMANN, Cath.	57	Langen	64-0782
Diedr. 26, Anna 21			
DEVERMANN, John	32	Louisville	63-1136
Dina 24, Helene 15, Meyer 9			
DEWALD, Henriette	17	Woerrstadt	66-0147
DEWAR, Johann	36	Bergheim	64-1053
DEWERMANN, Joh.	24	Nortrup	66-0576
DEXEROTH, Adam	33	Maryland	63-1136
Louise 32			
DEXHEIMER, C.	22	Marschheim	65-0974
DEYES, Jos.	50	Paris	63-1178
DEYHEE, Caroline	24	Gablenbergen	67-0007
DEYMANN, Eugen	30	Rees	66-0934
Appolla 24			
DEYMANN, John	30	Kl. Starern	63-0244
Henry 18, Ellen 21			
DICHE, Johs.	27	Kleinhausen	65-0151
DICK, Herm.	28	Ulm	64-1161
DICKE, Heinrich	22	Stolzenau	66-0577
DICKER, Clemens	36	Lengen	65-1030
Anna Adelh'd 34, Agnes 12, Clemens 10			
Heinrich 8, Caroline 6, Bernhard 1			
DICKERT, Magarit	20	Hemmen	64-0023
DICKMANN, Wilh'mne	29	Bexen	67-0353
DIEBALL, Carl	35	Kleinmasa-Lan	66-0650
Emilie 30, Gustav 4			
DIEBIG, Chr.	25	Pfungstadt	65-1189
DIEBOLD, Carl	29	Bieberach	66-1327
DIEBOLD, Seb.	22	Seeborn	65-0007
DIECKHAUS, Wm.	24	Neuenkirchen	64-0427
DIECKHOF, Chr.	15	Selbenfeld	64-0495
DIECKMANN, Carl	60	Lehe	66-1127
Meta 32, Hanchen 7			
DIECKMANN, D.H.	49	Vessendorf	65-0974
DIECKMANN, Elise	39	Cincinnati	64-0495
DIECKMANN, Ferd.	59	Kleinenberg	63-0296
DIECKMANN, G.	18	Bevensen	63-0917
DIECKMANN, G.M.	29	Varel	65-0713
DIECKMANN, Heinr.	30	Osnabrueck	64-0639
Anna 18			
DIECKMANN, J.W.	43	Bremen	64-0363
DIECKMANN, Rudolph	25	Brochterbeck	64-0199
DIECKMANN, W.H.	18	Bremen	63-1136
DIECKMANN, Wilh.	20	Bremen	65-0243
DIECKMANN, Wilhelm	23	Schwerin	67-0599
DIECKMANN, Wm.	36	Bremen	64-1053
DIEDERICH, Bernard	40	Preussen	64-0214
Catherine 27, Bernhard 6, Heinrich 3			
baby 9m			
DIEDERICH, Cacilie	26	Michigan	63-0821

NAME	AGE	RESIDENCE	YR-LIST
DIEDERICH, H.	29	Prussia	63-1003
DIEDERICHS, Peter	21	Hessen	66-0623
Johannes 16			
DIEDRICH, And.	40	Germany	63-0953
wife 36, Anna 12, Johan 9, Peter 7			
Georg 6, baby 6m			
DIEDRICH, Carl	24	Marburg	64-1053
DIEDRICH, Christ.	24	Frankenhausen	63-0953
Anna 21, Louise 4			
DIEDRICH, Ernst	29	Prussia	64-0432
DIEDRICH, Heinr.	17	Ellinghausen	64-0639
Marie L. 19			
DIEDRICH, Joh.	48	Radum	66-1248
Louise 45, Bertha 5, Wilhelm 4m			
DIEDRICH, Ludwig	35	Bockenhausen	64-0840
Therese 26, Elise 5, Helene 2			
Caroline 6m			
DIEDRICH. Caspar	28	New York	63-0244
Barbara 43, Benedict 9			
DIEDRICHS, Anton	23	Muenster	64-1053
DIEFENBACH, Heinr.	19	Minden	66-0934
DIEFENBACH, John	30	Speyer	63-0953
Josephine 29, Christine 25, Elise 21			
Charlotte 23			
DIEGMANN, John	29	Heuthen	63-0482
Anna Cath. 24			
DIEHICH, Peter	20	Altzeil	66-1327
DIEHL, Adam	45	Laubach	66-0704
DIEHL, Christine	20	Pfordt	64-0214
DIEHL, Elise	21	Ndr.Auerbach	64-0992
Christian 3m			
DIEHL, Fr.	24	Darmstadt	65-0189
DIEHL, Friedr.	23	Ruppertsburg	65-0116
DIEHL, Heinr.	16	Ruppertsburg	65-0594
DIEHL, Heinrich	21	Darmstadt	66-1031
DIEHL, Heinrich	43	Mittelsemen	65-0865
Margaretha 25, Casper 19, Margaretha 17			
Heinrich 14, Johannes 7, Elisabeth 6			
Heinrich 1			
DIEHL, Jacob	28	Coblenz	66-0734
DIEHL, Louise	31	Rupertsberg	66-1203
Jacob 8, Dorothea 6, Hary 5m			
DIEHL, Maria	17	Esslingen	64-0593
Cath. 16, Caroline 14, Sophie 13			
DIEHL, Robert	33	Lobsens	65-0865
Josephine 30, Bruno 6, Marie 2, Julius 4m			
DIEHM, Georg	25	Waldmichelbch	66-0668
DIEHM, Georg	25	Waldmichelbch	66-0668
DIEKEN, Egbertus	44	Ostfriesland	63-0752
Hiske 34, Antje 14, Meike 9, Cornelia 4			
baby 2m			
DIEKEN, Ibben	38	Visquard	66-1248
Alvine 21, Hilke 1			
DIEKEN, Siebert W.	47	Ostfriesland	64-0214
Stiemke 43, Wilke 14, Peter 12, Swantje 9			
Friedrike 1			
DIEKER, Anna Maria	22	Aslage	66-0704
DIEKHOFF, Peter	21	Rettum	66-1031
DIEKMANN, Ana	21	Lehe	66-0577
DIEKMANN, Carl	27	Hessen	66-0576
DIEKMANN, Chris.	26	Hovestadt	63-0752
DIEKMANN, Ferd.	28	Schinkel	66-1155
DIEKMANN, Heinr.	64	Hannover	64-0938
Minna 20			
DIEKMANN, Henry	20	Bremen	63-1136
DIEKMANN, Jac.	18	Bremen	65-0189
DIEKMANN, Mary	40	Bremen	66-0576
DIELER, Christine	27	Nienburg	65-1189
DIELING, Friedr.	23	Achim	66-0734
DIELS, Carl	22	Herschbach	66-0934
DIEM, Agathe	24	Dornbirn	66-1327
Marie 28, Emilie 12, Hermann 20			
DIEM, Friedrich	30	Neuenstein	66-0576
DIEMER, Ludwig	24	Cincinnati	66-0083
DIENER, Augusta	23	Wiesbaden	64-1022
DIENER, Wm. Jac.	27	Boehmen	64-0427
DIENST, Nicolaus	24	Baden	66-0109
DIENSTEL, Gustav	28	Schoenlinde	66-1373

NAME	AGE	RESIDENCE	YR-LIST
DIERCKS, G.(m)	20	Wedel	64-0331
DIERKEN, Gerhard	24	Osnabrueck	66-1093
Heinrich 14, Wilhelmine 16, Louise 22			
DIERKES, Gerhd.	63	Ruehlsford	64-0331
Johanna 21			
DIERKING, Sophia	20	Wendelbastel	64-0495
DIERKO, Dirk	27	Wengsel	66-0734
DIERKS, Ernst	40	Belgien	63-0168
DIERKS, Joh. D.	21	Ostfriesland	66-0704
DIERKS, Wilhelm	24	Oberstaedt	64-0456
DIERKSEN, Derckus	51	Nuttermoor	64-0886
DIERS, Heinrich	51	Varrel	65-1031
Mienchen 20, Marie 18, Hermann 16			
Caroline 14, Conrad 8			
DIERS, Hermann	19	Brockmuehle	66-0679
DIERSCH, H.W.	25	Elsterberg	63-1136
DIESCHER, Samuel	26	Peot	66-0147
DIESER, John	45	Sondelfingen	63-1218
Cathar. 43, Otto 9			
DIESTERWEG, August	23	Dillenburg	65-1031
DIETEL, Christ.	34	New Orleans	63-0953
Wolfgang 11			
DIETEL, Cunningund	24	Obernfranken	66-0221
DIETERICH, D.W.	25	Wolfhagen	65-0007
H. 27			
DIETERLE, Catha.	20	Jelingen	65-0189
Carl 17			
DIETERLE, Wilhelm	37	New York	66-0934
Wilhelm 9			
DIETERLEN, Emma	18	Wildentierbch	63-0097
DIETESHEIM, Paulin	19	Haegenheim	66-0576
DIETJEN, Martin	20	Vaaderude	66-1248
DIETMEYER, Eduard	19	Sasbach	64-1022
DIETRICH, Anton	27	Muenster	64-0639
DIETRICH, August	31	Washington	66-0934
DIETRICH, Chr.	34	New York	63-0168
DIETRICH, Chr.F.M.	26	Hirschberg	63-0821
DIETRICH, Christ.	29	Lorhaupten	65-0948
DIETRICH, D. Const	22	Wyhl	63-1038
DIETRICH, Friedr.	25	Landau	63-0398
DIETRICH, Friedr.	30	Osnabrueck	66-0412
Wilhelmine 30, Elise 9m			
DIETRICH, G.	34	Redingen	65-0974
DIETRICH, Herm.	29	Berlin	65-0055
DIETRICH, Joh.	20	Gleichen	66-1373
DIETRICH, John	43	Rastatt	63-1218
Cathar. 34, Wilhelm 16, August 9			
DIETRICH, Joseph	37	Meilau	66-0734
DIETRICH, Julia Ch	25	Neuenkirchen	63-0015
Bertha 4			
DIETRICH, Marie	18	Eschenstrudt	65-0038
DIETRICH, Michel	24	Brackingen	64-0331
DIETRICH, S.(m)	26	Eichberg	64-0331
DIETRICHS, Heinr.	29	Ildehausen	64-0199
DIETRICHS, Ma.(f)	23	Fuerstenau	64-0782
El.(f) 59, Heinr. 19			
DIETSCH, Carl Aug.	25	Netzekau	64-0073
DIETSCHI, Engelb.	19	Haardt	63-1085
DIETSCHLER, Caspar	18	Heidelbach	66-1327
DIETTER, Christine	18	Dusslingen	65-0189
DIETZ, Carl	14	Wildungen	64-0739
DIETZ, Casper	27	Hafenbreibach	66-0623
DIETZ, Cathrina	19	Ulple	67-0007
DIETZ, Diedr.	50	Gnidorf	65-0243
Marie 21			
DIETZ, Heinrich	13	Ganreweiler	66-1248
DIETZ, Marie	15	Daertzbach	63-1085
DIETZ, Michael	58	Eisenbach	63-0990
Ludwig 31, Amalie 26, Febronia 22			
DIETZ, Peter	18	Gauersheim	65-1030
DIETZ, Therese	21	Lohnsheim	66-0576
DIETZ, Valerie	21	Pymont	66-0576
DIETZEL, Johann	14	Marburg	66-0679
DIEZ, Margarethe	27	Bieberach	66-1327
Georg 5, Louise 4, John Abrah. 2, Carl 6m			
DILL, Dorothea	40	Leopoldshafen	65-0038
Louise 9			
DILLER, Johann	28	Gleissenberg	64-0739

NAME	AGE	RESIDENCE	YR-LIST
DILLING, Adam	18	Oberdieten	64-0687
DIMER, Ph. Jac.	23	Hochspeyer	64-0138
DIMLER. E.	19	Verden	67-0795
DINDEL, Melchior	28	Zurgberg	64-0456
DINIER, James	21	Baiern	64-0214
DINKEL, Joh.	24	Schwarzkolk	65-0974
DINKELACKER, Ernst	19	Sindelfingen	65-0189
Carl 18, Christoph 22			
DINN, Elisabeth	25	Oberheim	66-0346
DIONYS, Wilh.	24	Simmern	64-0214
DIPPACHER, Elise	17	New Orleans	63-0097
DIPPEL, Maria	24	Fuerstenhagen	64-0687
DIPPER, W.	27	Loxten	65-0974
Friderike 23, Lina 11m			
DIPPOLD, Georg	27	Hollfeld	65-1088
Anna 22			
DIPPOLD, Johann	42	Ebermannstadt	66-0412
Joh. Georg 34			
DIPPOLDER, Aug.	22	Wuerttemberg	63-0822
DIRIE, (f)	25	Rouen	63-0350
Francis 5m			
DIRIE, Benvit.	27	Rouen	63-0350
DIRK, Joseph	24	Ahlen	66-0413
DIRKEN, Otto	51	Vechta	65-1030
Helena 21, Franziska 18, Hermann 15			
Heinrich 13, Juliana 9			
DIRKES, Harm	22	Forlitz	66-0147
DIRKS, Albert	42	Holstrop	66-0668
Gretje 45, baby 2m, Jan 21, Harm 9			
Wilh 6, Antje 15, Gretje 2			
DIRKS, Gerhard	23	Jever	66-0668
DIRKS, Sophie	70	Erwitte	66-1313
DIRKS, Wilke	36	Oldenburg	64-0363
Trientje 29, J.H.(f) 12, G.A.(m) 10			
Frch.(m) 6, baby(m) 9m			
DIRKSEN, Dirk	34	Westermarsch	66-0984
Dirk 10			
DIRKSEN, Theodor	24	Emden	65-1031
DIRSUM, Philip	26	Neuenheim	66-0679
DIRTSCHIE, Franzka	26	Kobelwald	64-1108
DISCH, Car.(f)	23	New York	64-0214
DISCHMER, Johann	24	Cassel	66-0623
Margarethe 24, Georg 4			
DITHMANN, Rudolf	22	Marburg	65-0950
DITMAR, Carl	15	Herford	64-0992
DITMAR, Carl Heinr	19	Holzhausen	65-0243
DITMAR, Rudolph	25	Timpelberg	64-0639
DITSCHER, Michael	26	Rheinfelden	66-0221
DITTENBRAND, Carl	33	Berlin	65-0243
Johanna 32, Anna 6, Bertha 5, Carl 2			
Max 1			
DITTENHOEFER, C.	22	Mittlerweilbh	64-0782
DITTERS, Chr.	27	Diedesheim	65-1189
DITTMANN, Adolph	24	Bremen	64-0456
DITTMANN, Franz	28	Pforzheim	67-0007
Emma 22, Henriette 3			
DITTMANN, Vincent	23	Frankenhain	66-0349
DITTMAR, Cath.	25	Wabern	64-0840
DITTMAR, Christoph	18	Immelborn	63-0168
DITTMER, Anna	20	Volkmarsgruen	66-0679
DITTMER, Gertrud	51	Holzhausen	66-0679
Catharina 16			
DITTRICH, Joseph	38	Vienna	66-0837
DITZ, Michael	30	Trabelsdorf	63-0296
DITZ, Wm.	18	Nack/Hess.	65-0038
Maria 45, Caroline 17, Philipp 10, Carl 6			
Michael 4			
DIYSLAU, L. (m)	40	Switz.	63-0990
wife 30			
DIZ, Ludwig	14	Elisenbach	63-0990
DLOUHY, Charles	30	Frankfurt a/M	63-0990
DOANE, A.	25	Boston	63-0244
DOBBERN, Christine	33	Zeisersweiler	63-1038
DOBBERTSCHAN, Joh.	20	St.Margarethe	64-0433
DOBERER, Gottlieb	24	Baltimore	63-0862
DOBRAWA, Ign.	34	Tyrol	63-0862
DOBRINE, Helene	23	Krojanke	66-0704
DOCEN, Henriette	22	Hiller	64-0938

NAME	AGE	RESIDENCE	YR-LIST
Lina 17			
DOCHTERMANN, Paul	22	Bornholzhsn.	66-0221
DOCK, Claus H.	20	Neuenkirchen	64-0363
DOCKWEILER, Aug.	18	Hoerste	64-0073
DODANE, Zelima	23	Corney	63-0015
DODEN, Herm.	24	Jever	65-0713
DODENHOF, Peter	24	Freiburg	66-0623
DODENHOFF, H.H.	18	Rothenburg	65-0007
DOEBBERSTEIN, Mich	29	Liszkowke	66-0469
August 19			
DOEBLER, Elisab.	22	Beuren	65-0243
Dorethe 18, Martin 18, Cath. 54			
DOEBLER, Friedr.	26	Metzingen	64-0363
Maria 28, Fr. (m) 7, Franklin 7, Maria 4			
Gottfr. 6m, Magd. 63, Carl 34			
DOEBLING, Heinr.	21	Hoya	65-0116
DOEBRICH, Aug.	34	Preussen	63-0398
Michel 58, Hennriette 27, Friedr. 2			
Gustav 3m			
DOECKING, Anna	32	Preussen	63-0990
Marie 29			
DOEDING, Julius	28	Bremen	63-0990
DOEHL, Johann	25	Wuertemberg	66-0679
DOEHLE, Daniel	22	Bremen	66-1155
DOEHLEN, Henriette	22	Scholgau/S-M.	67-1005
DOEHLER, Laura	26	Appenzell	64-1053
Carl 2, Henry 9m			
DOEHLING, Johann	19	Morsum	66-1093
DOEHRING, Carl Frd	30	Meerane	64-0739
DOEHRING, Friedr.	40	Illinois	66-0734
DOEKEL, D.	16	Noertel	65-1088
DOELGER, Catharina	34	Aschaffenburg	65-1030
DOELGER, Eva	36	Liesenheim	65-1030
DOELKER, Ba.	20	Untermosbach	65-0974
DOELL, Caspar	28	Eichfeld	66-0346
DOELL, Cath.	20	Hesse-Darmst.	63-0822
DOELL, Cath.	21	Gilfershausen	64-0665
DOELLE, Jacob	47	Hessen	66-0734
Anna 47, Heinrich 23, Marie 18			
Elisabeth 15, Martha 9, Conrad 8			
Catharine 7, Jacob 4			
DOELLER, Andreas	23	Northeim	66-0623
DOELLER, Joh.	41	Aurich	66-0650
Julia 41			
DOELLING, Chr.	32	Rossbach	65-0898
Cath. 26, Ida 9m			
DOELLING, F.	20	Lienen	65-1189
DOELLINGER, Albert	17	Burgsteinfurt	63-0482
DOENGES, Johann	40	Worms	66-0679
DOENINGER, Ludw.	44	Durmersheim	66-0704
DOENNER, Wilhelm	20	Neuhaus	66-1127
DOEPEL, Augusta	20	Muenden	64-0840
DOEPFER, Hermann	13	Darmstadt	66-1093
DOEPNER, Heinr.	20	Grossluder	66-1203
DOEPPE, Christ.	24	Bueckeburg	65-0594
DOEPPE, Georg	17	Hatzfeld	66-0837
DOEPPNER, Chr.	25	Doehren	65-0974
DOERBECKER, Elisab	26	Dillich	65-0950
DOERER, Sebastian	21	Baden	66-0469
DOERGELOH, H.(m)	32	Sudweyhe	64-0495
C.(m) 79, A.(f) 59			
DOERGELOH, Herm.	20	Weyhe	65-0402
DOERING, Adolph	23	Lengsfeld	66-0577
DOERING, Anton	18	Geismar	64-0639
DOERING, Carl	25	Berlingrode	65-0116
DOERING, Ernst	26	Beverstedt	65-0594
DOERING, Ignatz	22	Geismar	64-1053
DOERING, Joh.	21	Dierlammen	65-0950
DOERING, Julius	26	Hannover	65-0055
DOERING, Lorenz	26	Erschhausen	65-0713
DOERING, S.	32	Prussia	63-1003
M. 20, C. 17			
DOERING, W.G.	19	Pittsburg	64-0687
DOERLE, Rosalie	53	Herbolzheim	64-0023
Gustav 32, Friederike 23, Flora 21			
Rudolph 15			
DOERMER, Christ.	25	Roetges	66-0704
DOERNACH, Daniel	24	Neckartenzlin	66-0734

NAME	AGE	RESIDENCE	YR-LIST
DOERNER, Carl	25	Saxony	66-1093
DOERNER, Wm.	38	Louisville	64-0432
DOERNSTE, Aug.	27	Scharpe	64-0840
DOERR, Amalie	32	Markelsheim	66-0704
Friederike 19			
DOERR, Georg	18	Speckwinkel	65-1030
DOERR, Georg Heinr	30	Wiera	65-0948
Catharine 35, Elisabeth 9, Cathrine 2			
DOERR, Heinr. Conr	28	Lantenhausen	66-0578
DOERR, Joh. Georg	20	Bessungen	64-0938
DOERRER, Sophie	21	Lauffen	66-0576
DOERSCH, Conrad	16	Kaltern	66-0623
Catharine 47			
DOERUH, Heinr.	26	Werda	64-0739
DOESAM, Getrud	24	Lorzenbach	66-1327
Marie 22, Johann 22			
DOESCHER, Ana Mar.	28	Ottendorf	64-0456
DOESCHER, Anna	20	Ringstedt	66-1093
DOESCHER, Anna	19	Stolp	66-0934
DOESCHER, Anna	30	Buchen	64-0427
DOESCHER, C.	27	New York	66-0934
DOESCHER, Chr'stne	17	Stotel	64-0739
Heinrich 14			
DOESCHER, Christof	16	Bramstedt	66-1128
DOESCHER, Claus	20	Kuehrstedt	63-0990
DOESCHER, Friedr.	32	San Francisco	63-0953
DOESCHER, H.F.	34	New York	64-0214
Anna 24, E.H.F.(m) 2, G.R.(m) 6m			
DOESCHER, Heinr.	23	Worbis	66-0734
DOESCHER, Heinrich	25	Dorum	66-0577
DOESCHER, Herm.	19	Lintig	65-0594
DOESCHER, Hinr.	19	Lintig/Hann	65-0038
DOESCHER, Louise	20	Koehlen	66-0934
DOESCHER, Marie	19	Lintig	63-1136
DOESCHER, Martin	35	New York	63-0990
DOESCHER, O.H.	20	Fressdorf	65-0974
DOESS, Gotlob Fr.	31	Rommelshausen	63-0244
DOETSCH, Nicolaus	41	Kitzebuettel	66-0623
Stina 41			
DOETSCHER, Bertha	16	Hannover	65-1088
DOETZEL, Joseph	28	Birnfeld	66-1373
DOGGE, Albert	14	Neumark	66-0734
DOHL, Adam	16	Berlin	64-0992
DOHLEN, v. Anna	16	Holftel	66-1031
DOHLEN, v. Heinr.	17	Northum	66-1031
DOHM, Joh.	39	Thedinghausen	65-0038
DOHME, Carl	56	Maryland	66-0679
Emma 16			
DOHMEYER, Anna	27	Osnabrueck	66-1093
DOHMSEK, Wm.	17	Phudershausen	64-0782
DOHNEHACKE, Fritz	18	Sothwalle	66-0623
DOHRMANN, Wilh.	22	Naton	65-0594
DOHRS, Wm.	20	Gr. Lobke	65-0038
DOLDERER, Rosalia	18	Schoenhardt	66-1373
DOLECK, Leopold	29	Kloesterle	66-0734
Josefa 25, Joseph 5, Anton 2			
Francisca 70			
DOLECK, Veit	34	Kloesterle	66-0734
Anna 23, Franz 2, Joseph 6m			
DOLKEMEYER, Gerh.	28	Ibbenbuehren	65-0898
DOLL, Louise	27	Bretten	64-0495
Friedr. 2			
DOLLAS, W.	27	Krakau	63-0821
DOLLETSCHEK, Peter	45	Petersdorf	66-0734
Anna 45, Peter 20, Franz 18			
DOLLINGER, Anna	21	Baden	66-0734
DOLPHO, Ludwig	45	Cassel	66-0984
Johanna 50, H. 19			
DOM, Nicolas	32	Rouen	65-0004
DOMANN, Emma	17	Pforzheim	66-1155
Marie 9			
DOMASZEK, Johann	27	Polen	66-0666
Catharine 21, Marianne 6m			
DOMCKE, Joh.	30	Posen	67-0795
Julie 25, Otto 3, Emil 8m			
DOME, Nicota	42	Liego	66-1093
Catharina 46, Melanie 19			
DOMES, Leo.	24	Lemberg/Pr.	65-0116
DOMMERICH, L.F.	24	Muehlheim	65-0055
DONATH, Hn. Oswald	22	Breitenau	66-0837
DONE, Joh. P.	14	Otterndorf	64-0432
DONG, Marye	23	Dorum	67-0600
DOOR, Maria	39	Riepe	63-0482
DOPMANN, Lena	50	Woemsdorf	66-0679
Diedrich 23			
DOPMEYER, C.G.(m)	34	Braunschweig	64-0214
DOPPELHAMMER, Geo.	38	Dietenhofen	66-0668
DOPPING, Emma	16	Hoexter	64-0023
DOPPLER, Louise	21	Edenkoben	65-0055
DORBECKER, Marie	57	Gilserberg	66-0984
DORENBERG, Julius	24	Vechte	66-0984
DORGELOH, Hermann	24	Weyhe	65-0402
DORHAUER, Aug.	44	New York	63-1136
DORLE, R.(m)	22	Herbolzheim	64-0331
DORMAN, Georg	26	St. Louis	63-0296
DORN, Bab.	18	Erlangen	66-0704
DORN, Heinrich	27	Heidelberg	66-1327
DORN, Lorenz	26	Crawford	66-0734
DORN, Richard	18	Chemnitz	66-0221
DORNBACHER, B.	28	Buhe	65-0402
DORNEKER, Joh.	18	Leeste	65-0974
DORNETTE, Heinr.	18	Lemke	66-1127
DORNFELD, Otto	18	Doebeln	65-0243
DORNHAUER, Heinr.	19	Hinterwaiten	66-0083
Caroline 20			
DORNHEIM, A.	44	New York	63-0953
DORNISS, Mrd.(f)	37	Coburg	64-0495
Bernh. 7, Frz.(f) 7			
DORNWALL, Rudolph	19	Goettingen	63-1178
DORP, D.	28	Sieheusen	65-1189
DORR, Julia	21	Osthofen	64-0073
DORRER, Jacob	29	Laufen	66-0576
DORRIES, Carl	43	Hardegsen	64-0331
Johanna 21			
DORRIES, Wilh'mine	18	Braunschweig	64-0331
DORSTEWITZ, Gust.	18	Kasckirchen	64-0639
DOSCHE, (m)	42	Hohefeldt	65-1189
Barbara 38, Andreas 18, Eva 17			
Valentin 7, Barb. 5, Georg 4, Wilhelm 2			
Maria 1			
DOSCHER, Helene	23	Wremen	64-0495
DOSTER, Catharina	20	Praitenberg	66-1327
DOSTER, Friedrich	34	Grafenberg	66-0147
Margarethe 31			
DOSTER, Georg	23	Grafenberg	66-0147
DOTGERT, Henriette	24	Darmstadt	66-1031
DOTT, Jacob	28	Mainz	66-0984
DOTTERPUHL, Aug.	30	Camitz	66-1327
DOTTERWEIER, Nicol	35	Hambach	63-1218
Dorothea 24			
DOTTLINGER, Mich.	20	New York	63-1136
DOTZAUER, Ferdin'd	28	Dotterweis	66-0679
DOTZAUER, Jacob	27	Muelsbach	66-0679
DOTZAUER, Ludw.	28	Undenheim	65-0243
DOUBRAVA, Barbara	32	Boehmen	63-0917
DOUPE, G.	19	Frankenberg	66-0413
DOWNS, Marie	26	Carlsruhe	64-1053
Helene 3			
DRACHE, Eugene	45	New York	63-0990
DRACHSLER, Dorothe	27	Clausthal	64-0886
DRAKE, Maria	15	Vlotho	65-1095
DRAKEN, Herm.	18	Leeste	65-0974
DRAKENFELD, Eduard	22	Erlangen	66-0147
DRANDT, Zacharias	33	Herbstein	65-1024
Franzisca 30, Constance 8, Marzala 6			
Elisabeth 10m			
DRANHARDT, Ernst	21	Grossenhain	66-0147
DRATH, Lor.	56	Waldau	65-0402
Frdke. 54, Math. 19, Louise 17			
DRAUTVETTER, Georg	58	Warsaw	63-0821
DRAZ, Carl	20	Nuernberg	64-0138
DREBLOW, Arnold	23	Gladbach	65-1031
DRECHER, Carl	22	Geisingen	66-0221
DRECHSEL, Margaret	30	Lindenhardt	63-0821
baby 9m			
DRECHSLER, Georg	23	Grindenhardt	64-0331

NAME	AGE	RESIDENCE	YR-LIST
Chst.(m) 7, Elis 5			
DRECHSLER, J. Geo.	32	Crofdorf	64-0138
DRECHSLER, W.	25	New York	66-0934
DREES, C.	26	Bersheim	64-0938
Fr. 9m			
DREES, Friedrich		Hannover	66-0984
DREES, Heinrich	22	Hannover	67-0007
DREES, Ph.	19	Erkenbrechtsw	64-0363
DREESE, Martin	17	Berne	66-0576
DREFFY, Carl	29	Brackenheim	66-0623
DREGEMEYER, Anton	27	Minden	66-0083
DREGER, Wilhelm	38	Leppien	66-0083
DREHER, Lorenz	36	Voehrenbach	66-0349
DREHER, Martha	29	Voehrenbach	66-0349
Adelheid 11m, Minna 16			
DREHER, Wilhelmine	22	Riedling	65-1095
DREICKEL, Casimir	38	Durmersheim	66-0704
DREIER, Emil Dr.	36	Chicago	63-0953
DREIER, Heinrich	24	Rahden	65-1088
DREIER, Louis	21	Bremen	65-0243
DREIFARTH, Ed.	25	Naumburg	64-1108
DREIFUSS, B.	17	Mannheim	64-1108
DREIFUSS, Moritz	17	Bieten	66-0576
DREIMEYER, Wilhelm	25	Natrup	66-0668
DREIS, Phil	32	Lorsch	65-0151
DREISS, A.A.(m)	32	Columbia	64-0214
baby			
DREISZLEIN, Leonh.	25	Treuchlingen	65-0594
DREME, Isaak	25	Zell	66-0576
DRERRES, Friedrich	32	Grefenberg	66-1031
Marie 35			
DRESCHER, Heinrich	21	Ahrenkamp	64-0920
DRESCHER, Richard	23	Altenburg	66-0623
DRESEL, Balthasar	25	Dippach	63-1038
DRESELAERS, Math.	34	Cincinnati	63-0953
DRESER, H. Wilhmne	24	Solingen	65-0038
DRESKE, Joachim	35	Krieheldorf	63-0614
DRESLER, Ottmar	33	Renderoth	63-0350
Adolphine 42			
DRESS, Wm.	36	Muenster	64-1053
Jacob 21			
DRESSEL, Bertha	26	Artern	66-0934
DRESSEL, Christine	28	Loebenstein	66-0734
Carl 8, Theodor 6			
DRESSEL, Heinr.	28	Bonn	65-0004
DRESSEL, J.	24	Ravensburg	63-1010
Joseph 23			
DRESSEL, Martin	31	Eisfeld	63-0482
DRESSELHAUS, John	27	Schale	66-0679
Anna 24, Regina 2, Marie 6m			
DRESSELT, Felix	21	Gr.Breitenbch	64-0432
DRESSING, Anna	21	Hannover	64-0739
DRESSLER, Joh.	17	Schondorf	65-0243
Gottl 15, Magdalena 18, Gottl. 49			
Magdal. 45, Louise 13, Wilhelm 7			
Friederike 5, Lidion 4, Lisette 19			
DRESSON, Leon	23	Paris	64-1053
DREUDT, Ludwig	26	Wetzberg	63-1218
Elisabeth 27			
DREWER, Adolph	29	Bielefeld	65-0713
DREWES, Joh.	20	Wenkeldorf	64-0992
DREWES, Peter H.	22	Otterndorf	66-1313
DREWING, Lewis	50	Marienstein	63-0350
Charlotte 51, August 24, Augusta 21			
DREYCINSKI, Joh.	26	Prust	66-0650
DREYER, Adolph	18	Eberswinkel	66-0984
DREYER, August	28	Bremen	65-1095
DREYER, Doris	15	Muneberg	65-0950
DREYER, Frd.	15	Dielingen	65-1024
DREYER, H.	20	Hannover	64-1206
DREYER, Heinr.	38	Folmhusen	65-0243
Gebke 38, Harm 15, Hendrik 12, Alfr. 7			
Jantje 5, Faabke 4, Dorothea 2			
DREYER, Henry	9	New York	66-0934
DREYER, Herm.	22	Neuenkirch	65-1031
Fr. 21			
DREYER, Margar.	19	Bremervoerde	66-0578
DREYER, Wiechen	16	Brinkum	64-0739
DREYFUSS, Rigge	19	Butterhausen	63-0953
DREYMELER, Wilh'e	25	Ledde	65-0948
DREZ, Emilie	28	New Orleans	63-1218
DRICHAUS, Heinrich	19	Welplage	66-0679
DRIEBENBACH, E.	24	Muehlhausen	66-0413
DRIEHAUS, Herm.	18	Driehausen	64-0214
DRIEMEYER, Christ.	31	Lengerich	64-0214
Henriette 28, Wilhelmine 1, Friedr. 28			
DRIESBACH, Geo.	39	Drebach	64-0687
DRIESCH, Ferd.	14	Madamuehle	64-0840
DRIESSHEIM, Chr.	35	Stuttgart	65-1088
DRIESTER, C.	25	Gernagenheim	65-0007
W. 21			
DRIEWER, A.(f)	24	Vechta	64-0427
DRINDING, B.	45	Papenburg	63-1003
DRISSNER, Isaac	31	Hausen	64-0495
DRIWA, Johann	26	Zaronnia	66-0666
DROEGE, August	19	Nienburg	66-1155
DROEGE, Hch. Fr.	26	Essern	66-0934
DROEGE, Nicolaus	16	Lehe	66-0734
DROESE, Heinrich	25	Gr. Groessin	66-0469
DROMMING, Peter	54	Zanne	66-1248
Emilie 17, Peter 20			
DROOP, Eduard	27	Osnabrueck	64-0331
DROSCH, Ferdinand	29	Poblotz	63-0614
Henriette 23			
DROST, Caroline	22	Eickhorst	64-0782
DROSTE, Bernh.	29	California	63-1038
Henry 18			
DROSTE, Diedrich	29	Stolzenau	64-0363
DROSTE, Gerhard	20	Haithoefer	66-1155
DROSTE, Louis	21	Hannover	66-0984
DROSTE, Reinhold	24	Born	66-1031
DROSTE, Wilhelm	36	Bueckeburg	63-0917
DRUEBBER, Elise	27	Stolzenau	66-1155
DRUECKER, Gerhard	27	St.Louis	66-0734
Diane 25			
DRUECKER, Mr.	60	London	63-1178
wife 48, Sarah 12, Joseph 10, Henriette 8			
Jannette 6			
DRUECKER, Wilh.	27	Ehrichsdorf	65-0243
DRUEHL, Chs.	20	Ruxte	64-0495
Elsb. 23			
DRUMMER, Franz	19	Zeitz	66-1128
DRUMMER, John G.	24	Weingarts	63-1038
DRUSCH, Jacob Fr.	37	Poblotz	63-0614
Charlotte 35, Mathilde 4			
DRUSCH, Johann Fr.	32	Poblotz	63-0614
Dorothea 39, Carl Aug. 28, Michael 66			
Henriette 19			
DRUSCHEL, Philipp	21	Kilidostetten	63-1038
DRUVENOWSKY, Franz	36	Lubna	66-1155
Anna 34, Anna 15, Rosalie 13, Sophie			
DRYER, Christian	50	Behren	66-1203
Caroline 23, Wilhelmine 21, Christian 29			
Louise 17			
DRZOWECK, Simon	37	Calinowa	65-1030
Wilhelmine 40, Ernst 15, Gottlieb 13			
Gustav 10, Wilhelmine 7, August 5			
Wilhelm 6m			
DUBAIS, L. (f)	19	Havre	63-0990
DUBBERSTEIN, Fr'dr	18	Friedrichshor	66-0578
DUBE, Johann	37	Midlum	66-0578
Catharina 43, Heinrich 13, Anna 10			
Hinrich 7, Meta 4			
DUBOIS, (m)	36	Havre	64-0214
DUCHANECK, John	33	Boehmen	63-1085
DUCHENAY, (f)	20	Paris	64-0214
DUCKHUS, Friedr.	17	Wietmarschen	64-0214
DUDDENHAUSEN, Jul.	21	Warendorf	63-0953
DUDEN, Bertha Paul	18	Nesse/Hann.	67-0599
Gust. Nic. G 15			
DUDENHAEFER, Georg	29	Rodheim	63-1218
Margarethe 25			
DUEBENER, Henry	21	Eisenach	63-1178
Elisabeth 21			
DUECKE, Carl	26	Hoexter	65-1088
DUECKMEYER, Joh.	19	Gruenenloh	66-0984

NAME	AGE	RESIDENCE	YR-LIST
DUEFFENBACH, Barb.	38	Berstadt	66-1327
Johannes 8, Heinrich 6, Wilhelm 4			
Caroline 1			
DUEHL, Friedr.	25	Oberflorsheim	66-1031
DUEKER, Friedr.	28	Westphalia	66-0469
Charlotte 32, Friedr. 3, Louise 9m			
DUEKER, Johann	18	Hannover	64-0432
DUELKEN, E.	22	Aachen	63-1218
DUEMCKE, Martin	30	Berlin	63-0350
DUEMLEIN, Georg	52	Cronach	65-0007
Jos. 50, Marie 44, Lina 15, Marg. 11			
Baptist 6, Joh. 2			
DUEMMING, Ch.	32	New York	64-0687
DUENNINGEN, Andr.	30	Leimbach	66-1373
DUENSING, H.	44	Nopke	64-0495
Alicia 43, Heinrich 16, Sophie 14			
Louise 8, Minna 5			
DUENSING, Henry	24	Neustadt	66-0109
DUENSING, Louise	20	Rodewald	66-0934
DUEREN, Heinrich	32	Iserlohn	66-1127
DUERENBERGER, Magd	33	Elsass	63-0693
Magdalena 10, Peter 8			
DUERIG, Babette	40	Bamberg	66-1373
DUERING, Ernst	33	Vandrum	64-1022
DUERING, Friedrke.	38	Helmstedt	66-0837
Minna 18, Theodor 13			
DUERING, Georg	21	Bremen	65-0948
DUERKS, Wilhelmine	24	Schessinghsn.	65-0948
DUERNER, Johannes	33	Weilhelm	66-1203
DUERNER, Margareth	24	Balzholz	66-1127
DUERR, Barbara	20	Gemaringen	67-0007
DUERR, C.	33	Dankenfeld	66-0413
DUERR, Carl	43	Endora	64-0687
Gustav 17			
DUERR, Georg	19	Schleidorf	66-1243
DUERR, Jacob	28	Derendingen	66-1127
Marie 30, Jacob 6m			
DUERR, Joh. Peter	16	Stadthausen	66-0623
DUERR, Louis	18	Leipzig	64-0938
DUERR, Magdalena	17	Schaffersheim	64-0886
DUERRBAUM, Heinr.	24	Hofgeismar	64-0456
Henriette 23			
DUERRWANGER, Anna	24	Muenchen	66-0679
Ludwig 30			
DUESCHER, Johann	20	Wedel	65-0950
DUESEL, Anna Marg.	23	Niederfuellb.	64-0456
DUESENBERG, Aug.	15	Eimbeck	64-0938
DUESENBERG, H.	25	Kirchheide	66-0413
DUESSEL, Carl	35	Oberhausen	65-1024
Anna 31, August 9, Lisette 7, Catharine 4			
DUEWEL, Friedr.	28	Bachholzhsn.	65-0950
Heinr. 28			
DUEWERNEY, Bertha	43	Stuttgart	63-0551
DUFELDORF, J.(f)	28	Seebergen	64-0495
DUFFRIN, F.	28	Malsch	65-0007
DUHM, Friedrich	32	Rastede	65-0770
Friederike 30, Elise 8, Sophie 6			
Louise 4, Marie 2			
DUISBURG, v. J.	39	Bremen	64-0840
DULITZ, Emil	25	Ottenhagen	64-0138
Heinr. 27			
DULS, Heinrich	15	Lehe	66-1031
DUMAS, Jean	26	Havre	64-1053
Marie 20			
DUMBECK, Godmar	41	Schorndorf	66-1155
Marie 32, Catharine 12, Hugo 7, Lisette 5			
Friedrich 2, Carl 6m			
DUMEL, Augustus	35	Brooklyn	63-0862
DUMEL, Elise	20	Muenster	66-0984
DUMMERAUF, Andreas	28	Bungeller	65-0713
Anna 26			
DUNGER, Lorenz	29	Dietendorf	64-0840
DUNGER, Wilhelm	23	Elschesheim	66-1131
DUNIAZEAU, Raymond	50	France	63-0862
DUNKAKA, Herm.	21	Bremen	64-0363
DUNKER, Adolph	16	Ahlerstedt	65-0116
DUNKER, Chr.	25	Hannover	63-0990
DUNKER, Friedr.	21	Huetbergen	65-0402
DUNKER, Gustav	30	Leipzig	64-1053
DUNKHORST, Hr.	25	Westrup	65-1031
Henriette 27			
DUNSTROP, Beta	16	Prussia	63-1218
DUNTZE, Charles	40	Bremen	63-1178
DUNTZE, Louise	40	Bremen	64-0331
Johanna 21			
DUNZIG, Carl	23	Moringen	65-1088
DUPKE, Carl Heinr.	29	Altdamm	65-0950
DURLACH, Georg	37	Stuttgart	63-0822
Johanna 42			
DURR, Catharine	22	Egenhausen	66-0147
DURSCH, Ullrich	25	Philadelphia	63-0482
Cath 19			
DURY, Anna	19	Trier	64-1053
DUSANEK, Anna	32	Kuttenberg	64-0170
Johann 9, Sophie 8, Joseph 6, Anna 8m			
DUSCHANEK, Joseph	41	Boehmen	66-0349
L. 21, P. 17, Marie 7			
DUSCHENES, Heinr.	17	Prag	67-0007
DUSCHER, Friedr.	29	Grebbin	63-0350
Sophie 25, daughter 2, baby 6m			
DUSCHINES, Philip	46	Prag	66-1093
Gustav 9			
DUSCHKE, Ernst	24	Ebersbach	66-1093
DUTMER, Antje	21	Uethusen	65-1095
DUTTMEIER, Franz	36	Harpendorf	66-1203
Maria 25			
DWERZADT, Franz	48	Boehmen	64-0023
Johanna 21			
DWORZECK, Ernestin	14	Klagenfurt	66-0109
DYKERHOFF, August	29	Mannheim	66-1127
DYONISIUS, August	27	New York	66-0221
Franz 23			
DZUR, Fr. Wilh.	26	Vizig	66-0650
Emilie 20			
De FRIESE, Reinke	19	Ost Friesland	66-0577
EBBEN, Wm.	36	Betzdorf	64-0992
Marie 34, Hubert 4, Charles 11m			
EBBIGHAUSEN, Aug.	26	Sievershausen	65-1030
Mathilde 10m			
EBBINGER, Telje	18	Manslagte	64-0331
EBBINGHAUSEN, H.	23	Oldendorf	64-0495
H. 7			
EBE, Rosalie	34	Magdeburg	64-0363
Martha 4, Albert 11m			
EBE, Rupert	28	Ehningen	66-0469
EBEL, Anton	29	Osterburken	64-0363
EBEL, Dorothea	34	Cincinnati	64-0138
EBEL, Heinr.	24	Runkel	64-1022
Henriette 23, Adolph 10m			
EBEL, Louise	18	Bremen	63-0006
EBELING, D.	20	Brinkum	65-1189
EBELING, Friedrich	45	Einbeck	64-0456
EBELING, Friedrich	16	Huelshagen	66-1031
EBELING, Heinr.	29	Bremen	65-0151
EBELING, Philip	17	Schornsheim	66-0221
EBENER, Caroline	27	Soal	64-0992
EBENSEN, Conr.	48	Adensen	65-0898
EBER, Catharina	54	Meissen	64-1053
EBER, Rosine	34	Lambrecht	64-1053
Christine 22			
EBERBACH, Wilhelm	15	Bretten	66-0576
EBERHARD, Herm.	24	Wuerttemberg	66-0221
EBERHARD, Joh.	31	Osnabrueck	64-1053
EBERHARD, Johanna	18	Misselwarden	65-0038
Eline 16			
EBERHARD, Johannes	29	Muelsen	66-1373
EBERHARD, Jos.	29	Neuler	66-1313
Lorenz 19			
EBERHARD, R.	23	Bromberg	64-1161
EBERHARDT, Anne M.	19	Hessloh	65-0770
EBERHARDT, Gottl.	44	Muehlhausen	66-0578
Johanna 35, Amalia 18, Emma 16, Carl 10			
Christoph 8, Gottfried 6			
EBERHARDT, Hy.	59	Brasach	63-1085
EBERHARDT, Jac.	21	Lauterbach	64-1161
EBERHARDT, Ursula	18	Heimingen	64-0687

NAME	AGE	RESIDENCE	YR-LIST
EBERHARDT, Wilhelm	36	Stuttgart	65-0594
Cath. 23, Wilhelm 3			
EBERHARDT, Wm.	24	Loccum	64-1161
EBERLE, Allois	43	Bicht	63-0693
Augustin 9			
EBERLE, Anna M.	33	Newton	63-0350
Carolina 7			
EBERLE, Anton	32	Soltuschen	64-0886
Maria 22, Marg. Mary 20			
EBERLE, Carl	40	Kurzell	65-0038
EBERLE, Elisabeth	23	Hessen	66-0109
EBERLE, Friedr.	36	New York	63-0015
EBERLE, Johann	23	Boesingen	66-0147
EBERLEHR, Cathrina	23	Berlsheim	66-0083
Margrethe 21			
EBERLING, Augustus	35	Bernsen	63-0168
EBERMEIER, F.W.	26	Osnabrueck	64-0331
Johanna 21			
EBERS, Christ. H.	41	Zwickau	63-0990
EBERS, F.J.	17	Hoexter	64-0639
EBERSBACHER, Carl	34	Esslingen	64-0427
EBERSTEIN, Heinr.	26	Hildesheim	63-0614
EBERT, Aug. Fr.	19	Barchfeld	66-0704
EBERT, Bertha	20	Olterwiek	65-1024
EBERT, Bonifacius	53	Hessenthal	63-1069
Jehava 47, Jakob 18, Justine 17			
Christian 15, Alexander 9, Therese 7			
EBERT, Caroline	22	Lobenhausen	64-0886
baby 6			
EBERT, Christ	24	Remlingen	66-0346
Catharina 31			
EBERT, Elisa	24	Klingenberg	64-0782
Margaretha 21			
EBERT, Greg.	21	Schleida	66-1313
EBERT, Heinrich	22	Brueckewerra	66-1155
EBERT, Lorenz	7	Ringersbrunn	63-1069
Johann 3			
EBERT, Margarethe	27	Biermunden	63-1069
EBERTH, Anna Kath.	19	Buegenwerra	65-1030
EBERTS, Wilhelm	20	Mariendorf	67-0007
EBERWEIN, Peter	35	Asch	66-0412
EBERZ, Andreas	26	Schenkelberg	67-0007
Cathrina 19			
EBINGER, Conrad	38	Herrenhof	64-0992
Catharine 40, Ida 7, Conrad 5			
EBINGER, Gottl.	15	Zwingerhausen	64-0138
EBKE, Ernst	23	Essen	66-0704
EBNER, Caroline	16	Stetten	66-0704
EBNER, Kasimir	33	Bayern	66-0147
EBRECHT, Louise	22	Muenden	66-1127
EBRI, Thobias	30	Rothweil	66-0221
Caroline 35, Theresia 5, Wilhelmine 3			
EBSTEIN, Isaac	47	Cincinnati	63-1136
EBSTEIN, Marcus	22	Sotsch	66-0623
ECHLE, Marie	21	Laufen	66-0984
ECK, Camillo	13	Eisenberg	64-0427
ECK, Peter	24	Ampferbach	66-1313
ECKARD, Ludw.	22	Sonnefeld	64-1053
ECKELMANN, Diedr.	18	Schwarme	66-1093
ECKELMANN, Johann	62	New York	66-0679
ECKEMANN, Lorenz	25	Eichfeld	66-0346
ECKENBERG, Fr. Aug	25	Bremen	63-1069
Anna 21			
ECKENBERG, Joh. Ch	46	Bremen	63-1069
Maria 35, Hen. Mar. 11, Wilhelm 16			
Christoph 3			
ECKENKRUSE, Gerd.	29	Hentrup	64-0639
ECKENSBERGER, B.	32	Margburg	64-0639
ECKER, Elisabeth	25	Dumwieler	66-1327
ECKER, Michael	31	Malsch	67-0007
ECKERLE, Friedr.	30	Landau	65-0594
ECKERLEBEN, Heinr.	30	Schewecke	64-1022
ECKERT, Adam	23	Bruchsal	66-1313
ECKERT, August	41	Altenau	66-0577
Augusta 36, Friederike 36, Friederike 18			
Louis 15, Louise 10			
ECKERT, Fr.(m)	28	Buchau	64-0363
ECKERT, Gertrud	21	Sorgenloh	66-1127
ECKERT, Johann	22	Bresslingen	65-0948
ECKERT, Karl Lud.	15	Heilbronn	63-1069
ECKERT, Louise	16	Jagsthausen	63-0990
ECKERT, Margarethe	23	Nuernberg	66-0679
ECKERT, T.	24	Nuernberg	63-1003
A. 15, H. 3, E. 1			
ECKERT, Victoria	62	Hirschbach	66-1373
Augusta 39, Hermine 35, Julie 26			
ECKHARD, Franciska	17	Gauersheim	66-1248
ECKHARD, H.	20	Uslar	63-1003
ECKHARD, Martin	14	Eisenach	66-1127
ECKHARDT, A.(f)	20	Henlau	64-0495
ECKHARDT, Chr'tine	28	Zufferhausen	65-0402
ECKHARDT, Conrad	24	Huenfeld	66-0349
Regina 27, Hildegard 3			
ECKHARDT, Edwin	25	Plauen	66-0934
ECKHARDT, Heinrich	33	Hesse-Cassel	63-0822
ECKHARDT, Jacob	44	Hessen	66-0469
ECKHARDT, Ma.(f)	18	Bonenfurt	64-0782
ECKHARDT, Therese	18	Duderstadt	66-1128
ECKHARDT, W.E.	25	Zittau	65-1088
ECKHARDT, Wilh'mne	19	Lintenhof	66-0578
ECKHARDT, Wilhelm	19	Wambeck	65-1030
ECKHARDT, Wm.	27	Lenn	64-0938
Henriette 29			
ECKHOFF, Adam	32	Hannover	66-0734
Caroline 26, Adam 6m			
ECKHOFF, Cath.	21	Bederkesa	64-0073
ECKHOFF, Cath.	32	New York	64-0214
ECKHOFF, Harms P.	45	Ihrhove	65-0243
Mecheltje 49, Peterke 18, Anros 16			
Aufka 14			
ECKHOFF, Heye	45	Holtrup	66-1128
Anna 30, Juergen 10, Anna 7, Bina 6			
Wilhelm 4, Catharina 6m			
ECKHOFF, Joh.	26	Etzel	66-1031
ECKJANS, Cath.	20	Toenningen	64-0938
ECKRODT, Elisabeth	25	Preussen	63-0990
ECKSTEIN, Andr.	30	Theyern	64-0170
ECKSTEIN, B.	18	Goettingen	65-1189
ECKSTEIN, Benj.	16	Goettingen	63-1038
ECKSTEIN, Charlott	25	New York	66-0147
Charlotte 6m			
ECKSTEIN, Gabriel	24	France	63-0953
ECKSTEIN, Joseph	25	Ndr.Wilstadt	65-1095
ECKSTEIN, Wolfgang	37	Wekorau	66-1373
EDEBOHLS, Hinr.	14	Wehrden	66-0704
Claus 21			
EDELER, Anton	29	Borghorst	66-0623
EDELMANN, A.	30	Schoeningen	65-0007
Marie 29			
EDELMANN, Carl	36	New York	63-0006
EDELMANN, Joseph	44	Wuerzburg	65-0713
EDELMUTH, Bettchen	58	Beuern	63-0693
Marianne 27			
EDELMUTH, Marens	19	Beuern	63-1178
Rachel 58, Hannchen 24			
EDEN, Helene	19	Hofe	66-1127
EDENHOFER, Simon	45	Sattan	66-0576
EDER, Cyrill	24	Breitenbach	66-0576
EDER, Emilie	19	Baden	66-0704
EDER, Joseph	26	Breitenbach	66-0576
EDERLE, Anton	28	Mengols	64-0073
EDERT, J. Jr.	40	Lupenburg	63-0990
EDERT, John	63	Lupenburg	63-0990
EDGAR, Louis	20	Appel	64-0593
EDINGER, Anna M.	22	Lippstadt	65-0243
EDLER, G.(m)	31	New York	64-0331
EDLING, Heinrich	16	Darmstadt	66-1031
Elise 17			
EDUARD, R.(m)	26	Berlin	64-0214
EDUARDS, C.	32	Chicago	63-0482
EDWART, Lambert	40	Hausen	63-1085
Marianne 34, Maria 3, John 11m			
EELZE, Fd.	25	Evenseh	64-0593
EFELT, Anton	50	Waldeck	63-1010
Marian 53, Franz 17, Johanna 16			
Therese 20			

NAME	AGE	RESIDENCE	YR-LIST
EFFENBERGER, Wenzl	49	Reichenberg	65-0713
EFFERTZ, Chs.	42	Epprath	64-0495
Gde. (f) 26, Jos. 6, Adam 3, Aa.(f) 3m			
Peter 29			
EFFINGER, Cathre.	22	Zimmern	63-0990
EFFINGER, Fr.(m)	20	Aldingen	64-0331
EFFINGER, Ignatz	18	Dotternhausen	64-0992
Columba 23			
EFFINGER, Mathilde	48	Frittlingen	64-1108
EFZINGER, Mat.(f)	19	Aixheim	64-0495
EFZINGER, Nart.	28	Trostingen	64-0495
EGBERT, Joh.Heinr.	37	Recke	63-0398
EGER, Adele	22	Warnsdorf	64-0495
Aa.(f) 3, Adele 2			
EGER, Carl	17	Meran	64-0427
EGER, David	51	Hohendorf	64-0170
EGER, Elisabeth	20	Franenbach	65-0189
Catharina 18			
EGER, Fuerchtegott	30	Muelser	66-1327
EGER, Herm.	17	Werdau	64-0427
EGER, Johanna	17	Weissenstein	66-1203
EGER, Jos.	30	Boehmen	64-0138
EGER, Louis	58	Bethlehem	63-1003
EGER, Mich.	40	Ob.Schwarzach	64-0170
EGERMANN, Barbara	21	Wassertruding	66-1131
EGETENMEYER, Jos.	22	Baldern	66-0679
EGGE, Anna M.	26	Fambach	66-1243
EGGELING, Ed.G.	45	Muenchen	64-0593
Dorette 23, Eduard 9m			
EGGEN, Anetha	25	Willstedt	66-0578
EGGEN, Mette	23	Lehe	65-1189
EGGER, Emma	23	Eberlettringn	65-0974
EGGERMANN, Joh.	30	Vechta	65-1088
Anna 20			
EGGERS, Alb.	32	Hooksiel	65-0402
EGGERS, Aug.	24	Eboldshausen	65-0402
EGGERS, Catharine	18	Bremerhaven	65-0055
EGGERS, Dorothea	17	New York	66-0679
Mary 15			
EGGERS, Dorothea	21	Holersen	66-1243
Johanna 27			
EGGERS, Ferdinand	16	Ritterhude	66-1155
Wilhelm 21			
EGGERS, Heinrich	25	Rotenburg	64-0739
EGGERS, Herm.	20	Ritterhude	66-1243
EGGERS, Margarethe	62	Neuenwalde	63-0693
Johanna 20			
EGGERS, Mary	20	Denwille	63-0551
child 2, child 11m			
EGGERS, W.	31	Muenster	63-0296
EGGERS, Wilhelmine	20	Ritterrode	65-0974
EGGERT, Alois	26	Magdeburg	64-1053
EGGERT, Johann	25	Linne	66-1373
EGGERT, Wilhelm	34	New York	66-0679
(f) 28			
EGGERT, Wilhelm	23	Osnabrueck	64-0739
EGLI, J.G.	17	Staefa	65-0007
EGNER, Conrad	32	Zischentshaus	64-0938
Marie 20			
EGNER, Nicolaus	21	Hessen-Darmst	66-0346
EGOLF, J.C.(m)	14	Rosenfeld	64-0331
EHLE, Friederike	16	Stetten	66-0704
EHLEBRECHT, Conr.	28	Oldorf	64-0214
EHLEN, J.	27	Westerstede	66-0413
EHLERDING, Herm.	26	Doehren	65-0974
EHLERMANN, Gustav	18	Hannover	66-1031
EHLERS, Amanda	16	Midlum	63-0398
EHLERS, Diedrich	20	Bremervoerde	63-0614
EHLERS, Francis	22	Halle	63-0752
EHLERS, Friedr.	26	Beckedorf	66-1155
EHLERS, Georg	33	Basel	64-1053
Cath. 28			
EHLERS, J.	22	Celle	65-1189
EHLERS, Martin	20	Nesse	63-1038
EHLERS, Rebecca	17	Deicke	63-1136
EHLERS, Sophie	32	New York	63-1218
EHLERT, Augusta	17	Dorum	66-1031
EHLERT, Hins.	63	Altenbruch	64-0593

NAME	AGE	RESIDENCE	YR-LIST
EHLERT, Joh. Ant.	33	Danzig	67-0795
Johanna 34, Rosalie 6, Franz 4, Johann 9m			
EHLERT, John E.	36	New York	66-0934
EHLING, Carl	18	Darmstadt	64-0992
EHMEN, Enne Jansen	23	Aurich	66-1128
EHMER, Johann	21	Dankmarshsn.	64-0433
EHNIS, Marie	21	Ebershardt	66-1131
EHRENHARD, Magd.	22	Hoesbach	64-0199
EHRESMANN, Adam	27	Havre	65-0004
EHRET, Peter	36	Dossenhiem	64-0170
Erica 38, Christoph 12, Friederike 9			
Adam 5, Cath. 3			
EHRGOTT, Elisab. A	30	Lemberg	67-0599
Jacob 8, Elisabeth 7, Friedrich 5			
Salome 3			
EHRHARD, Caspar	15	Mollau	63-0990
EHRHARDT, Aug. Fr.	59	Imshausen	65-0898
EHRHARDT, Chr.	23	Rembdendorf	63-1178
EHRHARDT, Emil	25	Passau	64-0593
EHRHARDT, Friedr.	56	Imshausen	65-0898
Emma 22, Auguste 18, Minna 14			
EHRHARDT, Georg	18	Goslar	63-0917
EHRHARDT, Henry	20	Guxhagen	63-0990
John H. 18			
EHRHARDT, Louis	23	Michelstadt	66-0679
EHRHARDT, Marie	25	Darmstadt	66-1327
EHRHARDT, Marie	16	Kirzel	64-0363
EHRICH, Caroline	22	Friedenwalde	63-1178
EHRICHS, H.	30	Bremen	65-0116
EHRLER, Wilhelmine	24	Langenbernsdf	66-0109
Arthur 9m			
EHRLICH, (f)	26	Germany	63-0482
EHRLICH, A.(m)	60	Boehmen	64-0495
Els. 54			
EHRLICH, Elisabeth	37	Sontra	66-0083
Marie 58			
EHRLICH, Fr.W.	28	Lewer	65-1024
EHRLICH, Helene	17	Weimar	66-0679
EHRLICH, Therese	23	Koenigswart	64-0427
Samuel 2, baby 9m			
EHRLINSPIEL, L.	32	Hegsen	65-0007
EHRMANN, Fr.	32	Winesburgh	63-0953
EHRMANN, Heym.	24	Hoechst	66-1031
EHRMANN, Joseph	24	Sulzschmid	66-0679
EHRMANN, Rosa	34	Dolitzschen	66-1327
EHRMANN, Sal.	17	Lichtenfels	63-0551
EHRT, Landolin	32	Ndr.Schopfhm.	66-0934
EIBEN, Christian	26	Jever	64-0170
Anna 21			
EIBER, Joh.	47	Aach	65-0402
Anna 46			
EIBERGER, Xaver	19	Dorfmerkingen	67-0795
EICHBERG, Jul.(f)	17	Stuttgart	64-0992
EICHBERG, Lena	19	Baiersdorf	64-0782
EICHBERG, S.	32	New York	63-0015
Caroline 23			
EICHBERGER, F.	40	Wien	64-0782
EICHE, Mathilde	30	Freiburg	63-0862
Amalie 31			
EICHELBERG, Gustav	16	Iserlohn	66-0934
EICHELBERGER, Benj	22	Esslingen	66-0083
Louise 13, Elise 18, Carl 8, Catharine 50			
EICHELBERGER, Jule	20	New Orleans	66-0984
EICHENBERG, Georg	28	Oberrieden	66-0346
EICHENBERG, Heinr.	18	Oberrieden	66-0346
EICHENBERG, John	36	Cassel	63-0296
EICHENGRUEN, J.	20	Zimmersroede	65-1088
EICHENSEER, Xaver	23	Berathshausen	64-0363
EICHER, Gottlieb	28	Eschenbach	63-0350
EICHERMANN, Carol.	25	Boesingfeld	66-0984
EICHERT, Peter	57	Wilburgsteten	66-0412
Marianne 58			
EICHHOFF, C.S.A.	25	Holthorst	66-0346
EICHHOLZ, Fritz	20	Rheda	64-0665
EICHHOLZ, Hannelei	14	Elsungen	66-1093
EICHHOLZ, Heinr.	27	Rheda	63-0752
EICHHORN, Cathrine	22	Hamburg	64-0885
EICHHORN, Franz	23	Lampoldshsn.	64-0687

NAME	AGE	RESIDENCE	YR-LIST
EICHHORN, Franz L.	27	Plauen	65-0713
EICHHORN, Heinr.	25	Schnei	66-0221
EICHHORN, John	28	Koepernick	63-0015
EICHLE, Carl	19	Bocholz	66-1031
EICHLER, Georg	40	Vache	66-0734
EICHLER, H.	25	Handschuhshm.	65-1088
EICHMANN, Bernh.	21	Altenburg	66-1203
EICHMANN, F.	24	Garbenhein	64-0782
Marg. 7			
EICHMEYER, Gerhard	18	Groenlohe	66-0984
EICHSTADT, Carl	26	Gifholt	64-1022
Charlotte 23, Johanna 9m			
EICHSTAEDT, Jac.	25	Czarnikau	65-0898
EICHWALD, S.	32	Carlsruhe	64-0782
EICKBUSCH, Carol.	24	Diepholz	65-0948
Fried. Joh'e 21			
EICKE, Marie	24	Landwehrhagen	64-0427
EICKEN, v. Hermann	56	Buenos Ayres	66-0934
EICKERT, Magd.	16	Rohrbach	65-0007
EICKHOF, Hermann	17	Jenscheim	67-0007
EICKMANN, P.	40	Cincinnati	63-0953
EICKS, Caspar H.	15	Osterholz	64-1108
EICKSCHEN, Gerhard	32	Moers	65-0950
Margarethe 38, Friedrich 10, Magdalene 4			
Elisabeth 2, Herrmann 8m, Magdalena 58			
EICKSTADT, Ferdin.	31	Preussen	66-0469
Caroline 35, Emil 8, Fritz 7, Ernst 5			
Marie 3, August 1			
EIDAM, Anna Cath.	25	Asbach	66-0623
EIDAM, Catharina	26	Marburg	63-0350
EIERS, Adam	29	Hessen	66-0109
Johannes 27			
EIFFERT, H.(m)	18	Tiefenort	64-0331
EIGELMANN, Maria	22	Riegel	63-0917
EIGENBROD, Chr'tne	28	Biermunden	63-1069
EIGENBRODT, Anna	3-	Ebersheim	66-1093
Franz 20			
EIGENBROT, Jacob	26	Berich	66-0469
EIGENMANN, Conrad	25	Flehsingen	63-0015
EIKEMA, Gerhard	23	Wendschoten	65-1088
Harmke 25			
EILERS, A.	24	Siellwarden	64-0665
EILERS, Alois	36	New York	64-0214
EILERS, Bernhard	38	Soegel	65-1024
Hermann 35			
EILERS, Conrad	69	Netzen	64-0886
Maria 7			
EILERS, Geerd	18	Ostfriesland	66-0704
EILERS, Heinrich	37	Altenberg	66-0623
Elisabeth 26			
EILERS, Herm. Hch.	44	Aurich	65-1030
Marie 46, Hermann 15, Caspar 9, Riecke 7			
Adelheid 5			
EILERS, Johann	21	Varel	66-0668
EILERT, Emilie	25	Fisshau	65-0770
EILING, Joh. H.	68	Ochtrup	64-1022
Elisabeth 62, Hermann 18			
EILKE, Juliane	18	Riege	65-0950
EILS, Emma	26	Midlum	65-0950
EIMER, Elisab.	23	Berka	64-0593
EIMERSTENBRING, H.	35	Buettendorf	65-0898
EIMKE, Dorothea	21	Doehnhausen	66-1203
EINHANS, Gesche	18	Osterholz	66-0221
EINHAUS, Carl	28	Listrup	65-0189
Anna 23, child bob			
EINHOLT, Anna M.	55	Zullig	66-1373
EININGER, Jacob	23	Wuerttemberg	63-0822
EININGER, Wilh'mne	19	Plieningen	65-0594
EINNERMANN, Carl	34	Darmstadt	65-0402
EINOLF, Carl	17	Biedenkopf	66-1093
EINSTEIN, Alb.	26	Buttenwiese	65-1024
EINSTEIN, Henr.(f)	58	Jebenhausen	64-0938
EINSTEIN, Henry	38	Philadelphia	64-0331
EINSTEIN, Mathias	20	Bachau	65-0402
EINSTEIN, Sam.	18	Buchan	65-0402
EINSTEIN, Siegf.	28	Buchau	64-0427
Rosa 22			
EINWAECHTER, Heinr	24	Merlen	65-0116

NAME	AGE	RESIDENCE	YR-LIST
EIPP, Ruppert	22	Gimsheim	63-1010
EIRICH, Joh.	30	Hassig	65-1189
Cathr. 25, Cathr. 3			
EISELE, Barbara	24	Pfeffingen	64-0433
EISELE, Barbara	15	St. Martin	66-1093
EISELE, Fr.(m)	20	Weilheim	64-0363
EISELE, Joseph	66	Emerfeld	64-1108
Caecilie 43			
EISELE, Louise	25	Rothenfels	66-0704
EISELE, Magdalena	23	Thieningen	64-0433
EISENACH, Carl Fr.	20	Rotenburg	65-0055
EISENACHER, Jos.	21	Vache	64-0992
EISENBERG, Etti	26	Sebes	65-1189
Simon 7, Adolph 5			
EISENFELS, Rud.	36	Pesth	63-0862
EISENFRESSER, Wm.	31	Bastadt	64-0886
EISENHARDT, Const.	25	Wuerttemberg	66-0109
EISENHARDT, Gustav	19	Wuertemberg	66-0984
EISENHARDT, Henr't	54	Muehlhausen	63-1218
Adolph 18			
EISENHART, Albert	29	Chicago	66-0679
EISENHAUSER, Mich.	23	Oberostern	66-0221
EISENHUTH, Chr.	30	Volkertshsn.	64-0363
EISENHUTH, Magdal.	40	Bietigheim	65-0243
EISENMANN, Carl	20	Weinsberg	66-1373
EISENMERGER, Wm.	37	Bridgeport	63-1218
EISENRING, Barbara	40	Weyl	66-1203
Agnes 9, Mathias 7, Caroline 6, Johanna 4			
EISENSCHMIDT, Emil	9	New York	66-0734
EISENSCHMIDT, Ida	39	New York	66-0734
Charles 9m			
EISENSTEIN, Carl	19	Wien	65-0189
EISENWUNER, Marg.	35	Heldburg	63-1010
EISER, Herm.	38	New York	63-0551
EISFELDER, Fr.	25	Muehlhausen	63-0482
EISFELDER, H.	21	United States	63-1136
EISINGER, Joh.	40	Kirchhausen	66-0704
Johanna 37, Franz 7			
EISINGER, Sebast.	14	Kirchhausen	66-0704
EISMANN, Heinrich	24	Wellingholzhs	67-0599
Wilhelm 18			
EISNER, Jacob	30	Boehmen	66-0349
EISWALD, F.L.	32	Providence	63-0350
EITEL, Christoph	24	Wildbach	66-0934
EITEN, Sophie	17	Lehe	65-0243
EITENBENZ, Eduard	35	Moeringen	63-0482
EITERMANN, Anna M.	29	Schapen	64-0363
EITZEL, Joseph	25	Ofzbach	66-0469
EITZEN, G.H.(died)	35	Bremen	65-1140
EITZEN, Heinrich	34	Bremen	66-0668
EKEL, Heinrich	15	Willershausen	66-0578
Thobia 41, Anna 41, Adam 18			
Eva Elisa. 16, Maria 14, Catharina 11			
Heinrich 9, Johannes 8, Margarethe 6			
Anna Elisa. 6, Johann Adam 4			
EKEL, Marie	22	Bringhausen	66-0578
EKING, Anton	35	Gescher	65-0948
ELBE, Gottlob Fr.	15	Vailangen	64-0073
ELBEL, Wolf	33	Harzberg	64-0593
ELBERDING, Charlot	22	Seese	66-0623
ELBERSHAUSEN, Char	27	Trippstadt	66-0668
ELBERT, Carl	27	Hamburg	64-0593
ELBERT, Fr. Joseph	28	Aschaffenburg	66-0837
Margarethe 28			
ELBES, Hr.	30	Hagen	66-0349
ELBRECHT, Chris.	25	Verden	63-0953
Gerhard 23			
ELBRECHT, Joh. Hr.	25	Goettingen	66-1127
ELBRECHT, Wilh'mne	20	Westrup	66-1373
ELBTHAL, Robert	20	Altona	67-1005
ELBUTH, Peter Ant.	58	Baiern	66-0469
Margarethe 24, Johann 20, Franz 18			
Emmerich 9m			
ELENZ, Adam	42	Baustert	63-1038
Simon 16, Anna 13			
ELERT, Frd.	60	Rodach	64-0495
Frz. 7			
ELFERICH, Bernhard	18	Emstedten	65-1088

NAME	AGE	RESIDENCE	YR-LIST
ELFERING, Anna	18	Schale	65-1024
ELFLEIN, Andreas	23	Heubach	63-0244
ELFLEIN, Andreas	23	Ebern	63-0244
H. 17, F. 16, R. 15			
ELGERT, K.	25	Friedrichsbrg	66-0413
ELIAS, Friedr.	27	Oedesheim	66-0704
ELIAS, Sally	19	Hoya	65-0594
Daniel 22			
ELIXMANN, Christ.	31	Hagen	64-0427
ELKAN, Alex	19	Berlin	64-1206
ELL, Johannes	44	Durmersheim	66-0704
ELLDORFER, Barbara	62	Renndorf	66-0984
Francisca 33			
ELLEBRECHT, Herman	30	Melle	66-1093
ELLENBECK, H.	23	Halle	66-1313
ELLER, Luise	20	Herstelle	66-1131
ELLERBROCK, Dina	16	Damme	66-1031
ELLERING, Heinr.	30	Schuettorf	66-0576
ELLERMANN, Carolin	20	Hummersen	66-0576
ELLERMANN, Carolne	23	Gronau	66-0934
ELLERMANN, F.W.	27	Bielefeld	65-0402
ELLERMANN, Friedr.	45	Humersum/Lppe	67-1005
Caroline 42, Wilhelmine 17, Friedr. 15			
Heinr. 12, Wilhelm 10, Hattwig 8			
August 5, Doris 2, Bertha 11m			
ELLERMANN, Heinr.	24	Battbergen	66-1373
ELLERMANN, Hippige	19	Waltershausen	64-0687
ELLERROT, Heinrich	24	Sieboldhausen	64-0433
Therese 22, Paul 9m, Carl 21			
ELLIGSEN, Johanna	17	Drueber	66-0704
ELLINGER, F.E.	18	Mittelhausen	63-0013
ELLINGHAUS, Doroth	21	Klus.	66-0221
ELLINGHAUSEN, D'dr	25	Syke	66-1155
ELLINGHAUSEN, Herm	17	Brinkum	64-0456
ELLINGHAUSEN, Lou.	24	Bremen	64-0665
ELLWANGER, J.G.	19	Schnaitz	64-0427
ELMENDORF, J.(m)	24	Broklin	64-0073
ELMER, Anna	27	Scharmbeck	66-0668
ELMER, Barbara	28	Raidwangen	66-1155
ELMER, Jacob	26	Schoenau	66-1373
ELMSHAEUSER, Elis.	25	Allnach	65-1024
ELPERT, Johann	36	Legden	66-0623
ELRICH, Alex.	22	Libau	65-0402
ELSAESSER, Adam	21	Groppingen	65-0007
ELSAESSER, Georg	24	Buttenhausen	66-1327
ELSAS, Joseph	28	Cannstadt	63-0953
ELSBACHER, Emilie	21	Langenberg	63-0821
ELSENHEIMER, Helen	33	Cincinnati	63-0821
Louise 11m			
ELSER, Louise	15	Hochberg	65-0151
ELSFELDT, Els.	36	Bremen	64-0495
Jos. 3m			
ELSHOFER, Levy	17	Allendorf	63-0482
ELSHOFF, Heinrich	35	Grouau	64-0840
Francisca 36, Franz 7, Hermann 5			
Engelbert 2, baby 6m			
ELSMAN, M.	58	Coburg	63-1003
W. 23, F. 1			
ELSNER, Albert	20	Plochingen	66-1313
ELSNER, Christ.	22	Seifhennersdf	64-0343
ELSOFFER, Josua	15	Allendorf	65-0402
ELSTER, Martin	22	Dahldorf	66-0704
ELSTER, Otto	23	Beushausen	66-0083
ELSTROH, Heinr.	45	Jawe	64-0886
Cath. Marie 63			
ELTZE, August	31	New York	63-1085
ELVANES, Jerome A.	30	Burlington	64-0023
ELY, Maria	18	New York	64-0363
ELZER, Adam	23	Eppenheim	65-0770
EMANUEL, Lazarus	47	Pruenstadt	66-1373
EMANUEL, Moritz	61	Berlin	66-1031
EMDE, Daniel	30	Marienhagen	65-0898
Cath. 32, Louise 1			
EMDEN, Fanny	22	Wassertrinken	64-0992
Emma 18			
EMDEN, v. Ocke	35	Leer	64-0739
Alje 36, Joh. Helene 7			
EMDER, Fanny	22	Wassertrink	64-0992
Emma 18			
EMERICH, Elisabeth	40	Bergen	63-1038
Emilie 16			
EMERSHORN, Minna	18	Hoerde	64-0886
EMKER, Eberhard	27	Nordei	63-0908
EMME, Heinrich	21	Preussen	66-0083
EMMEL, H.	29	Barstedt	65-1189
Anna 25			
EMMELHAINZ, Heinr.	25	Erbach	66-0934
Margarethe 21, Anna 4m			
EMMELMANN, Louis	22	Neuhoff	66-0349
EMMENECKER, Germ.	7	Rottweil	66-1155
EMMERICH, Alex	35	Frankfurt	63-0614
EMMERICH, Chr'stne	58	Wetterfeld	64-0938
EMMERICH, Chr.	27	Gera	66-1313
EMMERICH, Franz	44	New York	66-0704
EMMERICH, Friedr.	21	Hansbergen	63-0006
EMMERICH, Friedr.	22	Ickenhausen	65-0770
EMMERICH, Johannes	21	Schweinheim	66-0734
EMMINGER, Anselm	20	Deisfelden	63-0350
EMMIUS, Joh. Ubbe	25	Grimersum	66-0412
Stientje Har 31			
EMRICH, Magdalena	19	Moistadt	66-0679
Catharina 16			
EMRICH, Peter	38	Washington	63-1038
EMSHOFF, Carl	58	Levern	66-1155
EMSINK, Johannes	44	Wentersugk/Bo	63-1010
Bernhard 30			
EMTRESS, Andr.	42	Kretenbach	64-0170
ENDE, Emanuel	59	Pittsville	63-0752
ENDE, v. Friedr.	17	Cassel	66-1248
ENDEMANN, Wilhelm	57	Nussbaum	66-0412
Christina 48, Louisa 14, Peter 12			
Catharina 7			
ENDER, Eva	59	Schmalkalden	65-0402
Ferd. 26			
ENDERICH, Adolph	20	Nauheim	64-0214
ENDERLIN, Carl	18	Carlsruhe	64-0687
ENDERS, Ba.(f)	15	Wallenrad	64-0363
ENDERS, Ferd.	20	Angstedt	65-0898
ENDERS, Henry	21	Untersseibert	63-1218
ENDERS, Jots.	21	Alsfeld	64-0886
Louise 18, Caroline 13			
ENDERSCHEIT, Herm.	38	Goldapp	63-0244
ENDERT, Tobias	29	Hasselborn	65-0594
ENDLE, M.	31	Leinen	66-0413
ENDLER, Minna	22	Minden	66-0679
ENDLICH, Gabriel	22	Ndr.Saulheim	66-0221
ENDOVADT, Friedr.	26	Kalenbrok	65-1095
ENDREAS, Carl	26	Tuebingen	64-0023
ENDRES, Louis	18	Cassel	66-1031
ENDRES, Amalie	40	Schwabach	66-0576
Wilhelmine 38, Margarethe 22, Bianka 17			
Magdalene 60			
ENGBERT, Anna G.	60	Lingen	65-1030
ENGEL, Carl	20	Bingen	64-1022
ENGEL, Carl Hinr.	23	Voessingen	64-0427
ENGEL, Catharine	19	Altenbreitung	63-0006
ENGEL, Ce.(f)	30	Bingen	64-0363
ENGEL, Charlotte	19	Grossalmerode	64-0433
Elise 19			
ENGEL, Christ.	29	Ernsthausen	64-0214
ENGEL, Christian	21	Bernwinkel	66-1203
ENGEL, Friedrike	25	Neufen	66-0679
ENGEL, Henry	26	Eppingen	63-0990
ENGEL, Hrch.	33	Ernsthausen	64-0992
ENGEL, Jacob	32	New York	63-0917
Jacob 6			
ENGEL, James J	22	Wien	63-0551
ENGEL, Joh.(f)	24	Markstedt	64-0331
ENGEL, Johannes	38	Lauterbach	66-0147
ENGEL, Jul.	15	Hannover	65-0402
ENGEL, L.F.	21	Weiden	65-0007
ENGEL, Martin	28	Bebra	66-0469
Catharina 28, Johannes 3			
ENGEL, S.(m)	20	Sohlingen	64-0331
ENGEL, Sabine	30	Ebelsbach	66-1203
Leonhard 4m			

NAME	AGE	RESIDENCE	YR-LIST
ENGEL, Wilhelmine	24	Hannover	66-0734
ENGELBACH, Elisab.	15	Biedenkopf	66-0221
Georg 7			
ENGELBACH, Georg	41	New York	66-0221
ENGELBACH, Louis	26	Schneeren	65-0948
ENGELBACH, Marg.	24	Erkelshausen	66-1093
ENGELBARTS, Herm.	26	Schortens	63-0482
ENGELBERT, Wm.	28	Creuznach	64-0840
ENGELBRECHT, Joh.	45	Kornheim/Hann	64-0920
Friedrich 16, Wilhelm 9, Heinrich 6			
Rudolph 2			
ENGELBRECHT, Wilh.	26	Hannover	66-1327
ENGELBRECHT, Wm.	20	Dielingen	64-0920
ENGELERT, Gertrude	21	Steger	66-1203
ENGELHARD, Albert	29	Wilmershausen	63-0168
ENGELHARD, Anna M.	22	Weimar	64-0885
ENGELHARD, Seb.	28	Weissenberg	63-0862
ENGELHARDT, Ad.	29	Wetter	64-0214
ENGELHARDT, Cath.	56	Roth	66-1203
ENGELHARDT, Conrad	47	Genchet	64-0665
Sarina 47, Elisab. 22, Johannes 15			
ENGELHARDT, E.	18	Gieboldshsn.	64-0495
ENGELHARDT, Elise	41	Wehlheiden	63-0482
ENGELHARDT, Friedr	26	Wuertemberg	63-0822
ENGELHARDT, Gert.	15	Rosenthal	65-1030
ENGELHARDT, Heinr.	28	Hoheneggelsen	65-1030
ENGELHARDT, Herm.	21	Nordhorn	66-1243
ENGELHARDT, Paulus	28	Schwuerbitz	66-0704
ENGELHARDT, Rob.	31	Stollberg	64-0938
ENGELHARDT, Wilh.	21	Bremen	63-0482
ENGELHART, Friedr.	55	Bilcharchen	64-1022
Friedr. 22			
ENGELHART, Wilh.	22	Wahmbeck	63-0953
ENGELKE, Adolf	23	Hannover	65-0007
ENGELKE, August	29	Rotzlingen	63-1085
Doretha 24, Adolph 1			
ENGELKE, August	37	Strebloh	66-1248
Augusta 27, Wilhelmine 5m			
ENGELKE, Carl	48	Oldenburg	64-0687
ENGELKE, Christian	36	Bralenstein	66-1248
Louise 30, August 7, Wilhelmine 5			
Wilhelm 6, Augusta 6, Caroline 1			
ENGELKE, Diedr.	38	Hannover	65-0974
Marie 42, Heinrich 12, Minna 10			
Diedrich 7, Emilie 4, Johann 3			
ENGELKE, Friedrich	19	Benteln	66-0623
ENGELKE, Michael	38	Strebloh	66-1248
Emilie 34, Wilhelm 7, Emilie 2			
ENGELKE, Philip	27	Baden	66-0679
ENGELKEN, Conr.	20	Taken	65-0594
ENGELKES, A.C.	26	Eilgum	65-0004
ENGELKRAUT, W.	24	Quellitzhoff	65-1024
ENGELMANN, Bernh.	27	Wien	64-0427
ENGELMANN, E.	40	Homberg	63-0244
ENGELMANN, Hanne	23	Washington	63-0244
ENGELMANN, Henry	25	Hausen	63-0482
ENGELMANN, Herm.	38	Stetteritz	64-0665
ENGELMANN, R.	23	Koenigsberg	64-1161
ENGELN, W.(m)	49	Vincens	64-0331
ENGELN, Wilhelm	26	Leer	66-1093
ENGELSMANN, Gust.	29	Wien	64-0938
ENGEMANN, Alb.	24	Bern	64-1022
ENGEMEIER, Marie	18	Straubing	66-0576
ENGEMEIER, Zekla	23	Straubing	66-0576
Catharina 15			
ENGLBRECHT, Christ	18	Gottingen	64-0639
ENGLER, Caroline	28	Bremervorde	66-0679
ENGLERT, Charles	24	Hundsfeld	63-0244
ENGLERT, W.(m)	29	Gundelsheim	64-0331
ENKING, Clemens	27	Paderborn	65-1095
ENLER, Friedrich	59	Hailer	66-1327
Margarethe 30, Georg 20, Maria 8			
ENRICH, Andreas	47	Baden	66-0576
Marie 43, Andreas 14, Elisabeth 9			
Johann 8, Sophie 2			
ENSELMANN, G.H.	34	Melle	64-0840
ENSEMEIER, Whl'mne	23	Isenstedt	65-1030
ENSSLE, Georg	28	Welsheim	66-0679

NAME	AGE	RESIDENCE	YR-LIST
ENTERMANN, Carl	29	Baden	66-0109
ENZER, Charlotte	21	Geisslingen	66-0984
Emilie 19			
ENZIAN, Georg	23	Walldorf	66-1203
EPENSTEIN, Friedr.	59	Elbingerode	63-1085
Eva 17, Bertha			
EPHRAIM, Julius	19	Preussen	64-0331
EPP, Conr.	34	New York	64-0073
EPPELER, Wm.	30	Ermelshausen	64-0992
EPPING, C. Maria	24	Buende	63-0917
John Henry 3, Friedrich 9m			
EPPINGER, Dorothea	19	Bremen	63-0862
EPPSTEIN, Lina	20	Deftensee	64-0687
EPSTEIN, Leopold	20	Lichtenstadt	63-0693
EPSTEIN, Susanne	28	Boehmen	63-0693
EPTING, Fr.	32	Mannheim	63-0953
ERAI, Franz	25	Breisach	66-1373
ERB, Barbara	21	Pforzheim/Pr	64-1053
ERB, Friedr.	27	Gotha	66-0469
Theobald 14			
ERB, John August	28	Kirchhasel	66-1155
ERB, Joseph	23	Freisen	66-0623
ERB, L.M.	27	Fulda	63-1218
ERB, Margaretha	24	Stornfels	64-0593
ERB, Michael	16	Hambach	63-1136
ERBACH, Chr.	26	Truegleben	65-0898
ERBART, Carl	31	Ortsberg	66-1373
Margareth 27, Wolfgang 11m			
ERBE, Heinr. Fried	23	Kurhessen	66-0578
ERBE, Marie	24	Wernhausen	64-0840
ERBECK, Christoph	42	Roehrenfurth	64-0886
Anna 30, Christian 7, Anna 5			
Anna Cath. 4, Anna Maria 3, Conrad 2			
baby 11m			
ERBEN, Joseph	50	Boehmen	63-0862
Cathre. 41, Joseph 13, Emanuel 9, Mary 21			
Theresia 17, Josepha 11, Elisab. 4			
ERBENKOTTER, G.	18	Burscheid	64-0782
Helene 14, Elise 20			
ERBERGER, Salomea	29	Liestal	65-0189
Marie 5			
ERBERS, Ludw.	27	Hirschberg	66-1243
ERBERT, Franz	28	Damme	64-0593
ERBIN, Margarethe	59	Meiners	63-0990
ERBS, Heinrich	13	Padingbuettel	66-0679
ERBSEN, H.	26	Dorum	64-0495
ERCK, A.	25	Grumberg	65-0007
ERCKMANN, William	26	Bremen	63-0006
ERDEMANN, Bernh.	19	Stadtoldendrf	64-0170
ERDMANN, Fr'drke.	18	Gr.Breitenbch	64-0432
ERDMANN, Friedrich	28	Allershausen	63-0244
ERDRICH, Frantz A.	56	Petersthal	65-1030
ERFURTH, Anna	43	Pittsburg	66-0704
ERHARD, Dorothea	28	Suhl	65-1088
Otto 2			
ERHARDT, Joseph	25	Oestringen	63-0097
Mathilde 21			
ERHARDT, Marg.Barb	59	Gattersdorf	64-0938
Joh. Nic. 23, Anna Marg. 26			
ERHART, Magd.	30	Nuernberg	63-1085
ERICHS, Sophie	18	Dorum	66-1248
ERLANGER, James	26	Bingen	63-0752
ERLANGER, Leon	23	Bingen	63-0752
ERLEBACH, Ernstine	25	Bayreuth	63-0244
ERLEN, Herm. Max	22	Altenburg	66-0109
ERLENKOETTER, Gust	48	Magdeburg	64-1053
ERLER, Louis	24	Boehne	64-0938
ERLER, Pauline	17	Zuegelheim	66-0576
ERMEL, Elisabeth	56	Eudorf	66-0349
ERMELING, Anna	17	Nortrup	66-0576
Wilhelmine 15			
ERMELING, J.D.	23	Talge	65-1024
ERMETE, J.B.	36	Naumburg	64-0363
Maria 32, Franz 8, Carl 5, Conrad 3			
baby(f) 9m			
ERMOLD, Christine	19	Jaxthausen	65-0189
Caroline 16			
ERNA, Bernh.	18	Glettenberg	66-0349

NAME	AGE	RESIDENCE	YR-LIST
ERNE, Carl	38	Naila	66-1131
ERNE, John Ignatz	24	Vellkirch	63-1085
ERNENFRUTSCH, Jul.	21	Prussia	66-0109
ERNEST, Charles	52	Cincinnati	63-0821
wife 38			
ERNST, Adam Ernst	39	Sax.-Meiningn	64-0432
Marie 37, Moritz 11, Georg Fr. 6			
Georg Adam 3, Michael 9m			
ERNST, Adolph	6	Huttingen	65-0004
ERNST, Anna	35	Berlin	64-0593
ERNST, Carl	26	Preussen	66-0147
ERNST, Caroline	28	Nuertingen	64-0593
ERNST, Cathar.	24	Basel	65-0243
ERNST, Chr.	27	Haltenmondhm.	64-0331
ERNST, Constantin	23	Wuertemberg	66-0984
ERNST, Franz	26	Hannover	66-0934
Louis 23, Johannes 19			
ERNST, Friedr.	31	Jangershausen	64-0639
ERNST, Friedrich	27	Susbach	63-1178
ERNST, Gutman	18	Idwar	66-0679
ERNST, Heinr.	43	New York	64-0073
Maria 25			
ERNST, Heinrich	21	Osnabrueck	66-1127
ERNST, J.Erik Ludw	32	Beverstadt	63-0053
ERNST, Jacob	26	Illingen	64-0363
ERNST, Joseph	22	New York	64-1053
ERNST, Louise	23	Paine	66-0147
ERNST, Michael	29	Gauerstadt	66-0469
Bernhardine 23, Margarethe 2			
ERNST, Roman	29	Susbach	63-0244
ERNST, W.L. Martin	29	Braunschweig	66-0221
ERNSTDUFT, A.	19	Schwarzbach	66-0413
ERNSTINEDE, Joh'a.	48	Dunsenhausen	66-0413
ERNSTLING, Julius	30	Breslau	65-0116
ERNTGES, Gustav	23	Merlscheid	63-1010
ERSIG, Albert	18	Eichstetten	63-0551
ERTL, Aug.	30	Southhampton	66-0934
ERZBISCHOF, Camill	18	Wahningen	64-0639
ESCGEBAYER, Joseph	25	Ottenhausen	66-0221
Wilhelm 15			
ESCH, Jacob	22	Gruppenbach	64-0639
ESCHBORN, Betty	19	Fauerbach	64-0073
ESCHEN, Mrs.	28	New York	63-1136
Leonore 10, Philippine 4, Friederike 3			
ESCHEN, v. Stephan	29	Cheer	64-0427
Jacob 28			
ESCHENBACH, Alex	27	Alsleben	63-0350
Anna 21, Andreas 6m			
ESCHENBECK, Jos.	26	Auerbach	66-1313
ESCHENBRENNER, A	28	Sindlingen	64-0639
ESCHENFELDER, Mary	24	Schimborn	66-1243
ESCHER, Richard	29	Weida	64-0214
ESCHOCHER, Bernh.	26	Schloth	66-0679
ESCHWEGEN, R. Remm	22	Heppens	66-0412
ESPELAGE, Joh. H.	32	Oldenburg	66-0934
Gertrud 28, Johann 4, Josephine 2			
Wilhelmine 3m			
ESPELAGE, Joseph	24	Dinklage	65-0948
ESPEN, Samuel	27	Preussen	66-0221
ESPENSCHEID, Marg.	35	Siefenheim	66-1131
ESSELMANN, Johann	18	Alfhausen	66-1093
ESSELMANN, Ludwig	36	Senden	66-0704
ESSER, Herm.	38	New York	63-0551
ESSER, Mathias	44	V.D.Hoffung	63-0990
ESSIG, Christian	39	Stebbach	66-0147
ESSIG, Fr.	20	Lienzingen	65-1189
ESSIG, Johannes	29	Boenningen	65-0770
ESSLINGER, Cath.	43	Streschen	65-0594
ESSLINGER, Johann	26	Niederhofen	66-1248
ESSLINGER, Mayer	21	Carlsruhe	64-0593
ESSMANN, A.	18	Delmhorst	65-1189
ESSMANN, E.	28	Stadthagen	64-0782
ESSMANN, Ludwig	30	Wolfenbuettel	64-0433
ESSMUELLER, Fritz	21	Steinberg	66-1093
ESTEBEN, Paul	31	Schweiz	63-0953
ESTELMANN, Joh.	23	Battbergen	66-1373
ESTER, Johann	55	Hessen	63-0822
Friederike 21			
ESTERL, Joh.	36	Zwiesel	66-0109
ETHELMANN, Elisab.	33	Salmannsburg	66-0412
ETTER, Jacob	30	Busnang	65-0116
ETTER, Joh. Babt	25	Appenzell	65-0243
ETTLING, Cath.	42	Alsfeld	65-0007
ETTLINGER, B.A.	29	Carlsruhe	64-0992
ETTLINGER, Louis	20	Carlsruhe	66-0221
ETTLINGER, Selig	19	Eppingheim	66-0734
ETZEL, A.	26	Lautenbach	66-0413
ETZEL, Carl	21	Wangen	64-1161
EUBER, Friedrich	26	Kreutznach	65-0151
EUCHNER, Friedrich	25	Grafenberg	66-0147
EULBACHER, Johann	24	Roellbach	66-0734
EULER, Friedrich	59	Hailer	66-1327
Heinrich 8			
EULER, Nic.	38	Steinau	64-0495
Ce.(f) 32, Ph. 5, Gertrud 3			
EULER, Wm.	35	New York	63-1038
Marie 21, Wm. 11m			
EULMUS, Ce. (f)	16	Obernheim	64-0363
EURICH, Elisab.	21	Banneroed	64-0687
EUTENFELDT, Cath.	24	Bayreuth	64-0992
Rosalie 23, Caroline 2			
EVELD, Heinr.	30	Varenholz	64-0639
Gerh. 25			
EVEN, Joh.	44	Wietmarschen	64-0214
EVENS, Albert	17	Bremen	64-0739
EVERS, Gerd.	24	Blauhand	66-0221
EVERS, Heinr.	20	Bremen	64-0886
EVERS, Joh.	15	Dingen	65-0004
EVERS, Johann	38	Bremen	63-0614
EVERS, Lucie	34	Ronnebeck	65-0865
Heinrich 11, Lucie 7, Johann 1			
EVERS, Sophie	16	Borgentreich	65-0594
Caroline 41, Carl 14, Gussan 7, Amalie 7			
EVERSMANN, B.	26	Asgerberg	66-0413
C.W. 19			
EVERSMEIER, H.	27	Kappeln	63-1069
Wilhelm 19, Heinrich 11m			
EVERSMEYER, Friedr	21	Wersen	63-0614
EVERT, B.H.	24	Ochtrup	64-1022
EWALD, Cath.	17	Segnitz	65-0594
EWALD, Ferd.	21	Laubach	64-0840
EWALD, Johann	31	Hertzbach	63-1069
EWALD, Otto	21	Schoetten	66-1327
EWAN, Aug. Adolph	31	Janewitz	66-0650
EWEN, Johann	47	Mainz	66-0934
Anna 30, Conrad 4, Mathilde 3			
EWERS, Wilhelm	41	Atzendorf	64-0427
EWERT, Math.	18	Gandgesheim	65-0007
EXINGER, Marie	19	Rawitsch	64-0782
EYMANN, Rudolph	22	Hesepe	66-1373
EYRICH, Barb.	23	Tuttlingen	65-0402
EYSEL, Hermann	29	New York	63-0821
Elise 30, Helene 3, baby 3m			
FABER, (f)	30	Hamburg	63-1085
FABER, Chris.	21	Lorch	63-0862
FABER, Christ.	30	Wuertemberg	66-0734
FABER, Heinr.	26	Niederwesel	64-0138
FABER, J.H.(m)	33	Bremen	64-0138
H.(f) 33, Marie 8, Hr.(m) 6, Emil 7m			
FABER, Johann	26	Lamstedt	66-1327
FABER, Sus.	40	Nidda	64-0782
FABER, Wilhelm	28	Giessen	66-1203
FABERN, Ernst	15	Naumburg	66-1373
FABIAN, Abraham	18	Gehzeruh	65-0770
FABIAN, Peter	27	Hammelbach	66-0576
FABJEN, Herm.	24	Bruettendorf	66-0704
FABRICIUS, Adolph	23	Weilburg	66-1093
Wilhelmine 19			
FACH, Friedrich	23	Sachwann	66-0349
FACH, Jac.	32	Leissenwald	64-0023
FACH, John F.	30	New York	63-0015
FACH, Michael	20	Qualzheim	63-0693
FACKLER, J.	24	Haberslacht	65-0007
FADER, Marie	21	Mohringen	64-0331
FAEGER, Wilhelm	30	Bremen	66-0147
FAERBER, Christina	20	Stuttgart	65-1031

NAME	AGE	RESIDENCE	YR-LIST
FAERBER, Hermann	27	Willenroth	66-1248
FAESCHE, Heinrich	31	New York	66-0934
Louiza 33			
FAEUSTLIN, Anna	27	Freiberg	65-0055
FAHL, Catharine	32	Mannheim	66-0734
FAHLBUSCH, Friedr.	22	Bremen	64-0214
FAHLE, Heinr.	19	Schluesslburg	65-0950
FAHR, Christ.	14	Zaberfeld	64-0427
FAHRENHORST, Soph.	28	Brokum	66-0668
FAHRNER, Ambrosius	23	Oberndorf	65-1030
FAHRNER, Andreas	37	Roeth	64-0170
Maria 28, Chs. 3, Anna 8, Michael 6			
Mathias 5, Christ. 20			
FAIGEL, Carl	23	Tuebingen	65-0243
Mathilda 19, Mathilda 1, Henriette 23			
FAIGLE, Ferd.	30	Wuertemberg	66-0704
FAIR, Otto	48	America	63-1136
FAIST, David	45	Roeth	64-0170
FAIST, Magadalena	25	Bergzell	63-0168
FAISTER, Joseph	17	Hailtingen	63-0296
FAKE, Friedr. Wm.	65	Kappeln	63-1069
FAKE, Friedrich J.	40	Lengerich	63-1069
Friedrich A. 23, Ernst Fr. 20			
Ludwig W. 18, Marg. Elise 14, Lisette 7			
Bernhard 5, Kath. Louise 9m			
FALCK, Gottlieb	20	Schorndorf	66-1155
FALER, Richard	17	Gehrden	65-0898
FALK, A.C.	34	Hamburg	64-0687
FALK, Albert	26	Platow	67-0007
FALK, Bertha H.	21	New York	63-0168
FALK, Carl	23	Bockenheim	64-0639
Magdalena 18			
FALK, Ed.	39	Posen	66-0576
FALK, Eduard	28	Bueckeburg	65-0594
FALK, Elise	32	Steyerberg	66-1093
Minna 22			
FALK, Fr.	30	Wolchow	65-0402
Tina 28			
FALK, Jacob	38	Bergheim	66-0221
FALK, Joh.	21	Mainz	65-0402
FALK, Minna	30	Konitz	64-0495
Augusta 20, Elise 7m			
FALK, Salomon	67	Odenbach	66-1327
FALKE, Johann	42	Hildesheim	65-1140
Minna 44, Heinrich 15, (f) 12			
FALKE, Max	19	Steyerberg	66-1093
FALKENAU, L.	25	New York	63-1218
FALKENBERG, Marg.	25	Werda	65-0151
FALKENHAGEN, Franz	24	Berlin	65-0770
FALKENHAHN, Ferd.	21	Geismar	66-1313
FALKENHEIMER, Cath	20	Darmstadt	66-1031
FALKENMAYR, Martin	33	Wintzell	66-0704
Johanna 56			
FALKENSTEIN, H.K.	18	Altenbach/Han	63-1010
FALLER, Cath.	32	Haberschlacht	64-0886
FALLER, Clemens	24	Heimerdingen	64-0687
FALLER, Sophie	25	Hugstetten	64-0427
FALSENMAYER, Aug.	19	Westrup	66-0984
FALTER, Agnes	27	Cronach	65-0974
Johann 5			
FALZ, Conrad	25	Hausen	66-0412
FALZ, Heinrich	16	Tann	66-0623
FANGER, Jacob	23	Boehmen	63-0693
FANGMANN, Caroline	33	Stroehm	63-0693
Wilhelmine 3			
FANSCHE, Chr.Ernst	46	Crimmitzschau	63-0693
FANSEL, Albert	20	Cannstadt	65-0948
FANTA, Joseph	50	Malin	64-0433
Theresia 60			
FANTO, Joseph	17	Boehmen	66-0349
FARENHORST, Herman		New York	63-0917
FARNBACHER, Marian	24	Fuerth	63-0752
FARNZ, Maria	27	Boehmen	63-0693
Maria 3			
FARRENKOPF, Franz	32	Impfingen	66-0623
Marianne 27, Franz 7, Carl Joseph 10m			
FARRENKOPF, Philip	39	Buchen	65-0948
FASCHER, Framz	28	Ostenfeld	66-1127
FASKE, Joh. Herm.	32	Hannover	64-0432
FASNACHT, Cath.	25	Alpirsbach	64-0593
FASSBINDER, Ludwig	14	Wolf	64-0886
FASSBINDER, Magdl.	20	Bietigheim	65-0243
FASSBINDER, Peter	25	Euskirchen	63-1038
FASSERS, Ernst	19	Offenburg	66-1155
FASSHAUER, Gertrud	18	Witzenhausen	66-0704
FASSNACHT, Anton	32	Gruemstetten	66-0083
Marie 31			
FASTERLING, Josefa	21	Hohenassel	63-0693
FASTNACHT, Cyprim	37	Untermarchtal	66-1373
FASTONE, Gerhard	58	Lette	66-1248
Heinrich 38, Elisabeth 21			
FASTVIVE, John	26	Preussen	63-0990
Anna 28			
FATEITA, Adelbert	70	Heiligkilian	64-0433
FATH, Friedr.	21	Oberacken	66-1248
FATHA, Georg	28	Landwehrhagen	66-0934
FATTHAUER, Heinr.	25	Diepholz	66-0666
FAUBEL, Henry	17	Moistadt	66-0679
FAUFFELD, Ludw.	20	Burgholz	65-0007
FAULHABER, Bernh.	25	Schelmberg	64-0427
FAULHABER, Joh. Ch	58	Bietigheim	65-0243
FAULHABER, Mariana	44	Koenigheim	66-0412
Rosina 19, Michel Jos. 14, Ferdinand 9			
FAURE, Jacob	43	Immerath	66-1155
Elisabeth 39			
FAUSEL, Jacob	23	Erkenbrectwlr	65-0243
FAUSER, Marie	19	Oberwalden	66-1093
FAUST, Anton	26	Preussen	64-0363
FAUST, C.F.	21	Gr. Wieden	65-1024
FAUST, Phil.	27	Ndr.Ausheim	64-0938
FAUTH, Carl	24	Bueckeburg	65-0007
FAUTH, Jac. Fr.	32	Kleinheppach	65-0116
FAUTH, Joh.	30	Weissenfeld	64-0495
FAUTH, Marie	21	Grossiglabach	66-0934
FAUTZ, Silvester	49	Rodenberg	65-1189
FAUTZEN, Lina	25	Buehren	65-1088
FAWLER, John	28	Hohenzollern	63-0168
FAY, Antonia	20	Mackensell	66-1243
FEBBE, Emil	26	Dresden	65-0116
FEBBE, Gerhd.	31	California	64-0138
Christine 30			
FECHHEIMER, Marcus	38	Cincinnati	63-0953
wife 30, Anna 12, Emilie 10			
FECHKEIMER, C.	18	Matzwitz	64-0782
FECHT, Gustav	15	Stein	64-0593
FECHT, Hinrich	24	Aurich	66-0668
Antje 24, baby 9m, Motje 23			
FECHTER, Lisette	42	Paderborn	65-1189
Marie 7, August 6, Franz 4			
FECHTMANN, Wilhelm	32	Osnabrueck	66-1203
FECKEL, Ferd.	25	Ronneburg	66-0984
FECKMEYER, Friedr	25	Lengerich	64-0214
FEDDEN, Diedr.	15	Driftsethe	64-1108
FEDDEN, Elise	20	Hornknop	66-1313
FEDDER, Anton	34	Bremen	65-0770
Marie 29			
FEDELER, Heinrich	21	Bremen	64-0456
FEDER, Rosa	62	Pleschen	64-0840
FEDERMANN, Christ.	22	Zaberfeld	64-0639
FEDERMANN, Seligm.	27	Leipzig	66-0221
FEDERWITZ, Heinr.	19	Kuhstedt	63-0614
FEER, Franz	19	Schweiz	64-0138
FEGHT, Herm.	21	Esslingen	65-0116
FEGHTMANN, Th.	26	Rodenburg	65-0116
FEGTER, Peter	66	Pilsum	66-1248
FEGTHOF, Heinr.	34	Uldenrode	64-0687
FEHL, Elise	20	Wallroth	66-0623
Elisabeth 17			
FEHLE, Monika	50	Waldshut	66-1203
Carl 9			
FEHLHABER, Wilhelm	22	Bohmte	65-0948
FEHLING, Heinrich	33	Abertern	66-0623
Sophie 37, Sophie Just. 5, Heinrich 11m			
FEHMANN, Heinr.	32	Weinheim	64-0687
Marg. 26, Susanne 4, Philipp 3m			
FEHORN, Bernhardin	28	Borkum/Hann.	64-0920

NAME	AGE	RESIDENCE	YR-LIST
FEHR, Anna	25	Schweiz	63-1136
FEHR, Jas.	30	Schweiz	63-1136
FEHR, Susanne	22	Flach	66-0984
FEHRENBACH, A.(m)	29	Schoenewald	64-0331
Kr.(m) 3, Ja.(f) 1			
FEHRHOF, Wilhelm	19	Rheda	66-1373
FEHRING, Maria	25	Listrup	65-1095
FEHRMANN, Caroline	19	Rotenuffeln	64-0433
FEHRMANN, Louis	7	Oldenburg	65-1024
FEHSENFELD, H.	9	Nuremberg	65-1024
FEIDEN, Joseph	23	Alf	64-0639
FEIDNER, Heinr.	21	Dresden	65-0007
FEIFTEL, Mathilde	15	Redighausen	66-1031
FEIG, Margarethe	57	Asch	66-1031
Ernestine 24			
FEIGE, Maie	22	Prussia	64-0495
FEIGE, Math.(f)	30	Schiepzig	64-0495
FEIHL, John	27	Aalen	66-0934
FEIL, Diedr.	25	Holzum	65-0948
FEIL, G.	30	Oldisleben	65-0713
FEIL, Patriz	19	Ramsenstruth	65-1088
Josepha 15			
FEILENSCHMIDT, Cat	34	Sondelfingen	63-1218
John 9, Charles 4			
FEILER, Carl	20	Asch	66-1327
Margarethe 24, Carl 9m			
FEILER, Wilhelmine	23	Asch	66-0679
FEILKNECHT, Abrah.	39	Twaun	65-0243
FEILNER, Joseph	28	New York	63-0917
FEIN, Carl W.F.	30	Stuttgart	64-0073
FEIN, Max	21	Horb	66-1243
FEIND, F.	20	Fritzlar	64-0938
FEISS, Jacob	34	Taetern	64-0687
Emanuel 18, Ed. 18			
FEISSEL, Jacob	22	Darmstadt	66-0577
FEISSEL, Justus	37	Reddinghausen	66-0668
FEIST, Philippine	17	Oppenhiem	66-0668
Elisabeth 20			
FEIST, Walburga	42	Schuttersthal	66-0578
Franciska 3			
FEISTEL, Carl Frd.	22	Langenbernsdf	66-0109
FEITH, Heinrich	26	Bielefeld	66-1155
FELDBAUSCH, Joh. J	18	Speyer	65-0116
FELDER, Engelbert	46	Graefurth/Sul	63-0917
Carl 16			
FELDHAUS, Heinrich	22	Loehden	67-0007
FELDHAUSEN, Johann	23	Meppen	66-0412
FELDHOERSTER, Casp	23	Hannover	66-0576
FELDHOFER, Ferd.	17	Pest	64-0363
FELDHUSEN, Fritz	21	Oberhausen	66-0679
FELDHUSEN, Julie	21	Ritterhude	66-1243
FELDKAMP, John	40	Chicago	66-0734
FELDMANN, Anton	26	Warendorf	63-0551
FELDMANN, Anton	29	Wahrendorf	66-1155
FELDMANN, Aug.	30	New York	64-0363
FELDMANN, C.	33	Blumenthal	63-0551
FELDMANN, Casp.	24	Heidesheim	65-0974
Barbara 18			
FELDMANN, Eduard	20	Bremen	64-1053
FELDMANN, Elisab.	60	Hesel	63-0614
Wilhelmine 30			
FELDMANN, Fr'dke.	20	Prussia	64-0432
FELDMANN, Friedr.	36	Bunde	64-0427
FELDMANN, Friedr.M	21	Dissen	65-0950
FELDMANN, Helene	14	Giessen	66-0679
FELDMANN, Hermann	36	Muehlheim	63-0990
Anna 23, Arnold 9, Henry 7, Hermann 1			
FELDMANN, Johann	24	Steinfeld	63-0614
FELDMANN, John W.	45	Cincinnati	63-1038
FELDMANN, M.E.(f)	31	West Cappeln	64-0331
FELDMANN, Marianne	25	Dummelshausen	66-0984
FELDMANN, Sophie	30	Herzigerode	64-0593
FELDMANN, William	24	Muehlheim	63-0990
Maria 20			
FELDMEIER, Wilhelm	18	Nuertingen	66-1093
FELDNER, Anton	22	Neunburg	66-0083
FELDSCHER, Frdr.	57	Harpenfeld	66-0221
Marie 60			

NAME	AGE	RESIDENCE	YR-LIST
FELDSCHER, Herm.	27	Wittlage	63-0862
FELGER, J.C.	38	Melborne	64-0639
FELGHEDER, Hr.	27	Buer	64-0593
FELLE, Friedr.	40	Ingenau	64-0840
Friederike 37, Friederike 15, Friedr. 7			
Carl 2			
FELLER, Ernst	29	Altenburg	66-0984
Anna 19, Louise 6m			
FELLINGER, Fritz	24	Gruenenplan	63-0953
FELLJOHANN, H.	28	Ladbergen	64-1161
FELSBERG, Christ.	56	Unterellen	64-0593
Simon 13			
FELSCHER, Elisab.	13	Wittlage	63-0862
FELSENHELD, Eman'l	14	Marzbach	64-0938
FELSENHELD, L.(f)	16	Merzbach	63-0551
FELSENHELD, Ludwig	20	Merzbach	63-0990
FELTHEIM, Isaac	27	Szaboles	63-0551
FELZNER, Rosine	22	Aldorf	64-0687
FENCHEL, Christian	29	Gaildorf	65-0865
FENDLER, Ferd.	28	Fraustadt	64-1022
FENKEL, Jac.	25	Grieselbach	66-1243
FENKER, Wilhelmine	20	Rahden	65-1088
Christian 18			
FENKHOFF, Clara	37	Lingen	64-0495
Wm. 6, Bhd. 4, Christ. 11m			
FENKHOTT, F.	36	Lingen	64-0495
FENNEN, B.	22	Berge	63-1038
FENNLEIN, Heinr.	30	Wulfershausen	66-0704
FENSCHE, Henriette	43	Fisshau	65-0770
FENSTERMACHER, Wm.	25	Meisenheim	66-1127
FENZEL, Albert	26	Berlin	66-0413
FERBER, Amalie	17	Hessen	66-0576
FERBER, John	23	Buechenbach	66-1155
FERIE, Rosine	25	Elsass	63-0482
FERLING, Georg	16	St. Goar	65-0007
FERNSNER, John Fr.	25	Sulzbach	63-1038
FERTIG, Friedrich	28	New York	63-1218
FESCHER, Adelheid	24	Wohlert	66-0984
FESER, Eva	23	Halsheim	64-1022
FESMANN, Louise	29	Nuertingen	66-1313
FESSE, Michael	27	Lebenuke	66-0984
FESSEL, Henry	32	Hjoerring	63-0482
FESSLER, Carl	27	Duderstadt	66-1327
FESTNER, Th.	17	Prusia	63-1003
FETE, Josepha	47	Kuttenberg/Bo	64-0920
FETGER, Louise	16	Haubershausen	64-1108
FETT, Jacob	33	Muenster	66-0576
Catharine 30, Marg. 5, Jacob 10m			
Elisabeth 28, Marg. 3, Elisabeth 11m			
FETT, Johannes	29	Huser	65-0004
FETTE, Anna	30	Bremen	66-0984
Anna 6, Heinr. 4			
FETTE, C.	25	Bolschle	64-0992
FETTE, Friedr.	22	Minden	65-1031
FETTE, Gerhard	32	Joegel	64-0886
FETTE, Josephine	21	Loningen	64-1053
FETTER, Regina	19	Baden	66-0984
FETTGER, D.	33	Oldenburg	66-0413
Gesine 33			
FETTJE, Wilhelm	32	Delmenhorst	66-0666
Johanna 40			
FETZER, Carl	18	Baden	66-0734
FETZER, Dagobert	27	Baden	66-0734
FETZER, Friedrich	24	Freiberg	66-0576
FETZER, Lucinda	22	Gr.Breitenbch	64-0432
FETZNER, A.E.	29	Chemnitz	65-0402
FEUCHT, Cathar.	26	Weinsberg	66-1373
FEUCHTER, G.M.	26	Hagenhof	63-0821
FEUDEL, Carl	18	Germany	66-0666
FEUERBACH, Joseph	16	Rhina	66-0934
FEUEREISEN, Bernh.	26	Pest	64-0938
FEUERSTEIN, Rud.	35	San Francisco	63-0953
H. 26, Christ 6, Elisabeth 4			
FEUNER, M.	13	Gothharnstein	66-0413
FEUSS, Elisabeth	22	London	64-1022
FEUSSEL, August	27	Schleiz	63-0822
FEUSSNER, Heinrich	27	Ernsthausen	66-0412
FEUST, Sigmund	20	Fuerth	63-1038

NAME	AGE	RESIDENCE	YR-LIST
FEUSTEL, Leonore	36	Gotha	65-0004
Max 5, Elise 7, Hedwig 4, Paul 2			
Theobald 11, Louis 12			
FEY, John	28	Darmstadt	63-1038
Lewis 19			
FEYERABEND, Math.	24	Popenreuth	64-0639
Maria E. 9			
FHORST, Heinr.	15	Fhorst	66-0984
Caroline 25			
FIBBE, Catharina	25	Ruessel	63-0990
FIBKE, Claus	20	Ahlerstedt	65-0116
FICHTER, Alfred	17	Kenzingen	63-0551
FICK, Anton	20	Mainburg	64-0432
FICK, Fritz	24	Bremerhaven	66-1155
FICK, Henriette	15	Lehe	63-0953
FICK, Henry	32	New York	63-1218
Louise 30, Henry 9			
FICK, Joh. Theo.	31	Hannover	64-0432
FICK, Johannes	17	Lamstedt	65-0950
FICKE, Barbara	22	Holte	66-1327
FICKE, Erich	20	Lehnhorst	66-1248
Arend 18			
FICKE, Herman	27	Bremen	64-0938
Marie 25			
FICKEN, Chr. D.	27	Wulsbuettel	65-0402
FICKER, Carl	7	Mulmshorn	64-0992
Johannes 9			
FICKER, Friedr.	46	Rothenuffeln	64-0886
Carl Fr. 13, Heinr. Fr. 16			
Christ. Fr. 19, Marie Martha 41			
Carl Fr. W. 2, Caroline C. 7, John 11m			
FICKERT, Robert	30	Oelsnitz	66-0668
FICKERT, Wilhelm	30	Goettingen	64-0199
FICKERWIRTH, Moriz	23	Griesen	66-0734
FICKINGER, William	35	Meissenheim	63-0244
FICKS, Carl	21	Mannheim	66-0147
FICKWEILER, Chr. E	29	Dobareuth	64-0331
FICKWEILER, Ernst	25	Dobereuth	63-0990
FIDELDEI, Engel	17	Ledenberg	66-0679
FIDZMUC, Franz	48	Boehmen	66-0221
Barbara 43, Cathre. 15, Rosalia 5			
FIEBER, Wilhelm	22	Prag	64-0639
FIEDEKEN, Cathar.	23	Veenhusen	66-1031
FIEDELER, Fr'dr.Wm	51	Zeitz	63-0614
FIEDELER, Maria	24	Tarsis	64-0456
FIEDLER, Andr.	28	Maineck	63-0990
FIEDLER, Anton	41	Zella	65-1024
Christine 34, Anna 9			
FIEDLER, Carl	28	Mannheim	66-1127
FIEDLER, Georg	58	Maineck	63-0990
FIEDLER, George	18	Rittmarshsn.	63-0168
FIEDLER, Heinr.		Oster Cappeln	65-0950
FIEDLER, Hermann	28	Zuegelheim	66-0576
FIEDLER, Lina	20	Cassel	65-0007
FIEDLER, Theresia	24	Kuellendorf	63-0953
FIEGE, Augusta	20	Geestendorf	66-1327
FIEGENER, Maria E.	16	Eckmannshsn.	63-0168
FIEHEN, Diedr.	31	Nuernberg	65-1024
FIEKEN, Rudolph	44	Philadelphia	66-0984
Johann Heinr 18, Emmi 18			
FIEKERS, Marie Ad.	28	Lingen	25-0950
Euphemia M. 26			
FIEL, Adam	24	Unterwisheim	64-1053
FIELBRECHT, Carl	64	Minden	65-1095
August 19			
FIENHOLD, Bernhard	28	Erfurt	66-1155
FIENING, Maria	24	Essen	66-0668
FIENN, Louise	30	Hannover	42-0704
Caroline 17			
FIER, Peter	29	Remscheid	64-1053
FIFFARTZ, Robert	22	Mettmann	63-0482
FIGES, Wilhelm	23	Bielefeld	67-0353
FIGGE, Henriette	25	Helminghausen	66-0984
FIGGER, Barth	29	Salbi-Groskr.	66-0650
FILGE, Henry	59	Philadelphia	63-0917
Georg 18, Louis 16			
FILGE, Joh. H.	31	Philadelphia	66-0984
Francisco 27, Sally 25, Harry 6			
FILLEN, Christ.	23	Urrhausen	64-0023
Johanna 21			
FILLSHOEBER, Adam	6	Ndr.Berbach	66-0413
FINCKE, Carl	19	Goettingen	65-0770
FINCKE, Carl	20	Bremen	64-0593
FINCKEN, Herm.	36	New York	66-0734
FINGER, Fanny	27	Pirzen	66-1093
Ludwig 6, Mathilde 4, Julius 1			
FINGER, Joh.	25	Mainz	64-0920
FINIS, Ernst	27	Braunschweig	66-0221
FINK, Adam	38	New York	64-0170
Ricka. 28, Margarethe 6			
FINK, Amalie	25	Eckwarden	65-0055
FINK, Aug.	19	Muenchen	63-1218
Anton 15			
FINK, Aug.	21	Muenchen	65-0402
FINK, Cath.	19	Dorum	64-0456
Johanna 16			
FINK, Doris	30	Hulzeberg	64-1108
Catharina 3, Anna 11m			
FINK, Heinr.	40	Gundheim	64-0427
FINK, Ida	46	Gottingen	64-0782
Carl 4			
FINK, J.(m)	30	Oberneuland	64-0495
FINK, Magdalena	56	Vilsen	64-0331
Johanna 21			
FINK, Simon	25	Neresheim	64-0782
FINKBEINER, Gottl.	19	Hutzenbach	66-0147
FINKE, Anna	17	Lehe	63-0822
FINKE, Arnold	16	Norden	66-1203
FINKE, Charlotte	20	Rothenfelde	63-0917
FINKE, Elisabeth	26	Koenigshagen	66-0577
Heinrich 24, Wilhelm 22, Dorothea 18			
Carl 16, Christian 13			
FINKE, Elise	17	New York	66-0221
FINKE, Johannes	30	Koenigshagen	66-0577
Elisabeth 28, Johannes 6, Elisabeth 3			
FINKE, Ottilie	26	Clementinenhf	66-0704
FINKE, Rosine	31	Posen	64-0432
FINKELMANN, Clara	16	Wissingen	64-0427
FINKEN, G.(f)	23	Westerbeck	64-0495
FINKEN, Harry	4	New York	66-0734
FINKEN, Marg.	16	Hannover	64-0073
Heinr. 18			
FINKENSTEDT, Dina	22	Kellerberg	65-1031
FINKENSTEIN, Josef	39	Wien	63-0398
Marie 24, Leopoldine 2			
FINKWEILER, Louise	20	Kettelfingen	64-0170
FIRST, Christiane	24	Buechenau	64-0495
FISCHBECK, John	28	Bremervoerde	64-0639
FISCHE, Herm.	17	Wilkischen	66-1313
FISCHEL, Siegfried	18	Koenigswart	66-0934
FISCHER, Abraham	38	Prag	64-0938
Barbara 26			
FISCHER, Ad.	25	Dielingen	65-1024
Ludw. 27, Theod. 9, Julius 7			
FISCHER, Adam	26	Edingheim	64-0214
FISCHER, Alb.	18	Potsdam	66-1243
FISCHER, Alb.	24	Ziesar	64-0427
Lucia 3, Paul 1			
FISCHER, Albert	41	Redding	64-0170
FISCHER, Alois	32	New York	66-1031
FISCHER, Amalie	26	Rochlitz	64-0687
FISCHER, Anna C.	24	Tann	66-0349
FISCHER, Anton	22	Neukirchen	66-0679
FISCHER, Aug.	33	Rodenburg	65-1088
Charlotte 2			
FISCHER, Aug.	23	Eimsen	65-0898
FISCHER, Augusta	19	Bremen	66-0734
FISCHER, Barbara	54	Baiern	66-0469
FISCHER, Bernh.	25	Prussia	64-0073
Franz 20			
FISCHER, Bernhard	22	Ochtelbur	63-0482
FISCHER, C.	45	Bolschle	64-0992
Sophie 35, Caroline 12, Wilhelm 7			
Wilhelmine 5			
FISCHER, C.	19	Bollendorf	65-1189
FISCHER, C.W. Dr.	59	Cincinnati	63-0953

NAME	AGE	RESIDENCE	YR-LIST
Henry 35			
FISCHER, Carl	28	Seifershausen	64-0073
FISCHER, Carl	28	Elberfeld	63-0296
FISCHER, Carl	25	Esslingen	66-0221
FISCHER, Carl	22	Stuttgart	64-0840
FISCHER, Carl	30	Mannheim	66-1127
FISCHER, Carl Gotl	26	Moehringen	64-1108
Dorothea 21, Wilhelm 14			
FISCHER, Caroline	19	Nuertingen	64-0593
FISCHER, Catharina	15	Dudendorf	66-0837
FISCHER, Catharine	18	Hannover	63-0822
FISCHER, Charlotte	18	Marburg	66-1093
FISCHER, Chr.	33	Meiningen	66-0704
FISCHER, Chr. H.	22	Zelwitz	65-0713
FISCHER, Christian	27	Berg	66-0147
FISCHER, Christian	51	Hohenzell	66-1243
FISCHER, Const.	18	Frommerhausen	65-0007
FISCHER, Eduard	20	Boehmen	66-0147
FISCHER, Emil	20	Benig	66-0576
Bertha 14			
FISCHER, Emil	15	Mannheim	66-1373
FISCHER, Ernestine	18	Trogau	66-1127
FISCHER, Eva	27	Dettingen	66-0734
FISCHER, Eva	23	Gerricksheim	65-1030
FISCHER, Franz	29	Boehmen	63-0917
Theresa 24, Jos. 8, Anna 10m			
FISCHER, Franz	25	Wiesbaden	65-1189
FISCHER, Friedr.	28	Rosenfeld	64-1206
FISCHER, Friedrich	28	Coburg	66-0346
Sophia 27			
FISCHER, Friedrich	19	Marburg	65-1095
FISCHER, Fritz	20	Dalwigsthal	66-0469
FISCHER, Georg	27	Bayern	66-0147
FISCHER, Georg	31	Darmstadt	66-0221
FISCHER, Georg	23	Eckardts	66-0469
Rosine 24			
FISCHER, Georg	22	Hessen	66-0734
Heinr. 19			
FISCHER, Georg	30	Neresheim	64-0782
FISCHER, Georg	20	Bahlingen	65-0243
FISCHER, Gidion	30	Crumbach	63-1038
Doris 21			
FISCHER, Gottlieb	17	Nuerlelingen	66-1093
FISCHER, Gottlob	29	Reutlingen	63-0990
FISCHER, Heinr.	15	Marburg	63-0821
FISCHER, Heinr.	19	Scharmbeck	64-0427
FISCHER, Heinr.	65	Nordstemmen	64-1108
Engline 60, Dorette 26			
FISCHER, Heinrich	18	Eisenach	65-1030
FISCHER, Hermann H	30	Bremen	66-0412
Gesche Dorth 29, Georg 9m			
FISCHER, Hugo	21	Muenchen	64-1053
FISCHER, Jacob	19	Baiern	66-0469
FISCHER, Jacob	25	Oberfranken	66-0734
FISCHER, Joh.	28	York	64-0138
Frand.(f) 18, baby 6m			
FISCHER, Johann	27	Grafenberg	66-0576
FISCHER, Johann	24	New York	66-0679
FISCHER, Johann	22	Driespeck	67-0007
FISCHER, Johann	33	Tellen	66-1373
FISCHER, Johann	37	Trendelburg	65-1095
FISCHER, Johanna	24	Hessen	66-0734
Sophie 22			
FISCHER, Johanna	19	Muenden	64-0427
FISCHER, Johannes	25	Wenges	66-1093
FISCHER, Johannes	30	Marksuhl	64-0214
Anna B. 28			
FISCHER, John	29	Fellen	63-0244
FISCHER, Jos.	20	Rikken	66-1243
FISCHER, Joseph		Musonele	66-0984
FISCHER, Josepha	15	Steisslingen	64-0782
FISCHER, Jul.	26	Stuttgart	63-0482
FISCHER, Julie	25	Cincinnati	63-0953
Willy 11m			
FISCHER, Kunigunde	21	Unterfranken	66-0734
FISCHER, Ludwig	26	Baden	66-0679
FISCHER, Ludwig	22	Wuerttemberg	64-0687
FISCHER, Marg.	54	Lich	63-0551

NAME	AGE	RESIDENCE	YR-LIST
Sophie 16, Mary 14			
FISCHER, Marg.	54	Sich	64-0782
Sophie 17, Marie 15			
FISCHER, Margareth	19	Oberstetten	66-1155
FISCHER, Marie	23	Aurich	63-1178
FISCHER, Marie	45	Coburg	63-1038
Caspar 9			
FISCHER, Marie	22	Unterhausen	64-0639
Carl 2, Ernst 11m			
FISCHER, Marie	49	Schlessinghsn	65-1024
Louise 23, Friedrich 18, Caroline 15			
Heinrich 11			
FISCHER, Marie	24	Verden	65-0950
FISCHER, Martin	35	Grede	66-0837
Sophia 42, Lena 7, Jakob 5			
FISCHER, Meta	23	Scharmbeck	64-1053
FISCHER, Minna	24	Dielingen	65-1024
Louise 19			
FISCHER, Nicolaus	18	Siekenhofen	66-0679
FISCHER, Nicolaus	33	Weitesgruen	66-1327
Catharina 32, Johann 8			
FISCHER, Nicolaus	24	Altenbruch	66-1327
FISCHER, Otto	45	New York	63-0917
FISCHER, Otto	14	Greifenberg	65-0974
Paul 9			
FISCHER, Pierre	19	Trier	64-0938
FISCHER, Resi	26	Boehmen	66-0704
Bertha 23			
FISCHER, Samuel	35	Hamburg	66-0109
FISCHER, Sophie	16	Bohemia	64-0687
FISCHER, Sylvester	30	Buesslingen	65-1024
Judith 33, Anton 9m			
FISCHER, Th.	19	Visselhoerde	65-1024
FISCHER, W.	24	Wiesbaden	67-0795
Jenny 23			
FISCHER, Wilh'mine	21	Frantzberg	67-0599
FISCHER, Wilh'mine	38	Friedeburg	65-1031
FISCHER, Wilh'mne	42	Muenden	66-1373
FISCHER, Wm. Fr'dr	34	Pausa	64-0427
FISCHER, v. Andr.	29	Bremen	66-1248
FISCHL, Dora	19	Boehmen	66-0704
FISCHMANN, A.	31	Templin	66-0413
FISCHTER, Cath.	20	Gotha	66-1373
FISHER, John G.	29	Bahlingen	63-1136
John James 23, Christian 21, Anna M. 59			
FISKE, Daniel W.	26	Wien	63-0693
FISMER, Adolph	19	Minden	66-0934
FISSEL, Joh.	18	Mainz	65-1024
FITTSCHEN, J.C.	20	Selsingen	65-0402
FIX, Valentin	24	Kleestadt	66-0576
FLACH, Wilhelm	15	Zellerfeld	66-0704
FLACHMEIER, Wilh.	25	Flasmund	66-1128
FLACHS, Wilhelm	26	Spechback	66-0934
FLACHSBART, Heinr.	31	Gr. Munzel	63-0917
FLAD, Joseph	25	New York	66-0109
Sophie 25			
FLAGGE, J.H.	29	England	63-0953
FLAGMANN, Sophie	17	Dielingen	66-0704
FLAIG, Maria	26	Flotzingen	63-0006
Catharina 24			
FLAKE, Henry	43	New York	66-0679
FLAMM, Georg	28	Biedenkopf	65-0402
FLAMM, Georg	28	Biedenkopf	65-0402
FLANZ, Christiane	25	Fickenhausen	65-0151
FLASCHENRIEM, A.G.	27	Ravensburg	65-1088
FLATMANN, Frdr. W.	20	Bachholzhsn.	65-0950
FLAUDERMEYER, Fr.	26	Riemsloh	64-0593
FLECHSENHAAR, J.Fr	17	Zell	66-0704
Joh. Sim. 31			
FLECHSENHAR, Elisa	24	Zell	66-1327
FLECK, Julius	17	Bonitz	66-0837
FLECK, Michael	24	Zeilsheim	66-1327
FLECK, The. (m)	19	Jagstfeld	64-0363
FLECKE, John	32	Heimarshausen	63-0990
FLECKE, Maria	20	Waltershausen	64-0886
FLECKE, Marie	22	Heimirshausen	63-1136
FLECKENSTEIN, And.	27	Roedelsheim	66-1327
FLECKENSTEIN, Danl	29	Laufach	64-0363

NAME	AGE	RESIDENCE	YR-LIST
FLECKENSTEIN, Emil	20	Ellenbach	66-0650
Georg 18			
FLECKENSTEIN, Jul.	30	Baltimore	63-1136
FLECKENSTEIN, Thom	58	Kl.Blankenbch	63-0551
FLECKNER, Joh.	28	Auenhausen	66-1313
Helena 25, Joseph 9m			
FLEDDERMANN, Heinr	29	Essen	66-0221
Ida 18			
FLEIG, Alois	50	Heitersheim	65-0151
FLEIG, Emil	19	Grafenhaus	65-0007
FLEISCH, Regine	48	Raedelsheim	65-1088
Betti 22, Simon 21, Rosa 20, Rocha 18			
Nathan 19			
FLEISCHER, Wm. C.	26	Ulfa	64-0456
Caroline 26, Caroline 5, Wilhelm 2			
FLEISCHHAUER, Theo	42	Schnelt	64-0739
Wilhelmine 37, Caroline 17, Bernhard 15			
Emilie 13, Sophie Barb. 7, Elisabeth 5			
Augusta 2, Bertha 2m			
FLEISCHMANN, Anna	18	Nuernberg	64-1022
Cath. 7			
FLEISCHMANN, Bernh	20	Sonnenberg	66-1127
FLEISCHMANN, Clara	32	Fuerth	66-0734
FLEISCHMANN, Fanny	20	Mittelfranken	66-0679
FLEISCHMANN, Heinr	41	Nordhalben	64-0886
Maria 41, Heinr. 7, Elisabeth 5			
Johannes 4			
FLEISCHMANN, J.	22	Gunzendorf	63-0244
FLEISCHMANN, J.	35	Seibendorf	65-0007
FLEISCHMANN, Joh.	25	Gunzendorf	65-1024
FLEISCHMANN, Lebr.	38	Schweinsberg	64-0214
Johanna 35, John 20, Christ. 30			
FLEISCHMANN, Rosin	62	Offenbach	64-0992
FLEISCHMANN, Wilh.	28	Wallenheim	65-0116
FLEISCHNER, Sophie	20	Boehmen	63-0482
FLEISSNER, Margar.	26	Asch	66-0704
Johann 5			
FLEMING, Daniel	28	Rassitz	66-0413
Justine 20			
FLEMMING, J.	21	Raschitz	66-0413
Char. 19			
FLENTGE, Ludwig	42	Suisse	63-1010
FLESE, Heinrich	28	Osnabrueck	63-1069
FLESS, William	47	Frankfurt	63-0752
FLETRIG, Magd.	18	Hannover	64-0687
FLEURSHEIM, Bruno	16	Norden	64-0170
FLICK, Gottlieb	44	Rula	65-1030
FLIEGEL, Michael	36	Gr. Klonia	66-0469
Anna 29, Catharine 7, Anna 3, Martha 6m			
FLIEGEL, W.(m)	28	Kirchheim	64-0495
FLINKE, Conrad	40	Hotteln	66-0668
FLINTENFELD, David	20	Burgendorf	66-0679
FLITTNER, Anna M.	40	Erlenbach	67-0795
Eva 15, Val. 18, Andr. 21			
FLOCH, Maria	18	Wennings	64-0886
FLOCK, J.	41	Zischen	66-0413
Elisabeth 39, Katharine 17, Heinrich 14			
FLOEHR, Christoph	28	Marborssen	66-1093
FLOERKEN, F.	29	New York	63-0953
FLOERSCH, August	25	New York	63-1218
FLOERSCH, Joseph	38	Bloedesheim	66-0221
Wilhelm 9			
FLOERSHEIM, Henr't	20	Bottenberg	63-1085
FLOHN, Jac.	35	Heppenheim	64-0214
Phil. 39, Dorothea 32			
FLOHR, A. Wm.	35	Osnabrueck	64-0886
G.Eduard 15			
FLORECK, Carl	36	Liszkowke	66-0469
FLORENTZ, Victoria	30	Paris	63-0917
FLORIG, Christian	33	Flockenbach	64-1053
FLOTA, Amalie	20	Stuttgart	64-1206
FLOTEMESCH, Minna	14	Gehrde	66-1093
Elise 16			
FLOTO, August	35	Heinade	65-0243
George 18, Frdr. 23			
FLOTO, Heinr.	15	Cassel	65-0402
FLOTTMANN, Franz	22	Dissen	63-0917
FLOTTMANN, Heinr.	24	Bremen	66-1093

NAME	AGE	RESIDENCE	YR-LIST
FLUEGEL, Georg	55	Oberrieden	66-1327
Martha 23			
FLUEGEL, Marie El.	17	Kurhessen	66-0221
FLUEGERT, Charl.	18	Enshiem	64-0639
FLUEGGE, Sophie	27	Wustrone	66-1093
FLUEGGER, Herm.	18	Uhlenbrock	65-0402
FLUEGLER, Emil	15	Rothenfels	66-0704
FLUGHAUPT, Wilhelm	19	Kr.Salzwedel	67-0599
FLUHR, Christ.	20	Mainz	66-0109
FLUHR, Oswald	32	Cincinnati	66-0109
Margarethe 24, Johanna 11m			
FOCH, Juliane	16	Cassel	65-0402
FOCHE, Johanna	41	Middelsbach	64-0782
FOCHHEIMER, S.	23	New York	63-0752
FOCHHEIMER, Sigmnd	16	Mittwitz	64-0886
FOCKE, C.	37	Preussen	63-1003
FOCKE, Christian	17	Muenden	65-0950
Wilhelmine 17			
FOCKE, Eberhard	29	Bremen	63-0015
FOCKELE, F.(m)	21	Westfalen	64-0495
FOCKEN, Gerd	29	Muehlendorf	66-0668
Mantje 26, baby (f) 11m			
FOCKEN, Gesine	19	Dersum	66-0623
FOCKEN, Menno	26	Simonswolde	65-0151
FOCKENGA, Rixte	20	Aurich	66-0668
FOCKLELA, Heinr.	19	Bochum	66-0984
FOEBE, Friedr.	21	Volkmarshsn.	66-1243
FOECKE, Wilhelmine	34	Norden	66-0147
Meta 4			
FOECKEL, Heinr.	30	Langenheim	65-0189
FOECKEL, Ludwig	15	Schlotheim	65-1030
Wilhelm 18			
FOEDEL, Heinrich	25	Cloppenburg	65-0770
Hanne 30, Marie Cath. 9m			
FOEDER, Anna	40	Cloppenburg	65-0770
FOEGE, Wilh.	22	Steinau	65-1088
FOEHR, Ernst	30	Stuttgart	63-0168
FOELIX, John	23	Ndr.Saulheim	63-1178
FOELKE, Heinrich	35	Brueggen	66-0934
FOELKENING, Carl	58	St. Louis	66-0734
Carl 9			
FOELL, Barbara	21	Gomaringen	66-0679
FOELL, Caroline	20	Sulzball	65-0007
FOELSCH, Ludw.	25	Hannover	64-0432
FOELSKY, Paul	36	Soessnowd	66-0469
Elisabeth 33, Eva Rosine 8, Carl August 4			
Caroline 9m			
FOERDEN, Engel	27	Osnabrueck	67-0600
FOERDERER, Eduard	23	Frankenhausen	63-0482
Augusta 27, Robert 2, Ida 1			
FOERG, Anna	23	Wending	66-1203
FOERLING, C.	19	Vechta	65-1024
Josephine 17			
FOERNOFF, Peter	31	Cincinati	66-0147
FOERST, Herm.	26	Rawig/Pr.	64-0920
Hirsch 18			
FOERSTER, Carl	21	Baden	66-0679
FOERSTER, Cathrine	24	Hafenprepach	66-0623
FOERSTER, Friedr.	17	Grosslobigau	66-0934
FOERSTERMANN, Henr	20	Luethorst	66-0221
FOERSTIGE, Wilhelm	21	Brilon	65-0055
Otto 18			
FOESEL, Johann	24	Unt.Rochwiehh	66-1203
Catharina 48			
FOHR, Francis	24	Mannheim	63-0097
FOHT, Cathre.	24	Mitt.Eschenbh	63-0917
FOISTER, Ludwig	38	Dermbach	66-0679
FOKEROTT, Ferd.	52	Bleichrode	66-1243
Aug. 17			
FOKKEN, Herbert	47	Brinkum	66-1031
FOLDERTS, Ed.	28	Aurich	65-0402
FOLGER, Adolph	36	Berlin	64-0593
FOLKE, Henry	27	Blomberg	66-0109
FOLKERS, Diedrich	28	Wittmund	66-0576
FOLKERS, Sent.	26	Emden	65-1095
FOLKERS, Wilhelm	46	Oldenburg	66-0469
FOLKERTS, Renke	26	Oldendorf	66-1128
FOLL, Carl L.	19	Schulzbach	66-1243

NAME	AGE	RESIDENCE	YR-LIST
Gustava 19			
FOLLINGER, Franz	29	Asch	66-0679
Christiane 23, Simon 3			
FORDEN, Edw.	25	Ritzen	64-0023
FORDERER, Eduard	34	Frankenhausen	64-0363
FORDHMANN, Fr'drke	27	Bielefeld	66-1031
FORELLUN, Cat.	41	Mensingen	63-1085
Johannette 60, Henriette 27, Michael 51			
FORLING, H.(m)	27	Fohrling	64-0331
FORMAN, Fritz	25	Rosenfeld	66-0984
FORMANEK, Johann	40	Zdaslon	66-1131
FORSTER, Friedrich	22	Feldkirchen	63-1069
Xaver 27			
FORSTMANN, Franz	19	Rietberg	64-0687
FORTLAGE, Heinrich	21	Brockhausen	66-0668
FORTMANN, Joh.Fr'd	16	Crohne	64-0886
FORTMEIER, Wm.	19	Schlienworth	64-0593
FORTMUELLER, Lina	17	Muenden	63-0821
FOSS, Adolph	28	Ohrentrup	65-0402
FOSS, Fritz	26	Herford	66-0734
Dorothea 25, Mathilde 10m			
FOSSELMANN, Peter	25	Iggelheim	64-0023
FOSTER, Caroline	24	Switz	66-0679
Lina 3			
FOSTER, Hironimus	27	Sacharfenheim	66-0346
FOSZ, Ignatz	17	Otterswer	63-0693
FOULD, Fanny	26	Wullmars	64-0938
FOURIER, Aug.	34	France	64-0170
FOURIER, Henry	21	Zedel	63-1038
FRACK, Hermann	23	Fuerth	66-0679
FRAEDRICH, A. Ferd	28	Prillwitz	63-0296
Wilhelmine 24, Emma 2			
FRAENKEL, Nathan	24	Fuerth	63-1038
FRAENKING, Wm.	24	Hannover	63-1218
FRAENKLE, Elizab.	22	Schrotenthal	64-0023
FRAENKLE, Georg	25	Muenchweiler	66-0147
FRAENZEL, Ernst	27	Hamburg	63-0822
FRAGE, Conradine	28	Bremen	64-0739
Carl 6			
FRAKEN, Friedr. J.	38	Moorweg	64-0938
FRAME, Christ.	17	Libinthal	64-0992
FRANCIONY, Franz	49	Preussen	64-0214
Therese 22, Franz 18, Susanne 16			
FRANCIS, Jean	47	France	63-1038
FRANCK, James	16	Zwickau	63-0482
FRANCK, Johann	33	Mayen	66-0837
FRANCOIS, Jan	28	Rouen	65-0004
FRANDT, Herm.	28	Magdeburg	65-0594
Anton 2, Eleonore 7			
FRANK, Anton	25	Oberwalluft	66-1373
FRANK, Carl	20	Oberbahnstein	66-0109
FRANK, Carl	15	Laubach	65-0151
FRANK, Dorothea	30	Hannover	66-1327
Sophie 8, Margarethe 6, Louise 2			
FRANK, Elisabeth	31	Altmersleben	66-0623
FRANK, Friedrich	48	Wandersleben	65-0713
Barbara 55, johanna 23			
FRANK, G.A.	32	Falkenstein	63-1003
FRANK, Georg	21	Laubach	64-0138
FRANK, H.	24	Wien	64-0782
FRANK, Heinr.	23	Ahornberg	66-1327
FRANK, Hermann	26	Hagenow	66-0668
Marie 28, baby (f) 11m, Albert 3			
FRANK, Hermine	23	Neustadt	64-0687
FRANK, Isaac	32	Philadelphia	63-0551
FRANK, Jacob	20	Gervighofen	66-0704
FRANK, Jacob	30	Hildesheim	66-0934
FRANK, Jacob	35	Esslingen	66-1327
Christine 30, Carl 3, Sophie 9m			
FRANK, Jeannette	58	Burgkundstadt	64-0840
FRANK, Joachim	25	Oberwallet	66-1373
FRANK, Johanna	25	Conitz	63-1085
FRANK, John	24	Salzfeld	63-1136
FRANK, Louis	35	New York	64-0073
FRANK, Louis	30	United States	66-0679
FRANK, M.	19	Schwaabhausen	65-0974
FRANK, M.(m)	23	Wiseck	64-0495
FRANK, Marg. Magd.	29	Straas	64-0938
FRANK, Marie	24	Luxenburg	64-0495
FRANK, Mathias	27	Laubach	65-1088
Caroline 24			
FRANK, Michael	39	St. Gotthard	66-1155
FRANK, Nanny	26	Steinach	66-1248
FRANK, Rebecca	20	Schoenbach	65-0594
FRANK, Riet.	31	Gleidringen	66-1203
Hermine 18, (f) bob			
FRANK, Roeschen	45	Grossendorf	66-0734
Bertha 9, Emma 6, Henriette 4			
FRANK, Rosa	20	Fuerth	63-0953
FRANK, Samuel	24	Armenau	64-0687
FRANK, Schoenchen	37	Grossendorf	66-0734
FRANK, Theod.	31	Dransfeld	65-0898
FRANK, Theodor	26	Marienwerder	66-1373
FRANK, Theresia	22	Syke	66-0734
FRANKE, Aug.	28	Bremen	65-0189
FRANKE, Carl	35	Boehmen	66-0349
Barbara 55			
FRANKE, E.	15	Nuremberg	65-1024
FRANKE, Elise	24	New York	66-0934
FRANKE, J.	42	Luebbecke	64-1161
Hermann 18			
FRANKE, James	17	Wien	63-0917
FRANKE, Joh. G.	26	Wersen	64-0886
FRANKE, Louis	24	New York	64-0593
FRANKE, Louise Chr	20	Ob.Bauernschf	65-0898
FRANKE, M.	21	Steinach	63-1218
Caroline 18			
FRANKE, Marie	18	Weissensee	63-1178
Johanna 8			
FRANKE, Otto	22	Spiesinghol	66-1127
FRANKE, Philipp	42	Schwiesheim	64-1053
Charlotte 38, Adolph 7, Heinr. 4, baby 6m			
Magdalena 2, Wm. 12			
FRANKEL, N.	18	Eperies	65-0402
FRANKEN, Fr.	40	Niederbruch	66-0984
FRANKENBERG, Joh.	36	Rheda	64-0938
Clara 7, Wilhelmine 5, Ferdinand 6m			
FRANKENBERG, v. F.	18	Goettingen	63-0752
FRANKENBERGER, Dor	16	Culmbach	64-0886
FRANKENSTEIN, Adel	19	Neheim	66-1127
FRANKENSTEIN, Jac.	48	Neustadt	63-1136
Louis 21, Barbara 19			
FRANKENTHAL, Moriz	35	New York	63-0693
Carrie 26			
FRANKFURTER, Margr	29	Culmbach	66-0837
Margretha 4			
FRANKHAUR, Christ.	22	Thurn	67-0007
FRANKLE, Philipp	16	Wien	64-0214
FRANTZ, Christ.	25	Hohenfeld	63-0296
FRANTZ, Doroth.	25	Drahteren	63-0752
FRANTZ, Marg.	25	Duerkheim	63-0244
FRANTZEN, Hermann	21	Esens	66-0668
FRANZ, B.	19	Giessen	64-1161
FRANZ, Carl	42	Mittelbenbach	66-1327
Margarethe 39, Margarethe 8, Carl 6			
Elisabeth 4, Jacob 1			
FRANZ, Emilie	7	Solingen	64-1022
FRANZ, Johann	24	Hohebach	64-0938
FRANZ, John	25	Langgens	66-1327
FRANZ, Julius	25	Zeulenroda	66-1155
FRANZ, Magdalene	19	Hohenberg	66-1373
FRANZ, Marie	30	Oberhausen	66-1327
FRANZ, Martin	33	Unterleina	66-0704
FRANZ, Pauline	7	Frickenhausen	64-0427
FRANZ, Peter	30	Bermuthshaus	66-0679
Margarethe 26, Sibilla 4, Margaretha 12			
FRANZ, Regine	28	Darmroh	64-0456
FRANZ, Wilhelm	34	Ottenhagen	66-0578
Wilhelmine 34, Carl 3, Ernestine 2			
FRANZEN, Anna	30	New York	63-1085
Mathilde 1, Wilhelmine 52			
FRANZIG, S.	46	Lissa	66-0704
FRASCH, maria	17	Moehringen	64-1108
FRATZSCHER, Gustav	24	Weimar	65-0243
FRAUCKE, Catharine	23	Wuellen	66-0837
FRAUENBERGER, A.	26	Romhild	65-0974

NAME	AGE	RESIDENCE	YR-LIST
FRAUENDIENST, Hr.	46	Boernecke	65-0007
FRAUENPREISS, Gott	28	Feuerbach	63-0693
FRAUERNICHT, Joh'a	48	Magdeburg	64-0938
Anna 18, Augusta 16			
FRAUKE, Emma	24	Hannover	66-0934
FRAUKE, Ernst	24	Germany	66-0666
Anna 46, Heinrich 20, Hanne 14			
Caroline 42, Friedrich 14			
FREBING, Carl W.	22	Wannfried	64-0886
FRECHIE, Herman	36	London	64-0593
FRECKER, Adam	47	Hainhausen	63-0244
FRECKMANN, Anna	22	Desinghausen	63-1178
FREDE, P.	20	Hannover	66-0413
W. 18			
FREDE, Sophie	22	Rhoda	65-1031
FREDECKER, Henry	29	Lackheim	66-0221
Engel 17			
FREDER, Lena	18	Odenheim	63-1218
FREDERKING, J.F(m)	61	Hartum	64-0331
FREDERRIKSEN, Hans	27	Copenhagen	66-0666
Anna Maria 36, Sophia 7, Kund. 4			
FREEHAUF, Wilh.	63	Canada	63-1136
FREES, Henry	22	Esebeck	66-0109
FREES, Johanna	19	Wenzel	65-1030
FREESE, Herm.	27	Harpstadt	63-0953
FREESE, M.	28	Oldenburg	65-0974
FREESEMANN, Johann	33	Benningsfehn	64-0639
Hobbert 6, Johann 4			
FREESEN, Wilh'mine	20	Versmold	65-0974
FREHE, Lina	19	Peine	64-0886
FREHKLAU, Elisab.	24	Steinheim	64-0687
FREI, Franz Jos.	34	Weisbach/Bad.	65-0038
FREIBERG, Joseph	33	Walze	66-0679
FREIBERGER, Johann	20	Oelbronn	66-1203
FREIBISIUS, Martin	35	Oldenburg	66-0469
FREIBURG, Johanna	19	Allensdorf	66-0349
FREIBURG, Joseph	26	Allendorf	66-0704
Elisabeth 27			
FREIER, Carl	31	Werbelin	65-0402
FREIER, Ida	18	Altenburg	66-0984
FREIHAUF, Eva Dor.	18	Meiningen	63-0614
FREIMUTH, Louis	36	St. Louis	66-0984
FREIMUTH, W.	32	Minden	65-0950
FREISE, Jac. A.	35	Saalfeld	64-0214
FREISE, Wilh.	52	Kohlfeld	66-1243
Friederike 44, Conrad 6			
FREITAG, (f)	64	Hamburg	63-0862
FREITAG, August	26	Goestrup	63-0482
Simon 24, Fritz 23			
FREITAG, Joh. Marg	24	Bremen	63-0953
FREITAG, Leopold	22	Baiersdorf	64-0687
FREITAG, Wilhelm	18	Eisenach	63-0482
FREITAG, Wilhelm	28	Minden	66-1093
FREMONT, Lippert	30	Wien	66-0221
FREMYET, Eugenie	20	Paris	63-0917
FRENCK, Lina	16	Hungen	63-0350
FRENDENHAMM, Mesal	36	Hannover	64-1022
Ida 7, Blackin 5, Agnes 4, Martha 3			
Alfred 2, Rudolph 1			
FRERICHS, C.	35	Bremen	63-0097
FRERICHS, Friedr.	31	Bremen	63-0482
Caroline 23			
FRERICHS, Gerhard	24	Epe	65-0948
FRERICHS, Jac.	58	Rahde	64-0495
Ma. 47			
FRERICHS, Joh. Ed.	29	Sandel	65-0948
FRERICHS, Mr.	40	New Orleans	64-0170
Mrs. 30			
FRERICHS, Wilh'mne	22	Aurich	65-0402
FRERKS, Johann H.	29	Dupen	66-0623
FRESCHLE, Wilh'mne	17	Dinkedorf	66-0346
FRESE, Carl	62	Herford	64-0456
FRESE, Chr. H.	30	Bremen	63-0551
Anna 9, Louise 8			
FRESE, Heinr.	25	Hannover	64-0432
Engel 18			
FRESE, J.	21	Bremen	64-0427
FRESE, Julie	18	Bremen	64-0938
FRESE, Sophie	20	Haudorf	66-0934
FRESE, Weert	33	Rhaudermohr	64-0739
Hankeline 46, Lina 13, Friedrich 10			
Carl 7, Joseph 5			
FRESENIUS, Carl	17	Hartershausen	64-0023
FRESSNACK, Joh.	31	Sedlitz	64-0170
Cath. 27, Cath. 3			
FRETHOLD, Herm.	24	Osnabrueck	66-1127
FRETTER, Johanna	20	Lehe	66-1127
FREUDENBERG, Albrt	24	Rapperswil	67-0007
FREUDENBERG, De(f)	17	Lemke	64-0992
FREUDENBERG, Emily	22	Osten	63-1069
FREUDENBERG, H.	27	Rohrsen	66-0704
Fran. 20			
FREUDENHAMMER, Cnr	30	Hannover	64-0427
FREUDENSTEIN, Wilh	28	Cassel	65-0865
FREUDENTAL, Lorenz	22	Schleida	66-1313
FREUER, Gebh.	34	Rieden	65-0007
FREUND, Adolph	24	Marienwerder	66-0623
FREUND, Anna	7	Prag	66-1203
Jacob 5, Fritz 4, Moritz 2, Louise 30			
FREUND, Anton	36	Podebrad	66-1131
Franz 3			
FREUND, Aug.	17	Muenchen	64-0886
Sigmund 7			
FREUND, Cathre.	35	New York	63-0990
Cathre. 6m			
FREUND, Christian	23	Sachsenfloor	66-0346
Barbara 17, Georg 15, Adam 66			
FREUND, Daniel	34	Furth	67-0007
FREUND, Dorothea	19	Lengsfeld	64-1022
FREUND, Elise	14	Frankfurt	65-1024
FREUND, Friedrich	16	Bretten	66-0576
FREUND, Georg	17	Frankfurt	63-0752
FREUND, Herz	50	Grobenau	65-1088
FREUND, Julius	16	Augusta	66-1131
FREUND, Ludwig	26	Rockershausen	65-0189
FREUND, Rosalia	30	Loebau	66-1203
Jacob 3			
FREUNDT, Aug.	19	Seilauf	64-0331
FREUNDT, Ludwig	55	Lemke	66-1327
Marie 55			
FREVERT, Fr.	22	Asmussen	65-1088
August 29, Carl 25			
FREY, Adam	26	Schwarzenberg	66-1327
FREY, Andreas	18	Freisia	65-1024
Dorothea 9			
FREY, Anna B.	17	Geselbach	64-0073
FREY, Caroline	28	Schwarzenberg	66-0147
Andreas 9			
FREY, Caroline	28	Scbloth	66-0679
FREY, Caspar	17	Naila	66-1131
Conrad 15			
FREY, Catharine	35	Hollwangen	66-0147
Johann Georg 60, Christian 48			
FREY, Charles	18	Altensteich	63-1178
FREY, Christian	18	Hallwangen	66-0147
FREY, Christina	25	Baden	66-0704
FREY, David	36	Unterunsbach	64-0639
FREY, Diedr.	19	Ihlienworth	64-0427
FREY, Elisabeth	35	Hunenbach	66-0147
Sibilla 13			
FREY, Francis	41	Indianapolis	63-1178
FREY, Friederike	27	Groembach	64-0427
FREY, Friedrich	17	Hutzenbach	66-0147
Gottlieb 17, Andreas 19			
FREY, Heinrich	32	Darmstadt	65-0950
FREY, J.G.	38	Delmenhorst	63-0013
FREY, Jacob	42	Wisconsin	66-0734
FREY, Jacob	24	Groembach	66-0984
Mathilde 29, Wilhelmine 6			
FREY, Jacobine	28	Wuestenrod	66-0576
FREY, Johann	16	Hutzenbach	66-0147
Gottfried 23, Friederike 19			
FREY, Johann	18	Niclashafen	66-1327
FREY, Johann Georg	27	Groeppingen	66-1127
FREY, John	25	Hesselbach	63-0296
Christine 20			

NAME	AGE	RESIDENCE	YR-LIST
FREY, Marie	25	Kettelfingen	64-0170
Magd. 20			
FREY, Rosine	10	Darmstadt	66-1155
FREY, Sophie	22	Grosseichholz	66-0704
FREYE, Anna	31	Ostbevern	66-1327
FREYER, Robert	26	Meissen	63-0862
FREYMANN, Pauline	17	Buchau	64-0782
FREYMUTH, Alfred	21	Muenster	64-0639
FREYMUTH, Wilhelm	21	Emden	66-0837
FREYTAG, Amanda	20	Henbach	65-0151
FREYTAG, Carl F.	22	Ronneburg	65-0770
FREYTAG, Christ.	40	Annaberg	66-0577
Caroline 32, Bertha 10, Augusta 6			
FREYTAG, Ferd.	40	Trier	64-0840
Gertrude 46, Caroline 20			
FRIA, Carl	27	St Nicolai	64-0593
Josepha 28, Aloisia 11m			
FRICK, Adam	18	Aach	65-0402
FRICK, Anna	21	Lombach	65-0402
Georg 9m			
FRICK, Eduard	21	Gemmingen	65-0402
FRICKE, August	26	New York	63-0006
FRICKE, Carl	25	Ost Bovern	64-0073
FRICKE, Clara	29	Osnabrueck	65-0865
FRICKE, D.	54	Braunschweig	65-1088
FRICKE, Ernst	34	Platendorf	64-0904
Sophie 34, Ernst 15, Heinrich 9, Sophie 4			
Friedrich 2, Caroline 9m			
FRICKE, Fr.	20	Braunschweig	66-0109
FRICKE, Fr.	54	Eschenhausen	66-0934
Caroline 48, August 9, Caroline 6			
FRICKE, Friedrich	29	Riebau	63-0614
Dorothea 20			
FRICKE, Heinr.	48	Wolsdorf	65-0243
Marie 42, Andreas 11			
FRICKE, Heinrich	23	Steinbrink	66-0934
Catharine 16			
FRICKE, Henrich	29	Hehlen	66-0984
Louis 30, Henrich 3, Anna 3m			
FRICKE, Henry W.	59	Westbarthsn.	63-0917
FRICKE, Julius	58	Koenigslutter	64-0363
Louise 22			
FRICKE, Ludw.	29	Leiberdingen	65-0243
Anton 2, Eleonore 7			
FRICKE, Wilhelm	26	Lahde	65-0948
FRICKE, Wm.	20	Westrup	64-0782
FRICKENHAUS, Ernst	18	Elberfeld	66-1313
FRICKENSTEIN, Els.	23	Bielefeld	66-1093
FRIE, Anna	21	Langfoerden	66-1031
FRIEBEL, Gustav	25	Engeleben	64-1053
FRIED, Betty	20	Muessenheim	64-0214
FRIED, Caroline	25	Cassel	63-0821
FRIED, Ign.	24	Hunsdorf	63-0862
FRIED, Rosa	43	Karolinenberg	66-1127
Marie 9, Louise 7, Ignatz 5			
FRIEDBERGER, Berta	17	Laupheim	63-0953
Fanny 14			
FRIEDBERGER, Soph.	22	New York	64-0593
FRIEDE, Hugo	22	Gotha	66-0679
FRIEDE, Otto	20	Gotha	64-0886
FRIEDEBORNK, Albtn	22	Muenden	66-1093
FRIEDEL, Johann	29	Wunsiedel	64-0938
FRIEDEL, Leopldine	23	Wien	65-0055
Joseph 1			
FRIEDEL, Peter	35	Baltimore	63-0551
Edw. 11			
FRIEDEMANN, Christ	19	Brakenheim	65-0116
FRIEDERICH, Ernst	24	Altenburg	66-1203
FRIEDERICHS, Marie	24	Nutlar	66-0704
FRIEDHOFF, Wilhelm	23	Brinkum	66-0679
FRIEDLAENDER. S.	28	Kampen	65-0974
FRIEDLANDER, Isid.	20	Berlin	65-0038
Regine 50			
FRIEDLANDER, M.(m)	28	Pechynendorf	64-0495
Jul.(m) 28			
FRIEDLEIN, Johann	28	Nuernberg	66-0679
FRIEDLHUBER, J.(m)	33	Pothal	64-0170
FRIEDMANN, Amalie	22	Heinrichs	66-0934
FRIEDMANN, Bernh.	28	Wien	64-0427
FRIEDMANN, Jac.	18	Nuremberg	65-1024
FRIEDMANN, Johanna	22	Aschenhausen	66-0934
FRIEDMANN, Julius	19	Wien	65-0243
FRIEDMANN, Lazar	17	Trzutschau	66-0083
FRIEDMANN, M.	36	Newark	63-0953
FRIEDMANN, Minna	25	Waldorf	64-0938
FRIEDMANN, Sam.	25	Baltimore	63-0168
FRIEDMANN, W.	19	Pesth	64-0782
FRIEDOFF, Dorothea	24	Fartingen	65-1088
FRIEDRICH, Andreas	40	Boehmen	63-0917
Margaretha 49			
FRIEDRICH, Anna C.	17	Elvenhausen	67-0599
FRIEDRICH, Christ.	20	Else	66-1248
FRIEDRICH, Conr.	24	Freinsheim	65-0007
FRIEDRICH, Elisab.	28	Zella	67-0992
FRIEDRICH, Heinr.	31	Loebenstein	66-0734
Caroline 32, Anna 7, Carl 5, Heinrich 2			
Caroline 3m			
FRIEDRICH, Hermann	23	Leitz	66-0679
FRIEDRICH, Johanna	35	Germersreuth	66-1128
FRIEDRICH, Joseph	36	Riede	65-0189
FRIEDRICH, Julius	27	Glauchau	65-0770
FRIEDRICHS, (m)	22	Goettingen	63-1218
FRIEDRICHS, (m)	26	Friedland	65-0974
Anna 18			
FRIEDRICHS, Cath.	26	Bagband	65-0402
FRIEDRICHS, E.W.	22	Bagband	64-0363
FRIEDRICHS, F.W.	31	Aurich	66-0413
FRIEDRICHS, Friedr	29	Hannover	66-0577
FRIEDRICHS, Hugo	18	Gotha	64-0593
FRIEDRICHS, Joseph	13	Meschede	66-1093
FRIEDRICHSEN, Chr.	21	Kiel	64-1206
FRIEDRITZ, Bertha	29	Crimmitzschau	66-1373
FRIEGE, Clemens	18	Ludholz	64-0687
FRIEGELHOFF, Magd.	16	Kischbach	67-0007
FRIEMANN, Henry	40	Hestrup	66-0734
Anna 22, Henrike 19, Gerd 15			
FRIES, Carl	26	Desloch	65-0402
FRIES, Louis	24	Germany	63-1136
FRIES, Valentin	58	Coeln	66-0668
Caroline 54, Fritz 16			
FRIES, Wilhelm	18	Sommerkaal	66-0346
Johann 25			
FRIESS, Heinr.	32	Umstadt	65-0189
Elisabeth 24			
FRIESS, Malvine	21	Meerholz	64-0938
FRIESS, Margarethe	30	Beuren	66-1203
FRIESS, Martin	22	Doerndorff	63-0693
FRIEST, Niels P	26	Aarhuus	66-0666
FRILLING, Joseph	26	Steinfeld	65-0948
FRIMPIN, Alois	22	Petein	65-0151
FRINDIS, Cath.	19	Salzfeld	64-0886
FRINER, Jos.	18	Chluma	66-1243
FRISCH, Anton	24	Nowingen	66-1203
FRISCH, Emil	31	Aalborg	63-0953
FRISCH, Moritz	26	Dresden	66-1248
Anna 23, Gustav 1			
FRISCHE, J.	28	Bremen	63-1178
FRISCHE, Joseph	18	Neustadt	66-0109
FRISCHEMAYER, Fr.	51	Sudhagen	63-1038
Dina 19, Franz 16, Chrst. 14, Therese 11			
FRISCHEN, Friedr.	21	Bremen	66-0576
FRISCHHOLZ, Conrad	30	Rothendorf	66-0837
Katharina 28			
FRISCHMANN, Sigm.	22	Westphalen	63-1136
FRISSE, Cath.	45	New York	63-0551
FRISSEN, C.(m)	50	Mundenheim	64-0495
FRITA, Joseph	41	Niederhadamar	63-0398
Anna 46, Georg 9, Anna 8			
FRITSCH, Ferd.	16	Bregenz	63-1085
FRITSCH, H.	26	Arnstadt	65-0007
FRITSCH, Louis	22	Wundersleben	64-0593
FRITSCH, Martin	33	Aixheim	67-0007
FRITSCHE, Agnes	33	Dresden	63-0821
FRITSCHE, Amalie	26	Neustadt	65-0402
Franz 5, Martin 4			
FRITSCHE, Fr.(m)	29	Neustadt	64-0331

NAME	AGE	RESIDENCE	YR-LIST
FRITSCHE, Thekla	24	Grossenstein	64-0885
Clara 3m			
FRITSCHLE, Robert	27	Gera	66-1203
FRITZ, Adam	17	Obermoerle	64-1108
FRITZ, Caroline	22	Lindorf	66-1155
FRITZ, Catharina	20	Eppenstein	67-0007
FRITZ, Catharine	34	Lindorf	66-0147
FRITZ, Chr. Fr.	25	Sebenhausen	64-0073
FRITZ, Daniel	29	Hoeslinswarth	65-0007
FRITZ, David	48	Preussen	63-0990
Johanna 3, Christian 18, Ferdinand 15			
Louise 12, Marie 9, Hermann 7, Martha 3			
FRITZ, Emanuel	47	Poppenweiler	64-1108
FRITZ, Gottfried	22	Chur	64-0639
FRITZ, Jacob	23	Chemnitz	64-0639
FRITZ, Jacobine	19	Sulzfeld	64-0214
FRITZ, Marie	18	Giessen	66-0984
FRITZ, Nicol.	29	Ohio	64-0170
FRITZ, Philipp	20	Baestheim/Hes	65-0038
FRITZ, Richard	21	Wien	65-0402
FRITZ, Theresia	21	Messkirch	64-0593
FRITZ, Wm. Gottfr.	23	Kronau	65-0243
FRITZE, Clara	18	Bremen	64-0427
FRITZEL, L.(m)	25	Eschau	64-0331
FRITZGES, Georg	23	Petzenrod	65-0116
FRITZGES, Theodor	21	Goetzen	64-0840
FRITZSCH, William	36	Kiefenwald	63-0097
FRIZZI, Jean	48	New York	63-1136
FROBENSEN, John	28	New York	63-0990
FROBIETER, Marie	23	Harpenfeld	66-0221
FROCHTENICHT, Casp	37	Bremen	66-0984
FROEBER, Joseph	30	Netzthal	63-0482
Therese 30, Joseph 3			
FROEHLE, Gottfried	30	Bakum	63-0006
FROEHLICH, Eduard	38	Trampke	63-0990
FROEHLICH, Gottlob	20	Eberstadt	65-0055
FROEHLICH, Ignatz	19	Megyaszo	66-0679
FROEHLICH, Johann	45	Raboldhausen	66-0349
Anna 49, Adam 14, Christine 9, Heinrich 7			
Joh.Heinr. 3, Barbara 10m			
FROEHLICH, Johanna	43	Lobenstein	66-1313
FROEHLICH, Therese	26	Kirchhasel	66-0221
FROEHLICH, Wilhelm	17	Boehmen	66-0623
FROEHLIG, C.(m)	31	Eberstadt	64-0495
F.(m) 16			
FROEHLKE, Joseph	26	Slavensin	66-0469
FROELIG. Conrad	50	Halle	66-1093
FROENALE, Joseph	39	St. Louis	66-0984
Louise 36, Lina 10, Minna 9, Rudolph 6			
Theodor 4, Hugo 9m			
FROHBART, F.	25	Barsinghausen	63-0953
FROHBOESE, H.	27	Buerde	64-0782
W. 16			
FROHMUELLER, Rudo.	18	Tauberbischof	65-0004
FROHNHAEUSER, Aug.	24	Biedenkopf	64-0687
FROHRICH, Sophie	30	Wersabe	64-1108
baby 9m			
FROMM, Johannes	26	Bermersheim	66-0147
FROMM, Louis	37	Bassern	66-0577
FROMM, V.	43	Heitern	66-0413
Marie 38			
FROMME, Sophie	24	Hessia	66-0679
FROMMER, Catharine	28	Solingen	66-1131
FROMMER, Chrs. G.	21	Neuenburg	63-0953
FROMMER, S.(f)	21	Gessnitz	64-0495
FROMUTH, Christina	9	Laengsfeld	66-0734
FROSCH, Agnes	35	Philadelphia	66-0984
FROST, Carl	27	Hannover	66-1131
FROTHA, v. Claus W	23	Gaensefurth	63-0350
FROTTNER, Hermann	20	Worms	66-0679
FRUEHAUF, Levy	55	Eisenach	64-0331
Johanna 21			
FRUEHE, Theodor	34	Schmolnik	66-0668
Augusta 26, Hermann 3			
FRUEHLING, G.(m)	25	New York	64-0331
FRUEHSTUECK, Georg	26	Gilgelsdorf	66-0346
FRUEND, Eleonore	24	Lintorf	64-0170
FRUNKE, W.(m)	30	New York	64-0023

NAME	AGE	RESIDENCE	YR-LIST
FUCHINS, Emma	8m	Magdeburg	65-0594
FUCHMAN, Margareth	16	Hof	65-1095
FUCHS, Appolonia	50	Germersheim	65-1088
FUCHS, Carl	34	Leipzig	65-1088
FUCHS, Caroline	36	Wachtersbach	65-0974
FUCHS, Cathre.	23	Mowangen	63-0990
Margarethe 21			
FUCHS, Daniel	58	Orbis	66-0083
Dorothea 56, Johannes 12			
FUCHS, E.	19	Coburg	65-0007
FUCHS, F.(m)	31	St. Louis	64-0495
FUCHS, Franz	25	Graz	66-1155
FUCHS, Friedrike	22	Krumbach	65-0243
FUCHS, Gustav	28	Berlin	66-0469
FUCHS, Heinr.	26	Meyenborg	64-0427
Ad. 26, baby 3m			
FUCHS, Heinrich	16	Darmstadt	66-1031
FUCHS, Herm.	25	Burgkunstadt	64-0427
FUCHS, Hugo	44	New York	63-0350
FUCHS, Jacob	44	Pieningen	65-0594
FUCHS, Jacob	53	Germersheim	65-1088
FUCHS, Josepha	19	Waldurn	66-1203
FUCHS, Lina	27	Montingen	63-0990
FUCHS, Lina	28	Altenkessel	67-0007
FUCHS, Ludwig	29	Prag	63-0482
FUCHS, Marg.	19	Neuwied	64-1022
FUCHS, Maria	27	Fitzendorf	66-0837
Anton 5			
FUCHS, Marie	28	Sellirod	64-0782
FUCHS, Marie	24	Hannover	66-1031
FUCHS, Mich.	22	Beiengreis	63-0015
Elisabeth 33			
FUCHS, Michel	32	New York	63-1136
FUCHS, Pauline	23	Eisenach	66-0650
FUCHS, Philipp	29	Orbis	66-0083
Catharine 29			
FUCHS, Sophie	22	Pforzheim/Pr	64-1053
FUCHS, Therese	23	Wolfenshausen	65-0007
FUCHS, W.	21	Krumbach	66-0413
FUCHS, Wilhelm	18	Lueneburg	67-0954
FUCHS, Wilhelmine	25	Sachsen-Mein.	66-0623
FUCHS, Wm.	29	Lauterbach	64-1161
Cahtarine 25			
FUCHT, Abraham	23	Wilnow	66-0576
FUCHTER, Johann	19	Groeplingen	66-0984
FUCKENBERG, Marg.	25	Werda	65-0151
FUDE, Michael	30	Soessnowd	66-0469
Henriette 31, Carl 6, Louise 3, Anna 9m			
FUEFTEL, Mathilde	15	Redighausen	66-1031
FUEHR, Heinrich	27	Aufkirchen	66-0734
FUEHRER, Georg	27	Grewenau	66-0578
FUEHRER, Johs.	21	Herlau	64-0495
FUEHRING, Frz. W.	19	Gesmold	64-0840
FUEHRNAU, Carl	22	Hannover	66-1313
FUELLE, Aug.	43	Bremen	66-1243
FUELLING, Carl	38	Berlin	66-1093
Minna 33, Wilhelm 4, Paul 3			
FUELLING, H.H.	46	Clevinghausen	65-0898
FUENKE, Karl	33	Amelith	63-1069
Minna 24			
FUERGANG, John	30	Switz	66-0679
FUERK, Christ.	28	Bleistein	64-0214
FUERST, Blasius	30	Unterfranken	66-0147
Maria 23, Johann 45, Christine 27			
FUERST, Lina	22	Frankenberg	66-0984
FUERSTE, Heinrich	38	Gehrde	66-1093
FUERSTENAU, Ferd.	39	Preussen	63-1136
Johanna 37, Friedrich 13, Charles 9			
August 7, Francis 4			
FUESSE, Friedr.	28	Leipzig	66-0576
FUESSLE, Carl	19	Plochingen	66-0576
FUETHE, Johann	26	Flehingen	66-1155
FUGMANN, Peter	24	Bamberg	64-0886
FUHLHAGE, Ernst	21	Vossheide	63-1010
FUHR, Johann	21	Reinbach	66-0576
FUHRKEN, H.(m)	25	New York	64-0214
FUHRMANN, Carl	17	Duttenstaedt	65-0243
FUHRMANN, Charlott	21	Hessen	66-0734

NAME	AGE	RESIDENCE	YR-LIST
FUHRMANN, Franz	45	Schoenfeld	66-1128
Anna 40, Agnes 15, Joseph 10, Bertha 7			
FUHRMANN, Heinr.	19	Bremen	64-0214
FUHRMANN, J.	22	Elsoff	64-0782
FUHRMANN, Marie	17	Saxony-Weimar	66-0577
FUHRMANN, Roman	48	Schoenfeld	66-1128
Theresia 36			
FUISKE, August	29	Dissen	64-1053
FULBIER, Heinrich	33	Essen	66-1127
Gertrude 34, Joh. Heinr. 4			
FULD, Fanny	20	Willmaro	66-0704
FULD, Feist	58	Himbach	66-1327
Bettje 57, Dina 19			
FULDNER, Heinrich	17	Froeschheim	66-0666
FULLHERD, Wm.	30	Manil	64-1053
Therese 21			
FULLMANN, Frdr.	26	Pittsburg	66-0221
FUNCK, Mr.	30	New York	63-1136
wife 25			
FUNCKE, Franz Wm.	83	Solingen	63-0614
FUNG, Adam	22	Eisenach	66-1373
Alexander 18			
FUNGBLATT, Julius	26	Arolsen	66-1203
FUNK, (m)		Wuerttenberg	66-0221
FUNK, Conrad	18	Hachbour/Hess	65-0038
FUNK, Georg	59	Hetzbach	64-1206
Catharine 59, Heinrich 33, Adam 28			
Ludwig 15			
FUNK, Johannes	56	Sachsen	66-0221
Cathre. 36, Gottfried 11, Marie 2			
FUNKE, Elise Maria	26	Gesmold	63-1069
FUNKE, F.	24	Stuttrop	65-1088
FUNKE, Helene	28	New York	63-1085
Marie 10			
FUNKE, Hermann	22	Ostergrunberg	66-0934
FUNKE, Joh.	29	Ebersbach	65-0116
FUNKE, Lina	30	Elsfleth	65-1024
FUNKE, Louise	25	Wisbeck	64-0427
FUNKEN, K.C.	32	Cerwarda	64-0886
FUNST, Therese	30	Reichenbach	64-0427
FURCHT, Kellein	24	Carlstadt	64-0938
FURHMANN, Carl	26	Wolfenbuettel	63-0398
FURK, Heinr.	28	Wimmer	65-0189
FURMANN, A.(f)	22	Rincel	64-0495
FURMANN, Diedr.	16	Bremen	65-0402
FURMUEHLE, Babette	23	Schweiz	66-0147
FURTE, Anna	32	Schwabendorf	63-1178
FURTH, Ign.	33	Boehmen	64-0023
Rosa 36, Bertha 4, Rudolph 11m			
FURTWANGLER, Jos.	44	Gotterthal	65-0243
Benjamin 27, Mathias 17			
FUSS, C.	22	Annweiler	64-0495
FUSS, Carl	19	Zellerfeld	64-1108
FUSSNECKER, John	42	Cincinnati	63-0990
Louise 42, Amalie 15, Franzea 12			
FUTTERER, Joseph	12	Billafingen	65-0594
GAA, John Simon	40	Planekstadt	63-1178
Ottilia 38, John 14, Magdalena 7			
GABEL, H.	15	Heiligenstadt	65-0007
GABLER, Jacob	40	Besigheim	65-0189
GABRIEL, Anton	22	Maehren	66-0623
Marie 20			
GABRIEL, Johannes	30	Underseuch	66-0412
GABRIEL, Philipp	25	Trippstadt	64-0840
GACK, G.	56	Unt.Leimblein	63-1003
E. 50			
GAD, Leopold	21	Baden	66-0147
GADE, Aug. Heinr.	15	Wenjen	66-0650
GADE, Rebecca	15	Wanna	63-0482
GAEBELE, Math.	20	Selgartsweler	65-1030
GAEBLER, Johann	32	Schoenau	66-1373
GAEDE, Johann	58	Gesmold	63-1069
Konrad 23, Anna M. 32			
GAEDEKE, Joh. D.	33	Bremen	64-0665
Meta 32, J.G. 9, Helene 8, Johanna /			
Wilhelm 5, Mathilde 6m, Johann 58			
GAEDTKE, Friedr.	55	Pommern	66-0469
Jette 53, Carl 17			

NAME	AGE	RESIDENCE	YR-LIST
GAEFE, Gerhard	25	Hunteburg	64-0992
GAEHRING, Heinr.	26	Greiz	66-1373
GAEKE, Herm. Jos.	23	Lengerich	64-0343
GAERBER, Heinrich	19	Dortta	66-0083
GAERNER, Ignatz	17	Muenchen	64-1108
GAERTNER, August	27	Arheilingen	65-0151
GAERTNER, Carl	23	Allnach	65-1024
GAERTNER, Clara	16	Bensen	67-0599
GAERTNER, F.A.(m)	20	Borgholzhsn.	64-0331
GAERTNER, Fr.	23	Bensheim	65-0116
GAERTNER, Valentin	30	Kleinhausen	65-0151
Adam 17			
GAETJE, Gretchen	20	Bremervoerde	66-0679
GAETJERS, Emilie	16	Worms	64-1108
GAETZ, Chrs.	54	Wetzlar	66-0221
GAHLENBECK, Christ	57	Pommern	66-0469
Christine 49, Caroline 20, Carl 18			
Johanna 13, Wilhelm 16, Friedrich 8			
GAHN, Margarete	18	Rorbach	64-0433
Catharine 31, Wolfgeri 8, Eva 14			
Elisabeth 6			
GAHR, Johann	34	Groeningen	66-0083
GAHRE, Wilh.	42	Gestendorf	63-0168
Marie 38			
GAIBEL, Catharina	20	Suselberg	66-1327
Christine 21			
GAIDE, Jean G.	30	Cassel	65-0038
GAIL, Lisette	22	Bruetscheid	66-0576
GAIS, Marie	42	Neukirch	63-0482
Marie 14			
GAIS, St.(m)	26	Laufen	64-0495
GAISELMANN, Frnzka	22	Borsingen	63-0482
GAISSER, J. David	26	New Orleans	63-1178
GAITE, Marie	24	Bremen	64-0331
GAKREIS, Johann	16	Karlsbad	66-1128
GALFING, Michael	24	Wiesenthal	66-0349
GALITZ, Louise	19	Kappeln/Pruss	66-0577
GALL, Catharina	34	Wuestenrode	63-0614
Pauline 5			
GALLER, Wenzel	48	Chalowucik	66-1131
Maria 46, Joseph 15, Maria 7			
GALLHEBEN, D.	23	Bromskirchen	66-0934
GALLICHAU, Philip	37	Jersey Island	66-0147
GALLON, Luitgard	22	Boesingen	63-0482
GALLOT, Emile(m)	28	France	64-0363
GALLOT, Louis	29	France	63-0350
GALLSTERR, Marg.	18	Schwalbach	64-1022
GALLWITZ, Caroline	27	Berlin	65-0007
GALUBINSKY, Joh.	35	Posen	64-0432
Anna 33, Rosalia 6, Marinka 3, Pauline 2			
Franz 23, Mathilde 23			
GAMPFER, Saloman	19	Donseider	66-0221
GAMPP, Conrad	28	Culmbach	66-0576
GANDELL, Antonia	26	London	63-1085
GANDERMANN, Cath.	21	Heineburg	66-0623
Magdalene 15			
GANG, Fridolin	30	Enzingen	66-1093
GANGMUELLER, Aug.	20	Hochheim	66-1127
GANS, Aug.	18	Carlsbad	64-0170
GANS, Jacob	59	Langenschwarz	64-0214
Jette 52, Jette 13			
GANS, Johanna	23	Kleinbeck	64-0782
GANS, Minna	22	Edelshaim	66-1243
GANSBERG, Dorothea	19	Hoya	65-0898
GANSBERGER, J.D.	23	Eitzendorf	64-0495
GANTER, Christine	20	Simozheim	65-0189
GANTER, Domini	24	France	63-0990
GANTNER, J.(m)	19	Endingen	64-0495
GANZ, Charlotte	46	Doeringshagen	64-0433
Caroline 15			
GANZ, Joh.	17	Bremen	65-1189
GANZ, Louis	26	Thueningen	64-0593
GANZER, Margarethe	56	Hasburg	66-1031
Carl 9			
GAPPE, Michael	36	Soessnowd	66-0469
Antonia 26, Franz 8, Casimir 2			
GARBE, Joh. Gottl.	21	Goerlitz	63-0822
GARBEN, Adolph	14	Woelfel	64-0840

NAME	AGE	RESIDENCE	YR-LIST
GARBERS, Johann	26	Schwalingen	67-0007
Johann 18			
GARBES, Johann	29	Hoysinghausen	66-0147
GARCAN, F.(m)	62	France	64-0331
GARDIENT, John	25	America	63-0862
Barb. 20			
GAREFT, Kunigunde	18	Marktschargat	66-0576
GARLACH, F.	17	Herrenberg	64-0992
GARLING, Hermann	19	Ruessen	66-1031
GARLISCH, Aug.	19	Bremen	63-1136
GARLISCH, Frdr.	20	Susstedt	66-0221
GARLISH, Maria	23	Bremen	66-0623
Heinrich 9m			
GARRELL, Mathilda	36	Essen	64-0331
Johanna 21			
GARRELS, G.(f)	23	Ostfriesland	64-0495
GARRELS, Lena	7	Nuttermoor	64-0886
Elmina 5			
GARTELMANN, D.(m)	20	Kuhstedt	64-0138
GARTELMANN, Heinr.	20	Wallersole	66-1248
GARTHE, Herm.	32	Gera	64-1108
GARTMANN, Anton	23	Marschdorf	64-1108
GARTNER, H.	34	Oestereich	66-0934
GARTNER, Wilhelm	26	Rahden	65-1088
GARVES, A.(m)	23	Stuhr	64-0214
GARZ, Christian	46	Riebau	63-0614
Dorothea 48, Dorothea 18, Dorothea El. 22			
Wilhelmine 16, Friedericke 9, Albertine 6			
GASKAR, H.	35	Hameln	64-1022
GASMANN, Lorenz	23	Germerheim	64-0170
GASMUS, H.	30	Chemmitz	64-1206
Cathar. 25			
GASPARI, Agnes	32	Frankfurt/M.	64-0363
GASS, Louise	15	Malz	66-0623
GASSAU, Friedrich	16	Carlsruhe	66-0349
GASSENHEIMER, Joh.	17	Bibra	66-0679
GASSER, Joh.	27	Lienz	65-0898
GASSLER, Heinrich	25	Krossin	66-0469
GASSLER, Joseph	26	Ehningen	63-0350
GASSMANN, Magd.	36	Capsweyer	66-1248
GASSMEYER, C.	22	Lienzingen	65-1189
GAST, Gerh.	23	Badbergen	64-0073
GAST, Heinrich	18	Meiches	65-0950
GAST, Otto	20	Solothurn	64-1053
GASTMEYER, Heini	17	Bremen	66-0413
Herm. 25			
GASTORF, Carl Jos.		Chicago	64-0938
GASTREICH, Theodor	27	Olpe	63-0862
GATHMANN, Joh.Hch.	25	Wachendorf	63-0168
GATTERMANN, Wilh.	36	Naterberg	66-0623
GATTING, Ewa	20	Ettingen	66-0576
GATY, Wilhelm	28	Baden	66-0147
GAUCH, Elisabeth	19	Rossbach	63-0350
GAUDENBERGER, Walt	30	Pfungstadt	63-0296
GAUER, Catharina	21	Merlingen	64-0687
Sophie 30			
GAUL, Jacob	37	New York	64-0427
GAUS, Caroline	57	Laitbach	65-0594
Marie 16			
GAUS, Friederike	19	Neuhagen	67-0353
GAUS, H.	42	Braunschweig	64-0331
Johanna 21			
GAUS, Henry	23	Vollbuettel	63-1178
GAUS, Philippine	26	New York	66-0221
Emma 9m			
GAUSLMEYER, Sebas.	58	Epe	64-0639
Creszentia 59, Carl 13			
GAUSS, Albert	33	Aalen	64-0886
GAUTSCH, August	31	Davern	67-0599
GAYER, Jacob	23	Dirnstein	65-0189
GAYRING, Joh.	29	Schloth	64-0687
GAYRING, Leonh.	23	Huchen	64-0170
Ferd 44			
GEBAUER, Franz	24	D. Tscherbene	66-0109
GEBAUER, Henry	21	Oechsen	63-0917
GEBECKE, Dina	19	Egnord	66-0679
GEBELE, Afra	20	Megesheim	64-1108
GEBERS, Wilhelm	17	Schwalingen	66-1155

NAME	AGE	RESIDENCE	YR-LIST
GEBHARD, Eduard	30	New York	66-0734
GEBHARD, Elise	32	Coeln	64-1053
GEBHARD, Franz	38	Pforzheim/Pr	64-1053
GEBHARDT, Angela	18	Schoeningen	65-0007
GEBHARDT, Augusta	28	Bremerlehe	63-0350
GEBHARDT, Cathar.	28	Giengen	66-0704
Friederike 19			
GEBHARDT, G.	25	Duderstadt	64-0840
GEBHARDT, James	30	Ludwigshafen	63-1178
Emilie 28, Ludwig 20			
GEBHARDT, Johann	24	Weissenreuth	66-1373
GEBHARDT, Wilh.	25	Wuertemberg	63-0822
GEBHAUER, Carl	48	Unteralba	64-0782
Barbara 47, Marie 15			
GEBRECHT, Friedr.	27	Nordstemmen	66-0412
GEBS, John	31	Lehe	63-0168
GEBSER, Rudolph	28	Constantinopl	66-1093
GEERKEN, Anna	20	Hannover	66-1093
GEERKEN, Anna Soph	22	Brinkum	64-0456
GEERKEN, Claus	32	Nebischaffshm	64-0073
Mrs. 24, Mar.			
GEERKEN, Heinr.	20	Siefershausen	66-1373
GEERKEN, Henry	25	Bremen	63-0296
GEERKEN, Johann	18	Westerburg	65-0948
GEERKEN, Margar.	21	Zeven/Hann.	63-0822
GEERKS, Joh. H.	13	Norden	65-0594
GEES, Sophia	21	Mele	66-1248
GEESSMANN, Minna	18	Dissen	65-0950
GEFFKEN, Chris.	20	Ritterhude	66-1203
GEHAUF, Wilhelm	19	Minden	66-0083
GEHL, Anna	59	Dermbach	66-0679
GEHL, Catharine	56	Hoverstadt	66-0668
Sophie 21, Marie 16			
GEHLE, Albertine	20	Bremen	66-0576
GEHM, Philip	30	Sulzbach	65-0116
GEHNER, Wilhelm	21	Dissen	23-0865
GEHRE, Robert	21	Leipzig	65-0055
GEHRHARDT, Charles	41	New York	63-1136
GEHRICH, Ernst	28	Hemendorf	64-0593
GEHRING, Charlotte	20	Siedlar	65-1030
GEHRING, Jesias	26	Rickelsberg	66-0704
GEHRING, John	11	Hessenau	63-0953
GEHRING, Paul	35	Seggen	66-0679
Amalie 30, Mathaeus 5, Ida 3			
Marie Ursula 8m			
GEHRKE, Aug.	42	Helmstedt	64-0992
GEHRKE, Carl	37	Pommern	66-0469
Friedrike 37, Emilie 17, Caroline 12			
Bertha 9, Augusta 7, Carl 4, Hermann 9m			
GEHRKE, Gottlieb	44	Grossiejewe/P	66-0412
Louise 36, Pauline W. 18, Otilie E. 15			
Mathilde 5, Bertha 7, Gustav 9m			
GEHRKE, Joh.	23	Hannover	64-0739
GEHRKE, Wilhelm	28	Bernstein	66-1155
Henriette 33, Johanna 5, Ernst 3			
Augusta 9, Johanna 59			
GEHRKEN, Johann	17	Driftseth	64-0456
Catharina 20			
GEHRKEN, Trina	32	Axstadt	66-0934
GEHRONEY, Gottl.	22	Stuttgart	65-0770
GEIB, Conrad	40	New York	64-0427
GEIDT, Elsb.	15	Manburg	64-0495
GEIDT, H.(m)	24	Marburg	64-0331
GEIER, Anna	19		63-1085
GEIER, Bernhard	42	New York	66-0984
Bernhard 9			
GEIER, Hermann	30	Griestedt	65-0770
GEIER, Magdalene	24	Lindau	66-1327
GEIGEL, Ludwig	23	Essen	65-0004
GEIGER, A.	29	Noerdlingen	64-0495
GEIGER, Adam	22	Bavaria	63-0296
GEIGER, Albert	25	Norrick	67-0353
Cicilie 25			
GEIGER, Andreas	20	Hochdorf	66-0147
GEIGER, Barbara	31	Noerdlingen	64-0495
GEIGER, Conr.	27	Tittlingen	64-0331
GEIGER, Gottl.	27	Geisingen	63-0482
Christine 29, Christian 3, Friedr. 9m			

NAME	AGE	RESIDENCE	YR-LIST
Catharina 59			
GEIGER, Helene	36	Oberdorf	66-0679
Mathilde 5, Oswald 1			
GEIGER, Ma.(f)	25	Kappel	64-1161
GEIGER, Math.(f)	15	Aichsheim	64-0782
GEIGER, Max	20	Dielingen	64-0639
GEIGER, Meta	19	Wangen	67-0007
GEIGER, Sarah	40	Basel	64-1053
GEIGER, W.E.	30	Kirchheim	65-0007
GEIGER, Wm. Fr.	24	Megerkingen	66-1313
GEIGGENHEIM, Amali	20	Gailingen	63-0006
GEIGLE, Caroline	24	Baden	66-0469
GEILER, William	38	Westerstede	64-0593
baby 6m			
GEILKER, C.F.	25	Oberbeck	64-0023
GEIPEL, Joh.	20	Asch	65-0898
GEIS, August	40	San Francisco	66-0679
GEISE, Bernhard	24	Dammer Lohhsn	64-0170
GEISE, Elisabeth	16	Wora	65-1024
GEISE, Marg.	23	Pern	65-1024
GEISEL, Ferdinand	20	Giessen	66-1327
GEISEMEYER, Cathre	56	Dissen	63-0917
GEISENHEIM, Friedr	42	Frankenau	63-0168
Sophia 42, Alex 9, Emma 7, Lous 4			
GEISER, H.(m)	22	Steinfurt	64-0331
GEISERT, Joseph	22	Ulm	66-0083
GEISLER, Theod.	25	Borken	64-0170
GEISMANN, Bernhard	27	Preussen	63-1218
GEISSELMANN, Anton	18	Fockenhausen	64-0687
Joh. 16, Therese 24			
GEISSELMANN, Rudlf		Gnarrenberg	66-0704
GEISSERT, Cath.	65	Frauensee	64-0593
GEISSHIRT, Anna	23	Sachsen-Mein.	66-0349
GEISSLER, Alwine	18	Asch	65-0898
GEISSLER, Bertha	23	Pforzheim	66-1127
GEISSLER, Cath.	23	Eissfeld	64-1053
GEISSLER, Cath.	15	Herreshausen	65-0189
GEISSLER, Clara	25	Sachsen-Mein.	66-0349
GEISSLER, Eugen	18	Berg	64-0214
GEISSLER, Johanna	24	Fritzlar	66-1127
GEISSLER, Julius	29	Berlin	65-0004
GEISSLER, Leop.	26	Pforzheim	66-0734
GEISSLER, Lina	18	Altenburg	66-1155
GEISSLER, Louise	22	Mannheim	64-0687
GEISSMAR, N.	24	New York	63-1178
GEISSMAR, v. Chr.	23	Osnabrueck	63-1178
GEISTHARDT, Gottfr	28	Eisfeld	63-0482
Rosalie 22, baby 11m, Bertha 23			
Elisabeth 63			
GEISWEILER, Meta	28	Osterholz	64-0331
GEISWITZ, Joh.	18	Altenstadt	64-0170
GEITZ, Anna Martha	17	Rothendorf	66-0837
Katharina 17			
GEITZ, C.	26	Marienhagen	64-0782
GEITZ, Daniel	18	Broniskirchen	64-0886
GEITZ, Georg	29	Michelsbach	65-0038
Maria 19, Sophia 6m, Catharina 58			
GEITZ, Henriette	23	Harpe	66-0837
GEITZ, Johannes	23	Dinklage	64-0363
Michael 21			
GEITZ, Louise	20	Bremerhafen	64-0363
GELDERMANN, Heinr.	29	Hochstruss	65-0770
GELDERN, Otto	8	Berlin	66-1327
GELDHAEUSER, Cuno	20	Sonnenberg	66-1327
GELDMACHER, Heinr.	34	Grosmanrode	66-0623
Anna Marg. 33, Justus 3, Marie 2			
GELHAV, Marie	23	Steinau	66-0083
GELINEK, Wilh'mine	28	Wien	66-0576
Eduard 8, Johanna 6, Henriette 4			
Eduard 10			
GELKE, Cath.	19	Wolfhagen	66-1248
GELLERMANN, Doris	19	Koeln	66-0623
GELLERMANN, Eberh.	31	Iowa	63-0168
GELLMANN, Chr.	50	Neuhortz	63-1136
GELPKE, C.C.	32	Pennsylvania	64-0363
Charlotte 33, Caroline 3, Carl 6m			
GELSHORN, Herm.	22	Lingen	64-0456
Heinrich 17			
GEMTHE, Carl	31	Eisleben	64-0739
GEMUENHARD, Heinr.	28	Gesell	65-0770
GENEN, Heinr.	41	New York	64-0073
Cath. 36			
GENG, John	28	Heidenhofer	63-0296
GENIK, Adele	24	Elsass	63-0015
GENNER, Conrad	45	Frankfurt a/m	66-1093
Anna 45			
GENSLER, Caroline	25	Ostheim	66-0650
GENSLER, Caspar	20	Grossenbach	66-1155
GENSLER, Johanna	58	Cesseheim	63-0482
GENSLER, Joseph	40	Brombach	65-0713
GENTSCH, Johann G.	29	Germany	66-0666
GEORG, Cath.	24	Ludwigshafen	65-0594
Dorethe 21, Juliane 20			
GEORG, Heinr.	30	New York	64-0427
GEORG, James	24	Roden	63-1178
GEORG, Louise	21	Homburg	64-1108
GEORG, Peter	24	Luederstreit	64-0214
GEORGE, Georg	56	Lengeltach	63-1010
GEORGE, Johannes	52	Lengeltach	63-1010
Anna Cathr. 59, Conrad 19			
GEORGI, Adam H.	18	Weissenhausen	64-0456
GEORGIN, Carl	26	Bremen	66-1155
GERARD, Jean	42	Rouen	63-0350
GERATHWOHE, E.	24	Baltimore	63-1136
GERBER, Anna	22	Hostann	66-1373
Elenore 20			
GERBER, Charlotte	24	Kirn	63-0015
GERBER, Hinriette	56	Pr. Minden	64-0432
Mathilde 15			
GERBER, M.	25	Hannover	63-1178
GERBER, Robert	26	Luebbecke	65-1030
GERBERDING, W.	64	Husum	64-0992
H. 29, Caroline 30			
GERBITZ, Augusta	19	Preussen	63-0990
GERBRACHT, Phil.	37	Wabern	65-1140
Cathrine 36, Cathrine 7, Hannes 5			
Elisabeth 3, Maria 3m			
GERDEMANN, Phina	26	St.Mauritz	64-1053
GERDES, Alb.	26	Utah	65-1024
GERDES, Anton	32	Pr. Minden	65-0713
GERDES, Diedr.	27	Burg	66-1373
GERDES, Diedr.	35	Ruestersiel	65-1024
GERDES, Ed.	24	Cuxhaven	63-0244
Minna 25			
GERDES, Gretchen	21	Bremervoerde	64-0432
GERDES, Herm. J.	39	Matanzas	63-0990
F. 18, Maria 8, Florencio 20, Carlos 17			
GERDES, Hermann	28	Kl. Starern	63-0244
GERDES, Hermann	27	Norden	66-1243
Sophie 26			
GERDES, Johann	38	Oldenburg	65-0770
GERDES, Luer	60	Ritterlude	65-0004
Anna 57, Anna 15			
GERDTS, Fr.	22	Wieshausen	65-1024
GERDTS, Heinrich	20	Werningerode	66-1127
GERDUNG, Georg	21	Wunstorf	66-1248
GERECKE, Albert	23	Burg	65-0950
GERET, Franziska	22	Vechta	64-0920
GERFASS, Johann	22	Leinerholz	66-1203
GERFELDER, Theodor	30	Babenhausen	66-1093
GERHARD, F.	22	Weissenberg	65-1189
GERHARD, G.(m)	34	Langberg	64-0331
GERHARD, Jean	28	Rouen	63-0350
Elisabeth 25, Maria 5, Maria 3			
Antoinette 11m			
GERHARD, Martin	27	Darmstadt	65-0865
GERHARD, v. Ad.	26	Insterburg	64-0938
GERHARDT, C.	29	Bonn	65-0974
GERHARDT, Cathrine	23	Hessen	63-0614
Elise 18			
GERHARDT, Conrad	17	Bremen	64-0214
GERHARDT, Wm.	32	Gembeck	66-0837
GERHARDY, Wilhelm	23	Giboldshausen	66-0083
GERHENN, Charles	35	Stralsund	63-0862
GERHOFF, August	35	Rheinberg	66-1248
GERHOLD, Joh.Heinr	33	Dissen	66-0650

NAME	AGE	RESIDENCE	YR-LIST
GERICHTEN, v. A.M.	16	Langenkandel	63-1003
M. 18			
GERICHTEN, v. Cath	27	Herford	64-1206
GERICHTER, Phil.	29	Mannheim	64-0427
Cath. 23			
GERICKE, August	41	Marienwerder	65-0243
GERICKE, Heinrich	32	Legden	66-0623
GERICKE, Marie	18	Gr.Doehren	64-0138
GERISCH, Christ.	41	Querbach	64-0938
Friedr. 37			
GERKE, Julius	25	Wilkowa	66-0469
GERKE, Theodor	37	Runowo	66-0083
Wilhelmine 26, Amalie 6			
GERKE, Wilh.	23	Meyerhofer	65-1088
GERKEN, Bernhard	27	Drungstedt	66-1031
Catharine 22, Claus 10m			
GERKEN, Cathr.	18	Ellsen	63-1010
GERKEN, Johann	25	Friedrichsdrf	65-1031
GERLACH, Anna	17	Offenbach	66-1248
GERLACH, Annette	40	Grastorf	63-0693
GERLACH, Christoph	26	Nordhausen	64-0138
GERLACH, Georg	33	Weimar	65-0865
GERLACH, Gustave	34	Duesseldorf	64-0170
Friederike 24, Anton 25			
GERLACH, H.	19	Langendiepe	65-0151
GERLACH, J.J.	15	Litberg	65-0402
GERLACH, Joh.	22	Hommetshausen	65-0402
GERLACH, Juluis	22	Wuertenberg	66-0221
GERLACH, Marie	27	Soden	65-0948
GERLACH, Otto	17	Wetzlar	63-0015
GERLAND, Charlotte	25	Hessen	66-0734
GERLEN, Marie	52	Wachstadt	63-1085
GERLING, Johann	21	Prussia	63-0822
GERMANN, Arthur	21	Dresden	65-0007
GERMANN, Marianne	24	Claussen	67-0007
GERMAR, Carl	30	Wernigerode	64-1108
GERMER, Wilhelm	16	Luedersheim	65-0770
GERNAUD, Jos.	44	New York	64-0363
Wife 28, Marie 7, Louise 5			
GERNE, Regine	40	Philadelphia	66-0984
GERNEITEN, v. G.	20	Volkmarsen	63-1085
GERNER, Anna M.	41	Oidingen	65-0189
GERNER, Fr.(m)	36	Boehmen	64-0170
GERNING, Amalia	22	Heidelberg	65-0116
GERNOERSKY, V.	34	Kuttenberg	65-0116
GEROLD, Dorothea	44	Darmstadt	66-0221
Elisabeth 17, Dorothea 9, Henriette 6			
Philip 5			
GEROLD, Ludw.	18	Darmstadt	66-0221
GEROTE, Anton	36	Magdeburg	64-1161
GERPEN, v. Heikea	22	Upleward	64-0665
GERRARD, (f)	38	Bremen	65-0402
John 8			
GERSDORF, Robert	37	Schwarzenberg	66-0704
GERSIE, F.W.	33	Linen	64-0170
Ernst 29			
GERSMAN, Gertrude	24	Gesmold	63-1038
GERSMANN, Johann	18	Wellingholzh.	66-1203
GERSSINGEN, Johann	19	Unterkochen	64-0639
GERST, Jacob	32	Eglosheim	65-0151
GERST, Lisette	27	Cloppenburg	63-1038
Caspar 25			
GERSTEN, Minna	32	Hannover	64-0840
GERSTENSCHLAEGER,V	25	Habitzheim	64-1108
GERSTNER, Babette	20	Liesberg	65-0594
GERSTNER, Georg	22	Boehmen	66-0704
GERTELMANN, A.	21	Mettingen	65-1189
GERTES, Anna	24	Wittmund	66-1203
GERTH, Albin	22	Altenburg	66-0984
GERTH, Caroline	28	Switz	66-0679
Henriette 26, Natalie 18			
GERVEN, C.H.	23	Holsen	65-0898
GERWING, Marg.	22	Wirsum	65-1030
GERWISCH, Julie	23	Pforzheim	66-1373
GERZEN, Gerhard	29	Muehlheim	63-0990
GESCH, Ludwig	40	Goeln	66-0469
Christine 37, Mina 11, August 5, Anna 9m			
GESCKER, Chs. Hen.	28	Iowa	63-0693
GESELL, Ad.	24	Odessa	65-0189
GESELL, Barbara	32	Walpenreuth	63-0296
GESEN, Gerhard	26	Oldendorf/Old	64-0920
Anton 23			
GESSNER, August	17	Worms	66-0578
GESSNER, M.(m)	28	New York	64-0495
GESSNER, Paul Jul.	25	Loessnitz	66-1155
GETET, Alois	40	Ingolstadt	64-0363
Adelheid 40			
GETTING, Heinrich	18	Schlake	64-0739
GEVERS, Anna	19	Heppenheim	66-0734
GEYER, August	17	Asch	66-0679
GEYER, Babet	25	Neckarbischof	66-1373
GEYER, Christ.	28	Adelsdorf	66-1248
GEYER, Eduard	33	Baltimore	63-0862
Minna 27, Henry 4, Eduard 3, Charlotte 1			
Friedrich 5m			
GEYER, Ferd.	31	Asch/Boh.	65-0038
GEYER, Johann	20	Lindau	66-0412
GEYER, Nicolaus	24	Rothenberg	64-0343
GEYER, Wilhelm	32	Koethen	66-0412
GEYGER, Johann	25	Neigenmuenden	66-0734
GIBBEMEYER, H.	43	Berlin	66-1248
GIEBE, Cath.	18	Weimar	65-1189
GIEBE, Johann F.	25	Einbeck	66-1248
GIEBEL, Johann	26	Leimbach	66-1313
GIEBEL, Joseph	19	Kirchhassel	65-0243
GIECK, Georg	54	Dipport	66-1203
Georg 30			
GIEFER, Georg	29	Pumpe	66-0679
GIEHMANN, Johann	20	Becke	67-0007
GIELE, Gust.	31	Hannover	63-0398
Friedr. 28			
GIELOW, Charles	31	Luebz	63-1178
GIENGER, Johannes	21	Neidlingen	66-1248
GIERBICHS, Carl	29	Mersheim	65-0004
GIERENHAUS, John	27	Mettmann	63-0482
GIERING, Fr.	24	Bornstaedten	63-1085
GIERKE, Carl	36	Langhorn	65-0038
Lucinda 30, Louise 6, Elisabeth 4			
Adolph 2, Wilhelm 4m			
GIERSCH, Heinr.	17	Nenndorf	65-0402
GIERSE, August	30	Detmold	66-1203
Elisabeth 21			
GIES, Johann	19	Neustadt	66-0984
GIESCHEN, Claus	18	Achim	66-0734
GIESCHEN, H.	25	New York	63-1218
GIESE, Johannes	60	Wonra	66-0576
Elisabeth 52, Elisabeth 22, Johannes 14			
GIESECKE, August	25	Esperke	66-0109
Dorette 25			
GIESECKE, Heinrich	35	Schoeppensted	66-0412
GIESEKE, Heinrich	31	Braunschweig	63-1010
GIESEKE, William	28	St. Louis	63-0953
Albert 17			
GIESEKING, Heinr.		St. Louis	64-0214
Wilhelmine			
GIESEKING, Louise	18	Seese	66-0704
GIESEL, Barbara	51	Oberndorf	66-1313
Cath. 23, Anna 18			
GIESELER, Caroline	22	Kammerbon	66-1327
Friederich 4, Heinrich 17			
GIESELER, Friedr.	42	Eystrub	63-0398
Marg. 39, Herm. 14, Friedr. 9, Heinr. 4			
Christ. 1			
GIESELMANN, Herman	29	Werther	66-0704
GIESEN, Heinr.	24	Oftersheim	64-0214
GIESKE, Th.(m)	67	Oldenburg	64-0427
GIESLER, Martin	21	Meiningen	63-0953
GIESS, Joh. Georg	26	Eisenach	66-1128
GIESSELMANN, Casp.	36	Bielefeld	65-1030
Anna 36, Hanna 14, Friederike 8			
Hermann 4, Louise 6m			
GIESSLER, Georg	19	Cuxhagen	66-1248
GIESSLER, Wm.	26	Roringen	64-0992
GIESSMANN, Georg	30	Ohio	66-0734
GIESTING, J.(m)	21	Woltrup	64-0331
GIETZEN, Jos.	26	Neef	64-0214

NAME	AGE	RESIDENCE	YR-LIST
GIFFERT, Jac.	36	Eisenach	64-0331
GIG, Wilhelm	33	Muemelingen	66-0083
Elisabeth 26, Gertrude 6m			
GIGERICH, Cr.	28	Aschaffenburg	65-0950
Josepha 10			
GIGON, Francois	40	Paris	64-0073
Francois 9			
GILDEHAUS, Heinr.	28	St. Louis	66-0984
Charlotte 19			
GILDEMEISTER, H(m)	24	Bremen	64-0073
GILDEMEISTER, Hen.	22	Bremen	63-0244
GILDEMEISTER, Math	29	Bremen	63-0244
GILDNER, Marie	41	Erfurt	67-0795
Fritz 7			
GILKER, Johann	28	Bohnweiler	67-0007
GILLE, Joh. Heinr.	16	Cassel	67-0600
GILLER, Carl	30	Cassel	42-0704
GILLER, Otto	25	Gelnhausen	63-0168
GIMANN, August	19	Einbeck	66-0934
GIMBERGER, Sophie	23	Kroedel	64-0593
GIMENTEL, Rosa	16	Spain	63-0990
GIMMY, Peter	28	Prussia	63-0296
GIMS, Peter	25	Waldmichelbch	66-1248
GINDELE, Joseph	22	Aulendorf	66-1131
GINSELSBERGER, B.	14	Hausen	63-1085
GIPPERT, Phl.	18	Zell	64-0170
GIRAND, Annet	36	Frankfurt	65-1140
GISFELD, Louise	24	Weissenburg	64-0639
GISIN, Maria	29	Bernhausen	66-1131
GISPERT, Regina	25	Heppenheim	66-0734
GISSEL, Wm.	35	Duedelsheim	64-0886
Marie 35, Cath.Marie 7, Heinr. 5			
Wilhelmine 4, Maria 3, Wilhelm 11m			
GISSLER, Johann	35	Lautenbach	64-0433
Elisabeth 30, Johann 5, Franz 11m			
GISSLING, A.	23	Ladbergen	66-0934
GIZMOEHLE, Christ.	29	Kath.Hammer	65-1095
Anna 49, Karl Aug. 12, Susanna H. 7			
Karl Gottl. 6, Karl Ernst 3			
GLAAS, Ludwig	19	Garnika	66-0650
GLAATZ, Sophie	25	Bremen	65-0402
GLADE, Johann	31	Essen	65-0865
GLAENZER, Anna M.	21	Willingshain	64-0170
GLAESER, Heinrich	38	Schwabach	65-0948
Marie 39			
GLAHN, Heinr.	22	Cappeln	63-0398
GLAHN, v. Anna	19	Brameln	66-0577
GLAHN, v. Henry	22	New York	63-0693
GLAHR, Ludwig	16	Mannheim	67-0007
GLAMMANN, Wm.	32	Havre	65-0116
GLANDER, Louis	9	Verden	66-1031
GLANEN, Johann	40	Jungingen	64-0363
Anna 32, Maria 11m			
GLANGER, Wilhelm	27	Pommern	66-0469
Henriette 27			
GLASER, Elias	32	Wuerttemberg	64-0432
GLASER, Emma	20	Syke	66-0734
GLASER, Francisca	28	Edelsheim	66-0576
GLASER, Marie	38	Lorch	64-0639
Louise 15			
GLASER, Mathilde	30	Berlin	67-0007
Robert 9m			
GLASFORTH, Julie H	33	Berge	64-0886
GLASKOPF, Lazarus	22	Pilsen	64-0920
GLASS, C.F.	27	Baltimore	63-1218
GLASS, Friedrich	47	Charlston	66-0984
GLASSMEYER, J.F.	32	Hagen	64-0427
GLATLI, Elisabeth	30	Benstetten	63-0693
GLAUBITZ, J. Franz	32	Borgholzhsn.	64-0214
GLAUCK, Joh.	23	Dresden	64-0665
GLAUEN, Johann	40	Jungingen	64-0363
Anna 32, Maria 11m			
GLEB, Anna Martha	24	Hessen	64-0432
GLEBE, Johann	18	Oberngeis	66-0668
GLECHINGER, Rudolf	32	Grosseidingen	66-0083
GLEHM, Johannes	18	Mohre	66-1203
GLEIBER, Heinr.	22	Mittelstemmen	65-0189
GLEIBOGER, Joh. G.	21	Geeren/Hann	64-0920

NAME	AGE	RESIDENCE	YR-LIST
GLEIM, Georg	14	Rodenburg	66-0578
GLEIM, Jacob	32	Eschwede	64-1206
GLEIS, Gertrude	35	Epe	65-0948
GLEISENBERGER, Cth	60	Euskirchen	64-0427
GLENDEMANN, Christ	20	Riblerbuettel	66-0577
Henriette 51, Heinrich 17			
GLESCHNER, Friedr.	29	Dresden	66-1248
GLESER, Andreas	42	Sidesheim	64-1053
Anna 26			
GLINDEMANN, Conrad	46	Vollbuettel	64-0904
Dorothea 31, Heinrich 6, Louise 3			
Elisabeth 24			
GLINDMEYER, Sophie	23	Prussia	64-0432
GLINGKE, Carl H.	23	Sondershausen	64-1108
Louise 21, Hulda 3			
GLINSKI, Joh.	31	Posen	64-0432
Eva 25, Prince Slava 4, Valleria 1			
GLISS, Wm.	22	Schlitz	64-0992
GLISTER, Bernhard	32	Gloster	65-0948
GLIZ, Heinrich	28	Ndr.Liebersbh	64-0739
GLOCK, Ludwig II	29	Cassel	65-0116
Carol. 23			
GLOCKER, M.	26	Eilstetten	65-0007
GLOECKLE, Georg	20	Anterboringen	66-1373
GLOECKLER, Adolph	32	Kuppingen	65-0243
GLOECKLER, Hilarus	23	Taurendingen	65-0189
GLOECKNER, Mary	63	Carlsruhe	63-0551
GLOHM, v. Julia	25	Wallersole	66-1248
GLOR, John	50	Switzerland	63-0244
wife 30			
GLORG, Christian	24	Rabber	66-1373
Caroline 23, Christ. 4m			
GLORINS, Adam	62	Birkenfeld	64-0840
Christine 61, Regine 34, Heinrich 33			
Georg 6			
GLOYSTEIN, J.	15	Lehe	65-0189
GLUECK, Carl	14	Oetlingen	66-1327
GLUECK, Maria	30	Stuttgart	66-1093
GLUECK, Samuel	40	Arat	63-1038
GLUECK, Samuel	21	Preussen	66-0734
GLUECKAUF, Bertha	19	St. Lengsfeld	63-1178
GLUECKSELIG, Chr.	27	Berlin	66-1093
Martha 4			
GLUEPKER, Joh.	20	Hohenkoerbe	65-0402
GLUESENKAMP, Anna	17	Bohmle	65-0898
GLUNDER, Jos.	36	Bremen	64-0331
Johanna 21			
GLUTH, Eduard	25	Naseband	66-0469
GMESER, Anton	30	Boehmen	63-1136
GMUENDLER, Jacob	27	Gunden	66-0412
GNAEDIG, L.	26	Buesslingen	65-1024
GNAUTLE, Eduard	19	Stuttgart	64-0840
GNEITING, Michael	27	Linzenhofen	65-0948
GNETHLEIN, Nic.	37	Baltimore	64-0782
GNUTE, Wilhelm	22	Taerthausen	65-0950
GOBGERT, Elise	20	Gehrde	64-0886
GOBRECHT, Wilhelm	20	Wilhelmshaus	66-1093
GOCHELL, Kunigunde	54	Lohne	66-1131
GOCHER, Jac. D.	23	Hannover	66-1313
GOCKELER, Michel	28	Brucke	64-0331
GOCKER, Bernhard	25	Nordkirchen	66-1248
GOCOTKE, G.	30	Carnitz	65-0007
GODDERTZ, Nicol.	28	Anchenheim	64-0992
GODE, Christian	21	Precht	66-1248
GODT, Wilh.	19	Horste	64-0073
GOEBEL, Andr.	52	Laubach	64-0495
Cath. 38, Elis. G. 20, Elise 23, Hrch. 17			
Marie 15, Cath. 7, Wm. 5			
GOEBEL, Anna	18	Darmstadt	66-0221
GOEBEL, August	23	Wiesbaden	64-0886
GOEBEL, Catharine	23	Warzenbach	63-0398
Anna 29			
GOEBEL, Cathrine	70	Hessen	66-0469
GOEBEL, Christine	20	Lieselbach	65-0594
GOEBEL, Elise	24	Eisfeld	66-1093
GOEBEL, Eugen	27	Limburg/Pr.	65-0243
Anna 24, Wilhelm 10m, Cath 28, Friedr. 6			
Jac. 4, Wilhelmine 10m			

NAME	AGE	RESIDENCE	YR-LIST
GOEBEL, Heinrich	19	Grossalmerode	64-0433
GOEBEL, J.	58	Pfordt	64-0782
Valentin 16, Henry 14			
GOEBEL, Julius	20	Gr. Almerode	65-0004
GOEBEL, Louise	25	Osnabrueck	66-1031
GOEBEL, Sophie	39	Hannover	63-0482
GOEBEL, Susanne	28	Offenbach	66-0734
Philipp 6, Anna 2			
GOECKE, H.	21	Braunschweig	65-0974
GOECKELER, James	18	Reutlingen	63-0990
GOECKELER, John	24	Reutlingen	63-0990
GOECKELER, Ph.	28	Winnweder	64-0363
GOECKEN, Gerhard	26	Oldorf	64-0495
GOEDECKE, Oscar	19	Lage	64-0427
GOEDLICH, Ad.	21	Dresden	66-1243
GOEHLER, Heinrich	23	Hannover	66-0576
GOEHMANN, Justine	29	Polle	64-1022
GOEHRE, Bernhard	31	Leipzig	66-0679
Meta 24, Johanna 9			
GOEHRING, Herm.	32	Burgstedt	64-0904
GOEHRING, Justina	18	Diedelsheim	65-1088
GOEKE, Fritz	24	Hohenhausen	64-0456
GOELDEL, Carl	17	Breslau	67-0600
GOEMANN, August	19	Einbeck	66-0934
GOENERS, Anna M.	66	Elverdessen	63-1010
GOENNER, Louise	24	Borgholzhsn.	66-1031
GOEPEL, Anna	30	Wuerzburg	64-0639
GOEPEL, Charl. Ant	33	Pansa	66-0704
GOEPEL, Charles	17	Stuttgart	64-0593
GOEPEL, Christ. G.	21	Pansa	66-0704
Amalia Franz 19			
GOEPEL, Paul	20	Stuttgart	63-0917
GOEPFERT, Andreas	18	Kaltenlengsfd	63-0244
GOEPFERT, C.	21	Gerthausen	64-0665
GOEPFERT, Carl Fr.	27	Regenhausen	66-0650
GOEPFERT, Gottfr.	29	Fuechsen/S.-M	66-0412
Barbara 31			
GOEPPEL, Joh.	32	Hamburg	66-0837
GOEPPNER, Johann	27	Zedlitz	66-0668
GOERDER, Rob.	14	Celle	63-0482
GOERG, John	41	Nordhabben	64-0343
GOERGEN, Joseph	27	Gevenisch	65-0770
GOERGES, Julius	37	Nudersdorf	66-0147
GOERING, Johann	30	Diebach	66-1128
GOERKS, Gottlieb	28	Werderfelde	66-0679
Henriette 26			
GOERNER, Catherina	36	Boehmen	64-0427
GOERTEMUELLER, Aug	36	Duesseldorf	64-0433
GOERTZHAIN, Carol.	18	Alsfeld	66-0704
GOESCHE, Gustav	26	Berlin	65-0116
GOESSELN, v. Herm	20	Delmenhorst	67-0600
GOESSLING, Aug.	25	Halle	63-0821
GOESSNITZ, v. Ma.	56	Dresden	63-0990
GOETSCH, Augusta	33	Greifswald	66-0083
Clara 9m			
GOETTE, Elise	18	Baden Baden	64-0495
GOETTE, Fr.	23	Waldeck	66-0934
GOETTE, Wilhelm	25	Scharzhostolz	64-0433
Theresia 18			
GOETTIG, Christian	51	Betzisdorf/He	66-0412
Marie 53, Elisabeth 22, Anna Cath. 16			
GOETTLING, Theres.	17	Strassberg	63-0917
GOETZ, A.M.(f)	25	Schenklengsfd	64-0331
GOETZ, Adam	15	Ob.Mengelbach	64-0214
GOETZ, Anna M.	24	Ernsthafen	64-0886
GOETZ, Carl	27	Worms	66-1093
Anna 27			
GOETZ, Cathrine	30	Baden	66-0147
GOETZ, Herm.	23	Buehl	63-1085
GOETZ, Joh.	26	Frammersheim	64-0687
GOETZ, Joh. Christ	22	Ehrenfriedhof	65-0594
GOETZ, Leopold	20	Augsburg	64-0639
GOETZ, Louise	19	Flein	63-0482
GOETZ, Simon	16	Schleusingen	66-0734
GOETZE, Friedr. W.	38	Neustadt	64-0214
GOETZE, Friedrich	43	Teuchern	63-0482
Henriette 41, Ernst 18, Therese 16			
William 9, Hermann 8, Albert 6, Francis 4			
Amalia 9m			
GOETZE, Fritz	21	Osthofen	63-0953
GOETZE, Johann	40	Koehlen	64-0427
Cath. 30, Peter 3, Heinr. 9m, Marie 32			
Julius 7, Wilhelm 9m			
GOETZE, John C.	34	Saalfeld	64-0214
GOETZE, Julius	21	Jena	65-1030
GOETZE, Louis	31	New York	63-0482
Emmy 24, Helene 5, Henry 1			
GOETZE, Rud.	31	Neustadt	64-0023
Johanna 21			
GOETZE, Theobald	37	Nuernberg	65-0243
GOETZE, W.(m)	34	Hoboken	63-0244
M.(f) 32			
GOGOLL, A.C.T.(m)	35	Berlin	64-0331
GOHDE, Heinrich	22	Oldenstedt	67-0007
GOLD, Joseph	21	Wuertemberg	66-0147
GOLDACKER, August	39	Dernau	66-0413
GOLDBECK, Phillip	14	Hofgeismar	66-0837
GOLDBERG, Diedr.	25	Detmold	66-0984
GOLDBERG, Fettje	17	Hernighausen	66-0984
GOLDBERG, Is.	32	Neheim	66-1127
Hedwig 23			
GOLDBERG, Isaac	18	Vilbel	64-0904
GOLDBERG, Ludw.	22	Vilbel	64-0073
GOLDBERGER, Joseph	31	Prag	64-0886
Josephine 28, Elisabeth 2, Ferdinand 9m			
GOLDE, Elias G.	22	Schleitz	63-1010
GOLDENBERG, Joel	15	Kestrich	63-0917
GOLDENBERG, Kallm.	17	Hoeringhausen	66-0734
GOLDENBERG, Nathan	50	Kestriede	64-0639
GOLDENBERG, R.	21	Cincinnati	63-0482
GOLDFUSS, Margaret	20	Mistelgau	65-1031
GOLDHOFER, Theresa	23	Dietenheim	63-1136
GOLDMAIER, Sophie	34	Drainfeld	64-0687
Samuel 14, Alex 7, Isaac 5			
GOLDMANN, Caroline	18	Zeil	63-0482
GOLDMANN, Fanny	26	Hagen	63-0551
GOLDMANN, Jacob	22	Schoenlinde	67-0007
GOLDMANN, Therese	35	Schoenlinde	66-0984
GOLDNER, Simon	16	Zeitloss	66-1155
GOLDSCHMIDT, Bernh	25	Drelingen	65-0594
GOLDSCHMIDT, Bluem	18	Schenklengsfd	64-0920
GOLDSCHMIDT, Carl	13	Fuerth	63-0693
GOLDSCHMIDT, Carl	33	Osnabrueck	65-0770
GOLDSCHMIDT, Franz	36	Luzau	67-0806
GOLDSCHMIDT, Gottl	19	Harpstedt	66-0984
GOLDSCHMIDT, Heine	25	Lipperode	63-0953
GOLDSCHMIDT, Jette	27	Rimpen	66-1155
GOLDSCHMIDT, Jos.	21	Erdmannward	64-0687
GOLDSCHMIDT, Jos.	26	Lengerich	64-1108
GOLDSCHMIDT, Sam.	20	Darmstadt	64-0687
GOLDSCHMIDT, Sus.		Muehlberg	64-0495
GOLDSFUECKER, Otto	31	Baden	64-0427
GOLDSMITH, Betti	17	Romrad	64-0992
GOLDSMITH, Laz.	32	New York	63-0097
GOLDSMITH, Sara	18	Furth	64-0782
GOLDSMITH, Wilhelm	16	Posen	66-0221
GOLDSMITH, Wolf	19	Netra	66-1031
GOLDSTAECKER, Rosa	18	Posen	66-0221
GOLDSTEIN, Cathar.	27	Gaibach	66-1155
Wendelin 3			
GOLDSTEIN, Gust.	22	Berlin	64-0992
GOLDSTEIN, Jac.	38	Schrot	63-0821
GOLDSTEIN, Salom.	19	Bischwind	66-0650
GOLDSTEIN, Siegm.	29	Warren	63-1136
GOLDVOGEL, Math(f)	19	Weissbach	64-0639
GOLL, Johann	18	Weilheim	66-1203
GOLLA, Marie	24	Prussia	64-0432
GOLLMER, Jacob	28	Dettingen	66-1327
GOLLY, Marie Anne	47	Elsass	63-0482
Joseph 11, Leo 10, August 7, Nanette 3			
GOLOT, Adelheid	23	Bersede	65-0189
GOLTZE, Doroliese	36	Oettingen	64-0363
GOLZ, Johann Georg	43	Bodenbach	66-1128
GONDERMANN, Benj.	54	Hessen	66-0469
GONDORF, Philipp	24	Oberwallstadt	63-0693
GONERT, Philippine	20	Bezingen	66-1248

NAME	AGE	RESIDENCE	YR-LIST
GONNERMANN, Elisb.	18	Luederbach	65-0713
GONNERMANN, J.H.D.	17	Hainbach	64-0170
Conr. 18			
GOOS, H.(m)	28	West Cappeln	64-0331
GOOSEBRINK, Wilmne	25	Bockhorst	64-0331
GOOSMANN, Anna	18	Bremen	64-0992
GOOSMANN, Wilhelm	21	Bremen	66-0668
GOPF, Ludw.	21	Huttingen	65-0004
GOPPELT, Georg	27	Hofheim	66-0147
GORDAN, Hugo	32	Breslau	64-0938
GOREJKI, Anton	39	Prust	66-0650
Eva 29, Franz 6m			
GORENFLO, Caroline	35	Preussen	66-0221
GORENFLO, John Sam	35	Friedrichstal	63-0296
Francisca 38, Otto 5, Emilie 3			
Wilhelmine 2, Magdalena 63			
GORKS, Gerhard	29	Walle	65-0402
GORNER, Fr.(m)	25	Belleville	64-0363
GORNER, J.B.	24	Weingarten	64-0495
GOSE, Carol.	28	Stroehen	65-1031
GOSSELER, Erhard	26	Niederreit	65-1088
GOSSEN, Davis	18	Lehe	64-0938
GOSSER, Anot.	36	Redwitz	64-0639
GOTHE, Julius	21	Gr. Furra	64-0593
GOTHE, Marie	21	Leipzig	64-0023
GOTHEN, M.	26	Rosebeck	66-0704
GOTTBEHUET, D.	30	Geba	65-1189
Christine 30, August 4, Ludwig 1			
GOTTHELF, Nolan	35	Washington	66-0984
Julie 35, Sara 3			
GOTTHOLD, Pauline	48	Minden	63-0990
Charles 3			
GOTTING, G.	21	Stegenberg	63-0013
GOTTLIEB, Eduard	30	Steinbach	66-0679
GOTTLIEB, F.	24	Philadelphia	63-0953
GOTTLIEB, Louise	31	New York	66-0109
GOTTMANN, Andreas	24	Kuelte	66-0984
GOTTSALK, G.P.	30	Biedenkopf	64-0593
GOTTSCHALK, E.	33	England	63-0168
GOTTSCHALK, Joh.	15	Waldeck	66-0577
GOTTSCHALK, L.	48	Muehlhausen	66-1243
Hermann 12			
GOTTSCHALK, Selmar	33	Covington	63-0551
Rudolph 9			
GOTTSCHALK, Wilh.	17	Ottenhagen	66-1243
Friedr. 17			
GOTTSCHICK, Friedr	25	Tuebingen	66-0576
GRAAF, (m)	25	Vegesack	63-1038
GRAAT, (f)	37	Havre	63-0990
GRAB, Joh.	22	Eschelbronn	64-0138
GRAB, Margarethe	18	Pfordt	64-0214
GRAB, Simon	45	Baden	66-0109
GRABAU, Anna	19	Bremen	67-0007
GRABBE, Joh. Herm.	31	Schwagsdorf	65-0898
Marie Elise 23, Friedrich 6m			
GRABE, Minna	35	Lueneburg	66-0412
GRABENHEIMER, Max	17	Diedelsheim	66-0734
GRABENKAMP, Lisett	22	Hedern	65-1030
GRABENKRUEGER, Lse	17	Wolmerdingen	65-1030
GRABHER, Francisca	36	Hoechst	66-1031
Johanna 40, Anna 11m			
GRABOWSKY, Hada	17	Kempen	63-0953
GRACH, L.	41	St. Paul	63-1085
GRAEBE, Fr.	24	Boeninghausen	65-0007
GRAEBER, Lisette	35	Elberfeld	63-1038
Louis 4			
GRAEBER, Heinr.	25	Dielingen	66-1031
GRAEF, (f)	42	Aggersiefen	64-0593
Lina 22, Clara 14, Wilhelm 16, Walter 7			
GRAEF, Adolph	29	Ilmenau	65-0770
Amalie 21			
GRAEF, Francis	30	Eisenach	63-0168
GRAEF, Peter	46	Hessloch	66-0083
Elisabeth 46, Conrad Adam 14, Friedrich 8			
Elisabeth 7, Anton 3, Johannes 9m			
GRAEF, Peter	17	Funckstadt	66-1128
GRAEFENER, Carl	28	Roeda	64-0739
GRAEFF, Albrecht	20	Preussen	63-1136
Mathilde 18			
GRAEFF, Anna	25	Bliescartel	65-0055
GRAEFF, Anton	24	Mainz	65-0402
GRAEFF, Barthold	54	Culmbach	65-1024
Marg. 52, Elisabeth 16			
GRAEFINSTERN, Wm.	26	Indianapolis	64-0593
GRAEFT, Heinr.	23	Bueckeburg	65-0594
Sophie 26, Friedr. 25			
GRAEME, Cath.	18	Huernbach	64-1022
GRAETER, Mart.	36	Markgroeningn	64-0495
GRAETWA, Stanisl.	60	Posen	67-0795
GRAEWE, Johann	47	Bremen	66-1031
GRAF, Adam	18	Hessia	66-0412
GRAF, Amalie	19	Leuchtenberg	66-0679
GRAF, Christian	34	Ash	63-0006
GRAF, Christian	23	Oberensingen	66-1327
GRAF, Franz	24	St. Martin	66-1093
GRAF, Friedr.	25	New York	66-0984
Elise 21			
GRAF, Georg	27	Weissenburg	65-0243
GRAF, John	33	Mahlesreuth	63-1218
Christine 32			
GRAF, John	23	Heiden	63-1218
GRAF, Joseph	26	Baden	66-0734
GRAF, Lisette	24	Freyberg	66-0679
GRAF, Louise	20	Muenchweiler	66-0147
GRAF, Peter	28	Sauerburg	65-0189
GRAF, Rosina	23	Nuertingen	66-1203
GRAF, Thomas	51	Boehmen	63-1038
GRAFEMANN, F.(m)	30	Braunschweig	64-0331
Johanna 21			
GRAFF, E.	46	Baden	63-1085
GRAFFE, Joseph	19	Ostbevern	66-1327
GRAFSANG, Hermann	18	Augusta	66-1131
GRAGE, Ernst	25	Hannover	66-1131
GRAHL, Frd.	17	Doljesheim	66-1127
GRAHLFS, (f)	40	Brooklyn	63-0990
Caroline 7			
GRAHM, Emilie	30	Duesseldorf	66-1155
Nett. 2, Anna 10m			
GRAHMER, D.	30	Hannover	65-1189
D. 5			
GRAISCHEN, Louis	28	Werdau	66-0837
GRAM, Adam	34	Neustettler	66-0650
Joh. 39			
GRAMAN, Joseph	28	Fuerstenau	66-1373
GRAMBS, Julius	28	Prussia	64-0687
GRAMER, Wm.	38	New York	64-0214
GRAMM, Carl	18	Armsheim	66-0412
GRAMM, Franz	27	Wolbach	64-0904
GRAMMANN, Joh. Hr.	28	Bissendorf	64-0886
GRAMMEL, Friedrich	25	Hutzenbach	66-0147
GRAMS, Christoph	24	Preussen	63-0862
GRAMS, Gottfr.	26	Bromberg	64-0456
GRANAT, Jacob	31	Medosa	64-0840
GRANING, D.(m)	24	Stockstadt	64-0331
GRANINGER, Cathar.	24	Wohlhausen	63-0752
GRANTZAU, Friedr.	24	Cassel	65-0189
GRANZ, Amalie	20	Lengsfeld	65-1024
GRAS, Carl	15	Kippenheim	63-0006
GRAS, Johann	28	Runkerod	67-0007
GRASS, Adolph	28	Darmstadt	65-0038
GRASS, Barbara	24	Morolschweisc	66-0623
GRASSAU, J.(m)	43	Braunschweig	64-0331
Emil 7			
GRASSINGER, Lorenz	33	Lichtenfels	66-0469
Maria 31, Barbara 4			
GRASSO, Joseph	27	Mederalne	64-0214
GRATZ, John	21	Tiefenort	63-0862
GRAU, A.	36	Prussia	64-0495
GRAU, Adelheid	24	Bonn	63-0097
GRAU, Friederike	24	Bonn	65-1024
Anna 22			
GRAU, G.	40	New York	63-1085
GRAU, Hermann	17	Bonn	63-0917
Henry 14			
GRAU, Jacob	18	Owen	66-0109
GRAUE, Marie	18	Kirchdorf	66-0650

NAME	AGE	RESIDENCE	YR-LIST
Wilhelmine 19			
GRAUE, Sophia	19	Celle	65-1030
GRAUER, Maria	20	Enzberg	66-1093
GRAULARER, Carl	35	Zeulenrode	67-0806
GRAVE, E.	45	Simonswalde	66-0413
Gretchen 40, Tjarks 9, Adelheid 3			
GRAVE, Joseph	61	Ellenstedt	63-1010
Josephine 24, Maria 21, Bernhardt			
GRAVES, John M.	32	Boston	63-0693
GRAVEVEL, J.H.	24	Salzbergen	64-0331
GRAVIUS, Heinr.	24	Coeln	64-1053
GRAZE, Gottlieb Fr	21	Strumpfelbach	64-0433
GRAZLER, Joseph	33	Kachan	64-0938
Maria 31, Joseph 7, Rosalie 5, Stephan 6m			
GREB, Conrad	51	Oberohmen	63-0006
Catharine 58, Johannes 23			
GREBE, Anton Aug.	36	Cassel	66-1127
GREBE, Dittmar	23	Lohne	66-1031
GREBE, Jos.	23	Hildesheim	64-0073
GREBE, Sebastian	31	Buckenau	63-0097
GREBE, Wilhelm	65	Muehlhausen	65-0948
GREBEL, D.	27	Homershausen	64-0782
GREBENAU, Leopold	20	Hanau	66-0679
GREBER, Louise	17	Gernsbach	64-0840
GREEF, Emil	30	Barmen	64-0593
Wife 20			
GREENBAUM, J.H.	29	Cincinnati	63-0990
GREFE, Anna	34	Wanna	64-0363
Ma.(f) 4			
GREFE, Margar.	19	Zeven/Hann.	63-0822
GREFENKAMP, Bernh.	31	Cincinnati	66-0984
Agnes 31, Reinhard 7, Anna 3m			
GREGER, Bruno	15	Rueckerswalde	63-0244
GREGER, Johann	25	Moorschuetz	66-0412
GREGORIUS, Georg	23	Hoexter	64-0214
GREIBE, Elisabeth	35	Essen	66-0668
Engel 33			
GREIER, Wilh.	24	Hannover	65-0594
GREIF, Flora	26	Rikken	66-1243
GREIFENHAGEN, P.	27	Wollstein	65-0974
GREIFF, Adolph	34	New York	66-0679
Marie 22			
GREIFF, Andreas	30	Niederursel	64-0214
GREIL, Bernhard	18	Tachau/Boeh.	65-1030
GREILING, Agnes	30	Hopsten	65-0898
GREIM, Christina	21	Sparnek	66-0349
GREIM, Joh.	33	Hof	65-0116
GREINACHER, Jul.	20	Constanz	66-0147
GREINEDER, M.(f)	26	Staubing	64-0427
GREINER, Barbara	23	Albertshausen	65-0189
GREINER, Engelbert	41	Bohndorf	64-0023
Edward 44			
GREINER, Joh.	26	Stettin	64-0170
GREINER, John	21	Welzheim	63-0482
GREINER, Magdalene	27	Wichmansdorf	66-1127
GREINN, Elisabeth	14	Fraukirsch	66-1093
GREIPP, Peter	32	Worms	66-1131
Barbara 32			
GREIS, John	53	Wien	63-1136
Henr. 30, Editha 7			
GREISEL, George	24	Obermelzungen	66-0412
GREISSENBERG, J.	20	Biebergen	65-1189
GREITLER, Barbara	65	Baden	66-0576
GRELLE, Jos.	28	Cloppenburg	64-0938
GREMPLER, Philip	20	Breslau	66-0109
GRENAU, Christ.	26	Wullwieck	64-0639
Dorothea 49, Christ. 16, Joseph 17			
Emil 16, Urban 24			
GRENGER, Christian	22	Weilheim	66-1203
GRESE, Ferd.	28	Belkof	65-0713
Wilhelmine 23, Bertha 9m			
GRESER, Seb.	23	Zimmern	65-0007
GRESS, Johann Ad.	23	Mainz	66-1155
GRESSLER, Robert	32	Carlsruhe	64-0687
Elise 26, Robert 3			
GRESSMEYER, Chrlot	19	Grimminghsn.	63-0990
GRETHER, Fr.	40	Gundelfingen	65-0402
GREULE, Michael	21	Breitenberg	66-1203

NAME	AGE	RESIDENCE	YR-LIST
GREVE, Carl	15	Goedenstedt	65-1030
GREVE, Chr.	26	Braunschweig	66-1248
GRHEK, Johann	20	Posen	64-0432
GRIEB, Adam	17	Heiligenfels	66-0704
GRIEB, Gustav	24	Stuttgart	65-1140
GRIEB, Johann	23	Hall	66-1373
GRIEBEL, Friedrich	23	Coblenz	63-0693
GRIEBEL, Herm.	17	Henbach	64-0593
GRIEBEL, Michael	59	Veilsdorf	63-0482
Dorothea 58, Gustav 34, Catharina 26			
Jean 3, William 10m, Christ. 20			
GRIEFE, Heinr.	24	Herringhausen	65-0898
Elisabeth 29			
GRIEM, Heinr.	28	Matfeld	65-0713
Diedr. 23			
GRIEME, Herm.	24	Martfeldt	64-1108
GRIEME, Joh. D.	28	Martfeld	65-0055
GRIEMSMANN, Berth.	19	Balkan	66-1031
GRIEP, Albert	27	Henkenhagen	64-0665
GRIEP, Johann	18	Asselage	67-0007
GRIES, Hedwig	20	Bensingen	66-0083
GRIESBACH, Joh. Gg	27	Schaffhof	64-0739
Joh. Karol. 29, Joh. Christ. 11m			
GRIESBACH, Wilhelm	32	Marienau	66-0576
GRIESBAUM, Anna	21	Dorlenbach	65-0007
GRIESE, Carl	19	Mannheim	67-0007
GRIESE, Jobst. Hen	37	Bielefeld	63-0244
GRIESE, Johannes	33	Hainbach	64-0170
Dor. Elis. 27, Anna Cath. 5			
Cath. Elis 11m, Justus 56, Anna Elis. 56			
Anna Cath. 16, Amalia 13			
GRIESHABER, Albert	28	Niederwasser	63-0006
GRIESHABER, Barth	68	Freuenbrunn	64-0593
Andreas 23, Cath. 21, Christine 20			
GRIESHABER, Lisett	18	Wuerttemberg	64-0432
GRIESHALER, Chrtne	16	Tuttlingen	63-0917
GRIESHEIM, V.	19	Bemern	64-1161
GRIESMANN, Ma.(f)	18	Zeppenhahn	64-0495
GRIESMEYER, Carl	20	Hannover	66-1093
GRIESSAMMER, Conr.	22	Velmer	64-0687
GRIESSER, Ottilie	23	Wellendingen	65-0116
GRIESSHAMMER, G.	33	Muenchberg	65-0038
Margaretha 22, Louise 1			
GRIFFING, M.	40	New York	63-0097
GRIL, Adam	18	Baden	66-0147
GRILL, Peter	22	Ndr.Erlenbach	67-0007
GRILLENBERGER, Reg	23	Degersheim	66-1155
GRIMM, Edm.	27	Coburg	64-0687
GRIMM, Elise	18	Worpswede	65-0948
GRIMM, Friedr.	23	Neustadt	66-1243
GRIMM, J.A.	3-	Wernhausen	64-0495
GRIMM, Joh.	29	Wiesthal	64-0331
GRIMM, Josepha	22	Heimerdingen	64-0687
GRIMM, Moritz	21	Hessberg	64-0214
Francisca 36, Flora 9m, Joh. 17			
GRIMM, Rosine	26	Zepfenhahn	64-0331
GRIMM, Rudolph	25	Hinwyl	65-0243
GRIMME, Fr.	35	Girrwalde	65-0402
Johanna 28, Charl.(m) 56, Georgine 20			
Henr. 4			
GRIMMELBAUM, Gerh.	21	Haya	64-0456
GRIMS, Ricka	24	Loxstedt	65-0116
GRIPP, Wilhelm	29	Voersteum	67-0007
GROB, Paul	22	Obstalten	64-0214
GROBB, Conrad	39	Altdorf	66-0984
GROBE, Johann	26	Buchhausen	66-1243
Catharine 24			
GROEBEN, Carl	24	Stuttgart	66-1203
GROEHN, Johann	49	Brodden	66-1248
Julius 18, Wilhelmine 13			
GROELLE, Sophie	65	Riyenhagen	66-0650
GROENE, Georg	23	Verden	63-0953
GROENE, Herm.	28	Estwege	66-1373
GROENIG, Georg	62	Delbrinck	65-1095
Moritz 30			
GROENING, Albert	19	Hannover	64-0456
GROENINGER, Theod.	25	New York	63-1136
GROEPE, Barbara	32	Rottlersreuth	64-0886

NAME	AGE	RESIDENCE	YR-LIST
GROESCHEL, Sophie	20	Steinbach	66-1313
GROESE, James	20	Biebelshausen	63-1038
GROESLE, August	20	Stuttgart	64-1022
GROESSER, Cathrine	21	Schwiesheim	64-1053
GROETHER, Ludwig	17	Gleichen	66-1327
GROEZINGEN, Herman	17	Nuerlelingen	66-1093
GROFTFELD, Theodor	52	Esthof	66-1031
Elisabeth 55, Therese 20, Anna 16			
Engelbert 19, Marie 7, Amalie 5			
Theodor 6m, Elisabeth 6m			
GROHE, Eduard	36	Olmuetz	64-0886
GROHMANN, Friedr.	27	Potsdam	66-1243
Lotte 21			
GROLL, Friedr.	30	Reilingen	64-1022
GROLL, Ludwig	18	Gassen	63-0990
Clementine 21			
GROLL, Wilhelm	45	Neustadt	66-1373
Anna 33, Augusta 2, Wilhelm 6m			
GROLLMAN, v. H.	30	Darmstadt	64-0363
GROMMING, Peter	54	Zanne	66-1248
Emilie 17, Peter 20			
GRONEWEG, Carl	36	Lemfoerde	64-0840
GRONEWOLD, Eme Hrm	33	Holtrup	66-1128
GRONEWOLD, Enne	21	Holtrup	66-1128
Willm 17			
GRONING, Wm.	22	Bremen	65-0038
GROON, (m)		Hannover	66-0221
GROON, Margarethe	33	Blauhand	66-0221
GROOTE, Fokke	37	Wegnard	66-0704
Trientje 37, Jan 7, Antje 5, baby 9m			
GROSCH, Cathar.	29	Cassel	65-0116
GROSCH, Christ.	30	Kleinsachsen	66-0349
Cath. 9, Barbara 18			
GROSCH, Laurent	18	Markenzell	65-1030
GROSHANZ, Adam	20	Oberweiler	66-0147
GROSMANN, Fritz	46	Lingen	66-1203
Marianne 16, Fritz 12, Heinrich 9			
Caroline 6, Marianne 40, Diedrich 3			
Louis 6m			
GROSS, A.	21	Iggingen	63-1003
GROSS, Anton	26	Bachen	63-0821
GROSS, Carl Aug.	15	Salzungen	65-0594
Charlotte 35, Hinr. 7, Herman 5, Marie 19			
GROSS, Cathar.	20	Dousreider	66-0221
GROSS, Christ.	19	Weidelbrunn	66-1243
GROSS, Conr.	44	Stehlingen	63-1136
GROSS, Conrad	42	Cassdorf	66-1031
Elisabeth 37, Simon 7, Anna 5			
GROSS, David	69	Flouheim	65-0243
GROSS, Fr'ke. Mar.	19	Oberensingen	64-0433
GROSS, Fr.	16	Stuttgart	65-1088
GROSS, Georg	23	Daringsdorf	64-0639
GROSS, Heinr.	35	Fritzlar	66-1127
Lisabeth 36, Augusta 9, Friedrich 7			
Ernst 5, Moritz 9m			
GROSS, Heinr. L.	39	Bittersgruen	65-0713
GROSS, Herm.	23	Breitenworbis	65-0007
GROSS, Jacob	32	Wuerttenberg	66-0221
GROSS, Johann	22	Thurnau	64-0840
GROSS, Johs.	34	Geismar	65-0243
GROSS, Jos. W.	19	Muenden	64-0593
GROSS, Magd.	20	Heldenbergen	64-0138
GROSS, Robert	28	Werdau	64-0363
GROSS, Samuel	27	Zempelburg	66-0221
GROSS, Sigmund	26	Esslingen	66-1127
Margarethe 58, Heinrich G. 17			
GROSS, W.	34	Homburg	66-0413
Catharine 33, George 6, Heinrich 4			
Caroline 9m			
GROSS, W. Ernst	19	Winnenden	64-0170
GROSS, William	25	Ehringhausen	63-1218
GROSSE, A.L.	20	Bremen	65-0116
GROSSE, Ernst	41	St. Louis	65-0594
GROSSE, Heinrich	22	Bruchhausen	66-1203
GROSSE, Ida	38	Frankfurt/O.	67-0795
Clara 15, Mathilde 6			
GROSSE, Joseph	21	Loeningen	67-0007
GROSSE, Ludwig	30	Nienhagen	63-0862

NAME	AGE	RESIDENCE	YR-LIST
GROSSE, Maths.	28	Ballingen	64-0023
GROSSE, Waldemar	18	Hannover	66-0578
GROSSHAUPT, Chr.	26	Hemmingen	64-1161
Eva 26, Rosina 6m			
GROSSHAUS, Herm.	23	Calw	66-0984
GROSSKOPF, Ernst	28	Brichtenstadt	66-1203
GROSSLENRICK, Witt	25	Horndorf	63-1085
GROSSMANN, Aug.	35	Paren	67-0600
GROSSMANN, Fr.	24	Butzow	65-0898
GROSSMANN, Georg W	59	Biedenkopf	64-0687
Eva 57, Georg 46			
GROSSMANN, Marc	40	Ungarn	63-0917
Johanna 26, Mathilde 5, Rebecca 4			
Samuel 11m			
GROSSMANN, Ph.Wm.	21	Bremen	65-0116
GROSSMANN, S.	72	Dielesdorf	65-1189
GROSSTERLINDEN, T.	24	Prussia	65-0189
GROSTE, Wilhelm	36	Bueckeburg	63-0917
GROSZECK, Peter	51	Moschis	66-0578
Marianne 50, Anna 19, Joseph 16, Adam 13			
Johann 9, Ignatz 5			
GROTE, August	19	Lesum	65-0055
GROTE, Carl	23	Lemfoerde	66-0679
Marie 29			
GROTE, Caroline	16	Stolzenau	66-0577
GROTE, Cath. Elis.	20	Hannover	64-0920
GROTE, Domenicus	59	Oldenburg	66-1093
Catharine 59, Heinrich 22, Joseph 17			
Caroline 20, Anna 24, Clemens 9m			
GROTE, Doris	19	Liebenau	66-0578
GROTE, Friederike	55	Nordhausen	64-0886
Anna 19			
GROTE, Joh. Heinr.	30	Lerte	65-1030
GROTHA, Albrecht	36	Polen	66-0666
Catharine 40, Jacob 15, Pauline 6			
Julia 4			
GROTHAUS, Joh. D.	35	Arphofen	64-0938
GROTHENNE, Antonia	28	Braunschweig	66-1093
Elise 9			
GROTHHAUS, Herm.	24	Meissen	64-0782
Louise 25			
GROTHUSEN, Heinr.	24	Nordleda	66-1248
Nicolaus 21			
GROTJAN, Johann	41	Osnabrueck	64-0363
Wilhelm 12, Carl 9, Bertha 7, Johann 3			
Maria 6m			
GROVE, Chr.	30	Beelen	65-1024
GROZHOLZ, Hermann	21	Schwarzach	66-0679
GRUBE, Aug.	20	Goettingen	66-1243
GRUBE, Carl	66	Einbeck	66-1127
Minna 66			
GRUBE, Diedr.	19	Buschhausen	65-0116
GRUBE, F.(m)	29	New York	63-0551
GRUBE, Georg	29	Merseburg	66-1155
GRUBE, Herm.	33	Wehden	64-0214
GRUBE, L.	20	Lauenstein	66-0413
GRUBE, Michael	34	Nuernberg	67-0806
GRUBEND, Ludwig	44	Daubhausen	65-1024
GRUBER, D.(f)	48	Muenden	64-0427
Caroline 29, Anna M. 4, Wilhelmine 2			
baby 9m, Amalia 22			
GRUBER, Franz	30	Neufelden	66-0734
GRUBER, Heinrich	24	Freiburg	66-0934
GRUBER, John E.	48	New York	66-0934
GRUBER, Wilhelm	21	Wabern	64-0739
GRUBERT, M.G.	21	Fuerth	63-0862
GRUBERT, Norbert	37	Rippoldsen	66-0734
GRUBERT, Paul	22	Fuerth	65-0151
GRUBMEIER, Conrad	21	Amt Stolzenau	67-0599
Dorothea 18, Wilhelm 15			
GRUDOWSKY, J.	37	Schwetz	66-0413
Marie 33, Paulina 10, Augusta 7, Marie 1			
GRUEBER, Ida	18	Rauenstein	64-0170
GRUEBER, Ludwig	23	Freiburg	66-0679
GRUEDEL, Henry	21	Stade	66-1203
GRUEFELDER, James	17	Baltimore	64-0639
GRUEL, L.(m)	34	Stuttgart	64-0073
Julia 30, Albertine 2, Alfred 9m			

NAME	AGE	RESIDENCE	YR-LIST
GRUEN, Christ.	59	Zepfenhan	63-1038
Juliane 57			
GRUEN, Friedr.	29	Ossweil	64-0886
GRUEN, Julius	18	Berlin	64-0687
GRUEN, Sam.	23	Boljai	65-0007
GRUEN, Sigmund	42	Ungarn	65-0713
GRUENBAUM, Carolyn	21	Hellstein	64-0687
GRUENBAUM, Clara	24	Geisa	63-0917
GRUENBAUM, Henry	20	Polle	63-0244
GRUENBAUM, Lazarus	22	Kettenbach	65-1024
GRUENBAUM, Minna	17	Hettenhausen	66-0704
GRUENDT, Joachim	50	Spenden	66-1203
Marie 48, Heinrich 12, Johann 11			
GRUENE, Christ.	34	Gestorf	63-0097
GRUENEBAUM, Blume	28	Langsdorf	64-1053
GRUENEBAUM, Marcus	21	Hainchen	65-0055
Leopold 15, Lehnchen 23			
GRUENEFELD, Heinr.	25	Scheppingen	65-1030
GRUENEN, Maria	24	Zapfenhau	66-1373
GRUENER, Therese	20	Maroischweisc	66-0623
Bernard 9			
GRUENER, Wilhelm	19	Osnabrueck	66-1203
GRUENEWALD, Friedr	17	Brakel	63-0482
GRUENEWALD, L.	28	St. Louis	63-0917
GRUENEWALD, Leop.	30	Affoltrach	63-1136
GRUENEWALD, Rica	47	Brakel	63-0482
GRUENEWALD, Sophie	26	Ob.Breitenbch	66-0984
GRUENINGER, Christ	46	Reutlingen	66-1327
Caroline 17, Christiane 19			
GRUENKEMEIER, Bern	35	Bachholzhause	65-0950
GRUENTOW, Carl	25	Gmueden	66-1128
GRUESMEYER, Carl	16	Bremen	64-0593
GRUESS, Gerhard	54	Ehren	66-0934
Elisabeth 28			
GRUETSCH, Cathar.	13	Ipsheim	66-1031
GRUETTER, Carl Aug	21	Verden	63-0614
GRUETTER, Franz	18	Luzern	64-0456
GRUEWJES, H.G.	25	Westerstedt	66-0413
GRUMBACH, H.(m)	21	Hochenhain	64-0331
GRUMBEIN, Ernestin	24	Wallenburg	64-0687
GRUMBEIN, Fanny	21	Wallenberg	66-0734
GRUNAU, Wilhelmine	21	Wollin	63-0614
GRUNDGRIET, Christ	22	Hessen	66-0734
GRUNDLACH, Friedr.	21	Bremervoerde	65-0865
GRUNDMANN, C.(m)	28	Breslau	64-0138
GRUNDMANN, Rich.	18	Leipzig	64-0593
GRUNDMUELLER, Jos.	28	New York	66-0147
GRUNDNER, Carl	32	Bodenstein	64-0739
GRUNER, Andreas	39	Mittelbuchen	66-1373
GRUNER, Carl	19	Bremen	64-0331
GRUNER, Edm.	23	Zwickau	65-0402
GRUNER, Jacob	33	Waldangelbach	64-0073
Philippine 35, Fredr. 4, Cath. 3m			
Fredr. 31			
GRUNER, S.(m)	24	Osnabrueck	64-0331
GRUNEWALD, August	20	Cassel	65-0865
GRUNEWALD, Leonh.	25	Seckmann	63-0862
GRUNLER, Leander	38	Lenlenrode	66-1093
GRUNOW, Ferd. J.	30	Strotzewe	64-0687
GRUPE, Caroline	17	Bremen	65-0151
GRUPE, Heinrich	18	Osnabrueck	66-1093
GRUSSE, Friedr.	31	Paderborn	64-0840
GRUTNER, Paul	32	Sonneberg	66-1155
GSCHWIND, Caroline	21	Haardt	63-1085
GSCHWIND, Wilh'mne	25	Altstaedten	63-1085
GUAM, Ottilie	38	Schelbrun/Sw.	64-1053
Emilie 20, Bertha 17, Mathilde 15			
Elise 12, Wilhelm 10			
GUCKELSBERGER, Els	25	Rockenberg	63-0296
GUCKEMUS, Elisab.	20	Dudenhofen	63-0482
GUCKER, John	37	Moessingen	63-0296
Anna M. 27, Isaac 3, Marg. 1			
GUCKHARDT, Anna	31	Bloedisheim	66-0221
Adam 18			
GUDE, Catharine	22	Raine	66-0623
GUDEKUNST, Jacob	26	Heidelberg	67-0954
Christiane 21			
GUDEWILL, Herman	38	New York	66-0984

NAME	AGE	RESIDENCE	YR-LIST
GUDRIAN, Wilh.	27	Preussen	63-0398
GUECHNER, Sophie	19	Kobelwald	64-1108
GUEDEMANN, Herman	37	Quakenbrueck	64-0938
Anna 19			
GUEDERMANN, Melise	25	Hannover	63-0917
GUELDNER, Fritz	23	Rhenegge	66-0734
GUEMPEL, Ernst	26	Rotenburg	64-0639
Ernestine 18			
GUENDELACH, Ls.	21	Detmold	64-1161
GUENDER, Margareth	20	Zeiskau	65-0243
GUENSH, Christine	18	Oberhamm	66-1248
GUENST, Marg.	18	Altheim	63-1218
GUENTER, Johannes	19	Poll	65-1095
GUENTER, Joseph	42	Halsbronn	66-1203
Catharine 35, Wilhelmine 8			
GUENTERBERG, Emil	28	Kischkow	65-1030
Emilie 24			
GUENTERBERG, Joh.	48	Prussia	64-0427
GUENTERT, F.	22	Hornheim	64-1161
GUENTHER, Anna	45	Bechtolsheim	66-0837
GUENTHER, Anna	54	Uengsterode	66-1248
Anna 23			
GUENTHER, Anna El.	21	Regenhain	65-0116
GUENTHER, Aug.	19	Bichelhorst	65-0594
GUENTHER, Carl	17	Grumbach	66-0221
GUENTHER, Christ.	20	Moehringen	64-1108
GUENTHER, Christ.	35	Mohringen	64-0427
GUENTHER, Christne	24	Simmersfeld	66-0147
GUENTHER, Elise	28	Cramme	64-0782
baby 11m			
GUENTHER, Ernst	33	Hannover	66-0734
Friederike 27, Wilhelmine 3, Augusta 11m			
GUENTHER, Friedr.	43	Kahlwinkel	63-0614
Wilhelmine 38, August 15, Emilie 14			
Therese 12, Constanza 7, Louise 6			
Amalie 5, Carl 3, Robert 10m			
GUENTHER, Georg	26	Bellhorn	65-0116
GUENTHER, Helena	21	Hilgersdorf	66-1373
Theresia 23			
GUENTHER, Henry	46	Dayton	63-0752
GUENTHER, J.(m)	16	Boll	64-0495
GUENTHER, Jacob	45	New York	64-0170
Marg. 46			
GUENTHER, Joh.	39	Einortshausen	65-0116
GUENTHER, Margaret	18	Darmstadt	66-1031
GUENTHER, Philipp	20	Duesslingen	65-0189
GUENTHER, W.	22	Braunschweig	66-0704
Augusta 18			
GUENTZ, Albert	32	Weynona	63-0350
GUENTZER, Nicolaus	30	St. Paul	66-0221
GUERIN, (m)	31	Paris	64-0023
GUERTLER, Alb.	24	France	64-0782
Robt. 26			
GUESEFELD, W.	24	Zewenitz	65-0007
GUETEMANN, Christ.	27	Bischofsrode	66-0109
GUETENSLOH, F.(m)	27	Bremervoerde	64-0687
GUETERSLOH, H.	36	Beverstedt	65-0055
Rosa 36, Rosa 3			
GUETH, Heinr.	20	Gelnhausen	64-0938
Herm. 30			
GUETISCH, Peter	34	Rhein Duerkhm	65-1030
Catharina 28, Georg 5, Jacob 3, Bina 1			
Catharina 6m			
GUETZLAFF, Herm.	22	Coeslin	67-0795
GUGEL, Chrs.	20	Bettlingen	66-0221
Cathar. 16			
GUGEL, Gottfried	19	Wuertemberg	63-0822
GUGEL, Heinr.	25	Wien	65-0055
GUGELBERGER, Carl	40	Louisville	66-0109
GUGENHAHN, William	24	Ulm	63-0168
GUGGENHEIM, Amalie	21	Thiengen	66-0576
Baruch 9			
GUGGENHEIM, Elise	22	Gailingen	66-0704
GUGGENHEIM, Regine	23	Thiengen	66-0679
GUHL, W.(m)	27	Krauchenowis	64-0495
GUHMANN, Friedrich	42	New Orleans	66-0984
Louis 40, Marie 9, Friedr. 8, August 4m			
GUIGNARD, Alex	30	Paris	64-0073

NAME	AGE	RESIDENCE	YR-LIST
GULAN, Johann	18	Carlshaven	66-0679
GULAU, Joh.D.Gus.	15	Oldendorf	67-0599
GULBRECHT, Flor.	20	Rikken	66-1243
GULDE, Jean	33	Winzingen	66-0576
GULDEN, Carl	18	Esslingen	66-1093
GULDENFUSS, Ernst	31	Halle	64-0593
Lisette 19			
GULICH, Carl	18	Pforzheim	64-1161
GULL, Marie	26	Muenchen	66-0576
GULZ, Marie	31	Haschkanne	63-0350
GUMBEL, Isaac	22	Hoffenheim	65-0594
GUMPERT, Alex.	14	Schneidemuehl	64-0170
Ephr. 18			
GUMPERT, Lewis	18	Offenbach	63-0296
GUMSLACH, Friedr.	18	Almerode	66-1155
GUNDELACH, Carl	19	Schoenhagen	66-1327
GUNDELSMEYER, Joh.	24	Freinfeld	66-0349
GUNDENBERG, Georg	31	Pfingstadt	64-1053
Helene 24, Dorothea 6m			
GUNDERMANN, Cath.	20	Coblenz	66-0576
GUNDLACH, Marie	22	Hessen	64-0432
GUNDRUM, H.F.(m)	19	Alsfeld	64-0331
GUNKEL, Mar.	22	Worms	65-0402
GUNKELMANN, Joh. C	30	Windeberg	64-0214
GUNTERMANN, Peter	22	Darmstadt	65-0004
GUNTHER, Friedrich	27	Erzlingen	66-0346
Carl 17			
GUNTRUM, W.	23	Schlitz	65-1024
GUNZENHAUSER, Herz	20	Reichstein	64-0904
GUNZENHEIMER, Ba.	16	Gemuende	64-0782
GURAN, Mathilde	41	Berlin	65-0004
Hedw. 7, Marie 4, Martha 3			
GURTNER, Christ	25	Switz	64-0170
GUSCELLI, Maria	24	Triest	64-1053
Papina 24, Horinda 20, Alwina 6			
GUSS, M.	24	Behle	63-1003
GUSSMANN, Stephan	32	Coburg	67-0007
GUSSTEIN, Joseph	27	New York	66-0576
GUST, J.(m)	26	Preussen	64-0495
GUST, Julie	23	Werdum	67-0795
GUSTAHL, Betty	16	Furth	64-0782
GUSTAVS, August E.	32	Berum	63-1069
Sophie 34, Her. Heinr. 32			
GUSTRACH, G.(m)	21	Heiligenstadt	64-0331
GUT, Franz	25	Mohringen	67-0007
GUTH, Alexander	19	Herbolzheim	66-0147
Franz 16, Ignatz 22			
GUTH, Aug.	30	Stolp	66-0934
GUTHEIL, Adolph	30	Hamburg	66-1203
GUTHEIM, Friedrich	22	Rhoden	66-0984
GUTHHARD, Chr.	30	Goeppingen	65-1088
GUTHIMANN, Rud.	34	Chicago	66-0221
A.H. 30			
GUTHMANN, Herman	27	Hungary	64-0739
GUTJAHR, Johannes	16	Linzingen	64-0739
GUTKUNST, Gottl.	36	Hemerdingen	65-0243
GUTMANN, Beno	22	Schnei	66-0576
GUTMANN, Bertha	17	Bederkesa	66-1155
GUTMANN, Caroline	25	Wuerttemberg	66-0349
GUTMANN, Christine	29	Nordlingen	66-0734
GUTMANN, Emil	16	Brieg	64-0840
Mar. 14			
GUTMANN, Friedr.	23	Goettingen	66-0577
GUTMANN, Herm.	25	Ungarn	63-1136
GUTMANN, Isidor	22	Ungarn	66-0221
GUTMANN, Lena	23	Gemmingen	64-0593
GUTMANN, Leonh.	14	Michelsbach	65-0038
Georg 9			
GUTMANN, Marie	15	Scheinbach	63-0953
GUTOWSKY, L.(m)	39	Columbus	64-0331
Johanna 21			
GUTPERLET, Anna	20	Oversleben	65-1095
GUTTENSOHN, Mich.	50	Washington	63-1136
GUTZEN, Wm.	37	Duesseldorf	64-0886
GUTZLER, Geo.	29	Weinsheim	65-0974
GWINNER, C.(f)	34	Herrenberg	64-0331
GYSEN, F.	20	Unt.Steinbach	65-0898
HAABEN, Hr.	30	Levergte	64-0938
Anna 28, Hr. 5			
HAABERS, Lisette	20	Essen	64-0938
HAACKE, A.	31	New York	63-1038
Anna 24			
HAAF, Gottl.	19	Sieglingen	66-1313
HAAG, Augusta	23	Fuetzringen	66-1155
HAAG, Barbara	27	Mittelaurach	64-0739
HAAG, Engelbert	20	Hochnoessingn	66-1155
HAAG, Geo. Leonh.	35	Wettringen	67-0599
HAAG, Pauline	19	Osweil	66-1127
HAAG, Therese	19	Muenchen	64-0687
HAAG, Wilhelm	17	Wuertemberg	66-0679
HAAK, Marie	28	Adelsdorf	66-0679
HAAK, Peter	21	Lintig	65-0594
HAAKE, Friedr.	20	Bremen	63-0822
HAAKE, Friedr.	24	Warmsen	66-0650
HAAR, Marie	17	Neuenstein	65-0243
HAAR, Trina	14	Wackhausen	63-0953
HAAR, ter Herm.	32	Simonswolde	65-0151
HAAR, v.d. F. (m)	27	Fuerstenau	64-0363
HAARHAUS, Wm.	56	Dortmund	65-1024
HAARMANN, Friedr.	21	Bremen	63-0693
HAARMANN, Richard	21	Goslar	65-0950
HAARMANN, Sophie	21	Kappeln	65-1024
HAARMEYER, H. Aug.	28	Neunkirchen	63-0168
HAAS, Adam	16	Darmstadt	66-0576
HAAS, Aloisa	26	Mariazell	64-0687
HAAS, Andr.	53	Neunkirchen	65-0007
Eva 48, Caroline 19, Isaac 16, Simon 14			
Felix 10, Riekchen 9			
HAAS, Anna	18	Schweiz	66-0704
HAAS, Ar.	21	Erzig	64-0782
HAAS, Barth.	38	Herschau	64-1022
HAAS, Carl	52	Birkenfeld	64-1206
Wilhelmine 24			
HAAS, Catharine	20	Baden	66-0576
HAAS, Heinemann	14	Burgel	66-0679
HAAS, Heinrich	58	Voelkershsn.	66-1031
Caroline 48, Emilie 16, Marianne 14			
Minna 9, Malchen 7			
HAAS, Jacob	37	Lackersmuehle	66-0934
Elisabeth 36, Catharina 5			
HAAS, Jules	27	Baiern	64-0427
HAAS, Julius	18	Raegen	63-1085
HAAS, Katty	17	Rozgenz	65-0007
Siegm. 15			
HAAS, Lorenz	15	Sprendlingen	66-1155
HAAS, Louis	45	Eberbach	64-1053
HAAS, Louis	17	Ziegenhein	65-1031
HAAS, Nicolaus	39	New York	66-0668
HAAS, Peter	41	Hartford	66-1203
Marie 20, Martin 9			
HAAS, Silvester	25	Aichhalter	64-0023
HAASE, August	19	Frankenhausen	64-0687
HAASE, Bernhard	19	Muenden	66-1373
HAASE, Carl Fr.	37	Schoenebeck	63-0990
Anna 40, Emilie 14, Marie 9, Friedr. 8			
HAASE, Carl Victor	23	Oschatz	65-0948
HAASE, Christine	20	Hannover	63-0821
HAASE, Crl.	33	Oldendorf	64-0495
HAASE, Ferd.	22	Dagerode	65-0594
HAASE, Florentine	16	Weimar	66-0577
HAASE, Friedr.	23	Muenden	66-0704
HAASE, Heinr.	32	Olber	66-1131
HAASE, Robert	17	Muenden	66-1093
HAASE, Wilhelm	29	Duderstadt	66-1093
Elise 26			
HABBECK, Carl	53	Trutzlatz	64-0433
Wilhelmine 54, Hanna 25, Caroline 19			
Emilie 16, Friederike 10			
HABBECK, Gottlieb	28	Neugardt	64-0433
Charlotte 35, Maria 8, Wilhelmine 4			
HABBEN, Benjamin	23	Wiesens	66-1128
HABBERLE, John	43	Schmichen	64-0023
Johanna 21			
HABENICHT, Carl	17	Braunschweig	63-1010
HABER, John	24	Schluechtern	63-0350
HABERBOSCH, Joh.	25	Steinhilden	66-1313

NAME	AGE	RESIDENCE	YR-LIST
HABERER, Elisabeth	34	Rippoldsen	66-0734
Albertine 34, Otto 8, Bertha 5			
Crecentie 4, Albert 2, Philipp 9m			
HABERKAMP, Hermann	16	Borgholzhsn.	66-1031
HABERKORN, Peter	30	Eger	66-0704
HABERLE, Lorenz	33	Oggelshausen	66-0221
HABERLOH, Bernhard	35	Hannover	64-0432
HABERMANN, B.	30	Preussen	63-0990
HABERMANN, Babette	22	New York	63-1218
HABERMANN, Casp.	22	Huettengesess	66-1373
HABERMEHL, Elisa	21	Willofs	64-0214
HABERMEHL, Elise	15	Bellmuth	66-0668
Marie 19			
HABERMEHL, Louise	29	Stockheim	65-1088
HABERMEHL, Margar.	21	Lauterbach	65-1030
HABERS, Joh. Rud.	52	Aurich	65-1030
Margaretha 46, Rolph 19, Hermann 17			
Anna 10, Greta 7			
HABES, Gustav	28	Aachen	63-1038
Louise 25, Marie 1			
HABICH, Aug.(m)	28	Cassell	64-0331
Johanna 21			
HABICH, Carl	30	Eisenach	66-0221
Margarethe 27			
HABICH, Eduard	48	Boston	66-0576
Emma 42			
HABICH, Johs.	15	Bodenrod	64-0782
HABICHT, Philipp	35	Neustadt	64-0214
Jacob 28, Anna 43, Franz 9, Wilhelm 8			
HABLITZEL, Chr'tne	21	Wuertemberg	66-0984
HABMANN, Johann	17	Baden	66-0576
HACH, Dorette	24	Rineck	65-1024
HACHE, Hermann	22	Chemnitz	66-1203
HACHLAGE, Heinr	20	Tenstedt	66-1127
HACHMANN, Lena	57	Cappler	66-0734
HACHT, Marie Cat.	35	Marienjoest	66-0623
HACHTHAL, Georg	52	St. Louis	64-0023
Elisabeth 51, Catharina 16, Peter 9			
Carl 7, Elisabeth 6, Heinrich 5			
Christoph 4			
HACHTMANN, Henr'tt	9	Cappeln	66-0734
HACK, Marianne	18	Sigmaringen	66-0221
HACKE, Johannes	17	Heldenbergen	66-0679
HACKENBERG, Robert	26	Ronsdorf	66-0984
HACKER, Gottlob	16	Giglingen	65-0713
HACKER, Jos. Carl	25	Ansbach	63-0296
HACKMANN, Jos.	30	Bremen	63-1218
HACKMEISTER, Georg	30	Baltimore	63-0821
HADD, Julius	19	Otterndorf	66-0576
HADEL, Julius	19	Otterndorf	66-0576
HADEL, Rosalie	17	Otterndorf	66-0576
HADEPOHL, Goerg	19	Sudweyhe	66-0734
HADLER, Heinr.	15	Stroehm	64-0593
HADLER, Joh.	25	Hannover	64-0938
HADLES, Meta	20	Aschwarden	65-1024
HADON, William	24	Switz	66-0679
HADWIG, D.(m)	18	Rheda	64-0495
HAEBAHN, Adolph	27	Essen	65-0713
HAEBBELER, Minna	23	Osnabrueck	65-0007
HAEBERLE, Magnus	29	Eschenhausen	66-1131
Emma 23, Frieda 4			
HAEFELE, Math.	20	Betzgenrieth	64-0214
HAEFFENER, W.	28	Gehrde	63-0350
HAEFNER, John	23	Buckersdorf	66-0109
HAEFNER, P.	17	Carlsruhe	66-0413
HAEGE, Johann	16	Sulzfeld	66-1093
Maria 26			
HAEGELE, Gottfried	21	Mettingen	65-1031
HAEGELE, Jacob	23	Adelmannsfeld	65-1030
Caroline 18			
HAEGELE, Joh.	27	Eschach	66-1313
Regina 26			
HAEGER, Carl	30	Muenden	65-1024
HAEGLE, Ferd.	38	Prussia	64-0138
HAEHNERT, Carl	42	St. Louis	66-0704
HAEHNLEIN, Leopold	17	Weikersheim	63-0693
HAELBLEIN, Georg	19	Toenitz	66-1131
HAELL, Heinrich	20	Rohnshausen	63-0614

NAME	AGE	RESIDENCE	YR-LIST
HAELTEMANN, Bernh.	23	Osnabrueck	66-1031
HAEMEL, Jacob	30	Luetzewig	23-0865
Elisabeth 26, Andreas 14, Heinrich 4			
Catharine 1			
HAEMMER, Minna	32	Eisenach	64-1053
Friederike 59, Paul 12, Caroline 7			
Anna 5, Bruno 3			
HAEMMLER, Johann	26	Ohmenhausen	66-1243
HAENDEL, Kunigunde	31	Weissenohe	66-1248
HAENKHAUS, Ant.	22	Hedinghaus	65-0038
HAENLE, Jacob	32	Stuttgart	66-0934
Louis 23, Louis 2			
HAENTSCHEL, Joseph	40	Kaiserwalde	66-1373
HAEPER, Terese	59	Braak/Pr.	64-0920
HAERER, Maria	27	Pluderhausen	64-0687
HAERING, August	32	Beberstedt	64-0433
Maria Christ 40, Wm. Friedr. 5			
Friedr.Louis 6m			
HAERING, Friedrich	20	Asch	66-0679
HAERTEL, Wilhelm	20	Frankfurt	66-0469
HAESE, Johann	36	Moschitz	66-0578
Amalie 32, Charlotte 2, Augusta 1			
HAESLE, Matheus	29	Glotz/Switz	64-1053
HAESLER, Johann	38	Ronserwitz	66-1031
HAESLOOP, Georg	46	Bremen	65-0151
HAESLOOP, George	45	New York	63-0097
HAEUSER, Conr.	28	Frankfurt	63-0168
HAEUSER, Hr.	17	Lich	65-0594
HAEUSER, Peter	33	Werpelfelden	65-0974
Catharine 32, Louise 4, Elisabeth 14			
Balthasar 15, baby 11m			
HAEUSLER, Francis	42	Wien	63-0097
HAEUSLER, Johann	26	Primar	67-0007
HAEUSSLER, August	18	Loessnitz	66-1155
HAEUSSLER, Joseph	20	Ermingen	63-1178
HAFEMEYER, Elisab.	20	Lintorf	64-0170
HAFEN, David	34	New York	64-0593
HAFENSROCK, James	22	Kirchheim	63-0097
HAFERMANN, Bernh.	25	Dothen	65-0007
HAFERMEISTER, Emil	21	Roebe	66-0668
HAFFEN, Jacob	24	Weidenthal	66-0704
HAFFNER, Anton	30	Baiern	66-0704
HAFFNER, Louis	57	Pfalz	63-0990
HAFNER, C.A.	19	Untermunkheim	65-0402
HAFNER, Georg	28	Wegheim	64-0495
HAFNER, Maria	18	Schlichtum	66-0837
HAG, Lorenz	41	Steig	63-1085
HAGE, Eliza	17	Baden	66-0412
Catharina 19			
HAGE, Henry Ant.	15	Barnstorf	63-1178
HAGE, Rosine	18	Kentzingen	66-1093
Regina 23			
HAGEBAEKE, Maria	22	Isenstedt	66-1031
HAGEBOECK, Mina	26	Halver	63-0551
HAGEDORN, Bernard	31	Muenster	65-1095
Anna 35			
HAGEDORN, Carl	30	Carlsruhe	64-1108
Sophie 18			
HAGEDORN, Clara	22	Wittlage	66-1155
HAGEDORN, Heinrich	29	Glaue	66-0984
Mathias 32			
HAGEDORN, Rud.	35	Bremen	64-1161
HAGEDORN, Theorett	28	Pyrmont	66-1243
HAGELE, Eva	25	Horlochen	64-0427
HAGELE, Heinrich	26	Bokingen	66-0147
HAGELGANZ, Johanna	55	Sachs.-Weimar	66-0349
Emil 9			
HAGELMAIER, Christ	22	Beurtlingen	65-0189
HAGELUCKER, Jos.	23	Kleinenberg	65-1088
HAGEMANN, Anna	24	Garz	64-0363
HAGEMANN, Cathrine	22	Osnabrueck	67-1005
Conrad 15			
HAGEMANN, Chris.	22	Segelhorst	63-0482
HAGEMANN, Martha	17	Vegesack	67-1005
HAGEMEIER, Fr.	17	Pfullingen	66-1313
HAGEMEIER, Wilhelm	18	Dissen	66-1128
HAGEMEYER, Charles	33	New York	63-0990
Louise 27, William 1			

NAME	AGE	RESIDENCE	YR-LIST
HAGEMEYER, Friedr.	40	Haustenbeck	65-1088
Lina 18			
HAGEMUELLER, Vict.	18	Scheibe	64-0593
HAGEN, Carl	50	Oldenburg	66-1093
HAGEN, Clara Soph.	32	Lobenstein	66-0650
HAGEN, Ferd.	21	Olbersleben	64-0331
HAGEN, Hermann	28	Haseluene	66-1203
HAGEN, Licie	32	Koenigsheim	65-0865
HAGEN, N.	23	Zassdorf	63-1085
HAGEN, v. Peter	24	Elberfeld	64-0138
HAGENBERG, Albert	30	Osterrode	64-0433
HAGENBROCK, Adam	29	Rietberg	67-0007
Anton 28			
HAGENBRUCH, Franz	15	Muehlhausen	65-1030
HAGENDORN, August	35	Ilmhausen	65-0055
HAGENS, H.	27	Meiningen	66-1248
HAGENS, Joh.	19	Bremen	65-1088
HAGENSICK, C.W.	38	Iowa	63-0168
Amalie 36, Virginia 6, Charles 1			
HAGENWISH, J.	23	Quakenbrueck	64-0992
HAGER, Christiane	28	Asch	66-1031
HAGER, Louise	18	Asch	65-0898
HAGER, Ludwig	28	Ruedesheim	66-0083
Johanna 30, Ludwig 2			
HAGERMANN, Fritz	19	Steyerberg	66-0934
HAGERS, Gottfr.	15	Bremen	65-0402
HAGERSKAMP, Johann	25	Bremollen	66-1203
HAGGPIHL, Jos.	35	Meppen	63-1038
HAGHISCH, Heinrich	24	Lobenstein	66-1373
HAGIUS, A.R.	26	Rhauderfehn	64-0840
HAGIUS, Johann	35	Aurich	63-1136
HAGIUS, Ottoline	27	Erfurt	65-0151
Ottoline 4			
HAHLO, Herm.	40	New York	63-0752
wife 30			
HAHN, Adam	23	Kirchheim	65-0243
HAHN, Adolph	28	New York	64-0170
Peter 6, Anna 4, Mr.(f) 26			
HAHN, Albert	15	Hannover	64-0432
Gretha 19, Beta 22, Marg. 20			
HAHN, Amalie	24	Zweibruecken	65-0402
Babette 7			
HAHN, Anton	36	Westhausen	66-1327
HAHN, Appolonia	54	Treusdorf	65-0189
Magdalena 22, Barbara 18, Franz 15			
HAHN, Barbara	22	Schlotzen	66-1155
HAHN, Betty	18	Langen	63-0097
Anna 18			
HAHN, Carl	23	Meerane	64-0885
HAHN, Catharine	27	Bayern	66-0147
HAHN, Christian	26	Borken	66-0412
HAHN, Christiane	16	Untersteinsch	66-1327
HAHN, Dorothea	32	Brooklyn	64-0904
HAHN, Elisabeth	21	Polen	66-0704
Rosalie 19			
HAHN, Emma Emilie		Altengronau	64-0433
HAHN, Franz Jos.	30	Soesdorf	66-1313
HAHN, Friederike	27	Frickenhausen	63-0953
HAHN, Friederike	21	Gomaringen	66-0679
Leopold 19			
HAHN, Friedrich	18	Homberg	66-0083
HAHN, Friedrich	18	Westhofen	65-1030
HAHN, Georg	18	Halopes	66-0623
HAHN, Georg	26	Horchheim	64-1161
HAHN, Ha.(f)	22	Menzenheim	64-0495
HAHN, Heinrich	28	Huelben	65-1030
HAHN, Ida	24	Thedinghausen	65-0243
HAHN, Isaak	19	Baiern	66-0704
HAHN, J.L.	17	Bemflingen	64-0782
Carl 18, J.L. 26			
HAHN, Jos. G.	32	Ochsenwang	64-0331
HAHN, Julius	24	Stuttgart	64-0073
HAHN, Julius	8	Coburg	66-1327
HAHN, L.	22	Pattenzen	66-0413
HAHN, Martin	28	Oschelbronn	66-0147
HAHN, Otto	22	Weimar	64-0938
Anna 18			
HAHN, Richard	25	Breslau	65-0865
HAHN, Robert	26	Chemnitz	66-0704
HAHN, Samuel	22	Wien	66-0576
HAHN, Wilhelmine	19	Lehe	66-1127
HAHNE, Herm.	23	Kirchlangen	64-0214
HAHRTMAN, R.	36	Breslau	63-1085
Catharine 27, Maria 7, John 6			
Anastasia 2			
HAID, Anton	30	Neustadt	66-0413
Marg. 26, Karl 3, Allois 1			
HAIDBRUECK, Elise	26	Ludwighausen	66-1243
HAIDE, v.d. Ernstn	34	Hameln	64-0938
HAIER, Anselm	23	Camenz	66-1155
Louise 30			
HAIER, Jacob	20	Grafenweiler	66-0147
HAIGER, Meta	23	Lussen	65-0004
HAIL, Ludwig	27	Krummstadt	66-0984
HAILFINGER, Anna	20	Bitz	65-1024
HAIMANN, Minna	18	Waiblingen	63-1136
HAINBEL, Friedr.	21	Baden	66-0734
HAINEMUELLER, H(m)	52	Wiena	64-0495
HAINZ, Phil	36	Lorsch	65-0151
HAISCH, Jacob	32	Wuertemberg	66-0221
HAISCHER, Friedr.	29	New York	63-0482
HAISCHER, Maxm.	25	Berchhausen	66-1243
HAISER, Pauline	35	Wuertenberg	66-0221
HAJEK, Cathre.	59	Boehmen	63-0862
HAKE, Adolph	20	Lehr	63-0990
HAKE, Louis	30	Cincinnati	66-0934
HAKE, Sophie	21	Lauenvoerde	64-0363
HAKER, Maria	22	Drefhorn	66-1327
HALBACH, Ch.	25	Grafrath	63-1085
HALBACH, F.(m)	17	Borgholzhsn.	64-0331
HALBAUER, Johann	38	Glauchau	66-1131
Emilie 9, Julia 6			
HALBBORN, Marie	16	Bockenem	66-1127
HALBERSTADT, Dan'l	24	Baiern	66-0469
HALBFASS, H.C.(m)	31	Hollenstedt	64-0331
Johanna 21			
HALESSE, (f)	27	Magdeburg	64-0023
HALL, Anna	48	Worms	64-0331
HALL, H.(m)	16	Schottwarden	64-0170
HALL, Hugo	29	Aasen	63-0296
HALL, John	17	New York	63-0821
HALLATZ, Joh.	26	Pr. Friedland	66-0704
HALLE, Aug.	17	Lemgo	63-1010
HALLEBEN, Vanette	44	Dettelbach	64-0138
Emilie 17, Julius 14, Bertha 9, Theresa 8			
Hugo 5, Selma 6			
HALLENBERGER, John	28	Ober Hespe	66-1155
HALLER, Chr.(m)	22	Aldingen	64-0331
J.M.(m) 18			
HALLER, Fr.	28	Switz	63-0350
HALLER, Gerd.	20	Doetzingen	65-1088
HALLER, Joh.	25	Aldingen	65-0402
HALLER, Mary	48	Aldingen	63-0551
Anna 16			
HALLER, Max Julius	17	Baltimore	63-0822
HALLER, Peter	15	Trostingen	63-0990
HALLERBERG, H.	20	Lemgo	64-0992
HALOB, Max	18	Dub	66-1373
HALP, Heinrich		Eichelheim	65-0950
HALSINGER, Wilh.	29	Oldorf	64-0214
HALSKAMPER, Herm.	27	Menslage	64-0782
HALTENMEYER, Ma(f)	26	Hitzighof	64-1161
HALTERMANN, Jacob	52	Baden	66-0221
HALTMANN, Ad.	24	Hamburg	64-0992
HALVE, Carl F.	18	Luebbeke	65-1031
HALWIG, August	21	Hansbergen	63-1085
HAMANN, Carl	28	Bayern	63-0398
HAMANN, Georg	16	Umstadt	64-1022
HAMANN, J.C.F.	46	Havana	64-0432
HAMANT, Huber	32	Ihlingen	65-0007
Christine 30			
HAMBERGER, Georg	20	Truitsterangn	67-0007
HAMBRECHT, Georg	38	Neuhofen	64-0687
Christine 30, Friedr. 9, Johann 7			
Ludwig 5, Georg 4, Rosine 1			
HAMBURG, Adolph	28	Mainz	66-0984

NAME	AGE	RESIDENCE	YR-LIST
HAMBURGER, Aaron	43	Meppen	66-0650
HAMBURGER, H.	28	New York	64-0214
Regina 28			
HAMEL, Johanna	20	Kirchlotheim	67-0795
HAMEL, Margaretha	46	Goettingen	63-0244
HAMM, Conrad	22	Culmbach	65-0243
HAMM, Friderike	18	Islingen	65-1030
HAMM, Gustav	30	Braunschweig	67-0007
HAMM, Heinr.	17	Woffingen	64-0427
HAMM, Michael	34	Germany	63-0953
HAMMAN, Johanna	26	Breslau	66-0704
Agnes 6, Georg 5			
HAMMANN, Adam	37	Darmstadt	63-1218
HAMMANN, Cath.	20	Loeningen	65-0151
HAMMANN, Joh.	28	Oberndorf/Han	65-0038
HAMMECKE, Friedr.	28	Cincinnati	64-0214
HAMMEL, Adam	22	Kirchheim	65-0055
HAMMEL, Caroline	24	Kaiserslautrn	64-0782
baby 6m			
HAMMEL, Helene	18	Buergel	64-1053
HAMMEL, v. Gerh.	24	Cloppenburg	66-0221
HAMMELGARN, Agnes	45	Cincinnati	66-0984
HAMMER, Aug.	49	Nordhausen	64-1108
HAMMER, Daniel	28	Rheinbaiern	66-0072
Maria 25			
HAMMER, Fred.	24	Wildbach	63-0990
HAMMER, Friedrich	30	Kirschberg	66-1031
Caroline 25			
HAMMER, Heinr.	25	Lemertzsch	66-1373
HAMMER, J.	17	Westhofen	65-1189
HAMMERMANN, Gerhd.	29	New York	64-0170
HAMMERS, Margareth	61	Varensell	66-1203
Christine 18			
HAMMERSCHLAG, Blue	25	Launau	66-0984
HAMMERSCHLAG, Joh.	20	Minden	66-0576
Elise 22			
HAMMERSCHLAG, Ludw	19	Freuyse	64-0840
HAMMERSCHLAG, S.A.	60	Bederkesa	65-0402
Maria 32			
HAMMERSCHLAG, Sal.	30	Bruchhausen	66-0984
HAMMERSCHLAG, Ther	22	Boehmen	66-0147
Henriette 19			
HAMMERSCHMIDT, Ant	26	Buchholz	67-0600
HAMMERSCHMIDT, C.	20	Membris	63-0551
HAMMERSCHMIDT, Hr.	30	Wiesbaden	65-0055
HAMMERSCHMIDT, Mat	36	Buffalo	63-0482
HAMMERSTEDT, Aug.	22	Bremen	66-0734
HAMMERSTEIN, Eug.	24	Muenden	63-0953
HAMMEYER, Hin.	43	Graue	63-0693
Sophie 36, William 9, Mary 8, Henry 7			
Friedrich 4, Caby 4			
HAMMLER, Augusta	25	Battenberg	66-0734
HAMMS, Peter	19	Hammstedt	64-1022
HAMPE, Cath.	26	Linz	66-0934
HAMPEL, Franz	30	Lobendau	66-1373
Mathilde 30			
HAMPF, Johann	33	Eichfeld	66-0346
HAMPFLER, C.	42	Schoeningen	65-0007
HAMPFLING, Marg.	16	Weidmitz	65-1088
HAMSCH, F.	35	Sebnitz	64-0992
HAMSE, Marg.	17	Schiffdorf	64-0432
HAMZLIECK, Jos.	39	Oberbrois/Boh	65-0038
Barbara 33, Wenzel 6m			
HANCK, M.C.	24	New York	63-0752
HANCKE, Franz	21	Herstelle	64-0593
Augusta 21			
HAND, Carl	23	New York	66-0147
HAND, Gustavus	20	Stuttgart	64-0593
HANDEL, Rosina	33	Lemberg	64-0687
HANDLER, Sophie	28	Rinkers	65-1031
HANDNER, Wilh'mine	25	Duesseldorf	63-0551
HANDSCHIGL, Walb.	27	Zwarstruss	66-1373
HANDSCHUMACHER, H.	24	Lengsfeld	63-1178
HANDTKE, John G.	45	Prussia	63-0752
HANF, Christine	58	Ellwangen	67-0007
Emilie 23			
HANFELD, Sophie	18	Rulle	63-0953
HANG, G.	30	Berlin	65-0974

NAME	AGE	RESIDENCE	YR-LIST
HANG, Gottlieb	57	Freudenstadt	65-0243
HANG, Rosalie	29	Sigmaringen	63-0296
HANGER, Johs.	19	Neukirch	65-0402
HANGNER, Friedr.	19	Bahnfeld	67-0007
HANGSTORFER, Joh.	32	Gundelbach	65-0189
Caroline 32, Wilh. 5, Henriette 9m			
HANH, Catharine	22	Hanau	65-1189
HANITSCH, Georg	53	Lauterbach	64-0687
HANITSCH, Johann	24	Alsfeld	66-1248
HANK, Joseph	44	Wiesenfeld	67-0007
HANKE, August	32	Guenthorst	66-0412
HANNA, Franz	26	Melk	66-1031
Cecilie 22, Franz 11m			
HANNA, J.	32	Wien	65-1189
HANNA, Johann	48	Gundelsdorf	63-0614
Barbara 20, Margaretha 13			
HANNAHELL, John	74	Newark	63-0006
HANNAUER, Franz	31	Ruebelberg	66-0576
Elisabeth 23, Catherine 4, Mary 2			
Franz 6m			
HANNES, Heinrich	24	Einbeck	66-1131
HANNES, Jean P.	22	Holland	63-0350
HANNS, Wm.	33	New York	63-0917
Wm. 30			
HANNSBACH, Jacob	25	Frida	66-0668
Joseph 22, Elise 59, Betty 24			
HANRI, Elisabeth	19	Froschhauer	63-1178
HANSA, Alois	29	Tabor	66-0679
HANSBERGER, M.	40	Zell	64-0782
HANSCHEL, Edm.	29	New York	63-0990
Sophie 27			
HANSCHILDT, Christ	24	Achim	65-0007
HANSCHILDT, H.	25	Bremervoerde	65-0974
HANSEL, Catharine	32	Altenschlirf	63-1218
HANSEL. C.H.	19	Werfen	65-0402
HANSELMANN, Aug.	28	Cassel	66-1313
HANSEN, Anna	18	Frelsdorf	66-1248
HANSEN, Brasmus	25	Copenhagen	66-0666
HANSEN, Christian	28	Copenhagen	66-0666
HANSEN, Wilhelm	26	Copenhagen	66-0666
HANSEN, Wilhelm	14	Lamstedt	65-1095
HANSING, Annette	50	Hannover	66-0679
HANSING, Otto	18	Hannover	66-1128
HANSLE, Joh. Jacob	23	Waldenbach	66-0221
HANSLICK, Martin	37	Domislitz	66-0623
Anna 35, Maria 9, Johann 7, Barbara 5			
Martin 3, Catharina 1			
HANSON, Peter	20	New York	66-0679
HANTH, Appolonia	7	Pickeldorf	64-0938
HANTKOPF, Carl R.	25	Solingen	63-0614
HANTWIG, Friedr.	25	Wehrendorf	67-0007
HANWEG, Herm.	26	Ueken	64-0023
HANZEL, Nepho.	33	Boehmen	63-1218
HANZLIECK, Mart.	32	Oberbrois/Boh	65-0038
Maria 22			
HAPERL, Joh.	27	Haxbergen	66-0349
HAPPEL, Anna Cath.	21	Darmstadt	63-0614
HAPPEL, Cathar.	16	Roemershausen	66-0984
HAPPEL, Catharine	27	Kilianstede	65-0948
HAPPEL, Heinr.	44	Holzhausen	66-0221
Kunigunda 34, Catharine 7, Kunigunda 6			
Elisabeth 5, Margarethe 4, Henry 3			
Jost 2			
HAPPEL, Joh. Jac.	24	Dautpe	66-0934
HARBARTH, Emma	21	Flotho	65-1024
HARBECK, Gesche	23	Westerstede	64-0840
HARBERS, Heinrich	15	Stotel	64-0739
HARBURGER, Jette	17	Hurben	66-0576
HARCKE, Chr.	22	Voerden	64-1022
HARDELEN, Diedr.	34	Dorgeloh	65-0402
HARDENSTEIN, Fr'dr	18	Pforzheim/Pr	64-1053
HARDER, C.	30	Helle	63-1003
M. 35			
HARDEWIG, Anton	25	Frisoythe	63-0482
HARDNER, Carl Aug.	20	Lauffen	63-0006
HARDT, Christian	47	Rohrbach	65-0038
Johannetta 48, Georg 23, Johannes 16			
Friedrich 12, Heinrich 9			

NAME	AGE	RESIDENCE	YR-LIST
HARDT, Fr. Ad.	17	Simmern	63-1085
HARDT, Joh. Conrad	18	Wennings	64-0886
HARDT, Johann	28	Fuchsstadt	66-1327
HARDT, Wm.	38	New York	63-0752
wife 30			
HARDTER, Friedr.	20	Weinsberg	64-1053
Wm. 16			
HAREK, Joseph	34	Boehmen	66-0349
HAREN, D.	17	Valhingstedt	63-1085
HARERBECK, Conrad	33	Hannover	64-0433
HARERMANN, William	48	Berlin	63-0244
HARFNER, Marie	22	Klagenfurt	63-1178
Therese 18			
HARGINGA, Luika	29	Upleward	64-0665
Gesche 26, Marie 6m			
HARING, Margaret	28	Kirchhardt	64-0331
HARING, Wm.	17	Buchen	65-1024
Regine 9			
HARJE, Heinr.	21	Uterlande	66-1313
HARJES, Franz Jul.	23	Bremen	64-0456
HARJIS, Gesine	24	Fischerhude	66-1031
HARKE, Pauline	14	Coersbach	66-0984
HARKE, Woyciech	39	Durowa	66-0650
Rosalia 39, Stephan 5			
HARKEL, Elisab.	21	Schelbrun/Sw.	64-1053
HARLING, Joh. J.	20	Neustadt	64-0639
HARM, Anna	24	Ottenhausen	66-0221
HARM, Veronica	23	Thalheim	63-0482
HARMAR, Georg	40	New York	66-0221
HARMENING, Carl	19	Rinteln	65-0116
HARMENING, Christ.	70	Escher	66-0734
Christian 8			
HARMENING, Sophie	21	Hespe	66-0934
HARMENING, Wilhelm	23	Stolzenau	66-0577
HARMING, Carl	14	Hannover	66-1127
HARMS, Anna	20	Schuttischdin	66-0109
HARMS, Carl	30	Umeln	65-0402
HARMS, Ernst	32	Telgte	66-0147
HARMS, Friederike	7	Friedberg	65-0151
HARMS, Gerhard	26	Ost Friesland	66-0577
HARMS, J.	16	Ochsmaninn	64-0782
HARMS, Joh. Heinr.	15	Achim	66-0934
HARMS, Regina	20	Vegesack	64-0782
HARMS, Rieneld(f)	58	Thunum	63-0296
HARMS, Trinka	16	Bremervoerde	64-0639
HARMS, Weet	43	Aurich	64-0739
Harm 9			
HARMS, Wilhelm	28	Lehe	64-1108
HARMSEN, Jan	48	Nordhorn	66-1128
Hendrike 40, Berendina 12, Gerd 7			
Fenna 5, Evert 4, Harm 9m			
HARMSEN, Meta	21	Ritterhude	65-0950
HARNEY, Julia	30	Paris	64-0363
HARNISCHFEGER, Krl	14	Soden	63-1069
HARNISS, Otto	35	Burg	64-1053
HARNOP, Peter	31	Smogelsdorf	66-0412
Rosalie 25, Johann 6m			
HARNSBERGER, Brtld	44	Zell	66-1127
Johann 15			
HARO, J.A.	54	Massachusetts	63-0917
HAROTH, Theodor	25	Goettingen	66-1031
HARR, Fritz	37	Getrungen	63-0482
HARRE, Rosine	27	Rothenzimmern	66-0704
HARRENSTEIN, Jac.	30	Snurshusen	64-0331
Johanna 21			
HARRER, Adam	30	Duesseldorf	65-0950
HARRIGFELD, E.F.A.	30	Hannover	66-0221
HARRSCH, Lina	20	Heilbronn	64-0593
HARSCH, Bernhard	27	Abtsgwind	65-1030
HARSEMANN, Jost	21	Horinghausen	64-0782
Marie 25			
HARSKY, Ignatz	30	Boehmen	63-0917
Helene 22, Alois 4			
HART, Henry	26	Chicago	64-0170
HARTEN, Max	28	Altenburg	66-0984
Marie 24, Saly 9m			
HARTEN, v. D.	42	Bremervoerde	65-1024
HARTER, Gesine		Blumenthal	66-0984

NAME	AGE	RESIDENCE	YR-LIST
HARTH, Friederike	27	Grielow	66-0668
HARTH, Heinrich	49	Obermarkstadt	64-0456
HARTH, Philip	26	Ludwigshuette	65-0948
Cathr. 28			
HARTIG, Carl	29	Ruegen	66-0083
Sophie 30			
HARTIG, Ferd.	22	Halle	64-1108
HARTIG, Gustav	30	Goettingen	63-0693
HARTIG, Johanna	25	Goettingen	63-0693
HARTING, Eduard	19	Wallenbrueck	66-1031
HARTKEMEYER, H.	19	Pente	63-0953
Gerhard 25			
HARTKOPF, Gustav	28	Prussia	63-0822
HARTKOPF, Julius	29	Kattenberg	65-0189
HARTLAGER, Casper	29	Linen	65-1030
HARTLAUB, Franz	23	Cincinnati	64-0427
HARTLEB, Adeline	26	Veilsdorf	66-1131
HARTLEB, Anna	15	Worbis	66-0734
HARTLEBEN, Otto	25	Osterwald	63-0097
HARTMAN, Friedr.	23	Kochendorf	66-1327
HARTMAN, Hans	24	Horsten	63-1085
HARTMANN, Anna	16	Broschins	66-1203
Caroline 18			
HARTMANN, Anton	25	Dahlhausen	65-1030
Wilhelm 23			
HARTMANN, Aug.	36	Hodeshaim	66-1243
Christine 30			
HARTMANN, Aug.	23	Erfurt	65-0898
HARTMANN, August	42	Schneeren	65-0948
HARTMANN, Bernh.	22	Ankum	64-0938
HARTMANN, Bertha	19	Rezdican	64-0992
HARTMANN, Carl	20	Seifenheim	66-1131
HARTMANN, Carl	22	Ronneberg	66-1373
HARTMANN, Chr'tine	21	Langgens	66-1327
HARTMANN, Chr.Fr.	29	Eichelberg	64-0427
HARTMANN, Christ.	28	Bremen	63-0244
HARTMANN, Conr.	29	Schneeren	65-0948
Louise 28, Ernst 4, Wilhelmine 2			
HARTMANN, Ernestin	33	Hannover	66-0346
Albert 2			
HARTMANN, F.(m)	23	Algesdorf	64-0331
HARTMANN, Georg	22	Frutenhof	65-0402
HARTMANN, Georg	27	Bremen	67-0806
Helene 22, Augusta 11m			
HARTMANN, Georg	49	Wersau	65-0865
Auguste 17, Eva 11, Friedrich 7			
HARTMANN, Georg	40	Schneeren	65-0948
Louise 26, Caroline 2, Wilhelmine 6m			
HARTMANN, Gottlieb	41	Berwangen	64-0427
HARTMANN, H.	32	Gruenberg	64-0782
HARTMANN, Heinr.	28	Baden	66-0734
Sophie 21			
HARTMANN, Heinrich	24	Burhave	63-0953
HARTMANN, Heinrich	21	Neustadt	66-0734
HARTMANN, Heinrich	26	Neuenburg	66-0083
HARTMANN, Herm.	29	Quincy	66-0221
Louise 24			
HARTMANN, Hermann	23	Eistrup	67-0007
HARTMANN, Hubert	34	Bremen	63-0917
HARTMANN, Israel	29	Germany	66-0666
HARTMANN, James	26	Niederhadamar	63-0350
HARTMANN, Joh. Lev	44	Weberstedt	64-0456
Martha Maria 48, Johann Heinr 22			
Christine 10			
HARTMANN, Joh.Hin.	47	Ostfriesland	66-0704
Hinrich 24, Taalke M. 17			
HARTMANN, Johann	17	Meiningen	64-0885
Friedr.Heinr 30			
HARTMANN, Jos.	24	Mernes	66-1243
Cath. 22			
HARTMANN, Justus	18	Sachsen	66-0576
HARTMANN, Levy	15	Barchfeld	64-0938
HARTMANN, Lewis	46	Bremen	63-0097
HARTMANN, Marg.	23	Lorsch	63-0752
HARTMANN, Marg.	19	Stappenbach	66-1203
HARTMANN, Maria	17	Langgens	66-1327
HARTMANN, Martin	31	Fahrendorf	65-1095
HARTMANN, Peter	32	Albany	63-1218

NAME	AGE	RESIDENCE	YR-LIST
HARTMANN, Peter	24	Drammersheim	65-0004
Peter 23			
HARTMANN, Philipp	9	Weinhaim	66-1203
Dorothea 7, Heinrich 5, Jacob 2			
Catharine 31			
HARTMANN, Salomon	20	Maltitz	66-0576
HARTMANN, Sophie	42	Sulingen	66-0147
Bertha 16			
HARTMANN, W.	47	Bueckeburg	64-0023
Johanna 21			
HARTMANN, W.(f)	51	Wiesbaden	64-0427
HARTMANN, Wilh.	21	Frille	64-0214
HARTNER, John G.	41	Gibsbour	63-0953
Marie 6			
HARTSTEIN, A.(f)	40	Leipzig	64-0331
HARTUNG, Caroline	15	Milwaukee	63-0821
HARTUNG, Georg	31	Muehlhausen	66-1373
HARTUNG, Leopold	30	Weimar	63-0398
HARTUNG, Susanne	55	Bretten	66-0576
HARTUNG, Theodor	60	Prussia	64-0687
Moritz 27, Theodor 18			
HARTUNG, Wilh.	31	Eisenach	65-0189
Anna 28			
HARTWIG, Aug.	26	Dryburg/Pr.	65-0038
HARTWIG, August	28	Preussen	63-0917
HARTWIG, Ernst Fr.	19	Ndr.Moellrich	63-0296
HARTWIG, Friedrich	25	Zickwerder	63-0006
HARTZFELD, G.L.	21	Mannheim	64-0427
HASCH, Louise	30	Biedenkopf	65-0948
HASCHE, Bernardine	40	Bremen	67-0007
Marie 7, Heinrich 5			
HASE, Ernst	32	Gehrden	66-0469
Christine 29, Heinrich 7			
HASEKAMP, Diedrich	16	Wulften	66-1093
HASEKAMP, Herman	29	Wulften	64-0593
HASEMANN, Emilie	17	Appeln	65-0402
HASEMANN, Friedr.	18	Lindern	64-0023
HASEMEYER, Heinr.	24	Buchholz	66-0837
HASENJAEGER, Ad.	20	Bexterhagen	64-0214
HASENJAEGER, Aug.	22	Oldendorf	66-0934
HASENJAEGER, Wilh.	20	Bremen	66-1031
Maria 26			
HASENJAGER, Carl	24	Treptow	65-0038
Caroline 22			
HASENKAMP, Cath.	21	Wulften	66-0576
HASENPFLUG, Cath.	25	Mengsburg	65-0189
HASHAGEN, Beta	19	Blumenthal	65-1095
HASS, Jac.	17	Frauensee	64-0495
HASS, Joseph	24	Obernheim	63-1178
HASSE, Ernest E.	32	Yonkers	63-1038
HASSE, J.W.	30	New York	66-0934
HASSE, Johann	20	Preussen	66-0147
HASSELBACH, Fritz	25	Russelberg	66-0934
HASSELBACHER, Soph	21	Vessenbrggult	64-0782
HASSELBRING, Fr'dr	28	Lodesholz	67-0599
Marie 24, Friedrich 11m, August 21			
HASSELMANN, Ed.	15	Sieverdingen	63-0990
HASSENPFLUG, Barb.	21	Kipra	66-0623
HASSENPFLUG, Lor'z	19	Rohrbach	66-0623
HASSERT, Marie El.	22	Bremen	66-0412
HASSI, Maria	24	Wiesbaden	66-1327
HASSINGER, Loring	25	Koengernheim	65-0243
HASSLER, J.J.	22	Belzheim	64-1161
HASSLER, Marg.	17	Burgsbach	66-1203
HASSLINGER, Ludwig	27	Waldmichelbch	64-0214
Valentin 30			
HASSOLD, Johann	49	Offenbach	66-1128
HASTEDT, Carl Hr.E	24	Osterholz	67-0599
HASTEDT, Claus	19	Friedrichsdrf	64-0363
Jacob 18			
HASTOR, Catharina	24	Eppelsheim	65-0594
HATLACK, John	59	Boehmen	63-0752
Josefa 35, Pauline 9, Alois 8, John 5			
Wenzel 4, Jospeh 10m			
HATRY, Louis	23	Mannheim	63-0097
HATTENBACH, Th.	28	Rotenburg	63-0953
HATTERMANN, A.	47	Hannover	63-1003
HATTIEUR, Tina	24	Aachen	64-1108
HATZMANN, Marianne	29	Geisa	63-0917
HAUB, Ph.	37	Niederweisel	64-0782
HAUBEL, Catharina	25	Ruhlkirchen	66-0349
HAUBER, Christian	17	Metzingen	66-1327
Georg 22, John 15			
HAUBER, Paulina	32	Sigmaringen	66-0221
HAUBERT, Carl	23	Birkenfeld	64-0363
HAUBRICKE, G.(m)	25	Heinzrath	64-0331
HAUCH, Friederike	18	Eisfeld	63-0482
HAUCH, Joseph	24	Impfingen	66-0623
Louise 24, Emilie 11m			
HAUCK, Anna Martha	20	Moischeit	66-0623
HAUCK, Elise	21	Heubach	66-0984
HAUENSTEIN, Carl	16	Flechingen	63-0097
HAUENSTEIN, Mathia	32	Birk	66-0576
HAUER, Cresantia	59	Osterholz	64-0639
Rosa 24			
HAUER, Herm.	30	Herford	65-0243
HAUF, Borothea	19	Haufheim	64-0214
HAUF, Friedrich	18	Allstedt	63-0917
HAUF, Wilhelm	58	Wissen	66-0346
HAUF, Wilhelmine	44	Wissen	66-0346
HAUFER, Magdalene	23	Basel	66-1203
HAUFFE, Henry W.	28	New Orleans	63-0693
Josephine 20, Francis 3, Emily 1			
HAUFFLER, Christ.	21	Marbach	63-1136
HAUFLER, F.	25	Grunbach	64-0782
HAUFLER, Gottlob	28	Bainstein	64-0687
HAUG, Carl	37	Cannstadt	65-0007
HAUG, Christ.	18	Kaiserwiehr	64-0687
HAUG, Christ.	20	Fruthenhof	65-0402
HAUG, Gottfr	25	Siefertshofen	66-1373
HAUG, Johannes	22	Selgartsweler	65-1030
HAUG, Rosalie	29	Sigmaringen	63-0296
HAUGK, Cathar.	22	Pforzheim	66-0221
HAUK, Philippine	19	Muehlhofen	65-0402
HAULP, Barbara	22	Raidwanger	66-1093
HAUMANN, Francisca	22	Altheim	63-0482
Anna Maria 6m			
HAUPLER, Willibald	28	Wurzburg	67-0007
HAUPT, Elisabeth	35	Neukirchen	66-0934
HAUPT, Theresia	23	Ostercappeln	66-0984
HAUPT, W.	34	Weimar	66-0413
HAUPTMANN, Hugo	24	Paderborn	66-0147
HAURMANN, Johs.	6	Wabern	64-0840
HAUSCHILD, Joh.	36	Achim	65-0007
HAUSCHOPPE, Marie	23	Bork	66-0984
HAUSE, Carl	27	Sandhagen	66-1373
Friederike 27, Friedrich 10m			
HAUSEN, Ajette	18	Nessemergrobe	64-0938
HAUSEN, Emil	52	Tonnig	66-0734
Augusta 47			
HAUSER, Marie	50	Stadthagen	66-1093
Anna 14, Johnn 9, Doris 6			
HAUSER, Anna	18	Aldingen	66-1155
HAUSER, Augusta	59	Pruscht	64-0593
HAUSER, Babette	19	Niefern	63-0168
HAUSER, Ch.(m)	22	Aldingen	64-0331
HAUSER, Friedr.	26	Marbach	65-0151
HAUSER, Heinrich	20	Tuttlingen	64-0886
HAUSER, Joh.	44	Denkingen	64-0138
HAUSER, Joseph	22	Kappel	66-0469
HAUSER, Wilhelm	21	Rust	65-0007
HAUSERMANN, Cath.	64	Gruppenbach	64-0639
Christ. 26, Elisabeth 21			
HAUSERMANN, Heinr.	24	Eppingen	66-0221
HAUSHERER, Wilhelm	23	Friedland	66-0578
HAUSLER, Fredr.	23	Vaihingen	64-0138
HAUSLER, Joseph	33	Neudorf	66-0147
HAUSMANN, Chris.	23	Goenningen	63-0862
HAUSMANN, Christ.	17	Nuertingen	66-1093
HAUSMANN, Eduard	26	New York	63-0693
HAUSMANN, Salomon	36	Breslau	63-0917
HAUSMANN, Wilhelm	27	Heinsen	66-0734
HAUSMANN, Wilhelm	29	Iserlohn	66-1127
HAUSNER, Heinr.	29	Erlangen	66-0109
HAUSS, Louis	27	Schlitz	64-1161
HAUSSER, Veronica	30	Spaichingen	63-1136

NAME	AGE	RESIDENCE	YR-LIST
HAUSSERMANN, Chr.	25	Burgstall	64-0840
HAUSSMANN, Math.	23	Niederkath	66-0349
HAUSWIRTH, Helena	49	Erlangen	66-0704
HAUTH, Nicolaus	20	Gernsheim	64-0687
HAUWELKA, Maria	18	Boehmen	64-0427
HAVEKOST, Hermann	33	Oldenburg	66-0666
Beke 25, Gerhard 2, Hinrich 6m, Tonjes 25			
HAVEL, Rosalie	17	Otterndorf	66-0576
HAVENDICK, Anna	7	Varensell	66-1203
HAVERKAMP, Diedr.	26	Gronloh	66-0984
Heinrich 22			
HAVERKAMP, Herm.	18	Gronloh	66-0984
HAVERKAMP, Herm.	18	Gronloh	66-0984
HAVERSANG, Henry	45	Markruhe	63-1136
HAVIGHORST, Wm.	34	Hoerste	64-0886
HAWEMANN, H.W.	22	Ottendorf	66-1313
HAWIG, Peter	29	Kmargoss	64-0433
Catharine 28, Carl 7			
HAWLETSCHEK, Joh.H	38	Leipzig	67-0600
HAY, Christ.	29	Dettingen	65-0055
Wilhelmine 23, Carl 6			
HAYARDT, Heinrich	20	Nienburg	64-0456
HAYDKE, Ludwig	24	Marrow	66-0668
HAYEK, Jacob	26	Taus	67-0599
HAYEN, Luempke	22	Ostfriesland	66-0704
HAYLER, Christoph	26	Owen	66-0109
HAYLMANN, Philipp	34	Gehnhausen	65-0055
HAYM, Hermann	28	Haseluene	66-1203
HAYMANN, F.	25	Braunschweig	64-1108
HAZART, Ferd.	30	France	63-1178
HEBBEL, (f)	30	Kuehrstedt	64-0427
HEBBERLING, Aug.	21	New York	64-0495
HEBEB, Friedr.	45	Minden	65-0038
HEBELER, Martha	29	Luetzerach	67-0007
Nic. 5, Mathias 3, John 8m			
HEBER, Johanna	19	Berenbeck	66-0413
Caroline 16			
HEBERER, John	29	Grossumstadt	63-0917
HEBERLE, Otto	55	Deusberg	65-0974
Elisabeth 54			
HEBERMEHL, Philip	18	Brumstadt	66-1327
HECHE, Catharina	26	Brandoberndrf	63-1085
HECHELMANN, Adam	27	Pittsburg	66-0147
HECHINGER, Minna	20	Kuhbach	64-0363
HECHT, (f)	33	Metz	63-0551
HECHT, Ferdinand	3	Meerane	66-0679
HECHT, Gustav	32	Fahr	66-0147
HECHT, Her.	46	Orp	63-0244
Sarah 32, Simon 8, James 6, Nathan 4m			
HECHT, Johannes	22	Verden	64-0920
HECHT, Kappel	25	Lengsfeld	66-0679
HECHT, Louise	47	Darmstadt	66-1031
HECHT, Moritz	17	Curchin	66-0984
HECHT, Moses	23	Weimler	66-1093
HECHT, Salomon	41	Rhoden	65-0594
Elisab. 24, Hannchen 30, Jettchen 7			
Poli 6			
HECHT, Sophie	18	Rodenberg	66-0623
HECK, Doris	42	Bremen	63-0614
Meta 18, Marie 16, Diedrich 10			
Heinrich 12			
HECK, Emil	30	Kirchheimbol.	66-0109
HECK, Johannes	27	Eichesheim	66-0704
HECK, M.	25	Leibach	64-0992
HECK, Maria	27	Darmersheim	66-1373
HECKEL, Gottlieb	40	Buffalo	63-1136
HECKEL, John	22	Bahlingen	63-1136
G.Fr. 22			
HECKEL, Wilhelm	17	Stuttgart	66-1155
HECKEMANN, Johann	20	Nnutershausen	66-1127
HECKEMANN, Marie	18	Essen	66-1031
HECKEMEYER, G.C.	14	Lemvoerde	64-0495
HECKENBERG, Anna M	22	Buende	66-0934
HECKER, Hermann	27	Marburg	66-1093
Augusta 27			
HECKER, Johanna	24	Eppingen	63-0296
HECKER, Mathias	58	Muehlbach	63-1038
Maria 58, Thomas 19, Anna 14			

NAME	AGE	RESIDENCE	YR-LIST
Catherine 23			
HECKERMANN, Georg	61	Osnabrueck	67-0600
Catharina 61			
HECKEROTH, Michael	57	Blankenbach	63-0482
Anna 59			
HECKERT, Henry	38	Cincinnati	66-0984
Florentine 36, Florentine 8, Anna 10			
HECKMANN, Ch.	32	Waldbroel	65-1088
Oscar 18			
HECKMANN, Conrad	24	Dornhagen	65-1030
HECKMANN, Dorothea	18	Heinebach	66-1203
Elise 16, Caspar 23			
HECKMANN, Heinr.	20	Carlsheim	65-0243
HECKMANN, Heinrich	17	Wahrendorf	64-0739
HECKMANN, Johann	24	Waldkappel	66-0668
HECKMANN, Marie	19	Hannover	64-0739
HECKMANN, Wm.	15	Goettingen	65-0038
Augusta 55			
HECKSCHER, (f)	38	Woodside	64-0495
HECKSCHER, C.F.W.	42	New York	63-0097
Julietta 38, Richard 19			
HECKSCHER, Richard	19	Hannover	63-0097
HECKSTETTER, Jette	18	Fellheim	64-0331
HEDE, Ernst	21	Bremen	66-0469
HEDEMANN, Diedr.	27	Missouri	64-0073
Elise 28			
HEDEMANN, Hinr.	29	Helle	63-0821
Herm. 16			
HEDERICH, Elise	24	Hermanstein	64-0782
HEDSTROEM, O.G.	50	New York	63-0990
HEDWIG, Cornelius	14	Hessen	66-0734
HEEDT, Wilhelm	50	Preussen	66-0221
Wilhelmine 40, Lisette 7, Wilhelmine 6			
Fritz 5, Amalie 3, Heinrich 2			
Caroline 9m			
HEEGER, Bernardine	28	Bevergen	67-0007
HEEMANN, Bernardin	21	Prussia	64-0432
HEERBRANDT, G.	35	Altenburg	66-0469
HEERDEGEN, Martin	18	Volkmarsgruen	66-0679
HEERE, H.	19	Braatz	66-0413
HEEREN, Georg	20	Leer	65-0770
HEEREN, Toenjes	30	Kirchdorf	66-1128
HEEREN, Wilh.	18	Ostfriesland	66-0704
HEERING, A.	52	Emmerich	64-0495
HEERING, Gustav	18	Cassel	65-0948
HEESSMANN, Gerhard	18	Vehs	66-0349
HEETH, Elise	29	Sachsen	66-0576
Hermann 6, Georg 3, Carl 11m			
HEEVEN, v.d.Carol.	21	Braunschweig	63-0693
HEF, D.(m)	38	Boehmen	64-0495
HEFEL, Anna M.	22	Altenbamberg	63-0006
HEFELE, Eduard	19	Neuenheim	64-0840
HEFENER, Henry	17	Blumenthal	63-1136
Henrike 20			
HEFENTHAL, Henr'tt	32	Assenheim	63-1218
Jacques 11m			
HEFFLE, Babette	30	Mannheim	65-0594
HEFNER, Franziska	22	Malin	64-0433
HEGEL, Christian	21	Gefell	63-0990
HEGEL, G.H.R.(m)	15	Gefell	64-0331
HEGEL, Henry	27	Gefell	63-0990
HEGEL, Joh.	42	Hirschberg/S.	64-0432
HEGEL, Salome	53	Sulz	64-0593
HEGELAU, Johann	19	Waldhausen	66-0679
HEGELE, Ant.	18	Ittenhausen	63-1003
HEGER, Anna	36	Mainz	66-1093
Francisca 9, Joseph 5			
HEGEWISCH, G.W.	31	Quakenbrueck	63-1136
HEGGE, Bernh.	41	Freeven	65-0189
Herm. 20, Ernst 18, Elisabeth 14			
Servatius 12, Johanna 7, Caroline 5			
HEGNY, Johann	22	Erbach	64-0199
HEHGEMUTH, Therese	18	Schneeberg	63-0917
HEHMANN, Anton	19	Belm	66-1093
HEHMENN, A.C.	20	Loehne	66-0413
HEHNS, Bertha	33	Alzey	66-0109
HEHRE, Berthold	26	Brieg	64-0214
HEIBECK, Rud.	26	Darmstadt	65-0974

NAME	AGE	RESIDENCE	YR-LIST
HEICHARDS, Friedr.	27	Bremen	64-0023
HEICKEN, Joh.	16	Schooss	65-1024
HEID, John	41	Magdilshausen	63-0693
HEID, v.d. Adam	42	Schwickarthsn	64-0639
HEIDBREDER, Fr'drk	15	Elverdessen	63-1010
HEIDE, Joh.	48	Nicolaine	64-0782
Anna 53, Johanna 24, Catharina 21			
Pauline 19, Anna 1m			
HEIDE, Phil.	26	Helgenbach	64-1206
HEIDECKE, Emil	21	Ingenau	64-0840
HEIDECKE, Friedr.	20	Hasselfelde	63-0482
HEIDECKER, Georg	28	New York	63-0953
Cath. 31, Mariane 5, Joseph 3, Georg 7			
Willy 7m, Charles 11m, Conrad 30			
HEIDEGGER, Alois	35	Krumbach	64-0363
Marie 41, Elisab. 8, Marie 7, Engelbert 5			
Gottfried 3, Martin 22, Anton 27			
HEIDEGGER, Joseph	37	Ochsenberg	64-0363
Ba. (f) 30, Ambrosius 3, Chre. (f) 6m			
HEIDEKING, J.A.	28	Wietmarschen	64-0214
HEIDEL, Hermann	38	New York	66-0679
HEIDEL, Marie	19	Rheden	65-0948
HEIDELBERGER, Ant.	7	Fuerth	64-0938
HEIDEMANN, August	21	Varel	66-0147
HEIDEMANN, August	21	Fahrenholz	66-0934
HEIDEMANN, August	21	Vahrenholz	66-0934
HEIDEMANN, Reinh.	35	Wittmund	63-1069
HEIDEN, v.d. Hch.	24	Kitzebuettel	66-0623
HEIDENFELD, Daniel	47	Stressendorf	64-1053
Christine 45, Wm. 12, Hulda 7, Anna 4			
HEIDENREICH, Carl	27	Klosterbauers	63-1010
HEIDENREICH, Chr.	54	Ahlsen	65-0898
HEIDENREICH, Otto	22	Frieburg	64-0904
HEIDER, Christian	19	Orle	66-1093
HEIDER, Elise	21	Hessen	66-0734
HEIDER, Reinhardt	22	Merlscheid	63-1010
HEIDGERD, Herm.G	19	Hahlen	63-0821
HEIDGERT, Joh. Bh.	22	Hahlem	66-0984
HEIDLAGE, Regine	18	Oldenburg	66-1131
HEIDLER, Emil	21	Dabron	66-1373
HEIDORN, Elise	20	Versabe	63-0821
HEIDRICK, Ferdin'd		Grobengereuth	66-0984
HEIDT, Marg.	39	Homburg	64-1022
Ludwig 7			
HEIDT, Margareth	22	Bremervoerde	64-0433
HEIDTMANN, Ferd.	27	Schochtau	63-1085
HEIENGA, W.	35	Burnde	66-0349
HEIKE, Theresia	19	Davern	67-0599
HEIKEMANN, Laura	26	Rubsheim	64-0992
HEIKEN, Heike J.	60	Schoost	63-0482
HEIL, Adolph	23	Urasch	66-1093
HEIL, Ch. Peter	21	Philadelphia	63-0990
Margar. 20			
HEIL, Christian	24	Muenster	66-0083
HEIL, Elise	20	Chicago	64-0427
HEIL, Heinrich	17	Kurhessen	66-0704
HEIL, Heinrich	23	Crumstadt	66-1248
Helene 24, Elisabeth 4m			
HEIL, Maria	37	Boehmen	66-0623
HEIL, Maria	27	Schapen	65-0189
HEIL, Peter	23	Frankenbrunn	66-0576
HEILBRONN, Justus	16	Fuerth	66-0679
HEILBRONN, Mar.(m)	24	Fuerth	64-0138
HEILBRONNER, Lena	43	Buchau	64-0427
HEILBRONNER, Louis	18	Bienswangen	63-0953
HEILEMANN, Johanna	24	Braunscheweig	66-0221
HEILIGENSTEIN, Leo	28	Moscuta	64-0073
HEILIGER, Jac.	32	Butzbrunn	64-0495
Cath. 62, Ba.(f) 31, Cath. 9m			
HEILIGSETGER, Joh.	28	Babenhausen	64-0363
HEILLE, August Ed.	24	Freiburg	63-1069
HEILMAN, Damian	29	Hundsfeld	63-0296
Francisca 23, Juliane 1, Catharine 1m			
HEILMANN, Carl	34	Dinklage	66-0984
HEILMANN, Cath.	21	Schweinsberg	66-1313
HEILMANN, J.(m)	26	Ochsenwang	64-0331
HEILMANN, J.E.	22	Brandeis	64-0138
HEILMANN, Johann	30	Hausen	66-0221
HEILMANN, Marg.	25	Waechtersbach	64-0904
HEIM, Adolph	32	New York	63-1136
HEIM, Caroline	20	Rheinpfalz	63-0917
HEIM, Cath.	30	New York	63-0953
Anna 8, Friedr. 7			
HEIM, Daniel	40	Baidt	66-1031
Marie 25, Sophie 2			
HEIM, Elise	18	Bremen	64-0840
HEIM, Jacob	37	Eperies	65-0402
Tory 28, Olgar 5, Wilh. 3			
HEIM, Verona	52	Bottweil	66-0679
HEIMANN, Bernhard	30	Coesfeld	65-1030
Elise 24			
HEIMANN, Leopold	34	Milwaukee	66-0704
HEIMANN, Richard	18	Laibach	66-0679
HEIMBACH, Anton	42	Baldwinstein	64-0214
HEIMBACH, Carl	22	Furra	67-0600
Louise 21			
HEIMBACH, St.	24	Niederstein	64-0782
Maria 21			
HEIMBRUCH, Maria	15	Trennfurt	64-0782
HEIMBUCH, Ferd.	32	Frankfurt	64-1108
Jos. 39, Edmund 21			
HEIMBURGER, Aug.	66	Berga	64-0073
HEIMBUTH, M.	29	Trawfurt	64-0782
HEIMDEL, Sixtus	33	Reutweinsdorf	64-0840
Marg. 27, Marie 6m			
HEIMEL, Augusta	26	Bremen	63-1085
HEIMENROTH, M.	15	Ziegenhein	65-1031
HEIMERDINGER, Hch.	29	Washington	63-0953
Maria Barb. 57, Anne 25, Christine 2			
HEIMERZHEIM, Jos.	36	Essen	66-0666
HEIMFELDER, Friedr	27	Cassel	66-1203
HEIMGAERTNER, C.	34	Nuertingen	66-0413
HEIMS, Fr. Wm.	20	Bremen	64-0138
HEIMSAAT, Friedr.	44	Jahrsau	63-0614
Elisabeth 50, Elisabeth 7			
HEIN, Andr.	32		63-1136
wife 25			
HEIN, Anna M.	59	Wuerzburg	63-0862
HEIN, Chris	29	New York	63-0350
HEIN, Conrad	16	Fangenberg	66-0623
HEIN, Friedr. Wm.	43	Vendia/Pr.	64-0920
Caroline 26, Maria Mathd. 3			
Albert Ulr. 1			
HEIN, Friedrich	28	Grossiejewe/P	66-0412
HEIN, George	23	Schonstein	66-1155
HEIN, H.	15	Frankenberg	66-0413
HEIN, Isidor	20	Dorum	64-0343
Johanna 21			
HEIN, Joseph	39	Louisville	66-0147
HEINCK, Gertrud	26	Senden	66-0704
HEINDL, Joseph	43	Oberbrois/Boh	65-0038
Maria 40, Anton 13, Joseph 11, Maria 8			
Wenzel 6, Adam 32, Josepha 2, Joseph 9m			
HEINDSICK, Joh. H.	27	Brakewede	64-1022
Christiane 59			
HEINE, August	15	Lohne	66-0934
HEINE, Carl	31	Uslar	63-0398
Wilhelm 7			
HEINE, Caroline	60	Bolschle	64-0992
HEINE, Christian	20	Hannover	63-0693
HEINE, Ferdinand	28	Wolpe	66-1203
HEINE, Friedrich	20	Hannover	66-1327
HEINE, Gust.	17	Minden/Pr.	63-0822
HEINE, Herman	25	Hannover	65-0151
HEINE, Herrmann	17	Lohne	66-0934
HEINE, J.( )	31	Wetzlar	64-0073
HEINE, Joh. Friedr	21	Hagen	64-0456
HEINE, Josephine	26	Geisa	64-0687
HEINE, Victor	19	Hannover	66-1155
HEINECK, Ernst	36	Louisville	66-0109
Johanna 27			
HEINECKE, Johann	32	Grane	67-0007
HEINECKEN, Johanna	20	Bremen	64-1053
HEINEKE, Louise	33	Sidney	66-0934
Heinrich 30			
HEINEMANN, Albert	20	Dessau	63-0752

NAME	AGE	RESIDENCE	YR-LIST
HEINEMANN, Anne C.	17	Quentel	65-0865
HEINEMANN, Aug.	20	Breslau	63-0862
HEINEMANN, Christ.	45	Allendorf	66-0679
Wilhelmine 41, Georg 15, August 13			
Dorothea 9, Johannes 6			
HEINEMANN, Henry	17	Almstedt	63-0752
HEINEMANN, M.(f)	56	Schuctern	64-0495
F.(f) 24			
HEINEMANN, Marg.	19	Doringsdorf	64-0639
Cath. 18, Marie 14			
HEINEMANN, Peter	34	Opherdingen	63-0296
HEINEMANN, Thomas	22	Rubsheim	64-1108
HEINEMANN, W.D.	20	Cassel	65-0402
HEINEN, Elise	22	Jever	65-0402
Cath. 20			
HEINER, Joseph	18	Darmstadt	66-0576
HEINERT, Werner	41	Sachsen-Mein.	66-0349
Elise 40, Friedrich 9, August 6			
Louise 11m, Louis 9			
HEINKEN, Diedr.	22	Wiche	64-0687
HEINKEN, Ferdinand	17	Bremen	66-1093
HEINKEN, Wm.	19	Sottrum	64-0992
HEINKER, Joh. Wm.	26	Buer	64-0920
HEINKING, Peter	23	Osnabrueck	65-0865
HEINLE, J.	42	Woertlingen	65-0007
HEINLEB, Chr.	29	Weimar	64-0904
HEINLEIN, Betti	37	Gross Darmst.	64-0885
HEINOMITSCH, N.	37	Eperies	65-0402
Fannie 22, Etten 1			
HEINRICH, Gottlieb	21	Murhara	63-0752
HEINRICH, Isaac	23	Gross Zimmern	64-0138
Adam 16			
HEINRICH, Jacob	28	Bavaria	63-0822
HEINRICH, Joh.	38	Reuthlen	64-0938
Marg. 30, Joh. Nic. 3			
HEINRICH, Joseph	22	Untergrombach	66-1155
HEINRICH, Ludwig	30	Banfe	65-0402
HEINRICH, M.	45	Niederreuth	63-1003
HEINRICH, Math.	40	Breslau	65-0974
Gustav 18			
HEINRICH, Mathilde	25	Klagenfurth	66-1327
HEINRICH, Max	43	Klagenfurt	66-0109
HEINRICH, Paul	18	Murrhardt	65-0151
HEINRICH, Wilhelm	54	Darmroh	64-0456
Wilhelmine 49, Fritz 23, Carl 28			
HEINRICHS, August	18	Ahlfeld	66-1128
Dorothea 44, Louis 14, Sophie 9			
HEINRICHS, Eibe	30	Ost Friesland	66-0577
HEINRICHS, Herm.	26	Coeln	65-0898
HEINRICHSMEYER, Fr	17	Wulferdingsen	64-0214
HEINRITZ, Barbara	26	Bayern	64-0432
HEINRMANN, Georg	28	Holstein/Hess	65-0038
HEINS, Anna	20	Langen	63-1218
HEINS, Anna	29	Hannover	64-0427
HEINS, Carsten	19	Rhaddreichst.	64-0687
HEINS, Claus	20	Oehrdorf	64-0170
HEINS, H.	54	Darmstadt	66-0413
HEINS, Herm.	29	San Francisco	63-0953
HEINS, Hinze	32	Cuba	64-0938
HEINS, Philipp	40	Havana	63-0752
William 9, Louise 7			
HEINS, William	13	Muenden	63-0482
HEINSOHN, Cath.	22	Blumenthal	63-0752
HEINSOHN, Ferd'd.	28	Lohmuehlen	67-0007
HEINSOHN, George	40	Louisville	63-0752
wife 20, Mary 7			
HEINTZ, Jacob	31	Heckenfeld	65-0151
HEINTZE, Gustav	19	Syke	63-0862
HEINZ, Emil H.	27	Gehlberg	66-1313
HEINZ, Franz	20	Guentersdorf	67-0599
HEINZ, Johann	31	Moscontah	64-0427
HEINZ, Johs.	30	Barenhausen	64-0840
Juliane 48			
HEINZ, Phil.	24	Petersheim	65-0594
Carl 20, Eva 36, Philippine 7, Philipp 6			
Cath. 5, Jac. 2			
HEINZE, Clara	34	Kohla	66-0679
Clara 9, Anna 8, Eduard 3, baby 3m			
HEINZE, Elise	17	Eisfeld	63-0482
HEINZE, Emil	20	Eisfeld	63-0398
HEINZE, Emil	35	Coethen	65-0055
HEINZE, Emilie	53	Stettin	63-0482
Agnes 23			
HEINZE, F.	28	Woerlitz	65-0007
HEINZE, Friedr.	23	Salkendorf	65-0948
Caroline 19, catharine 29			
HEINZE, Helena	22	Lobendau	66-1373
HEINZELMANN, Jos A	28	Philadelphia	63-0482
HEINZER, Hermann	18	Cassel	66-0679
HEINZERLING, G.	48	Wichte	63-1003
E. 37, K. 43, M. 11, A. 8, J. 7, A. 4			
H. 3			
HEINZERLING, John	46	Licherod	64-0214
Therese 22			
HEINZERLING, Louis	32	America	63-0990
Elise 25			
HEINZIG, Paul	20	Meerane	64-0331
HEINZMANN, Ernstne	21	Asch	64-0840
HEINZMANN, Wilhelm	25	Hoechst	66-0734
HEISCH, Doris	28	Richmond	66-0984
HEISCHER, Robert	32	Chemnitz	66-1248
Augusta 36, Friedrich 7, Minna 6			
Friedr. 4, Max 3, Franz 10m			
HEISE, Christ.	36	Heimburg	63-1010
HEISE, Christ.	30	Hannover	66-0221
HEISE, Clamor	24	Stolzenau	66-1127
HEISE, Clamor	19	Stolzenau	64-0363
HEISE, Leop.	21	Evrode	66-1243
HEISE, Richard	19	Stolzenau	63-0482
HEISEL, Juliana	28	New York	63-0990
Adam 2			
HEISIG, Mina	24	Adenstaedt	66-1243
HEISINGER, Ja.	48	Oshkosh	65-1189
HEISKER, Wilhelm	28	St. Louis	63-0953
Dorothea 28			
HEISS, Elisa	26	Sul	66-1131
Gertrude 8			
HEISS, Jacob	34	Sprendlingen	65-1088
Anna M. 36			
HEISSE, Henriette	25	Gratznick	66-1248
HEISSENBUTTEL, Aug	22	Neumoring	66-1128
HEIST, Johann	36	Heilgenstadt	63-1069
HEIT, M.Cath	30	Wietmarschen	64-0214
HEITE, Elisa	9	Freisia	65-1024
HEITER, James M.	47	Baden	66-0576
Hanna 20, James 25			
HEITGERCHER, Gerh.	28	Stapelfeld	65-0116
HEITKAMP, Friedr.	20	Stocken	65-1031
HEITKAMP, Gerh.	31	Leschede	63-1178
HEITMANN, Ch.	25	Lienzingen	65-1189
Pauline 6			
HEITMANN, Heinr.	20	Hannover	64-0427
HEITMANN, Henr.	25	Strom	66-1373
HEITMANN, Hrch.	19	Wensebrok	64-0992
HEITMANN, J.A.	25	Lastrup	64-1053
HEITMANN, Johann	18	Waffensen	66-1203
HEITMANN, Marie	19	Hannover	66-0576
HEITMANN, Meta	30	Brooklyn	63-1085
Wilhelm 15			
HEITMEYER, Cathar.	36	Rheda	66-0576
HEITMUELLER, G.	30	Bremen	63-0752
HEITTEMEYER, Elis.	25	Herzebrock	66-1031
HEITZ, Fritz	25	Obergleen	64-1053
HEITZ, Katharina M	21	Gesmold	63-1069
HEITZMANN, Joh.	21	Donaueschingn	64-0363
HEIZENROEDER, Casp	15	Langendrehbch	63-1136
HEKE, Louise	18	Rahden	66-1093
HELA, Lorenz	49	Soessnowd	66-0469
Elisabeth 52, Anna 17, Andreas 16, Rosa 8			
HELBIG, Georg	31	Nentershausen	66-1127
HELBING, Friedr.	26	Dielingen	63-0990
HELBRONN, Roeschen	51	Luederbach	66-1155
Franciska 18			
HELBST, August	49	Hannover	66-0221
HELD, A.	26	Lippe	66-0413
HELD, Anton	42	Evansville	66-0147

NAME	AGE	RESIDENCE	YR-LIST
HELD, Bernh.	30	Wald	63-0862
Wm. 5			
HELD, Catharine	17	Baden	64-0432
HELD, Charlotte	23	Dalheim	66-0577
HELD, Clara	19	Wackensell	66-1131
HELD, Friedr.	29	Rhodt	66-1373
HELD, Gertrude	18	Hessen	63-0614
HELD, Gustav	21	Ulm	63-0821
HELD, Heinr.	17	Hohenhahnen	64-0687
HELD, Herrmann	24	Hortelhof	63-1069
Maria 22			
HELD, James	24	Ulm	63-0168
Bertha 22, Laura 11m			
HELD, Johann	24	Hohengehren	67-0007
HELD, Leonhard	30	Schweinach	63-0821
HELDENWANG, Ph.	23	Buttenhausen	64-0782
HELDT, Carl	34	Milwaukee	64-0138
HELDT, Friedr.	25	Verden	63-0953
Marie			
HELDT, Jacob	22	Friesenheim	66-0221
HELF, Ferd.	32	Steinach	64-0023
HELFENICH, Heinr.	20	Oestheim/Hess	65-0038
HELFER, Caroline	23	Rikken	66-1243
HELFERD, Babette	24	Heppenheim	65-0004
HELFERICH, Wilhelm	27	Braunschweig	66-0984
HELFERS, Heinrich	34	Stoeske	66-0578
Catharina 30, Catharina 5, Wilhelmine 2			
Wilhelm 29, Sophie 28, Sophie 12			
Wilhelm 5, Heinrich 3, Friedrich 6m			
HELFFERICH, Otto	28	Wurtenberg	66-0984
HELFMANN, Peter	27	Loehrbach	66-1373
Catharina 25			
HELFRICHT, Heinr.	20	Bernstein	63-0006
HELGANS, Johannes	34	Althattendorf	64-0456
Rosina 34, Elisab. 10, Elias 7			
Cath. E. 5			
HELGENBERG, Augta.	28	Cassel	66-1093
Richard 5, Gertrude 8			
HELGENS, Gerd	40	Bremerwoerde	64-0840
HELHAKEN, Joh.	19	Allendorf	65-0402
HELINUS, Wm.	28	Baltimore	63-0862
HELKE, Christian	34	Wilkowa	66-0469
Rosa 28, Theodor 6, August 4, Heinrich 2			
HELKE, Joh.	37	Klein Bislau	66-0469
Eva 30, Carl 11, August 7, Wilhelmine 4			
Marie 1			
HELLBACH, Heinrich	25	Limburg	66-1327
HELLBERG, Carsten	45	Franzenburg	67-0599
Cath. Marie 44, Marie 14, Minna 5			
HELLBERG, Heinrich	30	Franzenburg	67-0599
Catharine 28, Anna Dorothe 3			
Nicolaus Fr. 11m			
HELLBING, Julius	19	Weingarten	66-1155
HELLEMANN, Friedr.	18	Neukirchen	63-0398
HELLENBERG, Anna	18	Sparwiesen	66-0734
HELLER, Albert	31	Arnitzrin	66-0934
HELLER, Egidius	22	Sachsen-Mein.	66-0349
Eva 17, Bertha			
HELLER, Frd. B.	33	Wernshausen	64-0593
Anna Marg. 62			
HELLER, Friederike	17	Rimzeller	64-0992
HELLER, Gustav	25	Boehmen	63-1085
HELLER, Henry	46	Baltimore	63-1136
HELLER, Math.	23	Fambach	66-1243
HELLERMANN, Frz.	45	Buke	64-0593
HELLERMANN, Georg	25	Bischoffswerd	66-1248
HELLERMANN, Heinr.	30	Braunschweig	65-0151
Friederike 7, Amalie 35			
HELLFRICH, Joseph	25	Muenster	64-1053
HELLGERT, Cathrine	24	Nordhalber	66-0623
Barbara 26			
HELLING, Fr.	33	New York	63-1085
HELLING, Franz	25	Sondershausen	65-0770
HELLMANN, Aug.	25	Solingen	63-0752
HELLMANN, Isaac	19	Muehlhausen	63-0862
Meier 25			
HELLMER, Alex	18	Fallersleben	65-0950
HELLMER, E.H.	18	New York	63-0244
HELLMERS, J.R.	28	Varel	64-0427
HELLMICH, August	16	Rehute	64-1108
HELLMUND, Carl	41	Ichtershausen	66-0650
HELLMUTH, Anna	34	Grossmannsdrf	66-1373
Henrich 8, Carl 4			
HELLRIEGEL, James	20	Marbach	63-0168
HELLWEG, Caspar	32	Paderborn	64-0214
HELLWIG, Andreas	28	Grossenglis	66-1203
HELLWIG, Friedrich	22	Neustadt	66-0837
HELLWIG, Gertrude	18	Dorla	63-0006
HELLWIG, Henry	52	Friedberg	63-0693
Marie 22, Johannette 21, Elise 19			
Regine 18, Charles 16			
HELLWIG, Maria	23	Borken	66-0412
HELLWINKEL, Herman	26	Glandorf	66-1127
HELM, Ignatz	29	Boernau	63-0614
HELM, Wilhelm	26	Albany	66-1031
HELMBALD, Aug.	23	Oberweid	65-0950
HELMER, Ernst	21	Hannover	66-1128
HELMER, Wilh.	26	Preussen	63-0990
HELMERICH, C.J.	36	Schmalkalden	63-1003
HELMERS, Clemens	46	Louisville	66-0221
Marianne 42, Elisabeth 18			
HELMERS, Herm.	22	Hannover	65-0974
HELMICH, Caroline	20	Rahden	65-1088
HELMICH, G.H.(m)	26	West Cappeln	64-0331
HELMICH, Georg	49	Manil	64-1053
HELMKE, Anna	21	Neuenwalde	66-0576
HELMKE, Augusta	25	Stroit	63-1069
HELMKE, H.	21	Osterwald	65-1189
HELMKE, L.	33	Magdeburg	63-1003
HELMLING, Gottf.	34	Westhofen	66-1093
HELMLING, Sybilla	28	Westhofen	65-1030
Magdalena 23, Elisabeth 21			
HELMRICH, Anna M.	17	Hohnheim	66-0221
HELMRICH, Carl	19	Osnabrueck	66-1031
HELMS, Henry	24	Milwaukee	66-0109
HELMS, Herman	31	Sulingen	66-1093
HELMS, Sophie	58	Ludwalde	65-0402
HELMS, Wilhelmine	29	Stolzenau	66-0577
HELMUTH, Herm.	19	Wachenhausen	66-1127
HELWIG, Susanna	65	Mainz	66-0109
HEM, Augusta	23	Herzdorf	66-0704
HEM, Hermann	25	Herzdorf	66-0704
HEMANN, Friedr.	26	Osnabrueck	66-0704
HEMING, Elisabeth	56	Fehlen	66-0349
(f) 18			
HEMKER, Heinrich	24	Kellingholzh.	66-0349
Mary 33, Fanny 10			
HEMKER, Heinrich	58	Steyerberg	66-0934
Sophie 64, Fritz 9			
HEMLEB, Chr.	29	Weimar	64-0904
HEMLER, Christine	27	Raidwangen	66-1155
HEMME, Ad.	40	Hannover	64-0639
Antonia 34, Henry 3, William 6m			
HEMME, Catharine	23	Geestendorf	64-0886
Wilhelmine 3, baby 11m			
HEMME, Friedrich	47	Ylten-Ilten	66-0083
HEMMER, Casper	28	Bettinghausen	63-0917
HEMMER, J.F.	42	Oldenburg	66-0413
Frienchen 35, Franz Ernst 10m, Marie 3			
HEMMERLE, Anton	21	Marienrachdrf	67-0007
HEMMERLE, Conrad	32	Zeilsheim	66-1327
Elisabeth 28			
HEMMERLE, Xaver	19	Wuertemberg	66-0578
HEMMERS, Otto	19	Bielefeld	66-1155
HEMMERT, Joh.	55	Philadelphia	66-0984
Barbara 21			
HEMMETT, Theodor	40	Rheine	63-0551
HEMPEL, Ch. Gottl.	50	Seifhennersdf	64-0343
HEMPEL, Eduard	25	Gotha	63-0398
HENDEL, Jul. (m)	21	Boehmen	64-0138
HENDEL, Ludwig	36	Dresden	66-0734
Emilie 35, Anna 4, Margareth 2, Franz 3m			
Caroline 62			
HENDORFF, Friedr.	26	Damme	64-0170
HENDRICHS, Ch.Aug.	44	Wolfshaeusche	63-0990
Henriette 41, Emil 9, Augusta 6, Ernst 1			

NAME	AGE	RESIDENCE	YR-LIST
HENEISEN, Martin	20	Umollo	66-1373
HENES, Friedrich	40	Wertville	63-0296
HENGEL, v. Eckart	17	Ottmachau	63-0296
John 22			
HENGESBACH, Joseph	44	Eversberg	65-1095
HENGETULD, Fr. Wm.	26	Cincinnati	63-0917
HENGSTLER, J.A.	25	Aldingon	64-0331
Melchior 17			
HENGSTLER, Lewis	48	Stuttgart	63-0551
Lina 13			
HENING, Peter	29	Gagenholz	67-0007
HENJE, Marie	25	Oldenburg	65-0594
HENKE, Caroline	17	Cloppenburg	66-1093
HENKE, Christ. H.	17	Wedum	64-0920
HENKE, Heinr.	26	Colberg	67-0007
HENKE, Henry	26	New York	66-0221
HENKE, Louise	20	Hersfeld	65-1189
HENKE, Louise	23	Uchte	65-1088
Johanna 34			
HENKE, Reinhard	24	Hassseluenne	64-0886
HENKE, William	33	New York	63-1218
HENKEIN, Heinrich	26	Hessen-Kassel	66-0578
HENKEL, August	17	Darmstadt	66-0577
HENKEL, August	21	Dinklage	66-0984
HENKEL, Carl	24		65-0594
HENKEL, Elisabeth	21	Darmstadt	65-1140
HENKEL, Heinr.	56	Wichelshausen	66-1127
Charlotte 49, Anna 38, Lisette 20			
Wilhelm 9, Elisabeth 7			
HENKEL, Heinrich	17	Gutenbergs	64-0433
HENKEL, Heinrich	27	Quakenbrueck	66-0984
HENKEL, J.W.	28	Scheffelbach	64-0495
HENKEL, Valentin	22	Grossenbach	66-1327
HENKEN, Carl	34	New York	66-0984
Marie 28			
HENKEN, Carl W.	22	Berlin	66-0984
HENKEN, Henry	29	New York	66-0734
HENKEN, Lisette	18	Sievern	64-0938
HENKER, Gusta	32	Nordwedel	67-0795
Saviz 29, Bertha 4, Emilie 9m			
HENLEIN, Franz	14	Osterberken	66-1093
HENN, Adam	21	Stettin	66-1131
HENN, Peter	28	Seinschmidt	66-1203
HENN, Susanna	50	Pfalz	63-0862
HENN, Wilh.	25	Waldhausen	65-0594
HENNE, Christ.	28	Hannover	66-0984
HENNE, Joh.	27	Vornawaldhaus	64-0687
HENNEBERG, Reinhd.	30	Hannover	65-0116
Gustav 25			
HENNECKE, Heinrich	18	Rehme	66-0147
HENNEICH, Sophie	24	Bremen	63-0244
Ernst 10m			
HENNEMANN, Jos.	25	Gehrden	65-0898
HENNES, Elisabeth	36	Deiferode	63-0398
HENNIES, Alwine	18	Braunschweig	65-0974
Wilhelmine 7			
HENNIG, Caroline	23	Schoenlanke	66-0650
HENNING, Doris	20	Cappeln	66-1248
HENNING, E.A.	16	Buer	66-0934
HENNING, Elise	23	Heinfeld	63-0821
HENNING, Emilie	23	Barmen	63-1069
HENNING, Franz	27	Detmold	66-1128
HENNING, Geerd	30	Weener	64-0433
HENNING, Heinrich	26	Neumen	64-0433
HENNING, Joh. G.	34	Heilgersdorf	66-0349
Eva 63, Maria 34, Anna 7, Christian 3			
HENNING, Johann	24	Lang	63-1069
HENNING, L.	53	Landsberg	66-0413
Aug. 48, Hel. 6			
HENNING, Michael	21	Hohenzell	66-1243
HENNING, Robert	31	Burgedorf	63-0053
HENNING, Rudolph	25	Schloppe	64-0920
HENNINGER, Conrad	59	Neustadt	67-0007
Carl 41, Egerhard 28, Pauline 21			
HENNINGHAUS, Wm.	28	Kottendorf	67-0007
HENNINGS, August	32	Wollprehausen	66-0623
Jette 26			
HENNINGS, Chris.	30	Zezoch	63-0482

NAME	AGE	RESIDENCE	YR-LIST
HENNINGS, G.(m)	30	Liverpool	64-0363
HENNINGS, Joh.	19	Bremen	65-0038
HENNISCH, Albert	46	Chicago	63-0953
HENNRICH, Ludwig	17	Mainz	64-1022
HENNRIEGEL, Ed.	21	Nordhausen	63-0953
HENRICH, Christine	16	Langgoens	64-1108
HENRICH, Wm.	25	Heinchen	64-1108
HENRICI, Gustav	17	Suhlingen	66-0576
Carl 21			
HENRICI, Heinrich	33	San Francisco	66-0734
HENRICI, Wilhelm	24	Lehe	63-1136
HENRY, T.H.	39	Paris	63-0168
HENRY, Therese	36	Schmalkalden	65-0402
HENSCH, Carl	24	Ebersdorf	64-0331
HENSCH, Friedr.	37	San Francisco	63-0953
Helene 35, Johanna 9			
HENSCH, H.(m)	18	Bremerhafen	64-0363
HENSCHEL, Albert	38	Berlin	64-1022
Joseph 28			
HENSCHEL, Julius H	22	Dresden	66-0934
HENSCHEN, J.H.	23	Bremen	64-0427
HENSCHKE, Selma	15	Camenz	66-1131
HENSE, Theodor	27	Seringhausen	63-1038
Josephine 24			
HENSEL, A.	24	Zittau	64-1161
HENSEL, A.M.	32	Germany	63-0953
HENSEL, Anne Elise	23	Trauerbach	63-0296
HENSEL, Frdr.	28	Berlin	64-0495
HENSEL, Heinrich	30	Neunburg	66-0083
Clementine 26, Minna 3, Augusta 9m			
HENSEL, Oscar	25	Neunburg	66-0083
Minna 21, Carl 28			
HENSELL, Friedrich	21	Bremen	65-1140
HENSELMEIER, Heinr	22	Dissen	66-1128
HENSELMEYER, Frdr.	42	Dissen	66-1128
Wilhelmine 44, Wilhelmine 18, Wilhelm 7			
Franz 6, Heinrich 4, Charlotte 1			
HENSELMEYER, Wilh.	44	Dissen	66-1128
Anne Marie 40, Mina 17, Franz 13			
Charlotte 7, Louise 1			
HENSEMANN, Ursula	39	Oggelshausen	66-0221
Joseph 7			
HENSEN, Hermann	35	Aschendorf	65-1095
Maria 28, Margarethe 10m			
HENSING, Johanna	39	Arhold	65-0950
Marie 22			
HENTELMEIER, Frdr.	15	Dissau	65-0950
HENTZE, Georg	29	Osterode	65-0770
Auguste 34, Carl 9			
HENTZE, Heinrich	33	Hannover	66-0469
Leonore 28			
HENZ, H.(m)	45	Koch	64-0331
HENZE, Carol.	20		66-1313
Friederike 8m			
HENZE, Ch.(m)	19	Braunschweig	64-0331
Johanna 21			
HENZE, Siegfr.	18	Cassel	66-1313
HENZE, Wilhelm	21	Fredelsloh	67-0007
HENZEL, Heinrich	21	Wien	67-0992
HEPP, Elisabeth	19	Gaibach	64-0938
HEPPNER, Wm.	24	Tiefenort	63-1178
HEPS, Marg.	20	Salmsdorf	64-0840
HERALD, Antonia	24	Kuttenberg	64-0593
HERANT, Mary	32	Boehmen	63-0244
Caroline 11m			
HERB, L.	20	Bremen	64-0593
HERB, Peter	52	Baden	66-0578
Catharina 35, Peter 22, Carl 19			
Barbara 10, Joseph 9, Elisabeth 7			
Franz 4, Louise 1			
HERBEL, John	33	Lang Goens	63-0350
Elisabeth 45, Marie 9, John 7, Louisa 5			
Elis. 3			
HERBERMANN, Maria	30	Mauritz	66-1155
HERBERT, Augusta		Friedeloh	66-0734
HERBERT, Christ	31	Meerholz	64-0992
HERBERT, Engelbert	20		65-1095
HERBERT, Joh.	22	Hausen/Bav.	66-0577

NAME	AGE	RESIDENCE	YR-LIST
HERBERTS, Mag.	16	Rudisbronn	63-0013
HERBESTEIN, J.	28	Neustadt a/H	65-1189
HERBIG, Friederike	20	Lade	65-1095
HERBIG, Wilhelm	24	Petershagen	65-1095
Friedrich 50			
HERBIKE, W.(m)	16	Petershagen	64-0331
HERBOLD, Carl	27	Hessen	66-0734
Lisette 21			
HERBOLD, Georg	25	Hessen	66-0734
HERBRECHT, A.	19	Dortmund	65-0402
HERBST, Eva	66	Washington	64-0687
HERBST, F.(m)	15	Gelliehausen	64-0331
HERBST, F.(m)	23	New York	64-0331
HERBST, Geo.	37	Mestenfeldt	65-0974
Kinigunde 21			
HERBST, Heinrich	27	Kufenthal	65-0770
Dorette 26, Lina 18, Anna 3, Robert 2			
Bertha 3m, Dora 6			
HERBST, Hermann	40	Baltimore	63-0693
Ida 15			
HERBST, Justus	14	Curhessen	63-0822
HERBST, Otto	28	Magdeburg	65-0856
HERBST, Stephanie	24	Munderkingen	64-0433
HERBST, Theda	42	Muenchen	64-1022
HERBST, Theodor	33	Nordhausen	64-0739
HERBSTMANN, Anna	18	Dippach	66-1203
HERBSTREIT, Anna M	18	Wittenweiler	63-0296
HERCHENROEDER, Hh.	27	Radmuehle	65-0950
HERCHT, Friedrich	21	Vipachedethsn	64-0199
HERD, Friedrich	29	Oldenburg	67-0806
HERDA, Eduard	34	Gabitz	66-0147
Maria 31, Anna 4, Clara 10m			
HERDE, Joh.	19	Boehmen	64-0138
HERDE, John	45	Boehmen	63-0917
HERDER, Franziska	22	Maikamp	63-1085
HERDERER, Chr.	50	Rottweil	63-1085
HERDING, Georg	22	Limburg	66-0934
HERDLING, Marie	18	Luewersbach	65-0594
HERDT, Joseph	30	Borghorst	66-0679
HERFF, Joseph	40	Windischgruen	66-1327
HERFURTH, Aug.	30	Madison	63-0482
Ida 23, Emilie 11m			
HERGENROEDER, Adam	38	Duedelsheim	64-0886
Adam 58, Margaretha 56, Georg 22			
Heinrich 17			
HERHOLZ, Albert	30	Stressendorf	64-1053
Emilie 27, Hermine 4, Lidia 2			
Richard 10m			
HERICH, Caroline	19	Altenkronen	64-0433
HERIG, Joh. Ph.	40	Mannheim	64-0170
HERKE, Gottl. Carl	40	Altenburg	64-0432
Henriette 43, Carl 14, Herm. 9, Rosalie 5			
HERKES, Joh.	26	Echternach	64-0687
HERKLOTZ, Johannes	20	Bremen	66-0984
HERKMANN, Anna	16	Drehle	66-1093
HERLACKEN, Jacques	32	Switz	66-0679
HERLAN, Christine	20	Friedrichstal	63-0244
baby 6m, C. 30			
HERLAN, John	44	Friedrichstal	63-0244
Christine 43, Wilhelmine 22, Martha 18			
Pauline 15, William 9, Bertha 6			
Caroline 8, M. 33, M. 10, B. 8, Aug. 4			
HERLAN, Magdalene	54	Friedrichstal	63-0244
Isaac 16, Lewis 20, William 24, C. 18			
F. 16, B. 13, K. 44, L. 4			
HERLDT, Anthony	30	New York	64-0073
HERLIG, Michael	30	Bayern	65-0713
Barbara 25			
HERLITZ, Carl Gab.	19	Klintehamm	66-1127
HERLOTTE, Aug.	21	Mitteldorf	64-0331
HERLT, Anton	26	Schoenau	66-1373
HERM, Michael	23	Freinheim	64-1022
HERMANN, Adalbert	30	Gostysczyn	66-0578
Barbara 23			
HERMANN, Ann Marie	18	Westhofen	64-0073
HERMANN, August	23	Rheine	66-1155
HERMANN, Carl	16	Wuertemberg	66-0984
HERMANN, Charles	35	Deutz	63-0244

NAME	AGE	RESIDENCE	YR-LIST
HERMANN, Chs.	32	New York	63-0862
HERMANN, Elisabeth	28		67-0007
HERMANN, Elisabeth	56	Amsterdam	66-1248
HERMANN, Emil	23	Stargard	66-0668
HERMANN, Franz	27	Opperau	65-1088
HERMANN, Jacob	24	Baden Baden	64-1053
HERMANN, Johann	20	Leimbach	66-1327
HERMANN, Johanna	60	Stettin	66-1031
HERMANN, Ludwig	24	Neuenkirchen	67-0007
HERMANN, Philipp	26	Kreffelbach	66-1131
HERMANN, Pierre	24	Harve	63-0097
HERMANN, R.	19	Minden	63-0917
HERMANN, Sella	26	Giessen	64-0782
HERMANN, Th.	24	Trier	65-1024
HERMDING, Friedr.	49	Hahlen	64-0433
HERMERDING, Carl	19	Osnabrueck	64-0495
HERMES, Eman.	39	Boehmen	63-1136
HERMES, Georg	47	Gr. Mustadt	66-0576
Elise 49, Ludw. 13, Elise 9			
HERMSCHING, Bernh.	39	Wachtum	64-1053
HERMSTADT, Benno	33	Militsch	66-0576
HEROLD, Anna	18	Kuttenberg	65-0189
HEROLD, Carl	18	Castela	66-1327
HEROLD, Charles	30	Lohr	63-0917
HEROLD, Gustav	27	Gefries	63-0053
HEROLD, Heinr.	22	Mellrich	64-0840
Regina 20			
HEROLD, Joh.	29	Bohemia	64-0073
HEROLD, Johann	24	Lichtenfels	64-0214
HEROLD, John	41	New York	66-0221
HERPISCH, G.(m)	30	Frickendorf	64-0331
HERR, Elisabeth	67	Koenig	66-1203
HERR, Xaver	32	Baden	66-0576
HERRE, Christine	21	Laufen	66-0984
HERRE, F.	19	Strusberg	65-1024
HERRE, Franz	30	Hundeluft	66-1093
HERREILERS, Herman	26	Wardenburg	66-0734
HERRIG, John	46	Trier	63-0244
P.. 12			
HERRLEIN, Ernst	19	Frankfurt a/m	66-1248
HERRLINGER, Jacob	19	Schloth	64-0687
HERRMANN, Anna	18	Friedingen	66-1373
HERRMANN, Bertrand	17	Wuertemberg	66-0704
HERRMANN, Carl	25	Berlin	63-0244
Friedr. 23			
HERRMANN, Caroline	23	Walldorf	63-0917
Rosalie 22			
HERRMANN, Charles	30	Frankfurt	63-0990
Mathilde 20, Sophie 21, Caroline 9			
HERRMANN, Fanny	26	Barchfeld	66-0704
HERRMANN, Ferd.	24	Goppingen	64-0687
HERRMANN, Heinrich	19	Wuertemberg	66-0704
HERRMANN, James	30	Unterhausen	63-1038
HERRMANN, Joh. Geo	29	Steinfeld	66-0469
HERRMANN, Jos.	43	Bohemia	64-0687
Maria 24			
HERRMANN, Jos.	30	Mainz	64-0886
HERRMANN, Julius	38	New York	64-0023
HERRMANN, Margreth	44	Wernshausen	63-1069
HERRMANN, Nathan	23	Boehmen	66-0349
HERRMANN, Peter	40	Minikowa	66-0469
Catharine 30, Tomas 10, Franz 3			
August 6m			
HERRMANN, Wilhelm	42	Sievern	66-0349
Anna 28			
HERRSCHLER, Peter	32	Clusbach	64-0840
HERRWALD, Heinr.	34	Braunschweig	64-1022
HERSCHEL, Carl	24	Leipzig	66-1248
Oscar 14			
HERSCHEL, Carl Fr.	59	Frankfurt a/m	66-1248
Amalie 59			
HERSCHEL, Otto	19	Stuttgart	64-0593
HERSHENMUELLER, Fr	48	Wersen	64-0639
HERSTRIET, Anton	45	Baden	66-0147
HERT, Carl	30	Switz	66-0679
HERTEL, Edmund	23	Asch	66-0679
HERTEL, Georg	27	Neustadt	67-0806
HERTEL, Wilh.	17	Hessen	66-0221

NAME	AGE	RESIDENCE	YR-LIST
HERTENSTEIN, Fr'dr	18	Freisenheim	63-0990
HERTER, Jacob	55	Rothenzimmern	66-0704
Anna 46, Christine 23, Christian 16			
Gottlieb 14, Jacob 12, Leonhard 6			
HERTER, M.B.	33	Muehlheim	65-0402
Carl 5, Magdalina 2, Carl 30			
HERTH, Georg	22	Ohio	63-0097
HERTKORN, Joseph	23	Aldorf	64-0639
HERTLEIN, Christ.	19	Erlangen	66-1093
HERTSCH, Theo.	28	Meerane	64-0170
HERTSCHEN, Wilhmne	35	Meerane	64-0593
Julius 6m			
HERTWICH, Th.J.	22	Bollberg	64-0495
HERTWIG, Gust.	34	Steinkunzendf	66-1313
HERWALDT, Franzka.	24	Maenster	65-0950
Marie 18			
HERWEGK, Wilhelm	23	Darmstadt	65-0116
HERWIG, Anna M.	25	Rechtebach	64-0938
Anna C. 3, Martha 9m			
HERWIG, Christoph	28	Mederdunzebch	64-0170
Math. 40, Elisab. 38, Adam 9, Martha 7			
Fr. W. 5, Elise 2			
HERWIG, M.	36	Heiligenstadt	64-0665
Christoph 15, Wilhelm 8, Georg 3			
Louise 6m			
HERWIG, Math.	40	Hessen	64-0432
HERZ, Amalia	21	Dittenbein	64-0639
HERZ, Anna C.	23	Eichen	63-1010
HERZ, August	28	Dueseldorf	65-0151
HERZ, Bernhard	34	Megyaszo	66-0679
Therese 28, Victor 6, Bela 2, Juana 4			
HERZ, Friedrich	28	Lauenburg	67-0599
Henriette 26			
HERZ, Isaak	24	Crefeld	66-0734
HERZ, Jac.	25	Dierdorf	65-1024
HERZ, John C.	29	Bremen	63-1085
HERZ, Julius	26	New York	66-0734
HERZ, Nathan	17	Pforzheim	66-0221
HERZ, Ph.	19	Bremerhafen	64-0665
HERZBACH, August	25	Rothenstein	66-1131
HERZBERG, B.	17	Magdeburg	64-0495
HERZBERG, J.(f)	24	Magdeburg	64-0495
Aga.(f) 8m			
HERZBERG, Phil.	17	Coeln	65-0055
HERZFELD, Conrad	21	Insterburg	66-0412
HERZFELDER, Alb.	20	Burgkunstadt	64-0331
HERZING, Margareth	22	Wichsenstein	66-0083
HERZOG, Caroline	25	Worstadt	66-0984
HERZOG, Gottlieb	28	Geisingen	65-0594
HERZOG, Gottlieb	20	Giglingen	65-0713
HERZOG, H.	22	Kirchheide	66-0413
HERZOG, Joh.	29	Neuhausen	64-0073
Johanna 27, Carl 6			
HERZOG, Karl	16	Schollbrunn	66-1131
HERZOG, Paul	25	Munich	66-0412
Catharine 24			
HESPENHEIDE, Heinr	26	Renzel	65-1031
Marie 17			
HESPENHEIDE, Soph.	15	Hannover	65-0055
HESPERLEIN, Georg	30	Mistelgau	65-1031
HESS, Albert	18	Rottweil	66-0679
HESS, Alexander	32	Grossenbach	66-1327
HESS, Barbara F.	22	Hamelburg	63-1010
HESS, Benedikta	24	Rikken	66-1243
HESS, CLara	19	Salzdorf	64-0687
HESS, Carl	22	Vaihingen	64-0782
HESS, Catharina	15	Mailbach	63-0296
HESS, Christian	25	Weggum	64-1022
HESS, Conrad	37	Langgoens	64-1108
Elisabeth 7			
HESS, Fanny	18	Sulzdorf	63-0917
HESS, Franz	20	Oppershofen	66-1155
HESS, Friedr.	27	New York	63-0821
HESS, Georg	22	Zeviskausen	66-1203
HESS, Gottl.	54	Pommern	66-0469
Johanna 24, Caroline 22, Friederike 14			
HESS, Gottlob	38	Gosmanrode	66-0623
Anna Elisab. 37, Catharina An 10			

NAME	AGE	RESIDENCE	YR-LIST
Bernhard 6, Anna Maria 1			
HESS, Heinrich	27	Biberach	66-0412
HESS, Heinrich	66	Pfungstadt	66-0734
Christiane 64			
HESS, Jac.	17	Grunbach	64-0782
HESS, Joh. H.	15	Hersfeld	64-0593
HESS, Johannes	20	Kretzingen	66-0934
Friedrich 31			
HESS, Josepha	25	Breitendichen	64-0593
HESS, Jul.(m)	20	Lohr	64-0138
HESS, Julius	25	Marienwerder	65-1024
HESS, Phil.	31	Rehlingen	65-0402
HESS, Wilhelm	19	Gerbstadt	66-0679
HESSDORF, Philip	34	St. Louis	63-0953
HESSE, Anna Doroth	69	Lengenfeld	63-0482
HESSE, August	39	Seehausen	66-0679
HESSE, Bernhard	25	Sangerhausen	63-0953
HESSE, Caroline	20	Strasburg	65-0116
HESSE, Clemens	25	Beverstedt	65-0594
Friederike 26, Andreas 56, Josefa 52			
Joseph 22, Elisabeth 19, Clara 16			
Catharina 14, Victor 7, Juliane 6			
HESSE, Conr.	30	Marburg	63-0821
Elisabeth 27, Anna 2			
HESSE, Conrad	28	Frankfurt	66-0679
HESSE, Georg	21	Bremen	66-1093
Johann 28			
HESSE, H.(m)	15	Bothel	64-0331
HESSE, Heinr.	26	Minden	64-0363
Sophie 26			
HESSE, Henry	30	New York	63-0752
HESSE, Henry	25	Paris	63-1085
HESSE, Herm.	24	Chemnitz	66-0147
HESSE, Herm.	15	Gehrde	63-0350
HESSE, Johanna	30	New York	63-0953
Emma 5			
HESSE, Justus	29	Moischeit	66-0623
HESSE, Justus	18	Hannover	66-1031
HESSE, Theresia	20	Dollhausen	66-1128
HESSELBACHER, Frd.	21	Bressen	64-1022
HESSELMEYER, Chrlt	19	Osnabrueck	64-0886
HESSEN, Alex.	25	Haffen	65-0402
HESSENBRUCH, Herm.	17	Philadelphia	63-0482
HESSENMEYER, Herm.	26	St. Louis	64-0170
HESSINIUS, Peter	56	Schierum	64-0495
Me(f) 22, Talea(f) 20			
HESSLER, Joseph	45	Kogl/Ungarn	66-0346
Maria 34, Elisabeth 19, Andreas 15			
Mathias 9, Maria 1			
HESSLER, Michael	22	Laufach	63-1218
HESSLER, Ursula	30	Kogl/Ungarn	66-0346
HESSLING, Dora	21	Nentershausen	66-1127
HETSCHEL, Thecla	13	Buttstedt	64-0331
HETT, Anna	19	Wahlien	63-0398
Cath. 24			
HETTERER, Gregor	47	Bicht	63-0693
Rosa 17, Helena 15, Franz 9, Catharine 6			
Therese 3			
HETTERICH, Margar.	43	Stockheim	64-0687
Marie 7, Caroline 5			
HETTERLING, Cathr.	17	Karlstadt	63-1010
HETTERMANN, H.	22	Emsbuehren	63-1038
HETTIG, Fiedel	30	St. Louis	66-0679
HETTLINGER, John	14	Boehmen	66-0109
HETTRICH, Conrad	43	Stockheim	63-1218
HETZEL, Barbara	28	Ebern	66-0349
Franz 5, Peter 9m			
HETZEL, Joh. Geo.	27	Ebern	65-0898
HETZLER, Johannes	20	Wuerttemberg	64-0456
HEU, Elisabeth	67	Koenig	66-1203
HEU, Gertrude	32	Waldmichelbch	64-0214
HEUBOKY, Anton	37	Linglis	64-0170
HEUC, C.	52	Heiden	66-0413
HEUER, Aug.	29	Marientrelben	66-1243
HEUER, Carl	30	Giffhorn	64-0904
HEUER, Friedrich	23	Ostenholz	67-0599
HEUER, G.	26	Syke	65-0007
HEUER, Joh. Heinr.	22	Spieka	63-0614

NAME	AGE	RESIDENCE	YR-LIST
HEUER, Leo.	28	Bremen	63-0862
HEUGGELER, Anton	25	Unteragers	65-0151
HEUKE, Claus	23	Vickmuehlen	66-1373
HEUKE, Wilhelm	23	Strom	66-1373
HEUKET, Herm.	28	Battenberg	64-0593
HEULEIN, Max	23	Lohren	65-1024
HEUMANN, Erhard	33	Neustadt	66-1243
Johanna 32, Carl 8, Anna 5			
HEUMANN, Isaac	21	Cunrath	66-0221
HEUMANN, Jacob	60	Hildersberg	64-0885
HEURANG, August	26	Bastheim	64-0433
Gottlieb 46			
HEUSE, Johannes	25	Lauschroeden	64-0938
HEUSEL, Balthasar	23	Fauerbach	64-0214
HEUSELER, Heinr.	32	Laer	64-0840
Cath. 28, Franz 9m			
HEUSER, Daniel	22	Burkhardsfeld	64-0456
HEUSER, Elsb.	57	Ois	64-0782
HEUSER, Heinr.	27	Coppel	65-0974
HEUSER, Max.	48	Osnabrueck	65-1140
Wilhelm 25			
HEUSER, Peter	29	Gr. Kniegnitz	64-0665
HEUSHELT, Friedr.	43	Ruethersdorf	66-0934
HEUSING, Carl Frd.	25	Waldeck	64-0920
Charlotte 25			
HEUSLER, Herm.	17	Hingen	64-0840
HEUSMANN, Carl	15	Semmenstedt	65-1030
HEUSOHN, Heinr.	28	Weinegs	64-0214
HEUSS, J.(-)	29	New York	64-0331
HEUSS, Jac.	17	Worms	65-0402
Josephine 16			
HEUSSINGER, Chs(m)	39	Coburg	64-0363
HEUSSMANN, Heinr.	48	Wolfenbuettel	67-1005
Doris 43, Heinrich 13			
HEUSSNER, Augusta	27	Melsungen	65-0004
HEUTEL, Johann	36	Raboldshausen	66-0349
Margareth 31, Anna 5, Adam 10m			
HEUTER, Catherine	20	Darmstadt	66-1031
HEUTINGER, Christ.	45	Meiningen	65-0950
HEWESCHER, Wilhelm	15	Minden	65-1031
HEWIG, Marie	15	Hesse-Darmst.	63-0822
HEWINGHOFF, Rob.	25	Gleibltz	63-1010
HEY, Martin	29	Lehe	64-1108
HEYD, He.(f)	58	Gruenberg	64-0331
HEYDE, E.	23	Roushausen	65-0974
HEYDE, v.d. Geo.	26	Kleinenberg	64-0593
Caroline 24			
HEYDE, v.d. Hil.	39	Emden	66-0837
HEYDEMANN, Ferdin.	38	Ezernin	63-0693
HEYDEN, Heinrich	28	Goettingen	66-0668
HEYDEN, v.d. Gotfr	36	Calton	66-1327
HEYDUCK, Hugo	18	Hilders	66-0221
HEYE, Diedr.	36	Westerstede	64-0593
Anna 26, Herm. 14, Sophie 7, Ferd. 6			
Carl 5, Helene 4, Maria 3, Johanna 2			
Otto 1, baby 6m			
HEYE, Ernst	33	Bremen	66-1093
Emilie 22			
HEYEN, Gerd.	22	Strakholt	66-1128
HEYEN, Jann	32	Aurich	66-0668
Focke 24, baby 6m, Rixte 7, Gretje 3			
HEYEN, Koob Eden	31	Backband	66-0412
Margarethe 30, Edo 2			
HEYER, Carl Heinr.	28	Lang	66-0650
HEYER, Hermann	20	Sammerge	66-0412
HEYER, V.U.	40	Spalz	64-1053
HEYER, Wilhelmine	24	Kissow	66-0650
HEYKENS, H.G.	26	Campen	64-0331
HEYKENS, Zeljens	32	Campen	64-0331
HEYMANN, Abr.	22	Carlsheim	65-0243
HEYMANN, Augusta	32	Wuerzburg	66-1203
Therese 23			
HEYMANN, Wilh'mine	28	Oldenburg	66-0109
Carl 11m			
HEYMUELLER, F.C.	58	Louisville	63-0862
HEYN, Alex.	18	Bremervoerde	65-0402
HEYN, Daniel	15	Mannheim	66-1127
HEYN, Ferd.	20	Herborn	65-1031

NAME	AGE	RESIDENCE	YR-LIST
HEYN, Helene	17	Dorum	63-0917
HEYSE, Caroline	24	Duderstadt	66-1128
HICKEL, Adam	19	Winterscheid	65-0770
HICKMANN, Max	17	Muenster	65-1030
HIDDE, Minna	33	Berlin	63-0990
HIDISSEN, J.F.	31	Bremen	64-0214
HIEBEN, Franz	20	Crefeld	65-1095
HIEBER, Chr.	25	Kornthal	65-0974
Metta 29			
HIEBER, Otto	25	Freiburg	66-1327
HIECK, Wilhelm	23	Alfhausen	66-0679
HIEMKE, Sophie	24	Eldagsen	66-1327
HIERL, Ed.	35	Erfurt	66-0577
Friedr. 35, Christ 7, Ernst 6, Carl 10m			
HIERN, Friedrich	17	Ulm	66-0083
Catharine 16			
HIERONIMUS, J.	28	Zwittau/Boh.	65-0856
HIESSNER, Christ.	52	Jestedt	64-0687
Elisabeth 51			
HIFFMEYER, Johann	29	Gramberge	65-1095
HIFLEIN, Paul	46	Mit.Rainstadt	65-1088
Barbara 36, Eva 4, Anna 10			
HILB, Sophie	21	Landhusen	64-0331
HILB, Wolf	51	Eschelbach	65-0007
Sarah 41, Manasses 20, Leopold 14			
HILBER, Adam	22	Altmarschen	66-1327
HILBERG, Herm.	26	Wetter	66-0704
HILBERS, (f)	37	Geestendorf	65-0974
Hermann 4			
HILBERT, Chls.	32	Elberfeld	64-0992
HILBERT, Egar	14	Niederstedt	64-1022
Augusta 15			
HILBNER, Therese	26	Manil	64-1053
HILBRAND, Carl	23	Koenigsberg	66-1327
HILBRECHT, Fr.	37	Verden	65-0402
HILBURGER, Johann	42	Rindenheim	66-0679
HILCKEN, Doris	39	Troy	63-0244
HILD, Adam	20	Neubreitenbch	66-0083
HILD, Margaretha	19	Hersfeld	66-1155
HILD, Paulus	45	New York	63-0244
M. 35			
HILDEBRAAND, Ernst	26	Kaistorf	64-0904
HILDEBRAND, Cath.	25	Sievern	67-0795
HILDEBRAND, Conrad	27	Schlingenthal	64-0739
HILDEBRAND, H.W.	17	Osnabrueck	66-0934
HILDEBRAND, Heinr.	23	Armsen	65-1031
HILDEBRAND, Herm.	19	Riegel	63-1178
HILDEBRAND, Jacob	30	Frankenhausen	66-0934
HILDEBRAND, Joh.	25	Schweiz	66-0147
HILDEBRANDT, Anna	28	Lehe	66-0934
Anna 9, Catharina 7, Meta 4			
HILDEBRANDT, B.(m)	29	Westfalen	64-0495
HILDEBRANDT, Carl	28	Braunschweig	66-1248
HILDEBRANDT, F.W.	43	Hannover	63-0296
HILDEBRANDT, G.	32	New York	64-0593
Florentine 21, Hulda 20, Alwine 19			
Fritz 4m			
HILDEBRANDT, Heinr	22	Breslau	64-0073
HILDEBRANDT, Heinr	40	Detmold	67-0353
HILDEBRANDT, Heinr	18	Ebersdorf	65-1095
HILDEBRANDT, Joh.	30	Kuehrstedt	42-0704
HILDEBRANDT, Joh.	22	Orb	66-1031
HILDEBRANDT, Joh.	18	Jebenhausen	65-0594
HILDEBRANDT, Otto	15	Waldueren	66-1203
HILDEBRANDT, Ph.	27	Wieseck	64-1022
HILDEBRANDT, Wm.	16	Langendamm	63-0168
HILDEMANN, Carl A.	23	Fuerstenau	64-0214
HILDEMANN, Ludwig	18	Hessen	66-0469
Elise 19			
HILDINGER, John	39	Philadelphia	66-0704
HILFS, Carl	26	Lissberg	63-0006
HILGAERTNER, L.	30	Londorf	63-0244
HILGAERTNER, Val.	36	Havre	65-0004
HILGENBERG, Johann	23	Borken	66-0412
HILKER, Heinr.	25	Preussen	63-0398
Doris 24			
HILKMANN, Gertrud	26	Hoerstel	65-0402
Gertrudis 2			

NAME	AGE	RESIDENCE	YR-LIST
HILL, Elisab.	19	Ndr.Ufleiden	64-0639
HILL, Magdalena	19	Coeln	64-1053
HILL, Maria	17	Pfungstadt	66-0734
HILL, Ph.	23	Sickenbach	64-0992
HILLBERG, Heinrich	48	Hesse-Cassel	66-0837
Katharina 52, Elisabeth 22, Christoph 14			
Anna Kath. 10			
HILLE, Carl	22	Leesen	65-0189
HILLE, Elise	14	Lutterberg	66-1155
Marie 16			
HILLE, Heinrich	30	Indiana	66-0221
John 25			
HILLEBOLD, Werner	21	Wichdorf	66-1313
Joh. 17			
HILLEBRAND, August	24	Hoexter	66-1127
HILLEMANN, Hch.	24	Bavaria	64-0840
Sophie 22, Carl 3m, Carl 13			
HILLER, August	30	Braunschweig	66-1313
Rosine 40, Alvin 4, Augusta 4m			
HILLER, Cathre.	42	Baltimore	63-0821
HILLER, Friederike	59	Rommelshausen	64-1053
HILLER, Friedrich	21	Grossbettling	66-1373
HILLER, Georg	16	Weissenheim	66-0221
HILLER, Hermann	35	Woerlitz	64-1022
HILLERMANN, Doroth	50	Roetzlongen	64-0840
Ferdinanda 22, Otto 15, Ferdinand 12			
Hermann 7, Marie 8m, John 18			
HILLERT, Louis	46	Goetingen	65-0402
Minna 33, Aug. 7, Louis 6			
HILLKE, Carl	25	Bollensen	66-0469
HILLMANN, Aug.	25	Heidelberg	64-0495
HILLMANN, John	24	Osterholz	66-0221
HILLMANN, Matthias	36	Schwabach	66-1031
HILLMANN, Otto	28	Bremen	64-0593
Elise 24			
HILLMANN, Sophie	20	Steyerberg	66-0934
HILLMER, Christ.	21	Hoselingen	64-0214
HILLMER, Johann	18	Hannover	66-0734
HILLMER, Wm.	24	Langenbruggen	67-0007
HILLSMANN, Fr.	35	Braunschweig	65-0974
Christl. 26, Anna 9m, Friederike 60			
HILMER, Christian	15	Lenne	66-0469
HILMES, Anton	30	Rodenburg	66-0578
Christine 6, Heinrich 4			
HILPERT, Maria	32	Fischbach	66-1155
Caroline 4			
HILPOLTSTEIN, Sal.	19	Dirmstein	66-0734
HILSEMANN, Herm.	18	Varensell	66-1203
HILSMANN, Emil	20	Neuenkirchen	64-0363
HIMBER, Friedrich	24	Freiburg	66-0679
HIMELSKAMP, Lucia	30	Hannover	63-1218
HIMMEL, Franz	19	Stettin	65-1030
HIMMELMANN, Carl	19	Waldeck	64-0432
HIMMELSBACH, John	41	Philadelphia	66-0576
HIMMELSBBACH, Joh.	30	Schneeberg	66-0576
HIMMER, Franz	37	Pest	65-0007
HIMMER, Veitalis	36	Vienna	66-1093
HIMMERICH, Anna M.	57	Eyershausen	64-1108
HIMMLER, Leonhard	26	Grosshaslach	66-0704
HINARIK, Anton	19	Boehmen	66-0349
HINCK, Carsten	28	Hessel	65-1095
HINCK, Hinrich	29	New York	66-0679
Lorenz 22			
HINCK, J.W.(f)	20	Kluste	64-0363
HINCKE, Carl Wm.	16	Ihlienworth	64-0427
HINDERER, G. David	23	Aspergle	65-0189
HINICK, Mathilde	45	Bremen	64-0023
Marie 46			
HINK, Lucie	18	Bederkesa	66-0934
HINKE, H.	31	New York	63-0244
Christ. 20			
HINKE, J.(m)	29	Mederwies	64-0495
HINKEL, Johannes	18	Wohra	65-1024
HINKEL, Wilhelm	28	Vilbel	63-0990
Elisabeth 27, Henry 9m			
HINKEN, Julchen	20	Bremervoerde	66-0623
HINN, Eduard	22	Hardheim	66-0650
HINNERS, Anna	21	Lehe	66-0577

NAME	AGE	RESIDENCE	YR-LIST
HINRICHS, Anna	25	Bremen	64-0331
HINRICHS, Bern.Joh	24	Loquard	63-0614
HINRICHS, Cath.	22	Bremerhaven	66-1031
HINRICHS, Cathar.	25	Wohlert	66-0984
HINRICHS, Cathar.	25	Ahrenswalde	66-0984
HINRICHS, J.G.	40	Bremen	66-0221
HINRICHS, Johann	21	Hoeven	66-1373
HINRICHS, Wilhelm	36	Bourtscheid	66-1373
HINSCH, Carl	26	Hamburg	64-0639
HINSCH, Johann	20	Gieversdorf	65-1095
HINSCHE, Hermann	23	Segiln	66-0346
HINSCHT, Joh.	24	Sterzides/Boh	65-0038
Vincenzia 20			
HINSPETER, Gustav		Hann. Muenden	66-1127
HINTENLANG, Marie	30	New York	66-0679
HINTZE, J.	28	Neustrelitz	65-0007
HINTZEN, Maria	26	Aschendorf	66-0412
HINZ, Carl Hr.	37	Ikasgieren	64-0886
HINZ, Christoph	43	Posen	64-0432
Ernestine 29, Herm. 9, Juliane 6, Marie 3			
Sophie 1			
HINZE, Georg Diedr	37	Bentrode	66-0650
Catharine 31, Wilhelm 4, Louise 2			
Friedrich 6m			
HIPP, Lorenz	26	Tuttlingen	64-0639
HIPPOLD, Cathar.	29	Holzmaden	66-0221
August 6			
HIRCH, Math.	21	Wuerttemberg	65-0898
HIRNKAMP, H.	57	Langen	64-0782
HIRSCH, Babette	34	Kl. Gerau	63-1178
HIRSCH, Christoph	28	Sindelfingen	66-1203
HIRSCH, Friedrich	24	Sul	66-1131
HIRSCH, Isaac	52	Frankfurt	66-0734
Jorg 18			
HIRSCH, Jacob	40	New York	66-0679
HIRSCH, Joh.	17	Wurttenberg	64-0593
HIRSCH, Jos.	41	Santa Fe	64-0639
HIRSCH, Josef	34	California	66-0221
HIRSCH, L.(m)	25	Bohemia	64-0331
HIRSCH, Leon	40	Bechtheim	66-0679
Heinrich 21			
HIRSCH, Regine	20	Speyer	66-1155
HIRSCH, Roeschen	23	Waldgirmes	64-0687
HIRSCH, Rosa	18	Nordheim	64-0938
HIRSCH, Samuel	26	Tuebingen	63-1085
HIRSCH, Simon	17	Hessen	63-1085
HIRSCHBERGER, Soph	18	Welldingen	63-0990
HIRSCHEL, Samuel	53	Davenport	63-0953
HIRSCHFELD, H.	28	Prussia	63-0296
HIRSCHHEIMER, Falk	20	Lohren	65-1024
HIRSCHHORN, David	51	Friedberg	63-0015
HIRSCHLAND, Bai	9	Oberwiesse	65-1024
HIRSCHLAND, Hirsch	25	Hahnstadt	65-1024
Samuel 50, Helena 50, Betchen 18			
Jettchen 15, Julchen 5, Levin 12, Aron 9			
HIRSCHLAND, Lion	19	Linghofen	65-1024
HIRSCHLY, Louis	33	Switz.	63-0350
HIRSCHMANN, Anna	22	Preptitz	65-1189
Siegfried 2, baby 11m			
HIRSCHMOELLER, H.	27	Westercappeln	65-0974
HIRSEKORN, Hermann	30	Schwiebat	63-0168
HIRT, Amalie	25	Bandeg	66-1127
HIRT, Ernst	23	Paderborn	64-1206
HIRTE, Johann	30	Goslar	64-0687
HIRTH, John	59	Leisa	63-1136
HIRTZ, Georg	21	Muenster	65-0402
HISCHEMUELLER, Her	28	Kappeln	63-1069
Augusta 17			
HISMAIER, Joseph	21	Offenburg	63-0693
HISSLING, Carl	18	Dalwende	66-0734
HISTERBERG, F.	27	Bockeloh	65-1189
HITZEL, Gottfried	29	Moemmlingen	66-1031
HITZELBERGER, M.	21	Moringen	64-1161
HOBBIE, Th. A.	20	Varel	64-0214
HOBEL, A.	16	Harbarnsen	63-1085
HOBOLD, Elise	37	Hameln	64-0938
HOCH, Andreas	16	Wuertemberg	66-0679
HOCH, August	31	Muehlhausen	63-0693

NAME	AGE	RESIDENCE	YR-LIST
HOCH, Elise	26	Obernberg	66-0837
HOCH, Henrich	46	Schaddeback	64-0840
HOCH, Jacobina	21	Berghausen	66-1327
Carl 8			
HOCH, Joh.	31	Nokre	66-0704
Anna 22, Anna 2, Wenzel 9m			
HOCH, Johann	55	New York	66-0679
HOCH, Susanne	22	Hechingen	66-0984
HOCHBECK, Lisette	35	Bielefeld	65-0243
HOCHGREBE, Sophie	22	Lippstadt	66-0577
Louise 25			
HOCHGREVE, Aug.	26	Grenberg	64-0992
HOCHHEIM, Julius	28	Chemnitz	63-0990
Marie Th. 28, Marie 5			
HOCHMANN, Anna	30	Sorga	66-1093
HOCHREITER, Marie	21	Columbus	66-1131
HOCHSTAETTER, Wm.	30	Darmstadt	64-0938
HOCHSTEIN, Therese	22	Niederberndrf	66-0413
HOCK, Bernhard	16	Berlichingen	66-0576
HOCK, Pauline	18	Wuertemberg	66-0679
HOCK, Peter	22	Oberwefflingn	67-0007
HOCK, Philipp	51	Aschaffenburg	66-0837
Johann 24, Catharine 16, Joseph 15			
Franz 3, Maria U. 9, baby			
HOCKE, John	30	Riegel	63-0917
HOCKER, Johanna	59	Wien	63-0917
HOCKERJES, Sophie	25	Lahr	64-0593
HOCKMEYER, D.H.	23	Lemfoerde	64-0214
HODAPP, Caroline	21	France	63-1038
HODENBERG, v. H.	28	Verden	63-0862
HODES, Joseph	22	Heinfeld	67-0007
Eugen 7			
HODIAK, Wilh.	29	Hoerste	64-0073
HODINGHAUS, Joh.	54	Hagen	63-0398
Anna 49, Heinr. 19, Joh. 15, Bernh. 12			
Anna 2			
HODOWAL, Anton	40	Baschlow	66-0734
Kathar. 35, Francisca 14, Franz 3			
Joseph 11m			
HODRES, H.	18	Lippe Detmold	66-0413
HODUM, Carl	17	Wuertemberg	63-0398
HOE, Theresia	21	Breitendichen	64-0593
HOEB, Johann	23	Ruhlkirchen	66-0349
HOEBEL, Carl	22	Dersehen	65-1088
HOECHLER, Fanny	23	Angenrod	66-0704
HOECHSTER, Maria	66	Angenrod	65-1088
Jette 26, Henry 31			
HOECHSTETTER, Jos.	37	Geiselrohtit.	66-1093
HOEEHN, Seb.	42	Buffalo	63-0821
HOEFENER, Diedr.	24	Bersenbruck	66-0221
HOEFENER, Hermann	15	Dehle	64-1022
HOEFENER, Ludw.	23	Kurhessen	66-0221
HOEFER, Aug.	24	Walbach	64-0992
HOEFER, Caroline	17	Welzheim	63-0482
HOEFER, Christian	16	Hessen	66-0734
HOEFER, Fridolin	19	Hetschbach	66-0576
HOEFER, Hr.	52	Wahlbach	65-1189
Caroline 34, August 25, Sophie 19			
Emma 17, Heinrich 13			
HOEFER, William	27	Wahlbach	65-1189
HOEFERER, Philip	25	Lauterbach	66-1127
HOEFFLE, Chr.	38	Diedesheim	65-1189
Chr. 5			
HOEFFLE, Pauline	22	Albershausen	64-0687
HOEFFLER, Marie	21	Zweibruecken	64-0687
Catharine 17			
HOEFFNER, Michael	46	Erlinsbach	66-0109
Anna 48			
HOEFLICH, Christ.	21	Ostheim	66-0837
HOEFLING, Anna	20	Sackenbach	65-1031
HOEFLINGER, Georg	34	Neidlingen	66-0109
HOEFT, Bernhard	20	Quackenbrueck	64-0920
HOEGELN, Friedr.	19	Lorch	66-1248
HOEGER, Friedr. Wm	25	Heilbronn	66-1155
Wilhelmine 22, Friedr. Wm. 2			
HOEGES, Marie	24	Rheinbach	64-0992
HOEH, Theresia	22	Altenstadt	66-0668
Simon 19			

NAME	AGE	RESIDENCE	YR-LIST
HOEHEN, Peter	21	Lonsheim	64-0639
HOEHLE, Caroline	24	Bohne/Waldeck	66-0469
HOEHLE, Marie	44	Bessungen	66-0679
Elise 21			
HOEHN, G.	38	New Orleans	63-0917
HOEHN, Louis	19	Zostein	66-1327
Louise 21			
HOEHN, Mich.	28	Louisenthal	64-0138
HOEHNER, Jobst	21	Bremsen	65-1031
HOEHR, Christ.	20	Freudensdorf	64-0782
Joseph 39, J. 39			
HOEK, Philipp	54	Baden	66-0576
HOEKEL, Martin	26	Floersheim	66-1327
HOELAND, Caroline	19	Breitenbach	64-0432
HOELL, Georg	16	Goettingen	64-0495
HOELLE, Joseph	35	Ottweiler	66-0109
Marie Marg. 29			
HOELLEBOLD, Adam	27	Heimarshausen	64-1053
HOELLING, Carl	20	Berne	66-1155
HOELSCHER, Chr.	17	Hille	64-0214
HOELSCHER, Heinr.	21	Ossemissen	66-0984
HOELSCHER, Heinr.	27	Dissen	65-0004
HOELSCHER, Lisette	21	Prussia	64-0432
HOELTERMANN, Joh.	19	Wulfena	66-0984
HOENECKE, Adolph	28	Brandenburg	63-0006
HOENER, Peter	25	Bielefeld	65-1031
Friederike 24			
HOENES, Julius	35	Crumbach	63-1038
HOENNINGHAKE, Aug.	26	Damme	66-0413
HOEPER, A.	19	Bremen	65-0594
HOEPFNER, C.	21	Leipzig	66-0704
HOEPFNER, Christ.	34	New York	63-0990
HOEPKEN, Johann	30	Hannover	66-0734
Gerhard 20			
HOEPNER, Betti	25	Aschwarden	63-0953
HOERATH, Catharina	19	Stein	66-0666
Paulus 26			
HOERHOLD, Wilhelm	29	Elben	64-0739
HOERMANN, Heinrich	31	Emlinghausen	66-0668
Adelheid 28, baby (m) 11m			
HOERNBEIN, Ernst	35	Meiningen	64-1053
HOERSTE, Joseph	24	Bueckeburg	66-1127
HOERSTKAMP, Gert.	18	Leer	66-1131
HOERSTMANN, Carl	17	Huntsburg	66-1031
HOESS, Friedrich	17	Schollbrunn	66-1131
HOESSLI, Barbara	20	Andeer	64-0427
HOEVEL, (f)	40	Osterholz	66-0934
HOEVELKROEGER, Joh	35	Osterwiehe	64-1022
Cath. 32, Elisab. 11, Elisab. 7, Joseph 5			
Christ. 4, Georg 2			
HOEVEN, v. Carl	18	Wittmund	66-0837
HOEVER, Anna	23	Helgenbach	64-1206
HOEVER, Christian	24	Stocksdorf	66-1155
Marie 21			
HOEVERKAMP, John G	15	Gehrde	63-0990
Anne Cath. 39, Margarethe 9			
HOEVERMANN, Joh.	36	Platendorf	64-0904
Sophie 32, Sophie 9, Johann 7, Marie 6			
Dorothea 5, Wilhelm 2, Johanna 9m			
HOEXTER, Lina	20	Schweinsberg	64-0214
HOF, August	23	Heilbronn	67-0007
HOF, Friedr.	38	Oeterheim	63-0350
HOF, Joh.	30	Weidenhausen	65-0898
HOFACKER, Conrad	15	Soden	66-0623
Marie 22			
HOFELICH, John G.	21	Belsen	63-0006
HOFELICH, Matthias	31	Wuerttemberg	66-1031
HOFEN, Wendelin	25	Wahningen	64-0639
HOFER, Anna	50	Gilesdorf	66-0346
Johann 21, Therese 18, Vincenz 16			
Anna 14, Elisabeth 12			
HOFER, Jacob	20	Torgau	66-1373
HOFER, Joh.	30	Zoefingen	64-0840
HOFER, Margaretha	18	Bocksdorf	64-0687
HOFER, Marie	25	Aach	66-0679
HOFF, Alwin	18	Cusel	66-1327
HOFF, Anna	22	Wetzlar	64-0214
HOFF, Johann	24	Crefeld	66-0576

NAME	AGE	RESIDENCE	YR-LIST
HOFF, Louise	38	Oetsheim	63-0482
Johanna 4, Frida 2, baby 6m			
HOFF, Marie	23	Steinweiler	64-0782
HOFFA, M. (m)	35	Washington	63-0551
H. (f) 30, Henry 5, Franklin 4			
Rebecca 6m			
HOFFART, Gottlieb	17	Koenig	66-0704
HOFFELD, Otto	22	Gehrde	66-1093
HOFFELT, Anne	22	Holland	63-0350
HOFFER, Maria	27	Bohemia	64-0687
Maria 11m			
HOFFMANN, (f)	57	Denzlingen	63-0244
HOFFMANN, Adam	49	Neushausen	64-0992
HOFFMANN, Adolph	26	Unterheimbach	66-0679
HOFFMANN, Adolph	23	Pressburg	64-1206
HOFFMANN, Agnes	44	Herborn	65-0974
HOFFMANN, Anton	38	Eschenhadt	64-0886
HOFFMANN, Aug.	28	Cincinnati	66-0984
HOFFMANN, Aug.	28	Naumburg	65-0713
HOFFMANN, Aug. Ed.	21	Melis	66-0837
HOFFMANN, Augustus	31	Cassel	63-0244
HOFFMANN, C.	55	Herford	65-1189
Johanna 20, Martha 7			
HOFFMANN, C.(m)	57	Herningen	64-0495
HOFFMANN, Carl	28	Magdeburg	64-0023
HOFFMANN, Carl	18	Wuertemberg	66-0679
HOFFMANN, Carl	29	Hoxberg	64-0363
HOFFMANN, Carol. M	21	Schlarpe	64-0739
HOFFMANN, Cath.	22	Gruenberg	64-0073
HOFFMANN, Cath.	22	Gruenberg	64-0023
HOFFMANN, Cath.	21	Gerricksheim	65-1030
HOFFMANN, Catha.	17	Rhoda	65-1031
HOFFMANN, Cathar.	19	Ronnelshausen	64-1053
HOFFMANN, Cathrine	17	St. Leon	67-0353
HOFFMANN, Ch.	26	New York	63-1178
HOFFMANN, Christ.	26	Wresteck	66-0578
HOFFMANN, D.	35	Brooklyn	63-0990
Lise			
HOFFMANN, Doris	28	Fuerth	63-0990
HOFFMANN, Dorothea	45	Dorflis	66-0984
HOFFMANN, Ed.(m)	25	Oelskirchen	64-0363
HOFFMANN, Elisab.	20	Muenster	64-1053
HOFFMANN, Elisbeth	24	Engelhafen	65-0950
HOFFMANN, Elise	19	Wiesenthal	66-1203
HOFFMANN, Emilie	46	Stuttgart	66-1203
HOFFMANN, Eugen	21	Bremen	66-0221
HOFFMANN, F.	22	Weimar	65-1088
HOFFMANN, Ferd.	38	Massachusetts	63-0990
HOFFMANN, Friedr.	37	Nuernberg	63-0006
HOFFMANN, Friedr.	20	Worms	65-0038
HOFFMANN, Fritz	29	Wuerzburg	64-0023
HOFFMANN, G.	27	Lobejau	64-0495
HOFFMANN, Georg	25	Eppstein	66-0109
HOFFMANN, Georg	20	Gruenberg	66-0934
HOFFMANN, Georg	18	Hersfeld	65-1189
HOFFMANN, Georg F.	23	Freiensteinau	65-1030
HOFFMANN, H.	19	Wunstorf	64-0665
HOFFMANN, Heinr.	69	Iggelheim	64-0023
HOFFMANN, Heinr.	35	Sattelbach/B.	65-0038
HOFFMANN, Heinrich	33	Hanau	66-0083
Clara 28, Franz Anton 5, Carl Heinr. 3			
HOFFMANN, Heinrich	31	Liebenau	66-0934
HOFFMANN, Helene	20	Maineck	63-0990
HOFFMANN, Henry	23	New York	66-0679
HOFFMANN, Herman	24	Frankfurt	64-0739
HOFFMANN, Hermann	29	Basel	64-0073
HOFFMANN, Hermann	24	Frankfurt	64-0739
HOFFMANN, Herrmann	25	Engther	65-1095
Elisabeth 21			
HOFFMANN, Hugo	32	Russdorf	64-0886
HOFFMANN, James	32	Milwaukee	63-0953
HOFFMANN, Joh.	26	Lebach	64-0214
HOFFMANN, Johann	30	Wilsdorf	64-0433
Elisabeth 21, Emil 6m			
HOFFMANN, Johann	69	Froenstedt	66-0984
HOFFMANN, Johanna	44	Pest	23-0865
Rosa 23, Ignatz 31			
HOFFMANN, Johannes	30	Rheda	64-1053
Elise 30, Bernhard 9m			
HOFFMANN, Johannes	21	Mittelsemen	65-0865
HOFFMANN, John	31	Allendorf	63-0015
Marg. 27, John 6, Barbara 4			
HOFFMANN, Julius	32	Nienburg	66-1031
Louise 31, Louise 9m			
HOFFMANN, Ludw.	38	Hannover	65-0038
HOFFMANN, Margaret	27	New York	66-0704
Adam 6, Barbara 3, Veronica 10m			
HOFFMANN, Marie	10	Kaiserslauter	63-1218
HOFFMANN, Mathilde	20	Lippe-Detmold	65-1088
HOFFMANN, Michael	22	Goldmichl	64-0687
Heinr. 14			
HOFFMANN, Minna	15	Schlarpe	64-0739
HOFFMANN, Oscar	32	New York	66-0679
HOFFMANN, Philipp	27	Heuchelheim	64-0138
HOFFMANN, Rosa	21	Gorsdorf/Boh.	66-0650
HOFFMANN, Theod.	15	Feldkirchen	65-1030
Caroline 17			
HOFFMANN, Therese	18	Elmshorn	65-0402
HOFFMANN, Therese	18	Weissenberg	65-1024
HOFFMANN, Val.	30	Steinbach	66-0934
HOFFMEISTER, Georg	24	Wickersrode	67-0600
HOFFMEISTER, Louis	58	Ludwigsburg	66-0984
HOFFMEISTER, Math.	32	Odernheim	65-1189
Gg. 7, Sophie 6m			
HOFFMEISTER, Math.	20	Hasloch	65-1030
HOFFMEISTER, Meta	32	New York	63-0244
Friedr. 9			
HOFFMEYER, Chr.	20	Bremen	63-1085
HOFGESANG, Andreas	22	Laetzendorf	66-0469
HOFHAGEN, Christel	16	St. Maynur	66-0984
HOFHEIM, Carl	21	Baden	66-0734
HOFHEIMER, Isaac	47	Norfold	64-0427
HOFHER, Carl	18	Berlichingen	66-1373
HOFHERR, Anna	28	Frankenthal	64-0593
HOFINGER, Sebast.	45	Karlug	66-0147
HOFKER, Antoinette	22	Lehe/Hann	64-0920
HOFLINGEN, Marie	14	Wendlingen	65-0402
HOFMAN, Christine	26	Obergimpern	66-1155
HOFMAN, Joh. Nic.	26	Momart	66-1327
HOFMANN, Adolf	20	Heilbronn	66-1131
HOFMANN, Ana	20	Berghofen	66-1155
HOFMANN, Andreas	29	Hausen	66-0412
HOFMANN, Caroline	29	Thalheim	65-0004
Louise 9m			
HOFMANN, Charlotte	59	Brensbach	63-0953
HOFMANN, Chls.	33	Ossitz	65-0007
Jul.(m) 31, Pauline 24, Christine 60			
HOFMANN, Christian	23	Herbrechtingn	66-1155
HOFMANN, Elisabeth	18	Worstetten	66-1093
HOFMANN, G.	31	Thusbrun	64-0495
Kunigunde 21, M. 30			
HOFMANN, Georg	30	Launspach	64-0343
HOFMANN, Heinr.	27	Bessungen	65-0594
HOFMANN, J.(m)	32	Pittsburg	64-0495
HOFMANN, Jac.	31	Rohrheim	64-0073
HOFMANN, Joh.	43	Wintersbach	63-0398
HOFMANN, Joh.	24	Magdeburg	65-0898
HOFMANN, Joh. Phil	28		65-0243
HOFMANN, Johann	24	Tauchersreuth	66-0576
HOFMANN, Marie	21	Schropberg	66-1155
Margarethe 23			
HOFMANN, Ottilie	28	Neuerweiler	65-0402
HOFMANN, Peter	21	Hasselborn	65-0594
Caroline 41			
HOFMANN, W.	28	Tuerringen	63-0398
Jeremias 64			
HOFMANN, Wilh'mine	18	Bechtheim	65-0116
HOFMANN, William	44	Greiz	63-0693
HOFMEIER, H.	18	Rinteln	67-0600
HOFMEISTER, C.	25	Osnabrueck	64-0495
HOFMEISTER, Carl	24	Bremerhaven	66-1155
HOFMEISTER, Christ	21	Altwallenrode	63-0953
HOFMEISTER, Johann	27	Cassel	63-0006
HOFSKY, Maria	32	Pest	64-0427
Regina 19, Naina 17, Ida 7, Adolph 6			
HOFT, Friedr.	48	Wuerttemberg	66-0576

NAME	AGE	RESIDENCE	YR-LIST
Marie 42, Adolph 9, Friedrich 8, Marie 6m			
HOFZEL, Jacobine	16	Bayern	66-0221
HOG, Lorenz	42	Coburg	65-0243
HOGREBE, Meta	22	Wittloh	66-1031
HOGREVE, Heinrich	26	Markoldendorf	66-1373
HOH, Joh. Gottl.	30	Oberhemmitz	67-0795
Ant. Chr. 28			
HOH, Kunigunde	28	Unterleinleit	66-0412
HOHA, Hein.	17	Oberseemen	66-0984
HOHE, Carl	14	Bonn	64-0199
HOHE, Emil	45	Buffalo	63-1136
HOHE, Marie	22	Wachbach	65-0402
HOHEB, Maria	18	Baschlow	66-0734
HOHER, Herm.	14	Westrup	63-1136
HOHL, Wilhelmine	14	Spatzenhof	64-0427
HOHLACKER, Anton	22	Wendelsheim	65-0007
HOHLT, Henriette	19	Minden	65-1031
HOHLWEG, V.	58	Baltimore	63-0990
HOHMANN, B.	27	Wien	65-0007
HOHMANN, Carita	22	Hessen	63-0614
HOHMANN, Carl	25	Cassel	66-0934
HOHMANN, Eva	23	Hessia	66-0679
HOHMEIER, Johannes	69	Schlitz	66-1031
Johannes 36, Elisabeth 31, Barbara 3			
Johannes 3m			
HOHMEYER, John	26	Niederhome	63-1178
HOHNHEIM, Math.	24	Siegburg	63-1218
HOHNHOLZ, Abel	50	Dingstede	65-0038
Anna 26			
HOHNKIRCH, Heinr.	17	Luebbecke	65-0770
HOHNLE, Jacob	33	Herdmansmuel.	66-0221
Catharine 34, Caroline 7, Louise 5			
Rosine 3, Pauline 6m			
HOHNSTEDT, J.F.	26	Barnstorf	64-0331
HOICHENDORF, Marie	20	Moellen	64-0938
HOLD, Maria	21	Bavaria	66-0679
Joseph 24			
HOLDER, Paul	35	New York	64-0593
HOLDERMANN, John	54	Mosbach	63-0990
HOLDFOERSTER, Sus.	19	Hannover	66-1093
HOLFOGT, J.H.	35	New York	64-0427
HOLHUSEN, Gustav	16	Stottle	63-0614
HOLICK, Anna	41	Boehmen	66-0349
baby 1			
HOLKE, Hermann	22	Westerkappeln	64-0886
HOLKE, Steffen	54	Osterleda	64-1022
Cath. 41, Maria 7, Sophie 3			
HOLLABAR, Peter	25	Hammenitcha	64-0920
HOLLAENDER, Georg	22	Rheindurkheim	66-0623
Regine 24			
HOLLAENDER, Theod.	19	Dorum	64-1022
Friedr. 22			
HOLLAENDER, Wme.	26	Sievern	65-0974
Alwine 4			
HOLLAENDER, Wolf	25	Elsoff	63-0482
HOLLAND, Ferdinand	21	Steinbach	66-0934
HOLLAND, Joh. Fr.	16	Marburg	63-0244
HOLLAND, Johanna	62	Suhl	65-1088
HOLLAND, W.A.	20	Hansberge	66-0221
HOLLEBEN, v. (m)	26	Berlin	63-0015
HOLLECK, A.	38	Boston	63-1178
HOLLEMANN, Chris.	24	Esslingen	65-0116
HOLLEMANN, Friedr.	30	Schwichett	63-0244
HOLLEMANN, Ludw.	27	Schwiechet	63-0953
HOLLENKAMP, John	26	Ankum	63-0990
HOLLENSTEINER, Aug	40	Retzen	63-1010
Conradine 30, Aug. 6, Caroline 9m			
HOLLER, Hr.	24	Meldorf	65-1088
HOLLERBUSCH, Helen	22	Furth	67-0007
HOLLERING, Georg	29	New York	66-0734
HOLLERMANN, Franz	45	Stadtlohn	66-0984
HOLLEUFER, v. C.	19	Hannover	64-1053
HOLLMANN, Friedr.	30	Vechta	65-0402
HOLLMANN, Joh.	27	Rotenburg	64-0073
HOLLMANN, Joh. Fr.	36	Hannover	63-1069
HOLLNIDE, Wilhelm	26	Straatenn	66-1373
HOLLSTEIN, Christ.	23	Wickersrode	67-0600
HOLLSTEIN, Rud.	24	Rockensuess	63-0482
HOLLWEGS, M.	19	Bremervoerde	63-1003
A. 16			
HOLMBACH, Elisbeth	28	Eisenach	64-0885
HOLN, K.	32	Steuer	63-0551
HOLNHOLZ, Abel	50	Dingstede/Old	65-0038
HOLPP, G.	28	Obermotzbach	65-1024
HOLST, H.	44	New York	63-1218
HOLSTE, Friedrich	24	Rahden	65-1088
HOLSTEIN, Ferd.	44	Danzig	65-0770
Friedrich 34			
HOLT, Christ.	45	New York	66-0221
Emilie 7			
HOLTERMANN, Anna	26	Hannover	66-1031
HOLTERS, Johann	33	Ehren	66-0934
Herm. B. 32, Anna Marie 21			
HOLTHANS, Mathilde	27	Osnabrueck	65-0974
HOLTHAUS, Anna M.	59	Hoerste	66-1127
HOLTHAUSEN, A.E.	21	Stotel	63-0168
HOLTHUS, Joh.	29	Bruemsel	64-0840
HOLTHUSEN, G.	18	Stolzeln	65-1189
HOLTHUSEN, Johann	48	Bredstedt	66-0469
Christiana 40, Paul 15, Julius 4			
Heinrich 9m			
HOLTINGER, Joh.		Heidelberg	63-1218
HOLTKOETTER, Frz.	31	Pr. Minden	64-0432
HOLTMANN, Andreas	47	Holzhausen	66-0734
Elisabeth 19, Johannes 17, Peter 9			
Marie 5			
HOLTMANN, Heinrich	18	Rothenstein	66-1131
August 24			
HOLTMANN, Wilhelm	25	Osnabrueck	65-0865
HOLTZ, E.	25	Hannover	65-1189
Augusta 28, Augusta 9m			
HOLTZ, Marie	19	Bresbach	65-1189
Elisabeth 28			
HOLTZ, Philipp	28	Durlach	63-1178
HOLTZ, Sophie	50	Gamberg	66-1327
Jacob 16, Apollonia 7			
HOLUB, Franz	26	Boehmen	66-0349
HOLUB, Josepha	25	Buhnberg	64-0433
HOLWEGS, Hermann	20	Ringstadt	66-0679
HOLZ, Cath.	21	Unt.Groeningn	66-1313
HOLZ, Eva	58	Hessen	63-1069
Eva Elisa 26			
HOLZ, Friedr.	22	Pommern	66-0469
HOLZ, Gustav	19	Asch	64-0739
HOLZ, Jean	35	Otterstadt	63-1178
Catharine 32, Elisabeth 11, Anna 9			
Magdalene 7, Wilhelm 4, Catharina 1			
HOLZ, Joseph	58	Luzico/Boh.	65-0856
Joseph 20, Anna 22			
HOLZ, Ludw.	24	Wuerttemberg	66-0576
HOLZ, Wm. Friedr.	19	Hildrichhsn.	65-0004
HOLZAPFEL, Conrad	20	Melgershausen	66-0412
HOLZAPFEL, Friedr.	37	Cassel	65-0007
HOLZAPFEL, Leop.	18	Cassel	63-0953
HOLZE, Elise	20	Leese	67-0600
HOLZER, Christ	28	Muenchen	65-0116
HOLZER, Xaver	18	Tmolten	66-0083
HOLZGREFE, Heinr.	18	Alfhausen	66-1093
HOLZHAUER, Gustav	19	Aurich	66-0734
HOLZHAUER, Wilhelm	21	Cassel	66-1031
HOLZHAUSEN, Leopld	30	Ellerich	64-0886
HOLZHAUSEN, Rudolf	15	Fuhrse	66-0984
HOLZHAUSER, Georg	40	Hessen	63-0614
Elisabeth 25, Johannes 5, Jacob 3			
Anna Cath. 10m			
HOLZKAMP, Heinrich	29	Ostenholz	67-0599
HOLZMEISTER, Gerh.	40	Wien	67-0007
HOLZMER, Jacob	21	Bingen	64-0639
HOLZMEYER, Cath.	47	Erbhausen	64-0639
Eva 7			
HOLZMUELLER, Leop.	30	Zettwich	66-0934
HOLZSCHNEIDER, Wm.	50	Crefeld	63-0244
M. 20			
HOLZSTEIN, Adolph	16	Ungarn	63-1218
HOLZWARTH, Carl	23	Wuerttemberg	64-0687
HOLZWARTH, Maria	20	Wuertemberg	66-0679

NAME	AGE	RESIDENCE	YR-LIST
Caroline 28			
HOMANN, Aug.	31	Geismar	66-1243
HOMANN, Friederike	21	Adersleben	65-0007
HOMANN, Magnus	26	Soesdorf	66-1313
HOMANN, Marie	21	Bolschle	64-0992
August 68			
HOMANN, Marie Lou.	24	Oldendorf/Han	64-0920
HOMBERGER, Daniel	18	Moischeit	66-0623
Elisabeth 50			
HOMBERGER, Peter	33	Remscheid	63-0168
HOMEISTER, Anna	24	Eltmannshsn.	66-1203
HOMEYER, Carl	22	Lehe	66-0934
HOMEYER, Dietrich	70	Lahde	65-1030
Christine 56, Minna 23, Dietrich 15			
Carl 5			
HOMEYER, Fr. H.	18	Minden	65-1031
HOMEYER, Heinr.	21	Riemsloh	64-1053
HOMEYER, Joh.	34	New York	64-0495
HOMMANN, Heinrich	18	Westphalen	66-0469
Caroline 16			
HOMMEL, Anna Elise	39	Heringa	64-0433
HOMMEL, Christ.	31	Oppenhiem	64-0427
HOMMEL, Johann	21	Westernbach	66-1203
HOMRIGHAUSEN, Ludw	17	Wunderthausen	66-1031
HONER, Phil.	43	Elverdessen	63-1010
Marie 42, Joh. Heinr. 15, Friedr. Wilh 10			
August 9m			
HONIGHAUSEN, L.	21	Wundershausen	64-1022
HONING, Heinrich	30	Kellau	65-1095
HONNEGER, Gottfr.	35	New York	64-0427
HONNEMANN, Cath.	43	Ebersfeld	66-0679
HONNEN, Emma	20	Horsemuehlen	66-1127
HONNEN, Henrich	35	Langen	63-0097
HONOLD, Georg	23	Wasseralfingn	64-1022
HONOLD, Jeremias	37	Oterkochen	66-0576
HONS, Sophie	15	Misselwarden	63-0953
HOOFES, Peter	30	Schwalingen	66-0734
Anna 26, Peter 4m, Wilhelmine 217			
HOOFFLMAYER, Susan	57	Frankfurt	67-0954
HOOGLAND, M.	30	New York	63-0752
HOOL, Johannes	27	Erkshausen	66-0704
HOOLZER, John	26	Saarbrueck	63-0244
Marg. 26, John 4, Magdal. 3, Charles 7m			
C. 30, J. 54, Fr. 27, E. 25, F. 6, E. 1			
HOOPS, Claus	28	Rhaddreichst.	64-0687
HOOPS, Claus	28	New York	64-0427
HOOPS, J.H.C.	30	Tevel	65-0004
HOOSE, Friedr.	37	New York	66-0734
Elisabeth 64, Amalie 24, Marie 2			
HOPFENBERG, Anton	28	Amberg	64-1206
HOPFENMULLER, Mary	50	Meldburg	66-1327
HOPFF, Priska	25	Eisfeld	64-0840
HOPFFELD, John	28	Ostendorf	63-1218
HOPKINS, Jos.	18	Bremen	63-0821
HOPMANN, Ehlert	22	Schierholz	66-0934
HOPPE, Andr.	58	Bromberg	66-0577
Marie 18, Stanislaus 9, Stina 50			
HOPPE, Anna	42	St.Louis	66-0221
Elise 7			
HOPPE, Carl	20	Hanover	64-0138
HOPPE, Carl	29	Burgwedel	64-0138
HOPPE, Charles	40	Elmira	64-0593
Pauline 15, Eduard 7			
HOPPE, F.	19	New York	63-0168
HOPPE, F.	29	Polen	66-0413
HOPPE, Frdr. Herm.	50	St. Louis	66-0221
HOPPE, Joseph	19	Oberglogau	63-1038
HOPPE, Nicolas	27	Preussen	63-0398
Marie 36			
HOPPE, W.(m)	17	Bierbergen	64-0073
HOPPE, Wilh	22	Strom	66-1373
HOPPE, William	29	New York	63-0551
HOPPENSACK, Just.	20	Exter	66-0704
HOPPENSTOCK, Carl	58	Obernkirchen	64-0214
Louise 59			
HOPPENSTOCK, Fr.	27	Oberkirchen	64-0214
HOPPNER, Josefa	22	Boehmen	64-0427
HOPS, Herm.	16	Platendorf	65-0974

NAME	AGE	RESIDENCE	YR-LIST
HOPS, Joh.	21	Horstedt	64-0992
HOPT, Andreas	37	Zepfenhain	64-0363
Anna 28, Maria 7, Friedrich 5, Johann 3			
Catharina 6m			
HORACEK, Joh.	36	Boehmen	64-0427
HORACK, Marie	34	Vienna	65-0856
HORAK, Joseph	32	Wien	64-0886
child 6, child 4, baby 9m			
HORBACH, Wilh.	17	Lauterecken	64-0363
HORCH, Elise	26	Giessen	64-0687
Christine 19			
HORCH, Martin	41	Berlichingen	66-0576
HORCHHEIMER, Anna	35	Ledingworth	64-0593
HOREICH, Franz	24	Davritz	67-0007
Theresia 21			
HOREIS, Augusta	9	Wremen	66-1093
HORENBURG, C.W.	27	Hannover	66-0221
HORFF, Christian	21	Diedenbergen	66-1313
HORHAENDER, S(m)	28	Dudenhof	64-0331
A.M.(f) 23			
HORING, Franz	53	Rubsheim	64-0992
HORKHEIMER, Moritz	36	New York	66-0934
Minna 39, Isaak 9, Abraham 20			
HORLACHUM, Joh. M.	21	Oberohren	64-1108
HORMANN, Diedr.	21	Bremen	64-0456
HORMEL, John C.	52	Roth	63-0551
Malintha 38, John 50			
HORMEL, Ph.	25	Leberg	66-0650
HORMINGER, Jacob	19	Henchelheim	65-0189
HORN, August	21	Wiebelsbach	64-0886
HORN, C.H. Ferdin.	21	Lobenstein	66-0650
F.Gust. Alex 30, Christian 30			
Christiane 68, Hermann 12, Ernst 5			
Pauline 3			
HORN, Conrad	64	Gernheim	66-1093
Sophie 64, Elise 18, Minna 13			
HORN, Friedrich	25	Nordheim	63-1069
HORN, Georg	50	Heinersdorff	63-1218
Dorothea 50, Henniette 17, Anna 9			
Friederike 7, Bernhard 13, Louise 8			
HORN, Heinrich	37	Ndraberosch.	66-0349
HORN, Heinrich	23	Cassel	66-1248
HORN, Johann	29	Wermuthhausen	66-0650
HORN, Johann Fr.	27	Eplensbach	63-1069
HORN, Olje Wilm.	7	Aurich	64-0739
HORN, Wm.	16	Rehme	65-1189
HORN, v. Anna	20	Mohndorf	64-0456
HORNBERGER, Christ	21	Hannover	66-1131
Johann 18, Johannes 16			
HORNBERGER, Georg	46	Hallwangen	66-0147
HORNBORTHEL, Fanny	25		63-0990
HORNBOSTEL, Carol.	65	Parchim	65-1030
HORNICKEL, Christ.	19	Sindelfingen	65-0189
HORNIG, F.D.	51	Leer	64-0427
HORNING, Christine	43	Frachtenberg	65-0116
Christ. 19, Joh. 7			
HORNING, Johann	35	Fulda	64-1053
HORNKAMF, Wilh.	26	Werlei	63-1085
Marie 6m			
HORNSCHUH, Gottfr.	23	Heidersbach	64-0739
HORNSTEIN, Valent.	29	Olgreuth	66-1327
HORNUNG, Anton	37	Bayern	66-0221
HORNUNG, Anton	20	Westhausen	66-1327
HORNUNG, Caroline	26	Wuerttenberg	66-0221
Caspar 41, Catharine 45, Catharine 16			
Marie 7, Louis 6			
HORNUNG, Fr.	17	St.Wendel	64-0593
HORNUNG, Maria	24	Kirchhausen	64-0331
HORRAC, M.	27	Corinth	66-0413
HORSCHEL, Ernst	20	Eisfeld	64-0593
HORST, August	28	Hanau	65-0243
HORST, Heinrich	24	Melle	63-0614
HORST, Henriette	27	Hillern	66-0668
HORST, Wm.	31	Hanau	64-0495
HORSTKAMP, Ham.	28	Backelde	66-1203
HORSTMANN, Aug.	21	Glandorf	66-1373
HORSTMANN, Bertha	17	Bremenhaven	64-1108
HORSTMANN, Carl H.	35	Pr. Minden	63-0398

NAME	AGE	RESIDENCE	YR-LIST
Conradine 37, Christel 7			
HORSTMANN, Ernstne	16	Burgdamm	66-0984
Diedr. 7			
HORSTMANN, F.	24	Scharmbeck	64-1206
HORSTMANN, Ferd'd.	39	Oldenburg	66-0934
Marianne 32, Hermann 8, Josephine 9m			
HORSTMANN, Heinr.	44	Gruppenbuhren	66-0668
HORSTMANN, Heinr.	23	Nordstemmen	66-1327
HORSTMANN, Heinr.	56	Stocken	65-1031
Caroline 45, Wilhelm 25, Friedrich 20			
Maria 25, Sophie 14			
HORSTMANN, Heinr.	27	Kleekamp	65-0950
Marie 54, Cathar. 24, Heinrich O. 13			
HORSTMANN, Henry	20	Meesdorf	66-0221
HORSTMANN, Hinr.	23	Rahde	64-0432
HORSTMANN, Joh.	26	Bergheim	64-1053
HORSTMANN, Ludw.	18	Cluedhemme	64-0886
Christ 15, Christ.(f) 22, Caroline 20			
HORSTMANN, Ulrich	23	Soerlern	66-1373
HORSTMANN, W.	31	Vessendorf	65-0974
J.H. 6m			
HORSTMEIER, Fr. R.	28	Kappeln	63-1069
HOSE, Joh. Claus	32	Tockenrode	64-0433
HOSPE, Geo.	22	Hasburg	65-0898
HOSPER, Neinrich	37	Denkiehausen	66-0083
HOSPITAL, Mrs.	22	Paris	64-0073
HOSSFELD, John G.	58	Gehaus	63-1038
Elisabeth 55, Christiane 19, Caroline 8			
HOSTCHER, H.	32	Brachterbeck	66-0413
HOSTEN, Emilie	18	Hamburg	66-1093
HOSTEN, Heinrich	24	Kleinborstel	66-1093
HOTEMANN, Joh.	19	Hannover	64-0427
HOTENHOFF, Heinr.	24	Dreiburg	66-1248
HOTTELMANN, D.(f)	37	Engeln	64-0495
Frdr. 13			
HOTTENROTH, Chr.	27	New York	66-0704
Catharine 28, Emilie 2, baby 3m			
HOTZ, Christina	17	Crumbach	63-0953
HOTZLER, Josefa	31	Dornbirn	66-1327
HOVE, v. J.W.	30	Braunschweig	66-0221
HOXAMMER, And.	25	Meddersheim	65-0402
HOYE, Heinrich	24	Strom	66-1373
HOYER, Charles	29	New York	66-0147
HOYER, Elisab.	27	New York	64-0593
Ellen 7			
HOYER, Gottlieb	21	Kirchhaim	66-1243
HOYER, Joh.	32	Wasserknoten	65-0974
HOYER, Maria	20	Hannover	65-1024
HOYES, Friedr.	28	Zell	64-0639
HOYING, Aug.	32	Vechta	64-0495
HRDLICKA, Ferd'nd.	41	Boehmen	63-0917
Anna 24, Barbara 9, Maria 3, Anton 1			
HRUBY, Franz	30	Boehmen	66-0349
HRUBY, Katharina	20	Kroschowitz	66-1373
HUB, Dorothea	28	Weierbach	66-0734
Ludwig 8, Heinr. 1			
HUBAUR, Franc.	32	Tripstadt	63-0990
Adam 16			
HUBECKY, Joseph	46	Podebrad/Aust	66-0469
Maria 46, Kathrine 14, Anna 12			
Elisabeth 8, Wenzel 6, Franz 3			
HUBENSCHMIDT, Ba.	17	Muhlhausen	64-0782
HUBER, Agatha	56	Wittenberg	65-0007
HUBER, Alois	28	St. Louis	64-0138
HUBER, Alois	25	Klosterbeuern	66-0109
HUBER, Anna	30	Muenchen	63-0990
HUBER, Caroline	18	Stadelhofen	66-0469
Barbara 22			
HUBER, Christ.	19	Neckarthalfin	66-0934
HUBER, Cl.	28	Muehlingen	66-1031
Elisab. 18			
HUBER, Eleonore	26	Fuerth	63-0006
baby			
HUBER, Franz	34	Boehmen	66-0221
Anna 30			
HUBER, J.G.	40	Lienzingen	65-1189
Louise 39, Louise 14, J.C. 7, Marie 5			
Frd. 3			

NAME	AGE	RESIDENCE	YR-LIST
HUBER, Jacob	34	Busel	65-0189
HUBER, Johann	31	Cincinnati	66-0147
HUBER, Johannes	17	Wolfhart	63-1069
HUBER, John	33	Nussdorf	63-0482
HUBER, Joseph	36	Stratenport	64-1022
HUBER, Joseph	21	Aufhausen	65-0948
HUBER, Josepha	39	Riedlingen	66-0412
Maximiliana 14			
HUBER, Julius	18	Alleshausen	66-1373
HUBER, Mathias	23	Greissenbach	66-1327
HUBER, P.X.	44	Staubing	64-0427
HUBERT, Agnes	39	Teuchern	63-0693
Georg 2			
HUBERT, Emil	24	Poria	64-0886
HUBERT, Helene	19	Aichsheim	64-0782
HUBERT, Henriette	23	Clodgiessen	65-0189
Clara 11			
HUBERT, J.	20	Koechingen	66-0413
HUBERT, Jac.	36	Prussia	64-0170
HUBERT, Joseph	33	Rineck	64-0433
Margareth 29			
HUBERT, Pauline	31	Wuertemberg	66-0984
HUBERTUS, Marg.	27	Cochem	65-0402
HUBLER, Abrah.	30	Twaun	65-0243
HUBNER, R.	24	Boehmen	64-0495
HUCHTING, (m)	18	New York	63-0244
HUCHTING, Anna	26	Oldenburg	63-0482
HUCK, Bernd	22	Scheid	66-0734
HUCK, Lutgarde	20	Elschesheim	66-1131
HUCK, Paul	21	Varnholz/Bad.	63-0917
HUCKE, Conrad	31	Rotenburg	66-1031
Ernestine 29, Carl 7, Lina 2, Martha 19			
HUCKE, Juliane	24	Rotenburg	64-0363
HUCKE, Phil.	19	Rothenburg	63-1010
HUCKELRIEDE, Joh.	26	Nimmelage	66-0576
HUCKMANN, Louise	18	Eppendorf	64-0938
Anna 16			
HUCKRIEDE, C.	24	Lingerich	64-1161
HUDE, Pierre	33	Havre	64-1053
Seraph. Ros. 20			
HUDTWALLSER, AnCat	27	Hannover	64-0432
HUEBENER, Heinrich	32	Glauchau	65-0770
HUEBENTHAL, Christ	26	Gestedt	63-1178
HUEBER, Maria Mag.	27	Raitlingen	66-1243
HUEBER, Mathilde	25	Gloettwing	66-0934
HUEBLER, Pauline	20	Crimmitschau	66-1093
HUEBNER, Antonia	19	Friedland	66-0469
HUEBNER, Christ.	30	Duedelsheim	64-0886
Marie 26, Heinr. 2			
HUEBNER, Henry	29	Bremen	66-1155
HUEBNER, Johann	25	Koenigsberg	64-0739
HUEBNER, Johanna	19	Hannover	66-0704
HUEBNER, M.	24	New York	63-0752
HUEBNER, Martin	35	Posen	64-0432
Ernestine Wm 29, Gustav E. 2			
HUEBNER, Robert	24	Dresden	66-1155
HUEDEPOHE, Dina	25	Rieste	63-0953
HUEDEPOHL, Marg.	20	Horden	64-0593
HUEDEWITH, Aloys	28	Heck	66-1327
HUEFFNER, Leopold	37	New York	63-0350
Bertha 34, Herm. 9, Leopold 7, William 3			
HUEFNER, Edmund	21	Aschaffenburg	63-0398
HUEFNER, Otto	19	Cassel	64-0427
HUEGEL, Carl A.	17	Merlingen	64-0687
HUEGLER, Barnabas	28	Jottmadingen	64-1053
HUEHL, Johann	20	Schale	66-0679
HUELF, Georg	24	Asch	66-1031
HUELLEN, Henrich	18	Hambergen/Han	65-0038
HUELS, H.		Rheda	64-0840
HUELS, Nanke	25	Wiesens	66-1128
HUELSEMANN, Gerh.	25	Oldenburg	64-0938
HUELSHOFF, Bernhd.	21	Lingen	66-0704
HUELSHORST, Heinr.	26	Stocken	65-1031
HUELSING, Theodor	28	Bruemsel	64-0840
Johann 21			
HUELSMANN, E.	36	Hannover	63-0862
Marg. 30, Mary 10, Johann 5, John 3			
HUELSMANN, Herm. H	19	Osnabrueck	64-0938

NAME	AGE	RESIDENCE	YR-LIST
HUELSMANN, Lina	22	Oldenburg	66-1093
HUEMANN, John	52	Drefeld	64-0593
HUEMME, Julius	25	Oldenburg	63-0917
HUEMRICH, G.(f)	20	Unterrodach	64-0495
HUENECKEN, J.W.	21	Bremen	64-0214
HUENEFELD, Gerhd.	17	Oldenburg	64-1022
HUENEMANN, Franz J	24	Heuthen	64-1108
HUENERFELD, M.J.	25	Cochem	64-0639
HUENERING, Heinr.	52	Lingen	25-0950
Anna Marg. 51, Adelheid 17, Wenzel 15			
Helene 13, Maria 6			
HUENERLEIN, J.	43	Berlin	63-0013
HUENICKE, Hermann	34	Tedinghausen	63-0821
HUENKEN, Mary	25	Dorum	64-0593
Wm. 3, Adeline 2, baby 4m			
HUENORGART, Georg	24	Helbersheim	65-0948
HUERKAMP, Diedrich	18	Helle	66-1093
HUESGEN, Peter	40	Leavenworth	63-0244
C. 40, G. 17, K. 15			
HUESING, Hermann	21	Papenburg	66-1093
HUESINGS, Aug.	34	Elberfeld	65-0038
HUESMANN, Flora	25	Cloppenburg	63-0244
HUESMANN, L.(m)	22	Osnabrueck	64-0331
HUESSEBUCH, Johann	20	Hannover	66-0734
HUETHER, Elisabeth	23	Tiefenort	63-0862
Marg. 21			
HUETHER, Franz	46	Muenchweiler	66-0576
HUETHER, Geo.	26	Donndorf	65-0898
HUETTE, Gottl.	20	Leipzig	65-1030
HUETTENHEIM, Herm.	32	Hilchenbach	64-0687
HUETTENMUELLER, Hr	25	Heuthen	64-1108
HUETTER, Jeanette	15	Giessen	64-0343
HUETTINGER, Christ	27	Rothen	66-1131
HUEVE, Joh.	53	Hannover	66-0576
Adelheid 33, Carsten 27, Elisabeth 25			
HUFENDICK, Wm.	23	Heepenl	63-1010
HUFNAGEL, B.(m)	20	Steinau	64-0495
HUFSCHMIDT, F.G.	20	Rotenburg	64-0363
HUFSCHMIDT, Heinr.	17	Homburg	64-0886
HUG, Fanny	22	Engers	63-0953
HUGGEN, J.(f)	19	Schoenberg	64-0495
HUGGER, Martin	28	Willendingen	64-0214
HUGGER, Wend.	27	Simmern	64-0073
HUGO, Conrad	41	New York	63-0398
HUGOFETT, Carl	20	Hamburg	64-1161
HUHN, Heinr.	46	New York	66-0934
HUHN, P.		Schwabendorf	63-1003
HUHNHOLT, Theodor	29	Lippstedt	65-0865
HUHTI, Valentin	30	Waldaschhoff	65-0770
Agnes 26, Elisabeth 1			
HUI, Elisabeth	21	Bennhausen	66-0577
HUIBER, Franz	22	Boehmen	64-0432
HUINE, Joh.	34	Minderstadt	64-0840
HUISMANN, Jan	50	Strockholt	66-0668
Hindertje 50, Theile 23, Jann 18, Lena 17			
Mary 23, Anna 20, Hindertje 7			
HUISMANN, Meint.	36	Illinois	64-0363
HUITMANN, Joseph	56	Kreuzenhoff	66-1127
Reinhold 24, Anna 58			
HUITMANN, Wilh'mne	22	Krenzelhof	66-1127
Isabelle 20, Johanna 18			
HUIZING, Trientje	28	Spyk	66-0734
Trientje 2m			
HUKE, Therese	26	Schoenbueckel	66-1373
HUL, Joseph	21	Vorderburg	64-0433
HULDER, Gottlieb	24	Altschoningen	64-0639
HULF, Max	13	Oelsnitz	65-0898
HULL, Joseph	31	Hoevertshaus	66-0083
Therese 27			
HULLERMANN, Wilh.	19	Coesfeld	65-1030
Anton			
HULSBERG, Heinr.	17	Beverstedt	66-1248
HULSEBUSS, Ernst	20	Bremermoor	65-0243
HULSEBUSS, Peter	51	Bremermoor	65-0243
Johanna 24			
HULSMANN, Henry	24	Nellighof	63-0752
HUMERSEN, Adolph	25	Detmold	67-0353
Henriette 29			

NAME	AGE	RESIDENCE	YR-LIST
HUMMEL, Carl	20	Cannstadt	64-0639
HUMMEL, Carl	18	Offenburg	64-0427
HUMMEL, Chr.	23	Waiblingen	66-1313
Marie 16			
HUMMEL, Gottlieb	26	Buchhof	66-0576
HUMMEL, Johanna	18	Dietenhofen	65-1088
HUMMEL, John	32	Sondelfingen	63-1218
Cathar. 30, William 6m			
HUMMEL, Josepha	18	Weissenstein	66-1203
HUMMEL, Mathias	37	Oberbergen	66-1327
Veronica 34, Rosa 5, Therese 9m			
Fridolin 38			
HUMMELS, John H.	29	Blauhand	66-0221
HUMPETER, Ferdin'd	28	Hoechst	66-1031
HUNCKEL, Johann	17	Butzbach	65-0770
Wilhelm 7, Theodor 4			
HUND, Catharine	18	Gilsenberg	67-0992
HUND, Herm.	20	Frankenhausen	63-0482
Dorothea 59, Ella 9			
HUNDERTMARK, Jos.	58	Luetersheim	63-0168
HUNDERTMARK, Soph.	23	Ludersheim	66-1248
HUNDSHAGEN, Friedr	18	Walldorf	65-0594
HUNFELD, Johann	26	Heede	66-0734
HUNGELMANN, Anton	26	Lingen	63-0990
HUNGEMANN, Bernh.	21	Ibbenbuehren	65-0898
HUNING, Heinrich	24	Celle	66-0469
HUNKE, Friederike	25	Bischoffhagen	65-1030
HUNKE, Michael	26	Cercernitze	65-1095
HUNNING, F.	36	Mexico	63-0752
HUNSCHE, Friedrich	29	Lienen	64-0433
HUNSCHE, Friedrich	28	Lengerich	63-0168
HUNSCHE, Friedrich	21	Muenster	66-0469
HUNT, Michael	19	Otterswer	63-0693
HUNTEMANN, Carl	21	New York	66-0576
HUNTER, Jos.	28	Lichtenfeld	64-0023
HUNTING, Florentin	26	Buer	64-0920
HUNTMANN, Doris	16	Kellinghausen	63-1136
HUNZ, Cre.(f)	20	Loewenstein	64-0495
HUNZIGER, Jacob	28	Schweiz	63-1085
HUNZIKER, Maria	28	Lupfig	65-0243
HUPE, August	47	Leuenau	65-0948
Caroline 50			
HUPPE, Betty	24	Hannover	64-0432
HUPPERT, Philippe	42	Connecticut	63-1178
Henrike 27, Philipp 6m			
HUPPERTS, S.(f)	26	Geldern	64-0495
HURDELBRINK, Adolf	21	Osnabrueck	63-0482
HURTH, Herm.	33	Switz.	63-0350
HUS, Anton	25	Kuttenberg	64-0593
HUS, Magd.	19	Thomashardt	63-0990
HUSCHNOVITZ, Simon	34	Raschau	63-0990
Elias 15			
HUSEMANN, Chris.	58	Bodenfelde	65-1031
Caroline 56, Alwine 20			
HUSEMANN, Friedr.	19	Bodenfelde	64-0214
HUSEMANN, Heinr.	28	Kl. Lessen	65-1031
HUSEMANN, Herm.	19	Stolzenau	64-0363
HUSEMANN, Herrmann	54	Erwitte	66-1313
Louise 50, Therese 26, Joh. 19			
Elisabeth 16, Joseph 12, Anton 9			
HUSEMANN, Luise	24	Bremen	65-1189
Henriette 1			
HUSEMEYER, Ilsebin		Buettendorf	65-0898
HUSHAGE, Sophie	28	Bremen	64-0363
Friederike 28			
HUSING, Augusta	29	Barmen	65-0713
HUSLER, Margaretha	16	Hahlem	66-0984
HUSMANN, Heinrich	20	Hannover	66-1327
HUSMANN, Henriette	25	Wehdem	66-0668
Ernestine 21, Charlotte 17			
HUSMEIER, Henry	30	Kirchhorsten	63-0482
HUSS, August	21	Nuertingen	66-1093
HUSSCHMIDT, Anna	32	Lupfig	65-0243
Louise 8, Georg 6			
HUSSEN, G.	35	Osso	63-0752
HUSSING, Carl	29	Ernold	64-0593
HUSSMANN, Christ.	27	Oberbochingen	66-0734
Catharine 27, Christian 6, Johann 2			

NAME	AGE	RESIDENCE	YR-LIST
Catharine 9m			
HUSTER, Heinrich	46	Hilter	66-1128
Catharine 42, Franz 16, Wilhelmine 7			
Fritz 6, Caroline 9m			
HUSTIDDEN, Margret	25	Bischofspohl	64-0214
HUTER, Robert	19	Stuttgart	63-0917
HUTH, Marth.(f)	39	Manburg	64-0495
HUTINS, Leopoldine	50	Buende	66-1155
HUTMACHER, Anton	51	Gallen	64-0739
Josepha 49, Marie 11, Heinrich 6, Emma 7			
HUTMACHER, Edw.	22	Gahlenberg	64-0023
Gustav 18, August 16			
HUTSCHENREUTHER, O	14	Schney	66-0576
Catharine 45, Caroline 17, Babette 8			
HUTTELMEIER, Joh.	26	Hochhoffdorf	65-1030
HUWOLD, Ernst Hch.	34	Spiekau	64-0456
HYDE, Herm.	21	Gruenberg	64-1161
IBENTHALER, Christ	56	Baden	66-0576
Christian 34, Wilhelm 20			
ICKEN, Carl	35	Magdeburg	64-0782
baby 6m			
ICKENROTH, Wilhelm	22	Dueringen	66-1203
Christian 26			
IDE, Louis	27	Hoexter	64-0495
Lena 6			
IDEKER, Friedr.	20	Nienburg	66-0577
IDEKER, Hermann	16	Schneeren	65-0948
IDEL, August	24	Alten Donop	66-1327
IDZIOREK, Hilary	44	Posen	64-0432
Constanzia 40, Marianna 15, Agnes 3			
Anna 9m			
IFFELAND, Peter	24	Cassel	66-0837
IFFINGER, C.F.	19	Rastadt	66-0413
IFFLAND, Marie	21	Reutweinsdorf	64-0840
IGLAUER, Simon	23	Burgkundstadt	65-0055
Anton 24			
IGLECK, Jenny	14	Berlin	63-0953
IHLE, C.(m)	22	Carlsruhe	64-0331
IHLE, Rosine	18	Michelbach	67-0007
IHMS, Kate	9	New York	63-0821
IHNE, Amalie	36	Duisburg	63-1038
IHNEN, H.(m)	43	Leer	64-0170
Johanna 41, Harro 16, Henry 13, Feline 10			
Augusta 8, Ihno 7			
IHNEN, Onke	24	Aurich	65-1030
Tjark 29, Friederike 27, Gerhard 4			
IHRIG, Joh. Jacob	34	Lembaach	64-1053
IKEN, Mary	24	Bremen	63-0482
Johanna 17			
ILENFELD, Carl	33	Naddsetz	64-0433
Emma 24, Anna 3			
ILFELD, Lucia	20	Homburg	65-1088
ILG, Johannes	39	Bessbach	66-1327
ILLAUER, Marg.	20	Frailsdorf	65-0055
ILLIAN, Andreas	25	Hahnstein	66-0469
ILLIG, Benedicta	30	Gelnhausen	63-0953
ILLIG, Edmund	23	Middweida	66-1031
ILLIG, Johann	15	Darmstadt	66-1127
ILLIG, Jonathan	36	Kirnbach	64-1108
ILLJES, Elmar	24	Sandstedt	66-1093
ILSE, August	40	Ndr.Schenden	63-0821
Ernestine 38, Christian 5			
ILSE, Carl	15	Germany	66-0666
ILSE, Laurette	16	Niederscheden	64-1022
IMBLO, Henry	24	Algey	64-1206
IMGOLD, Joh.	44	Bavaria	64-0138
IMHOFF, Babette	19	Pfalz	64-0593
Maria 17			
IMHOFF, Cath.	20	Ernsthausen	64-0992
IMHOLZ, Wilhelm	31	Aschendorf	66-0837
IMMELMANN, Carolyn	50	Heidlingen	66-0934
IMMELMANN, J.	25	Hannover	63-0953
IMMEN, Minna	20	Sievern	66-0109
IMMENGHAIM, Bernh.	34	Ostebern	66-1243
Anna 40, Bernhardine 9			
IMMERMANN, B.	24	Coeln	63-1218
IMREKAR, John	19	Nacklo	63-0693
INACH, Ignatz	37	Cottenberg	66-0623

NAME	AGE	RESIDENCE	YR-LIST
INKERSTROTH, Liset	24	Engter	66-0734
INNOCENZ, Joseph	54	Kuesterdingen	63-0006
Marie 42, Barbara 9			
INSIEKE, Bernhard	26	Oldenburg	66-0221
INSSEL, Sicilia	26	Ochsenhausen	63-1085
INTERMANN, H.(m)	27	New York	64-0214
INZELMANN, Cathr.	18	Brockel	64-0073
IRION, Christian	23	Aldingen	66-1327
IRISON, Joh.(f)	24	Aldingen	64-0331
IRMSCHER, Louise	23	Dresden	66-0934
IRRER, Fides	37	Wendelsheim	66-0349
Thula 24, Carl 21, Elisabeth 19			
Agathe 13			
IRRER, Seb.	27	Wendelsheim	65-0007
IRTERMANN, Heinr.	30	Wisloch	65-0713
ISAACK, Fritz	22	Herford	64-1206
ISAACKS, Anna	17	Hochheim	64-1206
ISEMANN, Carl	41	Westfalen	66-0734
Anna 35			
ISENBERG, Jacob	20	Volkmarsen	63-0917
ISENBERG, Malchen	20	Ziegenhein	65-1031
Giedel 22, Salomon 17			
ISERLOH, R.	22	Schlingen	66-1243
ISLER, Robert	28	St. Gallen	66-1127
Rosa 20			
ISTEL, Friedr.	17	Ullmar	66-1373
ISTERKE, Z.	10	Pressburg	64-0782
ISTORK, Helene	29	Minden	65-1031
ITSCHNER, Werner	32	New York	63-0752
ITTEL, Friedr.	23	Grosskorbach	65-0055
Barbara 25, Helene 21			
ITTERMANN, Heinr.	30	Wisloch	65-0713
ITTERMEYER, P.	28	Riesenbeck	65-1189
Marie 20			
ITZEN, Anna	19	Bremerhaven	63-1178
IWAN, Carl	27	Doelgien	65-0770
JAAG, Fr.Jos.	19	Buchau	64-0363
JABIKOWSKI, Adalb.	25	Wiskittno	66-0578
JABURECK, Adalbert	44	Boehmen	63-0551
Anna 43, Thomas 5			
JACHMANN, J.G.	46	Oberneudorf	64-0363
Marie 32, Traugott 16, Gotthelf 14			
Anna 8, Johann 4			
JACK, Andreas	45	Polen	66-0666
Josephine 53, Franz 26			
JACKEL, Wiegand	21	Listberg	63-1178
JACKER, Jos.	30	Ellwangen	64-1022
JACOB, Anton	24	Wuertemberg	66-0413
Catharine 26, Gerhard 3, Michel 1			
JACOB, Betta	22	Stondorf	63-0482
JACOB, Catharine	23	Mussbach	63-0006
JACOB, Christoph	26	Hessia	66-0412
JACOB, Elias	20	Neigenmuenden	66-0734
JACOB, F.	19	Bremen	63-1003
JACOB, F.(m)	17	Cassel	64-0214
JACOB, Georg	24	Bachfeld	66-0576
JACOB, Gottfried	76	Laubau	66-0704
Cahrlotte 58, Adolph 25, Therese 33			
Paul 4, Anna 2, Marie Anna 6m			
JACOB, Jacob	23	Langsdorf	63-0822
JACOB, Johann	17	Lohnsheim	66-0576
JACOB, Marg.	36	Lispenhausen	64-0363
JACOB, Sophie	20	Gemuenden	65-1024
JACOB, Valentin	35	Lorsch	65-0151
JACOBER, Catharine	20	Linningen	66-0147
JACOBI, August	25	Rudolstadt	64-0199
JACOBI, August	25	Dodenau	64-0214
Catherine 23			
JACOBI, Ludwig	18	Dodenau	63-0482
JACOBI, Wilhelm	32	Hildburghsn.	66-1128
JACOBS, Carl	32	Salzwedel	64-0170
JACOBS, Chr.	26	Schwelm/Pr.	65-0038
JACOBS, F.	25	Zienau	65-0007
JACOBS, G.(m)	25	Cincinnati	64-0331
JACOBS, Gustav	28	Weimar	64-0886
Mathilde 23			
JACOBS, Julius	20	New York	63-0398
JACOBS, Marie	22	Ankum	65-0007

NAME	AGE	RESIDENCE	YR-LIST
JACOBS, Wilhelm	13	Chicago	63-1085
JACOBSEN, Augusta	29	Magdeburg	64-0593
Minna 9m			
JACOBSEN, Heinr.	21	Bremen	64-0593
JACOBSEN, Joh.	40	Copenhagen	65-0038
JACOBSOHN, Herm.	23	Berlin	65-0594
JACOBSON, J.	31	Stolen	63-1003
JACOBSON, Jacob	28	Muenster	64-0840
JACOBTORMEIER, El.	23	Varensell	66-1203
JACOBY, C.(m)	57	St. Louis	64-0363
JACOBY, Herm.	23	Berlin	63-0752
Therese 18			
JACOBY, J.W.	18	Quincy	66-0221
JACOBY, Susanne	26	Marburg	63-0244
JACOBY, Wilhelm	17	Darmstadt	67-0954
JACOT, Ferd.	32	Switz.	64-0170
JACSIC, Nic.	27	Prielicz	65-0007
JAECKEL, Conr.	66	Spenge	63-1010
JAECKEL, Friedr.	24	Prittag	63-1010
JAECKEL, Julius	25	Dresden	66-1155
JAECKEL, Wilh.	23	Neustadt	66-0704
JAEGELER, Bekka	27	Versmold	66-1127
JAEGELER, Friedr.	22	Cluvenhagen	66-0934
JAEGEN, Heinrich	24	Idenkopf	63-0097
JAEGER, Adolph	27	Riedern	64-0073
JAEGER, Amalie	7	Einortshausen	65-0116
JAEGER, And.	28	Wirthheim	66-0349
JAEGER, Anna	21	Davern	64-0427
JAEGER, Balthasar	18	Volkersheim	66-1248
JAEGER, Carl	25	Riblerbuettel	66-0577
JAEGER, Carl	23	Stuttgart	66-0704
JAEGER, Carl	24	Damene	64-0639
JAEGER, Caroline	22	Echterdingen	64-0687
JAEGER, Fr. Rich.	19	Schmalkalden	66-1373
JAEGER, Fr. Wm,	52	St. Goar	65-1140
Anna 38, Bertha 19, Pauline 15, Emil 12			
Otto 10, Carl 7, Emma 6, Louise 4			
Alexander 1, Arthur 6m			
JAEGER, Franz	24	Malges	64-0687
Gertrud 23			
JAEGER, Franz J.	53	Jasbach	64-0593
Anna M. 37, Joseph 18, Valentin 14			
Petronilla 7			
JAEGER, Fritz	24	Echterdingen	64-0687
JAEGER, Gerh.	24	Alstaden	63-0917
JAEGER, Heinr.	24	Hasseborn	65-0243
JAEGER, Henry	34	Baltimore	63-0097
JAEGER, Joh.	35	Steinfort	63-0398
Cath. 25, Johann 2			
JAEGER, Joh.	31	New York	64-0687
JAEGER, Johann	30	Grossmannsdrf	66-0221
JAEGER, Louise	15	Sachsen-Mein.	66-0412
JAEGER, Margarethe	21	Waldmichelbch	64-0214
JAEGER, Peter	25	Weiher	66-1093
JAEGER, Ph.	49	Pfungstadt	63-0350
Christine 45, Dorothea 9, Henriette 8			
Maria 1, James 6			
JAEGER, Philipp	24	Grombach	66-1155
JAEGER, Pierre	20	Belgien	63-0350
JAEGER, Robert	32	Duesseldorf	64-0214
JAEGER, Seb.	27	Eschenbach	64-0992
JAEGER, Sebastian	22	Neckartenzlng	64-0593
JAEGER, Thomas	22	Fressenfurt	66-1327
JAEGER, Wilhelm	20	Coeln	63-1218
JAEGGER, Anna	23	Malaus	64-0639
Anna 11			
JAEGGLE, Therese	27	Schlossenried	66-1327
JAEHN, Ignatz	52	Fulda	64-0363
JAENBOWICH, Gust.	25	Epperies	63-0862
JAENECKE, Ernst	23	Bremerhafen	64-0432
JAENICHER, Traugot	42	Kroppen	64-0938
JAENSCH, Heinr.	42	Koenigsberg	64-0840
JAGER, Anna	15	Wallenrad	64-0363
JAGER, Heinrich	27	Iburg	66-1128
Louis 20			
JAGER, Thomas	29	Trossendorf	66-1327
JAHELKA, Anna	43	Bohemia	64-0687
Joh. 7, Marg. 2			
JAHN, Elisabeth	38	Hessia	66-0679
JAHN, Heinr.	28	Merlingen	64-0687
JAHN, Julius	21	Meerane	66-0934
JAHN, Robert	18	Dresden	65-0055
JAHN, Wilhelm	34	Nassau	65-1030
Christine 38, Carl 14, Wilhelmine 9			
Johanna 5, Rudolph 9m			
JAHNKE, Alb.	25	Treptow/Pr.	65-0038
JAHNKE, Albert	18	Collberg	66-0668
JAHRSDOERFER, M.	22	Nienburg	64-0992
JAKLITSCH, Louise	32	Oberroch	65-0594
JAKOB, Elise	19	Halopes	66-0623
JAKOB, Wilhelm	31	Ruegheim	66-0623
JAKOBY, Christine	25	Kellau	65-1095
JANECK, Anna	34	Mainz	66-0147
JANETT, Heinr.	24	Gotha	66-0984
JANISCH, Anton	39	Boehmen	63-0917
JANISCH, Mathias	32	Carlsbad	65-0243
JANKA, Joseph	32	Soltuschen	64-0886
JANKE, Martin	29	Bichowe	66-0413
Theres 22, Augusta 5m			
JANKOSKY, Johann	24	Dzidne	64-0433
JANKOWSKI, Joh.	25	Preussen	63-0398
JANNECK, Louis	22	Madison	64-0073
JANNICKE, William	29	Leiha	63-0752
JANNING, Heinrich	29	Osnabrueck	66-1093
Louise 23, baby (f) 3			
JANNUSCH, Ferd.	19	Schwednitz	65-0713
Franz 31			
JANSELOW, Gottfr.	37	Delfusbruck	64-0665
Wilhelmine 37, Alwine 9, Pauline 9			
Bertha 6, Adeline 4, Herman 2, Anna 6m			
Elisabeth 58			
JANSEN, August	23	Oldenburg	66-0623
JANSEN, Joh.	30	Bockel	64-0427
JANSEN, Joh. W.	25	Warendorf	63-0551
JANSEN, Maria	52	Oldenburg	66-0578
JANSEN, Mathilde	26	Koch	64-0331
JANSEN, Peter	25	Carolinensiel	66-0413
JANSEN, Theodor	20	Hannover	66-0221
JANSEN, Wilhelm	22	Neubergen	66-0623
JANSING, Elisabeth	21	Wehbergen	66-1093
Theresia 15			
JANSSEN, Alida	18	Bremen	64-1022
JANSSEN, Ede	30	Burhave	66-0668
JANSSEN, Elisabeth	57	Kl. Starern	63-0244
Thecla 17, Catharine 21, Hermann 28			
Gerhard 16			
JANSSEN, Franz	31	Huiskirchen	64-0886
Marie 31, Heinrich 6, Alepda 2, Peter 31			
Maria 33, Heinr. 4, Anna 7			
JANSSEN, Gerh.	17	Mintewede	64-0938
JANSSEN, Gerhard	26	Oldenburg	65-0948
Margarethe 32, Johann 17, Cathrine 13			
JANSSEN, Helene	23	Neuboergen	64-1108
JANSSEN, J.(m)	29	Prussia	64-0495
JANSSEN, Joh.	22	Hannover	66-0576
JANSSEN, Joh.	21	Ost Friesland	66-0577
JANSSEN, Joh.	33	Tuhnum	65-1030
Anna Ch. 34, Johanna E. 3			
JANSSEN, Johann	23	Lastrup	67-0007
JANSSEN, L.(m)	29	Hastedt	64-0170
JANSSEN, M.	40	Brake	65-1088
Minna 8, Bernhard 3, baby 4m			
JANSSEN, Marg.	23	Ostfriesland	64-0214
JANSSEN, Maria	27	Sievern	63-1218
Hermann 3, Maria 2			
JANSSEN, Siebelt	22	Tuhnum	65-1030
Gretke 22			
JANSSEN, Tamma	27	Selvende	64-1053
JANSSEN, William	22	Louisville	66-0984
Wilhelm 28			
JANTZ, Wilhelm	36	Danzig	66-0578
Rosalia 34, Clara 10, Christoph 8, Otto 6			
Johanna 4, Elise 3m			
JANTZEN, Hermann	48	Steinhausen	63-0097
JANTZEN, Hintze	70	Aurich	64-0739
JANTZEN, Peter	22	Weine	66-0668

NAME	AGE	RESIDENCE	YR-LIST
JANZ, Carl	30	Werdamm	66-0623
JANZEN, Jack	32	Leewarden	63-0013
JAPP, Friedr.	16	Somrix	66-0576
JAPPEL, Marie	36	Worawitz	66-1031
Antonia 9, Wilhelmine 4			
JAQUIN, W.	22	Pforzheim	64-0639
JAROMERSKY, Joseph	36	Malin	64-0433
JASPER, Betty	26	Bremen	64-0840
JASPER, Cath.	58	Prussia	64-0432
Wilhelmine 28			
JASPERS, Berend	52	Loquard	64-1022
Alfke 26, Abraham 18, Berend 3			
JAUCH, J.M.	59	Mecterdingen	64-0593
Maria 27			
JAWASKI, Marianne	26	Jadno	66-0413
C. 26, Josepha 1			
JEAN, Caroline	24	Lehe	64-1053
JEANNOT, Aug.	29	Neuchatel	64-0495
JECKEL, Sara	59	Markt Erlbach	64-0214
JEDBICKA, Anna	16	Klizow	64-0593
JEDELE, Friedrich	36	Wolfenhausen	63-0350
JEDLICKA, Jos.	59	Kuttenberg	64-0214
Han(f) 7, Bernh. 5, Richard 6, baby 6m			
Antonia 49, Marie 23, Marie El. 9			
Albertine 3, Marie 6m			
JEGGLE, Pauline	30	Biberach	63-0482
JELBER, Reinhold	24	Neumark	63-1085
JELDEN, Hanke Brun	30	Buehren	64-0427
Gretje 28			
JELINEK, Antonia	24	Boehmen	64-0427
Maria 9m			
JELINEK, Maria	24	Leese	66-1327
JEMERICK Joh.	38	Lehe	64-0665
Heinr. 26			
JENNET, Mary	19	Paris	64-0593
JENNY, Jean (m)	22	Schwanden	64-0427
JENSCH, C.A.	41	Friechrichsdf	65-0402
JENSCH, Conr.	29	Baltimore	63-0551
JENSEN, Karen Mary	22	Copenhagen	66-0666
JENSEN, Louis P.	57	Radtjeburg	66-0666
Marta 54, Laurentine 7			
JENSEN, Niels P.	32	Copenhagen	66-0666
JENSEN, Soren	29	Copenhagen	66-0666
JENT, Chr.	42	Corboch	63-1085
JEOURES, Thera	26	Rouen	63-0350
Marie 24, Marie 2, Victoria 11m			
JERABECK, Carolin	27	Neustaedle	66-0734
JEREMIAS, Carl	40	Oldenburg	66-1093
Wilhelmine 34, Gesine 9			
JERER, Xaver	24	Wendelsheim	66-0349
JERRETTA, M.(m)	22	Ireland	64-0363
JESELSOHN, Phil	22	Neckarbischof	64-0687
Sophie 23, Johanna 2			
JETSCH, Hans	35	Hannover	64-0665
JETTER, Wilhelmine	25	Reutlingen	66-1155
JEUDE, James	29	Redinghausen	63-0990
JEUTTER, Christine	27	Unterschlecht	64-0687
JEZECK, Maria	25	Kuttenberg	64-0170
Joseph 4m			
JIRK, Joseph	24	Ahlen	66-0413
JOACHIM, Adam	26	Einortshausen	65-0116
JOACHIM, Margar.	37	Oppershofen	66-1155
JOB, Herm.	19	Mosbach	66-0734
JOBST, Christian	33	Kruszke	66-0578
Justine 28, Juliane 3, August 9m			
JOCH, Joh. Carl	52	Jena	63-0398
JOCHIM, Elisabeth	19	Krumbach	66-0734
JOCKERTS, Barbara	24	Schelbrun/Sw.	64-1053
JOECKEL, Joh.	24	Mardorf	66-1243
JOECKLE, Jacob	18	Schwenningen	66-0704
JOEGENSEN, Christ.	24	Radtjeburg	66-0666
Juliane 30, Christine 4, Peter 24			
JOEMEYER, Marie	18	Hannover	64-0739
JOERDING, Hartwig	23	Hannover	66-0576
JOERG, Jacob	28	Stolzenberg	65-0243
JOERGER, Carl	24	Illingen	64-0938
JOERGER, Theresia	20	Baden-Baden	67-0992
JOERREN, Louise	23	Hannover	66-0934
JOEST, Jacob	28	Asslar	66-0221
JOEST, Peter	33	Birkenau	64-1053
JOESTING, Augustus	28	Baltimore	63-0015
JOESTING, Gustav	17	Brockhausen	64-0639
JOHANNBOCKE, H.R.	28	Louisville	63-0917
Charlotte 26, Willy 3			
JOHANNES, A.	20	Altenbach/Han	63-1010
JOHANNES, Gerhard	27	Bassum	65-0243
JOHANNES, Heinr.	23	Cloppenburg	64-0427
JOHANNES, Leopold	26	Bastheim	64-0433
JOHANNES, W.	18	Poelgoenne	63-0350
JOHANNES, Wilh'mne	21	Oxhausen	65-0950
JOHANNS, F.W.	22	Elberfeld	65-0007
JOHANNTGER, Henr't	36	Solingen	66-1203
Clara 15, Emilie 8, Hermann 7, Carl 6			
Mathilde 5, Hugo 3			
JOHANNWEIER, Aug.	26	Broosen	63-1038
JOHANSEN, Chrst'ne	28	Gottenburg	66-0666
JOHELKA, Johann	15	Buhnberg	64-0433
JOHL, Caroline	58	Rust	65-0007
Rebecca 26, Leopold 21, Salomon 12			
JOHLITZ, Carl	25	Nennsdorf	65-0713
JOHN, Eduard	25	Culmbach	64-0886
JOHN, Marg.	28	Schlichter	64-1108
JOHN, Minna	52	Nordhausen	66-1093
JOKSCH, Louis	26	Poms	66-1128
JOLLIER, Wilhelm	32	Berlin	66-1093
Maria 25, Richard 7, Benno 5			
JONAS, Cath.	28	Scheppenbach	64-0331
JONAS, Johannes	27	Wiesbaden	65-0116
JONAS, K.	24	Deutschkrone	65-0950
JONAS, Minna	19	Stolpe/Pr.	65-0038
JONAS, W.(m)	14	Duesseldorf	64-0170
JONGSLERGERT, Corn	38	Paris	64-0687
JOOS, Jacob	29	Geschwendt	66-1373
JOPINA, Mathias	31	Bohemia	66-0469
Anna 25, Maria 9m			
JORDAN, Caspar	22	Alsfeld	65-0007
JORDAN, Chr.(f)	24	Leutenbach	64-0331
Johanna 21			
JORDAN, Wendel	26	Offenbach	64-0427
JORDAN, William	32	Lamstedt	63-0862
Meta 23, Mary 11m			
JORELLUM, Cath	41	Mensingen	63-1085
Cath. 13, Charles 9, Wolf 8, James 5			
Caroline 1, Emilie 3			
JOSCHT, Joseph	25	Wien	63-0614
Catharina 27, Josepha 4m			
JOSCHT, Joseph	52	Boehmen	63-0614
JOSEPH, Emil	20	Bestheim	65-0189
JOSEPH, Ernestine	16	Pleschen	66-0734
JOSEPH, Friederike	22	Hamburg	65-0151
Sara 23			
JOSEPH, Georg	50	Witzenhausen	64-0739
Sophie 48, Bernhard 23, Wilhelm 19			
Friederike 17			
JOSEPH, Heinr.	47	Berlin	66-0679
JOSEPH, Isaak	19	Gauersheim	65-1030
JOSEPH, Siegmund	31	Bechtheim	66-1203
JOSEPHTHAL, Louis	23	New York	63-0990
JOST, Carl	20	Hessen	64-0687
JOST, H.H.	28	Rodenburg	65-0974
JOST, Heinr.	25	Bueddelhagen	64-1206
JOST, Josepha	59	Kuttenberg	64-0214
Ad. 26, baby 3m, Anna 3			
JOST, Marie	20	Hessia	66-0679
JOST, Mathias	32	Kassel	65-0402
Anna 29, Peter 8, Mathias 6, Joh. 5			
Anna 1			
JOST, Philipp	23	Elmshausen	64-0687
JOST, Simon	16	Rabenheim	65-0594
JOSTEN, Franz	18	Waldulverheim	66-0083
JOSTES, Wilhelmine	24	Versmold	65-0974
JOSTSOHN, Johann	17	Koelbe	66-0412
JOTROWSKY, Wilhelm	29	Brodden	66-0578
Henriette 34			
JOUNGER, Henry	28	Marschale	66-0679
JUD, Emilie	24	Feldstetten	64-0363

NAME	AGE	RESIDENCE	YR-LIST
Rosine 26			
JUDAL, August	17	Hildburghsn.	64-0885
JUDD, N.B.	38	Washington	63-1136
son 18			
JUDENBERG, Meier	16	Leichtringen	66-1128
JUDIN, Matth.	39	Pittsburg	63-0990
JUEHNE, Carl	18	Goettingen	64-0886
JUELICHER, Ferd.	26	Wald	63-1038
JUENGLING, Barbara	23	Grossalmerode	64-0433
JUENGLING, Marie	28	Helmstedt	64-0992
JUERGEN, Carl	34	Mobile	66-1127
Anna 32, Henriette 9			
JUERGENS, Allerich	20	Langen	63-0168
JUERGENS, Anna	36	Steinau	66-1031
Heinrich 14, Anna 2			
JUERGENS, Behrend	38	Otterndorf	66-1031
JUERGENS, Clemens	25	Muenster	66-1313
JUERGENS, Friedr.	20	Kappeln	66-0668
JUERGENS, Friedr.	19	Hannover	66-1327
JUERGENS, Georg Fr	20	Lage	66-1373
JUERGENS, Heinr. W	42	Haldern	64-0920
Margaret 35, Louise 16, Aug. 3, Sophie 9m			
JUERGENS, Luehr	28	Williamsburg	63-0752
JUERGENS, Rudolph	24	Dingen	63-1178
Friedrich 22			
JUERGENS, Theodor	32	Tecklenburg	63-0990
JUERGENS, Wilhelm	32	Meschede	66-0934
JUETTE, B.	17	Borgenteich	66-0413
Helene 20			
JUETTING, Anna	26	Barge	65-1024
JUETTING, Heinrich	22	Detern	65-1024
Trientje 18			
JUNG, (f)	59	Malwitz	63-1085
JUNG, Adam	22	Wollman	64-1053
JUNG, Alexandra	18	Eisenach	66-1373
JUNG, Anna	29	Bremen	63-0482
Gerhard 7, James 10m			
JUNG, Anna	8	Oberneuland	66-1127
JUNG, Anna Marie	29	Dillheim	65-0243
JUNG, Anton	29	Mittelbach	66-1373
JUNG, Aug. L.	15	Malwitz	63-1085
Dorothea 59, Ella 9			
JUNG, Carl	18	Kirchberg	66-0576
JUNG, Carl L.	17	Lich	63-0398
JUNG, Casper	27	Scheitthal	65-0243
JUNG, Catharina	29	Hannover	64-0073
JUNG, Christine	20	Ziegenberg	64-0992
JUNG, Elisabeth	18	Trauerbach	63-0296
Catharine 9			
JUNG, Elisabeth	18	Unterfranken	66-0221
JUNG, Elisabeth	19	Bremen	64-0840
JUNG, Georg	22	Schmalkalden	65-0402
JUNG, Heinr.	22	Retterode	64-1053
JUNG, Jacob	31	Gensingen	64-0363
JUNG, Jeanette	19	Ebelsbach	65-0594
JUNG, Joh. Peter J	25	Quirnbach	66-0704
JUNG, Johann	29	Offenbach	66-1127
JUNG, Johanna	46	Creuznach	66-1131
Bertha 24			
JUNG, L.(m)	27	Steinfurt	64-0331
JUNG, Louis	36	California	66-0576
JUNG, Maria	21	Kersenhaim	66-0679
JUNG, Marie	33	Markgroeningn	66-1155
Marie 5, Wilhelmine 3, Caroline 2			
Louise 11m			
JUNG, Peter	27	Dornduerkheim	63-0551
JUNG, Philip	23	Aurich	66-0734
JUNG, Rabette	21	Wehrheim	65-0038
JUNG, Rudolph	25	Dresden	66-0221
JUNG, Wilhelm	31	Baden	63-0015
JUNGBLUT, Jacob	29	Pfungstadt	66-0109
JUNGBLUT, Johann	22	Underheim	66-0221
JUNGBLUTH, Carl	28	Arolsen	66-1203
JUNGE, Anna	13	Otterndorf	64-0456
JUNGE, Claus	30	Ordel	65-0402
JUNGE, Hermann	25	Cuxhaven	67-0007
Marie 22			
JUNGEN, Georg	24	Gomaringen	66-0679

NAME	AGE	RESIDENCE	YR-LIST
JUNGER, W.	40	Berlin	66-0413
Marie 30, Clara 39, Marie 12, Anna 12			
Bernhard			
JUNGHANS, Ernst W	23	Reinsdorf	63-0482
JUNGHANS, Adolph	18	Leibzig	65-0865
JUNGJOHANN, Sophie	17	Lehe	66-0576
JUNGKAMP, Anton	53	Vehlen	65-0948
Marie Chr 45, Christiana 9, Joh. Heinr. 7			
JUNGKURTH, Anna	38	Riehelsdorf	66-1373
Eckhardt 8, Anna 11m			
JUNGMANN, Alb.	25	Bremen	65-1024
JUNGMANN, Claus	21	Mittelste Nah	66-1373
JUNGMANN, Theodor	33	Boehl	65-0948
JUNGOLAS, H.	20	Rosenthal	63-1003
J. 18			
JUNKE, Melusine	23	Amelith	66-1031
JUNKEN, Caroline M	17	Pr. Minden	67-0599
JUNKEN, Herm.	18	Valhingstedt	63-1085
JUNKER, A. Cath	15	Gedern	63-1038
JUNKER, Arend R.	26	Oltmannsfehn	66-0469
Rolf R. 17			
JUNKER, Carl F.	18	Markendorf	64-0938
JUNKER, Caroline	56	Frankfurt a/m	66-1093
JUNKER, Georg	32	Neuenkirchen	63-0693
JUNKER, Philipp	23	Gedern	66-1373
JUNKERMANN, Carl	70	Helsen	66-0734
Louise 42			
JUNKMAN, Magdalene	20	Westheim	65-1095
JUNKMANN, Carl	19	Altkirchen	66-0984
Gustav 23			
JUNNETZBERGER, Hen	39	Darmstadt	64-1053
JURG, Georg	47	Berlin	67-0007
JURG, Joh. H.	30	Uhlenberg	64-0840
Cath. 28, Anna 10m			
JURGENS, Theodor	25	Westlevern	65-1088
JURGENSEN, S.(m)	20	Bremerhafen	64-0331
JURKA, Carl	51	Boehmen	66-0221
Josefa 46, Francisca 16, Antonia 9			
Anna 8, Therese 6, Joseph 4			
JURZIK, Wilhelm	26	Boehmen	66-0349
JUSTA, Carl	29	Berlin	66-0666
Alwine 23, Richard 27			
JUSTARIZS, Johann	18	Laibach	64-0687
JUTTING, Claus	30	Gruppenbach	65-0594
JUTZ, Christ.	45	Feldkirch	63-1218
Christiane 17			
JUTZE, Gustav	22	Suederbrock	64-1053
Christ 14, Minna 21, Elisa 29			
JUTZKY, Conr.	23	Althaningen	65-0007
Louise 18			
KAAKE, Ferd.	30	St.Louis	63-0168
KABELKA, Jos.	32	Liebentig	66-0576
Cath. 32, Carl 9, Joseph 7, Johann 6			
Wenzel 5, Marie 2			
KABLER, Oscar	18	Gr. Schoenau	64-0639
KACH, Rose	35	Philadelphia	63-0990
child 8			
KACHELHOFER, Mich.	36	Schoenenburg	63-1178
KACHELMANN, Joseph	25	Trabelsdorf	63-0917
KADE, Heinrich	16	Grafenweiler	66-0147
KADLITZ, Georg	36	Nemschlitz	65-0856
Barbara 36, Barbara 3			
KADTKE, Carl	31	Zamzow	66-0679
KAECHELE, Louis	24	Urasch	66-1093
Friederike 28			
KAEDING, Gottlieb	47	Arnswalde	66-1248
Christine 39, Bertha 14, Wilhelmine 7			
Friedrich 16, Carl 12, Gustav 6, Anna 10m			
KAEFER, Anna	18	Schwemmingen	65-0189
KAEFER, Marie	21	Schwenningen	64-0687
Catharina 19			
KAEFER, Nicolaus	23	Guetz	66-0734
KAEGLER, Karl	35	Steckenau	63-1069
Christine 27, Emilie 2, Gustav 1m			
KAEHR, Henry	36	France	63-0350
KAEHRS, Heinrich	25	Lilienthal	66-0666
A.Augusta 14			
KAELIN, Benedict	48	Baden Baden	64-1053

NAME	AGE	RESIDENCE	YR-LIST
Josepha 42, Ursula 20, Minrada 17			
Aloisa 15, Cathar. 10, Georg 5m			
KAELITZ, Heinrich	76	Zerbst	66-1093
KAELTERER, W.(m)	26	Rommelshausen	64-0331
KAEMENA, Margareth	18	Leeste	66-1127
KAEMMER, Eduard	38	Eisenach	64-1022
KAEMMERER, Heinr.	27	Duttenstaedt	65-0243
KAEMMERER, Henry	29	Bendeleben	63-0821
KAEMPE, Ferdinand	25	Schwieringen	66-0679
KAEMPF, Cacilie	21	Durbach	66-0679
KAEMPFER, Friedr.	27	Gotha	65-0004
KAEMPFF, Conrad	5	Durbach	66-0679
KAEMPFF, Sophie	34	Wasungen	64-0840
KAENGK, Seanna	48	Cincinnati	66-0221
KAENZEL, Marg.	18	Weinheim	64-0687
KAEPKE, Ferdinand	27	Preussen	66-0469
Johannes 20			
KAEPPEL, August	21	Giesberg	63-0990
KAERCHER, Marie	28	Nordheim	63-0006
Phillip 40			
KAERCHNER, Fr'dr.	37	Cannstadt	64-0639
KAERNER, Charlotte	19	Hueffe	64-0433
KAERSCHNER, Fritz	46	Philipsburg	65-1088
KAESSLER, Joh. Geo	29	Lachen	64-0433
Agnes 34			
KAESSMANN, Gottl.	19	Atsah	66-0679
KAESSMANN, Wilhelm	33	Asch	66-0679
Elisabeth 31			
KAESTLER, Bernard	19	Hessen	66-0109
KAESTNER, Hermann	18	Camenz	66-1131
KAFFENBERGER, Gott	27	Alsbach	66-0469
KAFFER, Heinr.	24	Glauchau	66-0576
KAFKA, Franz	16	Pormukel	66-0650
KAFNER, Anton	18	Fordkirchen	66-1248
KAHE, Heinr.	40	Osterweg	65-0950
Charlotte 30, Charlotte 3			
KAHL, Anna	20	Darmstadt	66-1031
KAHL, Heinrich	16	Schoenstein	66-0623
KAHL, Louise	19	Homberg	64-0433
KAHL, Robert	27	Glogau	64-1108
KAHL, Wilh.	28	Tenchern	63-1085
Henriette 41, Ernst 18, Therese 16			
William 9, Hermann 8, Albert 6, Francis 4			
Amalia 9m			
KAHLBAUM, Louis	22	Berlin	64-0073
KAHLE, F.	23	Bolschklee	64-0992
KAHLE, Lina	26	Altwalmoden	64-1053
KAHLES, Friedrich	30	Lengford	65-0948
Anna Maria 26			
KAHMEYER, Christ'e	18	Baden	63-0551
KAHN, Amalie	19	Cassel	65-0243
KAHN, Babette	19	Darmstadt	64-1053
KAHN, Eduard	18	Pathenheim	66-0576
KAHN, Eli	30	Strasburg	63-0990
KAHN, Frieda	22	Lichtenau	65-0189
Hanna 17			
KAHN, Johanna	22	Witzenhausen	64-0138
KAHN, John	31	Mitt.Eschenbh	63-0917
Barbara 59			
KAHN, M.(m)	25	Baltimore	64-0170
KAHN, Moses	22	Werba	66-0704
KAHN, Moses	15	Thuringen	64-0593
KAHN, Samuel	16	Weimar	66-0679
KAHN, Samuel	21	Basel	65-0243
Sarah 19			
KAHN, Sara	50	Gaudenbach	65-1024
Sara 27, Jettchen 14, Salomon 9			
KAHN, Wm.	18	Dietenbergen	64-0938
KAHR, Nannette	28	Liebenau	66-0734
KAHRE, H.Ch.	17	Doetzen	65-1088
KAHRENBERG, H.	25	Ovelgoenne	63-0482
KAHRS, Greta	19	Carlshafen	64-1022
KAHRS, Harm	21	Forlitz	66-0147
KAHRS, Meta	25	Habenhausen	66-1127
KAIBEL, Adolphine	21	Worms	63-0551
John C. 23			
KAIBEL, Carl Phil.	30	Mannheim	63-0614
KAIFEL, Alois	26	Donaustetten	66-1313

NAME	AGE	RESIDENCE	YR-LIST
KAIFFER, Fr.	28	Schweiz	63-1085
KAISER, Agatha	28	Gums	63-1085
KAISER, Anna	30	Hunshaven	65-0402
KAISER, Anna El.	21	Immelbrunn	63-0006
Christine 30			
KAISER, Auguste	35	Urrhausen	64-0023
Johanna 21			
KAISER, Augustus	32	Breslau	63-0168
KAISER, Berhd.	20	Vechta	64-0665
KAISER, Catharine	50	Buffalo	66-0679
KAISER, Christoph	28	Meiningen	64-0432
Anna Cae. 23, Anna Marg. 6m			
KAISER, Christoph	40	Baiern	66-0704
Catharina 26			
KAISER, Emilie	26	Breslau	63-0917
Emilie 2, Gustav 11m			
KAISER, Ferdinand	18	Nentershausen	66-1127
KAISER, Fritz	20	Doehren	65-0974
KAISER, Georg	18	Herzogsweiler	66-0147
KAISER, Georg	19	Zwesten	66-1313
KAISER, Gottlieb C	26	Rohracker	65-0055
KAISER, Heinrich	17	Hude	66-0412
KAISER, Heinrich	17	Kirchbracht	65-0402
KAISER, Jeanette	23	Hildburghsn.	66-1373
Maria 8			
KAISER, Johann	29	Ritze	63-0614
KAISER, Johann	23	Koburg	66-0083
KAISER, Johann	30	Obersein	66-1203
KAISER, Ludwig	18	Lauterbach	66-1127
KAISER, Martin	32	Posen	64-0456
Agnes 26, Maria 1			
KAISER, Martin	49	Marienwerder	65-0007
Marie 49			
KAISER, Pauline	19	Barchfeld	66-0704
KAISER, Philipp	25	Marienhagen	64-0639
KAISER, Wm.	25	Helmstedt	66-0837
Betty 44			
KALAS, Franz	26	Osick	66-0578
Catharina 18			
KALB, Adam	20	Kirchhasel	64-0214
KALB, Joh. Adam	38	Meiningen	64-0432
Eva Cath. 38, Christ.Marie 12			
Georg Adam 10, Eva Elise 7, Joh. Cath. 9m			
KALB, Peter	26	Geillastd	64-0639
KALB, Valentin	27	Melbes	64-0214
KALBER, Engelberta	16	Haardt	63-1085
KALBERT, Adolph	20	Rohmthal	64-0938
KALBFLEISCH, Heinr	24	Hessia	66-1093
KALBLAUB, Friedr.	38	Fulda	64-0639
KALCHEN, Michael	51	Weilburg	66-1093
Caroline 57			
KALDERWEIER, Aug.F	36	Bielefeld	65-1030
Amalie 36, Joh. Friedr. 11			
Friedr.Wilh. 9, Joh. Alwine 1			
KALDEWEY, Heinr.	35	Luedinghausen	65-1024
KALDYKIEWICZ, Flor	24	Posen	64-0432
KALE, George	27	Villingen	63-0097
KALENBERG, Pauline	29	Weinsberg	66-0413
KALENDER, Lewis	18	Coelln	63-0482
KALENLEIN, Fanny	17	Reyersbach	64-0639
KALETSCH, Johannes	42	Eltmannshsn.	66-1203
Maria 37, Gertrude 12, August 9, Julie 8			
Marie 60			
KALETSCH, Johannes	72	Eltsmannshsn.	66-1203
KALIESCH, Antonia	16	Schneidemuehl	65-0950
KALISCHER, Alphons	30	New York	63-0752
KALISKY, Jacob	21	Posen	65-0402
KALK, Heinr.	29	Raboldhausen	66-0349
wife 20			
KALKHOFF, Ad.	21	Frauensee	64-0495
KALKMANN, H.(m)	16	Verden	64-0363
KALL, Christoph	15	Willingen	66-1031
KALL, Johannes	33	Willingen	66-1031
Elisabeth 28			
KALLENBACH, Balbin	47	Neuenkirchen	63-1069
KALLENBACH, Valent	35	Meiningen	66-0704
Margarethe 35, Marie 12, Martin 6m			
KALLMANN, Fr'drke.	22	Berlin	66-1155

NAME	AGE	RESIDENCE	YR-LIST
KALLMANN, Sam.	25	Fuerth	65-0594
KALTENBACH, Carl	22	Lahr	66-0679
KALTENBACH, Christ	20	Grafenweiler	66-0147
KALTENBACH, Joh.	34	Switz.	64-0170
Mrs. 30, child 15, child 12, child 10			
child 9, child , infant 4m			
KALTHOF, Friedr.	31	Woden	64-0639
KALTHOFF, Ludolph	22	Hessen	66-0984
KALTWASSER, G.A.	14	Worms	64-0363
KAMEN, Isaac	22	Huever	64-0639
KAMING, W.(m)	45	Belleville	64-0331
KAMM, Barbara	29	Keidenzell	64-0938
Joh. 3			
KAMMER, Christian	17	Hallwangen	66-0147
KAMMER, Georg	19	Hutzenbach	66-0147
KAMMERER, Caroline	22	Epfendorf	66-0679
KAMMERER, Georg	31	Furth	66-0837
KAMMEYER, Caroline	26	Rahden	65-1088
KAMMINGER, Marg.	23	Schonweissenb	67-0007
Georg 3m			
KAMP, August	15	Bockhorst	66-1031
KAMP, Caspar Herm.	36	Buer	64-0920
Clara Maria 37, Florentine 13			
Cath. Louise 7, Clara Maria 9			
Heinr. Fr'dr 1			
KAMP, Elisab.	23	Hunbergen	65-1088
KAMP, Theodor	27	Prussia	65-0038
KAMPE, Aug.	26	Minden	64-0495
KAMPE, Augusta	25	Saustha	64-0495
KAMPEN, v. Heinr.	24	Bremerhaven	66-1155
KAMPER, Wilhelm	27	Melle	66-1093
KAMPEROW, Emil	18	Herford	65-1088
KAMPF, Anna	20	Ober Geiss	66-0668
KAMPHAUS, J.	25	Brockteich	65-1024
KAMPING, Hermann	25	Diepholz	65-0948
KAMPMANN, Henry	54	Overhagen	63-0917
Gertrud 39, Cathre 20, Friedrich 17			
Henry 13, Anton 10, Josephine 2			
KAMPMEIER, Minna	18	Kleekamp	65-0950
KAMPMEYER, Carl	18	Walldorf	67-0007
KAMPS, Augusta	25	Wremen	64-0665
KAMPS, Fr.(m)	25	Louisville	64-0073
KAMPS, Heinr.	27	St. Louis	64-0023
KAMPSER, Lina	22	Ottersberg	63-1218
KANAK, Anna	54	Boehmen	63-0990
John 31			
KANE, Johann	26	New York	64-0363
KANER, Magdalena	21	Nuernberg	66-1327
Georg 8, Johanna 7, Dorette 4, Barbara 3			
KANN, Adelheid	27	Oberheimbach	66-0704
KANN, Friederike	20	Kulte	65-0594
KANNENGIESSER, Lou	32	Brooklyn	63-0990
Louise 6, Marie 9m			
KANNER, Charles	28	Prussia	63-0752
Johanna 24			
KANNING, Dorothea	25	Lemke	66-0413
Louise 21, Elise 3			
KANNSTEIN, J.D.	39	Bremen	64-0363
Eleonore 40			
KANSAL, Johann	29	Wien	64-0687
KANT, J.H.C.	19	Dobareuth	64-0331
KANTER, Maria	19	Neustadt	64-0639
KANTH, Martin	23	Truttingen	63-0990
KANTZ, J. Philipp	30	Prussia	63-0296
Barb. 25			
KANTZ, Louis	22	Carlsruhe	64-0593
KANTZMANN, H.	24	Gr. Rohrstein	65-0402
KANTZOW, Fr. W.	47	Schweden	63-0752
KANZ, Caroline	22	Markgroningen	66-0679
KANZLEITER, Joh.	43	Frickenhausen	64-0427
Marie 45, Anna M. 12			
KAPAUM, S.	37	Boehemen	63-0752
KAPER, Johann	28	Hannover	64-1022
Elise 25			
KAPITAEN, Joseph	34	Oberbrois/Boh	65-0038
Barbara 24			
KAPITAN, Joseph	22	Cernowitz	66-0734
KAPLE, Marie	17	Besenfeld	63-1178

NAME	AGE	RESIDENCE	YR-LIST
KAPP, Anastasia	18	Seedorf	66-1155
KAPP, Ch. (m)	23	Versmold	63-0551
KAPP, Peter	24	Altheim	65-0189
Christine 20			
KAPPAUF, Friedrke.	20	Gr.Breitenbch	66-1203
KAPPAUF, Johanna	21	Grossbreitenb	66-0734
KAPPE, Hr.	21	Tehlen	66-0349
KAPPEIN, Juliane	58	Engelstedt	65-0948
KAPPEL, Anna	40	Boehmen	66-0349
Doretha 24, Adolph 1			
KAPPEL, Cath.	23	Heinershausen	63-0752
KAPPEL, Johann	43	Salmannsdorf	66-0346
Ursula 33			
KAPPELMANN, Sophie	31	Markt Heidenf	67-1005
KAPPEN, Rud.	28	Krusel	65-1030
KAPPENHOEFEN, Dan.	18	Frankenstein	66-0704
KAPPER, Christine	26	Kleinheubach	66-0934
KAPPES, Louis	32	New York	63-0917
Gertrud 27			
KAPPMEIER, Johanne	19	Oldendorf	66-1203
KAPSCH, Friedr.	23	Bremen	64-0938
KAPSCHINSKA, Soph.	56	Johannesthal	64-0456
KAPSER, Heinr.	18	Herstelle	64-0593
Aug. 28			
KARASEK, Joh.	30	Bohemia	64-0687
KARBER, Christine	26	Ruttershausen	64-0343
Johanna 21			
KARBOCHEWSKY, Rosa	22	Schloppe	64-0665
KARBUSICKY, Johann	28	Welim	65-0713
KARCH, Louise	38	Winnenden	65-1024
KARCHER, Jacob Fr.	21	Ruettpur	66-0704
KARDALSKY, August	33	Danzig	66-0666
Henriette 30, Friedrich 7, Marta 2m			
KARESCH, Alois	38	Bremen	63-0015
Anna 15, Otto 9			
KARG, Elisabeth	49	Herford	66-0734
Anna 23, Margarethe 20, Nicolaus 17			
Michel 9			
KARG, Henry	47	Dinkelsbuehl	63-1038
Wilhelmine 17			
KARGER, Friedrich	32	Weissweil	66-0412
KARGER, Marie	18	Posen	66-0221
KARHAU, J.	42	Briesen	66-0413
Justine 28, Hermann 10, Anna 7, Emilie 5			
August 3, David 8m			
KARL, August	17	Rauschenberg	66-1131
Louise 25			
KARL, Ignatz	21	Reichenbach	65-1024
KARLALEWSKY, Jac.	30	Prussia	64-0170
KARMEYER, Elisab.	52	Prussia	64-0432
KARNAPP, Friedrich	28	Petershagen	65-1140
Henriette 27, Frieda 9m			
KARON, Gottlieb	23	Rosmin	64-0739
KARPER, Robert	20	Pforzheim	66-0734
KARS, Meta	17	Soltrum	64-0456
KARSCH, Henry	54	Illinois	63-0350
KARSCHER, Christof	67	Spielberg	67-0007
KARSMEYER, Simon	39	Erder	63-0614
KARST, Anton	52	Augsburg	64-0456
Walburga 22, Ludowika 22, Anna 17			
Bernhard 11			
KARST, Friedr.	28	Burhave	63-0953
KARTHMANN, Hermann	36	Hannover	66-1093
KASEMEIER, H.	18	Bavaria	63-1003
KASMINSKY, Theoph.	31	Gottlanz	67-0007
KASPAR, Adolph	23	Boehmen	63-0953
KASPER, Everh.	20	Leden	64-0073
KASPERT, Franz	36	Schlichton	67-0007
Anna 37, Joseph 5			
KASS, Konrad	32	Delbrueck	65-1095
KASSEL, Joh. Wilh.	48	Schwarzenau	66-0578
Catharina 42, Wilhelm 20, Heinrich 17			
Catharina 14, Jacob 11, Christian 2			
Friedrich 6			
KASSELMANN, Rud.	18	Oesede	64-0687
KASSEN, Heinr.	38	New York	64-0214
Jeanette 24			
KASSENS, Trienka	21	Visquard	66-0349

NAME	AGE	RESIDENCE	YR-LIST
KASSLER, Julius	29	New York	63-0821
KASSMANN, Ernst	21	Leipzig	64-0343
KASSOW, Joseph	23	New Orleans	63-0752
baby 9m			
KASTEN, Amalie	23	Wohlenhausen	64-0992
KASTENS, Heinrich	25	Jever	67-0007
KASTER, Marie	22	Alsum	64-0992
KASTNER, Christian	32	Thiershein	65-1031
Lisette 33, Ernst 6, Adolph 3, Therese 6m			
KASYSCKE, August	28	Wilkowa	66-0469
KATE, George	27	Villingen	63-0097
KATENBRUN, Cath.	16	Kappel	66-0469
KATENHAUER, And.	36	Braunschweig	64-0331
Johanna 21			
KATER, Mathias	22	Naila	66-1131
KATERMANN, Bernh.	28	Holsten	66-1131
KATHALS, M.	41	Browenau	66-0413
Caroline 37, F.D. 13, Anna 9, Eva 6			
Johann F. 2, H. Leopold 3m			
KATHE, Johann B.	28	Twistringen	64-0886
KATHENBERG, Jans	56	Holstrop	66-0668
Thalcke 50, Johann 21, Altje 18, Baake 14			
Marie 9			
KATHENKAMP, Heinr.	25	Goldberg	66-0668
KATHMANN, Ferdin.	25	Dinklage	66-0576
KATHMANN, Gertr.	21	Essen	64-0938
KATHMANN, Josefina	22	Dinklage	65-0948
KATOW, Alfous	31	Paris	66-1373
KATSCH, Charles	42	New Haven	63-0015
Clara 16, Hedwig 9, Charles 7			
KATSCH, Chris.	46	Altenburg	63-1038
KATT, G.H.W.	17	Neuenkirchen	66-1313
KATTE, Abrah.	27	Langenselbach	64-0138
KATTENBRUNN, Ch.	30	Wegheim	64-0495
KATTENHORN, Anna	20	Uthlede	64-0593
KATTENHORN, Hch.	32	Cincinnati	64-0363
KATTENHORN, Lueder	16	Osterholz	64-0840
KATTSCHINPEL, Carl	24	Ischland	66-0413
KATZ, David	24	Geismar	63-0006
KATZ, David	16	Hatzbach	66-0679
KATZ, Ester	19	Hunfeld	64-0214
KATZ, Gotl.	21	Dudershein	64-0782
KATZ, H.C.	21	Lehe	66-0346
KATZ, Jacob	30	Paderborn	66-1155
Helene 27, Amalie 1			
KATZAK, Joseph	24	Boehmen	66-0349
KATZEMEIER, M.	39	Ndr. Berbach	66-0413
Elisabeth 18, M. 14, Elisabeth 65			
KATZENSTERN, H.	26	Cincinnati	63-1085
KATZMANN, Joh. W.	42	Reichelsdorf	65-1031
Anna Margar. 43, Heinrich 15			
Anna Margar. 13, Johannes 11, Wilhelm 9			
Anna Elis. 4, Adolph 2			
KATZWEILER, Simon	35	N. Carolina	66-0576
Alwine 28, Bettine 9, Milly 8, Therese 6			
Oscar 3, Robert 11m			
KAUBERT, Joseph	17	Bamberg	66-0668
KAUDMANN, Jac.	21	Duisburg	66-1243
KAUFER, Georg	14	Holzhausen	66-1155
KAUFFMANN, Jean	19	Frankfurt a/m	66-0704
KAUFFMANN, Louis	30	New York	63-1178
KAUFHOLD, Engelhd	27	Wustenterode	64-0023
KAUFMANN, Alex	18	Mannheim	63-0097
KAUFMANN, Bertha	19	Bremen	66-0413
KAUFMANN, C.C.(m)	29	Stetten	64-0495
KAUFMANN, Cathrine	20	Gaggstadt	63-0693
KAUFMANN, Diedr.	22	Tecklenburg	63-0953
KAUFMANN, Elisbeth	20	Weimar	64-0885
KAUFMANN, Ester	22	Riembach	65-0007
Therese 17			
KAUFMANN, Fannie	27	Baden	66-0734
KAUFMANN, Ferd.	48	Iowa	63-0752
KAUFMANN, Georg	19	Hannover	66-0668
KAUFMANN, Hch.	19	Hammstedt	64-1022
KAUFMANN, Helene	21	Bauerbach	64-0938
KAUFMANN, Isaak		Rinbach	66-1373
KAUFMANN, J. Dr.	40	New York	64-0495
KAUFMANN, Joh.	33	Hohenhausen	66-0837
KAUFMANN, Joh.	28	Waiblingen	66-1203
KAUFMANN, Jos. Sop	48	Zenkendorf	64-0886
Barbara 5			
KAUFMANN, Joseph	18	Naila	66-1131
KAUFMANN, Julius	24	Goslar	65-0865
KAUFMANN, K.(m)	16	Kirchorf	64-0214
KAUFMANN, L.(m)	18	Schney	64-0170
KAUFMANN, Lazarus	18	Leutershausen	64-0639
KAUFMANN, Margaret	21	Bissingen	66-1155
KAUFMANN, Martha	25	Tann	65-1088
Simon 6			
KAUFMANN, Minna	25	Duesseldorf	64-0170
KAUFMANN, Regina	19	Hildesheim	63-0350
KAUFMANN, S.	28	Prag	66-1243
KAUFMANN, Sara	50	Buffalo	66-0679
Adolph 16, Abraham 20			
KAUFMANN, Wilhelm	54	Quedlinburg	63-0752
KAUFMANN, Wilhelm	30	Frankfurt a/M	66-1203
KAUFMANN, Wm.	29	Helversdorf	64-0023
KAUKER, Christ.	28	Cassel	65-0116
KAUL, Johann	26	New York	64-0363
KAUL, Lisette	25	Wolbeck	66-1031
KAUL, Ludwig	38	Baiern	66-0704
Elisabeth 31, Elisabeth 9, Margar. 8			
Louis 6, Jacob 3, Friedrich 6m			
KAUPE, (f)	17	Crefeld	63-1085
KAUPIS, August	21	Guenthorst	66-0412
KAUPP, Valentin	28	Daum	65-1095
Susanna 23			
KAUPSCHAEFE, Herm.	51	Osterwiehe	64-1022
Elis. 49, Elis 7, Joseph 5, Anna 4			
Marg. 2, Georg 15			
KAURAT, Alwine	45	Baltimore	64-1022
Oline 17			
KAUSE, Catharina	17	Kruekum	64-0938
KAUSTEINER, Henr.	45	Hannover	66-0984
Margarethe 41, Henrich 7, Catharina 4			
KAUTER, Maria	19	Neustadt	64-0639
KAUTZ, Johann Jac.	33	Endbach	66-0083
KAUTZMANN, Fr.	50	Pennsylvania	63-0482
KAUTZMANN, Jacob	36	Weissenburg	65-0243
Jacob 24			
KAYMER, Henriette	54	Solingen	63-0822
Lebrecht 20			
KAYSER, Adam	30	Lengefeld	63-0296
KAYSER, Anton	37	Eisenach	64-0427
KAYSER, Aug.	24	Bielefeld	64-0456
Herm. 19			
KAYSER, Augustus	32	Breslau	63-0350
KAYSER, Carl	25	Obermochstadt	65-0007
KAYSER, Emil	27	Berlin	65-0007
KAYSER, Friedr.	30	Liln	64-0170
KAYSER, H.G.	40	Oldenburg	65-0594
KAYSER, J.A.	14	Herstelle	65-0402
KAYSER, Johann Eh.	22	Hildburghsn.	64-0456
Friedr.Elias 32			
KAYSER, Johannes	25	Herstelle	66-1131
KAYSER, Louise	21	Hannover	66-1128
KAYSER, Ludw.	17	Segnitz	65-0594
KAYSER, Paul	17	Rogasen	66-0469
KAYSER, Regina	21	Wuergassen	64-0593
KAYSER, Wilhelm	20	Oetlingen	66-1327
KAZNIK, Anton	37	Boehmen	66-0349
Julie 18			
KECK, Albert	31	Amelith	66-1031
Elise 27, Wilhelm 1			
KECK, Caroline	52	Dammin	63-0953
KECK, Catharine	34	Berge	64-0739
KECK, Christ.	31	Dammin	63-0953
KECK, Gottlieb	18	Wuertemberg	63-1069
KECK, Jacob	18	Seidringen	66-0704
Leonhard 17			
KECK, Sophie	22	Niederwaelden	66-0734
KECKEISEN, Jos.	26	Imenried	63-1178
KEDWITZ, Christine	35	Niefern	63-0168
Lewis 6, Charles 4			
KEEF, Elisabeth	23	Luste	66-0576
KEEPEN, Margaretha	23	Bremen	63-0398

NAME	AGE	RESIDENCE	YR-LIST
KEES, Carl	45	Friedrichshor	66-0578
KEESE, Heinr.	20	Alfeld	64-0904
KEESE, Louis	37	Aerzen	63-0482
KEFFEL, Enno	22	Braunschweig	64-0170
KEFKA, Caroline	15	Boehmen	63-1178
KEGEL, Louise	13	Wuertemberg	63-1069
Emilie 15, Christine 56			
KEGEL, Wilhelmine	22	Rumburg	64-0938
Oscar 11			
KEGELER, Franz	28	Boehmen	64-0495
Aa.(f) 24			
KEGELMANN, Carl	35	Ohrdrup	64-0427
KEHL, Cathr.	23	Bechtheim	63-1010
KEHL, Joseph	33	Rossbach	64-0343
Johanna 21			
KEHL, Louise	26	Hessen	64-0432
Marg. 30			
KEHLBECK, William	19	Bremen	65-0055
KEHLENBECK, Herm.	31	Hannover	64-1108
KEHR, Diedrich	18	Darmstadt	66-1031
KEHR, Johann	21	Gemuenden	65-1024
KEHRE, Mart.	27	Sondelfingen	63-1218
KEHRE, Peter	28	Ostheim	66-1093
KEHRER, Elisabeth	59	Sondelfingen	63-1218
KEHRET, Maria	23	Fresenbach	66-0623
Gertrude 15			
KEHRMANN, Statius	32	St.Louis	63-0917
KEHRY, Franz	46	Kreuznach	66-0221
Elisabeth 32, Rudolph 7, Clemens 4			
KEIBER, John G.	41	New York	63-1038
KEIDEL, Jacob	23	Gr. Burenweil	66-1155
KEIFEN, Ludwig	22	Duerkheim	65-1024
KEIGEL, Friedr.	24	Riegeln	64-0023
KEIL, Elis.	26	Ulrichstein	63-0482
KEIL, Georg	28	Wachendorf	65-0189
KEIL, Henry	20	Frankenberg	66-0109
KEIL, Henry	24	Kurhessen	66-0109
KEIL, Katharine	19	Lindenfels	66-0469
KEILBACH, Ludwig	26	Baiern	66-0704
KEILBAR, Heinrich	40	Schwarzenbach	63-0097
KEILHAUSER, Barb.	86	Gillersdorf	66-0650
KEIM, Georg	63	Nordhalben	67-0007
KEIMER, Ludw.	59	Langen	64-0782
Cath. 21, Friedr. 18			
KEINER, Philippine	47	Edingen	66-0576
Ludwig 24, Johanna 11, Wilhelmine 8			
KEINER, Rosine	20	Wuertemberg	63-1069
KEISEL, Hermann	24	Stuttgart	65-1031
KEISKER, Caroline	18	Dissen	65-0950
KEISSWENGER, Marie	21	Aalen	67-0795
KEITEL, Aug.	34	Bremen	64-0432
KEITEL, Joh.	16	Zahlbach	64-0593
KEITEL, Wilh.	25	Worms	64-0170
KEITZ, v. Maria		Grosenlueder	66-0469
KELB, Wilhelm	27	Leppien	66-0083
KELBEL, Thomas	26	Boehmen	66-0109
KELDENSTEIN, John	44	Lissa	64-0886
Amalie 7, Isidor 5			
KELIUS, Adelheid	37	Aumund	64-0593
Sophie 7, Friedr. 6			
KELKENBERG, Heinr.	30	Stolzenau	66-0577
Sophie 32			
KELKENBERG, Lotte	25	Steyerberg	66-0934
Sophie 20			
KELLAND, Catharine	18	Wennigen	66-1203
KELLENBERGER, Carl	30	Dallan	67-0007
KELLER, Adolph	30	Prag	66-0147
KELLER, Albert	32	Boehmen	66-0147
Bertha 3, Gabriela 11m			
KELLER, Aug.	4	Naundorf	64-0782
Joh. 44, Wilhelmine 18, Ernst 7, Emil 5			
Amalie 3			
KELLER, C.G.(m)	28	Crimmitschau	64-0331
KELLER, Carl	36	Boitzen	66-1127
KELLER, Charlotte	26	New York	63-0953
KELLER, Conrad	21	Frankenhausen	66-0221
KELLER, Elisabeth	21	Prussia	64-0363
KELLER, Fr.	30	Washington	63-1178

NAME	AGE	RESIDENCE	YR-LIST
KELLER, Fr. Wm.	40	Buer	64-1053
Wilhelmine 36, Rudolph 7, Amanda 5			
August 4, Frdr. 2, Marie 9m			
KELLER, Franzisca	19	Prag	66-0147
KELLER, Friedr. Wm	24	Heilsbach	64-0739
KELLER, Fritz	22	Buer	65-0594
KELLER, Heinrich	26	Ehringhausen	66-0576
KELLER, Heinrich	28	Hannover	66-1031
Caroline 23			
KELLER, Jacob	37	Lister	67-0007
KELLER, Jacob	23	Kaltenortheim	65-0151
KELLER, Jacob	21	Oberanstadt	64-0363
KELLER, Jul.	20	Hamburg	65-0038
KELLER, Louis	60	Heidermunden	65-0189
KELLER, Ludwig	25	Battenberg	66-0734
KELLER, Marie	22	Switz	64-0170
KELLER, Marie	17	Harpenfeld	66-0668
KELLER, Marie	26	Oetelfingen	65-0243
KELLER, Mary Magd.	59	Suhl	63-0482
KELLER, Pauline	28	New York	66-0109
Henry 11m			
KELLER, Pauline	22	Esslingen	65-0950
Christiane 9			
KELLER, Peter	40	New York	66-0679
KELLER, Sibilla	47	Augsburg	65-1088
KELLER, Victoria	34	Berenthal	67-0599
Susanne 4, Elisabeth 1			
KELLER, Wilhelmine	22	Vobel	66-1093
KELLER, Wm.	43	Lancaster	64-0687
KELLERHALS, Fr.	28	Friedrichshfn	64-0023
KELLERMANN, Abrah.	20	Langenthal	65-0770
KELLERMANN, Andres	27	Hessloh	65-0770
KELLERMANN, Frd.	25	Muenster	64-1206
KELLERMEYER, Herm.	24	Entruss	63-1010
KELLERT, Barbara	25	Willmersbach	64-0739
KELLERT, Friedr.	21	Schollbrunn	66-1131
KELLNER, Bernhard	45	Ungarn	63-1218
Moritz 16			
KELLNER, Fr.	35	Otterstedt	65-1031
KELLNER, Joseph	27	Ruthenberg	64-0433
KELLNER, Lisette	20	Aschmir	66-0668
KELLNER, Salie	28	Kellemes	65-1189
Henry 7, Simon 5, Martin 3, Caroline 2			
Heinrich 9m			
KELM, Eduard	36	Bernsee	66-1248
Christine 41, Carl 7, Friedrich 6			
Julius 5, Augusta 8, Anna 1			
KELM, Franz	21	Czarnikow	65-0898
KELM, Wm.	26	Czarnikau	64-0363
Ernestine 24, Wm. 3m			
KELTER, Alois	25	Wurttemberg	64-0593
Marie 20			
KEMLER, Siegm.	26	Meisenheim	66-1127
KEMMER, Franz J.	32	Arhaus	65-1030
KEMMLER, Joh. G.	17	Detzingen/Wrt	65-0038
Barbara 22, Martin 20			
KEMP, Sophia	32	Lautersbach	63-1038
KEMPEN, Wilhelm	23	Bermuthshaus	66-0679
KEMPER, Felitha	20	Alexandria	63-0862
KEMPER, H.	26	Detmold	64-0593
KEMPER, Heinrich	28	Westenhof	66-1155
KEMPER, Henriette	33	Brake	66-0984
KEMPER, Hermann	20	Freckenhorst	63-0953
KEMPF, Chr.	27	Ebersbach	65-1030
KEMPF, Joseph	40	Seelbach	65-0055
KEMPF, Lina	15	Darmstadt	66-1127
KEMPF, Martin	25	Landerieth	64-1108
Mathilde 23			
KEMPF, Oscar	28	Neustadt	64-0073
KEMPMEIER, Peter	20	Varensell	66-1203
KENHOEFER, J.	22	Ahlen	66-0413
J. 18, Anna 29			
KENK, Math.	18	Horgen	63-1085
Joseph 19			
KENKEL, August	21	Dinklage	66-0984
KENKEL, Heinrich	27	Quakenbrueck	66-0984
KENLEIN, Andr.	51	Themar	64-0840
Dorothea 42, Beata 23, Louise 11m			

NAME	AGE	RESIDENCE	YR-LIST
KENNER, Caroline	42	Esslingen	64-0427
Gottlieb 15			
KENNER, Jacob	18	Esslingen	65-0950
KENNERICH, Philip	30	Bayern	66-0221
KEPLER, Chr.	30	New York	63-1136
KEPPEL, Fr. August	55	Polkenstein	66-0666
KEPPLER, Georg	17	Pfullingen	66-1313
KEPPLER, Gustav.	24	Wuerttenberg	66-0221
KEPPLER, Jac.	22	Unterhausen	66-1313
KEPPLER, Joh.	29	New York	64-0170
KEPPLER, Jos.	40	Isnendingen	66-1313
KEPPLER, Lisette	17	Stuttgart	64-0639
KEPPLER, Ludwig	17	Grafenberg	66-0147
KEPPLER, Wilh.	23	Schondorf	64-0214
KEPPNER, Maria	35	New York	63-1218
Maria 2			
KERBART, Franz	39	Osik	66-1373
Anna 30, Anna 6, Sophie 11m			
KERBER, Maria	28	Rottweil	63-1038
KERKHOFF, Marie	28	Wabern	65-0950
KERKMANN, Ana	28	Beckum	66-1203
Anna 3, Henr. 3m			
KERLE, Leonhard	22	Jersey City	66-0679
KERN, August	20	Schleusingen	66-1248
KERN, Betty	28	Bremen	63-0917
KERN, Carl	18	Gera	66-1031
KERN, Felix	22	Wuerttemberg	66-0934
KERN, Friederike	20	Magdeburg	67-0992
KERN, Hermann	24	Uslar	66-1131
KERN, Jacob	57	Reichenbach	64-0687
Eleonore 7, Marie 4, Jacob 16, William 23			
Margarethe 15			
KERN, Joh.	39	Resenfeld	64-0073
KERN, Johann	16	Wuertemberg	66-1093
KERN, Philipp	32	Germany	63-0990
KERNAU, Ellen	19	Geneva	63-0551
Francis 21, Bernhardt 17, Thomas 15			
KERNBERGER, Geo.	21	Bruchsal	66-1313
Catharina 15			
KERNER, Martin	54	Wuertenberg	66-0221
Catharine 44, Melchior 17, Theresia 7			
Catharine 6, Fanny 4, Joseph 9m			
KERSCHER, Johann	23	Anspach	66-1203
KERSIN, Wilhelm	25	Neurese	66-0578
KERSTING, Aug.	18	Alf	64-0170
KERSTING, Wilhelm	27	Diepholz	64-0363
KERWER, Elisabeth	25	Waldbockelhm.	63-0482
KESEEL, Adolph	26	Lemberg	66-1373
KESEL, Juliane	47	Kempten	63-0350
KESLER, Sophie	19	Roedenau	66-0623
Elisabeth 23			
KESPOHL, Augusta	14	Borgholzhsn.	66-1031
KESSEL, v. Marie	28	Berlin	63-0990
Marie 9			
KESSELRING, G.	17	Ellestadt	65-0007
KESSLER, Anton	33	Langenheim	66-0576
KESSLER, Carl	24	Burzahn	66-1248
KESSLER, Caroline	18	Kaiseroda	63-0168
Hartmann 26			
KESSLER, Eduard	18	Cassel	66-1093
KESSLER, Heinr.	24	Osterholz	64-1206
KESSLER, J.	29	Klemsilheim	65-0974
KESSLER, Johann	18	Werschan	67-0007
KESSLER, Leopold	40	Baden	63-0752
Josepha 38, Marie 4, Joh. 1			
KESSLER, Magdalena	19	Ob.Schaffhsn.	66-1093
KESSLER, Paul	21	Lutzelhausen	64-0992
August 19			
KESSLER, Philipp	17	Everbach	66-0576
KESSLER, Philipp	28	Albach	63-0482
Eleonora 25			
KESSMANN, Johanna	23	Eimbeck	66-0577
KESSNER, Wilhelm	27	Maltitz	66-0934
KESTEN, Philipp	19	Thalfang	65-1030
KESTLER, Caspar	25	Sommerach	66-1373
KETERING, August	28	Rheims	64-1053
KETSCH, Lazarus	35	New York	64-0073
KETTELER, Philipp	23	Guentershein	65-1031

NAME	AGE	RESIDENCE	YR-LIST
KETTELER, Wm.	14	Papenburg	64-0938
KETTELKAMP, C.F.	30	Lengerich	63-1085
KETTENBEIL, E.(m)	24	Leipzig	64-0170
KETTERER, Frieder.	48	Urasch	66-1093
Rudolph 19, Emma 21, Rika 17			
Marthilde 16			
KETTERLE, Hr.	30	Gundersheim	65-0007
KETTERMEIER, Elise	28	Kappeln	63-1069
KETTLER, Anna Marg	23	Drivoerden	63-1038
J.P. 18			
KETTLER, Franz	38	Osnabrueck	65-0116
KETTLER, Georg	30	Linkershein	66-1031
KETTLER, Hy.	23	New York	63-1085
KETTMANN, Hermann	23	Bassum	66-1093
KETTNER, Carl Fr.	18	Rossdorf	63-0614
KETTNER, Chr.	56	Cincinnati	63-0482
KETTNER, Wilhelm	16	Stroseler Hau	65-0948
Wilhelmine 19			
KETZEL, Ph.	31	Weimar	65-1189
KETZSCHER, Carl	40	Crimmitschau	64-1022
Augusta 26			
KEUL, Catharina	22	Obergereuth	66-0147
KEUNECKE, Augusta	35	Braunschweig	65-0151
KEY, Agnes	20	Coblenz	64-0073
KEYSER, (f)	29	New York	64-0427
Regina 24, Friedr. 4, Friederike 1			
Mary 12, Henry 10			
KHAN, Joseph	42	Ludenburg	67-0353
Christine 29			
KIBITZ, Francisca	32	Pilsen	66-0734
KICK, Gust.	25	Sigmaringen	65-0594
KICKERITZ, Andr. C	33	Altenweddinge	64-0214
Marie 31, Ida 6, Anna 1, Marg. 15			
Marie 29, Marie 9			
KIEBEL, Nicolaus	17	Hohfeld	63-1038
KIEBEL, Peter	25	Buweiler	63-1038
KIEBELE, Pauline	21	Aichstetten	63-0752
KIEBLER, Regine	20	Wuestenroth	66-0679
KIECHLE, Anton	19	Muenchen	65-0594
KIEFER, Anna	19	Langgens	66-1327
KIEFER, Franz	29	New York	66-0576
Catharine 58			
KIEFER, Friedr.	18	Chemnitz	64-0639
KIEFER, Georg	28	Dietzenbach	64-0433
KIEFER, Louis	23	Carlsruhe	64-0073
KIEFER, Marie	29	Hausen	67-0007
KIEFER, Pierre	19	Belgien	63-0350
KIEFFER, Joh. Gott	23	Culmbach	65-0116
KIEHLHOZ, Aug.	44	Hannover	66-1031
KIEL, August	21	Wiesler	65-1095
KIEMEYER, Johann	24	Bremen	66-1203
Augusta 22, Friedr.W. 19			
KIENE, Emilie	19	Hannover	66-1031
KIENMEYER, Carl	21	Bremen	64-0456
KIENZEL, Emil	19	Balzholz	66-1127
KIENZLI, Victoria	33	Obernau	66-0349
KIEPE, A.(m)	16	Wollmershsn.	64-0331
KIEPER, Margaret	23	Gielert	64-0331
KIES, Jacob	36	Moehringen	65-0243
KIESELMANN, August	21	Muenden	65-1095
KIESEWETTER, Carl	21	Eisfeld	65-1024
KIESEWETTER, Herr.	26	Schotterthal	66-1203
KIESLING, Ernst	38	Greiz	66-0469
Ottilie 29, Otto 3			
KIESS, Theodor	26	Carlsruhe	66-1155
KIESSENBECK, Wm.	12	Kalbe	63-1218
KIESSLER, (m)	19	Solingen	66-0109
KIESSLING, Sophie	56	Zelwitz	65-0713
Johanna 22, Marie 19			
KIETER, J.F. (m)	52	Dresden	64-0170
KIKKER, Aug.	19	Segelhorst	66-1243
KILBEL, Albon(f)	23	Greiz	64-0495
Lena 9m			
KILIAN, Amand	23	Biedenkopf	65-0402
KILIAN, Elisabeth	22	Lobenhausen	64-0886
KILIAN, Rud.	32	Hassfurth	65-0898
Catharine 32, Geo. Bruno 8, Kunigunde 1			
KILIN, Johann	37	Alzenau	65-0151

NAME	AGE	RESIDENCE	YR-LIST
KILLHORN, Hy.	20	Dodenhausen	63-1085
KILLIAS, Joh.Fr.	26	Cheer	64-0427
KILLING, Christian	18	Vollmerdingen	66-1155
KILLING, H.Fr.	51	Rothfeld	64-0665
KILOMBERG, Diedr.	19	Bremen	67-0600
KIMM, Friedrich	24	Krombach	66-0147
KIMME, G.	28	Bremen	65-0116
KIMME, Johann	50	Wiemsdorf	66-1031
Johann 16			
KIMMEL, Joh. Mich.	47	Fuerth	66-0704
KIMMEL, Silvester	29	Kirchhasel	66-0221
KIMMER, Marie	22	Wuestegierdrf	64-0593
KINCKER, Philipine	19	Roecke	66-0934
KIND, August	30	Ottenessen	63-0482
Cath. 28, Augusta 3			
KINDER, Hermine	16	Bremen	66-0934
KINDERMANN, H.	35	Pressen	64-0427
Anna 31, Adam 5, Peter 6m, Emilie 25			
Marie 2			
KINDERVATTER, Carl	25	Witzenhausen	65-0865
KINDLER, Emil	24	Durbach	66-1093
KINDT, Joh. Friedr	47	Rebunke	67-0599
Henriette 43, Caroline 22, Wilhelmine 20			
Augusta 16, Charlotte 14, August 11			
Ferdinand 10, Bertha 11m			
KINEMANN, Heinr.	18	Wicklinghsn.	66-1327
KING, Anselm	27	Mariazell	64-0687
Christine 30			
KINKELDEY, Carl	31	Holzhausen	63-0053
KINNE, Catharine	25	Steinau	66-0576
KINNER, Hugo	25	Kenzingen	64-1022
KINNSCHUH, G.	26	Humboldstadt	66-1248
KINSKY, Rob.	22	Rikken	66-1243
KINSTLE, Joh. Mart	27	Bronnweiler	63-0296
KIPP, Minna	26	Emmerich	65-0402
KIPPUS, Andreas	40	Rothenzimmern	66-0704
KIRBERT, Henry W.	29	Markendorf	63-1218
KIRCH, Jost	28	Roemershausen	66-0984
KIRCHDOERFER, J.G.	43	Neckarems	66-0346
Christiane 41, Christian 8, Carl 5			
Ernst 2			
KIRCHEIS, Anna El.	27	Darmstadt	63-0482
KIRCHENBAUM, P'lne	24	Ulm	66-1093
KIRCHENDOERFFER, M	26	Eickenau	63-0693
KIRCHER, August	30	Dermbach	66-0679
Catharina 27, Marie 62, Ida 4, Adam 35			
baby 1m			
KIRCHER, Franz	38	Ulple	67-0007
Margarethe 37, Helene 16, Charles 15			
Johannes 7			
KIRCHER, Johannes	30	Eisenach	64-1053
KIRCHER, Otto	22	Carlsruhe	64-1053
Max 18			
KIRCHGESSNER, Sab.	19	Reinsheim	66-1327
KIRCHHOF, A.	38	Lahausen	64-0495
KIRCHHOF, Chr.	39	New York	63-1136
Catharina 62			
KIRCHHOFF, August	19	Rosenfeld	66-0984
KIRCHHOFF, Elise	25	Magdeburg	66-1155
KIRCHHOFF, Francis	33	Verl	63-0244
KIRCHHOFF, Friedr.	29	Oelsburg	66-0679
Heinrich 3			
KIRCHHOFF, Gustav	30	Chicago	63-0953
KIRCHHOFF, H.	24	Brinkum	65-0974
KIRCHHOFF, Paul	14	Berlin	63-0482
KIRCHHOFF, Rud.	30	Heiligenstadt	64-0214
KIRCHHOFF, Th.	35	Kiel	63-0350
KIRCHHOLD, Alb.	25	Duesseldorf	66-1313
KIRCHMANN, Heinr.	23	Grossmengels	66-0412
KIRCHMEYER, Friedr	32	Oldenburg	66-1373
KIRCHNER, Carl Jul	32	Erfurt	67-0795
KIRCHNER, Conrad	20	Grieselbach	64-0739
KIRCHNER, Friedr.	29	Germany	66-0666
KIRCHNER, Friedr.L	25	Suhl	63-1069
KIRCHNER, H.	21	Ludwigsburg	66-1313
KIRCHNER, Karl	16	Ostheim	66-0650
KIRCHNER, Michael	24	Gross Karben	66-0668
KIRCHNER, Philpine	30	Dermbach	67-0007
KIRCHNER, Regine	14	Himbach	66-1327
KIRCHNER, Sus.	37	Mannsbach	63-0551
William 6, Regina 3, Ferdinand 10m			
KIRKHAEFER, Carol.	37	Duenow	65-0038
KIRKMANN, August	27	Bachholzhsn.	65-0950
Charlotte 27, Wilhelmine 1			
KIRN, Christ.	23	Mainz	63-1178
KIRN, Theodor	18	Nehsaz	63-0693
KIRNBERGER, Franz	54	Neufurgweisen	64-0739
KIRNER, Jos.	28	Switzerland	64-0073
Nicolas 25			
KIRSCH, Therese	26	Prussia	64-0138
KIRSCHBAUM, August	23	Posen	66-0578
KIRSCHBAUM, Levi	72	Hoerste	66-1031
KIRSCHNA, W.	38	Weyer	63-1003
M. 38, P. 40, E. 9, M. 5			
KIRSCHNER, Ferd. P	30	Hersfeld	64-0886
KIRSTEIN, Emilie	30	Labes	66-1155
KIRSTING, Dina	30	Stadtlohn	66-0349
KISKER, Ernst Hch.	47	Buer	64-0920
Maria Elis. 46, Ernst Heinr. 19			
Joh. Friedr. 16, Heinr. Wm. 13, Louise 9			
Maria Elis 16, Carl Heinr. 6			
KISSEL, Babette	25	Worms	66-1031
KISSEL, Berthold	22	Aurich	66-0734
KISSEL, Robert	27	Preusskotten	66-0469
KISSLING, Anton	18	Huchelheim	66-0734
KISSLING, Chris.	57	Hochelheim	63-0953
KISSLING, Chrs.	28	Southhampton	66-0934
KISSLING, Hermann	29	Berlin	66-0934
Marie 24			
KISSLING, Hrch.	19	Hochelheim	64-0992
KISSLING, Johanna	24	Ebersdorf	65-0402
KISSNER, Johann	30	Sachsen-Mein.	66-0349
Anna 33, August 4, Louise 23, Oscar 4			
Emilie 1			
KISTER, Benedict	16	Steinbach	66-0221
KISTLER, Louis	33	Boston	64-0432
KITTEL, Richard	19	Uhlsteat	66-0984
KITTERER, Friedr.	27	Ludwigsburg	64-1053
Emilie 24			
KITTLER, A.	27	New York	63-1085
KITTLER, Carl	19	Schoenhagen	66-1327
KITTMANN, Joh.	21	Battbergen	66-1373
KITZ, Ernst	20	Langenhain	63-1038
KITZHAUPT, Friedr.	24	Wiesloch	66-1203
Bertha 24			
KITZMEYER, Michael	50	Erlbach	66-1203
Mathilde 27			
KLAAS, Elisabeth	19	Nuertingen	66-0413
KLAAS, Martin	26	Goulsheim	66-0704
KLAAS, Wm.	34	Sulingen	63-1003
KLABAT, Joseph	40	Oberbrois/Boh	65-0038
Anna 28			
KLABER, Joseph	25	Colmar/France	66-0346
Maria 21			
KLADEK, Anton	35	Kusenberg	66-1155
Anna 28, Anton 6, Joseph 4, Franz 2			
Anna 6m			
KLAEGER, Matthaeus	19	Engenhausen	66-0147
KLAG, Christine	27	Bavaria	63-0822
KLAGES, Diedr.	24	Verden	64-0992
KLAIBER, A.	25	Gauselfingen	63-1003
KLAIBER, Mathias	23	Wuerttemberg	64-0432
KLAKKENGA, Jjaak	23	Loquard	66-0349
KLAMMUENGER, Heinr	40	Cornbach	66-0666
Anna Susanne 22, Johann 14, Heinrich 11			
Catharina 7, Conrad 19			
KLANDER, Johann	25	Munkowatsch	66-0650
Marie 18			
KLANKE, Heinr.	19	Minden	65-1031
KLAPPENBURG, Fr'dr	20	New York	63-0015
KLAPPENBURG, Helen	28	Ellwuerden	65-0007
KLAR, C.O.	26	Leipzig	63-1003
KLAR, Moritz	17	Lengsfeld/Sax	64-0920
KLARE, Fr.	34	Indiana	66-0934
KLARE, Heinr.	28	Algermissen	64-0687
Josepha 25, Hr. 11m, H. 26			

NAME	AGE	RESIDENCE	YR-LIST
KLARZBACH, Christ.	18	Lengsfeld	66-1128
KLAS, Henriette	25	Amsweiler	64-0840
KLAS, Jacob	25	Kirnsulzbach	65-0116
KLASEN, Louis	22	Papenburg	66-1093
KLASING, Carl	22	Frille	64-0214
Carl 9, Friedr. 15			
KLASING, Sophia	21	Rahden	65-1088
KLASS, Hannchen	24	Tempelberg	64-0214
KLATANDA, Franz	17	Lutz	66-1155
KLATT, Carl	46	Mildenen	64-0992
Augusta 33, Carl 6, Albert 3, Wilhelm 3m			
KLATT, Heinrich	25	Borenberg	66-0837
KLATT, Pauline	19	Posen	66-0837
J. Michael 15			
KLATT, Rich.	20	Elbing	63-0168
KLATTE, G.	38	Varel	65-0974
Adelheid 30, Catharine 7, Heinrich 5			
Johann 3, Albert 9m			
KLATTE, Johann	17	Bremen	64-1022
KLATTENBERG, Gerh.	28	Thunum	63-0296
Ette 26			
KLATTENHOF, Joh.	27	Oldenburg	66-0469
KLATZ, Catharina	23	Reichenbach	64-0363
KLATZ, Franz	29	Heidelberg	63-1069
KLAUBER, L.(f)	31	Boehmen	64-0495
Aler. 13			
KLAUBER, Maria	16	Zubirow	66-0734
KLAUPRECHT, Emil	46	Cincinnati	63-0168
KLAUS, H.(m)	16	Steinau	64-0495
KLAUS, Heinr.	27	Stapelfeld	65-0116
Anton 31			
KLAUSING, Clara M.	59	Riensloh	63-1010
Marie 19			
KLAUSLI, Johannes	30	Hachfelden	65-0243
Adam 20			
KLAUSNER, Wilhelm	21	Ulm	67-0007
KLAUSS, Josepha	58	Biesendorf	65-1030
Leocadia 18, Emil 16			
KLAWITTER, Lorenz	21	Fuetz	64-0687
KLAYDA, Joh.	33	Posen	67-0795
KLEBER, Joh. Ad.	59	Kindenheim	65-0007
Marg. 57, Joh. 27, Marg. 22, Cath. 20			
Marie 16, Magd. 10, Joh.Phil. 30			
Cath. 28, Wilh. 9, Phil. 6, Adam 4			
KLEBER, Peter	22	Wuertemberg	66-0679
KLEBERG, Julchen	22	Silkerhausen	64-1053
KLEE, Cath.	21	Kleinstadt	64-0782
KLEE, Christian	40	Osterndorf	64-0992
Margrethe 21			
KLEE, Conrad	37	Luederbach	64-0739
KLEE, Doris	18	Dorum	66-0704
KLEE, Gesche	26	Nortauen	66-0666
KLEE, Heinrich	18	Bielefeld	66-1313
KLEE, Jacob	24	Reichenbach	64-0170
KLEE, Johannes	38	Hatzbach	66-0666
KLEE, Ludwig	33	Riedberg	64-0992
KLEE, Maria	26	Niederaula	63-0482
KLEEBOLTE, Fr.	26	Oestereiden	65-0038
Elisab. 23, Maria 11m			
KLEEKAMP, Heinr.	23	Detmold	64-1108
KLEEMANN, Jacob	30	New York	66-0704
KLEEMANN, Louis	32	Osthofen	63-0953
KLEEMEIER, Diedr.	26	Bremen	66-0072
KLEEMEIER, H.	36	Rottwalde	63-0953
KLEEMEYER, Adelh'd	21	Intschede	66-0704
KLEEN, Almt.	20	Holltrup	66-0578
KLEEN, Cath.	18	Langenhausen	65-0948
KLEENE, At.(m)	32	Withmund	64-0331
KLEENE, Louise	36	Wittmund	64-0331
KLEFFNER, Gertrud	23	Udorf	66-0734
KLEFORM, Elisabeth	7	Jawe	64-0886
KLEHER, Pierre	38	Holland	63-0350
Catharina 34			
KLEIBACKER, Adelh.	58	Hannover	64-0920
Cath. M. 16, Joh. Diedr. 14			
KLEIDER, Julius	39	Pferden	66-1128
KLEIER, Elisabeth	39	Cincinnati	63-1038
KLEIMANN, Aloys A.	19	Steele	66-0704

NAME	AGE	RESIDENCE	YR-LIST
KLEIN, Adam	42	Michigan	63-0752
KLEIN, Adolf	41	Mainz	65-0950
KLEIN, Anna	26	Naborn	65-0402
Niedas 28, Maria 32, M.(f) 10, Nic. 7			
Fannie 5, Cath. 3, Peter 11m			
KLEIN, Armin	19	Ungarn	63-1136
KLEIN, August	38	New York	63-0097
KLEIN, Cathr.	19	Nussbaum	65-0243
KLEIN, Charlotte	26	Detmold	66-0934
Marie 22			
KLEIN, Eleonore	55	Posen	64-0427
Caroline 27, Marie 9m, Fanny 29			
KLEIN, Elisabeth	53	Elsfleth	65-1088
KLEIN, Elisabeth	10	Niedermohr	65-0950
KLEIN, Elisabeth	24	Stockheim	64-0739
KLEIN, Emilie	21	Bremerhaven	63-1218
KLEIN, Garmer Harm	27	Sachcaldinne	66-0349
KLEIN, Heinr.	23	Donseiden	64-0023
KLEIN, Heinrich	36	Weimar	64-0433
KLEIN, Henry W.	25	Baltimore	63-0862
KLEIN, Herman	33	Hage	67-0806
Christine 38, Hermine 4, Friederike 1			
Maria 5m			
KLEIN, Isaac	30	Pesth/Ungarn	65-0898
Therese 21, Johann 9m			
KLEIN, Jacob	14	Bamberg	65-0189
KLEIN, Joh.	23	Reutlingen	65-0151
KLEIN, Joh. A.	55	Oese	65-0948
Margarethe 18			
KLEIN, Johann	22	Waldmanshofen	66-0083
KLEIN, Johannes	20	Wichmausdorf	66-1127
KLEIN, John	30	New York	63-1218
KLEIN, John Nic.	25	Thalboeckelhm	63-1178
KLEIN, Julie	19	Putzenried	66-0679
Juditha 25			
KLEIN, Louise	21	Neuenkirchen	66-1203
KLEIN, Ludmilla	17	Boehmen	66-0576
Elisabeth 24			
KLEIN, Marg.	15	Fuerth	63-0752
KLEIN, Marie	58	Schoonenburg	63-0006
Barbara 24, Antonia 17			
KLEIN, Marie	24	Posen	63-0990
Bertha 22			
KLEIN, Martin	35	Ockstadt	64-0739
KLEIN, Mathias	21	Brecin	66-0734
KLEIN, Moritz	32	Pest	64-0938
Anna 24, Nelly 3m			
KLEIN, Otto	32	Posen	64-0427
KLEIN, Peter	19	Merkelbach	67-0007
KLEIN, Peter	24	Saarburg	65-0189
Michel 30, Elise 25			
KLEIN, Wilhelm	26	Diepenau	66-0349
KLEINBAUER, Mich.	31	Demba	64-0433
Josepha 24			
KLEINBEIN, Ludwig	27	Aetluken	66-1248
Sophie 33, Emilie 1			
KLEINE, Christ.	59	Westphalen	66-0704
Marie 59, Caroline 23			
KLEINE, J.E.H.	31	Bettrup	65-1030
Wilhelmine 24			
KLEINER, Franz	17	Glandorf	66-1127
KLEINER, Samuel	58	Aargau	66-0412
Anna Cath. 63, Johannes 24, Johannes 3			
KLEINEWEBER, C.H.	25	Ahls	65-1088
KLEINFELDER, Heinr	40	Duedelsheim	64-0886
Anna M. 22, Dorothea 7, Carl 4			
Heinrich 10m			
KLEINHAMMER, Juerg	23	Neuenwolde	67-0007
KLEINHEIM, Anna	19	Wetter	66-0623
KLEINKE, Georg	17	Duderstadt	66-1128
KLEINKNECHT, Marg.	19	Bietigheim	63-0296
KLEINLEIN, Jonath.	36	Heidersbach	63-0398
Marie 36, Dorette 6, Jobst 2			
KLEINMAYER, Johann	34	Wuerttemberg	66-0083
Margarethe 31, Desidecius 3			
KLEINMEYER, Alwin	24	Oxxede	64-1206
Caroline 30			
KLEINPETER, Ferd.	9	Rastadt	63-1178

NAME	AGE	RESIDENCE	YR-LIST
KLEINSCHMIDT, Bern	55	Schale	65-0770
Catharine 54, Bernhard 32, Marie 22			
Joh. Heinr. 18, Adelheid 14			
KLEINSCHMIDT, Carl	3	Birkenfeld	64-0840
KLEINSCHMIDT, Carl	19	Cassel	65-0594
KLEINSCHMIDT, Chr.	27	Laudenbach	66-1248
KLEINSCHMIDT, Emil	24	Cassel	64-0782
KLEINSCHMIDT, F.	27	Seelenfeld	65-1024
KLEINSCHMIDT, Frdr	18	Groning	66-0469
KLEINSCHMIDT, G.L.	15	Schale	65-1024
KLEINSCHMIDT, Gust	18	Landeck	66-1373
KLEINSCHMIDT, Hch.	27	Prussia	63-0822
Marie 30, Bernh. H. 4, Elisabeth 22			
KLEINSCHMIDT, Joh.	16	Cobecke	66-1203
KLEINSCHMIDT, Marg	21	Reinheim	63-1069
KLEINSCHMIDT, Wilh	31	Nassau	66-0576
KLEINSCHREDT, C(m)	26	Oberkoch	64-0331
KLEINSINGEN, Andr.	24	Grosspura	64-0739
KLEINSINN, Friedr.	30	Bremen	63-0822
KLEISCHKA, Vinz.	28	America	63-0917
KLEIST, Wilhelmine	28	Niwer-Schleim	66-0650
Ewan 25			
KLEIT, Frz.	18	Steinheim	64-0170
KLEMM, Jacob	24	Gausengeim	64-0363
KLEMME, Christian	29	Hummersen	66-0576
Wilhelmine 28, Heinrich 4, Wilhelmine 5m			
KLENCKE, H.C.	23	Rehdingbruch	64-0073
KLENEKUTE, Marg.	22	Varensell	66-1203
KLENERT, Cath.	32	Willfahrtswlr	66-1313
KLENK, John	42	Creglingen	63-0953
Marie 33, Philipp 15, Leonhard 9			
William 8, Cathr. 3, Hermann 9m			
KLENK, Rosine	21	Ziegelbronn	66-1327
Catharine 29			
KLENKE, Johann	34	New York	64-0363
Cath. 24, Johann 7, George 5, Cath. 3			
Hch. 10m, Cath. 64			
KLENNER, Rob.	23	Freiburg	65-0189
KLENSCH, G.	42	Wuerttemberg	63-1085
KLENSKI, Elisabeth	35	Pozegnowa	66-0349
Johanna 4, Frida 2, baby 6m			
KLEPAT, Wenzel	23	Boehmen	66-0349
Caroline 35, baby 9m			
KLESS, Cresentin	26	Hanau	66-1093
KLETGE, Aug.	33	Ratha	66-0413
Henr. 33, Friedrich 4, Charlotte 10m			
KLETGE, F.	26	Ratha	66-0413
KLETH, Eugen	18	Dettingen	66-1155
K. 19			
KLETSCHEN, Henr'tt	25	Bromberg	64-0456
KLETT, Christine	21	Welzheim	63-0482
KLETT, Louise	24	Suhl	65-1088
KLEWES, Anton	29	Buehren	63-0953
KLEY, Gottlieb	20	Loewenstein	66-0576
KLEY, Gustav Fr'dr	16	Berkach	64-0433
KLEY, Harriet	17	Luebeck	64-0938
KLEYBOR, Franz	24	Preussen	63-0398
Constantine 24, Nathalie inf			
KLEYH, Johannes		Dettingen	66-1093
KLEYLA, Joh.	23	Bayern	64-0432
Babette 20			
KLEYNA, Marie	19	Nemish	66-1327
KLIE, Joseph	19	Heiligenstadt	64-0920
KLIEMANN, Fr'dke.	28	Hannover	66-1373
Dorette 7, Heinrich 6, Anna 2, Theodor 9m			
KLINCKERMANN, Frd.	28	Germany	66-0666
KLING, Elis.	23	Wieseck	64-0593
KLING, Heinr.	14	Umstadt	65-0189
KLING, Maria	24	Cassel	66-1248
KLING, Peter	26	Grosssachsen	64-0170
KLING, Peter	52	Loehrbach	66-1373
Barbara 50			
KLINGBLUM, Maria	55	Spengen	66-0623
KLINGE, A.	25	Cappeln	64-0665
KLINGE, Carl	59	Hessen	66-0734
Charlotte 54, Georg 9			
KLINGE, Catharina	17	Rhoda	65-1031
KLINGE, Louis	15	Cassel	65-0770

NAME	AGE	RESIDENCE	YR-LIST
KLINGEBEIL, Conr.	36	Adensen	64-0687
Heinr. 15, Hannchen 18			
KLINGEL, August	24	Pforzheim	64-1053
Louise 21, Carl 18			
KLINGEL, Karl	20	Heilbronn	63-1069
KLINGELHOEFER, C.	25	Marburg	65-1088
KLINGELHOEFER, Con	17	Rauschenberg	66-0412
KLINGELHOEFER, Wm.	20	Marburg	66-1327
KLINGENBERG, Fr'dr	31	Posen	64-0456
Theodor 8			
KLINGENBERG, Wm.	58	Mollenbeck	64-0343
Johanna 21			
KLINGENSTEIN, v.M.	26	Vienna	64-1022
KLINGER, Christ.	27	Waiblingen	66-0346
KLINGER, Rosa	28	Malsch	65-0007
KLINGERBERG, Aug.	40	New York	66-0984
KLINGERMEIER, Joh.	27	Heuchlingen	66-0083
KLINGMANN, Cather.	31	Sulzbach	63-0482
KLINK, Francisca	24	Basel	64-1053
KLINKA, Wenzl	32	Soltuschen	64-0886
KLINKER, Albert	17	Affinghausen	66-0704
KLINNERT, W.	24	Arensdorf	65-0974
KLINSCH, Elisabeth	57	Boehmen	63-1085
KLINZINGER, Mich.	18	Kaiserach	64-0639
KLIPFEL, Balthasar	32	Weixweil	66-0109
KLIPPER, F.(m)	24	Melsungen	64-0214
KLIPPER, Franz	29	Hannover	66-1155
KLITTICH, Wilhelm	18	Baden	66-1155
KLITZSCH, Carl	56	Callenberg	66-1327
KLIXMANN, Theodor	25	Osnabrueck	65-0594
KLOCK, Georg	25	Edingheim	64-0214
KLOCKE, Franz	19	Bruchhausen	66-1313
KLOCKE, Herm.	23	Kirchweyhe	64-0495
KLOCKE, Louise	19	Walldorf	67-0007
KLOCKZIEM, Wilhelm	50	Pommern	66-0469
Sophie 48, Caroline 22, Johanna 14			
Wilhelmine 7			
KLOECKER, Christ.	30	Wald	63-1136
KLOEDTMANN, Friedr	20	Hamm	66-1131
KLOEFER, Johanna	29	Bueckeburg	66-1127
KLOEPPER, Adelheid	14	Suestedt	66-0221
KLOER, Franz	58	Altenburg	66-0934
Ernestine 55, Mathilde 26, Ernst 15			
Hugo 13			
KLOER, Marie	26	Arnsberg	65-0189
August 9m, Francisca 23			
KLOES, Conrad	35	Hausen	65-1088
Anna 32, Catharina 5, baby 10m			
KLOES, Mathilde	22	Niederhessing	64-1108
Amalie 15			
KLOESS, Augusta	19	Steinfurt	63-0296
William 32			
KLOETZ, Christ	23	New York	66-0934
KLOETZ, Christ.	19	Marburg	63-0244
KLOHR, Philipp	23	Mussbach	65-0055
KLOOS, Alois	22	Hannover	66-0221
KLOOS, Peter	29	Putzbach	66-0412
KLOPF, Joseph	33	Krieselhausen	64-0343
Johanna 21			
KLOPFER, Christian	17	Laufen	63-1069
KLOPFER, Ernst	17	Verdame	64-0938
KLOPPENBURG, Elise	67	San Francisco	66-0734
Dina 40			
KLOPPENBURG, F.W.	29	New Orleans	64-0432
KLOPPER, Alfred	18	Muenchen	66-0147
KLOPPER, Bernhard	40	Vehlen	65-0948
Catharina 40, Elisabeth 11m			
KLOPPER, Hermann	26	Lengerich	66-1373
KLOPPNER, Ernst	28	Uslar	65-1024
Marie 25			
KLOSE, Carl	37	Frankfurt	65-0770
KLOSE, Hermann	22	Jauer	65-0004
KLOSE, Richard	24	Preussen	66-0147
KLOSTERMANN, Heinr	31	Muenster	66-0704
KLOSTERMANN, Otto	24	Goldenstedt	64-0920
KLOSTERMANN, Susan	19	Bentheim	66-1093
KLOTH, Alwine	24	Romansart	63-0614
KLOTH, Franz	20	Borgentreich	66-1327

NAME	AGE	RESIDENCE	YR-LIST
Carl 18			
KLOTZ, S.	24	Pforzheim	66-0109
KLOTZ, Sellin	18	Pforzheim	64-0023
KLOTZ, Wm.	20	Rudersberg	65-0189
KLOTZBACH, W.(m)	20	Cassel	64-0214
KLUBERG, Moses	18	Wilfhagen	66-1248
KLUEMPER, Elisabet	77	Cloppenburg	63-1038
KLUES, Anton	25	Wettrup	64-0343
KLUETER, Doris	35	Hannover	66-0734
KLUG, Albrecht	31	Dahl	66-1203
KLUG, Franz E.	36	Reichenbach	63-0821
KLUG, Georg,	24	Batten	67-0007
KLUG, Joh. (f)	20	Furnau	65-0189
KLUG, Johann	24	Tochen	66-1155
Friederike 24, Gottfried 3			
KLUG, Wilhelm	24	Groning	66-0469
Henriette 26			
KLUGE, Eduard	23	Gotha	65-0865
KLUGE, Friedrich	45	Hardisleben	63-0917
Therese 36, Alma 9, Char. 5, baby 10m			
Hermann 59			
KLUGE, Henriette	16	Cassel	66-1127
KLUGE, Hermann	19	Bramstedt	66-0221
KLUH, Wolfgang	26	Altenhof	66-0147
KLULL, Hedwig	18	Haste	63-1085
KLUMP, Bernhard	24	Baiersbronn	66-0679
KLUNDER, Heinr.	50	Luttorf	64-0495
Wilhelmine 47, Friedrich 18, Wilhelm 6			
Marie 5, Wilhelm 3			
KLUNE, Louise	36	Wittmund	64-0331
KLUNKEFORT, Carl	50	Bork	66-0984
KLUNT, Louis	16	Basel	64-1053
Suzanne 18			
KLUNZINGEN, Carl	28	Aufhausen	65-0948
KLUSMANN, Heinrich		Hoboken	66-1031
KLUSMANN, Louise	22	Bassum	63-1218
KLUSMANN, Rud.	21	Bassum	63-0482
KLUSMEYER, Carl	27	Uchte	66-1313
KLUSSMEYER, Friedr	29	Lohe	66-1313
Dorette 23, Wilhelm 6, Fritz 3, Doris 1			
KLUSSMEYER, Heinr.	18	Lohe	66-1313
Dietr. 16, Chr. 25, Marie 21, Heinrich 1			
KLUTE, Joh.H.	28	Wulften	65-0898
KLUTT, Franz	19	Deutsch Krone	64-0687
KLYSING, Rudolph	28	Weissenstein	66-1203
KNAB, Elise	21	Speyer	63-0097
KNAB, Marie	26	Baun	64-0138
KNABE, Emilie	25	Neumark	66-0734
KNABE, Fr. Bernh.	52	Altenburg	64-0432
Fr. Herm. 21			
KNABE, Heinrich	17	Rusfort	66-1093
KNABE, Philip	27	Gladenbach	65-0402
KNABEL, Jos.	34	Laneck	64-0073
KNACK, Ad.	34	Prussia	63-1003
Christine 43, Wilhelmine 22, Martha 18			
Pauline 15, William 9, Bertha 6			
Caroline 8, M. 33, M. 10, B. 8, Aug. 4			
KNACKE, J.	45	Oldenburg	63-0097
KNACKE, Sophie	24	Knickhagen	64-0214
KNACKSTEDT, Henr't	25	Hannover	66-1373
Heinrich 8			
KNAPP, Josephine	22	Neustadt	64-1022
KNAPP, Rudolph	29	Philadelphia	63-0244
Susanne 26, Anna 4, Frank 2, baby 9m			
KNAPP, Therese	18	Baden	66-0576
KNAPP, Valentin	22	Eppenheim	65-0770
KNAPPER, Emilie	23	Muscheid	63-1085
KNAPPLE, Joseph	20	Wimpfen	66-1248
KNAUE, Carl	17	Gehrde	64-1161
KNAUER, Elise	16	Gehrde	66-1093
KNAUFF, Nicolaus	18	Steina	66-1031
KNAUFT, J.W.A.	29	Soemmerda	63-0990
KNAUS, Christ. Got	35	Shorndorf	63-0482
Johanna 31, Christ. Gott 9m			
KNAUS, Christiane	26	Michelau	63-0482
KNAUS, Elise	33	Zeustern	65-0116
KNEBEL, H.(m)	24	Hose	64-0170
KNECHT, Ad.	28	Menzingen	65-0007
KNECHT, G.	24	Sulingen	64-0639
KNECHT, Gottlieb	19	Bempflingen	66-1203
KNEEB, Anna	30	Gang	64-0023
Johanna 21			
KNEF, Joseph	23	Bayern	63-0398
KNEIF, Dorothea	24	Rodenberg	67-0599
Engel 18			
KNEISEL, C.(m)	14	Blankenheim	64-0331
KNELL, Anton	26	Hundsfeld	64-0687
KNELL, John	36	Magdeburg	63-0990
KNERINGER, Jos.	42	Pfundt	65-0594
KNERR, Ernst	39	Baltimore	63-0244
KNEUER, Adam	29	Eltmann	66-0346
KNIDERA, Wenzel	35	Boehmen	66-0349
KNIEBEL, W.	25	Gaisberg	65-1189
KNIELING, Georg	30	Bremenhaven	65-0243
KNIELING, Marie	21	Meiningen	66-0576
KNIELING, Roselle	17	Gmuenden	66-0984
KNIERIM, Cath.	30	Alsfeld	64-0687
KNIPPENBERG, Emil	30	Osnabrueck	65-0865
Anna 19			
KNITTEL, Elisabeth		Tollnaishof	66-1373
KNITTEL, Friedrich	19	Constanz	66-0147
KNITTEL, Gustav	28	Gera	66-0934
Anna 23, Minna 5, Marie 2, Robert 6m			
KNIVEN, Franz	25	Klosterholte	65-1095
KNOBBE, Joseph	21	Meppen	65-0950
KNOBBE, Julius	29	Essen	65-0865
Gertrude 27			
KNOBEL, Reinhard	57	Ehler	66-1155
KNOBLAUCH, A.	17	Schorndorf	64-0782
Emilie 22			
KNOBLAUCH, Joh.	27	Bremen	66-1248
KNOBLAUCH, Johann	26	Coblenz	65-1031
KNOBLOCH, Anton	29	Selz	66-1203
KNOBLOCH, Carl	22	Lauba	66-1373
KNOBLOCH, Christ.	23	Knillingen	66-1203
KNOBLOCK, Cath.	25	Duerkheim	64-0331
KNOCHE, A.	26	Friedelsloh	66-0413
Martha 26			
KNOCHE, Ferd.	39	Zerssen	63-0482
KNOCHE, Fritz	25	Eistrup	67-0007
KNOCHE, Heinrich	17	Marienhagen	65-0898
KNOCHENHAUER, H.	36	Verden	63-0953
KNOCK, Caroline	30	Lauterbach	66-0412
Augusta 2, Elisabeth 6m			
KNOCKE, Wilh.	20	Schluesslburg	65-0950
KNOCKSTEDT, Ludwig	47	Bremen	66-1248
Maria 48, Adolphine 19, August 16			
Louis 12, Wilhelm 7, Anna 6, Georg 1			
KNODERER, Magd.	30	Kenzingen	64-1022
KNOEBEL, Diedr.	20	Warfleth	65-1024
KNOEDLER, Anna	24	Siefertshofen	66-1373
KNOEHN, Anna	23	Altdorf	66-1155
KNOEHR, Barbara	17	Stuttgart	66-1093
KNOEPFLE, Marie	30	New York	66-0576
KNOEPFLER, Emilie	18	Strasburg	63-0482
KNOEPKE, Agnes	26	Flatow	66-1327
Hugo 8			
KNOEPPEL, Daniel	35	Rosenthal	65-1030
Katharine 37, Adam 12, Anna Kath. 9			
Martha Elis. 7, Kath.Louise 2, Johann 60			
KNOERR, Charlotte	46	Soden	66-1327
KNOESEL, Julius	30	Altenburg	66-1373
Emilie 22			
KNOETLER, Rosine	18	Wetzheim	63-1085
KNOETTNER, Max	17	Asch	66-0679
KNOFF, Friedrich	33	Sachsen-Mein.	66-0349
Margareth 37, Louise 7, Ferdinand 2m			
Emil 4			
KNOFF, Joh. Valent	41	Sachsen-Mein.	66-0349
Christiane 34, Margarethe 59, Anna 12			
Ernestine 7, Margareth 9, Christiane 5			
Christian 1, wiife 30, John 5			
KNOKE, Friedr.	19	Osnabrueck	64-0363
KNOLL, Ant.	36	Rottweil	64-0782
KNOLL, Charles	19	Straubing	63-0821
KNOLL, P. Cyrillus	50	Staubing	64-0427

NAME	AGE	RESIDENCE	YR-LIST
KNOOP, Almer	18	Rechtenfleth	64-1108
J.H. 20			
KNOOP, Charles Hnr	27	Dresden	66-1155
KNOOP, Christiane	20	Bremen	63-0821
W ilhelmine 4m			
KNOOP, F.(m)	22	Bremen	64-0363
W.(m) 20			
KNOOP, Fritz	20	Rechterfleth	66-1155
KNOOP, Gerhard	26	Bremen	64-0363
KNOOP, Herm.	37	Bremen	63-1218
KNOOP, Johann	24	Eitelborn	66-1203
Jacob 36, Joseph 25			
KNOOP, Louise	30	Bremen	63-0752
Louise 9, Ludwig 8, Dorothea 6, Mathias 4			
Meta 9m			
KNOOP, Ludwig	39	Bremen	64-0363
Rebecca 33, Ludwig 8, Johann 6			
Wilhelm 9m			
KNOOP, Mathias	28	Bremen	64-0363
Ludwig 4m, Gesina 41, Gerhardina 9			
Hermann 8, Gustav 6, Helene 4, Mathias 9m			
KNOOS, Louise	17	Rudersberg	64-1206
KNOP, Hilke	53	Aurich	64-0433
Adolph 14			
KNOPF, Maria A.	15	Diehlheim	64-0687
KNOPP, Leopold	57	Pest	66-0984
KNORR, Barbara	21	Bettenhausen	66-1155
KNORR, Bernh.	23	Bassum	66-1373
KNORR, Henry	45	Eisfeld	63-0482
Caroline 38, Augusta 13, Eduard 9			
Emilie 7, Sophie 5, Caroline 3			
KNORR, Jacob Fr.	21	Barrenberg	66-0704
KNORR, Johanna	30	Stuttgart	65-0402
KNOST, Caspar	60	Altenmelle	64-0938
KNOST, Christian	19	Niedernrehnen	64-0739
KNOTECK, J.	36	Wien	64-0782
KNOTH, Doris	14	Uchte	64-0427
KNOTH, Maria	28	Tann	66-0349
Herm. 28			
KNOTHE, Emil	32	Salzungen	65-1088
KNOTT, Margarethe	56	Meiningen	66-0576
Nicolaus 24			
KNOTTE, John	58	Weckshaeusche	63-0990
Mathilde 22, Cuno 18, Bertha 25			
KNUBEL, Alb.	30	Burhave	63-0953
KNUEBER, J.	24	Wortfleth	63-1038
Louise			
KNUEBLER, Martin	17	Ueberberg	66-1373
Margarethe 27			
KNUEPER, Vitus	21	Hainigen	66-1243
KNUEVER, Gerhard	25	Schuettdorf	66-0666
Arend 23			
KNUMEYER, Marie	24	Herford	66-1031
KOBBE, Fr.	36	Vollbuettel	63-1178
KOBBE, H.	36	Braunschweig	64-0331
Johanna 21			
KOBELTISCH, Math.	27	Zerdiensdorf	65-0948
KOBER, Karl August	22	Sachsen	66-0578
KOBER, Laura	25	Coeslin	66-1203
Paul 1			
KOBERER, Georg	38	New York	63-0097
KOBERT, Carl	24	Lingen	66-1093
KOBIGER, Ernst	34	Coburg	67-0007
KOBLER, Catharine	22	Kugelwalt	63-1085
KOBLER, Christiane	16	Kobelwald	64-1108
Elisabeth 7, Bertha 5			
KOBLER, Joseph	32	New York	63-0752
KOBLER, Theo.	13	Haardt	64-1108
KOBLESCHECH, G.	47	Iggelheim	64-0023
Johanna 21			
KOBRISCH, Heinr.	20	Rotenburg	65-1031
KOCH, A.L.	41	Greuth	64-0593
KOCH, Andr.	22	Frossingen	63-0990
KOCH, Andreas	30	Euren	63-0990
KOCH, Anna	22	Lamstede	65-0402
KOCH, Barbara	23	Spielberg	66-1327
KOCH, C.H.	32	Braunschweig	66-1248
KOCH, Carl	16	Cassel	66-0221

NAME	AGE	RESIDENCE	YR-LIST
KOCH, Carl	21	Wollmershsn.	67-0007
KOCH, Catharine	21	Gelsungen	64-0433
KOCH, Chr.	26	Kuechheim	63-1085
KOCH, Christian	55	Pommern	66-0469
Christine 56			
KOCH, Christian	22	Rahden	65-1088
KOCH, Christian	27	Berga	64-0739
KOCH, Christine	29	Koesingen	66-0147
KOCH, Christopher	55	Haltenau	63-0693
Emma 41			
KOCH, Conrad	30	Bischofferode	66-1327
KOCH, D.B.	27	Sante Fe	64-0073
KOCH, E.(m)	25	Hansefeld	64-0214
KOCH, Elisabeth	30	Westhofen	66-1093
KOCH, Elisabeth	28	Cassel	65-0865
KOCH, Elise	35	Rossbach	66-0221
KOCH, Elise	21	Oberweimar	66-0469
KOCH, Ernst	19	Eschenhausen	66-1131
KOCH, Francis	25	Ludwigshafen	63-1136
KOCH, Franz J.	19	Boehmen	64-0593
KOCH, Frdr.	23	Halden	64-0138
KOCH, Friedr.	14	Stedessund	67-0599
KOCH, Friedrich	31	Kreiensen	65-0004
KOCH, Fritz	14	Rotenburg	63-0752
KOCH, Georg	59	Lobenhausen	63-0862
KOCH, Georg	27	Hessen	66-0469
KOCH, Georg	33	Minden	66-0984
KOCH, Georg	20	Verden	66-1373
KOCH, Gottfried	35	Prussia	63-0822
KOCH, Gottl.	32	Friedrichshde	64-0665
KOCH, Gottlob	20	Thieningen	64-0433
KOCH, Gregor	19	Hauswury	66-1248
KOCH, H.	50	Gielert	64-0331
Johanna 21			
KOCH, Heinr. Frdr.	38	Hannover	65-0950
KOCH, Heinrich	8	Minden	66-0984
KOCH, Heinrich	23	Hirden	64-0886
KOCH, Helene	25	Kressenbach	63-1069
KOCH, Hendrick	4	Nuttermoor	64-0886
KOCH, Henriette	20	Dissen	64-0023
KOCH, Herm.	30	Bremen	65-0007
Melia 24			
KOCH, Hermann	18	Hannover	66-0984
KOCH, J.	41	Prussia	63-1003
F. 40, R. 10, A. 12			
KOCH, J.(m)	26	Thedinghausen	64-0495
KOCH, Joh.	29	Trostingen	64-0495
KOCH, Joh. Frdr.	18	Hunibach	65-0243
KOCH, Joh. Heinr.	17	Brandert	64-0938
Ernst 16			
KOCH, Johann	24	Worms/Hessen	66-0346
KOCH, Johann	54	Grossvura	64-0739
KOCH, Johannes	49	Cassel	64-0739
KOCH, John	31	Fort Wayne	66-0679
KOCH, John Jos.	30	Olpe	66-1155
Marie Josefa 33			
KOCH, Katharina	29	Motgert	63-1069
KOCH, M.	38	Friederichshd	65-1088
Marie 5, baby 9m			
KOCH, M.	23	Strusberg	65-1024
KOCH, Marie	24	Bebra	66-1327
Anna Cath. 20			
KOCH, Mathias	19	Wuerttemberg	64-0432
KOCH, Mathias	18	Boesingen	66-0147
KOCH, Meta	19	Steinhausen	66-1248
KOCH, P.	20	Bremen	64-1022
KOCH, Peter	16	Ringshausen	66-0704
KOCH, Phil	42	Hattenbach	63-1010
KOCH, Rudolf	36	Goslar	65-0950
KOCH, Rudolph	31	Urach	66-1155
KOCH, Simon	25	Blausingen	64-0363
KOCH, Sophie	41	Philadelphia	63-0917
Marie 16			
KOCH, Theod.	24	Carlshaven	63-0953
KOCH, Theodor	6	Goettingen	66-1155
KOCH, Therese	28	Beelen	65-1024
KOCH, Wilhelm	22	New York	63-0917
KOCHE, Joh.H.F.	30	Borgloh	64-0938

NAME	AGE	RESIDENCE	YR-LIST
Anna M.C. 20, baby 11m, baby 11m			
KOCHEL, Maria	21	Hau	66-1127
KOCHELI, Georg	22	Leuchtkirch	66-1155
KOCHELMANN, Joh.	78	Trabelsdorf	65-1088
KOCHER, Alex.	49	Bueren	63-0752
Alex. 23, Hermann 19			
KOCK, M.	20	Wremen	66-0984
KOCK, Peter	23	Doese	66-0578
KOCKE, Hinrich	48	Curhessen	66-0984
KOCKE, William	24	Hannover	63-0862
KOEBEL, Michel	34	New York	63-0953
KOEBER, Elisabeth	19	Herbstein	64-0840
KOEBERICH, Anna	22	Reichelsdorf	65-1031
KOEBERICH, John	30	Rockenruess	63-0482
Emilie 30			
KOEBERLE, Johann	25	Boehmen	63-0917
Johanna 30			
KOEBERLE, Jos.	29	Insbruck	64-0840
KOEBIG, A.(m)	24	Homburg	65-0189
KOEGLER, Joh.	30	Gelnhausen	64-0938
KOEHER, Gottfr.	24	Dusslingen	65-0116
KOEHL, Catharina	19	Buch	63-0614
KOEHL, Flora	28	Grosenlueder	66-0469
KOEHLER, A.	25	Laubach	65-0974
KOEHLER, Agnes	17	Wiesbaden	64-0687
KOEHLER, Andreas	25	Ruedelern	63-0693
KOEHLER, Anna Cath	26	Bamberg	63-0482
KOEHLER, Augusta	23	Wasungen	66-0734
KOEHLER, Augusta	24	Altenburg	66-1243
KOEHLER, Barbara	32	Boehmen	63-0551
Mary 4, James 3			
KOEHLER, Carl	25	Gera	66-0623
KOEHLER, Carl	32	Nils	66-1155
Claudia 25			
KOEHLER, Caroline	26	Kurhessen	66-0576
Luise 7			
KOEHLER, Catharina	55	Dermbach	66-0679
Valentin 9, Catharina 5			
KOEHLER, Conrad	19	Allendorf	66-0349
KOEHLER, Ernestine	22	Limstein	66-1128
KOEHLER, Ferdinand	22	Oberstetten	66-1155
KOEHLER, Fr.	27	Heppenheim	64-0687
KOEHLER, Geo.	42	Rastadt	63-0168
wife 42, Theodor 2			
KOEHLER, Georg	28	Sax.-Meiningn	64-0432
Elisab. 26, Andr. 9m, Anna Elis. 23			
Johanna 19			
KOEHLER, Heinr.	25	Thedinghausen	64-0593
KOEHLER, Heinrich	46	Ottendorf	66-0837
Katharina 29, Bernhardine 15, Joseph 10			
Franz 8, Elise 18			
KOEHLER, Henni	19	Bremen	63-0482
KOEHLER, Herm.	15	Frienhagen	64-0840
KOEHLER, Joh.	19	Herstelle	64-0593
KOEHLER, John	20	Ostdim	63-0482
KOEHLER, Louis	20	Hildesheim	63-1178
KOEHLER, Ludw.	26	Frankfurt/M	64-0593
KOEHLER, Maria	23	Sachs.-Weimar	66-0349
Theresia 22			
KOEHLER, Maria M.	18	Angersbach	65-1031
Maria 14			
KOEHLER, Marie	24	Wuerttemberg	64-0432
Cath. 19, Cath. 20			
KOEHLER, Matilda	15	Rastede	63-0244
KOEHLER, Paul	16	Wuerttemberg	64-0432
Christ. 18			
KOEHLER, Robert	27	Neustadt	64-0687
KOEHLER, Wm.	19	Arnsberg	65-0116
Therese 26, Augusta 29			
KOEHN, Heinr.	24	Questzau	65-0402
KOEHNE, Andr.	37	Bergfeld	63-0482
Cath. 9, Barbara 18			
KOEHNE, Louis	23	Braunschweig	66-0704
KOEHNE, Therese	24	Luegde	63-0482
KOEHNE, Wm.	42	Fond du Lac	66-0704
KOEHNEN, Catharine	26	Coeln	66-0837
KOELLE, Heinr.	35	Burgstemmen	65-0038
KOELLE, Robert	27	Nuertingen	63-0244
KOELLER, Ferd.	33	Graetz	64-0427
KOELLER, Theresa	17	Stoermede	64-0433
KOELLING, Caroline	18	Kirchkamp	66-0623
KOELLNER, Carsten	41	Eschede	64-0214
Catherine 40, Sophie 9			
KOELLNER, Friedr.	38	Sax.-Meiningn	64-0432
Anna Marg. 37, Friedr. 17, Johannes 14			
Georg 6, Catharina 9m, Elisab. 15			
Johannes 21			
KOELNER, Heinr.	28	Geestendorf	65-0116
KOELSCH, Johann	30	Gilsa	64-0433
KOEMPEL, Conrad	23	Oberlimbach	66-1248
KOENCKE, Christ.	41	Waltinghausen	67-0795
Louise 46, Heinr. 16, Caroline 15			
Friedrich 7			
KOENCKE, Georg	25	Bremen	64-0938
KOENE, Friedrich	25	Hildesheim	66-0469
KOENECKE, H.	24	Pyrmont	65-1031
KOENERDING, Lisett	19	Vechta	66-0984
KOENIG, Alex	20	Augsburg	63-0990
KOENIG, Anna Mar.	25	Kirchheim	63-0097
Christine 11m			
KOENIG, B.	25	Westlevern	65-1088
KOENIG, Carl Aug.	30	Steinbach	66-0578
Ernestine 27, Elise 4, David 2			
August 11m			
KOENIG, Cath.	15	Obermerle	64-0840
KOENIG, Christine	36	Habenhausen	64-0782
baby 11m			
KOENIG, Elisabeth	19	Baiern	64-0214
KOENIG, Emilie	16	Schorndorf	63-1136
KOENIG, Eva	20	Obermarken	66-1155
KOENIG, Fr. Aug.	33	Coeln	65-0116
KOENIG, Friedr.	34	New York	63-0097
KOENIG, Friedr.	42	Preussen	66-0469
KOENIG, Fritz	15	Achim	64-0739
KOENIG, G. Joh.	24	Imsum	64-0840
KOENIG, Georg	57	Dettlingen	66-0349
KOENIG, Helene	20	Schwaren/Hann	65-0038
KOENIG, Joh.	39	Neustadt/Boh.	65-0856
Anna 37, Joseph 11, Therese 9, Marie 5			
KOENIG, Joh. G. Wm	19	Iba	64-0456
KOENIG, Ludwig	23	Wuerttemberg	66-0576
KOENIG, Margarethe	21	Elbersheim	66-1155
Friedr. 19			
KOENIG, Marie	29	Schwebenried	66-0704
KOENIG, Martin	17	Obermoerle	64-1108
KOENIG, Michael	25	Minden	64-1053
Emilie 21, August 4, Albert 1m, Emilie 16			
baby			
KOENIG, Peter	31	Hammerzell	63-0821
KOENIG, Peter	34	Friedrichstal	63-0693
Magdalene 33, Magdalene 2, Caby 1			
KOENIG, Rosine	47	Wien	67-0007
Anna 7, Wilhelm 3			
KOENIG, Wilh.	27	Wuertemberg	63-0398
KOENIG, Wilhelm	8	Erbach	66-0083
Babette 36			
KOENIGEL, Wm.	22	Muenster	64-1053
KOENIGHEIM, Henr't	19	Erkel	64-0739
Johanna 22			
KOENIGSBERG, Leop.	18	Ginesen	64-0992
KOENIGSKRAMER, Frd	22	St. Louis	66-0984
Wilhelm 40			
KOENIGSTEDTEN, Gg.	25	Bremen	67-0954
KOENING, Heinr.	42	New York	63-0551
Helene 42			
KOENKEN, Marie	21	Osnabrueck	65-0865
KOENNECKE, Franz	27	Wackensen	64-0687
KOENNEKER, Chr.	18	Hildesheim	63-1136
KOENNERMANN,		Koenigslutter	63-0244
KOEPKE, H.	14	Wulmsdorfe	66-0704
Wilhelmine 7			
KOEPP, Johann	34	Bromberg	64-0456
KOEPP, Rosalie	27	Bromberg	64-0456
Juliane 6, Johann 4, Herm. 2			
KOEPPING, David	50	Sontra	64-0938
Anna Elisa 49, Martha 7, Marie 5			

NAME	AGE	RESIDENCE	YR-LIST
Joh.Fr. 27			
KOEPPINGER, Friedr	29	Washington	63-0990
Willy 6, Henriette 4			
KOEPPS, Joseph	26	Hannover	66-0734
KOERBER, Elisabeth	68	Rothenburg	66-0704
KOERBER, Elise	38	Goettingen	64-0639
KOERBER, Ernst	22	Eboldhausen	65-0402
Wilhelmine 22			
KOERBER, Gust.	22	Sindelfingen	65-0189
KOERBER, Otto	20	Giessen	64-0904
KOERITZ, C.(f)	22	Nordbruch	64-0495
KOERMIKER, Henr'tt	24	Hildesheim	63-1136
KOERNER, Elias	22	Culmbach	64-0886
KOERNER, Maria	19	Drueber	65-1088
KOERNER, Moritz	17	Kaiserhagen	66-0109
KOERNER, Phil.	23	Hasenheim	65-0402
KOESINGER, Anna E.	24	Speckswinkel	64-0639
KOESTER, Bernh.	30	Schloppingen	65-1088
KOESTER, Carst.	30	Bremen	63-0953
KOESTER, D.(f)	23	Paderborn	64-1108
KOESTER, G. Joh.	65	Weillstadt	65-0594
KOESTER, Heinrich	52	Lengerich	65-1030
Anna Marie 42, Hermann 19, Wilhelmine 26			
Anna Marie 17, Hermann 15			
KOESTER, Henry	31	New York	63-1136
KOESTER, James E.	20	Bokel	63-0097
KOESTER, Jettchen	16	Zimmerrode	64-1206
KOESTER, Joha.Hel.	18	Midlum/Hann	65-0038
KOESTER, Johann		Bremen	66-1128
KOESTER, Johann	25	Lingen	25-0950
KOESTER, Lina	35	New York	63-0398
KOESTER, Nicolaus	36	New York	64-0432
KOESTERS, Wilhelm	20	Oldenburg	67-0007
KOETER, Aug.	21	Rothemitte	64-1108
KOETER, Carl	20	Neustadt	66-0349
Gerhard 52, Charlotte 46, Gerhard 17			
Caroline 15, Friedrich 9, Charlotte 8			
Louise 4			
KOETHE, Emilie	19	Osterode	64-0904
KOETHER, Johanna	31	Helmstedt	65-0189
Willy 2, Sevilla 9m			
KOETKE, Hermann	44	Ulzen	67-0599
Sop. Mar. D. 40, Joh. August 17			
Sop. Mar. D. 15, Ernst Joh. 13			
Christine D. 11, Dorothea 8			
KOETT, Ferdinand	25	Dermbach	66-0679
KOETTE, Anton	24	Asbeck	65-1095
KOETTE, Bernhard	15	Nienburg	65-1095
KOETTER, Anne M.	22	Bobenhausen	66-1313
KOETZEL, Anna	20	Landesbergen	66-1131
KOETZNER, J.	25	Lauter	63-1003
KOFF, Joh. Ph.	26	Ernsthausen	64-1022
KOFFMANN, Gustav	23	Bremen	66-0734
KOGELSCHATZ, Minna	30	St. Louis	64-0363
Bertha 11m			
KOHE, Eduard	54	Wald	63-0752
KOHERR, Rosa	22	Steisslingen	65-0594
Cath. 19, Johanna 18			
KOHL, Carl	32	Ofen	65-0898
KOHL, Johann	50	Altendorn	65-0950
Elisabeth 48, Carl 19, Amalie 18			
Anton 15, Johannes 14, Peter 11, Marie 9			
Franz 8			
KOHL, John	43	Weissenheim	63-0693
Juliane 37, William 15, Mary 12			
Juliane 8, Johanne 4, Gottfried 2			
KOHLBECHER, Alois	21	Rothenfeld	66-1155
KOHLBRECHER, Aug.	18	Pye	66-0668
KOHLE, Jac.	20	Thalheim	64-0331
KOHLENBECK, (f)	28	New York	64-0023
Johanna 21			
KOHLENBECK, Joh. P	70	Schenkelberg	66-0934
KOHLENBERG, Daniel	19	Lienbach	66-1248
KOHLENBERG, Sophie	40	Grunenplan	64-0593
KOHLER, Caroline	22	Baden	63-0990
KOHLER, Elis.	34	Rolfsbuettel	64-0331
KOHLER, Jac.	17	Dernbach	64-0782
KOHLER, Jos.	27	Binsdorf	64-0331

NAME	AGE	RESIDENCE	YR-LIST
KOHLER, Lisette	38	Gotha	66-1203
KOHLER, Marie	26	Kuppmannsfeld	66-0578
KOHLER, Martha	26	Godensberg/He	66-0412
KOHLGRUBE, Anna	36	Muenchen	66-0679
KOHLGRUBEN, Franz	40	Muenchen	66-0679
KOHLGRUBER, Jacob	15	Muenchen	66-0679
KOHLHAASE, August	37	Kolberg/Pr.	63-0822
Caroline 34, Auguste 10, Franz 1			
KOHLHAGEN, Gotth.	62	Langendorf	64-0938
KOHLHASE, Chr'tine	21	Gushagen	64-0687
KOHLHAUS, Carl	20	Erbach	66-1373
KOHLHEPP, Conrad	22	Heubach	65-1031
Elisabeth 9			
KOHLHEPP, Konrad	24	Gmuend	66-0837
KOHLI, Helene	17	Gr. Lobcke	65-0770
KOHLIEZEK, Mathias	26	Koeolau	66-1373
KOHLMANN, Chr.	24	Albersleben	63-0244
KOHLMANN, Conrad	28	Soesting	63-0244
KOHLMANN, Hr.	22	Bergedorf	67-0007
KOHLMANN, Mart.	22	Worbswede	65-0038
KOHLMANN, Meta	26	Oldenburg	63-0821
KOHLMEIER, Ludw.	27	Schoenberg	65-0007
KOHLMEYER, Friedr.	25	Husum	67-0007
KOHLMEYER, H.C.C.	24	Gestorf	65-0594
KOHLWECK, Sophie	24	Kirchhardt	64-0331
KOHLWEG, August	52	Deblinghausen	66-0934
Sophie 54			
KOHLY, Henry	26	New York	63-1136
wife 24			
KOHMANN, Moritz	29	Fischenbach	66-0412
KOHN, Ad.	25	Nakel	63-0990
KOHN, Armin	14	Ungarn	63-0917
KOHN, Bernhard	31	Hungary	64-0739
KOHN, Bertha	22	Neheim	65-0189
KOHN, Cacilie	27	Nakel	63-0990
KOHN, Catharina	55	Tereschau	63-0917
KOHN, Cathe.	26	Lancaster	63-0244
William 6, Cathe. 4, A. 30, F. 10, W. 8			
E. 6, H. 1			
KOHN, David	27	Burgkunstadt	64-0331
Johanna 21			
KOHN, Ernst	16	Boehmen	66-0704
KOHN, Hermine	16	Muttersdorf	66-0984
KOHN, Jeanette	15	Uhlfeld	65-0402
KOHN, Jos.	21	Tereschau	64-0427
KOHN, Julius	30	Zweibruecken	64-0687
KOHN, Math.(f)	30	New York	64-0593
Julie 5			
KOHN, Nanni	18	Pormukel	66-0650
Elisab. 16			
KOHN, Nathan	24	Minden	63-0482
KOHN, Salome	17	Bachau	65-0402
KOHN, Salomon	25	Bohemia	66-0109
KOHN, Wilh.	30	Boitzenburg	66-0577
Wilhelmine 38, Maria 7, Dorothea 58			
KOHNBURG, Wm.	22	Hannover	65-0055
KOHNEN, Johann	31	Alf	64-0639
KOHNFELD, Amalie	28	Bayern	64-0992
Eva 20			
KOHNLE, Jacob	22	Wetzheim	64-0433
KOHNSTAMM, Emil	25	Neustadt	65-0402
KOHNWANCKEN, Julie	32	Prag	66-1203
Mathias 14, Franz 18, Adelheid 9			
KOHOOT, Anna	29	Boehmen	64-0023
KOHOUT, Franz	28	Boehmen	64-0343
KOHRING, Ludwig	17	Hude	66-0412
KOHRN, Math.	25	Neunkirchen	63-0990
Maria 24, Adelheid 4, William 6m			
KOHRS, Diedrich	18	Marschkamp	65-1024
Trina 25, baby 9m			
KOHRS, Friedr.	22	Polle	67-0007
KOHRS, Heinrich	46	Oldenbuettel	64-0885
Sophia 26			
KOIDEL, Jacob	29	Goettingen	66-1243
Amalia 26, Minna 8, Augusta 3, Laurette 1			
KOKE, Franz	19	Borgenteich	66-0413
KOKEL, Maria	21	Neuhaus	66-1093
KOLASCHELL, Joh.	24	Schoenstadt	64-0840

NAME	AGE	RESIDENCE	YR-LIST
KOLB, G.C.	60	Aussig	66-0704
Agathe 52			
KOLB, Georg	18	Altengronau	64-0433
Michael 16			
KOLB, Johann	23	Ludwigsburg	65-0770
KOLB, Ludw.	18	Madamuehle	64-0840
Ferdinand 17			
KOLB, Margarethe	15	Neustadt	64-0739
KOLB, Martin	39	New York	64-0138
KOLB, Martin	30	Rassbach	65-0950
Lorenz 28			
KOLB, Nic.	23	Eschenbach	64-0992
KOLB, Nicolaus	24	Siggerfeld	66-0576
KOLB, Nothburg	40	Ried	65-0594
Hermine 14, Joseph 7			
KOLB, Peter	31	Hohenzelle	64-0433
Elisabeth 26, Johann 3, Adam 9m			
KOLB, Richard	19	New York	63-0482
KOLBE, August	36	Albany	66-0704
KOLBE, August	60	Wigheim	64-1053
Marie 63, Caroline 25, Aug.Ludw. 29			
Dorothea 47, Joh. 18, Fritz 4, Augusta 7			
Julie 1			
KOLBE, Maria L.	18	Herford	66-1243
KOLBE, Theodor	33	New Orleans	63-1178
Maria 31, Henriette 1			
KOLK, Gottfr.	45	Haver Co.	64-0073
KOLKE, Heinr.	39	Brake	63-1010
Henriette 39, Caroline 9m			
KOLLAS, Michael	35	Preussen	63-0398
Marie 30, Josephine 6, Joseph 4			
KOLLATZ, Anna	28	Berlin	64-0593
Alfr. 9m			
KOLLEG, Catharina	22	Bremen	66-0984
KOLLENBACH, G.	56	Meiningen	65-0007
KOLLER, H.F.	24	Moorsee	65-0594
KOLLER, Heinrich	25	Horst	66-1031
KOLLER, Pauline	26	Fruchtelfingn	66-0576
KOLLING, Heinr.	26	Oldendurf	66-1373
Wilhelmine 23, Wilh. Heinr. 2			
KOLLMANN, H.	50	Marienwer	66-0413
KOLLMANN, Maria	22	Holstein	65-1024
KOLLMANN, Marie	26	Bremen	63-0551
KOLLMAR, Conrad	26	Stebbach	64-0199
KOLLMAR, Pauline	22	Neustadt	66-0576
KOLLMEYER, Casper	18	Minden	65-1031
KOLLMEYER, Fr.	19	Elverdessen	63-1010
KOLLMEYER, Friedr.	17	Westphalen	66-0576
KOLLN, Emil	16	Dorum	64-0214
KOLLWOTZ, v. H.	25	Schlesien	64-0495
KOLOENAR, Elise	21	Hameln	66-0984
KOLTATSCHUNG, Jos.	44	Blumenau	64-0639
KOLTER, Albert	30	Seidenburg	65-0243
KOLTER, Simon	23	Alzey	65-1030
KOLZ, Robert	20	Volkmarsen	63-1085
KOMER, Heinr.	24	Kenzingen	65-0151
KONBA, Wenzel	45	Daberkreis/Bo	63-1010
Josephine 34, Caroline 9, Wenzel 7			
Therese 5, Franz 2, Johann 3m			
KONBECK, Anna	26	Zdaslon	66-1131
Antonia 18			
KONCKY, Wenzel	32	Beraua	66-1373
Anna 21, Maria 11m			
KONECNY, Franz	48	Boehmen	63-0398
KONIG, Rosina	24	Thalwenden	66-0734
Johann 2			
KONIGSHOFEN, Aug.	20	Muehlheim	66-0734
KONITZ, Carl	42	Wien	63-0398
KONITZKY, Fr.	24	Bremen	65-0116
KONRAD, Herrm.	28	Suedfelde	66-1313
KONTE, H.(m)	15	Heitjaden	64-0138
Fr.(f) 18			
KOOB, Margarethe	15	Niedernkirchn	66-0704
KOOP, Bernhard	15	Lehe	66-1031
KOOP, Eiland	73	Ardensberg	65-1030
KOOP, Jacob	21	Heppenheim	64-0639
KOOP, Joh. B.	53	Wardelohe	65-1030
Meika 56, Heinrich 28, Margarethe 24			
Wilhelm 15			
KOOP, Joh. Heinr.	18	Neuenwalde	67-0007
KOOP, Louise	17	Dielingen	66-0704
KOOPMANN, Aug.	19	Flatterlohaus	63-1038
KOOSMEYER, Hch.	15	Hoeverstedt	64-1206
KOPATSCH, Georg	31	Sachsenfeld	64-0938
KOPF, Elisabeth	20	Dinglingen	64-0023
KOPF, J.M.	15	Otterndorf	63-0953
KOPF, Joh. Georg	27	Bidringen	66-0704
KOPFF, Joseph	34	Germany	63-0953
(m) 30, Peter 12, Anne 10			
KOPISCHKE, Ludw.	23	Preussen	63-0398
KOPITSCH, Carl Rch	22	Neustadt	64-0938
KOPITSCH, Richard	24	Neustadt	66-1155
KOPMANN, Fr.(m)	36	New York	64-0073
KOPMANN, J.H.	28	Nortrup	67-0795
Maria 18			
KOPP, (m)	28	Hanau	65-1189
KOPP, Caroline	25	Idar	65-0594
Ida 22, Ida 52			
KOPP, Johann	22	Hessen	66-0984
KOPPEN, Wm. Conrad	12	Grossalmerode	64-0433
KOPPENHOLFER, Jam.	24	Cincinnati	63-0482
KOPPENROTH, B.H.A.	25	Hespe	64-0886
KOPPNER, August	21	Pottenhausen	64-0023
KORB, Kilian	27	Hessen	66-0147
KORBACH, Amalie	36	Lehe	64-0665
KORBEL, Fr.	48	Kirrweiler	66-0704
KORBEN, D.(f)	29	Horste	64-0331
KORBMACHER, Johann	24	Eyb	66-0469
KORDAN, Johann	22	Bodenheim	65-0402
KORDEL, Justus	20	Bohrenfurth	65-0974
Anna 19, Christine 4m			
KORDELER, Theod.	17	Alt Lueneberg	65-0950
Wilhelm 18			
KORDES, Gerhard	55	Haseldinnen	65-1030
Gesina 42, Margarethe 19, Bernhard 16			
Heinrich 11, Adelheid 6			
KORELL, Wilhelmine	17	Niederwiesen	66-0984
KORF, Eduard	37	Almena	64-0456
KORFES, Johann	18	Polle	66-1373
KORFF, Johanna D.	18	Berensch	64-0886
KORFF, Karoline	20	Unterlubbe	64-0331
KORHUMMEL, Ignatz	19	Neudingen	64-0687
KORLE, Ad.(m)	28	Himmelstadt	64-0331
KORMANN, Dorothea	22	Philadelphia	63-0862
KORMANN, Peter		Oberfleiden	66-0984
KORMEYER, Ae(f)	23	Osnabrueck	64-0331
Minna 6m			
KORN, Aloisia	26	Kirchen	66-1327
KORN, Caspar	36	Hersfeld	66-0623
KORN, Chs.	26	Ettlingen	63-1178
KORN, Johanna	9	Bremerhaven	66-0147
KORN, L.	34	Karsruhe	64-0639
KORNAHRENS, Claus	27	Wuestenwohlde	66-1031
KORNDOERFER, Guido	26	New Orleans	63-0168
KORNELIUS, Elisab.	26	Ebersdorf	66-0704
KORNEMANN, Dor. R.	7	Darmstadt	66-1127
KORNER, Friedrich	29	Elberfeld	66-0934
KORNERDING, August	23	Neuenkirchen	66-0984
KORNES, Marie	37	New York	63-1085
Cath. 28, Augusta 3			
KORNETT, Meta	19	Rinkstedt	64-0456
KORNMEYER, Kunig.	27	Wallenfelz	66-0650
KORNREUTER, Jeanet	18	Maineck	63-0551
KORNWEIN, August	15	Febenhausen	66-0469
KORTE, Joseph	30	Soest	64-0214
KORTEKAMP, Fr.	18	Oerninghausen	65-0038
KORTEN, John W.	20	Merscheid	63-1038
KORTENHAUS, Aug.	24	Barmen	65-0007
KORTER, Emilie	40	Carlsruhe	65-0974
KORTH, Carl	32	Berlin	66-0147
Augusta 37, Carl 2, Anna 6m			
KORTLANG, Mart.	20	Bremen	64-1161
KORTMANN, Josepha	20	Hambergen	65-1088
KORVES, Adolf	27	Lingen	66-1031
KORZYNESKA, Marian	23	Schanzendorf	66-0578
KOS, Anton	41	Kuttenberg	64-0170

NAME	AGE	RESIDENCE	YR-LIST
KOSCH, Carl	29	Schmisdorf	66-0083
KOSCHNICK, Wilh.	24	Charbrow	66-0650
KOSMI, Martin	47	Kochstedt	23-0865
KOSSE, Legien	35	Gimpelburg	64-0886
KOSSMANN, Georg	24	Creuznach	65-0007
KOSTE, Herm.	71	Minnelage	64-0992
Mavin 59, Heinrich 22, Anna 17, Helena 14			
KOSTEKA, Franz	35	Bohemia	64-0687
Marie 34, Joh. 7, Wenz. 2, Jos. 2			
Maria 6, Anna 9m			
KOSTENBADER, Heinr	28	Wuerttemberg	63-0822
Babette 26			
KOSTER, Marie	30	Bremen	64-0992
KOTH, Ferd.	22	Diedesdorf	64-0456
KOTHE, Fritz	21	Salzdetfurth	67-0599
KOTHE, Otto	20	Guckhagen	66-0984
Christiane 22			
KOTHMANN, Elisab.	24	Luedersheim	65-0770
KOTHRADE, Hr.	32	Suhlingen	65-1031
KOTKOWSKY, Joh.	24	Prust	66-0650
KOTOWSKY, Joseph	31	Pryerover	66-0349
KOTTER, Maria E.	24	Borkhausen	63-1218
KOTTKAMP, Carl	22	Bremen	66-1031
KOTTMANN, Bernhard	43	Cincinnati	64-0073
KOTTMANN, Cath.	25	Versmold	65-0950
Franz 19			
KOTTMANN, Wilh'mne	20	Osterleda	64-1022
KOTTMEIER, Carl	15	Huellhorst	65-0189
KOTTMEYER, Wm.	29	New York	63-0752
KOTZENBERG, Carl	20	Essen	65-0402
Aug. 37			
KOTZHIEVAR, Steph.		Sewa/Krain	66-0412
KOUTCKY, John	27	Boehmen	63-0990
KOUTSCHLADE, F.D.	38	Eisenach	64-0170
Charlotte 17, Eduard 9			
KOVESY, Wilhelm	28	Pest	64-0886
KOWALD, Bernhard	35	Ostbevern	66-1327
KOWASCHICK, Louis	24	Pest	64-0938
KOYEL, Ernestine	17	Heilbronn	66-1373
KOZLOWSKI, Michael	38	Posen	64-0432
KRACHT, Adolph	23	Hohenhausen	64-0456
Herm. 26			
KRACHT, C.	24	Lippe Detmold	66-0413
KRACHT, Franz	28	Lehmkule	67-0007
KRACHT, M.(f)	66	Olandorf	64-0782
KRACK, Antonia	23	Dieperz	67-0954
KRACK, Benedict	30	Hessen	66-0221
KRAECK, Eva	19	Teuschatz	67-0353
KRAEFT, Th.	45	Chicago	63-1085
KRAEGER, Leonhard	42	Koenig	66-1203
Elisabeth 42, Margarethe 17, Leonhard 15			
Heinrich 9m, Marie 7, Marie 7			
Christoph 5, Carl 3, Adam 8			
KRAEMER, Amalia	27	Windischfeist	64-1108
KRAEMER, Barbara	25	Washington	66-0623
Catharina 22			
KRAEMER, Carl	22	Solingen	65-0116
KRAEMER, Carth.	17	Berstadt	64-0639
Philippine 20			
KRAEMER, Charles	12	Strassburg	63-0990
Wilhelmine 35			
KRAEMER, Christian	17	Moehringen	64-1108
KRAEMER, Elisabeth	23	Gruenberg	63-0862
KRAEMER, Emma	24	Mihltoff	67-0599
KRAEMER, Ferd.	24	Coeln	64-0593
KRAEMER, Friedrich	24	Windhagen	66-0623
KRAEMER, Johann	32	Nordheim	65-0856
KRAEMER, John	58	Steinbach	63-0244
KRAEMER, Joseph	25	Rieste	63-0168
KRAEMER, Ludwig	34	Dudweiler	63-0693
KRAEMER, Marie	25	Nienburg	65-0856
Joh. 6			
KRAEMER, Matthias	23	Darmstadt	66-0704
KRAEMER, Reinhard	34	Altenburg	64-0593
KRAEMER, Rosine	22	Wachenheim	63-1178
KRAEMER, Rosine	20	Baiern	64-0214
KRAENZLER, Daniel	28	Adelberg	65-0189
KRAFFT, Barbara	24	Weinheim	64-0687

NAME	AGE	RESIDENCE	YR-LIST
KRAFT, Adam	31	Cassel	63-0821
KRAFT, Adam	30	Pfordt	64-0214
KRAFT, Adelbert	24	Regensburg	65-0151
KRAFT, Anna	43	Ebeleben	66-1093
Anna 16, Friederike 13, Hermann 9			
Ferdinand 8, Ottilie 6, Emilie 4			
KRAFT, Conrad	17	Pfordt	64-0782
KRAFT, Eduard	28	New York	63-0296
KRAFT, Elisabeth	24	Ammenau	66-1155
KRAFT, Elisabeth	33	Wallenroth	65-1030
KRAFT, Geo.	21	Schweinsberg	64-0331
KRAFT, George	26	Oberkaufungen	63-0551
KRAFT, Heinr.	24	Werda	64-0639
KRAFT, Henry	52	Trebur	63-0862
KRAFT, Joh.	23	Allnach	65-1024
Jac. 23			
KRAFT, Louis	16	Aalen	66-1327
KRAFT, Margarethe	24	Oberfranken	66-1131
KRAFT, Samuel	77	Heidringsfeld	65-1189
Pauline 24			
KRAFT, Siemon	31	Oberurbach	65-0116
KRAFT, Sophie	14	Schwabendorf	63-0482
KRAFT, Theodor	22	Baden	63-0862
KRAFT, Wilhelmine	58	Cassel	63-0821
Cathre. 34			
KRAHLING, Gustav	38	Ruegen	66-1248
KRAHLMANN, Helena	25	Dersum	66-0623
KRAHLMANN, Herm. H	46	Bielefeld	65-1030
Anna Cathar. 49, Joh. Heinr. 22			
Caspar Heinr 19, Friedr. Wilh 10			
KRAHN, Bertha		Schoenwitz	66-1248
KRAILING, Louis	22	Wieseck	64-0495
KRAISS, Wilh.	41	Schorndorf	64-0214
KRAKAUER, Friedr.	26	Bietigheim	64-0938
August 13			
KRAKE, Carl	26	Braunschweig	64-0840
KRAKENBERG, Carl	19	Volkmarsen	65-0948
KRAL, Adam	26	Bastlowitz	65-0713
KRAL, Simon	22	Sekkerschen	65-0713
KRALICECK, Joseph	25	Boehmen	63-0953
Anna 34, Catarina 9, Anna 8, Marie 5			
Wenzel 3, Friedrich 4m			
KRAMER, Albert	26	Baden	66-0576
August 23			
KRAMER, Alwine	20	Furra	67-0600
KRAMER, Bernhard	24	Lastrup	67-0007
KRAMER, Eduard	35	Biberach	63-0482
KRAMER, Emanuel	53	Biedenkopf	64-0687
Justine 24, Carl 18			
KRAMER, Ernst	22	Bremen	64-0363
KRAMER, F.	36	Wettin	65-1024
KRAMER, Fritz	27	Berga	64-0739
KRAMER, H.	19	Bremen	64-0593
KRAMER, Heinr.	26	Ems	63-1010
Johanna 27, Marie 9m			
KRAMER, Heinr.	17	Oppendorf	64-0456
KRAMER, Heinr.	24	Wulften	64-0593
KRAMER, Heinr.	42	Ekenhausen	65-1030
KRAMER, Heinz	27	Pfungstadt	66-0734
KRAMER, Herman	21	Wierup	66-1093
KRAMER, Hermann	27	Bueckeburg	66-0934
KRAMER, J.H.	26	Lorup	63-1003
J. 22, B. 18, M. 31, K. 58, H. 19			
KRAMER, Johann	24	Metzingen	66-1327
KRAMER, John	41	St. Clara	63-1085
Barbara 55			
KRAMER, Louise	39	Feklenburg	66-1248
Augusta 15, Maria 13, Martin 12			
Wilhelm 7, Johanna 6			
KRAMER, Ludwig	25	Groningen	66-0734
Anna 24, Anna 3m			
KRAMER, Marie	18	Willendingen	64-0331
KRAMER, Marie	30	Tittlingen	64-0331
KRAMER, Moritz	26	Wahlwies	67-0007
KRAMER, Philip G.	24	Roedersee	66-0221
KRAMER, Unke	31	Rhaude	64-0739
KRAMER, Wilhelmine	18	Brueninghast.	67-0806
KRAMER, Wilhelmine	59	Rothenfelde	65-0950

NAME	AGE	RESIDENCE	YR-LIST
KRAMER, William	23	Verden	63-0953
Cath. 24, Rud. 16			
KRAMER, William	32	Minden	63-0244
KRAMLICH, Margaret	17	Weiher	66-1093
KRAMM, Frz. Chr.	26	Grebenstein	65-0898
KRAMME, Henry Chr.	29	Steinhagen	63-1218
KRAMS, Michael	23	Kiedrich	66-0147
KRANICH, Jacob	23	Hemmingen	65-1030
KRANKARD, F.(f)	24	Frankenberg	64-0782
KRANTZ, Carl Heinr	20	Rinteln	65-0950
KRANTZ, Edeline	24	Linden	66-0679
Henriette 22			
KRANZ, Agnes	21	Remdau	66-0650
KRANZ, Carl	29	Basel	67-0007
KRANZ, Casp.	47	Hessen	64-0432
Elisab. 47, Heinr. 17			
KRANZ, Elisabeth	20	Grewenau	66-0578
KRANZ, Louise	20	Rotenkirchen	64-0433
KRANZ, Margarethe	40	Emperhausen	64-0885
Eduard 4, Ludwig 2			
KRAPFF, Gottl.	25	Baiereck	64-0073
KRAPP, Christ	34	Bremen	63-1178
KRAPP, Marg.	37	Pittsburg	63-1218
KRATOCHWILLE, Jos.	36	Dayton	64-0073
KRATOSCHWILL, Pet.	23	Posen	65-0402
KRATSCH, Wilhelm	27	Hannover	66-1031
KRATT, Dorothea	63	Schrembson	66-1203
KRATT, Is.	34	Trostingen	64-0495
KRATT, Martin	24	Frossingen	63-0990
KRATT, Thomas	24	Abdingen	64-1053
KRATZ, Aug.	34	Birklar	66-0704
KRATZ, Friederike	28	Lindheim	64-1206
KRATZ, Peter	36	New York	64-0593
KRATZENSTEIN, Bert	25	Hoeringhausen	66-0734
Sara 19			
KRATZENSTEIN, Jac.	26	Marienhagen	65-0898
Rosette 54, Herm. 17, Isaac 15, Sarah 19			
Marianne 26			
KRATZENSTEIN, Mary	20	Hoeringhausen	65-0038
Minna 15			
KRATZERLE, Jac.	32	Nauenheim	63-1010
KRATZERT, Valentin	33	Weinheim	64-0687
Peter 24, Eva 24			
KRATZMANN, Heinr.	49	Einbeck	66-1127
Minna 36, Carl 14, Marie 12, Ernst 9			
Robert 7, Minna 4, Louise 3, Johanna 1			
KRAUER, Hugo	22	Gr.Breitenbch	66-1203
KRAUS, Josepha	53	Boehmen	63-1218
Anna 22, Aloys 2			
KRAUS, Abraham	30	Stenowitz	66-0576
KRAUS, Anna	16	Duslingen	66-0576
KRAUS, Babette	60	Muenchen	66-1373
Teckla 29, Emma 8			
KRAUS, Cath.	23	Sachsen	66-0413
Marie 2			
KRAUS, Emilie	19	Altshausen	66-0576
KRAUS, Ernst F.			64-0023
KRAUS, Heinr.		Bederkesa	66-0934
KRAUS, Jacob	24	Graben	66-0576
KRAUS, Jacob	27	Coeln	64-1053
KRAUS, James	20	Brostdorf	63-1085
Mary 19			
KRAUS, John	32	Badendorf	64-0214
KRAUS, Margarethe	25	Baiern	66-0623
KRAUS, Martha Chr.	54	Solingen	65-0038
Ludwig 18, Ernst 15, Edmund 12, Otto 10			
KRAUS, Mathias	33	St. Martin	66-0984
Catharine 33, Georg 7, Adam 3			
Catharine 5m			
KRAUS, Wenzel	28	Boehmen	64-0023
Johanna 21			
KRAUSCHEN, Carl	16	Fulda	64-0170
KRAUSE, A.	35	Fuerstensee	66-0413
M. 33, Wil. 4			
KRAUSE, A.	22	Anleben	64-0495
KRAUSE, Charlotte	60	Berlin	66-0469
Adolph 21			
KRAUSE, Elise	19	Bockenheim	64-0938

NAME	AGE	RESIDENCE	YR-LIST
Fr. 9m			
KRAUSE, Ernst Lud.	50	Poblotz	63-0614
Constanza 45, Hermann 23			
KRAUSE, Florentine	36	Danzig	67-0007
KRAUSE, Franziska	19	Schwetz	64-0639
KRAUSE, Friedr.	37	Minikowa	66-0469
Anna 35			
KRAUSE, Friedr.	15	Rengershausen	66-0704
KRAUSE, Fritz	30	Berlin	66-0934
KRAUSE, Heinr.	48	New York	64-0023
Johanna 21			
KRAUSE, Herman	22	Wundersleben	64-0593
KRAUSE, Jacob	34	Gmuenden	66-1155
KRAUSE, Julius	39	Preussen	63-1136
KRAUSE, Melch.	25	Gmuenden	66-1128
KRAUSE, Peter	24	Karlisken	66-0413
KRAUSE, W.F.	30	Indianapolis	63-1085
Anna 33, August 4, Louise 23, Oscar 4			
Emilie 1			
KRAUSE, Wilhelm	25	Guenthorst	66-0412
KRAUSE, Wilhelmine	24	Wollin	63-0614
KRAUSE, Wm.	38	Magdeburg	65-0007
KRAUSER, Chr. Herm	18	Sax.-Meiningn	64-0432
KRAUSER, Nic.	28	Oberhohenwied	66-0704
KRAUSKOPF, Johann	26	Wallrode	66-0623
Eva 43, Peter 19, Anna 11, Elisabeth 7			
Georg 4			
KRAUSS, Babette	22	Baden	66-0576
KRAUSS, Carl Herm.	23	Dhum/Sax.	64-0920
KRAUSS, Caroline	20	Kotzhuette	64-0593
KRAUSS, Cath.	24	Ungstein	63-0551
KRAUSS, Cath.	25	Zellingen	64-0639
KRAUSS, Conrad	33	Altenorschen	64-0363
KRAUSS, Daniel	41	Philadelphia	63-0862
KRAUSS, Gottlieb	30	Heidenheim	65-1030
KRAUSS, Jacob	34	Tuebingen	64-0593
Johanna 33, Regina 25, Henry 11			
Pauline 1			
KRAUSS, Joh. Val.	34	New York	63-0296
KRAUSS, Kunigunda	31	Zeltingen	64-0639
KRAUSS, Leopold	23	Feschau	66-1327
KRAUSS, Leopold	25	Schwabach	66-1327
KRAUSS, Mathilde	24	Schwarzbach	63-0990
KRAUSS, Theodor	24	Hannover	66-0734
KRAUTER, G.	21	Heppach	64-0782
KRAUTER, Wilhelm	26	Waiblingen	63-1136
KRAUTI, Christine	22	Laubach	66-0704
KRAWIRYK, Casimir	46	Mirigin	66-0469
Maria 33, Anna 17, Julian 16, Franz 5			
Filia 9m			
KREBS, Abraham	40	New York	63-0097
KREBS, Gerhard	32	New York	63-0917
KREBS, Helene	24	Berleburg	63-0482
KREBS, Joh.(m)	19	Neumagen	64-0331
KREBS, Louise	48	Darmstadt	66-1127
KREBS, Marie	19	Drehle	66-1093
KREBS, Th.(m)	22	Goettingen	64-0331
KREBS, Wilhelm	23	Singershausen	66-0147
Friedrich 28			
KREBS, Wilhelm	40	Berlin	65-0898
KREBS, Wilhelmine	21	Posen	66-0578
Juliane 19			
KREE, Heinr.	22	Boerringhsn.	66-0221
KREEB, Cath.	26	Jebenhausen	64-0992
KREEB, Rosine	19	Bartenbach	66-1093
KREFT, Sophie	24	Mennighoefen	64-0938
KREG, Peter	37	Oldenburg	66-0578
Maria 27, Maria 2			
KREGE, Augusta	18	Posen	64-0432
KREHAUS, F.W.	45	Bockhorst	64-0331
Chath. 42, Wilhelmine 16, H.(m) 13			
Fr.(m) 4			
KREHE, Balthasar	59	Trommelsheim	63-0821
Amalie 58			
KREHLHUES, Fr.(m)	18	Detmold	64-0331
KREICH, Bernhard	44	Eisenach	66-1127
KREICH, Carl	16	Osnabrueck	66-1127
KREIDEL, Joseph	26	Wuertemberg	63-0693

NAME	AGE	RESIDENCE	YR-LIST
KREIENBORG, Heinr.	18	Oldenburg	66-1093
KREIENKAMP, Anna M	25	Harpenfeld	63-0862
KREILEIN, Amalia	19	Fritzlar	66-0984
KREILING, Gerhard	21	Helle	64-0886
KREIM, Lorenz	17	Helmbrecht	63-0244
KREIMANN, Arnold	17	Varensell	66-1203
Margarethe 19			
KREIMER, Herm. H.	63	Lingen	65-0038
KREIN, Barbara	19	Frankonia	66-0837
KREIN, Elisabeth	58	Ermsdorf	65-1031
KREISER, Aug.	30	New York	64-0331
KREIST, Christ.	27	Schonlieb	66-0984
KREITLEIN, Georg	56	Fuerth	66-1155
KREITMAIER, H.(m)	16	Nuernberg	64-0687
KREKE, Lisette	20	Neuenkirchen	66-1373
KREKELER, Carl	17	Oschershagen	66-0576
KRELL, Anna	21	Rendshausen	66-1327
Oswald 2, August 25			
KRELLWITZ, Julius	39	Ulfersleben	63-0482
Theresia 22			
KREMELBERG, J.D.	35	Baltimore	63-0482
Gertrude 20, Mathilde 22, Friedrich 9			
Ella 10, Dini 6, Meyer 34			
KREMELBERG, J.G.	25	Baltimore	64-0214
KREMER, Joh.	22	Preussen	64-0331
KREMER, Joseph	31	Winshausen	64-0023
KREMES, Fritz	28	Meschchied	64-0363
KREMS, Clamor	32	Essen	66-0668
Marie 31, baby , Eleonore 58			
KRENCKE, Rebecca	20	Lamstedt	65-1095
KRENKEL, Wilh'mine	38	Segelhorst	63-0482
KRENN, Wilh.	27	Nuertingen	65-1088
Caroline 32, Ernst 2			
KRENTZER, Leonh.	56	Muenchen	67-0806
KRENZ, John	27	New York	63-0862
KRENZ, Wilhelmine	24	Posen	64-0432
KREPCHER, August	16	Dobbestein	66-1203
KREPEL, Anna Elise	17	Tochen	66-1155
KRESCHKA, Mathilde	40	Bohemia	64-0593
Mary 28, Marie 1			
KRESS, Wilhelm	24	Brake	66-0147
Friedrich 28			
KRETSCHMAR, Lina		Philadelphia	63-0821
KRETSCHMER, Ernest	21	Zuegelheim	66-0576
Marie 28, Alma 6m			
KRETSCHMER, Joseph	28	Steindorf	66-0576
KRETZER, Theodor	36	Coblenz	64-0073
KRETZMEYER, Ludw.	27	Neustadt	64-1108
Caroline 20			
KRETZSCHMAR, Aug.	28	Saxony	63-0822
KREUDER, Carl	20	Gruenberg	64-0331
KREUDLER, Waldburg	50	Naukirch	63-0482
KREUTLER, Friedr.	21	Minsen	66-0984
KREUTZ, Peter	24	Hasseborn	65-0243
KREUTZBERG, Jos'a	22	Winzeln	63-1136
KREUTZBERGER, Chr.	22	Strahte/Hess.	67-0806
KREUTZER, Andreas	70	Willoss	63-1010
KREUTZER, Aug.	20	Messkirch	64-0593
KREUZ, F.	35	Madison	66-0704
KREUZER, Adolph	16	Messkirch	64-0593
Clara 9			
KREUZER, Carl	42	Plugrode	66-0623
Friederike 45, Robert 15, Wilhelm 12			
KREUZER, Magdalene	22	Weidenberg	66-1327
KREYBOHM, C. Jul.	25	Ahlsfeld	65-0898
KREYENBERG, Carl	22	Oldenburg	66-0984
KREYER, C.	26	Rochester	64-0687
KREYLING, Daniel	14	Rauschenberg	66-0412
KREYLING, Wilh'mne	50	Rauschenberg	64-0427
KREYMBORG, F.Jos.	27	Oldenburg	65-0007
KREYMEYER, Elisab.	21	Ibbenbuehren	65-0898
KREYSIMSKY, Anast.	23	Polen	63-0953
KREYSS, Philippine	21	Seilersbach	63-0482
KREYSSING, Aug.	27	Dresden	64-0363
KREZEK, Anna	26	Kuettenberg	66-1373
Emilie 3			
KRICH, maria	42	Grossarbbach	66-1373
Waldburga 7			
KRICK, Johann	16	Untersuhl	64-0739
KRICKHAUS, Wilh.	29	Evansville	63-0990
KRIECHE, Benjamin	26	Habendorf	67-0599
KRIEDE, Heinr	54	Rothenfelde	65-0950
Wilhelmine 56, Lina 16			
KRIEG, Fr.	37	Baden-Baden	63-1085
Caroline 35, baby 9m			
KRIEG, Friedrich	24	Grosseichholz	66-0704
KRIEG, Gustav	26	Schkoelen	67-1005
Henriette 24			
KRIEG, Heinrich	13	Lauterbach	66-1373
KRIEG, Jenny	32	Havre	64-1053
Louise 6			
KRIEG, Jenny	40	Genf	64-1022
Jenny 7			
KRIEGER, August	33	Carlsruhe	65-0243
KRIEGER, Augusta	20	Wedheiden	66-1327
KRIEGER, Frnz.	38	New York	64-0138
KRIEGER, Louise	29	Bremerhaven	65-1189
F.A. 11m			
KRIEGER, Otto	19	Sensburg	66-1243
KRIENKE, Joh. Lud.	26	Posen	66-0578
Justine 24, August 2			
KRIETE, A.	15	Rechtebe	63-1038
KRIETE, Joh.	18	Hannover	64-0427
KRIETE, Rebecca	24	Hannover	63-0398
KRIFTE, Joh. W.	24	Kattenkamp	64-0938
KRIMPHOFF, W.	49	Aurich	66-0413
KRINGS, Franz	35	Coblenz	65-0594
Joseph 17, Elisabeth 14, Maria 34, Joh. 5			
Franz 4, Maria 10m			
KRINSKI, Johann	27	Huttenberg	65-0004
KRISTELLER, Johann	48	Frankfurt a/O	63-1010
Caroline 23, Rosalie 20, Friedrike 16			
Minna 13			
KRIWANEK, Maria	24	Boehmen	64-0427
KRIZEK, Maria	20	Bohemia	64-0331
(f) 16			
KROBITSCH, Rud.	17	Leipzig	63-0482
KROCH, Elias	21	Preussen	63-1178
Hannchen 20			
KROCKE, Ludwig	19	Wunderthausen	65-0402
Marie 18			
KROCKER, Robert	14	Breslau	66-0837
KROEBER, Adm.	18	Crumbach	64-0495
Marie 16			
KROEBER, W.(m)	53	Washington	64-0331
Johanna 21			
KROECKEL, Augusta	37	Braunschweig	65-0594
Cathar. 35, Jacob 7, Ida 16, Oscar 15			
Caecilie 14, Carl 11, Clara 5, Maria 3			
KROEGER, Arnold Wm	21	Cassebrug	64-0456
KROEGER, Bernh.	21	Cloppenburg	65-0038
KROEGER, Cath.	23	Buettendorf	65-0898
KROEGER, F.	22	Baltimore	63-0244
KROEGER, Fr. W.	19	Buettendorf	65-0898
KROEGER, Heinrich	15	Luebbeck	66-1203
KROEGER, Joh. Gerh	24	Ellenstedt	66-0704
KROEGER, Johann	20	Arnsberg	67-0007
KROEGER, Lina	19	Lippstadt	66-0577
KROEGER, Theodor	38	Frohnhausen	63-0551
KROEGER, Theodor	27	Rotenburg	66-1127
KROEHLICH, Anna M.	16	Hoechst	67-0795
KROEHMER, Johannes	36	United States	64-0363
Franelin 9			
KROENCKE, H. Wm.	20	Hannover	64-0432
KROENER, D.(m)	25	New York	64-0331
KROENER, Frdr.	27	Eberbach	66-0221
KROGA, Heinrich	42	Kleinhorden	63-0053
KROGER, Lisette	21	Luebbecke	65-1189
KROGMANN, Joh.	25	Hude	64-0593
KROGMANN, Joh. Hr.	32	Osterburg	65-0950
Cath. 34, Georg 4, Johanna 4m			
KROHE, Louise	58	Gerendingen	63-0693
KROHN, Albert	26	Detmold	65-0402
KROHN, Lina	21	Berlin	63-0551
KROHNE, August	17	Bremen	64-0739
KROHNE, Friedrich	18	Nordheim	66-1248

NAME	AGE	RESIDENCE	YR-LIST
KROHNER, Johannes	26	Osweil	66-1127
KROLL, Johann	31	Zell	66-0576
Georg 23			
KROME, Fritz	19	Koppendorf	67-0007
KROME, Ludwig	23	Wolfenbuettel	63-0398
KROMER, Friedr.	27	Mezingen	66-1155
KRONACHER, Sophie	22	Eisfeld	64-0433
KRONAU, Heinrich	22	Rhoch	66-0349
KRONE, Ludwig	28	Fuerstenau	64-0938
KRONECK, Moritz	30	New York	64-0427
Carl Fr. 32, Anna 31, Wilhelm 3			
Ernestine 9m			
KRONENBITTER, Jos.	42	Glatt	66-0412
KRONICKE, Christ.	20	Westphalen	66-0704
KRONMUELLER, Soph.	20	Waldstrauss	66-1131
KRONSTEIN, P.H.(m)	29	Osnabrueck	64-0331
KROOG, v. Wilhelm	14	Odisheim	64-0456
KROP, August	26	Bramsche	65-0948
KROP, H.	30	Hameln	66-0413
KROPF, Franz	38	Vorarlberg	66-1127
KROPF, John	35	Lancaster	66-0221
KROPF, Mathilde	15	Fuerstenberg	66-1127
KROPKE, Herm.	32	Birnbaum	64-0363
KROPP, Casp. Wolfg	58	Germany	66-0666
Margarethe 58			
KROPP, Fr.	17	Osterholz	66-0704
KROPP, John	23	Fraenkskronbh	63-0752
KROPP, Louise	30	Magdeburg	64-0214
baby 9m			
KROPP, Pauline	19	Kilianstadt	64-0170
KROPPENHOFEN, Marg	22	Baiern	66-0704
Cathar. 19			
KROSCH, Johann	33	Zhier/Austria	66-0469
KROSE, Elisab.	20	Langensalza	64-0593
KROTLER, Mathilde	18	Meinsen	66-0984
KRUB, Carl	31	Boehmen	63-0398
KRUDOP, Martin	14	Holthorst	66-0934
KRUECK, Max	26	Osnabrueck	66-0984
KRUEGER, Anna	26	Muehlhausen	66-0221
Sophie 3, Christoph 5			
KRUEGER, Aug.	27	Posen	67-0795
KRUEGER, August	24	Buchwerder	65-0770
KRUEGER, Emil	18	Posen	66-0578
Johanna 21, Emma 15			
KRUEGER, Ernst	24	Herford	65-1024
KRUEGER, Folkert B	25	Eilsum	65-0189
KRUEGER, Friedr.	42	Schoenebeck	63-0990
Anna 41, Friedr. 16, Emilie 14			
Caroline 12, Wilhelm 9, Friederica 8			
Bertha 6, Johann 4, Emilie 11m			
KRUEGER, Friedr.	16	Beckstedt	64-0593
KRUEGER, Friedr.	48	Potsdam	66-1243
Wilhelm 12			
KRUEGER, Friedrich	23	Germany	66-0666
KRUEGER, Friedrich	18	Schaumburg	65-1030
KRUEGER, G.R.	31	Osnabrueck	64-0593
KRUEGER, G.W.	31	Bremen	64-0363
Jenny 25			
KRUEGER, Heinr.Chr	16	Varel	64-0739
KRUEGER, Heinrich	39	Rehburg	65-1095
KRUEGER, Heinrich	21	Herzberge	64-0739
KRUEGER, Herm.	14	Crimmitzschau	63-0482
KRUEGER, Herm.	24	Bremen	66-1203
KRUEGER, Hr.	18	Barmen	65-0594
KRUEGER, Joh.	32	Bornsen	65-0402
Cath. 30, Joh. 5, Chr. 9m			
KRUEGER, Julius	23	Minden	65-1024
KRUEGER, Louise	28	Bremen	64-0073
KRUEGER, Louise	21	Gera	66-0934
KRUEGER, Michael	25	Bensien	65-1095
Augusta 21			
KRUEGER, Peter	25	Wilkowa	66-0469
KRUEGER, Richard	25	Stressendorf	64-1053
Ottilie 47, Gustav 7			
KRUEGER, W.	45	Lippe Detmold	66-0413
Florentine 37			
KRUEGER, Wilh.	25	Rinteln	66-0469
KRUESEL, Helene	27	Wersuwe	65-1030

NAME	AGE	RESIDENCE	YR-LIST
KRUG, Adam	61	Godensberg/He	66-0412
Anna Cath. 62, Adam 28, Elisabeth 25			
Johannes 22			
KRUG, Barbara	59	Horas	66-0704
KRUG, Catharine	22	Cassel	66-0412
KRUG, Christian	27	Berka	64-0214
Anna Cath. 24, Christ. Fr. 3			
KRUG, Friedrich	24	Eisenach	66-0668
KRUG, Georg	42	Eichelheim	65-0950
Barbara 56, Margareth 22			
KRUG, Heinrich	20	Berka a/Werra	65-0948
KRUG, Jacob	23	Niederdieten	64-0687
KRUG, Marg.	21	Horas	63-1038
KRUG, Therese	19	Battenberg	66-0679
KRUG, Wilhelm	19	Wihlheiden	66-0412
KRUICKHAUS, Frd.	24	Wieweg/Blg.	64-1053
KRULICH, Aloisa	48	Kuttenberg	66-1093
Emanuel 14, Anna 7, Carl 5			
KRULISCH, Jos.	47	Boehmen	64-0427
Maria 22, Amalia 13			
KRULL, Anna M.	67	Bremen	67-1005
KRULL, Nicol.	28	Hannover	64-1022
Friedr. 26			
KRULL, Sophie Car.	16	Lieckwegen	63-0482
KRULL, Wilhelm	26	Hannover	66-0221
KRUMBACH, Wilhelm	24	Ofheim	64-1022
KRUMBIER, Ferdin'd	48	Moschitz	66-0578
Caroline 48, Emilie 20, August 17			
Ernst 9, Bertha 3			
KRUMDICK, Maria	16	Beckstedt	64-0593
KRUME, Friedrich	18	Rehme	66-0147
KRUMHOLZ, Cathrine	20	Culmbach	66-1327
KRUMM, Albertine	26	Lobsens	63-0990
Otto 5, Alma 4			
KRUMM, G.	21	Schotten	65-0713
KRUMM, Kunigunda	21	Wellenstadt	66-0349
KRUMM, Maria	18	Wellenstart	66-0349
KRUMME, Ahrend	30	Baltimore	63-0862
KRUMMEIER, Friedr.	46	Kirchweiler	64-0992
KRUMMINGER, Joh.	25	Hannover	64-0073
KRUNDMANN, Wilhelm	41	Langensalza	66-1155
KRUSCHKA, Joh.	34	Doldau	66-0704
Anna 34, Johann 9			
KRUSCHKA, Rosine	25	Budweiss	66-0837
KRUSCHKE, Johann	19	Neugedein	67-0007
KRUSE, Albert	30	Neugardt	67-0007
KRUSE, Anna	17	Hannover	63-0822
KRUSE, Chr.	20	Allendorf	64-0495
Hch. 17			
KRUSE, Diedr.	22	Mahndorf	64-0427
KRUSE, Engel	19	Friedewald	64-0331
F.W. 19m			
KRUSE, Franz	23	Brunswick	63-0822
KRUSE, Friedr.	23	Fuerstenau	66-1373
KRUSE, Georg	28	Wittmund	65-0950
KRUSE, Gerd. Ecken	29	Hentrup	64-0639
KRUSE, Gesche	16	Nenndorf	66-0413
KRUSE, H.(m)	23	Amsterdam	64-0331
KRUSE, Herm.	19	Bremen	64-0214
KRUSE, Hermann	18	Hintzendorf	66-0934
KRUSE, J.H.	26	Edewecht	65-0594
KRUSE, Joh. B.	36	Schapen	64-1022
KRUSE, Johann	23	Runkerod	67-0007
KRUSE, Johanna	19	Seebecke	65-0004
KRUSE, Maria	20	Westendorf	66-0984
KRUSE, Wilhelm	29	Diethe	67-0007
KRUSE, Wilhelm	20	Osterode	66-1127
KRUSENKLAUS, Chr.	60	Ladbergen	65-1024
Sophie 21			
KRUSKA, Jan	34	Bohemia	64-0593
Elisab. 34, Joseph 7, Johann 6, Mary 3			
Franz 39			
KRUSZA, Jacob	43	Klakomathe	66-0666
Marianne 43, Elsbita 15, Franciska 7			
Josephine 6, Joseph 5, Johann 9m			
KRUTINA, Ludwig	58	Schwetzingen	63-0990
Friedrike 57			
KUBACKI, Vincent	27	Posen	67-0795

NAME	AGE	RESIDENCE	YR-LIST
KUBEL, Friedr. Wm.	23	Stangenfeld	66-0934
KUBEL, Leonh.	23	Mainz	64-0023
KUBER, John	37	United States	66-0679
KUBES, Mathias	52	Mazic	65-0713
Anna 52, Marie 25, Catharina 17			
Elisabeth 13, Albert 8			
KUBISTA, Franz	26	Leschau	64-1206
KUBLER, Christine	26	Koesingen	66-0147
KUBLER, J.	17	Hornberg	64-0992
KUCERA, Barbara	24	Boehmen	63-0296
Francis 4, Barbara 4m			
KUCERA, J.	33	Krems	65-0007
KUCH, Johannes	34	Neidlingen	66-0109
KUCHANS, Henry	34	St.Louis	63-0917
Charlotte 9			
KUCHE, Christian	35	Lengerich	66-0668
KUCHEN, Wilhelm	19	Hannover	67-0007
KUCHLER, Anna	29	Nowak	66-0147
Toni 5, Lenni 3, Anna 2m			
KUCHLER, Casper	21	Aufhausen	65-0948
KUCK, A.C.	37	New York	63-0953
Bertha 25			
KUCK, Anna E.	25	Oldenburg	63-0917
KUCK, Cath.	20	Oldenburg	64-0363
KUCK, Cath. Elise	24	Lienen	66-0837
Katharina 52			
KUCK, G.	17	Hussendorf	64-1161
KUCK, Johann	30	Bremen	64-0363
KUCK, Marie	26	Lottbergen	66-1031
KUCKUK, Heinrich	27	Steinhude	64-0199
KUDEKUNST, Jacob	26	Heidelberg	67-0954
Christiane 21			
KUDER, Christian	40	Stein	63-0482
Fredr. 33, Conrad 18, August 15			
Caroline 13, James 8, Johanna 3			
KUEBA, Christian	17	Niederwald	66-1203
KUEBEL, Justine	20	Herbstein	65-1024
KUEBELING, Elisab.	24	Moischeit	66-0623
Catharina 22			
KUEBLER, Christoph	23	Bieberach	66-1373
KUEBLINGER, Joh.	23	Kreuznach	66-1373
KUECH, Eberhard	18	Steinfurth	64-1206
KUECH, Heinr.	18	Viech	64-0427
KUECHENMEISTER, L.	21	Heringen	64-0214
KUECHLE, Eugen	22	Roth	64-0886
KUECHLER, Chr.	43	New Orleans	63-0953
Wilhelmine 34, Oscar 6, Bertha 2			
KUECHLER, Christ.	37	Preussen	64-0214
Martha 33, baby 11m, Carl 9, Albert 7			
Adolph 5, Emilie 4			
KUECK, Anna	20	Willheim	66-0578
KUECK, Diedr.	17	Vich	65-0898
KUECK, Dorette	21	Hannover	66-0577
KUECK, Elise	16	Lehe	66-1373
KUECK, Gewert	23	Gerstdorf	67-0600
Trina 23			
KUECK, Herm.	18	Teufelsmoor	65-0898
KUECK, Hermann	24	Fendorf	66-0578
KUECK, Johann	19	Hannover	66-0734
KUECK, Martin	27	Lilienthal	66-0704
Heinr. 11, Anna 9			
KUECK, Meta	33	Gnauenburg	65-0948
KUEFEL, Rudolph	16	Herbstein	65-0189
KUEFER, Jockel	17	Hehnlein	63-0614
KUEGEL, Catharine	34	Ebermannstadt	66-0412
KUEHL, Claus	28	Neunbuster	64-0782
KUEHL, Eva	23	New York	66-0704
Ad. 5, Anna 10m			
KUEHL, Marie	24	Bremen	64-0427
KUEHL, Otto	25	Hildesheim	66-1031
KUEHLE, Anton	30	Naile	66-1131
KUEHLE, August	49	Duderstadt	66-1128
Rosalie 26, Heinrich 7, Minna 1			
Heinrich 56			
KUEHLKEN, Johanna	25	Hagen	64-0170
KUEHLWEIN, Genovev	22	Obergrunsbach	63-0990
KUEHLWEIN, Jos.	25	Oilingen	65-0189
KUEHMER, Hanna	25	Neustadt	66-0734

NAME	AGE	RESIDENCE	YR-LIST
KUEHN, Caspar	48	Saxony	63-0822
KUEHN, Franz	28	Weissenburg	65-0243
Peter 26, Barbara 25, Josephine 22			
KUEHN, Gottlieb	38	Preussen	63-0398
KUEHN, Lueppe	23	Thunum	63-0296
KUEHNE, Ernst	15	Grafelde	66-0704
Wilhelmine 21			
KUEHNE, Fritz	30	Wuertenberg	66-0221
KUEHNE, Heinr.	52	Rodewald	66-1203
August 17, Marie 19, Wilhelm 58, Maria 22			
Sophia 20			
KUEHNE, Joseph	22	Hannover	66-1373
KUEHNE, Wilhelm	30	Braunschweig	66-1155
KUEHNEMANN, Minna	28	Cassel	65-0038
KUEHNER, Adam	20	Gimmeldingen	66-0734
Peter 8			
KUEHNER, Wilhelm	62	Odernheim	65-1030
Anna Maria 53			
KUEHR, Heinrich	24	Wellendorf	65-1095
KUELMANN, Anton	30	Lingen	64-0639
KUEMME, Gustav	19	Finnelse	64-0687
KUEMMEL, Franz	32	Cassel	65-1031
KUEMMEL, L.	26	Wiesbaden	63-1003
KUEMMEL, Lisette	26	Heddesdorf	66-0576
KUEMMERLE, Marie	25	New York	66-0734
KUEMPEL, Ernst	26	Warnshausen	63-0482
Christiane 26			
KUENEKEN, Sabina	62	Bremen	64-1206
Johanna 20, Sophia 18			
KUENEMUND, Lisa	17	Schoenhagen	66-1327
KUENKER, Bernhard	23	Nentershausen	66-1127
KUENSTER, Friedr.	25	Kuppingen	65-0243
KUENSTLER, Carl	49	Berlin	64-1108
Hugo 17			
KUENSTNER, Friedr.	17	Nuertingen	66-1093
KUENY, Michael	21	Buehl	66-0704
Josephine 20, Jean 14			
KUENZEL, Ferdinand	17	Asch	66-0679
KUENZEL, Ferdinand	19	Atsah	66-0679
KUENZEL, Johann	23	Bohemia	66-0577
Casper 22			
KUENZEL, Margar.	29	Wildenau	66-0704
KUENZEL, Olga	16	Breslau	66-1203
KUENZEL, Oskar	25	Oelsnitz	66-0668
KUEPPER, Carl W.	29	Solingen	63-0822
KUEPPER, Christine	24	Schuettorf	66-0734
KUEPPER, Wilhelm	80	Barmen	66-1093
Ewald 28, Wilhelmine 10m			
KUERLES, Em.(m)	63	Bollberg	64-0495
L.(f) 17, Agnes 2, J.G.(m) 32, Franz 21			
Ida 6m			
KUERN, Marie	19	Bayern	66-0221
KUERS, Tekla	26	Freisenburg	66-0623
KUERSTER, John	20	Rechternfleth	66-1155
KUERTEN, F.	51	Merscheid	65-1024
Marie 54, Emma 9			
KUESTER, Chr. Ludw	21	Hannover	64-0886
KUESTER, Christ.	51	Hannover	65-0116
Dorethe 31, Carl 11, Wm. 6			
KUESTER, Eva	48	New York	63-0990
child 9			
KUESTER, F.	42	Lando	66-0413
KUESTER, Friedr.	28	Langen	64-1108
KUESTER, Heinrich	23	Yebes	66-0083
KUESTER, Heinrich	17	Peine	64-0840
KUESTER, Joh. Conr	32	Hessen	64-0432
Christine 28, Marie 4			
KUESTER, W. (m)	49	Altenweldinge	64-0331
(m) 7			
KUESTNER, Maria	20	Darmstadt	64-0886
KUFFER, Heinr.	24	Glauchau	66-0576
KUGEL, Ch.(m)	17	Esslingen	64-0495
KUGELER, August	29	Flehingen	66-1155
KUGELER, Wilh'mine	16	Cappel	66-0083
KUGELMANN, Julie	20	Wagenfeld	64-0992
KUGELMANN, Levy	19	Altenstadt	66-0668
KUGLER, Chr. Jul.	19	Minden	63-0482
KUGLER, Lothar	28	Flehingen	63-0482

NAME	AGE	RESIDENCE	YR-LIST
KUGPERS, Adamina	40	Rotterdam	66-0984
Joseph 10			
KUHFUSS, Georg	58	Luethorst	66-0221
Caroline 43, Georg 14, Regina 7			
Bertha 20, Lina 4			
KUHFUSS, W.(m)	40	New York	64-0363
KUHL, Andreas	27	Asch	66-0704
KUHL, Euphrosine	50	Altenschlirf	63-1218
KUHL, Margaretha	19	Hesse-Cassel	66-0837
KUHL, Marie	24	Schale	64-0363
Rika 15			
KUHL, Phil.	18	New York	66-0704
KUHLBACH, Christ.	54	Luedolfsheim	66-0083
Friderike 49, Friedrich 27, Wilhelm 16			
KUHLE, August	32	Hannover	65-0770
KUHLENKAMP, Joh. H	19	Hiddensdorf	65-0189
KUHLENKAMPF, C.G.	20	Bremen	64-0331
KUHLES, Wilhelm	22	Scheebach	66-1327
KUHLGAMBERGER, Mar	17	Tafingen	66-0412
KUHLMANN, Aug.	19	Brake	63-0482
Simon 16			
KUHLMANN, Caroline	30	Stapelfeld	65-0116
KUHLMANN, Cath.	18	Loehne	66-0413
KUHLMANN, Ch.(m)	16	Bremen	64-0343
KUHLMANN, Chr.	29	Bega	64-0840
KUHLMANN, Christ.	17	Bueckeburg	63-0953
KUHLMANN, Conrad	27	Meerbeck	65-0770
Heinrich 29			
KUHLMANN, Fr.	35	St. Louis	63-0953
KUHLMANN, Friedr.	21	Spengen	66-0623
KUHLMANN, Friedr.	19	Vehrte	66-1031
KUHLMANN, Georg	25	Battbergen	66-1373
KUHLMANN, Heinr.	25	Glaue	66-0984
KUHLMANN, Heinr. W	35	Piqua	63-0990
KUHLMANN, Herm.		Todtemann	64-0214
KUHLMANN, Joseph	19	Lippstadt	66-1131
KUHLMANN, Marie	21	Stapelfeld	64-0938
KUHLMANN, Theod.	32	Lemgo	63-0953
KUHLMANN, Theodor	24	Stapelfeld	65-0116
KUHLMANN, Wilhelm	20	Rahden	65-1088
KUHMANN, Theod.	30	Ochtrup	64-1022
KUHN, Arnold	31	Corbach	66-1373
KUHN, August	20	Bayern	66-0221
KUHN, Carl	24	Switz	64-0170
KUHN, Ch.	22	Daertzbach	63-1085
KUHN, Eugen	19	Muehlhausen	66-0221
KUHN, F.(m)	25	Hersfeld	64-0331
KUHN, Flora	24	Frankfurt a/O	63-1010
KUHN, Georg	25	New York	66-0147
KUHN, Hchn(f)	25	Ilversheim	64-0782
KUHN, Jean	23	Otterstadt	63-1178
KUHN, Joh. G.	21	New York	65-0004
KUHN, Johann	22	Niederwald	65-1030
KUHN, John C. Aug.	17	Friedrichsfld	63-0296
KUHN, M.	22	Linsenhofen	63-1003
KUHN, Maria	23	Beuren	65-0243
KUHN, Nathan	32	Obertsheim	66-0221
KUHN, Robert	31	Magdeburg	64-0840
KUHN, Samuel	62	Ebersheim	66-0221
Caroline 60			
KUHN, Tobias	36	Hersfeld	63-1178
KUHN, Wilh.	22	Hardheim	66-0650
KUHNER, Joachim	25	Pilsen	64-0886
KUHNERETT, Carl	20	Berlin	65-0770
KUHNERT, Carl	30	Berlin	65-0770
KUHNLE, Alb.	30	Schwieberding	64-0427
KUHNLE, Ludwig	5	Treschklingen	65-0594
KUHNLE, Virginie	28	Baden	66-0578
Rudolph 35, Lisette 5, Elphia 3			
Friedrich 2, Jacob 9m			
KUHR, G.H.	56	Cincinnati	63-0953
KUHSIEL, Augusta	25	Hochberg	64-0593
KUJAETH, Wilh.Aug.	32	Kuestrin	66-0578
Wilhelmine 32, Gustav 9, Emilie 4, Mine 1			
KUK, Ernst	23	Salzdettfurt	66-1243
KULAGE, Heinrich	19	Varensell	66-1203
Joseph 15			
KULEN, Friedr. Wh.	22	Meerbeck	65-0950

NAME	AGE	RESIDENCE	YR-LIST
Eberhard 26			
KULFEIFER, Wm.	23	Natzungen	66-1313
KULING, Wilhelm	21	Hochus	63-1010
KULL, Caroline	18	Stuttgart	66-0984
KULL, Joh. Jac.	25	Schoenberg	65-0007
KULL, Johannes	25	Hundelshausen	66-0934
KULLE, Cath.	33	Hameln	66-1313
Wilhelmine 10, Carl 9, Heinrich 4			
KULLMAR, Angelina	22	Hessia	66-0412
KULOGE, Herrmann	26	Petershagen	65-1095
KULP, Regina	20	Buedingen	64-1053
KUMBACH, Gustav	21	Landerhut	65-1030
KUMME, Dorothea	21	Salzwedel	66-1127
KUMME, Kilian	39	Eisenach	64-0138
Magdalene 26, Anna 4m			
KUMMICH, Johann	19	Bergfelden	66-1373
KUMMING, Johann H.	23	Schledehausen	63-0006
KUNA, Jacob	35	Boehmen	66-0578
Maria 33, Joseph 7, Marie 5			
KUNA, Johann	34	Boehmen	66-0349
Martha 27			
KUNATH, Hugo	28	Louisville	64-0687
KUNCKEN, Meta	33	Bremen	66-1313
Minna 12, Meta 8			
KUNDMUELLER, Cath.	16	Halbendorf	66-1203
KUNEMEYER, Heinr.	30	Ledde	65-0948
KUNG, Philipp	35	Muthmershafen	65-0243
Creszencia 35, Ludw. 15, Wilh. 15			
KUNIG, Peter	30	Blechlingen	66-0221
KUNISCH, William	46	Prussia	63-0752
Juliane 40			
KUNKEL, Andreas	16	Wiesthal	66-0704
KUNKEL, Balthasar	24	Rothenbuck	64-0456
KUNKEL, Carl	33	Uslar	65-1024
Hanne 62, Heinrich 34			
KUNKEL, Christoph	19	Damme	66-0837
KUNKEL, Martha	41	Damme	66-0837
Eva 21			
KUNKEN, A.(m)	26	Lingen	64-0331
KUNKLER, Adam	23	Muenster	64-1053
KUNOTH, G.H.(m)	48	New York	64-0073
KUNSCH, Christian	44	Magdeburg	65-0865
KUNSCHER, Paul	35	Moshietz	66-0413
Agnes 30, George 7, Marie 4, Joseph 2			
KUNSEMUELLER, Gust	20	Hilter	66-1031
Lina 18, Fritz 9			
KUNST, Friedrich	33	Brake	66-0147
KUNSTMANN, Helene	29	New York	63-0097
baby(f) 11m			
KUNSTMANN, Richard	22	Gera	66-1031
KUNTER, Friedr.	25	Dielingen	66-1031
KUNTH, Oscar	20	Bremen	63-0990
KUNTZ, Jean	30	New York	63-0752
KUNTZ, Sophie	36	Umstadt	66-0679
KUNTZBER, Jacob	16	Suhl	63-1069
KUNTZE, Herm.	24	Altenburg	66-1155
KUNTZE, Wilhelm	17	Muenden	66-1031
KUNZ, Albert	42	Pecknow	66-1373
Barbara 45, Adalbert 22, Anna 20			
Antonia 17, Joseph 5			
KUNZ, Franz	28	Buhlenberg	64-0593
KUNZ, James	28	Philadelphia	63-0296
KUNZ, Louise	18	Muenchweier	65-0898
KUNZ, Philippine	20	Muenchweiler	66-0147
Catharine 27			
KUNZE, Aug. F.	25	Breitenbronn	65-0055
KUNZE, August	44	Patschkau	65-1095
KUNZE, Carl	30	Nordhausen	64-0593
Dorothea 27, Friedr. 9, Anna 3m			
KUNZE, Chr. Gottf.	56	Wernsdorf	65-0948
Wilhelmine 37, Helene 2			
KUNZE, Fz.	23	Thalster	64-0782
KUNZE, Jac. F.	39	Stemenberg	64-0214
KUNZE, Johanna	35	Berlin	67-0599
Bertha 4, Anna 2, Louise 11m			
KUPER, Hermann	30	Hannover	66-1093
KUPFE, Joh. Gottl.	36	Neustadt	65-0713
Pauline 34			

NAME	AGE	RESIDENCE	YR-LIST
KUPFER, Anton	60	Ringsheim	63-0862
Mariane 21			
KUPFER, Bertha	37	Leipzig	66-1203
Friedr. 9, Anna 8, Clara 7, Emil 5			
Alfred 4			
KUPFER, Maria		Culvorden	66-1373
KUPFERSCHMIDT, A.	25	Spaichingen	64-0782
KUPFERSCHMIDT, M.	28	Durkheim	64-0495
KUPKA, Joh.	30	Kris	65-1088
Marie 31, Josepha 3, Anna 11m			
KUPPEL, Lorenz	22	Bottmer	64-0495
KUPPENHEIM, E.(m)	28	Havre	64-0214
KUPPER, Carl	32	Libenthal	66-0650
Helene 30, Gustav 4, Carl 2			
KURERVA, Franz	24	Polen	63-0953
KURHARDT, Carl	35	New York	66-0734
KURITZ, Paul	32	New York	66-0221
KURRE, Johann	19	Vertatsche	64-0427
KURSECK, Le. (f)	19	Kirzel	64-0363
KURSTNER, M.	30	Frankfurt	65-0007
KURTH, Bernhard	20	Duderstadt	66-1093
KURTH, Johann	28	Montabaur	65-1030
KURTH, Lina	25	Darmstadt	66-1127
KURTZ, Adam	27	New York	64-0214
KURTZ, Julius	29	Clausthal	65-0594
KURZ, Barbara	20	Laudenhausen	66-1248
KURZ, Ferd.	42	Kirzel	64-0363
Michael 76			
KURZ, Friedr.	28	Balzholz	66-1127
Johannes 25			
KURZ, Gottlob	23	Grafenberg	66-0221
KURZ, Isaac	37	Petzingen	64-0992
KURZ, Jacob	26	Ossweil	64-0886
KURZ, Joh. H.	22	Schwarzenbach	65-0189
KURZ, Louise	14	Osweil	66-1031
KURZ, Martin	8	Lehe	66-0109
KURZ, Mary	29	Horn	64-0343
KURZ, Mathilde	18	Cassel	66-1248
KURZ, Michael	22	Grossenaspach	64-0170
Christian 18			
KURZ, Sara	21	Gailingen	66-0704
KURZ, Wm.	25	Moehringen	64-0495
L.(f) 30, M.(f) 18, C.(f) 7			
KURZKNABE, Ludwig	36	Philadelphia	63-0953
KURZROCK, H.	58	Altmorschen	63-1003
K. 48			
KURZROCK, Heinr.	27	Altenorschen	64-0363
Gesine 30, Maria 4, Anna 3m			
KURZROCK, Joh.	17	Lendorf	64-0665
KUSER, Friederike	54	Duderstadt	66-1128
KUSEWITT, Marie	37	Melle	65-1031
KUSSERLE, Agnes	23	Klagenfurt	63-1218
KUSSROW, Henry	34	Freiburg	63-0296
KUSTERLE, Cath.	26	Bohemia	64-0782
Gab. 20			
KUTNOWKOWSKY, Ad.	9	Kuttenberg	64-0170
KUTSCHER, Friedr.	55	Wettin	63-0551
William 19, Anna 14			
KUTSCHERA, J.	33	Krems	65-0007
KUTZMANN, Wm.	30	Lubasch	64-0456
Juliane 25, Heinrich 6m			
KWAPIL, Josef	38	Probese	66-0734
Francisca 40			
KWITZ, Mathilde	50	Boehmen	66-0349
Julie 39, Ida 17, Alice 14, Trewer 12			
KYBURG, Veronica	26	Aargau	66-0412
KYDERKA, Barbara	24	Lutz	66-1155
Maria 2, Barbara 11m			
KYPTA, Augustin	27	Boehmen	63-0953
LAABS, Friedr.	19	Zamow	65-0038
Wilhelmine 45, Wilhelm 11			
LAABS, Johann	52	Suerrowshoff	66-0469
Wilhelmine 42, Emilie 11, Bertha 8			
Albert 6, Augusta 4			
LAAKE, H.B.	57	Baltimore	64-0138
LAAR, Adolph	17	Rodheim	66-0984
LAAR, Jacob	24	Limborg	66-0984
LABAUSEUR, Joh. N.	46	New York	66-0934

NAME	AGE	RESIDENCE	YR-LIST
Dorette 52			
LACH, Carl	30	Leuchen	64-0331
Johanna 21			
LACHENMAN, William	48	Reutlingen	63-0296
Rosine 37, Babette 17, Sophie 2			
LACHENMEYER, Fr'dr	19	Oppelsbohm	64-1022
LACHMANN, Herm.	66	Edelsen	64-0639
Margaretha 62, Herman 21, Adelheid 27			
LACHMANN, Heymann	18	Wirsitz	66-0578
LACHMUND, Johann	18	Osterholz	63-0398
LACHS, Kunigunde	26	Cronach	66-0734
LACHS, Theresia	28	Seegedin	66-1327
Julius 11m			
LACINA, Maria	18	Sedlitz	64-0170
LACKAMP, Hermann	25	Ostenfelde	65-1031
LACKE, Charles	29	Cincinnati	63-0693
LACKEMEIER, Friedr	14	Heidelberg	67-0954
LACKMANN, Hinrike	18	Eckwarden	64-0073
Johanna 21, Johanna 21			
LACKMANN, Margaret	24	Hannover	63-0822
LACKMANN, Wilh.	21	Wertenwisch	63-1136
LADDEY, Wilhelm	29	Horbke	65-0007
Louise 30, Wilhelm 4, Herm. 3			
LADENBURGER, Jos.	22	Zobingen	66-0679
Moritz 26			
LADENSACK, C.	18	Querfurth	63-1010
LADES, Joh.	32	Hohenlinsberg	64-0495
LADNER, Johannes	21	Dieslingen	66-0668
LAEGE, T.	31	Prussia	63-1003
Dorothea 21, C. 34, H. 8, M. 6, E. 4			
LAEMMERHIRT, Magd.	19	Salzungen	63-0168
LAENNEKER, G.A.	18	Varel	63-1085
LAESSING, Carl	23	Wuertemberg	66-0734
Christiane 17			
LAEUFER, Louise	22	Mecterdingen	64-0593
LAGE, B.(m)	46	Philadelphia	64-0331
LAGE, Benedict	24	Halwerde	65-0189
LAGE, zur Hermann	38	Gr. Drehle	66-1127
Maria 24, Maria 1			
LAGEMANN, Joh.	38	Prussia	65-0038
LAGER, Johann	27	Lengerich	65-1030
LAGESCHNETE, Cath.	24	Schale	66-0679
LAHAUS, Anton	25	Gaxel	66-0349
Anna 59			
LAHAY, Joseph	45	Wieweg/Blg.	64-1053
LAHM, Carl	26	Wentelshain	64-0782
Elis. 16			
LAHM, Christ.	30	Wetter	63-0398
LAHM, Friedrich	23	Wetter	65-1095
LAHMANN, Henriette	27	Detmold	63-0097
LAHMEYER, Ernst	19	Wedehorn	66-0704
LAHMEYER, F.W.	27	Eschenhausen	66-0704
LAHN, Louis	16	Werden	63-0752
LAHNER, Johann	19	Oberdingeshm.	66-1203
LAHR, Cath. Elisab	55	Steinbockheim	64-0456
LAHR, Christoph	36	Singles	64-1053
LAHRMANN, Friedke	34	Lintorf	64-0170
LAHRS, W.	28	Oldenburg	65-1024
LAHUSEN, Fr.	32	Bremen	65-0243
LAILER, Bernhardin	22	Vimbruch	63-0244
LAISTNER, C.J.	25	Wildbad	63-1003
LAITLIN, Anna	18	Lingen	64-0639
LAKONY, Felix	33	Bromberg	66-0577
Ferdinand 23			
LAMAC, Adelbert	38	Mazic	65-0713
Catharina 32, Maria 10, Catharina 5			
Anna 1			
LAMAC, Joseph	26	Bohemia	64-0593
LAMACH, Anna	34	Lomitz	63-0053
LAMB, Charlotte	21	Gangloff	67-0007
LAMBART, Josepha	19	Obergunzburg	65-0402
LAMBEIN, Georg	19	Steinfeld	66-0576
LAMBERT, Agnes	30	Staten Island	63-0244
Anne 9, Charles inf			
LAMBERT, Joh.	32	Marseille	64-0432
LAMBERT, Susanne	19	Elmshausen	64-0687
LAMBRECHT, Anna	17	Bremen	64-0992
LAMBRECHT, Carl	62	Stressendorf	64-1053

NAME	AGE	RESIDENCE	YR-LIST
Friederike 54, Bertha 7, Gottlieb 23			
Charlotte 19			
LAMM, Salinger	23	Sprottau	65-0189
LAMMEL, F.	28	Auscha	64-0992
LAMMENEN, C.	29	Waldkappeln	66-0413
Martha 23, Wilh. 3m			
LAMMER, Herm.	25	Salzbergen	64-0331
LAMMERFELD, Johann	32	Elberfeld	64-0495
Arthur 12, Ewald 9			
LAMMERMANN, Louise	18	Seligenstadt	64-0214
LAMMERS, Cath.	26	Nienburg	65-1030
LAMMERS, Gerhard H	25	Ruhle	66-0412
LAMMERS, J.	18	Bremen	63-1003
LAMMERS, Leonhard	26	Aschbach	66-0704
LAMOTTE, H.	24	Bremen	63-0244
LAMPACH, Elisabeth	58	Reiskirchen	64-0782
LAMPART, Babette	17	Kellmuenz	66-0679
LAMPE, Carl	43	Ankum	64-0427
Cath. 27, baby 6m, Fr.(f) 30			
LAMPE, Caspar Hch.	37	Buer	64-0920
Maria Elis. 23, Maria Elis. 1			
LAMPE, Emil	26	Braunschweig	66-0984
LAMPE, Heinrich	26	Redwin	67-0007
LAMPE, Henry	35	Bremen	63-0350
LAMPE, Hermann	18	Wedem	65-1031
LAMPE, J.	28	Bremen	65-0007
LAMPE, Johann	34	Indiana	66-0221
LAMPE, Sophia	21	Rahden	65-1088
LAMPERT, August	47	Wangen	64-0687
Augusta 20			
LAMPERT, Heinrich	18	Meinbreun	65-1031
LAMPERT, Jacob	26	Reichenbach	66-0679
LAMPING, Elisabeth	22	Dummelshausen	66-0984
LAMPING, Hermann	27	Grabow	67-0007
LAMPRECHT, Barbara	26	Busenweiler	66-0704
LAMSTER, Eduard	29	Frankfurt	66-0668
LANDA, Anton	31	Tabor	66-0679
LANDAGE, Heinr.	30	Exter	66-1203
Louise 26, Louise 1			
LANDAU, Anna	25	Rockensuess	65-1030
LANDAUER, Jette	23	Crailsheim	64-0639
LANDAUER, William	20	Neuenstadt	63-1136
LANDENBACH, John	16	Boehmen	63-1085
LANDENBERG, Christ	17	Elsingen	64-0782
LANDER, Anna	19	Neustadt	63-1085
LANDER, Wilhelm	25	Dahlskamp	64-0023
Johanna 21			
LANDES, Eugen	3	Uhlbach	66-0349
LANDGRAF, Victor	24	Fritzlar	66-1127
LANDGREBE, Marie	16	Marburg	66-0679
LANDMANN, Anna	23	Langen	65-0189
LANDMANN, Carl	27	Pirremhee	66-0469
LANDMANN, Marie	42	Wienershausen	65-1030
Ludwig 14, Georg 13, Elisabeth 12			
Conrad 10, Caroline 7, Heinrich 5			
LANDOCKER, Adolph	17	Bischberg	66-0984
LANDRE, Dorothea	34	St. Louis	63-0693
LANDSCHNEIDER, Con	24	Cassel	65-0865
LANDSIEDEL, Heinr.	36	Dietershausen	65-0402
LANDSIEDEL, Peter	19	Curhessen	63-0822
LANDSKRON, C.(f)	36	Prussia	64-0495
LANDT, Cath.	32	Oberkleen	64-0593
LANDVOGT, G. Louis	29	St.Louis	63-0821
LANDWEHR, Clemens	19	Bohlarn	66-1373
LANDWEHR, Gottlieb	17	Elberdissen	66-0837
LANDWEHR, Heinr.	23	Schaale	64-0782
Bernh. 63, Charlotte 30			
LANDWEHR, Herm. H.	32	Gehrde	63-0862
LANDWEHR, Johann	26	Schinkel	66-1131
LANG, Andreas	37	Breitenbach	66-0412
Kunigunde 43, Gabriel 2			
LANG, Anna	16	Michelstadt	66-0679
LANG, Babette	20	Ebern	66-1127
LANG, Christian	22	Darnsfetten	67-0007
LANG, Christoph	47	Mannheim	63-1069
Louis 21			
LANG, Fr. F.	37	Esslingen	64-1161
Margaretha 34, Wilhelm 7, Julius 5			
Ferdinand 4, Johann 1, baby bob			
LANG, Friedr.	33	Frankfurt	65-0594
LANG, Friedrich	23	Ochsenbach	66-0679
LANG, G.C.A.	19	Meiningen	66-1127
LANG, Georg	32	D'Niederrad	66-1203
LANG, Georg	28	Arzberg	67-0806
Catharina 28, Catharina 7			
LANG, Gottl.	27	Philadelphia	63-0168
LANG, Heinrich	23	Brauerschwend	66-0837
LANG, Jacob	25	Bachshausen	66-0984
LANG, Johann	34	Breitenbach	66-0412
LANG, Johann	28	Hopfigheim	67-0007
LANG, John	33	Reichelsheim	63-0953
LANG, Lisette	18	Richen	64-0593
LANG, Louise	16	Neustadt	65-0116
Joh. 7			
LANG, Ludwig	40	Bingen	66-1127
Maria 32, Hermann 11m			
LANG, Margarethe	26	Hauba	64-0739
LANG, Maria	20	Angersbach	65-1030
LANG, Mary	24	Philadelphia	66-0734
LANG, Pauline	26	Dudolsheim	63-0990
Emma 27			
LANG, Peter	21	Kuenderheim	66-0679
LANG, Ph.	22	Neuenkirchen	64-0331
LANG, Theodore	18	Wiesbaden	63-0917
Chris. 16			
LANG, Wilhelmine	30	Kleinbastar	65-0151
Caroline 7, Elise 2			
LANGBEIN, Georg	38	Stuttgart	66-0679
LANGBEIN, Sophie	17	Marburg	66-0623
LANGE, (f)	42	Eisenach	63-0168
LANGE, Anna	16	Osnabrueck	67-0600
LANGE, Anna	20	Udeborn	65-1024
LANGE, Bernhard	26	Dorum	66-0679
LANGE, Carl Heinr.	46		65-0948
LANGE, Caroline	25	Poole	66-0623
LANGE, Catharine	22	Durbach	66-0679
LANGE, Christ.	33	Hallensen	63-0244
Dorothea 21, C. 34, H. 8, M. 6, E. 4			
LANGE, Christian	30	Meerane	65-0770
LANGE, Elisabeth	22	Wabern	66-1127
LANGE, F.H.	20	Boitzen	66-1248
LANGE, Frand.(f)	27	Leavenworth	64-0138
sister 22			
LANGE, Friedr.	34	Oldenburg	66-0984
Heinr. 22			
LANGE, Friedr. Chr	20	Pr. Minden	67-0599
Sophie Wm. E 14			
LANGE, Friedrich	24	Ob.Murschnitz	66-1248
Louise 21, Eduard 2, baby (f) 3m			
Dorothea 63			
LANGE, G.A.	20	Dorum	65-0402
LANGE, H.(m)	21	Preussen	64-0331
LANGE, H.B.	26	Bohmte	64-0639
Johannes 24			
LANGE, H.W.	23	Brunsen	66-0704
LANGE, Heinrich	23	Soerlern	66-1373
LANGE, Henry	24	Lackheim	66-0221
LANGE, Herm.	30	Dietz	65-0007
LANGE, Joachim	26	Velgau	64-0665
Elisabeth 32, Friederike 8			
LANGE, Johann	21	Weyhe	66-1031
LANGE, L.	31	Prussia	63-1003
LANGE, P.N.	30	Otterndorf	65-0402
LANGE, Sam.	21	Schaffhausen	64-0427
LANGE, Wilh.	14	Ahausen	63-1010
LANGE, Wilhelm	29	New York	66-0734
LANGE, Wilhelm	22	Belle	66-1203
LANGE, Wm.	30	Thedinghausen	63-1038
LANGEFELD, Christ.	17	Rosenthal	66-0578
LANGEHOF, Carl	28	Iserlohn	65-0004
LANGEMANN, Charltt	23	Hannover	66-0984
LANGEMANN, Hr.	19	Prussia	64-0432
LANGENBACH, Carol.	24	Genslach	63-1178
LANGENBACH, R.	34	New York	63-0482
LANGENBERG, Friedr	19	Osnabrueck	64-0427
Louise 25			

NAME	AGE	RESIDENCE	YR-LIST
LANGENBERG, Louis	17	Osnabrueck	66-0934
LANGENDORF, W.(m)	19	Weingarten	64-0495
LANGENHAGEN, Herm.	37	Wolfenbuettel	64-0687
Elise 25			
LANGENHAHN, Georg	16	Wichelshausen	66-1127
LANGENHEIM, Will.	22	New York	66-0109
LANGENSEN, Lina	21	Roedelheim	66-1327
LANGER, Anton	22	Pollritz	66-1373
LANGER, Johannes	23	Weschersbach	64-0073
LANGGOESSER, Georg	23	Mainz	66-1155
LANGGUTH, Friede.	15	Meiningen	66-0679
LANGGUTH, Georg	57	Brettendorf	65-0594
LANGHAGEN, G.	17	Sulingen	64-0593
LANGHAUS, Ernst	42	Gehrden	66-0469
Dorothea 41, Sophie 8, Caroline 9m			
LANGHEIM, E.	27	Braunschweig	65-0974
LANGHEINEKEN, Emil	21	Oldenburg	64-0938
Georg 3m			
LANGHEINIKE, Carl	20	Hannover	65-0243
LANGHEINZ, Elis.	56	Darmstadt	63-0551
LANGHENNING, Henry	28	Havingstedt	66-0221
LANGHOFF, Johann	31	Preussen	66-0147
LANGHOFT, A.(m)	21	Hamburg	64-0023
LANGHORST, Wilhelm		Rahden	65-1088
LANGMEYR, Josef	37	Crajowa	66-0576
LANGSDORF, Emil	15	Bottenfeld	65-0402
LANGSDORF, Sigm.	16	Rattenfeld	63-0482
LANGSLAHNE, W.	16	Westrup	64-0886
LANGSTADT, Bertha	30	Vosswinkel	64-1053
LANGSTADT, Susanna	25	Vosswinkel	64-1053
Adolph 8			
LANGSTROTH, James	28	Hamburg	66-0679
LANGUILLETTE, de E	45	Hickville	63-0862
Henry 12			
LANHARST, Ba.(f)	25	Bonames	64-0992
LANKEN, Doris	27	Rangstedt	66-1031
LANTING, John B.	29	Coesfeld	63-0990
LANTZ, Adam	27	Oberwalluft	66-1373
LANTZ, Dorothea	26	Darmstadt	66-1127
LANTZ, Nic.	33	Werchweiler	65-0007
LANZ, Catharina	21	Arnshain	66-1327
LANZMANN, Jos.	47	Milwaukee	66-0934
LAPP, Georg F.	19	Famberg	66-1243
LAPP, Heinr.	19	Erxdorf	64-0639
Elise 52			
LAPPE, Egan	21	Paderborn	64-0433
August 18			
LARAMBA, Katharina	33	Philadelphia	63-1069
Maria 6			
LARCH, Babette	22	Frankenthal	63-0862
LARSEN, Carl Ch.	22	Copenhagen	66-0666
LARSEN, Hans	21	Copenhagen	66-0666
Sophie 18			
LARSEN, Jens P.	22	Copenhagen	66-0666
LARSEN, Johann	36	Copenhagen	66-0666
LARZINGER, Wilhelm	23	Lenach	66-0221
LASCHEID, Peter	45	Eistorf	64-0331
Johanna 21			
LASE, Anna Cath.	24	Obervorschutz	64-0433
LASS, Diedrich	28	Hannover	66-1243
LASSELMANN, Chr. L	22	Hessen	63-1069
LASSEN, Carl	19	Pommern	66-0623
LASSER, Valentin	30	Klagenfurt	63-0990
LATERMANN, A.	21	Peine	63-1136
LATHMANN, Hannchen	24	Norden	66-1127
LATINNE, H.	21	Buessel	63-0953
LATSCH, Josephine	21	Kinzel	66-1243
LATT, Marianne	20	New York	63-0752
LATTMANN, Marie	28	Hessen	66-0734
LAU, Boniface	26	New York	63-0752
LAU, Henriette	29	Otterndorf	63-0990
LAU, Johann	31	Soessnowd	66-0469
Christine 24, Emilie 9m			
LAU, Johann	19	Elmslohe	66-0576
LAUB, Josefa	25	Boehmen	64-0427
LAUBENHEIMER, Wm.	17	Carlsruhe	65-0055
LAUBER, A.	30	Buesslingen	65-1024
LAUBER, Lisette	22	Meschede	63-0350
Minna 26			
LAUBER, M.	27	New York	63-0752
wife 22, baby 3m			
LAUBER, Peter	27	Dornholz	63-0821
Cathre. 25, John 2			
LAUBER, Rudolph	39	Ingenhain	66-0147
LAUBERSHEIMER, Ad.	23	Oldenburg	64-1108
LAUBIS, Frida	21	Schweiz	66-0934
LAUCHNER, Bernhard	26	Aue	64-1053
LAUDECKER, Hanni	22	Oberfranken	66-0984
Fanny 18			
LAUDENBACH, Cathr.	24	Oberweid	65-0950
LAUE, Diedrich	16	Schlusselberg	63-0614
LAUE, Heinrich	53	Platendorf	64-0904
Dorothea 40, Heinrich 30, Wilhelmine 23			
Friedrich 20, Christian 9, Wilhelm 7			
Ernst 6, Dorothea 2			
LAUENSTEIN, Carl	25	Bisperode	66-1313
Louise 34			
LAUER, Gertrud	33	Oberbessenbch	65-0038
LAUER, H.	30	Bremen	65-0116
LAUER, Henry	18	Muehlhausen	63-1038
LAUER, Jacob	30	Sailhofen	66-0221
LAUERMANN, Elisab.	20	Rheinhessen	63-0990
LAUF, Christian	27	Balduinstein	65-1030
Catharine 26, Anna Maria 3, Philippina 5			
Anna 3, Catharina 9m			
LAUFER, Friedr.	25	Zuerich	63-0350
LAUFER, Henriette	32	Hersfeld	63-0296
LAUFER, Louise	23	Esslingen	66-1203
LAUFER, Ulrich	35	Eglisau	63-0350
LAUGSHEIM, Heinr.	38	Brannschweig	64-0938
LAUKE, Wilhelmine	25	Heinade	65-0243
LAUMANN, Johann	17	Melle	66-1093
LAUMEYER, Frd. Wm.	34	Lotte	63-1069
LAUN, Cath. Elisab	23	Obermelrich	66-0412
LAUNER, Joseph	23	Glaubendorf	65-0950
LAUNSBACH, Carl	56	Hausen	65-0898
LAUPE, Hermann	26	Vollage	66-1203
LAUPERT, C.	33	Neustadt	64-1161
LAURENT, Rud.	19	Zweibruecken	64-0687
LAUSER, Carl	26	Stuttgart	65-0594
LAUSTER, Carl	22	Sternfels	66-0412
LAUTEN, Max H.	18	Rheda	64-0639
LAUTENBACHER, Joh.	47	Sachundorf	67-0795
LAUTENSCHLAEGER, A	26	Bechtheim	66-0679
LAUTENSCHLAEGER, J	10	Barmen	65-1024
LAUTENSCHLAEGER, M	30	New York	63-0752
LAUTER, Monika	29	Glatt	66-0412
LAUTERBACH, Anna E	25	Untershausen	65-0243
LAUTERBACH, Carl	34	Hausen	63-0398
LAUTERBACH, Georg	44	Heinbach	67-0007
LAUTERBACH, John W	18	Stotternheim	63-0693
LAUTEREN, C.L.	22	Mainz	65-1088
LAUTNER, Charles	50	Pittsburg	66-0934
LAUTNER, Kunigunde	22	Fischbach	66-0576
LAUTZ, Alexander	48	Gotha	66-1248
LAUTZER, H.	25	Ingenheim	64-0992
LAUX, Chs.	20	Gimbach	64-0495
Catharine 18			
LAUX, Ph.	18	Neustadt	63-1085
LAWALL, Philipp	21	Eppelsheim	63-1038
LAWANIC, W.	18	Brake	66-0413
LAX, Ed.	22	Minden	65-0594
LAY, Maria	19	Heidelberg	65-0151
LAYER, Gotthard	26	Reichenbach	67-0007
LAYER, Marie	30	Romgen	64-0495
LAYSE, Heinr.	25	Eisenberg	64-0023
LAZANSKY, Lewis	21	Kolinetz	63-0168
LE CAPPELLAUS, Joh	30	New York	63-1136
LEBER, Adolf	26	Coblenz	66-0147
Susanna 33, Susanna 6m			
LEBER, Ed.	24	Germany	64-0363
LEBER, Joseph	30	Aschaffenburg	66-0837
LEBER, Martin	34	Shehlingen	63-1136
Babtist 9m, Rosine 9m			
LEBOLD, David	15	Allendorf	65-1024
LEBRECHT, M.(m)	15	Memelsdorf	64-0782

NAME	AGE	RESIDENCE	YR-LIST
LEBRECHT, Simon	17	Hohenstein	63-0482
LEBSANFT, Wilhelm	18	Weil	67-0007
LEBSCH, Mathias	27	Proesingen	66-0679
Antonia 24, Catharine 11m			
LECHE, Zechiel	26	Duesseldorf	67-0954
LECHNER, Geo.	38	Chicago	64-0427
Magdalena 37			
LECKBRANDT, Wilh.	28	Gueglingen	63-0350
LECKE, Heinrich	49	Breitenbach	66-0412
Martha 19, Maria 17, Philippina 15			
Anna Cathar. 7, Christina 4			
LECKMANN, J.(m)	40	Bremen	64-0331
LEDEBUR, Adolph	19	Dissen	63-0953
LEDER, John	19	Oberflachs	63-1218
LEDER, Joseph	22	Sobotka	66-1373
LEDER, Maria	17	Boehmen	64-0427
LEDERER, Barbara	18	Koenigswart	66-0934
LEDERER, Caroline	20	Geroldstetten	66-1093
LEDERER, Christian	24	Atzberg	66-0346
LEDERER, Jacob	27	Arzberg	66-1031
Catharine 23, Margarethe 2, Catharine 11m			
LEDERER, Moses	16	Boehmen	63-0482
LEDERLE, Joh.	32	Switzerland	64-0170
LEDERMANN, M.	28	New York	64-0427
Henry 5			
LEDIG, Elise	42	Harsheim	64-1053
Charlotte 10m			
LEDING, Joh.	28	Lengstedt	64-0495
LEDOSQUET, Magd.	28	New York	64-0073
Eva 5, Marg. 4, baby 10m			
LEE, Andreas L.	36	California	63-0917
LEE, August	20	Sulzbach	66-0984
LEE, Meta	27	New Orleans	63-0990
Margaretha 9, Gustav 7, Hermine 5			
Benjamin 3			
LEEDE, Johann	18	Zainingen	67-0007
LEESEKAMP, Jacob	33	Emden	66-0349
LEESER, Franz	60	Dielingen	64-0920
Elisab. 53, Sophie Wm. 13, Heinr. Wm. 19			
LEESER, Henriette	28	Uthlede	63-0917
LEESMANN, Wilh.	32	Lotte	63-0953
Marie 28, John Rud. 58, Catharine 59			
Bernhard 2			
LEFFERT, Aug.	27	Burgsteinfurt	65-1088
LEGEL, Joh. Georg	16	Schwenningen	64-0687
LEGEL, Martin	31	Bavaria	66-0679
LEGENHAUSEN, Hain	18	Wachtendorf	66-0221
LEGER, Georg	23	Moscow	65-0402
LEHE, v. Henning	33	Padingbuettel	66-0704
Mathilde 29, Eide 9, Franz 7, Louis 5			
LEHFELD, Adelheid	22	New York	63-1085
LEHING, Friedrich	49	Wagenfeld	63-0006
LEHMAIER, G.	37	Forst	63-0551
LEHMAIER, Lewis	22	Leipzig	63-0752
LEHMAIER, Stephan	39	New York	63-0097
Sirela 33			
LEHMANN, Abrah.	19	Oberurbach	65-0116
LEHMANN, Adelb.	28	Oldenburg	63-0350
LEHMANN, Adolf	24	New York	66-0576
LEHMANN, Caroline	22	Altenkirchen	64-0639
LEHMANN, Catharina	28	Oldenburg	63-0350
LEHMANN, Christine	22	Bichelhorst	65-0594
LEHMANN, Hele	18	Furth	64-0782
LEHMANN, Henry	25	Wiedenbrueck	63-1218
LEHMANN, Joh.	25	Driburg	64-1206
Rebecca 18, Jettchen 20			
LEHMANN, Joseph	30	Fussgruenheim	63-1178
LEHMANN, Joseph	31	Burlington	63-1178
Babette 23, Maurice 9m			
LEHMANN, Julius	30	Rohschack	64-0138
Mrs. 24			
LEHMANN, Maria	21	Meerane	64-0331
LEHMANN, Marianne	30	Oldenburg	64-0840
Albert 5			
LEHMANN, Marie	22	Posen	66-0576
LEHMANN, Maur.	13	Zempelburg	63-1085
Elise 40, Friedrich 9, August 6			
Louise 11m, Louis 9			
LEHMANN, Minna	26	Dissen	65-0950
LEHMANN, Robert	23	Staffa	66-0576
LEHMKUHL, H.W.	20	Bremen	64-0214
LEHMKUHL, Henry	35	New York	63-0953
LEHMKUHL, Wilh'mne	25	Bremen	65-0243
LEHNARD, August	15	Hansbergen	63-1085
LEHNEMANN, Anna	19	Pommerfelden	64-0840
LEHNER, Gustav	26	Illingen	64-1053
LEHNER, Heinr.	22	Preussen	66-0221
LEHNER, Johann	35	Nuernberg	66-0147
LEHNER, Louise	30	New York	66-0576
Wilhelm 9			
LEHNERT, Joh.	22	Luewersbach	65-0594
Cath. 19, Johanna 18			
LEHR, Elisabeth	24	Rupertsberg	66-1203
LEHR, Friedrich	20	Neuhausen	66-1327
LEHR, Georg	30	Michelstadt	66-0679
Julie 28, Sophie 4			
LEHR, Hein.	22	Ruppertsburg	66-0984
LEHR, Heinrich	22	Dietzenbach	66-0679
LEHR, J.G.	26	Heslof	65-0007
Joh. 23			
LEHR, Peter	26	Hessloh	65-0770
LEHRACH, Barbara	29	Luhbritz	67-0007
Cecilie 7, Marie 6, Wenzel 2, Emanuel 11m			
LEHRBERGER, Amalia	26	Wetter	64-0904
LEHRBERGER, Lina	23	Fuerth	63-0752
LEHRIAN, Joh. Ph.	24	Zwingenberg	66-1313
Dorothea 31			
LEHRKIND, Friedr.	30	Milwaukee	63-0693
LEHRMANN, H.	40	Braunschweig	64-0432
Dorothea 31			
LEHTERT, Anton	31	Effelsberg	64-0992
LEIB, Georg	15	Horschheim	66-1093
LEIBER, Wolfgang	44	Hemstedt	64-0432
LEIBFARTH, John	46	Pittsburg	63-1218
Anna Marie 41			
LEIBOLD, W.(f)	40	Staubing	64-0427
LEICHEN, Hedwig	39	Aschwarden	63-0953
Emy 4			
LEICHEN, T.W.	17	Aschwarden	63-0953
LEICHER, Chr.	30	Philadelphia	63-0752
LEICHT, Jacob	42	Alteislingen	66-1373
Louise 26			
LEICHTENMEIS, (m)	21	Funkstadt	63-1085
LEICHTLE, Franz'ka	38	Baden	66-0576
LEIDECKER, Philipp	27	Pfaffenwierbh	64-0639
LEIDEDKER, August	28	Idenkopf	63-0097
LEIDEG, Cash.	33	Gruningen	65-0402
LEIDEL, Joh.	58	Zeitz	64-0886
LEIDENDECKER, J.H.	23	Illinois	64-0138
LEIDHAUSER, Ed.	16	Alt Buseke	64-0782
LEIDHAUSER, H.(m)	31	Ana	64-0331
LEIDHEISER, Dan.	17	Fritzlar	66-0837
LEIDNER, August	44	Bueringen	66-0576
Francisca 34, Joseph 9, Maria 7			
Josephine 4, Elizabeth 7m			
LEIDOLFS, E.(f)	18	Naunheim	64-0782
LEIENACKER, John	18	Sinzig	63-0693
LEIKERT, Caroline	19	Bavaria	63-0822
LEIMBACH, Cath.	36	Blankenheim	64-0331
LEIMBACH, Christ.	20	Cassel	66-0576
LEIMBACH, H.	22	Hildburghsn.	63-1003
LEIMBACH, Johann	28	Fraurambach	65-0713
LEIMBERGER, D.	23	Rexingen	64-1161
LEIMKE, Carl	30	Welkenried	66-0349
LEIMKOEHLER, Heinr	34	Dissen	66-1128
Charlotte 27, Marie 3			
LEIMKUEBLER, Henrt	25	Dissen	65-0950
LEIMKUEHLER, Minna	34	Melle	65-0402
LEIMKUHLER, F.W.	29	Aachen	64-0023
LEIMPOHL, Elisab.	24	Nienburg	65-1030
LEINBACH, Wilhelm	26	Wilhelmshsn.	65-0189
LEINER, Therese	9	Baden	66-0576
LEININGEN, Joh.Frd	26	Mickelbach	64-0427
LEINKUEHLER, Chr1t	27	Aschen	63-0917
LEIP, Charlotte	47	St. Louis	64-0593
Elise 16			

NAME	AGE	RESIDENCE	YR-LIST
LEIPALD, Jacob	48	Salzburg	64-0363
Wenzel 9			
LEIPERT, Joseph	27	Kirchheim	66-1248
LEIRE, Henr.	27	Melle	66-0984
LEISCH, Ludw.	22	Leidelsheim	64-0331
Che(f) 23			
LEISER, Andreas	27	Margelsheim	64-0214
LEISING, Theo	43	Ahrnsberg/Pr.	64-0432
Cath. 36, Franz 10, Casp. 7, Theod. 5			
Joseph 3m			
LEISLER, B.	24	Marburg	64-1161
LEISMANN, Cathrine	21	Ostbevern	66-1327
LEISS, Th.	16	Scholtte	65-0007
LEISSEN, Wubbe	32	Holtgaste	65-0594
LEISSLER, Martha	26	Cassel	66-1127
LEISSNER, Zerline	23	Walldorf	63-0244
M.(f) 32			
LEIST, Albert	18	Tantfeld	66-1327
LEITH, v.d. H.	25	Ritzebuettel	67-0007
LEITHARF, And.	28	Richach	65-0974
LEITHEUSER, Elise	26	Rotterod	64-1053
Mary 4m			
LEITMANN, Johannes	30	Frischborn	65-1030
Marie 22, Catharine 20			
LEITSCHUB, Wm.	42	Meiningen	64-0432
Marg. 39			
LEITZ, Salomon	40	Koenigswart	64-0427
Francisca 36, Flora 9m			
LEIWERS, H.(m)	31	Gr. Verne	65-0189
LEKER, Johann	25	Melle	66-0984
LELEWER, Isidor	27	Lessa	65-0055
LEMBERG, Johann B.	33	Scheppingen	66-0623
Johann 27, Wilhelm 19			
LEMCKE, F.	42	Ramanisch	66-0413
Gustav 17			
LEMCKE, Joh.	25	Freisenheim	65-0007
LEMHERTZ, Anna	23	Bremen	66-0072
LEMIKE, Henry	28	Herringhausen	63-0917
LEMINIL, Clotex	35	France	63-0350
Adele 28, Johan 7, John 1, Deni. 60			
LEMK, Franz	24	Neustadt	64-0363
LEMKE, Adolph	33	New York	63-0693
LEMKE, Peter	37	Bremervoerde	66-0984
Heinr. 7			
LEMKUHL, Lueder	25	Bremen	63-0917
LEMME, Fr.	22	Almersleben	65-1024
LEMMEN, Buttges	32	Aachen	64-1108
LEMMER, Helene	53	Solingen	66-1373
Wilhelmine 18, Carl 10, Helene 9			
LEMMERMANN, Anna	18	Loxstedt	66-1093
LEMMERT, Heinrich	19	Germersheim	65-1088
LEMMERT, Joh.	37	Lentzendorf	66-0469
Barbara 22, Pauline 10, Friedr. 8			
Joh. Georg 1			
LEMMLER, Ad.	50	Louisville	66-0704
Agnes 48			
LEMON, August	32	Darmstadt	66-1127
LEMPP, August	35	Rommelsbach	64-0427
LEND, Cathar.	36	Mainz	64-1053
LENDEMAN, Carsten	37	Nehrstedt	63-0296
LENDMEYER, M.E.(f)	33	West Cappeln	64-0331
LENERT, C.W.	21	Elstra	65-1030
LENG, Pauline	19	Cassel	64-0639
LENGER, Christ.	23	Siefenheim	66-1131
LENGFERMANN, Bernh	18	Oldenburg	66-1031
LENGK, J.(f)	36	Trostingen	64-0495
LENHARDT, Engelh.	21	Willmer	66-1203
LENI, Joh. Carl	28	Schwarzenbach	66-0666
LENK, Cunigunde	34	Mandel	66-1131
LENNEMANN, Paul	25	Prussia	64-0170
LENNEPPER, Joseph	30	Stelborn	66-0109
LENSCHAU, Fd.(m)	38	Luebeck	64-0495
Ma.(f) 6, A.(f) 4			
LENT, Caroline	34	Preussen	63-1218
Agnes 15, Oscar 10, Arnold 4			
LENT, Marie	23	Ninderheim	64-0170
LENTY, Carl	25	Mannheim	66-0679
LENTZ, Wilhelm	45	Preussen	64-0363
Wilhelmine 43, Anna 36, Anna 13			
Henriette 10, Maria 8, Anna 5			
LENTZSCH, Aug.	32	Glauchau	64-0495
Augusta 26, Aa.(f) 3			
LENZ, August	36	St. Louis	66-0679
LENZ, Christ.	16	Kuppingen	65-0243
LENZ, F.	23	Behle	63-1003
LENZ, Louis	17	Urbach	67-0007
LENZ, Susanne	42	Trier	64-0938
Johanna 32, Carolina 30			
LENZ, W.	27	Zug	64-0639
LENZE, Emma	18	Coeln	65-0055
LENZING, Andreas	36	Sielen	64-0739
Louise 34			
LEO, E.(m)	19	Wien	65-0189
LEO, Marie	43	Ebersbach	63-1136
Conrad 9, Ernst 8			
LEONARDT, Philipp	46	Dayton	63-0862
Charles 9			
LEONHARD, Conrad	35	Baden	66-0934
LEONHARD, Fr.	23	Heilbronn	64-0687
LEONHARDT, Charltt	30	Gibichenstein	65-0243
Reinhold 6			
LEONHARDT, Kath.	30	Lauran	65-0594
LEONHARDT, Ph.	30	Osthofen	64-0073
LEOPOLD, Agatha	40	Durchhausen	64-0639
LEOPOLD, James	23	Bestheim	63-1178
LEOPOLD, James	19	Louisville	63-0990
LEOPOLD, Joh.	23	Vihringen	66-1243
LEOPOLD, Johanna	17	Rechtenfleth	64-0456
LEOPOLD, Roeschen	22	Barchfeld	66-0704
Babette 20			
LEOPOLD, Salomon	18	Barchfeld	66-0934
Michael 19			
LEOPOLD, Wilh.	31	Steinau	65-1088
Casp. 31			
LEOPOLD, William	33	New York	63-0168
LEPP, Lina	27	Neckarbischof	66-1373
LEPPER, H.	33	Piken	65-0974
LERCH, Ca.(f)	15	Wallenrad	64-0363
LERCH, Eduard	24	Baden	63-1218
Emil 22			
LERCHE, Emil	18	Saalfeld	66-1131
LERCHE, Johanna	26	Bremen	64-0073
LERCHE, Th.	29	Saalfeld	65-0007
LERNER, Georg	21	Wuerttemberg	63-0822
LERNER, Johann	30	Germany	66-0666
LESCHINGER, Franz	27	Boehmen	63-0917
LESEMANN, Carl	25	Uslar	64-0687
LESER, Heinrich	26	Baden	66-0679
LESER, Sophie	16	Frankfurt/M.	64-0886
Emma 18			
LESS, (f)	24	Lippdo	66-0413
LESSER, Carl	21	Kopenhagen	65-0898
LESSER, Wilhelm	29	Paris	67-0007
LESSING, Christian	24	Bremen	64-0456
LESSING, Christian	26	Bremen	65-1030
Margarethe 30			
LESSING, H.	27	Lupow	63-1003
LESSJACK, Therese	25	Mieger	66-1327
LETSCHE, Christoph	28	Undingen	66-1155
Barbara 31, Johannes 1			
LETSCHE, Friedr.	22	Eibersbach	65-0948
LETZING, Catharina	18	Borgheim	64-0214
LEU, M.	23	Laskunitz	66-0413
LEUCKART, Elis.	24	Freiburg	64-0593
LEUDENBACH, Mich.	39	Zettlitz	66-0666
LEUPOLD, Conrad	27	Almbranz	64-0886
Catharine 24			
LEUPOLD, Pauline	28	Neustadt	64-0938
LEUPOLD, William	26	Schlesien	63-0693
LEUTNER, Philip	19	Hanau	65-0116
LEVI, Aug.	19	Aufhausen	63-1136
LEVI, August	23	Esslingen	66-1155
LEVI, Fanni	22	Laitbach	65-0594
Magdalena 35, Cath. 7, baby 10m, Lina 20			
LEVI, Fanny	18	Deftensee	64-0687
LEVI, Henriette	22	Esslingen	64-0938

NAME	AGE	RESIDENCE	YR-LIST
LEVI, Henriette	18	Worms	65-0402
LEVI, Herman	16	Adelsdorf	64-0639
LEVI, Leib	17	Oberwurst	66-0221
LEVI, M.	25	Waiblingen	63-1136
LEVI, Marcus	29	Boehmen	63-1136
LEVI, Minna	27	Moehringen	65-0594
LEVI, Sp.	17	Laudenbach	63-0693
LEVINTASS, Matilda	17	Emmendingen	63-1178
LEVIS, Aron	14	Eppelsheim	63-1038
LEVISOHN, A.	24	New York	63-0862
LEVY, Abraham	67	Braunfels	66-0679
LEVY, Anna	22	Burweis	66-0679
LEVY, Arthur	32		63-1136
LEVY, B.(m)	20	Worms	64-0023
LEVY, B.S.	36	New York	66-0934
LEVY, Bertha	18	Lauheim	63-0917
LEVY, Bertha	21	Preussen	64-0214
LEVY, Berthold	29	Frankenberg	65-0974
LEVY, Clara	18	Ihlingen	65-0007
LEVY, Emilie	35	Duesseldorf	64-0170
LEVY, Fanny	22	Kurhessen	66-0704
LEVY, Francisca	30	Bremen	66-0576
LEVY, Georg	24	Burgsteinfurt	66-0984
LEVY, Gottfried	45	London	63-0015
LEVY, Gustav	15	Berlin	63-0821
LEVY, Israel	18	Erdmansrode	66-0679
LEVY, Itzig	33	Burgsteinfurt	67-0795
Julie B. 22, Veilcherr 9m			
LEVY, J.	30	Neukirch	63-0752
LEVY, Jos.	17	Ilhingen	65-0007
LEVY, Lesser	20	Schonlande	64-1206
LEVY, Siegf.	18	Lindenberg	64-0992
LEVY, Simon	36	Aufhausen	66-0734
Marie 18			
LEWALD, Feist	15	Borgfeld	64-0593
LEWI, J.	22	Hannover	65-0055
LEWIN, Lazarus	32	Berlin	64-0840
LEWIS, Ann	35	Germany	63-1178
LEWITZ, Leopold	34	Ostein	66-0734
LEYHE, Fritz	27	Twiste	66-1327
LEYHOLD, Friedrich	22	Schuerwitz	66-1327
LEYKOFF, Nicolaus	32	Fort Wagne	66-0679
LEYMANN, Heinrich	18	Bruchmuehl	66-0147
LEYRER, Pauline	15	Affalterbach	64-1022
LEZING, August	23	Berchheim	65-1095
Christian 17			
LIAS, L.(m)	42	New York	64-0170
LIBAS, Jacob	23	Berlin	66-0734
LIBAS, Theophil	41	Berlin	66-0734
Anna 36, Emil 1			
LICHER, Math.	31	Eppendorf	64-0938
LICHINS, Margareth	22	Atzenbach	63-0551
LICHT, Adrian	26	Rummels	65-0713
LICHT, Carl	22	Hanau	65-0004
LICHTENBERG, Joh.P	27	Cassel	67-1005
LICHTENSTEIN, Lou.	18	Menne	65-0898
LICHTLECHTER, Frz.	30	Osnabrueck	66-1131
LICKTEIG, Franz	24	Dinsieders	64-0138
Catharine 24, Marie 2, Joseph 3m			
LICKUEBER, Silvest	19	Riegel	63-1178
LIEB, Frz Jos.	20	Istern	64-0363
LIEB, Simon	25	Ottenhausen	66-0576
LIEB, Thomas	23	Flehsingen	63-0015
LIEBCHEN, Mathias	33	Wennigloh	64-1206
Sophia 28, Anton 2, Sophia 2m			
LIEBECK, Joseph	45	Woelf	66-0349
LIEBENBERG, Moses	22	Lippoldshsn.	65-0402
LIEBER, Jacob	16	Ranitz	64-0593
Julius			
LIEBERMANN, Anna	27	Roehrburg	66-0623
LIEBERMANN, Ba.(m)	25	Diesslingen	64-0782
LIEBERMANN, Bab.	18	Alt.Kundstadt	63-0551
LIEBERMANN, Louise	24	Rottweil	66-1155
LIEBERUM, Georgina	17	Herrnbreitung	66-0349
LIEBES, Louis	20	Preussen	63-1178
Augusta 21			
LIEBHARD, Cathrine	19	Stuttgart	66-0083
Wilhelmine 23			

NAME	AGE	RESIDENCE	YR-LIST
LIEBICH, Mina	33	Gera	63-0693
Penny 9, Alice 8, Arthur 7, Rosa 6			
LIEBIG, Joh. G.	22	Niederhausen	65-0038
Joh.Jacobina 21, Cath. Marg. 16			
LIEBIG, Nath.(f)	25	Aachen	64-0495
Carl 11m			
LIEBING, Fr.(m)	16	Lengerich	64-0170
LIEBING, Hy.	39	Lengerich	63-1085
LIEBMANN, Ag.	18	Erfurt	64-1161
LIEBMANN, Ida	21	Cassel	63-1085
LIEBRANZ, Mad.(f)	23	Loquard	64-0331
LIEBREICH, Sophie	31	Bernhausen	66-1131
Caroline 9			
LIEDECKER, Theo.	15	Ihlienworth	64-0427
LIEDER, Joh. H.	19	Herleshausen	64-0593
LIEGFELD, Flor.	26	St. Louis	63-1136
LIEKER, Johanna	23	Versmold	65-0974
LIEKS, Ferdinand	24	Kempten	66-0147
LIERE, John H.	39	Gehrde	63-0350
LIERMANN, L.	40	Albertinhof	66-1248
Bertha 30, Helene 7, Anna 3, Wilhelm 1			
LIES, Friedrich	31	Dippach	66-1155
LIESBERGER, Daniel	26	Lisberg	66-0734
LIESCH, Andreas	23	Graubuenden	63-0693
LIESCHMER, Wensel	26	Boehmen	66-0221
Franz 32			
LIESE, C.	15	Limmer	66-0413
LIESE, Friederike	21	Rotenburg	66-1031
LIESE, Julius	21	Rothenburg	64-0938
LIESENDAHL, F. (f)	28	Burscheid	64-0495
LIESKE, Aug.	29	Putzighauland	63-1003
LIESTMANN, Ludw.	26	Dessau	65-0189
LIETH, Juergen	20	Elmslohe	66-0576
Catharine 17			
LIETH, Martin	22	Hannover	64-0432
LIETSCHY, Jacob	26	Switz	63-0350
Caspar 21			
LIETZ, v.d. W.	24	Messelwarden	64-0495
LIFKE, Christoph	24	Sunkendorf	63-0482
LILBAY, F.W.	21	Portland, Me.	64-0495
LILIENFELD, Amalie	18	Hannover	64-1022
Henriette 25			
LILIENFELD, D.	29	Diepenau	64-0938
LILIENFELD, Wilhm.	30	Diepenau	66-0984
LILIENKAMP, Ernst	30	Unterluebbe	64-1108
LILIENSTEIN, Guede	20	Grossenfelden	66-0934
LILIENSTROEM, v. G	34	Anklam	65-1030
Gust.A. 34			
LILIENTAL, Matilda	21	Braunschweig	66-0934
LILIENTHAL, Hanke	43	Wolpeln	66-0704
Catharina 37, Anna 8, Dorothea 6			
Margaretha 5, Rebecca 4, Mathilde 10m			
LILIENTHAL, Her.	15	Holzel	65-1088
LILIENTHAL, M.	29	Berlin	65-0007
LILLE, Lina	18	Rastatt	66-1243
LILLIE, Jacob	16	Meisenheim	64-0363
LIMBACH, Elisabeth	29	Wabern	64-0840
LIMBERG, Casper	36	Britzmuehle	65-1031
Anna 31, Carl 8, Heinrich 2, Ferdinand 2m			
LIMBERG, Rheinhard	26	Lippe Detmold	65-1031
LIMMER, G.H.(m)	20	Leipzig	64-0170
LIMONT, Adolphe	26	France	64-0170
LIMPRECHT, Ferd.	48	Berlin	64-1206
LINCK, Heinr.	25	Pfordt	64-0214
LINCKOGEL, Mariann	26	Woehle	64-0214
LIND, Georg C.	16	Nidda	65-0594
LINDAU, Anna	60	Schale	64-0363
Lambert 34, Anna 30, L.H. 3, J.G. 3m			
LINDAUER, Carl	23	Lienzingen	67-0007
LINDEMAN, Marie	18	Barkhausen	64-0433
LINDEMANN, Ange.	26	Rotenburg	64-0992
LINDEMANN, Anna	52	Emden	63-0917
LINDEMANN, Casp.	20	Langsfeld	66-1243
LINDEMANN, Caspar	54	Emperhausen	64-0885
Anna 50, Andreas 20, Caspar Adam 18			
Christian 14, Margaret El. 9			
LINDEMANN, Casper	40	Eckhardts	66-0469
Dorothea 28, Elisabeth 14, Ernst 5			

NAME	AGE	RESIDENCE	YR-LIST
LINDEMANN, Charltt	17	Dissen	65-0950
LINDEMANN, Chrs.	34	New York	66-0221
LINDEMANN, G.H.	25	Osnabrueck	64-0432
Maria 23			
LINDEMANN, H.	15	Bolschklee	64-0992
LINDEMANN, Harm	38	Rhauderfehn	64-0739
Jan 28, Elsina 5, Engeline 2, Hermann 4m			
LINDEMANN, Heinr.	19	Wahn	66-0469
LINDEMANN, Theod.	26	Kohlenfeld	66-1243
Theod. 6			
LINDEMANN, Wm.	32	Marzell	65-0055
LINDEN, Johann	29	Mayen	66-0837
LINDEN, v.d.Herm.	35	Baltimore	64-0138
LINDENBAUM, Hannch	25	Eschwege	67-0007
LINDENKOHL, Wilh.	26	Messina	66-1203
LINDENLAUB, Carol.	32	Lahr	64-0427
LINDENSTRUTH, Elis	25	New York	66-0934
LINDER, Jacob	29	Ufingen	66-1155
LINDER, Robert	24	Scharrenberg	63-0614
LINDERER, Wm.	30	Aschern	64-0687
LINDERORTH, Heinr.	19	Osterkappel	66-1031
LINDHEIM, Anton	26	New York	66-0679
LINDHEIM, Moses	16	Rennertehsn.	63-0482
LINDHORN, N.(m)	30	Bremen	64-0214
LINDHORST, Heinr.	18	Siedenberg	66-1093
LINDIG, Peter	38	Limburg	66-0934
LINDLAGE, Sophie	23	Neunkirchen	66-1248
LINDLAU, Barbara	24	Coelln	64-0199
Sibilka 1			
LINDLOFF, Heinrich	20	Roiskielde	66-0666
LINDNER, Alb.	47	Freiburg	65-0007
LINDNER, Anna	19	Gera	66-0412
LINDNER, Gottf.	36	Prussia	63-0752
Maria 30, Pauline 6, Johanna 11m			
LINDNER, Heinr.	14	Eisfeld	64-0593
LINDNER, Jul.	30	Osterburg	64-0992
LINDNER, L.	25	Wienheim	65-1189
LINECK, Jacob	36	Trostingen	63-0990
LINENFELSER, Mart.	34	Darmstadt	64-1053
LING, Fr.	32	Altengerecke	66-0704
LINGEBACH, Ferdin.	20	Cincinnati	66-0679
LINGEN, v. G.A.	25	Baltimore	64-0214
LINGENFELDER, Theo	26	Gemmeldingen	65-0055
LINGNER, Carl	21	Schoenau	66-0083
LINK, Carl	17	Wiesbaden	64-1022
LINK, Cath.	28	New York	63-0482
Mary 4, Chris 11m			
LINK, Georg	19	Herrenzimmern	64-0023
LINK, J.F.	30	Grottingen	64-0363
Andreas 20			
LINK, Johannes	29	Mittelbuchen	65-1030
Caroline 28, Heinrich 1			
LINK, Peter	19	Hessia	66-0679
LINK, R.	23	Leimbach	66-0734
Maria 21, Maria 2m			
LINKE, Amalia	32	Berlin	65-0594
Clara 3, Marie 2			
LINKE, Wilhelmine	41	Carlsruhe	64-0886
Joseph 13, Wilhelm 12, Gustav 4, Carl 1			
LINKER, Lisette	21	Braungesheim	63-1136
LINKER, W.(m)	22	Wingershausen	64-0331
LINKER, Wilhelm	23	Leer	66-1131
LINKGRAF, Elisab.	22	Neustadt	66-0734
Wilhelm 4, Christian 32, Carl 2, Elise 6m			
LINKHORST, Christ.	34	Luderstadt	64-0687
child 7			
LINKOGEL, Marianna	26	Woehle	64-0214
LINN, Carl	40	Ohio	63-0990
LINN, Carl	27	Neuwied	64-1161
Wilhelmine 29, Max 3, Anna 9m			
LINN, Christine	28	Tripstadt	63-0990
Carl 18, Jacob 18			
LINN, Peter	30	Lippstadt	65-0243
Eva 26, Philipp 4, Charlotte 9m			
Cathar. 59, Cathar. 16			
LINNE, Sus.	23	Wolfgruben	65-0402
LINNEMEIER, Heinr.	40	Rehburg	66-0576
Heinr. 9			
LINNEMEYER, Joh.	32	Hannover	63-0398
LINS, Cath. Elis.	22	Oberzelle	66-0650
LINS, Marie	22	Altenstadt	63-1085
LINSENMAYER, James	41	Stettin	63-0693
LINSKY, Nathalie	20	Prussia	64-0432
LINTIG, Helene	19	Wremen	66-1127
LINZ, Cath.	30	Eschingen	64-0639
LINZ, Chr.	35	Aach	65-0402
LINZ, Georg	28	Bremen	63-0614
LINZ, Georg	19	Fuerth	65-0594
LINZ, Johann	19	Fuerth	65-0713
LINZ, Nicolaus	24	Eichfeld	66-0346
LINZE, W.	28	Muenden	64-0840
LINZHEIM, Alex'dr.	20	Calbe	64-1022
LINZL, Samuel	26	Pest	65-0594
LION, Daniel	30	Prag	66-1031
LIPERMANN, Robert	20	Sachsen	66-0147
LIPFELD, Wilhelm	29	Ostheim	66-0984
LIPKE, Christian	29	Hetzdorf	66-0578
Charlotte 25, Augusta 1			
LIPKOW, Wilhelm	31	Wirchow	65-0770
LIPOWITZ, Max	24	Berlin	65-0004
LIPP, Adam	27	Carlsruhe	64-1022
LIPPE, Theodor	30	Lobmachtersen	64-0739
LIPPER, Jul.	16	Fuerstenau	65-0898
LIPPER, W. .	27	Loxten	65-0974
Friderike 23, Lina 11m			
LIPPERT, August	32	Newark	64-0138
LIPPERT, August	22	Eudorf	64-0023
LIPPERT, Catharine	20	Hessia	66-1093
LIPPERT, Christine	19	Hoff	65-1024
LIPPERT, Conrad	20	Kleba	63-0097
LIPPERT, Edmund	20	Leipzig	64-0343
LIPPERT, Helene	41	Leipzig	66-0576
Carl 2, Paul 10m			
LIPPMANN, Aug. F.	53	Stengendorf	64-0023
Johanna 53, Emilie 25, Wilhelmine 23			
Herrman 17, Leberecht 12, Ernst 12			
Sophie 9, Emma 8m			
LIPPMANN, H.G.	22	Bremen	64-0427
LIPPMANN, Henriett	33	Wankheim	66-0734
LIPPODT, Joh. Aug.	47	Meissen	64-1108
Christine 41, Anna 20, Maria 13			
Augusta 7, Heinrich 18, August 15			
Oswald 11m			
LIPPOLD, George	38	Langensalza	64-0593
Friederike 28, Augusta 4			
LIPPOLD, Joseph	26	Thedinghausen	64-0593
LIPPOLD, Richard	26	Zwickau	64-1206
LIPSKE, Jacob	33	Kunitz	65-0713
LIPSTADTER, J.	21	Heddenhausen	64-0495
LIRINGER, Anna	24	Freinsheim	64-1022
LISIUS, Franz	50	Danzig	66-0666
LISNER, Selig	53	Walldorf	64-0938
Amalie 54, Johanna 17, Abraham 13			
LISTMANN, Carl	22	Lauterbach	63-0398
LITSCHGI, Leonhard	17	Pfafenweiler	66-0679
LITT, Matth.	30	New York	63-0350
LITTAU, Joseph	27	Lich	63-0990
LITZ, John B.	18	Emsbuehren	63-1038
John G. 22			
LITZAU, Joh. Heinr	21	Spiekauenfeld	63-0614
LITZENBERGER, Hch.	50	Neustadt	64-1108
LIVONI, Peter	24	Sonderburg	63-0398
LIWAN, Bertha	28	Sangershausen	63-0953
August 9m			
LOB, C.(m)	16	Philippsberg	64-0495
LOB, Otto	28	Coeln	64-0073
LOB, Rud.	54	Dehren	65-1189
Taub. 48			
LOBE, F.W.(m)	35	New York	64-0495
Mess.(f) 25			
LOBE, Ferdinand	20	Odenwald	65-0004
LOBEJAEGER, Louise	22	Berlin	66-0934
baby 9m			
LOBL, Regina	18	Pesth/Ungarn	65-0898
LOBOKISKY, Andreas	29	Zochnoc	64-0433
LOBSTEIN, Fanny	19	Brueck	64-0782

NAME	AGE	RESIDENCE	YR-LIST
LOCHER, Rud.	26	Bechtolzweilr	66-0704
LOCHIER, Diedrich	21	Offenbach	66-1248
LOCKEMANN, C.	40	Herbenhausen	64-0992
Gustav 41			
LOCKEWITZ, Justus	30	Burgen	64-0885
LOCKMANN, Jacob	24	Gunnersblum	64-1022
LODDE, W.H.	27	Asgerberg	66-0413
LODERHOSE, H.A.	18	Frankenberg	64-0363
E.J. 20			
LOEB, Aron	35	New York	66-0576
LOEB, Aug.	20	Bechtheim	64-1161
LOEB, Christine	63	Schweppeshaus	64-0639
Caroline 28, Caroline 7			
LOEB, Goetz	26	Gedern	63-1218
LOEB, Gustav	17	Buchtheim	64-0214
LOEB, Joseph	23	Bechtheim	66-0679
LOEB, Marens	24	New York	63-0990
LOEB, Regine	21	New York	66-0576
Regine 6m			
LOEB, Rosa	25	Obertshausen	63-1178
LOEB, Rosalie	19	Darmstadt	66-0576
LOEB, S.	16	Dehren	65-1189
S. 7, Sophie 5			
LOEB, S. (m)	35	New Orleans	64-0073
LOEB, Sophie	24	Sloesheim	66-0679
LOEBE, E. Otto	20	Troeben	64-0432
LOEBEL, Marcus	37	Falkenau	66-1373
LOEBENSTEIN, Lob.	22	Heringen	65-1024
LOEBER, Anna	21	Dienstag	66-0623
LOEBER, Aug.	14	Giessen	65-0038
LOEBER, Conr. Emil	34	Cassel	64-0739
LOEBER, Friedrich	23	Neuhoff	63-0990
Hermann 17			
LOEBER, Johannes	19	Niehnstein	65-1095
LOEBER, Marie	25	Langenstein	65-1030
LOEBLE, Paul	16	Shirendorf	67-0007
LOEBLIN, Elisabeth	24	Schaurheim	65-0004
LOEBMEIER, Sophie	26	Ibbenbuehren	66-1127
LOEBNER, Gust.	32	New York	66-0704
LOEFEL, Jacob	25	Ortenburg	66-0837
LOEFFLER, C.	24	Wuertemberg	63-1085
LOEFFLER, Christ.	13	Kleebronn	64-0427
LOEFFLER, Ernst	44	Washington	66-0109
LOEFFLER, Fritz	30	New York	67-0007
Lina 20			
LOEFFLER, Heinrich	21	Darmstadt	65-0865
LOEFFLER, Henry	42	New Orleans	63-1085
Mary 33, Fanny 10			
LOEFFLER, Johann	21	Blankenbach	66-0576
LOEFFLER, Sophie	32	Eibigheim	66-0734
LOEFFLER, Wilhelm	35	Oberrad	65-1095
LOEFLED, Caspar	30	Reichenbach	66-1327
LOEH, Philipp	29	Varel	66-0704
Johanne 21			
LOEHFINK, Frank	20	Rossbach	66-1327
LOEHNER, Anton	40	San Francisco	63-0693
LOEHNER, Carl	23	Fuerth	65-0151
LOEHR, Andr.	32	Cairo	64-0138
Catharine 27, Hermine 6			
LOEHR, Margrethe	28	Pottenstein	66-1327
LOEHR, Sebastian	65	Baden Noedles	66-1031
Kunigunde 63, Joseph 28			
LOEL, August	25	Pfungstadt	66-0668
LOELKAMP, Ebenhard	42	Poeckinghsn.	64-0840
Ilsabein 26, Catharine 4, Wilhelm 11m			
Marie 11m, Joh. 17			
LOELL, Johannes	41	Werdorf	66-1031
Elisabeth 36, Johanna 10, Wilhelmine 7			
LOELLE, Kaspar	23	Louisville	64-0170
LOEN, Bernhard	28	Seegedin	66-0734
Peter 8			
LOENCKER, Heinr.	25	Blasheim/Pr.	65-0038
LOENE, Gottlieb	20	Barnstein	67-0007
LOEPPER, Wilhelm	25	Liszkowke	66-0469
LOERRY, Fanny	22	Boehmen	66-0221
LOERS, T.J.	35	Bueckeburg	66-1127
Franke 30, Johann 8, Franke 9m			
LOERSCH, Christine	26	Oppenheim	66-0668
LOES, Anna Martha	20	Verna	65-0898
LOESCH, Joh.	21	Pfullingen	66-1313
LOESCHE, Herm.	14	Wehden	63-1136
LOESCHE, Wilhelm	20	Wehrder	66-1127
LOESCHEN, Albert R	27	Grossefehn	66-1128
Rolf R. 23			
LOESCHER, Fr. Aug.	20	Frankerhausen	65-0402
Clara 26			
LOESCHER, Robert	28	Frankenhausen	66-1327
LOESE, Carl	25	Goeln	66-0469
Maria 28, Mini 9m, Daniel 62			
LOESEN, Aug.	29	Gruenenplan	64-0886
LOESER, Ernestine	23	Habichtswald	63-0693
LOESKING, Hr.	19	Varrel	65-1031
LOEW, Jac.	18	Stuttgart	65-0594
LOEW, Siegmund	22	Wien	66-1373
LOEWE, Chr.	25	Peskelsheim	66-1203
LOEWE, Ernst Aug.	19	Siebenlehn	63-0953
LOEWE, Moritz	29	Reichenbach	66-1093
LOEWENBEIN, Judith	56	Liebeschuetz	63-0482
LOEWENBERG, Emma	24	Vorarlsberg	64-0992
LOEWENFELS, Jeanet	29	Raubenheim	64-0687
Babette 24			
LOEWENHERZ, Joseph	27	Lauenvoerde	64-0363
LOEWENSOHN, Gust.	33	Schwerin	63-0953
LOEWENSOHN, Mons.	9	Oberwiesse	65-1024
LOEWENSTEIN, Bernh	18	Fuerth	66-1373
LOEWENSTEIN, Bernh	17	Hoeringhausen	65-0898
LOEWENSTEIN, Chs.	18	Lichtenstadt	64-0593
LOEWENSTEIN, David	18	Schoenbrunn	65-1024
LOEWENSTEIN, Flora	22	Altenstadt	66-0704
LOEWENSTEIN, Fr'ke	21	Salzwedel	66-1127
LOEWENSTEIN, Fr.	17	New York	63-0551
LOEWENSTEIN, G.	21	Hadamar	65-0007
LOEWENSTEIN, Gudul	19	Elsdorf	63-0990
LOEWENSTEIN, Heinr	20	Cassel	66-0679
LOEWENSTEIN, Isaac	36	Elsdorf	63-0990
LOEWENSTEIN, Isaak	33	Kronhausen	65-1031
Jette 31, Jacob 3			
LOEWENSTEIN, L.	26	Jever	64-0938
LOEWENSTEIN, Liebm	17	Haringshausen	64-1206
LOEWENSTEIN, M.	18	Busack	65-0594
LOEWENSTEIN, Minna	30	Mollenfeld	66-0984
Moses 5, Magnus 8m			
LOEWENSTEIN, Moses	25	Bredenbach	64-0687
Michael 22			
LOEWENSTEIN, Otto	17	Berlin	65-0770
LOEWENSTEIN, Sabin	25	Angerod	65-0594
LOEWENSTEIN, Sara	23	Rutershausen	64-0593
LOEWENSTEIN, Soph.	26	Wachbach	64-0687
LOEWENTHAL, Daniel	17	Brubach	66-0679
LOEWENTHAL, Herm.	27	Berlin	63-1178
LOEWENTHAL, Isaac	18	Laupheim	64-0593
LOEWENTHAL, Moritz	25	Hannover	64-1022
LOEWER, Valent.	19	Homberg	63-0862
LOEWI, Valentin	34	Fuerth	63-0953
LOEWY, Marens	35	Wien	66-0576
LOEWY, Sigmund	20	Elbogen	66-0704
LOGARDE, Emil	25	New York	63-0752
LOGEMANN, Conr.	30	Cabre	64-0073
LOGEMANN, Conrad	36	Hannover	66-0734
Margarethe 24			
LOGEMANN, Cord	44	Gesche	42-0704
Hinrich 14, Dorothea 8, Sophie 7, Marie 5			
Hermann 2			
LOGEMANN, D.W.G.	19	Geestemuende	65-1031
LOGEMANN, Heinr.	19	Bremerhaven	64-0170
LOGES, Johanna	20	Bremen	64-0073
LOGGEMANN, Friedr.	25	Wagenfeld	65-0950
LOGUS, Carl	35	Fuerth	64-0938
Julius 25, Amalie 23, Henriette 21			
Fuerchtegott 25			
LOH, Anna	32	Konitz	64-1022
LOHER, K.	24	Leine	66-0413
LOHEYDE, Oscar	24	Lingen	66-1093
LOHF, H.	22	Haltern	63-0482
LOHLE, B.	30	Buesslingen	65-1024
LOHMAELTER, Chryso	26	Berg	63-0482

NAME	AGE	RESIDENCE	YR-LIST
LOHMANN, Albert	18	Holzminden	64-0639
LOHMANN, Anna	25	Goettingen	66-1155
LOHMANN, Carl	18	Ottenstein	64-1108
LOHMANN, F.(m)	26	Westfalen	64-0495
LOHMANN, G.	15	Brinkum	65-1024
LOHMANN, H.	27	Osterwelde	65-0402
LOHMANN, Herm.	29	Verden	64-0456
Cath. M. 27, Heinrich 4, Johann 3m			
LOHMANN, J.H.	21	Hassendorf	64-0214
LOHMANN, Joh. F.	29	Bielefeld	66-0577
Anna 29			
LOHMANN, Leopold	22	Muenchehoff	65-0151
LOHMANN, Salom.	14	Baiersdorf	63-0862
Babette 15			
LOHMANN, Wilh'mine	24	Dissen	66-1128
LOHMEIER, H.	45	Nienburg	66-0413
Marie 45, Sophie 17, August 14			
LOHMEYER, Carl A.H	36	Haldern	63-0006
LOHMEYER, Fr.	33	Lashorst	65-0898
Wilhelmine 26			
LOHN, Hannchen	16	Pleschen	64-0840
LOHNER, Anton	35	Posthof	66-1031
LOHNS, Anna	19	Epplingen	64-0840
LOHR, Eduard	45	Anweiler/Bav.	66-0837
LOHRENGEL, Carl	18	Bilshausen	64-0433
LOHRMANN, M.	54	Frielendorf	66-0704
LOHRMANN, Nic.	34	Feldstetten	64-0363
LOHSE, Carl Julius	53	Kamentz	64-0433
LOHSE, Metta	42	New York	64-0593
Christ.(f) 15			
LOHSE, Peter	29	Osterbruch	65-0594
Wilhelmine 23			
LOMER, Emil	26	Leipzig	65-0055
LOMPA, Emanuel	35	Zuetz	65-0189
LONICKER, Marie	60	Rodenberg	67-0600
LONTAF, Caroline	39	Boehmen	64-0023
Gustav 18			
LOOCK, H.E.A.	23	Netze	65-0402
LOOS, Henriette	35	Wien	65-0055
LOOS, T.	25	Laspberg	66-1248
LOOS, Wilhelm	22	Liesenwold	64-0886
LOOSCHEN, Johann	32	Hoechst	66-0679
Lina 26			
LOOSE, Conrad	21	Bremen	64-1022
LOOSE, Diedr	23	Neuenwalde	66-1373
LOOSE, Joh.	20	Berlin	65-0004
LOOSER, Friedr.	34	Baden	66-0734
LOPFS, Folina	39	Leer	63-1136
Henno 15, Meta 13, Bernhard 9, Theodor 7			
LOPPIN, A. (m)	39	New York	63-0821
wife 30, Anna 10, Louise 8, Alex 7			
Edward 6, Albert 2			
LORBEER, Ferd.	40	New Leixin	63-0482
LORBEER, R.(m)	18	Boehmen	64-0495
LORBER, Maria	27	Klagenfurt	63-1218
LORCH, Joh.	32	Tuttlingen	65-0007
Magd. 24			
LORENTZ, August	37	Hagendorf	67-0599
LORENZ, Aug.	21	Maningen	64-0639
LORENZ, Carl Otto	20	Weimar	64-1022
LORENZ, Friedr.	38	Muenster	64-0214
Gottl. 17, Jacob 8, Friedr. 6			
LORENZ, Henriette	20	Wremen	66-1093
LORENZ, Henry	42	Baltimore	63-1136
LORENZ, Ludmilla	25	Tojanov	67-0007
LORENZ, M.F.	31	New York	63-0752
LORENZ, Mathias	40	Weimar	66-0469
Johannes 16			
LORENZ, Paul	20	Westhausen	66-1373
LORENZ, Wm.	16	New York	64-0495
LOREY, Anton	26	Alsfeld	66-1248
LOREY, Heinrich	24	Hessia	66-0679
LOREY, Wilhelm	16	Iselburg	66-1327
LORG, Margaretha	32	Hessfurth	66-1155
baby 3m, Aloys 7, Nicolaus 14, Joseph 2			
LORIC, Jacob	18	Stapna/Boh.	64-0920
LORINI, Vera	28	London	63-1085
LORWICH, Wm.	21	Paris	67-0007

NAME	AGE	RESIDENCE	YR-LIST
LOSCH, Carl	29	Nuertingen	66-1327
LOSCH, Ignatz	17	Gratz	67-0992
LOSCHER, Jacob	20	Bueren	66-1127
LOSEKAMM, J.C.	17	Worms	64-0363
LOSEMANN, G.H.(m)	52	West Cappeln	64-0331
LOSER, Mathias	62	Germany	63-0350
Magdalene 56			
LOSSIUS, Franz	25	Kribitzen	66-0623
LOSTE, Christian	30	Baltimore	64-0363
LOTGE, Johann	53	Oberwald	63-0917
Martha 47, Emilie 26			
LOTH, Caroline	17	Bruenn	65-1088
LOTH, Joh.	28	Niederafleidn	64-0214
Gottfr. 20			
LOTH, Philip	44	Cleveland	66-0734
LOTHE, Friedrich	46	Koenigsberg	67-0353
Wilhelmine 46, Albert 17, Louise 14			
Fritz 8			
LOTTE, Anton	26	St. Louis	64-0687
LOTTIG, John	32	Steinfurt	63-0296
LOTZ, Anna Cath.	19	Heidelbach	66-0412
LOTZ, Elise	22	Herzhausen	65-1189
LOTZ, Jacob	23	Lich	63-0398
LOTZ, Maria	25	Kurhessen	64-0432
LOTZ, Martin	17	Niederzell	64-0639
Catharina 21			
LOTZE, Aug.	16	Muenden	64-0840
LOTZE, Soph.	22	Diedesheim	65-1189
LOUIS, Emma	20	Cannstadt	66-1031
LOVET, Philip	27	Boehmen	66-0221
Henriette 24, Ludwig 9m			
LOWENSTRASSE, Ern.	33	Muehlhausen	66-0147
LOWENTHALER, Louis	33	Unruhstadt	63-1136
LOWI, Julius	30	Berlin	66-0679
LOWY, Katy	21	Boehmen	66-0704
LUAM, Joh.	22	Niederklein	64-0840
LUBACH, Louis	23	Hessen	66-0109
LUBERWIRTH, Bernh.	22	Schleitz	63-1010
LUBIENS, Fr.	39	Hannover	65-0402
LUBIN, Ch.M.	25	Paris	63-0821
LUBRANCZYK, David	25	Pudewitz	63-0953
Roeschen 39, Cacilie 19, Maurice 8			
Lene 6, Abraham 11m			
LUCAS, Anton	48	Osnabrueck	67-1005
LUCAS, Ludwig	20	Darmstadt	65-0055
LUCAS, Ludwig	21	Darmstadt	65-1189
LUCH, Marie	25	London	64-0593
LUCHS, Jos.	17	Buttenwiesen	65-0007
LUCHSINGER, Jacob	28	Endy/Switz.	66-0412
Adelheid 31, Magdalene 4			
LUCIUS, Herm.	31	Braunschweig	65-1140
LUCK, Friederike	45	Eisenach	63-1178
LUCK, Heinr.	18	Preussen	66-0469
LUCKEMEYER, Heinr.	24	Ahden	63-0398
LUCKEN, G.(m)	28	Oldenburg	64-0495
LUCKHARDT, Amalie	25	Ziegenhain	64-0138
LUCKMANN, Heinrich	20	Wossendillen	63-1010
LUDECKE, H.	38	Osterwald	65-1189
Lena 28, Heinr. 3			
LUDEMEIER, Carol.	18	Schlusselburg	65-0950
LUDERS, Carst. H.	37	Vorbruecke	64-0639
Cath.M.Soph. 27, Dorothea 4			
LUDESCHER, Franz	20	Berum	63-1069
Therese 55, Catharine 26, Marianne 19			
LUDEWIG, L.	18	Wunstorf	64-0665
LUDOLF, Georg	32	Munden	66-1128
LUDOVICI, Hermann	21	Waldkappel	66-1031
LUDRA, Maria	17	Sedlec	66-1373
LUDWICI, D.	38	Gandenheim	63-1085
Margareth 37, Louise 7, Ferdinand 2m			
Emil 4			
LUDWIG, Afra	27	Steinbach	66-0984
LUDWIG, Caroline	26	Wittenberg	66-0109
LUDWIG, Emma	20	Grossbreitenb	66-0704
LUDWIG, Ernestine	28	Asch	66-1031
Johann 5			
LUDWIG, Gottlieb	72	Baden	66-0576
Catherine 63, Christian 19, Adolf 21			

NAME	AGE	RESIDENCE	YR-LIST
LUDWIG, Heinrich	18	Laudenbach	66-1203
Gustav 19			
LUDWIG, Jos.	26	Prussia	64-0363
Jos. 24			
LUDWIG, Julius	31	Kahla	63-0015
LUDWIG, Julius	27	Osnabrueck	66-1127
LUDWIG, Philippine	20	Detroit	66-0576
LUDWIG, Wm.	30	Wolferode	64-0427
LUEBBE, Anna	17	Cloppenburg	65-1189
LUEBBE, Hr.	20	Cloppenburg	65-1189
LUEBBEN, Albert	10	New York	63-1136
LUEBBERS, Bernard	21	Evenkamp	65-0974
LUEBBERS, G.A.	19	Bremen	64-0363
LUEBBES, Stephan	29	Manil	64-1053
LUEBE, Franz	20	Detmold	66-1031
LUEBKE, Carl	24	Bernsdorf	66-0469
LUECHEFELD, E.	27	Muenster	65-1024
LUECK, Johann	42	Zuhlsdorf	66-1248
Wilhelmine 44, Henriette 22			
Wilhelmine 20, Augusta 17, Julie 14			
Albertine 7, Emilie 5, Julius 16			
LUECK, Peter	22	Bierbach	67-0599
LUECKE, Christian	17	Essen	63-1218
LUECKE, J.(m)	18	Westfalen	64-0495
LUECKE, Joh. Aug.	22	Poeckinghsn.	64-0840
LUECKE, Regina	37	Notzungen	65-0594
Joh. 7, Therese 6, Franz 5, Jos. 4			
Luke(f) 51, Marg. 21, Teuke(m) 18			
LUECKEMEYER, Joh.	45	Sammern/Hann	65-0243
LUECKEN, August	21	Lohnau	23-0865
Heinrich 23			
LUECKEN, C.	21	Ladbergen	66-0934
LUECKEN, Friedrich	53	Aurich	65-1030
LUECKENHEIL, Chr.	23	Wildbad	66-1313
LUECKENS, Heinr.	35	Wimmer	65-0189
LUEDECKE, Herm.	40	Hannover	64-0687
LUEDECKE, Lena	18	Stocksdorf	66-1155
LUEDEKE, August	23	Hagenow	66-0668
Marie 23, baby (f) 11m			
LUEDEKE, Eduard	29	Braunschweig	66-1248
LUEDEKING, Conrad	26	Lippe	66-0576
LUEDELING, Gerh.	37	New York	63-1136
LUEDEMANN, Heinr.	18	Hannover	66-1031
LUEDEMANN, Henry	9	Everisen	63-0482
LUEDERS, Gesina	7	Bremen	65-0243
LUEDINGER, Gerh.	24	Groothusen	64-1022
LUEDKE, Gottlieb	22	Kazemierzelso	63-0821
LUEDKE, Ludwig	30	Motkowo	66-0578
LUEHKE, Minna	20	Coppenbruggen	66-0934
LUEHNING, F.(m)	25	Bothel	64-0331
LUEHNING, Joh.Conr	23	Verden	65-0948
LUEHNING, Julie	26	Czarnikau	64-0363
LUEHNING, Louise	60	Halle	64-0427
LUEHR, C.A.(m)	32	New York	64-0331
Johanna 21			
LUEHR, Elise	20	Osnabruck	66-1031
LUEHR, Ernst	23	Lackheim	66-0221
LUEHR, Martin	21	Baden	66-0109
LUEHRMANN, Henrich	25	New York	66-0984
LUEHRS, Albert	35	New York	66-0934
Anna 35			
LUEHRS, Georg	22	Messling	66-1243
Catharine 20			
LUEHRS, Joh. Heinr	21	Hannover	64-0432
LUEHRS, Metha	24	Hethorn	66-0668
Nancy 2, Amalie 14			
LUEHRS, Minna	21	Moorsee	65-0594
LUEHRSEN, Wilhelm	24	Otterndorf	66-1031
LUEKEN, Heinrich	9	Quakenbrueck	64-0739
LUEKER, Wilhelmine	16	Hille	66-1031
LUEMMANN, Hindrik	27	Frensdorf	66-1203
LUENBURG, Johann	25	Voelkershsn.	66-1031
LUENING, Anna	28	Stolzenau	66-0984
LUENING, Lorenz	20	Erwitte	66-1313
LUENSTROTH, Cath C	21	Hesselteich	63-0917
LUEPKE, Aug.	26	Aldameroh/Pr.	65-0038
Louise 26, Caroline 3, Emilie 2			
LUERDING, W.(m)	25	Hannover	64-0432
LUERMAN, Christ.	58	Neustadt	66-1243
Marie 54, Wilh. 17			
LUERMANN, Friedr.	15	Hanover	66-0577
LUERMANN, George	24	Lima	63-0244
LUERS, Heinrich	17	Holtrup	66-1031
LUERS, Joh. H.	35	Luningen	64-1053
LUESCHER, Friedr.	46	Duerrenesch	66-0109
LUETJE, Wilh.	19	Luedingworth	66-0576
LUETJEN, Heinrich	30	Hannover	64-0199
LUETJOHANN, Teresa	17	Verlar	66-0934
Anton 15			
LUETKEHNS, Johanna	58	Eilsfedt	66-1155
LUETS, Catharina	20	Wremen	66-1327
LUETTGENS, August	23	Solingen	63-0822
Amalie 26, Carl Gustav 9m			
LUETTING, F.F.(m)	23	Detern	64-0331
Johanna 21			
LUETZEMEYER, Joh.	22	Hessen	66-0934
LUETZEN, Hinrich	30	Hamburg	63-0015
LUETZER, John	30	Huettenbusch	63-1136
LUGENBERGER, L.(m)	36	Obergessenhsn	64-0170
LUHMANN, Johanna	18	Lobenstein	64-0687
LUHN, August	35	Theresia	66-0650
Erstine 43, Herm. Julius 9, Aug. Emilie 7			
Aug. 2			
LUHN, Johann	18	Untersuhl	64-0739
LUHNIG, Ernst	38	Meissen	64-0782
Christiane 38, Marie 7, Ernst 6			
LUIDENSTAEDT, Bern	27	Berlin	66-1243
LUIKART, Wm.	23	Unt.Lenningen	65-0055
LUIS, Maier	75	New York	64-0073
LUITZ, Clemens	29	Oggersheim	65-1088
LULY, Catharina	24	Bremen	67-0007
LUMP, Joseph	45	Ganth	63-0614
Josepha 40, Maria 12, Anna 7, Barbara 3			
LUNENSCHLOSS, Ad.	24	Neuborn	66-1155
LUNG, Adam	20	Frankenberg	67-0007
Cathrine 19			
LUNGERMANN, Adam	37	Liebenzell	64-0639
LUNGFINGER, Jacob	44	Muehlhofen	65-0402
Cath. 51, Marg. 15			
LUNGHEIM, Peter	20	Selters	65-0770
LUNKAU, Heinr.	30	Bremervoerde	66-0984
Martin 18, Sophie 16			
LUNSACK, Cresentia	45	Bayern	64-0432
Bertha 25			
LUPINCK, Franz	28	Boehmen	64-0343
LUPINEK, Johann	29	Boehmen	66-0349
Mary 6m			
LUPP, Caspar	42	Wuertemberg	63-0990
LUPP, Joh.	29	Gundelfingen	65-0402
LURASKI, Francesco	24	Italy	63-1136
LURK, Friederike	45	Eisenach	63-1178
LURSCH, J.B.	21	New Orleans	63-0862
LURSING, H.(m)	25	Burfort	64-0331
LURZ, Georg	24	Wiesentheit	65-0116
LUSKER, Anna	16	Salzberg	66-1203
LUSS, Caroline	14	Kurhessen	66-0704
LUSSIECK, Louise	49	Herford	64-1206
Diedr. 19, Wilhelm 7, Carl 7m, Louise 45			
LUST, H.	20	Bamberg	63-0953
LUST, Petronella	17	Rosely	66-0679
LUSTFELD, Ludwig	44	Rehburg	65-1095
Sofie 32, Marie 7			
LUSTIG, Hannchen	24	Unsleben	66-0984
LUTE, Wilhelmine	30	Muenden	66-1127
LUTHER, Caecilia	13	Selchow	67-0795
Fr. Wilhelm 23			
LUTHER, Emil	34	Neudiedendorf	63-0953
Bertha 28, Max 7, Alexander 9, Eugenia 5			
LUTHER, Richard	22	Goldisthal	66-1248
LUTKY, Rosa	20	Switz.	64-0170
LUTSCH, Elisabeth	26	Birschwind	63-0244
Elisabeth 6m			
LUTTER, Anna	15	Ritterade	66-0934
LUTTER, Aug. Henry	23	Hamburg	66-0109
LUTTER, Casp.	45	Frankfurt/M	66-1243
LUTTER, Louise	28	Muenden	63-0990

NAME	AGE	RESIDENCE	YR-LIST
LUTTGER, Joh.	28	Emmerich	65-1088
LUTZ, Andreas	70	Racken	63-0821
wife 63			
LUTZ, Anna	17	Grafenweiler	66-0147
LUTZ, Anna	22	Gunzelhausen	64-0782
LUTZ, August	19	Braunschweig	65-1031
LUTZ, C.	25	Wildbad	63-1003
K. 19, E. 46, M. 23, M. 12, F. 8, A. 8			
C. 1			
LUTZ, Carl	40	Freiensen	66-0734
Elisabeth 35, Conrad 14, Carl 9			
Christian 8, Heinrich 5, Emma 4, Marie 1			
LUTZ, Carl Hr.	28	Philipsburg	65-1088
LUTZ, Catharine	23	Oberwaldach	66-0147
LUTZ, Emil	20	Pforzheim	65-0243
LUTZ, Geo.	24	New York	63-0752
LUTZ, Herm.	21	Steinheim	64-1022
LUTZ, J.	33	Langenrozeld.	66-0413
Marie 21			
LUTZ, Jacob	22	Bettingen	66-0221
LUTZ, Jacob	30	Augum	65-0243
LUTZ, James Fr.	48	America	63-0990
LUTZ, Joh.	27	Kastel	65-0402
LUTZ, Johannes	20	Oeschingen	66-1373
LUTZ, John	29	Aichsdorf	65-1189
LUTZ, Maria	21	Gutweiler	66-0623
Magdalene 16			
LUTZ, Matthias	19	Waldorf	66-0147
LUTZ, Robert	20	Wagenfeld	66-1127
LUTZ, Wilhelm	24	Ludwigburg	66-1155
LUTZ, Wilhelm	17	Mittelsorf	66-1243
LUTZENBERGER, Ch.	21	Gomaringen	65-1189
Ch. 22			
LUTZENBERGER, L.	36	Ob.Gessenhsn.	64-0170
LUTZER, Johann	35	Grafenweiler	66-0147
Barbara 28			
LUY, Edward	38	Sachsen	66-0221
Margareth 38, Catharine 13, Johannes 6			
Jacob 3			
LUYTIES, Fritz	19	Bremen	64-0885
LYGATHYF, Alexand.	48	Kaschau/Hung.	64-0920
Franz 14, Alexander 12			
LYMANN, D. Th.	47	Pittsburg	63-0821
LYNAKER, v. Lator	26	Berlin	66-0221
LYVARTH, Carl	20	Oldenburg	64-0920
Le NOIR, Jerome	18	Cassel	66-0576
MAAG, Caspar		Locherbuelach	63-0551
MAAG, Caspar		Locherbuelach	63-0482
MAAS, A.	26	Memphis	63-0168
MAAS, Caroline	17	Pfalz	66-0576
MAAS, H.	38	Mexico	63-0168
Trini 28			
MAAS, Heinr.	24	Muenchen	65-0402
MAAS, James	18	Dolgesheim	63-1178
James 16			
MAAS, Jeannette	24	New York	63-0953
MAAS, Salm	24	Hattenbach	64-0782
MAASS, Carl	21	Eimersleben	65-0770
MAASS, Johann	44	Thedinghausen	64-0456
Marg. 38, Henry 9, Marg. 6			
MAASSEN, J.F.	36	Cincinnati	64-0073
MACH, Ignatz	27	Boehmen	64-0331
MACHMEYER, Heinr.	24	Sandhausen	65-0007
MACHOWINSKY, Alex	25	Ginow	65-0770
MACIEJEWSKI, Mich.	32	Bromberg	64-0432
Rosalia 28, Anastasia 4, Johann 2			
Magdalena 9m			
MACK, A.(m)	25	Weilheim	64-0331
MACK, Ferdinand	24	Kemderod	66-1373
MACK, Jac.	22	Fuerth	63-0752
MACK, Johann	39	Radhoscht	67-0007
MACK, Philomene	16	Obergenzburg	66-0576
MACKE, Bernhard	34	Bueschendorf	66-1031
Caroline 29, Bernhard 24, Anna 4			
Bernhard 6			
MACKE, Franz	33	Damme	66-0934
Lisette 32, Heinrich 8, Franz 6, Agnes 4			
Carl 3, Werner 9m, Bernhardine 18			
MACKE, Fritz	22	Offenbach	64-0214
MACKEBEN, Christ.	47	Rehburg	66-0576
Lisette 46			
MACKENBERG, Franz	22	Venninghausen	64-0214
MADEMANN, Fr. Wm.	29	Lunau	64-0920
Louise 26, Fr. Wm. 11m			
MADER, Margarethe	23	Weserdeich	66-1127
MADLAGE, Bernh.	28	Essen	64-0938
MADRIAN, Maria	21	Nebischoffshm	64-0073
MADROW, August	43	Minden	64-1053
Juliane 42, Wilhelmine 17, Emilie 7			
Friedr. 5, Mathilde 4, Bertha 9m			
MAEDER, Peter	31	Unterseen	63-1218
MAEFERT, Wilh'mine	28	Stemmen	65-0950
Wilhelmine 9, Friedrich 7, Ernst 4			
MAEGLE, Marie	59	Wichtenstein	66-1031
MAENDEL, Louis	36	Oldorf	64-0214
MAERKEL, Anton	28	Aufhausen	65-0948
MAERTENS, (f)	2	Veracruz	66-0934
Guillermo 2, Eduarde 6			
MAERTENS, Carl	45	Raacon	66-0469
MAERTENS, Christ.	30	Riebau	63-0614
MAERTENS, Johann	37	Riebau	63-0614
Marie 17			
MAERZ, Cath. Elis.	27	Geiss Nidda	64-0938
MAERZ, Herm.	21	Weilsdorf	64-0992
MAERZ, Joan(m)	30	Chicago	64-0023
MAERZ, Joh.	31	Trappstadt	64-0593
Reg. 42, Ant. 9, Jos. 7, Ph. 4			
MAERZ, Johann	34	Asch	66-0679
Louise 26, Lisette 8, baby (f) 10m			
MAERZ, Paula	22	Nuernberg	66-0577
MAESEL, Christoph	33	Fuerth	63-0482
MAESEL, Walburga	34	Fuerth	64-0427
Carl 7, Lisette 5, Bernhard 3			
MAEUERER, Peter	33	Coblenz	64-0432
Christine 24			
MAEULLEN, Friedr.	23	Stuttgart	64-0433
MAEUSER, Ernst	22	Willmer	66-1203
MAGAI, Johann	22	Laibach	65-1095
MAGDEBURG, F.W.	33	Berthalsdorf	64-0170
Pauline 26, Gustav 9m			
MAGDZINSKY, M.	41	Prussia	63-1003
M. 43, M. 9, J. 8, A. 4			
MAGENHEIMER, Ludw.	16	New York	66-0576
MAGER, Catharina	25	Rodan	66-1327
MAGER, Louis	22	Luettich	67-0007
MAGER, Sebastian	42	Zimmern	67-0007
MAGNUS, J.(f)	24	Herbsen	64-1161
MAGNUS, Joseph	44	Libenau	64-0456
Riecke 39, Elise 13			
MAGNY, Ernest	24	New York	63-1218
wife 20			
MAGRAW, A.R.	22	Dresden	64-1161
MAHER, Henry	16	Geneve	64-0073
MAHLA, Christian	24	Babenhausen	66-1093
MAHLAN, Wm.	27	Berlin	64-0840
MAHLAND, Fr.	17	Luedingworth	63-1010
MAHLE, Gottfried	60	Backnang	66-1031
Christiane 59, Friedrich 23			
MAHLE, Maria	59	Ebenbach	66-1327
Friederike 31			
MAHLENBROCK, Wmne.	20	Rockhurst	63-0917
MAHLER, Anton	26	Luzar	64-0992
MAHLER, Friedr.	24	Rust	65-0007
MAHLER, Metta	9	Bremervoerde	64-0639
MAHLER, Victor	26	Luzern	63-0168
MAHLMANN, Elise	52	Quakenbrueck	63-0482
MAHLMANN, Heinr.	26	Quakenbrueck	64-0739
Johanna 28, Elise 11m			
MAHLMANN, Wilhelm	23	Rehburg	65-1095
MAHLSTEDT, Johann	17	Elmlohe	66-0934
MAHLY, Leopold	25	Carlsruhe	66-0704
Albert 19			
MAHN, Carl	33	Rossdorf	66-0934
Ludwig 29			
MAHN, Johanna	27	Clausthal	66-1031
MAHNEKE, Fr.	26	Lengerich	66-0934

NAME	AGE	RESIDENCE	YR-LIST
MAHNKEN, Anna	22	Frelsdorf	66-1248
MAHNKEN, Henry	26	Bremen	66-0679
MAHNKEN, Meta	22	St. Juergen	63-1178
MAHNKEN, Wm.	23	Zuchholz	65-0402
MAHRER, Adam	31	Nagy Ida	65-0007
Phil. 19			
MAHRGANG, Heinrich	21	Darmstadt	66-1031
Catharina 41			
MAI, Anna Cathar.	22	Godensberg/He	66-0412
MAI, Johannes	58	Hessia	66-0679
Elise 24			
MAI, William	22	Heidelberg	63-0296
MAIBAUM, Ricke	32	Silberhausen	64-1053
Felix 5, Regina 3, Jacob 9m			
MAIER, Anton	69	Wehling	63-1069
MAIER, Bertha	19	Esens	63-0752
MAIER, Bettchen	21	Kirchgoens	65-0594
MAIER, Chr.	19	Keinnath	65-0007
MAIER, Christine	25	Belsen	63-0821
MAIER, Conrad	18	Eppingen	66-0221
MAIER, Ernst	28	Seefelden	63-0350
MAIER, Ernst Fr'dr	22	Maburg	66-1128
MAIER, Friedrich	47	Hameln	66-0679
MAIER, Garrels	26	Au	67-0007
MAIER, Gottlieb	18	Reutlingen	63-0296
MAIER, Hermann	21	Pforzheim	66-0109
MAIER, J.(m)	18	Steinau	64-0495
MAIER, Jeanette	18	Buchau	66-0576
Maria 15			
MAIER, Johann	31	Dessingen	66-1327
Catharine 33			
MAIER, Joseph	20	Neuler	66-1203
MAIER, Julie	17	Rottweil	66-0704
MAIER, L.(f)	20	Tittlingen	64-0331
MAIER, Maier	22	Bavaria	66-0679
MAIER, Marie	24	Sterbfritz	64-0495
MAIER, Moritz	31	Waldshut	63-1085
Maria 54, Wenzel 25, Maria 24			
Maria Magd. 23, Therese 21, Francisca 19			
Vincens 15, Aloisia 12, Alois 9			
Francis 31, Ludmilla 34			
MAIER, Sophie	21	Carlsruhe	65-1024
MAIER, W.	24	Borgenteich	66-0413
MAILLARD, Jacq.	54	Switzerland	63-0990
MAINE, Lorenz	20	Borgenteich	66-0413
MAINE, M.	36	Darmstadt	63-0097
MAINZ, Joseph	36	Baden	66-0083
MAINZ, Rosalie	22	Friedberg	66-0083
MAINZER, John	36	Cleveland	64-0331
MAIRINGER, Alex	25	Felixdorf	63-1218
MAISCH, John	26	Laichingen	63-0551
MAISENBACHER, Joh.	20	Wissbaden	65-0004
MAITROFF, Johs.	20	Reicheldorf	67-0007
MAJER, Johann	59	Wuertemberg	66-0679
Maximiliane 58			
MAKENBERG, Heinr.	28	Preussen	64-0138
MAKOWSKY, Mathias	25	Lankowitz	66-0469
MALARD, Emilie	17	Havre	64-1053
MALCHOW, Otto	19	Bremen	65-0898
MALDFELD, Georg	30	Niederwitten	65-0055
MALECKA, Thomas	37	Bohemia	64-0593
Anne 27, Johann 12, Maria 2, Wenzl 5			
MALER, Georg	21	Sudderbruk	64-0495
MALER, Joh.	25	Thedinghausen	64-0495
MALER, Ludwig	15	Wichelshausen	66-1127
MALITZKY, Augusta	20	Kempten	65-1088
MALKE, Aug.	28	Preussen	64-0170
Augusta 20			
MALKMES, Magd.	15	Ansbach	63-0862
MALKOMES, Joh. H.	19	Neuerode	64-0687
MALL, Jacob	49	Dossenheim	64-0170
Cath. 18, Anna 19, Peter 14, Pankratz 9			
Jacob 7			
MALLECK, Pauline	17	Kuttenberg	64-0214
MALLY, Johann	18	Unterlakowitz	66-1373
MALMO, Edmund	14	Lobenstein	66-0650
MALSCH, Anna	29	Salzungen	66-1248
MALSCH, Anna Marg.	33	Meiningen	64-0432

NAME	AGE	RESIDENCE	YR-LIST
MALTZ, Friedrike	30	New York	63-1038
MALWITZ, Christina	56	Eissfeld	64-1053
Anna 19			
MALY, Carl	39	Bohemia	64-0687
Maria 39, Anna 7, Franz 11m			
MALY, Johann	29	Schoenweid	64-0593
MALY, Wenzel	19	Luhbritz	67-0007
MALZER, Fr'dke.A.	47	Treben	65-0055
MAMBERGER, Elisab.	22	Ulple	67-0007
MAMEL, Anna	25	Zwickau	65-1024
MANAS, Franz	26	Teschvietz	67-0007
MANCH, Gottlieb	29	Teufelsthal	65-1088
Elisabeth 29, Gottfried 4, Theod. 3m			
MANCHENHEIMER, P.	27	Goellheim	65-1189
MANDE, Jacob	18	Beverstedt	66-1093
MANDEL, H.M.	36	New York	63-0244
MANDEL, Heinr.	24	New York	64-0665
MANDEL, Jeannette	22	New York	63-0990
Ida 11m			
MANDLER, Adam	54	Giessen	66-1327
Elise 50, Charlotte 20, Carl 18			
Ludwig 16			
MANGELS, Christ.	23	Ringstedt	63-1136
MANGELS, Johann	22	Hainmuehlen	66-1031
MANGERICH, Cathre.	27	Brettnach	63-0990
MANGLES, Maria	27	Hannover	66-0412
MANGOLD, Barbara	33	Mutterstadt	66-0704
Eva 5, Max 2, Sebastian 4m			
MANGOLD, Cresenza	18	Oberiffingen	66-1327
MANGOLD, Ernst	25	Eschach	66-1313
MANGOLD, Johann	33	Bislinghausen	65-0770
MANHEIM, Meier	27	Birkenau	66-0083
MANKE, Alb.	21	Koenigsberg	65-0038
MANKE, Aug.	29	Bielefeld	65-1030
Henriette 28, Carl 2, Louise 1			
MANKE, Ferdinand	37	Cratzig	66-0578
Caroline 37, Wilhelmine 17, Caroline 9			
Carl 7, Friederike 5, Ludwig 3, August 1			
MANKE, Karl	32	Plimenhagen	66-0578
Friederike 33, Ferdinand 9, Ludwig 6			
Carl 3			
MANN, Gustav	18	Vaihingen	66-0109
MANN, Heinr.	28	Eckelsheim	66-1127
Catharina 26			
MANN, Jacob Fr.	18	Weisbach	65-0243
MANN, Julius Alb.	21	Dresden	66-0934
MANN, Louis	34	Trymeszno	66-0679
MANN, Louise	22	Osterkappel	65-0151
MANN, Minna	21	Washington	64-0687
MANN, Moses	19	Carltburg	65-0770
MANNAVAL, Chrs.	27	Gr. Umstadt	66-0221
MANNECKE, Fr.	28	Almersleben	65-1024
MANNEL, A.W.	32	Cassel	63-1085
MANNIERE, C.	34	Altdorf	64-1161
MANNS, Albert	28	Pekum	64-1022
MANNS, Catharina	31	Hersfeld	66-0679
Johannes 8, Gertrud 5			
MANSHOLT, Focke G.	23	Buehren	64-0427
MANSHOLT, Mootje	45	Brinkum	66-1031
Antonia 9			
MANSLAGT, R.G.	23	Hannover	64-1022
MANTEL, Alvin	36	Berlin	67-0353
MANTEL, Caspar	32	Hellmershsn.	66-0346
MANTHEY, Joh.	28	Prussia	63-1003
M. 38, P. 40, E. 9, M. 5			
MANTINI, Hugo	17	Engelheim	64-0593
MANTZ, Marie	20	Ulm	66-1093
MANTZ, Matth.	22	Dettingen	63-0551
MANUEL, Theresia	22	Matanzas	66-0934
MANZ, Johannes	30	Darmstadt	66-0734
MANZ, Jos.	36	Newark	64-0138
MANZEL, Carl	7	Elmershausen	64-0886
MAR, Ammon	58	Neufrach	63-0296
MARAHRENS, Friedr	22	Braunschweig	63-0350
MARBACH, Georg Fr.	30	Schwarzbach	66-0469
Hanna L. 24, Heinrich 6m			
MARBERT, Caroline	26	Hafenhohr	66-1031
MARBURG, Jeanette	28	Duedelsheim	65-0594

NAME	AGE	RESIDENCE	YR-LIST
MARBURG, Liebm.	21	Hessen	66-0221
MARBURG, Michael	34	Nashville	66-0221
MARBURGER, August	34	Schwarzenau	66-0578
Louise 29, Daniel 7			
MARCHBANG, Friedr.	24	Minden	64-1053
MARCHESINI, Beatr.	16	Forella	63-1178
MARCHESINI, Girola	24	Vicenza	63-1178
MARCINKIEWITZ, Mar	22	Dzidzennek	64-0665
MARCK, Karel	29	Boehmen	63-0862
MARCORECK, Johann	18	Boehmen	66-0349
MARCUS, (m)	24	Geestemuende	64-0495
MARCUS, A.	33	Louisville	66-0934
Sabine 30, Sidanie 6, Clara 4			
MARCUS, Ph.	24	Krauchenowis	64-0495
Ra.(f) 4			
MARCZINK, Johann	39	Zulz	67-0007
MARESCH, Jacob	34	Laritz	66-1373
MARHAN, Anna	54	Boehmen	64-0427
MARHANG, Johanna	60	Gillersheim	66-1155
MARHOFFER, Elisab.	20	Maisenheim	66-0984
MARIACHER, J.	24	Zell	64-0782
MARK, Antonia	18	Crauder	66-1155
MARK, Eva	35	Orb	64-0938
Ph. Jac. 5			
MARK, Georg	19	Langenau	64-0938
MARK, Joseph	15	Reichenbach	66-0679
MARK, Solomon	48	Grambach	64-0687
Therese 40, Caroline 12, Siegmund 7			
Abramam 5, Jeanette 3, Fanny 58			
Augusta 52, Bernhard 12			
MARKEMES, Conrad	25	Curhessen	63-0822
MARKERT, Carl	17	Grossalmerode	64-0433
MARKERT, Carl	16	Dermbach	66-0679
MARKERT, Franz	51	Grossamersde	65-0004
Josephine 39, Marie 7			
MARKERT, Joh. G.	60	Bayern	64-0639
MARKERT, Lorenz	49	Weichersheim	65-0713
Theresia 38, Friedrich 14, Margretha 15			
Barbara 12, Christina 10, Mathaeus 8			
Johann 2			
MARKETS, Hr.	27	Gefelde	64-0593
MARKGRAF, Gustav	26	Brambach	66-1155
MARKMANN, C.Wm.	31	Elberfeld	64-0138
MARKS, Ferdinand	38	Eidinghausen	65-1095
Louise Chr. 37, Christian 14			
Carl Heinr. 11, Carl Friedr. 7			
Karolina 6			
MARKS, Gottlieb	36	Posen	66-0578
Louise 32, Ernestine 10, Emil 8, Albert 3			
Ottilie 1			
MARKS, Sussmann	19	Griesen	66-0984
MARKT, Mart.	34	Waldshut	63-0350
MARKTAMMEN, Aron	14	Norfolk	64-0427
MARKUS, Dorothea	58	Bamberg	64-0456
MARKUS, Jos.	21	Lemere	64-0840
MARKWALD, Ernst Fr	25	Zellgenerwo	66-0578
MARKWALD, Julius	22	Lindenwerder	66-0577
MARKWARD, Aug.	22	Soessnowd	66-0469
MARLINECK, Rosalie	19	Malin	67-0007
MARMONT, Pia	20	Rottweil	63-1038
MAROWIE, Franz	50	Klonk/Austria	66-0469
Maria 48, Joseph 21, Anna 15			
MARQUARD, Adam	14	Sandbach	66-0679
MARQUARD, Carl	38	Pammin	66-0469
MARQUARD, Chr'stne	39	Pammin	66-0469
Wilhelmine 11, Emilie 9, Augusta 2			
MARQUARD, Gottfr.	16	Unterjessingn	64-0593
MARQUARD, Phil	18	Landbach	64-0170
MARQUARDT, Joh.	15	Aldingen	65-0402
MARQUARDT, Marg.	19	Elmershausen	64-0886
MARQUARDT, Marg.	50	Muenchen	64-0593
MARQUART, Andreas	26	Lindenwerder	64-0456
MARSCH, Lorenz	33	Basdach	64-0886
Georg 30			
MARSCHALL, Balthas	29	Bliesscastel	66-0349
MARSCHALL, Jacob	58	Baumbach	64-0687
Anna 53, Conrad 16, Barbara 24			
Eve Elise 18, Anna Maria 14			

NAME	AGE	RESIDENCE	YR-LIST
Anna Martha 7			
MARSCHLOT, Margret	24	Klus.	66-0221
MARSCHNER, Benj.	21	Schoenau	66-1373
MARSCHUETZ, (m)	23	Cincinnati	63-1038
wife 18			
MARSCHUTZ, Max	16	Muehlhausen	65-0151
MARSUCHEK, Jacob	32	Schweinitz	66-0837
Marie 21			
MARTEN, Friedr.	25	Schonau	67-0007
MARTENS, D.(m)	26	Bremen	64-0214
MARTENS, Doris	16	Bremervoerde	65-0974
MARTENS, Her.	25	Dicksterhsn.	65-1030
MARTENS, Joh.	19	Dungen	64-1161
MARTENS, Maria	16	Oerel	65-1095
MARTENS, Peter	23	Ebersdorf	65-1095
MARTFELD, Wm.	40	California	66-0934
Augusta 35			
MARTH, Dina	28	Nordkirchen	66-1093
MARTH, Peter		Altenlotha	66-0412
MARTI, Anna M.	26	Rauchwill	63-1085
MARTIN, Adam	22	Armsheim	66-0412
Catharina E. 26			
MARTIN, Anna Marg.	30	Heldorf	64-0427
MARTIN, Capt.	35	Germany	63-0350
MARTIN, Carl	16	Hessen	66-0109
MARTIN, Carl Fr.	33	Frankenberg	64-1108
MARTIN, Edm.	27	Basel	65-0243
MARTIN, Eugen	30	Dirlenwang	63-1085
MARTIN, Gottlieb	29	Borruchoeon	66-0413
Ludwig 22			
MARTIN, Joseph	22	Bruckenau	65-1030
Elisabeth 23			
MARTIN, P.	22	Oberhait	64-0782
MARTIN, Pauline	19	Stangenfeld	66-0934
Ernestine 18			
MARTIN, Philippine	19	Rossbach	63-0350
MARTIN, Rosine	23	Urasch	66-1093
Fritz 9			
MARTINE, Garrelt	39	Kampen	66-0668
Marie 39, Jacob 15			
MARTING, Herm. Th.	29	Lingen	65-0950
Marg. Adelh. 32, Joh. Gerh. 4			
Bernh. Herm. 9m, Joh. Gerh. 50			
MARTINI, Jacob	27	Gruenstadt	64-0593
MARTTES, Johann	25	Zunsweier	66-0346
MARUSCHKE, John	30	Thomaskirch	63-0168
MARX, B.	31	New Orleans	63-0953
MARX, David	22	Grossenlinden	63-1085
MARX, Fr.	35	Cannberg	65-0007
MARX, Gustav	26	Hessen	66-0221
MARX, Jeanette	60	Ober Mendig	64-0593
Joseph 14			
MARX, Joseph	36	Basel	64-1053
Louise 40, Margarethe 18, Elisabeth 15			
Josephine 13, Peter 9			
MAS, Bernhard H.	44	Prussia	63-0822
Ana Adelheid 37, Bernh. H. 13, Carl H. 11			
Caroline 9, Friederike 6, Friedrich 2			
MAS, Lambert H.	32	Prussia	63-0822
Anna Elisa. 23			
MASBAUM, A.	25	Wahn	63-1003
MASCHKE, Franz	30	Lank	64-1161
MASCHKE, P.	32	Fuerstenwalde	66-1373
MASERT, Anna	19	Lorsch	65-0151
MASKE, Emil	29	Czarnikau	64-0840
Julius 33			
MASLEIN, Adolph	36	Lohrt	64-0920
MASS, Alma	22	Rawinkel	64-0687
MASS, Johann	30	Mengsberg	66-0837
MASSBACHER, Phlpne	24	Gleicherwiese	63-0917
MASSCHMIDT, Heinr.	17	Dissen	66-1128
MAST, Christian	26	Engthal Kette	64-0170
Maria 23, Nich. 20, Christine 22			
MAST, Christine	19	Untermosbach	65-0974
MAST, Theodor	19	Gruenenplan	63-0953
MATEBKA, Barbara	30	Miletz	66-0623
MATELING, Rudolph	25	Twixlum	64-0456
MATHAI, Christine	23	Marburg	63-0821

NAME	AGE	RESIDENCE	YR-LIST
MATHAI, Diedr.	27	New York	63-0821
Helene 24			
MATHAIS, Ferdinand	25	Hamburg	65-0004
MATHEN, Mrs.	30	New York	63-0953
Anne 6, F. 4			
MATHES, H.(m)	28	Neustadt	64-0331
MATHEUS, Bernhard	28	Edenkoben	65-1024
Elisabeth 33, August 1, Sigmund 1m			
MATHEUS, Johann	26	Smolnick	64-0433
MATHEZ, Paul	23	Neudingen	64-1022
Alexander 26			
MATHIAS, Carl	17	Peckelsheim	65-0898
MATHIAS, Casp.	17	Saas	64-0427
MATHIAS, Joh. H.	48	Nenndorf	64-0639
M. Dorothea 40, Conrad H. 7			
Engelb. Mar. 6, Carl Wm. 6, Hans Conr. 4			
Fr. Conr. 11m			
MATHIAS, Wm.	17	Goettingen	64-0432
MATHIE, Noel	19	Havre	64-1053
MATHIES, Franz	26	Kemnath	64-0343
MATHIES, Johanna	36	Hannover	66-0346
Sophia 27			
MATHIS, Ernst	21	Harbarnsen	63-1085
MATHUSEK, Adolph	24	New York	63-1218
MATJEA, Barbra	15	Prague	65-0038
MATLAGE, Louise	20	Versmold	63-0953
MATSCHALKA, Paul	24	Goldberg	63-0015
MATSCHENBACHER, Ad	28	Cronach	64-0687
MATT, Crescens	26	Raukwyl	64-1108
Elisabeth 38			
MATTAN, H.(m)	18	London	64-0170
MATTERN, Heinr.	65	Oberhausen	64-0456
MATTERN, Heinr.	16	Alsfeld	64-1206
Elis 14			
MATTERN, Otto	9	Dammin	63-0953
MATTES, Johann	18	Bietz	65-1095
MATTES, Robert	27	Schoenau	66-0083
MATTFELD, Carsten	25	Posen	64-0456
MATTFELD, Theod.	20	Verden	63-0015
MATTHEY, Carl	30	Marburg	65-1189
Anna 28, Carl 6			
MATTHIAS, Fr.	24	Rodenberg	66-0934
Wilhelm 22, Conrad 21			
MATTHIESEN, Erich	27	Seestermuchen	63-0296
MATTHISEN, Frdr. W	16	Maenster	65-0950
MATYA, Joh.	58	Sterzides/Boh	65-0038
Boranca 50, Leopold 20, Barbara 10			
Joseph 14, Broka 9, Anna 3			
MATYK, Peter	40	Probese	66-0734
Maria 38, Anna 15, Maria 9, Anton 8			
Franz 2			
MATZ, Gottlieb	48	Hammersdorf	65-0865
Ernestine 37, Marie 19, Ernestine 16			
Ferdinand 11, Ottilie 7			
MATZENBACHER, Anna	23	Kussel	64-0363
MATZKE, Anna	48	Boehmen	63-1010
Ana 21, Anton 18			
MAU, Dorothea	18	Schloppe	64-0665
MAUCH, Aloys	29	Neukirch	64-0992
MAUCK, Gottliebin	28	Philadelphia	63-1069
MAUER, J. Chr.	16	Heiligenstadt	64-0170
MAUER, Lorenz	21	Zimmern	66-1203
MAUER, Maria	20	Reutlingen	65-0898
MAUERMANN, Andreas	40	Carlshafen	66-1248
MAUL, Elise	49	Bindsachsen	63-0482
MAUL, Ferd.	25	Wohlfelder	64-0840
MAUL, Hugo	24	Eisenach	66-1031
Augusta 18			
MAUL, Louise	19	Schlichtum	66-0837
MAUL, Moritz	59	Grossenheim	63-0917
Amalie 50			
MAUL, Wilhelmine	24	Frischborn	66-0679
MAULBACH, Christin	19	Goettelfingen	66-0147
Magdalene 17			
MAULHARD, Franz	23	Mingerode	66-1313
MAULLE, Lisette	15	Michelburg	63-1218
MAULPRETCH, Barbra	19	Gottelfingen	63-1085
MAUN, Sophia	30	Wien	63-1136

NAME	AGE	RESIDENCE	YR-LIST
MAUNTZ, Elisabeth	25	Hessen	66-0109
MAUPAT, Chrs.	27	Assler	66-0221
MAURER, Marie	36	Mannheim	66-0576
MAURER, Andr.	18	Wuerttemberg	64-0432
Paul 11, Christ. 15, Anna 17			
MAURER, Barbara	20	Waldenburg	66-0704
MAURER, Chr.	23	Darmstadt	66-0577
MAURER, Ernst	16	Heinriss	66-1128
MAURER, Friedr.	23	Friedrichstal	63-0244
MAURER, Gottl.	29	Lauffen	66-0349
MAURER, Heinr.	27	Karlbach	64-1022
MAURER, Jacoba	52	Burgstadt	65-0007
MAURER, Johann	48	Gimbsheim	65-1095
MAURER, Marg. Magd	17	Stuttgart	63-0822
MAURER, Nicolaus	27	Huttingen	65-0004
MAURER, Otto	16	Wurtemberg	63-0822
MAURER, Paul	51	Wuerttemberg	64-0432
Elisab. 48, Ursula 11, Johann 6			
Elisab. 4			
MAURER, Peter	26	Eitelborn	66-1203
MAURER, Rudolph	32	Switz	63-0350
MAURER, Wilhelm	25	Waldenburg	66-0704
MAURER, Wilhelm	30	Minden	66-0934
MAUS, Elisabeth	22	Pehl	63-0015
MAUS, Elisabeth	17	Grossmoor	66-1093
MAUS, Johannes	18	Niederzell	64-0639
Philipp 20			
MAUS, Lorenz	29	Sieglas	64-0687
MAUSBACH, Theodor	19	Luebbecke	66-1131
MAUSCHNER, Chr.	63	Sebritz	65-0007
MAUSCKE, John	30	Schweinsburg	63-0350
MAUSER, Clara	37	Bavaria	63-0822
Heinr. 6			
MAUSGEIER, Marg.	35	Lichtenfels	64-0495
E.(m) 7			
MAUT, Ignatz	25	Wittenberg	66-0578
Marianne 30			
MAUTH, Joh.	20	Boll	64-0495
MAUTHE, Aug.	30	Prussia	63-1003
Antonia 44, Anne 13, P. 28, C. 8, D. 5			
A. 2			
MAUTHET, Patrise	20	Istein	66-0668
MAUZEL, Carl	7	Elmershausen	64-0886
MAVRIN, Jos.	34	Boehmen	63-0917
Anna 22, Jos. 11m			
MAX, Friedr.	27	Pessingen	67-1005
MAXMEIER, Friedr.	24	Bielefeld	66-0704
MAY, Adam	25	Bischhausen	64-1022
Martha 25, Adolph 7			
MAY, Christian	22	New York	66-0083
MAY, Edward	23	Bremen	67-0600
Julius 19			
MAY, Heinrich	27	Braunschweig	66-0469
MAY, Jeanette	24	Eschhorn	64-0938
MAY, Julius	28	Goettingen	65-0151
MAY, Leonhard	21	Heidelberg	63-0821
MAY, Marie	21	Neukirch	65-0189
MAY, Martin	17	Villmar	67-0007
MAY, Nicolaus	30	Cincinnati	63-0990
Cathre. 29, Marie 17			
MAY, P.(m)	10	Neukirch	64-0495
MAYER, Andreas	24	Drehsendorf	66-1031
Conrad 21			
MAYER, Antohony	25	Eichstadt	63-0168
MAYER, Blasius	19	Zephenhun	63-0990
MAYER, Carl	32	Schonau	66-1373
Theresia 21			
MAYER, Carl	24	Worms	64-0363
MAYER, Cath.	30	Spachbruecken	64-0138
Marg. 3			
MAYER, Christian	27	Owen	66-0109
MAYER, Constant	35	Besancon	64-1053
MAYER, Daniel	25	Lisberg	66-0734
H. 13			
MAYER, Dav.	16	Osthofen	66-0704
MAYER, F.	21	Neufra	64-0782
MAYER, Frd.	29	Wien	65-1189
MAYER, Friedr.	32	Pittsburgh	64-0214

NAME	AGE	RESIDENCE	YR-LIST
MAYER, G.A.	37	New York	64-0331
MAYER, Georg	59	Sondelfingen	63-1218
MAYER, Georg	25	Spachbruechen	64-0687
MAYER, Gertrude	30	Williamsburg	63-1178
Clara 4, James 3			
MAYER, Heinrich	22	New Orleans	63-0862
MAYER, Herm. Joh.	43	Lesum	64-0885
Meta 43, Antonia 15, Friedr. 10, Arnold 6			
MAYER, J.G.	19	Owen	63-1003
MAYER, Jac.	34	Goelesdorf	64-0495
MAYER, Jacob	43	Telgte	66-0934
Fanny 34, Johanna 20, David 9, Naphtali 6			
Bertha 3, Alexander 1			
MAYER, Jacob	46	Gundersheim	64-0214
MAYER, Jean	21	Hildesheim	66-0704
MAYER, Joh.	23	Kaisersbach	64-0687
MAYER, Johann	22	Baden	66-0576
Marie 25			
MAYER, Johann	24	Neustadt	66-0734
MAYER, Juliane	24	Neukirchen	66-0934
MAYER, L.	23	Iven	64-0782
MAYER, Leopold	16	Ndr.Ingelheim	63-1178
MAYER, Leopold	34	Carlsruhe	64-0782
MAYER, Louise	26	Worms	66-0576
MAYER, Marie		Cloppenburg	65-0116
MAYER, Michael	18	Bibra	63-0917
Nathan 15			
MAYER, Michael	40	Wuertenberg	66-0221
Ursula 19, Joh. Jacob 16, Paul 14			
MAYER, Nicolaus	16	Breidenbach	66-0576
MAYER, Regina	18	Bretzenhain	63-0862
MAYER, Rosalia	20	Verden	66-0984
MAYER, Sigm.	34	Bavaria	64-0593
MAYER, Theresia	23	Bapau	66-1373
MAYER, Wilhelm	29	Boll	64-0363
Christian 20, Anna 23, Lina 20			
MAYERER, Jac.	15	Pfeddersheim	64-0170
MAYWALD, Wenzel	35	Wien	66-0934
Therese 34			
MAYWITSCH, Carolne	17	Espe	63-1085
MAZEAND, F.P.	32	France	63-1178
MAZISCH, (m)	25	Boehmen	64-0495
MEBUS, Frd.	17	Hahnstadt	65-1024
MEBUS, Heinrich	25	Bonn	64-0199
MECHAN, Hugo	27	Lobenstein	63-0953
MECHEL, Elise	49	Rosenheim	65-0243
MECHELKE, Anna	24	Chicago	64-0427
MECKE, Carl	29	Norden	63-0614
MECKEL, Wmne.	23	Herborn	64-1161
MEDDELMANN, Herm.	37	Louisville	63-0990
Cathr. 38			
MEDEFENDT, Emilie	35	Braunschweig	64-0170
Minna 8			
MEDER, Friederike	22	Bolier	66-1128
MEDER, John	26	New York	66-0109
MEDER, Jos.	27	Aasen	63-0296
MEDICUS, Joseph	44	New York	64-0687
Maria 31, Jos. 7, Emilie 5, Heinr. 3			
Ludwig 2			
MEDLIN, Barbara	25	Pellnsen	66-0623
MEECKE, Gesine	23	Sievern	66-0984
Alwina 6			
MEECKELKEN, Bernh.	19	Lehe	63-0693
MEELE, Gustav	59	Bremen	64-0992
Regina 58			
MEENTS, J.J.	25	Wittmund	64-0665
MEENTS, Jamken	21	Berdum	66-1093
MEENTS, Johann Rem	28	Heppens	66-0412
MEENTZEN, Eduard	28	Bremerhaven	64-0199
MEES, Margar.	24	Boehingen	65-1088
MEESE, Emilie	25	Osnabrueck	66-1093
MEESE, Joh.	39	Soegelin	65-0151
MEESE, Oscar	21	Elze	66-1327
MEESMANN, Gerhd.	17	Vahs	65-0151
MEETH, Bernhardt	27	Hanau	66-0577
MEETH, Joh. Jos.	45	Trier	66-0577
Maria 40, Johann 14, Peter 13, Maria 12			
Mathias 7, Joseph 3			
MEFFERT, Paulus	24	Suhl	66-1327
MEGERLE, Johann	35	Werrenwar	65-1030
MEHL, Anna Marg.	50	Grosmanrode	66-0623
Georg 21			
MEHLBURGER, Georg	24	Melzungen	66-0412
MEHLE, Regina	22	Cassel	65-0116
MEHLHOP, Diedr.	18	Hannover	65-0974
MEHLHORN, Friedr.	25	Schvenau	63-0482
MEHLMANN, Wilhelm	75	Neuhausen	66-1093
MEHNERT, Elisa	22	Berlin	64-0427
MEHNERT, F.(m)	35	Meerane	64-0331
Johanna 21			
MEHNERT, Herm.(f)	57	Gich	64-0331
MEHRING, Caspar	41	Hamm	66-1313
Antonette 37			
MEHRLE, Carl	38	Fuerfeld	67-0007
Josephine 35			
MEHRSTEDT, Christ.	23	Koerner	65-1030
MEHRTENS, C.Adelh.	25	Harderstedt	66-1128
Peter 9m			
MEHRTENS, Cathrine	30	San Francisco	63-0097
MEIBERGER, Peter	21	Orb	66-1031
MEIBOOM, Eduard	30	Wesel	63-0482
MEIBORG, Lisette	23	Essen	64-0938
MEICHAU, Elise	19	Ovelgoenne	63-0752
MEICHLE, St.	30	Melchingen	64-0782
MEIDLING, E.E.F.	17	Bremen	64-0427
MEIDNER, Isidor	40	Namslau	66-0109
MEIER, A.(m)	32	New York	64-0363
Louise 22			
MEIER, Alois	29	Friedlingen	63-1038
MEIER, Anton	28	Poepinghausen	64-0840
Leonore 20			
MEIER, August	28	Salzderhelden	63-1069
Sophie 28, August 2			
MEIER, August	32	Berlin	65-0770
MEIER, C.	30	Oldendorf	65-0007
MEIER, Chr.	4	Elze	65-0402
Marie 3			
MEIER, Chr.	43	Elze	65-0402
Ma. 23			
MEIER, Christ	16	Bexhoevede	64-0363
MEIER, Conrad	24	Ritterhude	65-0950
Friedr. 18			
MEIER, Franz	29	Minden	65-0865
MEIER, Fried.	28	New York	63-1136
MEIER, Friedr.	70	Huelsen	66-1128
Maria 55, Hein 22, Friedrich 15			
MEIER, Fritz	25	Bueckeburg	67-0600
MEIER, Georg	32	Weissweil	66-0412
MEIER, Gesche Soph	19	Hannover	66-0934
MEIER, Heinr.	25	Lafringen	64-0214
MEIER, Henriette	62	Mechenstein	66-0346
Albert 23			
MEIER, Herm.	27	Alfeld	64-0073
MEIER, John	17	Fischerhude	64-0593
MEIER, Josephine	19	Zuebrick	66-1203
MEIER, Louis	24	Buer	63-0862
MEIER, Martin	20	Rutihof	66-1093
MEIER, Meta	16	Roennebeck	65-1095
MEIER, Otto	16	Walsrode	66-0934
MEIER, Otto	23	Bassum	64-0363
MEIER, Paul	30	Detmold	66-0109
Marie 26, Marie 9m			
MEIER, Rud.	21	Bremen	64-0593
MEIER, Sophie	28	Diepholz	66-0577
MEIER, Sophie Elis	26	Hannover	66-0934
MEIER, Toenjes	22	Pilsum	66-0623
MEIER, Ursula	26	Schwenningen	65-0402
Betti 4			
MEIER, Wilhelm	22	Versmold	23-0865
MEIER, Wm.	43	New York	64-0495
MEIERHOF, Raphael	29	Melbach	63-0350
Emanuel 19			
MEIERHOLZ, John	28	Braunschweig	66-0221
MEILE, Jos.	23	Hohenstaat	66-1313
MEILENHAUS, Christ	24	Dransfeld	64-0782
MEILER, Sebast.	25	Windischenbch	67-0795

NAME	AGE	RESIDENCE	YR-LIST
MEIM, Carl Joh.	21	Kirchhasel	66-1155
MEIN, Heinrich	30	Worms	66-0679
Catharine 25			
MEINANDE, H.S.	49	Ostfriesland	64-0495
Gulke 37, Hanke 6, Antje 7, Isache 4			
baby 11m			
MEINE, Friedrich	66	Dueshorn	65-0770
Sophie 19, Diedrich 17			
MEINE, Robert	24	Clausthal	66-1248
MEINECKE, Elise	60	Harbesse	64-0331
MEINECKE, Fred.	37	Ringstedt	63-1136
Johanne 30, Amalie 7, Willy 5, Agnes 1			
Minna 6m			
MEINEKE, John H.	32	New York	66-0221
MEINEN, A.	38	Jaderaltend.	66-0668
MEINEN, G.D.	35	New York	63-0821
MEINERS, Heinr. D.	14	Lehe	64-0427
MEINERS, Theodor	23	Langwarden	66-0577
MEINERTS, Henry	24	Thunum	63-0296
MEINHAEUSER, Adam	24	Trabelsdorf	66-1373
MEINHARDT, Conrad	19	Schoenau	66-1373
MEINHARDT, Ludw.	15	Lieblos	64-0992
MEINHARDT, Margret	57	Bergheim	67-0954
Margret 22, Catrina 1, Johannes 16			
MEINHARDT, Michael	27	Berkach	66-1131
MEINHOLD, Alex'der	36	Berlin	63-0693
MEINKEN, Friedr.	25	Balben	65-0055
MEINKEN, Marie	32	Rangstedt	66-1031
MEINKING, W.	31	Nienburg	64-0992
Sophie 30, Caroline 7			
MEINS, H.(m)	24	Hohenkirchen	64-0214
MEINZ, Friedr.	25	Rieden	67-0007
MEISE, Friedr.	17	Dissen	66-0984
MEISENDRATH, Benj.	26	Darsten	63-0917
Marianne 19, Bruenette 17			
MEISING, Bertha	59	Wallerstein	63-0917
Charles 9			
MEISNER, Anna	28	Boehmen	63-0551
Rosalie 5, John 3			
MEISNER, Frz.	33	Miltenberg	64-1022
MEISNER, Robert	16	Teuchern	63-0693
MEISSAR, Charles	25	Cleveland	66-0984
MEISSEL, Joh. P.	55	Worms	64-0886
Anna Maria 53, Emilie 20, Sophia 7			
MEISSEL, Simon	14	Marktegast	64-0433
MEISSENBACH, Wm.	28	Thiesengarten	63-0693
MEISSENBACHER, Ul.	33	Pforzheim/Pr	64-1053
MEISSERT, Gerd.	19	Luckau	66-1248
MEISSNER, Adolph	26	Goettingen	63-1178
MEISSNER, Ales.	30	Berlin	66-0346
Augusta 29, Clara 7			
MEISSNER, Fr'dke.	58	Burg	65-0856
Heinrich 28, Amalie 23			
MEISSNER, Franz	44	New York	64-0023
MEISSNER, Friedr.	30	Hessberg	64-0495
Friederike 23, Chrls. 3			
MEISSNER, Jacob	28	Friedrichshal	66-0346
Friedericke 25, August 9m			
MEISSNER, Jul.(m)	20	Teuhern	64-0214
MEISSNER, Louise	31	Sondershausen	66-0221
Lily 7, Albert 9m			
MEISTEL, Friedrike	17	Dorzbach	64-0992
MEISTER, A.		Dietz	63-1003
MEISTER, An Marie	28	Curhessen	63-0822
MEISTER, Chr.	18	Armorsgruen	65-0898
MEISTER, Dorothee	30	Teleschhausen	66-0413
MEISTER, E.	24	Tauchau	65-0189
MEISTER, Georg	24	Wetzlar	63-0006
MEISTER, George	32	Daertzbach	63-1085
Marie 14			
MEISTER, J.W.	42	Mederdunzebch	64-0170
M.Elise 40, Matheus 16, M.Elise 9			
MEISTER, John	35	Riegel	63-0917
Cathrel 40, Maria 36			
MEISTER, John	19	Waldau	66-1031
MEISTER, Peter	18	Olmbach	66-1243
MEISTERLING, John	28	Odenbach	63-0350
Elisabeth 22, John 3, Elisabeth bob			

NAME	AGE	RESIDENCE	YR-LIST
MEKEL, Joseph	23	Asmanshausen	63-0953
MELA, Ludw.	26	Pforzheim	64-1053
MELCHE, Margar	37	Baltimore	66-0704
Margar. 8			
MELCHING, A.	21	Sievershausen	66-0413
MELCHINGER, Christ	62	Menzingen	65-0007
Christ. Fr. 24			
MELCHIOR, Heinrich	28	Schadenbach	66-1155
MELCHIOR, Ra. (f)	31	Osterburken	64-0363
MELCHIOR, Wilhmine	16	Adelsfeld	64-0073
MELETTA, (m)	30	Mainz	65-0189
(f) 23			
MELGES, Gottlieb	32	Hoerste	65-0898
MELGES, Lina	27	Leopoldshoehe	65-0898
MELHUISH, J.H.	26	England	64-0363
MELING, Kilian	20	Himmelstadt	64-0639
MELIS, Donne	26	Rouen	63-0350
MELITZER, Caroline	17	Westphalia	66-0469
MELKE, Arthur	20	Leipzig	66-1248
MELKE, Theodor	22	Widenburg	64-0456
MELL, Christian	37	Witzenhausen	64-0739
Fritz 9, Heinrich 7, Carl 6			
MELLEN, Fritz	23	Switz.	64-0170
MELLERT, Friedrich	31	Boetzingen	63-0296
wife 34			
MELLERT, Xaver	29	Steinach	64-0023
MELLOH, Doris	21	Sulingen	66-1313
MELLOH, Doris	20	Stroehen	65-1031
MELLOH, Louis	21	Suhlingen	64-0992
MELZER, David	17	Cotterschin	65-0038
MEMERS, Hy.	16	Espe	63-1085
MEMKING, Louis	2	Nienburg	64-0992
MEMMLER, Anna	26	Oberkachen	66-0668
MENCH, Gottlieb	29	Teufelsthal	65-1088
Elisabeth 29, Gottfried 4, Theod. 3m			
MENCKE, Hermann	21	Bremen	66-0413
MENDE, Ferdinand	26	Corbecke	63-0953
MENDE, Wilhelm	29	Greiz	66-1248
MENDEL, Betty	36	New York	63-0917
MENDEL, Gustav	26	Cincinnati	66-0984
Hanni 18			
MENDELSOH, J.	55	Hohenems	64-0992
MENDLER, Joach.	46	Kempen	65-1030
Cath. 34, Elisabeth 7			
MENDLICK, Theresia	32	Pibruch	67-0007
MENDLIK, Franz	34	Teschvietz	67-0007
Marie 34, Marie 7, Anna 5, Joseph 3			
Anna 6m			
MENEBROEKER, Frdr.	19	Ledde	65-0948
MENG, Friedr.	25	Aulenbach	64-0170
MENGE, Carl Fr.	24	Zchechnitz	64-0073
MENGE, Henr.	24	Peine	63-1136
MENGE, L.	28	Solschen	63-1003
MENGEL, Catharine	20	Bunghofen	66-0668
MENGER, Peter	24	Herbsthal	65-0243
MENINGER, Wilhelm	20	Hemelingen	67-0007
MENKE, Charlotte	21	Westrup	64-0639
MENKE, Chr.	17	Bremen	66-1248
MENKE, Heinr.	17	Rechtenfleth	64-0456
MENKE, Johannes	25	Dahlhausen	65-1030
MENKE, Sophie	23	Kuepperzell	65-0004
baby bob			
MENKE, Theodor	23	Bielefeld	66-0109
MENKEL, Gertrud	58	Marburg	64-0170
MENKEMEYER, Wilh.	38	Eschenhausen	66-0934
MENKEN, Georg	33	New York	63-0693
Henry 32			
MENKEN, Heinr.	18	Schamstuden	66-1243
MENKHAUS, Wilh.	28	Laer	64-0639
MENKING, Heinr.	21	Bueckeburg	66-1243
MENLO, Fr.	22	Havre	64-1053
MENNE, Joseph	19	Corbecke	66-1203
MENNING, Louise	20	Wehdem	63-1136
MENNY, Julius	40	New York	66-0221
MENSCHING, Dorothe	19	Lauenhagen	66-1031
MENSCHING, Mesulin	46	New York	63-0006
MENSINCK, Guido	24	Bochold	65-1095
MENSING, Bernhard	20	Bockold	64-0199

NAME	AGE	RESIDENCE	YR-LIST
MENSING, Diedr.	25	Stolzenau	66-0577
MENSING, Wilh'mine	25	Stolzenau	66-0577
MENSINGER, Diedr.	19	Oese	64-0593
MENTEL, Johann	26	Roboldshausen	66-0668
MENTEL, John	20	Allmutshausen	63-0551
MENTERS, D.(m)	18	Amsterdam	64-0331
MENTRUP, Franz	25	Spelle	66-0679
MENTZE, Gottlieb	28	Volksdorf	65-0950
MENZ, Mich.	42	Albress	66-1243
Anna Maria 30, Louis 13, Ferdinand 7			
Bernard 10			
MENZA, Jacob	36	Nemschlitz	65-0856
Marie 31			
MENZE, Diedrich	20	Leese	66-1031
MENZE, Herm.	20	Ostercappeln	66-0984
Bernhard 18, Mathias 15			
MENZEL, A.	17	Wingershausen	65-0713
MENZEL, J.(m)	25	Leipzig	64-0331
MENZEL, Wm.	36	Altenburg	64-0432
MENZER, Simon	43	Ostercappeln	66-1127
MEOMERT. Chr.	31	Stemmer	64-0331
H.(m) 7, W.(f) 4, Ce.(f) 3, F.(f) 1			
MEPPEN, N.	24	Werdum	63-1085
MERGELMANN, Aug.	19	Detmold	66-1031
MERGERLE, Peter	22	Neuenstein	66-0704
MERHOLZ, Reinhard	46	Neunburg	66-0083
MERK, Heinrich	29	Bamberg	65-0713
MERKATER, Carl	24	Waldueren	66-1203
MERKEL, Conradine	17	Stadtoldendrf	66-0469
MERKEL, Minna	28	Keierde	66-0650
MERKER, Julius A.	23	Zierenburg	63-1010
MERKHARDT, John	46	Hagen	66-1031
Catharine 40, Catharine 22			
MERKLE, Christ	27	Michelau	64-0214
MERKLE, Heinrich	28	New York	66-0147
MERKLEIN, Babette	23	Pommersfelden	66-1203
MERNICK, Mary	54	Springfield	63-1085
MERSE, G.	53	Bieste	63-1003
M. 56			
MERSFELDER, Isak	28	Lorneksmuehl	64-0495
Ph.(f) 22, Ghd.(f) 23, C.(f) 21			
August 6m, Louis 6m			
MERTEL, Heinrich	28	Baltimore	66-0147
MERTEN, J.	30	Muenster	63-0296
MERTENS, Aug.	19	Rhoden	65-0594
MERTENS, Heinr.	25	Bruetscheid	66-0576
MERTENS, Heinr.	19	Uthfelde	66-0934
MERTENS, Philipp	20	Alzey	65-0151
MERTES, Franz	26	Alf	64-1108
MERTZ, Reb.	22	Endringen	65-1189
MERTZ, Theodor	13	Marburg	66-1093
MERUNKA, Josepha	53	Boehmen	63-1218
Anton 18			
MERZ, Anton	37	Sackenbach	65-1031
MERZ, Barbara	22	Oterkochen	66-0576
Barbara 5m			
MERZ, Geo.	31	Hanau	63-0482
MERZ, Georg	8	New Orleans	63-1038
MERZ, Georg	27	Altenhain	65-0116
MERZ, Gottlieb	33	Altdorf	66-1093
MESCH, Hermann	18	Alfhausen	66-1093
MESCHEDE, F.Fr'dr.	24	Duesseldorf	65-0038
MESCHENDORF, O.	17	Lechterke	65-0402
MESEDLICK, Anna	24	Pibruch	67-0007
MESH, Adolph	24	Hohausen	66-0984
Caroline 25			
MESICKE, Mary	36	Baltimore	63-0821
Mary 14			
MESKE, Carl	43	Potsdam	66-1243
Sophie 43, Minna 17, Carl 14, August 6			
MESLE, Francisca	24	Duerkheim	65-0007
MESLOH, Lena	18	Stocksdorf	66-1155
Wilhelm 9			
MESNER, Cresenz	22	Durbach	66-0679
MESS, Bernhard	22	Hannover	66-0679
MESSAER, Hermann	27	Meppen	64-0886
MESSELHANSER, Mar.	27	Muehlhausen	63-1218
MESSEN, Gottlieb	25	Schwabach	64-0739

NAME	AGE	RESIDENCE	YR-LIST
MESSER, Adam	20	Hessen	63-0614
Conrad 18			
MESSER, Chrltt Sph	28	Krummendeich	66-0147
MESSER, Ellias	34	Connecticut	63-0350
MESSER, Heinr.	18	Gilfenshausen	65-0713
MESSER, Joh.	37	Aixheim	64-0495
MESSER, Johann	30	New York	66-0083
Jacob 28			
MESSERSCHMIDT, E.A	18	Loccum	64-0433
MESSERSCHMIDT, Mar	17	Nassau	66-0576
MESSINGER, Cathar.	35	Hessen	66-0109
Carl 9, Conrad 9, Theodor 7			
MESSLER, A.	23	Borlachshein	64-0495
MESSLER, Conrad	21	Nannenroth	66-0704
MESSLER, Joseph	26	Koblenz	65-0856
MESSMANN, Joh.	56	Pommern	66-0469
Sophie 53, Ernst 22, Sophie 20, Johann 18			
MESSMER, Peter	17	Grosselfingen	66-1313
MESSMER, Philipp	16	Coblenz	64-0214
MESSNER, Christ.	26	Frossingen	63-0990
Gottlob 16, John 23, Matthias 22			
MESSNER, Friedr.	18	Trostingen	63-0990
MESSNER, Mathias	22	Trassingen	63-0917
MESSNER, Mich.	27	Trottingen	65-0402
Anna 27, Johann 32, Johann 21			
MESSNER, Paul	28	Trostingen	64-0495
Ch.(f) 21			
MESSNER, Paul	44	Trossingen	64-0363
MEST, Gust.	25	Muenchen	65-0402
MESTER, Heinrich	20	Bremen	64-0456
MESTER, Joseph	37	Elspehausen	63-0350
METJE, Carl	19	Bremervoerde	67-0007
METJEN, Caroline	41	Kufenthal	66-1243
Caroline 15, Heinrich 15, Heinrich 10			
METSCHNABEL, Mich.	34	Beckendorf	66-0623
METTE, Anton	30	Dorlar	66-0576
METTE, John	33	Durlar	66-1155
Joseph 16, August 16, Theresia 22			
Johann 21, Adam 25			
METTHOEFER, Joh.	20	Wittlage	65-1031
METTWEG, Franz	25	Werden	65-0007
METZ, Conrad	17	Gontershausen	66-1155
METZ, Eva D.	16	Rothenhoff	65-1024
METZ, G.	25	Sondershausen	66-0413
H. 22			
METZ, Johann	21	Hersfeld	66-1248
Catharina 22, Georg 6m			
METZ, Peter	26	Hirschnitz	64-0331
METZ, Wilhelmine	24	Hoyna	65-0007
METZ, Wm.	43	Gruenberg	64-0331
Mart. 15			
METZE, Heinr.	34	Celleda	65-1030
METZENHEIM, Bernh.	21	Veilsdorf	63-0482
METZER, Louis	18	Berlin	66-1155
Simon 21			
METZGER, Abraham	27	Barlingen	65-1031
METZGER, Augusta	17	Halsdorf	65-0948
METZGER, Cath.	23	Halsdorf	64-0782
METZGER, Cath.	19	Gambach	65-0007
H. 17, Marg. 9			
METZGER, D.	34	Philadelphia	64-0331
Johanna 21			
METZGER, Emilie	21	Gehrde	66-0704
METZGER, Emilie	18	Speyer	64-1108
METZGER, Gottlieba	24	Dermsheim	63-0953
Marie 58			
METZGER, Jacob	60	Rohl	64-0023
METZGER, Jacob	15	Wuertemberg	66-0984
METZGER, Jacob	18	Birkenau	66-1373
METZGER, Joseph	40	Kirchhausen	64-0886
Wilhelmine 25, Maria 7, Franz 6, August 4			
METZGER, Martin	58	Darmsheim	63-0482
METZGER, Rosine	16	Gaildorf	66-1203
METZGER, Sabine	23	Cassel	64-1053
METZGER, Wm.	36	Buffalo	64-0495
METZLER, Heinrich	23	Mainz	66-1373
METZNER, Augusta	28	Drenzig	63-0551
METZNER, Philipp	42	Menthausen	66-0412

NAME	AGE	RESIDENCE	YR-LIST
Anna Cathar. 52			
MEUBERGER, M.(m)	20	Hainstedt	64-0495
MEUEL, Felix	45	Mundbach	64-0687
Sophie 40, Theo. 7			
MEULEN, A.	24	Berlin	65-0898
MEURER, Charles	44	Philadelphia	66-0984
Saali 43, William 18			
MEUSER, Ludwig	31	Reizenwagen	65-0948
Heinrich 18			
MEUSER, Marie	21	Schwelm	66-0837
MEUSER, Wm. Fr.	24	Carlsbaum	63-1003
MEUSNEST, Marie	24	Holzhausen	64-1053
MEVES, Carl	25	Abstshagen	64-0840
MEWES, Henry	19	Ritaebuettel	63-0990
MEY, Herm.	37	Rurdorf	63-0752
Clara 10m			
MEYBORG, B.	21	Gehrde	64-1161
MEYENBORG, Adele	26	Neuende	64-0214
MEYER, (m)	16	Osnabrueck	67-0600
MEYER, A.C.L.(m)	35	Delmenhorst	64-0331
Johanna 21			
MEYER, A.G.	21	Twistringen	65-1088
MEYER, Abraham	23	Luebbecke	64-0938
MEYER, Adolph	24	Utzupoenen	63-1178
MEYER, Alois	24	Neustadt	64-1022
MEYER, Andreas	36	Bremke	64-1053
Heinrich 32			
MEYER, Anna	20	New York	63-0990
MEYER, Anna	20	Lehe	65-0189
MEYER, Anna	18	Bremen	65-0974
MEYER, Anna Maria	21	Ostercappeln	65-0950
MEYER, Aug.	17	Attendieck	63-0953
MEYER, Aug.	19	Osnabrueck	64-0687
MEYER, Aug.	20	Coblenz	64-1206
MEYER, Aug.	18	Terschau	64-1022
MEYER, Aug.	25	Evenhausen	65-0898
MEYER, August	21	Esbaeck	65-0004
MEYER, August	14	Einbeck	66-0934
Otto 18			
MEYER, August	31	Neuenkirchen	65-0974
MEYER, August	18	Reinhausen	64-0593
MEYER, B.H.	27	Ostfriesland	64-0495
MEYER, Barbara	24	Kitzingen	66-1127
Barbara 8m			
MEYER, Berh.	19	Cloppenburg	65-0116
Marg			
MEYER, Bernhard	22	Wierlte	67-0007
MEYER, Bernhard	34	Fuerstenau	66-0934
MEYER, Bernhd.	38	Detmold	65-1088
MEYER, C.(m)	19	Einbeck	64-0331
MEYER, C.R.	19	Ritzebuettel	63-1010
MEYER, Carl	18	Kirchheim	64-0073
MEYER, Carl	31	Gera	64-0023
MEYER, Carl	24	Dinklage	66-0576
MEYER, Carl	25	Glauchau	64-0593
MEYER, Carl	18	Carlshafen	64-0938
MEYER, Carl	16	Bremen	65-0004
MEYER, Carl	15	Coeln	64-0886
MEYER, Carl Diedr.	28	Wertheim	67-0599
MEYER, Carl Fr.	22	Bulsten	66-0469
MEYER, Carl Herman	18	Leipzig	66-1248
MEYER, Caroline	48	Bruessel	66-0221
Elise 18, Arthur 9, Emanuel 7			
MEYER, Caterine	20	Kirchhaukum	64-0214
MEYER, Ch.	22	Hellebach	66-1243
MEYER, Charles	50	Hildesheim	63-1178
MEYER, Charles	50	Berlin	63-0693
MEYER, Charlotte	17	Hannover	64-0739
MEYER, Chr.	22	Riemsloh	64-0593
MEYER, Chr.(m)	33	Poll	64-0170
MEYER, Christ. F.	32	Luebbecke	65-0713
Anna 31, Marie 6, Louise 4m			
MEYER, Christian	22	Bremen	66-0984
MEYER, Christian	21	Twistringen	64-0920
MEYER, Christian F	19	Bremen	63-0168
MEYER, Christoph	34	New Orleans	64-0138
Catharine 31, Marie 3, Catharine 11m			
MEYER, Claus	23	New York	63-0398
MEYER, Claus	25	Hollenstedt	66-0083
Meta 20			
MEYER, Claus	20	Fahrendorf	65-1095
MEYER, Cord	20	Tramstedt	66-1093
MEYER, D.	63	Bruessel	65-1088
Be. 26			
MEYER, Dan. M.	34	Schwarza	63-0168
MEYER, Daniel	48	Amsterdam	63-0482
MEYER, Diedr.	19	Dedendorf	63-0168
William 17			
MEYER, Diedr.	18	Halle	65-0151
MEYER, Diedrich	34	Indiana	63-1136
MEYER, Diedrich	20	Lankenau	66-0679
MEYER, Dorothea	21	Nebischaffshm	64-0073
MEYER, Dorothea	22	Rahden	65-1088
MEYER, E. Ff.	24	Lehe	64-0495
MEYER, Ed.(m)	26	Bremen	64-0331
MEYER, Eduard	26	Nordstaetten	65-0151
MEYER, Eduard	23	Antonina	65-1030
Rudolph 20			
MEYER, Edw.		New York	63-1136
Marg. , Edward 6, Henry 3, baby 6m			
MEYER, Elisabeth	20	Lemfoerde	63-1085
MEYER, Elisabeth	11	Osnabrueck	67-0600
MEYER, Elisabeth	29	Lengsfeld	64-1053
MEYER, Elisabetha	24	Neuscharrel	66-0984
MEYER, Elise	18	Minden	63-0862
MEYER, Elise	34	Philadelphia	66-0984
MEYER, Erich	30	Memphis	66-0934
MEYER, Ernst	18	Altendorf	64-0433
MEYER, Eva	16	Steinach	63-1218
Saly 12			
MEYER, Everhard	45	Gruensburg	64-0593
MEYER, F.	24	Honnrol	66-0934
MEYER, F.H.J.	36	Twistingen	64-0687
Franz 21			
MEYER, F.W.	38	New York	64-0427
Christine 15, Louise 18, wife 30			
MEYER, F.W.A.	28	Calmstedt	64-0593
MEYER, Ferd.	20	Oberhofen	63-1136
MEYER, Fr.	23	Pr. Minden	64-0639
MEYER, Fr. A.	18	Bremen	64-0665
MEYER, Fr. Wm.	33	Bremen	63-1003
MEYER, Fr.(f)	16	Utlede	64-1108
MEYER, Francisca	43	Bremen	66-1373
MEYER, Franz	30	Berlin	66-1327
MEYER, Friederike	19	Liesberg	65-0594
MEYER, Friedr.	23	Hilbe	64-1108
MEYER, Friedr.	28	Barkhausen	65-0038
MEYER, Friedr. Aug	40	Bremen	66-0577
Emma 39			
MEYER, Friedrich	25	Hannover	64-0199
MEYER, Friedrich	30	Bremen	63-0551
MEYER, Friedrich	23	Nordhemmern	63-0917
MEYER, Friedrich	43	Seesen	63-0006
Catharine 43			
MEYER, Friedrich	19	Kappeln	66-0668
MEYER, Friedrich	42	Minden	66-0083
MEYER, Friedrich	17	Bosteln	66-1031
MEYER, Friedrich	19	Bueckeburg	66-1031
MEYER, Friedrich	36	Erfurt	65-0950
MEYER, Fritz	19	Bremen	66-0576
MEYER, Fritz	28	Niederaula	63-0482
MEYER, Fritz	14	Oiste	64-0739
MEYER, Fritz	25	Preuss	67-0007
MEYER, Fritz	16	Hechingen	65-1024
MEYER, Fritz	20	Bremen	64-0363
MEYER, G.	38	Lankenau	63-0990
Behrend 15			
MEYER, G.	21	Zuerich	66-0413
MEYER, Georg	39	New York	64-0782
Maria 26, Anna 7, Georg 5, Salm. 4			
MEYER, Georg	38	Rossbach	64-1053
Margarethe 34, Conrad 14, Betti 12			
Julie 10, Georg 7, Margarethe 3			
MEYER, Georg H.	26	Haren	63-0006
MEYER, Gerh. H.	20	Gesede	65-0189
MEYER, Gerhard	26	Nieort	63-1038

NAME	AGE	RESIDENCE	YR-LIST
MEYER, Gerhard	18	Osnabruck	66-1031
MEYER, Gerhard	34	Oslebshausen	64-0363
Marie 25, baby(f) 10m			
MEYER, Gesche	75	Leer	63-0551
MEYER, Gesche	17	Abbehausen	64-0840
MEYER, Gesche	22	Mahndorf	66-1093
MEYER, Gesche	18	Bremen	64-0214
MEYER, Gesine	49	Hastedt	63-0015
MEYER, Gesine	18	Linden	66-0679
MEYER, Gesine	24	Oldenburg	65-0038
MEYER, Gesine	23	Bremen	65-0038
MEYER, Gustav	22	Reinsdorf	66-1373
MEYER, H.	36	Bremen	63-0752
MEYER, H.	25	Oldenburg	66-0413
F. 21			
MEYER, H.	21	Leeste	65-0974
MEYER, H.(m)	26	Preussen	64-0331
MEYER, H.(m)	31	Bremen	64-0331
Johanna 21			
MEYER, H.(m)	32	Osnabrueck	64-0363
MEYER, H.F.A.	18	Messingen	64-0331
MEYER, Ham.	66	Bremen	66-0349
MEYER, Hannchen	28	Altenstadt	65-0594
MEYER, Hch.	30	Holtum	64-0495
MEYER, Heinr.	25	New York	64-0170
MEYER, Heinr.	24	Cincinnati	64-0023
MEYER, Heinr.	29	Damme	64-0593
MEYER, Heinr.	25	Ndr.Auerbach	64-0992
Ernst 20			
MEYER, Heinr.	21	Behren	66-1203
MEYER, Heinr.	20	Webbergen	65-0189
MEYER, Heinr.	17	Helmichhausen	65-1030
MEYER, Heinr. W.	48	Eschede	64-0214
Marie 48, Heinr. 9, Marie 7			
MEYER, Heinrich	23	Hegewede	64-0433
Rudolph 43			
MEYER, Heinrich	22	Bruchmuehle	66-0147
MEYER, Heinrich	27	Herford	66-0412
MEYER, Heinrich	28	Kuhlen	66-0578
MEYER, Heinrich	18	Haidengruen	66-0679
MEYER, Heinrich	22	Buende	66-0837
MEYER, Heinrich	30	Williamsburg	64-0687
Lisette 25, Elise 2, baby 11m			
MEYER, Heinrich	18	Osnabrueck	66-1093
MEYER, Heinrich	19	Ritterode	66-1155
MEYER, Heinrich	30	Bremen	66-1031
MEYER, Heinrich	31	Gehlenbeck	66-1127
MEYER, Heinrich	19	Nordenbeck	65-0948
MEYER, Henrich	26	Hannover	66-0734
MEYER, Henriette	26	Gladenbach	65-0594
MEYER, Henry	17	Bremen	63-1136
MEYER, Henry	55	Reckum	63-1178
Anna 58, Christoph 15			
MEYER, Henry	47	Newark	63-0953
MEYER, Henry	31	New York	63-0015
MEYER, Herm.	38	New York	63-0752
MEYER, Herm.	26	Dorumjahmsfld	64-0687
MEYER, Herm.	19	Bremen	64-0739
MEYER, Herm.	28	Ingenau	64-0840
Emilie 28, Bertha 2			
MEYER, Herm.	19	Verden	64-1206
MEYER, Herm.	22	Boilen	65-0055
MEYER, Herm.	21	Hagenburg	66-1373
MEYER, Herman Hch.	24	Rotenburg	64-0739
MEYER, Hermann	21	Riede	66-0221
MEYER, Hermann	22	Woemsdorf	66-0679
MEYER, Hermann	23	Schweringen	66-0704
MEYER, Hermann	20	Wedehorn	66-0704
MEYER, Hermann	18	Bocksdorf	66-1031
MEYER, Hr.	24	Suchen	65-0007
MEYER, I.	38	France	63-0350
MEYER, Ibo. Rolfs	33	Emden	64-0739
Robino 32, Rolf 4, Peter 10m			
MEYER, Isaak	17	Honsheim	66-0349
MEYER, J.	56	New Orleans	63-1003
MEYER, J.	17	Alten Solheim	64-0639
MEYER, J.A.W.	35	Oldenburg	63-1218
MEYER, J.C.(m)	30	Alton	64-0331

NAME	AGE	RESIDENCE	YR-LIST
MEYER, J.F.(m)	30	West Cappeln	64-0331
MEYER, J.G.	30	Epterode	64-0665
MEYER, J.H.	58	Iowa	63-0097
MEYER, J.H.	18	Leeste	64-0495
MEYER, Jacob	28	Wolfenbuettel	64-0138
MEYER, Jacob	28	Bayern	63-0398
MEYER, Jacob	21	Hessen	66-0109
MEYER, Jacob	36	Dessenbach	66-1093
MEYER, Jacob	25	Borgholzhsn.	66-1373
MEYER, Jacob	28	Weimtingen	64-0363
MEYER, Joh.	38	Starnitz-Lab.	66-0650
MEYER, Joh.	20	Neustadt	64-0687
MEYER, Joh.	29	Gruppenbach	64-0639
MEYER, Joh.	29	Cloppenburg	65-0038
MEYER, Joh.	16	Rahde	65-0116
MEYER, Joh. Fr.	20	Unteraichen	64-0639
Fr. Wm. 20			
MEYER, Joh. H.	21	Rechtenfleth	64-0432
MEYER, Joh. Heinr.	44	New York	63-0398
Gertrude 37, Marie 3, Joseph 11m			
MEYER, Joh. Heinr.	25	Buer	64-0920
MEYER, Johann	28	Adolphshaus	66-1093
Diedrich 15			
MEYER, Johann	30	Sandstedt	66-1093
MEYER, Johann	22	Marschholtum	66-0934
MEYER, Johann	22	Pforzheim	66-1131
MEYER, Johann	29	Olber	66-1131
MEYER, Johann Herm	28	Bremen	66-1248
MEYER, Johanna	24	Chemitz	64-0639
MEYER, Johanna	15	Bremen	66-1031
Johanna 16			
MEYER, Johanna	15	Schweiburg	66-1313
MEYER, Johanna	21	Gr. Bockenhm.	63-0862
MEYER, Johannes	25	Altenstadt	65-0189
MEYER, Johannett	25	Darmstadt	64-0739
MEYER, John	26	Prussia	63-0296
MEYER, John	25	New York	63-0168
MEYER, Jos.	32	New York	63-1136
MEYER, Joseph	47	Rodersdorf	63-0862
MEYER, Joseph	48	Menslage	65-0243
MEYER, Julie	20	Beverstedt	65-1088
MEYER, Julius	33	Wetten	64-0023
MEYER, Julius	26	Hildesheim	63-0482
MEYER, Julius	24	Hannover	64-0840
MEYER, Justus	27	Osten	63-0862
MEYER, L.	53	Hamburg	66-0734
MEYER, Lina	25	Emden	65-1095
Margarethe 25			
MEYER, Lorenz	40	Bremen	66-0934
MEYER, Louis	34	Oldendorf	65-0055
MEYER, Louis	24	Oberessen	65-0402
J.G. 36			
MEYER, Louise	16	Ovelgoenne	63-0953
MEYER, Louise	19	Loehne	66-0413
MEYER, Louise	16	Schweringen	66-0704
MEYER, Lucas	24	Bilsum	64-0904
MEYER, Ludwig	16	Ilsenworth	66-0704
Eduard 14			
MEYER, Luetje	30	Fischerhude	63-0821
MEYER, M.	30	Braunschweig	65-1189
August 29, B. 2			
MEYER, M.	15	Grebenau	65-1189
MEYER, M.	20	Bueckeburg	65-1088
MEYER, Mar.	27	Schlingen	66-0349
MEYER, Margaretha	24	Schotten	63-0350
MEYER, Margarthe	25	Ohsen	65-0243
MEYER, Marie	30	Sulingen	64-0593
MEYER, Marie	20	Gruenbach	65-0151
MEYER, Marie	28	Diepenau	65-1189
MEYER, Marie	20	Eichstetten	65-0770
MEYER, Marie	6	Quakenbrueck	64-0739
MEYER, Marx	31	Lebach	64-0214
MEYER, Mathias	24	Bremen	66-0734
MEYER, Maurice	25	Coburg	63-0168
MEYER, Meta	21	Bremerhaven	64-0432
MEYER, Meta	17	Wersabe	64-0739
MEYER, Michael	24	Thalheim	65-0713
MEYER, Minna	20	Grosskreutz	64-0170

NAME	AGE	RESIDENCE	YR-LIST
MEYER, Minna	24	Minden	66-0934
MEYER, Minna	30	Vechta	65-0948
Dina 20			
MEYER, Nicolaus	17	Eschenhausen	66-1131
MEYER, Olb.	16	Kreinsen	64-0782
MEYER, Philip	22	Wuertemberg	66-0679
MEYER, Raphael	70	Mutterstadt	63-1178
MEYER, Rebecca	55	Boderkesa	66-0984
MEYER, Rebecca	14	Hannover	66-1313
MEYER, Ricus	30	Nord Georgfeh	64-0433
Hermine 11m, Elisabeth 5m, Ricka 28			
MEYER, Rosalie	30	Hannover	64-0992
MEYER, Rud.	31	Frankfurt a/M	65-1088
MEYER, Rudolph	14	Fedderwarden	66-0984
MEYER, S. (m)	15	Bayersthal	64-0331
MEYER, Sophie	19	Bremen	63-0917
MEYER, Sophie	21	Bremen	66-1203
MEYER, Sophie	18	Holtrup	65-1088
MEYER, Therese	18	Hameln	64-0992
MEYER, Theresia	28	Schlungen	64-0138
MEYER, Ths.	21	Ruppin	65-1024
MEYER, Valentin	33	Lancaster	63-0752
MEYER, Walburga	30	Stauf	63-0693
Therese 31			
MEYER, Walburga	21	Baden	66-0576
MEYER, Wilh.	25	Hofherrnweilr	66-1313
MEYER, Wilh.	37	Burg	65-0950
MEYER, Wilhelm	35	Neuenkirchen	66-0734
Magdalena 26, Wilhelmina 3, Magdalene 11m			
MEYER, Wilhelm	30	Lage	66-0668
MEYER, Wilhelm	29	Hoya	64-0456
MEYER, Wilhelm	27	Dielingen	64-0920
MEYER, Wilhelm	20	Mehnen	66-1155
MEYER, Wilhelmine	27	Ihlienworth	64-0427
Wilhelm 7, Eleonore 4, Anna Marg. 28			
MEYER, William		Bueckeburg	63-0953
MEYER, William	22	Glatten	63-1218
MEYER, Wm.	23	Fischbeck	64-0495
MEYER, Wm.	25	Detmold	64-1053
MEYER, Wm.	25	Manil	64-1053
MEYER, Wm.	47	Altenbruch	64-0593
MEYER, Xaver	25	Rottweil	64-0782
MEYER, Z.(m)	25	Luttorf	64-0495
MEYERER, Rosine	20	Hagenbach	66-0109
MEYERFELD, Amalie	29	Goedens	65-1024
MEYERHOFEN, Alois	39	Donauwoerth	64-0840
Anna 33, Cath. 7, Alois 8, Anton 5			
Wilhelm 12			
MEYERHOFF, Heinr.	18	Thal	64-0840
MEYERHOFF, Henry	29	Boehmen	63-0752
MEYERHOFF, Julie	25	Medebach	63-0917
Marie 24			
MEYERHOFF, Moses	16	Medebach	65-1031
Benjamin 19			
MEYERHOLD, Fr. A.	18	Bremen	66-0837
MEYERHOLZ, Emma	20	Hannover	66-1031
MEYERHOLZ, Heinr.	28	Uslar	66-1327
MEYERRIECKS, Anna	19	Bremen	66-0934
MEYERS, Evelyn	16	Charleston	64-0170
MEYFURTH, Joh.	47	Gotha	66-0576
MEYN, L.(m)	16	Lehe	64-0170
MEYN, Pet.H.	24	Otterndorf	64-0456
MEYNERT, H.(m)	27	Evansville	64-0331
MEZIS, Barbara	29	Bohemia	64-0782
Maria 1m			
MIAHM, Mathilde	27	Borsch	65-0594
MICHAEL, C.Fr.	33	Schortan	64-0427
Wilhelmine 33, Emilie 6			
MICHAEL, F.A.(m)	22	Grossneuhsn.	64-0363
MICHAEL, Friedr.	19	Wolf	64-0886
MICHAEL, Georg	27	Eugen	66-0984
MICHAEL, Johann	24	Wuerttemberg	64-0687
Elisabeth 18			
MICHAELIS, August	28	Clausthal	66-1031
MICHAELIS, Diedr.	18	Gruppenbuhren	66-0668
MICHAELIS, Dorothe	71	Schoenhagen	66-0934
MICHAELIS, Georg	20	Rauenstein	64-0170
MICHAELIS, Georg	17	Lilienthal	66-1031
MICHAELIS, Gretchn	22	Queckhorn	66-1127
MICHAELIS, Luetje	20	Eckstedt	64-0495
MICHAELIS, M.(f)	24	Luechte	64-0495
MICHAELIS, v. Eug.	39	Berlin	66-1248
MICHAELS, Minna	38	Potsdam	66-0679
baby (f) 6m			
MICHALOVITZ, J.	41	Eperjis	63-1003
S. 27, B. 17, D. 13, J. 11, P. 9			
MICHEL, Andreas	25	Bergfelden	66-1373
Johanna 23, Johannes 2, Johanna 1			
MICHEL, Barbara	24	Niederwiesen	63-0006
MICHEL, Barbara	43	Igersheim	65-0189
MICHEL, Fanny	23	Jorgenbach	64-0938
MICHEL, Ferdinand	25	Bueckeburg	66-0221
MICHEL, Harm	42	San Francisco	66-0734
MICHEL, Heinrich	25	Guterheim	66-1373
MICHEL, Herm. H.	57	Schledehausen	65-0898
Anna M. 26, Catharina 22, Christoph 20			
Joh. Friedr. 18, Joh. Adam 16			
MICHEL, Jacob	20	Mersheim	65-0004
Leopold 14			
MICHEL, Joh. Georg	23	Rheinheim	65-0189
MICHEL, Johann	27	Goennern	66-0221
MICHEL, Johann P.	25	Geismar	66-0623
MICHEL, Julie	20	Elberfeld	63-0917
Arthur 11m			
MICHEL, Lena	24	Worms	64-0427
Anna 19			
MICHEL, Leopoldine	47	Wien	64-0840
Amalie 20, Adalbert 19, Emilie 9			
MICHEL, Wilhelm	18	Guentersdorf	67-0599
MICHELS, Louise	25	Eppendorf	66-1155
Loettchen 19			
MICHELS, Margareth	4	Germany	63-0350
MICHELSEN, Andreas	39	Gottenburg	66-0666
MICHLER, Friedr.	27	Leipzig	66-0221
MICHLER, Hugo	35	Braunschweig	63-1069
Karoline 33, Elisabetha 7, Paul 6			
Oscar 3, Alfred 9m			
MICKA, Maria	18	Crastau	66-0934
MICKE, Jes.	36	Zell	64-0782
MICKEL, Conr.	38	Obermockstadt	64-0073
MICKEL, Elis.	21	Deckenbach	64-0639
MICKENS, Henry	17	Butze	65-0402
MIDDELKAMP, Fr.	22	Borringhausen	64-0593
MIDDENDORF, Franz	26	Fuerstenau	64-1053
MIDDENDORF, Herman	19	Helle	66-1093
Catharine 17			
MIDDENDORF, Herman	31	Dinklage	65-0948
MIDDENDORF, John	16	Bremen	67-0600
MIDDENDORF, L.	43	Schale	65-1024
Johanne 34, Johann 19, Johanne 16			
Georg 12, Marie 6, Anna 1			
MIECKEN, Henry	16	Grebbin	63-0350
George 25			
MIEDEL, Georg	30	Rotenburg	63-0990
MIEDING, Rudolph	30	Hildesheim	63-0168
MIEGEL, Gottlieb	25	Hartha	63-0614
MIEHLE, Joseph	19	Lesum	65-0116
MIELEVAN, Georg	43	New York	66-0109
MIELKE, Hermine	28	Danzig	66-0666
MIERDEN, van der M	14	Holland	63-0821
Josephine 36, Gerhardine 17			
MIESSENER, E. Leo.	33	Baden	66-0109
MIHM, Gertrude	24	Kirchhasel	66-0221
MIHM, Susanne	16	Darmspach	65-1030
MIKOTA, Franz	33	Nepomuk	66-1327
MIKOWOSKY, Wenzel	33	Boehmen	63-0953
Elisabeth 36, Joseph 9, Maria 8, Anna 5			
Catharina 3, Elisabeth 3m			
MIKULA, Ph.	52	Klagenfurt	65-0402
Agnes 45			
MIKUS, Carl	25	Natzungen	66-1313
MILAN, Henry	24	Paris	63-0917
MILCHENBERGER, Jos	39	New York	64-0593
MILDENBERGER, Aug.	33	Duesseldorf	65-0402
Magd. 30, Heinr. 8, Carol. 6			
MILDENSTEIN, J.	20	Schleswig	65-1189

NAME	AGE	RESIDENCE	YR-LIST
MILFS, Jan. F.	58	Kl. Sander	64-1053
Adolphine 55, Gesche 21, Minna 14 Angela 11			
MILFTENBERG, Wilh.	26	Detmold	66-1127
MILKE, Julius	50	Steinbach	66-1128
MILL, Margaretha	18	Gambach	63-0015
MILLEK, Pauline	22	Biesen	66-1313
MILLER, Adam	20	Sebenhausen	64-0073
MILLER, Caspar	40	New York	63-0244
A. 25, J. 8, A. 2			
MILLER, Dorothea	57	Washington	63-0917
MILLER, Louis	23	New York	63-0097
MILLER, Louis	23	Pyrmont	64-0495
MILLER, Marg.	29	New York	63-1038
Eduard 2			
MILLER, Wm.	39	New York	64-0170
Wilhelmine 21			
MILLERET, (f)	27	Switzerland	63-0990
MILLIKAN, Jos.	24	Cincinnati	64-0495
MILLZ, C.	30	Rohschuetz	66-0413
Julie 19, Rudolph 3m			
MILTENBERG, Raphin	28	Obenburg	63-0953
MILZ, Friedrich	21	Rothen	66-1131
MILZ, Marie	21	Helsen	64-0214
MIMISCH, C.	27	Hahn	66-1327
MINDACK, Johann	29	Dzidzinnek	64-0433
Eva 30			
MINDACK, Michael	32	Dritznik	64-0433
Josepha 27			
MINDEMANN, Anton	30	Gomariugen	66-0679
MINDEN, Caroline	15	Unterluebbe	64-0433
Gottlieb 46, Marie 56			
MINDER, Johann	33	Butau	66-0413
Josepha 27			
MINDERMANN, H.(m)	21	Oberneuland	64-0331
MINGER, Simon	30	France	64-0170
MINGES, Carl Jos.	26	Laudon	64-0427
MINGST, W.A.	30	Bederkesa	65-0402
wife 24, child 9m			
MINIX, Friedrike	28	Wuertenberg	66-0704
MINK, Eduard	32	Friedrichswld	65-1024
MINK, Franz	42	Carlsruhe	64-0687
Catharina 46			
MINK, Magdalena	40	Ippingen	64-0782
Maria 7, Veronica 6, Joh. G. 5			
MINK, Maria	24	Reichenbach	66-0679
MINK, Xaveria	30	Thchenhausen	66-0679
Rosa 8			
MINNER, Cath.	35	New Orleans	63-0168
Oscar 6, Albert 3, Adaline 1			
MINZ, Marie	44	Metzingen	64-0073
MIRKEL, Ludwig	38	Corbach	64-1022
Marie 33			
MISCH, Babette	27	Heppenheim	67-0007
MISCHINO, Martin	43	France	63-0015
MISEGARS, Anna	27	Vave	66-1248
MISSBACH, Malhans	38	Hesse-Darmst.	66-0623
Margarethe 36			
MISSNER, Cord	29	Horstedt	64-0992
MITCHELe, Emanuel	22	Sindelfingen	65-0189
MITCHERLING, Paul.	15	New York	63-0006
MITH, Heinr.	48	New York	64-0363
MITHAEFER, Herm.	14	Melle	64-0840
MITSCHEL, Francis	8	Ruth	63-1136
MITTELBERGER, J.	50	Vorarlberg	66-1127
MITTELHOKAMP, Han.	31	Stedefreund	63-1010
MITTELSTAEDT, Joh.	29	Vostronka	64-0938
MITTELSTAEDT, Ludw	32	New York	63-0990
MITTHOFF, Henry	25	Einbeck	63-0244
MITTLER, August	23	Thalitter	66-0934
MITTRACH, Herm.	30	Dresden	66-0704
MITZEHEIM, Hilmar	17	Veilsdorf	66-0576
MOCK, Christ.	19	Westcreten	65-0116
MOCK, Johannes	20	Speyer	65-0116
MOCK, Theresia	24	Rebbeke	64-0433
MOCKE, Antonia	36	Bremen	64-0886
Richard 9, Johannes 6			
MOCKEL, Ph.	54	Baltimore	64-0782
MODENBACH, Fern.	25	Kudolphschau	66-1373
MODERSOHN, Lisette	33	Lippstadt	63-0862
Julius 14, Louise 12			
MODRI, A.	43	Kralowitz	66-0413
Rosalie 41, Wentzel 14, Franz 12, Marie 3			
MOEBIUS, Theodor	25	Boitzen	66-1127
Gustav 22			
MOEBS, Wilh.	23	Echzell	65-1031
MOECKEL, Joseph	42	Gottmansgruen	66-1093
Christine 45			
MOEHLE, Christ.	22	Gruppenbach	65-0594
Carl 20, Dorothea 15			
MOEHLE, Jos.	31	Algermissen	64-0687
MOEHLENBECK, Heinr	42	Wolbeck	66-1031
MOEHLENDERP, Aits	28	Simonswolde	65-0151
MOEHLER, Joh.	26	Eggersheim	64-0170
MOEHLMANN, Augusta	25	Bremen	65-1095
MOEHLMANN, Brnh.	27	Wersuwe	65-1030
MOEHR, Augusta	25	Mennewitz	66-0679
MOEHRING, H.	19	Lohe	66-1313
MOEHRING, Sophie	18	Stroehen	65-1031
MOEHRLE, Christ.	22	Gruppenbach	65-0594
Carl 20, Eva 36, Philippine 7, Philipp 6 Cath. 5, Jac. 2			
MOEHRLING, Mag.	48	Minden	65-1031
Christine 18, Wilhelmine 16			
MOELL, Paul	31	Ludwigsburg	65-1095
MOELLENKAMP, Gerh.	30	Tecklenburg	64-0886
Wilhelm 24			
MOELLER, Alfred	27	Niedeck	66-1031
MOELLER, Anton	18	Fulda	66-1128
MOELLER, Bernard	28	Badendorf	66-0623
MOELLER, Bernh.	30	Fuerth	64-0073
MOELLER, Caroline	28	Bliehausen	63-0482
Sophie 15			
MOELLER, Casper	25	Wagenfeld	67-0007
MOELLER, Cath.	22	Gehau	64-0665
MOELLER, Chris.	51	Cincinnati	63-0862
MOELLER, Constant.	18	Grossentaft	66-1155
MOELLER, D.	30	Frankenhausen	65-0007
A. 18			
MOELLER, Elise	28	Oberursel	63-0821
MOELLER, Ernst	17	Isenstedt	65-1030
MOELLER, Fr.	57	Mineral Point	63-0990
MOELLER, Heinrich	23	Eissen	67-0007
MOELLER, J.G.	34	Marksuhl	64-0214
Anna Cath. 28			
MOELLER, J.M.	24	Schelesburg	65-0402
Elise 23			
MOELLER, Jacob	29	Zimmerode	66-1127
MOELLER, Joh.	26	Lauterbach	64-0593
MOELLER, Joh.	22	Altenschlirf	64-0992
MOELLER, Joh.	30	Darmstadt	65-1140
Elisab. 23			
MOELLER, Johann	17	Dodenhausen	66-0083
MOELLER, Johann	19	Lohne	66-1131
MOELLER, Joseph	21	Nellighof	63-0752
MOELLER, Joseph	44	Cappeln	65-0116
MOELLER, Martin	17	Brunhausen	64-0433
MOELLER, Peter	26	Weilerbach	65-0116
MOELLER, William	28	St. Louis	63-0953
MOELLER, Wm.	35	Riede	64-0433
Maria 33, Ernst 13, Jacob 8, Sophie 7 Heinrich 5, Maria 2, Elisabeth 11m			
MOELLER, Wm.	20	Schoenstein	64-0687
MOELLMANN, Heinr.	29	Rulle	63-0953
MOELLMANN, Mar.	19	Rieste	63-0953
MOELLMANN, Rudolph	24	Hessia	66-0679
MOENCH, Jacob	18	Limmersfeld	64-0170
MOENCH, Tob.	16	Dieterweiler	65-0402
MOENDERMANN, Joh.	25	Bassen	65-0189
MOENK, A.	28	Fahr	66-0679
Sophie 27			
MOENNICH, Adolph	33	Welflingen	66-0083
Marie 37, Emil 7, Adolph 6, August 4 Joseph 9m			
MOENNICH, Folke L.	40	Emden	66-0837
MOENNIGHOFF, Jos.	23	Muenster	65-1030

NAME	AGE	RESIDENCE	YR-LIST
MOENNIL, Otto	18	Zeitz	66-0576
MOEOS, Martha	27	Fritzlar	64-1022
MOERCHEN, Fr.	20	Brunshaus	65-1024
MOERK, Philipp	27	Hagen Donop	66-1327
MOERMANN, Euphemia	26	Wietmarschen	64-0214
MOERSCHEN, Franz	30	Hallenberg	65-1030
MOERSZBUEHR, H.	13	Calumburg	64-0782
MOESCHLER, Carl	27	Kaegna	66-0576
MOESE, Gottfried	29	Berlin	66-1327
MOESER, John Val.	59	Darmstadt	63-1178
Philipp 16			
MOESER, Ludwig	22	New York	63-0821
MOESER, Philippine	35	Langenheim	64-0687
Elise 8, Marg. 5, baby 9m			
MOESLIN, Conrad	25	Batten	67-0007
MOESSINGER, Joh.	16	Aichenberk	65-1030
Cath. 17			
MOESSNER, Friedr.	24	New York	66-0576
MOETZ, Friedrich	26	Oversleben	65-1095
MOGGER, Engelb.	35	Neukirch	64-0214
MOHLENHOFF, B.(m)	18	Gehrde	64-0331
MOHLENKAMP, Christ	27	Loyel	66-1373
MOHLMANN, A.(m)	23	Alfhausen	64-0023
MOHLMANN, Carol.	33	New York	63-1218
John 9			
MOHLSTEDT, Herta	21	Elmlohe	66-1203
MOHN, Friedrich	18	Durlach	66-1373
MOHN, Johannes	27	Duedelsheim	64-0886
Marg. 27, Dorothea 5, Heinr. 9m			
MOHR, Anne Marg.	17	Hochweisel	63-0296
MOHR, C.	23	Schlitz	65-1024
Christine 17			
MOHR, Claus	22	Barmstedt	65-0948
MOHR, Ernestine	20	Bremerhaven	66-1155
MOHR, Ernestine	23	Veilsdorf	66-1131
MOHR, F.C.	27	Stuttgart	65-1024
MOHR, Georg	24	Mainz	64-1161
MOHR, Jacob	22	Eltville	66-0221
MOHR, James	19	Eltville	63-0752
MOHR, Johannes	33	Hessen	66-0221
MOHR, Jost	65	Bisses	67-0007
Heinrich 28			
MOHR, Nicolaus	25	Lamstedt	66-1031
Peter 18			
MOHRBACH, Adam	22	Ruebelberg	66-0576
MOHRENSTECHER, Fr.	22	Guetersloh	66-1155
MOHRFELD, G. Henry	20	Quackenbrueck	66-0221
MOHRFELD, Henry	43	Trenton	66-0221
MOHRHOFF, Sophie	18	Rahden	65-1088
MOHRLAND, Carl	29	Mengeringshsn	66-1243
Caroline 34, Friedrich 7, Minna 5			
Philippine 3, Carl 11m			
MOHRLAND, Chr'stne	59	Mengeringshsn	66-1243
MOHRLOCH, Christ.	27	Roth	64-0170
Friederike 23, Anna 1			
MOHRMANN, An.Elis.	22	Hessen	64-0432
MOHRMANN, Andr. P.	26	Loxstedt	64-0456
MOHRMANN, Heinr.	15	Zeven	64-0739
MOHRMANN, Heinrich	24	Neuenkirchen	23-0865
MOIGG, B.	52	Zell	64-0782
MOLITOR, John	33	Ittendorf	66-1327
MOLITOR, Otto	21	Ebern	67-0795
MOLL, Ab.	22	Lissa	64-0782
MOLL, Cath.	21	Plochingen	66-1313
MOLL, Florian	35	Gunzheim	66-1373
MOLL, Jacob	27	Unterheimbach	66-0679
MOLL, Johann	20	Wichmansdorf	66-1127
Christoph 18			
MOLLAST, Juliane	28	Werdamm	66-0623
MOLLENBAUER, John	24	New York	63-0917
MOLLENHAUER, Fritz	24	Gronau	65-0594
MOLLENKOPF, Joh.	19	Pfullingen	66-1313
Ursula 58, Christiana			
MOLLER, John	17	Saasen	63-1218
MOLLER, Marie	23	Hainbach	64-0170
MOLLMANN, Wilh'mne	18	St. Louis	66-0679
MOLLUS, Johann	44	Schwargendorf	64-0433
Anna 39, Marianne 19, Eva 14, Elisabeth 8			
Mathias 7, Appolonia 3			
MOLTEN, Jacob	55	New York	66-0679
Margarethe 58			
MOLTENBREY, John	45	Sindelfingen	65-0189
MOLTERS, Christian	24	Portentragen	66-1327
MOMBERG, Christian	20	Gudamsberg	65-0151
MOMMBERGER, Conr.	30	Langwasser	64-0593
Elis. 29, Chs. 6, Elis 5, George 73			
Phil. Jost 53, Adelheid 19, Elise 19			
MONERI, Eduardo	30	Russow	63-0821
MONFORT, Dorothe	24	Coeln	66-0109
MONGIN, (f)	18	Suisse	64-0214
MONSEES, Anna	20	Huettendorf	65-0898
Ger. 22			
MONSEES, Chr.	21	Schiffdorf	64-0432
MONTAG, Ferd.	25	Scheid	66-1248
MONTAG, Jacob	18	Darmstadt	66-0576
MONTAG, John	36	Cassel	66-1327
MONTANDON, Ph.	25	Mannheim	65-1140
MONTEGNIEUL, M.J.	28	Paris	64-0593
MONTOUX, Chris.	15	Herdille	63-0482
MONTOUX, Friedrich	17	Schwabendorf	63-0482
MONTZ, Henry	29	New York	66-0109
Lina 22			
MOORKAMP, Elisab.	27	Helminghausen	65-0974
MOORKAMP, Theodor	38	Loningen	64-1053
Cath. 42, Johanna 7, Gerhard 5, Elise 4			
MOORLOK, Christian	28	Wuerttemberg	63-1178
MOORMANN, Cathrine	60	Bueschendorf	66-1031
MOORMANN, J.	28	Holsdorf	64-0782
MOORMANN, Jos.	27	Damme	64-0593
MOORSTADT, Rudolph	31	Kuelsheim	65-0713
MOOSBACH, Heinrich	46	Wallenrod	66-0679
Catharina 16			
MOOSER, Xaphir	18	Otterswer	63-0693
MORANCECK, Johanna	49	Wodurau	66-1093
Catharine 40			
MORAST, G.A.	24	Schrinsheim	64-1161
MORATH, Jacob	24	Switz	63-0350
MORAWETZ, Wenzel	37	Buhnberg	64-0433
MORBUSCH, Sophie	27	Herford	66-0984
MORCE, v. Lewis	26	Boppard	63-0168
MORCHE, Carl	34	Berlin	65-0243
Marie 29, Clara 4, Max 2, Edw. 9m			
MORDAU, Marie	23	Rouen	63-0350
MORE, John	30	Binningen	63-0015
MORELLI, (m)	44	London	63-1085
MORGENROTH, Carl	19	Grossbreitenb	66-0734
MORGENSTERN, Carol	18	Quirnbach	64-0214
MORGENSTERN, Jac.	17	Duedelsheim	65-0594
MORGENSTERN, Phil.	22	Fuerth	65-0594
MORGENSTERN, S.	39	San Francisco	63-0244
MORGENTHAL, Julian	17	Soden	66-0623
MORGENTHAL, Martha	28	Luederbach	65-0713
MORGENTHAL, Maxim.	18	Mannheim	66-0147
MORGENTHAL, Wlhmne	15	Mannheim	66-0147
MORGENTHUM, Louis	50	Mannheim	66-0576
Babette 40, Bertha 21, Pauline 16, Ida 9			
Becka 8, Gustav 10, Heinrich 8, Julius 7			
Mengo 5			
MORGES, Philip	16	Hessen	66-0109
MORGNER, Gottl.	21	Goeppingen	66-0469
MORIAL, (m)	51	Paris	63-0990
MORIS, Heinrich	19	Duderstadt	63-0006
MORISSE, Hermann	24	Duderstadt	66-1327
MORISSE, John	37	New York	63-0097
Catharina 31, Pauline 1			
MORITZ, Anton	22	Hannover	66-1373
MORITZ, Gottlob	28	Schorndorf	66-0221
MORITZ, J.D.(m)	28	Baltimore	64-0214
MORITZ, Johann	26	Beverstedt	66-1093
Meta 18			
MORITZ, Moses	22	Langenseebald	64-0138
MORITZ, Peter Jos.	16	Bonn	63-0482
MORITZ, Simon	22	Bremen	64-0495
MORITZ, Wm.	32	Buer	64-0739
Marie 27			
MORNEBURG, Andrea	18	Fuerth	63-0821

NAME	AGE	RESIDENCE	YR-LIST
MOROF, Jacob	18	Flacht	66-1373
MORROCK, Carl	34	Brooklyn	64-0427
MORSCH, Johann	26	Asch	66-1031
MORSCHHAUSER, Frz.	19	Bachern	63-1136
MORWITZ, Louis	33	Philadelphia	66-0984
MOSCHE, Ernst	27	New York	63-0990
Marie 25			
MOSCHE, Sal.	26	Preussen	64-0214
MOSCHEL, Catharina	15	Welenheim	65-0189
MOSEBACH, Ernst B.	36	Burgstadt	64-0214
MOSEBACH, Wilhelm	17	Bueckeburg	65-1030
MOSEL, Christiane	40	Klueckhof	64-0992
Louis 3			
MOSEL, W.(m)	42	Werthal	64-0331
MOSENTHAL, Marcus	24	Eisenach	64-1022
MOSER, Alfred	23	Schwitz	64-0023
MOSER, Andreas	26	Baden	66-0578
MOSER, Carl	24	Hungen	66-0934
MOSER, Caroline	17	Hungen	66-0679
MOSER, Fr.	26	Stettin	66-1313
MOSES, Abraham	20	Reden	65-0007
MOSES, Bernhard	18	Ostercappeln	66-1127
MOSES, Hanne	21	Felchne	63-0482
MOSES, Joseph	59	Ndr.Gemuenden	63-0752
MOSES, Moritz	17	Wirsitz	66-0578
MOSES, Samuel	26	Ndr.Gmuenden	63-0752
MOSI, Ernst Ludwig	37	Bruesshof	66-0578
Augusta 24, Ernst 4			
MOSSENDORP, Janna	41	Nuttermoor	64-0886
MOST, Elise	16	Fuerstenhagen	65-0038
MOST, Ferdinand	30	Baden	63-0822
MOST, Johann	25	Cassel	65-0865
Elisabeth 22, Elisabeth 3, Anna 9m			
MOSTER, Agnes	42	Alfern	64-1108
Franz 16			
MOTIG, Emilie	13	Cincinnati	66-0576
MOTSCHENBACHER, Ph	25	Bayern	64-0427
MOTZ, Edw.	26	New York	63-1085
MOTZECK, Hermann	31	Zuelz	65-1030
MOUTUELLI, Casino	26	Mailand	63-0398
MOZEL, Fr.	21	Reichweil	63-1218
MROZ, Stephan	31	Preussen	63-0398
Marie 34, Joh. inf, Joseph 5			
MUBERT, Frdr.	65	Loth	65-0243
MUBUS, August	34	Boehmen	64-0138
MUCHA, Heinrich	25	Dratzig	65-0770
MUCHAU, Franz	22	Berlin	66-0734
MUCK, O.	26	Treptau	63-1178
MUCKE, Friedr.	26	Bitterfeld	64-0427
MUCKER, Carl Th.	17	Bitterfeld	63-0614
MUDDELMANN, Heinr.	25	Suhlingen	64-0023
MUDEKING, A.	15	Marl	63-1085
MUDRACK, A.(m)	49	Breslau	64-0214
MUEBUS, Anna	32	Boehmen	63-0917
Theresa 8, Barbara 6, Aug 11m			
MUEDEKING, Georg L	20	Diepholz	64-0456
Heinr. Fr'dr 17			
MUEGGE, Albert	15	St Louis	63-0917
MUEGGE, Catharina	26	Belum	64-0456
MUEGGE, Claus	25	Bevern	64-0170
MUEGGE, Johanna	38	St. Louis	63-0917
Louise 8, Anna 6			
MUEHE, Elisabeth	47	S. Francisco	63-1136
MUEHLBACH, Carl	33	Bremen	65-0189
Elise 22, Johanna 6m			
MUEHLBACH, John	46	New York	66-0934
Josephine 36			
MUEHLBECK, Math.	48	Illinois	63-1178
Cath. 32, Cath. 59			
MUEHLBERT, Joh.	21	Ndr.Lichersbh	65-0007
MUEHLEISEN, Eberh.	40	Feuerbach	64-0363
MUEHLENHOFF, Herm.	29	New York	66-0109
Sarah 24			
MUEHLER, John	33	New York	63-1218
MUEHLHAEUSER, Chr.	23	Mugendorf	65-1088
MUEHLHAUSEN, Johan	18	Wuerttemberg	66-0576
MUEHLING, Heinrich	24	Grosmanrode	66-0623
MUEHLKE, C.		Prussia	63-1003
MUEHLMANN, Wilhelm	19	Badbergen	64-0992
MUEHLMEIER, Elise	35	Vienna	66-1093
MUEHLSIEPEN, Heinr	29	Prussia	63-0821
MUELDAUER, Emil	32	Posen	63-0862
MUELDEN, Ed. Albr.	25	Emden	66-0577
MUELDENER, Ida	32	New York	63-0990
Ernst 10, Louise 9, Anna 7, Henry 5			
Ida 2			
MUELDER, Bernhard	49	Oldenburg	65-1031
MUELE, Otto	17	Carlsruhe	64-0687
MUELKER, Friedr.	54	Volmerdingsen	64-0214
Friedrike 17, Ernst 17, Ludwig 14			
MUELLER, (m)	25	London	63-0482
wife 20			
MUELLER, A.C.(m)	69	Bockenem	64-0331
Johanna 21			
MUELLER, Adam	34	Neudorf	66-0984
MUELLER, Adam	29	Asch	64-0639
MUELLER, Adam	24	Kleinsbach	64-1161
MUELLER, Adolf	30	Ysenburg	65-0950
MUELLER, Adolph	42	Hildesheim	63-1069
MUELLER, Adolph	16	Nuertingen	66-1093
MUELLER, Agnes	26	Leipzig	65-0007
Paul 3, Johanna 2			
MUELLER, Albert	19	Holseln	64-0023
MUELLER, Albert	20	Oberesslingen	63-1136
MUELLER, Albertine	40	Halle	64-0363
MUELLER, Albin	23	New York	63-0693
MUELLER, Andreas	29	Umstadt	66-0679
MUELLER, Andreas	17	Oberlimbach	66-1248
Barbara 20, Valentin 1			
MUELLER, Anna	15	Oberhond	64-0138
MUELLER, Anna	22	Rauenstein	64-0170
MUELLER, Anna	33	Ebersbach	63-1136
MUELLER, Anna	27	Erfurt	63-0006
Dorothea 3, Julius 6m			
MUELLER, Anna	30	Kulm	66-0109
MUELLER, Anna	21	Schluechtern	66-1373
Kung. 19			
MUELLER, Anna Dor.	36	Willersdorf	66-0578
Marie Elisa 14			
MUELLER, Ant.	31	Wagenritz	64-0992
Joseph 32			
MUELLER, Anton	20	Kauzagh	66-0576
MUELLER, Anton	27	Haselune	66-0679
MUELLER, Anton	35	Weichenzell	64-0886
Genovefa 37, Jacob 6, Tobias 5, Xaver 4			
Benedict 3, Wilhelm 2			
MUELLER, Anton	55	Rhens	65-0402
MUELLER, Apollonia	15	Bonn	66-1031
MUELLER, August	23	Bremerhaven	64-0023
MUELLER, August	31	Fuerstenwalde	63-0752
MUELLER, August	24	Reddinghausen	66-0668
MUELLER, August	26	Langensalza	67-0599
MUELLER, August	42	Dessau	65-0243
MUELLER, Augusta	26	Iserlohn	64-1022
Helene 2, Elisabeth 10m			
MUELLER, Augusta	50	Coeln	65-0974
Helena 19, Mathilde 18, Caroline 14			
MUELLER, Babbette	23	Wirthheim	67-0007
MUELLER, Babette	16	Altenkunstadt	64-0331
MUELLER, Barbara	13	Weinheim	63-0752
MUELLER, Barbara	44	Hechingen	66-0837
Katharina 16			
MUELLER, Becka	23	Brockhausen	64-0456
MUELLER, Benjamin	16	Hinnebeck	65-0898
MUELLER, Bernhard	17	Wettewarden	66-0623
Heinrich 19			
MUELLER, Bernhard	45	Posneck	66-0109
MUELLER, Bernhd.	25	Neusaatz	65-0402
MUELLER, Brunett.	35	Buehren	64-0427
Antje 25, Heinr. 15, Maria 2, Heye 9m			
MUELLER, C. Otto	41	New York	63-0015
Mary Louise 30, July 3, Mathilde 1			
MUELLER, Carl	28	Nordhausen	64-0331
Johanna 21			
MUELLER, Carl	21	Kirchberg	66-0576
MUELLER, Carl	21	Roellfeld	66-0650

NAME	AGE	RESIDENCE	YR-LIST
MUELLER, Carl	22	Jellenrod	64-0593
MUELLER, Carl	20	Lobmen	66-1203
MUELLER, Carl	18	Gladenbach	65-0402
MUELLER, Carl	31	Dessau	65-0770
MUELLER, Carl Fr.	19	Muenchingen	64-1108
MUELLER, Carl Jos.	32	Koeln	66-0412
MUELLER, Carl Rein		Solingen	63-0822
MUELLER, Caroline	15	Halgenhausen	63-0953
MUELLER, Caroline	17	Eberstadt	63-0693
MUELLER, Caroline	28	Wilkowa	66-0469
MUELLER, Caroline	21	Falkenstein	63-1085
MUELLER, Caroline	22	Schlusselburg	65-0950
MUELLER, Caspar	50	Mitt.Steinbch	65-0189
Friedr. 29			
MUELLER, Cath.	39	Reichenberg	63-0953
MUELLER, Catharina	32	Ilsfeld	63-0244
MUELLER, Catharine	24	Roedenau	66-0623
Maria 22			
MUELLER, Catharine	9	Bremervoerde	66-0934
MUELLER, Catharine	63	Luetzeldorf	65-0713
MUELLER, Cathre.	38	Coburg	63-1038
Johanna 12, Marie 9			
MUELLER, Ch. F.	54	New York	66-0934
MUELLER, Charles	33	Nuertingen	63-0244
MUELLER, Chr.	20	Melle	63-0990
MUELLER, Chr.	30	Zienau	65-0007
MUELLER, Chr.	40	Bremen	65-0898
MUELLER, Chr.	23	Rastede	64-0739
MUELLER, Chr. Ed.	16	Neide	66-0934
MUELLER, Christ.	48	Heimburg	63-1010
MUELLER, Christ.	50	Toenninghsn.	65-0007
MUELLER, Christine	19	Windebach	65-1030
MUELLER, Christoph	25	Stemshorn	66-0412
MUELLER, Christoph	73	Wesch	67-0007
MUELLER, Cohrs	36	Eisebergen	66-0221
MUELLER, Conr. Rbt	20	Pigau	64-0904
MUELLER, Conrad	22	Bingenhert	64-0073
Jacob 4			
MUELLER, Conrad	58	Kleinern	63-0693
MUELLER, Conrad	21	Beckedorf	66-0934
MUELLER, Conrad	24	Broel	66-1203
Peter 37			
MUELLER, Const.(m)	69	Biengen	64-0363
Rosa 31, Maria 9m			
MUELLER, D.	22	Schlesinghsn.	64-0992
Louise 33, Caroline 33, Wilhelmine 7			
Fritz 4			
MUELLER, Diedrich	32	Hannover	66-0934
MUELLER, Dorothea	24	Heidigsfeld	63-1038
Catharina 23			
MUELLER, Dorothea	21	Sievern	64-0687
MUELLER, E. Milf	34	Kl. Sander	64-1053
MUELLER, E.G.F.(m)	24	Groningen	64-0331
MUELLER, Ebeline	21	Mannslagt	64-1022
MUELLER, Ed.	28	Pforzheim	64-0170
MUELLER, Eduard	28	Coburg	66-0147
MUELLER, Eduard	25	Hannover	63-0953
MUELLER, Eduard	22	Neunburg	66-0083
MUELLER, Eduard	15	Michelsdorf	66-1155
MUELLER, Eduard	36	Breese	66-1373
MUELLER, Elis.	18	Wolfskehlen	65-1189
MUELLER, Elisabeth	28	Holzhausen	66-1155
MUELLER, Elisabeth	20	Alsfeld	64-0885
MUELLER, Em.	21	Vihringen	66-1243
MUELLER, Emil	20	Bockenheim	63-1136
MUELLER, Emma	38	Stuttgart	63-0551
MUELLER, Engelf.	25	Preussen	64-0214
Catherine 25			
MUELLER, Ernst	30	Zicker	63-1218
Ludwig 27			
MUELLER, Ernst	15	Alsfeld	64-0687
MUELLER, Ernst	22	Kaufungen	65-0038
MUELLER, Ernst	30	Jankowo	65-1030
Louise 20			
MUELLER, Ernst	30	Altenweddinge	64-0214
Heinr. 20			
MUELLER, Erst	25	Helgenbach	64-1206
MUELLER, F.	22	Zicker	63-1218
MUELLER, F.(m)	22	Etzendorf	64-0495
MUELLER, F.R. Aug.	24	Saxony	63-0822
MUELLER, F.W.	21	Bremen	64-0495
MUELLER, F.W.	26	Reichstadt	65-1088
Christine 22, Hulda 1			
MUELLER, Fanny	17	Kunterheim	66-0679
MUELLER, Fr.	18	Camberg	63-0752
MUELLER, Fr.	44	Prussia	63-1003
D. 48, K. 15, A. 13			
MUELLER, Fr.	14	Pertheim	65-0007
Marie 19			
MUELLER, Fr.(m)	29	Kl. Aspach	64-0138
MUELLER, Francisca	21	Muebringen	64-1161
MUELLER, Franz	28	Flurlingen	66-0576
Conrad 22			
MUELLER, Franz	30	Wolfenbuettel	66-0109
MUELLER, Franz	31	Marbach	66-0083
MUELLER, Franz	20	Ebringen	66-1327
MUELLER, Frd.(m)	27	Istern	64-0363
MUELLER, Friedr.	46	Leiferde	64-0904
Henriette 40, Heinrich 17, Louise 15			
Minna 9, Caroline 6, Fritz 2			
MUELLER, Friedr.	23	Flain	64-0840
MUELLER, Friedr.	49	Doelme	64-1108
Charlotte 48, Friedr. 14, Wilhelmine 20			
MUELLER, Friedr.	26	Frille	66-1131
MUELLER, Friedr.	21	Lebach	64-0214
MUELLER, Friedrich	48	Neuenburg	66-0577
MUELLER, Friedrich	21	Hofgeismar	66-0679
MUELLER, Friedrich	33	Glolzin	64-0456
MUELLER, Friedrich	25	Varensell	66-1203
MUELLER, Friedrich	15	Echenstruth	65-0865
MUELLER, Friedrike	34	Hoboken	66-1327
Margarethe 10, Rudolph 9, Amalie 8			
Josephine 6, Lina 2			
MUELLER, Fritz	22	Cassel	66-1248
MUELLER, Fritz	16	Kamme	64-0214
MUELLER, G.	25	Bremen	63-0953
MUELLER, G.	47	Prussia	63-1003
Isaac 16, Lewis 20, William 24, C. 18			
F. 16, B. 13, K. 44, L. 4			
MUELLER, G.	42	Wahlbach	65-1189
So. 39, Eleonore 13, Herm. 11, Matth. 7			
J. 4, Emma 1m			
MUELLER, Georg	22	Worms	64-0170
MUELLER, Georg	45	Meiningen	64-0432
MUELLER, Georg	29	Worms	66-0679
Catharine 18			
MUELLER, Georg	18	Darmstadt	66-0837
MUELLER, Georg	20	Riesendorf	64-0495
MUELLER, Georg	27	Schlussendeid	67-0007
MUELLER, Georg	19	Burguffeln	65-0038
MUELLER, Georg	19	Bempflingen	66-1203
MUELLER, Georg	24	Gerricksheim	65-1030
MUELLER, Georg	18	Warburg	65-1088
MUELLER, Georg	30	Arolsen	65-0974
MUELLER, Georg	28	Schweinsthal	65-0713
Margretha 33, Joh. G. 9m			
MUELLER, Georg M.	24	Rottenburg	65-0055
MUELLER, George	25	Melsungen	64-0433
MUELLER, Georgine	28	Herbertswind	63-0006
Emil 4			
MUELLER, Gertrude	30	Bierbach	67-0599
Nicolaus 5, Johann 3, Philipp 11m			
MUELLER, Gottliebe		Wuestenroth	65-1095
MUELLER, Gustav	17	Paderborn	63-1038
Sophie 39			
MUELLER, Gustav	48	Jena	64-0885
MUELLER, H.	59	Bremen	64-0593
MUELLER, H.(m)	26	Thedinghausen	64-0495
MUELLER, H.C.	44	Maningen	65-0007
Johanna 40, Johann 9, Johanna 7			
Heinrich 5, Wilhelm 30			
MUELLER, H.O.	18	Leer	63-0693
O.L. 16			
MUELLER, Heinr.	30	Uldenrode	64-0687
MUELLER, Heinr.	20	Wolfenbuettel	66-0984
MUELLER, Heinr.	16	Osnabrueck	64-0639

NAME	AGE	RESIDENCE	YR-LIST
MUELLER, Heinr.	40	Luebbecke	64-0639
MUELLER, Heinr.	38	Stuttgart	64-0639
MUELLER, Heinr.	33	Loensburg	66-1373
MUELLER, Heinr.	27	Kohlgrund	64-0214
MUELLER, Heinr. D.	22	Osnabrueck	64-1053
MUELLER, Heinrich	45	Philadelphia	66-0147
MUELLER, Heinrich	25	Bieberach	66-0576
MUELLER, Heinrich	28	Coeln	66-0679
MUELLER, Heinrich	46	Birklar	66-0704
Margarethe 44, Margarethe 18, Elise 13			
Johanna 9, Heinrich 8, Ludwig 5			
MUELLER, Heinrich	17	Cuxhafen	67-0007
MUELLER, Heinrich	23	Langgens	66-1327
MUELLER, Heinrich	29	Burgsinn	66-1313
Amalia 25, Hubertus 10m			
MUELLER, Heinrich	23	Neuenstein	66-1373
MUELLER, Heinrich	25	Steinhude	66-1373
MUELLER, Heinrich	64	Sellnrod	65-0713
MUELLER, Henriette	30	Mannheim	66-1127
Henriette 3m			
MUELLER, Henry	23	Weilheim	63-1178
MUELLER, Henry	40	Dayton	63-0953
MUELLER, Henry	46	Dresden	63-0244
MUELLER, Henry		Sievern	63-1218
MUELLER, Henry	22	Reddighausen	63-0482
MUELLER, Herm.	56	Horn	63-1085
MUELLER, Herm.	20	Verden	66-1373
MUELLER, Hermann	39	Batzdorf	63-0917
MUELLER, Hermann	24	Marienberg	66-0578
MUELLER, Hermann	40	Osnabrueck	66-0984
Charlotte 81, Marie 56			
MUELLER, Herrmann	23	Hanover	66-0577
MUELLER, Isaac	16	Steindorf	64-0170
MUELLER, J.	32	Rudolfingen	63-0551
Mary 31, James 5, Rosina 3, John 2			
Elisabeth 9M			
MUELLER, J.	56	Havanna	63-1085
MUELLER, J.A.B.	22	Buchheim	64-0992
MUELLER, J.D.	15	Hassendorf	64-0214
MUELLER, Jac.	42	Simonswalde	64-0495
E.(f) 40, Claas 10, Weeke 7, Heike 5			
Gretje 3			
MUELLER, Jacob	21	Istein	66-0668
MUELLER, Jacob	25	Grosssachsen	66-0109
MUELLER, Jacob	26	Morchen	66-0083
MUELLER, Jacob	19	Homburg	65-0004
MUELLER, Joh.	23	Muenderstadt	64-0687
MUELLER, Joh.	27	Oidingen	65-0189
MUELLER, Joh. G.	45	Rhauderfehn	64-0840
wife 39, Almuth 16, Johann 14, Anton 12			
Georg 7, Hermine 5, Emma 4, Minna 3			
Hokes 6m			
MUELLER, Joh. Rolf	25	Dornum	66-0578
MUELLER, Joh.(m)	35	Oberkoch	64-0331
MUELLER, Joh.Fr'dr	19	Nordheim	63-0053
MUELLER, Joh.Henry	25	Offenbach	63-1038
MUELLER, Johann	32	Kail	66-0734
Marie 27, Christoph 4, Margarethe 2			
Marie 4m			
MUELLER, Johann	30	Zelp	66-0623
MUELLER, Johann	33	Barbach	66-0679
Maria 32, Sophia 7, Catharina 5			
Susanne			
MUELLER, Johann	30	Bremen	66-0679
Adolphine 25			
MUELLER, Johann	24	Wohlerst	66-0984
MUELLER, Johann	25	Berlin	64-1053
MUELLER, Johann	20	Osnabrueck	66-1327
MUELLER, Johann	32	Nordhalven	66-1203
Catharina 25			
MUELLER, Johann	20	Hannover	66-1203
Diedrich 18			
MUELLER, Johann	35	Loeben	66-1203
Elisabeth 32, Dorothea 9, Joachim 6			
MUELLER, Johann	23	Aurich	65-1030
MUELLER, Johann	25	Smilowa	23-0865
Rosalie 23			
MUELLER, Johann	48	Elbkorn	64-0593
MUELLER, Johanna	19	Wederwarden	64-0739
MUELLER, Johannes	28	Niederafleidn	64-0214
MUELLER, John	36	New York	63-0350
Friedrich 11m			
MUELLER, John	45	Chicago	66-0984
Barbara 40			
MUELLER, John Chr.	22	Marktlauthen	63-0693
MUELLER, Jos.	19	Wurgassen	64-0840
MUELLER, Jos.	27	Cassel	66-1313
MUELLER, Jos.	23	Frauenhofen	64-0214
MUELLER, Joseph	55	Nussdorf	63-0693
MUELLER, Joseph	16	Boesingen	63-0482
Mary 19			
MUELLER, Joseph	27	Faurndon	64-0639
MUELLER, Joseph	21	Ottenhofen	66-1155
MUELLER, Joseph	16	Poria	64-0886
MUELLER, Joseph	25	Fulda	64-0363
MUELLER, Julius	28	Lingen	65-0402
MUELLER, L.G.H.	28	Hannover	65-0898
MUELLER, Leonhard	23	Bayern	66-0147
MUELLER, Louis	28	Schoendorf	66-0576
MUELLER, Louis	22	Saxony	66-0577
MUELLER, Louise	57	Hannover	63-0482
MUELLER, Louise	27	Darmersheim	66-1373
Maria 24			
MUELLER, Louise	22	Oedinghaas	65-1024
MUELLER, Ludwig	25	Hassbach	63-0862
MUELLER, Ludwig		Schwackheim	66-0221
MUELLER, M.	36	Dachsenhausen	63-1003
MUELLER, M.	24	Neuenburg	66-0413
MUELLER, M.E.	32	Leipzig	65-1088
MUELLER, Magdalena	49	Chicago	63-1136
Cath. 9			
MUELLER, Margar.	19	Bavaria	63-0822
Barbara Eva 17			
MUELLER, Margareth	18	Grefenhausen	66-1327
MUELLER, Maria	23	Reckenhausen	66-0704
Margar. 19			
MUELLER, Maria	17	Laubach	65-1088
MUELLER, Maria	37	Worms	64-0363
MUELLER, Marie	39	Schoenau	63-1178
MUELLER, Marie	20	Ilbertshausen	66-0650
MUELLER, Marie	22	New Orleans	66-0984
MUELLER, Marie	24	Neustadt	64-0938
MUELLER, Marie	21	Alze	65-0007
MUELLER, Marie	16	Babenhausen	65-1189
MUELLER, Martin	41	Pommern	66-0469
Caroline 32, Minna 10, Carl 9, Marie 5			
MUELLER, Max	27	Trier	66-0221
MUELLER, Meta	23	Herford	63-1010
MUELLER, Meta	25	Lehe	66-0734
Meta 4			
MUELLER, Mich.	36	Gr. Asbach	65-0189
MUELLER, Michael	23	Bayern	64-0432
Marg. Cunig. 19			
MUELLER, Michael	24	Wuertemberg	66-0147
Caroline 2			
MUELLER, Michael	46	Hassbach	63-0862
MUELLER, Minna	18	Zeven	64-0739
MUELLER, Nicolaus	18	Spahn	64-0739
MUELLER, Paul	21	Ohio	63-0244
MUELLER, Peter	18	Fischerhude	66-1031
MUELLER, Peter	22	Lamstedt	65-1095
MUELLER, Regina	22	Aldefeld	65-0402
MUELLER, Reinhard	58	Merscheid	66-1093
MUELLER, Rob.	25	Ohligs	65-0189
MUELLER, Rosalia	26	Wangen	63-1085
MUELLER, Rosalie	37	Muenchen	65-0594
MUELLER, Rosine	19	Ebersbach	64-1053
Barbara 58			
MUELLER, Rosine	24	Untermusbach	65-0402
MUELLER, Salomon	25	Ungarn	63-1136
Maria 21, Henni 9			
MUELLER, Samuel	22	Preussen	66-0221
MUELLER, Seb.	20	Gleichlingen	65-0898
MUELLER, Sophia	17	Heeste	64-0639
MUELLER, Sophie	18	Langendahnbch	65-0402
MUELLER, Sophie	25	Almersleben	65-1024

NAME	AGE	RESIDENCE	YR-LIST
Emma 4m			
MUELLER, Stephan	22	Heppenheim	63-1010
MUELLER, Th. Fr.	22	Vechta	65-0116
MUELLER, Theod.	38	Oranienbaum	66-1313
Louise 34, Albert 4, Emil 10m			
MUELLER, Theodor	19	Kalm	66-0704
MUELLER, Therese	32	Roesebeck	63-1136
MUELLER, Therese	26	Braunschweig	65-0974
MUELLER, Theresia	14	Freiburg	66-0934
MUELLER, Traugott	22	Goldisthal	66-1248
MUELLER, Ullrich J	26	Osnabrueck	66-0412
MUELLER, Victor	18	Rottweil	66-0734
MUELLER, Victoria	36	Duddenhausen	64-0023
Wm. 26, Lucia 24			
MUELLER, W.	67	Guttenberg	64-0992
MUELLER, W.(m)	30	Meisenheim	64-0363
MUELLER, Werner	26	Wehrenberg	67-0007
MUELLER, Wilh'mne	28	Sindelfingen	65-0189
MUELLER, Wilh.	32	Goettingen	64-0432
Marie 21			
MUELLER, Wilh.	24	Prussia	63-0296
Louis 28			
MUELLER, Wilh.	18	Germersheim	65-1088
MUELLER, Wilhelm	25	Bremen	63-0614
MUELLER, Wilhelm	28	Niedermending	64-0639
MUELLER, Wilhelm	30	Drueber	66-1155
Amalie 28, Wilhelm 7, Wilhelmine 3			
August 9m			
MUELLER, Wilhelm	41	Altenhagen	66-1243
Mina 36, Wilhelm 7, Augusta 5			
MUELLER, Wilhelm	32	Glandorf	66-1127
Fritz 30			
MUELLER, Wilhelm	24	Kemderod	66-1373
MUELLER, Wilhelm	19	Hoheneggersen	65-1030
MUELLER, Willhelm	17	Oberzelle	66-0650
MUELLER, Wm.	23	Wehden	64-0138
MUELLER, Wm.	22	Celle	64-0170
MUELLER, Wm.	22	Melle	64-0593
MUELLER, Wm.	45	Leipzig	64-0840
MUELLICH, Johann	22	Niederdorf	66-0679
MUELWERT, Heinrich	17	Darmstadt	66-1327
MUENCH, (f)	26	New York	63-1085
baby 1			
MUENCH, Ch.	23	Hohebach	64-0938
Cath. 19			
MUENCH, Conrad	29	Weissenborn	66-0147
MUENCH, Franz	22	Seaton	66-0576
Pauline 22			
MUENCH, Gertrude	74	Freisenheim	65-0007
MUENCH, Sarah	16	Heidelberg	64-0938
MUENCH, Theod.	26	Wetterfeld	64-1022
MUENCH, Wilhelmine	53	Crimitzschau	66-1093
MUENCH, Wm.	22	Darmstadt	64-0432
MUENCHEN, Pauline	24	Gritschnow	65-0713
MUENDER, Wilhelm	20	Bremen	66-0679
MUENDORF, Philip	24	Moistadt	66-0679
MUENK, Adam	28	Cassel	64-1053
MUENNICH, Carl	23	Heidelberg	66-1093
MUENNINGHOF, Clem.	19	Kretebeck	66-0623
MUENRING, James	36	Ohio	63-0990
Catherine 30, Friedrich 4, Wilhelmine 1			
MUENSBERG, Gustav	27	Rawiez	66-0083
MUENSTER, Carl	19	Berlichingen	67-0007
MUENSTER, Johann P	16	Berlichingen	66-1373
MUENSTER, Louise	18	Birnbaum	64-0456
MUENSTER, Martin	20	Berlichingen	66-0083
MUENSTER, Simon	19	Pera Schauzst	66-0623
MUENSTERMANN, Lou.	82	Gellersen	66-0934
MUENZ, Simon	18	Pilsen	63-1085
MUES, H. (m)	23	Hannover	64-0214
MUESMANN, Herm.	22	Fladerlohhaus	66-0984
MUESS, Marie	22	Sandstedt	64-0840
MUESSIGBORD, Carl	33	Dresden	63-0296
MUESTIG, Franz	20	Ziegenhals	66-0576
MUETZE, Carl	30	Louisville	66-0934
MUETZE, Emma	25	Marburg	64-0886
MUFF, Marg.	23	Maineck	63-0990
MUHLER, F.(m)	35	Baltimore	64-0331
MUHLHAUS, Conrad	23	Hilberhausen	66-0679
MULHER, Crescentia	27	Sauldorf	65-0243
MULICH, Friedrich	15	Enzweihingen	64-0433
MULL, Andreas	52	Haverlah	64-0363
Christine 56			
MULLEN, Therese	16	Liebenburg	66-1127
MULLER, Carl	32	Bensburg	66-1248
MULSS, Marie	22	Sandstedt	64-0840
MULTHAUP, Rieke	21	Broosen	63-1038
MULTHAUPT, A.	20	Lippe	66-0413
MUMME, Georg	35	Cincinnati	66-0221
MUMME, Wilhelm	24	Olber	66-1131
MUND, Doris	17	Dextel	64-0138
MUND, Sophie	20	Husum	64-0992
MUNDELIUS, Eduard	18	Neumarkt	66-0934
MUNDER, Julius	20	Bremen	64-1022
MUNDHENK, Christ.	41	Bentheim	65-0189
MUNDIGE, Johannes	15	Aschbach	66-0704
MUNDT, Franz	29	M. Friedland	66-1313
MUNDT, Gustav	25	Hamburg	66-0934
MUNDT, Joh. Dav.	24	Hannover	66-1313
MUNGST, S.H.	20	Cuxhaven	63-0244
MUNKEWITZ, Elis.	16	Lauchroeden	65-0950
MUNSCHER, George	40	Hersfeld	63-0482
MUNSTERMANN, Georg	47	Hudebeck	66-0072
MUNTER, Elisab.	18	Hamburg	64-0593
Anna 55			
MUNTZ, Marcus	31	Coeln	66-0109
MUNZ, Chr. Cath.	21	Untermbach/Wt	65-0038
MUNZEL, Chr.	24	Gedern	66-0984
MUNZEL, Friedr.	24	Hannover	66-1131
MUNZERHEIM, Moritz	23	Baden	66-0734
MURCKEN, Henry	29	Lilienthal	63-1178
MURICH, Caroline	30	Wuertemberg	66-0576
MURKEN, Georg Pr.	30	Lilienthal	66-0666
MURMANN, Georg	17	Darmstadt	64-0885
MURRAY, John H.	22	Schweiz	63-1085
Emilie 30			
MURRBACH, Elise	29	Tuttlingen	65-0007
Marie 4, Elise 6m			
MURSE, Hermann	25	Nortup	65-1024
MUSBACH, George	59	Beiertheim	63-0244
Elisabeth 56, Magd. 57, Mary 11			
Christine 9, Magd. 8, Louis 6, Georg 5			
Charles 2, Hermann 11m			
MUSELMANN, Magdal.	22	Waldmansdorf	66-0083
MUSER, John	31	Anten	63-0693
MUSKE, Ernst	25	Koestlin	66-0578
Wilhelmine 28			
MUSKE, Fr.	53	Stade	64-0665
Friederike 47, Marie 18, Emilie 16			
Bertha 5			
MUSS, E.	20	Hannover	65-0007
MUSSEL, Anna	29	New York	63-1038
Chris 3, Susanne 11m			
MUSSEL, W.(m)	29	Hildesheim	64-0495
MUSSLER, Leopold	46	Schwarzach	63-0482
Augusta 46			
MUSTERMANN, Cath.	16	Drehle	66-1093
Catharine 16			
MUTH, Adam	43	Hadamar	66-0576
Gertrude 37, Elise 15, Anna 13, Helene 8			
Jacob 2			
MUTH, Anna	38	Wabern	66-1127
Heinrich 12, Marie 9			
MUTH, Christian	15	Wabern	64-0739
MUTH, Gustav	32	Nordhausen	64-0639
MUTH, Karl	24	Stuttgart	66-0668
MUTH, Louis	30	Baltimore	64-0593
Christine 20			
MUTH, Margarethe	18	Freiensteinau	65-0950
MUTH, Maria	33	Leiningen	64-1053
Jacob 7			
MUTH, Maria	24	Neisen	65-1088
MUTH, Marie	26	Bresbach	65-1189
MUTH, Tobias	26	Darmstadt	66-1031
Heinrich 12, Sybilla 15			
MUTH, Wilh.	25	Darmstadt	65-1140

NAME	AGE	RESIDENCE	YR-LIST
MUTH, Wilhelm	19	Wiesen	66-1243
MUTSCHLECHNER, Geo	18	Sandersdorf	63-0821
MUTSCHLECHNER, Oto	20	Chicago	63-0296
MUTSCHLER, Am.	21	Baden	66-0147
MUTSCHLER, Friedr.	16	Wuertemberg	66-0679
MUTTER, Catharine	26	Hatbolingen	66-0083
MUTTERER, Barbara	24	Freiburg	66-0934
MUTTERER, Christ.	27	Wildbad	66-0147
MUTTERER, Christ.	19	Wuertemberg	66-0221
MUTTERER, Joseph	32	Wildbad	66-0147
MUTZ, Robert	26	Muscheid	63-1085
John 22, Richard 36, Amalie 40			
Christian 14, August 12, Robert 9			
Julius 7			
NACHHOLZ, Robert	26	Marienwerder	65-0243
NADEBAUER, Johanna	26	Baukweil	63-0917
NADIG, Chris	14	Odernheim	63-0482
NAEGEL, Elisabeth	17	Cassel	65-0865
NAEGELE, Fried'ke.	60	Bietigheim	66-1131
NAEGELE, Karl	27	Stuttgart	63-1069
NAEGELEIN, F.	27	Kaltenwesthm.	65-0007
NAEGLI, Louis	26	Paris	67-0007
NAEHRMEYER, (m)	17	Osnabrueck	67-0600
NAGE, Wilhelm	27	Gescher	65-0948
Elisabeth 26, Anna Cath. 58			
NAGEL, Anna Marg.	30	Hochheim	64-1108
NAGEL, Anton	28	Glandorf	66-1127
NAGEL, Caroline	39	Dortmund	64-1053
Heinr. 4, Friedr. 11m			
NAGEL, Christ.	28	Furstenau	64-0782
Heinrich 18			
NAGEL, Frd.	38	Werther	64-0782
Wm 37			
NAGEL, Friedr.	33	New York	66-0984
NAGEL, Heinrich	51	Otterndorf	64-0456
Rosetha Mary 52, Anna C. 26			
Maria Marg. 22, Joh. Wm. 13			
NAGEL, J.C.	42	Carlsruhe	65-1024
Frd. 27			
NAGEL, Johann	14	Unt.Hellingen	66-0934
Margaretha 17			
NAGEL, John G.	37	Philadelphia	63-1178
John 8			
NAGEL, Johs.	36	Eichelsdorf	64-0593
NAGEL, Julius	18	Stafforth	65-1024
NAGEL, Lisette	24	Fuerstenau	64-0782
NAGEL, Louis	20	Langenberghm.	65-1088
NAGEL, Ludwig	38	Darmstadt	66-1127
NAGEL, Maria V.	28	Tyrol	66-0221
NAGEL, Marie	20	New York	64-0427
NAGEL, Sebastian	29	Grossaspach	64-0170
NAGEL, Sebastian	29	Grossasbach	63-0482
Margar. 21			
NAGEL, Wilh.	17	Friedberg	65-0243
NAGENGAST, Eva	28	Treuschendorf	66-1327
NAGENGAST, Georg	27	Drenschendorf	65-0007
NAGGEN, Cath.	19	Glueckstadt	64-0840
NAHRING, H.	24	Gr. Varlingen	64-0992
Wilhelmine 39, Louise 11, Wilhelmine 7			
Christine 2			
NAHRUNG, Louise	24	Buedingen	66-0984
NAIVER, R.	24	Pirmens	66-0413
NALBACH, Baptist	29	Zuetzen	64-0938
NALBMANN, Heinr.	32	Silberhausen	64-1053
Marie 23			
NALEEN, Lisette	17	Oldenburg	66-1093
Gertrude 20			
NAMANN, C.L.	41	Gerar	65-1189
Catharina 39, Cathrina 13, Marie 7			
Elisabeth 2, Heinrich 5, Ludw. 3			
Adolph 3m			
NANNINGA, Thomas	30	Wuethausen	64-0456
Antja 45, J.(f) 16, Durtje 10, Nanneke 5			
Joh. 11m			
NANTING, Chr. Gotf	20	Kumburg	67-0599
NARBEI, Johannes	25	Tiefenort	64-0886
NARDELLI, A.G.	51	Muenchen	65-0594
Caroline 41			

NAME	AGE	RESIDENCE	YR-LIST
NARR, Andr.	32	Wuerttenberg	66-0221
NARR, Louise	19	Berg	63-0350
NASER, Christine	26	Heilbronn	66-1327
NASITS, Wm.	21	Arad	64-0138
NASITZ, J.L.	38	New Orleans	63-1178
wife 30, (m) 24			
NASSAUER, Hermann	33	Philadelphia	66-0679
Adelheid 27, Ottilie 5, baby 10m			
NATERMANN, Sophie	28	Beckstedt	64-0593
NATHAN, Adolph	18	Kuersterheim	66-0679
NATHAN, Adolph	18	Mannheim	65-0402
NATHAN, Babette	22	Sandhausen	63-0693
Caroline 19			
NATHAN, Feist	66	Ruenkel	66-0679
NATHAN, G.(m)	19	Bruecken	64-0495
NATHAN, Heinr.	18	Mannheim	64-0427
NATHAN, L.	24	Mannheim	65-0974
NATHAN, Max	23	Iloesheim	66-0576
NATHAN, Max	32	Krakau	65-0004
NATHASON, Adolph	20	Berlin	66-0668
NATZ, Ernestine	28	Gotha	67-0599
Louise 22			
NATZ, Ferdinand	29	Baden	66-0221
Hedw. 26, Pantalon 2, Franz 3m			
NAU, Carl	26	Darmstadt	66-1155
NAU, Const.	21	Schreck	66-1243
NAU, Henrich	22	Schrock	66-1373
NAU, Johannes	22	Ohmes	66-1127
NAUE, Fr.	17	Hildesheim	65-1140
NAUMANN, A.	20	Bispingen	63-0168
NAUMANN, Agnes	29	Neuschoenfeld	66-1203
Richard 3m			
NAUMANN, C.	23	Bispingen	63-0482
Maria 20			
NAUMANN, Catharine	21	Mohre	66-1203
NAUMANN, Elisabeth	19	Lohr	66-1203
NAUMANN, Johann	19	Marburg	65-1024
NAUMANN, Lina	20	Bieber	66-0576
NAUMANN, Rudolph	25	Ilfeld	66-1155
Augusta 19			
NAUNDORF, Carl	35	Werdau	64-0363
NEBEL, Joseph	42	Elzheim	64-0886
Anna Maria 43, Cathrina 7			
NEBEL, O.	16	Berlin	63-0013
NEBELUNG, H.	30	Osten	63-0013
Doris 26			
NEBER, Rudolph	33	Gemmersdorf	67-0007
NEBER, Wilhemine	22	Koenigsberg	65-0950
NEDDE, Ludwig	30	Pattensen	66-0469
Louise 35			
NEEDERWIESEN, Henr	24	Mainz	66-0984
NEEF, Georg F.	31	Degenbach	63-0990
NEEF, Johann	19	Loquard	64-1022
NEEF, Sieverdina	30	Loquard	64-1022
Tolea 18			
NEES, Joh.	32	Krombach	66-1243
Cath. 21			
NEESE, Ludwig	21	Westen	65-0402
NEESEN, Emil	22	Cleve	63-1085
NEFF, Johann	20	Degarloch	66-1243
NEGER, Franz	19	Weilerbach	64-0432
NEGGERMANN, Heinr.	30	Neumuehlen	65-0116
NEHER, Lorenz	36	Musbach	63-0244
NEHLS, Franz	16	Bernstein/Pr.	66-0577
Pauline 18			
NEHMEN, Jacob	24	Neigenmuenden	66-0734
NEHREN, Gertrude	3m	Kail	66-0734
NEHREN, Philipp	40	Pommern	66-0734
E. 31, Margareth 12, Gertrude 8, Peter 6			
Joseph 4, Catharine 2			
NEHRER, Georg	28	Ravensburg	66-1031
NEHRING, Adolph Fr	21	Thomsdorf	63-0006
NEID, Christ.	31	Birkenried	65-0594
NEIDEL, Amalie	21	Sachsen	66-0576
NEIDEL, Franz	31	Werdau	64-0427
NEIDEL, Gotthard	29	Werda	65-1088
NEIDEL, Oswald	25	Verdame	64-0938
NEIDHOEFER, Philip	30	Kreffelbach	66-1131

NAME	AGE	RESIDENCE	YR-LIST
NEIDINGER, Helene	56	Buesslingen	65-1024
Sigmund 13, Martha 25			
NEINASS, Heinrich	26	Annaberg	66-0577
Charlotte 28, Tina 6m, Wilhelmine 2			
NEINER, Philippine	22	Insbruck	64-0840
NEIPP, Christ.	19	Trostingen	63-0990
NEIPP, Joh.	42	Schurra	64-0495
NEIS, Adolph	26	Stamos/Hung.	65-0038
Rese 28			
NEISS, Wilhelm	22	Weilar	66-1128
NEITZ, Salom.	42	Raeding	63-0752
NEJEDLI, John	43	Boehmen	63-0482
Anna 38, Anton 19, Francis 9, Joseph 2			
NELK, Bernhard	19	Varensell	66-1203
NELLE, Friedrich	25	Corbach	66-1031
NELLER, Carl	28	Freiberg	66-0679
NELSON, Moritz	30	Carlsruhe	63-0917
Augusta 18			
NEMECEK, Joseph	34	Boehmen	66-0221
Elsle 25, Wilhelm 27			
NEMECEK, Wenzel	48	Boehmen	66-0221
Rosalia 41, Catharine 13, Wenzel 7			
Elisabeth 5, Wenzel 3			
NEMETZ, Franz	39	Wier	64-0023
NENDORF, Jacob	16	Oberflorsheim	66-1031
NENNBERGER, E.	19	Calumburg	64-0782
NENSCHUEBER, L.	27	Rhaunen	64-0782
NENSS, Carl	24	Braunschweig	65-0974
NEPNUTH, And.	23	Schlitz	64-0992
NERBERLE, M.(f)	25	Bayern	64-0495
NERERS, Carl	29	Hochhausen	66-1155
NERN, Conrad	31	Ebergoens	64-0593
Cath. 28, Conrad 2, Martin 60			
NESEMANN, Diedr.	37	San Francisco	66-0734
Lisette 30, Elisa 6, Enno 5, Carl 2			
NESS, v. J.	20	Osnabrueck	64-0495
NESSELBUSCH, Fran.	32	Graefrath	63-0168
Charles 35			
NESSLAGE, Herm.	27	Mimmelage	64-0593
NESTER, Cyprian	21	Coelsdorf	66-1327
NESTERMANN, Gert.	20	Heggen	66-0704
NESTLER, H.O.	31	Rosswein	64-0170
NESTOR, Barthol	20	Herren Zimmer	63-0097
Margarethe 17			
NETHE, Abraham	40	Brakel	66-1093
NETSCH, J.	35	Asch	63-1003
NETTE, Carl	28	Waldeck	64-0938
NETTLER, Math.(m)	18	Trostingen	64-0687
NETTLING, Henry	27	Braunschweig	63-0953
NETZ, Wilhelm	27	Nordheim	64-0214
W.(f) 69			
NETZDE, Carl	20	Berlin	65-0004
NEU, Andreas	39	Leistadt	65-1030
Catharina 39, Maria 12, Catharina 7			
Peter 9, Friedrich 5, Carl 3, Fritz 6m			
NEU, Jacob	22	Weissenburg	65-0243
NEU, Joh. Hinrich	42	Altenbruch	66-0837
NEUBAUER, Carl	18	Nuernberg	66-0679
NEUBAUER, Dorothea	18	Regendorf	66-0704
NEUBAUER, Johann	39	Oberheimbach	65-1095
Susanna 33, Peter 6, Anna M. 4, Johann 7m			
NEUBAUER, Ludwig	31	Wien	65-0151
NEUBER, Franz	26	Reichenbach	65-0055
NEUBER, Theresia	27	Berlin	65-0116
NEUBERGER, M.(f)	20	Bustan	64-1161
NEUBOURG, Marie	21	Weiden	65-0007
NEUBRAND, Caroline	18	Riedlingen	64-0992
NEUBRAND, Xaver	31	Riedlingen	64-0992
NEUBURGER, Fanni	23	Bachau	65-0402
NEUBURGER, Rosa	32	Buchau	64-0427
NEUCKE, Ernst	27	Elmlohe	64-0938
NEUCKS, Constantin	21	Bederkesa	65-1088
NEUDIECK, Johanna		New Orleans	63-0990
NEUENDORF, W.L.	50	Wiesbaden	64-0886
Louis 14			
NEUENDORF, Wilh.	18	Wiesbaden	63-1136
NEUER, Marie	20	Eberbach	63-0693
NEUFELD, Wilhelm	29	Weichselburg	66-0083
NEUFFER, M.	26	Greuth	64-0593
NEUFFER, Natalie		Aalen	66-0984
NEUFFER, Wilhelm	17	Neufen	66-0679
Hans 15, Max 19			
NEUFUSS, Werner	28	Ob.Duenzebach	64-0170
NEUHARDT, Magd.	22	Homburg	64-1161
NEUHAUER, Jul.	28	Neulewin	64-0782
Aug. 35			
NEUHAUS, Anton	26	Coeln	65-0402
NEUHAUS, C.	32	San Francisco	64-0593
Wife 26			
NEUHAUS, Caroline	25	Borgholzhsn	64-0170
NEUHAUS, Elisab.	26	Oberluebbe	64-0886
Marie 22			
NEUHAUS, Heinr.	34	Isenstedt	65-1030
Caroline 32, Louise 3			
NEUHAUS, Heinr.	17	Utlubbe	64-0214
NEUHAUS, Johann	27	Bokel	65-0713
NEUHAUS, John	37	St. Louis	66-0576
NEUHAUS, Moritz	17	Bremke	23-0865
NEUHAUS, Philipp	26	Elben	66-1248
Wilhelm 24			
NEUHAUS, Wilhelm	34	Hannover	63-1038
NEUHAUSEN, W.(m)	24	Amsterdam	64-0331
NEUHERR, Fr.	29	Rechnitz	65-0189
NEUHOFF, Doris	28	New York	63-0990
Johanna 7, Christian 1			
NEUKAMP, W.A.	27	Schwertz	65-1030
NEULINGER, Friedr.	20	Braunschweig	66-0734
NEUMANN, Adam	22	Obenburg	63-0953
NEUMANN, Carl	24	Hirschberg	64-0363
NEUMANN, Catharine	23	Syke	66-0734
NEUMANN, Christine	72	Potsdam	66-1243
NEUMANN, Dav.	32	Doerdorf	65-1024
NEUMANN, Elisabeth	25	Allnach	65-1024
NEUMANN, F.W.	36	Wchte	64-0687
NEUMANN, Francis	28	Dobern	63-1218
NEUMANN, Friedr.	46	Pommern	66-0576
Charlotte 44, Wilhelmine 16, Justine 10			
NEUMANN, G.	17	Kaschau	65-0007
NEUMANN, Heinr.	19	Hannover	66-1313
NEUMANN, J.	31	Wien	65-0007
Marie 27, Marie 6, Caroline 11m			
NEUMANN, John	40	Posen	67-0600
Marie 14			
NEUMANN, Lothar	22	Wuerzburg	65-0243
Caroline 19, Christine 2			
NEUMANN, Louise	13	Krasnitz	65-1095
NEUMANN, Ludw.	31	Posen	64-0432
Justina 27, Johann 6, Ernestine 4			
NEUMANN, Marg.	57	Bremervoerde	65-0974
NEUMANN, Otto	12	Dorum	64-0331
NEUMANN, Philipp	30	Bechtheim	66-1203
NEUMANN, Rebecca	19	Lehe	65-1024
NEUMANN, Rosa	18	Schrozberg	66-0734
Eugenia 15			
NEUMANN, Rosie	45	Eperies	65-1024
Charl. 21, Jac. 9			
NEUMANN, Samuel	42	Eperico	64-0840
NEUMEISTER, Maria	21	Sugenheim	64-0427
NEUMUELLER, Carol.	17	Pfatter	63-1085
NEUNABER, Caroline	25	Lehe	64-0456
NEUNHAGEN, John	36	Ndr.Kaufungen	63-1136
NEUNOLD, Marg.	17	Stangenrod	64-1022
NEUPERT, Gustav	16	Doerendorf	66-1203
NEUSCHAEFER, Frdr.	28	Kohlgrund	64-0214
Helene 25, Aug. 23			
NEUSCHWANDER, Barb	26	Kleebronn	64-1108
Christ. 4, Ludwig 1, Hendrike 25			
NEUSCHWANDER, Lse.	17	Kleebronn	64-0427
NEUSE, Conrad	42	Freidorf	64-0739
Dorothea 42, Wilhelmine 15, Johann 13			
Elisabeth 9, Emilie 7, Dorothea 6			
August 4			
NEUSSEL, G.	15	Bellesheim	66-0413
Helene 28, Marg. 18			
NEUSSER, Carl	78	Westhoven	66-1093
NEUSTADEL, (m)	25	Frankfurt	65-0007

NAME	AGE	RESIDENCE	YR-LIST
NEUSTADT, Chr'stne	18	Bussford	66-1093
NIBEL, Anna M.	21	Reinergau	63-0296
NICALAS, Margareth	15	Ostheim	63-0015
NICKEL, N.	24	Leeheim	65-1189
NICKELS, Louise	37	Helgoland	63-1136
Anna Marie 12, James 4, Anna Cath. 52			
NICKELS, Peter	24	Wintzert	66-0412
NICKLAUS, Georg	28	Uchtelhausen	65-0770
NICOL, Barbara	19	Kamach	63-0053
NICOLA, Valentin	28	Eppstein	65-0189
NICOLAI, August	17	Veltheim	66-1373
NICOLAI, Diedr.	22	Giessen	66-1327
NICOLAI, Friedr.	36	Wyszinhae	64-1206
Caroline 29			
NICOLAI, Friedr. C	33	Weberstedt	64-0456
Eva Dorothea 44, Martha Carol 17			
Wm. Heinr. C 9, Louise Chris 6			
NICOLAI, Friedrike	28	Kossdorf	66-1203
Maria 26, Margarethe 7, Friederich 6			
Catharine 4, Elisabeth 2, Johannes 6m			
NICOLAI, Gertr.	21	Bavaria	63-0822
NICOLAI, Ludwig	48	Sprendlingen	66-1155
NICOLAUS, Andreas	18	Hambach	63-1218
NICOLAUS, Franz	51	Hambuch	64-0886
NICOLAUS, Julius	19	Nowingen	66-1203
NICOLAY, John	21	Rossdorf	63-0168
NICOLAY, Wilh'mine	24	Sophienburg	66-0650
NICOLAY, Wilhelm	36	Bromberg	64-0456
NICOLETT, Sarette	18	Switz.	63-0482
NICTOR, Simon	22	Alze	64-0495
Bertha 18			
NIDDA, v. Carl	24	Schwetzingen	64-0938
NIEBAUM, Marie	25	Borgholzhsn.	66-1093
NIEBELING, Peter	18	Wuerzburg	65-1030
NIEBERLEIN, Elise	17	Cassel	65-0865
NIEBUHR, Th.	30	San Francisco	63-0953
NIED, Julius	15	Krautheim	63-1085
NIEDERBRACH, Wilh.	28	Rusbend	65-0950
Phillippine 25, Ernestine 9m, Engel 21			
Ernst 15			
NIEDERBURSTER, Lse	20	Hannover	64-0739
Margarethe 17			
NIEDERHOEFER, Anna	18	Weiterhausen	66-0083
NIEDERHOEFER, Joh.	45	Wieterhausen	66-1313
Marg. 48, Cathar 48			
NIEDERLUCKE, F.H.	20	Bockhorst	63-0917
NIEDERMAYER, Aug.	23	Eschenhausen	66-1131
NIEDERMEYER, Heinr	18	Alten Donop	66-1327
NIEDERSCHULT, Mary	26	Osnabrueck	67-0600
NIEDERWIESEN, Bert	18	Mainz	64-0886
NIEDERWIESS, Joach	68	Augsburg	65-1088
Jacob 16			
NIEDERWISER, Franz	16	Augsburg	65-1088
Barbara 14			
NIEDING, Jacob	18	Heiner	66-0679
NIEDNER, Hermann	35	Hohenstein	63-1136
Chris.Henry 27, Christine 27, Auguste 9m			
Aug. Hermann 25			
NIEDNIG, Conrad	26	Altmanshausen	64-0992
NIEHAUS, Anna M.	17	Beten	66-0109
NIEHAUS, Heinrich		Osnabrueck	66-1373
NIEHE, Marg.	17	Fresenburg	63-0953
NIEHOF, Joh.	26	Daenenkamp	64-0214
NIEHOFF, A.	26	Bremen	65-1189
NIEHOFF, C.	23	Werningerode	64-1053
NIEHOFF, Heinrich	20	Ahaus	66-1327
NIEHOFF, Loiuse	27	Muehlhausen	65-0004
Martha 22			
NIEHUS, Carl W.	16	Steinbrueck	64-0214
NIELSEN, Christ.	20	Radtjeburg	66-0666
NIELSEN, Jerg	22	Copenhagen	66-0666
NIELSEN, Niels Clr	29	Copenhagen	66-0666
NIELSEN, William	18	Copenhagen	66-0666
NIEMAND, Heinrich	14	Markendorf	64-0433
NIEMANN, A.	31	Oldenburg	65-1024
J.F. 26			
NIEMANN, Adolph	25	Oysthe	64-1022
NIEMANN, Albrecht	21	Hoehentrupp	64-0886
NIEMANN, August	23	Delmenhorst	64-1053
NIEMANN, Bernhard	24	Heissum	66-0934
NIEMANN, Christine	20	Todsenhausen	64-0840
NIEMANN, Conr. H.	25	Solten	64-0427
NIEMANN, Eduard	33	Baltimore	66-0734
NIEMANN, F.	35	Loehne	66-0413
Louise 36, Heinrich 9m			
NIEMANN, Friedrich	25	Schildesche	63-0006
NIEMANN, Gerhard	25	Wulften	66-0704
NIEMANN, Heinr.	30	Hoesseringen	64-0214
Marie 30, Christine 6, Wilh. 6m			
NIEMANN, Heinr.	18	Russbenden	64-0214
NIEMANN, Heinrich	16	Affinghausen	66-0704
NIEMANN, Joh.	17	Schleptrup	65-1031
Amalie 15			
NIEMANN, Joh. Chr.	60	Bachholzhsn.	65-0950
August 16, Maria 57, Charlotte 27			
Cathar. 20, Minna 13			
NIEMANN, Justus	38	Bremen	65-0004
NIEMANN, Marie	17	Hannover	64-0840
NIEMANN, Wilhelm	19	Hannover	66-1131
NIEMEIER, Herm.	20	Bielefeld	66-0109
NIEMENKAMP, Carl	18	Minden	65-1031
NIEMER, Gustav	38	Missingen	66-0984
Fanny 8			
NIEMEYER, Anton	18	Lippstadt	66-0577
NIEMEYER, Bernhard	24	Lingen	25-0950
NIEMEYER, Cathrine	30	Cappeln	66-1031
NIEMEYER, Fr.	29	Lingen	65-1088
NIEMEYER, Heinr.	30	Boerringhsn.	66-0221
Agnes 22			
NIEMEYER, Heinz	30	Kirchdorf	66-0650
NIEMEYER, Jos.	26	Muenster	65-0189
NIEMEYER, Marg.	25	Schole	64-0023
NIEMEYER, Simon	27	Schnorbeck	65-1088
NIEMEYER, Wilhelm	19	Rahden	65-1088
NIENABER, B.	18	Bassum	63-1136
NIENABER, Diedr.	31	Uchtinghausen	64-0593
NIENABER, Franz	41	Haverbeck	66-0984
NIENHUESER, H.F.	18	Bohmle	65-0898
NIENKAMP, Heinrich	39	Dedendorf	66-0469
NIENKAMPF, Joh.Mic	23	West Cappeln	64-0331
NIENOECKL, Engelb.	32	Boehmen	63-0862
Franzisca 33, Wendelin 8, Francis 9			
Marie 6, Anton 5, Engelbert 3			
NIENSTADT, Franz	19	Hannover	66-1373
NIERE, Henry	42	St. Louis	66-1031
NIERMANN, Carl	65	Isenstedt	66-1031
NIERMANN, Carl	16	Isenstedt	65-1030
NIERMANN, Elise	25	Klosterveseld	64-0343
NIERNGARDT, Anna	21	Masskirch	63-0917
NIERSTE, Anna M.	24	Ob.Bauernschf	65-0898
NIERUECKER, Amalia	39	Biberach	66-0412
Heinrich 14, Caroline 12, Louise 10			
NIES, Marg.	25	Wolfskehlen	65-1189
NIESCHWITZ, Th. Wm	18	Mannheim	63-0917
NIESING, M.	50	Cincinnati	63-0953
NIESLER, Mathias	35	Kriegshaber	66-1093
NIESSE, Wm.	19	Voerden	64-0840
NIESTEL, Joseph	23	Muenster	66-0221
NIET, Barb	19	Meslingen	65-0007
NIETENSTEIN, Joh.	19	Hagewede	66-0704
NIETFELDT, J.F.	49	Washington	63-0953
NIETHFELD, Carol.	20	Uchte	65-0713
NIETZER, Adam Carl	20	Bopfingen	65-1030
NIEWOEHNER, Cath.	31	Angelwodde	66-1031
NIGGER, Hr.	24	Cloppenburg	64-0938
NIGTST, Wilhelm	60	Menchholz	66-1155
NILSCH, Rosine	18	Oetlingen	65-0402
NIPPER, (baby)	18m	Cloppenburg	65-1189
NIST, Michael	58	New York	63-1085
Caecilie 23			
NITZSCHE, Henr'tt.	65	Freiburg	67-0007
NITZSCHMANN, Rich.	22	Germany	66-0666
NOACK, Adolph	24	Kemberg	66-1327
NOACK, August	30	Berlin	67-0353
NOACK, Wilhelm	43	Muskau	66-0623
NOAK, Julius	44	Lippe	66-0577

NAME	AGE	RESIDENCE	YR-LIST
Henriette 46, Carl Julius 12			
Henriette 10, Wilhelmine 6, Johanna 20			
NOAK, Wilhelm	31	Breslau	66-0734
NOBEL, Georg	25	Schweinheim	66-0734
NOBLING, Adam	18	Salzungen	66-1248
NOCE, Rennigio	22	Italia	63-0015
NODRICKEN, M.	31	Duehren/Pr.	65-0038
NOE, Mathias	30	Noedroth	63-0350
NOEHER, Wilhelm	16	Altenbach	66-1203
NOEHL, Joh.	17	Niederstedin	64-0687
NOEHRING, Joachim	40	Zella	65-1024
Maria 30, Joseph 9, Georg 4, Edmund 11m			
NOEHRINGEN, Martin	20	Urasch	66-1093
NOELL, Georg	25	Nassau	66-0576
Henrica 23, Daniel 4, Friederike 2			
Max 8m			
NOELLE, Fritz	15	Wallenbrueck	66-1327
NOELLER, David	25	Erfurt	63-0822
NOELTING, W.(m)	8	New York	64-0331
Johanna 21			
NOERR, Joh. Fr.	19	Muenchen	64-1053
NOETZLI, Gusto.	23	Oetweil	65-0243
NOFTI, Adam	30	Worms	64-0840
NOHL, Louis	58	Paras	65-0055
H.(f) 55			
NOLKE, Maria Ilsab	41	Markendorf	64-0433
Joh. Heinr. 16, Carol. Luise 13, Ernst 8			
Clara 7, Carl 4			
NOLKEMEYER, Adolph	24	Wehte	67-0007
NOLL, Amanda	19	Gr. Almerode	65-0004
NOLL, Charles	25	Neuwier	63-0917
NOLL, Conrad	28	Rosenthal	64-1108
NOLL, Franz A.	36	Hansen	65-0189
NOLL, Fritz	28	Esterdorf	65-1088
NOLL, Jacob	19	Hugsweier	66-0704
NOLL, Jacob	37	Coblenz	67-0599
Anne Maria 47, Catharina 14			
Margaretha 12, Wilhelm 8, Marianne 5			
NOLL, Johann	37	Weidenau	64-0433
Magdalina 29, Wendlin 6, Catharina 3			
Peter 9m			
NOLLER, Carl	18	Kl. Ebach	64-0138
NOLLMANN, (f)	26	Louisville	63-0917
child 3			
NOLTE, Aug.	35	Heidelberg	65-0055
NOLTE, August	31	Empede	65-1031
NOLTE, Carl	23	Dehnsen	66-0934
NOLTE, Cath. Elis.	27	Rothendorf	66-0837
NOLTE, E.H.	55	Bremen	65-1024
Auguste 38			
NOLTE, Heinich	20	Dalbke	66-0412
NOLTE, Heinrich	27	Algesdorf	67-0599
Sophie 28			
NOLTE, Hy. R.	32	Dresden	63-1085
Adelene 24, Emilie 24, Alfred 2			
Caroline 22, Leeser 9			
NOLTE, Louise	20	Germany	66-0666
Sophie 27			
NOLTENIUS, E.	28	Brooklyn	66-0934
NOLTENIUS, F.E.(m)	30	St Helena	64-0214
NOLTING, Hartw.	35	Barrduttingd.	63-1010
Bernhard 30			
NORD, Carl	16	Michelstadt	66-1155
NORD, Louise	20	Biedenkopf	65-0948
NORDBROCK, Augusta	21	Driftsethe	66-0934
NORDBRUCH, J.D.	24	New York	64-0073
Maria 15			
NORDECK, v. Ed. Fr	47	New York	64-0432
NORDEN, Cath. Soph	27	Hannover	64-0432
NORDEN, Heinr.	34	Holthaus	65-0402
Anna 20			
NORDENHOLZ, Bernh.	18	Vegesack	64-0073
NORDHAUS, Joh. Fr.	24	Kl. Sottrum	66-0109
NORDHEIM, F.A.	59	Gehaus	63-1038
Marie 59			
NORDHOF, Heinrich	23	Oldenburg	66-0221
NORDHOFF, Joseph	28	Schuetterzell	64-0639
NORDHOFF, Martin	49	Covington	66-0109

NAME	AGE	RESIDENCE	YR-LIST
NORDHOFF, Peter	43	Vorhelm	65-0402
NORDLINGEN, Sam	21	Coeln	66-0109
NORDLOCH, Albert	25	Gudesdorf	66-0221
NORDMANN, Bernhard	40	Cloppenburg	63-1136
NORDMANN, Bernhard	28	Goldenstedt	64-0920
NORDMANN, Franz'ka	24	Rietberg	67-0007
Marie 3			
NORDORF, F.	27	Amenhausen	64-0992
Carl 22			
NOS, Maria	26	Duedelsheim	64-0886
NOSECK, F.(f)	36	Bohemia	64-0331
NOSS, F.	23	Lagau	63-1003
NOTH, Anton	24	Alverdissen	66-0984
Fr. 65, Wilhelmine 64			
NOTH, August	58	Alverdissen	65-1088
Louise 55, Friederich 24, August 22			
Emilie 19			
NOTH, Heinr.	24	Milwaukee	66-0984
NOTHDURF, Aug.	21	Osterode	65-0402
NOTHOLT, Amanda	28	Bremerhaven	66-1093
baby (f) 9m			
NOTMEYER, Heinr.	26	Feldheim	64-0214
NOTZHAPER, Joseph	27	Baiern	66-0623
NOVER, Friedrich	21	Giessen	65-1030
August 19			
NOVIS, Carl V.	24	Thalheim	65-1095
Johanna 45, Anna A. 21, Maria 16			
Anna M. 11, Louis B. 7, Friedrich 6			
NOWACK, Adam	31	Wilkowa	66-0469
Marianne 27, Rosalie 9m			
NOWACK, Anton	30	Boehmen	63-1218
NOWACK, Moritz	51	Wien	64-0073
NOWACK, Thaly	31	Kuttenberg	64-0170
Maria 11m			
NOWAK, Josef	28	Bohemia	66-0469
Johanna 28, Wenzel 1			
NOWAK, Vincenz	26	Kunitz	65-0713
Stephan 24			
NOWOITNY, Franzka.	14	Wien	67-0007
NOWRING, Johann	50	Priovat	66-1203
Veronika 44, Anton 14, Johann 7			
NUELSEN, Clemmens	16	Cincinnati	66-0984
NUELTEN, H.	42	Cincinnati	63-0821
Clemens 13, H. 9			
NUERNBERGER, Anna	25	Aschach	66-0147
NUERNBERGER, H.	49	Reiskirchen	64-0782
Cath. 59			
NUERNBERGER, Joh.	31	Reisenkirchen	64-0593
Ludw. 23, Elisab. 25, Phil. 9m			
NUERNBERGER, Jul.	24	Wieselsheim	66-1327
NUHN, Cls.(f)	27	Freyes	64-0495
Marg. 4			
NUHN, Elisab.	19	Hattenbach	64-0456
NUHN, Emmeline	31	New York	63-0953
NULLER, Jacob	29	Wuertemberg	66-0413
Marie 26, Sophie 4, Emilie 10			
NUN, Anna Cathar.	22	Herzdorf	66-0623
NUP, Wilhelm	18	Schoningen	66-0469
NUSMANN, Clemens	21	Lengerich	67-0007
NUSS, Adam	27	Heuschelheim	65-0189
NUSS, August	20	Bruckenau	66-1155
NUSSBAUM, Bertha	18	Burghann	64-0214
NUSSBAUM, Henry	30	Switz.	64-0170
NUSSBAUM, Koppel	16	Burghamm	65-1024
NUSSBAUM, M.	36	Erdmannsrode	65-0974
Veilchen 27, Mathilde 65, Caroline 5			
Aron 3, Malchen 9m			
NUSSBAUM, Meyer	14	Erdmannsdorf	66-0679
Bertha 15			
NUSSBAUM, Re.(f)	23	Ulmbach	64-0495
NUSSBAUM, Schoench	21	Neukirchen	65-0594
NUSSBAUM, Veilche	18	Hatzbach	66-0679
NUSSBAUMER, Louis	22	Pouchy	63-1218
NUSSER, Anton	23	Guendsburg	65-1030
NUSSER, Wilhelmine	18	Ernstbach	65-0189
NUSSMEYER, H.	28	Rehme	65-1189
NUTTELMANN, Wilh.	33	Deblinghausen	66-0934
Charlotte 30, August 9, Wilhelm 4			

NAME	AGE	RESIDENCE	YR-LIST
Marie 1			
NUTTREY, Emil	26	New York	63-0752
OACKMEYER, Gerhard	18	Groenlohe	66-0984
OAT, Josepha	24	Hessen	66-0469
OBBERNDORF, Leonh.	47	Frederick	63-0752
Maria 29, Samuel 9			
OBENAUER, Susanne	28	Darmstadt	66-1127
OBERDICH, Hy.	27	Altendorf	63-1085
OBERER, Theresia	21	Empfingen	66-1327
OBERFELDER, Isaac	19	Muehlhausen	63-0862
OBERFELDER, Max	17	Muehlhausen	66-1031
OBERGLOCK, Gottl.	22	Gingen	66-0083
OBERGUENNER, F.W.	45	New York	63-0168
OBERHEIM, Lorenz	30	Gedern	64-0363
OBERKRAMER, Carl	18	Minden	65-1031
OBERLE, Benedict	22	Friedrichshfn	63-0551
OBERLEH, Johann	38	Breitenfeld	66-0083
OBERLIS, Carl	24	Ludwigshafen	66-0837
OBERLOHMANN, Jobst	26	Niederjoellen	63-0244
OBERMAID, Wolfgang	20	Bremen	63-0614
OBERMANN, Anna	52	Varel	65-0950
OBERMEIER, Heinr.	23	Iburg	66-1128
OBERMEYER, Fr.	26	Schnathorst	65-0594
OBERMEYER, Heinr.	19	Oeringhausen	65-1088
OBERMEYER, Peter H	22	Hannover	66-1313
OBERMUELLER, Aug.	18	Meiningen	66-1031
OBERMUELLER, Carl	30	Zell	66-0679
Severin 25			
OBERNDORF, Abraham	14	Rimbach	63-0953
OBERNDORFER, Ed.	15	Fuerth	65-0402
OBERNDORFER, Jacob	25	Fuerth	66-0934
OBERSCHELB, F.W.	27	Soelbenbeck	64-1022
Friedr. 34, Maria 9m			
OBERST, Magd.	40	Unterwisheim	65-0402
Joh. Mich. 8, Adolph 5, Christine 1			
Carl Alex 27			
OBERST, Michael	40	Weyhe	65-0402
Magd. 40, Joh. Michael 9			
OBERT, Joh.	24	Offenbach	64-1206
OBERT, Therese	20	Rust	65-0007
OBERWARTH, Leo	24	Berlin	65-0402
OBITZ, William	30	Mohrin	63-0953
OBREN, Michael	26	Hungary	64-0363
Wife 20			
OBST, William	33	Philadelphia	63-1136
OCH, Conrad	46	Bayern	63-0398
OCH, Johann	29	Bamberg	65-0038
OCHS, Adolph	26	Eisenach	64-0886
Mathilde 27, Otto 9m			
OCHS, Balthasar	18	Kurhessen	66-0704
OCHS, Elise	20	Hessia	66-0679
OCHS, Frdr.	32	Muehlhausen	65-0004
OCHS, Herm.	19	Wedelsdorf	64-0138
OCHS, Myer	27	Ulmbach	64-0886
OCHS, Sara	20	Ulmabch	64-0495
Johanna 16			
OCHS, W.	28	Walkening	64-0639
Therese 29, Ida 9m			
OCHSE, Henriette	23	Zueschen	63-1038
Friedr. 2m			
OCHSENDORF, Wm.	19	Wrisbergholzn	65-0116
OCHSENHIRT, Casper	31	Hainchen	67-0007
OCHSENHIRT, Heinr.	20	Selters	64-0886
OCHSENHIRT, Marg.	15	Duedelsheim	64-0886
Johannes 30, Marg. 30, Heinr. 7			
Wilhelm 3m, Maria 5			
OCHTE, Catharina	22	Wonra	66-0576
OCKEL, Casp.	18	Themar	64-0886
OCKELS, Johann	19	Lehe	65-1024
OCKER, Louise	25	Kiel	64-1022
OCKERSHAUSEN, Mina	33	Kirchheim	66-1155
Adolph 7, Elise 4, Margaretha 61			
OCKINGA, Rikus	21	Ostfriesland	63-0752
ODE, August	28	Emsdetten	66-0576
ODENWAELDER, Heinr	27	Friedrichstal	66-0934
ODERWALD, August	28	Willegassen	66-0469
ODERWALD, Theresia	28	Willegossen	66-0469
OEBECKE, Adolph	26	Warburg	65-1088
OECHSLE, G.(m)	24	Stuttgart	64-0331
OECHSLE, Sophia	20	Schoenberg	63-0990
OECHSLI, John	19	Schaafhausen	63-1136
William 14			
OEHLBAUM, Bruno	22	Gotha	65-0948
Amalie 30			
OEHLER, Johannes	23	Frankenbach	66-1327
OEHLER, Louis	19	Scheiba	66-0934
OEHLER, Otto	33	La Crosse	64-0495
OEHLMANN, Johanna	18	Hannover	65-0402
OEHM, Heinrich	20	Waltersbrueck	65-1031
OEHRI, Marianne	36	Feldkirch	63-1218
OEHRING, Johann	27	Bentheim	25-0950
Anna Maria 21, Marianna 2			
OEHSEN, v. H.	27	Mulsum	63-0908
OEHSLER, Daniel	22	Gmuend	66-1131
OEKER, Aug.	27	Bremen	63-1136
Friedr. 24			
OELBERMANN, R.	26	Philadelphia	63-0821
OELERT, Franziska	24	Pickelsheim	66-0984
OELFKEN, Wm.	25	St. Louis	64-0687
OELKE, Gottlieb	18	Eckcyn	66-0413
OELKE, Wilhelm	30	Bromberg	64-0456
Louise 24, Otilie 1, Joh. Aug. 2m			
OELKER, Aug.	18	New York	63-0752
OELKER, August	19	New York	63-0953
OELKERS, Caroline	24	Polle	64-1022
OELMANN, Fr'derike	24	Oldenburg	65-0007
OELMANN, Gerhard	39	Herringhausen	63-0917
Gertrud 39, Elisabeth 59, maria 7			
Gertrud 5, Henry 3			
OELSNER, Gustav	17	Friesack	66-0668
OELVELMANN, Franz	18	Thiene	66-1093
OENNING, Heinr.	30	Allendorf	65-0402
OENNING, Heinrich		Quincy	66-0349
OERTEL, Henry	36	Litzen	66-0109
OERTEL, Marg	27	Horlochen	63-0296
Cunigunde 4, Leonh. 7, Nic. 9			
OESELEIN, Joh.	29	Gerolzhoefen	66-1373
OESEN, v. Beta	20	Wohlhoefen	66-0934
OESEN, v. Hermann	14	Elmlohe	66-0934
OESER, Carl	28	Taucha	66-0934
OESSNEIEN, Johann	25	Haert	67-0007
OESTE, Jos.	24	Cassel	65-1031
OESTERLE, Georg	20	Roth	64-0170
OESTERLEIN, Wilh.	18	Offenburg	66-1031
OESTERREICH, Conr.	38	Ober Lais	63-0350
OESTLING, Joh.	23	Elsfeld	66-0984
OESTREICH, Andreas	27	Stockhausen	65-1031
OESTREICH, Georg H	22	Almenrod	65-0189
OESTREICH, Heinr.	20	Lauterbach	65-1030
OESTREICHE, Anna	19	Carlsbad	66-0734
OESTREICHER, Ern.	21	Zuerndorf	63-0862
OETJEN, Fr.	39	Riepe	65-1024
Engel 35, Joh. 2			
OETKER, Wilhelm	19	Delmenhorst	66-0679
OETKING, Heinr.	28	Minsen	66-0934
OETTING, Charlotte	24	Bremen	64-0782
OETTING, F.	24	Langwedel	64-0992
OETTKER, Heinr. A.	24	Bachholzhsn.	65-0950
Wilhelm 20			
OETZEL, Georg	21	Cassel	65-0865
OFFENBAND, Anna	54	Blumenthal	63-1218
OFFENHAUSEN, Otto	22	Noerdlingen	66-0109
OFFER, Anna	18	Wippershain	66-0679
OFFERMANN, August	29	Mohe	67-0007
OFFERMANN, Marg.	18	Bremervoerde	65-0974
OFFINGER, Jacob	18	Trostingen	63-0990
OGROSKY, Wilhelm	26	Masleschhamer	65-1095
OHLAND, Heinr. Fr.	37	Hartem	66-0704
Dorothea 37, Conrad H. 6, Hinr. W. 3			
OHLAND, Johann	9	Ringstedt	66-1327
OHLAND, Meta	20	Bremerhaven	66-0704
OHLEN, Harry	27	New York	63-0990
OHLENDORF, Carl	27	Holzen	67-0600
OHLENDORF, Heinr.	45	Adenstaedt	66-1243
Mina 41, Bertha 13, Gustav 8, Emil 3			
OHLENDORF, Heinr.	23	Hannover	65-0116

NAME	AGE	RESIDENCE	YR-LIST
OHLENKAMP, C.	42	Nienburg	66-0413
Sophie 45, Sophie 19, Marie 14			
Dorothea 9, Diedrich 7, Wilhelm 5			
Sophie 19			
OHLER, Nicol.	22	Gimeldingen	64-0687
OHLINGER, Frdr.	40	Kattenberg	66-0109
OHLINGER, Valentin	42	Edingheim	64-0214
OHLMANN, Helene	29	Zetel	66-0576
OHLMANN, Max	25	Freudenthal	65-0055
OHLROGGE, F.W.	19	Westphalen	66-0704
OHLSEN, Christine	19	Dedesdorf	66-1327
OHLSSEN, Johannes	36	Kopenhagen	65-1088
OHLWAERTER, M.(f)	36	Thuisbrunn	64-0495
OHM, Augusta	22	Merkshausen	65-0243
Augusta 6m			
OHM, Fritz	32	Vlotho	65-1095
OHM, Julia	19	Hannover	64-0920
OHMSTEDT, Emil	33	Havanna	63-0990
OHMSTEDT, Gesine	19	Neunkirchen	65-0950
OHNING, Heinr.	30	Geestendorf	65-0116
OHNLEITER, Jakobin	s6	Rhein Duerkhm	65-1030
Valentin 18			
OKOLSKI, Heinrich	46	Danzig	67-0992
OLDEDING, Heinrich	18	Steinfeld	66-0623
OLDEHOF, Fr'derike	22	Bassum	64-0904
OLDENBURG, Ferdr.	22	Kirchdorf	66-0109
OLDENBURG, Georg	21	Landesbergen	64-0433
OLDENBURG, Herm.	48	Sulwarden	64-0665
Meta 32			
OLDIGES, Anna	22	Wahn	65-1024
OLFENIUS, Friedr.	34	New York	63-0990
OLFERDING, Adam	26	Hoelene	64-0687
OLGES, Herm.	24	Oldenburg	66-0984
OLLANIER, Xavier	24	France	63-0350
Francisca 21, Julius 2, Agathe 1			
OLLROGGE, Claus	20	Hannover	66-1313
OLRODET, Franz	17	Sieboldhausen	64-0433
OLSEN, Gerd	28	Bergen	64-0904
OLSEN, Thorsten	26	Wooge	67-0992
Gansine 22			
OLT, Georg	20	Breitenbaum	66-0576
OLTHUES, Tecla	29	Hueven	64-0739
OLTHUM, Frdr.	22	Bornholzhsn.	66-0221
OLTMANN, Friedr.	29	Meerenburg	65-0950
OLTMANN, H.(m)	42	Heppens	64-0331
OLTMANNS, G.C.L.	29	Jever	65-0713
OLTMANNS, Hajo	32	Carolinensiel	63-0482
OLTROGGE, Friedr.	45	Armbackhausen	66-0623
OLTROGGE, Johann	59	Seegelhorst	66-1203
Sophie 56, Dorothea 49, Dorothea 18			
Conrad 16, Heinrich 13, Sophie 8, Marie 5			
Dorothea 1			
OLVESTE, v. R.	18	Riste	63-1085
ONEBEMANN, Gerh.	25	Gerde	64-0886
Cath. 21, Gerh. 16			
ONKELBACH, Anton	36	Launstein	66-1327
OPALANT, J.(m)	33	Berlin	64-0023
OPEL, Josephine	22	Richmond	64-0023
OPERMANN, Theodor	21	Meiningen	66-0577
OPFER, Cathar.	25	Wehrhausen	66-1127
Heinrich 9m			
OPFER, Johannes	23	Hersfeld	66-0984
OPHAEBER, Wilh.	30	Herfort	66-1243
OPITZ, Carl	44	Luchtenwalde	65-0770
OPKING, Engel M.	27	Rusbend	65-0950
OPLATKA, Joseph	34	Karolinenberg	66-1127
OPPE, Ignatz	29	Bruchsahl	66-0679
OPPEL, Christ.	27	Veilsdorf	66-0576
OPPELT, Johann	24	Zeil	67-0806
Bartel 31, Barbara 26, Adam 3			
Michael 11m			
OPPENHEIM, Ferd.	17	Oppenheim	64-1206
OPPENHEIM, Minna	16	Heidelberg	64-0938
OPPENHEIMER, (f)	55	Baiern	66-0934
Sam. 25, Isaak 23			
OPPENHEIMER, J.	24	Amousgruen	66-1031
OPPENHEIMER, John	24	Barntrup	66-1031
Pauline 22			
OPPENHEIMER, K.	20	Augenrod	65-1088
OPPENHEIMER, Mary	27	Frankfurt	63-0551
OPPENHEIMER, Mos.	30	Heimbach	66-0704
OPPENHEIMER, Moses	15	Baltimore	63-0917
OPPENHEIMER, Regin	17	Hettenhausen	66-0704
OPPENHEIMER, Taub.	23	Angenrod	66-0704
OPPER, Herm.	28	Gruenberg	64-0739
Marie 30			
OPPER, Margarethe	58	Gruenberg	64-0739
OPPERMANN, George	27	Mengelrode	64-0023
OPPERMANN, Heinr.	36	Gehrden	66-0469
Caroline 38, Ernst 7			
OPPERMANN, Helmine	19	Braunschweig	65-0116
OPPERMANN, J.H.	29	Adenstedt	65-0402
OPPERMANN, Jacob	17	Kaltenholzhsn	66-1373
OPPERMANN, Louise	21	Bremen	65-0243
OPPERMANN, Me.(f)	22	Hochborn	64-0331
OPPOLD, Anton	18	Westhausen	66-0984
ORB, J. Chr.	32	Berghausen	63-0168
wife 34			
ORDING, Heinr.	28	Quincy	64-0687
ORDNER, Johann	40	Dinkelsbuehl	66-0668
Barbara 38, Friedrich 48			
ORDNER, Louise	59	Neuenstadt	65-0055
ORLEMANN, Peter	50	Alzey	63-1136
Catharine 50			
ORLOB, Heinrich	40	Wingerode	66-0469
OROOM, Doris	24	Bremen	66-0147
Rudolph 3			
ORSCH, Maria	21	Dolgersheim	65-0402
ORTEL, Andr.	59	Stettin	65-1088
Emilie 25, Traugott 7, Moritz 4, Ida 9m			
ORTEMEYER, Wilhelm	22	Schoetmar	67-0353
ORTENSTEIN, Carlne	22	Walldorf	63-0244
ORTH, C.(m)	28	Ockersheim	64-0331
ORTH, Heinr.	27	Brighton	64-0170
ORTH, John	18	Luetzelwiebel	63-0862
ORTH, Justus	15	Gudenburg	64-0886
ORTH, Mart.	34	Gothenburg	63-0862
ORTH, Nicolaus	51	Wichelsbach	65-0189
Sybilla 43, Joh. E. 19, Elisabeth 19			
Joh. W. 16, Adam. 14, Joh. Phil. 7			
Anna 5			
ORTH, Peter	44	Michigan	64-0214
ORTHEY, Mathilde	23	Neuwied	64-0023
ORTLUEFF, Carl	21	Exteve	66-1127
ORTMANN, Heinrich	39	Diepholz	65-0948
Caroline 38, Hermann 12, Friedrich 10			
Dorette 7, Ernst 4			
ORTWEIN, Joseph	20	Tantfeld	66-1327
OSAN, Adam	44	Hessen	63-0614
Elisabeth 31, Peter 4			
OSIANDER, Robert	24	New York	63-1136
OSLOB, Oscar	27	Berlin	66-0679
OSMEN, Joh.	21	Osterholz	64-0687
OSMERS, Philipp	23	Bremen	66-0413
OSNER, Ferdinand	38	Erenheim	64-0886
OSS, v. Mortiz	16	Beverstedt	65-1088
OSSENFORT, Heinr.	26	Pr. Minden	67-0599
OSSENHEIMIER, Ludw	63	Dettensee	64-0840
Babette 66			
OSTEMEYER, Heinr.	32	Osterwiehe	64-1022
Marg. 30, Anna Cath. 7, Elisabeth 5			
Joseph 3			
OSTEN, Wilhelm	28	Goslar	64-1053
OSTENDORF, B. Henr	40	Baltimore	63-1218
OSTENDORF, W.	38	Chicago	63-0752
OSTERDORF, Henr'tt	22	Hausau	64-0885
OSTERHAGE, Franz	26	Talle	67-0007
OSTERHUES, H.R.(m)	57	Osnabrueck	64-0331
OSTERHUISEN, Wilh.	64	Osterwiland	65-1095
Wilhelm 30			
OSTERING, Antonett		Riesenbeck	63-0917
OSTERLOH, Minna	17	Schlahe	65-1031
OSTERMANN, Christ.	45	Bremervoerde	63-0350
Justine 44, Friedrich 25, Christian 18			
Fr. Conrad 14, William 9, Henry 7			
August 5, Wilhelmine 9m, Caroline 54			

NAME	AGE	RESIDENCE	YR-LIST
Wilhelmine 50			
OSTERMANN, Ferd.	50	London	64-0023
OSTERMANN, Friedr.	20	Borgholzhsn.	66-1373
OSTERMEIER, Theod.	38	Cincinnati	63-1085
OSTERTAG, F.W.(m)	24	Krehwinkel	64-0331
OSTERWALD, Chr.	22	Ferderstedt	64-0639
OSTERWALD, H.	25	Plauen	66-0934
Selma 23			
OSTERWALD, Wilh.	26	Lemgo	63-1136
OSTEYDA, Claus	33	Osterdorf	64-0992
OSTFELD, Aug. F.	19	Cloppenburg	64-0427
OSTFELDERN, v.Hugo		Koenigsee	66-1203
OSTHOFF, C.H.	26	Brake	65-0189
OSTHOFF, Franz	33	Muenster	66-0109
OSTHOFF, H.H.(m)	27	West Cappeln	64-0331
OSTING, Joh. N.	26	Osterfeine	64-0593
OSTMANN, (f)	49	Bielefeld	64-0427
OSTMANN, Aug.	29	Gr. Ferra	64-0593
Johanna 27, Aug. 1			
OSTMANN, Aug.	28	Damme	64-0593
OSTREICH, J.	23	Ressewo	65-0007
OSTWALD, Carl	20	Coblenz	66-1155
OSTWALD, Ch.	21	Laubach	64-0782
OSWALD, Anna M.	21	Gimsheim	65-0116
OSWALD, Carl	15	Umstadt	64-1022
OSWALD, Christine	56	Wuerttemberg	63-0822
Christian 25, Christina 21, Caroline 18			
Wilhelmine 16, Louise 1			
OSWALD, Nicolas	52	Lupenburg	63-0990
Cath. 59, Jean 18, Peter 16, Bernhard 8			
Elisabeth 20			
OTERSEN, Bruno	14	Wunstoaf	64-0739
OTT, Abraham	25	Auenstein	66-0109
OTT, Anton	25	Membach	63-1136
OTT, Car. Sophie	17	Lobenstein	66-1313
Joh. Chr. 24			
OTT, Caroline	18	Wuerttemberg	66-0109
OTT, Elisabeth	23	Hoechst	63-1218
OTT, Franz	28	Schneeberg	66-0576
OTT, Joseph	22	Fuerstenau	66-1373
OTTE, Eduard	25	Steindorf	64-0170
OTTE, Friedrich	27	Schoenhagen	66-1327
OTTE, Ludwig	24	Dinklage	66-0412
OTTEN, Cath.	23	New York	63-0398
OTTEN, Claus	18	Esterwegen	66-1131
OTTEN, Gesche	22	Exteve	66-1127
OTTEN, Heinrich	19	Syke	66-0734
OTTEN, Hermann	18	Narpen	66-1031
OTTEN, Johann	39	New York	66-0984
OTTEN, Louis	40	New York	63-0693
Margarethe 30, Margarethe 9, Wilhelm 7			
Emy 5, Louis 3, Caby 6			
OTTEN, Meta	23	Tharmstadt	66-1031
OTTEN, Wilh.	38	Burhave	63-0953
OTTENBACH, Michael	26	Heuchlingen	66-0734
OTTENDORFER, Elias	28	Stein	66-0666
Catharina 34, Barbara 2, Catharina 54			
Barbara 34, Catharina 17, Friedrich 11			
OTTENDORFER, Goerg	31	Stein	66-0666
Catharina 24, Johann 10m			
OTTENHAUSEN, Wilh.	38	Hanzighausen	65-1030
OTTENHEIMER, Janet	27	Nordstetten	63-1178
Mar. 17			
OTTENHEIMER, Jete	56	Nordstetten	66-0704
Riecke 22, Augusta 18, Immanuel 14			
OTTENHEIMER, Juls.	26	New York	63-0097
OTTERHEIM, Clemens	20	Grossluder	66-1203
OTTERMANN, Chr. H.	59	Hunteburg	63-1038
Fritz 13			
OTTING, Anna Marie	17	Oldenburg	66-0221
OTTING, Minna	26	Bielefeld	66-0578
Mathilde 6, Hermann 6m			
OTTINGER, Magd.	21	Nebischaffshm	64-0073
OTTLOF, Andr.	48	Boernecke	65-0007
OTTMEIER, Heinrich	22	Emsdetten	66-0412
OTTO, Adam	7	Wabern	64-0840
OTTO, Augusta	22	Verden	66-1373
OTTO, Catharina	20	Rheime	64-0214

NAME	AGE	RESIDENCE	YR-LIST
OTTO, Dorette	28	Hannover	64-1161
Ernst 5, Bernhard 3, Fritz 9m			
OTTO, Eva	22	Zell	66-0349
OTTO, Fr. Carl	21	Gr. Esserig	64-0840
OTTO, Franz	33	Wansdorf	64-0427
OTTO, Hermine	24	Bremen	63-0482
OTTO, Joh.	19	Freisbach	66-1313
Cath. 21			
OTTO, Julius	18	Warmbrunn	64-0886
OTTO, Margaret	32	Berlin	64-0427
Marg. 32, Philipp 3, Emilie 1			
OTTO, Marie	18	Delmenhorst	63-0917
OTTO, Marie	28	Wischinheulan	66-0934
Marie 4, Albert 6m			
OTTO, Michael	42	Bromberg	64-0456
Henriette 41, Gotthelf 11, Michel Ernst 6			
Joh. Juliane 3, Fr'dr.Otilie 11m			
OTTO, Philipp	29	Neustadt	66-1155
OTTO, Rud.	28	Alsfeld	64-0495
OUATMANN, Heinrich	18	Bevera	65-1088
OULIF, Alexis	26	Paris	64-0023
OVER, Maria Anna	25	Bakum	65-1030
OVERBECK, D.(m)	48	Lohringen	64-0331
OVERBECK, H.	25	Lippstadt	64-0687
OVERBECK, Helene	32	Emden	64-0456
Joh. Frdk. 9, Louise 6, Georg 4, Helene 2			
Friedrich 3m			
OVERBECK, Wilhelm	25	Aschendorf	66-1128
OVERBERG, Gertrude	36	Muenster	66-1155
OVERMANN, F.N.	20	Wehbergen	65-1024
OVERMANN, Georg	26	Koettingen	64-0456
OVERMEYER, J.B.	19	Steinfeld	64-0665
OVERSTE, zur Anna		Loyel	66-1373
OWERGARD, Christ.	35	Copenhagen	66-0666
OXMANN, Julia	20	Kellingholzh.	66-0349
OZERWINSKI, Anton	30	Salna	66-0578
Josephine 32, Ludwig 9, Catharina 4			
Marianne 1			
PAAR, A.	30	St. Paul	63-1085
PAAR, Johann	24	Altendorf	66-0623
PABST, Jacob	54	Langenheim	66-0679
PABST, Johannes	58	Felda	64-0739
Elisabeth 58			
PABST, Wm.	28	Gran	65-0007
PACHER, F.	26	Bohemia	64-0782
PACKWITZ, Friede.	58	Hannover	66-0679
PACOLE, Jettchen	19	Langenschwanz	63-0917
PADE, Heinrich	27	Dissen	65-0865
Henriette 25			
PAEHLER, Heinrich	23	Kaunitz	63-0006
PAEHLIG, J.G.	30	Dresden	65-0898
PAEPKE, Caroline	27	Nuernberg	65-0038
PAETTING, Heinr.	19	Bachholzhsn.	65-0950
PAETZ, Charles	41	Eisenberg	63-1178
PAETZEL, Fr.	48	Muggeburg	64-0665
PAFFE, Fr.	19	Westfalen	63-1003
PAGEL, Christian	40	Gneisenau	66-0578
Charlotte 39, Wilhelm 18, Wilhelmine 13			
Carl 10, Friedrich 8, Anna 1			
PAGENSTECHER, (m)	22	Hanover	63-1218
PAGENSTECHER, H.	22	Lochtingen	65-1088
PAGERS, Carl	24	Holstein	65-0898
Adelheid 24			
PAGNER, Marie	40	Taus	67-0599
Rosine 7, Anna 3			
PAHL, Anna	20	Braunschweig	64-1053
PAHL, Frz. Wm.	8	Westbarthsn.	63-0917
PAHL, Hermann	23	Brodden	66-0578
PAHL, Louis	39	Pyrmont	64-0840
PAHL, Martin	23	Hildesheim	66-0412
PAHLMANN, J.(m)	18	Riste	64-0073
PAHNCKE, Johanna	22	Pommern	63-0614
Hermine 20, Ferdinand 18			
PAHNCKE,Rrobert	31	Pommern	63-0614
Johanna 31, Julius 6, Robert 3, Eugen 10m			
PAJER, Veit	35	Konitz	66-0704
Marie 37, Joseph 4, Adelbert 2			
PALIWKA, Emil	18	Bremen	67-0007

NAME	AGE	RESIDENCE	YR-LIST
PALKING, Heinrich	20	Oldenburg	65-0770
PALM, Henr.	26	Clausthal	66-1203
PALM, William	39	Hamilton	63-0953
PALMER, Christine	22	Schrembson	66-1203
PALMER, Daniel	47	Wuertemberg	66-0221
Eva Dorothe 44, Cathr. 16, Emanuel 7			
PALZ, L.	19	Frankenberg	66-0413
PALZIN, Peter	25	Bromberg	66-0577
PANCKERT, Franz	44	New York	63-0614
Anna 45, Caecilie 15			
PANE, Anna	22	Kirchheim	65-0594
PANGEL, F.L.U.	25	Homburg	66-0413
PANGELMEYER, Carol	27	Gmuend	63-1218
PANGER, Conrad	29	Gross Bersen	64-0739
PANITZ, Franziska	22	Salzgitter	64-0363
baby (f) 9m			
PANK, August	19	Hessen	66-0221
PANKE, A.	52	Neudorf	66-0413
Wilh. 48, Pauline 13, Louise 8			
PANKRATZ, Hed. W.	63	Cloppenburg	63-0244
PANRATZ, William	16	Clpppenburg	63-0244
Ferdinand 14			
PANZER, H.	20	Herford	64-0639
PAPE, Behrend	18	Hannover	66-1031
PAPE, Carl	24	Nienstedt	65-1095
PAPE, Carl	24	Nassau	65-1030
PAPE, Caroline	24	Quakenbrueck	63-1038
PAPE, Friedr.	28	Gadenstedt	64-0427
PAPE, Gerhard	25	Bremen	64-0331
Johanna 21			
PAPE, Heinrich	14	Nenndorf	66-0837
PAPE, Joh. H.	19	Weierdehlen	66-1373
PAPE, Johanna	33	Lobach	65-0594
Adolph 23, Johanna 26, Friedr. 24			
Carl 21, Wilhelm 4			
PAPE, Ludwig	36	Linden	63-0752
Heinrich 27			
PAPE, Maria	22	Kloetze	67-0599
PAPE, Marie	18	Zeven/Hann.	63-0822
PAPE, Rudolph	18	Burgdorf	64-1022
PAPENDIECK, Chr'e	33	Bremen	63-0551
PAPENDIECK, F.W.	23	Frankenhausen	65-0898
PAPER, Diedrich	17	Affinghausen	66-0704
PAPERNO, A.	29	Triest	63-0821
PAPITZ, L.(f)	37	Dessau	64-0495
H.(f) 7, Robert 6, Fanny 5			
PAPKE, Fr.	40	Stade	64-0665
Hinriette 40, Franz 5, Christian 3			
Carl 6m			
PAPKE, Friedr.	31	Quakenbrueck	63-0244
PAPPE, J.	58	Prussia	63-1003
PAPPENHAUS, H.(m)	18	Amsterdam	64-0331
PAPPERT, Constant.	20	Wisen	66-1243
PAPST, Ernst	34	Lipprechtrode	66-1243
PAPST, Heinrich	30	Hintersteinh.	66-0623
Gertrude 27, Heinr. Casp. 3, Melchior 6m			
PAPST, Heinrich	23	Wintersteinau	66-0623
Catharine 19			
PAPT, Alex.	17	Insbruck	64-0840
PARDALL, Friedrich	25	Stadtoldendrf	66-1031
PARDECLY, Elisbeth	56	Boehmen	66-0349
Anna 42			
PARDICK, Dorette	18	Osnabrueck	66-1093
PARENT, Francis	28	France	63-0244
PARFUERST, Ernst	59	Neustadt	64-0938
Wm. 60			
PARGMANN, Fr.	27	Ordinghausen	66-0704
PARISETTE, Louis	20	Muenster	65-0055
PARISOT, (f)	16	France	63-1038
PARULEY, C.W.	32	Jacobsdrebber	64-0495
PARZEFALL, Max	27	Regensburg	63-0398
PASCH, Anna	16	Celle	63-0990
PASCH, Friedrich	45	Craatz	66-0469
Caroline 42, Wilhelmine 9, Wilhelm 6			
August 9m			
PASECCA, Jos.	30	Prag	64-0593
PASKER, Joseph	48	Preussen	63-0990
Gertrud 43, Marie 12, Anna 9, Albert 7			
Henry 4, Bernhard 11m			
PASSCHEN, Franz O.	27	Muenster	66-0349
PASSE, Wilhelmine	29	Linden	66-0734
Friedrich 3, Lina 8m			
PASSECK, Anna	26	Kuttenberg	66-1093
PASSMANN, Joseph	19	Stoecker	66-1327
PASTUNINK, Josina	31	Bentheim	66-0734
PATRCZEK, Hedwig	53	Schweinitz	65-1030
PATSCHKE, August	16	Zeitz	66-0576
PATTNER, Fr.	16	Volldorf	65-1189
PATTRI, Carl W.	18	Haan	65-0116
PATZ, Carl	23	Neugardt	67-0007
PATZE, W.	31	New York	66-0413
PATZER, Daniel	24	Kl.Klonia	66-0349
PAUER, Friedr.	28	Madorf	66-1243
PAUER, Joseph	37	Boehmen	66-0147
PAUKERT, Albert	26	Wintersdorf	64-0432
PAUL, Conrad	20	Obergees	65-0243
PAUL, Friedrich	25	Clewitzdorf	66-0668
Beate 24			
PAUL, James	23	Membach	63-1136
PAUL, Jantne	63	Bunde	66-1203
Christoph 20, Heinrich 17			
PAULI, Catharina	64	Weinsburg	66-1327
Magdalena 30			
PAULI, Clemens	28	Luebeck	63-1038
PAULI, Elisab.	32	Alsheim	64-0992
PAULI, F.W.	21	Cassel	65-0898
PAULI, J.	27	Prussia	63-1003
Th. 25, A. 1			
PAULI, Johanna	58	Ortenberg	63-0990
PAULI, Marie	20	Bremen	63-1038
PAULICH, Ag.(f)	35	Gratz	64-0495
PAULING, Friedr.	21	Hannover	66-0469
PAULISCHKA, Joseph	14	Prodozow	66-0734
PAULL, Hermann	43	Oldendorf	66-0837
PAULMANN, C.	23	Hannover	65-0055
PAULO, Friedrich	26	Wittlage	66-1373
PAULS, Bertha	21	Merscheid	65-0007
Carl 10m			
PAULS, Christ.	19	Bremen	64-0427
PAULS, Henning	28	Dorum	66-0578
Anna 22, Helene 6m			
PAULSEN, Nic.	17	Lockstedt	64-1161
PAULSEN, P.F.	58	United States	63-0013
PAULUS, Joh.	25	Prinzkostel	65-0402
PAULY, (f)	45	Preussen	64-0214
Franz 22			
PAULY, Ad	22	Hungen	65-0151
PAUS, Dina	22	Prussia	63-0822
PAUSEL, Chs.	20	Wuerttemberg	64-0593
PAUSEWANG, C.	24	Prussia	63-1003
W. 23, L. 1			
PAUSS, Fr.	25	Bernstein	65-0898
PAWELSKY, Franz	27	Klakomathe	66-0666
PAWLIK, Johann	50	Taus	67-0992
Anna 49, Georgine 17, Catharine 10			
Johann 8			
PEACK, Bernhard	23	Posen	66-0072
PEAK, Johann	21	Bonn	63-0006
PECHAN, Anna	19	Klatten	67-0007
PECHER, Cath.	39	Horlochen	63-0296
PECHER, Elisab.	58	Mainz	65-0594
PECK, Bernh.	21	Kneheim	63-1038
PECK, Bernh.	40	Quincy	66-0349
PECK, Conrad	17	Seelenfeld	65-1024
PECK, H.	40	Gruenenplan	64-1206
PECK, H.(m)	42	New York	64-0170
PECK, Heinr.	45	Gruenenplan	64-1022
PECK, Henry	48	Gruenenplan	63-0482
PECK, Oscar	23	Riga	65-0004
PECKA, Johann	27	Gr. Klonia	66-0469
Marianne 24			
PECKEN, Ulrich	28	Hannover	66-1127
PECKER, Anth.	18	Krombach	66-1243
PECKER, Herm. A.	32	Gr. Stavern	64-0886
PECKERING, John	66	England	66-0734
Ann 66			

NAME	AGE	RESIDENCE	YR-LIST
PECKHAUS, John	32	Mettmann	63-0482
PECKNER, W.	27	New York	63-1218
PEDAL, Carl	17	Eisenach	66-0576
PEDERIT, Maria	21	Goettingen	63-0398
Amalia 19, Bertha 17			
PEECK, H.	40	Gruenenplan	63-0990
PEECK, H.	40	Grunenplan	65-0055
PEETER, Claas	27	Ihrhorn	64-0495
Fe.(f) 27, Aa.(f) 3, baby 5m			
PEGER, A.	25	Nordnach	65-0007
PEHLE, Wilhelmine	23	Oldentrup	66-0934
PEHLING, Christ.	17	Hannover	64-1108
Maria 22			
PEHLMANN, Anne	42	Grothe	66-0984
Anna 29			
PEHRENS, Fried'ke.	27	Kohlfeld	66-1243
Augusta 25			
PEHRINGER, F.	25	Steyer	63-0862
PEIFFER, John N.	36	Cincinnati	63-0953
PEIL, Georg	32	Sample	64-0886
PEIL, J.(m)	24	Hochborn	64-0331
Johanna 21			
PEIN, Anna	48	Sontra	66-0668
Conrad 20, Anna 22, Caroline 16			
PEIN, Joh.	19	Bremen	66-0576
PEIN, v. Rudolph	39	Emden	66-0837
PEINE, Friederike	28	Koerbicke	66-0412
PEIPER, Wilhelm	52	Belderwang	63-0350
PEIPERS, Carl F.	43	St. Louis	63-1085
Anna 42			
PEISER, F.	30	Nuernberg	65-1189
PEISKER, Gottlieb	32	Prussia	63-0752
Anna 30, Caroline 9, Elisabeth 7			
William 5, Friedrich 11m			
PEITER, Adam	20	Mohre	66-1203
PEKAUSCHKE, Hedwig	29	Bischdorf	63-0053
PEKENROTH, J.	28	Heddesheim	65-1189
Margar. 21			
PEKERSCH, Cath.	24	Bohemia	64-0593
PEKLO, Marie	16	Taus	67-0992
Anna 22			
PEKNEY, Franz	42	Daberkreis/Bo	63-1010
Barbara 32, Franz 3, Anna 9			
PELLE, Carl	40	Cincinnati	66-0984
PELSTRING, Cath.	21	Freeren	65-0189
PELTIES, Maria	22	Lingen	65-1140
PELTRUP, Meta	25	Bremen	63-0168
PELTZER, Joh.	21	Duderstadt	63-0821
PELZER, Mich.	31	Jeissen	64-0938
PENDEL, J.	35	Wuertemberg	66-0413
PENINA, C.	25	Bremen	64-0665
PENKER, Hermann	46	Sachsen-Altb.	66-0623
PENNER, Ferd.	21	Berlin	65-0151
PENNING, Za.(f)	27	Haidhof	64-0495
PENTZEL, Joh. Frd.	25	Berndorf	66-1128
PENZEL, Cath.Carol	20	Markneukirchn	64-1108
PEPER, Anna	25	Seedorf	66-1243
PEPER, Catherine	22	Fischerhude	66-1031
Johann 17			
PEPER, Heinr.	20	Osnabrueck	66-1155
PEPERKORN, Fr. Dan	27	Borgholzhsn	64-0170
Cath. 21, Caspar 14			
PEPLER, Ernst	20	Ulrichstein	65-1024
PEPPERSACK, Heinr.	16	Osterfeine	64-0593
PEPPING, Hermann	29	Crefeld	64-1053
PEPPLER, Georg	17	Laubach	64-1022
PEPPMUELLER, A.	31	Hooksiel	65-1088
PERCH, John	25	Schelsen	63-0752
PERINA, Marie	24	Boehmen	63-1085
Elise 18			
PERK, Ellen	27	Kl. Starern	63-0244
PERKE, Ludwig	27	Hillbethak	66-1131
Anna 22, Anna 4			
PERL, Simon	34	Gluedingen	64-0593
PERLEWITZ, Augusta	25	Czarnikau	64-0363
PERLEWITZ, Gustav	23	Magdeburg	65-0865
PEROUSKA, Thomas	65	Bohemia	64-0593
Anna 28, Wenzel 28, John Jares 40			

NAME	AGE	RESIDENCE	YR-LIST
Cath. 40, Anna 14, Cath. 11, Elisabeth 7			
Mary 6, Rosalie 3, John 1			
PERSUA, Wilhelmine	23	Bremen	66-0984
PERTGEN, Jac.	27	Buedesheim	64-0992
PESCHAN, Eduard	26	Altenbruch	65-0243
PESCHEL, Selma	17	Pr. Minden	66-1127
Marie 16			
PESCHIK, Franz	27	Boehmen	66-0221
PESCHL, Franz	38	Swratkow	66-0734
Theresia 20, Emilie 6m			
PESCHL, Josef	33	Swratkow	66-0734
Francisca 28, Anton 4, Maria 9m			
PESKER, Charles	32	Prussia	63-0752
Johanna 30, Anna 5, John 6m			
PESSELES, J.	23	Fuerth	66-0934
A. 16			
PESTEL, Christiane	43	Balsar	66-1248
Helene 18, Alban 12, Lina 9, Albin 7			
Bernhard 5			
PESTORIUS, H.	23	Vasbeck	65-1189
PESTRUP, Joh.	18	Leest	66-1373
PETER, Aug. Friedr	40	Pommern	66-0469
Henriette 30, Wilhelm 6			
PETER, August	30	Havre	64-0427
Caroline 27, Ag.(f) 9m, wife 28			
PETER, Bertha	21	Magdeburg	64-0495
V.(f) 11m			
PETER, Carl	25	Unterwisheim	65-0402
PETER, Caspar	25	Unteralba	64-0782
PETER, Claus Joh.	35	New York	66-0704
PETER, G.W.	20	Ringenheim	65-1189
PETER, Heinrich	30	Gruenenplan	63-0097
PETER, Jacob	28	Bavaria	63-0822
PETER, Joh.	57	Cloppenburg	65-0038
PETER, Johanna	25	Herford	65-0004
PETER, John Wolf	22	Fuerth	63-0862
PETER, Louis	24	Gotha	65-0004
PETER, Ludw.	25	Lauterbach	65-0594
PETER, Martha	20	Cassel	66-0412
PETER, Martin	58	Kolberg/Pr.	63-0822
August 19, Justine 54, Gottlieb 16			
PETER, Minna	24	Frankfurt/O.	67-0795
Max 6, Anna 9m			
PETER, Sophie	19	Rastatt	66-0934
PETER, Thomas	29	Schrothaus	66-0650
PETERAN, Ludwig	33	Ottenhagen	64-0456
Wilhelmine 9, Friederike 33, Friederike 7			
Wilhelmine 1			
PETERMANN, Adam	27	Haschenheim	65-1024
PETERMANN, August	30	Uslar	63-0398
Friedricke 29, August 6, Heinr. 1			
PETERMANN, Friedr.	15	Syke	66-1093
PETERMANN, Henry	31	San Francisco	66-0147
Maria 25, Minna 1			
PETERMANN, J.	19	Rumpenheim	64-0495
PETERMUELLER, Adlf	22	Iburg	65-0116
PETERS, Aug.	29	Schortens	63-0482
PETERS, Betty	22	Bremen	66-1313
PETERS, Carl	45	Rodenburg	66-0147
Johanna 17, Heinrich 15			
PETERS, Caroline	23	New York	64-0593
PETERS, Chr.	30	New York	63-1136
PETERS, Dorothea	42	Rheda	63-0350
William 13, August 9, Minna 5, Conrad 11m			
PETERS, Ferd.	30	Neuruppin	65-0055
PETERS, Franz	16	Hannover	66-0984
Ernst 14, Charlotte 24			
PETERS, Gottlieb	18	Dortmund	65-0713
PETERS, H.	40	Jever	65-0402
Maria 32, Elise 7, Florenz 6, Julius 5			
PETERS, Heinrich	27	Rechtenfleth	63-0822
PETERS, Heinrich	18	Lienen	66-1031
PETERS, Henricke	18	Rechtenfleth	63-0822
PETERS, Hermann	35	New York	66-0576
PETERS, J.F.	18	Versmold	65-0974
PETERS, Jan	30	Manschlagt	64-1022
PETERS, Johann	25	Brakel	66-1327
PETERS, Johanna	26	Brake	63-0614

NAME	AGE	RESIDENCE	YR-LIST
PETERS, Lina	14	Rothenfelde	63-0917
PETERS, Marie	42	Weinheim	63-1178
PETERS, Nicolaus	17	Bramstedt	64-0456
PETERS, Nicolaus	18	Lehe	66-1031
PETERS, S.	24	Visquard	65-1189
PETERS, Sophie	26	Iffezheim	66-0704
PETERS, Theodor	30	Brake	63-0614
PETERS, Therese	30	Emsdetten	66-0576
PETERS, Wm.	27	Cassel	65-0116
PETERSEN, Anna	58	Bremen	63-0244
PETERSEN, Christ.	33	Floren	63-1010
PETERSEN, Erik	17	Gottenburg	66-0666
PETERSEN, Jens	32	Copenhagen	66-0666
PETERSEN, John H.	26	New York	63-0917
PETERSEN, Ole	39	Copenhagen	65-0004
Catharine 27			
PETERSHAGEN, Bernh	30	Linteln	64-0170
PETERSILIE, Emil	35	Langensalz	64-0456
Johanna 36, Wilhelm 12, Friedr. 9			
Herm. 5, Anna 4, Emma 10m, Heinr. 39			
PETERSOHN, Wilhelm	29	Coerlin	64-0433
Minna 29			
PETERSON, H.	29	Gamberg	65-1189
Marie 27			
PETGEN, John G.	23	Saarburg	65-0189
PETH, Elisabeth	20	Westhofen	66-1093
PETMECKY, H.	19	Wiesbaden	65-0007
PETRAM, Wilh'mine	20	Rheine	64-0170
PETRE, Anna Maria	33	Neustadt/Weim	65-0950
PETRI, Anton	63	Lanzheim	66-0083
Marie Joseph 42, Joseph 8, Michel 12			
Margarethe 6, Christian 4			
PETRI, Friedr.	18	Goettingen	64-0432
PETRI, Friedrich	33	New York	63-0990
PETRI, Fritz	39	New York	63-1218
PETRI, Herm.	21	Marburg	64-1161
PETRI, Jacob	20	Holzhausen	66-1155
PETRI, Regina	36	Neuenkirchen	65-0974
Ferd. 25			
PETRI, W.	22	Hannover	64-0432
PETRIE, Martha	55	Eisenach	63-0862
PETRING, Mart.	20	Dahlingen	65-1088
PETROUSKY, Bta.	24	Pasenack	64-0782
PETRY, Joh.	30	Schweiz	63-1136
PETRY, Matthias	24	Heinzrath	64-0331
PETS, Margaretha	21	Bueckel	65-1030
Elisabeth 17			
PETSCH, Carl	34	Querfurth	63-1010
PETSCH, Julius	40	Linden	66-0576
Leonore 38, Lina 9, Franz 8, Bertha 7			
Anna 2			
PETSCH, Pauline	36	Alsenben	66-1203
Louise 6, Marie 3			
PETSCH, Susanne	26	Neuwied	64-0214
PETT, Gustav	49	Klakomathe	66-0666
Caroline 59, Berta 22, Hermann 20			
August 17			
PETTELKOW, Johann	26	Wiederausmass	66-0469
PETTER, Margarethe	18	Fambach	63-0006
PETTERSCH, Carl	27	Wien	64-0687
PETTKER, Heinr. A.	24	Bachholzhsn.	65-0950
Wilhelm 20			
PETZ, Adam Friedr.	34	Bavaria	64-0739
Margarethe 34, Elisabeth 9			
Geo. Gottfr. 7, Cath. Sophie 5			
Margarethe 3, Maria magd. 11m			
PETZ, H.	22	Wallenhausen	66-0413
F. 23			
PETZ, Marg.	38	San Francisco	63-0953
Henry 12, Peter 9, Marie 8, Anna 2			
PETZACHEK, John	34	Boehmen	66-0221
Maria 34, Cathr. 7, Wenz. 5			
PETZER, Carl	34	Magdeburg	66-1127
PETZOLD, Emil	24	Altenburg	66-0837
PETZOLD, Fr.Moritz	21	Besswein	64-0433
PETZOLD, Friedr.	60	Pressen	64-0427
PETZOLD, Heinrich	27	Koerlitz	66-1373
PEUPELMANN, Fr.	21	Eisenach	66-0934

NAME	AGE	RESIDENCE	YR-LIST
PEUSER, Friedr.	38	Nassau	65-0243
Martha 38, Cathar. 2			
PEYSER, Max	30	Boston	64-0023
PEZOLD, Andr.	35	Grafengeheich	64-1108
PEZOLD, H. Aug.	65	Schoenfeld	64-0593
PFAEFFLIN, Paul	34	New Orleans	63-1136
Caroline 29, Bertha 5, Clara 4			
PFAELZER, Simon	20	Heinbach	66-0704
PFAFF, Franz	28	Paris	67-0007
PFAFF, Herm.	17	Cassel	64-1161
PFAFF, James	26	Mariabronn	63-0551
Theresia 38			
PFAFF, Joh.	44	Ndr.Stammstdt	65-0594
Elise 29, Christine 15			
PFAFF, Johanna	27	Darmstadt	63-0953
Regine 1			
PFAFF, Justus	29	Oberapperfeld	66-0349
Elisabeth 21			
PFAFF, Louise	22	Fritzlar	66-0984
PFAFF, Marie	21	Hersfeld	65-1189
PFAFF, Theresa	23	Waldburg	66-0577
Magdalena 25			
PFAHLER, Carl	25	Elwangen/Pr.	65-0004
PFANDER, Fritz	20	Plattenhardt	67-0007
PFANDER, Jeremias	57	Frickenhausen	64-0427
Marie 58, Rosine 23, Cathrine 21			
Friedrike 19, Caroline 17			
PFANN, Caroline	20	Sulzdorf	64-0687
PFANN, Jacob	22	Mainz	66-0984
PFANNKUCH, H.(m)	28	Bremen	63-0296
PFANNKUCH, Wilh.	28	Melsungen	64-0170
PFANNKUCHEN, Carl	17	Brockhausen	66-1248
PFANNKUCHEN, Chr.	39	Cincinnati	66-0734
Rosa 28, Elise 5, Friedrich 31			
Adelheit 30			
PFANNKUCHEN, Meta	23	Burg/Bremen	65-0950
PFANNSTIEL, Caspar	40	Kurhessen	66-0349
Maria 42, Georg 9, Siegmund 7			
PFANNSTIEL, Valtin	6	Kurhessen	66-0349
George 1			
PFANSTIE, Elisabet	19	Urrhausen	64-0023
PFARBECK, Wilhelm	19	Dissen	66-0984
PFAU, C. (m)	25	Vogt	63-0482
PFAU, Heinr.	25	Neustadt	66-0349
PFAU, Joseph	60	Kirchhausen	65-0594
PFAU, Mathias	37	Igersheim	64-0170
PFEFFER, Cathar.	24	Rottenburg	65-0055
PFEFFER, Conrad	38	Breitenbach	66-0578
Marie 39, Heinrich 11, Berthold 9			
Justus 7, Catharina 5, Marie 1			
PFEFFER, Friedrich	32	Bruckenau	66-1155
PFEFFERLE, Jean	40	Baden	64-0170
Mrs. 36, child 6, child 7, infant 4m			
PFEIFELE, Bernh.	31	Gernbach	64-0170
PFEIFER, Doroth.	24	Gomaringen	64-0992
PFEIFER, Elisabeth	18	Heppenheim	64-0639
PFEIFER, Hermann	24	Hersfeld	66-1248
PFEIFERLING, Louis	18	Ludersheim	66-1248
PFEIFFER, Adam	10	Fruthenhof	65-0402
Barb. 42			
PFEIFFER, Anton	29	France	63-1038
PFEIFFER, August	20	Cassel	66-1203
PFEIFFER, Balthas.	25	Switz	63-0350
PFEIFFER, Barbara	15	Mit.Rainstadt	65-1088
PFEIFFER, Carl	21	Bremen	64-0170
PFEIFFER, Caroline	27	Schwarzach	63-0482
PFEIFFER, Cath.	13	Niederhausen	63-1136
PFEIFFER, Cathrina	19	Oberfleiden	66-0984
PFEIFFER, Christ	27	Lannsbach	64-1053
PFEIFFER, Emil	30	Mexico	66-0576
PFEIFFER, Franz	24	Tuebingen	64-0639
PFEIFFER, Friedr.	36	Tuebingen	66-1373
Caroline 27			
PFEIFFER, Georg	62	Schornweisack	66-1093
Peter 13, Paulus 9			
PFEIFFER, Gotth.	26	Goppingen	65-0974
PFEIFFER, Heinrich	23	Baden	66-0984
PFEIFFER, Jacob	22	Friedelhausen	64-0363

NAME	AGE	RESIDENCE	YR-LIST
Caroline 25			
PFEIFFER, James	35	Boehmen	63-0551
Amma 33, John 9, James 3, Rosina 6			
Theresia 8m			
PFEIFFER, Joh.	23	Braunschweig	66-1313
PFEIFFER, Johannes	21	Wellendingen	66-0679
PFEIFFER, John E.	30	Washington	63-0990
Elisabeth 59			
PFEIFFER, Joseph	17	Zepfenheim	63-0482
PFEIFFER, Julius	31	Meerane	64-0433
PFEIFFER, Maria C.	27	Maulbach/Hess	65-0038
PFEIFFER, Martin	31	Barlingen	65-0770
PFEIFFER, William	6	Ettlingen	66-1155
PFEIFFLER, Cathre.	22	Ellenberg	63-0990
PFEIFLE, Eva	16	Untermosbach	65-0974
PFEIFLE, John	22	Kretzingen	66-0934
PFEIFLER, John	36	Pennsylvania	64-0073
Michel 32, Frederik 20, Carl 23			
PFEIL, Barbara	20	Knillingen	66-1203
PFEIL, Georg	29	Marburg	66-0109
PFEIL, Jacob	34	Burg Gmuenden	66-1155
Lisette 28, Wilhelm 4, Heinrich 2			
PFEIL, Johannes	24	Riehelsdorf	66-1373
PFEIL, Nannette	16	Giessen	66-0704
PFEILMEIER, Steph.	21	Elchingen	66-1327
PFENDLER, Georg	28	Waben	65-0189
PFENNIG, Joseph	34	Uberlingen	64-0639
PFETZNIG, Paul	30	Rotenburg	66-0984
PFIFFER, Joh.	29	Buhlenberg	64-0593
Henriette 25, Jacob 3, Cath. 10m			
PFIFFERLING, Zebor	12	Hatzbach	66-0679
Her. 9, Mendel 7, Bertha 6			
PFINGSTAG, Cath.	24	Altenrieth	64-0593
PFINGSTEN, Ernst	21	Hameln	67-0007
PFINGSTEN, Heinr.	21	Cersen	66-1243
Charlotte 27, Caroline 24			
PFINGSTEN, Joseph	16	Coeln	65-1088
PFISTEN, Bernhard	23	Kuelzberg	63-1136
PFISTER, Anton	15	Wuertemberg	66-0679
PFISTER, Fr.	29	Ettenheim	64-0687
PFISTER, J.(f)	36	Brokenheim	64-1161
PFISTERER, Chr.	18	Oethlingen	65-1088
PFISTNER, Carl	40	Rastatt	66-0934
Friedrich 28, Wilhelmine 24			
PFITZENMEYER, Chr.	21	Rietenau	66-0576
PFLAESTERER, Phil.	24	Weinheim	64-0687
PFLAUM, Barbara	19	Emerthausen	65-0594
PFLAUM, Joh.	25	Weyhe	65-0402
PFLAUME, John	24	Erbach	66-0109
PFLIEGER, Chr. Hr.	24	Sindelfingen	65-0189
PFLOCH, Sophia	43	Anstadt	67-0599
Fried.Amalie 22			
PFLUEGER, Johannes	24	Battenhausen	64-0639
PFLUEGER, John	33	Illinois	63-0821
PFLUEGER, Johs.	37	Duenkirk	64-0138
PFLUG, Carl	14	Glauchau	66-0576
Gottl. 9			
PFLUG, Joseph	29	Buchau	66-0109
PFLUMM, Mich.	17	Hinterweiler	64-0073
PFORR, Maria	27	Haeringen	64-0363
PFORSICH, Conrad	25	Pfeffingen	64-0433
PFROMM, Anna	16	Malcomes	66-0349
PFROMMEN, Peter	19	Schenkburgfld	66-0984
Jacob 17			
PFUETZ, Bernhard	24	Veilsdorf	64-0433
PFUETZENREUTER, M.	19	Schoeneberg	64-0138
Jacobine 29, Carl 17			
PFUND, Jacob	43	California	66-0109
John 9			
PFUNDER, Nic.	32	Muehlheim	65-0007
PFUNDT, August	20	Stuttgart	66-1203
PHILIP, Theodor	18	Duerrenesch	66-0109
PHILIPP, Carl	21	Bainingen	64-0840
PHILIPP, Gerhard	28	Oberhausen	65-1024
Ludw. 27			
PHILIPP, Heinr.	32	Harra	66-1155
PHILIPP, John	24	Schlankweiler	63-1038
PHILIPP, Martin	54	Oldenburg	65-0770

NAME	AGE	RESIDENCE	YR-LIST
Helene 48, Helene 23, Marianne 14			
PHILIPPI, Johns	24	Hasseborn	65-0243
PHILIPPI, Louis	23	New York	66-0679
PHILIPPI, Marg.	40	Ruppertenrode	65-0116
PHILIPPS, Adolph	18	Bremen	66-1127
PHILIPPS, August	16	Laer	66-0576
PHILIPPS, Fd.(m)	21	Osterburken	64-0363
PHILIPS, Friedr.	39	Leer	63-0398
Heinr. 9			
PHILIPS, Joseph	18	Bremen	66-1127
PHILLIPP, Georg	39	Darmstadt	65-1088
Elisabeth 34, Georg 12, Anna Marg. 10			
Anna 7, Hermann 3			
PHILLIPP, Jos.	45	Darmstadt	65-1088
Babette 53, Pauline 19, Saul 16, Samuel 7			
Emil 6			
PIATZECK, Aug.	50	Burg	65-0950
PICHELBERGER, Phil	18	Kupferberg	66-1327
PICK, Adolphus	46	Milwaukee	63-0862
PICK, Martin	34	San Francisco	63-1178
Anna 29, Anna 5, Martin 3, Georg 2			
PICKEL, Johann	25	Neidhartshsn.	65-1030
Amalie 22, Reinhold 9m			
PICKER, Marg.	26	Iburg	65-1088
PICKER, Sophia	17	Seekirchen	66-1093
PICKERT, Elise	24	Sarstedt	66-1127
PICKERT, Heinrich	32	Niete	66-0576
PICKHARDT, Isaac E	38	Constanz	63-0693
PIEGLER, Jac.	25	Crefeld	64-0138
PIEGORSCH, Friedr.	40	Scharschof	66-0650
Augusta 28, Charlotte 58, Augusta 3			
Albert 6m			
PIEKER, Heinr.	17	Isenstedt	65-1030
PIEL, Augusta	19	Lemburg	65-0402
PIELENZ, Emil	25	Calmbach	63-1136
PIELLER, Anna	27	Tatzmansdorf	63-0953
PIENING, Bernhard	24	Oldenburg	66-0221
PIENING, Fr. Heinr	26	Sandbrink	66-0704
PIEPENBRUECK, Fr.	18	Kleinhagen	64-0840
PIEPENBURG, Minna	29	Salzgitter	64-0363
Gustav 2, baby 6m			
PIEPER, Amalie	22	Oerlinghausen	66-1327
PIEPER, Ernst	20	Rothenfeld	64-0886
PIEPER, Ferd.	25	Rondsdorf	65-0055
Heinr. 20			
PIEPER, Franz	22	Houkhausen	66-1373
Melchior 18			
PIEPER, Heinrich	20	Oldenburg	66-0668
PIEPER, Herm.	27	Niederlangen	64-1108
PIEPER, Jobst	45	Wiembeck/Boh.	63-1010
Amalia 33, August 9, Fritz 5, Wilhelm 3			
PIEPER, Leo.	34	Ragnit	65-0038
PIEPER, Ludwig	24	Minden	65-1031
PIEPMEYER, Joseph	20	Rieste	64-0593
PIEROTTO, Lisette	19	Darmstadt	65-0594
PIESBACH, Peter	25	Prussia	64-0363
Nicolaus 20			
PIESROCK, Johann	31	Neunburg	66-0083
PIETSCH, Catharine	38	Homburg	65-0004
Louise 4, Heinr. 1m			
PILANZ, Carl	32	Stornberg	64-0782
PILGER, Friedr.	30	Nalune	64-0687
PILGRAM, Johann	53	Allemberg	65-1030
Dorothea 52, Maria 24, Anna Martha 22			
PILGRIM, Wilhelm	19	Osnabrueck	66-0668
PILZ, Eduard	26	Loebenstein	66-0734
PILZ, Julie	26	Coburg	66-0934
PINDER, Heinr.	33	Asselage	67-0007
PINGER, Heinr.	22	Escholbruecke	65-0402
PININGER, Eva	21	Geisenbach	64-0073
PINSCHOWER, Bertha	28	Kempen	65-1088
Caroline 9, Simon 9			
PINSK, Hedwig	30	Breslau	64-0687
Angelica 8, Elisabeth 7, Hermann 2			
Gerry 9m			
PINTA, Anna	40	Boehmen	66-0349
Lina 6			
PIOKA, Anna	12	Buhnberg	64-0433

NAME	AGE	RESIDENCE	YR-LIST
PIPENBRINK, Friedr	17	Wolmerdingen	65-1030
PIPER, Dina	30	Langwedel	66-0984
PIPMEIER, Herm.	17	Riste	63-1085
PIPP, Peter Wilh.	29	Giessen	66-1127
Elisabeth 32, Wilh. 3, Heinrich 9m			
PIQUE, Ernst	16	Rindeln	65-1030
PIQUET, Rod.	26	France	63-1136
PIRKL, Joseph	25	Maltitz	66-0576
PIRYTZ, Carl Heinr	35	Petersburg	64-0886
PISTER, Conr.	59	Hassbach	63-0551
PISTOR, Anna Elise	25	Kerstenhausen	65-0243
PISTOR, Chr.	23	Herborn	65-0402
PISTOR, Conr.	22	Weissenburg	65-0243
PITALIK, Lukas W.	29	Schweinitz	66-0837
Katharine 40, Marie 12			
PITOL, Apollonia	26	Mayen/Pr.	65-0038
PITSCHAU, Lina	22	Miltelstenau	65-1095
PITSCHLER, Rosine	53	Reichstadt	65-0116
Amalie 19, Louis 22			
PITTERSON, Hch.	25	Eitze	63-0908
PITTOLL, Joseph	22	Maien	65-0948
Gertrude 36, Johann 7			
PITTRUFF, Friedr.	24	Schallersdorf	66-1327
PITZ, Gertrude	23	Betzisdorf	66-0412
PIVONKA, Franz	30	Boehmen	63-0862
Anna 19, Mathias 5m			
PLAAS, Wilhelm	42	Heidullendorf	66-1243
PLACK, Wilhelmine	29	Biedenkopf	66-0221
PLACKE, Christian	23	Osnabrueck	65-1030
PLACKE, Gerhard	24	Osnabrueck	65-1030
Anna Maria 25, Elise 3, Gerhard 1			
PLAFF, Cathr.	20	Herlach	63-1136
PLAG, Christian	30	Knittlingen	63-1136
Friedr. 21			
PLAG, Joh. T.	28	Emden	65-0856
PLAGERS, Hermann	32	Harburg	66-1373
PLAGGENBURG, Nicol	59	Nofries	63-1038
PLANCHAUD, Jos.	30	Marseille	64-0073
PLANK, Emil	18	Giessen	65-0189
PLANT, Friederike	22	Neustadt	64-0593
PLANTH, Hannchen	26	Willingshsn.	63-0693
PLAPPERT, Doris	20	Goslar	66-0083
PLASS, Lina	28	Erfurt	64-0639
PLASS, Wm. Louise	23	Ilse	67-0599
Marie Sop. L 23, Maria Aug. C 20			
PLATE, A.(m)	21	Bremen	64-0331
PLATE, Becka	24	Worbswede	65-0038
PLATE, Friedrich	19	Stuhr	66-0578
PLATE, H.C.	27	Paese	65-0055
PLATE, Joh. H.	46	Delmenhorst	64-1053
Meta 45, Joh. 19, Margarethe 16			
Heinr. 13, Friedr. 9, Wm. 2			
PLATE, Lueder	25	Bremen	63-0917
PLATHNER, Marie	23	Zitterode	66-0221
PLATT, Jac.	14	Kleinthal	64-0992
Daniel 13			
PLATTER, Michael	38	Bermerdingen	66-0679
PLATTNER, Ferd.	25	Gronau	64-0886
PLATTNER, Heinr. A	54	Osterode	64-0593
Bertha 19			
PLATZ, Adam	46	New York	66-0679
PLATZ, J.T.	45	Philadelphia	64-0073
PLATZ, Lisette	45	Erfurt	66-1031
PLATZ, Robert	22	Leipzig	67-0806
PLAUT, Abraham	25	Spangenburg	66-0083
PLAUT, Emma	22	Schenklengsfd	66-0934
PLAUTH, Hannchen	26	Willingshsn.	63-0693
PLEICKHARDT, Georg	23	Hessen	63-0822
PLENGE, H.	29	Nienburg	66-0413
PLENKER, Wilhelm	46	Essen	66-0221
Maria 45, Marie 22, Wilhelm 21, Johann 20			
Caroline 19, Augusta 17, Emilie 16			
Carl 9			
PLESNER, Clemens	25	Ankum	64-0214
PLETSCH, Jacob	46	Niederjosha	66-1093
PLETSCH, Reinhardt	14	Ernsthausen	65-1030
PLETSCHEL, Michel	17	Schaffhausen	66-0623
PLETTNER, Chrs.	34	Horenburg	65-0116
Otto 5			
PLETZ, Johann H.	29	Ernsthausen	66-0666
Anna Ch. 20, Margarethe 10m			
PLEU, H.	25	Angermuende	63-1178
PLITT, Justine	19	Biedenkopf	64-0687
PLOCK, George	56	Ernsthausen	66-0666
Anna Ch. 50, Anna Ch. 13, Friedrich 16			
Anna Ch. 21			
PLOCK, Heinrich	19	Wonfeld	65-0713
Dorothea 24, Margretha 14			
PLOCK, Philipp	21	Ernsthausen	65-1030
PLOEGER, Heinrich	26	Nienhagen	66-1127
PLOESS, Nicolas	26	Asch	64-0840
PLOETZ, Joh.	26	Zetendorf	66-1313
PLOG, G.(m)	56	Ankum	64-0214
Bertha 54, Emma 28, Anna 15, H.(m) 30			
Catherina 57			
PLUEMER, Augusta	21	Cassel	63-0953
PLUEMER, Franz	40	Dissen	66-1128
Wilhelmine 30, Wilhelmine 18, Fritz 7			
Elise 5, Louise 9m			
PLUEMER, Heinrich	58	Dissen	66-1128
Elise 50			
PLUESCH, Friedr.	24	Vechte	66-0984
PLUMDORF, H.(m)	26	Nopke	64-0495
PLUMP, Diedrich	15	Ritterhude	66-1327
PLUMP, Gg.	22	Kettelfingen	64-0170
PLUMP, Hermann	24	Ewers	63-0908
POBANZ, David	43	Preussen	63-0398
Louise 38, Friedr. 21, Marie 18			
Augusta 4			
POBE, Minna	30	Berlin	63-1136
Wilhelmine 27			
PODER, Josepha	21	Boehmen	63-1218
PODESTA, Pasquale	25	Italien	63-0990
Bartolomeo 24			
POEHL, Louise	23	Siefershausen	66-0650
POEHLER, Friedr.	29	Leresen	64-0639
POEHLER, Heinr.	32	Lage	64-0840
POEHLER, Sabine	24	Wiescheid	66-1093
POEL, v.d. Sim.	27	Arnheim	66-0734
POELER, Georg	58	New York	63-0917
POEPKE, Augusta	19	Moerenberg	66-0679
POERCHER, August	24	Schweinsberg	64-0840
Catharine 20			
POERTNER, Chris.	38	St. Louis	63-0752
POERTNER, Otto	19	Walldorf	67-0007
POERTNER, Robert	26	Alexandria	63-0862
Felixine 19			
POESCHEL, Joh.	18	Wuestritz	64-0665
POESNECKER, J.	26	Hoff	65-1024
POESTNER, Franz	59	Schildesche	63-0990
POETTCHER, Sophie	58	Linden	63-0752
Chris. 26			
POETTLER, Friedr.	34	Braunschweig	64-0427
POETZSCH, Leopold	25	Dresden	65-0189
POGGEMANN, John	30	Salzbergen	63-1178
Marie 28, John 2m			
POGGEMANN, Wilhelm	33	Handorf	66-0576
POGGEMUELLER, Anna	13	Alsen	65-0898
POGGEMUELLER, Lse.	51	Alsen	65-0898
POGGENBURG, Chr.	20	Bremen	64-0886
POGGENBURG, Friedr	34	Bremen	63-0244
POGGENBURG, Marie	30	Bremen	63-0953
Cath. 7, twins 7m			
POGGENMEYER, H.W.	22	Buer	66-0934
POHL, E.	21	Wahn	63-1003
POHLE, Eduard	33	Magdeburg	65-0865
Marie 30, Gustav 4, Robert 1			
POHLE, Joh. Ph.	39	Erfurt	65-0038
POHLIG, Moritz	17	Bremke	23-0865
POHLMANN, C.	24	Goldkronach	64-0992
POHLMANN, Ignatz	33	Neustadt	63-1178
Anna 27			
POHLMANN, Joh.	35	Asch	64-0495
Johanna 35, Christ. 6, Adolph 7, Emma 2			
POHLMANN, John	28	Malbergen	64-0343
POHLMEYER, Anton	25	Reuhenberg	66-1327

NAME	AGE	RESIDENCE	YR-LIST
POHLMEYER, Louise	21	Brockum	65-1024
POHN, Lotte	58	Potsdam	66-1243
POIESZ, Antonia	18	Ibbenbuehren	65-0898
POIESZ, Wilhelm	24	Ibbenbueren	65-0898
POLACZIA, Andreas	31	Silcze	64-0433
POLANSKY, Joseph	27	Boehmen	66-0349
POLASCHEK, Henry	17	Karschau	63-0551
POLCHAR, Wilhelm	30	Hannover	64-1022
POLDARID, Heinr.	23	Osterwiehe	64-1022
POLEMANN, Alex	34	Braunschweig	64-0886
POLENSKE, Ludw.	27	Prokenhauland	66-0650
POLENY, Theodor	29	Breslau	63-1010
POLH, Franz	25	Bessungen	66-0346
POLHAUS, Auguste	30	New York	63-0821
Mathilde 5, Emmy 3			
POLKERTS, Zieden	45	Lintermarsch	67-0007
Anna 54, Heinrich 7, Fritz 6, Louis 3			
POLLACK, Nathan	24	Weener	64-0593
POLLACK, Wenzel	67	Boehmen	64-0427
Barbara 61, Maria 23			
POLLAF, Simon	19	Weirich	66-0984
POLLAK, Joseph	20	Prag	67-0007
POLLAK, Leopold	45	New York	66-0109
POLLATSCHECK, Magd	38	Wien	67-0007
Magdalene 7, Juliane 5, Bernhard 3			
Wilhelm 9m			
POLLATSCHEK, Jac.	24	Wien	63-0862
POLLATSCK, Ad.	22	Tallgan	64-0782
POLLATZ, Wm.	30	Oderberg	64-0593
POLLER, Louise	23	Southhampton	63-0821
POLLKLOESENER, Ann	20	Varensell	66-1203
Catharina 20, Eberhared 7			
POLLMANN, Anna M.	44	Ibbenbuehren	65-0898
Heinr. Jos. 23, Bernhard 14, Aug. 10			
POLLMANN, Fritz	28	Billinghausen	66-1093
Emilie 22			
POLLMANN, Heinrich	40	Rees	66-0934
POLLMANN, Philipp	19	Varensell	66-1203
Caspar 16			
POLSTER, Christine	43	Bruetzfeld	66-0412
POLY, Anton	32	Koenigswart	64-0427
POLZER, Francis	49	Tropplowitz	63-0482
POLZIN, Mathias	24	Bromberg	64-0432
POMMERICH, Wm.	27	Rheinbach	64-1053
POMMERING, Carl	30	Wolsk	66-0412
Louise 31, Dorothea 58			
POMPLUM, Friedrich	46	Neuendorf	66-0666
Henriette 38, Wilhelm 12, Hermine 7			
Berta 6, Maria 1			
PONE, Wilh.	27	Marburg	66-1243
PONNAZ, Friedr.	18	Braunschweig	63-0821
PONNITZ, J.L.	18	Frankenhausen	65-0898
PONS, M.(m)	26	France	64-0170
PONTEKOCK, Anton	36	Loquard	65-1030
Otje 34, boy 7, Berend 5, Everdine 6m			
POOS, Henry	42	Haevern	63-0821
Louise 39, Caroline Mar 4, Hermann 2			
Ernst 6m			
POOZ, Heinrich	17	Messlingen	66-0734
POPE, Johann	29	New York	66-0934
POPITZ, Louis	36	Dessau	63-0821
POPOWITSCH, Marcus	32	Maline/Aust.	66-0412
POPP, Andreas	60	Welzdorf	64-0433
Theresia 8, Regina 24, Maria 19			
Caroline 16			
POPP, Betine	27	Zettlitz	66-0666
POPP, Elisabeth	21	Hohenberg	64-0433
POPP, Friedrich	15	Haesselrieth	64-0433
POPP, Margarethe	28	Burgklesan	66-1373
POPPE, Adolf	27	Zeitz	66-0576
POPPE, Anna	24	Linteln	66-0934
POPPE, August	19	Osnabrueck	63-0917
POPPE, Betty	24	Bremen	66-0578
POPPE, Emil	20	Bremen	64-0214
POPPE, Ernst	21	Wildehausen	64-0214
POPPE, Friedr.	49	Artern	65-0151
POPPE, Friedrich	23	Melle	67-0007
POPPE, Heinrich	39	Cassel	65-1095
POPPE, Joh. Casp.	26	Muenchen	67-0599
POPPE, Joh. Henr.	35	Lilienthal	63-1178
POPPE, Mangels	34	Bremen	66-0412
POPPE, Nicolaus	22	Oldenburg	66-0668
POPPENHUSEN, C.	45	New York	63-1136
POPPENHUSEN, C.	46	New York	64-0427
Marie 33, Bernhard 7, August 9m, wife 39			
Georg 3, Frd. 2			
POPPER, Cath.	52	Tereschau	64-0427
Christine 32, Adolph 8			
POPPER, Stefan	18	Prag	66-1243
POPPER, Wilhelm	58	Diepholz	64-1022
POPPINGA, Jacob G.	44	Hinte	66-0412
Amalia 44, Geertje 16, Johann 14			
Ettje 13, Tertje 5, Gerd. 3			
POPPLER, Marie	22	Aulendiebach	64-0427
PORCHE, Joh.	19	Westhofen	66-1243
PORGES, Henry	20	Boehmen	63-0862
PORGES, Julius	25	Prag	63-1038
PORSCHNER, Friedr.	28	Buhlendorf	64-0593
PORTH, Carl	19	Pappewerder	66-0650
PORTH, Ernestine	26	Wichmansdorf	66-1127
PORTH, Gottfr.	48	Papenwerder	66-0650
Leonore 49, Wilh. 16, Wilhelmine 13			
PORTMANN, Aug.	25	Minden	65-1031
Angel. 50, Henriette 15, Wilhelmine 9			
PORTMANN, Maria	32	Oldenburg	64-0920
Lena 22			
PORTNER, Henrich	19	Hannover	66-0984
PORTUETSCH, Julian	18	Ebermannstadt	66-0412
PORUBSKY, Emil	21	Wien	63-0953
POSCH, Joh.	29	Boehmen	66-0109
Rosalia 24, Anna 11m			
POSLUSCHNI, Eber.	27	Maltitz	66-0576
POSNAUCKI, Juda	26	Lubrance	64-0639
POSSEL, Claus	27	New York	64-0363
POSSELS, Joh.	23	Willstedt	65-0402
POST, Albert	18	Hessia	66-0679
POST, H.G.	37	Milwaukee	63-1178
POST, Ludwig	29	Ostfriesland	66-0577
Trientje 30, Friedr.F. 15, Johann 10m			
POST, v. A.M.	21	Bremen	65-1024
POTEN, A.H.	40	Washington	64-0687
POTHOFF, Henry	20	Dannesberg	64-0343
POTT, Francisca	24	Borwalz	65-0594
POTT, Louis	27	Eschwede	64-1206
POTT, Otto	23	Linde	66-1327
POTTENBORN, C.(m)	20	Vackenrod	64-0023
POTTHART, August	26	Osterhagen	67-0007
POTTKAMPER, Ewald	19	Froendenberg	66-1313
POTTMANN, G.G.	42	Stuttgart	64-1206
POUR, Johann	23	Zubirow	66-0734
POWELLSCHOCK, Jos.	29	Staren	66-0578
Marianne 28, Andreas 4, Anna 11m			
POWICHILL, Moritz	26	Asch	66-0412
POWUNSKY, Barbara	19	Schotta	66-1131
PRACHT, Th. w.	16	Herborn	65-1031
PRACK, Eva	54	Buechenau	64-0495
Cathr. 19, Brhd. 19			
PRAEGER, Sophie	22	Waldsbach	66-0734
PRAEMINGER, Georg	24	Lenkerstetten	66-1155
PRAETORIN, Hermann	38	Schotten	66-1031
PRAETORIUS, Otto	30	Tostedt	63-0097
PRAETZ, Carl Conr.	36	Soehne	67-0007
PRAGER, D.L.	25	Hamberg	64-0687
PRAGER, Herm.	21	Ronneburg	65-0898
PRAGER, Wilhelmine	27	Thairnbach	64-0687
PRAIKSCHATIS, L.	27	Muehlheim	63-0296
PRALLE, Lina	24	Bremen	65-1024
PRANGER, Anton	23	Carmen	64-0840
PRANGER, Lambert	46	Kl. Stavern	64-0886
PRANKARD, (m)	30	Havre	65-0007
PRATSCHNER, Johann	36	Gersdorf	66-0346
Rosalia 36, Anna 7, Maria 2			
PRAU, Wenzel	39	Muenchen	67-0806
PRAUTWEIN, Barbara	14	Heidesheim	65-0974
PRAZAK, Josepha	39	Lutz	66-1155
Elisabeth 14, Josefa 9, Anna 66			

NAME	AGE	RESIDENCE	YR-LIST
PRECHT, Daniel	25	Redwin	67-0007
PRECHT, Emma	48	Bremen	63-0482
Willy 14			
PRECHT, H.	26	Carlsbaum	63-1003
PRECHT, H. (m)	22	Bothel	64-0331
PRECHT, Heinr.	22	Verden	66-1373
PRECHT, Sophie	15	Schlusselburg	65-0950
PRECKEL, Johanna	20	Mainz	66-0734
PREGER, Wilhelm	23	Napen	66-1031
PREHL, Heinr.	28	Rudersberg	67-0007
PREIS, Rosalie	20	Ottersberg	64-0992
PREISE, Wilh.	52	Kohlfeld	66-1243
Catharine 26			
PREISLE, Frank	30	St. Louis	63-0821
PREISS, Ferd.	35	Zwickau	64-0073
PRELL, E.(m)	23	Boehmen	64-0495
PRENZEL, Conrad	31	Wabern	64-0739
PRESS, Adam	25	Gross Aspach	64-0138
Jacob 24, Christine 18			
PRESSEN, Margareth	24	Baden	66-0679
PRESSER, Elisab.	20	Rodenbach/Bav	65-0038
PRESSER, Juliane	18	Bodenbach	66-0679
PRESSLER, Louise	24	Hundelshausen	66-0668
PRESUMLEH, Ph.	14	Reef	64-0170
PRETSCH, heinr.	19	Darmstadt	64-0840
PRETTIG, Michael	25	Neustadt	66-0704
PRETZFELD, M.(m)	40	Burgkunstadt	64-0331
Johanna 21			
PREUSSE, Dan.	21	Nordheim	64-0138
PREX, Joh.	35	Wehrheim	64-0639
PREY, Mathias	23	Aixheim	67-0007
PRIBE, Christoph	31	Schneidemuehl	65-0950
PRIECK, Louise	35	Alsbach	64-1161
PRIEM, Hilke	31	Ihrhove	65-0243
PRIEMEYER, Heinr.	17	Oppenwehe	64-0170
PRIGGE, Catharine	18	Huettendorf	65-0898
PRIGGE, Joh. Heinr	17	Osterode	65-0898
PRIGGE, Louis	16	Appensen	66-0221
PRIGGER, Martin	28	Brooklyn	66-0934
Helene 27, Anna 1			
PRILL, Wilhelm	39	Liszkowke	66-0469
Caroline 44			
PRILLAR, Franz	30	Brunowo	64-0456
PRILLER, James	59	Hitzelrode	63-1218
Sophie 58			
PRILLWITZ, Carl Th	38	Strussow	63-0006
Augusta 33, Bertha 14, Augusta 13			
Minna 11, Eduard 9, Mathilde 7			
Franzisca 3			
PRIMAVESI, Hugo	26	Gravenhorst	64-0886
PRINER, John	26	Boehmen	63-1218
PRINKE, Joh. H.	17	Hellerwestery	64-0023
PRINS, Friedr.	23	Kirchheim	64-0363
PRINZ, Abraham	42	Jelet	64-0840
Rosa 30, Bernhard 4, Fanny 9m			
PRINZ, Catharina	40	Warzenbach	64-1053
Catharina 7m			
PRINZ, Theo.	27	Breslau	65-0055
PRINZ, Wilhelm	32	Rossbach	64-1053
Charlotte 32, Wilhelm 6, Caroline 4			
Heinrich 5m			
PRINZEL, Johann	41	Kurhessen	66-0623
PRIOR, Carl G.	21	West.Oldendrf	65-1088
PRITSCH, Carl	30	Hehlen	64-0938
PROBST, Anna Barb.	28	Breitenau	67-0599
Anna Rosine 38, Rosine Marg. 14			
PROBST, Anton	25	Uechtingen	64-0073
PROBST, Caroline	37	Bockenems	64-0363
PROBST, Georg	24	Lamspringe	65-0898
PROCHASKA, Elisab.	24	Gang	66-1373
PROCHASKA, Francis	43	Kuttenberg	64-0593
PROCHASKA, Maria	25	Liebentig	66-0576
PROCHASKA, Maria	22	Boehmen	64-0427
Emilie 3m			
PROCHASKA, Wensel	32	Opocwitz	66-1131
Veronica 33, Heinrich 9, Aloisa 6			
Maria 9m			
PROCHASKA, Wenzel	35	Boehmen	63-0398

NAME	AGE	RESIDENCE	YR-LIST
PROCHAZKA, Franz	52	Boehmen	63-1178
PROCHNOW, August	34	Corling	66-1248
Caroline 28, Julius 2, Bertha 5m, Anna 58			
PROEHL, Fr.A.	22	Helmdorf	65-0898
PROEHLE, Heinrich	19	Nuernberg	66-0679
PROEL, H.	19	Bonenfurt	64-0782
PROELIL, Joh. Hch.	26	Dueshorn	64-0456
PROEPFKE, Joh. Fr.	65	Ueckermark	66-1313
Carl 25			
PROESSEL, Louise	21	Bevern	63-0482
PROESSLER, Caspar	59	Ulrichstein	63-0990
Eliza 54			
PROHASKA, Maria	36	Kuttenberg/Bo	64-0920
Antonia 4, Emilie 10m			
PROKATE, D. Chr.	18	Uchte	64-0363
PROKOP, Franz	35	Bohemia	66-0469
Maria 30, Franz 8, Maria 4			
PROKOPP, Wenzel	38	Prodozow	66-0734
Anna 29, Francisca 9, Joseph 7, Johann 3			
Wenzel 11m			
PROMMEL, Caroline	22	Sindelfingen	66-1203
PRONOLD, Georg	44	Tiefenbach	64-0427
Anna 40, Anna Marie 15, Barbara 11			
Siegm. 7, Georg 6, Bernh. 4, baby 6m			
PROPHETEN, Heinr.	24	Mossbach	65-1031
PROPPER, Mich.	21	Prag	65-0402
PROSCHAK, Joseph	46	Boehmen	64-0427
Anna 41, Joh. 16, Maria 14, Franz 7			
Geo 6, Anna Cath. 5, Cath. 4			
PROSCHEL, Julius	31	Czarnikau	64-0886
PROSCHER, Charles	29	New York	63-0244
PROSDORFF, Josep'e	32	Goessaitz	64-0593
Bertha 7			
PROSEK, Albertina	22	Boehmen	64-0427
PROSS, Jac. Fr.	42	Calmbach	64-0214
Dorothea 30, Christine 11, Wilhelm 3			
Louise 3, Jacob 1			
PROT, de Benjamin		Niemoschaus	66-0984
PROTHE, Anna	18	Lemvoerde	66-1373
PROTRASCHKI, Wilh.	24	Pohlatz	66-1128
PROTT, Carl	21	Neuhaus	64-0886
PROTZ, Martin	17	New York	63-0990
PROTZIG, Fr. Heinr	33	Waldsachsen	64-0593
Heinr. 3			
PROTZMANN, Maria	7	Wittjenborn	64-0456
PROX, Charles	33	Wellingholzh.	64-0687
Elise 31			
PRUBE, Friedr.	30	Weidenhausen	63-1218
PRUESCH, Christ.	24	Laxstedt	65-0116
PRUNER, Eduard	43	Gratz	67-0992
PRUSER, Carl	26	Achim	66-0934
PRUSING, Daniel	25	Linglis	64-0170
PSOTTA, Paul	40	Bohemia	64-0073
PUCK, Wm.	24	Oppendorf	64-0138
PUDENZ, Carl	17	Erdhausen	64-0639
Joseph 32, Regina 24			
PUDER, Cath.	52	Cassel	64-1053
Elisabeth 26			
PUETTER, C.	24	Dedesdorf	63-1085
PUETZ, William	23	Muehlheim	63-0990
PUFAHL, Christ. C.	30	Moschitz	66-0578
Wilhelmine 29, Wilhelm 3, Emilie 3m			
PUFE, Chas.	33	Siebis	63-0917
PUFF, Johann	19	Themar	64-0886
PUFF, Peter	49	Hessberg	64-0495
Marg. 49			
PUGGE, Emil	14	Giessen	66-0679
PUHL, Bernhard	27	Preussen	63-0990
PUHLMANN, Wilhelm	19	Riste	66-1203
PUHN, Conrad	30	Culmbach	65-0402
PUKROP, Marianne	3	Schlandorf	64-0433
PULL, G.H.	18	Birichum	64-0495
PULLITZ, Wilhelm	28	Ohlendorf	66-0623
PULS, Jan B.	25	Holstein	65-1024
PULVERMACHER, Rosa	29	Dyrenfurth	66-1031
PUMP, Gesche	18	Bardert	66-1248
PUND, Beta	58	Ritterhude	65-1189
Johann 19			

NAME	AGE	RESIDENCE	YR-LIST
PUNDSACK, Heinr.	30	Geiste	64-0687
PUNDT, Aug.	32	Lingen	64-0992
Elisab. 27, Anna 4, Bernhard 10m			
PUNDT, Joh.	24	Thedinghausen	65-0189
PUNTMANN, F.W.(m)	41	West Cappeln	64-0331
Johanna 21			
PUPELMANN, Marie	28	Gross. Lessen	64-0023
PUPP, Ernst	24	Sulz	66-1031
PURFUERST, Anna	17	Dresden	63-0296
PURFUERST, Ida	22	Neustadt	63-0990
PURK, Joh. Gerh.	25	Abeldorn	65-1030
Maria G. 22			
PURRNECKER, Wm.	29	Wunsiedel	64-0938
Verona 30			
PURRNEKEN, Joh.	22	Sparnecke	64-0938
PUSCH, Georg	18	Echzell	65-1031
PUXONKA, Franz	27	Boehmen	66-0349
QUACK, E.	30	Toledo	64-0593
QUADE, Carl Fr.	19	Selchow	67-0795
QUADE, Jul.	16	Wechold	64-0687
QUADE, Wilh.	23	Ositha	63-0482
QUANDT, Andr.	18	Wetzlar	63-0296
QUANTE, Elisabeth	25	Obern Tudorf	64-0739
QUANTZ, Ant.	40	Baltimore	63-0551
QUANZ, Heinr.	31	Schlottau	64-1022
QUAPPE, Augusta	18	Posen	64-0427
QUATHAMER, Jans	21	Wiesens	66-1128
QUECKBORN, Charltt	67	Atzenhain	65-0116
Catharine 33			
QUELL, Peter	19	Muehldorf	66-1243
QUELLE, Heinrich	19	Wohlsbuttel	66-1093
QUENTIN, Joh. Wilh	28	Hannover	66-0469
QUETIN, Henriette	35	Covington	64-0073
Adolph 12, George 9, Marie 5, Marion 2			
QUIDDE, Gunther	35	Braunschweig	63-1010
QUINNSTEDT, Fr'dke	25	Danzig	66-1155
QUINTER, Longinus	37	Muenster	63-0482
QUINTING, Joseph	24	Niesen	63-1136
QUINTKOWSKY, Joh.	25	Selchow	67-0795
QUINZMEYER, Anton	25	Detmold	65-0594
RAAB, Adam	20	Asch	65-0898
RAAB, Albert	14	Frankfurt/M	64-0782
RAAB, Anna	21	Ungarstein	64-0782
RAAB, Dan.	26	Petersaurach	66-1313
RAAB, Heinr.	29	Muenster	64-1053
RAAB, Maria	21	Waismar	64-0782
RAABE, Carl	21	Mardorf	66-1243
RAABE, Friederike	24	Minden	65-0007
RAACKE, Victor	24	Salzkotten	66-0109
RAASCH, Gottlieb	43	Treptow	66-0668
Friederike 44, Auguste 14, Friederike 5			
Wilhelmine 3, Martin 12			
RAASKE, Ferd.	30	St. Louis	63-0168
RABACH, Wenzel	51	Boehmen	63-1136
Cath 36, Wenzel 8			
RABAND, Edmund	36	Worbis	66-0734
Anna 32, Marie 2			
RABATH, Florentine	25	Rawolesko	66-0413
RABBE, Veit	25	Chottischau	65-0713
Catharine 27			
RABBER, Cornelius	23	Oldenburg	66-0221
RABE, Carl	30	Hannover	66-0934
RABE, Carl	30	Hannover	66-0934
RABE, Cathar.	60	Hessen	66-0934
Heinr. 33, Louise 28, Gretchen 36			
Elisabeth 7, Elisabeth 26, Sophie 20			
Margarethe 5, Anna 3m			
RABE, Christine	25	Schleswig	66-1031
RABE, Ferdinand	28	Steinfeld	65-0948
RABE, Heinr.	16	Schierholz	64-1053
RABE, Johann	21	Emden	63-0614
RABE, Julius	34	New York	64-0687
Ernestine 26			
RABE, Sophie	19	Bergen	66-0984
RABENAU, Philipp	24	Darmstadt	64-0992
RABENBERG, Gerhard	22	Benningsfehn	64-0639
RABENBERG, Joh. G.	48	Benningafehn	65-0189
Ecke 46, Thete 20, Anka 16, Stephan 14			

NAME	AGE	RESIDENCE	YR-LIST
Rheinder 11, Heinr. 7			
RABENG, Wilh.		Kohlenfeld	66-1243
RABENSTEIN, Marg.	21	Herzberg	64-0593
RABIG, Christiane	60	Langensalz	64-0456
RACH, Wilh.	41	Kleisch	66-1243
Maria 43, Minna 20, Aug. 12			
Friederike 12, Caroline 8, Marie 8			
Ernestine 6			
RACHE, Hermann	24	Brockum	65-1024
RACHEL, Anna	60	Muenster	64-0886
RACHEL, M.	24	London	64-0593
RACHMEYER, C.(m)	27	Oestringen	64-0495
RACK, Georg	50	Hessen	66-0576
Regine 47, Georg 44, Wilhelm 9, Georg 8			
RACKEL, Cajetan	39	Bianz	64-1108
RADE, Wenzel	21	Schauerslau	64-0920
RADEHOFF, Marie	66	Gr.Poisdorf	64-0593
RADEKE, Friedrich	56	Dagestaff	65-0713
Johann 27, Friederike 19, Christine 55			
RADELOFF, Jacob	30	Gr. Bisdorf	64-0593
Christine 27, Johann 28			
RADEMACHER, Johann	23	Estorf	66-0469
Johann 19			
RADEMACHER, Nanke	28	Grethausen	66-0623
Sophie 25			
RADEMACHER, Wilh.	30	Preussen	63-1136
Wilhelm 22			
RADIMERSKY, John	30	Boehemen	63-0917
Katha. 26			
RADKE, Martin	45	Bromberg	64-0456
Ernestine W. 38, Emilie 19, August 14			
Wilhelm 9, Ottilie 6, Adolph 5, Pauline 1			
Friederike 1			
RADLOFF, W.(m)	25	Hannover	64-0331
RADONITZ, v. B.	30	Belgard	63-1136
RADOWITSCH, Nicol.	25	Welsberg	65-0948
RADTKE, Rudolf	22	Samorzin	65-0950
RADWITZKY, Franzka	26	Wien	63-0917
RAEBEL, Francis	29	New York	66-0109
RAEDER, Louis	26	France	63-1085
Julie 18			
RAEDLEIN, Nicolaus	64	Ebern	63-0693
RAEMMER, Anna	22	Neustadt/m	67-0795
RAESCH, Nicolaus	17	Ritzebuettel	67-0599
RAETTIG, Carl	27	Berlin	66-1203
RAEUBER, Catharine	20	Grafenberg	66-0147
RAEUSCHER, Johanna	49	Mittelsemen	65-0865
Gertrude 48, Elisabeth 20, Heinrich 16			
RAEVERMANN, August	20	Rieste	66-1131
RAFF, Wilhelm	20	Heiligenzell	66-1327
RAFFEIN, Camilla	9	Camenz	66-1131
RAGNE, v. Louis	26	Olde	64-1108
RAGNET, Philipp	23	Landstuhl	64-1108
RAHE, Wilhelm	64	Markendorf	64-0433
Maria 26			
RAHM, Adam	51	Boehmen	63-0917
Margarethe 51, Eva 18, John 15			
RAHN, Carl August	26	Pommern	66-0469
Friederike 27			
RAHN, Johanne	26	Coblenz	66-0413
Pauline 27			
RAHRS, Harm	21	Forlitz	66-0147
RAIN, Margareth	19	Goennern	66-0221
RAINER, Fr.	22	Oestereich	66-0934
RAISCH, Magd.	30	Hannover	65-1024
Anna 5, Louise 11m			
RAISMAIER, Fried.	25	Salzdettfurt	66-1243
RAITH, Jacob	32	Ndr.Reichbach	65-0055
RAITH, Wilhelm	25	Weissweil	66-0412
RAITHEL, Jacob	28	Aschenberg	65-0948
Johann 31			
RAKE, Johanna	24	Versmold	65-0974
RALIESS, Aug.	32	Preussen	63-0398
Cath. 25, Christiana 11, Friedr. 57			
RALL, Elisabeth	42	Neukirch	63-0015
Albertine 14, John N. 12, Simon 9			
Elisabeth 5, Mary 3			
RAMELKAMP, Gustav	18	Paderborn	66-1093

NAME	AGE	RESIDENCE	YR-LIST
RAMELLI, Pierre	36	Italy	63-1136
RAMKE, Herrmann	22	Biene	65-1095
RAMMENSTEIN, Amaly	23	Ettingen	64-0687
RAMPE, Albert	19	Liegenhagen	66-0679
RANDEGGEN, Aug.	14	Paris	65-0402
RANDEGGER, Agathe	21	Boettingen	66-0147
RANGE, Louise	31	Thalister	64-0593
RANKE, Heinr.	16	Dielingen	64-0920
RANKE, Heinrich	26	New York	66-0934
RANKE, Henry	22	New York	63-0821
RANKER, Ernst	30	Apolda	64-0138
RANSCHOLB, Valent.	17	Wachenheim	65-1095
RANSICK, Herman	16	Riemsloh	65-0402
RANSTEIN, Fr.	29	Horste	64-0073
Cath. 20			
RANT, George	29	Schoenau	63-1178
Sophie 41			
RANTZAU, Theod.	21	Voehrum	63-0752
RANTZE, Joh. H.	32	Groenloh	65-0189
RAPHAELSOHN, Paul.	24	Herford	66-0576
RAPIERA, Franz	28	Preussen	66-0083
Juliane 27, Theresia 5, Catharine 1			
RAPLE, Marie	17	Besenfeld	63-1178
RAPP, Carl	24	Hobitzheim	64-1108
RAPP, Carl Wm.	19	Schieferstadt	65-0116
RAPP, Conrad	32	Dissen	64-1053
RAPP, Emil S.	28	Berlin	64-0023
RAPP, Jacob	19	Wuestenrod	66-0576
RAPP, Johann	17	Darmstadt	66-0576
RAPP, Magdalena	30	Sigmaringen	66-0221
Gustav 4			
RAPPAFORT, Heinr.	26	Fuerth	66-0576
RAPPE, Christian	34	Nussdorf	63-0693
Anne Mary 43, Catharine 9, Christian 2			
RAPPENECKER, Carl	23	Kuhbach	64-0363
RARUM, Julie	22	Werdum	66-0413
RASCH, Augusta	24	Leipzig	66-1327
Therese 3			
RASCH, Christine	30	Wulsdorf	66-1093
RASCH, Jacob	20	Holzkerlingen	65-0189
RASCH, Johann	23	Baden	66-0734
RASCH, O.	26	Volldorf	65-1189
RASCHE, Eduard	28	Damme	64-0214
RASCHEN, H.(f)	23	Zwischenohn	64-0593
RASCHKE, Anna	21	New York	63-0821
RASEMEIER, H.	18	Bavaria	63-1003
RASMUSSEN, Jens A.	28	Aalburg	66-0666
RASP, Jac.	57	Epprath	64-0495
RASSENACK, Emilie	18	Bismark	65-1030
RASSMANN, Fr. Aug.	24	Ernsthafen	64-0886
Johannes 3			
RASTEDE, J.W.	29	Neuende	64-0214
Cath. 26, Maria Magd. 4, Albert H. 1			
RATAZZI, Battista	28	Mailand	66-0679
RATERMANN, Herm.	20	Alfhausen	65-0189
RATH, Barbara	25		64-0331
RATH, C.F.E.(m)	16	Gefell	64-0331
Johanna 21			
RATH, Carl	14	Stolzenau	67-0600
RATH, G.(m)	27	Gefelden	64-0331
RATH, J.H.(m)	63	Wildbad	64-0495
H.(f) 43, W.(f) 15, R.(f) 6, P.(f) 7			
RATH, Marie	20	Schwickarshsn	64-0687
Dorothea 19			
RATHGEBER, Maria	29	Oppelsheim	65-0594
Adolph 23, Johanna 26, Friedr. 24			
Carl 21, Wilhelm 4			
RATHJEN, Bernhard	50	Blumenthal	67-0007
RATHJEN, H.	26	New York	63-1085
RATHJEN, Hch.	31	Hammstedt	64-1022
Cath. 26, Johann 3, Hch. 6m			
RATHLIN, Georg	33	Unterfranken	66-0734
Margarethe 23, Nicolaus 7			
RATHMANN, Friedr.	30	Okel	64-0639
RATHS, Herm.	32	Kettwich	64-0992
RATHSAIN, Friedr.	25	Truchlingen	65-0594
RATJE, Wm.	22	Wagenfeld	64-0495
RATJEN, Elise	27	Deedesdorf	64-0495

NAME	AGE	RESIDENCE	YR-LIST
Anna 3, Anna 4m			
RATTELMANN, Sophia	20	Rahden	65-1088
RATTENBERGER, Isak	14	Waldorf	63-0917
RATZ, Gustav	23	Friedrichstal	64-0214
Carl 25			
RAU, Carl	20	Wieseck	66-0109
RAU, Catharine	19	Mittelsemen	65-0865
RAU, Charles	18	Giessen	64-0343
RAU, Gottl.	24	Backnang	65-0116
RAU, Heinr.	56	Colbach	64-1108
Dorothe 52, Margaretha 24, Friedrich 22			
Maria 20, Peter 18, Heinrich 7			
RAU, Heinrich	17	Wiessek	67-0007
RAU, Heinrich	56	Bisses	67-0007
Charlotte 24			
RAU, Jacob	28	Tuebingen	66-0704
RAU, Jette	20	Flaunloch	65-1030
RAU, Louise	28	Calmbach	66-1373
Jacob 33			
RAU, Margarethe	22	Cohnweiler	66-1093
RAU, Thomas	29	Simmern	64-0214
RAUBENHEIMER, Henr	32	Friedbourg	66-0984
RAUBITSCHEK, Edu'd	23	Wien	65-1095
RAUCH, Christ	30	Madamuehle	64-0840
RAUCH, Friedr. A	27	Alterstadt	65-0594
RAUCH, Henriette	34	Gillersdorf	66-0650
RAUCH, Margarethe	14	Bearden	64-0687
RAUCHER, Maria	37	Leipzig	63-0350
Anna 12, Emma 9, Frances 6m			
RAUCHHOLZ, Emma	14	Siegen	66-0984
RAUCHHOLZ, Marie	39	Siegen	64-0938
RAUCHLE, Wilhelm	19	Heilbronn	66-1155
RAUCK, Christ	20	Langsfeld	66-1243
RAUFHER, Raimund	26	Untergrombach	66-1155
RAUFT, Marie	24	Buchenau	64-1206
RAUH, Barbara	18	Doebschen	65-0713
RAUH, Jacob	27	Huelben	65-1095
RAUH, Louise	19	Hessen	63-0822
RAUHE, Heinrich	27	Kirchdorf	66-0650
RAUHEN, H.	26	New York	63-1136
RAULBACH, G.	41	New York	66-0679
RAULF, Wilh.	28	Gr. Freeden	66-0704
RAUNEGGER, Andreas	23	Dorfmertingen	66-1373
RAUPER, Wolfgang	30	Franken	63-0822
RAUPES, Ernst	22	Baden	66-0734
RAUSCH, Amalie	23	Carlhafen	64-0739
RAUSCH, Anna	41	Dudelsdorf	66-1327
Josephine 16			
RAUSCH, Carl	23	Eisenach	66-0221
RAUSCH, Jacob	26	Oldenburg	66-0109
RAUSCH, Joh. Carl	25	Bavaria	66-0577
Catharine 26, Johann 3			
RAUSCH, Jos.	23	Eichenheim	65-0950
RAUSCH, Leonhardt	30	Karlshafen	63-1010
RAUSCH, Nicolaus	40	Pfeddersheim	66-0469
Maria 38, Nicolaus 15, Johann 16			
David 10, Catharina 8, Conrad 7			
Friedr. 6, Carl 5, Jacob 2			
RAUSCH, Otto	24	Texas	63-1178
RAUSCH, Wilhelm	21	Gornstein	66-0109
RAUSCHEN, C.	30	Rennerod	65-0007
RAUSCHENBACH, Elis	24	Auen	63-1178
RAUSCHENBERG, Hil.	36	Malges	64-0687
Anna Marie 29, Joh. Adam 7, Christian 5			
Hilarius 3			
RAUSCHENBUSCH,	23	Nordhausen	63-0614
RAUSCHER, Anna	23	Brinkum	66-0576
Augusta 16			
RAUSCHER, Anton	20	Schoenfeld	66-1128
RAUSCHER, Heinr.	18	Oberturkheim	66-0984
RAUSCHER, Joseph	24	Metzingen	66-1327
RAUSCHER, Ma.(f)	33	New York	64-0495
RAUSENBERGER, Ja's	56	Philadelphia	63-0862
RAUSS, Anna M.	32	Wolfenhausen	63-0350
Christine 30, Magdalene 27			
RAUTENBERG, Elise	42	Bremen	64-0433
Carl 8			
RAUTER, Fr.	23	Niessen	63-0990

NAME	AGE	RESIDENCE	YR-LIST
RAUTH, Anna	25	New York	63-0398
RAUX, August	22	Friedrichstal	65-0243
RAVE, Ludwig	22	Ramsdorf	66-1203
RAVE, N.	49	Bueude	66-0349
Mathilde 1, Wilhelmine 52			
RAVEN, Herm.	34	Affinghausen	64-0363
Heinr. 29, Elise 23			
RAVENSBERG, Bernh.	21	Cloppenburg	63-1218
RAVER, Joh.	25	Hannover	65-0974
RAWE, W.	36	Wersen	64-0639
Friedrich 61			
REBEL, Emanuel	26	Fayette	63-1218
Amalie 35, Amalie 10, Lina 9, Saly 6			
REBELING, Heinrich	17	Neukirchen	65-1095
REBER, Dorothea	24	Aspach	66-0147
REBER, Jacob	23	Mussbach	65-0055
REBER, John	46	Danmuehle	63-0953
REBHAHN, Eva	34	Wallendingen	64-1206
Alfred 9m			
REBHAHN, Johann	26	Coburg	66-0679
Elisabeth 27, Barbara 4			
REBMANN, Anna Mar.	22	Beusen	66-0221
REBMANN, Johann	18	Wuertemberg	66-0984
Gottf. 22			
REBSTOCK, Gust.	21	Jingelfingen	64-0593
REBSTOCK, Joh.	19	Michelbach	64-0427
Louise 24			
RECH, Barbara	19	Kirrweiler	66-0704
RECH, Daniel	28	Quirnbach	64-0214
RECHBERG, Johannes	57	Curhessen	66-1155
Adam 7, Johannes 6			
RECHBERG, Mar.	21	Leimbach	66-0734
RECHINGER, Therese	22	Oberfranken	66-0679
RECHLIN, August	25	Schillersdorf	66-0083
RECHLINGER, Johann	30	Cekenhard	67-0007
RECHOHAIDT, Alex.	16	Linda	64-0885
RECHTERMANN, Aug.	24	Heede	63-0862
RECHTERN, Charles	17	Achim	63-0244
RECHTMEYER, Aug.	16	Varenholz	64-0639
Friedrich 15			
RECK, Alois	22	Naila	66-1131
RECK, Carl	21	Bremen	64-0840
RECK, Jacob	32	Quirnbach	64-0639
RECKA, Adelhaid	20	Bremen	63-0006
Johanna 25			
RECKA, Anna	66	Muhlhausen	64-0992
RECKE, Louis	17	Vorberg	63-0752
RECKER, Georg	27	Riedberg	65-0243
RECKER, Louis	27	Osnabrueck	66-1093
Fritz			
RECKESNIGER, Heinr	27	Aarholzen	66-1128
Friederike 17, Wilhelm 2, Augusta 6m			
RECKMEYER, Gottl.	16	Minden	66-0984
RECKNAGEL, Albert	16	Paderborn	64-0886
Hermann 18			
RECKNAGEL, Julius	26	Reutlingen	63-0822
RECKOORTH, Jan	55	Kesebe/Hann.	66-1128
Hinnerke 44, Gesche 24, Harm 7			
REDATZKI, Anna	18	Hannover	66-0934
Friedrich 25			
REDDEHASE, Maria	17	Braunschweig	67-0007
REDDERSEN, Wilhelm	30	Rodenburg	64-0665
REDECKER, Lisette	30	Melle	63-1069
REDEL, Math.	36	Wellingholzhs	65-0594
Cath. 21, Elisab. 44, Math. 10, Elisab. 7			
Cath. 6, Conrad 9m, Elisab. 60			
REDER, Margarethe	54	Mittelstreu	65-0948
Franz Bernh. 29			
REDER, Michael	39	Mittelstreu	65-0948
REDER, Peter	58	Bollendorf	65-1189
Catharine 59, Joh. 27, Susanne 25			
Jos. 18			
REDIELFS, L.	24	Wittmund	64-0665
REDMANN, Carl	21	Birsitz/Pr.	65-0038
REDMANN, Caroline	23	Zeckwerder	65-0038
REDMANN, Friedrich	32	Zickwerder	63-0006
REDWITZ, Christine	35	Niefern	63-0168
Lewis 6, Charles 4			

NAME	AGE	RESIDENCE	YR-LIST
REEG, Georg Peter	24	Zell	66-0704
REEG, Kunigunde	21	Obermotzbach	65-1024
R. 15			
REENKEN, Conrad	21	Angersbach	65-1030
REES, Johannes	22	Wuerttemberg	64-0432
REESE, Heinrich	52	Emden	65-1024
Trientje 47			
REESE, Joh.	25	Neudorf	66-0221
Ferdinand 23			
REESING, Anna	19	Diepholz	66-0734
REETZ, Gustav	34	Strahlsund	63-0398
REETZ, Wilhelm	16	Erpel	66-0578
Caroline 18			
REEZ, Ludwig	20	Zell	66-1327
REFFELD, August	26	Bramsche	66-0837
REGELEIM, John	64	Pittsburg	64-1022
REGELMANN, Carl	34	Wuertemberg	63-0398
REGELMANN, Joh. G.	32	Blochingen	65-0948
Barbara 32, August 4			
REGENSBURGER, J.	22	Freudenstadt	63-1178
REGENSBURGER, Joh.	16	Eisenach	65-0950
REGENSBURGER, John	50	Stadtilm	63-0953
Christ. 39, Marie 18, Richard 9			
Friedrich 7, William 5, baby 10			
REGENSBURGER, S.	25	Meiningen	64-0363
REGENSPURGER, Carl	32	Berlin	66-0469
REGENTANZ, Felix	24	Solingen	64-0343
REGER, Fr.(m)	17	Wilflingen	64-0331
REGER, Louise	25	Dielingen	64-0920
REGLIN, Anton	19	Hespenthal	64-0023
Joseph 21			
REGLING, Joseph	23	Engen	67-0007
Anton 24			
REGNET, Chr.	24	Schweiz	63-1136
REHBEIN, Wm.	14	Lauenfoerde	63-0752
REHBURG, Wilhelm	19	Rahden	65-1088
REHDER, H.	30	Vegesack	64-0665
Johanna 20, H. 18			
REHKOPF, Georg	29	Dissen	63-0917
REHLENAER, Carl	17	Wasensell	66-1203
REHLIS, Carl	29	Rastatt	66-1243
REHLKEN, H.(m)	21	Bremen	64-0214
REHM, Leonhard	19	Schloth	64-0687
REHMANN, John	25	Heidhorn	64-0073
REHME, Charlotte	31	Linderbruck	66-1093
REHNELT, Franziska	27	Habendorf	67-0599
Anna 17			
REHOR, Henriette	19	Taubhausen	66-0576
REHORST, H.W.	39	Loxstedt	63-0168
REHORST, Johann	14	Geestendorf	66-0668
Ferdinand 15			
REHRS, Christian	22	Nentershausen	66-1127
REI, Philipp	37	Planekstadt	63-1178
Elisabeth 41			
REIBELD, v. W.	29	Wuerzburg	64-1108
REIBER, Augusta	18	Kurnick	65-1030
REICH, Bernhard	28	Nehren	66-1093
REICH, David	37	Meiningen	64-0432
REICH, Ernestine	20	Libinfrauland	66-0578
REICH, Fanny	38	Tachau	66-1031
Bertha 9, Ludwig 8			
REICH, Israel	17	Zeitlofs	66-0679
REICH, Johann	30	Saulgau	65-1030
REICH, Simon	14	Gottschau	66-1031
REICH, W.	32	Gruenenplan	63-0917
REICHARD, August	28	Wolmerstedt	65-0243
REICHARD, Fr.	19	Pfullingen	66-1313
REICHARD, Richard	23	Scheifreisen	66-0147
REICHARDT, Julius	17	Ohio	64-0170
REICHBERT, Peter	18	Gedern	66-0984
REICHE, Henry	59	Gruenenplan	63-1038
Adolph 20			
REICHE, J.H.	29	Meerane	64-0331
Johanna 21			
REICHE, Joh. Wm.	34	Gruenenplan	63-0097
REICHE, W.	34	New York	63-1136
REICHE, Willi	37	New York	66-0109
REICHEL, Anna	19	Holzhausen	65-0055

NAME	AGE	RESIDENCE	YR-LIST
Elisabeth 18, Heinrich 14			
REICHEL, Carl	26	Marienburg	66-0668
Caecilie 53, Louise 23			
REICHEL, Emma	28	Antonlust	64-0170
REICHEL, Friedrike	23	Offenbach	66-0984
REICHEL, Jacobine	18	Lobenstein	64-0433
REICHELT, Joseph	30	Wien	63-0693
Adele 31, Sidonic 9			
REICHENBACH, Chrlt	28	St. Peter	63-0350
REICHENBACH, Josef	24	Cassel	66-0221
REICHENBACH, Phlpp	18	Birschheim	66-1127
REICHENBACH, Soph.	22	Oberbergen	66-1327
REICHENBACH, Wilh.	59	Thueringen	63-1010
Johanna Chr. 39, Johanna Wilh 14			
Georg Gottf. 2			
REICHENBERGER, Mar	24	Unternfranken	66-0221
Therese 2			
REICHENBERGER, Rub	58	Bayern	66-0221
REICHENECKER, A.	32		64-0331
REICHERT, Adalbert	24	Duetchau	65-0243
REICHERT, Adam	43	Wuerttemberg	64-0739
REICHERT, Adam	50	Rohrdorf	64-1161
REICHERT, Bertrand	20	Koengernheim	65-0243
REICHERT, Christ.	30	Rothenstein	66-1131
REICHERT, Friedr.	18	Bechtheim	65-0151
Gustav 16			
REICHERT, Heinrich	20	Warmbrunn	66-1327
REICHERT, Joh.	28	Biswang	66-1313
REICHERT, Joh. Er.	27	Hunibach	65-0243
REICHERT, Peter	35	Coblenz	66-0679
REICHERT, Sophie	17	Hegstfeld	66-0934
REICHHARDT, Jacob	17	Neuenkirchen	64-0639
REICHL, Wilh.	34	Gruenenplan	65-0189
REICHLE, Friedr.	21	Neckarems	63-1136
REICHLE, Marie	25	Endersbach	66-0083
REICHLE, Wilhelm	20	Neckarems	66-0083
REICHMANN, August	18	Bamberg	66-1127
REICHMANN, Gustav	26	Calne	66-1131
REICHOW, Carl	30	Cratzig	66-0578
Wilhelmine 33, Marie 2, Caroline 6			
Bertha 22, Henriette 36			
REICK, F.(m)	20	Berg	64-0331
REICK, Heinr.	29	Essen	66-0576
REICKE, W.(m)	36	Gruenenplan	64-0331
REICKS, Joseph	35	Preussen	63-0990
Anna 34, Caspar 9, Elisabeth 5, Franz 3			
Anna 11m			
REIDEL, Georg	21	Neckarau	64-0687
REIDT, Conrad	15	Marburg	63-0244
REIER, Heinrich	17	Allendorf/Hes	67-1005
REIF, Franz Jos.	32	Leimgraben	64-0739
Anna 34, Franz 12, Aloys 15, Emilie 8m			
REIF, Henriette	23	Hof	63-1178
REIF, Justine	25	Meckenheim	65-0038
REIFEGERST, Olga	22	Magdeburg	64-0214
REIFF, Johann	33	Neckartenzlng	64-0593
Friederike 31, Caroline 7, Rosine 6			
REIFTMUELLER, Bern	42	Gmuenden	66-1031
REIGELSBERGER, Wmn	16	Insbach	64-0886
REILING, Joseph	23	Manil	64-1053
REILLINGER, Friedr	24	Wuertemberg	66-0984
REIM, Heinrich	36	Niederklein	64-0840
REIM, Magdalene	22	Weppersdorf	66-0109
REIM, Th.	40	Ernsthausen	64-0992
Wm. 34			
REIMANN, Catharina	21	Crefeld	66-0576
REIMBOLZ, Anton	30	Baden	66-0221
Adolphine 26, Pauline 6, Caroline 4			
Adolph 6m			
REIMER, (m)	46	New York	63-1178
REIMER, August	30	Burg	66-0147
REIMER, C.H.	26	Lausiek	64-0495
REIMER, C.H.	18	New York	66-0704
REIMER, Doroth.	47	Kirchheim	63-0168
REIMERING, Joh.	34	Loster	64-0840
REIMERS, Beta	24	Aschwarden	66-0576
Beta 10m			
REIMERS, Herm.	45	New York	63-1085

NAME	AGE	RESIDENCE	YR-LIST
Simon 24, Fritz 23			
REIMERS, Herm.	21	Bremen	64-0363
REIMKE, Michael	22	Zickwerder	66-0578
REIMLER, Chr.(m)	29	Hille	64-0214
Fr.(m) 29, Wilhelmine 17			
REIMLER, Friedr.	19	Hilbe	64-1108
REIN, Carl L.	23	Undingen	66-1313
REINARD, Franz	30	Warendorf	64-1053
REINAUER, Bonifac.	36	Buffalo	66-0679
Marie 24			
REINAUER, Louise	9	Buffalo	66-0679
REINBAUER, F.	20	Cassel	65-0974
Albert 18			
REINBOLD, Ludwig	33	Hannover	66-0577
Dorothea 29, Dorothea 1, Friedr. 26			
Chr. 36			
REINBOLD, Ludwig	43	Baden	66-0984
REINDEL, Georg	24	Muenchen	63-0015
REINDEL, Ursula	19	Hohenkemnath	65-0950
REINDERS, Aug.	28	Amsterdam	63-0862
REINDERS, Emma	19	Langenberg	63-0821
REINDERS, Joh. D.	34	Hannover	63-0398
Marg. 32, Dietrich 7, Otto 5, Johanna 2			
REINECKE, Alb.	20	Braunschweig	65-0055
REINECKE, August	43	Kirchbraak	66-0412
REINECKE, Joh. H.	52	Riblerbuettel	66-0577
Dorothea 22			
REINEKE, Johannes	31	Ohio	66-0704
Therese 28, Therese 3, Bertha 1, Maria 1m			
REINEKE, Ludwig	22	Meiningen	66-0704
REINER, Anton	48	Bamberg	63-0917
REINER, Anton	26	New York	66-0109
REINER, Br.	35	New York	63-1085
Christiane 34, Margarethe 59, Anna 12			
Ernestine 7, Margareth 9, Christiane 5			
Christian 1, wiife 30, John 5			
REINER, Carl	24	Nuerlelingen	66-1093
REINER, Helene	26	Gratz	64-0687
REINER, Rosine	50	Urasch	66-1093
REINERS, H.(f)	24	Bremen	65-0189
REINERS, Helene	23	Blexen	64-0456
REINERS, Rich.	25	New York	63-0350
REINERT, C.	28	Steinberg	65-0007
REINERT, F.	23	Plauen	63-0953
REINES, Grietje	54	Ihrhorn	64-0495
Ella 28, Lana 23, Johanna 22, Hajo 20			
Ma.(f) 17, Ra.(f) 11			
REINEWALD, Carl	30	Limburg	64-0363
Johanna 25			
REINGEL, Christian	20	Wuertemberg	66-0734
REINHARD, Carl	25	Ritzebuettel	67-0007
REINHARD, Ch.	23	Helmhoff	63-0551
Emma 8			
REINHARD, Chr'tine	23	Itzenheim	65-0055
REINHARD, Conrad	22	Grossenbach	66-1155
REINHARD, Emma	17	Meiningen	66-0577
REINHARD, Friedr.	28	Amelith	63-1069
Friedrich 59, Wilhelm 51, Georgine 27			
Emma 11m			
REINHARD, Henr'tt.	28	Teuchern	63-0693
Emilie 7, Hermine 5, Elisabeth 3			
Marie 11m			
REINHARD, Joh.	17	Heemes	64-0331
REINHARDT, Apollon	26	Niederkirchen	63-0917
REINHARDT, Edw.	29	Hohlborn	65-0974
REINHARDT, F.	36	Schochtau	63-1085
Caroline 38, Augusta 13, Eduard 9			
Emilie 7, Sophie 5, Caroline 3			
REINHARDT, Fred.	24	Prussia	63-0296
REINHARDT, John F.	58	Noeda	63-0693
William 17, Robert 9			
REINHARDT, Justus	45	Heiner	66-0679
Anna 45, Justus 16, Jacob 14			
REINHARDT, Martin	26	Markelsheim	63-1038
REINHARDT, Otto	29	Apenstadt	65-0007
REINHARDT, Rosine	24	Cutsamg	64-0886
REINHOLD, Henry	60	Beckum	63-0482
Elise 18			

NAME	AGE	RESIDENCE	YR-LIST
REINHOLD, Jacob	13	Weruesheim	64-0593
REINICKEN, R. (m)	39	Schinznach	64-0331
REININGA, August	24	Hannover	64-0199
REINKE, Aug.	29	Posen	64-0432
Wilhelmine 29, Augusta 4, Ernestine 2			
REINKEN, Ludwig	25	Bremen	64-0920
REINKER, Friedrich	16	Brockhausen	66-0668
REINKING, C.F.	18	Strohen	65-0402
REINKING, Chr.	20	Geestendorf	64-0432
REINKING, Diedrich	23	Seese	66-0704
REINKING, Em. Ed.	30	Stuttgart	65-0116
REINKING, Marie	18	Stadthagen	66-1031
REINKMEYER, Anna	29	Bischofshagen	63-0990
REINLE, G. Peter	30	Schweitzingen	66-0934
REINMANN, F. Th.	43	Goritzsch	66-0221
REINMOELLER, Anton	17	Friedewald	64-0433
REINMUELLER, Elis.	20	Friedewald	64-0433
REINMUTH, Emilie	28	Glanchau	63-0752
Anna 5, Clara 10m			
REINSCH, Berthold	29	Zuellichau	63-0821
REINSCH, Eduard	34	Indianopolis	66-0984
Marie 32, Emma 7			
REINTANZ, Emilie	21	Muehlhausen	64-0214
REINTANZ, Friedr.	16	Muehlhausen	63-1069
REIPERT, J.H.	18	Micklar	64-0495
REIS, Adolph	24	Preussen	66-0221
REIS, Amalia	28	Essen	66-0221
REIS, C.	37	Fuerth	64-0639
REIS, Georg	22	Curhessen	66-0577
REIS, John	18	Hessen	63-0350
REISCH, Eleora	22	Buehl	63-0006
REISCH, Franz	19	Heiligenzell	66-1327
REISCH, Joh. Conr.	30	Nuremberg	66-0412
REISER, Creszencia	38	Carlsruhe	66-1327
Joseph 8			
REISER, Johann	25	Neuenwalde	67-0007
REISIG, Erdmunde	21	Saxony-Weimar	66-0577
REISKY, Joh.	37	Boehmen	63-0398
REISLER, Caroline	20	Marbach	63-1136
REISS, B.	25	Fuerth	63-1136
Jette 19			
REISS, Conrad	27	Coburg	65-0243
REISS, Elisse	26	Eltmannshsn.	66-1203
REISS, Henrich	26	Eltsmannshsn.	66-1203
REISS, Henry	38	Horsten	66-0679
REISS, Lazarus	25	Eberstadt	64-1022
Caroline 65, Sara 21			
REISS, Sab.	21	Ulrichstein	63-0482
REISS, Wilhelm	20	Batten	67-0007
REISSENWEBER, Rosi	24	Coburg	64-0170
REISSER, Wilhelm	24	Pfullingen	67-0007
REISSHEIMER, Peter	19	Rohrbach	66-0623
REISTERER, Johann	28	Gronen	66-0083
Caroline 27, Hermann 1			
REITEMEYER, Carl W	19	Ritterhude	65-0950
REITENBACH, Philip	28	Berweidler	63-0482
REITER, Barbara	21	Darmstadt	66-0221
REITER, Carl	16	Breslau	65-0974
REITER, Henriette	22	Prussia	64-0432
REITH, Ignatz	22	Oberlimbach	66-1248
REITHER, Vorina	58	Makelsberg	65-0948
REITSCHMIDT, J.B.	25	Philadelphia	63-0862
REITZ, Appolina	21	Cassel	66-1313
REITZ, C.	27	Geislingen	66-0413
Agatha 21			
REITZ, Elisab.	25	Kornstein	65-0402
REITZ, F.	28	Rossbach	66-1248
REITZ, Jac.	40	Hochelheim	64-0992
REITZ, Johannes	32	Quadshausen	66-1093
REITZ, Marie	22	Redighausen	66-1031
Wilhelm 25			
REITZ, Peter	39	Hasseborn	65-0243
REITZ, Peter	49	Hasseborn	65-0243
Conrad 21			
REIZ, Carl	30	Liebrich	66-1243
Augusta 30			
REIZER, Alois	59	Etgrade	65-0402
Aug. 7			

NAME	AGE	RESIDENCE	YR-LIST
RELLER, Heinrich	28	Hannover	66-1031
Caroline 23			
RELLINGER, J.L.	17	New York	63-0821
REMBORD, Johanna	31	Laufen	63-1069
REMER, Math.	26	Aasen	63-0296
REMILLION, H.	40	Italy	63-1136
daughter 12, daughter 7			
REMMEL, Anna Elise	27	Dielfen	64-0938
REMMERS, Henry	22	Bremerhaven	63-1218
REMMERS, Louis	22	Duslingen	66-0576
REMMET, Elisabeth	30	Wiesbaden	66-0934
REMPE, Jos.	51	Cloppenburg	64-0938
REMPEL, Elise	18	Cincinatti	66-0576
REMPEL, Heinrich		Bielefeld	66-1031
REMPEL, Max	17	Bielefeld	63-0752
REMPP, Friedrich	24	Heimendingen	63-0097
REMPT, Albert	26	Mannheim	64-0886
RENARD, Victor	29	France	63-0350
RENCIN, John	38	Boehmen	63-0917
Cath. 31, Barbara 7, Franzisca 5, John 1			
RENDETZEN, John A.	44	Steinbach	63-0244
RENFERT, Elisabeth	78	Duelmen	66-0704
Anna 23			
RENK, Joh. Th.	20	New York	63-1178
RENKEN, Anna	16	Ritterhude	64-0331
RENKEN, Gerd.	38	Bremervoerde	64-0639
Maria 25, Louise 15			
RENKEN, Heinrich	30	Angersbach	65-1031
RENKEN, Johanna	36	Charleston	63-0953
RENKER, Catharine	32	Oberlais	66-1248
RENKER, Gustav	32	Dhum/Sax.	64-0920
RENKER, Joh.	25	Lauterbach	63-0398
RENKS, Anna	20	Hildesheim	63-1178
Otto 9			
RENNE, Julius	24	Horstenbeck	66-1031
RENNER, August	19	Heilbronn	66-1131
RENNER, Friedr.	18	Schoeneck	64-1022
August 35			
RENNER, M.(f)	56	Scheffelbach	64-0495
RENNER, Rich.	23	Meiningen	64-0432
RENNERT, Conrad	24	Reckendorf	66-0349
RENNESS, Martin	47	Soessnowd	66-0469
Elisabeth 42, Eva Rosine 13, Anna 8			
Carl 6			
RENNISLAND, Herm.	19	Gleichen	66-1373
RENNWANZ, A.	18	Friedrichsbrg	66-0413
RENSCH, Johann	25	Hundsangen	66-1373
RENSCH, Nikolaus	27	Heilbach	63-1069
RENTER, Bernhard	30	Cassel	66-0679
RENZ, Caroline	22	Mohringen	66-0221
RENZELMANN, Diedr.	58	Stolzenau	65-1031
REOMECL. Carl	21	Ulm	64-0687
REPLER, Christ.	60	Wetzlar	66-0221
Christ. 22			
REPLER, Jacob	32	Wetzlar	66-0221
REPP, Adam	24	Steinberg	63-0006
REPP, Carl	34	Hessen	63-0398
REPPENHAGEN, Anna	20	Lehe	66-1127
REPPERT, Christ.	35	Washington	63-0917
RESENER, Ernst	24	Luhbau	66-0413
RESIGER, Pauline	20	Zeitz	64-0363
RESK, J.	19	Posen	66-0413
RESLER, Gottlieb	30	Prussia	64-0363
Michael 21			
RESSE, Heinr.		Eisbergen	64-0214
RESSING, Wilh'mine	21	Diepholz	63-0693
RESTEMEYER, Joh. F	24	Oelingen/Hann	65-0038
RESTLE, Martin	22	Ueberlingen	64-0593
RESTOCK, C.	34	Meridau	64-0593
RETHMANN, Anton	24	Damme	65-0770
RETHMANN, B. Heinr	32	Oldenburg	66-0934
Marie 27, Franz 6, Marie 4, Anton 1			
RETHORST, Cath.	24	Missouri	64-0073
RETTER, Carl	26	Eltingen	65-1088
Therese 25			
RETTIG, Chr.	26	Buerstadt	63-1136
Susanna 22, Francis 2, Susanna 6m			
RETTIG, Eva	23	Niederringelh	63-0482

NAME	AGE	RESIDENCE	YR-LIST
RETTIG, Philippine	22	Burgstadt	66-1248
RETTIG, Rosa	18	Rastadt	63-1178
RETTINGER, Marg.	36	Brooklyn	63-1038
Peter 15			
RETZER, Georg	53	Rhodt	63-1136
RETZING, Conrad	18	Wallrode	64-0433
RETZNER, Carl Frdr	49	Berka	65-0948
REUB, Fr. Louis	23	Waldenbach	66-0221
REUE, Carl	18	Cassel	66-1031
REUKS, Anna	20	Hildesheim	63-1178
Otto 9			
REULE, Philipp	20	Kretzingen	66-0934
Magdalena 22			
REUM, Karl	23	Steinbach	66-1128
REUMANN, Joh.	21	Frankfurt/M	64-0170
REUNER, Me.(f)	40	Neugedein	64-0495
REUNS, C.A.	28	Altenbreitung	64-0023
REUSCHLE, Chr'tine	22	Mannheim	67-0806
REUSCHLER, Johann	46	Obernbach	64-1108
Cath. 33, Rosine 4, Cath. 3, Louise 1			
REUSER, Fr.	30	Hannover	64-0665
REUSING, Dina	19	Nienburg	65-1030
REUSINGER, Sophie	24	Schneppenbach	63-1038
REUSS, Francis	40	Bremen	63-0097
REUSS, Magd.	44	St. Louis	63-0482
REUSS, Peter Karl	35	Frankfurt	66-0109
REUSSNER, J. Barb.	21	Haula	64-0739
REUTER, Andreas	51	Guetershausen	66-0412
Christine 45, Gottfried 18, Philipp 7			
REUTER, Anton	23	Rheinpfalz	66-0221
REUTER, Carl	30	Weissenburg	65-0243
REUTER, Christine	25	Stemmer	65-0948
REUTER, Dorothea	23	Garbsen	66-0934
Conrad 16, Minna 17			
REUTER, Friedrich	19	Oberhamm	66-1248
REUTER, G.(m)	47	Bamberg	64-0138
Marguerite 23			
REUTER, Georg	26	Arolsen	64-0199
Fredrich 28			
REUTER, Lewis	19	Schoenhagen	63-0244
REUTER, Nicolaus	38	Bergheim	64-1053
REUTER, Ph.	30	New York	63-1136
wife 28, child 4, baby 9m			
REUTHER, Louise	53	Striegann/Pr.	65-0004
REUTLER, Ernst	19	Rauschenberg	66-0576
REUTLINGER, Salom.	25	Zuerich	63-0953
REUTTER, Gottlieb	24	Denkendorf	66-1203
Johannes 25, Joh. Jacob 27			
REUTTER, Robert	19	Boblingen	66-0734
REVER, B. (f)	17	Lupenburg	63-0990
REVIL, (f)	28	New Orleans	63-1178
REWER, Caroline	17	Niederwehnen	66-1155
REWERTS, Tamme	28	Aurich	66-0668
Johann 29			
REXEROTH, John	24	Pferdedorf	63-1136
REYGEROW, Bertha	16	Rutlitz	66-0668
Ulricke 21			
REYHER, Louise	17	Kiel	64-0363
REYMANN, Wenzel	23	Carlsbad	66-0734
REYMER, Heinr.Math	24	Ihlienworth	64-0427
REYNERS, Heinr.	21	Uthfelde	66-0934
REYTER, C.O.	26	Bremen	66-0934
REZ, Adam	26	Merzbach	66-1327
Joh. Georg 24			
RHEDER, F.W.	30	New York	64-0073
RHEIMER, Wilh'mine	25	Pirmasens	66-1131
RHEIN, Caroline	58	Pyrmont	66-0704
RHEIN, Otto	24	Speyer	64-0214
Ab. 36, Elisaeth 58, Caroline 43			
Christine 9			
RHEINSMANN, Henry	19	Altenur	64-0639
RIBOCK, Adelbert	22	Borkowitz	65-0713
RICHARD, Herrm.	34	Minden	66-1313
Anna M. 31, Maria 3			
RICHARD, Marie	18	Gruenberg	65-0594
RICHARD, Therese	36	Leobschuetz	66-0083
RICHARDS, Gust.	25	Solingen	63-0822
RICHARTZ, Chr'stne	35	Duesseldorf	66-1093
RICHE, Peter	46	Ohio	64-0170
Marg. 18, Phlipp 23			
RICHET, Jeanne	36	San Francisco	64-0073
Augusta 14, Berthe 5, Charles 4			
RICHT, Rosine	24	Stammheim	67-0007
RICHTER, Ad.	33	Hohmelser	65-0007
Christine 35, Alwin 8, baby 9m			
RICHTER, Ad.	26	Cassel	64-0593
RICHTER, Aug. Herm	31	Freiberg	65-0948
RICHTER, C.E.	27	Sachsen	66-0109
RICHTER, Carl F.	1	Noerdlingen	64-1108
RICHTER, Carolina	29	Durlach	66-1131
Barbara 32			
RICHTER, Christian	28	Hof	66-1155
RICHTER, Conr.Carl	41	Braunschweig	66-1243
RICHTER, Elis.	37	Neuenkirchen	65-0974
Catharine 19, Joseph 27, August 14			
RICHTER, Elisabeth	29	New York	63-0990
Constance 9, Elisabeth 5			
RICHTER, Elise	20	Zwickau	66-1373
RICHTER, Emma	24	Zeitz	66-1248
Otto 4, baby (m) 10m			
RICHTER, F.(m)	22	Steinfurt	64-0331
RICHTER, Fr.(m)	30	Breslau	64-0687
RICHTER, Franz	27	Muntinghausen	63-1038
RICHTER, Heinrich	19	Ebsdorf	65-0865
RICHTER, J.G.A.L.	26	Berlin	64-0023
RICHTER, John G.	59	Siebenlehn	63-0953
Theresia 21			
RICHTER, Julius	30	Bautzen	63-0482
RICHTER, Maria	35	Lamspringe	63-1069
Augusta 17			
RICHTER, Minna	22	Oldenburg	66-1131
RICHTER, Titus	34	Grossentaft	64-0343
RICHTER, Traugott	46	Dresden	66-0934
RICHTER, Wilhelm	19	Kirchhasel	66-1155
RICHTER, Wilhelm	20	Marburg	66-0934
RICHTERING, Gerd.	21	Nordhorn	66-1128
RICHTERS, Hugo	25	Haudorf	66-0576
RICKART, Friedr.	19	Flein	63-0482
RICKE, C.J.	46	Ahnebeck	64-0170
RICKE, Catharina	23	Elsfeld	64-1053
RICKEISEN, Andres	42	Thaldorf	63-0551
RICKEL, G.A.	25	Eichenrode	63-1085
RICKEL, Wm.	35	Neustadt	64-1022
Wilhelmine 27			
RICKENBERG, Minna	22	Hagen	65-0898
RICKERS, Trine	16	Thedinghausen	64-0495
RICKERT, Francis	40	New Orleans	63-0953
RICKERT, Joh.	38	Untersalzbach	65-0116
RICKERT, Michael	35	Talheim	65-0770
Magdalene 36			
RICKERT, W.	30	Wertheim	66-0413
RICKING, Heinr.	26	Matzfeld	64-0687
RICKLING, Andr.	38	Letzlingen	67-0007
RICKMERS, Herm.	25	Edelsen	64-0593
RICKWEG, Christine	24	Lesum	64-0885
RIDDEL, Anna	16	Philadelphia	64-0170
RIDDERBUSCH, Carl	20	Braunschweig	63-1010
RIDER, Christian	40	New York	63-0097
RIEB, Wm.	22	Braunschweig	65-0116
RIEBE, Andreas	16	Kschent	67-0007
RIEBECK, Marie	28	Boehmen	64-0023
RIEBEL, Jacob	26	Bodenheim	65-0151
RIEBEL, Katharine	22	Lindenfels	66-0469
Kaetchen 18			
RIEBELING, H.	39	Brellshausen	66-0413
RIEBELMANN, Joh.	51	Tettnang	63-0013
Joseph 12			
RIEBLE, Jacob	27	Wuertemberg	66-0413
RIECHENMEIER, F.H.	36	Blomberg	64-0593
Friederike 57			
RIECHERS, Joh.	33	Oyten	65-0151
Johann 15			
RIECHERS, Joh.	44	Hannover	65-0974
Margarethe 44, Dorothea 16, Diedrich 14			
Adelheid 23, Johann 5, Georg 7			
Margarethe 4, Heinrich 2			

NAME	AGE	RESIDENCE	YR-LIST
RIECHERS, Nic. H.	23	Ritzebuettel	67-0007
RIECHMANN, C. Hch.	30	Nordhemern	64-0456
RIECHMANN, Ch.	27	Pr. Minden	63-0398
RIECHMANN, Gustav	22	Wuertemberg	66-0734
RIECK, Aug. Carl.	36	Moschis	66-0578
Pauline 27, Eduard 1			
RIECKER, August	35	Crefeld	63-0917
Sophie 24, August 9, Albert 8			
Clothilde 2, baby 4m			
RIECKMANN, W.A.(m)	19	Hartum	64-0331
RIEDEL, A.	36	Cincinnati	64-1206
RIEDEL, Elisabeth	20	Reichenheim	66-0576
RIEDEL, Franz	30	New York	63-1218
RIEDEL, Franz	36	Elsnitz/Sax.	65-1030
Margarethe 40, Emilie 9m, Marie 9			
RIEDEL, Friedrich	28	Schleid	67-0007
Heinrich 23			
RIEDEL, Georg C.	35	Oppenheim	66-0704
Marie 32, Elisabeth 4, Henriette 3			
RIEDEL, Henriette	41	Saxonia	66-1093
RIEDEL, J.S.	23	Boehmen	64-0495
Magd. 25			
RIEDEL, Leonhd.	20	Muenchen	64-0138
RIEDEL, Paul	23	Leipzig	64-0433
RIEDEMANN, Herm.	14	Twistringen	63-1038
RIEDEMANN, Louise	58	Hille	66-1155
Friedrich 30, Maria 30, Friedrich 3			
RIEDER, Sigmund	24	Baltimore	63-0168
RIEDESEL, G.	21	Wunderthaus	65-1024
RIEDIG, Theodor	20	Chemnitz	66-1127
RIEDING, A.	41	Heinichen	64-1022
Peter 28			
RIEDINGER, Wilhelm	21	Rothenfeld	66-1155
RIEDL, Joseph	22	Boehmen	66-0704
RIEDL, Theodor	17	Muenchen	66-1373
RIEDLE, G.	30	Bremerlehe	63-1003
RIEF, Conrad	24	Eschenbach	64-0992
RIEFER, John	32	Nordstetten	64-0331
RIEGE, Agnes	19	Steinau	66-0576
RIEGEL, Ottomar	35	Werthausen	64-0363
RIEGELMANN, J.F.	30	Bremen	64-0432
RIEGELMANN, Max	22	Fuerth	65-0594
RIEGELMANN, Sim	18	Adelsdorf	64-0427
RIEGER, Caroline	25	Kirchdorf	63-0482
RIEGER, Charles	26	Mittelbruden	63-1178
RIEGER, Frd.	24	Laupheim	64-1161
RIEGER, Georg	23	Affalderrich	65-1030
RIEGER, Johanna	23	Bochingen	64-0214
RIEGER, Xaver	33	Esslingen	66-0679
RIEGLER, John	20	Schwabhausen	63-0693
RIEHM, Wm.	17	Schlichtum	66-0837
RIEKE, Heinrich	22	Germany	66-0666
RIEKE, Ernst	29	Osserweg	66-0469
RIEKE, Gustav	20	Minden	63-1085
RIEKELMANN, Heinr.	22	Ankum	66-1373
RIEKEMANN, Heinr.	45	Suhlingen	66-0934
Sophie 26, Elise 6m			
RIEKENS, Rieke	54	Loquard	64-1022
Antje 47, Antje 22, Dettje 19			
Jacobine 16, Rieke 14, Gesche 11			
Wilhelmine 7, Ankea 5			
RIEL, Joh. Ph.	20	Mardorf	66-1243
RIEMANN, Wilhelm	22	Bremen	63-1010
Elise 20			
RIEMENSCHNEIDER, A	45	Oldorf	64-0214
Marie 27, (f) 20			
RIEN, Mr.	40	New Orleans	63-0953
Anna 46			
RIEN, Otto	26	Elbingerode	64-0214
RIEPE, Caroline	23	Koerbicke	66-0412
RIEPE, Friedrich	14	Werther	66-0704
RIEPEN, Anna	30	Lackheim	66-0221
RIEPENHAUSEN, Hch.	45	Ballenhausen	64-0456
RIEPENS, Johanna	23	St.Louis	64-0495
RIES, Anna Marie	24	Geisenbach	64-0073
RIES, Johann	16	Ritterhude	66-0576
RIESBERG, Gerhard	57	Preussen	63-0990
Anna 44, Maria 13, Caspar 15, Bernhard 9			

NAME	AGE	RESIDENCE	YR-LIST
William 8, Anna 3, Dina 3m			
RIESBERG, Theodor	30	Preussen	63-0990
Anna 34			
RIESCH, Wilhelm	16	Rheinpfalz	66-0984
RIESE, Joh. Heinr.	15	Schwaningdorf	64-0433
RIESE, Johannes	21	Kleinpurschiz	66-0679
RIESENER, Louis	23	Berlin	66-0984
Minna 20			
RIESER, Elise	19	Oberdorf	64-1022
RIESSNER, Anna	23	Fuerth	63-0990
RIESTER, Georg	31	Dunzingen	64-0363
RIETES, Carl	28	Hoexter	66-0704
RIETHAUER, Fride	26	Hannover	66-0221
RIETMANN, Bernhard	26	Coesfeld	66-1327
RIFFERT, Anna Elis	20	Hesrode	64-0433
RIGLING, Catharina	25	Engen	65-0055
RIHA, Franz	27	Bohemia	66-0469
Maria 22			
RIKLI, Arthur	19	Wangen	66-1327
RILGER, Carl	15	Aalken	64-0639
RILLING, Christian	26	Gomaringen	66-0679
RILM, Carline	18	Braunschweig	65-0974
RIMBACH, Johann	25	Unhausen	64-0433
RIME, Anton	28	New York	63-0097
RINCKER, Carl	30	Breslau	66-0734
RINDER, Christoph	24	Vihringen	66-1243
RINDER, Julius	56	Rochester	63-0953
Louise 52			
RINDERKNECHT, Joh.	47	Oelbersheim	64-0992
Barbara 37, Christian 10, Barbara 7			
Maria 4, Friedrich 2			
RINECKER, Carl	24	Gieselbach	64-0073
RING, Augusta	15	Salzungen	64-0665
RING, Friedr.	40	Salzungen	67-0795
Christine 31, Wilhelm 9, Marie 7			
Christian 4, Georg 3, Caspar 8m			
RING, Jacob Ludw.	23	Schierloch	66-0221
RING, Samuel	18	Fuerth	64-0938
RING, Valentin	32	Otzbach	66-0349
RINGE, Christ.	49	Lehe	65-0038
Julius 16, Heinrich 17			
RINGEL, Elisabeth	19	Gruenberg	65-0594
RINGEL, Georg	56	Schierbach	67-0007
Margarethe 19			
RINGEL, Ludw.	38	Cincinnati	64-0073
RINGER, S.	52	Fuerth	65-1189
RINGERS, (m)		Kr.Salzwedel	67-0599
Elisabeth 25, Bernh. Herm. 2			
Joh. Petrus 2			
RINGERT, Carl	23	Liskastel	66-0650
RINGHOFF, Wilh'mne	18	Westerende	67-0599
RINGHOFFER, Johann	37	Guens/Ungarn	66-0346
Therese 39, Joseph 9, Therese 4			
Stephan 7			
RINGSHAUSEN, Fr.	21	Belmuth	65-1031
RINGSWALD, Apold.	26	Insbach	64-0593
RINGWALD, An Marie	16	Pfeffingen	64-0433
RINGWALD, Cath.	23	Buchsol	66-1243
RINKEL, Aug.	18	Quikershausen	64-0495
RINKEL, Frd.	34	Platendorf	64-0904
Friederike 38, Louis 14, Minna 8			
Frieda 3, Emma 9m			
RINKER, Philipp	38	Minnesota	63-0482
RINNE, A.	20	Osnabrueck	63-1218
RINNE, Christiane	60	Vorwohle	66-0147
Minna 17			
RINNE, Friedrich	22	Ronneberg	66-1248
RINNE, Heinrich	22	Liebenau	66-0734
RINNEKE, Johann	53	Essen	66-0221
Amma M. 51, William 24, Epha 19			
Cathre. 7, Niclas 6			
RINNEKEN, John	25	New York	66-0221
RINSCHLER, Johs.	38	Kettelfingen	64-0170
RINTELN, Fr.	26	Paderborn	65-1088
RIPENHAUSEN, Joh'a	23	Bremen	63-0350
RIPKA, Katha.	22	Boehmen	63-0990
RIPKE, Hermann	49	Oetzen	66-0704
Johann 47, Adelheid 23			

NAME	AGE	RESIDENCE	YR-LIST
RIPP, Philip	25	Duerkheim	66-0734
RIPPE, Adelheid	27	Rothenuffeln	64-0886
RIPPE, Heinr.	29	Werse	64-1206
RIPPE, Justus	40	Vlotho	65-1095
Henriette 42, Eduard 10, Susanne 7			
Karoline 5, Minna 2			
RIPPEL, Carl	34	Kroschowitz	66-1373
RIPPELMEYER, Louis	54	Pr. Minden	64-0432
Caroline 27			
RIPPENHORST, Wilh.	26	Otterndorf	66-1127
RIPPENTROPP, Eiler	34	Hinte	66-0412
Gesche 32, Jann 7, Johann 3, Geertje 6m			
RIPPENTROPP, Frank	39	Warsingfehn	66-0412
Johann 7			
RIPPER, Peter	16	Bierbach	63-1069
RIPPLE, Vi.	35	Muehlenbach	66-0083
RIPPMANN, Carl	28	Bietigheim	66-1131
RISCH, Wilhelm	45	Berlin	66-0221
RISCHEBUSCH, Gust.	15	Carlshafen	64-0739
RISCHMUELLER, C.	24	Rumbeck	64-0427
RISCHMUELLER, Edw.	16	Hieligenstadt	64-0639
Elisab. 19			
RISKE, Hermann	22	Dissen	66-0578
Charlotte 18			
RISKEN, Bernh.	40	Wersuwe	65-1030
Gesine 36, Margarethe 59, Anton 14			
Joh. Gerh. 13, Joh. Heinr. 9			
Bernh. Jos 7, Joh. Bernh. 4			
RISKUS, Juliane	18	Worms	65-0402
RISO, Marie	14	Loehne	66-0413
RISSOW, Carl	31	Wuerehowa	66-0469
Emilie 36, Caroline 56, Reinhold 25			
Wilhelm 24, Ulrike 18, Augusta 14			
Augusta 15, Bertha 8, Ida 6, Friedr. 4			
Anna 9m			
RISTENPADT, Aug.	24	Aerzen	63-0482
RITH, James	44	Rouffach	63-0551
RITHMULLER, Ce.(f)	19	Branau	64-0331
Frd.(m) 15			
RITSCHEL, Jos.	32	Reichenberg	63-0953
Hermann 9			
RITSCHER, Elise	22	Liebenau	66-0679
RITSCHIE, Cathrina	43	Raukwyl	64-1108
RITT, Gust.	22	Freiburg	63-0244
Caroline 51, Cath. 25, Christine 25			
William 11			
RITTER, August	21	Birkert	63-1069
RITTER, Caroline	24	Kennade	66-0469
Christian 22			
RITTER, Franz	26	Baden	66-0576
RITTER, Friedr.	16	Kennade	66-0469
RITTER, Friedr.	17	Cassel	66-1203
RITTER, G.	21	Illinois	64-0138
RITTER, Georg	20	Darmstadt	65-0004
RITTER, Heinr.	28	Kirchheim	65-0055
Philippine 54, Elise 20			
RITTER, Heinrich	28	Neckarbischof	66-1373
RITTER, John	62	Spaichingen	63-0482
Jacobine 18			
RITTER, Lazar	60	Zubirow	66-0734
Rosalie 58, Emilie 23			
RITTER, Maria	18	Balsbach	63-1069
RITTER, Therese	26	Herstelle	63-0482
RITTER, Wm.	22	Ziegelrodt	64-0992
RITTERBUSCH, Frd'r	27	Alten Donop	66-1327
RITTERBUSCH, Fritz	23	Oldendorf	64-0199
August 17			
RITTERBUSCH, W.	30	England	63-0953
RITTERHAUS, J.A.	24	New York	66-0109
RITTERSBACH, Conr.	29	Dericum	66-1327
RITTERSBACH, Wilh.	26	Rheinpfalz	66-0576
RITTERSOHN, Fr.	17	Rohrsen	66-0704
RITTETT, Werso	33	Pest	65-0007
RITTLINGMAYER, Got	20	Fluederhausen	67-0007
RITTMANN, Elisab.	24	Bloedesheim	66-0221
RITZ, Augustin	22	Rossbach	66-1327
RITZEL, Anna	19	Lehe	63-1085
RITZER, Joseph	16	Hohenschangen	64-0343
RITZERT, F.W.	45	New York	63-0551
wife 40			
RITZI, Eduard	25	Ingenhain	66-0147
RITZI, Joseph	28	Buesslingen	65-1024
Magdalene 59, Maria 25, Barbara 10m			
Wend. 22, Jacob 16			
RITZMANN, August	22	Ebersbach	66-0221
ROBBERS, Carl	31	Cloppenburg	64-0427
ROBE, Emil Wilhelm	19	Berlin	63-0006
ROBERDT, Adrian	26	Havre	64-0886
ROBERT, Franz Ant.	43	Obernhuisen	64-0639
Eva Cath. 37, Valentin 20, Eva Cath. 16			
Anna 7, Philipp 4			
ROBRECHT, Jos.	28	Hamern	64-0593
ROBYN, (f)	49	Emmerich	65-0402
ROCACEK, Wenzel	58	Caslau	64-0593
Anna 45, Vincens 26, Adelbert 22, Anna 20			
William 7			
ROCHLITZ, August	27	Erfurt	66-0577
ROCHOLL, Fritz	22	Bremen	65-0116
ROCHS, Carl	28	Duesseldorf	64-0687
ROCHTS, Theresia	20	Pilsen	64-0886
Anna 55			
ROCKENBACH, Gusto	32	Mersheim	65-0116
ROCKENFELDER, Phil	35	Wallendorf	66-0147
ROCKWITZ, Carl L.	21	Hannover	64-0886
RODACH, Julius	24	Gimpelburg	64-0886
RODDERT, Marie	42	Muenden	64-0639
Louise 16			
RODE, H.	19	Wallburg	65-0974
RODE, Heinrich	41	Lutter	65-1095
Maria 33, Louis 7			
RODE, Herm.	36	Blandern	64-1161
RODE, Sophie	31	Bremen	66-1327
RODEFELD, William	23	Rothenfelde	63-0917
RODEKOPF, Heinr.	17	Herste	64-0214
Heinr. 19			
RODEKOPF, Heinr.	19	Utlubbe	64-0214
Heinr. 17			
RODELHEIMER, Ca(f)	27	Laupheim	64-1161
RODEMEYER, Diedr.	21	Stolzenau	66-0577
Sophie 57, Caroline 23, Friedrich 18			
RODEN, Cathr.	56	Soden	65-0948
Christian 16			
RODEN, Fr.	30	Eisenach	64-0687
RODENBECK, Conrad	45	Garspens	65-0151
Christ. 18			
RODENBENDER, Anton	24	Schrock	65-0007
RODENBIK, W.	25	Eggeberg	65-1189
RODENBOHL, William	49	New York	63-0990
Henriette 44, William 3			
RODENBURG, Lidia	38	Leipzig	64-0593
J.G. 16, F.H. 15, Mary 3			
RODENBUSCH, Heinr.	9	Weinheim	66-0679
RODER, Martin	22	Remlingen	66-0346
RODEWALD, H.(m)	21	Edelsen	64-0331
RODEWALD, Hermann	25	Hagensburg	67-0007
RODIUS, Carl	25	Heilbronn	64-1022
RODOWE, C.A.(m)	33	Osnabrueck	64-0331
RODRIGE, Ernst	23	Schwalingen	66-0734
RODUTZ, Caroline	29	Flensburg	65-0974
ROEBB, Marg.	21	Stedem	64-1022
ROEBEN, D.G.	28	New York	64-0687
E.G. 27			
ROEBEN, Frdr.	33	Varel	65-0243
ROEBER, Aug.	29	Veersen	65-0402
Emilie 29, Wm. 5, August 10m, Cath. 60			
Chr. 24			
ROECK, Caspar	23	Bolstern	66-1155
ROEDEL, Friedrich	41	Michigan	63-0693
ROEDER, Carl	25	Rothenkirchen	64-0427
ROEDER, Elisb.	22	Crumbach	64-0495
ROEDER, Elise	29	Niederhausen	63-1136
ROEDER, Friedrich	28	Bergmansreuth	67-0806
Margaretha 20			
ROEDER, Henry	20	Ulm	64-0639
ROEDER, Joh.	33	Untersalzbach	65-0116
Joseph 56, Anna 58			

NAME	AGE	RESIDENCE	YR-LIST
ROEDER, Johann	55	Altengronau	64-0433
ROEDIGER, Chr. O.	39	Armstadt	64-0639
ROEGGE, Herm.	18	Wimmen	63-1085
ROEGGE, Wilhelm	17	Essen	66-0668
ROEGNER, Susanne	22	Oberschlingen	64-0427
ROEHL, Bernhard	27	Magdeburg	66-1155
ROEHL, Carl	24	Querfurt	65-0116
ROEHL, Heinrich	41	Ostheim	66-0650
Christian 40			
ROEHLER, Heinr.	30	Hoesseringen	64-0214
Dorothea 30, Heinr. 6m			
ROEHLER, wilhelm	16	Wuertemberg	66-0679
ROEHLING, Caroline	28	Voltlage	66-0984
ROEHLING, H. W.	55	Oppendorf	64-0840
ROEHNER, Carol.	25	Frieburg	65-0402
Elis. 5, Barb. 3			
ROEHR, Bertha	16	Scheitz	67-0599
ROEHRIG, Fr. Wilh.	50	Bornden	63-0862
ROEHRING, Fritz	20	Nordhorn	66-1243
ROEHRING, Joh.Geo.	29	Ostheim	66-0650
Dorothe 31, Heinr. 5, Friedr. 3			
ROEHRS, Anna	25	Brackel	65-0116
ROEHRS, Johann	18	Hastedt	63-0614
ROEHRS, Meta	23	Otterstedt	66-1031
ROEHRS, T.C.	29	Stuckenbostel	64-1161
ROEKER, Carl	34	Hulben	65-0974
ROELFS, Jacob	16	Groothusen	64-1022
ROELKER, August	54	New York	63-0953
Friederike 40, August 20, Bertha 19			
Emma 16, Hedwig 14, Hermann 15			
Charles 10, Joseph 8, Edward 7, Henry 4			
Bernhard 1			
ROELOFSZ, Georg	60	Pella	66-0734
ROEMANN, Aron	7	Oberdorf	64-1022
ROEMEHILD, Marcus	19	Wagenfeld	66-1127
ROEMER, August	18	Neuertingen	66-1203
ROEMER, Berthold	26	Baltimore	63-0953
Anna 9			
ROEMER, Charl.	33	Iftershausen	63-0551
ROEMER, Conrad	33	Rechlitz	66-0679
Carl 34			
ROEMER, Conrad	36	Carlissen	66-0984
Christiana 30, Elisabeth 20, Susanne 7			
ROEMER, Heinr.	24	Darmstadt	65-0189
ROEMER, Hermine	31	Petershagen	65-1095
ROEMER, Herrmann	24	Ettenstein	66-0679
ROEMER, Wm.	36	Illinois	63-0752
ROEMHELD, Justus	18	Marburg	66-0934
ROEMING, Carl	18	Herbsen	64-1206
ROEMOLIN, Louis	60	Zevenitz	65-0007
Elise 60			
ROEMSCHILD, Georg	23	Sachsen-Mein.	66-0349
ROENER, Julius	24	Sauerburg	65-0189
August 9m			
ROENKER, Caroline	20	Oldenburg	66-0934
August 6m			
ROENN, Ludwig	36	Bromberg	64-0456
Caroline 32, Emilie Otil. 7			
Caroline W. 4, Ernst 1, Christine 60			
Wilhelm 28			
ROEPKE, William	19	Braunschweig	66-1155
ROERIG, Jacob	33	Steinfeld	66-1093
Francisca 28, Johann 6m			
ROERIG, John	16	Hambach	63-1136
ROERIG, Philip	16	Schnei	66-1127
ROES, Ludw.	21	West.Beverst.	63-0551
ROES, Stina	15	Lensing	63-0693
ROESCH, Friederike	19	Liedolsheim	63-0244
ROESCH, Jacob	44	Lieboldsheim	64-0363
Catharina 47, Sophia 18, Jacob 16			
Caroline 14			
ROESCH, Rudolph	22	Werthen	65-1088
ROESCHE, Franz Frd	32	Oldorf	66-0984
Bernhardine 27			
ROESCHE, Johannes	22	Engelbach	66-0221
ROESEKE, Augusta	43	Berlin	66-1248
ROESEL, Wilhelmine	29	Augusta	66-1131
Herm. 23, Caroline 9, Maria 7			

NAME	AGE	RESIDENCE	YR-LIST
ROESELER, Joh. Got	26	Muelhoff-Rad.	66-0650
Rosalie 26			
ROESER, Pierre	28	Belgien	63-0350
ROESING, B.	18	Neustadt	64-0639
ROESING, Joh.	30	Coehn	64-0073
Mrs. 17			
ROESS, Johann	41	Mannheim	66-1127
Franz 9			
ROESSE, Friedr. Wm	51	Zuerich	64-0739
Johanna Jul. 46, Maria 9, Anna 6			
ROESSER, Carl	28	Klingen	66-1031
ROESSER, Doris	15	Schweinsberg	66-0679
ROESSER, Elisabeth	26	Gehaus	63-1038
ROESSINCK, C.	24	New York	63-0482
ROESSLE, Cathar.	21	Korb	66-1373
ROESSLER, Emilie	47	Boehmen	63-0752
ROESSLER, Minna	24	Erwitte	66-1313
ROESSLER,G.	21	Pirmenz	66-0413
ROESSNER, Aug.	14	Bauerbach	65-0007
ROESSNER, Frd.	45	Baltimore	64-0904
ROETER, B.	24	Brachterbeck	66-0413
ROETERIGGE, Gert.	25	Leer	66-1131
ROETGER, H.W.	33	Dielingen	64-0639
ROETH, Peter	29	Sul	66-1131
ROETHGEN, C.	28	Bremen	64-0840
ROETHGEN, Wm.	15	Muenster	64-1053
ROETHLE, Magdalena	21	Wehningen	66-1327
ROETTER, Ernst	43	Erfurt	67-0795
Louise 41, Louis 15, Friedr. 13, Carl 10			
Emilie 6, Emil 3, Alma 1			
ROETTERING, Anna M	21	Lengen	65-1030
ROETTGER, Carl	24	Braunschweig	63-1010
ROETTIGEN, Gustav	23	Bourscheid	63-0482
ROETTJER, Sophia	42	Kochstedt	23-0865
ROETZ, Wilhelm	31	Potsdam	66-1243
Caroline 32, Minna 6, August 5			
Wilhelm 11			
ROETZEL, Peter	32	Manil	64-1053
ROEVER, (m)	35	St. Louis	63-0862
ROEVER, H.C.	50	Kustedt	65-1088
ROEVER, Hermann	18	Kuhstedt	63-0614
ROEVER, Philipp	25	Marburg	64-0739
ROEWEKAMP, Anna	23	Amelsbueren	66-1031
ROFFERT, Christ.	22	Cannstadt	64-0840
ROGALLE, M.		Wilde	63-1003
ROGGE, F.	16	Lienen	65-1189
ROGGENBACH, Carl	23	Breitenstein	65-0243
ROGGENKAMP, Heinr.	25	Neuenkirchen	65-0038
ROGLER, Gottlob	26	Asch	64-0073
ROGLER, Louis	16	Asch	66-0704
Alleina 23			
ROHACH, John	33	Boehmen	63-0752
Josefa 31, Maria 7, John 5, Anna 9			
ROHDE, Friedr.	47	Bromberg	64-0456
Antonia P. 47, Caroline P. 18			
Wilhelmine A 16, Emil 5			
ROHDE, Gertrude	22	Hoelsa	65-1030
ROHDE, H.M.	18	Schlienworth	64-0593
ROHDE, Heinr.	25	Geestendorf	63-0990
ROHDE, Heinr. W.	19	Luedingworth	64-0687
ROHDE, Henriette	24	Meineringhsn.	66-0934
ROHDE, Theod.	45	Preussen	63-1136
Johanne 37, Marie 2			
ROHDERS, (m)	16	Boehmen	64-0495
ROHE, Carl	26	Trebnitz	66-1327
ROHE, Christ.	30	New York	63-0953
Thecla 28, Joseph 14, Anna 9, Anna 3			
baby 11			
ROHLE, Joh.	16	Heslach	64-0782
ROHLEDER, Nicolaus	36	Lobenhausen	66-1248
Catharina 30, Georg 9, Conrad 5, Anna 7			
baby (f) 9m			
ROHLFFS, H.C.	21	Hoya	64-0782
ROHLFING, August	32	Baltimore	63-1178
ROHLFING, Heinr'tt	19	Essen	66-0668
ROHLFING, Wilhelm	33	Osnabrueck	63-0917
Emma 31, Ch. 6, William 4, baby 4m			
ROHLFINGMEIER, Fr.	26	Meetrecht	63-1069

NAME	AGE	RESIDENCE	YR-LIST
ROHLING, Georg	31	Weidenbach	64-0023
ROHLING, Wilh'mine	16	Burgdamm	66-0984
ROHLINGER, Elisa	20	Istein	66-0668
ROHLOFF, (m)	25	Prussia	64-0138
ROHM, Maria	23	Ndr.Wilstadt	65-1095
ROHMANN, Heinrich	26	Plauen	64-0433
ROHMER, Heinr.	24	Nordhoff	65-0116
ROHMEYER, Friedr.	27	Newark	66-0221
Wilhelm 25, Louise 18, Marie 59			
ROHR, Friederike	45	Frandenbach	64-0138
Friedr. 18, Wilhelmine 17			
ROHR, Josepha	20	Eltville	67-0007
ROHRBACH, Johannes	39	Giessen	66-1127
ROHRBACH, Margaret	22	Oppenheim	66-0147
Catharine 25			
ROHRBACH, Maria	16	Kirschenhsn.	66-0412
ROHRBECK, Gustav	23	Bromberg	65-0151
ROHRCHEN, Caroline	29	Prussia	63-0752
Louise 4, August 11m			
ROHRER, Philipp	22	Herzogsweiler	66-0147
ROHTE, Emil	30	San Francisco	64-0023
ROI, Friedrich	31	Dissen	66-1128
Wilhelmine 32, Wilhelmine 7, Wilhelm 5			
Heinrich 4, Franz 2, Caroline 9m			
ROIEL, Oltmann	24	Westerstede	64-0920
ROJERS, Anton	24	Wersuwe	65-1030
ROJERS, Gerhard	23	Abbemuehle	65-1030
ROLAND, Anna	16	Altenburg	66-0934
ROLEICK, Ignatz	30	Kuttenberg	64-0593
ROLF, Herm.	21	Wolfenbuettel	65-0038
ROLF, Melchior	41	Lehe	66-1031
Therese 39, Gertrude 59, Therese 7			
Anna 4, Georg 2, Gertrudis 10m			
ROLFE, Math.	30	Paris	67-0007
ROLFFS, H.(m)	30	Muehlheim	63-0296
ROLFS, Heinr.	28	New York	64-0214
ROLFS, J.	31	Oldenburg	65-0974
Mrs. 23			
ROLL, Ludw.	16	Ruppertsburg	65-0116
ROLL, Ludwig	26	Ruppertsberg	66-1093
ROLL, Robert	19	Emendingen	66-0734
ROLLAND, Adam	36	Pennsylvania	63-1136
ROLLAND, Friedrike	21	Rechborn	63-1136
ROLLBERG, J.Th.	21	Scherbda	65-0898
ROLLER, Eva Barb.	35	Euppingen	63-0862
ROLLMANN, F.(m)	20	Berlin	64-0023
ROLOFF, Ferdinand	21	Bockenau	64-0433
ROLTGER, Conrad	32	New York	63-1218
Elisabeth			
ROMBERG, Anna L.	23	Eininghausen	65-0038
ROMBERG, Jan	25	Bentheim	64-0363
ROMEISEN, Conrad	20	Steinau	67-0007
ROMER, Max	23	Eitenheim	66-0221
Anna 20			
ROMETSCH, Wilh'mne	50	Basel	66-1131
Wilhelm 8			
ROMMEF, Ed.	35	Beinstein	65-1030
ROMMEL, Erasmus	52	Sachsen-Mein.	66-0349
ROMMEL, Gottlieb	20	Schwieden	66-1327
ROMMEL, Joh. B.	21	Gr. Esslingen	64-0886
ROMMEL, Wilhelmine	25	Ossweil	64-1022
RONDIG, Caspar	25	Meiningen	64-1108
RONDSTADT, Charltt	23	Hannover	63-1136
RONNACK, Johann	33	Danzig	67-0795
Albertine Ch 22, Maria 9m			
RONNEBAUM, Agnes	18	Oldenburg	66-0221
RONNERS, P.	20	Zeithern	66-0413
RONSTADT, Johanna	19	Leer	64-0170
ROOLFS, R.J.	28	Norden	65-0594
ROOLVINK, Gerh.	22	Oldenzaal/Hol	64-0904
ROOS, Ad.(f)	23	Mernheim	64-0782
ROOS, Albert	21	Plochingen	64-0593
ROOS, Babeth	18	Speyer	66-1155
ROOS, Balthasar	46	Drummersheim	65-0004
ROOS, Friedrich	21	Carlsruhe	63-0551
ROOS, Maria	25	Astheim	66-1327
ROOS, Martin	28	Messkirch	64-0593
ROPERS, Johann	21	Bremervoerde	66-0934

NAME	AGE	RESIDENCE	YR-LIST
ROPKE, Heinrich	19	Morsum	66-1093
ROPSACK, W. Adelb.	23	Loebau	63-1010
ROPTKE, Charlotte	27	Silberhausen	64-1053
RORODE, Theo.	31	Ober Brake	63-0168
ROS, Margarethe	27	Emden	64-1161
ROSCHE, Friederike	18	Esslingen	66-0412
ROSCHKA, Johann	30	Bohemia	64-0363
Franziska 28, Johann 7, Marie 5, Anna 9m			
ROSCHMANN, Balt.	26	Wuerttemberg	64-0782
ROSE, Aug.	36	Eisen	65-1189
ROSE, Charlotte	27	Bremen	66-1248
ROSE, Chr.	53	Gruenenplan	63-0244
ROSE, J.F.	46	Brilon	65-0974
ROSEBROCK, Heinr.	23	Visselhovede	66-1373
ROSELAND, Maria	32	Achim	66-1093
Heinrich 9m			
ROSELIUS, Aa.(f)	16	Thedinghausen	64-0495
ROSELIUS, Herm. H.	15	Thedinghausen	65-0189
ROSEMEYER, Ad.	45	Insterburg	63-1003
ROSEMEYER, Sophie	18	Frille	66-1131
ROSEMUELLER, Natan	27	Hannover	66-0984
ROSEN, Chrs.	36	Oldenburg	63-1085
Friederike 59			
ROSEN, G.	24	Sommerwalden	63-1003
ROSENAU, Hirsch	15	Diespeck	65-0402
ROSENBAUER, Conrad	32	Washington	66-0984
ROSENBAUM, Carl	33	Schoenheide	66-1327
ROSENBAUM, Christ.	54	Chamberburg	66-0346
ROSENBAUM, Gerhd.	35	Broning	64-1022
Antje 33, Berend 7, Harm 3, Peter 9m			
ROSENBAUM, Gottl.	59	Milezhauland	65-1095
Anna 50, Gustav 20, Justina 23, Augusta 3			
Wilhelm 1			
ROSENBAUM, Johann	47	Bromberg	64-0456
Wilhelmine 50, Anna Justine 22			
Gottlieb Joh 16, Michael Gott 18			
Anna Justine 22			
ROSENBAUM, Samuel	28	Kalamazoo	66-1155
Henriette 24, Louis 2, Caroline 2m			
ROSENBECKER, Wm.	29	Steinfurt	63-0296
Catharine 27, Eberhard 59			
ROSENBERG, Adolph	22	Nordenburg	64-0214
ROSENBERG, Anna	25	Liebenic	66-0576
ROSENBERG, Benj.	48	Louisville	63-1178
ROSENBERG, F.	19	Dorum	65-0974
ROSENBERG, Felix	25	Koesen	64-0433
ROSENBERG, R.	22	Dorum	63-0168
ROSENBERG, S.	19	Langendiebach	65-0402
ROSENBERG, Simon	42	Zerbst	66-1155
Augusta 34, Gustav 9, Clara 8, Albert 6			
Hedwig 4, Leopold 2, baby (m) 10m			
ROSENBERGER, Georg	20	Exdorf	65-1030
ROSENBERGER, Hirsh	20	Alldingen	63-1085
ROSENBERGER, Teres	18	Unterfranken	66-0221
ROSENBLATT, Heinr.	31	Cassel	65-0594
Rebecca 21, Sara 7, Joh. Fr. 14			
ROSENBLATT, Lena	37	Geisa	63-0917
Aron 9			
ROSENBROCK, Johann	18	Wellstedt	66-1031
ROSENBROOK, Joh.	22	Fischerhude	64-0363
Heinr. 16			
ROSENBRUCK, Rebeka	29	Bremen	63-0097
ROSENBURG, L.	46	Bamberg	63-0990
ROSENER, Peter	20	Hessloch	66-0083
Heinrich 37			
ROSENFELD, Ad.	32	New York	63-0551
ROSENFELD, G.	28	Cincinnati	63-0917
Catharina 18			
ROSENFELD, L.	44	Nassau	63-1178
Caroline 22			
ROSENFELD, Wolf	14	Hohnbach	63-0953
ROSENGARTEN, H.(m)	18	Gehrde	64-0331
ROSENGARTH, M.	25	Buttenhausen	63-1218
ROSENHAEUSER, Cath	60	Mannheim	66-1127
ROSENHEIM, Ferd.	30	New York	66-0704
ROSENHEIM, M.	30	Jebenhausen	64-1161
Simon 15			
ROSENKRANTZ, Henry	39	Weilburg	63-0990

NAME	AGE	RESIDENCE	YR-LIST
ROSENKRANZ, Frdr.	50	St. Louis	66-0109
ROSENKRANZ, James	46	Wollschrogler	63-0862
ROSENKRANZ, Otto	20	Bremen	65-0189
Carl 18			
ROSENKRANZ, W.	22	Rotheburg	65-1024
ROSENROTH, Cathar.	28	Fickenbuettel	66-0984
Ernst 4			
ROSENSTEIN, Franz	17	Ungarn	63-1136
ROSENSTEIN, Herman	25	Lipsringe	64-1022
Riekchen 23, Bertha 21, Johanna 18			
ROSENSTEIN, Jos.	22	Beverungen	64-0495
ROSENSTEIN, Meyer	22	Buehne	64-0687
ROSENSTEIN, v. Fr.	27	Coblenz	63-1085
ROSENSTOCK, Malche	20	Beuern	65-0594
ROSENTHAL, Abraham	29	San Francisco	63-0953
Minna 18			
ROSENTHAL, Abraham	17	Roth	64-0992
ROSENTHAL, Alois	42	Peeth	63-1085
ROSENTHAL, Anna	27	Heldringen	65-0974
ROSENTHAL, C.	34	Gruenenplan	63-1038
C. 14			
ROSENTHAL, C.	35	Gruenenplan	64-1108
ROSENTHAL, C. (m)	30	Gruenenplan	64-0138
ROSENTHAL, C.(m)	34	New York	64-0023
ROSENTHAL, C.L.(m)	17	Gruenenplan	64-0073
ROSENTHAL, Carl	18	Hannover	66-0734
ROSENTHAL, Conrad	18	Alfeld	66-1093
ROSENTHAL, Francis	59	Olpe	63-0862
ROSENTHAL, Hanne	18	Nagelsberg	63-0693
ROSENTHAL, Helene	20	Fellheim	64-1161
ROSENTHAL, Henry	20	Gruenenplan	63-0482
ROSENTHAL, Herm.	25	Gandersheim	64-0427
ROSENTHAL, Lazarus	23	Berleburg	66-0679
Moses 18			
ROSENTHAL, Louise	31	Odisleben	64-0593
ROSENTHAL, Moritz	37	Pyrmont	63-1218
Caroline 34, Ferdinand 8			
ROSENTHAL, Moses	17	Nassau	66-0679
ROSENTHAL, Nachman	28	Martfeld	64-0433
Jonas 28			
ROSENTHAL, S.	30	Malsingen	63-0990
ROSENTHAL, S.(m)	24	Liedolsheim	64-0495
ROSENTHAL, Sarah	22	Mattfeld	66-1313
ROSENTHAL, Willy	15	Osnabrueck	65-1088
ROSENTRETER, Aug.	28	Stangenfort	65-0713
ROSENTRETER, Fr.	18	Drifsethe	66-0934
ROSENTRETTR, Peter	46	Driftsethe	66-0934
Louise 40			
ROSENWASSER, Sam	25	Ungarn	63-1218
ROSENWINTHER, Hch.		Bagern	64-0023
ROSETT, Meta	36	Lehe	66-1127
Anna 1			
ROSMAN, Julia	19	Aurenberg	66-1203
ROSMEYER, Max	32	Germany	63-1136
ROSS, August	41	Philadelphia	63-0917
ROSS, Eduard	24	Weimar	65-0770
Elise 24			
ROSS, Ferd.	24	Lingen	66-1243
ROSS, Hermann	35	Philadelphia	63-0015
ROSS, Joseph	19	Nassau	67-0007
ROSS, R.	17	Gruenberg	65-1024
Emma 21			
ROSSBACH, Heinrich	57	Marburg	63-0006
ROSSBACH, J.	30	Frankfurt	65-0007
ROSSBACH, Jacob Fr	22	Kreuzburg	64-0739
ROSSBACH, Th.(m)	28	Hirschfeld	63-0482
ROSSE, Elise	55	Kriegsheim	63-1069
Barbara 16			
ROSSERT, Christ	39	Reichenbach	64-0170
Agatha 28, Peter 3, Christine 4			
ROSSNER, Theodor	22	Altenburg	63-1038
ROST, Johannes	25	Mahlberg	66-0346
Jacob 28			
ROST, Louis	29	Wuerttemberg	66-0576
ROSTENSTEIN, J.	24	Steinach	63-1218
ROSTOSIL, Anton	20	Wrof	67-0007
ROTENBAUER,	22	Gaertenrode	63-1003
ROTENBERG, Marcus	33	Blichhawka	63-1178

NAME	AGE	RESIDENCE	YR-LIST
ROTERT, Lisette	22	Damme	64-0214
ROTH, Adam	42	Curhessen	63-0822
ROTH, Adam	19	Ungarn	63-1218
ROTH, Adam	28	Finley	64-0687
ROTH, Adolph	20	Boehmen	66-0221
ROTH, Adolph	18	Michten	66-1203
ROTH, Adolph	18	Miehlen	66-1373
ROTH, Albert	27	Soest	64-0199
ROTH, Amalia	23	Bremen	65-1024
ROTH, August	33	Hochnoessingn	66-1155
ROTH, Barbara	19	Voehringen	67-0806
ROTH, Cath.	22	Altheim	64-0840
ROTH, Catharina	20	Frankonia	66-0837
ROTH, Catharine	22	Hornbach	66-1093
ROTH, Chr. F.	40	Kirchheim	63-0097
ROTH, Conrad	20	Robenhausen	63-1218
ROTH, Crescentia	38	Kirchhausen	65-0594
Caroline 19, Christine 2			
ROTH, Eleonore	20	Carlissen	66-0984
ROTH, Elisabeth	23	Salzungen	66-1031
ROTH, Elise	22	Wolfsgrube	65-1189
ROTH, Fr. (m)	52	St. Goar	64-0363
Elise 16			
ROTH, Franz	22	Lindau	66-1155
ROTH, Friedrich	38	Luedolfsheim	66-0083
Sophie 31, Sophie 7, Christine 5			
Friederike 3, Louise 11m			
ROTH, Georg	27	Weissenburg	65-0189
ROTH, George	53	Chicago	63-0350
ROTH, Henry	25	Altenhasslau	63-0015
ROTH, Henry	23	Hessen	66-0221
ROTH, Henry	20	Erlinsbach	66-0109
ROTH, Joh.	14	Grattstadt	64-0427
ROTH, Johann	29	Bayern	66-0221
Margarethe 30, Sebastian 5, Margareth 9m			
ROTH, Johann	28	Hausen	66-0469
Catharina 21			
ROTH, Johann	22	Oberbessenbch	65-0038
ROTH, Johann	33	Matten	64-0363
ROTH, John	27	Baltimore	63-1218
ROTH, John	19	Rheinpfalz	66-0984
ROTH, John A.	19	Langendrehbch	63-1136
ROTH, Lendelin	54	Duemmingen	64-0687
Catharina 22, Wendelin 20, Sophie 11m			
ROTH, Magdalena	22	France	63-0990
ROTH, Margarethe	20	Niedergrundau	65-0948
ROTH, Marie	50	Dermbach	66-0679
Bonifacius 16			
ROTH, Martin	41	Boehmen	63-1038
Sal. 31, Abraham 9, Schendel 7, Moses 5			
baby 11m			
ROTH, Michael	28	Bavaria	63-0822
Franziska 50, Victoria 20			
Marie Ursula 18, Margar. 16, Marie 3			
ROTH, Peter	22	Bavaria	63-0822
ROTH, Philipp	50	Kleestadt	66-0576
Marie 31			
ROTH, Sophie	21	Markdorf	66-0704
ROTH, Wilhelm	25	Liederheim	67-0007
ROTHAERMEL, Cath.	22	New York	63-0244
ROTHAERMEL, Nicol.	17	Niederfleiden	64-0639
ROTHAMMEL, Elisa.	25	Friedewald	64-0433
ROTHBART, Paul	27	Garz	64-0363
ROTHE, Adolph		Bremen	64-0343
ROTHE, Benjamin	64	Indianapolis	64-0687
ROTHE, Dorothea	57	Gotha	66-1373
ROTHE, Louis	40	Walsrode	66-0934
Elise 22, Diedrich 3			
ROTHEMEL, Marie	20	Lamstedt	66-0704
ROTHENBERGER, Gust	21	Reinsheim	66-0413
ROTHENBURGER, Cel.	23	Reinsheim	66-1327
Franziska 20, Caroline 18			
ROTHENHABER, Eva	18	Heppenheim	64-0639
ROTHER, Jos.	27	Frankenstein	65-1189
ROTHERMEL, Therese	19	Lamstedt	66-0704
ROTHERMUND, Joh.	25	Hannover	66-1131
ROTHERT, Heinrich	18	Rothenstein	66-1131
ROTHFOS, H.(m)	25	St. Magnus	64-0427

NAME	AGE	RESIDENCE	YR-LIST
ROTHFUCHS, Carolyn	29	Schweiz	66-0704
ROTHGANGEL, Carl	42	Thueringen	64-0687
Gottlieb 17, Conrad 7, Bernhard 3			
ROTHGANGEL, Christ	37	Coburg	64-1022
Anna 7, Johanna 5, Helene 2			
ROTHMEIER, Heinr.	18	Westphalen	66-0469
ROTHSCHED, Abraham	21	Butzbach	66-1093
ROTHSCHILD, Adolph	36	Voehl	66-0734
Cathinka 26, Hermine 5, Augusta 3			
Reinhard 2			
ROTHSCHILD, Alb.	18	Pforzheim	64-0073
ROTHSCHILD, Aug.	23	Rottweil	65-1189
ROTHSCHILD, Carl	19	Goettingen	65-0055
ROTHSCHILD, E.	22	Iven	64-0782
ROTHSCHILD, Fr.	28	Detroit	64-0886
ROTHSCHILD, Hirsch	17	Nordstetten	66-0704
ROTHSCHILD, Lazar	30	Hattersheim	64-0427
ROTHSCHILD, Louis	30	Terre Haute	66-0734
ROTHSCHILD, M.	26	Wuerttemberg	63-1136
Henry 20			
ROTHSCHILD, Max	19	Mainz	66-0679
ROTHSCHILD, Minna	28	Nordstetten	66-0704
Maier 23			
ROTHSCHILD, Ruben	18	Hessen	64-0639
ROTHSCHILD, Samuel	16	Osthaim	64-0904
ROTHSCHILD, Simon	16	Werlau	66-0704
ROTHSCHILD, Zulche	17	Oberaula/Hess	64-0920
Joseph 14			
ROTKO, F.	25	Stolzenau	66-0413
ROTLT, Caroline	16	Ottersdorf	66-0984
Marie 7			
ROTTENBACHER, El.	24	Altheim	67-0007
ROTTENSTEINER, Joh	39	Dillingen	64-0687
ROTTER, Eduard	28	Wien	65-0402
ROTTHOFF, Johann	31	Niederklein	64-0840
Maria 32, Anna 58, Maria 20, Anna 7			
Cath. 5, Joseph 3			
ROTTLER, Caspar	24	Schelmberg	64-0427
Marie 27			
ROTTLER, Conrad	20	Schoeberg	64-0214
ROTTMANN, Frederic	36	Indianapolis	63-1178
ROTTSTEIN, G.	25	Hildburghsn.	63-1003
ROUCHED, Caroline	47	Neushausen	64-0992
ROUGET, Emil	30	Giessen	66-0577
ROUSSEAU, Fr'drich	19	Minden	64-0199
ROUX, W.	25	Carlshaven	63-0953
ROVE, K. (f)	18	New York	63-0821
L. (m) 29			
ROWLAND, Lipmann	33	New York	64-0593
ROX, Philipp	22	Wirschhausen	64-0840
RUAFF, Moritz	27	Altenburg	66-0734
RUB, Johann	27	Basel	64-1053
RUBE, Catharine	32	Uhrbach	66-1093
Johann 3, Gottlob 11m			
RUBE, Joh. Chr.	47	Unteruhrbach	64-0739
RUBEL, Ferdinand	17	Steinbach	66-0679
RUBEN, Ernst	19	Burchhausen	64-0363
Albert 15			
RUBENBERGER, Georg	41	Eysolden	64-0363
RUBERT, Joseph	18	Sonda	66-0623
RUBNER, Johann	29	Asch	66-0679
RUBS, Alexander	41	St.Petersburg	63-0015
RUCH, Heinr.	24	Rollsted	64-0886
RUCK, Marie	33	Reckum	63-1178
RUCKEN, Marg.	20	Eichloch	66-0412
RUCKER, Simon	25	Hohenberg	64-0138
RUCKERT, Georg	18	Gr. Zimmern	64-0782
RUCKERT, J.	24	Garbenheim	64-0782
RUCKGAUER, Peter	29	Nagelsberg	64-0427
RUCKLE, A.G.	20	Waldenbuch	64-1206
RUDDE, Joseph	18	Braetz	64-1053
RUDECK, Henry	38	Blumenau	64-0593
Rosine 21, Henry 12, baby 3m			
RUDERT, Ernst	16	Gefell	64-0938
RUDIN, Albert	22	Muttenz	64-0456
Marg. 53, Maria 17			
RUDKE, Herrmann	37	Westphalen	66-0349
Elisabeth 34, Christine 6, Sophie 3			

NAME	AGE	RESIDENCE	YR-LIST
RUDLAFF, Heinerich	19	Sachs.-Weimar	66-0349
RUDOLF, Johann	28	Oberbuechen	67-0007
RUDOLPH, Adolph	24	Rothenburg	65-0116
Francisca 28			
RUDOLPH, Anna	14	Rhoda	65-1031
RUDOLPH, August	24	Landshut	63-0053
RUDOLPH, Charles	37	New York	63-0917
William 6			
RUDOLPH, Franz	24	Meerane	65-0770
RUDOLPH, Georg	24	Rohrbach	66-0623
Anna Cath. 24, Johann 9m			
RUDOLPH, Isaac	42	Bohemia	64-0782
RUDOW, Carl	27	Bulge	66-0576
RUDWIG, (m)	30	Mengsburg	65-0189
RUEBEL, Carl	24	Rosenbach	64-0782
RUEBEL, Jacob	24	Reichenbach	64-0639
RUEBELING, Elisab.	24	Moischeit	66-0623
Catharina 22			
RUEBENAPF, Louise	16	Sattenhausen	66-1031
RUEBER, Peter	36	New York	64-0687
RUEBSAM, Amalie	30	Cassel	66-1093
RUECKE, Heinrich	28	Bruemmerloh	65-1031
RUECKERSFELD, C.F.	20	Minden	63-1010
RUECKERT, Marg.	20	Gamberg	65-1189
RUECKGABER, Math.	33	Rotenburg	63-1218
RUECKLOS, William	19	Landau	63-0296
RUEDEBUSCH, F.	29	Astede	64-1161
RUEDER, Gottfried	23	Asch	64-0739
RUEFLER, Georg	22	Hohenzell	66-1243
RUEGER, Ed.J.	28	Bremen	64-0363
RUEGER, Heinrich	32	Niederasphe	63-0097
RUEGLE, Johs.	18	Buchlingen	67-0007
RUEHE, Heinrich	29	Lanbach	67-0007
RUEHE, Johannes	24	Achim	64-0639
RUEHL, Carl Emil	18	Rudkers	67-0007
RUEHL, Cath.	48	Brengesheim	64-0593
Cath. 20			
RUEHL, Johannes	31	Herbstein	65-1024
RUEHL, John	23	Rohna	65-1024
Hans 23			
RUEHL, Johs.	51	Rainrod	64-0593
RUEHL, Mina	36	Wiesbaden	66-1131
Francisca 6, Paul 3			
RUEHLING, Gustav	30	Osnabrueck	63-0953
RUEHLMANN, Anna	35	Offenbach	66-0734
Philipp 9, Wilhelm 6			
RUEHNKE, Zita	26	Aachen	63-1218
RUEHR, Wilh.	45	Gotha	65-0713
RUEHRS, Harm.	22	Willstedt	64-0593
RUELLE, Friedr.	18	Brakel	64-0593
RUEMMELE, Ed.	33	Dornhirn	64-0639
RUEMMLE, Marie	38	Dornbirn	66-0734
Anna 28			
RUEPPEL, Emil	15	Bremen	64-0885
RUEPPEL, Friedr.	22	Oberlaub	64-0687
RUEPPEL, Maria	19	Herbstein	65-1024
RUESCH, Chr. H.	24	Osterbruch	65-0594
RUESSEL, St.(f)	26	Soehlingen	64-0331
RUESSER, Johann	22	Rotenburg	66-0623
RUESSLER, Jacob	59	Treschklingen	65-0594
Pauline 22, Marie 2m, Maria 59			
RUESTER, Max	14	Pfungstadt	66-0734
RUETE, Georg	20	Verden	66-1327
RUETE, Marie	15	Westphalen	66-0576
RUETER, Gerh.	26	Hannover	65-0038
Catharina 19, Theodor 11m, Joh. Gerh. 56			
RUETER, Hemine	33	Upleward	65-0594
Sophie 23, Gobke 27			
RUETER, Joh.	24	Brockum	65-1024
Sophie 24, baby 9m			
RUETER, Ludw.	20	Wolmersdingen	65-0974
RUETER, Sophia	22	Obernkirchen	66-0576
RUETER, Sophie	17	Stroehen	65-1031
RUETH, Franz	46	Oberseun	66-1373
RUETHING, Maria	18	Manil	64-1053
RUETICHER, Ph	31	Graefendorf	66-0413
Elise 22			
RUETTINGER, Melch.	28	Gerchsheim	64-0687

NAME	AGE	RESIDENCE	YR-LIST
RUF, Carl	26	Graben	66-0576
RUF, Zacharias	31	Weiler	63-1010
RUFF, August F.	19	Rohracker	65-0055
RUFF, Carl	23	Rottweil	65-0402
RUFF, Caroline	24	Oberhofen	64-0840
RUFF, Hermann	26	Burg	63-0013
RUFF, Mathias	66	Jungingen	64-0363
RUFF, Rosine		Nuertingen	66-1327
RUFFNER, Minna	20	Kaltenthal	66-1093
RUGE, Hermann	15	Scharmbeck	63-0693
Juergen 16			
RUGGE, Johann	14	Wersabe	64-0739
RUGGLES, Ed.	30	Dresden	64-1022
RUH, J.	29	Pirmens	66-0413
RUH, Michael	24	Buerstadt	63-1136
Apollonia 59			
RUHEN, Chs.(f)	28	Messlingen	64-0331
(f) 5			
RUHER, Maria	26	Stoermede	64-0433
Johann 28, Elisabeth 26, Joseph 11m			
Catharina 20, Theresia 18			
RUHER, Theodor	22	Stoermede	63-0398
RUHL, A.H.(m)	21	Schale	64-0363
RUHL, Carl Ludwig	19	Neustadt	66-0984
RUHL, Euphrosine	50	Altenschlirf	63-1218
RUHL, Joh.	28	Neuenkirchen	65-1088
RUHL, Johann	39	Rotenburg/Hes	66-0469
Elisabeth 33, Margaretha 9, George 1			
Sophie 61			
RUHL, Johannes	59	Sundheim	65-0594
RUHL, Maria	24	Kirchheim	64-0840
RUHL, Nic.	18	Herbstein	64-0992
RUHL, Pauline	19	Engethal	64-0073
RUHLAND, D.(f)	59	Loccum	63-0917
Dora 22, Augusta 20, Hermann 30			
RUHLE, Re.(f)	22	Endersbach	64-0782
RUHLING, Lisette	22	Dorzbach	64-0992
RUHLMANN, Andre	24	Pennsylvania	64-0023
RUHLMANN, C.F.(m)	27	Osnabrueck	64-0331
RUHMANN, Aug.	27	Schwelm	66-1373
RUHMANN, Wm.	22	Helwartshsn.	64-0427
RUHOLA, Joseph	21	Emsteck	66-1373
RUHR, Maria	26	Stoermede	64-0433
Johann 28, Elisabeth 26, Joseph 11m			
Catharina 20, Theresia 18			
RUHRAED, Fritz	23	Scharnhausen	66-1373
RUHSTAAT, Friedr.	20	Oldenburg	66-1155
RUIGER, John	28	Assler	66-0221
RUIZ, Ric.	17	Cardenas	64-0331
RULAND, Wm.	22	Dueringen	64-0687
RULENDER, Conrad	28	Kirchheim	65-0243
RULL, Gottlieb	21	Sulzbach	66-0984
RULLMANN, J.H.	52	Oberholstein	65-0594
Dorethe 18, Martin 18, Cath. 54			
RUMBHOLTZ, Gottl.	24	Wildbach	66-0934
RUMKORF, Frankelin	25	Leer	63-0398
RUMMEL, Johann	18	Hayengen	65-1095
RUMMEL, Josephine	23	Hoheneggelsen	64-0886
RUMP, Bernard	44	Covington	63-0953
RUMP, Bernh.	38	Essen	64-0938
RUMP, Carl	22	Bremen	65-1189
RUMP, Gerh.	30	Uptoh	65-1088
RUMP, Wilhelm	24	Loeningen	65-1030
RUMPEL, Johanna	26	Hildra	64-0840
RUMPERNICK, J.	54	Zell	64-0782
RUMPF, A.(m)	22		64-0331
RUMPF, Carl	25	Magdeburg	64-0639
RUMPF, Georg	19	Angerod	64-0782
RUMPF, Peter	29	Rosenholt	64-0782
Catharine 29, Georg 2, Marie 23			
RUMPP, Adolph	35	Nuettingen	66-0679
Margarethe 31, Margarethe 9			
RUNDENBERG, Ernst	48	Hildesheim	64-0433
RUNDSHEIMER, John	27	Friebertshsn.	65-1095
Johannes 30			
RUNEKE, J.(m)	30	Westfalen	64-0495
RUNG, Wilhelmine	26	Mettstetten	64-0639
Pauline 3, Benedict 3m			
RUNGE, August	21	Freschlunebrg	65-0713
RUNGE, Chr.	30	Gruenenplan	64-1206
RUNGE, Chrs.	21	New York	66-0221
RUNGE, Diedrich	21	Hessen	66-0734
RUNGE, Dorette	30	Minden	64-0427
RUNGE, Dorothea	24	Voigtle	66-0934
RUNGE, Eduard	28	Bassum	66-1093
RUNGE, Fr.	26	Bremen	64-0593
RUNGE, Friederike	23	Bremen	64-0456
RUNGE, Friedr.	29	Giessen	66-0577
Marie 28, Maie 2, Carl 6m			
RUNGE, Heinr.	28	Bassum	65-0243
RUNGE, Herm.	28	Beckstedt	64-0593
RUNGE, Hermann	21	Wuellen	66-0837
RUNGE, Johann	27	Sukershoff	65-0713
RUNGE, Ludw.	35	Oesterhaiden	65-0038
Elisabeth 35, Bernhard 6, Theresia 4			
Franziska 1			
RUNGE, Wilhelm	23	Siedenburg	64-0023
RUNKEL, Adam	22	Grolsheim	63-1010
RUNKEL, Henriette	27	Rodenberg	66-1127
RUNKY, Ottilie	14	Cassel	65-0402
Johanna 18			
RUNNER, Sophie	21	Uthlede	64-0456
RUNNER, Wilhelmine	35	Rockel	63-1038
Wilhelmine 9, Juliane 7, Martha 5			
RUNSE, Wilh.	28	Neuhaus	64-0214
RUPERTI, Carl	16	Hemtten	66-1031
RUPERTI, Gustav	24	Oldenburg	66-0469
RUPP, Christian	30	Hannover	66-1131
RUPP, Clemens	28	Muensingen	64-0363
RUPP, Heinrich	17	Unterrodach	66-0221
RUPP, Jacob	20	Rodach	64-0687
RUPP, Marie	23	Wuertemberg	63-0822
RUPP, Regine	23	Leisenwald	65-0713
RUPP, Rudolph	18	Untersdach	66-0221
RUPP, Wilh.	27	Baurnberg	64-0214
RUPPEL, Conrad	50	Nita	66-1128
Catharina 48, Caroline 17, Carl 7			
RUPPEL, Georg	30	Bettenhausen	66-0412
RUPPEL, Karl	29	Soden	66-1128
RUPPERSBERG, Gust.	27	Biedenkopf	63-0097
RUPPERT, Anna Elis	19	Hessia	66-0412
RUPPERT, Johannes	57	Weisenhausen	66-0934
Catharina 57, Joh. Jost 32, Sophie 34			
Helene 18			
RUPPERT, Joseph	31	Karlsbad	66-1128
Joseph 16			
RUPPERT, Michael	33	Washington	66-0704
RUPRECHT, C.W.	31	New York	64-0331
Johanna 21			
RUPRECHT, Joh.	36	Neustadt	64-0938
RUPRECHT, Sophie M	18	Salzungen	66-0412
RUPRECHT, Wilhelm	25	Haling	65-0948
RURF, Georg	26	Irslingen	64-0214
RUS, J.(f)	24	Billingheim	64-0495
C.(f) 25			
RUS, Joseph	20	Boehmen	66-0704
RUSCHE, Anna	26	Cassel	65-1031
Henriette 5, August 1			
RUSCHMEIER, Joh.	17	Fischerhude	64-0593
RUSS, Agnes	34	Boehmen	63-0862
RUSS, Johann Conr.	39	Herford	66-0412
Johana Luise 40, Johana Clara 14			
Peter Robert 12, Christian Th 9			
Johanna Hedw 8, Christian Em 6			
Louise Soph. 3			
RUSS, Sophie	18	Wuertemberg	66-0734
RUSSMANN, Carl	30	Eisfeld	64-0073
RUST, Chr.	40	Rodenberg	67-0600
Dorothee 33, Julie 10, Wilhelm 8			
Sophie 6, Heinrich 2			
RUST, Dirk	24	Oldendorf	66-1128
RUST, Heinrich	26	Huelshagen	66-1031
Dorothea 19, Anna 17			
RUST, Jan	39	Norden	64-1022
Alwina 30, Johanna 6			
RUST, Pauline	23	Baden	66-0147

NAME	AGE	RESIDENCE	YR-LIST
RUST, Pauline	25	Ruethersdorf	66-0934
Traugott 9			
RUSTE, T.	22	Busserk	63-0013
RUSTEMEYER, Wm.	17	Uslar	65-1024
RUSTIGE, A.	23	Westfalen	64-0495
RUTEMEYER, Herm.	16	Osnabrueck	65-1030
Louis 22			
RUTH, H.	14	Langenberghm.	65-1088
RUTH, Maria	19	Niederstadt	63-1136
RUTH, Robert	22	Wilsbach	63-1136
RUTH, Valentin	26	Obernburg	64-0363
RUTHFUS, Henry	30	St. Francisco	66-0984
RUTZ, Elisabeth	24	Horbach	66-1373
RUTZEL, Anna	32	Orb	63-1010
RUTZEN, Carl	43	Hammersheim	64-0687
RUWE, Heinrich	29	Lintern	66-0934
Catharina 20			
RUYHAVEN, Conrad	19	Oldenburg	66-0679
RUYTERS, Catharine	19	Otterndorf	66-1031
RYBARSYK, Michael	18	Rommanshof	64-0456
RYCHLY, Joch.	34	Boehmen	64-0427
RYMUS, Wilh.	22	Kirchdorf	66-1243
SAAK, Friedrich	49	Brake	63-0482
SAALFELD, August	32	Stadthagen	66-1031
Marie 29, Louis 5, Carl 16			
SAALMANN, Ernst	21	Saalfeld	66-1131
SAALMANN, Johann	24	Nexdorf	66-1373
SAATHOFF, Anke	35	Holltrup	66-0578
Gerd 10, Einke 8, Motie 7, Almt 5, Lina 3			
Maria 1			
SAATHOFF, Weert	41	Hesel	66-1031
Gesche 32, Rindert 12, Heere 8, Tamme 6			
Ruebka 2			
SABEL, Ph.	27	Bremen	64-0427
SABISCH, Josefa	33	Sedlitz	64-0639
SACHERS, Franz	48	Boehmen	64-0432
SACHS, Carl	29	Frankfurt	67-0954
Elisabeth 27			
SACHS, Fr. (f)	40	Rochester	64-0687
SACHS, Johannes	17	Waldmichelbch	64-0214
SACHS, Robert	40	Washington	66-0704
Rosalie 23, Antonia 3, Emma 10m			
SACHS, Samuel	30	Boston	64-0639
SACHS, Wilhelm	25	Warburg	66-0349
SACHS, v. H.	38	New York	63-0015
Elisabeth 38, Julius 9, Willy 6			
SACK, Carl	36	Helmstedt	66-0837
SACK, Conrad	25	Rauschenberg	66-0412
Dorette 22			
SACKARND, Lucas	45	Emstetten	66-1031
SACKARUT, Georg	38	Emsdetten	66-0576
SADLER, Elisabeth	20	Ostheim	66-0650
SAEDTELD, Julie	19	Rindsheim	66-1127
SAEGER, Henry	41	Walle	63-1136
Cath. 31, Marie 9, Minna 8, Sophie 4			
Henriette 2			
SAEGER, Johannes	19	Woeglingen	66-0147
SAEGER, Wilh.	20	Bremerhaven	63-1136
SAEHNKE, Antonia	58	Saarbruecken	64-0331
Johanna 21			
SAENGER, Georg	18	Lauterbach	65-1031
SAENGER, James	14	Buttenwiesen	63-1218
Pauline 19			
SAENGER, Sarah	18	Laupheim	63-0953
SAETTLE, Max	39	Sulzbach	66-0984
Nathalie 22			
SAEUBERLICH, F.	34	Wirthheim	63-0015
SAFAR, Joseph	28	Bostock	66-1155
Franziska 25, Franz 4, Anna 22			
SAFFER, Andreas	39	Bamberg	63-0398
SAFFER, Conrad	27	Neuss	65-0055
SAFTIG, H.	28	Andernach	65-1189
SAFTJE, J.	24	Leeste	65-1189
SAGE, Anton	52	Cette	63-0097
SAGEMUEHL, Wrauke	25	Klost.Heiligr	65-0948
SAHLBERGER, Herman	22	Steyerberg	66-1093
SAHLE, Hch.	23	Bremen	64-0331
SAHULZ, Martin	24	Weilar	66-1128

NAME	AGE	RESIDENCE	YR-LIST
SAIGGER, Anton	17	Rottweil	63-1038
SAILER, Bernhardin	22	Vimbruch	63-0244
SAKE, Christine	30	New York	66-0984
SALACK, Antonia	17	Kuttenberg	67-0007
Carl 21			
SALARI, Catharina	19	Italia	63-0015
SALBE, Maximilian	16	Insbach	64-0886
SALBERGER, August	20	Steuerberg	66-0679
SALCHERT, Augusta	24	Brietzig	66-1373
SALELLAND, Juliet	14	France	63-0693
SALGE, Heinrich	24	Seelenfeld	65-1024
SALINGER, Rosl.	24	Schiefelbein	64-0495
SALLERT, Wilhelm	39	Fehlen	66-0349
Cath. 24, Georg 18			
SALM, Helene	24	Steinberg	65-1024
SALOMO, Sophie	40	Bremen	66-1327
Emma 4			
SALOMON, Carl	18	Quetgen	65-0151
SALOMON, Jos.	35	Amberg	64-0073
SALOMON, Nathalie	24	Pfaffweiler	63-1085
SALTE, Ellen	24	Arsten	63-0350
SALTER, Capt.		New York	64-0170
Mrs. , child , child			
SALTZMANN, Henry	33	Hopffelder	63-1178
Elisabeth 28, Wilhelmine 55, Friedrich 2			
baby 9m			
SALTZWEDEL, Gottl.	38	Liszkowde	66-0469
Henriette 34, August 5			
SALZ, Cath.	22	Rezdican	64-0992
SALZENSTEIN, Wolf	14	Halsdorf	64-0639
Amalia 23			
SALZER, David	26	Neufen	63-1136
SALZER, Moses	25	Ermershausen	66-0704
SALZMANN, Peter	25	Badenauheim	66-0412
SALZMANN, Salome	32	New York	63-0953
William 14, Franz 10, Anna 3			
SALZMANN, Valentin	26	Hirschberg	64-0170
Elisab. 21			
SAMANN, Catharine	29	Freudenthal	66-1093
SAMBERG, Louis	41	Delitzsch	63-0953
SAMECK, Cathar.	68	Baschlow	66-0734
SAMEIER, Agnese E.	30	Soeste	66-1128
SAMER, M.(m)	22	Monbach	64-0495
SAMISCH, Fanny	54	Carlsbad	66-1093
Rosa 21			
SAMISCH, Robert	19	Lichtenstein	66-0679
SAMMELMANN, Diedr.	21	Quakenbrueck	64-0739
SAMOIT, Eugenio	39	France	63-0015
SAMSON, Jos.	18	Paderborn	64-0432
SAMUEL, Prosper	18	Paris	64-0023
SAND, Georg	25	Eisenach	63-1178
SANDER, Anna Maria	15	Oster Cappeln	65-0950
SANDER, Bernhardin	18	Neuhaus	64-0433
SANDER, Caroline	21	Osnabrueck	66-0984
SANDER, E.	32	Carlshafen	64-0782
Emma 6			
SANDER, E.	26	Kobylin	65-0007
Hannchen 23, baby 10m, Pauline 31			
SANDER, Fritz	25	Braunschweig	65-0004
SANDER, H.	25	Frankfurt	65-0007
SANDER, H.E.	19	Harste	64-0495
SANDER, Heinr.	17	Lemvoerde	66-1031
SANDER, Heinrich	20	Varensell	66-1203
SANDER, Heinrich	21	Paderborn	65-1095
SANDER, John	49	Boehmen	63-0953
SANDER, Minna	27	Bermten	66-0650
SANDER, Sophie	27	Stolzenau	66-1155
SANDER, Theodor	19	Lemforde	64-0214
SANDER, Wilh.	17	Berenbusch	64-0214
SANDER, Wm.	14	Wagenfeld	63-0482
SANDERS, Albert	41	Galena	66-1093
SANDERS, Aug.	15	Schwarzburg	65-0974
SANDERS, Hermann	17	Bremen	64-0199
SANDERS, Hermann	48	Bremen	64-1053
SANDERSFELD, Carst	37	Weserdeich	67-0599
Anna Margr. 34, Marie Gesine 7, Johann 4			
Nic. Gerhard 11m			
SANDES, Bernhard	45	Uhlbach	66-0349

NAME	AGE	RESIDENCE	YR-LIST
Theodore 45, Josefa 15, Julius 9			
Albert 5			
SANDFURTH, Fr.	29	Braunschweig	65-0007
SANDGREBE, Paul	20	Nentershausen	66-1127
SANDHEIMER, Julius	22	Barsteden	64-0687
SANDHERR, Wilh'mne	59	Blaubeuren	66-1327
SANDKUHL, Herm.	24	Herbergen	64-0593
Anna 19			
SANDMANN, Therese	33	Recke	66-1093
Heinrich 5, August 3, Marie 2, Johanna 60			
SANDSTEIN, Nathan	26	Kostalar/Boeh	66-1128
SANDT, Emil	22	Elberfeld	66-1313
SANDVOSS, Ernst	28	Salzdetfurth	64-0840
SANG, Henry	32	Lieblos	64-0992
Amalie 23, Christian 10m			
SANG, Wilh.	23	Kirchheim	65-0243
SANGSTUECK, Herm.	20	Bremen	66-1203
SANKER, Diedr.	26	Drangstedt	66-0221
SANNE, Heinr.	23	Culbe/Saale	65-1088
SANNING, John	18	Leschede	63-1178
SANSON, Johannes	23	Hessen	66-0109
SAPPENHORN, G.	23	Vechta	64-0992
SARG, Sophie	30	Stuttgart	66-0679
SARITZ, Thomas	18	Boehmen	66-0109
SARNTGET, Michael	26	Boehmen	63-0693
Catharine 28, Catharine 11m			
SARTORIUS, Casper	28	Hontheim	67-0007
SARTORIUS, Heinr.	31	Hontheim	67-0007
SARTORY, Andreas	30	Baden	64-0432
SASE, Meta	18	Sandstedt	63-0398
SASSAMANN, Wilhelm	26	Rodenberg	67-0599
SASSE, (f)	17	Germany	63-0990
SASSE, David	31	Havanna	63-0990
SASSE, Johann	16	Spiker	66-0083
SASSE, Sebastian	41	Frankenberg	65-0770
SASSE, Theodor	34	Kistenhausen	64-1022
Emma 22			
SATHOFF, Gerh. H.	30	Wietmarschen	64-0214
SATTERER, John	23	Hasselbach	66-0734
SATTLER, Friedrich	21	Mannheim	64-0739
SATTLER, Hugo	28	Allstedt	65-1024
aline 21, Hans 2, Georg 3m			
SATTLER, Ludwig	30	Reda	66-0147
Ludwig 4			
SAUER, Adam	17	Lohne	66-0934
SAUER, Adam	20	Lohne	66-1131
SAUER, Albert	21	Stuttgart	65-1088
SAUER, Apollonia	38	New York	63-1136
SAUER, Apollonia	19	Hessloche	63-0693
SAUER, Carl	28	Marburg	66-1127
SAUER, Catharina	25	Urach	66-1155
SAUER, Catharine	26	Freinsen	66-0984
SAUER, Christ.	36	Hundshagen	64-0214
SAUER, Elisabeth	27	Berleburg	66-0734
SAUER, Ernestine	14	Cannstadt	64-0938
SAUER, Francis	34	Luetz	63-1136
Josepha 32, John 9, Francis 7			
Ferdinand 3, Florian 6m			
SAUER, Francisca	39	Wien	64-0687
Julius 7, Emil 6			
SAUER, Gg.	64	Wahlbach	65-1189
SAUER, Henr.	24	Lanthausen	66-1203
SAUER, Isaac	30	Heischbach	64-0782
SAUER, Joh.	17	Stangenrod	65-0116
SAUER, Joh.	17	Maecklinghsn.	65-0948
SAUER, Johann	23	Steinau	66-0623
SAUER, Johannes	20	Gleichen	66-1373
Eckardt 8, Anna 11m			
SAUER, Joseph	20	Nust	66-1373
SAUER, Julius	25	Pforzheim	63-0752
SAUER, Michael	24	Neuses	64-1108
SAUER, Reinhard	41	Solingen	63-0822
Gertrude 41, Wilhelmine 9, Stephan H. 8			
Leopold 5, Johanna Jos. 11m			
SAUER, Wilhelm	30	Reichensachsn	64-0170
SAUER, Wilhelm	25	Hersfeld	63-0482
SAUERLAENDER, Wilh	25	Dortmund	66-0083
SAUERWALD, Aug.	26	Stuttgart	64-0886
SAUERWEIN, Martha	26	Mecklar	63-1010
Anna C. 46			
SAUL, Nathan	24	Kockerhausen	64-1108
SAUPE, Christian	55	Poehla	63-1038
Sophia 55, Rosina 20			
SAURBIER, Franz	21	Sondershausen	65-0402
SAUSELE, David	26	Besigheim	65-0594
SAUSTMANN, Friedr.	27	Steierberg	66-0083
SAUTER, Anna	36	St. Gallen	65-0151
SAUTER, Frdr. Carl	33	Hochheim	66-1127
SAUTER, Friedr.	24	Neufra/Pr.	65-0116
SAUTER, Joh.	26	Laufen	64-0495
SAUTTER, Anna M.	25	Reusten	63-0693
SAUTTER, H.(m)	34	New York	64-0331
Johanna 21			
SAUTTER, Johann	21	Feldstetten	67-0806
SAWALL, Gottlieb	47	Bromberg	64-0456
Henriette 45, Johann 18, Eduard 6			
SAX, Caroline	23	Posen	65-0594
SAXE, Paul	36	Baden	67-0007
Rosine 26, Rosine 4, Anna 2			
SAXOVSKY, Louise	20	Lade	65-1095
SAY, Ida	16	Dicktelhausen	67-0007
Stephanie 19			
SAYCHORN, Henr.	22	Scheier	66-0984
SCHAAB, Catharina	35	Kaltlengsfeld	64-0023
SCHAAF, Anna	21	Rauschenberg	63-1085
SCHAAF, Caroline	20	Leimersheim	63-0006
SCHAAF, Georg	55	Eichelhain	64-0992
SCHAAF, Joh.	20	Arnshausen	66-1313
SCHAAF, Ludw.	17	Luebberstedt	65-1024
SCHAAF, Magdalene	22	Neustadt	63-1178
SCHAAKE, Elisab.	25	Thalitter	67-0795
SCHAAL, David	40	Muddelsbach	64-0214
Friedrike 16			
SCHAAL, Friedr.	37	Miedelau	64-0023
SCHAAL, J.	14	Gerartstadt	64-0782
SCHAATE, Caroline	24	Dunsenhausen	66-0413
Wilh. 10m			
SCHAATZ, Elisabeth	15	Rothendorf	66-0837
SCHABECKER, Christ	46	Weissenborn	66-0704
SCHABERT, Hermann	41	Prussia	66-0984
SCHACHT, H.H.(m)	25	Berghausen	64-0331
H.F.(m) 20, H.L.(m) 17			
SCHACHT, Louise	18	Bachholzhsn.	65-0950
Charlotte 26			
SCHACK, Adolph	20	Wiesbaden	66-1373
SCHACK, Barbara	22	Schelbrun/Sw.	64-1053
SCHAD, Conrad	19	Hessen	64-0432
Anna Martha 24			
SCHAD, Francis	48	Louisville	66-0704
Mathilde 28, Carl 9, Francis 8			
SCHAD, Math.	54	Schwarza	63-0398
Susanne 51, Georg 15			
SCHAD, Philip	18	Ruppertsberg	66-1093
Johannes 23			
SCHAD, Pierre	30	Switz.	64-0170
SCHADE, Adolph	25	Wulfspringe	64-0023
SCHADE, Christian	55	Coeslin	66-1203
Pauline 33, Christian 9m, Oskar 8			
SCHADE, Joh. M.	27	Erdhausen	64-0639
SCHADE, Marg. M	27	Netra	64-0886
SCHADE, Maria	26	Falkenberg	66-0412
SCHADE, Robert	21	Altkirchen	66-0984
SCHADELE, Michael	11	Hildersberg	64-0885
SCHADEWITZ, George	19	Cassel	66-0934
SCHADOWITZ, Heinr.	61	Berlin	65-0243
SCHAECHTER, Hinri.	16	Wester Cappel	65-0948
SCHAECK, Gustav	17	Wuerttemburg	66-0109
SCHAED, Friedr.	23	Sundtheim	66-0704
SCHAEDDEL, Geo.	24	Lauterbach	65-1030
SCHAEDEL, Carl	20	Oehlingen	66-1327
SCHAEDEL, E.	23	Oberlais	64-0782
SCHAEDEL, Johann	37	Bavaria	63-0822
Regine 37, Elisabeth 3			
SCHAEDEL, Therese	27	Werda	66-1203
B. 10m			
SCHAEDLER, Louise	23	Wuerzburg	66-1327

NAME	AGE	RESIDENCE	YR-LIST
SCHAEFER, Heinr.	20	Darmstadt	66-1031
SCHAEFER, A.C.(m)	16	Eudorf	64-0023
SCHAEFER, Adam	22	Brooklyn	64-0214
SCHAEFER, Andreas	20	Carlsheim	65-0243
SCHAEFER, Andreas	18	Halberstadt	65-0950
SCHAEFER, Anton	36	Braak/Pr.	64-0920
Lisette 32, Therese 8, Minna 6, Anna 2			
SCHAEFER, B.	24	Hildburghsn.	63-1003
SCHAEFER, Barbara	56	Oberschuept	64-0840
SCHAEFER, C.	22	Oettinghausen	64-0782
SCHAEFER, C.L.	25	Schrock	65-0007
SCHAEFER, Carl	20	Cassel	67-0600
SCHAEFER, Carl	24	Alsfeld	64-1022
SCHAEFER, Carl	26	Merchlbach	65-0402
SCHAEFER, Casp.	32	Echzell	66-1243
SCHAEFER, Caspar	21	Frohnhausen	66-1155
SCHAEFER, Cath.	22	Luetzel-Wieke	65-0116
SCHAEFER, Cathar.	20	Laisa	65-0974
SCHAEFER, Cathrine	20	Eberstadt	66-0668
SCHAEFER, Cathrine	24	Koenig	66-1203
SCHAEFER, Charlott	44	Burkhardt	63-1038
SCHAEFER, Chr.	32	Duderstadt	63-0821
SCHAEFER, Chr.	22	Wolfskehlen	65-1189
SCHAEFER, Christ.	18	Oberlshausen	66-0623
SCHAEFER, Christof	18	Coburg	64-0593
SCHAEFER, Conrad	21	Densburg	65-0948
Margarethe 32			
SCHAEFER, Doris	19	Hainbach	64-0170
Anna C. 15			
SCHAEFER, Ernst	42	Philadelphia	63-0917
SCHAEFER, F.	33	Cincinatti	63-0821
SCHAEFER, Franz	20	Pietersheim	66-0650
Carl 16			
SCHAEFER, Franz'ka	28	Nenndorf	63-0821
SCHAEFER, Friedr.	17	Brockenheim	66-0984
SCHAEFER, Fritz	20	Esslingen	66-1093
SCHAEFER, G.Melch.	22	Steinberg	63-0168
SCHAEFER, Georg	27	Memphis	63-0953
SCHAEFER, Georg	25	Geottingen	66-0984
SCHAEFER, Gerturd	19	Ahrenkamp	64-0920
SCHAEFER, Gustav	21	Willenroth	66-1248
SCHAEFER, H.	30	Washington	63-0015
Bertha 27, Helene 22			
SCHAEFER, H.	25	Prussia	63-1003
SCHAEFER, Heinrich	25	Alsfeld	63-1069
Margaretha 22			
SCHAEFER, Heinrich	24	Mosbach	66-0734
SCHAEFER, Heinrich	18	Darmstadt	66-1031
William 21, Elisabeth 17			
SCHAEFER, Henriett	17	Boehne	66-0469
SCHAEFER, Henriett	25	Barterode	66-0666
SCHAEFER, J. Ph.	25	Nassau	65-0007
SCHAEFER, Jacob	18	Schlaildorf	64-0593
SCHAEFER, James	21	Steinbach	63-0244
SCHAEFER, Joh. Jac	27	Kassel	66-1128
SCHAEFER, Johann	18	Hessia	66-0679
SCHAEFER, Johanna	21	Ludwigslust	66-0934
SCHAEFER, Johannes	26	Weimar	66-0469
SCHAEFER, Johannes	17	Densberg	66-0623
SCHAEFER, John	34	Esselbach	64-0170
Maria 42, Johann 7, Maria 23			
SCHAEFER, Johns	26	Hofken	65-0243
Cathar. 26			
SCHAEFER, Jos.	33	Gamberg	65-1189
Josepha 30, Anna 22			
SCHAEFER, Joseph	22	Pilgersdorf	65-0948
SCHAEFER, Jost	26	Heinertshsn.	64-0687
Cathar. 23, baby 6m			
SCHAEFER, Justine	52	Carlshafen	66-1243
Augusta 20			
SCHAEFER, K.	45	Busserk	63-0013
SCHAEFER, K.	24	Weitenthal	66-0413
SCHAEFER, Lina	17	Coburg	65-0243
Hermine 14, Joseph 7			
SCHAEFER, Louise	16	Stuttgart	64-0138
SCHAEFER, Louise	28	Bremen	66-0704
Carl 5			
SCHAEFER, Ludwig	29	Wiedermehre	64-0363

NAME	AGE	RESIDENCE	YR-LIST
SCHAEFER, Marg.	58	Eistorf	64-0331
SCHAEFER, Maria	20	Heidelberg	65-0116
SCHAEFER, Marie	22	Ernsthausen	64-0938
SCHAEFER, Marie	24	Baerrenborst	65-1031
SCHAEFER, Martin	22	Cassel	66-0934
Mathilde 24			
SCHAEFER, Minrad	24	Wendelsheim	65-0007
Marianne 26, Helene 20, Victorie 15			
SCHAEFER, Moritz	35	Westfalen	66-0734
Anna 56, Caroline 19, Ernst 17			
SCHAEFER, Paul	17	Willingshsn.	66-1373
SCHAEFER, Peter	25	Asslar	66-0221
SCHAEFER, Peter	31	Muehlheim	66-0650
SCHAEFER, Peter	32	Ndr.Durrenbch	65-1095
SCHAEFER, Philipp	22	Wieseck	64-0343
Johanna 21			
SCHAEFER, Philipp	22	Markobel	64-0739
SCHAEFER, Rosa		Nambach	66-1373
SCHAEFER, Rosine	22	Metzingen	66-1327
SCHAEFER, Theobald	19	Waldborn	65-0151
SCHAEFER, Wilh.	24	Anndorf	66-0221
SCHAEFER, Wilhelm	36	New York	66-0221
SCHAEFERS, Herrman	24	Ickenhausen	65-0770
Albert 17			
SCHAEFFER, Heinr.	21	Vegesack	64-0456
SCHAEFFER, Jacob	33	Germany	63-1136
SCHAEFFER, Marie	21	Angersbach	66-0578
SCHAEFFER, Marie	24	Lutzel-Weibel	65-0116
SCHAEFFLER, Wilh.	30	Notringen	63-1038
SCHAEFFNER, Jac.	23	Wiesloch	65-0007
Theodora 21			
SCHAEFLEIN, Leopld	23	Pirmasens	66-0412
SCHAEFNER, Marie	22	Werther	66-0704
SCHAEPER, Bernhard	17	Luedinghsn.	66-0412
SCHAEPERS, Anna	29	Bremen	65-0402
Anna 2			
SCHAER, Adolph	20	Verden	65-0948
SCHAERER, Marie L.	18	Basel	64-0214
SCHAERTL, Aug.	30	Koenigshaber	63-0296
SCHAETER, Joseph	19	Durlar	66-1155
SCHAETTLE, William	17	Weilheim	63-0990
SCHAFENBURG, Liset	28	Suhl	65-1088
SCHAFER, Fr.	25	Brauingsweilr	63-1010
SCHAFER, Joh.	30	Bleidenroed	64-0214
SCHAFER, Johs.	44	Helversdorf	64-0023
SCHAFFNER, A.	17	Wolfskehlen	65-1189
SCHAFFNER, C.	14	New York	63-1085
SCHAFFNER, Elisab.	23	Bledesheim	64-0214
SCHAFFNER, Heinr.	53	Pfingstadt	64-1053
Dorothea 50, Friedr. 14, Wm. 9			
SCHAFFNER, Johanna	20		66-0576
SCHAFFNER, Johanna	42	Ippelsheim	64-0886
Bertha 17, Salomon 7, Helene 5, Ida 4			
Pauline 6m			
SCHAFFNER, John P.	27	Edesheim	63-1085
SCHAFFNER, Leander		Wien	66-0934
SCHAFFNER, Louis	15	Pfungstadt	63-0350
SCHAFFNER, Peter	33	New York	63-1218
Elisabeth 26			
SCHAFFNER, Siemon	14	Epelsheim	64-0886
Hermann 18			
SCHAFFNIT, Adam	28	Preussen	66-0221
SCHAFFNIT, Fr'dr.	17	Preussen	66-0221
SCHAFFNIT, Leonh.	18	Brembach	66-0679
SCHAFFNIT, Lina	30	Darmstadt	66-1127
SCHAFNERT, Georg	21	Breusbach	64-0782
SCHAIBE, Chris.	21	Wettershausen	64-0495
SCHAIBLE, Joh.Mar.	19	Koenigshofen	66-0349
SCHAICH, Louise	24	Reitwangen	64-1108
SCHAIRTELL, Maria	21	Dorum	65-0007
Cath. 20			
SCHAKE, Catharine	21	Ludersheim	66-1248
SCHAKEL, Rosa	23	Stuttgart	64-1161
SCHAKENBERG, Hinr.	22	Fenndorf	66-0578
SCHALK, Adolph	40	Carlsruhe	63-0953
SCHALK, Carl	34	Vizig	66-0650
SCHALK, Emma	28	Philadelphia	63-0862
Lili 8, Rudolph 6			

NAME	AGE	RESIDENCE	YR-LIST
SCHALLER, Johanna	20	Platendorf	64-0904
SCHALLER, Theodor	21	Bremen	64-0904
SCHALLER, anna	17	Calbe	65-0713
Oscar 15			
SCHALLMANN, Ernst	26	New York	64-0138
SCHALLMEYER, Josef	55	Beverstedt	65-0594
Caroline 26, A.M. 55			
SCHALM, Augusta	34	Czarnikau	66-1327
Friederike 14, Juliane 8, Ernst 4			
Carl 9m			
SCHALUPNICIK, Joh.	43	Rielo	66-1131
Anna 42, Anton 8, Johann 5, Rosalia 3			
Joseph 4m			
SCHALWE, Gerd	41	Neermoor	64-0363
Frauke 50, Geeske 18, Claas 15, Jan 9			
Hinderk 6			
SCHALZE, Carl Aug.	27	Vinnenien	66-0349
Ernst 17, Johanna 24, Wilhelmine 40			
SCHAMBACHER, Ferd.	21	Weiler	67-0007
SCHAMBACHER, Gottl	28	Philadelphia	64-0138
SCHAMBACHER, H.	49	Geradstetten	63-1003
SCHAMETSCHECK, Joh	24	Dachau	65-0898
SCHANDA, Joseph	32	Strobulos	66-1373
Maria 31, Maria 11m, Maria 21, Anna 6			
SCHANK, Carl	17	Kirchardt	67-0007
SCHANKWEILER, G.El	20	Meisenheim	65-0038
SCHANNINGER, Jos.	20	Schramberg	66-1327
SCHANOM, Anton	28	Elberfeld	66-0109
SCHANTZ, Maria C.	19	Niederhamm	64-0886
SCHANZ, Johann	20	Hauswurtz	66-1327
SCHANZ, Paul	26	Dietingen	64-0214
SCHANZ, Phil	44	Webern	63-0821
SCHAOFLER, Hermine	26	Stuttgart	67-0007
SCHAPER, August	26	Halle	66-1031
SCHAPER, Clemens	35	Louisville	66-0576
SCHAPER, Fritz	40	Ringelheim	66-0668
SCHAPER, Heinrich	42	Odenstedt	66-0734
Johanna 41, Johanna 16, Heinrich 12			
Wilhelm 9, Hermann 7, Dorette 5, Minna 3			
SCHAPER, Joh.	24	Ahstedt	66-1131
SCHAPER, Joh.Steph	22	Sommersdorf	67-0599
Eva Barbara 28, Eva Margr. 10m			
SCHAPPACH, B.	19	Hundheim	65-0007
SCHAPPACH, Carl	22	Bleichheim	66-1131
SCHAPPE, August	35	Gruenenplan	63-0917
SCHAPPERLE, Alb.	19	Hochdorf	64-0593
SCHARD, Charles	28	Tenesee	66-0934
SCHARDIN, Carl	32	Germany	66-0666
Cahrlotte 45, Hermine 19, Julius 7			
Berta 14, Otto 28, Henriette 29			
SCHARDT, Anna	25	Hollfeldt	65-1024
SCHARDT, Cath.	24	Diedelskopf	64-0214
SCHARDT, Marie E.	32	Lich	66-0934
Wilhelmine 26			
SCHARELL, D.	22	Muenchen	65-0007
SCHARENHORST, Hans	16	Hohenhorst	65-1095
SCHARF, Cath.	16	Baltmansweilr	65-0402
SCHARF, John	27	Ohio	63-0244
SCHARF, Rosine	43	Hohengeren	65-0402
Maria 18			
SCHARFENBERG, Wilh	50	Suhl	63-0482
SCHARFF, Gustav	32	Milwaukee	66-0704
SCHARFFENBERG, Dan	25	New York	63-0168
SCHARFRING, Johann	22	Friedrichshor	65-1095
SCHARGES, Otto	24	Muenchen	65-0402
SCHARLACH, Heinr.	23	Northeim	66-0346
Magdalena 27			
SCHARMANN, Theodor	28	Hessen	66-0576
SCHARMHORST, Aug.	18	Quackenbrueck	65-1189
Anna 20			
SCHARPF, Joseph	24	Weissenstein	66-1203
SCHARPF, Michael	43	Hohmigchen	64-1053
SCHARPSNACH, Herm.	27	Elberfeld	67-0007
SCHARRER, Wilh.	19	Moehringen	65-0402
SCHARTZ, Julius	26	Megyaszo	66-0679
SCHASSLER, Heinr.	23	Praschewitz	66-1373
SCHATZ, Christel	20	Rothenzimmern	66-0704
baby 1			

NAME	AGE	RESIDENCE	YR-LIST
SCHATZ, Wm.	20	Langenberghm.	64-0170
SCHAUB, Adelh.	21	Suisdorf	66-1243
SCHAUB, Bonavent	19	Yosa	65-1030
SCHAUB, Gustav	27	Pieringen	66-1327
SCHAUB, Kunigunde	60	Poppenheim	66-1373
SCHAUB, Margarethe	23	Syeckmuehl	66-0576
SCHAUBEL, Walpurga	20	Bavaria	66-0679
SCHAUBERG, Hermann	17	Darmstadt	66-1031
SCHAUBERGER, Carl	25	Kirchdorf	66-1031
SCHAUDA, Joseph	32	Strobulos	66-1373
Maria 31, Maria 11m, Maria 21, Anna 6			
SCHAUER, Carl	26	Soessnowd	66-0469
SCHAUFELE, Joh.	23	Ebingen	64-0138
Ludwig 21			
SCHAUFELL, Friedr.	24	Cannstatt	66-0679
SCHAUFFLER, Emil	16	Stuttgart	66-1203
SCHAULBACH, Wilh.	23	Schmalkalden	66-1127
SCHAULBERGER, Phe.	30	Niederell	64-0495
SCHAUM, Jacob	32	Hausen	65-1088
Margarethe 29, Anna 6, Margarethe 3			
baby 10m			
SCHAUMBERGER, Geo.	18	Niederzell	64-0639
SCHAUMBURGER, R(m)	23	Breslau	64-0138
SCHAUMEL, Gerhard	76	Mistelgau	65-1031
Kunigunde 40, Michael 9			
SCHAUMLOEFFEL, A.C	24	Vorschuetz	66-0412
SCHAUPP, Wilh'mine	24	Hagelloch	66-1131
SCHAUSEIL, J.A.(m)	58	Eisenach	64-0170
Charlotte 47, Antonia 20, Henriette 17			
Helena 12, Dora 4			
SCHAUTZ, Georg	34	Mergelstedten	66-1243
SCHAWEL, Johanna	32	Zdaslon	66-1131
Maria 23, Wenzel 9m			
SCHAWN, Jos.	40	Ohio	63-0296
SCHAXEL, Theresia	21	Herbolzheim	63-0862
SCHEBE, W.	50	Loehne	66-0413
Anna 50, Engel 18, Louise 15, Helene 7			
SCHECKINGER, Luise	45	Calbe	65-0402
Elise 13, Wilhelmine 15			
SCHEDELICH, Gustav	24	Pierschendorf	66-1128
SCHEEL, Cath.	57	Cassel	63-0482
Cath. 26			
SCHEEL, Clara	25	Frankfurt	65-0038
Margaretha 18			
SCHEELE, Friedrich	27	Hofgeismar	64-0456
SCHEELE, Hinrich	14	Rotenburg	63-0614
SCHEELE, Johann	52	Eberschuetz	65-0770
Emilie 19, Herrmann 12, Caroline 7			
SCHEELE, Wilhelm	26	Hamburg	66-0934
SCHEELING, August	20	Walsrode	66-0934
SCHEEPER, Andr.	22	Langen	63-0990
SCHEER, Adam	21	Matzfeld	64-0687
SCHEER, Adolph	20	Gailingen	65-0243
SCHEER, Elisabeth	28	Preussen	64-0214
SCHEER, Emilie	21	Diefmut	65-1030
SCHEER, Georg Ad.	15	Motzfeld	63-0862
SCHEER, Johann	44	St. Louis	64-0023
SCHEER, Minna	16	Huitsburg	66-1373
SCHEER, Rosine	23	Schloth	64-0687
SCHEER, Wm.	46	McConsville	64-0138
SCHEER, v.d. Helen	23	Weddewarden	64-1053
SCHEERER, Martin	18	Betzingen	64-0331
SCHEERMANN, Louis	33	Baltimore	63-0917
Margarethe 33, Paul 9, Martha 8, August 7			
SCHEFE, Hermann	27	Loeningen	66-1031
SCHEFFLER, Joseph	24	Fort Wayne	66-0576
SCHEIB, Christian	20	Ramersberg	66-1327
SCHEIB, Franz	17	Oppenweiler	67-0007
SCHEIBEL, Andreas	57	Auberg	67-0806
SCHEIBENER, Martin	22	Callies	63-0053
SCHEIBERT, Wilhelm	29	Grimmen	66-0578
Wilhelmine 41, Johann 15, Wilhelmine 13			
August 11, Wilhelm 9, Ernst 2			
SCHEIBLE, Thomas	25	Dietingen	66-1155
SCHEIBNER, Carl	28	Washington	63-0917
Marie 24			
SCHEID, Louise	15	Rothenburg	67-0007
Cathrine 19			

NAME	AGE	RESIDENCE	YR-LIST
SCHEID, Peter	33	Kiesweiler	66-1373
SCHEIDERICH, Ther.	27	Lippstadt	65-0974
Fritz 4, Wilhelm 2, Georg 4m			
SCHEIDING, Friedr.	24	Mana	66-0679
SCHEIDING, H.C.	25	Bromberg	64-0432
SCHEIDLE, Franz	46	Elbingalte	67-0007
SCHEIDLER, Aug.Cl.	25	Peketsheim	65-1030
SCHEIDT, Barbara	27	Woerstadt	65-0116
SCHEIDT, Ernst	26	Crefeld	63-0053
SCHEIFER, A.C.(m)	16	Eudorf	64-0023
SCHEIKING, Pauline	29	Untertuerkhm.	67-0007
SCHEINER, Ernstine	23	Asch	66-0704
SCHEINUS, Johann	24	Sonnawitz	67-0806
SCHEIPEL, Math.(f)	24	Ochsenweg	64-0331
SCHEITER, Ludw.	22	Verden	64-1161
SCHEITERLEIN, Barb	22	Wuertenberg	66-0221
SCHEITH, Johannes	15	Rothsilberg	65-1024
SCHEITHER, Albert	17	Beixen	65-0770
SCHEKRER, B.	31	Wetter	65-1088
Maria 27, Chr. 9m			
SCHELD, Cathrina	25	Mittelsumen	66-0469
SCHELD, Johannes	28	Sinkershausen	66-1327
SCHELDBERG, Fr'dke	28	Bremen	63-0614
SCHELDT, Augusta	15	Cassel	63-1178
SCHELDT, Rupert	20	Allna	63-0990
SCHELE, Heinrich	39	Kufenthal	66-1243
Wilh. 21			
SCHELE, Maria	18	New York	63-0752
SCHELER, Heinr.	21	Coburg	64-0432
SCHELL, Amalie	19	Impfingen	66-0623
SCHELL, Jean	16	Neusenberg	64-0363
SCHELL, John E.	19	Conzberg	63-1085
SCHELLE, Casp.	25	Stuttrop	65-1088
SCHELLENBERG, G.	76	Woerth	64-0782
SCHELLENBERGER, Gg	21	Mannheim	64-0739
SCHELLENTRAEGER, F	18	Eisenach	63-0482
Emil 9			
SCHELLER, Doctorin	18	Braunschweig	65-1088
Adele 38			
SCHELLER, James	26	Homburg	63-0990
SCHELLERMACHER, C.	42	Neuenkirchen	64-0433
Catharine 13, Sophia 7, Anna 3			
Christina 4m			
SCHELLERS, Christ.	57	Mittelsemen	65-0865
Gertrude 19			
SCHELLHAAR, Anna C	20	Roden	64-0593
SCHELLHAAS, Joh.	19	Niederhausen	66-1243
SCHELLHARN, August	21	Sonneberg	66-0934
SCHELLHORN, Johann	22	Horsten	65-1095
SCHELLING, Diedr.	25	Diepholz	66-1373
SCHELTENTRAEGER, J	44	Eisenach	64-0170
Ernst 9, Ludw. 7, Ricka. 5			
SCHELTI, John	29	Obersimenthal	63-0097
SCHELVER, Herm.	28	Osnabrueck	64-0593
SCHEMBER, Carl	23	Kirchardt	64-0427
SCHEMMERICH, Elisa	18	Schwarza	66-0469
SCHEMPF, Wilhelm	20	Oelbronn	66-1203
SCHEN, Johann	19	Sterzhausen	66-0734
SCHENK, August	24	Biberach	66-0412
Emma 17			
SCHENK, Carl Aug.	24	Aalen	63-0006
SCHENK, Dorothea	21	Ansbach	63-1136
SCHENK, Eduard	15	Schlagpfuetze	66-1373
SCHENK, Fr.	11	Wuertemberg	63-1085
SCHENK, J.(m)	38	Philadelphia	64-0331
SCHENK, Ludwig	19	Wiesbaden	65-0594
Aug. 29			
SCHENK, Marie	24	Cassel	65-1031
SCHENK, Natalie	21	Neubrunn	63-0990
SCHENKBIER, Louise	20	Bockhorst	66-1031
SCHENKE, Johann	19	Schale	66-0679
SCHENKEL, Fr.(f)	40	Boston	64-0214
Jos.(f) 10, Pauline 2			
SCHENKER, Heinr.	26	Gretzenbach	64-0363
SCHEPER, Heinrich	15	Lohne	66-0984
SCHEPERS, Heinrich	28	Raine	66-0623
SCHEPPACH, Rud.		Weilsdorf	64-0214
SCHEPPECK, W.	58	Reschitz	66-0413

NAME	AGE	RESIDENCE	YR-LIST
Anna 55, Wentzel 32, Jacob 28, Marie 24			
Anna 21			
SCHEPPERLE, Christ	40	Baltimore	64-0593
SCHERBEL, Isidor	22	Lissa	63-0752
SCHERCHLICHT, Marg	4	Kail	66-0734
SCHERER, Adam	52	Kl.Gladenbach	64-0687
Elisab. 32, Cathar. 24, Eva 18, Adam 15			
Adam 3			
SCHERER, Babette	23	Bayern	66-0147
SCHERER, Carl	20	Cassel	66-0704
SCHERER, Catharina	19	Neuburg	66-0147
SCHERER, Christ	18	Alzey	63-1178
SCHERER, G. Friedr	25	Obstwind	63-0296
SCHERER, Heinr.	37	Creuznach	64-0427
Wilhelmine 30, Heinr. 3, baby 6m			
SCHERER, Heinrich	24	Ankum	66-1373
Gerhard 24			
SCHERER, John	22	Aasen	63-0296
SCHERER, Joseph	32	Baiern	64-0214
Marie 24, Magdalena 24			
SCHERER, Math.	33	Trier	63-0168
SCHERER, Otto	18	Darmstadt	66-1127
SCHERER, Wilh'mine	18	Lahr	66-0934
SCHERF, Marie	25	Thaliter	66-0984
SCHERF, Wilhelm	28	Marienhagen	65-0898
SCHERFF, Elisab.	12	Ulm	65-0402
Marie 37			
SCHERIBBE, Gottl.	49	Esslingen	63-0551
SCHERLE, Magd.	18	Tuttlingen	65-0007
SCHERLING, Johann	24	Gonsberg	66-0083
SCHERMANN, Franz	40	Boehmen	66-0221
Josefa 26, Josefa 11m			
SCHERMANN, Johann	46	Boehmen	66-0349
John 22, Richard 36, Amalie 40			
Christian 14, August 12, Robert 9			
Julius 7			
SCHERMANN, Joseph	17	Gerresdorf	66-0346
SCHERMER, Henry	44	Curhessen	63-0862
SCHERMEYER, Carl W	18	Hannover	66-0469
SCHERPEN, Maria	24	Buhlerweit	66-0984
SCHERR, Bruno	16	Zuerich	63-0482
SCHERR, Heinrich	15	Nolle	66-1128
SCHERRICH, Johann	24	Cell	66-0349
SCHEU, Catharina	25	Sturtzhausen	66-0623
SCHEU, Jean	26	Schwitz	64-0023
SCHEU, Johann	22	Grafenweiler	66-0147
SCHEUDEWOLF, Wilh.	29	Cassel	66-0984
SCHEUER, H.	16	Mittwitz	64-0886
SCHEUER, Joh.	14	Schechtiz	66-0576
SCHEUER, Moses	30	Abenheim	66-0576
Johanna 36			
SCHEUERLE, Christ.	36	Stuttgart	65-0948
Rosine 31, Adolph 7, Albert 6, Wilhelm 4			
Friedrich 9m			
SCHEUERLE, Gottfr.	20	Hausen	63-0990
SCHEUERMANN, Georg	22	Minden	66-1203
SCHEUERMANN, J.	21	Gocheringen	64-0782
SCHEUFLER, Albrect	20	Bernhardsmuhl	66-0704
SCHEURE, Joseph	33	Geislingen	66-0734
SCHEURER, Fr.	17	Weyer	63-1003
SCHEURIG, Jette	21	Waldurn	66-1203
SCHEURING, Valent.	36	Richmond	63-0821
Barbara 24, John 34, Angela 23			
SCHEUZLEBEN, Jos.	29	Bollingen	64-0840
SCHEVER, Catharine	27	Guntersblum	63-1218
SCHEYER, Mathilde	19	Schwarza	64-0938
Louis 13			
SCHIBALL, J.	17	Schwartz Kost	66-0413
SCHIBLO, Barbara	32	Bohemia	64-0073
Jos. 32			
SCHIBLO, Jos.	32	Boehmen	64-0427
SCHICK, Chr. Gottl	29	Britz	63-1178
SCHICK, Christ.	64	Enzweihingen	65-0594
Elise 29, Christine 15			
SCHICK, Christian	17	Wuestenrod	66-0576
SCHICK, Geo.	28	Bleistein	64-1022
SCHICK, Gottl.	24	Hochdorf	64-0782
SCHICK, Hermann	18	Stuttgart	66-0934

NAME	AGE	RESIDENCE	YR-LIST
SCHICK, John	23	Bitz	63-1178
William 19			
SCHICK, Joseph	27	Wuerttenberg	66-0109
SCHICK, Karl	32	Feilbinger	66-0668
SCHICKEMUEHLE, C.A	32	Oldenburg	66-0934
Caroline 25, Elisabeth 59, Josephine 20			
Josephine 3, Wilhelmine 9m			
SCHICKWEST, Conrad	24	Mardorf	66-1243
SCHIEBEL, Otto	20	Plauen	66-1203
SCHIEBER, Georg	38	Prag	67-0007
SCHIEBRAM, Ch.	24	Baltimore	63-0551
SCHIECK, Gottl.	26	Bitz	64-0782
SCHIECK, Gottl.	26	Oberurbach	65-0116
SCHIECK, Joh. Jac.	21	Oberurbach	65-0116
SCHIECK, Philip	27	Strasburg	65-0116
Marie 26, Marie 4			
SCHIED, Joseph	27	Bavaria	66-0679
Theresia 23, Jacob 2			
SCHIEDEL, Dorothea	7	Wiesenfeld	67-0007
SCHIEDER, Georg	25	Pegnitz	65-0713
SCHIEDER, Johann	29	Altheim	66-0221
SCHIEFER, Anton	27	Reichenberg	66-1373
SCHIEFER, Chr. F.	19	Kirchheim	63-0097
SCHIEFER, Peter	28	Hilbe	64-1108
SCHIEFERSTEIN, C.	34	Hochheim	64-0331
SCHIEFERSTEIN, Hch	28	Lichtenau	65-0402
SCHIEFERSTEIN, Hr.	27	Lannsbach	64-1053
SCHIEFERSTEIN, Joh	21	Odenhausen	64-0593
SCHIEKERCKEN, Joh.	30	Krukow	66-0413
Just. 25, Stephan 11m			
SCHIEL, Joh Mart.	31	New York	63-0482
SCHIELE, Sab.	16	Lichtenau	65-1024
SCHIELE, Schann	22	Adelmannsfeld	66-0349
Margar. 22			
SCHIELE, Wilh'mine	23	Czarnikau	64-0363
SCHIEMER, Ferdiand	42	Altfeld	63-0821
SCHIENEN, Franz	35	Karlsbad	66-1128
SCHIENLE, Ed.	24	Kettenacker	63-1003
SCHIER, Johann	36	Bremen	64-0840
Mathilde 35			
SCHIER, Johann	18	Mingsberg	66-0934
SCHIER, Joseph	9	Paderborn	66-1093
SCHIERBAUM, John	27	Linne	63-0551
SCHIERBRAND, Adolf	21	Weimar	66-0577
SCHIERENBECK, Hch.	24	Emshoop	65-0402
SCHIERENBECK, Rich	19	Martfeld	66-0704
SCHIERENBEK, Arend	19	Leeste	66-1127
SCHIERENBEK, Gust.	9	Bremen	64-0363
SCHIERER, Caspar	23	Unterfranken	66-1327
SCHIERLOH, Margar.	42	Etutinghausen	64-0886
Mathilde 23			
SCHIERMANN, Chta.	44	Neuenhaus	64-0992
Caroline 36, Caroline 7, Aloisius 5			
Anna 3, Elise 2			
SCHIERMEYER, Frdr.	22	Sundern	64-0138
SCHIERMEYER, John	17	Wellendorf	65-1095
SCHIERSTER, Anna M	34	Acken	63-1085
SCHIESLER, Cath.	18	Nussbaum	66-0413
Cath. 56			
SCHIESSER, Caspar	27	Markelseim	63-1038
SCHIFF, David	22	Altensolheim	64-0639
SCHIFF, Ed.	26	Detmold	65-0594
SCHIFF, Herm.	33	Detmold	64-0840
SCHIFF, John	37	Euren	63-0990
Marg. 24			
SCHIFF, Ludw.	21	Pforzheim/Pr	64-1053
SCHIFF, Moritz	27	Frankfurt	66-0576
Nanny 50			
SCHIFF, Peter	33	Euren	63-0990
SCHIFF, Peter	38	Volkmarsen	66-0984
SCHIFFER, Ferd.	21	Fuerth	64-0073
SCHIFFERT, Maria	24	Boehmen	63-1136
SCHIFFLIN, F.A.	24	New York	63-0821
SCHIFFMANN, Simon	27	Kissingen	63-0917
SCHIFFNER, Louis	23	New York	64-0214
SCHILBACH, Carl	20	Neufuerstenh.	66-0576
SCHILD, Anna	42	Quincy	63-1010
SCHILD, Babette	22	Hillerig	66-0704

NAME	AGE	RESIDENCE	YR-LIST
SCHILD, Christian	25	Amsweiler	64-0840
SCHILD, Gertrude	17	Koelbe	66-0412
SCHILD, Heinr.	24	Pfalz	66-0221
Anna M. 22, Magdalene 59			
SCHILD, Henriette	32	Celle	63-0990
Henry 3, Emil 11m			
SCHILD, P.(m)	28	Buttenhorn	64-0495
SCHILD, Peter	32	Taubhausen	66-0576
SCHILDBORN, Chrtne	60	Hahlen	65-1030
SCHILDERN, Herm.	35	Reis	64-0023
SCHILDGER, Conrad	16	Stockheim	63-1218
Marie 23			
SCHILDMACHER, Bern	28	Paderborn	66-0734
SCHILDT, Josephine	22	Polen	66-0666
Thomas 21, Marianne 16, Johann 7			
Josephine 5, Anna 4, Pauline 2			
SCHILDWAECHTER, W.	26	Philadelphia	63-0862
SCHILL, Aug.	21	Zahringen	63-0244
SCHILL, Lucia	21	Oberbergen	66-0109
SCHILL, Rosine	23	Birken	66-0679
SCHILLIG, Aug.	34	Braunschweig	65-1189
Augusta 7, Alwine 5, Alwina 31, Clem. 3			
SCHILLING, Anna	17	Glueckstadt	64-0840
SCHILLING, Ca.	20	Fehenbach	66-1203
SCHILLING, Chr.	19	Unterlemnitz	66-1313
SCHILLING, Christ.	28	Neukufstein	66-1031
SCHILLING, Dina	20	Schweinsdorf	66-1203
SCHILLING, Emil	16	Schlitz	65-1088
SCHILLING, Ernest.	15	Unt.Fuellbach	64-0639
SCHILLING, Friedr	30	Cassel	65-0865
SCHILLING, Gottf.	62	Meiningen	63-0614
Marg. Elisa. 48, Emma 13, Veronika 11			
Ernst 8, Anna 7, Robert 3			
SCHILLING, Jacob	33	Mittelsberg	64-0427
SCHILLING, Joseph	35	Neudingen	64-1022
SCHILLING, Marie	22	Oldenstadt	65-0243
SCHILLING, Theodor	25	Muenster	66-0221
Ferdinand 23			
SCHILLINGER, Andr.	27	Rotenburg	64-0073
SCHILLINGER, Marie	34	Nienburg	65-1189
Fr. 7			
SCHILT, Jacob	24	Switz	63-0350
SCHIMA, Frz.	44	Boehmen	64-0495
Ma.(f) 38, Ge.(f) 14, Aa.(f) 7, Jos. 6			
Frz. 5, Cthe. 1			
SCHIMEK, Franz	37	Rielo	66-1131
Anna 30, Anna 8, Wenzel 28, Anna 33			
Anna 2, Barbara 3m			
SCHIMM, Christian	19	Niederstetten	66-1155
SCHIMMEL, Carl	39	Rietzig	66-1248
Albertine 35, Wilhelmine 7, Louise 3			
Augusta 6, Gustav 4, Julius 11m			
SCHIMMEL, John	43	Poehlgoens	63-1218
Christina 59			
SCHIMMEL, Pauline	27	Prokenhauland	66-0650
SCHIMMER, Val.	55	Schereishaim	66-1243
Marg. 50, Catharina 21, Friederike 19			
Andreas 15, Philip 13, Elisabeth 8			
SCHIMPF, Cath. R.	13	Neuweiler/Wrt	65-0038
SCHIMPF, Johann G.	59	Niederweisel	63-0015
SCHINCK, Carl	59	Schoenberg	63-0990
Victoria 21			
SCHINCK, Otto	19	Obernkirchen	66-1131
SCHINDEHUETTE, El.	19	Breitenbach	66-1313
Joh. 16, Friedr. 13			
SCHINDEHUETTE, J.G	18	Breitenbach	66-0412
SCHINDEL, Joseph	26	Carlsbad	66-0679
SCHINDELE, J.	22	Hohengehren	63-1003
SCHINDEWOLF, Chr.	28	Helmarshausen	66-0934
SCHINDLER, Cath.	30	Bremen	63-1085
SCHINDLER, Fridol.	46	Switz	63-0350
SCHINDLER, Heinr.	22	Kappel	64-1108
SCHINDLER, Joachim	71	Switz	63-0350
Fridolin 28, Eduard 10, Rosine 19			
Marie 14, Sophie 9			
SCHINK, Johanette	21	Biebrich	63-1218
SCHINKMAIER, Josef	39	Maltitz	66-0576
Barbara 26			

NAME	AGE	RESIDENCE	YR-LIST
SCHINMUELLER, Mary	22	Suedenborn	64-0427
SCHINNEL, Peter	23	Brechtheim	66-1203
SCHINSSLER, Gottf.	24	Gerstungen	66-1327
SCHINTENHANS, Bern	21	Einbeck	66-1127
SCHINZER, Adam	29	Niederdunzebh	64-0170
Anne Marg. 24, Elisab. 5, Louise 3			
SCHIPF, Johann	28	Reichenberg	66-1327
SCHIPPER, Jacob	18	Loquard	64-1022
SCHIPPER, Joh. Fr.	25	Wundel/Pr.	65-0116
SCHIPPLOCH, Carol.	16	Kissow	66-0650
SCHIRDING, Herman	22	Wehdel	66-1327
SCHIRM, Peter	40	Veilsdorf	64-0214
SCHIRMANN, Barbara	19	Zeiskam	65-0243
SCHIRMER, Christ.	43	Dielingen	64-0639
Engel 37, Heinr. 7, Wilhelm 5			
SCHIRMER, Francis	25	Membach	63-1136
SCHIRMER, Johann	31	Baiern	66-0623
SCHIRMER, John	26	Allfeld	63-0482
Kunigunde 23			
SCHIRP, Nic.	20	Halpen	63-1085
SCHISLER, Jacobine	26	Nussbaum	65-0243
SCHISSMAYER, Theo.	20	Selz	64-0992
SCHITTELKOPF, Ant.	42	Carolensthal	66-1373
SCHLAAK, Gottl.	25	Bromberg	65-0950
SCHLAAR, Carl	26	Freiburg	63-0482
SCHLACHTER, Cresc.	48	Aspach	66-1243
SCHLACHTER, Friedr	30	Osnabrueck	66-1243
SCHLACHTER, Johann	37	Chidam	63-0006
SCHLACKER, Friedr.	34	Rheine	66-1131
SCHLAEFER, Carl	20	Prussia	63-1218
SCHLAEFER, Elisab.	28	Bennhausen	66-0577
Elisabeth 6, Marie 4, Barbara 2m			
SCHLAEFER, Philipp	34	Bennhausenia	66-0577
SCHLAEGEL, Elsle	25	Boehmen	66-0221
SCHLAEGEL, Martin	56	Babendorf/Ung	66-0346
Therese 48, Elisabeth 24, Franz 20			
Michael 12, Maria 9, Georg 5, Martin 18			
SCHLAERF, An. Cath	30	Allendorf	64-0343
SCHLAGER, Johann	22	Jatschamneck	63-0053
SCHLAGER, Johann	26	Ilscheunick	66-0704
SCHLAGHECK, Henry	49	Preussen	63-0990
Elisabeth 46, Caspar 21, Anna 9			
Bernhard 6			
SCHLAGHECK, Herm.	23	Gosfeld	65-0948
SCHLAKE, Franz	22	Markendorf	66-0469
SCHLAKE, Justine	24	Wenohagen	66-1155
SCHLATTER, Cath.	21	Petershagen	65-0974
SCHLATTER, Jacob	32	Oetelfingen	65-0243
SCHLAUERSLACH, M.	30	Nuernberg	65-0007
Babette 5, baby 1m			
SCHLEBANEK, Anton	21	Bohemia	64-0363
SCHLECHENMAIER, W.	17	Mittelbruden	66-1203
SCHLECHT, Carl	39	Wolfenbuettel	63-1010
SCHLECHTE, Died.	40	Pennsylvania	63-0350
SCHLECHTE, Wilhelm	21	Rahden	65-1088
SCHLECHTER, Chr.	33	Wabern	67-0600
Catharine 28, Friedrich 4, Elisabeth 10m			
SCHLECHTWEG, Ernst	25	Urnshausen/H.	63-1010
SCHLECKRIEDER, Lse	19	Rahden	65-1088
SCHLEE, Joh. Aug.	38	Lingen	65-1030
SCHLEER, Franzisca	14	Kenzingen	63-1038
SCHLEG, Charlotte	52	Zowen	66-0469
Johannes 20			
SCHLEGEL, Agathe	25	Mahlstetten	66-0679
Amalie 21			
SCHLEGEL, Elisab.	30	Wigheim	64-1053
SCHLEGEL, Flora	27	Stuttgart	64-0639
SCHLEGEL, Friedr.	25		66-1203
SCHLEGEMILCH, Otto	18	Suhl	67-0795
SCHLEGER, Anna	19	Jena	64-0593
SCHLEGER, Michael	18	Trabelsdorf	66-1373
SCHLEICH, Johannes	24	Burg Gmuenden	66-1155
SCHLEICHER, Doroth	23	Hessen	64-0432
SCHLEICHER, Elisab	21	Hafenprepach	66-0623
SCHLEICHER, Eva El	27	Engelhelmi	66-1373
Anna 11m			
SCHLEICHER, Friedr	27	Wichelshausen	66-1127
SCHLEIERMACHER, C.	23		64-0433

NAME	AGE	RESIDENCE	YR-LIST
SCHLEIFER, Carolne	22	Eisenach	63-0821
SCHLEIK, Johann	26	Ndr.Grenzbach	66-0083
SCHLEINING, Cath.	28	Hoffmansfeld	65-0950
SCHLEININGEN, Cren	17	Soden	66-0623
SCHLEISS, Wilhelm	24	Wuerttenberg	66-0221
SCHLEIZER, Henr'tt	27	Gera	66-1093
SCHLEMBECKER, Ludw	18	Rodheim	63-1218
SCHLEMM, Anton	23	Danzig	63-1218
SCHLEMM, Carl	26	Clausthal	66-1248
SCHLENDORG, L.H.A.	60	Bremen	65-0038
SCHLENGLENBORG, J.	39	Holland	63-0168
SCHLENGMANN, Johan	15	Borghorst	66-0623
SCHLENK, Heinr.	69	Rheda	64-1053
Francisca 63, Louis 19			
SCHLENKER, Georg	26	Windeureuthe	66-1093
SCHLENZIG, Franz	32	Zeitz	63-1010
Emilie 25, Franz Paul 5, Anna 2			
Louise 7m			
SCHLEPPACHER, Isak	34	Baltimore	63-0917
SCHLESINGER, Jeane	18	Aufhausen	64-1108
SCHLESINGER, Ph.	26	Berlin	64-1108
SCHLESSLER, Christ	27	Auenda	65-0713
SCHLEUER, Friedr.	23	Solingen	63-0822
SCHLEUNING, Theod.	40	Darmstadt	65-0116
SCHLEUS, Fr.	21	Bremen	64-0639
SCHLEWING, Minna	47	Dissen	65-0950
Albine 8			
SCHLEWITZ, Leopold	25	Rodenberg	65-0898
SCHLEYER, Aug.	22	Midlum	64-0343
SCHLEYER, Mathilde	19	Schwarza	64-0938
Louis 13			
SCHLICHTE, Heinr.	18	Schlake	64-0739
Heinrich 22			
SCHLICHTERT, Gottf	59	Unterkochen	64-0639
Mariane 50, Mariane 27, Franziska 13			
Joseph 21			
SCHLICHTHORST, Fr.	59	Dorum	63-0908
E. 37, K. 43, M. 11, A. 8, J. 7, A. 4			
H. 3			
SCHLICHTIG, Wilmne	25	Posen	66-0578
SCHLICHTING, M.	19	Vegesack	64-0782
SCHLICHTING, Wilh.	26	Bremen	65-0004
SCHLICHTING, v.E.	20	Hirschberg	64-0214
SCHLICHTMACHER, C.	26	Waldstrauss	66-1131
SCHLICHTWEG, Cr.W.	18	Freiburg	64-0739
SCHLICKE, Robert	28	Naumberg	65-1088
SCHLICKEN, Cath.	26	Mannheim	64-0840
SCHLICKER, Heinr.	55	Wenjen	66-0650
Justine 45, Augusta 10, Minna 6, Wilh. 3			
SCHLICKER, Heinr.	24	Wenzel	65-1030
SCHLIEF, F.	17	Elberfeld	63-0752
SCHLIEKER, Johann	60	Baden	66-0147
Margarethe 58			
SCHLIEM, Ludwig	30	Preussen	63-0990
Ana 30, Wilhelmine 7, Minchen 5			
SCHLIESSER, Georg	22	Hanau	66-0837
SCHLIEWERT, Christ	58	Preussen	63-0990
SCHLINGEL, Anton	22	Dambach	66-0679
SCHLINGHOFF, A.Els	26	Kurhessen	66-0221
SCHLINGLOFF, Franz	18	Rinteln	63-1038
SCHLINGLOFF, Nicol	19	Schuechtern	66-0679
SCHLINGMANN, Aug.	14	Buer	64-0687
SCHLINGMANN, Hr.A.	29	Bachholzhsn.	65-0950
SCHLINGMANN, Luise	18	Dissen	63-0917
SCHLINGMANN, Wilh.	18	Dissen	66-1128
SCHLINGSOG, August	27	Kathol.Hammer	65-1095
SCHLINKER, H.	36	Braunschweig	65-0974
SCHLINSOG, Wilhelm	42	Kath.Hammer	65-1095
Helena 36, Gottlieb 8, Friedrich 7			
Gustav 5			
SCHLIPF, Franz Xav	37	Ludwigsburg	63-0917
Marie 30, Marie 6, Franz 3, Lina 11m			
SCHLIPF, Joseph	24	Gromberg	66-1327
SCHLIPF, Sebastian	38	Westhausen	66-0984
SCHLITT, Conrad	29	Frischborn	65-1030
Wilhelm 23			
SCHLITTER, Wilhelm	20	Meiningen	66-1131
SCHLITTLER, Caspar	54	Niederurnen	65-0189

NAME	AGE	RESIDENCE	YR-LIST
Balthasar 23			
SCHLITZ, M.J.(m)	24	New York	64-0023
SCHLOBOHM, Ernst	16	Dorum	64-1022
SCHLOBOHM, Joh. H.	15	Ottersberg	65-1030
Catharina 20			
SCHLOBOHM, Louise	18	Ottersberg	64-0992
SCHLOEMANN, Henry	15	Bremen	63-0350
SCHLOENDORF, J.G.	23	Bremen	63-0244
SCHLOEPCKE, Anna	18	Nesse	67-0599
SCHLOERB, Elisabet	20	Shotten	63-0244
SCHLOESSER, H.D.	18	Worms	64-0363
SCHLOESSER, Johann	32	Worms	64-0170
Caroline 36			
SCHLOETKER, He.(f)	24	Hettringen	64-1161
SCHLOHMANN, Bernh.	24	Schleida	66-1313
SCHLOHMANN, Heinr.	27	Dehme	65-0007
SCHLOSS, Jacob	23	Duderhofen	66-0934
Salomon 24			
SCHLOSS, Julius	24	Stuttgart	66-1093
SCHLOSSER, Georg	23	Visselhoevede	66-1373
SCHLOSSER, Gertrud	63	Detmold	66-1203
Gertrude 42, Johann 19, Joseph 16			
Gottfried 14, Lisette 9, Caspar 7			
SCHLOTH, Leopold	26	Grossenbach	66-1327
SCHLOTHAUBER, Mina	17	Hannover	66-1155
SCHLOTMANN, Fr.	26	Bremerhaven	65-0243
SCHLOTTER, Heinric	18	Tuttingen	66-1313
SCHLOTTERBECK, Agn	21	Markt Heidenf	67-1005
SCHLOTTERER, Frd.	17	Wuertemberg	66-0984
SCHLOTZ, Andreas	62	Hohengehren	66-1031
SCHLOTZ, Sophie	40	Bremen	65-0189
SCHLUCKEBIER, Henr	19	Warholdern	66-0984
SCHLUCKSBIER, Lud.	20	Ehrsten	65-0974
SCHLUEHLEIN, Heinr	30	Pflaumbach	65-0004
SCHLUEHLING, Henry	22	Diemerode	63-0990
SCHLUERMANN, Anton	24	Steinfeld	65-0948
SCHLUETER, Anton	20	Osnabrueck	64-0739
SCHLUETER, August	26	Bevern	65-1088
SCHLUETER, Emil	42	Polzin	64-0639
SCHLUETER, Ernst	23	Celle	63-0990
SCHLUETER, Frdr.	26	Oppendorf	66-0109
Hermann 29			
SCHLUETER, Friedr.	21	Alten Donop	66-1327
SCHLUETER, Heinr.	43	Lamspringe	63-1069
Wilhelmine 44, Heinrich 9, Karl 6			
Louise 4, Maria 11m			
SCHLUETER, J.H.(m)	29	New York	64-0023
SCHLUETER, Johann	19	Schmolnik	66-0668
SCHLUETH, Carl	48	Schinher	65-1095
Emilie 32, Albert 16, Anna 6, Mina 4			
Ottilie 9m			
SCHLUETTERBURG, C.	34	Hofgeismar	63-0614
SCHLUGMANN, Babett		Freiberg	66-1093
SCHLUMPF, Ludw.	17	Breusbach	65-0189
Catharina 25			
SCHLUMPS, Magd.	33	Ebhausen	63-0953
SCHLUPFER, John	57	Schweiz	63-1085
Marie 45, Friederike 1			
SCHLUTERJAHN, Bern	21	Ochtrup	64-0214
SCHLWETER, Heinr.	20	Breinen	66-1373
SCHMACK, Joh. Fal.	21	Melbers	66-0650
SCHMACKENBERG, H.	20	Bremen	64-0331
SCHMAEDEKE, Diedr.	20	Wenden	63-0398
SCHMAEDEKE, H.(m)	56	Wenden	63-0398
SCHMAGGER, Jeramy	50	Augum	65-0243
SCHMALD, Barbara	27	Feldberg	65-0007
SCHMALE, Friedrike	49	Bromberg	65-0974
Pauline 17, Hedwig 7, Emilie 2			
SCHMALENBERG, Barb	3	Bavaria	66-0679
SCHMALENBERG, Marg	32	Triebstadt	66-0679
SCHMALING, Wilh.	26	Oschersleben	63-0990
SCHMALL, Cath. El.	19	Hessia	66-0412
SCHMALSTICH, Wlmne	23	Dannhausen	67-0007
SCHMALZ, Anton	33	Muehlhausen	65-0856
SCHMALZ, C.(m)	20	Boehmen	64-0331
SCHMALZ, Catharina	21	Hungen	66-0934
SCHMALZ, G.	30	Shiepjarre	66-0413
Henriette 37, Eduard 16, Otielge 14			

NAME	AGE	RESIDENCE	YR-LIST
Friedrich 10, Albertine 7			
SCHMALZRIED, Georg	20	Fluederhausen	67-0007
SCHMANN, Heinr.	27	Ahausen	64-1022
SCHMECKEPEPPER, D.	24	Duedinghausen	66-0577
SCHMEDEKE, Marg.	16	Hoya	65-0898
SCHMEDER, Hermann	29	Cloppenburg	66-0221
SCHMEHL, Antonia	31	Iburg	64-0782
SCHMEISER, Jul.(m)	30	Altenbreitung	65-0007
SCHMEISSER, Ern. C	45	Kl.Schmalkald	63-0693
SCHMEL, Wilh.	66	Westofen	65-0594
SCHMELLBACKER, J.	44	Wersand	65-1189
Joh. 44, Wilhelm 18, Fr. 16, Jacob 7			
Aron 5, Johanna 14, Marie 3			
SCHMELZ, Catharina	41	Dermbach	66-0679
Sidonia 12			
SCHMELZ, Heinrich	17	Lienbach	66-1248
SCHMELZLE, Anna	20	Rottweil	65-1189
SCHMERSAHL, Henry	62	Hethorn	66-0704
Carl 13			
SCHMET, A.(m)	28	Willindorf	64-0495
Crl.(m) 18			
SCHMICH, Georgia	36	Luccimin	64-0433
Josephine 24, Catharina 2m			
SCHMID, Christ.	20	Schwitz	64-0023
SCHMID, Elisab.	21	Ensingen	64-0170
SCHMID, Florian	27	Weissenstein	66-1203
SCHMID, John	29	Flawill	63-0482
SCHMID, Lorenz	18	Mecklar	64-0363
SCHMID, Ludwig	25	Sendling	64-0073
SCHMIDHUBER, Jacob	68	Zillhausen	66-0704
Anna 35, Jacob 3			
SCHMIDING, Wilhelm	19	Minden	66-0934
SCHMIDLIN, Richard	25	Uhebach	64-0593
SCHMIDT, (f)	35	Geestendorf	65-0974
Bertha 4, baby 2m			
SCHMIDT, Adam	54	Laubach	63-1038
Georg 9			
SCHMIDT, Adam	60	Laubach	65-0594
SCHMIDT, Adam	47	Eilsheim	65-0770
SCHMIDT, Adolph	30	Stoermede	63-0398
SCHMIDT, Albert	24	Strassdorf	64-0363
Ce. (f) 19			
SCHMIDT, Alfred J.	29	Gotha	64-0886
SCHMIDT, Amalie	32	Neu Ronnebeck	64-1053
SCHMIDT, Andr.	30	Germany	63-0990
SCHMIDT, Andreas	43	Darmstadt	63-0398
Catharine 42, Cath. 46, Elisabeth 9			
SCHMIDT, Andreas	48	Waldgirms	66-0576
Ludwig 34			
SCHMIDT, Andreas	37	Blasbach	64-0639
Cath. 30, Cath. 7, Elise 6, Georg 4			
SCHMIDT, Angela	31	Stoermede	65-0189
SCHMIDT, Anna	16	Freisen	66-0623
SCHMIDT, Anna	30	Gross Habersd	66-0668
SCHMIDT, Anna	24	Oberlimbach	66-1248
SCHMIDT, Anna	23	Damshausen	65-0055
SCHMIDT, Anna	17	Wremen	66-1327
SCHMIDT, Anna	29	Kl. Grabow	65-1189
C. 31, Marie 28, Dorothea 4, Johann 3			
Christian 28			
SCHMIDT, Anna	22	Fuerth	66-1373
SCHMIDT, Anna	47	Blasbach	64-1161
Cathar. 22, Heinrich 19, Joh. G. 15			
Caspar 7, Elisabeth 12, Catharine 6			
SCHMIDT, Anna E.	21	Oesede	64-0687
SCHMIDT, Anna Elis	16	Langgoens	64-1108
SCHMIDT, Anton	55	Buffalo	66-0734
SCHMIDT, Anton	32	Heiligenbuth	66-1327
SCHMIDT, Apolonia	25	Bellheim	65-0594
SCHMIDT, Arend E.	37	Ostfriesland	66-0469
Wybka 37, Ede 9, Jantje 5			
SCHMIDT, Aug.	31	Prussia	63-1003
William 6, Cathe. 4, A. 30, F. 10, W. 8			
E. 6, H. 1			
SCHMIDT, Aug.	29	Wuergendorf	64-0687
Augusta 34			
SCHMIDT, Aug.	27	Bremen	64-1206
SCHMIDT, Aug.	18	Mainz	65-0116

NAME	AGE	RESIDENCE	YR-LIST
SCHMIDT, August	20	Lutter	64-0138
SCHMIDT, August	18	Baden	66-0109
SCHMIDT, August	15	Osterwald	66-0934
SCHMIDT, August	27	Ebersbach	66-1327
SCHMIDT, Baldwin	20	Goldisthal	66-1248
Laura 21			
SCHMIDT, Barb.	17	Merner	64-0593
SCHMIDT, Barbara	23	Dingfeld	65-1030
SCHMIDT, Benedikt	20	Grossenlueder	66-0469
SCHMIDT, Benjamin	38	St. Louis	66-0934
SCHMIDT, Bernh.	24	Jentheim	65-0116
Rosine 27			
SCHMIDT, Bernhard	27	Melchriebest.	66-0984
SCHMIDT, Bernhard	20	Homberg	65-1030
SCHMIDT, C.	37	Mosheim	64-0593
SCHMIDT, C.	47	Meiningen	65-0007
Anna 45, Eva 18, Marg. 15			
SCHMIDT, C. Ernst	27	Lich	63-0398
SCHMIDT, C.A.(m)	19	Um	64-0023
SCHMIDT, Carl	32	Breslau	64-0138
SCHMIDT, Carl	23	Sachsen-Mein.	66-0349
SCHMIDT, Carl	29	Cleishoe	66-0578
Friederike 29, Ernestine 4, Augusta 2			
Emilie 6m			
SCHMIDT, Carl	33	Greiz	66-1093
SCHMIDT, Carl	27	Luebeck	66-1248
SCHMIDT, Carl	30	Schmaldalden	66-1127
Friederike 23			
SCHMIDT, Carl	25	Flechtdorf	65-0948
Catharine 26			
SCHMIDT, Carl F.	23	Rosenfels	63-1010
SCHMIDT, Carl H.	27	Stepnitz	64-1053
SCHMIDT, Caroline	40	Grafenweiler	66-0147
SCHMIDT, Caroline	10	Hannover	66-1093
SCHMIDT, Carsten	31	Stolzenau	66-0578
SCHMIDT, Carsten	34	New York	66-1031
SCHMIDT, Cath. El.	54	Dorlar	66-0704
Elise 22			
SCHMIDT, Cathar.	32	Damshausen	66-0984
Anna 28, Joh. Christ. 15			
SCHMIDT, Cathar.	24	Darmstadt	64-1053
SCHMIDT, Catharina	26	Rippoldsan	63-0296
SCHMIDT, Catharina	22	Schliessheim	66-0679
Maria 24			
SCHMIDT, Catharina	21	Schlapphausen	66-1248
SCHMIDT, Catharina	21	Emden	66-1373
Henriette 18			
SCHMIDT, Catharine	21	Woehl	66-0734
SCHMIDT, Catharine	24	Brechtheim	66-1203
SCHMIDT, Catuna	23	Philippsburg	67-0007
SCHMIDT, Charles	25	Strumpfelbrun	64-0593
SCHMIDT, Charles F	30	New York	64-0073
SCHMIDT, Chr.	42	Messlingen	64-0331
SCHMIDT, Chr. W.		Rahden	65-1088
SCHMIDT, Chr.(f)	2	Oberseenen	65-0402
Marie 9, Chr. (f) 7			
SCHMIDT, Christ.	29	Stuttgart	64-0138
SCHMIDT, Christ.	22	Kretzingen	66-0934
SCHMIDT, Christ.	30	Landsbergen	65-0038
SCHMIDT, Christ.	23	Dirnstein	65-0189
SCHMIDT, Christ. F	22	Schotten	66-1127
Christine 19			
SCHMIDT, Christian	16	Stetten	66-0704
SCHMIDT, Christian	28	Carlsberg	66-1248
Henriette 28, Ernestine 3, Emilie 2			
Hermann 3m, Ernestine 19			
SCHMIDT, Christine	19	Feldernach	63-0953
SCHMIDT, Christine	27	Mandel	66-1131
SCHMIDT, Christoph	26	Weingarten	63-1178
SCHMIDT, Christoph	33	Stein	65-1030
SCHMIDT, Conr.	47	Burgdamm	65-0007
SCHMIDT, Conr.	50	Hasselhorn	65-0243
SCHMIDT, Conrad	24	Stoermede	64-0433
Franziska 28			
SCHMIDT, Conrad	16	Langgoevs	63-0015
Christine 14			
SCHMIDT, Conrad	30	Wittjenborn	64-0456
Elisabeth 25, Carl 1			

NAME	AGE	RESIDENCE	YR-LIST
SCHMIDT, Conrad	20	Rohrhausen	66-1093
SCHMIDT, Conrad	36	Tuebingen	64-1022
Cath. 34			
SCHMIDT, David	29	Hessenhaus	65-0243
Emilie 28			
SCHMIDT, E.	21	Kaltern	65-1189
SCHMIDT, Ed.	21	Braunschweig	65-0974
SCHMIDT, Edw.	30	Bremenhaven	64-0023
Sophie 20, Lissy 9m			
SCHMIDT, Ehrentz	28	Osterburken	64-0363
SCHMIDT, Elisabeth	37	Bremen	63-0097
SCHMIDT, Elisabeth	18	Goennern	66-0221
SCHMIDT, Elise	25	New York	66-0576
SCHMIDT, Elise	21	Sievern	66-0349
Maria 30			
SCHMIDT, Elise	22	Volnsberg	64-0687
SCHMIDT, Elise	19	Achim	66-0934
SCHMIDT, Emlie	21	Fuerth	63-1218
SCHMIDT, Ernst	29	Curhessen	63-0693
Margarethe 32, James 11m			
SCHMIDT, Ernst	32	Oberohmen	63-0006
Catharine 49, Marie 23, Catharine 20			
Georg 17, Marie 7, Elisa 4			
SCHMIDT, Ernst	46	Weltprechsrod	66-0083
SCHMIDT, Eva	18	Lauran	65-0594
SCHMIDT, Ewald	32	Preussen	66-0147
SCHMIDT, F. (m)	26	Braunschweig	64-0331
Johanna 21			
SCHMIDT, F. Gerdes	23	Logabirum	65-0898
SCHMIDT, F.C.	26	Frankenhausen	65-0898
SCHMIDT, Felix	31	New York	66-0984
SCHMIDT, Ferd.	14	Lunsen	63-0821
SCHMIDT, Ferd.	30	Berlin	65-0004
SCHMIDT, Fr.	55	Furra	67-0600
Aug. 15, Herm. 9, Friedr. 52			
SCHMIDT, Fr.	36	Allendorf	65-0402
Therese 33, Franz 4, Anton 1			
SCHMIDT, Fr.	23	Burgstemmen	65-1088
Georg 17			
SCHMIDT, Frank	34	St. Louis	63-0752
SCHMIDT, Franz	26	Grabow	67-0007
SCHMIDT, Franz Jos	28	Bruchhausen	66-1313
SCHMIDT, Frd,	24	Preussen	66-0221
SCHMIDT, Frdr.	18	Hamm	64-0992
SCHMIDT, Friedr.	57	Weilburg	66-0984
Kaetchen 27			
SCHMIDT, Friedr.	21	Lutter	64-1053
SCHMIDT, Friedr.	24	Obergen	66-1243
SCHMIDT, Friedrich	31	New York	63-0350
SCHMIDT, Friedrich	24	Werderfelde	66-0679
SCHMIDT, Friedrich	26	Zamzow	66-0679
Friederike 34, baby 3m			
SCHMIDT, Friedrich	18	Mehnen	66-1155
SCHMIDT, Friedrich	43	New York	66-0934
SCHMIDT, Friedrich	20	Oberfranken	66-1131
Heinrich 28			
SCHMIDT, Frz.	16	Sulzthal	66-1243
Adalb. 20			
SCHMIDT, G.(m)	18	Wien	64-0073
SCHMIDT, G.A.(m)	25	Sailauf	64-0073
SCHMIDT, G.M.	26	Ditzum	64-0886
Trientje 29			
SCHMIDT, G.W.	39	New York	63-1085
SCHMIDT, Geo.	22	Attenheim	63-0990
SCHMIDT, Geo.David	27	New York	63-1178
SCHMIDT, Georg	25	Bremen	63-0614
SCHMIDT, Georg	25	Erlangen	66-0668
SCHMIDT, Georg	40	Wuerttemberg	66-0109
SCHMIDT, Georg	34	Biedenkopf	64-0687
SCHMIDT, Georg	20	Paunach/Bav.	65-0038
SCHMIDT, Georg	18	Bueckeburg	66-1127
SCHMIDT, Georg Ad.	54	Oberlustadt	65-0243
Marie 45, Cath. 20, Johann 13			
SCHMIDT, Gerhard	22	Rinteln	67-0007
SCHMIDT, Gesina	18	Lehe	66-1093
SCHMIDT, Gottfried	54	Limbach	66-1248
Margarethe 17, Christine 14			
SCHMIDT, Gottlieb	24	Heerstein	67-0007

NAME	AGE	RESIDENCE	YR-LIST
SCHMIDT, Gottlieb	22	Heiligenzell	66-1327
SCHMIDT, Gustav	17	Braunschweig	66-0147
SCHMIDT, Gustav	33	Schlotheim	65-1030
Dorothea 33, August 9, Mathilde 7			
Gustav 3, Augusta 5, Kaethe 9m			
SCHMIDT, H.	25	Eschenbach	64-0992
SCHMIDT, H.	24	Weener	65-1088
SCHMIDT, H. (f)	32	Wertheim	63-0990
Friedrich 9, Michael 6			
SCHMIDT, H.(m)	26	Hainbach	64-0170
SCHMIDT, H.(m)	31	Braunschweig	64-0331
SCHMIDT, Heinr.	23	Stoermede	63-0398
SCHMIDT, Heinr.	25	Kirchheim	64-0992
SCHMIDT, Heinr.	13	Oldenburg	64-0938
Anna 22			
SCHMIDT, Heinr.	38	Gilfenshausen	65-0038
SCHMIDT, Heinr.	24	Bremen	65-0151
SCHMIDT, Heinr.	26	Diepholz	66-1373
SCHMIDT, Heinrich	58	Riebau	63-0614
Anna Marie 58, Ermina 21, Caroline 19			
Dorothea 13			
SCHMIDT, Heinrich	32	Muenden	66-1093
SCHMIDT, Heinrich	24	Amt Stolzenau	67-0599
SCHMIDT, Heinrich	18	Ritterhude	64-0886
SCHMIDT, Heinrich	22	Steinhude	66-1373
SCHMIDT, Henry	35	Kiel	66-0221
SCHMIDT, Herm	30	Panna	64-0495
SCHMIDT, Herm.	16	Gohrau	63-1136
Alwine 21			
SCHMIDT, Herm.	25	Hugelsheim	65-0402
SCHMIDT, Herm. L.	37	Sangershausen	65-1030
Therese 37, Carl Aug. 10, Marie 3			
SCHMIDT, Hermann	17	Hoysinghausen	66-0147
Doris 21			
SCHMIDT, Hermann	19	Glamhau	66-1327
SCHMIDT, Hiram	27	Saal	64-0593
SCHMIDT, J.A.(m)	38	Altenmuhr	64-0170
SCHMIDT, J.C.	32	Grossenmoor	64-0170
Anna Maria 27, Anna Maria 9m			
Elisabeth 18, Anna Maria 15			
SCHMIDT, Jac.	41	Rosenfeld	64-0331
Johanna 21			
SCHMIDT, Jacob	25	Oltershausen	63-0398
SCHMIDT, Jacob	22	Nussbaum	66-0413
Peter 46			
SCHMIDT, Jacob	24	Osnabrueck	67-0007
SCHMIDT, Jacob	25	Lenbach	66-1373
SCHMIDT, Jacob	60	Hohscheit	65-0243
Ottilie 58			
SCHMIDT, James H.	24	Baltimore	63-1038
SCHMIDT, Joachim	32	Molitz	67-0599
SCHMIDT, Joh.	23	Hoechstadt	65-0116
SCHMIDT, Joh.	18	Bremen	66-1128
SCHMIDT, Joh.	28	Windecke	66-1373
SCHMIDT, Joh. Mich	58	Giessen	66-0577
Henriette 33, Elise 25, Wilhelmine 2m			
SCHMIDT, Joh.Heinr	37	Lauterbach	63-0398
SCHMIDT, Johann	30	Dettingen	64-0199
SCHMIDT, Johann	29	Kolberg/Pr.	63-0822
Wilhelmine 24, Wilhelmine 24			
SCHMIDT, Johann	17	Preussen	66-0469
SCHMIDT, Johann	39	Pommern	66-0577
Hanna 39, Bertha 11, August 5, Marie 11m			
Augusta 11m			
SCHMIDT, Johann	22	Darnsfetten	67-0007
SCHMIDT, Johann	39	Potsdam	66-1243
Friederike 37, Emilie 7, Wilhelm 4			
Christian 68			
SCHMIDT, Johann	28	Speyer	65-0055
SCHMIDT, Johann	23	Treichtlingen	65-1024
SCHMIDT, Johann H.	25	Gesmold	63-1069
SCHMIDT, Johannes	15	Heidelbach	66-0412
SCHMIDT, Johannes	33	Schotten	64-1161
SCHMIDT, John	32	Gruenberg	63-1038
Elise 22, Friedr. 9m			
SCHMIDT, John	37	Ebersfeld	63-0482
Maria 30			
SCHMIDT, John	25	Neuchatel	65-0898
SCHMIDT, Jos.	24	Oettingen	64-0073
SCHMIDT, Joseph	28	Wuertemberg	66-0147
SCHMIDT, Joseph	23	Boehmen	63-0862
SCHMIDT, Joseph	46	Rock Island	63-0862
SCHMIDT, Joseph	28	St. Louis	63-0917
SCHMIDT, Joseph	28	Eschenbach	63-0097
SCHMIDT, Joseph	47	Boehmen	63-0990
Barbara 57, John 18			
SCHMIDT, Joseph	20	Westhausen	66-1373
SCHMIDT, Jost	23	Breidenbach	64-0687
SCHMIDT, Juliane	24	Waldshut	63-0350
SCHMIDT, L.	18	Herbstein	64-0992
SCHMIDT, Leonh.	30	Hoboken	64-0170
SCHMIDT, Leonhard	22	Hofheim	67-0007
SCHMIDT, Louis	59	Allentown	63-0953
SCHMIDT, Louis	17	Rodelsheim	66-1248
SCHMIDT, Louis	29	Meschchied	64-0363
SCHMIDT, Louise	20	Cunar	65-0189
SCHMIDT, Ludw.	16	Dorlar	64-0782
SCHMIDT, Ludwig	17	Bremerhafen	64-0343
SCHMIDT, Luer	19	Leeste	66-1127
SCHMIDT, Ma.	53	Nurnberg	63-1085
SCHMIDT, Marg.	22	Hohenschwarz	64-0495
SCHMIDT, Marg.	26	Frohnhausen	65-0974
Heinrich 15			
SCHMIDT, Margareth	36	Hoellrich	66-0576
Margaretha 16			
SCHMIDT, Margareth	19	Krumbach	66-0734
SCHMIDT, Marie	23	Roedelheim	66-0576
Anna 10m			
SCHMIDT, Marie	18	Roenneberg	67-0007
SCHMIDT, Mart.	23	Vihringen	66-1243
SCHMIDT, Martin	18	Dermsheim	63-0953
SCHMIDT, Martin	29	Ulm	65-0007
Regina 21			
SCHMIDT, Martin	50	Ihlpohl	64-0886
SCHMIDT, Martin	24	Cassel	65-0865
SCHMIDT, Mary	19	Eisenach	66-1031
Minna 18			
SCHMIDT, Math.	31	Crailsheim	63-0990
SCHMIDT, Math.	35	Naborn	65-0402
Elisab. 28, Nicol. 7, Elisab. 6, Maria 4			
Peter 3, Maria 9m			
SCHMIDT, Mathilde	20	Oehringen	66-1093
SCHMIDT, Max	30	Insbach	64-0593
SCHMIDT, Michael	23	Mundestadt/Bo	64-0920
SCHMIDT, Mrs.	34	Pittsburg	63-1136
Oscar 8, Eugenie 9			
SCHMIDT, Mrs. G.	40	New York	63-0953
Amanda 24, Henry 7, Alfred 1, Gustav 2m			
SCHMIDT, Nicolaus	21	St. Gallen	65-0243
SCHMIDT, Paul	28	Prust	66-0650
SCHMIDT, Peter	39	Naborn	65-0402
Martha 32, Maria 10, Cathr. 7, Elisab. 4			
Peter 2, Nicol. 9m			
SCHMIDT, Peter	27	Hochweisel	64-0214
Cath. 23, baby 6m			
SCHMIDT, Ph.	24	Schwesheim	66-0413
SCHMIDT, Phil.	22	Breitenbach	65-0402
Cath. 19			
SCHMIDT, Philip	28	Asslar	66-0221
Cathar. 25, Wilhelmine 5m			
SCHMIDT, Philippin	21	Detroit	66-0576
SCHMIDT, Pierre	24	Schweiz	63-1136
SCHMIDT, R.	23	Neustadt	65-1189
SCHMIDT, Regine	22	Magstadt	65-0594
SCHMIDT, Ros. Cne.	22	Dettenhausen	65-0038
SCHMIDT, Simon	30	Baltimore	63-1010
Maria 21, Ida 2			
SCHMIDT, Sophia	25	Thedinghausen	66-0679
SCHMIDT, Sophie	40	New York	63-0614
Herbert 11			
SCHMIDT, Sophie	15	Bretten	66-1155
SCHMIDT, Stephan	58	Edenkoben	65-1024
Catharine 59			
SCHMIDT, Theodor	22	Bersenbrueck	66-1093
SCHMIDT, Theodor	28	Muenster	65-0770
SCHMIDT, Therese	23	Sax.-Weimar	64-0938

NAME	AGE	RESIDENCE	YR-LIST
SCHMIDT, Theresia	26	Durlar	66-1155
Georg 30			
SCHMIDT, Valentin	19	Wimmweiler	66-0576
SCHMIDT, Valt.	20	Wuerzburg	65-0038
SCHMIDT, Victor	21	Ndr.Zeitheim	66-0984
SCHMIDT, Victoria	28	Arnstadt	66-1093
SCHMIDT, W.(m)	21	Gr.Eisslingen	64-0331
SCHMIDT, Wendel	33	Gr.Rohrheim	64-0214
SCHMIDT, Wihelmine	32	Ruppersdorf	66-1093
Rahel 2			
SCHMIDT, Wilhelm	27	New York	63-0015
SCHMIDT, Wilhelm	20	Marburg	66-0623
SCHMIDT, Wilhelm	24	Damerow	66-0578
Carl 29			
SCHMIDT, Wilhelm	19	Darmstadt	66-0679
Henriette 17, Friedrich 14, Ludwig 5			
SCHMIDT, Wilhelm	28	Goslar	64-1053
SCHMIDT, Wilhelm	19	Freeren	65-0055
SCHMIDT, Wilhelm	20	Backnang	66-1373
SCHMIDT, Wilhelm	25	Muelsen	66-1373
SCHMIDT, Wilke	15	Ihrhove	66-1127
SCHMIDT, William	26	Basel	66-1203
SCHMIDT, Wm.	21	Boston	63-1003
SCHMIDT, Wm.	25	Philadelphia	64-0495
SCHMIDT, Wm.	49	Insbach	64-0593
Rosa 50, Carl 20, Wm. 18, Franz 17			
Magdalena 14, Hermanna 9			
SCHMIDT, Wm.	17	Rumbeck	64-0593
SCHMIDT, Wm.	38	Ottersberg	66-1313
Lucie 32			
SCHMIDT, Wm.	28	Jettingen	65-0594
SCHMIDT, Wm.	28	Schmiedefeld	65-0898
SCHMIDTHEIMER, Ph.	24	Leun	65-0004
SCHMIDTMANN, Carl	55	Lueneburg	66-0412
Hannchen 15, Carl 5			
SCHMIDTMANN, Heinr	48	Clarion Co.	64-0073
SCHMIDTS, Augusta	19	Wildeshausen	64-0073
SCHMIDTZ, Samuel	28	Muenster	64-1053
SCHMIED, Christian	36	Arbor	66-0147
SCHMIED, Joh.	26	Herschbach	64-1108
Gertrud 26			
SCHMIED, Rub.(m)	24	Oberstalzingn	64-0495
SCHMIEDEBERG, v. A	34	United States	64-0593
SCHMIEDEKAMP, Lou.	28	Lage	64-0687
SCHMIEDEL, Eduard	55	Regensburg	66-0837
SCHMIEDER, Ernst	28	Wetter	66-0704
SCHMIEDER, Gottl.	28	Hutzenbach	66-0147
Sabina 19			
SCHMIEDER, Hugo	18	Carthausen	66-1093
SCHMIEDER, Mr.	24	New York	64-0073
SCHMIEDERBUR, Wm.	40	Herringhausen	63-0917
Gertrud 45, Franz 20, Henry 16, Casper 13			
John 11, Maria 8, Elisabeth 3			
SCHMIEDESKANN, Aug	18	Lage	64-0593
SCHMIEDLIN, Rosali	26	Dittingen	64-1108
SCHMIEDT, Carl	35	Friedrichshor	65-1095
Justine 39, Gustav 14, Albertine 12			
Maria 6, Amalie 4			
SCHMIEG, Christ.	27	Doessenheim	64-1206
SCHMIET, Jacob	41	Wehrendorf	66-0679
SCHMIETTEN, Adam	26	Leimbach	66-0734
SCHMIPF, Emilie	55	Muehlenhausen	64-0886
Emil 7			
SCHMIT, Jan	52	Stappelmoor	66-0668
Reinh. 17			
SCHMITS, Wilhelm	15	Nentershausen	63-0006
Heinrich 14			
SCHMITSCHULTE, Wm.	19	Emstedt	66-0576
SCHMITT, Fred	35	Switzerland	64-0138
SCHMITT, Johann	45	Oberelsbach	66-1203
SCHMITT, Julius	33	Mellrichstadt	66-0704
Dorothea 27, Fritz 7, Max 3, Agnes 9m			
SCHMITTGALL, Ros.	31	Adolzfurth	66-1327
SCHMITTGER, Wm.	16	Lengerich	65-1189
SCHMITTING, Marie	20	Salingen	64-0023
SCHMITTKNECHT, Bar	20	New York	63-0752
SCHMITTKONZ, Rosin	24	Prichsenstadt	66-0147
SCHMITTLE, Ph.	34	Kleinsbach	64-1161

NAME	AGE	RESIDENCE	YR-LIST
SCHMITZ, (m)	22	Holten	65-0974
SCHMITZ, Agnes	54	Prussia	64-0432
Elis. 18, Cath. 15, Magdalena 11			
SCHMITZ, Arnold	20	Braken	66-1093
SCHMITZ, Augusta	21	Messcheid	64-0639
SCHMITZ, Carl	20	Darmstadt	65-0865
SCHMITZ, Fritz	22	Meschede	66-0679
SCHMITZ, G.(m)	40	New York	64-0138
SCHMITZ, Martin	27	Bremen	64-0214
SCHMITZ, Richard	18	Frankfurt/M	64-0363
SCHMITZ, Th.	40	Merscheid	65-1024
SCHMITZER, Adolph	21	Dahlenfeld	65-0243
SCHMOELLER, Robert	26	Magdeburg	66-1155
SCHMOKELBERG, Ant.	18	Lage	66-1373
SCHMOLDE, Wilh'mne	23	Mildenen	64-0992
SCHMOLDT, Hermann	36	Preussen	64-0363
Caroline 27, Wilhelmine 7, Emilie 6			
baby (f) 6m, Marie 4			
SCHMOLL, Heinr. W.	37	Melsungen	65-0713
Marie E. 38, Heinr. A. 4			
SCHMOLL, Louise	19	Huellhorst	65-0189
SCHMOLL, Pauline	21	Nuertingen	64-1053
SCHMOLLER, Joh. W.	21	Kleinkundorf	66-0934
SCHMOLLINGER, Gott	26	Lienzingen	64-0840
Regina 22			
SCHMOLT, Jos.	30	Nieort	63-1038
SCHMONSEES, M.	20	Katzeweschbch	63-0296
SCHMUCK, Nicolaus	32	Phalheim	66-1203
SCHMULACH, Friedr.	24	Gross Lubs	65-0713
SCHMUSCHER, H.	17	Buttenwiesen	65-0007
SCHMUTZLER, Friedr	34	Glauchau	66-0576
Henriette 32, Martha 3			
SCHMUTZLER, Wm.	30	Bremen	64-0427
Marie 24			
SCHNABEL, Wichand	42	Oberursel	66-0666
Wilhelmine 32, Elisabeth 13, Eva 10			
Margareth 7, Wilhelmine 4, Elisabetha 2			
SCHNACKENBERG, Mta	19	Osterode	65-0898
SCHNAFELIUS, Herm.	23	Offenbach	67-0007
SCHNAKE, Friedr.	14	Huellhorst	65-0189
SCHNAKENBERG, Ant.	19	Bremervoerde	65-0865
SCHNAR, Marie	50	Schluechtern	64-1206
SCHNARR, Barbara	28	Jachheim	65-0116
SCHNARR, Peter	52	Grewenau	66-0578
Elisabeth 55, Elisabeth 9			
SCHNATZ, Magdalena	32	Gernsheim	66-1093
Elise 8, Jacob 6			
SCHNAUE, Henry	40	New York	63-1218
SCHNAUFFER, Adolph	18	Magstadt	64-0214
Marie 20, Wilhelm 18			
SCHNECH, Ernst Fr.	19	Stetten	66-0704
SCHNECK, H.D.(m)	25	Stettin	64-0170
SCHNECKE, Charles	50	Leipzig	63-1178
SCHNECKENBURGER, J	30	New York	63-0990
SCHNECKER, Sophie	24	Kl. Borssel	66-1127
SCHNEEBECK, H.	17	Aldrup	65-1189
SCHNEEBERG, Maria	27	Boehmen	66-0623
SCHNEEBERGER, Elis	22	Lindheim	63-0006
SCHNEEGANS, Heinr.	40	Bielefeld	65-1030
Anna Cath. 40			
SCHNEFIE, Edw.	27	Braunschweig	66-0221
Caroline 25			
SCHNEIBER, F.	25	Vreckenhorst	64-0782
SCHNEICHT, Theo. P	25	Stuttgart	65-1031
SCHNEIDEEISEN, Jos	26	Katlach	66-0413
SCHNEIDEL, Elisab.	52	Arnsberg	63-0614
SCHNEIDEMANN, H.	19	Fraustadt	64-0593
SCHNEIDER, Adam	57	Derksheim	65-1030
Dorethe 55, Matthias 24, Georg 17			
Peter 14, Johann 12			
SCHNEIDER, Anna	23	Antwerp	65-0004
Margarethe 21, Peter 18			
SCHNEIDER, Anna	25	Hohenfels	66-1131
SCHNEIDER, Babette	14	Hof	64-0214
SCHNEIDER, Barbara	25	Hessen	63-0350
Agnesia 5, Margarete 2			
SCHNEIDER, Brigitt	20	Insbach	64-0886
SCHNEIDER, Cacilie	19	Krojanke	66-0704

NAME	AGE	RESIDENCE	YR-LIST
SCHNEIDER, Carl	25	Pforzheim	66-0576
SCHNEIDER, Carl	39	Breitenthal	67-0007
SCHNEIDER, Carl F.	23	Frauenpriestn	65-0055
SCHNEIDER, Cath.	57	Darmstadt	63-1178
Caroline 20			
SCHNEIDER, Cathar.	40	Breidenbach	64-0687
SCHNEIDER, Cathar.	36	Cassel	66-1093
Dora 6, baby 10m			
SCHNEIDER, Cathar.	18	Schlen	66-1155
SCHNEIDER, Cathar.	20	Coeln	66-1155
SCHNEIDER, Chr'tne	24	Hochstellen	63-0244
SCHNEIDER, Chr'tne	30	Hildesheim	66-1131
Marie 2			
SCHNEIDER, Chr'tof	18	Armsheim	66-0412
SCHNEIDER, Christ.	23	Hof	63-1178
SCHNEIDER, Christ.	17	Hergershausen	66-0469
SCHNEIDER, Christ.	22	Giessen	66-0679
SCHNEIDER, Elisa	27	Oberkaufungen	63-0551
SCHNEIDER, Elisab.	19	Gr. Umstadt	66-0221
SCHNEIDER, Elisab.	27	Weikerbier	66-0576
SCHNEIDER, Elisab.	26	Stettin	64-0639
Rosine 9m			
SCHNEIDER, Elisab.	36	Herbstein	65-0189
SCHNEIDER, Emma	21	Osnabrueck	66-1031
SCHNEIDER, Ernst	22	Puplitz	63-1010
SCHNEIDER, Ernst	23	Plauen	65-0713
SCHNEIDER, Eug.	15	Herbstein	64-0992
SCHNEIDER, Ferd'd.	18	Orb	66-1031
SCHNEIDER, Ferd.	29	Ndr.Althoven	65-0594
SCHNEIDER, Ferdin.	26	Hachenburg	66-1127
SCHNEIDER, Florian	20	Baden	66-0576
SCHNEIDER, Fr'drke	24	Leidesheim	66-1093
SCHNEIDER, Friedr.	27	Rheda/Pr.	63-0822
Anna 21			
SCHNEIDER, Friedr.	25	Laaspe	63-0862
SCHNEIDER, Friedr.	20	Mannheim	65-0151
SCHNEIDER, Friedr.	23	Hesepe	66-1373
SCHNEIDER, Fritz	17	Zeven	63-0244
SCHNEIDER, G.	24	Wolfskehlen	65-1189
SCHNEIDER, Georg	29	Windecken	64-0170
Cath. 20			
SCHNEIDER, Georg F	20	Coburg	66-0109
SCHNEIDER, Gottl.	25	Wilmas	66-0650
SCHNEIDER, H.	23	Ruppertsweilr	66-0413
C. 2, Ph. 1			
SCHNEIDER, Heinr.	17	Philadelphia	66-0704
SCHNEIDER, Heinr.	23	Birklar	66-1155
SCHNEIDER, Heinr.	28	Durlar	66-1155
SCHNEIDER, Heinr.	26	Wolfhagen	66-1373
SCHNEIDER, Heinr.		Oberkaufungen	65-0950
SCHNEIDER, Helene	23	Udenheim	66-1093
SCHNEIDER, Henr(f)	22	Thalitter	67-0795
SCHNEIDER, Herm.	22	Itzenheim	65-0055
SCHNEIDER, Hermann	26	Saalfeld	66-0666
SCHNEIDER, Jacob	41	New York	64-0199
SCHNEIDER, James	39	Landau	63-0821
SCHNEIDER, Joh.	33	Radlus	65-0007
SCHNEIDER, Joh. D.	29	Ostheim	66-0650
SCHNEIDER, Joh.Alb	32	Hamstrup	65-1030
SCHNEIDER, Johann	23	Bodenheim	66-0147
SCHNEIDER, Johann	32	Waettgendorf	66-0576
Ernestine 26, Anna 6, Minna 2, Hermann 4			
Ida 9m			
SCHNEIDER, Johann	22	Schleu	66-0984
SCHNEIDER, Johanna	18	Weedingen	63-0990
SCHNEIDER, Johanna	40	Leipzig	65-0055
SCHNEIDER, John	56	Darmstadt	63-0953
Philip 25			
SCHNEIDER, Johs.	22	Wahlen	66-0147
SCHNEIDER, Josephi	32	Louisville	63-1218
Louis 8, Marie 6, Julie 4, John 9m			
SCHNEIDER, Julie	17	Burgkundstedt	66-1093
SCHNEIDER, Justine	26	Werdum	66-0413
SCHNEIDER, L.	23	Mollenfelde	63-1003
SCHNEIDER, L.	25	Gunzelhausen	64-0782
SCHNEIDER, Laura	30	Bremen	64-0427
Han. (f) 7, Bernh. 5, Richard 6, baby 6m			
SCHNEIDER, Leo	38	Herbstein	64-1053
Therese 32, Wm. 2, Gotthard 6m			
Albertus 18			
SCHNEIDER, Leo.	24	Waldberg	65-1095
SCHNEIDER, Leonh.	26	Kirchhardt	66-0109
SCHNEIDER, Lorenz	23	Untergrombach	66-1155
SCHNEIDER, Louis	45	Milwaukee	64-0363
Hugo 12, Bertha 31, Adelheid 14, Oscar 9			
Louis 9m			
SCHNEIDER, Ludw.	27	Mindelheim	65-0038
SCHNEIDER, M.	19	Scherenbach	64-0639
SCHNEIDER, Magdal.	32	Freinfeld	64-0593
Margaretha 5			
SCHNEIDER, Magdal.	34	Foehrden	64-0363
SCHNEIDER, Maria	58	Herbstein	64-0840
Elisabeth 15			
SCHNEIDER, Marie	22	Kirchheim	64-1206
SCHNEIDER, Martin	30	New York	63-0752
SCHNEIDER, Mathias	22	Hochwissen	66-0679
SCHNEIDER, Minna	21	Freisenheim	65-0007
SCHNEIDER, Ottilie	23	Cassel	66-0221
SCHNEIDER, Peter	33	Gandersheim	64-0363
SCHNEIDER, Phil	24	Schloss Neuse	63-1136
SCHNEIDER, Philipp	58	Wetzlar	66-1155
Therese 56			
SCHNEIDER, Rosine	24	Laufen	66-0679
SCHNEIDER, Rudolph	19	Burgsteifurt	65-1030
SCHNEIDER, Sebast.	20	Goelsdorf	66-0734
SCHNEIDER, Sophie	24	Graslitz	66-1243
SCHNEIDER, Susanne	24	Darmstadt	66-1031
SCHNEIDER, Tha.	19	Koenigswart	64-0427
SCHNEIDER, Thee	24	Firrel	66-0668
Johanna 21			
SCHNEIDER, Wilh.	27	Altenberge	66-0679
SCHNEIDER, Wilhelm	31	Rodenberg	67-0599
SCHNEIDER, Wilhelm	29	Strathe	66-1155
Heinrich 22			
SCHNEIDER, Wilh.	14	Esslingen	66-0469
SCHNEIDERMANN, Jan	36	Simonswolde	64-0363
Beefke 34			
SCHNEIDERS, Wilh.	25	Hannover	63-0398
SCHNEIDHELM, Bernh	22	Sonnenberg	66-1127
SCHNEIDIG, Eva	28	Creuznach	66-1203
SCHNEITHORST, Herm	34	Verden	63-0953
Elise 8, Henry 5			
SCHNELL, C.A.	22	Windelberg	64-0665
SCHNELL, Friedrich	20	Muehlbach	66-0576
SCHNELL, Rosalie	26	Coburg	63-1038
SCHNELLER, Georg	30	Schlitz	65-0007
SCHNELLER, J.B.(m)	26	Uchtingen	64-0023
SCHNELLI, Anton	17	Preussen	66-0221
SCHNEPEL, Cast.	23	Aschwarden/Pr	65-0038
SCHNEPEL, Charltt.		Doehren	66-1127
SCHNEPF, Christian	21	Weilar	66-1248
SCHNERKE, Dorothea	23	Riebau	63-0614
Catharina 22			
SCHNIBGER, Rosine	24	Grossbettingn	66-0576
SCHNICK, J.H.	34	Heidelberg	65-0055
SCHNIDLER, Lorenz	40	Amshausen	64-0840
Barbara 39, Louise 13, Anna 7			
Christine 4			
SCHNIEDER, Richard	25	Insbach	64-0593
SCHNIEDERS, Johann	65	Coesfeld	65-1030
Elisabeth 44, Johann 19, Elisabeth 17			
Anna 14, Gertrude /			
SCHNIEDLER, Alma	21	Lanzenau	64-0687
SCHNIETZMEYER, Joa	16	Muntinghausen	63-1038
SCHNIRRING, Heinr.	30	Ahausen	65-1024
H. 23			
SCHNITGER, A.	34	Saxony	63-1003
SCHNITTGER, J.Siem	25	Neermoor	67-0600
Margarethe 27, Janette 3			
SCHNITTGER, Johann	23	Eschwege	66-1093
SCHNITTHENNEN, Jac	14	Bavaria	63-0822
SCHNITTJER, John W	53	Louisville	63-0862
SCHNITTKER, Gerh.	21	Altenkamp	66-0734
SCHNITTLER, Georg	17	Meiningen	64-0432
SCHNITTLER, Johann	16	Weinsheim	66-1327
Margarethe 17			

NAME	AGE	RESIDENCE	YR-LIST
SCHNITZEL, Jacob	23	Speier	66-0734
SCHNITZER, Henry	30	Minden	63-0244
SCHNORBUS, Heinr.	39	Preussen	64-0214
Cath. 34, Franz 9, Joseph 7, Fr. (m) 5			
Cath. 3, baby 11m, Elisabeth 22			
SCHNORS, Hinr.	16	Garrelstedt	64-0432
SCHNUERDREHER, Bab	20		63-0693
SCHNUERLE, Christ.		Gaarweiler	66-0147
Barbara 20			
SCHNUR, Caroline	15	Baden	66-0576
SCHOBER, L.	18	Darmstadt	65-1189
SCHOBER, Marg.	30	Bromberg	64-0432
SCHOCK, Catharine	27	Rippoldsen	66-0734
Amalie 29, Agnes 5			
SCHOCK, Johann	37	Moschis	66-0578
Rosine 36, Albertine 11, Augusta 2			
SCHODEL, Joh. Ed.	19	Gmuenden	65-0950
SCHOE, H.	27	Schuettorf	66-0704
SCHOEDER, H.(m)	26	Bremen	64-0495
SCHOEFFEL, Hr.	34	Saalfeld	65-0007
SCHOEFFLER, Friedr	32	Grossenwasen	65-1088
Conrad 29			
SCHOEFT, August	40	Wien	63-1085
SCHOEGERT, Wm.	20	Goedberg	64-1161
SCHOEIBER, Aug.	35	Wien	64-0840
Leopoldine 23			
SCHOELKOPF, Christ	39	Buffalo	66-0734
Alfred 6			
SCHOELL, Christoph	23	Mezingen	64-1206
SCHOELL, Friedr.	24	Metzingen	66-1327
SCHOELLKOPF, Fr'dr	46	Wuertemberg	66-0734
Gottl. 17			
SCHOEN, Aug.	21	Werda	64-0363
SCHOEN, Elisabeth	24	Ellnrode	66-0668
SCHOEN, Friederike	22	Wilssassen	66-1203
SCHOEN, Isaac	17	Ob.Waldbehrun	66-1373
SCHOEN, Jacob	41	Staten Island	66-0109
Anna 38, John 19			
SCHOENAUER, E.	25	Heddesheim	65-1189
SCHOENBERG, Isaac	18	Burg Grafenrd	66-1031
Isaac 15			
SCHOENBERGER, Conr	18	Vielbrunn	66-1155
SCHOENBERGER, Joh.	38	Schenkelberg	66-0934
Marie 38, Margaretha 3, Christian 9m			
SCHOENBERGER, Otto	19	Buchau	64-0363
SCHOENBURG, Georg	27	Wabern	64-0840
Conrad 22			
SCHOENDORFF, J.A.	66	Lehe	65-0974
SCHOENDUBER, Carl	47	Schoningen	66-0412
SCHOENE, Johann	40	Bosfurt	66-0666
Elisabeth 50, Christian H. 14			
Johann Gerh. 9, Elise 7, Johann Heinr 73			
SCHOENE, Margareth	23	Herbergen	66-0349
SCHOENEBERGER, Csp	44	Tapke	65-0243
SCHOENECK, Fr.	56	Prussia	63-1003
Marg. 26, John 4, Magdal. 3, Charles 7m			
C. 30, J. 54, Fr. 27, E. 25, F. 6, E. 1			
SCHOENEFELD, Diedr	20	Bromkamp	66-0083
SCHOENEN, Marie	20	Talge	64-0886
Adelheid 24			
SCHOENEWEG, L.	26	Essnerberge	63-1003
SCHOENFELD, Aug.	26	Friedrichshor	65-0038
Juliana 29, Augusta 8, Albertine 5			
Caroline 3, Adolph 5m			
SCHOENFELD, August	18	Fangenberg	66-0623
SCHOENFELD, David	14	Frankenberg	66-0984
SCHOENFELD, F.W.	31	Detmold	64-0170
Virgine 17, Susette 2			
SCHOENFELD, Gustav	33	Reutlingen	66-0934
Lisette 30, Lisette 3m			
SCHOENFELD, Julie	27	Nordhausen	64-0593
SCHOENFELD, Livi	27	Hamburg	63-0482
Adelene 24, Emilie 24, Alfred 2			
Caroline 22, Leeser 9			
SCHOENFELD, Marg.	24	Bremen	64-0170
SCHOENHALS, C.	35	New York	63-0296
SCHOENHALS, Henr't	29	New York	63-0990
Augusta 7m			

NAME	AGE	RESIDENCE	YR-LIST
SCHOENHAUS, Julie	19	Pickelsheim	66-0984
SCHOENHERR, Oscar	27	New York	63-0752
SCHOENHUTH, Albert	18	Steppingen	66-1203
SCHOENHUTH, C.	24	Goppingen	65-0974
SCHOENROCK, Gottl.	25	Preussen	66-0623
SCHOENTHAL, Heinem	23	Sielen	66-0679
SCHOENWOLFF, Fr'dr	18	Hessia	66-0679
SCHOEPFER, Wilhelm	38	Reichenbach	66-0734
SCHOEPPNER, C.	23	Burgpreppach	63-1003
SCHOERRING, Wilh.	24	Hasebeck	63-1010
SCHOESSER, Friedr.	26	Durlach	67-0007
SCHOETT, Carl	35	Ilbertshausen	66-0650
Catharine 26, Maria 8			
SCHOETT, Robert	18	Plauen	67-0806
SCHOETTE, Joh. G.	23	Ebhausen	64-1108
SCHOETTELKUTTE, F.	28	Ochtrup	64-1022
Marianne 25			
SCHOETTLE, Christ.	29	Rottweil	63-1038
SCHOFFLER, Carl Ag	24	Pohr Crome	64-0433
SCHOFRANK, Franz	31	Boehmen	66-0221
Anna 25, Anna 5, Carl 3, Franz 6m			
SCHOFRANK, Johann	26	Boehmen	66-0221
Maria 24, Joseph 6m			
SCHOKLITSCH, Urban	34	Untergorbach	66-1327
Marie 36			
SCHOLASTICA, E.	25	Schoenberg	63-0990
SCHOLBORG,	27	New York	63-0752
SCHOLER, John	38	Derendingen	66-1155
Catharina 33, Johannes 6, Carl 3			
SCHOLER, Marg.	19	Armheim	64-0782
SCHOLL, Christian	58	Krumbach	63-1069
Maria 54, Peter 28, Christina 22			
Christina 23			
SCHOLL, Conrad	34	Deckenbach	64-0639
Louise 22, Catharina 1, Ludwig 1m			
SCHOLL, Heinr. W.	18	Monhausen	66-1155
SCHOLL, Herm.	40	Bremerhaven	63-1178
SCHOLL, Joh.	25	Ob.Lichtenbch	65-1088
SCHOLL, Ludwig	21	Deckenbach	65-0402
SCHOLL, Wm.	30	Weinheim	64-0495
SCHOLLENBERG, Cath	20	Limbach	66-1248
SCHOLTZ, Jacob	22	Olmuetz	66-0623
SCHOLTZ, Joh.	1	Hohengeren	65-0402
SCHOLVIEN, Alb.	20	Quakenbrueck	63-1136
SCHOLVIN, Helene		Gruenloh	64-0938
Cath. M. , Herm. H.L.			
SCHOLZ, August	31	Kath.Hammer	65-1095
Christiana 25, Herrmann 2m			
SCHOLZ, Gottf.	24	Prussia	63-0752
Johanne 22, Chr. 9, Wm. 5, Ernst 9m			
SCHOMAKER, Diedr.	29	Neuenmarhorst	66-0934
SCHOMAKER, Euphem.	14	Wietmarschen	64-0214
SCHOMAKER, Joh. G.	54	Huven	64-0639
Bernh. 17, Adelheid 17, Anna 24			
SCHOMAKER, Johann	33	Buhlerweit	66-0984
SCHOMBURG, Elise	16	Verna	65-0898
SCHOMBURG, Frnz'ka	21	Hannover	64-1053
SCHOMBURG, Helene	16	Hamburg	63-0482
SCHOMMEL, Christ.	42	Baltimore	66-0679
SCHOMMINGER, Alois	20	Lautlingen	65-1088
SCHOMPERT, Fr.	15	Quekborn	65-0898
SCHONE, Anna	20	Osterberken	66-1093
SCHONE, Herrm.	21	Hahlen	66-0349
Maria 19			
SCHONHOFF, B.	32	Lingen	64-0495
Sophie 27, Anna 6, Heinr. 3, Clara 2			
Clemens 1m			
SCHONING, Daniel	49	Berlin	66-0147
SCHOO, Herm.	59	Lingen	64-0992
Anna 59			
SCHOON, Jaan	27	Warsingsfehn	64-0495
Geske 33			
SCHOONER, Ludw.	33	New York	63-0097
SCHOPF, Franz	19	Neorthen	63-0990
SCHOPF, Phil.	19	Neustadt	64-0938
SCHOPFLIN, Jacob	33	Auggen	65-1088
SCHOPPE, Aug.	31	Gruenenplan	64-0023
SCHOPPE, Aug.	39	Gruenenplan	63-0244

NAME	AGE	RESIDENCE	YR-LIST
SCHORB, Friedr.	23	Schotten	64-0363
SCHORBACH, Fr.	25	Mengsbach	65-0189
SCHORECK, Albertin	38	Breslau	66-0679
Eugen 18, Olga 14, Martha 9			
SCHOREGGE, Heinr.	18	Melle	66-1093
SCHORMANN, Georg	14	Schoningen	66-0469
SCHORNBURG, Cath.	31	Lienen	65-1189
SCHORNDORFER, Val.	19	Thalheim	66-0576
SCHORNER, Anna	26	Staubing	64-0427
SCHORR, Jacob	17	Schwabach	66-1031
SCHORS, Christian	21	Spangenberg	66-1243
Elise 27			
SCHORSCH, Caroline	38	Hannover	66-1243
SCHORT, Louise	75	Elze	65-0402
SCHORTEMEYER, Hch.	25	Lengerich	66-0934
SCHOTER, Gustav	15	Carlsruhe	66-0679
SCHOTT, Catharine	25	Muenchhausen	63-0398
SCHOTT, Ernst	19	Kirchheim	66-0704
SCHOTT, Jac.	30	Krughuel	63-0821
SCHOTT, Jacob	30	Weissenburg	65-0243
SCHOTT, Jos.	17	Kronach	64-0495
SCHOTT, Julius	20	Dermbach	67-0007
SCHOTT, Margarethe	28	Bayern	66-0147
SCHOTTE, Joh. Ch.	45	Gernbach	64-0214
SCHOTTES, Matthias	37	Prussia	64-0427
Gertrude 36, Anna M. 7, Jacob 5, Peter 3			
SCHRACK, Marie	18	Wurmberg	64-0593
SCHRADE, Anton	24	Leipolt	63-0482
SCHRADER, Augusta	15	Peine	63-0990
SCHRADER, Carl	17	Celle	64-0938
SCHRADER, Carl	27	Schoenhagen	66-1327
SCHRADER, Eduard	27	Ahnsberg	64-0432
SCHRADER, F.	22	Osterwald	65-1189
SCHRADER, Fr.	27	Braunschweig	65-0974
SCHRADER, Friedr.	25	Coeln	66-0221
SCHRADER, H.	28	Oldenburg	65-0974
SCHRADER, Heinrich	21	Schiffdorf	65-0950
SCHRADER, Jacob	50	Wuertingen	66-1155
SCHRADER, Johs.	30	Gruentershsn.	64-0138
SCHRADER, Wilhelm	24	Obernkirchen	65-0243
SCHRAEG, Marie	16	Gr.Sachsenhm.	64-0840
SCHRAFFER, Herm.	27	Meerenburg	65-0950
SCHRAGE, F.	27	Vlotho	65-1189
SCHRAM, Wilhelm	36	Redwitz	66-1373
Henriette 25, Berthold 4			
SCHRAMM, A.F.(m)	28	Ohio	64-0073
SCHRAMM, Carl	34	Hexenschrot	66-1248
SCHRAMM, Fritz	13	Gr. Himstedt	65-1030
Sophie 18			
SCHRAMM, Gottlieb	25	Berlin	65-0770
SCHRAMM, Heinrich	34	Branndorf	66-0576
SCHRAMM, Mathias	19	Wasserangert	67-0007
SCHRAMME, Louis	28	Allfeld	63-0917
SCHRAND, Joh. Alb.	59	Liender/Old.	65-1030
Helena 55, Joh. Heinr. 20			
Joh. Wilhelm 17, Anna Maria 15			
SCHRANTEMEYER, Aug	26	Westenhof	66-1155
SCHRAPP, Marie	20	Budenhausen	65-1030
SCHRAUB, Carl	46	Mainz	67-0007
Franz 44			
SCHRAUT, Kilian	26	Durlach	66-1131
SCHREBER, Eduard	26	Herford	63-0917
SCHREBER, Wih.	26	Quackenbrueck	65-1189
SCHRECK, Gerhard	27	Wester Cappel	66-0469
SCHREI, Cath.	21	Weiterspan	66-0413
SCHREIBER, Ant.	30	Quackenbrueck	63-1085
SCHREIBER, August	30	Leipzig	63-0168
SCHREIBER, August	19	Bremen	66-0469
Heinrich 18			
SCHREIBER, Bertha	25	Albany	63-0990
SCHREIBER, Casper	27	Mittelsemen	65-0865
SCHREIBER, Elisab.	59	Zweibruecken	66-1373
Minna 18, Maria 15			
SCHREIBER, Eva Dor	28	Unhausen	65-1030
SCHREIBER, H.G.	21	Minden	65-1024
SCHREIBER, Joh.	28	Waburg	64-1108
Marg. 62			
SCHREIBER, Joseph	25	Birkendorf	66-1155
SCHREIBER, Marg.	33	Wiesenfeld	67-0007
SCHREIBER, Margar.	23	Ronshausen	63-0614
SCHREIBER, Marie	21	Dissen	65-0950
SCHREIBER, Meta	21	Bremen	66-0734
SCHREIBER, Raimund	9	Ulm	63-0482
SCHREIBER, Rudolph	20	Elzach	64-0023
SCHREIBER, Sebast.	39	Meiningen	64-0432
Elise Betta 34, Elisab. 7, Adam 4			
Joh. Andr. 9m			
SCHREIBER, Wm.	19	Celle	64-0138
SCHREIBNER, Sophie	17	Hoff	65-1024
SCHREIBVOGEL, Chr.	46	Schoenbeck	64-0433
SCHREIER, August	33	Crimmitschau	64-0992
Ernestine 29, Agnes 7, Oswald 4, Anna 10m			
SCHREIER, Fr.	59	Crimmitzschau	63-0482
Friederike 59			
SCHREIER, Michael	33	Worms/Bayern	66-0346
Charlotte 32, Anna 8, Carl 2, Philipp 9m			
SCHREINER, A.	43	New Orleans	63-0015
SCHREINER, Heinr.	34	Hermsdorf	63-1010
SCHREINER, Kunig.	25	Silberhof	66-1128
Anna Marie 49, Antonia 15			
SCHREINER, Paul	29	Rissingen	66-1313
SCHRENK, Christ.	29	Philadelphia	64-0432
SCHRENK, Jos.	22	Medwisch/Aus.	65-0038
SCHREPFER, Joachim	25	Hardergroen	64-0739
SCHREPPER, Barbara	18	Bamberg	66-0109
SCHRERLING, J.	29	Worms	64-0495
L.(f) 23			
SCHRICK, Ch.(m)	27	Eggersheim	64-0170
Clara 26			
SCHRICK, Friedrich	54	Solingen	63-0822
Wilhelmine 59			
SCHRIEFER, (f)	28	Brooklyn	63-0752
Henry 4			
SCHRIEFER, Cath.	23	Osterholz	64-0904
SCHRIEFER, Friedr.	28	Zeegendorf	66-0109
SCHRIEFER, Hermann	25	Cuxhaven	67-0007
Christine 21			
SCHRIERHOFF, Joh.	26	Mellen	64-0938
Maria 25, Joh. Herm. 9m			
SCHRIEVER, Martin	16	Huettenbusch	65-0898
SCHRIMKER, Heinr.	25	Ochtoup	64-0214
SCHRIMPF, Barbara	21	Grosenlueder	66-0469
SCHROCK, Eva	29	Wasserlos	64-1161
SCHRODT, Michael	32	Albany	66-0147
SCHROECK, C. (m)	22	Bremen	64-0214
SCHROEDER, Adele	29	Osterholz	65-1088
Wilhelmine 15			
SCHROEDER, Ag.(m)	30	Kollrechthaus	64-0495
SCHROEDER, Albert	32	Hinterpommern	64-0138
SCHROEDER, Albert	17	Ndr.Florsheim	63-1218
SCHROEDER, Amalie	22	Blomberg	65-1031
SCHROEDER, Anna	23	New York	66-1031
SCHROEDER, Anna M.	20	Reichelsdorf	65-1031
SCHROEDER, Aug. W.	26	Grenzhausen	66-1373
SCHROEDER, B(m)	24	Hannover	64-0432
SCHROEDER, Cacilie	48	Magdeburg	65-0865
Hedwig 16, Julius 14, Ida 7			
SCHROEDER, Carl	19	Wagenfeld	66-0576
SCHROEDER, Carl	25	Langensalza	67-0007
SCHROEDER, Carl	18	Hannover	66-1031
SCHROEDER, Carl	39	Tiefenort	64-0886
(f) 39, (f) 11, (m) 7			
SCHROEDER, Carl	26	Lingen	66-1203
SCHROEDER, Carst.N	16	Schiffdorf	64-0432
SCHROEDER, Carsten	20	Tramstedt	66-1093
Gretje 18			
SCHROEDER, Cath.	36	Philadelphia	63-0953
SCHROEDER, Cath.	18	Worbswede	65-0038
SCHROEDER, Cath.	26	Eschwege	65-1189
SCHROEDER, Cathar.	20	Dorum	66-0934
SCHROEDER, Charles	17	Tiefenort	63-0862
SCHROEDER, Chr.	35	Dorrberg	66-1313
Christiane 30, Carl R. 5, Agnes 2			
SCHROEDER, Christ.	21	Raldernstead	66-0984
SCHROEDER, Christ.	25	Norberg	66-1093
SCHROEDER, Christ.	24	Taubach	65-0007

NAME	AGE	RESIDENCE	YR-LIST
SCHROEDER, Claus	22	Neuhaus	66-0623
SCHROEDER, Dirk	17	Ditzum	65-1024
SCHROEDER, Doris	27	Bremen	67-1005
SCHROEDER, Eduard	28	St. Louis	63-0821
Mary 24			
SCHROEDER, Elisab.	28	Braunau	64-0433
SCHROEDER, Elise	21	Handorf	65-0594
SCHROEDER, Emil	25	Schelzten	64-0920
SCHROEDER, Ernst	22	Hamburg	63-0693
SCHROEDER, F.(m)	20	Bremen	64-0214
SCHROEDER, Fr.	22	Braunschweig	64-0331
SCHROEDER, Fr.(m)	25	Bremen	64-0427
SCHROEDER, Franz	24	New York	66-0984
SCHROEDER, Friedr.	28	Worbtwede	63-1178
SCHROEDER, Friedr.	34	New York	66-0147
SCHROEDER, Friedr.	19	Lissen	66-0704
SCHROEDER, Friedr.	28	Darmstadt	66-1127
SCHROEDER, Friedr.	35	Bederkesa	65-0948
Marie 23			
SCHROEDER, Georg	16	Ertzen	65-1031
Caroline 21			
SCHROEDER, Gustav	15	Tiefenort	64-0427
SCHROEDER, H.	21	Oldendorf	64-0665
SCHROEDER, H.	26	Dinklage	64-0782
SCHROEDER, H.	24	Scharmbeck	64-1206
SCHROEDER, Heinr.	17	Riedberg	66-0346
SCHROEDER, Heinr.	24	Kurhessen	66-0576
SCHROEDER, Heinr.	19	Bremen	64-0687
SCHROEDER, Heinr.	18	Wehbergen	66-1093
SCHROEDER, Heinr.	40	St. Paul	66-0934
Adelheid 37, Heinrich 5, Wilhelm 3			
Anna 9m			
SCHROEDER, Heinr.	29	Laibach	66-1131
SCHROEDER, Heinr.	23	Suhlingen	65-1031
SCHROEDER, Heinr.	19	Lamstedt	65-0865
SCHROEDER, Heinr.	15	Lamstedt	65-0950
SCHROEDER, Herm. F	23	Diepholz	65-0948
SCHROEDER, Hermann	18	Stadthagen	67-0007
SCHROEDER, Hinr.	29	New York	63-0862
SCHROEDER, Joh.	43	Gans	66-0650
Johanna 35, Augusta 20, Albert 4			
Theodor 2, Rudolph 6m			
SCHROEDER, Joh.	50	Strozewo	64-0938
Anna 45, Ottilie 17, Ernestine 13			
Julie 7, Reinhold 5, Bertha 2, Emma 9m			
SCHROEDER, Joh.	20	Hannover	64-0427
SCHROEDER, Joh. Fr	17	Bremen	65-0950
SCHROEDER, Joh. H.	30	New York	63-0097
SCHROEDER, Johann	46	New York	66-0734
SCHROEDER, Johann	22	Altheim	66-1093
SCHROEDER, Johann	23	Osnabrueck	66-1031
SCHROEDER, Johanna	30	Calcutta	66-1127
SCHROEDER, Lisette	22	Rethern/Old.	65-0038
SCHROEDER, Louise	34	Ballenstedt	63-0168
SCHROEDER, Louise	27	Bremen	65-0594
SCHROEDER, Maria	22	Bueschen	66-1127
SCHROEDER, Marie	17	Bremen	66-0413
SCHROEDER, Marie	20	Deplinghausen	66-0577
SCHROEDER, Marie	19	Lilienthal	66-0734
SCHROEDER, Marie	15	Helminghausen	66-0984
SCHROEDER, Marie	22	Osnabrueck	67-0600
SCHROEDER, Marie	54	Osnabrueck	65-0865
Marie 16			
SCHROEDER, Matilda	53	Braunschweig	66-0679
SCHROEDER, Michael	25	Lindingen	67-0007
SCHROEDER, Paul	23	Leuwarden	66-0734
Johann 17			
SCHROEDER, Peter	21	Durlar	66-1155
SCHROEDER, Theod.	25	Vernlage	65-0151
SCHROEDER, Theodor	24	Osnabrueck	66-1031
SCHROEDER, Wilh.	27	Cuelk	65-0713
SCHROEDER, Wilhelm	13	Tiefenort	63-1178
SCHROEDER, Wilhelm	17	Midlum	63-0398
SCHROEDER, Wilhelm	49	Renneroth	66-1327
Margarethe 42, Margarethe 42, Helene 8			
Caroline 6			
SCHROEDER. Caspar	57	Riehelsdorf	66-1373
Elisabeth 62, Anna 24, Conrad 18			

NAME	AGE	RESIDENCE	YR-LIST
SCHROEPPEL, Wm.	19	Eisfeld	64-0593
SCHROER, D.A.(m)	29	Wietmarschen	64-0214
Anna 9, (m) , (f) , (m) , (f) 17			
G.H.(m) 55			
SCHROER, Wilh'mine	29	Westercappeln	63-0953
SCHROETER, A. Carl	24	Eisleben	63-0296
SCHROETER, Adolph	19	Lieberose	66-1327
Anton 17			
SCHROETER, Carl H.	31	Goldberg	63-0053
SCHROETER, Otto	52	Latowice	66-1327
SCHROFF, Gu.	25	Zell	64-0782
SCHROPPMEYER, A.C.	24	Bremen	64-0073
baby 9m			
SCHROTH, Chs. H.	27	Langen	64-0138
SCHROTH, O.	32	Berlin	65-1088
SCHROTT, Wilh'mine	19	Moesbach	64-1053
SCHROTTER, Samuel	22	Bierbergen	64-0138
SCHRUENDER, August	24	Hamilton	66-0704
Caroline 7, Albert 4			
SCHRUMPF, Richard	22	Kurhessen	66-0349
SCHUBART, Adolph	19	Eisfeld	63-0482
SCHUBART, Robert	33	Schonfeld/Boh	66-1128
Julie 30, Constantin 7, Joseph 5			
Wenzel 3, Karl 9m			
SCHUBERT, B.	24	Prussia	63-1003
C. 25, C. 2			
SCHUBERT, C.	24	Rotenkirchen	64-0782
SCHUBERT, Carl	20	Mulersch	64-0433
SCHUBERT, Fr.	26	Tschoerne	65-0243
SCHUBERT, Fr.Mart.	53	Nossen	65-0898
SCHUBERT, Frances	31	Williamsburgh	64-0170
SCHUBERT, Heinr.	26	Tscherne	65-0243
SCHUBERT, Joh. Ad.	19	Echkats	66-1243
SCHUBERT, Julius	60	New York	64-0495
SCHUBERT, Magd.	53	Wunsiedel	65-0898
SCHUBERT, Martin	25	Northeim	66-0623
SCHUBERT, O.R.	19	Welsdorf	64-0138
SCHUBERT, Pauline	24	Zeitz	66-0934
SCHUBERT, Wilhelm	16	Camenz	63-1136
SCHUBRING, Adolph	31	Elbing	64-0938
Louise 29, Robert 5, Adolph 11m			
SCHUCH, Jac.(f)	25	Mannheim	64-0331
SCHUCHARD, A.	28	Eschenrott	65-1189
SCHUCHARDT, Alex.	35	Kirchhain	65-1030
SCHUCHARDT, Georg	58	Iba	63-1010
SCHUCHARDT, H.(m)	43	Eschwege	64-0170
Elisabeth 26			
SCHUCHARDT, Heinr.		Wollbrandshsn	65-1030
SCHUCHMANN, Fr.	30	Darmstadt	65-0038
SCHUCHMANN, G.P.	19	Modau	63-0013
SCHUCHT, Friedrich	14	Lohne	66-0679
SCHUCHTER, Franzka	23	Lingen	65-0189
SCHUCKMANN, Aug.	34	San Francisco	63-0482
Augusta 24			
SCHUDITER, Franz	34	Fraudingen	64-0840
Catharine 29, Crezentia 4, Josepha 44			
SCHUDT, Ludwig	33	Gutenberg	65-0402
Wilhelmine 20			
SCHUEL, Adam	23	Heppenheim	64-0639
SCHUELE, J.M.	37	Schwackheim	66-0221
Christine 23			
SCHUELE, Louis	25	Baden	66-0221
SCHUELER, Alfred	25	Cassel	63-0693
SCHUELER, August	38	Bellinchen	67-0353
Ernestine 30, August 9, Carl 7, Emma 5			
SCHUELER, Carl	20	Nidda	64-1108
SCHUELER, Conr.	19	Bretten	66-0576
SCHUELER, Georg	23	Hall	65-0243
Dorethe 21, Juliane 20			
SCHUELER, Jean D.	43	New York	63-0821
Jean 7			
SCHUELER, Margaret	16	Schenklengsfd	66-0934
SCHUELER, Maria	17	Cassel	66-1093
SCHUELER, Max	23	Roemheld	64-0495
Erich 21			
SCHUELER, Sara	38	Scheppenhauer	64-0639
SCHUELER, Wilhelm	20	Gerdorf	63-1010
SCHUELKE, Heinr.	24	Klein Bislau	66-0469

NAME	AGE	RESIDENCE	YR-LIST
Wilhelmine 22			
SCHUELZ, Val.	42	Buernstadt	64-0495
B. 42, Johs. 17, Carl 12, Franz 7			
Valt.(f) 4, B.(f) 3, S.(f) 2, A.M.(f) 9m			
SCHUENEMANN, Conr.	19	Hannover	66-1327
SCHUENEMANN, G.H.	34	Rodenberg	65-0974
Angel. 36			
SCHUENPP, Andr.	25	Holzmaden	64-0363
SCHUEPPERT, Carl A	28	Elberfeld	65-0594
SCHUERENBECK, Anna	19	Luste	66-0576
SCHUERLE, Christ.		Gaarweiler	66-0147
Barbara 20			
SCHUERMAN, Fr.(m)	18	West.Oldendrf	64-0170
SCHUERMANN, Anton	25	Oldenburg	65-1024
SCHUERMANN, Ernst	21	Buer	64-0938
Louis 16			
SCHUERMANN, H.F.	36	Baltimore	63-0296
Augusta 29, Martha 2, Annette 22			
SCHUERMANN, Ha.	30	New Orleans	64-0138
Sophie 27, Henry 4, Diedrich 2			
SCHUERMANN, Heinr.	26	Daenenkamp	64-0214
SCHUERMANN, Julie	27	Neukirchen	66-0668
baby 10m			
SCHUERMANN, Wilmne	38	Lengerich	64-1206
SCHUESEBURG, Doris	26	Bramsche	64-1022
SCHUESSLER, Adam	39	Densberg	63-0752
Anna 34, Mary 9, Emilie 8, Louis 7			
SCHUESSLER, Herm.	22	Oldenburg	64-0687
SCHUESSLER, Joseph	20	Kaladey	66-0576
SCHUESSLER, Magd.	22	Kurhessen	63-0398
SCHUESSLER, Peter	19	Brennings	64-0433
Christian 20			
SCHUETER, Franzka.	20	Varensell	66-1203
SCHUETLE, Albertin	32	Minden	64-0992
SCHUETT, Barbara	28	Bonn	66-0623
SCHUETT, F.	30	Hannover	63-0551
SCHUETT, Gottl.	20	Salzbach	65-0007
SCHUETT, Johannes	15	Bannerot	67-0599
SCHUETTE, August	24	Ippensen	66-1155
SCHUETTE, Charles	14	New York	66-0679
SCHUETTE, H.(m)			64-0073
SCHUETTE, Herm.	22	Bremen	64-0992
SCHUETTE, Hermann	38	Lehrte	65-1030
Elisabeth 50, Bernhard 21, Hermann 18			
Elisabeth 15, Gesine 13			
SCHUETTE, J.C.	30	New York	63-1136
SCHUETTE, Lisette	40	Rendsburg	63-0693
Martha 14			
SCHUETTE, Therese	25	Arnsberg	65-0189
Helene 3			
SCHUETTENHELM, Chr	20	Poll	65-1095
Mathias 16			
SCHUETTLER, August	35	Puschwitz	66-1248
SCHUETZ, C.	21	Vietsgoth	65-0007
SCHUETZ, Conrad	20	Densburg	65-0948
Anna Martha 26			
SCHUETZ, Heinr.	26	Herbsleben	65-0898
SCHUETZ, Heinrich	24	Hannover	66-1155
SCHUETZ, Hermann	19	Hannover	66-0984
SCHUETZ, J.	23	Bueckeburg	63-1003
SCHUETZ, Kaspar	28	Gotha	63-1069
SCHUETZ, Louis	21	Bietigheim	66-1131
SCHUETZ, Philipp	24	Itzenheim	65-0055
SCHUETZ, Willi	22	Wuerttemberg	66-0109
SCHUETZE, Cath. El	50	Lotterbehr	66-1243
SCHUEYER, Ernst	48	Diedelsheim	67-0007
Philippa 49			
SCHUFELE, Jacob	17	Brette	64-0427
SCHUFFLE, Marg.	21	Weilerbach	65-0116
Cath. 17			
SCHUH, Anna	22	Oberbergen	66-1327
SCHUH, Joseph	34	Louisville	66-0704
Elise 26, Josephine 5, Adolph 3			
Albert 10m			
SCHUH, Margarethe	18	Washington	66-0623
SCHUH, Ph.	24	Dortweil	66-1243
SCHUHKNECHT, L.	59	Jago	66-0413
SCHUHMACHER, Barb.	16	Darmstadt	66-0109

NAME	AGE	RESIDENCE	YR-LIST
SCHUHMACHER, Carl	25	Bekedorf	65-1088
SCHUHMACHER, F.W.	30	Bremen	64-0331
SCHUHMACHER, Georg	34	Vorstaetten	66-0412
SCHUHMACHER, Heinr	57	Sinoegel	64-0433
Hermann 23, Heinrich 18, Wilhelmine 13			
Friedrich 34, Johanna 33, Carl 4			
August 11m, Hermannn 9m			
SCHUHMACHER, Jo. G	20	Hall	63-0006
SCHUHMACHER, Joh.	26	Mainz	65-0402
SCHUHMACHER, Luise	20	Diepenau	65-1024
SCHUHMANN, Friedr.	25	Homberg	65-0770
SCHUHMANN, Heinr.	22	Kurhessen	66-0623
SCHUHMANN, Louise	37	Potsdam	63-1010
Georg 9, Arthur 8, Wilhelm 7, Johanna 4			
August 2, Adolph 9m			
SCHUHWERK, A.	33	Buesslingen	65-1024
SCHUL, Adam	27	Pfordt	64-0214
SCHUL, Elsb.	43	Pfordt	64-0782
Marg. 27, Marg. 4m, Elisabeth 20			
Elisabeth 14, Andreas 7, George 26			
SCHULDHEISS, John	21	Froeschheim	66-0666
SCHULDT, Agatha	21	Essen	66-0221
SCHULDT, Doroth.	26	Bohr	66-0984
Dorothea 4			
SCHULEIN, D.(m)	21	Bavaria	64-0593
SCHULENBERG, Chr.	20	Bremen	65-0594
Gesina 37, Liena 7, Gesina 5, Frdr. 5			
Henni 10m			
SCHULENBURG, Aug.	25	Rotenburg	65-1088
SCHULENBURG, J.H.	26	Barnsen	64-0363
SCHULENKORF, Henr.	36	Borbau	66-0984
SCHULER, Christoph	42	Luedolfsheim	66-0083
Christine 36, Christine 14, Friederike 12			
Sophie 3, Louise 9m			
SCHULER, J.(m)	27	Trostingen	64-0495
SCHULER, Johann	24	Pfeffingen	64-0433
Jacob 22			
SCHULER, Philipp	24	Bretten	64-0427
Conrad 18			
SCHULHAUS, Jettche	31	Herleshausen	63-0953
Loeb 11, Fanny 8, Michel 6			
SCHULHERR, Louis	16	Marsbach	66-1203
SCHULHOF, Malchen	24	Hoeringhausen	66-0734
SCHULKE, Wilhelm	23	Hagenow	66-0668
Caroline 23, baby (f) 11m			
SCHULLER, Adolph	30	Hannover	66-0734
Emilie 30			
SCHULT, Herm. Hch.	16	Wanna	64-0456
SCHULT, Pet. T.	17	Otterndorf	64-0456
SCHULTE, A. Marie	35	Riemsloh	63-1010
A. Marie 10, August 9			
SCHULTE, August	21	Bachholzhsn.	65-0950
SCHULTE, B.	23	Herringhausen	65-0007
SCHULTE, Fr.	21	Dissen	63-0917
SCHULTE, Franz	20	Leer	64-0886
SCHULTE, Friedrike		Osnabrueck	66-1031
SCHULTE, H.W.	16	Rothenfeld	64-0023
SCHULTE, Heinr.	17	Ankum	65-0594
SCHULTE, Heinrich	27	Wersuwe	65-1030
SCHULTE, Henry	40	Houston	66-0221
Ernestine 35, Henry 7, Anna 6			
SCHULTE, Herm H.	20	Rattenkamp	64-0938
SCHULTE, J.T. (m)	35	Ahlde	64-0331
SCHULTE, J.W.	25	Brilon	65-0974
SCHULTE, Joh.	20	Papenburg	65-1024
SCHULTE, Otto	28	New York	64-0331
SCHULTE, Rud.	24	Langerich	64-0214
SCHULTE, Rudolph	15	Osnabrueck	66-1093
SCHULTE, Th. (f)	20	Wehbergen	64-0331
SCHULTE, Wilhelm	22	Muenster	66-0469
SCHULTES, v. F.	26	Meiningen	65-0055
SCHULTES, v. Hugo	30	Coburg	63-0990
SCHULTHEISS, John	33	Roelshausen	65-1030
SCHULTHEISS, Wm.	25	Stuttgart	63-0693
SCHULTZ, C.A.	21	Meschede	64-0495
SCHULTZ, Carl	28	Elbing	66-1248
SCHULTZ, Christian	29	Arolsen	66-1031
SCHULTZ, Christlib	53	Pustamin	66-0650

NAME	AGE	RESIDENCE	YR-LIST
Johanna 23			
SCHULTZ, Friedr.	24	Leipzig	67-0007
SCHULTZ, Fritz	43	Altmersleben	66-0623
Anna 38, Friederike 8, Friedrich W. 6			
August Otto 4			
SCHULTZ, Joh. C.	49	Osnabrueck	65-0038
SCHULTZ, Julius	25	Friedrichsbrg	64-1108
SCHULTZ, Julius A.	21	Kreuzschubin	64-0739
SCHULTZ, Martin	39	Brooklyn	63-0862
Charlotte 33, Wilhelmine 9			
SCHULTZ, Robert	37	Kiszewo	65-0898
Pauline 24, Wilhelm 5, Otto 3, Robert 6m			
Wilhelm 24			
SCHULTZ, Theodor	30	Boskraden	66-1093
SCHULTZ, Victor	22	Hannover	66-0623
SCHULTZE, Adolph	28	New York	64-0495
SCHULTZE, Ant.	30	Berlin	66-1248
SCHULTZE, Friedr.	20	Wagenburg	66-1373
SCHULTZE, Marie	19	Upen	64-0138
SCHULWATER, Moritz	15	Berlin	63-0821
SCHULZ, A.	22	Behle	63-1003
SCHULZ, Adeline	22	Bederkesa	63-1178
SCHULZ, Alexander	32	Breslau	66-0469
SCHULZ, Anna	30	Berlin	65-0151
Otto 7, Albert 4, Hedwig 2, Augusta 9m			
SCHULZ, Annette	25	Fuerstenberg	65-1189
SCHULZ, Aug.	21	Volkertshsn.	64-0363
SCHULZ, Carl	28	Stein	66-0147
SCHULZ, Chr.	30	Boehmen	64-0495
Magd. 26, Ernst 2			
SCHULZ, Chr.	44	Claushagen	66-1313
SCHULZ, Conrad	57	Roth	63-0551
John 22, Henry 20, Cathar. 18, Conr. 9			
SCHULZ, Elisabeth	32	Pasau	63-0614
SCHULZ, Ernst	28	Niebruch	66-0666
SCHULZ, Ernst	23	Baden	66-0984
SCHULZ, Ferd.	33	Port au Princ	64-0073
SCHULZ, Ferd.	36	Berlin	64-0593
Lisette 35, Richard 7			
SCHULZ, Fritz	24	Lemmersdorf	66-0578
SCHULZ, Georg	27	Lingen	64-1108
SCHULZ, Gustav	30	Bromberg	64-1053
SCHULZ, Heinrich	38	Riebau	63-0614
Dorothea 33, Wilhelmine 7, Friederike 4			
Dorothea 2			
SCHULZ, Henry	26	New York	64-0593
William 17			
SCHULZ, Herm.	42	Bremen	63-0752
SCHULZ, Herm. W.	32	Wittstock	64-0639
SCHULZ, Joh Valent	27	Nagelsberg	63-1178
SCHULZ, Joh.	34	Berlin	65-0007
Anna 5, Arthur 8			
SCHULZ, Joh. Gottl	29	Bromberg	64-0456
Juliane 28, Ludwig 7m			
SCHULZ, Johann	40	Langhorn/Meck	65-0038
Karoline 29, Minna 1, Maria 19, Sophia 60			
SCHULZ, Lina	38	Frisach	64-0593
Clara 3			
SCHULZ, Lisette	20	Mauer	64-0840
SCHULZ, M.	43	Shiepjarre	66-0413
Wilhelmine 32, Carl 16, Julius 8			
August 6, Amalie 4, Pauline 11, D. 58			
SCHULZ, M.	38	New Wien	66-0413
Wilhelmine 7, Eduard 5			
SCHULZ, Margarethe	23	Darmstadt	64-1053
SCHULZ, Martin F.	59	Buchhal	63-1010
Christine 56, Martin 31, Ida 24			
Caroline 25, Hermann 19			
SCHULZ, Minna	31	Dortmund	63-0614
Edmund 6, Albert 10m			
SCHULZ, Rosine	21	Schrothaus	66-0650
SCHULZ, Theodor	26	Weinheim	64-0687
SCHULZ, Wilh.	29	Soessnowd	66-0469
Johanna 35			
SCHULZ, Wilhelm	61	Mangfeld	64-0886
Charlotte 55, Carl 30, Wilhelmine 24			
Therese 16, Otto 2			
SCHULZ, Wilhelm	17	Holzhausen	65-1189

NAME	AGE	RESIDENCE	YR-LIST
Lina 40			
SCHULZE, Adolph	47	Muehlhausen	66-0147
SCHULZE, Adolph	28	Wollshausen	63-0244
SCHULZE, Anna	23	Dortta	66-0083
SCHULZE, Augustus	22	New York	66-0109
SCHULZE, C.F.	27	Kuehrstedt	64-0427
SCHULZE, Christian	39	Pittsburg	66-0576
Catharine 30, Bernhardine 9			
SCHULZE, Eduard	17	Kassel	66-1128
SCHULZE, Fr.	42	Geestemuende	65-0116
SCHULZE, Heinrich	26	Quedlinburg	66-0349
SCHULZE, Joh. D.	22	Bremen	67-0954
SCHULZE, Otto	21	Lueneburg	66-0576
SCHULZE, Pauline	30	New York	64-0073
Julius 6			
SCHULZE, Rudolph	23	Mennewitz	66-0679
SCHULZE, Wm.	22	Stade	64-0665
SCHUMACHER, Adalb.	36	Gauerkon	64-0885
SCHUMACHER, Albert	17	Sprum	66-0704
Friedr. 20			
SCHUMACHER, Alfred	22	Buchau	66-0576
SCHUMACHER, Anna	31	Brooklyn	63-1085
Theresa 15			
SCHUMACHER, Ant.	28	Vechta	63-1218
SCHUMACHER, Aug.	30	Damitz	64-0665
Friederke 28, Caroline 56, Gustine 28			
Wilhelmine 17, Ferdinand 20, Hanne 6m			
SCHUMACHER, August	33	Wiesbaden	66-1155
Anna 7, Carl 5			
SCHUMACHER, August	39	Hamburg	65-0116
SCHUMACHER, Carol.	46	Hille	66-1031
Marie 25, Louise 23, Elisabeth 17			
SCHUMACHER, Dietr.	37	Warfleth	65-0038
Margarethe 35, Henrich 9, Hermann 5			
SCHUMACHER, Franz	15	Damme	66-0984
SCHUMACHER, Friede	22	Schlusselburg	66-0984
SCHUMACHER, Friedr	24	Grimminghsn.	63-0990
SCHUMACHER, G.	16	Bitz	65-1024
C. 15			
SCHUMACHER, Gesine	20	Hannover	63-1136
SCHUMACHER, H.	31	Cincinnati	66-0984
SCHUMACHER, H.W.G.	23	Oeynhausen	64-0938
SCHUMACHER, Herm.	22	Brockhausen	65-1140
Rebecca 19			
SCHUMACHER, J.D.	14	Hassendorf	64-0214
SCHUMACHER, Jacob	38	Wismar	64-1053
Magdalena 36, Franz 4, Charlotte 6m			
SCHUMACHER, Joh. H	20	Oberheimbach	64-0639
SCHUMACHER, Joh. M	40	Magstadt	65-0594
Caroline 41, Carl 14, Gussan 7, Amalie 7			
SCHUMACHER, Meta	19	Bremerhaven	65-0243
SCHUMACHER, Nicol	23	Belgien	63-0168
SCHUMACHER, Peter	31	Lorsch	64-0456
SCHUMACHER, Philip	28	Offenbach	66-1031
SCHUMACHER, Reinh.	23	Baden	66-0576
SCHUMACHER, Rosine	24	Esslingen	63-1218
SCHUMACHER, Theres	23	Philadelphia	64-0023
SCHUMACHER, W.(m)	23	Grosssachsen	64-0170
SCHUMANN, Anton	19	Muenchen	66-1203
SCHUMANN, C.	36	New York	63-0168
Louise 31			
SCHUMANN, Georg	18	Lohne	66-1131
SCHUMANN, Johanna	22	Rossack	63-0482
SCHUMANN, Julius	19	Altenburg	66-1155
SCHUMANN, Ludwig	24	Grossheimth	66-0679
SCHUMANN, Moritz	31	Muenchen	63-0482
SCHUMANN, Wil'mine	45	Crimmitschau	64-0170
SCHUMER, Jos.	24	Steinau	64-0170
SCHUMM, Magdalena	54	Wuertemberg	63-1069
Charlotte 21			
SCHUPP, Friederike	25	Oberbergen	66-0109
SCHUPPE, C.(m)	22	Gruenenplan	64-0073
SCHUPPE, Ch.	25	Gruenenplan	64-0687
SCHUPPE, Charles	24	Gruenenplan	63-1178
SCHUPPER, Carl	26	New York	66-0147
SCHUPPERS, Aug.	30	Duesseldorf	64-0992
SCHUPPERT, Carl	28	Antwerp	65-0004
SCHUPPERT, Chr'tne	24	Gueglingen	63-0862

NAME	AGE	RESIDENCE	YR-LIST
SCHUR, Wilhelm	17	Bockhorst	65-0243
SCHURBECK, Diedr.	23	Burcher	66-1248
SCHURBROCK, Ant. R	46	Mellen	64-0938
Crilla 35			
SCHURER, Johann	20	Crefeld	64-1108
Anna 24			
SCHURER, Wm.	28	Schweiz	63-1085
Friederike 25			
SCHURK, Jacob	22	Preussen	66-0221
SCHURMANN, Joh. P.	40	Stedefreund	63-1010
Wilhelmine 33, Louise 6, Zacharias 4			
Gottlieb 9m			
SCHURUCK, Conrad	57	Freysa	64-0593
Catharina 55			
SCHUS, Julius	57	Birschweiler	65-1024
SCHUSTER, Aug.	27	Prussia	63-1003
M. 26, C. 4, E. 2			
SCHUSTER, Carl	19	Driburg	65-1024
Elise 21			
SCHUSTER, Cathar.	54	Stuttgart	66-1327
SCHUSTER, Eduard	20	Hirschberg	64-0938
SCHUSTER, Emilie	35	Gera	66-0109
SCHUSTER, Heinrich	22	Holtrup	66-1128
SCHUSTER, Joh.	25	Lienz	65-0898
SCHUSTER, John	33	Fuerth	63-0990
Margarethe 28, Augusta 5			
SCHUSTER, Joseph	30	Linden	66-0221
SCHUSTER, Joseph	31	Wien	66-1203
SCHUSTER, Many	23	Meinhard	66-0934
SCHUSTER, Max	29	Zempelburg	66-1127
SCHUTHE, William	27	St. Louis	63-0917
SCHUTTE, Hermann	36	Oldenburg	66-0469
SCHUTTMEIER, H.	16	Solehue	66-0413
SCHUTZ, J.G.	15	Cassel	64-0992
SCHUTZ, J.N.	21	Birkenau	64-0687
SCHUUR, V.D.(m)	53	Holthusen	64-0331
Johanna 21			
SCHWAAB, Elise	24	Uhlfeld	65-0402
SCHWAAB, Josefine	18	Hemmstadt	66-1243
SCHWAB, Dorothea	14	Moehringen	64-1108
SCHWAB, Friedrich	38	Asch/Bohemia	66-0412
Anna Margar. 34, Catharina 5, August 9m			
SCHWAB, Heinrich	18	Buchen	65-0950
Ernestine 14			
SCHWAB, Margarethe	19	Orbis	66-0083
SCHWAB, Michael	24	Remlingen	66-0346
SCHWAB, Peter	27	Harmbach	63-0693
SCHWAB, Seb.	31	Amerbach	64-0214
SCHWABACHER, He(f)	26	Fellheim	64-1161
SCHWABACHER, Jette	16	Oberdorf	63-1136
SCHWACH, Maria	40	Kuttenberg	66-0704
Johanna 15			
SCHWACHLER, Cath.	31	Basel	66-0934
Dorothea 2, Marie 8, Joseph 5			
SCHWACKE, Heinr.	23	Rodenberg	66-0934
SCHWAEGERL, Elise	26	New York	66-0576
SCHWAERER, Appolon	31	Sollach	64-0687
SCHWAGER, Carl	37	New York	64-0427
SCHWAIBOLDT, Steph	19	Pizheim	66-1373
SCHWALB, Nicolaus	26	Kotzau	66-1128
SCHWALBE, C.	26	Quedlinburg	64-0886
SCHWALBE, Emil	26	Preussen	66-0221
SCHWALKE, Rudolph	21	Hagewede	64-0433
SCHWALWE, Gerd	41	Neermoor	64-0363
Frauke 50, Geeske 18, Claas 15, Jan 9			
Hinderk 6			
SCHWALZ, August	18	Cappeln	65-1088
SCHWALZ, Heinr.	35	New York	64-0214
SCHWAMB, Friedrich	19	Mainz	66-1155
SCHWAN, Wilh.	20	Bremerhafen	66-1243
SCHWANBECK, Benja.	59	Berlin	65-0770
Christine 58			
SCHWANECK, Heinr.	30	Hannover	64-1108
SCHWANEWEDE, Reg.	24	Wremen	66-0934
SCHWANGER, Barb.	27	Dreschitz	65-0402
SCHWANGER, Franz	35	Olmuetz	64-0886
Josephine 27			
SCHWANKE, August	36	Smolnik	66-0666
Caroline 33, Eva 59, Ernestine 7			
Eduard 6, Emilie 4, Augusta 2			
SCHWANN, Louise	20	Frankfurt	65-0007
SCHWANTKE, August	44	Liszkowke	66-0469
SCHWANWEYER, Cath.	24	Bottenheim	63-1085
SCHWANZ, Goerg	27	Wahlwies	67-0007
SCHWAPPACH, M.(m)	18	Veilsdorf	64-0495
SCHWARS, Heinrich	28	Gessel	65-0713
SCHWARTE, Joh. Her	18	Groenlohe	66-0984
SCHWARTING, Elis.	20	Oldenburg	63-1136
SCHWARTING, Friedr	19	Linteln	64-0886
SCHWARTING, Heinr.	32	Hude	66-1093
SCHWARTJE, R.(m)	20	Bremen	64-0363
SCHWARTZ, Adele	20	Meyyaren	66-0679
SCHWARTZ, Adolph	22	Delmenhorst	63-0097
SCHWARTZ, Bernh.	19	Vestrup	66-1031
SCHWARTZ, Gottlieb	23	Wurtemberg	63-0822
SCHWARTZ, Heinr.	23	Gruenberg	64-0138
Ann Marie 28			
SCHWARTZ, Heinr.	25	Baiern	64-0214
SCHWARTZ, Johann	30	Warburg	63-0015
SCHWARTZ, v. Jos.	21	Coeln	63-0752
SCHWARTZE, Ludwig	25	Gensekirchen	65-1030
SCHWARZ, Cath.	20	Neububach	63-1003
SCHWARZ, Adam	21	Essenheim	66-0221
SCHWARZ, Adam	16	Sebenhausen	64-0214
SCHWARZ, Andreas	26	Ulmingen	64-0687
SCHWARZ, Anna	28	Frankenthal	63-0917
SCHWARZ, Babette	21	Creuznach	66-1155
SCHWARZ, Barbara	24	Egenhausen	65-0402
SCHWARZ, C.(f)	23	Unterweissach	64-0495
SCHWARZ, C.A.	24	Hansberge	66-0221
SCHWARZ, C.H.	21	Ottendorf/Han	63-1010
SCHWARZ, C.W.V.	21	St.Petersburg	63-0015
SCHWARZ, Carl	33	Posen	66-0578
Henriette 34, Wilhelm 11, Erdmann 9			
Friedrich 6, Carl 3, Augusta 1			
SCHWARZ, Carl	33	Bremen	66-0907
Johanna 25			
SCHWARZ, Casimir	40	Mittelsheim	66-0984
Maria 49, Philippina 7, Emilie 6			
SCHWARZ, Ed.	29	Prussia	63-1003
SCHWARZ, Eduard	28	Oedesheim	66-0704
SCHWARZ, Emil	40	Weimar	64-0433
SCHWARZ, Ernst	27	Ingersleben	64-0840
SCHWARZ, Ferdinand	22	Oberbochingen	66-0734
SCHWARZ, Franz	24	Braunkirchen	64-0214
SCHWARZ, Friedr. W	31	Elberfeld	67-1005
SCHWARZ, Gottl.	45	Bietigheim	65-0038
Albert 14			
SCHWARZ, Heinrich	21	Austria	66-0679
SCHWARZ, James	22	Hettlingen	63-0990
SCHWARZ, Johann	20	Wuertemberg	66-0984
SCHWARZ, Johann	23	Simmern	64-0214
Blandine 27, Genoveva 20, Josephine 17			
SCHWARZ, Johannes	23	Epfendorf	66-0679
SCHWARZ, Johannes	24	St. Gallen	65-0243
SCHWARZ, Johannes	45	Kasselborn	65-0594
Cath. 21, Elisab. 44, Math. 10, Elisab. 7			
Cath. 6, Conrad 9m, Elisab. 60			
SCHWARZ, John	48	Misskolez	63-0752
Maria 38, Antonia 6, Alexdra 4, Rudolph 1			
SCHWARZ, Joseph	18	Rosolup	66-1155
SCHWARZ, Jul.	32	Magdeburg	64-0593
SCHWARZ, Ludwig	16	Bavaria	66-0679
SCHWARZ, Margar.	28	Frankenthal	66-1327
Anna 8			
SCHWARZ, Marie	19	Kenzingen	64-1022
Albert 38			
SCHWARZ, Melchior	19	Schinkel	66-1131
SCHWARZ, Mich.	22	Wiesenthal	64-1022
SCHWARZ, Michael	20	New York	64-0687
SCHWARZ, Peter	24	Hannover	66-0623
SCHWARZ, Ph.(m)	38	St. Louis	64-0214
B.(f) 26			
SCHWARZ, Regina	38	Cleveland	63-0551
SCHWARZ, Robert	30	Coln	63-0053
Henriette 29			

NAME	AGE	RESIDENCE	YR-LIST
SCHWARZ, Sophie	17	Eislingen	66-1327
SCHWARZ, Susanna	19	Bremervoerde	65-1088
SCHWARZ, Theresia	22	Balig	64-0992
baby 11m			
SCHWARZ, Wm.	24	Brinkum	65-0974
SCHWARZAUER, Ar.	20	Schwarza	63-0482
SCHWARZAUER, M.	20	Schwarza	64-1161
SCHWARZAUER, Max	24	Dresden	65-0116
SCHWARZBACH, Chr.	14	Rotenburg	66-1031
SCHWARZE, Ferdin'd	22	Uchte	65-1088
SCHWARZEBACH, John	29	Viessen	63-1178
SCHWARZEN, Carl	17	Minden	65-0974
SCHWARZENBACH, Har	33	Zuerich	63-0296
SCHWARZENBACH, Hch	36	Schweiz	63-1136
SCHWARZENBERG, Ert	35	Glauchau	66-0984
SCHWARZER, Minna	32	Sebeskellem	65-0402
Jette 7, Isaac 6, Esti 5, Jani 9m			
SCHWARZMANN, Ad.	23	Ochsenwang	64-0331
SCHWARZMANN, Georg	26	Bamberg	65-0865
SCHWARZMEIER, Fr.	30	Bremen	63-0097
Anna 29			
SCHWARZWAELDER, Ad	19	Sulz	66-1327
SCHWARZWAELDER, M.	23	Hambach	63-1218
SCHWARZWALDER, Gg.	24	Weissenburg	65-0243
SCHWARZWALDER, Got	25	Vachingen	66-0934
SCHWARZWOLLEN, L.	39	Halle	64-1108
SCHWAWAINI, W.	20	Herrenhausen	64-0782
Frz. 20			
SCHWEBEL, Sophia	19	Sturbach	67-0007
SCHWEBRING, Christ	18	Diepholz	64-1108
SCHWECK, Friedrich	26	New York	66-0109
SCHWECKE, Friedr.	46	New Orleans	64-0432
Anna 47, Aleck 14, Ernst 6, Anna 3			
SCHWECKENDIK, Wilh	20	Hildesheim	65-1088
SCHWED, Ernestine	18	Roeckendorf	63-0482
SCHWED, Meyer	17	Aschenhausen	66-0934
SCHWEDA, Joh.	39	Prust	66-0650
Marianna 34, Paul 6m			
SCHWEER, Carl Ludw	22	Remsen	66-1155
SCHWEER, Christian	18	Frille	66-1131
SCHWEER, Maria	20	Oldenburg	66-0934
SCHWEER, Sophia	17	Colenfeld	67-0007
SCHWEERS, Conrad	23	Rengel	65-1031
SCHWEGLER, Joseph	34	Wohlhausen	63-0752
Anna 24, Julius 4, Francis 1, Peter 45			
SCHWEGMANN, Hinr.	28	Langwarden	64-0665
Henriette 22			
SCHWEICKHARDT, X.	36	Schoenberg	64-0495
A.(f) 38, P.(f) 4			
SCHWEIDEL, Johann	28	Schlesien	66-0147
SCHWEIGER, Gottf.	31	Elldingen	66-1248
SCHWEIGER, J.	50	Zell	64-0782
SCHWEIGER, J.F.	30	Minnesota	63-0990
SCHWEIGER, Therese	29	Regensburg	64-0687
SCHWEIGMANN, Jul.	29	Essen	65-0402
SCHWEIKER, Ernstin	19	Berlichingen	66-0576
SCHWEIKER, Minna	19	Philadelphia	63-0862
SCHWEIN, Catharina	50	Sandusky	63-0917
Eduard 22			
SCHWEINBINZ, John	27	Wiesenstetten	64-0363
SCHWEINFURT, Math.	25	Lungrindel	67-0599
SCHWEINFURTH, Frz.	28	Wiesloch	65-0007
Marg. 24			
SCHWEINFURTH, Jac.	46	Helgenbach	64-1206
Cath. 47, Johanna 7			
SCHWEINFURTH, Ph.	34	New York	64-0331
Johanna 21			
SCHWEINITZER, Ant.	22	Schoenfeld	66-1128
SCHWEINKERT, John	36	Prussia	64-0363
Marie 28, baby (f) 6m			
SCHWEINLER, Meinrt	27	Haechhingen	65-0004
Const. 24, Magd. 22, Jenne 10m			
SCHWEINSBERG, Chr.	43	Simmershausen	65-1095
Justus 7			
SCHWEINSBERG, Joh.	24	Retterode	64-0433
SCHWEINSBERG, Nic.	19	Fuerstenhagen	66-1248
SCHWEISS, Heinr.	37	Chicago	63-0862
SCHWEITGER, Moritz	22	Breslau	64-0456

NAME	AGE	RESIDENCE	YR-LIST
SCHWEITZER, A.	46	Wenzi	64-0840
SCHWEITZER, Adam	24	Hensheim	64-0214
SCHWEITZER, Christ	23	Blinpflingen	66-1327
SCHWEITZER, Joh.	29	Aalen	67-0795
Anna 27, Barbara 2			
SCHWEITZER, Marg.	67	Geisslingen	64-1022
SCHWEITZER, Phil.	15	Offstein	63-1010
SCHWEITZER, Rich.	22	Neustadt	63-0693
Minna 23, Ed. 21			
SCHWEITZER, Wilh.	32	Reichenbach	66-0576
Peter 9, Henriette 7			
SCHWEITZER, Wm.	30	Neustadt	63-0693
SCHWEIZER, Anna	29	Dusslingen	65-0189
SCHWEIZER, Bernh.	20	Cassel	65-0116
SCHWEIZER, Carl	33	Lemberg	64-0687
SCHWEIZER, Christ.	16	Ulm	66-0083
SCHWEIZER, Georg	41	Wuertemberg	66-0984
Margarethe 19			
SCHWEIZER, J.	50	Zell	64-0782
SCHWEIZER, Math.	18	Thalheim	65-0038
SCHWEIZERT, Elisab	19	Preussen	66-0221
SCHWELLKOPF, Joh.	16	Bunzwangen	65-0007
SCHWENCKERT, Aug	22	Magdeburg	63-1218
SCHWENDEL, Wilhe.	25	Darmstadt	66-1127
SCHWENHER, Magdal.	42	Hamburg	65-0151
August 7			
SCHWENK, David	22	Wetzlar	66-0109
SCHWENK, Friedr.	20	Homburg	65-0594
SCHWENK, Jac.	27	Aach	65-0402
SCHWENK, Leonhard	32	Pekin	64-0938
SCHWENKE, Hermann	18	Westereite	64-0433
Sophie 18			
SCHWENKE, Louis	40	Meyerndorf	66-0837
Philippa 35, Philipp 22			
SCHWENKE, Wilhelm	29	Iburg	66-0679
SCHWENKER, Elise	57	Hille	64-0456
Elise 25			
SCHWENKER, Fritz	18	Hille	64-0456
SCHWENKER, Rudolph	23	Vegesack	63-0614
Elise 22			
SCHWENNINGER, Vict	30	Vildenmoor	64-1108
SCHWENZNER, Gotth.	27	New York	63-0482
Maria 24			
SCHWEPFINGER, Carl	21	Eisenberg	64-0427
Bertha 54, Emma 28, Anna 15			
SCHWEPPE, Anna	28	Enger	64-1022
SCHWEPPER, Friedr.	28	Osnabrueck	65-0594
Friederike 26, Andreas 56, Josefa 52			
Joseph 22, Elisabeth 19, Clara 16			
Catharina 14, Victor 7, Juliane 6			
SCHWER, Bernhard	29	Logabirum	66-1031
Anna 36, Georg 6m			
SCHWER, Heinrich	25	Pr. Minden	65-0948
SCHWER, Ludwig	44	Beerlage	64-1206
SCHWERDTMANN, H.	26	Covington	64-0782
Margaretha 7, Erich 2, Joseph 29			
SCHWERDTS, Gefke	40	Leiste	65-0007
Anton 45, Antonia 9			
SCHWERTFEGER, Carl	63	Sievershausen	65-1030
SCHWERTMANN, Carl	23	Halle	64-0427
SCHWERZEL, August	25	Kirzl	65-1095
Louise 28, Emma 1			
SCHWESING, Paul	18	Baiern	66-0623
SCHWESINGER, Joh'a	19	Roth	66-0623
SCHWETZ, J.(f)	35	Wien	64-1161
SCHWICHTENBERG, J.	35	Lobehn	66-0668
Mathilde 34, baby (f) 3m, Adeline 6			
SCHWIDELT, J.	19	Dukenschild	64-0782
SCHWIDT, Nicolaus	20	Lehr	67-0007
Margarethe 18			
SCHWIED, Anna	18	Bremen	66-0984
SCHWIENING, Wm.	22	Stadthagen	67-0600
SCHWIER, Caroline	19	Dudenstadt	64-0840
SCHWIERJOHANN, Hch	19	Weese	65-0055
SCHWIES, Anton	32	Freren	64-0687
SCHWIETING, Bernh.	15	Arhaus	65-1030
Elise 18			
SCHWILL, Elisab.	7	Koenigsberg	64-0992

NAME	AGE	RESIDENCE	YR-LIST
SCHWIN, Peter	26	Eberstadt	66-0668
Gretchen 19, baby 4m			
SCHWIND, Felicitas	59	Schifferstadt	64-0739
Peter 16			
SCHWING, Christ	20	Pforzheim/Pr	64-1053
SCHWING, Louis	31	Mosbach	63-0917
SCHWINGER, Gottl.	22	Alfdorf	64-0495
SCHWINN, Wm.	24	Bergfeld	64-0495
SCHWIRING, Heinr.	28	New York	66-0083
SCHWITZER, Friedr.	25	Magdeburg	65-0856
Caroline 22			
SCHWOB, Maurice	24	Hegenheim	65-0004
SCHWOERER, Xaver	29	Schoenenbach	66-0083
SCHWOON, Fr.	23	Bremerhafen	64-0639
SCHWOONE, August	38	Hohnerode	64-0427
Johanna 24, Johanna 24			
SCHWOPE, Chris.	32	Prussia	63-0752
Marie 26			
SCIO, Peter	18	Oberkinzig	65-0189
SCOLES, A.B.	57	New York	63-0862
SCONCZYK, Joseph	31	Johannesthal	64-0456
Constancia 27, Franz 1			
SCROTH, Jacob	36	Pforzheim	65-0151
Jacob 63			
SEBALD, Christ.	35	Eisenberg	64-0639
SEBALD, Julius	27	Kronach	64-0433
SEBECK, Geo.	23	Uterlande	66-1313
SEBRANTKE, G.	31	Posen	64-0427
SECHSER, Rudolph	49	Wien	65-0243
SECKEL, Moritz	17	Dietz	64-0687
SECKER, Christ.	31	Varrel	65-1031
Wilhelmine 23			
SECKER, Wilhelm	30	Ebersbach	66-0221
SECKINGEN, Barbara	56	Rothenburg	64-1206
SEDLACZECK, Franz	34	Pilgensdorf	64-0840
Theresia 33, Franz 11, Francisca 7			
Maria 5, Robert 3, baby 10m			
SEDLAK, John A.	27	Boehmen	63-0551
Sabaldina 27			
SEDLER, Jos.	57	Milwaukee	66-0934
SEDLETZKY, Mary	23	Boehmen	63-0551
SEEBACH, Doroth.	37	Eisenach	65-1189
August 7, Margarethe 5, Otto 3			
SEEBACH, Friedr.	32	Zweibruecken	64-0023
SEEBECK, D.	18	Driftstedt	64-1161
SEEBERT, August	27	Schlede	64-1053
SEEBOHM, Carl B.	32	Oldendorf	64-0214
Louise 32, Otto 9, Anna 7, Wilhelm 5			
Carl 3, Helena 3m			
SEEBOHM, Julius	19	Lemfoerde	64-0456
Gustav 20			
SEEBURGER, Franz	31	Altoberndorf	65-0594
SEEDORF, Cath.	16	Beverstedt	65-1088
SEEFELD, August	23	Neuschoenwald	66-0679
SEEGEL, Juliane	50	Bruchsal	66-1373
Anna 22, Theresia 18			
SEEGER, Friedrich	34	Tuebingen	63-0953
Cath. 25, Chs. 4, Friedrich 11m			
SEEGER, R.(m)	39	Sacramento	64-0495
SEEGFRIED, B.(f)	26	Tittlingen	64-0331
SEEHAUS, (m)	36	Berlin	65-0594
SEEHAUSEN, Friedr.	33	Bielefeld	64-0885
SEEKAMP, H.	34	New York	63-1085
SEEKAMP, Henrich	20	Malendorf	66-1373
SEEKAMP, Joh. T.	28	Honstedt	64-0456
SEEL, Anton	41	Danna	66-0984
Eva 41			
SEELIN, Fritz	30	Bebra	63-0296
SEELING, Cath.	27	Hersfeld	64-0331
baby 9m, (m) 2			
SEELO, S.C.(m)	29	Philadelphia	64-0331
SEELRICH, Anna	23	Loer	65-1031
SEEMANN, Bertha	20	Buckershaus	65-1024
SEEMANN, Carl	30	Pr. Minden	67-0599
Sophie Wm. 32			
SEEMANN, Friedr.	37	Schlonowe	66-0650
Pauline 24			
SEEMANN, Johann	34	Nettenahrberg	65-0243
SEEMS, Meta	28	Hassendorf	64-0214
SEEMUELLER, Joh.	32	Haubersbronn	64-0495
Magd. 49			
SEERING, Heinrich	23	Dietzenbach	66-0679
SEERING, Henry	28	Hirschfeld	63-1069
SEETBALL, J.	43	Maehren	66-0413
SEETZ, Joh.	37	Ingelfingen	64-0992
SEEWARD, Marie	20	Nuernberg	64-1108
baby 2m			
SEGAR, Hermann	38	Koeln	63-1069
Bernharda 35, Hermann 10, Katharina 8			
Edeltrud 4, Klara 9m			
SEGELHORST, Carol.	27	Stoehen	65-0594
Carl 20, Dorothea 15			
SEGELKE, Heirnich	18	Buelkau	67-0599
SEGELKEN, C.	14	Heilshorn	66-0413
SEGELKEN, Diedr.	40	Niederbuehren	64-0840
Meta 20			
SEGELKEN, Friedr.	23	Visselhoevede	66-1373
SEGELMANN, Jos	34	Ungarn	63-1136
SEGENHAUSEN, Heinr	22	Inschede	66-0704
SEGER, H.	58	Lippe	66-0413
F. 24, Wilhelmine 22			
SEGERS, J.Fr.	23	Bremen	64-0432
SEGESENMAN, F.	30	New York	63-0953
SEGGEL, Albert	17	Bernhausen	66-1131
SEGGEL, August	26	Oberfranken	66-0934
SEGGEL, Louis	21	Oberfranken	66-0221
SEGGERN, v. H.	33	Falkenburg	64-1108
Anna 54			
SEHL, Heinr. Wilh.	24	Echzell	65-1031
SEHLE, Conrad	36	Hessia	66-0679
Catharine 59, Martin 22, Marie 24			
Michael 34, Adelheid 26			
SEHLE, Joseph	30	Kempten	66-0679
SEHLE, Max	46	Rieden	66-0147
SEHR, August	33	Berlin	63-0752
SEHRT, Otto	21	Wetzlar	63-0862
SEIBERT, August	30	Coeln	66-1127
SEIBERT, August	11	Wetter	65-1088
Carl 13			
SEIBERT, Conrad	27	Fraukirsch	66-1093
SEIBERT, E.	49	Alsdorf	63-1003
C. 40, G. 17, K. 15			
SEIBERT, Heinrich	16	Hungen	66-0934
SEIDE, Eduard	24	Prodozow	66-0734
SEIDE, Ernst	22	Dresden	67-0007
SEIDECKER, Friedr.	28	Goettingen	66-0934
SEIDEL, E.(f)	28	Herbsen	64-1161
SEIDEL, Joh.	27	Grafenroth	65-1031
SEIDEL, John	26	Boehmen	63-0917
Margaretha 51			
SEIDEL, Margretha	25	Obernfranken	66-0221
SEIDENBERG, Elias	74	Schlesien	66-0679
SEIDENFADEN, Wilh.	27	Bachleben	64-0214
Ferd. 24, Emilie 15			
SEIDENSPINNER, Mar	24	Kohlberg	66-0221
SEIDENSTICKER, Mna	24	Indianapolis	64-0363
George 6			
SEIDLER, Gustav	27	Koenigsberg	63-0296
SEIDLER, Martha	28	Cassel	66-1127
SEIFER, Jacob	19	Neuler	66-1203
SEIFERHELD, Alois	24	Halle	66-0147
SEIFERT, Adolph	31	Michigan	66-0576
SEIFERT, Ernst	26	Rosenthal	63-0551
SEIFERT, Maria	20	Dietershausen	66-1327
SEIFERT, Marie	33	Dermbach	66-0679
baby 2m			
SEIFERT, Marie	21	Langenberg	66-0934
SEIFERT, Peter	30	Braunschwieg	64-0363
SEIFFER, Christine	25	Kirchheim	67-0992
SEIFFERT, Chr.	23	New York	63-1136
SEIFFERT, Christ.	38	Wuerzburg	66-0734
Marie 28			
SEIFFERT, Elise	20	Winsterkassen	66-0469
Eva 17			
SEIFRIED, Conrad	30	Kaichen	65-0594
SEIFRIED, Georg	35	Kettelfingen	64-0170

NAME	AGE	RESIDENCE	YR-LIST
SEIFRIED, Johann	39	Schwarzach	66-0412
SEIHOLD, Rud.	26	Unterjessingn	64-0593
SEILER, Carl	21	Sandhausen	63-0168
sister 18			
SEILER, Carl	22	Gera	66-1093
SEILER, Conrad	24	Kentucky	63-0168
SEILER, Emma	45	Bern	66-1031
Marie 21			
SEILER, Louise	21	New York	63-1085
SEILER, Robert	25	Leuchtkirch	66-1155
Catharina 24, Elisabeth 3			
SEILERT, Engelbert	28	Frankenhausen	66-0147
SEIM, Casper	35	Ndr.Gemuend	65-1030
Anna Elise 44, Anna Elisab. 5			
Anna Marie 2			
SEIP, Friedr.	16	Friedrichstal	65-1031
SEIP, Math. (f)	21	Vegesack	65-0055
SEIPEL, Anna Marg.	16	Trauerbach	63-0296
SEIPEL, Anton	37	Eichelsachsen	66-1093
SEIPEL, Conrad	30	Philadelphia	64-0363
SEIPEL, Juliane	16	Eichelsachsen	63-0551
Louise 14, John 11			
SEIPELT, Eduard	25	Michelsdorf	65-0865
SEIPHEIMER, Edw.	33	Balzheim	64-1053
SEITINGER, Andreas	24	Gratz	66-0221
SEITTER, Caroline	25	Gaisberg	66-1093
SEITZ, Adolph	17	Lindolsheim	63-0990
SEITZ, Carl	21	Unterkochen	64-0639
SEITZ, Conrad	26	Windecken	65-0151
SEITZ, Conrad	19	Mettingen	65-1031
SEITZ, Friedrich	17	Laubach	66-1093
SEITZ, G.	18	Cassel	65-0974
SEITZ, George	23	Groerenbach	63-0296
SEITZ, J.	30	St .Louis	64-0495
SEITZ, James	30	Hambach	63-1218
SEITZ, Joh.	23	Gamburg	65-1189
SEITZ, Magd.	22	Lorsch	65-0151
SEITZ, Marie	74	Lorch	64-0639
Catharina 46			
SEITZ, Oscar	25	Columbus	63-1178
SEITZ, Otto	23	Buer	63-0862
SEITZ, Regina	48	Philadelphia	63-0990
SEITZ, Stephan	29	Jelbrueck	66-1093
Elisa 20			
SEITZ, Wilhelm	59	Windecker	64-1108
Wilhelmine 37			
SELBHAUSEN, August	42	Washington	66-0109
SELDNER, Johanna	20	Heimstadt	65-1024
SELHORST, Hermann	17	Loxten	65-0243
SELIG, Agnes	16	Hersfeld	64-0992
SELIGE, Henry	31	Springfield	66-0221
SELIGER, Helena	58	Babenhausen	63-0990
SELIGMANN, Joseph	18	Dorsau	66-0984
SELIGMANN, Joseph	45	Crenznach	65-0594
SELIGMANN, Mary	16	Boehmen	63-0482
SELIGMANN, Nath.	20	Fuerth	65-0594
SELIGMANN, Salomon	21	Baden	66-0734
Isaac 16			
SELINEK, Franz	22	Boehmen	66-0349
SELKE, Bernhard	37	Voerden	64-1022
Elise 25, Johann 3, Friedr. 9m			
SELL, Gottlieb	25	Bromberg	67-0599
SELL, J.	39	Katznisekerwe	66-0413
Jenestine 29, E. , Aug. 4			
SELL, Johann	24	Hodamshausen	66-1203
Elisabeth 26, Catharina 9m			
SELL, Ludwig	40	Bromberg	64-0456
Henriette 30, Christ. Frd. 7, Herm.Aug. 4			
Wilhelmine C 4m			
SELL, Wilhelm	35	Rabenstein	66-1248
Caroline 26, Emilie 7, Albertine 4			
Augusta 3			
SELLEMANN, Frdr.	27	Eberbach	66-0221
SELLHORST, Joseph	37	Langenberg	65-0713
SELLINGEN, Gottl.	30	Altenburg	64-0593
Rosalie 26, Leopold 3, Hildegard 1			
Carl 9m			
SELLMANN, Dorette	24	Muehlhausen	65-0007

NAME	AGE	RESIDENCE	YR-LIST
SELTENREICH, Ludw.	22	Kandern	63-0862
SELTMANN, Herrm.	28	Talge	66-0349
SEMAR, James	37	Zweibruecken	63-0168
SEMKE, Johann	22	New York	63-0097
SEMLE, Raimund	22	Ulm	66-0412
Catharine 23			
SEMLER, H.	37	Olisack	64-0665
Albertine 28, Emma 9, Magde.			
SEMM, Catharine	18	Pfersdorf	65-0770
SEMMLER, Johannes	25	Heinebach	67-0599
SEMMLER, Martin	28	Aasen	63-0296
SEMSEN, Geske	27	Weserberg	65-0974
SEMSKY, Anna	40	Naumburg	64-1022
Hedwig 7, Ernst 5, Carl 3			
SENAC, Jean	40	Paris	63-1178
SENDZZISKA, Lorenz	27	Polen	63-0953
SENF, Chr.	56	Gera	65-0402
SENF, Eduard	18	Altkrichen	66-0984
SENF, Heinr.	26	Ober Saalheim	64-1108
Jacob 16			
SENF, Wilhelm	20	Niersen	67-0795
SENFELDER, Chr.	50	Reichau	64-0782
Nanette 45			
SENGER, Aurelius	25	Lubozin	64-1206
SENGER, Francisca	21	Nettelrode	66-1031
SENGER, Louis	27	Germany	66-0666
SENGSTACK, Aug. C.	20	Hannover	64-1022
SENGSTACK, Rudolph	27	Pilgersdorf	64-0840
Josefa 34, Rudolph 3			
SENGSTAKE, J.(m)	24	Bremen	64-0331
SENGSTAKE, Marg.	17	Michelstadt	66-1327
Heinrich 8			
SENKENBERG, Chris.	59	Darmstadt	63-0862
Georg 7			
SENKRECHT, Ad.	36	Osch	64-0782
SENN, August	28	Speyer	63-0953
SENNE, Aug.	47	St. Island	63-0953
SENNLICH, Fr.	25	Kappeln	63-1069
SENT, Catharina	29	Dausenau	65-1030
SENZER, Johanna	24	Karschau	63-0551
SEPPEL, Marg.	18	Hutsdorf	63-1010
SEPPER, Maria	14	Weissenstein	65-0402
SEPPLER, Rich.	29	Bueckeberg	64-0495
SERFLING, Hulda	24	Eisenberg	64-0331
SERR, Barbara	27	Rhodt	66-1373
SERVIERE, Horace	20	Heiligenstadt	63-0097
SESSLE, Catharina	31	Sontheim	64-1108
SETTER, Joh. Herm	20	Rietberg	64-0199
SETTLER, Siegmund	22	Hockenheim	66-0576
SETZER, Fanny	36	New York	63-1136
August 9			
SEVER, Gumpel	18	Curhessen	66-0934
SEVERLOH, Aug.	57	Eschede	64-0214
Marie 50, Dorothea 20			
SEWING, Hanna	28	Herford	65-0594
SEXANER, Louis	26	Sulzfeld	66-0679
Minna 24			
SEXER, P.	17	Wien	65-1189
SEXTRO, Julius	35	New York	66-0934
SEY, Helene	20	Distelhausen	66-0576
SEYBOLD, Barbara	31	Hagelloch	66-1131
SEYBOLD, Joh.	19	Ramsenstruth	65-1088
SEYDEL, Carl	43	Glauchau	66-0576
SEYDEL, E.	30	Berlin	65-0007
SEYDEL, Moritz	28	Thurgau	63-0752
SEYER, Friedrich	41	Gustendorf	63-0614
Elisabeth 37			
SEYFANF, Johannes	43	Heinichen	64-1053
SEYFANG, Jacob	56	Schloth	64-0687
Math. 28, Gottlob 19, Johann 17, Maria 25			
Barbara 15, Ursula 10			
SEYFORTH, Meta	17	Stadteln	65-0007
SEYFRIED, Cathrine	24	Cohnweiler	66-1093
Louise 2, Friedrich 6m			
SHANKLAND, Ths.		Hannover	63-0482
SHORT, Cath.	20	Switz.	64-0170
SIARECK, Martin	30	Brunowo	64-0456
SIBBEL, George	43	Grossalmerode	66-0650

NAME	AGE	RESIDENCE	YR-LIST
Martha 41, Martha 14			
SICHEL, Emilie	22	Kl. Schuettig	66-1031
Sophie 20			
SICHEL, Joseph	18	Langenschwarz	66-1327
SICHER, Franz	29	Maltitz	66-0576
SICHERN, Louis	35	Marburg	65-1189
wife 34, Elise 8, Elise 7, Charles 5			
Emmi 3, Emmi 6m			
SICHLER, Hugo	19	Heilbronn	66-1093
SICHLER, P.(f)	30	Schelerstadt	64-1161
SICHMANN, Johannes	15	Braunhaus	66-1093
Martha 18			
SICHTIG, Carl	25	Braunschweig	65-0594
SICKERMANN, Louis	21	Oehnhausen	65-0950
SIDECK, Johann	36	Prag	64-0938
Marie 30, Anna 4, Marie 3			
SIDENBURG, Cathar.	20	Sandstedt	67-0600
SIEBEL, Carl	23	Hesse-Darmst.	66-0984
SIEBEL, Henrich	20	Muenden	66-0984
SIEBEL, P.D.	40	Solingen	64-0363
SIEBELS, Joh.	25	Nordunum	66-1243
SIEBEN, Heinr.	22	Goergenloh	64-0938
SIEBENBORN, Bertha	20	Fuerstenberg	65-0594
SIEBENHORN, Carol.		Bisses	65-1024
SIEBENS, Trina	24	Holtrup	66-1128
SIEBENSOLD, Georg	36	Schweinfurth	66-1243
SIEBER, W.	32	Hannover	65-0189
SIEBERSCH, Metha	23	Enschen	66-1243
SIEBERT, Amalie	22	Langensalz	64-0456
SIEBERT, Barbara	18	Darmstadt	63-0398
Valentin 15			
SIEBERT, C.	34	Bremen	65-0189
SIEBERT, Caroline	27	Everbach	66-0576
SIEBERT, Caspar	52	Hungen	63-0350
SIEBERT, Cathar.	20	Isberg	66-0934
SIEBERT, Chs.	19	Philadelphia	63-0862
SIEBERT, Conrad	25	Hellmershsn.	66-0346
SIEBERT, E.W.(m)	30	Baltimore	64-0214
SIEBERT, Elise	26	Braunschwieg	64-0427
baby 6m			
SIEBERT, Ernst	23	Berreshausen	63-1069
SIEBERT, Ernst	40	Jessperg	65-0594
SIEBERT, Friedr.	22	Offenburg	64-0687
Amalie 17			
SIEBERT, Georg	22	Hessen	66-0734
SIEBERT, George	30	Breitenbach	66-0412
SIEBERT, Heinrich	56	Illinois	66-0934
SIEBERT, Peter	21	Rheinpfalz	66-0576
Johanna 19, Peter 6m			
SIEBKE, C.	20	Rinteln	64-1161
SIEBOLD, Chr.	23	Otterndorf	66-1313
SIEBOLD, Henry	35	New York	63-0990
son 4			
SIEBOTT, Henry W.	21	Buettenberg	63-1136
SIEBRANDT, Herm.	47	Hoya	65-0898
Heinrich 14, Fritz 8			
SIEBRECHT, August	17	Niedenstein	64-0199
SIEBRECHT, August	17	Goettingen	66-1093
SIEBRECHT, Chr.	20	Hannover	65-0402
SIEBRECHT, Julius	17	Niehnstein	65-1095
SIEBRING, Barteit	24	Simonswolde	65-0151
SIECKMANN, Otto	18	Herford	64-0138
SIEDENBERG, W.	36	Nienburg	66-0413
SIEDENBURG, Friedr	20	Minden	64-1108
SIEDENBURG, Hedwig	54	Scharmbeck	66-0221
Meta 7			
SIEDENBURG, J.G.	37	New York	63-0296
SIEDENBURG, Marie	33	Scharmbeck	64-1022
Elise 7, Heinrich 6			
SIEDENHOP, Chr.	30	Harbesse	64-0331
(f) 34			
SIEDER, Aug.	28	Engstein	67-0795
SIEDLER, Carl	55	New York	66-0109
SIEFKEN, Adolph	19	Varel	66-0221
SIEFKEN, Theodor	35	Germantown	64-0739
SIEFKES, H.	40	New York	63-0990
SIEGEL, Carl	20	Bethlehem	66-1327
SIEGEL, Christine	25	Unterschlecht	64-0687

NAME	AGE	RESIDENCE	YR-LIST
SIEGEL, Conrad	22	Wickersrode	67-0600
SIEGEL, Francisca	18	Berlin	65-0594
SIEGEL, Heinr.	22	Wichmansdorf	66-1127
SIEGEL, Johann	19	Weinheim	66-1327
SIEGEL, Louis	25	Waldorf	64-0938
SIEGEL, Magnus	21	Regensburg	63-0614
SIEGEL, Mathilde	24	Wuertemberg	66-0734
SIEGELE, August	40	Chicago	63-0296
Catharina 35			
SIEGELE, Caroline	32	Chicago	63-0990
child 1			
SIEGELMANN, Kathy	31	Sebeskellem	65-0402
Cath. 8, Johanna 6, Jac. 5, Nani 3			
SIEGERT, August	28	Berlin	64-1053
SIEGFRIED, Frz.	29	Pfeddersheim	64-0170
Cath. 23, Franz 6m			
SIEGFRIED, Maria	17	Muehlhausen	63-1010
SIEGLE, Gottlieb	19	Grossheppach	66-0469
SIEGLER, Barb.	27	Bleningen	65-1030
SIEGLER, Carl Lud.	44	Wollin	63-0614
Wilhelmine 39, Albert 19, Hermine 15			
Friedrich 13, Hermann 9, Richard 3			
Franz 9m			
SIEGLER, Christian	23	Biig	66-0837
SIEGLER, F. (m)	48	Praschnow	64-0427
SIEGMANN, Carl	26	Minden	63-0015
SIEGMUND, Christ.	19	Sindelfingen	65-0189
SIEGMUND, Franz	59	Reichenberg	63-0953
SIEGRIST, Cath.	22	Steinheim	64-0170
SIEHLING, Sophie	20	Bremen	63-0398
SIEK, Friederike	26	Grambergen	65-1088
SIEKEL, Ge.	58	Baltimore	63-1136
SIEKENDIECK, Frdr.	28	Versmold	65-0950
Charlotte 25, Charlotte 3m			
SIEKMANN, Heinr.	37	Herford	64-1206
SIELBECK, Marie	56	Nienburg	66-0413
SIELJUCS, Marie	20	Ahrberg	66-0413
SIELKA, Ludwig	36	Lippe Detmold	66-0413
Wilhelmine 7, Heinrich 4			
SIELKE, Ernst	34	Klivenau	66-0413
Justine 26, Emil 7, Gustav 10m			
SIELKEN, Joh.	18	Scharmbeck	65-0974
SIELSHOT, Georg	18	Osnabrueck	66-1093
SIEMANDEL, Wm.	21	Aldameroh	65-0038
SIEMER, Bernh.	17	Petersfeld	65-0594
Gottl 15, Magdalena 18, Gottl. 49			
Magdal. 45, Louise 13, Wilhelm 7			
Friederike 5, Lidion 4, Lisette 19			
SIEMER, Clemens	20	Backum	66-1127
SIEMER, Heinrich	23	Soerlern	66-1373
SIEMERING, Diedr.	22	Bruchmuehle	66-0147
SIEMERMANN, Friedr	30	Oldenburg	66-0576
SIEMERS, Diedr.	29	Dedesdorf	63-0953
SIEMERS, Friedr.	17	Driftseth	64-0456
SIEMERS, Heinr.	28	Brinkum	65-0402
SIEMON, Caspar	19	Reinbolderode	64-0886
Franz 23			
SIEMS, Anna	19	Buchholz	65-1030
SIEMS, Diedr.	17	Buchholz	66-0666
SIEMSBACHER, Cresc	18	Muenchen	65-0007
SIENER, Diedr.	20	Hannover	66-0734
SIERICH, Heinrich	65	Nesse	66-0934
Heinrich 31			
SIERKE, Carsten	44	New York	63-0953
SIERKEN, Hannah	22	Spika	66-0837
SIERS, Betty	22	Midlum	63-0990
SIESEL, Isaac	18	Aberheim	64-0495
Sam. 15			
SIESKE, Fr.	28	Germany	63-1136
SIESSFELD, Henr'tt	22	Wuerzburg	66-1203
SIEUL, Joseph	23	Oldenburg	64-1022
SIEVER, Hermann	27	Ruhrbach	66-0623
SIEVERDING, Elise	42	Lohne	63-0953
SIEVERET, Alb.	32	Oberkirchen	64-0073
Elisabeth 32			
SIEVERS, A.(m)	23	Hildesheim	65-0055
SIEVERS, Adeline	18	Wersabe	64-0739
SIEVERS, Aug.	30	Pyrmont	64-0138

NAME	AGE	RESIDENCE	YR-LIST
SIEVERS, Ferdinand	19	Hessia	66-0679
SIEVERS, Giesche	17	Thedinghausen	64-0495
SIEVERS, J. Louis	22	Elberfeld	66-0221
SIEVESBERG, Teresa	30	Veracruz	66-0934
SIEWE, Franz	36	Fhorst	66-0984
Dina 66			
SIEWERSEN, Christ.	18	New York	63-0244
SIEWESKE, Augusta	18	Luebbecke	66-1127
Herm. 22			
SIGEL, Georg	35	Maxdorf	66-0837
SIGL, Kres.	23	Augsburg	64-0782
SIGLE, Christ.	13	Romershausen	64-0782
SIHOEN, Anna Maria	35	St Gallen	64-0456
Christian 1			
SILBER, Daniel	17	Schnaits	64-0214
SILBERBLATT, Getti	21	Oberfranken	66-0984
SILBERHORN, Joh. F	21	Oberthal	65-1031
SILBERMANN, Marian	30	Oberasbach	66-0984
SILBERMANN, Moritz	18	Lemforde	66-1248
SILBERN, Helene	20	Baden	66-0147
SILBERSCHMIDT, Sam	22	Geisa	63-0917
SILGE, Agness	26	Glandorf	66-1127
SILKE, Heinrich	19	Vorden	66-1203
SILLES, Marie	40	Lingen	65-0950
SILLIES, Th. H.	24	Drivoerden	63-1038
SILMANN, Andreas	36	Weidmes	64-0433
Andreas 35			
SILVER, N.	17	Bernstockheim	63-1085
SIMA, Catharina	25	Seifritz	66-1327
SIMENES, Justo	25	Havana	64-0170
SIMMEN, Joh.	22	Frankfurt	66-1128
SIMMENDINGEN, Fr'd	32	Killer	65-0402
SIMMERER, Georg	36	Schwarzenbach	66-1313
SIMMONDS, Henr'tt.	15	Pyrmont	64-0840
SIMMONDS, Sigismun	17	Pyrmont	63-1218
SIMMRODT, Ma.(f)	19	Weimar	64-0331
Ae.(f) 17			
SIMON, Anne Maria	29	Steinwiesen	66-0934
SIMON, Anton	27	Marbach	66-0576
SIMON, August	18	Gensingen	66-0704
SIMON, August	28	Giessen	65-0948
SIMON, Catharine M	19	Altenbreitung	63-0006
SIMON, Charles F.	46	Altenburg	63-0917
SIMON, Conrad	21	Langgoens	66-1327
SIMON, Conrad	20	Melsungen	65-0713
SIMON, Elisabeth	18	Ensheim	64-0456
SIMON, Friedr.	28	Pittsburg	66-0576
SIMON, Friedrich	19	Mickelhorn	63-0917
SIMON, Heinrich	28	Altenbreitung	63-0006
SIMON, Heinrich	32	Evinghausen	66-0576
Henriette 55, Henriette 24			
SIMON, Henriette	24	Ritterhude	65-0770
SIMON, Johannette	27	Gross Gerau	66-0984
SIMON, Lottie	56	Prag	66-0147
SIMON, Louis	33	Louisville	66-0984
SIMON, Louise	20	Philadelphia	66-0147
SIMON, Marie	25	Damme	65-0055
SIMON, Nannchen	17	Altenstadt	65-0594
SIMON, Phil.	20	Stolpe/Pr.	65-0038
SIMON, Philipp	20	Giessen	66-1131
David 16			
SIMON, Salli	19	Bielefeld	64-1161
SIMON, Samson	17	Eberstadt	66-1127
SIMON, Wenzel	45	Boehmen	66-0349
Marie 6m			
SIMON, Wilhelm	40	Conitz	63-0097
SIMONS, F.	35	Germany	64-0495
SIMONSEN, Salomon	22	Gottenburg	66-0666
SIMPER, Christ.	36	Quakenbrueck	66-0984
Christine 26, Gerhard 2, Eberhard 9m			
SIMRING, Georg	24	Rothenditmold	65-0038
Anna G. 49, Joh. Heinr. 18, Martin 16			
SIMSBEIMER, Magd.	59	Neckarsteinn.	63-0482
SIMSHAEUSER, Conr.	26	Worms	64-0073
Dorothea 20			
SIMSHAEUSER, Val.	25	Hessen	66-0221
Caroline 36, Franzisca 31, Barbara 6			
SINDA, Thomas	35	Moncowasch	64-0433
Marianna 26			
SINDEL, Julie	35	San Francisco	64-0073
Mariette 7			
SINECKY, Franz	29	Boehmen	64-0687
SINEL, Peter	24	Horn	66-0221
Georg 23			
SINGE, Js.(m)	19	Freienhagen	64-0495
SINGER, Jacob	19	Sickingen	66-1155
SINGER, Martin	28	Dettlingen	64-0331
SINGLE, Christ	32	Duerrwangen	65-0116
SINIDRO, Giovanni	25	Havre	64-1053
SINN, Chr.	29	Ohlendorf	64-0427
SINNER, Henry	29	Bindsachsen	63-0482
Cath. 20, Caroline 25, Sophie 29			
SINNING, Conr.	24	Altenbauslar	64-0687
SINNING, Heinr.	31	Kuehnbach	65-0055
SINRAM, Hch.	28	Oldendorf	64-0495
SINSEL, Adam	23	Cassel	66-1313
SIPPACH, Carl	18	Leidenroda	66-0934
SIPPEL, Agnes	22	Meiningen	66-0704
SISENDOP, Wilh.	23	Lutte	63-1010
SITTEL, Ed.	23	Westhausen	64-1108
SITTEL, Heinr.	37	Chemnitz	64-0073
SITTIG, Wm.	17	Hegelheim	65-1189
SITTING, Heinrich	28	Bremen	64-1022
Marg. 25			
SIVERT, Bartha	19	Plathe	64-0639
Emilie 24			
SIXTER, Wenzel	40	Boehmen	66-0221
Barbara 30, Maria 6m			
SKALITZKY, Franz	29	Boehmen	63-0917
Anna 26, Emily 3m			
SKANDERA, Fr.	23	Wien	65-0189
SKLENAR, Jos.	24	Bohemia	64-0687
Aug. 36			
SKOREPA, Johann	24	Precek	64-0593
Anna 24, Joseph 3m			
SKORSCH, Joseph	15	Lutz	66-1155
SKORST, Dina	18	Oldenburg	64-1022
Kath. 15			
SLAWICK, Xaver	31	Kipfenberg	63-1038
Josefa 32, Marie 2m			
SLEZACK, H.(m)	18	Boehmen	64-0495
SLUNSKY, Franziska	17	Domislitz	66-0623
SMECKE, Heinr.	16	Sandstaedt	67-0600
SMIDT, Georg	22	Marburg	64-0138
SMIDT, Louise	18	Ottersberg	64-0992
SMIT, Ba.(f)	65	Rorichum	64-0495
SMIT, Luitje	30	Spyk	66-0734
SMITH, Louis	35	Pittsburg	63-0693
SMITH, Marg	24	Basel	64-1161
SMITH, Teis	37	Pekin	64-1022
SMITTEL, H.	29	Canada	64-0495
SNASCHOLLER, Anna	33	Winterscheid	64-0331
Johanna 21			
SNATTERBECK, Magd.	22	Uppstadt	66-1155
SNEYDA, Joseph	36	Schweinitz	66-0837
Catharina 35, Joseph 6, Andres 3			
SOBBE, v. H.		Minden	63-0244
SOBICEK, Emanuel	30	Bohemia	64-0687
SOCKA, Joseph	25	Chalowucik	66-1131
Anna 24			
SOCKEL, L.(m)	30	Cincinnati	64-0363
SOCKFELD, Angel	20	Muenster	66-1313
SOCKMANN, Friedr.	25	Lippe Detmold	63-0350
SODT, B.H.	21	Scharr	64-0495
SOEDLES, Minna	20	Carlsbad	64-0992
SOEFFKER, William	22	Segelhorst	63-0482
Gerhard 52, Charlotte 46, Gerhard 17			
Caroline 15, Friedrich 9, Charlotte 8			
Louise 4			
SOEFKER, Carl	38	Staude	66-0576
Marie 57, Carl 5, Marie 3			
SOEFKER, Charlet	23	Staude	66-0576
Anna 19			
SOEFKER, Greta	29	Geestendorf	65-0007
Carl 7, Gust. 6			
SOEHL, Johann	21	Niendorf	65-1095

NAME	AGE	RESIDENCE	YR-LIST
SOEHLMANN, Heinr.	15	Mehringen	64-1053
SOEHNLEIN, Ludw.	22	Basel	65-0243
SOEKELAND, Wilhelm	31	Muenster	66-1373
SOEL, Moses	23	Tusgenheim	65-1024
SOELLIG, Emil	50	Bremen	64-0199
SOELTER, Wilhelm	20	Elbingerode	66-1373
SOENNKER, H.A.	20	Hannover	64-0593
SOERG, Leonhard	26	Grossheimth	66-0679
SOHELKA, Ant.	46	Boehmen	63-1136
SOHL, Barbara	70	Steinfeld	66-1093
SOHL, Fr.	19	Darmstadt	64-0432
SOHLMANN, Louis	25	Hannoram	64-0495
SOJKA, Joseph	26	Boehmen	63-0614
Maria 26			
SOLDAU, Franz Ludw	23	Frankfurt	63-0614
Ottilie 18			
SOLDAU, Gustav	26	Giessen	64-0938
SOLDAU, Theod.	28	Cincinnati	66-0984
SOLDMANN, Anton	23	Rothenburg	66-1243
SOLINGER, John	40	Rheinkirchen	66-0109
SOLLE, Carl	19	Detmold	66-1127
Hermine 27			
SOLOMON, Rosa	21	Beerfelden	65-0007
SOMMER, Anna	21	Hildesheim	66-1093
SOMMER, Anton	33	Podmohl	66-1373
SOMMER, Astor	53	Gambach	65-0594
Rebecca 21, Sara 7, Joh. Fr. 14			
SOMMER, August	29	Indiana	66-0934
SOMMER, Babette		Amrichshausen	63-1218
SOMMER, Carl Heinr	41	Langensalz	64-0456
Sophie 39, Heinr. 18, Sophie 10, Carl 8			
Friedr. 1			
SOMMER, Christian	23	Hannover	66-0469
SOMMER, El.	44		63-0917
SOMMER, Friedr.	37	Zaberfeld	64-0427
Cath. 35, Louise 7, Fr.(m) 6			
Friederike 16			
SOMMER, Fritz	16	Northeim	63-0006
SOMMER, Fritz	26	Corbach	66-1031
SOMMER, Gerhard	17	Oldenburg	66-1093
SOMMER, Gottlieb	23	Muddelsbach	64-0214
SOMMER, Heinr.	27	Detmold	65-0189
SOMMER, Henry	35	Sevelten	66-0221
SOMMER, Johann	51	Moellenfeld	66-0984
Margarethe 48, Gerhard 20, Adelheid 18			
Catharine 16, Margarethe 14, Helene 7			
Anna 6, Thekla 5, Heinrich 3			
SOMMER, Marie	21	Ludwigsburg	64-0427
SOMMER, Martin	18	Nonnenwerth	66-0837
SOMMER, Minna	18	Grebbin	63-0350
SOMMER, Moritz	21	Sulzburg	66-0734
SOMMER, S.	19	Rottweil	64-0992
SOMMER, Wilhelmine	20	Detmold	66-0934
SOMMERER, Cath.	22	Miedelsbach	65-0189
SOMMERFELD, Christ	18	Bromberg	64-0456
SOMMERFELD, Friedr	28	Weissenspring	66-0412
SOMMERKAMP, H.	18	Dissen	63-0953
SOMMERKAMP, Minna	25	Melle	66-0934
SOMMERLAD, John	35	Wieseck	64-0343
Johanna 21			
SOMMERLAND, Conrad	18	Frais	66-0679
SOMMERLAND, J.	45	Wieseck	64-0495
Marg. 15, Georg 2			
SOMMERMANN, Caspar	42	Horwagen	66-0083
SONDA, Johann	18	Piseck/Aust.	66-0837
SONDER, Clara	25	Murkdorf	63-1085
SONDERHOF, Richard	15	Eisenach	66-0668
SONDERMANN, J.	30	Mettingen	64-0495
Regina 20			
SONDERMANN, Wilh.	32	Herrnhut/Sax.	65-0038
SONNABEND, Joh.	32	Achim	66-0650
SONNE, Louise	62	Windheim	66-0650
SONNEBURG, Heinr.	25	Fangenberg	66-0623
SONNEMANN, Cathar.	17	Quakenbrueck	66-0984
SONNEN, Peter H.	32	Wittlar	66-1203
SONNENBERG, Fanny	18	Oppach	63-0953
SONNENBERG, Johann	26	Krojanke	65-0004
Justine 24			

NAME	AGE	RESIDENCE	YR-LIST
SONNENSCHEIN, A.	22	Bohemia	64-0782
SONNENSCHEIN, Mart	20	Kerstenhausen	64-0665
SONNLEITER, Marie	19	Berlichingen	66-0576
SONNTAG, Ottilie	57	Altdorf/Bad.	65-0950
SONNTAG, Philipp	47	Schoenhagen	66-0934
Friederike 40, Marie 21, Pauline 18			
Wilhelm 16, Ferdinand 13, Alma 9			
Susanne 8, Anna 7, Lisette 6, Bernhard 4			
Bertha 2, Emma 1			
SONTERMANN, August	18	Erfurt	65-0713
Ernst 27			
SOOSTEN, v. Cath.	19	Koehlen	64-0427
SOOSTEN, v. Luede	17	Koehlen	66-0668
SORGE, Wilhelm	42	Rudolstadt	67-0600
SORGER, Carl	32	Everrode	66-0109
SORTE, de la T.	23	Steinfurt	63-1038
SOST, Martin	15	Ringstedt	63-0614
SOTHEN, v. Louis	32	Gieboldehsn.	66-1203
SOUDHEIMER, Fanny	20	Baiern	66-0704
Hannchen 19			
SOUTER, Georg	54	Warsau	63-0862
SOYER, J.M.(m)	25	Markelsheim	64-0170
SOYER, Joh.	26	Kleinensee	66-0349
SPACZELL, Anna	25	Vienna	66-1093
Emilie 3			
SPAER, Jac.	30	Chemnitz	65-0974
Catharine 26			
SPAETH, Johannes	16	Oterkochen	66-0576
SPAETH, Marie	22	Wuertemberg	63-0822
SPAHL, Joh. Ad.	46	Hausen	67-0795
Barbara 43, Marie 15, Marg. 14			
Michael 12, Anna M. 9, Andreas 7			
Maria Anna 6, Catharina 5, Johann 9m			
SPAHLER, Charles	21	Bremen	63-0693
SPAHN, E.O.	24	Lanhusen	64-0495
Chte. 23			
SPAHN, Elise	21	Frankfurt	66-0679
SPAHN, John	26	Fulda	63-0693
SPAHN, Otto	20	Obernburg	65-1030
SPAHN, Theodor	34	Breslau	65-0038
SPAHNER, W.	17	Bremen	63-0006
SPAHR, Joh. Caspar	29	Schnaithain	64-0427
SPAHR, Michael	39	Wirtheim	63-0015
SPALLING, Rud.	24	Breslau	64-0073
SPANGENBERG, C.J.	25	Springe	63-0350
wife 22			
SPANGENBERG, Carl	9	New York	66-0934
SPANGENBERG, Carl	40	New York	66-0934
SPANHAKE, Hermann	23	Baltimore	66-0147
SPANIEN, Joh.	28	Ost Friesland	66-0577
SPANJER, Elske	47	Riepe	63-0482
Forke 14			
SPANJER, Elske	48	Emden	64-0687
SPARENBERG, H.H(m)	28	West Cappeln	64-0331
SPARFELDT, Carl	34	Pessnitz	64-0593
Friederike 35, Cornelia 9m			
SPARK, Emil	28	Barmen	65-0594
SPARNECHT, Wm.	32	Ihlienworth	64-0427
Gottl. 17			
SPARR, David	26	New York	63-1178
SPATH, Katharina	15	Luetzenbach	66-0837
SPATH, Marg.	25	Miltenberg	65-0007
SPATH, Wilhelmine	19	Rothweil	66-0221
SPATT, Maria	32	Wundshuh	64-1108
SPECHT, Bernh.	18	Lilienthal	65-0038
SPECHT, Fr. Wilh.	19	Wittmund	65-0856
SPECHT, J.H.	23	Gumpelstadt	66-0221
SPECHT, Jac.	31	San Francisco	64-0593
SPECHT, Jerem.	47	Gilfershaus	63-1010
Justine 35, Elisabeth 20, Anna Cathr. 6			
Elisabeth 7m			
SPECHT, Johannes	21	Heinade	65-0243
Carl 18			
SPECHT, Lorenz	36	Boehmen	64-0495
M.(f) 38, L. 7, Lisette 6, Joh. 21			
SPECHT, Margaretha	27	Asch	66-1155
SPECHT, Marie	24	Berlichingen	66-0576
SPECHT, Martin	25	Meiningen	64-0432

NAME	AGE	RESIDENCE	YR-LIST
SPECHT, Martin	28	Meiningen	66-0704
Gertrud 56, Eva 22			
SPECK, Johann	34	Wurmlingen	66-0576
SPECK, Joseph	23	Hitzkopfle	67-0007
SPECK, Therese	23	Tuttlingen	66-0576
SPECKART, Adolph	25	Meschede	66-0679
Francisca 22			
SPECKLEE, Marie	30	Rauchwill	63-1085
SPECKMANN, Ch. Fr.	21	Stroehen	64-0343
SPECKMANN, Christ.	26	Rahden	65-1088
SPECKMANN, D.	25	Offenwarden	66-0934
SPECKMANN, Heinr.	14	Rheda	64-0456
SPEES, John	31	New York	63-1218
SPEIDEL, F.	34	Wachbach	64-0992
SPEIDEL, Theod.	19	Bahlingen	65-0243
SPEIDEL, Tobias	27	Bahlingen	63-1178
SPEISER, Arnold	23	Vechta	66-0704
SPEISER, Marg.	59	Laudau	63-1218
SPEITEL, Joh.Georg	36	Rattenberg	66-0349
SPELMEYER, Johanna	13	Gothe	64-1206
Heinr. 20			
SPENDLER, Nepomuc	26	Switz.	64-0170
SPENGLER, Chr.	20	Boll	64-0363
W. (m) 9			
SPENGLER, Leopold	28	Achern	64-0886
SPENGLER, Philipp	15	Pferdersheim	66-1031
Julie 14			
SPERIG, John	32	Schmichen	64-0023
Johanna 21			
SPERKOWSKIE, John	25	Schanzendorf	66-0578
SPERLING, Johann	23	Witzenhausen	64-0023
SPERRSCHNEID, Frd	52	Haidengruen	66-0679
Kunigunde 54, Caroline 12			
SPERRY, Sophie	22	Ettenheim	64-0886
SPERZEL, Adam	32	Sterbfritz	66-1243
Catharine 26			
SPETH, Rosalie	21	Breslau	66-1093
Bertha 3			
SPETTEL, Michael	34	Marktheidenfd	66-1327
Andreas 22			
SPEXARTH, Wilhelm	20	Varensell	66-1203
SPEYER, Emma	16	Frankfurt/M	64-0886
SPEYER, Meyer	14	Volkershausen	64-0593
SPEYER, Oscar	22	Bielefeld	63-0917
SPEYER, Siegmund	24	Kalamazoo	63-0917
SPEYER, Therese	33	Dresden	65-0007
SPIECKER, Henry	40	Leer	63-0693
Henriette 33, Gesine 7, Cathrine 6			
Hinrich 4, August 3, John 2			
SPIEGEL, Elise	24	Hannover	66-0576
SPIEGEL, Moritz	36	California	66-0704
SPIEGEL, Paul	29	Beiengreis	63-0015
SPIEGELBERG, A.	18	Bremen	65-0974
SPIEGELHALTER, Jos	19	Baerenthal	64-1206
SPIEKERMEYER, Herm	61	Westenholz	64-0433
SPIELER, Johann Ch	40	Pennsylvania	63-0006
SPIELMANN, Doroth.	59	Schweitz	63-1136
SPIELMANN, Henry	38	Zsadary	66-0109
SPIER, Berle	18	Schrecksbach	66-0984
SPIER, Carl	22	Willebadesse	65-0950
SPIER, Isaac	32	Calcar	64-0331
SPIER, Isaak	59	Wiedelsberg	64-0427
SPIER, Ludwig	30	Germany	63-0953
SPIER, Pauline	16	Gr. Hessen	66-0704
SPIEREK, Peter	28	Boehmen	66-0349
SPIEREN, Henry	18	Achim	63-1038
SPIERS, Jette	26	New York	66-0934
SPIES, Carl	40	Frankfurt	65-0594
SPIES, Caspar	22	Mannheim	63-0015
SPIES, Heinr.	44	Grossbadungen	64-0170
SPIES, Lewis	18	Dittelheim	63-0350
SPIESS, Elisabeth	29	Dillheim	65-0243
SPIESS, Frd.	68	Guerbelsdorf	64-1161
SPIESS, Heinr.	22	Darmstadt	66-0577
SPIESS, Pauline	19	Hohenfels	66-1131
SPIESS, Peter	38	Castel	63-0862
SPILE, Bernh. H.	23	Wostendetten	64-0427
SPINDLER, Anna	22	Otternberg	63-0990

NAME	AGE	RESIDENCE	YR-LIST
SPINDLER, Hermann	21	Eisenberg	66-1093
SPINNLER, Math.	29	Ebersbach	65-1030
SPINTER, Carl	30	Moritzfeld	66-0576
SPITAL, Ernst	40	Engersleben	65-0948
SPITHOEVER, Theod.	17	Wolbeck	66-1031
SPITNAGEL, Carl	16	Ruedingen	64-0886
SPITZ, Adalbert	22	Boehmen	63-0482
SPITZMESSER, Walb.	21	Moos	66-0704
SPIZENBERG, L.(m)	31	Joehlingen	64-0495
SPOEDE, Heinr.	20	Gruenenloh	66-0984
SPOEDE, Marie	36	Helle	63-0990
SPOERER, Fr. Jul.	22	Osterode	66-1155
SPOERER, Friedr.	26	Amorbach	63-0862
SPOERER, Marie	21	Ruderhausen	65-0402
SPOERHAS, Elisab.	19	Marburg	65-1088
SPOERL, Friedr.	24	Rastede	64-0739
Heinr. 24			
SPOERL, Marg.	52	Naila	64-0938
SPOHN, Eduard	28	Pommern	66-0469
Friederike 26, Caroline 5, Wilhelm 3			
Bertha 2, Friederike 6m			
SPOHN, Helene	23	Bockenhausen	64-0840
SPOHN, Ursula	70	Laichingen	63-0551
Walpurga 40			
SPOHR, Aug.	42	Lehe	66-0577
Johanna 41			
SPOHR, Gottlieb	22	Mitt.Fischbch	64-1053
Georg 18			
SPONHOLZ, Bertha	18	Rueban	64-1053
SPONHOLZ, Carl F.	49	Claushagen	64-0886
Marie Elisa. 42, Friedr. W. 16, W. Fr. 14			
Carl Fr. A. 19, Friederike A 11			
Herman Alb. 7, Albert Aug. 5			
Anna Marie 3, Marie Louise 9m			
SPOOHR, Caroline	29	Salzgitter	63-0953
Emma 6, Louis 2, Hermine 10, Bertha 31			
SPORE, Henriette	21	Unterstetten	66-0412
SPORER, Anna	59	Wuertemberg	66-0679
SPORK, Johann	26	Ostheim	66-0469
SPRADEL, Rosine	25	Grafenberg	66-0147
SPRADER, J.	23	Elwangen	63-1003
SPRECKELSEN, Dor.	22	Cappeln	65-0038
SPREEN, Wilhelmine	28	Luebeck	66-1203
SPREITZER, Paul	39	Offenbach	66-0109
SPRENGER, Anton	41	Missouri	63-0917
Sophie 22			
SPRENGER, Elisab.	26	Schwabendorf	63-0482
SPRENGER, Friedr.	46	Eickelborn	63-0917
Sophie 41, Anton 12, Caspar 10			
Antoinette 7, Joseph 5			
SPRENGER, Herman	26	Klosterholte	65-1095
Anna 18			
SPRENGER, J.	26	Hesse-Darmst.	64-0456
SPRENGER, Jacob	35	Ostringen	64-0433
SPRENGLER, Carl H.	44	Altenburg	65-1140
Ernestine 38, Robert 13, Alvin 10, Carl 7			
Franz 3, Max 9m			
SPRENGLER, Heinr.	26	Berghausen	66-1031
SPRENGLER, Louise	17	Egeln	63-0990
SPRETER, Xaver	16	Rothweil	66-1155
SPREYER, G.	23	Angenrod	64-0992
SPRICK, Louise	30	Dissen	65-0950
Anna 4m			
SPRICK, Mina	19	Beckhorst	65-0950
SPRING, Franz	30	Zeitz	66-0576
SPRING, Gottl.	23	Stuttgart	64-0495
SPRINGER, Hermann	17	Hirschburg	67-0007
SPRINGER, Lina	9	Hohenems	63-0953
SPRINGER, Marg.	56	Epplingen	64-0840
SPRINGER, Math.	17	Deitersweiler	65-0402
SPRINGER, Siegm.	29	Fuerth	64-0073
SPRINGER, Wilhelm	34	Osnabrueck	63-1069
SPRINGMANN, Johann	26	Hallwangen	66-0147
SPRINGMANN, Ludw.	23	Hannover	66-1243
SPRONSTY, Barbara	29	Ameikosit	67-0007
SPROTBAUM, Chr'tne	23	Iburg	65-0116
SPRUNGK, Bernhard	32	Philadelphia	63-0244
Josephine 25, Dorothy 3			

NAME	AGE	RESIDENCE	YR-LIST
SPRUNK, Lothar	53	Trier	63-0822
SPRUTE, Heinr.	45	Schonemack	64-0840
SPUCK, Begatha	59	Langenberghm.	65-1088
Cath. M. 32			
SPUDE, Rosalia	34	Berlin	66-1203
Rickchen 2			
SRIKA, Ignaz	16	Bersmen	67-0007
STAAL, Jenstt.	31	Copenhagen	66-0666
Christine 25			
STAAS, Johanna	20	Oster Cappeln	65-0950
STAATS, Caroline	20	Bremerhaven	64-0593
STAB, Dorothea	37	Unterlinach	66-0469
Anna Maria 10, Margaretha 9			
STABLEIN, Simon	20	Nordheim	63-0398
STACHLEY, Rh.	35	Milwaukee	63-1085
STACHLIN, Lorenz	32	Huttingen	65-0004
STACKMANN, Marie	20	Stadthagen	66-1127
Anna 16			
STADE, Wilhelm	20	Winden	67-0007
STADEMANN, Adolph	16	Geismar	64-0639
STADEN, Rosina	23	Aadorf	66-0984
STADEN, v. Diedr.	35	San Francisco	66-0984
Anna 28			
STADEN, v. Henry	16	Bremervoerde	63-0482
STADLER, Conrad	66	Wonsess	65-1024
Marg. 55, Barbara 16			
STADLER, John	38	Schmalkalden	66-1155
STADTFELDT, Elis.	30	Meiserich	63-1136
STADTLER, John	37	Altstaedten	63-1085
STAECKEL, Wm.	25	Basel	64-1053
STAEGLE, Leo.	19	Wyhl	64-0427
STAEHLE, Ernst	21	Jebbenhausen	65-0007
STAEHLI, Helene	25	Switz.	64-0170
Rosine 15, Joel 16, Jos. 10, Susette 9			
Jean 4			
STAEHLI, Jean	45	Switz	64-0170
Rosa 40, Sona 16, child 14, child 12			
child 10, child 9, child 1			
STAEHLI, Joel	22	Switzerland	64-0170
Lina 18			
STAEMMER, Theresia	17	Stoermede	64-0433
STAERK, Louise	22	Masskirch	63-0917
STAEUTERMANN, Joh.	26	Wellendorf	64-0938
STAFF, Franz	33	Deutschederit	66-0623
STAFFERSMANN, Els.	20	Almersloh	66-1031
STAFFREGEN, Carl	19	Lippstadt	66-1031
STAHE, Maria	34	Bayreuth	63-0752
Eleonore 5			
STAHL, (f)	35	Guetersloh	64-0427
STAHL, Balthasar	16	Moischeit	66-0623
STAHL, Carl	29	Jena	63-0398
STAHL, Ernestine	25	Hoboken	66-0734
STAHL, Ferd.	25	Madamuehle	64-0840
STAHL, Ferdinand	24	Madenmuehle	66-0221
STAHL, Friedr.	27	Alsheim	64-0138
STAHL, Geo.	40	Kronach	64-0495
Marg. 40, Cath. 7, Nata 5, Lorenz 11m			
STAHL, Gorg	65	Markstadt	64-0840
Christina 64			
STAHL, Jacob	18	Worms	64-0214
STAHL, Marg.	23	Vorstetten	63-0551
STAHL, Theodor	30	New York	64-0593
STAHL, Wilhelm	25	Baden	66-0221
STAHLBERG, Ferdin.	48	Germany	66-0666
Augusta 17			
STAHLHUT, Ernst	42	Stadthagen	66-1093
Sophie 28, Sophie 6, Marie 3, Ernst 3			
STAHLMANN, Ernst	23	Bielefeld	65-1030
STAHLMANN, Marie	21	Bielefeld	65-1030
STAHMER, Dietr.	23	Cloppenburg	65-0038
STAHOL, Caspar	36	New York	63-1136
STAIB, Conr.	20	Rissingen	64-0331
STAIB, Johann	14	Neckartenzlin	66-0734
STALLEY, Charles	25	Neumuenster	63-0693
STALLMANN, Regine	24	Oldenburg	65-1024
STALMANN, Heinr.	22	Eisbergen	64-0214
STALZER, Marie	37	Laibach	64-0687
Joseph 14			

NAME	AGE	RESIDENCE	YR-LIST
STAMM, Carl	30	Wuerzburg	66-0083
Catharine 26, Catharine 4, Adam 6			
Jacob 9m			
STAMM, Johanna	18	Schney	64-0639
STAMM, Joseph	17	Buke	65-0402
STAMM, Joseph	22	Ladenberg	64-0427
STAMM, Mary	42	Lancaster	63-0244
STANDEMEYER, Luise	20	Esslingen	65-1088
Meyer 26			
STANDFULD, Edmund	24	Pretford	66-1373
STANDINGER, Maria	26	Klagenfurth	65-1088
Heinrich 29			
STANDT, Georg	40	Riesenbeck	66-0679
Eva 45, Elisabeth 5			
STANFT, Ferdinand	34	Kupferzell	64-0885
STANG, Georg	19	Marburg	65-1088
STANGE, Julius	37	Leipzig	65-0007
STANGLER, Franz	45	Boehmen	63-0917
Rosa 42, Anna 16, Franz 21, Rosa 9			
Therese 6			
STAPENHORST, Fr'dr	15	Lengerich	66-0679
STAPENHORST, Jan	34	New York	66-0679
STAPENHORST, W'mne	18	Lengerich	64-0199
STAPNIKO, Wenzel J	46	Boehmen	66-0349
Marie 45, Friederike 1			
STAPP, Aug.	22	Biedenkopf	64-0687
STARF, Friedr.	21	Neuenstein	66-0704
STARK, Friederike	16	Unt.Weissbach	65-0151
STARK, Heinrich	50	Frankfurt a/m	66-1093
Louise 17, Robert 9			
STARK, J.H.	31	Wolchow	65-0402
STARK, Joh. Adam	18	Koengernheim	65-0243
STARK, Josefa	22	Beraun	66-1327
STARK, Joseph	19	Westhausen	66-1327
STARK, Matth.	42	Niederremmel	64-0427
Marie 30			
STARKE, Adolph	24	Jena	64-0687
STARKE, Gesine	21	Bremen	64-0920
STARKE, Regina	21	Bremen	66-0147
STARKLOFF, Carl	20	Weimar	64-1022
STARMANN, John	36	Boehmen	63-0917
Anna 24, baby (f)			
STARRY, Geo.	33	Boehmen	64-0495
STARSBERG, Aug.	24	Merlscheid	63-1010
Julius 20			
STATICK, Joh.	24	Flatow	65-0950
STAUB, Johann	20	Gelnhausen	66-0934
STAUBACH, Conrad	42	Herbstein	65-1024
Agathe 21, Lowa 19, Maria 15, Benedict 9			
Heinrich 8, Moritz 6			
STAUDEMEYER, Cath.	25	Stuttgart	65-0038
Wilhelm 9m			
STAUDENMAIER, Carl	26	Heidenheim	66-1031
STAUDT, G.(m)	50	Maubach	64-0331
STAUDT, Georg	28	Schwetzingen	64-0427
Johanna 25			
STAUDTE, Rob.	25	Kaina	65-0189
STAUFENBERG, Carl	16	Reichelsdorf	65-1031
STAUFFENBERG, Joh.	32	Riehelsdorf	66-1373
Magdalena 31, Magdalena 7, Johannes 5			
Anna 9m			
STAUTER, Barbara	34	Stambach	63-0244
John 16, Marg. 9, James 7, Elisabeth 27			
STAY, Maria	24	New York	63-1178
STEAZNER, Ernstine	26	Bennersdorf	67-0599
STEB, Franz Jos.	18	Bremen	66-1313
STECHMANN, Herm.	18	Mainburg	64-0432
STECHMANN, Val.	27	Streyda	64-0023
STECKENER, Moritz	19	Dreilingen	66-0221
STECKER, Joh. H.	39	Bremen	64-1053
Emilie 34, Fr. 7, Johanna 5, Elise 3			
STECKLING, Hermann	34	Guetersloh	64-0433
Catharina 13			
STECKMANN, Meta	24	Bastahl	66-0578
STECKMANN, Whl'mne	40	Greiz	64-1161
STECKMERT, Henry	19	Bramstedt	63-1136
STEDE, Ernst	38	Waldeck	66-1248
STEDTFELDT, Emil	33	Sulingen	64-0593

NAME	AGE	RESIDENCE	YR-LIST
Wilhelmine 31, Sophie 8, Heinrich 6			
Marie 4			
STEDTMEISTER, Ed.	52	Helmstedt	66-0934
STEEB, Georg	25	Engenhausen	66-0147
STEEFENS, Maria	15	Stade	63-0990
STEEGER, John	59	New York	66-0734
Friedrike 56			
STEEGMANN, J. Chr.	32	Stoevern	63-0482
STEEL, Michael	17	Hallwangen	66-0147
STEENBRINK, Wilhe.	16	Gutenberg	64-0992
STEENKAMP, H.	26	Asgerberg	66-0413
STEENKEN, A.	28	Montreal	65-0116
STEENLUND, Chr'tne	21	Helsingford	66-1031
STEEPPLER, Helene	25	Angersbach	65-0950
STEER, Bernh.	15	Brenken	66-0576
STEFFEK, James	18	Boehmen	63-0990
STEFFEN, Arnold	28	Bentheim	64-0904
STEFFEN, Franz	23	Gerdtshagen	66-0679
Sophie 23			
STEFFEN, G.	27	Luehling	66-0413
STEFFEN, Ivany	24	Northen	63-1085
STEFFEN, Jost.	29	Lundenroth	66-0413
STEFFENS, Cath.	30	Bremen	65-0594
Caroline 30, Augusta 23, Maria 19			
August 8, Louise 3, Robert 9m, Mathilde 5			
Minna 10m			
STEFFENS, Franzka.	26	Bremen	65-1088
Fritz 29, baby 10m			
STEFFENS, Gottfr.	25	Bremen	65-0243
STEFFENS, H.	20	Mittlung	66-0413
STEFFENS, Hch.	21	Achim	64-0363
STEFFENS, Joh Hch.	39	Neuhaus	64-0432
Meta 50			
STEFFENS, Johann	55	Moellenfeld	66-0984
Maria 55, Johann 24, Maria 22, Gerhard 20			
Adelheid 18, Hermann 15, Heinrich 8			
Margaretha 6			
STEFFENS, Wm.	23	Bremen	64-0427
STEGE, Diedr.	59	Lage	63-0953
Elisabeth 9			
STEGE, Juluis	25	Posen	66-0578
Ernestine 23			
STEGEMEIER, Diedr.	21	Brueninghast.	67-0806
STEGEMEIER, Steph.	55	Soeste	66-1128
Catharine 50, Catharine 22, Wilhelmine 17			
Hermann H. 14, Johann Fr. 7, Friedrich 3			
Christine 4			
STEGEMUELLER, Matt	31	Muenchen	66-1313
STEGER, Cath.	56	Elsleben	65-0007
STEGER, Wm.	21	Bramsche	66-0837
STEGERER, Wenzelin	21	Sulzen	63-1218
STEGMANN, Conr.	51	New York	63-0953
STEGMANN, Dorothea	32	Coeslin	66-1203
Sophie 9, Minna 8, Friederike 4			
Alwine 9m			
STEGMANN, Hermann	22	Stroehen	66-1031
Heinrich 18			
STEGMANN, J.(m)	19	Bremen	64-0331
STEGMANN, Johann	9	Driftsethe	66-1127
STEGMANN, Margaret	23	Heppenheim	65-0770
STEGMANN, Wilhelm	19	Waldeck	66-0934
STEGMANN, Wm.	27	Buchholz	66-0837
STEGMEIER, Friedr.	27	Stuttgart	64-0427
STEHL, Elise	48	Mohre	66-1203
Anna 22, Elisa 17			
STEHLE, Christ.	40	Neuenheim	66-1131
Friederike 38, Sophie 23			
STEHLE, Friedr.	20	Oberndorf	66-1155
Louise 20, baby 3m, Louise 20, baby 3m			
STEHLICH, Franzka.	24	Bohemia	64-0363
STEHLING, Liolea	21	Dermbach	66-0679
STEHMANN, Ignatz	18	Schapen	64-0687
STEHN, Heinr.	33	Otterendorf	67-0007
STEICK, J.	25	Waldkappel	65-1189
STEIDEL, Leopold	32	Constanz	64-0992
STEIDLER, P.	22	Hechingen	63-1136
STEIFFLER, Wil'mne	24	Stuttgart	67-0007
STEIGENWALD, Elis.	34	Sonderkahl	64-0023

NAME	AGE	RESIDENCE	YR-LIST
Johanna 21			
STEIGER, Elise	28	Limburg	64-0214
Wolff (f) 66			
STEIGER, Lucas	16	Poria	64-0886
STEIGER, Rud.	25	Uetka	64-0427
STEIGER, Sabine	14	Halbingen	64-0138
STEIL, Anna Maria	50	Belsheim	67-0599
Carl 23, Christina 20, Franz 15			
Nicolaus 5			
STEIL, Julius	19	Bremen	66-0221
STEIN, Adolph	27	Kremmer	67-0353
STEIN, Anton	21	Wuerttemberg	64-0687
STEIN, Barthold	29	Lenningen	64-1053
STEIN, C.	31	Melle	65-0974
STEIN, Carl	25	Hungen	66-0704
STEIN, Carl	35	Pesth	65-0974
STEIN, Cath.	39	Herford	63-0752
Herm. 5, Minna 4, Emilie 9			
STEIN, Catharine	22	Drammersheim	65-0004
STEIN, David	23	Brumgesheim	63-0350
STEIN, Doroth.	30	Brooklyn	64-0495
Heinr. 9m			
STEIN, Elis.	27	Oberahmen	64-0593
STEIN, Elisabeth	59	Beuern	63-1178
STEIN, Elise	35	Ob. Scharbach	66-1243
STEIN, Felix	21	Sondershausen	64-0782
STEIN, George	25	Herford	64-0593
STEIN, Gesine	20	Hannover	63-1218
STEIN, Gottl.	30	Torgau	67-0600
STEIN, H.	45	Neukirch	63-0752
STEIN, Hannchen	22	Geismar	64-0639
STEIN, J.	32	Berlin	64-0593
STEIN, J.	16	Brenngesheim	65-0007
STEIN, Jacob	24	Nonnweiler	64-0687
STEIN, Joseph	39	Louisville	66-0147
STEIN, Leopold	21	Baden	66-0734
STEIN, Mathias	32	Eitelborn	66-1203
STEIN, Max	21	Horb	66-1243
STEIN, Michael	19	Eschbach	67-0007
STEIN, Rebecca	26	Willmars	66-0704
STEIN, Ros.	36	Bohemia	64-0782
Anna 16, Emanuel 13, Nathan 11, Adolph 7			
Wm. 6, Hermann 15			
STEIN, Samuel	49	Terischau	64-0427
STEIN, Sara	17	Freudenthal	64-1161
Caroline 16			
STEIN, Simon	24	Thaleischweil	63-1136
STEINACKER, Ernstn	17	Hanau	65-0243
STEINBACH, Friedr.	25	Eisenach	64-1022
STEINBACH, Frz.	21	Weyda	64-0170
STEINBACH, Georg P	32	Baltimore	63-0917
Caroline 21, baby 11m			
STEINBECK, Anna	19	Neuenkirchen	63-0953
STEINBECK, Elisab.	17	Bremen	66-0837
STEINBECK, Franz	24	Dissen	67-0007
STEINBECKER, Heinr	18	Hannover	66-0984
STEINBERG, A.B.	51	Trappau	64-0687
STEINBERG, Georg	25	Dessigen	66-0413
STEINBERG, H.	28	Kl. Wilken	65-0594
STEINBERG, Pauline	25	Rawitsch	66-0984
STEINBERG, S.	24	Dehren	65-1189
STEINBERG, Sortina	29	Vlotho	64-0427
Eva 32, Phil. 6, Heinr. 9m, baby 6m			
STEINBERGER, Adam	30	Baltimore	63-0168
STEINBERGER, B.	57	Angenrod	66-0704
STEINBERGER, Georg	36	New York	63-0168
STEINBERGER, Marg.	27	Soden	66-1128
STEINBRECHER, Anna	16	Schoenstadt	64-0840
STEINBRECHER, Karl	17	Fritzlar	63-1069
Amalia 15			
STEINBRENNER, Adlf	17	Vahs	65-0151
STEINBRINK, Babett	58	Minden	63-0917
Emma 8			
STEINBRUCH, Christ	24	Koenigsbrunn	65-1030
STEINBUCK, (m)	24	Stettin	63-1038
STEINBURGER, Marie	26	Staubing	64-0427
STEINCKER, Marie	30	Leavenforth	63-0953
Anna 11m			

NAME	AGE	RESIDENCE	YR-LIST
STEINDLER, Simon	31	Nagi	65-0594
STEINEL, C.T.	14	Baden Baden	64-0495
STEINEL, Josephine	19	Oestringen	66-0109
STEINENBREY,	19	Boston	63-0244
STEINER Charlotte	65	Delischen	64-0938
STEINER, A.	36	Karlsbad	64-0495
STEINER, Abraham	17	Boehmen	63-0551
STEINER, Anna Mary	26	Tierbingen	64-0739
STEINER, Augusta	26	Baden	66-0147
STEINER, Chami	16	Boehmen	66-0704
STEINER, David	37	Holitz	67-0007
STEINER, Georg	30	Cincinnati	64-0687
STEINER, Johann	36	Martinszell	64-0593
STEINER, Joseph	55	Fronstetten	63-0296
Francisca 27, Josepha 19, Joseph 4			
Peter 9m			
STEINER, Julius	20	Reinerstadt	67-0795
STEINER, Kathi.	18	Hohenneuss	65-0243
STEINER, Ludwina	22	Rottach	64-0992
STEINER, Salomon	22	Ganaritz	66-0679
STEINER, Susanne	16	Grittlingen	66-1248
STEINER, Therese	40	Wels	66-1373
Leopold 5, Maria 4			
STEINERD, Johann	25	Altenstein	66-0346
STEINERS, H.	24	Asgerberg	66-0413
STEINERT, An Marie	23	Laetzendorf	66-0469
STEINERT, Johann	29	Pommern	66-0469
Bernhardine 27			
STEINERT, Th.	31	Binzen	65-0007
STEINERT, Wilh'mne	23	Schwarzenau	66-0578
STEINFELD, Friedr.	34	Altendorf	66-0576
Christine 29, Heinr. 3, Catharine 54			
STEINGRABER, C.	36	Sonneberg	66-1155
STEINGRAEBER, C.	33	Prussia	63-1003
John 18, Lewis 22, Christian 17, E. 34			
J. 8, H. 3			
STEINHAEUSER, Els.	24	Wittenberg	64-0593
STEINHAEUSER, Hch.	20	Heinebach	66-1203
STEINHAEUSER, Henr	47	Baltimore	63-0482
STEINHARD, Anna	18	Waldorf	64-0938
STEINHARD, Jette	24	Essenfeld	64-0782
STEINHARDT, Babett	26	Riegel	63-0917
STEINHARDT, Jette	34	Flouheim	65-0243
Caroline 65, Bertha 7, Siemon 5, Gusto 3			
Leo 2, Salomon 27			
STEINHAUER, Conrad	60	Weissel	65-0770
STEINHAUER, Friedr	48	Westphalen	66-0469
Caroline 47, Caroline 13, Heinrich 17			
Ernst 9, Louise 4			
STEINHAUER, Henry	27	New York	66-0109
STEINHAUER, Margar	21	Muenster	66-0576
STEINHAUS, Alex.	19	Breslau	65-0243
STEINHOF, Oscar	26	Madison	63-0821
Johanna 24			
STEINHOFF, Ernst	26	Moringen	63-0953
STEINHOFF, G.	31	Schoenhagen	66-0704
STEINHOFF, Gesine	28	Grappenbuhrin	64-1206
STEINHOFF, H.	15	Lehe	66-0577
STEINHOFF, H.C.(m)	31	New York	64-0331
Johanna 21			
STEINHOFF, Johanna	16	Wenjen	66-0650
STEINHOFF, William	22	Bishausen	63-0482
STEINHOLZ, Ed.	42	Philadelphia	63-0168
Anna 24			
STEINICKE, Maria	30	Sedlitz	64-0170
STEININGANS, Pet.	36	Bech	65-0402
STEINITZ, Math(f)	22	Schiefelbein	64-0495
Solma 9m			
STEINKAMP, Anna M.	25	Alsen	65-0898
STEINKAMP, C.H.	35	Ahls	65-1088
STEINKAMPF, J.	24	Willinghof	64-0782
STEINKE, Albert	32	Lurzmin	64-0433
Josephine 28, Catharina 7, Stanislaus 6			
Ladislaus 3, Johann 1			
STEINKE, Joh.	30	Arhaus	65-1030
STEINKE, Johann	42	Soessnowd	66-0469
Elisabeth 36, Anna 7, Mina 5, Emilie 9m			
STEINKE, Julius	32	Stangenfeld	66-0934
Anna 27, Augusta 4, Albert 2, Gustav 1			
baby bob			
STEINKEMPER, Franz	24	Westenholz	64-0433
STEINKUEHLER, Wm.	23	Hilter	66-1128
STEINLAGE, Arnold	25	Wersenbrueck	65-1031
STEINLAGE, Georg	25	Osnabrueck	66-0984
STEINLARZ, Franz	32	Mannheim	67-0007
STEINLE, Martin	26	Nordstetten	64-0331
STEINLEIN, Michael	37	Goldberg	65-0243
STEINLEIN, W.	24	Krautostheim	65-0055
STEINMANN, Carl	18	Hildburghsn.	66-1155
STEINMANN, Elisab.	46	Niedermiesau	66-0704
STEINMANN, Frd.	29	Braunschweig	64-0904
STEINMANN, Jacob	18	Heidelberg	66-0837
STEINMANN, Sophie	56	Schmedenstedt	63-0990
STEINMANN, Wilhelm	25	Gifhorn	64-1206
STEINMEIER, Anna	18	Lehe	67-0806
STEINMETZ, Caspar	26	Herleshausen	64-0739
STEINMETZ, Elisa	19	Rudisbronn	63-0013
STEINMETZ, Juliane	26	Herteshausen	64-0593
STEINMETZ, Louise	19	Elberfeld	66-0221
STEINMETZ, Michael	23	Schwebenried	66-0704
STEINMETZ, Wilhelm		New York	66-0576
STEINMEYER, Bertha	21	Bremerlehe	64-0885
STEINMEYER, Henr't	26	Brokhausen	67-0353
STEINNAGEL, Mina	16	Eschelsbrueck	64-0214
STEINSILBER, J.	22	Altdorf	64-1161
STEINSIPEN, Aug.	38	Hoechscheide	65-0151
STEINWARTZ, Ludwig	22	Horst	66-0934
STEINWEDE, Heinr.	38	Cincinnati	66-0984
Caroline 39			
STEINWEDEL, Bernh.	18	Ahrlingen	64-0170
STEINWEDEL, J.C.	30	Neubrandenbrg	63-1010
STEINWEG, Cathinka	20	Borgentreich	63-0551
STEINWEG, S.	52	Posentreich	63-0551
STEINWEG, Theod.	39	Braunschweig	64-0363
Anna 29			
STEINWENTER, Joh.	25	Wien	65-0243
STEITZ, Aug.	24	Missouri	63-0244
STEITZ, Fritz	20	Butzbach	66-1248
STEITZ, Heinrich	24	S. Francisco	63-1136
STEITZ, Johann	22	Rheinpfalz	66-0576
STELJES, Hermann	21	Scharmbeck	63-0693
STELLHORN, Carl	49	Prss. Muenden	66-1243
Elise 48, Caroline 14, Minna 8, Fritz 8			
STELLING, Caroline	31	Husum	65-0038
Wilhelmine 6, Heinrich 3			
STELLING, Caroline	17	Stolzenau	64-0363
STELLING, Fritz	21	Dorum	66-0704
Augusta 21			
STELLING, Heinrich	27	Niendorf	65-1095
STELLING, Johanna	20	Bremervoerde	66-0623
STELLING, Minna	17	Calumburg	64-0782
STELLING, P.H.	15	Otterndorf	64-0432
STELLJES, Carl	36	Vegesack	66-1243
Elise 31, August 3			
STELLJES, Diedr.	21	Frischersdorf	66-1243
STELZER, Johann	36	Bruch	66-1373
STEMAUER, Dominic	39	Orth	64-0138
STEMLER, Wm.	20	Hessen	64-0432
STEMME, Johann	26	New York	66-0934
STEMME, Martin	33	St. Louis	66-0934
STEMME, Wilhelm	28	Wenthal	66-0412
STEMMER, Therese	25	Sonderhart	63-1136
STEMMERMANN, Georg	16	Lingenfeld	67-0600
STEMMERMANN, Jurg.	62	Lehe	66-1327
Anna 50, Catharina 19			
STEMMLER, Gottfr'd	25	Mislen	67-0007
STEMMLER, Peter	24	Muelsen	67-0007
STEMPEL, Adolph	26	Sternsberg	63-1085
STEMPELMANN, H.	37	Zuerich	65-0151
STEMPF, Wm.	20	Carlsruhe	65-0116
STEMPFEL, Anna	19	Jena	64-0433
STEMSIEK, Anna	21	Essen	66-1127
Bertha 20, Louis 12			
STENAD, Matthias	36	Daberkreis/Bo	63-1010
Barbara 26, Alice 3, Anton 9m			
STENBECK, Johanna	20	Barmen	63-0862

NAME	AGE	RESIDENCE	YR-LIST
STENDEL, Johann	22	Bruecken	64-0363
STENDER, Minna	24	Neudorf	64-0904
STENGEN, Conrad	27	Schollkrippen	66-1327
STENGLE, Wilhelm	20	Oberensingn	66-1155
STENIGKE, Reinhold	27	Berlin	67-0353
STENTER, Dorette	19	Neudorf	63-1178
STENZEL, Caroline	19	Breslau	63-0015
STENZER, Georg	38	Braunschweig	66-0934
STENZIG, Heinr.	32	Hannover	65-0116
STENZIG, Maria	23	Hohenhameln	66-0679
STEPANEK, Wenzel	57	Bohemia	66-0469
Theresia 42, Mathias 19, Franz 18			
Jacob 17, Mathias 8			
STEPHAN, Carl	30	Markoldendorf	66-1155
STEPHAN, Casper	24	Groningen	67-0007
STEPHAN, Ferdinand	19	Roda	65-0116
STEPHAN, Fr.	21	Fritzlar	64-0593
STEPHAN, Friedrich	27	Flannhausen	66-1127
STEPHAN, H.	28	Brunslar	64-0665
Elisab. 22, Martin 5			
STEPHAN, Wm.	18	Zerwig	64-0840
STEPHANY, Chls.	28	Mainz	64-0495
STEPPACHER, Carol.	18	Noerdlingen	66-1203
STER, Xaver	42	Bachberg	63-1085
STERBEL, Catharine	40	Wimreuden	66-1203
Rosine 9			
STERN, Alex	24	Langendarmbch	64-0687
STERN, Amalia	32	Hartford	63-0482
July 4			
STERN, Amalie	22	Bayreuth	64-0938
STERN, David	18	Creuznach	64-0170
STERN, Emanuel	14	Gumbweiler	64-0495
D.(m) 16			
STERN, Emilie	18	Bergen	63-0168
STERN, Hanchen	21	Ziegenhain	66-1203
STERN, Hannchen	17	Habitzhain	64-0593
STERN, Heinr.	24	Ernstbach	64-0073
Rachel 18			
STERN, Helene	26	Westphalen	66-1031
STERN, Herm.	22	Alberndorf	64-1206
STERN, Hermann	31	Woldau	63-0917
STERN, Hirsch	17	Darmstadt	65-1088
Rosa 15, Amalia 14			
STERN, Isaac	59	Gemmden	64-0593
Front 47, Jacob 15, Sueskind 9			
Baetchen 7, Roeschen 4			
STERN, Isaac	16	Brakel	66-1093
Johanna 18			
STERN, Jacob	13	Hochberg	64-0938
STERN, Jette	24	Ulrichstein	65-0594
STERN, Johann	25	Gr.Bettlingen	66-1203
Friederike 23			
STERN, Johs.	19	Dietershausen	65-0402
Wm. Wigand 19			
STERN, Joseph	20	Sommerhausen	63-0168
STERN, Joseph	38	Budweiss/Hung	66-0837
STERN, Joseph	15	Gr. Hessen	66-0704
STERN, Joseph	39	Pest	66-1373
STERN, Julie	23	Duesseldorf	64-0170
STERN, L.	20	Eisenach	65-1024
STERN, Leopold	18	Niederklein	65-0594
STERN, Leser	24	Niederklein	64-0840
Herzog 19			
STERN, Lina	21	Ziegenhein	65-1031
STERN, Louis	21	Baiern	64-0214
STERN, Ludwig	16	Heddesheim	66-0984
STERN, M.	18	Homberg	63-1178
STERN, Marg.	27	Czarnikau	64-0363
STERN, Mayer	55	Mainzlar	64-0593
Jette 54, Rebecca 24, Sam. 18, Isaac 13			
Loebsommer 17			
STERN, Moses	17	Mellerich/Pr.	64-0920
STERN, Nathan	23	Wetzlar	66-0221
STERN, Rebecca	25	Rothenkirchen	64-0214
Salomon 18, Betty 21			
STERN, Rosa	16	Tachau	66-1031
STERN, Rosa	25	Eperies	65-0402
Moritz 3, Frdke. 10m			
STERN, Rudolph	17	Mannheim	66-0679
STERN, Salomon	17	Hannover	66-0734
Hannchen 20			
STERN, Sebastian	40	Dossenheim	64-0170
Barbara 29, Maria 20, Adolph 12			
Barbara 9, Erica 7, Anna 4			
STERN, Therese	19	Harburg	65-0594
STERN, Tobias	19	Oberasphe	64-0639
STERNBERG, Carl	18	Berlin	66-1155
STERNBERG, Gunter	31	Innsbruck	66-0734
STERNBERG, Lisette	26	Versmold	66-1327
STERNBERG, Moses	20	Koerbecke	63-0168
STERNBERG, v. Ert.	15	Cassel	66-0704
STERNE, David	29	Schluechtern	64-0886
STERNFELD, Albert	20	Labian	63-0990
STERNZEE, Ignatz	25	Polen	63-0953
STERZEL, Marie	40	Breslau	63-1010
Marie 16			
STESCH, Bertha	25	Breslau	65-1095
Max 1			
STETTHEIMER, James	41	New York	63-1136
Lina 27, Francis 7, James 4, Lewis 5			
Charles 3, Georg 1, Max 4m			
STEUB, Gustava	22	Elberfeld	64-0992
STEUBE, Johann	44	Rengshausen	63-1069
STEUBER, Johannes	28	Bronskirchen	64-1022
Marie 20, baby 6m			
STEUBER, Wilhelm	24	Eisenach	65-1140
STEUERBERG, Christ	24	Autendorf	66-0623
STEUERER, Anton	32	Wien	64-0073
STEUERMANN, Ferd.	24	Biblis	63-0482
STEUERNAGEL, Cath.	28	Eidorf	66-0412
STEUERNAGEL, Marie	28	Freiensel	64-0214
STEUERWALD, Adam	28	Heide	66-0083
Marie 25, Catharine 1, Elise 3m			
STEUNER, Albert	19	Ovenstedt	66-1093
Emilie 24			
STEVE, Berend	28	Dinklage	66-0984
STEVENS, Angela	22	Spahn	64-0938
STEYSKAL, Maria	26	Boehmen	66-0147
Sophia 5, Josef 11m			
STEYSKEL, Anton	29	Boehmen	64-0073
STIBBE, G.	42	Prussia	63-1003
K. 34, G. 10, O. 6, W. 2			
STICHT, Heinr.	22	Hannover	66-1313
STICKEL, Elisabeth	45	Brandoberndrf	63-1085
Dorothea 58, Gustav 34, Catharina 26			
Jean 3, William 10m, Christ. 20			
STICKEL, Joh.	26	Unterjessingn	64-0593
STICKEL, Johanna	24	Spielberg	66-1327
STICKHAR, A.	35	Braunschweig	65-1189
Minna 26			
STICKLE, Adam	41	Baltimore	63-1218
Therese 41			
STICKLING, Heinr.	31	Verl	64-1022
Marg. 32, Conr. 7, Heinr. 5, Elisab. 3			
Anna 6m			
STICKRATH, Cath.	22	Waldangelbach	64-0073
STICKRATH, Wiegand	26	Cassel	65-0865
STIEBEL, Sophie	23	Lengsfeld	64-0938
STIEBELING, Conr.	30	Hessen	64-0432
Anna Elis. 24, Maria 9m			
STIEFEL, Carl	27	Blautzenloch	66-1203
Caroline 32, Carl L. 8m			
STIEFEL, Joh.	28	Unterheimbach	64-0427
STIEFEL, Karl	28	Unterheimbach	63-1069
STIEFEL, Moses	16	Vockerode	63-0551
STIEFVATER, Jos.	21	Ehrenstetten	64-0138
STIEGELMEIER, Marg	31	Kuppingen	65-0243
Margarethe 1, Johann 35			
STIEGER, Hedweg	26	Kugelmalt	63-1085
STIEGLER, Francois	30	Strassburg	63-0990
STIELER, Clara	22	Annaberg	66-1373
STIELER, Daniel	20	Magdeburg	66-1127
STIENKER, Chr.	30	Rahden	65-1088
Caroline 26, Dorothea 20, Sophie 8			
Dorothea 26			
STIER, C.H.	19	Sonneburg	65-0974

NAME	AGE	RESIDENCE	YR-LIST
STIERER, Mrs.	31	Bremerhafen	64-0073
Anna 7, Emma 5, baby 1			
STIETZ, Catharine	23	Dezenrode	66-1248
STILKENBOHM, Jean	24	Nordgeorgsfhn	66-1031
Gretje 22			
STILLER, Johann	43	Darmstadt	67-0992
Catharine 34, Johann 4, Elisabeth 6m			
STILLGER, Adam	27	Villmar	67-0007
STILTGER, Guillaum	30	France	63-0953
STING, Friedr.	20	Balingen	65-0007
STING, Gottlieb	27	Kirchheim	64-0427
STIR, Henry	34	Cincinnati	63-0953
wife 30, Julie 9, Emma 5			
STIRM, David	24	Rudersberg	64-0199
STIRN, Anna	23	Dielershausen	66-1248
STISSER, Christian	40	Clausthal	64-0886
Emilie 38, Philipp 16, Wilhelm 14			
Mathilde 7, Augusta 5, Meta 2			
STOCK, August	29	Kaldorf	66-0412
Florentine 21, August 6m			
STOCK, Bernhard	16	Orb	66-1327
Alex 32			
STOCK, Casp.	25	Rixfeld	65-0950
STOCK, Catharina	24	Maiches	64-0456
STOCK, Christine	21	Hannover	64-0432
STOCK, Conrad	15	Alzey	63-1136
STOCK, Engelke	48	Mordorf	66-0668
Caroline 38, Wilhelmine 12, Wilhelm 7			
STOCK, Friedrich	33	Bremen	66-0984
STOCK, Heinr.	48	Ludwigshafen	66-1155
STOCK, Louise	26	Walldorf	67-0007
STOCK, Maria	26	Herbolzheim	66-1093
STOCK, S.	27	Kirchheide	66-0413
Emilie 20			
STOCK, Wilh.	21	Flacht	64-0214
STOCK, Wilhelm		Warsingfehn	66-0412
STOCK, Wilhelmine	25	Altenbruch	64-0992
STOCKEL, Engelbr.	30	Trebnitz	64-0886
STOCKER, Chr.	24	Cuelk	65-0713
STOCKER, Constant.	26	Wahlwies	67-0007
STOCKERT, Joh.	37	Homburg	67-0795
Christ (f) 45, Wilhelm 13, Elisabeth 10			
Catharina 6, Eva 1			
STOCKERT, Leonh.	29	Deydon	63-0862
John 25, Eva Cathre. 26, Leonh. 11m			
Georg 17			
STOCKFISCH, Heinr.	16	Osterbruch	66-1127
STOCKINGER, Berth.	25	Kapperodeck	63-0244
STOCKKAMP, F.	26	Loquard	64-0331
Johanna 21			
STOCKKAMP, Wilh.	29	Versmold	65-0950
Heinrich 36			
STOCKLE, Marie	57	Leonberg	64-1022
STOCKLER, Anna	19	Marburg	64-0886
STOCKMANN, Ant. F.	24	Greiz	63-0482
STOCKMANN, Christ.	20	Speyer	65-0116
STOCKMANN, Gustave	27	Ortrand	66-0412
STOCKMEYER, C.	21	Bremen	63-1136
STOCKMEYER, Heinr.	31	Bardert	66-1248
STOCKROTH, Carolne	29	Birkenfeld	64-0170
STODDARD, A.H.	24	Paris	63-0168
STOEBER, Pauline	21	Obermeter	65-1030
STOEBERANDT, Marie	16	Nienburg	64-1022
STOECKENBRINK, Ann	20	Varensell	66-1203
STOECKER, Ana Mary	20	Rodenburg	66-0578
STOECKER, Carl	36	Helgenbach	64-1206
Caroline 30			
STOECKER, Cornelis	38	Wesseling	63-0917
STOECKER, Maria	23	Roemershausen	66-0984
Eduard 16			
STOECKICHT, Heinr.	20	Goettingen	63-0006
STOECKMANN, David	32	Prussia	63-0822
Louise 38, Jacob 9, Marie 2			
Wilhelmine 20, Anna 17			
STOEHR, Cath.	25	Bunde	64-0073
STOEHR, Christ.	31	Feuerbach	64-0687
STOEHR, Christ.	20	Freudensdorf	64-0782
Joseph 39, J. 39			
STOEHR, Conrad	30	Altmarschen	66-0623
Anna Cath. 26, Dorothea 12, Hermann 6m			
STOEHR, Georg	24	Dingfeld	66-0576
STOEHR, Louis	26	Elschesheim	66-1131
STOEHR, Marie	22	Wuertemberg	63-0822
STOEHR, Moritz	28	Eggolsheim	63-0693
STOELL, Catharina	16	Langgoens	64-1108
Wilhelmine 7			
STOELPING, Ernst	24	Rotenburg	66-1031
STOELTING, Herm.	26	Zellerfeld	65-0594
STOEPEL, August	27	Wieken	66-1093
STOERINGER, Fritz	19	Wildbad	66-0984
STOERMER, Henr'tt.	14	Oetinghausen	66-1093
STOERMER, Lorenz	56	Suhl	65-1088
Lisette 52, Emilie 16, August 2			
STOERZ, Christian	32	Floezlingen	64-0687
Barbara 42, Maria 36, Catharina 35			
STOESSEL, F.	22	Eisenach	65-0974
STOETZEL, Antonia	19	Oelsnitz	65-0898
STOEVER, Gretchen	15	Wanne	63-0693
STOEVER, Hermann	20	Leeste	66-0650
STOEVER, Johann	21	Riede	66-1031
STOEVESANDT, Lenor	30	Hannover	65-1088
STOFENER, F.	18	Elverdissen	64-0782
STOFFERS, Caroline	19	Altenbruch	66-0837
STOFFREGEN, Carl	24	Evensch	64-0593
Ernst 15			
STOFFREGEN, Gustav	20	Hannover	64-0904
STOGEMOELLER, Frd.	59	Markendorf	64-0433
Heinrich 21, Carl 17, Marie 15			
Wilhelm 13, Margarethe 8, Catharina 8			
Caroline 6			
STOHLER, Marg.	50	Basel	65-0189
STOHR, Gustav	23	Prussia	63-0296
STOLAR, Johann	20	Bohemia	64-0363
STOLBERG, Max	27	Langensalz	64-0456
Joh. Maria 28			
STOLL, Carl	18	Bitz	65-1024
STOLL, Eva Cath.	21	Wallrode	66-0623
STOLL, Friedr.	29	Weilheim	64-0363
STOLL, Georg	64	Reichenbach	64-0170
Barb. 32, Friederike 5, Doroth. 3, Eva 25			
STOLL, Georg	31	Nidda	65-1030
STOLL, Gustav	29	Kirchheim	66-1313
STOLL, Heinrich	24	Zeisenhausen	66-0679
STOLL, Joh.	38	Reichenbach	64-0170
STOLL, Joh.	58	Lauterbach	63-0398
Elisabeth 17			
STOLL, John G.	27	Unteraichen	63-1136
STOLL, John J.	34	Weingarten	63-0551
STOLLE, Emma	22	Oldenburg	63-0296
STOLLE, Heinrich	25	Detmold	66-1127
STOLLE, Sophie	28	Hannover	66-1131
STOLLMANN, M.	32	New York	63-0862
STOLTE, Diedr.	28	Rohrsen	64-0739
Marie 30, Louise 3, Heinr. 11m, Marie 17			
Heinr. 12, Henriette 10			
STOLTING, Lisette	21	Soegel	65-1024
STOLTZ, C.	14	Mergentheim	64-0992
STOLZ, A.C.(m)	22	Bodenteich	64-0363
STOLZ, Heinrich	21	Neuenstadt	66-0576
STOLZ, Johanna	16	Holzmaden	65-0974
STOLZ, Philipp	16	Meissenheim	63-1136
Henriette 18			
STOLZ, Seb.	26	Camberg	64-0214
STOLZE, Louis	51	Philadelphia	66-0934
STOLZENBERG, John	33	Otterndorf	64-0639
STOLZENBURG, P.(m)	10	Steinau	64-0495
STONELMANN, A.Mar.	22	Theilfingen	66-0837
STOPPERT, Joseph	24	Arnsberg	64-1206
STOPS, Carl	38	Merseburg	66-0679
STORCH, Christian	28	Waesungen	66-0679
STORCH, Franz	18	Bensen	67-0599
STORCH, John	21	Tiefenort	63-1178
STORCH, V.(m)	36	Eisenach	64-0331
Marie 31			
STORCK, Agnes	26	Anspach	66-1155
STORCK, Johs.	30	Bernstadt	64-0782

NAME	AGE	RESIDENCE	YR-LIST
Elise 25, Catharine 3, Jog. 60 Elisab. 58			
STORDTMANN, Jurg.B	18	Lesum	64-0885
STORER, E.	46	London	63-0551
wife 35, child 4, child 2			
STORET, J.D.	17	Bunte	64-0495
STORK, Francis	25	Hermersberg	63-0296
STORK, Joh. Georg	20	Widdershausen	64-0433
STORK, Peter	28	Hermersberg	63-0296
STORKAMP, F.H.	24	Asgerberg	66-0413
STORM, Johann	37	Flachslanden	64-0739
STORM, Wilhelm	34	Hagenow	66-0668
Ulrike 34, baby (f) 9m, Franz 4 Mathilde 2, Marie 21			
STORRE, H.	38	Baltimore	63-1136
STORTZER, Baltazar	26	Sachsen Gotha	66-0221
STORZ, John	37	Philadelphia	63-0168
Sophie 38, Gustav 2			
STOSS, Adolph	46	Boehmen	66-0349
Cath. 13, Charles 9, Wolf 8, James 5 Caroline 1, Emilie 3			
STOSS, W.	19	Wuertemberg	66-0413
STOSSBERG, August	34	Lennep	66-1031
Laura 24, Laura 3m			
STRAASS, Aug.	26	Schlusselburg	63-0398
STRAATMANN, Carl	16	Bremerlehe	64-0432
STRACH, Heinrich	20	Cassel	65-0770
STRACK, Magdalena	17	Muenster	64-1053
STRACK, Vincent	30	Oberweier	63-0244
STRACKER, Jac.	20	Binau	64-0331
STRACKHEIN, Heinr.	27	Wunderthausen	65-0402
Marie 25			
STRACOWSKY, Carl	27	Boehmen	63-0398
STRADTNER, Johann	27	Diedenhofen	66-0734
Georg 25			
STRAECKER, Georg	14	Ruetfort	66-0576
Catharine 57, Catharine 17			
STRAEHLE, Joh. Jac	26	Durnau	63-0917
STRAETJER, Hermann	21	Dissen	23-0865
STRAHLMANN, Chr.	47	Oldenburg	64-0343
STRAIBLE, Conrad	25	Schernbach	63-0296
Math. 17			
STRAKA, Anna	55	Boehmen	66-0147
STRAKA, John	47	Boehmen	64-0782
Anton 16			
STRANAD, Wenzel	43	Stradernitz	65-0038
Anna 41, Joseph 20, Barbara 9, Thomas 3			
STRANGE, Edwin	55	New York	66-0147
Josephine 54			
STRANGMAN, Pauline	15	Alexandria	63-0862
STRANKMEYER, Heinr	29	Lemfoerde	65-0948
STRASBURGER, W.	30	Coburg	64-0593
STRASSBURG, August	21	Bremen	63-0917
STRASSBURGER, Malc	18	Lautershausen	63-1178
STRASSBURGER, Mary	14	Lahr	66-0934
STRASSENFISCHER, T	27	Muenster	66-0576
STRASSER, Justus	22	Micheldorf	66-0221
STRASSER, Ulrich	27	Benken	63-0551
Anna 25, Ulrich 9m			
STRATEMEIER, Fr'dr	52	Iowa	63-1069
STRATEMEYER, C.H.	21	Hellern	65-0898
STRATEMEYER, Ernst	15	Markendorf	64-0920
Louise 12, Clara Elis. 25			
STRATEMEYER, Ernst	17	Osnabrueck	67-0600
Caroline 4			
STRATEMEYER, Soph.	20	Steinheim	63-0053
STRATHMANN, Heinr.	29	Herringhausen	63-0168
STRATHMANN, Wilh.	17	Hagenow	66-0668
STRATHOFF, G.	19	New York	63-0693
STRATMANN, August	17	Beleche	66-0346
STRATMANN, Gert.	37	Herringhausen	63-0917
Therese 31, Gertrud 59, Henry 4, baby 1			
STRATMANN, Lisette	3m	Detmold	66-1203
STRATZ, August	23	Baden	66-0109
STRAUB, Adam	16	Brick	63-0244
STRAUB, Chr.	20	Lienzingen	65-1189
STRAUB, Georg	26	Preussen	66-0221
Ludw. 23			
STRAUB, Heinr.	36	Wasseralfingn	65-1030
Sirene 34, Robert 14, Richard 10 Adolph 9, Anna 7, Casper 6, Rudolph 3 Marie 4, Friedrich 2			
STRAUB, Joh. Pap.	50	Brueckenau	63-0244
Antonia 44, Anne 13, P. 28, C. 8, D. 5 A. 2			
STRAUB, Johanna El	52	Sax.-Meiningn	64-0432
Elisab. 14, Emma 9, Friederike 7			
STRAUB, Ludwig	29	Hessia	66-0412
STRAUB, Peter	21	Buerkhardt	64-0593
STRAUBE, Fr.	23	Furra	67-0600
STRAUBEL, Albin	26	Dresden	66-0147
STRAUBEL, Henriett	29	Saalfeld	66-0469
STRAUBER, Franz	30	Querfurt	64-0687
STRAUCH, Carl	36	Oberensingen	66-0734
STRAUCH, Johannes	43	Gaismieden	65-1095
STRAUS, Adolph	16	Pilsen	64-0920
STRAUS, Johannes	26	Cassel	64-0593
STRAUSKY, Barbara	19	Rielo	66-1131
STRAUSS, Anna	51	Boehmen	64-0687
Eva 18			
STRAUSS, Benjamin	18	Grambach	64-0687
STRAUSS, David	17	Niederstetten	63-1136
STRAUSS, Elise	32	Koenigsberg	65-1088
STRAUSS, Emil	25	Heilbronn	66-0147
STRAUSS, Felix	56	Steier	63-0953
STRAUSS, Franz	22	Beerwalde	66-1155
STRAUSS, Friedr.	18	Dedendorf	63-0168
STRAUSS, Hanna	68	Langenselbach	64-0938
STRAUSS, Hanna	26	Leichtersbach	65-0007
STRAUSS, Hannchen	54	Bierstadt	63-0953
STRAUSS, Henriette	16	Manburg	64-0992
STRAUSS, Isaac	25	Dolgenheim	65-0151
STRAUSS, Isaak	23	Ammenburg	65-0770
STRAUSS, Jac.	25	Wittlich	64-0782
STRAUSS, Joh. Gg.	24	Mettingen	65-1031
STRAUSS, Joseph	25	Basel	66-0679
STRAUSS, Julius	28	Geisleheim	66-0934
STRAUSS, Juluis	21	Buerstadt	63-0953
Regine 17, James 12			
STRAUSS, Lazarus	32	Kronach	64-1108
Minna 28, Lucia 2, baby 7m			
STRAUSS, Leopold	21	Cronberg	65-0594
STRAUSS, Lippmann	20	Altenaslau	64-0214
STRAUSS, Marie	53	New York	63-0821
STRAUSS, Martin	25	Sonnerstadt	66-1031
STRAUSS, Moses	18	Bodenheim	65-0151
STRAUSS, Raphael		Mt. Morrisch	63-0693
STRAUSS, Regina	59	Rohrbach	64-1108
STRAUSS, Rosalie	21	Markelsheim	63-0693
STRAUSS, Salomon	19	Niederwurzen	64-0639
STRAUSS, Sara	20	Kirchheim Bol	64-0138
Simon 18			
STRAUSS, Simon	16	Niederwiesen	66-0984
Regina 16			
STRAUSS, Sophie	22	Dedesdorf	63-0953
STRAUT, Philipp	30	Hamelroth	64-0433
STRAYBAL, Mart.	34	Apolda	64-0992
STRECK, Dorothea	43	Lengers	66-0668
baby (f) 10m, Ernest 9, Peter 6 Gretchen 7			
STRECKER, Daniel	17	Grossenaspach	64-0170
Carl 19			
STRECKER, Edward	23	Alsfeld	64-1206
Wilhelmine 19			
STRECKER, Gottl.	24	Rabensville	64-0138
STRECKER, Heinr.	17	Sollingen	64-0138
STRECKFUSS, P.	25	Lauterbach	64-1161
baby			
STRECKHAHN, Marie	19	Unen	64-0138
STREHLEN, Carl	35	New Yord	66-0734
Marie 30, Carl 6, Alfred 11m			
STREHLOW, Ferdin'd	35	Pommern	63-0614
Emma 28, Maria 3, Therese 2m			
STREHLOW, Robert	21	Peoria	63-0821
STREIB, Carl	24	Unt.Vorschutz	66-0109
STREIB, Sebastian	30	Moesingen	63-0296

NAME	AGE	RESIDENCE	YR-LIST
Agnes 30, Martin 3, Rosine 1			
STREICH, Carl	27	Ebingen	66-1155
Marie 26, Carl Fr. 4m			
STREICH, Gottlieb		Uebingen	66-1243
STREIDINGER, Carol	19	New York	64-0593
STREINER, Christ.	57	Wuertenberg	66-0704
Rosine 23, Gottlieb 9m			
STREINER, Philipp	40	Sonneberg	64-0885
STREIT, Eduard	18	Sontheim	66-0650
STREIT, v. Matilda		Bonn	66-0984
STRELAU, Johann	37	Konitz	64-0739
Emilie 28, Carl 5, Augusta 4, Paul 1			
Anna 6m			
STREMMING, Friedr.	18	Westphalen	66-0469
STRESSE, J.(m)	36	New York	64-0363
STRESSER, Cathrine	59	Ostweiler	64-1108
STRETZ, Anton	34	New York	63-0097
Sophie 31			
STREUTER, Joh Hch.	23	Buer	64-0920
STREWAN, Ignatz	31	Boehmen	66-0349
Robert 10, Eugen 5			
STRICHOW, Martin	50	Hagenow	66-0668
Friederike 43, baby (m) 5m, Wilhelm 17			
Bertha 4, Emilie 2			
STRICKER, F.F.	30	Reselage	64-0593
STRICKER, Franz	18	Rothenfelde	64-0593
STRICKER, Jacob	18	Gundersheim	64-0214
STRIEBECK, Wm.	23	Kettwig	63-1038
STRIETELMAYER, Wm.	20	Lienen	63-0862
STRIETHORST, Casp.	40	Varensell	66-1203
STRIKKER, Louise	18	Greifswald	63-1038
STRIPPEL, Conrad	28	Eisenach	66-1127
STROBACH, Johann	36	Schoenau	66-1373
Anton 40			
STROBEL, Aug.	24	Ziegenhausen	64-0427
STROBEL, Theod.	26	Heimstetten	63-0296
STROBEL, Wilh.	28	Wuertemberg	66-0469
STROCKA, Moritz	28	Tetschen	66-0984
STRODBAUM, Daniel	42	Hardewinkel	65-0116
STRODICK, Hinr.	23	Boke	65-0948
STRODT, Anna M.	27	Tecklenburg	64-0886
STRODTMANN, Minna	30	Versmold	65-0950
STROEBEL, Georg	18	Lauf	66-0576
STROEGEL, Gabriel	30	Breitenbach	66-0412
STROEKER, Caroline	38	Buhr	65-0974
Marie 7			
STROELE, Friedr.	18	Coersbach	66-0984
STROEMER, Hch.Euk.	17	Esens	66-1128
STROENING, Louis	33	Wittringen	66-0578
Dorothea 42, Carl 7, Ewald 5, Emma 4			
Pauline 1			
STROGBEL, Marg. C.	54	Wustenselbitz	64-0687
STROHAECKER, Magd.	18	Stetten	66-0083
STROHBACH, Carl	30	Merseburg	66-0576
STROHBACH, Joh. G.	22	Opfingen	67-0806
STROHEIDE, Heinr.	21	Versmold	65-0950
STROHFUSS, Anna	27	Boehmen	63-0752
STROHHACKEN, Magd.	31	Steeden	63-1010
Christine 7, Friedr. 2, Louise 9m			
Louis 30			
STROHM, Chr.	48	Trostingen	64-0495
E.(m) 45			
STROHM, Elise	29	Trottingen	64-0363
Johann 20			
STROHM, Philippine	23	Virlach	64-0073
STROHMAKER, E.(m)	20	Esslingen	64-0331
STROHMEYER, August	20	Yebes	66-0083
STROHMEYER, Carol.	30	Aumund	64-0739
Elisabeth 26			
STROHMEYER, Conrad	65	Schmahlnbruch	65-0713
STROM, Jacob	20	Trostingen	63-0990
STROMBERG, David	23	Seligenstadt	64-0073
STROPP, Wilhelm	20	Versmold	66-1127
STROSS, Salomon	20	Schoenlinde	66-0984
STROSSNER, Jos.	29	Eppingen	65-1030
Rika 19, Moritz 9m			
STROYCK, v.d. Anna	20	Debstedt	66-1203
STRUBE, Theodor	28	New York	63-0398

NAME	AGE	RESIDENCE	YR-LIST
STRUBEL, Cath.	19	Iggelheim	64-0023
STRUCKER, Therese	22	Waldersdorf	66-0734
STRUCKERT, Georg	25	Umstadt	65-0189
STRUCKHOFF, Becka	15	Moorsum	65-0243
STRUCKMANN, Carol.	25	Schneeren	65-0948
STRUCKMANN, De.(f)	18	Bolschle	64-0992
STRUCKMEYER, Fr'dr	24	Behren	66-1203
STRUCZ, Rebecca	20	Heddesdorf	66-0576
STRUEKENBERG, Mina	25	Vechta	66-1031
STRUENKEL, F.(m)	14	Fallingbostel	64-0495
STRUEWER, Joseph	28	Mauritz	66-1155
STRUM, Ernst	36	Mainz	64-1161
STRUMPF, Adolf	22	Culm	65-1095
STRUMPF, Charlotte	22	Laengsfeld	66-0734
STRUMPF, P.	22	Wien	63-0752
STRUMPF, Wilhelm	24	Weiler	66-1248
STRUNK, Johann	19	Steinau	66-1248
STRUNZ, Albrecht	56	Hof	63-1069
STRUNZ, Gustavus	26	Philadelphia	64-0593
STRUPEL, Joh.	42	Boehmen	63-0398
Anna 36, Joh. 13			
STRUSCH, Marie	13	Zuerich	66-0576
STRUVEN, Cath.	18	Bremen	65-0402
STRYDORP, V.(m)	29	Belgium	64-0495
(f) 24			
STUBBE, Henry	13	New York	63-0990
STUBBE, Marie A.	58	Twistringen	63-1038
STUBBE, Martin W.	23	Pommern	66-0469
Friederike 22			
STUBBE, Wilhelm	44	Gabatke	65-0770
Gustav 2, Caroline 43, Amanda 3m			
Wilhelm 18, Caroline 16, Ludwig 13			
August 9, Bertha 7			
STUBBEMANN, Luder	33	Storhausen	64-0363
STUBE, Cath. Elise	29	Steinke	66-1248
STUBENHEBER, Georg	34	Darmstadt	64-1053
STUBENRANCH, Henr.	36	Berreshausen	63-1069
Jakob 13, Mathias 16			
STUBENRAUCH, Joh'a	18	Karlshafen	63-1069
STUBENS, Jacob	18	Arnsheim	64-0840
STUBER, Henry	22	Ihlsfeld	63-0482
Regine 30, Friedr. 11m			
STUBER, Louise	22	Gruenstadt	66-0704
STUBINGER, Hch.	66	Melkendorf	64-0331
Johanna 21			
STUCKEL, Georg	37	Jatschamneck	63-0053
STUCKEL, Joh.	20	Sodendorf	64-0665
STUCKENBERG, A.N.	20	Luedingworth	64-0363
STUCKENBERG, Wilh.	21	Thiene	66-1093
STUCKENBURG, Heinr	28	Vechta	63-0953
STUCKENDROETZ, Mar	26	Holzhausen	64-0840
STUCKMANN, E.	22	Lippe-Detmold	65-1031
STUCKWIESER, Heinr	24	Hunteburg	67-0007
STUDE, H.(m)	23	Illinois	64-0331
STUDER, Loseli	23	Reinfelden	65-1088
Hermine 5, Elise 3			
STUDT, Caroline	22	Schargen	66-0679
STUEBBE, Cath.	19	Muenster	25-0950
STUEBBE, Eleonora	15	Harpenfeld	66-0221
Johann 19			
STUEBEL, Roeschen	20	Langenschwanz	63-0917
STUEBNER, August	19	Hellmarshsn.	66-0734
STUECKLE, Wilh'mne	33	Ulm	63-0168
STUECKLIN, Cath.	40	Freudenstadt	65-0950
STUECKRATH, Just.	33	Ronsdorf	67-0795
Elisabeth 29, Anna Martha 3m, August 3m			
Anna 23			
STUEHLER, Conrad	19	Hessen	63-0822
STUEHRENBERG, Frd.	18	Rottinghausen	64-0214
STUEMPEL, Joh. Ger	30	Plautime	64-0938
STUENKEL, Maria	21	Borg	64-0593
STUENKEL, William	25	Stoeckel	63-1136
STUER, Carl	27	Kepersheim	67-0007
STUERENBERG, Dina	27	Rottinghausen	64-0593
Elisab. 26			
STUERKE, Sophie	16	Hannover	64-0432
STUERKEN, August	14	New Orleans	63-1038
STUERKEN, Gesche	10	Lensing	63-0693

NAME	AGE	RESIDENCE	YR-LIST
STUERKEN, Johann	18	Koehlen	66-0934
STUERKEN, Johanna	20	Dorum	66-0083
STUERMER, Barbara	18	Aschaffenburg	66-0837
STUERMER, Caroline	21	Muenchen	63-0990
STUERMER, Joh.	36	Frankfurt	65-0948
STUERMER, Salomon	40	Pittstown	66-0679
Valleria 30			
STUESS, Theodor	19	Asch	64-0639
STUEVE, Elv.	27	Rahden	65-1095
STUEVEL, Grete	41	Wengsel	66-0734
Gesche 15			
STUEVER, Henriette	39	Mandelbeck	65-0948
STUEWE, Aug.	40	Prussia	63-1003
baby 6m, C. 30			
STUEWEN, Christine	34	New York	66-0984
Wilhelmine 6, Eduard 4, Anna 7, Marie 8m			
STUHL, Ferd.	21	Geisslingen	64-0427
STUHL, Joseph	24	Philadelphia	63-0015
STUHLMANN, Caspar	31	Wetter	65-1088
STUHLMANN, F.(m)	15	Detmold	64-0331
STUHRHAHN, Ernst	47	Aspe	63-1010
Henriette 35, August 18, Hermann 15			
Henriette 16, Leopold 13, Wilhelmine 10			
Pauline 6, Carl 9m, Johanna 4			
STUHRHANN, Johann	57	Walldorf	67-0007
Justine 58			
STUHRS, Wilhelm	25	Rinzeln	67-0007
STULZEL, Albert	19	Aasen	67-0007
STUMM, Wm.	18	Dukenschild	64-0782
STUMME, Ernst	25	Harzgerode	65-0898
STUMME, Theodor	24	Ndr.Sachswerf	65-0004
STUMMEL, Sybilla	18	Guentersblum	66-1093
STUMP, Juliane	15	Lautlingen	66-1327
Rosalie 41			
STUMPE, Adolph	19	Pr. Minden	66-1127
STUMPE, Heinrich	15	Dissen	66-1128
STUMPE, Wilh.	20	London	63-0168
STUMPF, Ferdinand	20	Ostheim	66-0650
Friederike 24, Karl 6m			
STUMPF, Franz	16	Bachern	63-1136
STUMPF, Georg H.	27	Bavaria	63-0822
Margarethe 22, Cunigunde 5m			
STUMPF, Lisette	29	Washington	66-0623
Catharina 26			
STUMPF, Robert	20	Braunschweig	66-0147
STUNKEL, A.(f)	23	Fallingbostel	64-0495
STUNTEBECK, Carl J	29	Steinfeld	66-0623
Marie 24			
STUNZ, Carl	38	Bodenfelde	65-0974
Louise 35, Friedrich 16, Maria 14			
Georgine 4, Charles 6m			
STURBAUM, Elisabet	27	Stadtlohn	66-1127
STURKE, G.H.	35	New York	63-1178
STURM, Alois	35	Wittlislingen	67-0007
STURM, Elise	22	Aalfeld	66-0577
STURM, Joseph	23	Baden	66-0147
STURM, Margaretha	18	Baden	66-0147
STURM, Paul	29	Freudenstadt	64-1108
STURM, Robert	27	Indianapolis	63-1178
A. 33, Malvina 22, Cath. 58, Henriette 8			
Fritz 3m			
STURM, Valentin	26	Planekstadt	63-1178
STUSSDT, Herm.	18	Horste	64-0073
Heinr. 20			
STUSSMEYER, Minna	20	Heinsen	66-1155
STUTEMUND, Louis	50	Bremen	64-0885
STUTENBERG, Fritz	22	Hannover	66-1155
STUTTERER, Georg	28	Affenburg	63-0296
Elisabeth 26			
STUTTWOLD, R.	24	Jever	63-0752
STUTZ, Mathilde	26	Seimen	63-0953
STUTZMANN, C.	28	Baiern	64-0214
Regina 19, Maina 17, Ida 7, Adolph 6			
(f) 22			
STUTZMANN, Heinr.	23	Cassel	64-0170
SUBROECK, Heinrich	29	Hamburg	66-1093
SUBTHUT, Maria	22	Lehringen	66-1031
SUCHART, Gertrude	21	Solz	65-1030

NAME	AGE	RESIDENCE	YR-LIST
SUCHOW, Hermann	33	New York	63-0097
Mathilde 28			
SUCHSLAND, Maria	53	Unterabba	64-0687
Augusta 27, Catharine 30			
SUCK, Mathias	44	Boehmen	63-0551
Maria 43, Christian 18, James 16			
Thomas 14			
SUDE, Philipp	16	Mengeringhsn.	67-0806
Pauline 19			
SUDEN, P.H.	24	Otterndorf	65-0402
SUDHEIMER, Louise	23	Illinois	63-0953
Louis 4			
SUDHEIMER, Nic.	36	Bielesheim	64-1022
SUDHOLMER, Heinr.	20	Schotten	66-1127
SUDHOLTER, Henry	46	St Louis	66-0679
Louise 30			
SUDINA, John	40	Klagenfurt	63-0990
SUDKAMP, H.A.(m)	25	Ahorn	64-0170
SUDLOW, Herm.	36	Baltimore	66-0221
SUEDBROCK, Carolyn	41	Oldenburg	66-1093
SUEDEN, Anna	23	Varlohe	65-1030
An. Helena 63			
SUEDEN, Marie	28	Vorloh	65-1030
SUENKE, Heinr.	38	Baltimore	66-0147
SUENKEL, Marie	19	Schreckenlohe	65-0594
SUESS, Christian	20	Oetlingen	66-1327
SUESS, Marie	26	Minden	65-1024
SUESSKRAUT, G.A.	36	Bueng	64-0363
Math.(f) 24			
SUESSMANN, Joh.	24	Riehelsdorf	66-1373
SUESSMILCH, Ludwig	21	Halmgerode	64-0886
SUETTERLIN, Carl F	24	Switz.	64-0170
Marie 19			
SUFFA, Johann	20	Toenitz	66-1131
SUHR, Anna	37	Otterndorf	63-0752
SUHR, John J.	27	Bremen	63-0953
SUHRBECK, Christ.	42	Dorum	64-0214
Johann 13, Johanna 7			
SUHRKE, Joh.	26	Hannover	64-0432
SUING, H. Frdr.	22	Holzhausen	66-0221
SUKAMP, Herm.	21	Schambeckslit	66-1243
SULGER, Wilhelm	28	Constanz	66-0704
SULZ, Matilde	32	New York	64-0495
SULZE, Louise	46	Zeitz	65-1095
Augusta 17			
SULZER, Gustav	26	Uelzen	66-1128
SULZER, Johanna	21	Wetzlar	65-1024
SUMANN, Chr.	29	Tecklenburg	64-0427
SUMAR, Ehrhard	24	Oberusee	66-0221
SUMMANN, Louise	19	Rahden	65-1088
SUMMER, Henriette	16	Gumbach	64-0687
SUMP, Heinr.	22	Emtinghausen	64-1161
SUNDERMANN, Anna	20	Hilter	66-1128
SUNDERMANN, August	29	Betzen	64-1053
SUNDERMANN, G.H.	18	Wellingen	65-0898
SUNDERMANN, Georg	25	Orb	66-1031
SUNDHEIMER, Wilh.	17	Worms	64-0170
SUNDORF, Lisette	22	Wallbergen	64-0938
SUNGHEN, Henry	27	Darmstadt	66-0109
SUNKER, A. Cath.	15	Gedern	63-1038
SUNNEBOOM, Maria	25	Cannum	65-0402
SUNNEN, Luehr	26	New York	63-0693
SUNNEWALD, Heinr.	29	Ilmshausen	64-0782
SURBECK, Zacharie	36	Schwitz	64-0023
SUSCHANKA, Jos.	21	Boehmen	63-1038
Katharine 9			
SUSSEGGER, G.	37	Mimmenhausen	65-0007
SUSSEKIND, Rich.	19	Eilenburg	64-0363
SUSSMANN, Eleonore	41	Gruenberg	64-0331
Pauline 7, G.(m) 7			
SUTTER, F.(m)	27	Mainz	64-0495
(f) 25			
SUTTER, Georg	23	Albenheim	65-0116
Christine 19			
SUWALD, Emil	24	Breslau	64-0687
SUWALSKY, Andreas	17	Posen	64-0456
SWABADE, Joseph	33	Boehmen	66-0349
SWART, Johannes		Aurich	66-0412

NAME	AGE	RESIDENCE	YR-LIST
SWATOS, Jos.	42	Boehmen	63-1136
SWATOS, Joseph	43	Kuttenberg	64-0593
Josepha 32, Antonia 7			
SWOBADA, Vinzent	18	Bohemia	64-0363
SWOBODA, Eduard	40	Asch	66-0679
SWOBODA, Elisabeth	27	Verona	66-1155
Joseph 3, Anton 9m			
SWOBODA, Josefa	39	Boehmen	64-0495
SWOPERDAM, K.	38	Wobieseck	66-0413
SXHREIER, J.	46	Wolfegg	63-1003
SYHRE, Carl	25	Berlin	66-0679
SYISKA, Simon	32	Soltuschen	64-0886
SYKORA, Franz	38	Boehmen	63-0990
Josefa 36, Franz 9, John 8			
SYKORA, John	34	Boehmen	63-0990
Emilie 27, Anna 6, Emilie 5, Rosalie 11m			
SYKORA, Joseph	23	Boehmen	63-0953
SYKORA, Rosalie	42	Boehmen	63-0990
Franz 20, Francisca 17, Rosalie 9			
Anton 8, John 7, Barbara 10m			
SYLVESTER, Claus	22	Oerel	65-1095
SYPMINSKY, (f)	44	Altona	64-0687
(f) 13			
SYRER, Barbara	22	Hafenprepach	66-1327
SZABLOWSKY, Gottl.	27	Bromberg	64-0456
Caroline 23			
SZELLGAG, Anna	42	Lucmin	64-0433
Antonia 20, Lucia 8, Leo 6, Josephine 4m			
SZENCSEN, Julie	36	Seegedin	66-1373
Elenore 8, Elisabeth 7, Hermann 6			
Wilhelm 5, Carl 4, Helene 3, Rosalia 10m			
SZWIRSCHINA, Franz	50	Dillingen	66-0704
Marie 48, Marie 19			
SZYLERESKA, Nicol.	32	Polen	63-0953
SZYMIKOWSKY, Jacob	46	Klakomathe	66-0666
Juliane 19			
TABEL, Aug.	25	Tetzlau	63-0908
TABEUS, Heinr.	27	Moersen	64-0593
TABLER, Elisabeth	19	St. Gallen	66-1127
TACHA, Francis	31	Boehmen	63-0551
Cath. 31, Francis 6, Francisca 4			
Gottlieb 9m			
TACK, Theodor	58	Niedergeckler	67-0600
Valentin 27, Lucia 52, Veronica 24			
Amalie 21			
TACKELMANN, Samuel	34	Berlsheim	66-0083
Catharine 5, Georg 4			
TACKENBURG, Anton.	32	Bremen	66-1373
Augusta 11m			
TADDICKEN, J.B.	25	Jeverland	63-0953
TAEHR, Johann	18	Wallrode	64-0433
TAEUSCHLE, Johann	30	Mittelstadt	67-0992
Anna 31, Johann 9m			
TAIKST, Marie	21	Schmichen	64-0023
TAKELMANN, Peter	24	Dunbeck	67-0007
TALLER, Conr.	31	Baltimore	64-0170
TAMA, Maria	23	Prag	64-0920
TAMKE, Louise	47	Peine	64-0363
Maria 9, Dora 7			
TAMM, Joh.	21	Altenbruch	65-0151
Geo. Ph. 31			
TAMMAEUS, Wilke	23	Ostfriesland	63-0752
TAMMEN, Willm	23	Aurich	66-1128
TAMMENS, Aye	22	Emden	64-1022
TAMMESS, Martin	53	Upleward	65-0594
Joh. 7, Therese 6, Franz 5, Jos. 4			
Luke(f) 51, Marg. 21, Teuke(m) 18			
TAMPKE, Hermann	21	Wittorf	66-0934
TANDLER, Jos.	25	Wien	64-0687
Eduard 23			
TANHEUSER, Aa.(f)	17	Laar	64-0782
W.(m) 31			
TANNEBAUM, Joseph	23	Weimar	66-0679
TANNENBAUM, Isac	28	Nagy Ida	65-0007
TANNER, Anna	39	Herisau	64-0331
TANNER, Ludwig	18	Duderstadt	66-1128
Josephine 23			
TANNINGER, Paul	30	Naugard/Pr.	65-0116

NAME	AGE	RESIDENCE	YR-LIST
TANRATH, Friedrich	28	Waimar	65-1095
TAPKE, Johanna	25	Heinade	65-0243
TAPKIN, Theodor	25	Jever	66-1248
Charlotte 25			
TAPP, Antje	17	Norden	65-0594
TAPPE, Carl	64	Bederkesa	64-0593
TARESCH, Joseph	32	Boehmen	66-0349
Joseph 11, Leo 10, August 7, Nanette 3			
TARNER, Wilhelm	31	Aschendorf	63-0953
TARNICH, Emil	19	Solingen	63-0006
TASCHE, Wilhelm	22	Lippe	66-0147
TASCHNER, Michael	38	Garben	66-0668
TASTANE, Franz	22	Lette/Pr.	65-0038
TAUBERT, Dorothea	33	Rheda	64-0456
Emilie 10, Friedr. 8, Elise 9m			
TAUBOLD, Friedr.	24	Gefell	63-0990
TAUD, H.	54	Himbach	66-0413
TAUFKIRCH, Barbara	21	Detroit	63-1218
TAUSCH, Marie	19	Oberkochen	65-1030
TAXIS, Otto	28	Maulbronn	64-0214
TEBBENS, C.P.	42	Leer	66-0413
Johanna 40, Christoph 15, Johann 12			
Gerhard 7, Henrich 6, Wilhelmine 3			
TEBBENS, G.C.	30	St.Louis	66-0413
Margarethe 24			
TEBCKER, Johann	16	Ahrenswalde	66-0984
TECHERT, Heinr.	30	Ulrichstein	63-1010
TECKENBROCK, Rud.	20		63-0862
TECKLENBURG, Frdke	21	Oesde	63-0917
TEDDERWEH, Carsten	31	Wallhof	66-1248
TEEBE, Louise	25	Brinkhausen	66-0623
TEGMEIER, Doris	22	Rodenberg	67-0599
TEGTMEIER, Christ.	21	Lohe	65-1095
TEGTMEYER, W.(m)	22	Westfeld	64-0331
TEICHER, Alexander	28	Arzburg	63-0006
TEICHERT, Carl	47	Schoenburg	66-0668
Friederike 40, Wilhelmine 18, Ernst 14			
TEICHERT, Ernstine	59	Striegau	64-0593
Pauline 24			
TEICHERT, Johannes	28	Pinneberg	63-1010
TEICHFUSS, Louis	23	Gera	63-0053
TEICHMANN, Franzka	22	Leipzig	63-0614
TEIG, Richard	16	Goettengruen	63-0990
TEIKNER, Sophie	56	Cincinnati	64-0023
TEIS, Anna	20	Bederkesa	63-0244
TEISEL, Anna	27	Nennerstorf	66-1031
TEITZ, Friedr.	23	Coeln	66-0984
TEKENER, Peter	32	Osnabrueck	65-0865
TELGER, Johann	24	Barnstein	67-0007
TELKAMP, Anna	20	Bersenbrueck	64-0170
TELKEN, Margarethe	28	Schwefingen	65-1030
TELLER, Joseph	23	Boehmen	63-0917
TELLY, Friedrich	20	Hermsdorf	66-1373
TEMME, Friederike	23	Bockhorst	66-1031
TEMME, Heinr.	26	Versmold	65-0950
TEMME, Margar.	27	Warburg	66-0349
TEMMEN, Berah	40	Soegel	66-1127
Mathilde 42			
TEMPEL, Chr.	30	Steinheim	64-0170
Johs. 16			
TEMPEL, Heinr.	23	Forstmuehle	64-0840
TEMPELMEIER, Charl	28	Wehden	65-1024
TEMSFELD, C.F.	15	Hasslingshsn.	65-0007
Wilhelmine 12			
TEN, Julius	23	Bicken	66-1155
TENBILT, Joseph	32	Ottenstein	65-1095
Gertrude 31			
TENIE, Anton	25	Paderborn	65-1095
TENNE, Armin	18	Mischenbach	64-0170
TENNEMEYER, W.	19	Rahden	65-1088
Wilhelmine 19			
TENT, Chr.	42	Corbach	63-1085
TENZEL, Carl	34	Scheibe	64-0593
Georgine 33, Oscar 4, Friedr. 2, Emma 6m			
TEPE, Minna	18	Wersenbrueck	65-1031
TEPEL, William	25	Corbach	63-0990
TERBECK, Simon	24	Ostfriesland	63-0752
TERHOFFSTEDDE, H.A	24	Rothenburg	64-0639

NAME	AGE	RESIDENCE	YR-LIST
TERNES, Mathias	26	Brinkhoff	65-0865
TERNOW, Theod.	24	Berlin	63-0350
TERPPE, Marie	18	Prussia	64-0687
TESCH, Carl	29	Berlin	65-0770
Friederike 21			
TESCHE, Daniel	56	Prussia	64-0432
Amalie 27, Abraham 9m			
TESCHLER, Genofeva	28	Wielingen	65-0948
Friedr. 21			
TESKE, Martin	23	Bromberg	64-0456
Ernestine 23, Emma 1			
TESS, Wilhelm	27	Neudorf	65-0770
TESSNER, Johann	35	Preussen	63-1069
Charlotte 21, Juliane 6, Gustav 3			
Emil 3m			
TETTEL, F.(m)	32	Lorch	64-0331
TETZEL, Augusta	21	Bamberg	66-1127
TETZLAFF, Theodor	26	Pommern	65-0713
TEUBERT, August	21	Hannover	66-1131
TEUBERT, Ernst	32	Mana	66-0679
TEUBNER, Carl Fr.	22	Kribitzen	66-0623
TEUFEL, Gerh.	32	Beinstein	65-1030
TEUKELMANN, Samuel	34	Berlsheim	66-0083
Catharine 5, Georg 4			
TEUSCH, Ernst	50	Bremen	64-0593
TEUSCH, Heinr.	52	Leer	65-0038
TEUSSEL, August	27	Schleiz	63-0822
TEUSSNER, Heinrich	27	Ernsthausen	66-0412
TEUTERBERG, Heinr.	14	Brinkum	64-0739
TEVES, Friedr.	29	Iserlohn	66-1127
Carl 19			
TEWES, Heinr.	23	Buchholz	66-1243
TEWES, Ludwig	23	Zamzow	66-0679
Wilhelmine 34, baby 2m			
TEWS, Joh.	53	Neustrelitz	66-0576
Louise 50, Augusta 23, Caroline 18			
Marie 9, Carl 6			
TEXTOR, Theodor	25	Hofgeismar	63-0862
TEZLAFF, August	37	Cincinnati	66-0679
THADEN, Claus	52	New York	63-0006
THAETE, Heinrich	22	Lemberg	67-0599
THALECKER, Georg	43	Erfurt	67-0795
Christine 42, Louis 12, Carl 9			
Reinhold 7, Adulbert 1			
THALER, Georg	29	Lemgo	65-0974
THALHEIMER, Leon	25	Baden	66-0576
THALMANN, Bhd.	21	Passneck	64-0214
THAME, Joh.	21	Ispringen	64-0170
THAMFORDE, Johann	25	Hagenau	65-0948
THANHAUSER, Salom.	28	Paris	64-0886
Fanny 21			
THANNER, Henry	25	Saasen	63-1218
THANNHAUSEN, J.(f)	21	Ischenhausen	64-0427
THARMANN, Marie	25	Bremervoerde	66-0934
Anna 23			
THAU, Albert	18	Eisfeld	64-0593
THEDICK, Joseph	32	Hannover	64-0023
THEE, Heinr.	23	Groenloh	66-0576
THEES, Cord.	28	Brunsbrock	66-0668
THEES, Napoleon	50	Hoeckweiler	64-0214
THEES, Rudolph	19	Nuertingen	66-1093
THEESSEN, Jantje	27	Pewsume	64-0886
THEIL, Therese	24	Reudmitz	66-0934
THEILMANN, Appolon	22	Mechtersheim	67-0007
THEIMER, Wenzel	33	Boehmen	63-0917
Katar. 31, Emil 9, Wenzel 6, Victor 2			
Maria 8, Emilie 7			
THEIS, Ferd.	45	Merscheid	66-1243
THEIS, Ferdinand	25	Ludersheim	66-1248
THEISNER, Johann	28	Menslage	66-0668
Marie 30, Catharine 7			
THEISS, Christ.	21	Braunsen	64-0427
THEISS, Conrad	26	Schaddebeck	64-0840
THEISSBACH, Sophie	22	Wolferode	64-0639
THEISSEN, H.A.	24	Burhaven	64-0214
THEMPEL, Chr. Hch.	27	Schwarzenbach	66-0704
THEN, Kunnigunde	25	Stettfeld	66-0221
THEOBALD, Joh.	31	Ottweiler	66-0109

NAME	AGE	RESIDENCE	YR-LIST
THERKAUF, Andr.	35	Basel	64-0687
THESFELD, Heinrich	24	Rahe	66-0984
THESING, Angela	21	Aschendorf	64-0938
THESING, Wilhelm	31	Quakenbrueck	64-0739
Elisabeth 30, Wilhelm 4			
THEUERBACH, Marg.	26	Erlangen	64-1206
Elise 18			
THEUERSBACHER, Aug	35	Chemnitz	64-0639
Bluno 4, Louise 2			
THEUERSBACHER, Con	28	Chemnitz	63-1010
THEURER, Cath.	20	Eisenbach	64-0639
Joh. G. 14			
THEURER, Cathar.	30	New Orleans	63-1136
THEURER, Chr.(f)	27	Aichelberg	64-0495
THEURER, Christina	17	Hallwangen	66-0147
THEURER, Gottl.	60	Gomaringen	64-0992
THEURER, Joh. Gg.	18	Speilberg	66-1327
Johann 16			
THEURER, Rudf.	29	Tuebingen	64-0138
Carl 2			
THEWYS, Sophie	19	Stolzenau	64-0938
THIAS, Wilhelmine	22	Hannover	66-0984
THIBAUT, Carl	52	Rastadt	67-0007
THIE, Anton	50	Haffnigton	63-0350
Engel 40			
THIEBES, Franz	26	Cologne	63-0822
Johanna 24, Minna 2			
THIEL, Anton	25	Grottau	66-0934
Joh. Carl 24, Georg Wilh. 30			
Joh. Andr. 32, Heinrich 34			
THIEL, C.W.	27	Godlau	65-0402
THIEL, Frd.	29	Prussia	64-0782
THIEL, John	58	Lamstedt	63-0862
Marg. 52, Friedrich 15			
THIEL, Louis	54	Carlsruhe	65-0974
Barbara 47			
THIELE, Celeste	20	Bremen	64-0363
Sophie 2, Anita 1			
THIELE, Elise	22	Bremen	64-0427
THIELE, Ferd.	29	Berlin	65-0151
THIELE, Friedrich	18	Moischeit	66-0623
THIELE, Heinr.	24	Steinhude	66-0984
THIELE, Heinrich	30	Harunstein	64-0739
THIELE, Herm. H.	32	Oytel	64-0665
Marie 20, Elisabeth 6m			
THIELE, Otto	27	New America	64-0639
THIELE, Paul	26	Schweckhausen	64-0593
Anna 19			
THIELE, R.	25	Bremen	64-0886
THIELE, Valentin	24	Herford	66-0469
THIELERT, A.(m)	30	Frankenstein	64-0331
THIELICKA, Wm.	35	Neuen	65-0151
Johanna 36, Louise 5			
THIELMANN, Franz	23	Speyer	65-0116
THIEM, Jos.	24	Heiter	64-1108
THIEMANN, Heinrich	18	Diepenau	66-0934
THIEMANN, Margaret	60	Osnabrueck	65-0950
Johanne 16			
THIEMANN, Peter	36	Topolinken	65-0713
Barbara 25			
THIEMEYER, Sophie	19	Isenstedt	66-1031
THIEN, Wenzislaus	28	Muenster	66-0934
Herbert 22			
THIENES, John	30	Eisweiler	63-1038
THIENS, Sus. Cath.	17	Nuernberg	64-0886
THIERENFELD, W.	26	Glashuette	65-0402
THIERMANN, Henry	29	Wunsiedel	63-1038
THIES, Aug.	20	Altenplatow	66-1327
THIES, Christine	19	Osnabrueck	66-1031
THIES, Friederike	20	Papenburg	64-0363
THIES, Friedr. Wm.	30	Buer	64-0920
THIES, Friedrich	33	Germany	66-0666
THIES, Joh. Friedr	55	Markendorf	64-0920
Maria Elis. 44, Joh. Friedr. 23			
Caroline 12, Minna 7, Maria Elis. 4			
Catharine 1			
THIES, Johann	18	Ahrenswalde	66-0984
THIES, Marie	26	Luetersheim	66-0704

NAME	AGE	RESIDENCE	YR-LIST
THIES, Robert	16	Hessia	66-0679
THIESE, D.(m)	36	Gruenstadt	64-0495
THIESFELD, Diedr.	29	Schierholz	64-1053
Charlotte 37, Elisabeth 7, Dorothea 5			
Heinrich 4, Charlotte 3, Johann 9m			
THIESMEYER, Whlmne	25	Menningtrufel	64-0023
THIESS, Fr.	18	Gifhorn	63-0862
THIESS, Joach.	21	Bremen	65-0038
THIESS, Joh. Henr.	50	Bremen	66-1373
THIESSEN, Fr.(m)	21	Bremen	64-0331
THIETKER, Wilhelm	25	Deplinghausen	66-0934
THILO, Adolph	39	Treffurt	63-1178
Augusta 30			
THOBEN, Dominicus	35	Brameln	66-0577
Marie 29			
THODE, Caroline	21	Otterndorf	63-0752
THODE, Chr. John	21	Bremen	63-1038
THOELE, Jos.	30	Wildeshausen	64-0992
Bernhardine 21, Wilhelmine 9m			
THOELKE, Joh.	15	Herbergen	64-0593
THOLE, Gerh. Heinr	20	Holthausen	64-0456
Anna Chr. 50			
THOMA, Carl Johann	27	Braunschweig	63-0614
THOMA, Felix	34	Haslach	66-1203
THOMA, George	34	Graz	63-0350
THOMA, J.L.(m)	24	Durnberg	64-0363
THOMA, Jacob	28	Neuses	66-0679
THOMAS, Adolph	30	Tyrol	66-0221
THOMAS, Cath.	64	Schaidt	65-0116
Magd. 26			
THOMAS, Cathre.	22	Philadelphia	63-0862
THOMAS, Elisabeth	51	Oberdresselnd	63-0006
Earl 21, Elisabeth 18, Reinhard 10			
THOMAS, Gerhard	19	Ueffeln	63-0953
THOMAS, Henriette	19	Huisterberg	66-0576
THOMAS, Julius	12	Fuerstenberg	64-0639
THOMAS, L.	40	Michigan	63-0862
THOMAS, Mart.	40	Illinois	64-0023
Elise 18			
THOMAS, Wilhelm	35	Braunschweig	65-0974
Christl. 26			
THOMASS, Georg	24	Underheim	66-0221
THOMEIER, Henry	20	Bremen	66-0679
THOMS, Johann	25	Eschwege	66-1373
THOMSEN, Arnold	23	Bremen	64-0456
THONEMANN, Aug.	27	Schwedt	66-0576
Marie 24			
THONER, Franz	24	Hunteburg	67-0007
THONET, Philip	28	Belgium	64-0170
Mrs. 20			
THONNIES, W.	62	Oldenburg	64-0495
THORIN, Louis	40	Paris	64-0073
Mrs. 37, Eugene 16			
THORMAEHLEN, H.	18	Bremen	63-1003
THORMANN, F.	29	Braunschweig	65-0974
THORMEIER, D.	20	Bremen	64-0593
THORNER, Justus	11	Geestendorf	63-0917
THORNER, Lisette	18	Geestemuende	64-0427
THORRING, Niels	24	Copenhagen	66-0666
THORSPUKEN, Julius	21	Bremen	63-0990
THREWER, B.	17	Coburg	64-0782
THRO, John	28	St. Charles	63-0990
Cathre. 27			
THROENE, Anton	30	Canstein	64-0214
Adelheid 26, Emilie 4			
THROLICHT, Anna	20	Langenberg	63-0821
THRONER, Anna	25	Dorfbauersch.	66-0934
THRUSCHKA, Joh.	34	Doldau	66-0704
Anna 34, Johann 9			
THRUSCHKA, Joseph	38	Marokote	66-0704
Franziska 34			
THUEMANN, Gerhard	19	Sudlahn	66-0349
THUEN, F.	29	Heiden	66-0413
THUENER, Caroline	27	Gerlachsheim	64-0363
THUERINGER, Wilh.	27	Chicago	66-0576
THUERNAUER, Ch.	22	Burgkunstadt	66-0576
THUERVOGEL, Carl	38	Nils	66-1155
Barbara 34			

NAME	AGE	RESIDENCE	YR-LIST
THUERWACHTER, Frz.	26	Frickenfeld	65-0151
THUMANN, Anna Marg	28	Otterndorf	64-0456
THUNHORST, Heinr.	18	Huesede	66-1373
THUNIUS, Alma	17	Eisenberg	64-0331
THURINGEN, Martin	30	Eitrich	64-0427
THURMANN, John	24	Lippstadt	63-1136
Charles 29			
THURNAUER, Jos.	30	Paris	64-0427
THYARKS, Henry	34	San Francisco	65-0055
THYSSEN, Anke	30	Campen	64-0331
Johanna 21			
THYVISSEN, Otto	26	Aachen	66-0109
TIARKS, G.B.	24	Schortens	65-1024
Anna 20			
TIDDEN, Hibbe	58	Ditzum	65-0402
Gebke 56, Jemme 25			
TIDEMANN, H.	23	Bermen	63-0168
TIEBERMANN, Otto	24	Posen	63-0990
TIEBRING, Anna	22	Vechta	66-1031
TIEDECKEN, Theodor	19	Twistringen	66-0934
TIEDEMANN, Albert	21	Bremen	64-0904
TIEDEMANN, Anna	14	Holftel	66-1031
TIEDEMANN, August	20	Hagen	63-0917
TIEDEMANN, Carl	21	Haldemar	64-0639
Sophie 20			
TIEDEMANN, Claus	42	Vorst	65-0948
TIEDEMANN, D.	17	Sottrum	64-0992
TIEDEMANN, F.A.(m)	19	Hagen	64-0170
TIEDEMANN, Johann	26	Bevegstedt	66-1248
TIEDEMANN, Johann	35	Mittelstenau	65-1095
Anna 30, Heinrich 1, Johann 25			
TIEDGEN, Ilse	25	Hannover	66-0679
TIEGEL, Julius	34	New York	65-0243
TIEGS, Johann	41	Hagenow	66-0668
Marie 40, baby (m) 2m, Albert 13, Otto 2			
Caroline 10, Bertha 6, Emilie 4			
TIELITZ, Ferd	38	Hornburg	64-0687
Minna 24, baby 11m			
TIELKEN, Malwina	24	Elsfleth	63-1136
TIELKEN, Sophie	26	Elsfleth	63-1038
TIEMANN, Chr.	17	Hille	64-0214
TIEMANN, Friedrich	29	Oldenburg	65-0770
TIEMEIER, Heinr.	16	Isenstedt	65-1030
TIEMEYER, Cathrine	22	Osnabrueck	66-1093
TIEMEYER, J.C.	46	St.Louis	63-0862
TIESING, Louise	28	Meyerhoefer	65-1024
TIETIG, A.	20	Bremen	64-0432
TIETIG, Heinr.	27	Bremen	66-0984
TIETJE, Diedr.	25	Weberhamm	63-1136
TIETJEN, Beta	19	Mahndorf	66-1093
TIETJEN, Catharina	21	Mohndorf	64-0456
TIETJEN, Elisabeth	24	Willardhausen	64-0687
TIETJEN, Friedr.	19	Bremen	66-1155
TIETJEN, Heinr.	22	Vich	65-0898
TIETJEN, Heinrich	27	Hannover	67-0007
TIETJEN, Henry	29	Ueberhamm	63-1178
TIETJEN, Hermann	20	Hannover	67-0007
TIETJEN, Johann	20	Fiehe	64-0904
TIETJEN, Johann	21	Wiste	66-1093
TIETJEN, Johann	20	Offenwarden	66-1327
TIETJEN, Marie	22	Hannover	66-1031
TIETJEN, Martin	18	Teufelsmoor	67-0600
TIETZE, Geo.	25	Hannover	66-1313
Emilie 26, Emilie 9m			
TIETZEN, Augusta	39	Fuerstenwalde	66-0934
Helene 5, Hulda 2			
TIETZEN, Th.(m)	20	Thedinghausen	64-0495
Geesche 22			
TIFFARTZ, Robert	22	Mettmann	63-0482
TIKUS, Paul	42	Prussia	64-0363
Anna 37, Thekla 12, Maria 9, Paul 7			
TILGE, Heinrich	37	Ehmen	64-0739
TILKING, Caroline	28	Oberlippe	67-0599
TILLAR, Bhd.	18	Emsbuehren	65-1024
TILLE, Ludw.	23	Rachhausen	63-1085
TILLING, Adam	40	Bischhausen	64-1022
TILLMANN, Johann	21	New York	63-0990
TILLNER, Ernst	44	Dresden	64-0023

NAME	AGE	RESIDENCE	YR-LIST
Anna 18, Malvine 15			
TIMKEN, Betty	36	New York	63-1085
Henry 1			
TIMLING, Chris.	37	Baltimore	63-0015
TIMM, Hinr. Herm.	24	Dissen	65-0950
TIMM, J.	28	Mecklenburg	63-0244
TIMM, Louise	22	Grebbin	63-0350
TIMMEL, E.(m)	28	Kreubach	64-0495
TIMMEN, Jan	19	Bentheim	64-0363
TIMMERMANN, C.L.	38	New York	63-1136
wife 23			
TIMMERMANN, Lis.	23	Riesch	64-0782
TIMMERMANN, W.	18	Oldenburg	66-0413
TIMMERMANN, Wm.	24	Stade	66-0109
TIMMERMANN, Wm.	26	Manil	64-1053
TIMMERMEISTER, Ch.	20	Klekamp	63-0917
TIMMERS, Carol.	24	Burgsteinfurt	63-0953
TIMPE, Heinr.	41	Berlin	66-1327
TIMPE, Heinr.	22	Soerlern	66-1373
Hermann 25			
TIMPE, Heinrich	38	Bielefeld	66-1248
Amalie 37, Wilhelm 15			
TIMPE, Louise	18	Stemshorn	64-0433
TIMPKE, Philip	27	Nordholz	63-1136
TINNEMANN, Ernst	21	Wolfke	65-0898
TINNEN, Diedr.	15	Hannover	66-0734
TINSCH, Elisabeth	58	Geestendorf	65-0865
TISCHER, Anna C.	19	Gich	64-0331
Elis. 22			
TISCHLER, G.(m)	18	Messlingen	64-0331
TITJEN, Catharina	16	Ritterhude	64-0886
TITTEL, Bernh.	22	Zwickau	63-1178
TITTEL, Crezentia	33	Mannheim	66-0679
Joseph 29, Albert 9			
TITUS, Joh. P.	27	Marklengast	65-0038
Kunigunda 28, Nicolaus 9m, Johann 21			
TITZEN, Albert	24	Weinheim	64-0687
TJADEN, Alb. Lamm.	25	Holsdorf	66-0349
Margar. 21			
TOBECK, Christian	56	Matfeld	65-0713
Dorothea 56, Anna 24, Margretha 17			
Louise 14			
TOBECK, Fritz	19	Martfeld	64-0433
Heinrich 25, Johann 20			
TOBECK, Heinr.	45	Martfeld	64-0363
Dorothea 42, J.D. 30, Marg. 32, Heinr. 6			
baby (m) 11m			
TOBERGTE, Georg	21	Ostenfelde	66-1127
TOBIAS, Aug. Berh.	29	Harburg	64-0886
TOBIAS, Camille	17	Wien	63-1085
TOBIAS, J.G.	23	Brake	64-0363
TOBIAS, Michael	49	Bodenbach	66-0346
TOBIASEN, B.(m)	18	Friedeberg	64-0214
TOCH, B.(m)	36	Wien	64-0073
E.(m) 34			
TOCHTERMANN, J.	34	Bayern	63-1003
TODENBIER, Car.	26	Neustadt	65-1088
TODENFELD, Gertrud	20	Wulften	66-0704
TODORFF, Nicolaus	19	Petersburg	64-0639
TODT, Gustav	27	Bromberg	64-0073
TODTS, Georg	19	Bremen	64-0199
TOEBELMANN, G.	23	Wagenfeld	63-1085
TOEBELMANN, Gustav	21	Delmenhorst	66-0934
August 19			
TOEBELMANN, Johann	19	Dreye	67-0007
TOEGEL, H.	35	Hilbe	64-1108
TOEKING, Maria	25	Suedlohn	66-0349
TOELKE, Carl	33	Wuldefka	66-0469
Eva Rosine 27, Michael 7, Wilhelmine 9m			
TOELKEN, Hen.	22	Bremen	66-1155
TOELL, Ad.	18	Sulzbach	65-0007
TOELL, Friedrich	36	Siebenknie	66-1327
Dorothea 32, Gottfried 6, Christine 3			
TOELL, Louise	21	Westheim	65-0189
TOELL, Robert	22	Heilbronn	66-1131
TOELLE, Wilhelm	25	Gutsbueren	65-0948
TOELPE, Carl	26	Coswitz	64-1022
TOEMANECK, Franz	13	Luhbritz	67-0007

NAME	AGE	RESIDENCE	YR-LIST
TOENJES, Anna	20	Gnarrenburg	64-0363
TOENJES, Diedr.	26	Mooshusen	66-0576
TOENJES, Wilhelm	15	Cappel	66-0083
TOENNISSEN, Marie	40	Amsterdam	64-0840
TOENSING, Franz	25	Neuenkirchen	66-0984
TOEPEL, Wilhelm	27	Flechtdorf	65-0948
Chr. Friedr. 32			
TOEPELMANN, Frdr.	20	Kirchweicke	65-0243
Heinr. 18			
TOERING, Minna	20	Emsdetten	66-0576
TOERKE, Heinr.	33	Lage	63-0168
TOLL, Friederike	29	Ukerwala	65-1030
TOLL, J.T.W.	36	Thonsdorff	65-1030
Wilhelmine 38, Hermann 10, Wilhelm 6			
TOLLE, Friedrich	22	Niederspier	65-1095
TOLSCHER, Joh.	22	Preussen	64-0331
TOMACZIK, Jacob	42	Posen	64-0432
Marba 40, Anna 4			
TOMEK, Catharina	24	Boehmen	66-0349
TOMEK, Joseph	30	Boehmen	66-0349
Julie 39, Ida 17, Alice 14, Trewer 12			
TOMISCHKA, Elisab.	28	Boehmen	66-0109
TOMME, Ludwig	20	Leese	66-1031
TONDORF, F.	18	Kuchenheim	65-1088
TONN, Franz	24	Frankenhausen	65-0974
TONNE, Fr.	22	Schmalfoerden	63-0551
TONNENMACHER, Jul.	19	Hessia	66-1093
TONNES, Eduard	26	Hannover	66-1131
TONNIES, Georg	19	Hannover	66-0984
TONNIES, Louise	16	Gnarrenburg	66-1031
TOPKEN, Henry	31	Nieort	63-1038
TOPP, Georg	31	Hehnershausen	63-1136
TOPP, James Ignatz	28	Boeckerndorf	63-0482
TORNOFF, Georg	18	Wichelsbach	65-0189
TORWEIHE, Jacob	30	Neuenkirchen	64-0433
TOSCHNER, John	24	Boehmen	63-0551
Sophie 23			
TOSS, Johanna	18	Solingen	66-1373
TOSTMANN, Louis	30	San Francisco	64-0073
TOTH, H.A.W.	19	Offerndorf	65-0007
TOTTEL, Marie	19	Sebaldsbrueck	64-0639
TOUZELIN, Fred.	33	France	63-0350
TRABANT, Marie	18	Schluchter	64-0427
TRABLER, J.	24	Eickerswiel	63-1085
TRAEN, Wm.	30	Erfurt	64-0432
Dorothea 22			
TRAGBRODT, Carl W	36	Dresden	65-1030
TRAGESSER, F.	19	Wasserlos	64-1161
TRAME, Friedrich	20	Hollage	66-0668
August 18			
TRAMMEN, Anna	18	Buehren	64-0427
Tanne C. 25			
TRAPMANN, William	34	Haseluenne	63-0168
TRAPP, Eleonore	64	Giessen	64-0992
TRATTNER, E.	34	Mischholz	65-0898
TRAUB, Herm.	19	Meschelfeld	65-0007
TRAUB, Joseph	19	Oberlemmingen	67-0007
TRAUBE, Maria	21	Wrikenrode	65-0004
TRAUBE, Matthias	42	Wildbach	66-0934
TRAUE, Friedr.	54	Maaslingen	66-0576
Herm. 34			
TRAUERNICHT, W.	18	Bornum	64-1022
TRAUFNER, Wilhelm	20	Leipzig	66-0221
TRAUM, Heinr.	18	Sellenrod	65-0116
TRAUPE, Friedrich	29	Edemissen	63-0482
Freiderike 24, Minna 2			
TRAUPE, H.	32	Braunschweig	65-0974
Caroline 28, Caroline 7, Wilheline 5			
August 9m			
TRAUSHEIM, Joh.	19	Rhoda	65-1031
TRAUSIL, Johann	32	Senomatz	66-1373
TRAUT, Margarethe	20	Grossaspach	64-0170
TRAUTA, Johann	33	Maltitz	66-0576
TRAUTBETTER, Dorth	24	Meiningen	66-0576
TRAUTH, Anna	17	Hoechst	66-0668
TRAUTH, E.	24	Wilgenroth	63-1003
TRAUTMANN, Samuel	38	Merseburg	66-0679
TRAUTMANN, Siegm.	22	Worms	64-0427

NAME	AGE	RESIDENCE	YR-LIST
TRAUTMANN, Theda	21	Worms	65-0402
TRAUTMANN, Wilhelm	31	Bremen	64-0199
Emilie 19			
TRAUTNER, Joh.	23	Walkersbrunn	64-0495
TRAUTSCHKE, August	18	Kerzdorf	66-0704
TRAUTVELLER, Elisa	22	Sachsen-Mein.	66-0349
TRAUTWEIN, Gottlob	18	Bernhausen	66-1131
TRAUTWEIN, H.	64	Worms	63-0990
wife 57			
TRAUWETTER, Heinr.	17	Meiningen	64-0432
TREBING, Carl W.	22	Wannfried	64-0886
TREBING, Martin	20	Gr. Almerode	66-1248
TRECKMANN, Becca	14	Achim	66-0934
TREFTZ, Jacob	20	Siefenheim	66-1131
TREFZ, Joh.	25	Grossenaspach	64-0170
Maria 22			
TREFZ, Marie	34	Stuttgart	66-0704
Augusta 9			
TREFZG, Joh.	22	Wuerttemberg	64-0687
Georg 20			
TREIBLER, Carl	32	Lippich	66-1203
TRENCK, Lina	16	Hungen	63-0350
TRENNEPOHL, Friedr	30	Ledde	65-0948
Bernadina 23			
TRENNEPOHL, Georg	46	Ibbenbuehren	65-0898
Ricke 49, Heinrich 23, Wilhelm 15			
Hermann 13, Dina 11, August 8			
TRENTELMANN, Chris	24	Indianapolis	63-0953
TRENTMANN, Friedr.	31	Oster Cappeln	65-0950
Franz 24			
TRENTMANN, John H.	26	Ostercappeln	63-0953
Magd. 23			
TRESCHER, Andreas	19	Densburg	65-0948
TRESSELT, Adolph	19	Breitenbach	64-0432
TRETTIN, August	25	Romansart	63-0614
TREUERNICHT, Juett	54	Aurich	66-0668
TREUKAMPF, Heinr.	45	Neuenkirchen	64-0782
Wilhelmine 15			
TREUSCH, Cath.	35	Hungary	64-0687
Eduard 16, Maritz 9, Netti 7, Mandi 5			
Therese 2			
TREUSCH, E.	39	Peeth	63-1085
Anna Maria 6m			
TREUSCH, Therese	26	Pest	64-0938
Fanny 1, Josephine 9			
TREUTMANN, John H.	26	Ostercappeln	63-0953
Magd. 23			
TREVERT, Gesine	28	Bremen	64-0073
TREVIRANUS, C.	40	Bremen	63-0752
TREVIRARUS, C(m)	40	Bremen	64-0023
TREWERT, Henry	25	Asmissen	63-0168
TRIBLER, Ernst	25	Oelbe	64-0938
TRIBOLET, Jean	27	Rouen	63-0350
TRICHLINGER, Marie	42	Trostingen	63-0990
Cathre. 13			
TRICHT, Wm.	32	Halifax	64-0023
TRIEBEL, Robert	24	Ophausen	63-0015
TRIEBNER, Jacob	41	Philadelphia	63-0015
TRIEFENBACH, G.	47	Illinois	66-0679
TRIER, Caroline	20	Wilsdorf	66-0576
TRIER, Elisabeth	18	Pfatter	63-1085
TRINKBEINER, Joh.G	21	Gutach	63-0482
TRINTEN, G.	50	Blankenheim	64-0331
Johanna 21			
TRINTHAMMER, Emily	30	Hanau	64-1206
TRIPP, Johannes	34	Ernsthausen	64-1053
TRIPPEL, Adolph	21	Sickenhofen	66-0984
TRIPPENHAHN, Fr'dr	25	Pommern	66-0469
Maria 19			
TRIPPER, Benjamin	38	Boston	63-0097
TRISK, Friederike	19	Sulzbach	66-0679
TRITSCHLER, Paulne	19	Bubenbach	65-1030
TRITT, Chr.	20	Zell	65-0594
TRITT, Hendrike	48	Zell	65-0594
Charlotte 18			
TROCHNER, Wm.	22	Oldenburg	65-0116
TRODER, Th.	58	Prussia	63-1003
TROEBNER, Wm.	22	Oldenburg	65-0116

NAME	AGE	RESIDENCE	YR-LIST
TROEGER, Marg.	28	Stambach	63-0953
TROHWARDT, Joseph	43	Wuestenfelde	66-0837
TROLL, Joseph	28	Fautenbach	63-0244
TRONCH, Anna	18	Darmstadt	66-1093
TROOST, Caspar	73	Preussen	63-0822
TROPPEL, Ery	23	Rothenburg	66-0413
TROST, Heinr.	18	Siggerfeld	66-0576
TROST, Joh.	30	Oberlemsen	64-0687
TROST, Joh.	31	Wiesbaden	65-1088
TROST, Leopold	31	Baden	66-0576
Marie 28, Marie 4			
TROST, Wm.	18	Frankenberg	64-0363
TROY, Christ.(f)	21	Metternich	65-0189
TRUBE, S.	27	Klagenfurt	64-1161
Franz 34			
TRUCKENBROD, Joh.	18	Coburg	67-1005
TRUEMPIN, Cathar.	21	Istein	66-0668
TRUEVERANNS, C.	44	Bremen	63-0013
TRUHLAR, Joh.	34	Bohemia	64-0687
Anna 33, Jos. 7, Franz 6, Marg. 5, Joh. 3			
Wenz. 10			
TRUMMER, Michael	57	Goessnitz	66-0679
Johanna 54			
TRUMPIN, Joh.	30	Istern	64-0363
TRUMPP, Emilie	34	Wuerttemberg	66-0576
TRUNK, Salomone	24	Coeln	66-1093
TRUNK, Therese	42	Klagenfurt	63-1178
Anna 16			
TRUNZER, Joseph	23	Kalsbach	64-0992
Walpurga 25			
TRUNZER, Ludwig	18	Answanz	65-1024
TRUSHEIM, Eberh.	36	Ernsthausen	64-0214
Cath. 18			
TRUZIL, Jos.	46	Boehmen	64-0427
Anna 41			
TRUZLA, Peter	30	Polen	66-0666
Juliane 19			
TSCHAKERT, Vincenz	39	Meilerliebich	63-1010
TSCHIRGE, Alois	25	Mels	63-1178
TSCHUDI, Fridolin	24	Schwanden	64-0938
TUCHAN, Christina	24	Laaspe	66-0668
TUCHSCHERER, Franz	20	Bremen	65-1140
TUCHSCHERER, Wm.	36	Niederweiha	63-0350
TUEBBEN, Bern. Ant	24	Binstrup/Old	64-0920
TUECHERSFELD, Soph	24	Horb	63-0953
Margarethe 25			
TUGER, Adam	30	New York	63-0168
Eva 30, Francis 2, Mary 2m			
TUITE, Elisabeth	18	Ireland	63-0990
TULAFOUS, Carolina	26	Schotta	66-1131
TUSCH, Heinrich	28	Gesmold	65-0948
Marie Elisab 25			
TUXHORN, Wilhelm	18	Amshausen	64-0840
TWACHTMANN, L.	28	Holtorf	64-0992
Eleonore 27, Louise 4, Wilhelmine 1			
Marie 6m			
TWAROCKA, Antonia	22	Kuttenberg	64-0170
TWEBE, Pp.	27	Volkmarshsn.	66-1243
TWEITMANN, Theod.	16	Dorum	64-1022
Elise 25			
TWELKEMEYER, Heinr	22	Farsmuth	65-1030
TWICKLER, Elisbeth	25	Emstetten	66-1031
TWIETMEYER, H.(m)	22	Eigendorf	64-0363
TWIETMEYER, Heinr.	34	Hessen	66-0934
TWILD, Joseph	40	Hodern	67-0007
Marie 30, Marie 6, Joseph 3, Franziska 6m			
Barbara 18			
TWINEBENG, Bernh'd	16	Sielen	64-0739
TWISTERA, v. Gg.	20	Otterndorf	66-1203
TWORKE, Carl	29	Roschitz	66-0650
Emilie 22			
TYARKS, Henry	36	St. Francis	66-0934
Helene 31, Bertha 6, Hermann 4, Emma 2			
TYDMANN, H.	25	Tettens	64-0992
TYLECK, Wenzel	37	Boehmen	66-0349
TYSLICK, Carl	28	Preussen	66-0083
Caroline 28, Florentine 5			
UBER, Gottlieb	19	Grafenberg	66-0147

NAME	AGE	RESIDENCE	YR-LIST
UBHAUS, Johann	20	Kirchweil	65-0770
UCHMANN, Minna	9	Merxhingen	64-0938
UCHTMANN, Elise	35	Oldenburg	64-0456
UDE, Johanna	34	Braunschweig	65-0007
UDE, Th.	18	Braunschweig	65-0974
UDEMANN, Henry	29	Herzford	63-1038
UDRICH, J.	23	Netschen	65-1189
UEBEL, Marg.	59	Hohenschwaerz	63-1038
Anna 32			
UEKER, Christian	58	Fuersdorf	66-1248
Sophie 57, Ernetine 22, Wilhelmine 21			
UEKERMANN, August	19	Buende	66-1203
UELLENBERG, W.(f)	31	Barmen	64-0495
UELTZ, Augustus	37	Goettingen	63-0168
UFFELMAN, Claus H.	39	Horstedt	63-1085
UFFELN, Georg	21	Nordheim	66-1128
UFFKES, Lammert	59	Pilsum	66-0623
UGING, Maria	35	Gronau	64-0840
UGOREK, Mathias	27	Wuldefka	66-0469
Anna 25			
UHDE, H.	52	New York	63-0953
UHDEN, Carl	19	Bevern	65-1088
UHE, Fr.	18	Obernkirchin	63-1085
UHER, Theresia	24	Klizow	64-0593
UHING, Carl	27	Cleve	64-0433
UHL, Adam	18	Uslar	64-0938
Franz 16			
UHL, J.G.	26	Arnheim	64-0782
UHL, Michael	24	Aurheim	64-0886
UHLBRAND, Ferd. W.	30	Oldenburg	66-0934
Sophie 24			
UHLENBRAND, Heinr.	37	Duesseldorf	65-0402
Elisab. 33			
UHLENBRINK, Herm.	37	Wirsum	65-1030
UHLENBUSCH, Herman	33	Kirchhassel	65-0243
Charlotte 35, Hinr. 7, Herman 5, Marie 19			
UHLENKAMP, Herm.	29	Osnabrueck	64-0427
UHLFELDER, Jacob	19	Furth	67-0007
UHLHERR, Marianne	22	Horlingen	65-0189
UHLHORN, Gerhard	20	Wittlage	66-1093
UHLICH, Paul Gerh.	22	Magdeburg	63-1069
UHLIG, Robert	21	Berlin	66-0346
UHLMANSIEK, Heinr.	22	Markendorf	64-0433
Marie 24, Fredrich 3, Heinr. 6m			
UHMANN, Leopold	18	Hessen	66-0109
UHR, Joseph	28	Menzingen	66-0221
UHRBACH, C.	53	Matanzas	66-0934
Josefa 45, Josephine 14, Alfred 10			
Louis 5, Rosalia 5			
UHRELACHER, Christ	35	Hinterwaiten	66-0083
Magdalene 33, Philipp 8			
UHSEMANN, Gotlieb	33	Ndr.Zirkka.	64-0456
UKENA, Uke	25	Velde	64-0331
ULBACHARI, Jac.	19	Sofia	63-1038
ULFERS, Peter	26	Uppgaul	66-0349
ULFES, J.	25	Ochsiel	66-0413
ULKE, Henning	18	Cappeln	65-1030
August 15			
ULLFELDER, Fr.	25	Nuernberg	65-1024
ULLMANN, Anton	18	Stuttgart	65-0594
ULLMANN, Conrad	27	Fromershausen	66-0679
Magdalena 35			
ULLMANN, Gustav	25	Joh.Georgenst	66-1203
Anna 23			
ULLMANN, Joh.	43	Breisbach	66-1248
ULLMANN, Leopold	22	Constadt	66-0109
ULLMANN, Ludwig	20	Fuerth	66-0934
ULLMER, Fr.(m)	23	Almeloo	64-0214
ULLRICH, Barbara	50	Ritzingen	63-1178
Margarethe 22			
ULLRICH, Gottf.	49	Alschofki-Kat	66-0650
Johan 43, Helena 18, Dorothea 16			
Fr. Wilhelm 12, Gottfried 8			
ULLRICHS, Friedr.	32	Bremen	63-0097
ULM, Henry	48	Haggerweila	64-0073
Geo. 25			
ULMANN, Ad.	44	New York	64-0495
ULMANN, M.	20	Erlangen	65-0402

NAME	AGE	RESIDENCE	YR-LIST
ULMER, Ernst	17	Stuttgart	64-1108
ULMER, Georg	23	Schaffhausen	66-1327
ULMER, Gottlieb	30	Asch	64-0840
ULMER, Joh. Geo.	28	Ruetlingen	66-1313
ULMER, Moses	27	Langenfeld	66-1373
ULPT, Nicolaus	39	Hannover	66-1093
ULRICH, Adam	22	Waldeck	64-0938
Wm. 22, Phil. 17, Louise 24			
ULRICH, Anna	31	Kuttenberg	64-0593
ULRICH, August	26	Egel	66-0668
ULRICH, C. (m)	26	Gruenenplan	64-0138
ULRICH, Carl	30	Alfeld	66-1031
ULRICH, Carl	60	Wichmansdorf	66-1127
Dorothea 58, Emilie 22, Carl 16			
Bertha 19, Wihelm 13			
ULRICH, Carl	49	Veilsdorf	64-0214
ULRICH, Gustav	29	Seligenthal	65-0004
ULRICH, Jean	17	Germany	63-0990
ULRICH, Joh.	24	Chicago	64-0170
Louise 22			
ULRICH, Louise	29	Duderstadt	64-0331
ULRICH, Martin	32	Veilsdorf	63-0953
ULRICH, Richard	32	Veilsdorf	66-1131
Eduard 22			
ULRICH, Thiebaut	28	Louisville	63-0990
ULRICHS, Clara	28	Hannover	63-0551
ULRICHS, Dr.	40	St. Louis	63-0953
ULRICHS, Jette	14	Ihrdigshagen	65-0713
Louise 16			
ULRICHS, Marie	17	Nienburg	63-0398
ULRIKE, Adolf	22	Leopoldhafen	66-1131
UMBACH, Conr.	27	Waben	65-0189
UMBACH, Lorenz	23	Marburg	65-0713
UMLAND, Heinrich	18	Ebersdorf	65-1031
Gertrude 15			
UNDEUTSCH, Johanna	19	Weddewarden	64-0840
UNGAR, C.	34	New York	63-1085
Lina 6			
UNGER, Ad.	54	Magdeburg	65-0898
Herm. 22, Wilhelm 16			
UNGER, Adam	20	Heppenheim	66-0083
Louise 13			
UNGER, Albert	19	Wuerttenberg	66-0109
UNGER, Aron	25	Muenster	64-1053
UNGER, C.	32	Sachaffhausen	65-1189
UNGER, Emilie	24	Clansfeld	64-0886
UNGER, Joh. Georg	25	Holzmaden	66-0221
Anna 30, Marie Cath. 2			
UNGER, John M.	36	Ohio	63-0821
UNGER, Leopold	24	Kaschau/Hung.	66-0346
UNGER, Marcus	36	Pleschen	64-0840
Caecilie 36, Nathalia 4, Herm. 3			
Abraham 11m			
UNGER, Sophie	18	Blasheim	66-0984
UNGERECHT, Valent.	45	Kellbach	64-0639
Eva 30, Carl 7, Georg 4, John 59			
Margaretha 58, Friedrich 36			
UNGERER, A.	22	Fuerth	64-0782
UNGERER, Petronela	24	Tiefenbach	66-0469
UNGEWITTER, Anton	29	Eisleben	64-0456
UNLAND, Gerhard	20	Harpenfeld	66-0221
UNRATH, Aug.	27	Neuerlingen	63-1085
Clara 37, Clara 7, Ottilie 5			
UNRUH, v. A.F.St.	17	Blumenhagen	64-0214
UNTERBAENDER, Magd	15	Zeiskam	65-0243
UNZICKER, Helene	26	New York	63-0006
Emil 3			
UPHEBER, Heinrich	17	Getmold	66-0668
UPHOFF, Gerhard	32	Damensen	66-0984
Margaretha 31, Anna 7, August 3, Fritz 1			
UPHUS, Friederike	40	Schale	65-1024
Marie 12, Joh. Fr. 9, Ludw. 6			
UPMANN, Carl	20	Bremen	64-1022
UPPENKAMP, Carl	17	Wuellen	66-0837
Elise 27			
URBAN, Dominic	28	Boehmen	63-1085
URBAN, Jacob	47	Rheinboellen	67-0599
Eva 39, Philipp 22, Juliane 20			

NAME	AGE	RESIDENCE	YR-LIST
Catharine 15, Eva 7, Jacob 5			
URBAN, Valtin	47	St. Louis	63-1069
URBANOWICS, Alfons	31	Baltimore	66-0934
URBANOWSKI, Johann	22	Sakolitz	66-0577
URLAU, Wm.	26	Louisville	64-0023
Johanna 21			
URSPRUNG, Cathar.	20	Waldeck	64-0938
USHARY, (m)	70	Texas	64-0214
(m) 23			
USSLAR, v. W.	34	Adelaide	64-0073
USSNER, Henriette	17	Bavaria	63-0822
UTHARDT, Henry Chr	27	Dachrieden	63-0296
UTHE, John	20	Bischhausen	63-1136
UTZ, Caspar	22	Weppersdorf	66-0109
VABER, Lorenz	36	Hohenkemnath	65-0950
Martin 25, Lorenz 59, Margarethe 29			
Kunigunde 19			
VAGEDES, Bernhard		Loeningen	66-0984
Marie 24			
VAGER, Herm. Heinr	28	Neunkirchen	65-0950
Maria 28, Herm. 4m			
VAHLKAMP, Henry	23	Quakenbrueck	63-0551
VAHLSING, Heinr.	34	Stolzenau	66-0577
Louise 34, Wilhelmine 7, Heinrich 6			
Friedrich 3, Diedrich 10m			
VAHRENKAMP, Doroth	20	Isenstedt	66-1031
VAHRENKAMPF, Wilh	24	Saarbruechen	63-0168
VAIT, Friedrich	22	Fuerth	66-1031
VAKERT, Catharina	56	Espa	66-1155
Heinrich 18, Elisa 4			
VALENTIN, Albert	42	Berlin	66-0679
VALENTIN, Philppne	20	Umstadt	65-0189
VALENTIN, William	53	Muenchen	63-0244
VALER, Peter	22	Graubuenden	63-0296
VALETITSCH, Marc.	19	Tschoeplach	64-0427
VALK, Adam	18	Cassel	66-1031
VALLENTIN, Carolyn	37	Hamburg	66-1127
VALLER, Maria	17	Vielingen/Pr.	64-1053
VALLET, Marianne	32	Impfingen	66-0650
VANDAME, Mag. Ils.	30	Minden	63-1010
VANDERWORT, M.A.	40	New York	63-0821
VANIER, Johann	24	Bach	67-0007
VARK, Maria	23	Bockhorst	64-0331
VARTMANN, August	30	Horste	66-0934
wife 25, baby 1			
VASEL, Carl	17	Luebbeke	65-1031
VASEL, Theala	24	Wuerttemberg	66-0109
VASTEEN, Meta	16	Delmenhorst	66-0934
VATER, Friedr.	23	Heilbronn	65-0950
VAUBELL, Geo. W.	31	Chicago	63-0482
VAUPEL, Anna M.	23	Strasburg	64-0170
VAUPEL, Christiane	20	Arolsen	66-1248
VAUPEL, Wilhelmine	24	Arolsen	66-1248
VAZTO, Peter	18	Achim	66-0734
VECHTMANN, Diedr.	26	Osterholz/Br.	65-0038
VECKERT, Caroline	20	Prussia	64-0170
VEHIGE, J.	30	Westenholz	65-0974
VEICKER, H.	30	New York	63-0953
wife 26			
VEIL, Aloisia	24	Wuertemberg	66-0147
VEIT, Leopold	40	Pest	66-0984
VEITH, Georg	30	Eberbach	63-0693
Philippine 33, Henry 4			
VEITH, J.	49	Texas	66-0934
VEITH, Lud.	20	Buchsol	66-1243
VEITH, Robert	28	Lockwitz	67-0795
Albertine 26, Anna 1			
VELDE, v.d. H.	19	Wirdumerland	65-0116
Trienke 19			
VELKER, Andreas	23	Daum	65-1095
VELLENS, Christian	22	Lorup	66-1203
VELTE, Wilhelm	27	Stuttgart	64-0639
VENCENT, (f)	40	Berlin	66-0934
VENNE, Gottlieb	70	Muehlberg	65-0007
VENNEMANN, Anton	19	Loeningen	64-0938
VENS, Cathar.	26	Gescher	65-0948
VERBSKY, Wenzel	34	Boehmen	63-0398
Catharina 24, Magdalena inf			

NAME	AGE	RESIDENCE	YR-LIST
VERCH, Gottl.	22	Bromberg	64-0432
VERCLAS, Cornelius	28	Lautenberg	67-0007
VERI, Emilie	7	Philadelphia	63-0953
Charles 5, Friedr. 4			
VERING, Heinr.	19	Oesede	64-0687
VERING, Johann	22	Klosterode	66-1093
VERSPOHL, Anton	22	Muenster	65-1030
VERTEN, Joseph	21	Doeblitsch	63-0053
VESLAGE, L.B.	33	Suttrup	66-1127
VESPERMANN, Friedr	24	Hasteneck	66-0083
VESPERMANN, Heinr.	25	Suedweyhe	64-0214
VESTER, Gottfried	30	Hebsack	64-0739
VETH, Adam	27	Golschheim	64-0886
VETH, Heinr. W.	18	Marburg	64-0639
VETTEL, Babara	21	Heppenheim	65-1088
VETTEL, Therese	23	Heppenheim	67-0007
VETTER, Adam	29	Gleisberg	63-0398
VETTER, Carl Hr. A	18	Hille	67-0599
VETTER, Conrad	35	Winterkasten	65-1088
Elisabeth 33, Anna 9, Elisabeth 5, Adam 2			
VETTER, Conrad	30	Stockhausen	65-1031
Catharine 21			
VETTER, Gustav	43	Lulingen/Hann	64-0920
VETTER, Jacob	35	Behla	65-0950
VETTER, Joh.	29	Lindenfels	64-0992
Adam 25, Agnes 22			
VETTER, Johann	24	Schlierbach	66-0679
VETTER, Marg.	20	Bledesheim	64-0214
VETTER, Peter	24	Weissenheim	66-0221
VETTERLE, Johann	30	Wodnien	67-0007
VIAL, Felix	33	France	64-0170
VICHEG, Catharina	29	New York	63-0015
VICTOR, Albert	21	Varel	66-0984
VICTOR, Carl	21	New York	66-0109
VICTOR, Georg Fr.	26	New York	66-0109
VICTOR, Heinrich	22	Eberstadt	66-1127
VICTOR, Josepha	26	Neustadt	65-1088
VICTOR, Simon	22	Alze	64-0495
Bertha 18			
VICTORY, Marie	2	Grosmanrode	66-0623
VIDAVER, Henry	31	Berlin	64-0938
Alva 19			
VIEBROCK, Claus	20	Balkenwede	66-0984
VIEDINGHOFF, F.(m)	44	Wilmington	63-0551
VIEHBROCK, Cathar.	21	Zeven	64-0739
VIEHMEYER, Louis	27	Wildungen	67-0600
VIELHAUER, Joh.	73	Berwangen	65-0402
VIENOP, Ernst	17	Luebbeke	65-1031
VIENOP, Fr.	21	Minden	65-1031
VIEREGG, H.	57	Lippe	66-0413
Wilhelm 58			
VIEREGGE, Simon	18	Harchheide	63-0482
VIERENZ, Heinrich	21	Landau	66-0346
VIERHELLER, J.Adam	59	Rodau	63-0053
VIERHELLER, Johann	40	Busenborn	64-0885
Maria Anna 26			
VIERING, Ernst	28	New York	63-0013
VIERING, Wilh.	29	Cuelk	65-0713
VIESEL, Conrad	17	Remmingsheim	66-1155
VIESER, Elisabeth	32	Havre	64-0214
VIESING, Friedr.	33	Mengeringhaus	66-0837
VIESS, Friedr. Wh.	32	Velbert	65-0948
VIESS, Math.	42	France	63-0350
Marie 40, Franz 7, Escaville 13, Henry 5			
Joseph 1, Cathrina 69			
VIETH, Christian	34	Owieczeck	65-0770
VIETH, Wilh.	18	Obernkirchen	64-0214
VIETS, Joachim	50	Hartefeld	66-1128
Rebecca 46, Engel 17, Joachim 19			
Hinrich 12, Rebecca 7, Johann 6			
VIEWEGER, Bernhard	19	Zeulenroda	66-1155
VIGEKSABGM Adela	17	Hannover	64-0432
Mathilde 15			
VIGETOR, D.	25	Buende	66-0349
VIGNE, de la M.	21	Bohemia	64-0593
VILBROCK, Heinrich	18	Kasefeld	66-1128
VILLMANN, Wilhelm	26	Giessen	66-1155
VINKE, Carl	16	Isenstedt	65-1030

NAME	AGE	RESIDENCE	YR-LIST
VIOL, Wm.	30	Danzig	63-0752
VIRESS, Cathar.	42	Cincinnati	63-0752
Cathar. 21			
VISEL, Martin	59	Derendingen	66-1155
Catharina 21			
VISKER, Berend	56	Wegnard	66-0704
VISSELMEYER, Wilh.	19	Luebbeke	65-1031
VISSER, Johanna	26	Bremen	64-0840
VITT, Kansten	15	Stotel	64-0739
VOECKER, Joseph	36	Stadtlohn	66-0349
VOECKLER, Elise	19	Lohne	63-0953
VOECKS, Wilhelm	20	Wauderig	65-1140
Dorothea 54, Friedrich 18, August 16			
Emilie 12			
VOEGE, Joh.	15	Emtinghausen	65-0189
VOEGELIN, Johann	28	Basel	66-1093
VOEGTLE, Friedr.	40	Baden	66-0221
Cathar. 27, Adolph 7m			
VOEHL, Johann	32	Haina	66-0576
VOEHRING, A.B.(f)	18	Rissingen	64-0331
VOELCKER, Maria	22	Darmstadt	64-0885
VOELKEL, Margareth	34	Pennsylvania	66-0349
Conrad 4			
VOELKENING, Carl	68	Luebbecke	66-0083
VOELKER, Georg Val	57	Gibichenstein	65-0243
Eva 53, Cathar. 7, Eva 19			
VOELKER, George Ch	46	New York	63-0168
VOELKER, Jacob	23	New York	63-0752
VOELKER, Margareth	30	Duerkheim	66-1155
Helene 22			
VOELKERS, Meta	25	Rahde	66-1127
VOELLING, Carl	20	Bohmte	65-0948
VOELLM, Marie	22	Asperg	66-0083
Catharine 15			
VOELZING, Conrad	43	Arnshain	66-0349
VOERBRUCK, Gerh.	21	Wengsel	66-1127
VOEREST, Bernard	31	Eppe	66-0623
VOETSCH, Math.	35	Engstlatt	63-0168
VOGE, Ida	21	Braunschweig	66-0934
VOGEL, August	30	Ritterode	66-1155
Heinrich 36, Friederike 24			
VOGEL, Carl	26	Helminghausen	66-0984
VOGEL, Carl	18	Nuertingen	66-1203
VOGEL, Carl Aug.	23	Solingen	63-0822
VOGEL, Caroline	22	Hessen	63-0614
VOGEL, Caroline	55	Oberlongwitz	63-0482
VOGEL, Christine	22	Daertzbach	63-1085
VOGEL, Ernst D.	21	Ebstorf	66-1155
VOGEL, Franz	23	New York	63-0990
VOGEL, Friedrich	17	Darmstadt	66-1031
VOGEL, Geo.	25	Gersprenz	65-0594
VOGEL, Heinr.	31	Jaxthausen	65-0189
VOGEL, Heinrich	20	Scharmbeck	66-1327
VOGEL, Henriette	33	Berlin	65-1024
Oscar 6, Rud. 4, Paul 9m			
VOGEL, Hugo	23	Lichtenfein	67-0007
VOGEL, J.A.	28	Nemmersdorf	64-0687
VOGEL, J.G.(m)	26	Lotschen	64-0495
VOGEL, Jacob	41	St. Louis	64-0023
VOGEL, Jacob	22	Nienburg	66-0577
VOGEL, Joh.	25	Kirchberg	64-0138
VOGEL, Joh.	25	Rohden	65-0116
VOGEL, Joh.	32	Eisenheim	65-1030
Eva 27			
VOGEL, Joh. Aug.	53	Berlin	64-0886
VOGEL, Lina	21	Ludwigsburg	64-0938
VOGEL, Louis	23	St. Louis	63-0917
Mary 20			
VOGEL, Ludwig	22	Reinsdorf	66-1373
VOGEL, Marianne	19	Schenklengsfd	66-0934
VOGEL, Regine	18	Sohlingen	64-0331
VOGEL, Sophie W.	40	St. Louis	63-0168
VOGELE, Adolph	17	Bruchmuhlbach	64-0782
Heinrich 7, Caroline 21			
VOGELER, Gerhard	8	Sontra	66-0083
VOGELER, Joh.	34	Cassel	66-1313
VOGELFAHL, Heinr.	29	Verden	65-0950
VOGELHUND, Jacob	49	Gemuend	64-0886
Pauline 36			
VOGELKAMP, Ernst	19	Lippstadt	66-1031
VOGELMANN, F.(m)	24	Gmuend	64-0170
VOGELMANN, Gottfr.	28	Uttenhofen	64-0433
Anna 23			
VOGELMANN, Marie	31	Heilbronn	66-1131
Carl 7, Adolph 4			
VOGELSANG, Heinr.	35	Arhaus	65-1030
VOGELWOHL, Regina	32	Rieste	66-1373
VOGES, Fritz	28	Hannover	65-1088
VOGES, Leonhard	22	Braunschweig	67-0007
VOGHT, Claus	22	Ahlerstedt	65-1030
VOGL, Lotti	20	Eger	64-0886
VOGLER, Baptist	24	Krauschemaus	64-0170
VOGLER, Catharina	15	Mainz	64-1206
VOGLER, Catharine	22	Schnaid	63-1178
VOGLER, Cunigunde	25	Windischgrun	66-1327
VOGLER, Henry	26	Truelicon	63-0551
VOGRIN, Catharine	52	Boehmen	63-0693
Catharine 17			
VOGT, Anna	34	Ersingen	65-1024
Fanni 6, Marie 26			
VOGT, Arnold	30	Bremen	64-0639
Catharine 30, Johanna 3, Frierich 1m			
VOGT, Carl	28	Fabbenstadt	64-0886
VOGT, Caroline	20	Eberschutz	64-0782
VOGT, Caspar	21	Gesmold	63-0350
VOGT, Caspar	19	Dossenheim	66-1313
VOGT, Ernst Heinr.	42	Minden	66-1128
Anne Marie 39, Caroline 7, Friederike 6			
Ernst 4, Louise 9m			
VOGT, H.(m)	36	New York	64-0363
VOGT, Heinr.	39	Hagenburg	65-0038
VOGT, Hr. Ludw.	28	Bunde	64-0073
VOGT, Lorenz	28	Otterndorf	66-1031
VOGT, Therese	22	Oberhof	63-1085
VOGT, Theresia	22	Hessen	64-0432
Elise 24			
VOGT, W.	55	Essen	63-0990
VOGT, Wilhelm	27	Hamburg	66-1128
VOGTE, Joh. Ph.	14	Kattenkamp	64-0938
VOHL, Fr.	21	Leipzig	65-1088
VOIGT, (f)	23	Peoria	66-0934
VOIGT, Anna	21	Strasburg	65-0116
VOIGT, August	25	Hannover	66-1203
VOIGT, Bernhard	24	Behndorf	66-1093
VOIGT, Carl	15	Lubbeke	65-0713
VOIGT, Carol.Agnes	51	Frankfurt/O.	67-0795
Mathilde 22			
VOIGT, Emil	24	Limbach	66-1203
VOIGT, Friedrich	24	Una	66-1127
VOIGT, Herm.	31	Magdeburg	65-0950
VOIGT, Hugh	27	Berlin	63-0168
VOIGT, Therese	58	Leipzig	66-1327
VOIGT, Wilh.	22	Burg	65-0950
VOIGT, Wilhelm	51	Bayern	66-0221
VOIGT, Wilhelmine	33	Magdeburg	64-0593
VOLAND, Casp.	21	St. Louis	63-1136
VOLCK, Paul	28	New York	66-0934
VOLDERAUER, Rich.	24	Constanz	64-0432
VOLHARDT, Ernst W.	31	Fahrnau	65-0898
VOLK, Barbara	19	Waldurn	66-1203
VOLK, James	26	New York	63-0551
VOLK, Johann Adam	20	Schmalkalden	66-1373
VOLKENING, Ludwig	41	Oeynhausen	64-1108
VOLKENS, Diedr.	35	Osternbruch	64-1053
Cath. 21			
VOLKHARDT, Friedr.	20	Lienbach	66-1248
VOLKHARDT, Heinr.	19	Salzungen	66-1248
VOLKITZ, Gerh.	33	Leipzig	66-0221
VOLKMANN, Albert	21	Bremen	67-0600
VOLKMANN, C.(m)	19	Preussen	64-0331
VOLKMANN, Carl	18	Bremen	67-0600
VOLKMANN, Ferdin.	30	Mechenstein	66-0346
Henriette 33, Albert 6, August 3			
Bertha 6m			
VOLKMANN, H.(m)	19	Hahlen	64-0331
VOLKMANN, Jacob	28	Heuchelheim	64-0138

NAME	AGE	RESIDENCE	YR-LIST
VOLKMANN, Marie	17	Rothenuffeln	64-0214
Ernst H. 15			
VOLKMANN, Richard	16	Zwickau	64-0687
VOLKMANN, Wm.	19	Petersburg	64-1053
VOLKMAR, Chr.	28	Herfurt	64-1206
VOLKMAR, Emilie	29	Herford	65-0243
VOLKMAR, Max	20	Frankenstein	66-0576
VOLL, Cordula	24	Urrhausen	64-0023
VOLL, Valentin	39	Philadelphia	64-0593
Caspar 31, Johann 34			
VOLLAND, G.F.(m)	19	Tuebingen	64-0138
VOLLAND, Joh.	25	Pfaffenhofen	64-0427
VOLLBRECHT, Whlmne	27	Thedinghausen	65-0189
VOLLE, Carl Fr.	18	vollmerdingen	66-1155
VOLLERS, Beka	25	Lehe	66-1327
VOLLGRAF, Georg	18	Rotenburg	64-0639
VOLLIN, J.	23	France	63-0350
VOLLKAEMPFER, Chr.	27	Borgholzhsn.	64-0214
VOLLMECKE, Franz	38	Preussen	64-0214
VOLLMER, Agnes	26	Osterode	64-0840
Lise 4, Anna 1			
VOLLMER, Anna	24	New York	63-1069
VOLLMER, Ernst	18	Lauenhagen	66-1031
VOLLMER, Franz	26	Baden	66-0469
VOLLMER, Gottlieb	20	Geradsfehn	67-0007
VOLLMER, Gottlieb	23	Bielefeld	65-1030
VOLLMER, Magdalena	57	Ainheim	66-1155
VOLLMER, Philipine	28	Niedermohr	65-0950
Jacob 3m			
VOLLMER, William	23	Rieningen	63-0693
VOLLMERSHAUSEN, J.	30	Bracht	66-0412
Anna Cath. 32, Heinrich 3, Elisabeth 3m			
VOLLRATH, Adolph	34	Zeitz	64-0170
VOLLWEITER, Cath.	18	Baden	66-0576
VOLMARING, Joh.	30	Soegel	65-1024
Maria 31			
VOLMER, Anton	31	Meschede	66-0704
VOLMER, Mathias	28	Golsdorf	66-1373
VOLS, Wilh.	34	Schrevenhagen	66-0650
Margareth 42, Heinz 14			
VOLTE, Hinrich	28	Bissendorf	65-0948
Chr. Hinrich 24			
VOLTERS, Marg.	58	Inschede	65-0974
Gretchen 22, J.H. 19			
VOLTZ, Marie	35	Nuernberg	65-0007
F.C. 11, C.F. 9			
VOLTZ, Valentin	23	Hornstein	63-1085
VOLWERT, Ludwig	23	Kirchhain	66-0984
VOLZ, Catharine	20	Hoernstein	65-0189
VOLZ, Heinr.	15	Barenhausen	64-0840
Anton 39, Cath. 23			
VOMBRE, Anna	31	Heffen	65-1030
VONWEILER, Jac.	22	Malans	65-0007
VONWILLER, J.Bernh	45	St Gallen	64-0073
VORAN, V.	43	Kotsch	66-0413
VORBACH, Caspar	21	Altenbrueck	64-0840
VORBACH, Friedrich	24	Heidelberg	63-1178
VORDERBRUEGGE, Joh	16	Barstingdorf	66-0734
VORENBERG, Jettche	20	Greben	63-0821
VOREUTER, Eva E.	24	Gormern	63-0006
VORHANER, Martha	16	Hofgeismar	66-0221
VORHOLD, Bernhard	21	Benstrup	66-0934
VORHOLZ, Adolph	19	Berg	64-0214
VORK, Eberhard	32	Herford	66-0109
VORLANDER, M.	24	Minden	64-0495
VORNDRAU, Christ.	24	Laubach	64-0840
VORRATH, J.G.(m)	20	Luedingworth	64-0363
VORRATH, J.H.	23	Bodenworth	64-0992
VORRATH, Joh.	24	Bereusch	65-0151
VORRATH, Margareth	19	Bederkesa	66-0934
VORRATH, P.D.H.	26	Berensch	64-0886
VORRAUTER, Matilda	19	Salzdorf	64-0687
VOSACKE, Jos.	25	Hopsen	64-0687
VOSHAGE, Christ.	27	Vollbruch	64-0456
VOSS, Albert	26	Ohlendorf	64-0886
Catharina 23			
VOSS, Anna	24	Quakenbrueck	64-0739
VOSS, Carl	52	Solingen	64-0992
Franz 23			
VOSS, Columba	24	Aachen	63-1218
VOSS, Franz	20	Iburg	66-1128
VOSS, Friedr.	15	Hiddingen	66-0734
VOSS, Friedr. G.	36	Cassin	64-0840
Marie 40, Wilhelmine 7, Marie 9m			
VOSS, Georg	29	Westenholz	64-0433
VOSS, Gustav	23	Prussia	64-0170
Mathilde 15			
VOSS, Heinrich	21	Fuerstenau	66-1373
VOSS, Lewis	37	Potsdam	63-0482
VOSS, Louis	29	Braunschweig	65-0974
VOSS, Marie Carol.	20	Hameln	65-1031
VOSS, Norman	41	Kreiensen	66-1327
VOSS, Sophie	18	Cassel	64-1053
VOSS, Theodor	22	Sutrup	66-1093
VOSSEL, Johannes	35	Wellingholzhs	65-0770
Catharina 40, Mathias 13, Johann David 8			
Casper Heinr 9m, Casper 9m			
VOSSELER, Johann	26	Thueringen	66-0679
VOSSELER, W.(m)	37	Laufen	64-0495
S.(f) 26, M.(f) 2, Jac. 9m, Xaver 28			
P.(f) 20			
VOSSKOETTER, Heinr	45	Cincinnati	64-0073
VOSSLER, Dan.	22	Mietersheim	64-0427
VOSSLER, Kaspar	28	Osnabrueck	63-1069
VOTEL, Anna Marie	19	Listrup	65-0189
VOTZ, Carl	26	Wuerttemberg	66-0083
VOWATNY, Ignatz	27	Boehmen	66-0221
Marie 24, Stanislaus 3m			
VRAUT, Christine	22	Laubach	66-0704
VREHL, Heinr. Chr.	29	Osterkappeln	64-0687
VRIES, de Cath.	25	Vegesack	64-1108
VRIES, de Henry	60	Vegesack	66-1155
Anna 55			
VRING, v.d. D.	30	Oldenburg	64-0363
VULLMEYER, Jacob	39	Karlshafen	66-0413
Johanna 39			
WABERT, August	46	Oberorle	65-1088
Cath. 41, Cath. 20, Maria 18			
Magdalena 10, Jacob 8, Elisabeth 6			
Catharine 3, Catharine M. 2			
WACH, Louis	21	Bielefeld	66-0934
WACH, Louis R.	17	Bielefeld	63-0350
WACHA, Matthias	39	Boehmen	66-0349
Marie 10			
WACHER, Georg	26	Williamsburg	65-0007
WACHES, Emma	19	Sul	66-1131
WACHHOLZ, Fr.	32	Warrenton	64-0073
WACHLER, Wilhelm	24	Wasseraffnign	66-1203
WACHMANN, David	14	Cincinnati	63-0350
WACHNER, Waldburga	23	Buchau	66-0221
WACHS, Aug.	19	Bockenheim	64-0427
WACHSMUTH, (f)	25	Magdeburg	64-0782
Mch. 22			
WACHSMUTH, G.	25	Soden/Hess.	65-0038
WACHTEL, Marianne	18	Gehaus/Sax.	64-0920
WACHTEL, Peter	41	Bezdekau	66-1373
WACHTER, Albert	30	Strasburg	65-0116
Francisca 28			
WACHTER, Maria	36	Waltershalm	63-1085
WACK, Friedr.	27	Darmstadt	66-1203
WACKER, Dorothea	26	Dorflis	66-0984
Roeschen 4, Georg 2			
WACKER, Fr.	59	Grunbach	64-0782
WACKER, Fr.	18	Moehringen	65-0402
WACKER, Heinr.	33	Ostenfelde	66-0984
WACKER, Henry	24	Hannover	66-0109
WADEL, Chr.	36	Bremen	64-0363
An. (f) 9			
WADHIACK, Johann	25	Smogelsdorf	66-0412
Anna 26, Catharine 6m			
WADTGE, G.	24	Baltimore	63-0013
Heinrich 26, Maria 20			
WAECHTER, Augusta	30	Jersey City	63-1069
WAECHTER, Carol.	55	Hanan	64-0639
WAECHTER, Georg	29	Fuchsstadt	66-1203
Eberhard 34			

NAME	AGE	RESIDENCE	YR-LIST
WAECHTER, Johann	17	Northeim	66-0623
WAEGER, Anton	30	Krefeld	66-0469
WAEGLER, Anton	23	Muenchweiler	66-0147
WAEHRE, Dorette	24	Ingeln	66-0734
WAELLENSTEIN, Mary	17	Sand	64-0433
WAEPER, Hartmann	54	Siefenshausen	64-0433
Anna Cath. 50, Ludwig 19, Johann Peter 13			
Johann Adam 7			
WAETJEN, Diedrich	20	Gomaringen	66-0679
WAETJEN, H.	22	Bremen	63-0482
WAETJEN, H.	24	Sudweyhe	64-0214
WAETJEN, Oltmann	20	Walle/Bremen	66-0704
WAGEMEYER, Heinr.	49	Paderborn	65-1095
Katharina 48			
WAGENBAUER, Chr.	30	Kalm	65-0402
WAGENER, Augusta	20	Magdeburg	64-0639
WAGENER, Elisabeth	22	Winterscheid	65-0770
WAGENER, Franzisca	21	New York	63-0862
WAGENER, Julius	45	Reichenbach	66-0704
WAGENER, Martin	29	Borruchoeon	66-0413
WAGENER, Nic.	28	Hindheim	64-0639
Margarthe 11m			
WAGENER, Peter	35	Muehlheim	63-0990
Ana 36, John 5, Marie 3, Juliana 6m			
WAGENHEIM, Johanna	24	Lenne	66-0469
WAGENSCHWANZ, Frdr	30	Ratspert	66-0147
Elisa 31			
WAGNENER, Albert	42	Giebenhalle	64-0363
WAGNER, A.	24	Sellbach	65-0007
WAGNER, Alb.	20	Carlsruhe	64-1022
WAGNER, Anna	23	Worms	66-1093
Otto 2			
WAGNER, Augusta	21	Penig	66-0984
WAGNER, Balthasar	23	Coburg	65-0243
WAGNER, Brodasius	43	Neukirch	65-0189
WAGNER, Carl	64	Darmstadt	64-0170
Cath. 38, Carl 9, Eva 7, Ludw. 5			
WAGNER, Carl	17	Bicken	64-0593
WAGNER, Carl	19	Roecke	66-0934
WAGNER, Caspar	30	Einortshausen	65-0116
Elise 57, Joh. 33			
WAGNER, Caspar	39	Moehringen	65-0402
WAGNER, Catharina	17	Lohne	66-0679
WAGNER, Chr.	31	Bielefeld	63-1038
Sophie 21			
WAGNER, Chris.	46	Mengringhsn.	63-0013
John 9m			
WAGNER, Christ.	22	Moehringen	64-1108
WAGNER, Christian	41	Giessen	64-1206
WAGNER, Chs.	64	Neustadt	64-0495
Johann 26, Wilhelmine 3m, Julie 30			
Lucia 28, Jette 9m			
WAGNER, Elisabeth	21	Gmuenden	66-0679
WAGNER, Elisabeth	38	Giessen	66-0934
WAGNER, Elisabetha	34	Giessen	64-0840
baby 1			
WAGNER, Elise	22	Darmstadt	66-1031
WAGNER, Ernst	21	Bremen	65-0770
Georg 18			
WAGNER, Fr.	33	Marburg	64-0938
WAGNER, Francis	35	New York	63-0752
WAGNER, Franz	28	Freinsheim	67-0007
Cathrine 25			
WAGNER, Franzisca	40	Giessen	66-0934
WAGNER, Friedr.	32	Kaiserslauter	64-0840
WAGNER, Georg	31	Boston	64-0073
WAGNER, Georg	31	Obergereuth	66-0147
WAGNER, Georg	31	Washington	63-0953
WAGNER, Gertrude	23	Bonn	64-0199
WAGNER, Heinrich	26	Bayern	66-0147
WAGNER, Heinrich	28	Barmen	66-0837
WAGNER, Helene	24	Tiessen	64-0840
WAGNER, Henry	41	Friedrichstal	63-0244
John 18, Lewis 22, Christian 17, E. 34			
J. 8, H. 3			
WAGNER, Herm.	24	Duesseldorf	64-0938
WAGNER, Hermann	18	Eberstadt	66-1327
WAGNER, Joh.	32	Friedewalde	63-1003
A. 25, J. 8, A. 2			
WAGNER, Joh.	19	Grebenstein	65-0974
WAGNER, Joh. A.	31	Aurich	65-0189
WAGNER, Joh. Conr.	48	Fauerbach	65-1030
WAGNER, Joh. Math.	59	Baiern	63-1069
WAGNER, Johann	39	Duerkheim	66-0837
Eva 42, Wilhelm 10, Dorothea 8, Hannes 5			
Jacob 3			
WAGNER, Johann	66	New York	64-0427
WAGNER, Johann G.	19	Simmershausen	65-1095
Geo. Wilhelm 17			
WAGNER, Johannes	31	Oberzelle	66-0650
Kunigunde 30, Heinr. 5, Louise 3			
Wilhelm 9m			
WAGNER, John	27	Welsenbrunn	63-1085
Augusta 27, Robert 2, Ida 1			
WAGNER, Jos.	20	Boehmen	63-0821
WAGNER, Josepha	28	Ober-Hausdorf	63-0693
WAGNER, Jost	47	Reinbolderode	64-0886
Elisabeth 46, Bernhard 22, Hermann 7			
Louise 5, Margarethe 9m			
WAGNER, Julius	17	Altenburg	66-0984
WAGNER, Julius	31	Plauen	66-1373
WAGNER, Karl	38	San Francisco	63-0350
Wilhelmine 24, William 4, Alex 3			
Emilie 1			
WAGNER, Louise	41	Stuttgart	66-1093
WAGNER, Ludwig	46	New York	63-0953
Antonia 43, Georg 4			
WAGNER, Ludwig	33	Paderborn	66-1127
WAGNER, Marg.	30	Kassel	65-0402
WAGNER, Margaret	21	Gielert	64-0331
WAGNER, Maria	31	Fritzlar	63-1069
Elise 33			
WAGNER, Maria	24	Heppenheim	66-0679
WAGNER, Maria	25	Himbach	66-1327
WAGNER, Marie	22	Heimendingen	63-0097
WAGNER, Mary	22	Wollman	64-1053
WAGNER, Math.(f)	24	Pochingen	64-0495
WAGNER, Peter	44	Kollbach	64-0739
elisabeth 43, Margareth 24, Friedrich 7			
WAGNER, Philipp	22	Alsfeld	63-0168
WAGNER, Sophie	21	Wuerttemberg	64-0687
WAGNER, Stephan	31	Cassel	65-0594
Heinr. 19, Johanna 21			
WAGNER, Susanna	14	Fuerfeld	63-1136
WAGNER, Theodor	26	Stuttgart	66-0934
WAGNER, W.(m)	31	New York	64-0593
WAGNER, Wilhelm	21	Wollmer	66-0984
WAGNER, Wilhelm	28	Minden	64-0840
WAGNER, Wilhelm	22	Ruppertsberg	66-1093
WAGONER, Mathilde	26	Chicago	63-0917
WAGSTAFF, A.(f)	42	New York	63-0015
WAHL, Adam	18	Holzhausen	23-0865
Johannes 24			
WAHL, Apolonia	19	Darmstadt	66-0221
WAHL, Christ.	26	Salzungen	64-0782
WAHL, Franz	35	Buchholz	63-0990
Louise 34, Louis 2, Richard 6m			
WAHL, Goerg	28	Ullerhausen	64-0214
WAHL, H.(m)	40	Williamsburg	64-0073
WAHL, Joseph	30	Riegel	63-1178
Rosa 23			
WAHL, Josephine	18	Bersenbrueck	65-1024
WAHL, Philip	19	Odenstein	66-0679
WAHL, W.A.G.	26	Ebersberg	65-0402
WAHLBAUM, J.H.	17	Gehrde	65-1024
WAHLDIEK, August	23	Neunburg	66-0083
WAHLE, Carl Andr.	18	Ziegelbronn	65-0007
WAHLEMEYER, Maria	52	Aspergle	64-0687
Friedr. 23, Wm. 18, Carl 17, Heinr. 17			
WAHLENMEYER, John	21	Aspegle	63-0482
WAHLHEIMER, Cath.	50	Neustadt	63-1178
WAHLMANN, Heinrich	32	Einbeck	66-1131
WAHNSCHAFFE, Rud.	34	New York	63-0168
WAHRENDORFF, Georg	41	Diepenau	65-0770
WAIBEL, Ludwig	14	Treschklingen	65-0594
WAIBLIN, W.(f)	18	Baden Baden	64-0495

NAME	AGE	RESIDENCE	YR-LIST
WAIDELICH, Joh. G.	36	Wildbad	64-0214
Dorothea 32, Joh. G. 70, Cath. 65			
Joh. 26			
WAITERSHAUSEN,Lina	23	New York	64-0073
WAITROTT, George	23	Riehelsdorf	66-1373
WALBAUER, Julie	24	Preussen	63-1218
WALBRACH, Conr.	28	Cassel	65-0594
Elise 26, Emma 11m			
WALBRECHT, Wm.	28	Osterode	64-0904
WALCHER, Barbara	21	Gloris	65-0243
WALD, Johanna	45	Krojanke	66-0704
Adam 9, David 8, Bertha 7			
WALDBART, Alex	20	Carlsruhe	66-0984
WALDBAUM, Cathrine	20	Gehrde	65-1024
WALDE, Herm.	22	Oldenburg	66-0221
WALDE, Lisette	23	Lohne	66-0984
WALDECK, Elisabeth	24	Alsfeld	66-1248
WALDECK, Ernst	19	Alsfeld	66-1248
WALDER, C.	32	Grossdorf	66-0413
Christ. 32			
WALDERMANN, Wilh.	41	Freienwalde	67-0353
Justine 40, Wilhelm 12, Friedrich 10			
Carl 7, Theodor 3			
WALDHEIM, Charles	45	Troy	63-0244
Dorothea 39, Helene 10, Louis 9, Johann 6			
Louise 9			
WALDIGE, Johanna	30	Hannover	66-1327
WALDIN, Anton	42	Heinrichshall	64-0886
Johanna 35, Olga 14, Paul 13, Bernhard 6			
Walter 2			
WALDMANN, Conrad	18	Fuerth	66-0934
WALDMANN, Heinrich	19	Bonames	66-1248
WALDORF, Jos.	25	Mannheim	65-1189
WALDOW, Friedr.	30	Groning	66-0469
Marie 25, Johanna 2			
WALDREI, Fr.	30	Molenban	65-0007
WALDSCHMIDT, A.Cth	26	Hessen	64-0432
WALDSCHMIDT, J.	17	Wora	65-1024
WALDSTEIN, Henr'tt	20	Berlin	63-0350
Ernestine 22			
WALENFELDT, Robert	16	Giessen	63-1218
WALENTA, Maria	24	Buhnberg	64-0433
WALERS, Michael	26	Dermbach	65-1088
WALISCH, Cecilie	52	Lorsch	66-1203
Alex 20			
WALJE, Wilh.	22	Ibbenbuehren	65-0898
WALKASS, Johann	49	Zewonin	66-0666
Josephine 29, Pauline 7, Anton 10m			
WALKER, Adam	19	Boulanden	66-1373
WALL, Anton	35	Hiskow	64-0433
Anna 34, Anna 2m, Maria 6, Antonia 5			
WALL, Christian	24	Altheim	66-1373
WALLACH, A.	40	New York	63-1178
WALLACH, Betty	25	Oberaula/Hess	64-0920
WALLACH, Bones	27	Schwarzenborn	64-0639
Roeschen 21			
WALLACH, E.	16	Ahlfeld	64-0639
WALLACH, Jonas	36	Schwarzenborn	65-0402
Rickchen 26, Dina 3, Joseph 1			
WALLACH, Salomon	64	Neukirchen	64-0938
Sarah 27			
WALLENHORST, Franz	24	Osnabrueck	66-1131
WALLENSTEIN, Fanny	19	Busack	65-0594
WALLER, G.C.	42	Stade	64-0427
Conr. 18, Cath. 39, C.(f) 15, Marie 7			
WALLER, Maria	24	Fritzlar	65-1088
WALLERSTEIN, Herm.	36	Buchau	65-0402
Betty 26, Joseph 5, Clara 3, David 9m			
WALLHOF, Louise	24	Wiedeswehre	64-0639
WALLING, Heinr.	27	Ritzebuettel	67-0007
WALLMANN, Georg	23	Beverstedt	66-1373
WALLMANN, Johann	19	Schinkel	66-1131
WALLMANN, Paul	38	Havre	64-0214
WALLMANN, Wilhelm	28	Nauheim	66-0221
WALLOCH, Joseph	27	Flatow	65-0950
WALLRAFF, Anton	30	Oberhausen	66-0679
WALLRAND, Gertrud	18	Trier	64-0938
WALLSCHMIDT, Heinr	54	Wohra	66-0666
Elisabeth 45, Heinrich 5, Conrad 14			
WALLSTEIN, Griakus	30	Eisenach	67-0795
Elise 27, Elise 2			
WALPER, Elise	31	Darmstadt	66-0469
Wilhelm 6			
WALRAWE, Wilhelm	32	Stadtlohn	63-0482
Anna Marie 34, Maria Agnes 14			
Maria Cath. 9, Berh. Wm. 5			
WALSER, Emilie	16	Constanz	64-0363
WALTEMATH, P.(m)	21	Bremen	64-0170
WALTER, Anna	21	Hannover	66-1127
WALTER, C.G.	54	Thalheim	64-0331
Johanna 21			
WALTER, Cathar.	23	Ofterdingen	63-1218
WALTER, Catharine	48	Worms	67-0599
Carl 28, Peter 23, Anna 15, Philipp 9			
Conrad 8			
WALTER, Cora	21	Langel	64-1161
WALTER, Emil	24	Hohenbra	66-0934
Adeline 19			
WALTER, Georg	60	Dettingen	66-1327
WALTER, H.	30	New York	63-1136
WALTER, Henry	30	Oberodenbach	66-0109
WALTER, Joh. Alois	59	Ruelsheim	65-0713
Anna 24			
WALTER, Johann	49	Moschitz	66-0578
Henriette 48, Wilhelm 20, August 15			
Wilhelmine 9			
WALTER, John	35	America	63-0917
Cath. 37, John 2			
WALTER, John	22	Heidesheim	66-1327
WALTER, Martin	23	Auggen	65-0116
WALTER, Paul	23	London	66-0147
WALTER, Steinnach	25		66-0650
WALTERMATH, W.(m)	23	Bremen	64-0138
WALTHEIM, Heinrich	30	Bergheim	65-1140
Luise 31, Minna 10, Caroline 5, Maria 3			
Luise 6m			
WALTHER, Alois	54	Grossheubach	66-0469
Therese 48, Lothar 19, Benedicta 15			
Pauline 10, Julius 8, Lorenz 6			
WALTHER, Angela	14	Arnstadt	65-0007
WALTHER, Christ.	32	Girard	64-0073
WALTHER, Henry	31	New York	63-1136
WALTHER, Henry	23	Lindheim	66-0109
Anna M. 24			
WALTHER, Joh. Fr.	55	Altenburg	64-0432
Hanne Ros. 43			
WALTHER, Jul.	23	Landau	66-0704
WALTHER, Karl	24	Stuttgart	66-0576
WALTHER, Maria	58	Darmstadt	63-1178
WALTHER, Philipp	44	Langenberghm.	65-1088
WALTHER, Susanne	26	Offstein	66-1155
WALTHER, Wilhelm	26	Wuerttemberg	66-0576
WALTHER, Wilhelm	44	Glashuetten	65-0770
WALTHMANN, Barbara	32	Wasserlosen	67-0795
Barbara 7, Alisius 6, Mathius 5			
Donathus 3, Maria 1m			
WALTJEN, Elise	20	Bremen	66-1203
WALTKE, Wilhelmine	21	Brueninghast.	67-0806
WALTZ, R.(m)	24	Prussia	64-0495
WALTZING, Conrad	24	Hannover	66-1373
WALZ, Carl	25	Carlsruhe	64-1022
Caroline 24, Christ.(f) 27			
WALZ, Eduard	19	Haeussen	65-0770
WALZ, Friedr.	30	Heilbronn	63-0990
WALZ, Heinrich	22	Heiterbach	63-0006
WALZ, Joseph	22	Wetringen	66-1327
WALZ, Kunigunde	25	Waltershausen	66-0576
WALZ, Leopold	28	Griesheim	66-0679
WALZ, Louise	20	Carlsruhe	66-1093
WALZ, Maria	39	Wuertemberg	63-0398
Martin 8			
WALZ, Maria	26	Herstelle	66-1131
WALZ, Martin	14	Mittelsdorf	66-1243
WALZ, Sophie	22	Carlsruhe	66-0679
WALZ, Wilhelm	24	Ohnenhausen	66-1155
WAMBACH, Anna	16	Fritzlar	66-0934

NAME	AGE	RESIDENCE	YR-LIST
WAMBACH, Conrad	39	Rauschenberg	65-1030
Margaretha 33, Anna Gertrud 9, Clara 5			
Conrad 3, Anna Martha 1, Conrad 17			
WAMBACH, Johann	27	Prussia	64-0363
WAMBACH, Leo	20	Cassel	65-0865
WAMMES, Adelheid	30	Wuerzburg	63-1178
WAMSLER, Louise	25	Strassdorf	63-0821
WANAUS, Johann	59	Posik	66-1131
WANAUS, Jos.	34	Boehmen	63-0917
Marianne 31, Jos 5, Anna 1			
WAND, Friederike	17	Erfurt	64-0432
Wilhelmine 15			
WANDERER, Eugen	33	Scheibe	64-0593
Emilie 30, Oscar 6, Laura 5, Wm. 3			
Emma 2, Albin 6m			
WANDMACHER, Wlhmne	17	Oxstedt	63-0614
WANDNAGEL, Christ.	30	Esslingen	64-0363
WANDNER, Carl	19	Muenchen	65-0594
WANECK, Franz	38	Crastau	66-0934
Mathilde 9, Anna 32, Franz 6, Johann 4			
Marie 7, Joseph 10m			
WANEK, Franz	33	Wamburg	66-1373
WANETSCHEK, Carol.		Bruenn	66-0704
WANGE, Ludwig	14	Duderstadt	66-1128
WANGLER, Conrad	15	Schweighausen	66-1327
WANICEK, Maria	30	Boehmen	63-0296
Antonia 7			
WANKERMANN, Fritz	23	Heldesheim	64-0495
WANKMEISTER, Meta	25	Vegesack	63-1085
WANNER, Gottlob	17	Ulm	63-0350
WANNER, Johann	29	Schweitz	66-0623
WANTROP, Justine	24	Pyrmont	66-1243
Mathilde 18			
WANZURA, J.(m)	32	Bohemia	64-0331
Anna 29, Maria 10m			
WAPLA, Franz E.	59	Neustadt	63-1085
Kunigunde 23			
WAPMANN, Gretchen	28	Degendorf	66-1093
Dorette 2			
WARANETZ, Josepha	26	Boehmen	64-0023
WARASEK, Elisabeth	26	Lutz	66-1155
baby 11m			
WARDELICH, Adam	33	Kettelfingen	64-0170
WARENS, Poppa	50	Suedenburg	63-0752
WARKER, Th.	48	New York	63-0482
WARKNER, Carl	36	Bega	65-0151
WARNCKE, Henry	54	Columbia	63-0244
WARNECK, L.	26	Gittelde	65-0007
Augusta 22, Bertha 10m			
WARNECKE, August	25	Rehburg	66-1093
WARNECKE, F.	31	Roschitz	66-0413
J. 28, Gustav 4, Gottl. 24			
WARNECKE, Friedr.	32	Alfeld	66-0083
WARNECKE, Friedr.	18	Oberfranken	66-1131
WARNECKE, Heinrich	21	Rotenburg	64-0739
WARNECKE, Hy.	32	Lilienthal	63-1085
WARNECKE, John	36	Ritzebuettel	63-0168
WARNECKEN, S.	23	Braunschweig	65-0974
WARNEKE, Gustav	15	Elze	66-1327
WARNEKEN, H.A.(m)	47	Bremen	64-0073
WARNER, Rosa	44	Pised	64-0170
Regine 22, John 19, Edward 9			
WARNER, Wilhelm	24	Osnabrueck	66-1093
WARNING, Fr. Aug.	33	Wisconsin	66-0704
WARNKE, F.	32	Bremen	64-0665
WARNKE, Heinr. Chr	14	Hannover	64-0432
WARNKE, Heinrich	18	Klumpeln	67-0007
WARNKE, J.H.	24	Sudweyhe	64-0214
WARNKEN, Aug.	45	New York	64-0073
WARNKEN, Fr.(m)	27	New York	64-0363
WARNKEN, Friedr.	31	Bremen	64-0214
Wilhelm 7, Eleonore 4, Anna Marg. 28			
Johanna 23, baby 6m, Claus 21			
Diedrich 29			
WARNKEN, J.H.	20	Sudweyhe	64-0495
WARNKEN, Joh. Frdr	52	Bremen	66-0221
WARNKEN, Johann	18	Weihe	66-1127
WARNKES, Eilt	24	Walle	66-1128

NAME	AGE	RESIDENCE	YR-LIST
WARNSMANN, H.G.	25	Hagen	64-0427
WARNSTORF, A.	37	Hannover	63-1003
WARREN, Harriet	20	Springfield	63-1085
Mary 6m			
WARTENBERG, Cath.	32	Kuttenberg	64-0170
WARTENS, August	25	Hannover	66-1131
WARTH, Chr. Fr.	25	Zuerich	63-0953
WARTH, Dorothea	23	Unterturkheim	66-0221
WARTH, Ph. Ch.	41	Birkenfeld	64-0343
WARTMANN, J.G.	29	Gesumbach	64-0073
Mrs. 25			
WARVERKA, Joseph	36	Boehmen	63-0006
Barbara 34, Franz 10, Jean 9, Anna 7			
Maria 5, Bertha 6m			
WARZELHAHN, Jacob	23	Geisenheim	65-0713
WASCH, Friedrich	20	Dorum	66-1248
WASCHE, Wenzel	32	Neschkardisch	64-0593
WASDEMUENDE, Heinr	42	Neumuenster	66-0666
Margarethe 50, Catharine 19			
WASEK, Anna	22	Carlsbad	66-0734
WASEL, Heinrich	26	Luebbecke	66-1127
WASKA, Ignatz	24	Cappeln	66-1203
WASKOW, Albert	34	Guedenhagen	66-0469
Wilhelmine 33, Hulda 6, Emil 3			
Mathilde 1			
WASKOWIAK, Rosalie	26	Moschietz	66-0413
J. 32, Johanna 5			
WASMANN, Anna	26	New York	63-0482
Ellen 3, Hugo 5			
WASMUTH, Johannes	20	Rhoda	65-1031
WASMUTH, Jul.	27	Daseburg	65-0402
WASS, Harry	38	Rouen	63-0350
WASSENEBERT, John	17	Manil	64-1053
WASSENPFLUG, Just.	29	Zimmerode	66-1127
WASSERBACH, Joh.	38	Horheim	66-0650
WASSERER, Marie	23	St Etienne	64-0023
Johanna 21			
WASSERMANN, C.	35	Fuerth	65-0974
WASSERMANN, Casmir	19	Gotthardt	66-0349
WASSERMANN, Chr.	40	Lauchheim	63-1136
WASSERMANN, Conrad	29	Schwarzbach	66-0349
WASSERMANN, Herman	37	Fuerth	64-0639
WASSERMANN, Jeanet	21	Aufhausen	65-0594
WASSERMANN, N.	19	Paris	63-1178
WASSERMANN, Victa.	25	Kurhessen	64-0432
WASSERVOGEL, Louis	30	Breslau	64-0782
WASSINE, Nicl.	18	Breitenbrenen	64-0886
WASSMER, Bernh.	42	Milwaukee	66-0734
WASSMUTH, Andreas	24	Teckelsheim	64-0433
WASSMUTH, Marie	16	Rhoda	66-0109
WATERMANN, Christ.	20	Behren	66-1203
Charlotte 23			
WATERMANN, H.	32	Leer	66-0413
Minna 28, Linchen 1			
WATERMANN, Wilhelm	22	Hessia	66-0679
WATERMEYER, Bertha	17	Welstorf	63-0482
WATERMEYER, H.R.	24	Bremen	66-0934
WATERSHAUSEN, Lina	23	Gruenberg	64-0023
WATJEN, Herm.	25	Lehrte	63-0350
WATTENBERG, Heinr.	17	Walldorf	67-0007
WAUANST, Wenzel	23	Boehmen	63-0917
Theresa 20			
WAUKE, Johann H.	21	Roschern	66-0934
WAULKER, Friedr. C	25	Buer	64-0920
WAUSCHAUER, J.	7	Krotsheim	64-1161
WAVRIN, Jos.	34	Boehmen	63-0917
Anna 22, Jos. 11m			
WAWRICK, Martin	54	Boehmen	63-0752
Anna 49, Maria 24, Antonia 9			
WAYGAND, Johann	41	Esslingen	66-0679
WAYNING, Carl	26	Ahdorf	66-1131
WEBBS, Robert	29	Cosel	66-1327
WEBER, A.	23	Gross Floethe	66-0413
WEBER, Andreas	18	Darmstadt	65-0865
WEBER, Anna	20	Dildershaus	64-0593
WEBER, Anna	24	Fritzlar	64-0938
WEBER, Anna	20	Sollenberg	66-1248
WEBER, Anna C.	17	Hainbach	64-0170

NAME	AGE	RESIDENCE	YR-LIST
WEBER, Anton	29	Thorn	66-0837
WEBER, Anton	27	Anzefahr	66-0837
WEBER, Anton	24	Koenigshafen	65-1031
WEBER, Barbara	55	Zeiskam/Boh.	65-0243
WEBER, Bernh.	17	Hermanstein	64-0782
WEBER, Bernhard	24	Hemelingen	65-0402
WEBER, Carl	45	Philadelphia	66-0412
Magdalene 50, Carl 10			
WEBER, Carl	19	New York	66-0577
WEBER, Carl	38	New York	66-0109
WEBER, Carl	20	Solingen	66-1128
WEBER, Carl	33	Stettin	65-0594
Louise 22, Otto 3, Marie 1			
WEBER, Carol.	27	Zweibruecken	66-1313
Ludwig 7			
WEBER, Caspar	21	Helfershe	64-0840
WEBER, Catharine	21	Etzingen/Wrt.	66-0469
WEBER, Catharine	20	Klingemunster	63-1085
WEBER, Ch.	19	Wetzheim	63-1085
WEBER, Chr.	33	Buer	64-0739
WEBER, Chris.	20	Wetzheim	63-0482
WEBER, Christian	17	Corbocke	66-1203
WEBER, Christian	29	Besigheim	65-0189
WEBER, Diedr.	17	Alsfeld	64-1206
WEBER, Diedr.	21	Bremen	66-1373
WEBER, Dorette	22	Cassel	65-0865
WEBER, Doris	27	Buer	64-1053
Wm. 39			
WEBER, Dorothea	22	Diepholz	66-1031
WEBER, Eduard	30	Baden	66-0469
WEBER, Elisabeth	22	Fellinghausen	63-1218
WEBER, Elisabeth	22	Buhlenberg	66-0083
WEBER, Elisabeth	57	Anzefahr	66-0837
Heinrich 17			
WEBER, Emilie	25	Coburg	63-0244
WEBER, Ernst	22	Cannstadt	64-0363
WEBER, Eva	26	Staudenheim	63-1178
WEBER, F.	22	Hannover	64-0593
WEBER, Fr.	25	Osterwald	65-1189
Ludeke 11m			
WEBER, Franz	34	Switzerland	64-0170
WEBER, Franz	34	Cansas	64-0782
Heinr. 28, Heinr. 7			
WEBER, Friedr.	23	Friedrichstal	64-0687
WEBER, Fritz	19	Wildbad	66-1155
WEBER, Georg	18	Elsoff	64-0782
WEBER, Georg	38	Neuenhain	66-0934
WEBER, Georg	20	Leimbach	66-1327
WEBER, Gottibia	19	Koenigsbrunn	65-1030
Anna 36			
WEBER, Gottlieb	26	Wuerttemberg	66-0576
WEBER, H.	20	Rheydt	64-0938
WEBER, Hedwig	30	New York	63-0015
WEBER, Heinrich	25	Hohmuelbach	66-0147
WEBER, Heinrich	21	Rohnshausen	63-0614
WEBER, Heinrich	17	Moischeit	66-0623
WEBER, Heinrich	29	Elberfeld	66-0837
Martha 39, Louise 7, Heinrich 4			
WEBER, Heinrich	18	Wehden	65-1024
WEBER, Henry	40	Lamersheim	63-0551
WEBER, Herm.	23	Troiseau/Aust	65-0898
Regine 22, Fanny 9m			
WEBER, Heymann	45	Breslau	63-0862
Ernestine 19, Johanne 17, Isidor 15			
WEBER, Jacob	18	Lich	66-0704
WEBER, Jacob	40	Rothenburg	67-0007
Caroline 26, Amalie 5, Jacob 9m			
WEBER, Jacob	54	Zeiskam	65-0243
Friedr. 27, Cath. 19			
WEBER, Joh. Jac	36	Bretzwyl	64-0023
Daniel 9			
WEBER, Johann	26	Germany	66-0666
WEBER, Johann	17	Rauschenberg	65-1030
WEBER, Johann Geo.	27	Heilbronn	66-0083
WEBER, Johannes	29	Evansville	66-0221
WEBER, Johannes	24	Kurhessen	66-0221
WEBER, Johannes	20	Lingen	64-0886
WEBER, Johannes	21	Rewal	65-0402

NAME	AGE	RESIDENCE	YR-LIST
WEBER, Joseph	32	Berlin	64-0023
WEBER, Joseph	29	Fulda	66-1128
Veronica 24, Rudolph 23			
WEBER, Joseph B.	56	Wuerttemberg	63-0168
WEBER, Julius	24	Haiger	66-0147
WEBER, Louis Mart.	31	Baltimore	63-1178
WEBER, Louise	15	Moehringen	64-1108
WEBER, Ludw.	18	Lich	63-0398
WEBER, Maria	25	Leese	66-0734
WEBER, Marie	22	Baden	66-0147
WEBER, Mart.	25	Lanzhausen	63-0953
WEBER, Mathias	48	Heinebach	66-1203
Anna 48, Cathrina 23, Elise 16, Martha 14			
Wilhelm 8			
WEBER, Michel	28	France	63-1038
WEBER, Oskar		Berlin	66-0666
WEBER, Paul	25	Lingen	67-0007
WEBER, Ph.	16	Erlau	64-0495
M. 25			
WEBER, Philipp	36	Salzschlief	65-0770
WEBER, Regina	16	Bissingen	66-0221
Marie 39			
WEBER, Rosalie	40	Berlin	64-1022
Daniel 4, Wilhelm 9m			
WEBER, Theodor	30	Ruessel	63-0990
WEBER, Thomas	59	Geissenbach	64-0687
WEBER, W.(F)	19	Rauschenberg	64-0938
WEBER, Wilh.	23	Wildungen	66-0221
WEBER, Wilhelm	23	Lemfoerde	66-1155
WEBER, Wilhelmine	31	Baden	66-0147
WEBER, Wilhelmine	17	Altenhof	66-0147
WEBER. Gertrud	25	Muenster	66-0349
WEBERLING, Friedr.	44	Osterholz	64-0639
WEBSTER, William	30	New York	66-0109
WECHART, W.	23	Bergheim	64-0782
WECHMAUER, T.	21	Esens	66-1248
WECHSELBERGER, Alb	20	Lahr	64-0138
WECHSLER, Henr'tt.	22	Mittelfranken	66-0984
WECHSUNG, Wm.	34	Ballenstedt	64-1161
WECHT, Adam	18	Munschbacht	66-0576
WECK, Anna	15	Werningerode	66-0934
WECK, Marie	26	Malin	67-0007
WECKBACKER, Barb.	25	Mietenberg	64-0214
WECKE, Fanni	26	Braunschweig	65-1024
WECKER, Armin	26	Gotha	66-1313
WECKER, Friedrich	29	Eimsheim	63-1218
WECKERBAUER, Jos.	31	Briloka	64-0433
WECKESGER, R.	24	Meckmeel	66-0413
WECKWERTH, Ferd.	28	Elzin	65-1030
Jule 26			
WEDDE, Albertine	22	Borreck	66-0666
WEDDINGEN, Ferd.	24	Ueberdingen	64-0687
WEDDINGER, C.	24	Barmen	65-1189
WEDEKAEMPER, Heinr	28	Dissen	66-1128
Anne Marie 40			
WEDEKIND, George	15	Lamstedt	63-0862
WEDEKING, Caroline	19	Cassel	66-0734
WEDEKING, F.	30	Sievershausen	66-0413
Dorothe 25, Minna 10m			
WEDELER, Siegmund	31	Nuernberg	67-0007
WEDELING, Albertin	19	Osterholz	65-0055
WEDELKING, Georg	33	Osterholz	65-0055
Amalie 26			
WEDEMEYER, H.	28	Neuenkirchen	65-0974
WEDEMEYER, Henry	36	Lehe	66-1155
WEDEMEYER, Herm.	45	New Orleans	63-1178
WEDEMEYER, Wilhelm	20	Dissen	66-1128
WEDIG, Henriette	30	Gruenstadt	64-0593
WEDLER, Philipp	27	Sandhofen	67-0007
Maria 28, Peda 5, Andreas 11m			
WEDMANN, Ed.	31	St Andreasbrg	65-0038
WEDMANN, Mich.	26	Biebgarten	63-1218
WEEBKING, H.	26	Schneeren	64-0992
WEEKING, Fr.	16	Tepenbrok	65-1031
WEELAGE, Heinrich	23	Ostenwald	66-1131
WEENER, Johanna	21	Lingen	64-0214
WEERMANN, Chr.	25	Stucken	65-0243
WEERTS, Georg	34	Hollogue a/P.	66-0734

NAME	AGE	RESIDENCE	YR-LIST
Josephine 31, Josephine 9, Anna 8			
Antoinette 7			
WEFLING, Diedrich	14	Brueninghast.	67-0806
WEG, v. Abrah.	18	Barmen	64-1108
WEGE, Cath.	28	Wolfgruben	65-0402
WEGE, Elisabeth	23	Frieberthsn.	66-1155
WEGE, Joh.	25	Weitershausen	63-0398
WEGE, Ludwig	16	Frohnhausen	66-1155
WEGENER, Carl	24	Schernebeck	65-0116
WEGENER, Christian	52	Pommern	66-0469
Johanna M. 48, Christian 22, Johann 20			
Fritz 19, Wilhelm 8			
WEGENER, Christian	45	Lubasch	64-0456
Caroline 30, Heinrich 4, Emil 9m			
WEGENER, Ernestine	24	Posen	64-0432
WEGENER, G.H.	28	Hannover	64-0432
WEGENER, Johann	27	Osterberken	66-1093
WEGENER, July	35	Margonin	64-0886
Emma 5			
WEGERLE, G.	14	Ulm	64-1161
WEGGEMANN, F.(m)	25	Buchau	64-0495
WEGHE, Henry	35	Memphis	63-1038
Marie 28, John 9, Hermann 7, Theodor 5			
Helene 9m			
WEGHORST, Wilh.	39	Indianapolis	63-1136
Hermann 9, Charlotte 5			
WEGLEIN, Sophie	26	Unterfranken	67-0007
WEGMAIER, Joh.	32	Aschet	65-0116
WEGMANN, A.(m)	35	Bottmer	64-0495
A.(f) 31, Ma.(f) 20, B.(f) 7, Jos.(m) 9m			
WEGMANN, Elise	18	Wuertemberg	66-0734
WEGMANN, Gerhard	25	Emsdetten	66-0412
WEGMANN, Joh. H.	25	Gauthe	64-0427
WEGMANN, Martin	31	Kempten	66-0221
WEGWARTH, Sophie	64	Freienwalde	67-0353
WEHE, Dorette	26	Goettingen	64-0073
WEHLAU, Johann	15	Freyberg	66-0679
WEHLE, Georg	22	Nordstetten	64-0331
WEHLE, M.(m)	50	New York	64-0170
WEHLING, Friedr.	25	Plaggenburg	64-0992
WEHMAIER, William	21	Schwarzenmoor	63-0917
WEHMANN, Hermann	49	Neuenbande	65-0243
Gerhard 37			
WEHMANN, Joh. E.	17	Burgdamm	65-0189
WEHMANN, Johanna	19	Vegesack	63-0862
WEHMANN, John	23	New York	64-0170
WEHMANN, Meta	25	Burgdaman	65-0713
WEHMEYER, Conrad	30	Fabenbueren	66-1373
WEHMEYER, Fr.	21	Pr.Laengerich	65-0189
WEHMEYER, Frdr. W.	36	Hefer	65-0948
WEHMEYER, Henr'tt.	16	Wehden	64-1022
Wilhelmine 14			
WEHMEYER, S.F.	28	Talle	63-0990
WEHMEYER, Sophie	21	Dielingen	65-1024
WEHN, Georg	26	Biedenkopf	65-0948
Emilie 27, Carl 1			
WEHNER, Edmund	22	Huenfeld	66-1155
WEHNER, Justine	26	Peoria	63-0244
William 9m, Charles 18			
WEHNER, Lucretia	25	Oberlimbach	66-0469
WEHNER, Ludw.	36	Erlbach	67-0795
Maria 24, Magdalena 3m			
WEHNER, Wm. Adolf	24	Fulda	66-1128
WEHRENBERG, Diedr.	17	Drehle	66-1093
WEHRHAHN, Heinrich	27	Sievershausen	67-0007
WEHRKAMP, Adolf Ld	17	Dissen	23-0865
WEHRMANN, Anna	20	Achim	65-0974
WEHRMANN, J.	26	Bremen	65-1189
WEHRMANN, Johann	24	Upleward	66-0679
WEHRMANN, Paul	21	Berlin	64-0073
WEHRS, Christian	30	Suhlingen	66-0934
Minna 33, Marie 4, Sophie 2			
WEHT, Betti	21	Dettingen	66-0734
WEHULL, Cresc.	24	Steig	63-1085
WEIBEL, Jacob	38	Otzenhausen	65-0402
Helene 38, Joh. 7, Jacob 6, Marg. 1			
WEIBLER, Louis	18	Reutlingen	66-0934
WEIBRECHT, Dorothe	16	Mainz	64-0432
WEICHEL, Elisabeth	19	Altenkronen	64-0433
WEICHELT, Johann	56	Ronnenberg	65-0770
WEICHMANN, Carl	23	Hannover	66-0734
Sophie 54			
WEICHSEL, Heym.	70	Rimbach	64-0427
Anna 39, Maria 7, Us. 5, Anna 9m			
Hannchen 23, Fanny 21			
WEICK, Friedrich	19	Graben	66-0083
WEICK, Ludw.	27	Heidelberg	64-0687
WEICKARD, Anna	25	Rheinpfalz	63-0917
Helene 20			
WEICKERT, Friedr.	25	New York	66-0147
WEIDEHAUS, Jos.	15	Norten	63-1010
WEIDEL, Gottfried	29	Schaffhausen	66-0083
Louise 34			
WEIDEMANN, August	43	Luerdissen	66-0083
WEIDEMANN, Engel	22	Bolinghausen	66-1155
WEIDEMUELLER, Ed.	22	Auerbach	66-1155
WEIDENER, Anton	15	Coln	66-1248
WEIDENFELD, Sigm.	59	New York	63-1038
WEIDER, Joh. Mich.	18	Fulda	66-0704
WEIDER, Joseph	31	Dermbach	66-0578
Josepha 27, Franciska 4, Adam 2			
WEIDIG, Emilie	26	Giessen	66-1327
WEIDIG, J.	16	Hassbach	65-0007
WEIDIG, Wilhelm	18	Stoltel	66-0668
Henriette 22			
WEIDLE, Carl	38	Ossweil	64-0886
Anna 42, Mathilde 7, Anna 3			
WEIDLICH, Benjamin	42	Duesseldorf	66-0837
WEIDMANN, Eduard	24	Asch	64-0739
WEIDMANN, Marg.	23	Sendelbach	64-0840
WEIDMANN, Wm.	22	Zweibruecken	64-0687
WEIDNER, Carl	36	Heilbronn	66-1093
Pauline 30, baby (f) 8m			
WEIDNER, Juliana	20	Bromberg	64-0432
Carl Aug. 26, Anna C. 48, Ernestine P. 17			
Augusta 13, Ernestine 9, Gottl. 8			
WEIERMUELLER, Carl	32	Pansa	66-0704
WEIGAND, Joh.	38	Hessen	66-0469
Elisabeth 42, Catharine 8, Johannes 6			
WEIGAND, Kilian	29	Ellenbach	66-0650
WEIGAND, Steph.	26	Ellenbach	66-0650
WEIGEL, Barbara	18	Zettlitz	66-0666
WEIGEL, Carl	20	Speyer	64-0363
WEIGEL, Josephine	20	Bretten	63-1218
WEIGEL, Wilhelm	31	Davern	67-0599
Franz 20			
WEIGEL, Wilhelm	22	Zschocken	66-1155
Pauline 24, Anna 6m			
WEIGELE, Chr.	18	Unterdingen	65-1189
WEIGELE, L.(f)	35	Altendorf	64-0495
WEIGELT, August	33	New York	66-0679
WEIGELT, Robert	17	Hellefeld	66-0837
WEIGERT, Augusta	46	Philadelphia	64-0495
WEIGERT, Wilhelm	21	Coeln	66-1093
WEIGMANN, Ludw.	43	Hannover	65-0594
Christine 43			
WEIHER, Balthasar	31	Mursbach	64-0593
WEIHING, Jonas	27	Gemaringen	67-0007
Barbara 25			
WEIHRAUCH, Fr'drke	41	Rudersdorf	66-0934
Augusta 17			
WEIK, Christine	18	Langentrand	66-0412
WEIKAM, Therese	19	Berlin	65-0116
WEIKLING, Dorothea	44	Oberssetten	65-0713
WEIL, Amalie	18	Frankfurt/M.	64-0886
WEIL, Anton	27	Wasenbach	66-1128
WEIL, Bernhard	7	Rezdican	64-0992
WEIL, Ernst	19	Berlin	64-0214
WEIL, F.	32	Holsdorf	64-0782
Cath. 7, Bernhard 17			
WEIL, Franz	32	Birschheim	66-1127
Cathrina 28, Marie 2, Emma 6m			
WEIL, Ida	25	Buchau	66-0704
WEIL, James	45	Mutterstadt	63-1178
Caroline 43, Adolph 16, Marcus 13, Rosa 9			
Mathilde 6			

NAME	AGE	RESIDENCE	YR-LIST
WEIL, Johannes	26	Affalterbach	64-1022
WEIL, Joseph	25	Hoppstaedten	66-0109
WEIL, Ludolph	21	Nordleda	63-0350
WEIL, M.	16	Kanndegg	63-1136
WEIL, Marcus	36	Evansville	63-0917
WEIL, Minna	25	Laupheim	64-1161
Jette 16			
WEIL, Pauli	21	Hannover	66-1093
WEIL, Peter	30	Worms	63-0296
WEIL, Rosalie	21	Hannover	63-0917
Alfred 14			
WEIL, Samuel	19	Havre	65-0004
Ida 18			
WEIL, Victor	28	London	64-0073
Rosalie 20			
WEILAGE, Heinr.	14	Gerde	64-0886
WEILAGEN, Lisette	22	Gehrde	63-1136
WEILAGEN, W.	28	Schweiz	63-1136
WEILAND, Louis	25	Louisville	66-0221
Christine 64			
WEILAND, Louis	34	Ulm	64-0840
WEILER, Cath. Elis	16	Wabern	64-0739
WEILER, Ernst.	28	Frohnhausen	63-0821
WEILER, Richard	25	Paris	63-1178
WEIMANN, Bernhard		Vechta/Oldenb	66-0346
WEIMANN, Ferdinand	17	Bremen	66-0083
WEIMANN, Gottlob	19	Wuertemberg	66-0984
WEIMANN, Johann	35	Rigland	66-0666
Anna 28			
WEIMANN, Louis	23	Gunsenhausen	66-1203
WEIMAR, Carl	19	Gotha	65-0004
WEIMAR, Magdalene	18	Weilheim	66-1203
WEIMBACH, Jacob	16	Bloedesheim	66-1093
WEIMER, Adolph	27	Pesth	63-1038
WEIMER, Josepha	26	Glasshofen	66-0623
WEIMER, Leonh.	35	Geisslingen	66-1313
Mathilde 25, Louise 9m			
WEIMER, Michael	39	Bohndorf	66-0412
WEIMER, Peter	22	Villmar	67-0007
WEINANG, Augusta	36	Cassel	66-1313
Adolphine 9			
WEINBERG, Aron	32	Luebbecke	64-0938
WEINBERG, Caroline	24	Rhina	66-0679
Hanchen 22			
WEINBERG, Ernstine	22	Schweinshsn.	65-0594
WEINBERG, Heinrich	23	Seele	65-1031
WEINBERG, Jacques	25	Wagenfeld	64-0687
WEINBERG, Johanna	27	Luebbecke	64-0886
WEINBERGER, Margr.	18	Rinteln	66-0679
WEINBRECHT, Ludw.	16	Suhl	66-0668
WEINBRICH, Christ.	24	Regensburg	64-0992
WEINER, Carl	47	Kahla	66-0668
Dorothea 50, Wilhelmine 20, Marie 20			
Louise 18, Carl 16, Adolph 14, Hermann 9			
WEINER, Cath.	22	Boehmen	63-0482
WEINER, Julie	30	Naumburg	64-0331
WEINERT, Adolph	40	Mainz	64-1022
WEINERT, Dorothea	49	Preussen	66-0469
Carl 19, Wilhelmine 14			
WEINFELD, Ester B.	53	Bartfeld	64-1108
Aide 14			
WEINGAERTNER, Frz.	30	Durmersheim	66-0704
baby 3m			
WEINGAERTNER, Theo	32	Hubern	66-0704
WEINGARTEN, Mart.	33	Troiseau/Aust	65-0898
Betty 26, Adolf 9m			
WEINGARTNER, Roman	27	Pfaffenrode	66-0576
WEINHARDT, Chr'tne	26	Deidelau	65-0950
WEINHARDT, Ernst	31	Schoenberg	65-0950
WEINHEIMER, Christ	19	Streschen	65-0594
WEINHEIMER, Sophie	36	Philadelphia	63-0990
WEINHOLT, G.(m)	34	Munsterberg	64-0331
WEINKAUF, Pauline	34	Offenburg	66-0704
Louise 31			
WEINLAND, Peter	35	Linden	64-0687
WEINMANN, Elisab.	15	Schwarzwald	65-0189
WEINMANN, Emilie	9	Pforzheim	65-0189
WEINMANN, Jac.	28	Wuerttenberg	66-0221

NAME	AGE	RESIDENCE	YR-LIST
WEINMANN, Joseph	48	Zepfenhan	63-0482
Caecilie 23			
WEINREICH, A.Marth	56	Hessen	64-0432
WEINREICH, Johanna	23	Burbach	65-1189
Marie 33			
WEINRICH, J.H.	23	Altenritte	65-0402
WEINSTEIN, August	43	Hannover	64-0920
WEINSTEIN, Louise	17	Cassel	65-0038
WEIRICH, Cath.	22	Spoonhain	66-0413
WEIRIUS, M.(m)	40	Germany	64-0170
WEIS, Herm.	28	Ruchenberg	64-0992
WEISBURGER, Valent	48	San Francisco	66-0147
WEISE, Marie	18	Thueringen	64-0687
WEISE, Robert	38	Weimar	64-0170
WEISHAUS, Fr.	22	Marburg	66-1243
WEISHEIT, Georg F.	56	Strahte/Hess.	67-0806
Elisabeth 17, Christoph 7			
WEISKOPF, Georg	44	Mit.Rainstadt	65-1088
Maria 31			
WEISLEIN, Maria	17	Joxberg	63-0752
WEISNER, Therese	43	Guerbelsdorf	64-1161
WEISREUTER, U.	29	Woiswalde	66-0413
WEISS, Adam	24	Obergereuth	66-0147
WEISS, Adam	25	Heppenheim	66-0734
WEISS, Ana	27	Trostingen	63-0990
WEISS, Anna M.	57	Hagenau	65-0594
WEISS, Aug.	32	New York	63-0862
WEISS, August	30	Fritzlar	66-0412
WEISS, C.B.(f)	20	Hauhafen	64-0331
WEISS, Carl	26	Frankfurt/M	64-0199
WEISS, Carl	14	Holzhausen	66-1155
WEISS, Cath.	33	Philadelphia	63-1178
Louise 6, Charles 5, Lisette 8m			
WEISS, Emil	15	Mainz	66-0576
WEISS, Ernestine	19	Ensberg	63-1085
WEISS, Ernst Frdr.	33	Goldlauter	64-0456
Augusta 28, Clara 5, Hedwig 3			
WEISS, Georg	28	Hofheim	66-0147
WEISS, Georg	30	Wuerttemberg	66-0576
WEISS, H. Anton	23	Jeverland	63-0953
WEISS, Helene	17	Hirschberg	63-0953
WEISS, Henriette	17	Ruwivez	66-0984
WEISS, Jacob	34	Cincinnati	66-0734
WEISS, Johanna	24	Smiprechtshsn	64-1108
Theresa 19			
WEISS, John	35	Boehmen	63-0482
Marianne 34, Maria 3, John 11m			
WEISS, Julie	18	Karschau	63-0551
WEISS, Julie	28	Bielefeld	64-0886
WEISS, Liebe	24	Kempen	63-0953
WEISS, Ludwig	18	Eichelsachsen	65-0189
WEISS, Margar.	19	Weisbenreuth	63-0482
WEISS, Maria	32	Suhl	65-1088
Aug. 5, Wilhelm 3			
WEISS, Matth.	33	Frossingen	63-0990
WEISS, Mich.	18	Neustadt/Bav.	65-0038
WEISS, Michael	18	Trossingen	64-0363
WEISS, Nathan	21	Lengsfeldt	63-1178
WEISS, O.T.(m)	36	Hofgeismar	64-0331
WEISS, Olga	18	Ulm	65-1024
WEISS, Sigmund	37	Seegdain	66-0679
WEISS, Theodor	18	Strassbourg	63-1178
Constanz 16			
WEISS, Ularia	28	Groezingen	66-1131
WEISS, Valentin	24	Wagenschwedt	64-0433
WEISS, Wilhelm	43	Westerende	66-1093
Dina 40, Ecke 17, Wilhelm 15, Johanna 13			
Julie 13, Wilhelm 9, Johanna 7, Dina 5			
Andreas 2, baby (m) 9m			
WEISS, Xaver	19	Gosheim	66-1327
WEISSBECKER, Cresc	25	Salmuenster	63-1178
Augusta 19			
WEISSBURGER, Jeane	19	Neunkirchen	63-1038
WEISSEL, Georg	17	Laubach	64-0138
WEISSENBACH, Mart.	26	Cassel	65-0189
WEISSENBORN, Aug.	26	Weissenborn	64-0886
WEISSENBORN, Johan	32	Gilfershausen	64-0433
WEISSENBORN, M.El.	24	Creuzburg	65-0950

NAME	AGE	RESIDENCE	YR-LIST
Marie L.J. 5			
WEISSENBURGER, Ad.	19	Deutschland	63-0168
Joh. 19			
WEISSENSTEIN, Jac.	29	Frankfurt	66-0109
WEISSENSTEIN, John	24	Hanau	66-0109
Cathr. 21			
WEISSER, Bernhard	27	Nordwalde	64-1206
WEISSER, Fr. Carl	18	Remderoda	66-1127
WEISSER, Johann	23	Waiblingen	66-0704
WEISSGERBER, Marg.	29	New York	63-0296
WEISSHAAR, August	24	Chemnitz	67-0007
WEISSHAAR, Johs.	36	Luederbach	65-0713
Magdalena 23, Ernst 9, Martha 7, Jacob 3			
WEISSHEIT, Jacob	23	Schmalkalden	66-0349
WEISSINGER, Georg	22	Wichmansdrof	66-1127
WEISSKOPF, Hannche	23	Walldorf	63-0917
WEISSMANDEL, Joh.	23	Obersinn	66-1373
WEISSMANN, Franz	17	Rothselbug	66-0469
Marie Elise 22			
WEISSMANN, Franz	20	Wuertemberg	66-0984
WEISSMANN, Jacob	21	Unterschiff	66-0346
WEISSMANN, Leopold	26	New York	66-0679
Sophie 19			
WEISSMUELLER, J.G.	20	Fulda	66-1128
WEISSNER, Cath.	24	Alsfeld	64-1053
WEISSNER, Joh.	19	Besenfeld	64-0170
WEIT, Juliane	16	Bergkirchen	65-0594
WEITNER, James	20	Viernheim	63-1136
Eva 17			
WEITZ, Joh.	45	Nack/Hess.	65-0038
WEITZEL, Adam	30	New York	63-0953
WEITZEL, Johannes	21	Kalkobes	66-1093
WEITZELL, Anna	25	Sondershausen	65-0007
WELBROCK, J.H.	37	New York	63-0953
Anna 46			
WELDE, Elisab.	28	Eppingen	65-0402
WELDERT, Friedr.	30	Rupelrath	66-0349
WELFER, Jacob	29	Osweil	66-1127
WELGE, Fritz	27	Borsum	65-0402
WELHEFER, Elisab.	25	Falkendorf	64-1022
Marg. 5, Johanna 3			
WELK, Wilhelmine	30	Neudorf Albau	67-0795
Julie 8, Wilhelmine 8m			
WELKER, Gottlieb	18	Thuebingen	66-0346
WELLAGE, Franz	28	Neuenkirchen	63-0752
WELLAGE, Friedrich	29	Neuenkirchen	63-0752
WELLBROCK, H.	30	New York	63-1136
WELLBROCK, Mangels	17	Osterholz	67-0599
WELLBRUECK, Diedr.	20	Linteln	66-0934
WELLE, Catharina	25	Aschen	64-0427
Wm. 3m			
WELLEN, Heinrich	55	Moellenfeld	66-0984
Maria 44, Bernhard 16, Helena 7			
Catharina 6			
WELLEN, Johann	41	Moellenfeld	66-0984
Marie 37, Marie Adelh. 7, Marie Helene 6			
Gerhard 5, Bernhard 4			
WELLENBROCK, Heinr	22	Glaue	66-0984
WELLENBURG, Jacob		Vechte	66-0984
WELLENKAMP, Meta	39	Norden	66-0147
WELLENKAMP, Meta	27	Hannover	63-0398
WELLER, Gertrude	47	New York	63-0006
WELLER, Gottfried	28	Geldorf	64-0639
WELLER, Joh. Mich.	25	Nagelsburg	65-0189
Magda. 18			
WELLER, Wm.	24	Garbenhein	64-0782
WELLHAKE, Anton	19	Allendorf	66-0349
WELLHAUSEN, Georg	22	Perthausen	66-1243
WELLHAUSEN, Wilh.	14	Schoningen	66-0469
WELLINGHORST, Gerh	24	Menslage	66-0576
WELLMANN, Cath.	29	Wellingen	65-0898
WELLMANN, J.E.(m)	18	Osnabrueck	64-0023
WELLMANN, Joh. Hr.	25	Buer	64-0739
WELLMANN, Jos.	36	Lichtenfeld	64-0023
WELLNER, Anna Mar.	24	Bohmte	63-1069
Louise 2, Joh. Heinr. 5m, Christoph 16			
Herrmann 19, Lud. Christ. 59, Juliane 26			
WELLNER, Christoph	23	Bohmte	63-1069

NAME	AGE	RESIDENCE	YR-LIST
WELLNER, Fritz	27	Osnabrueck	63-1069
WELLNITZ, Friedr.	26	Plagow	66-1327
WELLNITZ, Juliane	17	Heleodrobo	63-0614
WELLS, Meta	17	Bremen	66-0934
WELLSANDT, Ludwig	37	Waldau	65-0402
Carol. 36, Johanna 7, Gust. 6, Ida 4			
Ludw. 3, Johanna 11m			
WELSBACH, Carl	32	Fahr	66-0147
WELSCH, Adam	22	Bamberg	64-0886
WELSCH, Wilhelmine	20	Lintenhof	66-0578
WELSCHER, Johann	55	Cranach	65-1088
Margarethe 59			
WELTER, Barbara	25	Schoenberg	64-0023
WELWARSKY, Barbara	27	Schotta	66-1131
Constantin 9, Christine 8			
WELZ, Anna	23	Dobeschau	65-1095
WELZ, Christ. G.	22	Lippoldsweilr	64-0214
WEMHOEFER, Sophie	17	Bolinghausen	66-1155
WEMHOFF, B.	21	Muenster	64-0782
WEMMER, Friedr.	22	Adelmannsfeld	66-0349
WENDEHORST, Heinr.	23	Hildesheim	66-0704
WENDEL, Carl	22	Lemberg	64-0687
WENDEL, Elisabeth	30	Muenster	66-0576
WENDEL, Franz	19	Kuttenberg/Bo	64-0920
Barbara 16			
WENDEL, Georg	37	Worms	66-0679
WENDEL, James	24	Homberg	63-0244
WENDEL, Nicolaus	29	Baden	66-0576
WENDEL, Simon	15	Wendelsheim	66-0984
WENDELE, Catharina	18	Gernsheim	64-0687
WENDELER, Joh. W.	25	Gr. Staven	64-0639
WENDELMAN, Pauline	15	Doetzingen	65-1088
WENDFELDER, Barbra	43	Bamberg	64-0886
WENDIG, Samuel	32	Sembach	63-1178
Amalie 22			
WENDL, Josefa	47	Boehmen	66-0221
Joseph 46			
WENDLAND, Friedr.	55	Brunowo	64-0456
Leonora 52, Henriette 21, Emilie Berth 15			
Rudolph 12, Theodor Carl 8			
WENDLAND, Gustav	28	Breslau	64-0920
WENDNAGEL, Louis	28	Esslingen	63-0917
Johann 22			
WENDT, Augusta	40	Bernburg	65-0898
Robert 7			
WENDT, Becka	17	Deichshausen	66-1203
WENDT, Carsten	18	Bremen	66-1127
WENDT, Emil	17	Koethen	65-0189
WENDT, Fritz	26	Yedingen	66-1155
WENDT, Heinrich	47	Horsens	67-0806
WENDTLAND, Louise	39	Stettin	64-0363
WENERKA, Joseph	23	Manth/Bohemia	65-0856
Anna 33, Joseph 12			
WENGEL, Minna	18	Heilbronn	66-0934
WENGENROTH, Heinr.	40	Grosseifen	66-1093
WENGER, Barbara	19	Eschenhadt	64-0886
WENIBERG, Marcus	23	Silixen	66-0984
WENIGE, Herrmann	29	Hildburghsn.	64-0885
WENIGER, Moritz	22	Sartowitz	64-0639
WENK, F.(m)	23	Mullheim	64-0495
WENK, Felix	48	Lichtensteig	65-0007
Isabelle 21			
WENKE, D.	36	Vegesack	63-0350
WENNEKOHL, L.(f)	23	Hesum	64-0495
WENNER, Augusta	21	Dresden	64-0938
WENNER, Peter	50	Crammstadt	64-0639
Cash. 34, Susanna 21, Marie 20, Jacob 17			
Margareth 13, Louise 7, Elise 5			
Barbara 2			
WENNER, Peter	18	Crummstadt	64-0214
WENNERS, Theresia	18	Emstetten	66-1031
WENNET, Bernhard	44	Emsdetten	66-0576
Therese 40, Therese 12			
WENNET, Gertrud	30	Emsdetten	66-0576
WENNINGER, Andr.	27	Zufferhausen	65-0151
WENSCH, Aug.	18	Nuertingen	65-0402
WENSDORFER, Barb.	20	Halbendorf	66-1203
WENSON, Anna	20	Schiffdorf	64-0432

NAME	AGE	RESIDENCE	YR-LIST
WENSTHOF, Amalie	26	Hannover	66-0576
WENTHE, Heinrich	62	Borstel	66-0734
Sophie 21			
WENTZEL, B.	18	Ellhuthen	66-0413
WENZEL, Anna	21	Boettingen	65-0007
WENZEL, Carl	30	Hannover	66-0734
Wilhelmine 25, Dorothea 3			
WENZEL, Emma	9	Ruppersdorf	66-1093
Alvin 7			
WENZEL, Franz	37	Boehmen	66-0349
WENZEL, Henry	30	Malkomes	63-0296
Martin 31			
WENZEL, Jac.	25	Kaltenborn	64-0495
WENZEL, Joh.	17	Langgoens	64-1108
WENZEL, Joseph	33	Boehmen	66-0221
Elisabeth 30, Theresia 5			
WENZEL, Ludwig	21	Dresden	63-0693
WENZEL, Ludwig	33	Kirchgoens	64-0739
WENZEL, Peter	33	Pittsburg	63-1136
WENZEL, Peter	34	Bohemia	66-0469
WENZEL, Sarah	50	Curhessen	63-1136
Anna Lise 19, Elise 9			
WENZEL, Val.	52	Kaufungen	66-0934
Anna Elisab. 50, Dorothea 28, Maria 22			
Fr.Caspar 20, Georg Friedr 17			
WENZEL, Wilhelm	27	Bremen	66-1248
WENZIG, Herman	26	Steinberg	64-0639
Carl 24			
WENZLER, Gottfried	40	Muehlburg	66-1243
WENZLER, Gottfried	30	Raidwangen	64-0739
WENZLER, Jordan	19	Wuerttemberg	64-0432
Joh. 27			
WENZLER, Pauline	37	Grittlingen	66-1248
WEPEL, Herm.	42	Ostfriesland	63-0822
Antje 42, Bertha 12			
WEPPLER, Nicolaus	25	Oberlustadt	65-0243
WEPPNER, Christ.	30	Spangenberg	65-0038
WERDE, Damil	34	Kischkow	65-1030
WERDER, John	26	Nienhagen	64-0840
Emilie 21, Heinr. 9m			
WERFELMANN, Joh.	26	Bremen	65-1024
WERFF, de Brunke	42	Hessel	65-0243
Hanke 43, Bertha 21, Rentsche 20			
Thomas 18, Gesche 15, Th.(f) 13, Gebke 7			
Anke 4			
WERHLS, Francis	22	Riegel	63-1178
WERK, Casimir	22	New York	63-0953
WERKMANN, Martje	19	Spyk	66-0734
WERLER, Johanna	32	Greiz	66-1093
Paul 9, Rodolph 7, Max 3, Albin 9m			
WERMUTH, Hans	38	Signau	63-0752
WERN, Catharina	35	Biebach	66-1373
WERNDE, J.	32	Steuer	63-0551
WERNEFELD, Cathar.	17	Grothe	66-1093
WERNEFELD, Joh.	20	Grothe	64-0593
WERNEKING, Heinr.	26	Schlusselburg	64-0363
WERNER, Alw.(f)	21	Ohrdorf	64-0782
WERNER, Aug.	23	Heidelberg	65-0189
WERNER, C.	33	Rachitz	66-0413
Amalie 24			
WERNER, C.	34	Trier	65-1024
WERNER, Carl	40	Hannover	64-0170
WERNER, Catharine	28	Baden	66-1031
WERNER, Conrad	20	Wichdorf	66-1313
WERNER, Dorothea	22	Buetenfeld	66-0083
WERNER, Emilie	45	Merseburg	65-0713
WERNER, Fr. Ch.	50	Bitterfeld	64-0427
Johanna 49, Sarah 16, Maria 7, Johanna 6			
Paul 5, Louise 3			
WERNER, Franziska	36	Waldeck	63-1010
WERNER, Friedrich	17	Suhl	66-0668
WERNER, Fritz	26	Frankfurt	66-0109
WERNER, Georg	28	Hannover	66-0734
WERNER, Gust.	25	Ballenstedt	65-0038
WERNER, H.	54	Homburg	66-0413
C.G. 22			
WERNER, H.A.	23	Frankenhausen	65-0898
WERNER, Heinrich	33	Hummersen	66-0576
WERNER, Henry	21	Wien	63-0917
WERNER, James	24	Zempelberg	63-1085
WERNER, Joseph	25	Schney	66-0576
WERNER, Julius	34	Breiten	65-0713
Christiane 36			
WERNER, Ludw.	26	Schnelrode	64-1108
WERNER, Martin	56	Sondheim	64-0214
WERNER, Mr.	54	Saarbruecken	63-1178
wife 30, (f) 1			
WERNER, Otto	20	Altkirchen	66-0984
WERNER, Philippine	24	Graben	66-0576
WERNER, Sara	57	Wien	66-0147
Maria 19, Jacob 9			
WERNER, Sarah	59	Zempelburg	63-1085
WERNER, W.	17	Winth	66-0413
WERNER, W.	28	Gechingen	66-0413
WERNER, Wilhelm	28	Kurhessen	66-0349
Margareth 23, Susanne 58, Ferdinand 9m			
WERNER, William	25	Albany	63-0296
WERNKE, Bernhardin	22	Recke	66-1093
WERPUP, Ella	22	Bremen	64-0331
WERR, Amalia	23	Rittmarshsn.	67-0007
WERSCHINA, Joseph	18	Kirchhausen	66-1155
WERSELMANN, E.	49	Holste	64-0782
Dorothea 5, Heinr. 13, Marie 11, Sophie 7			
Louise 5			
WERSENBROCK, Dorot	18	Lingen	64-0886
WERTENBERG, Heinr.	27	Gildehaus	66-0576
WERTER, Ernst	43	Pyrmont	64-1022
Math. (f) 7			
WERTH, Carl	15	Luebbecke	66-0577
WERTHEIM, Amalia	19	Hatzbach	64-0639
WERTHEIM, Dorette	17	Imshausen	64-0170
WERTHEIM, Fanny	23	Angerod	64-0687
WERTHEIM, Fanny	22	Angenrod	66-0704
WERTHEIM, Lina	16	Erdmannsdorf	66-0679
WERTHEIM, Moses	23	Wesel	65-0948
WERTHEIMER, Michel	19	Carlsruhe	64-0687
WERTHHEIM, Hanna	23	Angenrod	63-0752
WERTHHEIMER, Helen	23	Rimpen	66-1155
WESCHE, Gustav	34	Magdeburg	67-0992
WESCHE, Heinr.	40	Gr.Doehren	64-0138
Caroline 30, Sophie 6, Auguste 4			
WESEL, A.	36	Joehlingen	64-0495
Cath. 52, Joh. 44			
WESELEY, Adalbert	31	Boehmen	63-0482
Catharine 27, Maria 7, John 6			
Anastasia 2			
WESELMEYER, Herm.	19	Bremerhaven	66-1155
WESEMANN,		Rothenfeld	66-1155
WESEMANN, August	23	Muenchenhagen	65-0948
WESEMEIER, Wm.	39	St Andreasbrg	65-0038
WESS, Magdalene	30	Niederhadamar	63-0398
WESS, Nicolaus	16	Niederhadamar	64-0363
Ludwig 62, Peter 19, Maria 23			
WESS, Philippine	21	Mainz	66-1243
WESSDY, Joseph	30	Napehn	64-0433
WESSEL, Friedr.	27	New York	63-0990
WESSEL, J.D.(m)	42	Lehe	64-0023
WESSEL, Johann	19	Langen	65-0151
Catharine 48			
WESSEL, Therese	18	Franzinbar	66-1155
WESSELES, A.	16	Fuerth	66-0934
WESSELES, J.	23	Fuerth	66-0934
WESSELI, Joseph	21	Luebbecke	64-0886
WESSELMANN, Bernh.	31	Liener	65-0116
WESSELS, Betty	25	Bremen	65-0594
WESSELS, Christel	20	Hilbe	64-1108
Elise 18			
WESSELS, Diedrich	26	Twistringen	64-0920
WESSELS, Dorothea	55	Bremen	65-1189
Johanna 15, Dorothea 20, Meta 11m			
WESSELS, Fritz	21	Vechte	65-1030
Hermann 43			
WESSELS, G.L.	23	Kirchhuchting	64-0427
WESSELS, Heinr.	29	Schale	64-0363
WESSELS, Heinrich	23	Halem	66-0109
WESSELS, Helene	7	Wremen	66-1203

NAME	AGE	RESIDENCE	YR-LIST
WESSELS, Hermann	21	Bremen	66-0668
WESSELS, Meta	53	Schremmror	66-1031
WESSELS, Meta	31	Bremen	65-1189
Regina 7, Almevet 5, Johann 3, Carl 11m			
WESSELS, Theod.	19	Aarsten	65-1024
Geisne 19			
WESSELY, Aloisius	21	Bohemia	64-0331
Maria 28, Franz 10m			
WESSENFELDER, Joh.	25	Baden	66-0469
WESSING, Wilhelm	53	Vehlen	65-0948
Christina 52, Berd. 20, Elisabeth 17			
Marianne 16, Heinrich 9, Catharina 7			
WESSLING, Anna	24	Oldenburg	66-1093
WESSLING, Bernhard	18	Woltrup	66-1093
WESSLING, Georg	32	Burgsteinfurt	65-0974
Mrs. 30			
WESSLING, J.F.	32	Wallenbrueck	64-0170
Cath. 24			
WESSTRUPP, Johann	44	Teggen	65-1095
Katharina 44, Maria L. 14, Wilhelmine 4			
WESTENBORG, Emilie	40	Germany	63-0350
Louise 4, baby 1			
WESTENDIEK, August	15	Borgholzhsn.	66-1031
WESTENDORF, Bernh.	28	Loeningen	63-1038
Doris 35			
WESTENDORF, Deb.	29	Schwege	66-0984
WESTENDORF, Theod.	20	Quakenbrueck	66-0984
WESTENGRAD, Cicily	19	Copenhagen	66-0666
WESTENHOF, A.Chrlt	24	Grevenwiese	63-0917
WESTER, Julie	19	Solingen	65-0116
WESTERHEIDE, Maria	59	Borgloh	63-1038
WESTERHOLD, Elsab.	20	Amelsbueren	66-1031
WESTERMANN, Aug.	34	Ringstedt	64-1022
Elisab. 28, Emma 4, baby 6m			
WESTERMANN, Carl	23	Nieder Weser	66-1243
WESTERMANN, Ferd.	28	Bielefeld	66-0734
Agnes 26, Hugo 1			
WESTERMANN, Lisett	18	Levergen	66-1093
WESTERMANN, Louis	25	New York	63-1136
Emma 20			
WESTERMEIER, Andr.	42	Paderborn	65-1095
WESTERMEYER, Cath.	24	Cappeln	66-1031
WESTERNHAGEN, v.W.	16	Muehlhausen	67-0600
WESTERRUF, Bernh.	28	Buehren	64-0427
WESTERWELLER, Els.	23	Fauerbach	65-1030
WESTHAUS, Heinr.	25	Muenster	64-0886
Elisabeth 25			
WESTHEIM, Joseph	20	Lissinghausen	66-0984
Johanna 28			
WESTHEIMER, Jeanet	50	Bavaria	63-0822
Fanny 26, Koppel 28			
WESTHEYMANN, Ph.	28	Versmold	65-0974
WESTHOFF, Christ.	23	Varensell	66-1203
WESTHOFF, Eglb.	23	Ahlen	63-0168
WESTHOFF, H.	26	Steinhausen	63-0097
WESTPHAL, August	33	Minden	64-1053
Emilie 24, Marie 7, Otto 5, Johann 4			
Martha 9m			
WESTPHAL, C.	22	Stendal	64-0992
WESTPHAL, E.	24	Gotha	65-1024
WESTPHAL, Herm.	19	Samyn	64-0363
WESTPHAL, J.F.	20	Bremen	63-1136
WESTPHAL, Jac.	48	Neushausen	64-0992
WESTPHAL, Joh. B.		Osnabrueck	66-0934
WESTPHAL, W.(m)	27	New York	64-0331
WETJEN, H.	48	Pennigbuttel	63-0482
WETJEN, Heinr.	18	Sudweyhe	66-0734
WETNER, Catharina	24	Heimirshausen	63-1136
WETTELHUT, August	28	Nassau	66-0578
Wilhelmine 28, Bertha 1			
WETTEMEYER, Maria	19	Hilbe	64-1108
WETTER, Genoveva	32	Appenzell	64-1053
Emilie 7, Alois 3			
WETTER, Georg	20	Gera	66-1203
WETTER, Gustav A.	18	Mainz	63-0015
WETTERAN, Simon	28	Blankenbach	66-0576
WETTERAU, John B.	57	Richelsdorf	63-0482
Cath. 24, Georg 18			
WETTERAUER, Louise	18	Gr.Eicholzhm.	64-0639
WETTERLIN, Cath.	24	Basel	63-0244
Magd. 19			
WETTERROTH, Georg	25	Darmstadt	63-1038
WETTIG, Anna Marie	19	Sorgenloch	66-0221
WETTLAUFEN, Otto	18	Cassel	64-0073
WETTMUELLER, Ed.	27	Oberelsbach	66-0679
WETTRUP, Dina	23	Emstetten	66-1031
WETTSTEIN, Baron	28	Venedig	64-0073
WETTSTEIN, Henry	25	Zuerich	64-1206
WETZ, Cathr.	58	Dagersheim	63-0953
WETZEL, Anna Elis.	20	Hessen	64-0432
WETZEL, Bertha	22	Frankenstein	64-1022
WETZEL, Chr.	20	Altenrieth	64-0593
WETZEL, Clara	25	Darmstadt	66-1127
WETZEL, Heinr Jac.	15	Kleinwelsbach	64-0938
WETZEL, Joh. Chr.	34	Leipzig	67-0599
Carol. Ber. 31, Amalie Anna 9			
Maria Hedwig 6			
WETZEL, Johann	19	Schwarzenberg	66-0147
WETZEL, Leonhard	27	Gornheim	66-1155
Valentin 22			
WETZEL, Math.	30	Wattenheim	64-0427
WETZLAR, A.(m)	37	Rottenbern	64-0495
WETZLER, Albert	41	New York	63-1038
WETZLER, Marie	25	Saatz	63-1038
WETZSTEIN, Heinr.	20	Gettenau	65-1095
WETZSTEIN, Joh.	19	Eichwoge	65-0713
WEUMANN, Jos.	36	Lichtenfeld	64-0023
WEUNING, Hermann	29	Schuettorf	65-0243
WEUSTMANN, Heinr.	25	Burgsteinfurt	65-1088
WEWER, Cathar.	28	Handorf	64-1053
WEWERKA, Martin	56	Heckoritz	66-0734
Maria 22, Elisabeth 19, Joseph 17			
Wenzel 15, Catharina 13, Eva 8, Franz 7			
Johanna 5, Johann 3, Mathias 11m			
WEWERS, Joh. W.	29	Schwefingen	66-1313
WEY, Ernestine	24	Maden	64-0433
WEY, Georg Aug.	19	Solz	63-0990
WEYDEKAMP, Gustav	24	Iserlohn	64-0665
WEYER, Elisabeth	21	Neubrunn	63-0990
WEYL, M.	24	Hadamar	65-0007
WEYLING, Ursula	13	Gomaringen	66-0679
WEYRAUCH, Oscar		Freysa	66-1373
WEYRICH, Friedr. W	41	Creuzburg	65-0950
Anna Barbara 43, Ludwig Barb. 14			
Heinrich Asm 11, Carol. Asmus 9			
Dorothea 6			
WEZEL, Georg	22	Goelsdorf	66-0734
WEZSTEIN, Joh.	19	Eichwoge	65-0713
WHITE, Wilhelmine	59	Charlestown	66-0704
WIBBELER, Adolph	49	Ladbergen	63-1178
WIBBEN, Henry	45	Louisville	63-1038
Caroline 45, Anna 9			
WIBBOLDING, B.J.	27	Alfhausen	63-0953
WIBER, Eva	31	Kaltennordhm.	64-0992
Alwin 4			
WICH, Georg	24	Unterrodach	66-0221
WICH, Peter	13	Rodach	64-0495
WICHELHANS, Aug.	18	Neuscheid	63-1218
WICHELS, Cath.	14	Taken	65-0594
WICHERT, Chr.	28	Magdeburg	63-1038
WICHMANN, August	24	Oldenburg	66-1031
WICHMANN, Carl	35	Geestemuende	64-0938
wife 30, baby			
WICHMANN, Carl	60	Innbuettel	66-0934
Wilhelmine 58			
WICHMANN, Caroline	35	Crefeld	66-1127
Louis 3, Marie 6m			
WICHMANN, Elise	28	Geestemuende	64-0938
Ludw. 4			
WICHMANN, Hans	35	Eilsdorf	64-0687
Cath. 33, Catharina 7, Maria Cath. 17			
WICHMANN, Heinr.	34	Hasbergen	65-0055
WICHMANN, Heinrich	35	Recke	66-1031
Louise 31, Marie 11m, Therese 24			
Heinrich 60			
WICHMANN, J.	25	Wiedenbrueck	65-1088

NAME	AGE	RESIDENCE	YR-LIST
WICHMANN, Marg	54	Lamstedt	63-0862
WICHTRUP, Elisab.	25	Preussen	63-0990
WICKE, Franz	26	Fritzlar	64-0639
Johanna 23, Marie 6m			
WICKE, Helene	24	Cassel	66-0984
WICKE, Wh.	24	Oldendorf	65-0974
WICKE, Wilhelm	21	Stadthagen	66-1373
WICKENTRAEGER, Hch	21	Celle	66-0469
WICKER, Philipp	19	Darmstadt	66-0576
WICKERS, Thomas	31	Heidelberg	66-1327
Caroline 30, Elisabeth 10m			
WICKERT, Heinrich	16	Westphalen	66-0469
WICKLER, Marie	19	Rosenberg	64-0782
WICKY, Jos. P.	21	Freiburg	64-1108
Alphons 19			
WIDMAIER, Wm.	45	Wasseralfingn	64-1022
WIDMANN, Isaac	25	Zweibruecken	64-0992
WIDMER, G.	27	Baden	63-0296
WIDMEYER, Wilhelm	25	Scranton	66-1327
Wilhelmine 24, Margarethe 21			
Wilhelmine 4			
WIDONE, Ostrop	66	Essen	66-1127
WIEBEL, Wm.	27	Imgen	64-1053
WIEBER, Heinr.	30	Osnabrueck	64-0639
WIEBOLD, Herm.	28	Rieste	66-0734
WIEBUSCH, Heinrich	20	Zeven	66-0704
WIEBUSCH, Marie E.	17	Lintorf	66-1373
WIECHERATH, Cath.	9	Klagenfurt	63-1218
WIECHMANN, Carl	22	Uslar	65-1024
WIECHMANN, Wm.	36	Loquard	64-1022
Berend 13, Heinr. 7, Ette 5			
WIECKMANN, F.(m)	27	Hoya	64-0331
WIEDEMANN, Anton	35	St. Leon	65-0402
Ignatz 32			
WIEDEMANN, Aug.	30	Stuttgart	65-0402
WIEDEMANN, Bernh.	29	Dresden	66-0934
WIEDEMANN, G.M.	19	Herbrechtinge	63-0551
Elisabeth 21			
WIEDEMANN, Georg	28	Lebach	64-0214
WIEDEMANN, Jacob	19	Sulzbach	66-0984
WIEDEMANN, John	58	Martinhausen	63-1218
WIEDEMEYER, Alb.	17	Borgentreich	67-0795
WIEDENBACH, Leopld	21	Birgen	65-0151
WIEDENHOFER, Matth	39	Oterkochen	66-0576
Marie 44, Georg 9, Hermann 6			
WIEDERECHT, Heinr.	20	Cassel	66-1373
WIEDERSPECKER, Ad.	22	Suhl	65-1088
Anetta 24			
WIEDFELDT, Fr.	31	Braunschweig	63-1010
WIEDMANN, August	17	Wuertemberg	66-0679
WIEDMANN, V.	29	Balingen	63-1003
WIEDMAYER, John	29	Schaafhausen	63-0862
WIEFELMEYER, Aug.	21	Bremerhaven	66-1155
WIEGAND, A.F.(m)	29	Nordhausen	64-0138
WIEGAND, Anna	15	Lengsfeld	66-1128
WIEGAND, Anna M.	29	Malges	64-0687
WIEGAND, Carl	27	Voigtsberg	64-1206
WIEGAND, Chrst'ne.	37	Philadelphia	66-0704
WIEGAND, Conrad	23	Linglis	64-0170
Wiegand 16			
WIEGAND, Elise	27	Lorsch	63-0015
Margareth 6			
WIEGAND, Friedrich	38	Gestedt	63-1178
WIEGAND, Georg	17	Darmstadt	65-0004
WIEGAND, Gunterine	24	Breitenbach	64-0432
WIEGAND, H.	24	New York	63-0244
WIEGAND, Heinr.	18	Verna	65-0898
WIEGAND, Heinrich	19	Heiner	66-0679
WIEGAND, Hermann	23	Melle	66-1373
WIEGAND, Johann	21	Motgert	63-1069
WIEGAND, Johann	29	Wertheim	66-0934
WIEGAND, Margareth	25	Hessia	66-1093
WIEGAND, Wm.	21	Jestedt	64-0687
Heinr. 18			
WIEGEL, Bernhard	22	Holdorf	64-0363
WIEGER, Wilh.	22	Essdorf	63-1038
WIEGERD, Marie	19	Steinbach	66-0578
WIEGERS, Wilh.	19	Zeven	66-0704

NAME	AGE	RESIDENCE	YR-LIST
WIEGHARDT, Georg F	20	Minden	64-1108
WIEGMANN, Anna	47	Felgte	66-1031
Clara 16, Catharina 9, Louise 7			
WIEGMANN, Aug.	29	Dueringen	64-0687
WIEGMANN, Helene	20	Beverstedt	66-1093
WIEHE, H.(m)	32	Stemmer	64-0331
Fr.(m) 21			
WIEHNERS, G.J.	45	Leer	64-1053
WIEKING, Diedr.	18	Bramsche	65-0948
WIEKING, Hermann	18	Bramsche	66-1031
WIELAGE, Aug. Rud.	22	Oldenburg	66-0984
WIELAND, Christian	57	Siebertbach	63-1069
WIELAND, Christian	15	Sulzbach	65-0713
WIELAND, Christine	16	Oberohren	64-1108
WIELAND, Joh. Gg.	27	Halle	65-0004
WIELAND, Johanna	20	Endersbach	66-0083
WIELAND, Octavia	26	Stuttgart	64-0023
WIELATZ, Friedr.	27	Pommern	66-0469
Caroline 29, Marie 4, Carl 9m			
WIEMANN, August	25	Osnabrueck	66-1031
Joseph 23			
WIEMANN, Bernhard	47	Hannover	66-1093
WIEMANN, Franz	16	Braamsche	66-0679
WIEMANN, Heinr.	19	Versmold	64-0023
WIEMANN, Heinrich	30	Providence	66-1031
WIEMANN, Marie A.	17	Osnabrueck	66-1127
WIEMANN, Wilhelm	64	Frankenhausen	66-1155
Friederike 73			
WIENBERG, H.(m)	29	Langenschwarz	64-0214
WIENBERG, Julie	40	Meiningen	63-1085
Adelheid 11m, Minna 16			
WIENBERG, Martin	24	Altstadt	66-0623
WIENBERG, Minna	17	Himberg	63-0917
WIENECKE, Justine	21	Hornburg	64-0992
C. 28			
WIENER, Christian	23	Saarbruecken	63-1178
wife 19			
WIENER, E.	38	Coeln	66-0576
WIENER, Leibschlig	16	Cotterschin	65-0038
WIENER, Robert	17	Wien	66-1373
WIENER, S.	37	Bochholt	66-0934
Rosalie 27, baby 7m, baby 7m			
WIENERS, William	36	New York	63-0953
Maria 9, Lina 6			
WIENHOLT, Heinr.	17	Reus	67-0600
WIENHOLZ, Carl	14	Goettingen	63-0693
WIENICKE, Albert	24	Schoningen	66-0469
WIENKE, Wilhelm	39	Minden	66-1155
WIERHACKE, Marie	35	Wimmen	63-1085
WIERSING, Georgine	24	Veilsdorf	66-0576
Georgine 1			
WIES, Aug.	27	Kleinsbach	64-1161
WIESBADER, Samuel	19	Michelstadt	64-0938
WIESCHEN, August	18	Osnabrueck	66-1093
WIESE, Andreas	51	Preussen	63-0398
Anna 30			
WIESE, Anna	20	Ringstedt	66-1093
WIESE, C.(f)	16	Schwarzbach	64-0495
WIESE, Christian	68	Liskowe	65-0770
WIESE, Friedrich	18	Kaselia	66-0666
WIESE, H.	30	Luebbeck	65-1189
WIESEHAHN, Johann	18	Oerle	65-1031
WIESEL, Friedrich	42	Sachsen	66-0221
WIESEL, Maria	52	Dessau	66-0469
Eduard 18, Minna 16, Friedrich 14			
Herrmann 12, Emma 9			
WIESELS, Friedrich	19	Wertheim	66-1127
WIESEN, Bernard	36	New Orleans	63-0953
Julie 15, Anna 8			
WIESENER, Wilh.	30	Ibbenbuehren	65-0189
WIESEPOHL, Wilhelm	15	Wehdem	66-1373
WIESING, Heinrich	26	Coesfeld	65-1030
WIESMANN, Emilie	19	Backnang	66-1155
WIESNER, Gotthelf	40	Glauchau	64-0593
WIESNER, Hermann	21	Carlsruhe	66-1093
Anna 27			
WIESSNER, Friede.	20	Bremervoerde	66-0704
WIEST, Heinrich	18	Stebbach	64-0199

NAME	AGE	RESIDENCE	YR-LIST
WIETERER, Geo.	23	Algermissen	64-0687
WIETERMANN, Georg	32	Wenningen	66-1155
WIETGEN, Franz	39	Oestorf	64-0687
Aug. 18			
WIETHOELTER, Wilh.	24	Hessia	66-0679
WIETHORN, E.	18	Osnabrueck	64-0782
WIETING, Heinr.	29	Estwege	66-1373
WIETSCH, Jacob	30	Fritzlar	64-0432
WIETZEL, Jac.	29	Dietenshausen	65-0402
WIETZKE, Wilhelm	28	Pommern	66-0578
Rosette 24, Bertha 2			
WIEVINNER, Elise	19	Gaste	66-0668
WIEWEL, Heinrich	43	Almersloh	66-1031
Elisabeth 41, Ana 6, Heinrich 3, Johann 2			
WIGAND, Carl	18	Gudamsberg	65-0151
WIGAND, Friedrich	25	Hannover	63-0614
WIGAND, Ludasica	42	Pyrmont	63-0693
WIGANS, Friedr.	16	Neukirchen	63-0398
WIGEMANN, Anna	28	Obergogesheim	66-1203
WIGGE, Joseph	36	Preussen	64-0214
Marie , Jenny 6, Antonia 5, Caspar 9m			
WIGGENHAUSEN, Herm	22	Wahlwies	67-0007
WIGGER, Herm.	24	Stachelau	63-0821
WIGMANN, Caroline	16	Hannover	64-0432
WIKA, Joseph	25	Willemitz	66-1155
WIKOBIL, Aloysia	22	Boehmen	63-1218
WILBERDING, Agnes	20	Rueshendorf	66-0984
WILBERS, Christ.	36	New York	63-1218
Herm. Henry 6, Alb. Henry 6			
WILCKENS, A.	27	Bremen	63-1003
WILCKENS, Wilh'mne	19	Bremen	63-0350
WILCYNSKY, Leopold	15	Gnesen	63-1038
Wilhelmine			
WILCZZEWSKY, H.	17	Gnesen	64-0593
WILD, Chris	42	Luetisburg	63-0482
WILD, Franz	21	Loebenstein	66-0734
WILD, Johann	27	Oettigheim	64-0840
Victorine 6			
WILDA, Theodor	28	Belgardt	63-0614
WILDBERG, L.(m)	16	Mottgers	64-0495
WILDE, Henriette	27	Breslau	66-1243
WILDERMUTH, Julius	21	Ulm	64-0886
WILDEROETHER, L.	53	Schweiz	63-1085
L. 21, P. 17, Marie 7			
WILDFANG, Heinrich	31	Berlin	66-0346
WILDFUEHR, Heinr.	18	Hannover	65-0116
WILDHACK, Anna	22	Beckedorf	66-0147
WILDMANN, Ad.	36	Schwerin	63-1178
WILDMANN, Friedr.	29	Leipzig	64-1053
WILDNER, Joseph	40	Libenau	67-0007
Francisca 38			
WILDNER, Joseph	56	Reichenberg	66-1155
WILDSCH, Leopold	28	Ratibor	64-0343
WILER, Caspar	45	Frauenfeld	63-0953
WILFERT, James	33	Hochenbug	63-0482
Margar. 31, Marg. 9, Cath. 3, John 8			
WILFERT, Rosalie	25	Schoenfalk	66-1155
WILGENBUSCH, Joh.	27	Fehlen	66-0349
Eleonora 25			
WILHELM, Anna	59	Otzenhausen	65-0402
WILHELM, Aug. E.F.	23	Bernau	64-0073
WILHELM, Barbara	58	Naborn	65-0402
WILHELM, Carl	30	Schweiz	63-1136
WILHELM, Christ.	42	Reinerstadt	66-0576
WILHELM, Dorothea	21	Wuerzburg	63-0862
WILHELM, Eduard	20	Kurhessen	66-0734
WILHELM, Heinr.	13	Willerdorf	64-0170
WILHELM, Hermann H	59	Oerlinghausen	63-0917
WILHELM, Jacob	29	Bambach	65-0770
Marie 25			
WILHELM, Johann	47	Zullig	66-1373
WILHELM, Joseph	30	Gerstengrund	66-0679
WILHELM, Josephine	16	Worms	66-0576
WILHELM, Louise	17	Schorusheim	66-0083
WILHELM, Ludwig	16	Lehse	63-1218
WILHELM, Philip	23	Dermbach	66-0679
WILHELM, Wilh. Chr	32	Steinbach	66-0578
WILHELME, Charltt.	19	Eldagsen	65-0770

NAME	AGE	RESIDENCE	YR-LIST
WILHELMI, Anton	75	Weichenzell	64-0886
Angelika 67			
WILHELMI, Max	21	Schoenstein	66-0109
WILHELMS, Clemens	26	Natzungen	66-1313
WILHELMS, J.	26	Sponheim	65-0007
WILHELMSDORF, Ern.	32	Cincinnati	63-0097
WILHELMY, Louise	18	Obersheim	63-1085
WILHORN, Hermann	50	Vechte	65-1030
WILK, Valentin	42	Empfertshsn.	64-1161
WILKE, Bertha	19	Hagenow	66-0668
WILKE, Carl	20	Rinteln	64-0170
WILKE, Carl	45	Berlin	64-0593
WILKE, Heinr.	24	Woldorf	65-0007
WILKE, Hermann	22	Poldewin	66-0679
Carl 17			
WILKE, Wilhelm	20	Witzenhausen	66-1203
WILKELOH, Ernst	23	Heilshorn	66-0413
Louise 20			
WILKEN, Conrad	30	Ostfriesland	66-0704
Dorothea 25			
WILKEN, Gertrud	24	Emsdetten	66-0576
Lisette 26			
WILKENEK, Wilh.	19	Kreuzreh	66-1243
WILKENING, Christ.	20	Sellstein	66-1327
WILKENS, Heinrich	18	Bremerhaven	64-0456
WILKENS, Johann	25	Lessum	63-0614
Heinrich 22			
WILKENS, Marie L.	18	Otterstedt	65-1031
WILKENS, Mathias	27	New York	63-0482
WILKENS, R.F.	22	Delmenhorst	64-0427
WILKER, Andreas	20	Bremen	64-0199
WILKES, Wilhelm	22	Oloesberg	65-0189
WILKING, Elise	51	Louisville	64-1053
WILKING, Joh. Hch.	17	Harpendorf	66-0704
WILKINS, A.M.(f)	22	Drehle	64-0331
WILKOWSKY, Johann	40	Schlaugendorf	36-0433
Wilhelmine 36, Carl 11, Mathilde 7			
Emilie 4m			
WILL, Adolph	15	Sulzbach	66-0984
WILL, Anna	26	Lihn	65-0713
WILL, Catharine	21	Oberhilbershm	66-1248
WILL, Heinrich	25	Magdeburg	65-0898
WILL, Johann	19	Leutesdorf	63-0821
WILL, Johann	28	Woffendorf	66-1203
WILL, Louis	24	New York	63-1136
WILLE, Adolf	18	Disten	66-0576
WILLE, Caroline	29	Wolfenbuettel	63-1010
WILLE, Christ.	19	Buxtehude	66-1373
WILLE, Frd.	30	Bremen	63-0168
(f) 29			
WILLE, Friedr.	24	Hoefken-Neuk.	66-0650
Wilhelmine 23, Bertha 9m			
WILLE, Friedrich	46	Lippe Detmold	66-0623
WILLE, Fritz	48	Goettingen	65-1140
Henriette 44, Helene 15, Georg 10			
Heinrich 10, Charlotte 7, Louise 7			
Martin 4			
WILLE, Ottilie	28	Wuertemberg	63-0398
WILLE, Robert	18	Ruelte	64-0840
Wilhelm 15			
WILLE, Wilhelm	28	Disten	66-0576
WILLEMANN, John	30	Westenhof	66-1155
WILLEMSEN, Lars	56	Copenhagen	66-0666
Anna 44, Hans 22, Karen Maria 22			
Sophia 18			
WILLEN, Joh. B.	29	Ehren	66-0934
WILLEN, v.d. Hr.	29	Westerroden	66-0704
WILLENBORG, Friedr	43	Dinklage	66-0984
Marie 22			
WILLERDING, C.	25	Hildesheim	66-0413
WILLGRUBS, Itje H.	70	Nessemergrobe	64-0938
Antje 39			
WILLHORM, Wilh.	27	Nordsehl	64-0214
Sophie 37, baby 1			
WILLIAMS, Th. A.	26	New York	63-1178
WILLICH, Georg	21	Iba	66-0668
Dorothea 47			
WILLICKY, Jarost.	28	Zhitomir	64-1206

NAME	AGE	RESIDENCE	YR-LIST
WILLIEB, Wilh.	23	Rotenburg	66-0984
Maria 26, Sophie 24			
WILLIEN, Leo	24	St Marie Ill.	64-0023
WILLIG, Cath.	25	Osbis	65-0950
WILLIG, Ernst	31	New York	63-0350
WILLIMOVSKY, Ther.	47	Boehmen	64-0023
WILLINGER, Jacob	45	Bohemia	66-0469
Mathias 16, Jacob 14, Joseph 8			
WILLMANN, M.N.	30	New York	66-0934
WILLMANN, Marie	18	Langenhausen	65-0948
WILLMS, Joh. Heere	19	Esens	66-1128
WILLMS, Joh. Pet.	59	Coeln	66-0349
Margar. 21			
WILLMY, Anna	33	New York	63-0821
WILLNS, Ferd.	29	Mainz	63-1178
WILLON, Emilie	30	Frankenberg	64-0073
WILLSCHAU, Casp.	30	Olzbach	66-0349
WILLWERTH, Carl	26	Sohlingen	64-0331
WILMANNS, Charlott	35	Milwaukee	63-1136
WILMERING, Heinr.	20	Ahausen	65-0243
Elise 22			
WILMET, R.	23	Burgsteinfurt	65-0974
Elisabeth 25			
WILMS, Caecilie	28	Strohhausen	63-0614
Georg 7, Charlotte 3			
WILMS, Carl W.	29	New York	66-0221
WILMS, Hilke	30	Proothusen	66-1327
Mente 8, Otto 7			
WILMS, Joh.	29	Eckwarden	64-0665
WILMS, Johanna	26	Solingen	65-0116
(m) bob			
WILRAUS, Georg	30	Braunschweig	66-0109
WILSHUSEN, Henry	21	Kuehrstedt	66-0221
WILSTAEDTER, Emil	24	Bruchsal	66-0679
WILTS, Jan	22	Hannover	66-0577
WIMMEL, Carl	15	Cassel	66-0576
WIMMER, Chr.	14	Kirchhausen	65-0594
WIMMER, Pauline	16	Heilbronn	63-0990
WIMMER, Theodor	28	Cassel	66-1031
WIMPFHEIMER, Jette	29	Baden	66-0576
WINCKELMANN, Joh.	31	Brunswick	66-0837
Caroline 27			
WINCKLER, Conr.	45	Woelflingen	63-0990
Elisabeth 42, Elise 7, Barbara 4			
Charles 6m			
WINCKLER, Sophie	24	Dezisau	66-1155
WINDEISSEN, Gotlob	24	Meylau	64-0433
WINDELMUTH, Theo.	26	Tonndorf	64-0433
WINDELN, Bern. Hnr	23	Grossenstam	64-0639
WINDELS, Martin	24	Hasbergen	66-0679
WINDHEIM, Wilhelm	24	Schotte	64-0886
WINDHORN, H.	29	Nienburg	66-0413
Marie 33			
WINDHUS, Heinr.	21	Ibbenbuehren	65-0898
WINDICK, Carl	30	Jastrow	64-1053
WINDISCH, Friedr.	26	Pommerfelden	64-0840
WINDORFF, Friedr.	21	Dalwende	66-0734
WINDT, August	24	Rensin	64-0433
WINDWEK, Herm.	30	Thedinghausen	65-0950
WINECKE, C.	28	Hamburg	64-0992
WINGESS, Friedr.A.	20	Fambach	66-1243
WINK, Cath.	17	Schwabendorf	63-1178
WINKE, Friedr.	17	Lohne	66-1131
WINKELFOS, Aug.	15	Eboldhausen	65-0402
WINKELMANN, C.(m)	27	Goettingen	64-0331
WINKELMANN, C.F.C.	28	Braunschweig	65-0594
Margarethe 1, Johann 35			
WINKELMANN, Cath.	16	Gutweiler	66-0623
WINKELMANN, Christ	22	Lehe	66-1248
WINKELMANN, Fr.	27	Mecklenburg	64-0593
WINKELMANN, Friedr	27	Markoldendorf	66-1373
WINKELMANN, G.H.	29	Klus.	66-0221
WINKELMANN, Heinr.	23	Sandwisch	66-0679
Louise 14			
WINKELMANN, Joh.	19	Thedinghausen	65-0189
WINKELMANN, John	28	Achim	63-0482
Dorothea 26, Henry 9m			
WINKELMANN, Me.(f)	21	Thedinghausen	64-0495

NAME	AGE	RESIDENCE	YR-LIST
WINKELMANN, Rich.	18	Walsrode	65-0898
WINKELMANN, Wm.	16	Leese	67-0600
WINKELMEYER, Aug.	32	Berlin	64-0885
WINKELS, Rebecca	56	Depstedt	63-1069
Helene 15			
WINKELSELZ, Hch. F	28	Delmenhorst	64-0739
Doris 27			
WINKELSTERN, Joh.	19	Cassel	65-1140
WINKLER, Carl	32	Sachsen	64-0432
WINKLER, Emilie	24	Clausnitz	64-0363
WINKLER, Franz	39	Elsnitz/Sax.	65-1030
Marg. 37, Franz E. 14			
WINKLER, Frd.	27	Maulbronn	64-0495
WINKLER, Heinr. B.	19	Leipzig	66-0934
WINKLER, Heinrich	28	Schweiz	66-0147
Margarethe 30, Verena 5, Heinrich 3			
Johann 2			
WINKLER, Joh.	38	Buernstadt	64-0495
Elsb. 34, S.(f) 14, Wal. 7, Ther. 4			
Marg. 3, Geo. 11m			
WINKLER, Joh. W.	22	Malans	65-0007
WINKLER, Johann	35	Bremen	66-0666
Anna 35, Johann 7, August 6, Gustav 5			
Sophie 3			
WINKLER, Maria	26	Brixen	64-1108
WINKLER, Theodor	24	Czarnikau	63-0551
WINNEN, Carl	33	Gladbach	66-0623
WINNER, G.D.	21	Langen	65-1024
WINNIG, Aug.	45	Blankenburg	63-0244
C. 25, C. 2			
WINNING, Johann	28	Ahrhaus	66-0623
WINNINGEN, Marie	19	Staubing	64-0427
WINOBST, Joh. Jos.	24	Cloppenburg	65-0038
WINOWIECKI, Jacob	36	Posen	64-0432
Anna 42, Marianna 5, Joseph 6m			
WINTEL, Marg.	21	Mengsbach	65-0189
WINTER, Albrecht	19	Bahlum	65-0243
WINTER, Anton	44	Dortmund	66-0147
Bertha 27, Carl 9			
WINTER, August	29	Emsdetten	66-0576
WINTER, Caroline	41	Berlin	64-1022
WINTER, Chr.	27	Untermusbach	65-0402
WINTER, Claus	17	Hannover	64-0427
WINTER, Dina	30	Prussia	64-0432
WINTER, Ernestine	23	Stoenach	66-0469
WINTER, Ernst	20	Weil	66-0704
Wilhelm 18, Jacob 16			
WINTER, Franz	27	Blocknitz	66-0679
WINTER, Friedr.	24	Daenenkamp	64-0214
WINTER, Georg	28	Otterndorf	63-0482
WINTER, Georg	17	Schafheim	66-1327
WINTER, Heinr.	45	Echzell	66-1243
Elise 35, Henriette 8, Lisette 6			
Catharina 30			
WINTER, Heinr.	28	Osterode	65-0189
WINTER, Heinrich	67	Braunschweig	63-0168
WINTER, Henry	24	Minden	66-0221
WINTER, Joseph	32	Leutschau	66-0221
WINTER, Michael	30	Eiderhagen	66-0412
WINTER, Rud.	21	Otterndorf	63-0953
WINTERBALD, Anna	27	Bruchsal	66-1203
WINTERBERG, Anna	24	New York	66-0704
WINTERER, Ludwig	38	Schlutterdahl	66-0934
Augusta 38			
WINTERHOFF, Fritz	27	Hoesseringen	64-0214
WINTERNITZ, Marcus	32	Weitzen	66-1327
WINTERS, Catharina	22	Burgdamm	63-0350
WINTERS, Edward	40	Moskau	64-1022
WINTISCH, Joseph	39	Salmannsdorf	66-0346
Therese 30, Christine 9, Joseph 6			
Catharine 1			
WINTSCH, Regula	22	Switz	65-0007
Rudolph 19			
WIPPERLING, A.	20	Bremen	66-0704
WIPPERMANN, Louise	18	Duderstadt	66-1128
WIRKLER, Georg	16	Behmingen	66-1243
WIRSING, Ever.	34	Belleville	64-0782
WIRSING, Julius	35	Falzdorf	64-0433

NAME	AGE	RESIDENCE	YR-LIST
WIRSSENBERG, Joh.	21	Bremen	64-0665
WIRSUM, Johanna	17	Urasch	66-1093
WIRTENSOHN, Leopld	23	Meschede	66-0679
Elise 23, baby 6m			
WIRTH, Charles	32	Chicago	63-1178
wife 20			
WIRTH, Charles	46	Philadelphia	66-0934
WIRTH, Christian	32	Wittenburg	64-0433
WIRTH, Friedr.	66	Philadelphia	63-0953
WIRTH, John	32	Iowa	64-0170
Barb. 25, Franz 3, Johann 9m, Carl 35			
WIRTH, John	30	Rochester	63-0693
WIRTH, Joseph	26	Boehmen	63-1085
Mary 29			
WIRTH, Sicilia	26	Ochsenhausen	63-1085
WIRTHS, Cuno	17	Solingen	63-0822
WIRTHS, Hugo	19	Solingen	63-0822
WIRTZ, Wil.	42	Altenhof	67-0795
Elisab. 38, Conrad 4			
WIRZ, A.	39	Lissach	64-1161
WIRZ, Catharina	46	Cologne	63-0015
Caroline 9			
WISCH, Marg.	18	Unterrodach	64-0495
Joh. 39			
WISCHMANN, Carl	35	Geestemuende	64-0938
wife 30, baby			
WISCHMEYER, Ernst	18	Hannover	64-0739
WISCHMEYER, Heinr.	25	Oesede	64-0938
WISCHMEYER, Wm.	19	Steinum	64-0938
WISCOCIL, Joseph	40	Boehmen	63-0398
WISKOVIL, Anna	19	Zubirow	66-0734
WISKUS, Bernhard	29	Darup	65-1030
WISMANN, Conrad	34	Leer	63-0398
Anna 35			
WISMANN, Ph.	24	Gr. Rohrstein	65-0402
WISSEL, Louise	54	Altwallmoden	64-0363
WISSENBACH, Louis	21	Burg	65-0594
WISSERT, Valentin	59	Appershausen	65-0948
susanne 34, Johanne 9m			
WISSIG, Johannes	20	Nauerbach	65-0189
WISSING, Johann	41	Westphalen	66-0734
WISSINGER, Jac.	18	Ruppin	65-1024
WITFELD, Heinr.	22	Crefeld	64-0363
WITHMER, Hannchen	32	Rossbach	64-1053
WITKOWSKY, G.	31	Nashville	64-0687
A. 21, Alice 2			
WITMERSHAUS, Dietr	46	Pennigseel	65-0189
WITPEN, Johann	21	Westerbeck	66-1093
WITT, Friedrich	19	Lamstedt	63-0862
WITT, Peter	13	Ebern	63-0693
WITTBERGER, John	44	Rodersdorf	63-0862
WITTBOLDT, Friedr.	58	Hannover	66-1031
Wilhelmine 42, Helene 28, Julius 2			
WITTE, Carl	28	Rueden	65-0402
WITTE, Clara	18	Angermuende	63-0821
WITTE, Ed.	22	Haugen	66-0934
WITTE, Heinr.	19	Cincinnati	63-0097
WITTE, Heinrich	25	Hannover	66-1031
WITTE, Heinrich	34	Berlin	65-0770
Louise 28, Wilhelm 4			
WITTE, Joh. Aug.	25	Wussow	65-0948
WITTE, Johann	23	Brachdorf	65-0004
WITTE, Johanna	18	Bremen	64-0214
WITTE, Johannes	19	Bremen	65-1024
WITTE, John B.	31	Beckum	63-0482
Mary 29			
WITTE, Louise	9	Haevern	63-0821
WITTE, M.C.G.	49	New York	63-0953
Marie Elise 31, Melchior 11, Parker 8			
Elise 7, Sarah 4, Allehe 10m			
WITTE, Rike	23	Hannover	63-0862
WITTE, Sophie	20	Bremen	65-0950
WITTEBERG, Anna	70	Paderborn	66-1155
WITTEBERG, Heinr.	18	Soest	66-0704
WITTEFELD, Gustav	24	Osnabrueck	66-1127
WITTENBERG, Minna	17	Vollbuettel	64-0904
WITTER, Anton	34	Neustadt a/H	66-1327
WITTER, Heinr.	19	Oberneubrunn	64-0593

NAME	AGE	RESIDENCE	YR-LIST
WITTER, Tobias	24	Vinen	67-0007
WITTEROCK, B.	26	Neukirchen	66-0413
WITTFELDER, Anton	55	Wuerzburg	66-1313
Elise 55, Gottfr. 16, Augelina 15			
WITTGENSTEIN, Aler	15	Liebenau	64-0593
Julie 21			
WITTGENSTEIN, Dav.	21	Ibenau	66-0221
WITTGIS, Nicolas	43	Prussia	64-0427
WITTHAUT, Fr.	32	Miste	63-1038
WITTHOFER, C.	23	Preussen	63-1003
WITTIG, (f)	65	Berlin	63-0551
WITTIG, C.	26	Hannover	63-0296
WITTIG, Ludw.	18	Auenstern	64-0427
WITTIKIND, Johann	46	Fischbach	67-0007
Johann 25, Heinrich 21, Joseph 5			
Johann 19, Elisabeth 23, Isabelle 9m			
WITTINGEN, Lina	21	Boll	64-0363
WITTJEN, Johanne	16	Stindstedt	66-1031
WITTKOETTER, Anna	15	Minden	65-1031
WITTLAGER, Peter	22	Elz	66-1203
WITTLAND, Wm.	40	St. Louis	64-0495
WITTLER, Ernst	32	Rauschenberg	66-1131
WITTLER, Sophie	19	Lichtenbaum	64-0687
WITTLINGER, Joh.	20	Unterboehring	64-0687
WITTMAIER, Severin	19	San Francisco	64-0687
Francisca 26, George 1			
WITTMAN, Barbara	28	Resenfeld	63-1085
WITTMANN, Caspar	21	Gaggenau	63-1178
WITTMANN, Caspar	26	Hofheim	66-0147
WITTMANN, Eva	23	Friesenheim	65-0243
Emilie 4, Franz 9m			
WITTMANN, H.(m)	24	Coburg	64-0331
WITTMANN, Johann	27	New York	64-0363
WITTNEBERT, Heinr.	27	Erfurt	66-0734
Emilie 23, Wilhelmine 21			
WITTNER, Elisabeth	21	Frankfurt	64-0739
WITTOR, Robert	22	Sonneberg	66-0679
WITTPENER, H.	22	Drifseth	64-0495
WITTWER, Wilhelm	29	Bielefeld	64-0427
Lina 7, Edmund 6, Francisca 24			
WITZ, Johann	23	Ilvesheim	65-0243
WITZEL, Anna Cath.	56	Wifterhude	64-0427
Anna M. 23			
WITZEL, Augusta	22	Hasselfelde	64-0593
WITZEL, Elise	23	Cassel	64-0886
WITZIG, Friedr.	20	Plochingen	66-1203
WITZLEBEN, v. (f)	60	Miltenburg	64-0427
Marg. 2, Friedr. 28, Elise 32, Philipp 5			
WITZLER, Andreas	27	Herford	64-1206
WLPRODA, Franz	52	Dobrka	66-1155
Barbara 47, Catharina 7, Franciska 5			
WOBESER, Herm.	39	Potzdam	63-0350
WOCASEK, A.(f)	20	Bohemia	64-0331
WOCASIK, Catharina	42	Opocwitz	66-1131
Wensel 20, Franz 16, Anna 6			
WOCHE, Marie	37	Asch	66-0704
Margar. 9, Marie 7, Johann 5			
WODRICH, Marie	30	New York	63-1010
WODTKE, Johann	40	Pommern	66-0578
Johanna 38, Wilhelm 18, Bertha 14, Carl 9			
Hermann 7, August 5, Henriette 64			
WOEBER, Anton	23	Rettinau	64-0593
WOEBKE, Nicolaus	41	Bremerfoerde	65-1030
WOEHLKE, Joh.	25	Leeste	65-0974
WOEHR, Adam	20	Meisenheim	66-1127
WOELCHER, L.	25	Oldenburg	63-0097
WOELFEL, Anton	12	Weisskirchen	65-0402
WOELFEL, Georg	39	Bayreuth	65-1031
WOELFEL, Johannes	27	Bavaria	66-0577
Elisabeth 30			
WOELFFLER, Frdke.	20	Bremen	64-0363
WOELFLE, Urban	23	Oeffingen	66-0704
WOELLMANN, Bernh.	27	Oldenburg	66-1131
Catharine 19			
WOELLNER, Heinrich	64	Linden	66-0679
Sophie 61			
WOELTJEN, Charlott	22	Oldendorf	66-1031
WOELTJEN, Gustav	20	Bremen	64-0938

NAME	AGE	RESIDENCE	YR-LIST
WOELTJEN, John	20	Bremen	63-0821
WOEMER, Friedr.	23	Plochingen	66-0576
WOEPPEL, M.	58	Gamberg	65-1189
Elisabeth 50, John 14, Carl 7			
WOEPPNER, Diedr.	34	New York	66-0984
Marie 28			
WOERDE, v. Gesine	19	Dorum	65-1189
WOEREBACH, Johanna	22	Wuestenroth	66-0679
WOERMANN, Heinr.	32	Rueshendorf	66-0984
Lisette 21			
WOERMER, Joh. Geo.	32	Balingen	64-0433
WOERNER, Elisabeth	42	Lohne	66-0679
WOERNER, Friedr.	23	Plochingen	66-0576
WOERNER, Sophie	36	Baden	64-0363
WOESSNER, Jacob	59	Rothenburg	64-1206
Barbara 23, Catharina 38			
WOEST, Sophie	21	Altenbruch	64-0456
Julie 20			
WOESTEWALD, C.	49	Niederberndrf	66-0413
Louise 48, Caspar 23, Johann 18, Hugo 13			
WOESTMANN, Elisab.	23	Varensell	66-1203
WOGT, Peter	46	Bueringen	66-0576
Caroline 32, Margarethe 4, Genoveva 2			
WOGTE, Heinr.	40	Malges	64-0687
Justine 28, Pauline 5, Marie 3			
Georg A. 10m, Gertrude 34, margarethe 29			
WOHLBRINK, Clemens	28	Prussia	64-0138
WOHLENBERG, Chr.	26	Gadenstedt	64-0427
WOHLER, Jacob	32	Weissweil	66-0412
WOHLER, Minna	28	Bremen	64-0023
WOHLERS, A. (m)	23	Bremerhafen	64-0331
WOHLERS, B.	18	Bremen	65-1024
WOHLERS, Johann	33	Lobe	66-1203
Anna 30			
WOHLFAHRT, John	21	Siebenknie	66-1327
WOHLGREEN, Anna	25	New Jersey	66-0668
WOHLHAUPTER, Luise	28	Nuertingen	65-0402
WOHLIDKA, Joh.	29	Bohemia	64-0363
WOHLMANN, Anna	20	Jersey City	66-0984
WOHLMUTH, Adolph	18	Bahlenwarsleb	63-0168
WOHLTMANN, Jacob	29	Axstedt	65-0594
WOHLTMANN, P.N.	25	Wannen/Hann	65-0038
WOHN, Andr.	43	Naila	64-0938
WOHNER, Cths(f)	35	Blaiswald	64-0495
WOISIN, Barbara	22	Mannheim	66-0679
WOKER, Heinr.	50	Dortmund	63-1010
Caroline 54			
WOKER, Louise	18	Wulferdingshs	65-1095
WOLBERT, Cath.	19	Miltenberg	64-1022
WOLBERT, Christ.	26	Altenstock	64-0214
WOLF, Ad.M.(f)	27	Pfoehne	64-0331
S.(f) 3m			
WOLF, Adolph	30	Louisville	67-0007
WOLF, Aloys	22	Socken	65-0038
WOLF, Anna Elisab.	24	Lobenhausen	64-0886
WOLF, August	35	Trebdorf	66-0221
WOLF, Bernhard	41	Immelborn	63-0168
Paul 27			
WOLF, Carl	22	Wehrsdorf	66-1373
WOLF, Caroline	20	Grossaschbach	66-1031
WOLF, Charles	52	Corning	63-0296
WOLF, Christian	44	Pisterfeld	66-1243
Fritz 19, August 13			
WOLF, Cora	50	Dresden	65-0594
WOLF, Estar	19	Geisa	63-0917
WOLF, Ferdinand	18	Erfurt	66-1031
WOLF, Georg	21	Bayern	66-0147
WOLF, Georg	44	Neuwiedermus	64-0639
WOLF, Gertrude	23	Marienjoest	66-0623
WOLF, Gottlieb	20	Drohne	65-0898
WOLF, Jocob	59	Zweibruecken	64-0886
WOLF, Joh. Reinh.	42	Bengenheim/He	67-1005
WOLF, Johann	32	Olenhausen	66-0623
WOLF, John P.	22	Sinzig	63-0917
WOLF, Joseph	33	Boehmen	66-0349
Friederike 25			
WOLF, Joseph	35	Fond du Lac	66-0704
WOLF, L.	58	Nuernberg	63-1003
WOLF, L.	20	Diemsbach	65-0007
WOLF, Lazarus	28	Oestwalde	67-0353
WOLF, Mathilda	19	Cassel	66-0221
WOLF, Minna	18	Goudelsheim	66-0704
WOLF, Nathan	28	Stebbach	64-0214
WOLF, Nic.	20	Neufra/Pr.	65-0116
WOLF, Philipp	29	Altheim	65-0189
WOLF, Robert	30	Stressendorf	64-1053
Charlotte 32, Bertha 6, Gustav 3			
WOLF, Sebastian	19	Buchen	64-0427
WOLF, Veronica	17	Orb	65-0948
WOLF, Wm.	21	Hildesheim	65-0038
WOLFER, Friedrich	26	Hohenzollern	66-0704
WOLFERMANN, David	15	Barchfeld	66-0934
WOLFERT, And.	26	Duisburg	66-1243
WOLFERT, Maria	55	Feldberg	63-1069
Wilhelm 15, Johanna 21			
WOLFERTZ, Christ.	19	Wald	63-1136
WOLFERTZ, Rud. W.	30	Danse	63-1218
WOLFES, Gerhard	27	Hannover	66-0679
WOLFF, (f)	66	Stebbach	64-0214
WOLFF, (m)	37	Iowa	63-1218
WOLFF, Anton	28	Limberg	64-1022
WOLFF, August	19	Asch	66-0679
WOLFF, Barbara	25	Wuertemberg	66-0679
WOLFF, Bertha	28	Berleburg	65-1088
Henriette 25			
WOLFF, C.(m)	32	New York	64-0495
WOLFF, Carl	34	Mohringen	64-0138
WOLFF, Charlotte	19	Laltern	64-0782
WOLFF, Chr.	28	Detmold	63-0482
Bertha 24			
WOLFF, Conr.	18	Bamberg	64-0363
WOLFF, Elisa	17	Graever	64-0214
WOLFF, Elisabeth	19	Herford	66-0734
WOLFF, Ferdinand	40	Berlin	66-0576
WOLFF, Franz	29	Krautheim	64-1206
WOLFF, Franz	24	Osnabrueck	66-1031
WOLFF, G.	59	Koenigslutter	63-0244
WOLFF, G.A.(m)	35	Ilion	64-0331
WOLFF, Gerhard	40	Lungerhausen	63-0953
WOLFF, Heinr.	36	Unshausen	64-0023
WOLFF, Herm.	23	Coeln	63-0990
Norbert 20			
WOLFF, Hermann	15	Kirchheimbol.	66-0109
WOLFF, J.(m)	38	New York	64-0495
WOLFF, Johann	63	Illinois	66-0679
Maria 61			
WOLFF, Johanna	22	Hanau	64-1022
WOLFF, John C.	32	New York	63-0990
Mary 25			
WOLFF, Jonas	20	Elmshausen	65-0055
WOLFF, Lehmann	24	Koenigsbach	66-0679
WOLFF, Louis	15	Duerkheim	65-1024
WOLFF, Maria	14	Hundsweiler	65-1024
WOLFF, Nathan	20	Kollstadt	65-0402
WOLFF, Ph.	24	Monsel	64-0782
WOLFF, Robert	19	Nordleda	63-0482
WOLFGANG, Friedr.	23	Ahdorf	66-1131
WOLFORT, Heinrich	38	Amelahne	66-0349
Henry 1			
WOLFRAM, Aa.(m)	19	Hof	64-0363
WOLFRAM, Christine	21	Marktuhl	65-0007
WOLFRAM, Friedr.	32	Marksuhl	64-0214
Caroline 28, Elise 9, Wilhelm 6			
WOLFRAM, Wm.	22	Silberhausen	64-1053
Felix 5			
WOLFS, Annette	37	Peoria	63-0693
WOLFSCHMIDT, Heinr	29	Biedingen	66-1128
WOLFSHEIMER, Lina	26	Alt.Schoenbch	64-0840
WOLFSKEIL, Valent.	18	Hoenebach	65-0004
WOLFSKOEHL, Johann	21	Limburg	65-1024
WOLFSOHN, Wm.	25	Gleiwitz	65-0007
WOLFSTEIN, W.	26	Minden	65-0974
WOLKE, Anna	22	Berge	65-1024
WOLKE, Helene	19	Berge	66-1093
WOLKEN, Wendel	26	Vabarg	66-1128
WOLLBECK, Heinrich	20	Nienburg	65-1095

NAME	AGE	RESIDENCE	YR-LIST
WOLLBERG, David	31	Mahnde	63-1218
Joseph 23			
WOLLEBEN, Friedr.	23	Mellendorf	66-1031
WOLLENHORST, Aug.	31	Glandorf	64-0782
Arthur 12, Bernhard 25, Bertha 20			
WOLLENSACK, Johann	19	Heiligenzell	66-1327
WOLLENWEITER, Henr	25	Switz	66-0679
WOLLF, A.	43	Hannover	65-0856
Lina 38, Minna 16, Therese 12, Marg. 8			
Lina 6, Moses 6			
WOLLFAHRT, Georg	30	Zollbach	67-0599
WOLLMANN, Chr'tine	19	Osnabrueck	66-0668
WOLLMANN, Henry	35	Schlienworth	64-0639
WOLLNER, Adolph	23	Szenitz	63-1218
WOLLNER, Mali	22	Eperies	65-0402
Marcus 2			
WOLLRAR, Ludwig	26	New York	66-0147
Margarethe 38			
WOLLRATH, Theodor	21	Gotha	66-1373
WOLLWINKEL, Heinr.	16	Osterholz	67-0599
WOLNAP, Ludwig	21	Oberflorsheim	64-0363
WOLNY, Joseph	32	Malin	64-0433
Theresia 24			
WOLSCHENDORF, Adlf	20	Frankfurt	63-1069
WOLTARY, Jean	36	Rouen	63-0350
WOLTER, Ad.	45	Berlin	65-0594
WOLTER, Bernh.	39	Coesfeld	64-0170
WOLTER, Chr.	26	Moringen	63-0482
WOLTER, G.	27	Brietzig	65-1024
H. 24			
WOLTER, Johanna	56	Portenhagen	66-1327
WOLTER, P.		Coeln	63-1003
wife , child			
WOLTER, Peter	39	Abtweiler	63-1136
WOLTERS, Christoph	21	Bohemia	66-0984
WOLTERS, Herm.	24	Wellen	64-0782
WOLTERS, Steven	24	Langenberg	66-0679
WOLTERS, Wilh'mine	58	Westrup	63-1136
WOLTERS, Wilhelm	47	Tonnenheide	66-0984
WOLTHER, Joh.	35	Weitereid	63-1010
WOLTMANN, Lueder	18	Cattebruch	63-0990
WOLTMANN, Marie	19	Hannover	67-0795
WOLZ, Rudolph	36	Kuppingen	65-0243
Cathar. 35, Jacob 7, Ida 16, Oscar 15			
Caecilie 14, Carl 11, Clara 5, Maria 3			
WOLZENDORF, Teresa	17	Bremen	66-0576
WONASEK, Adalb.	22	Bohemia	64-0073
WONASEK, Franciska	2	Lutz	66-1155
WONASEK, Maria	20	Schotta	66-1131
WONDRASEK, Sieg.	27	Camehl	66-1373
WORBROOK, Otto	21	Neustadt	65-0974
Ida 23, Paul 3m, Auguste 53			
WORBUSCH, Wilhelm	30	Herford	66-0734
WOREL, Johann	34	Lubna	66-1155
Rosalie 32, Anna 9, Marie 7			
WOREL, Wenzel	50	Boehmen	63-0482
Maria 54, Wenzel 25, Maria 24			
Maria Magd. 23, Therese 21, Francisca 19			
Vincens 15, Aloisia 12, Alois 9			
Francis 31, Ludmilla 34			
WORFELS, Gesine	36	Bremen	65-0402
Herm. 7, Wm. 5, Wilhelmine 4, baby 9m			
WORGANG, Sebastian	18	Indiana	66-1093
WORMS, Carl J.	29	Wollin	65-0189
WORMSCHLAY, Peter	19	Ernsthausen	64-0938
WORNDIECKE, A.	17	Neuenkirchen	64-0782
WORRISHOFER, C.F.	22		65-0594
WORTHE, Brd.(m)	18	Gross Zimmern	64-0138
WORTHMANN, Alb.	28	Wachendorf	64-0427
WORTHORST, Franz	19	Birkenfeld	66-1127
WORTMANN, (f)	32	Oberkirchen	64-0214
WORTMANN, Christ.	26	Bremen	66-1243
Sophie 32, Tini 11m, Augusta 11m			
WORTMANN, Henry	17	Dorum	64-0343
WORTMANN, Marie	19	Arbergen	66-1093
WOSATKA, Anna	24	Bohemia	64-0687
WOSSELS, Gerd.	19	Diele	66-1373
WOSTERMANN, Rudolf	30	Waldhoeve	65-0950

NAME	AGE	RESIDENCE	YR-LIST
WOTAPEK, Alois	22	Bohemia	64-0687
Aloisa 22			
WOTAPKA, Marg.	21	Bohemia	64-0687
WOTAPKA, Petrolina	18	Boehmen	63-1218
WOTHE, Christian	28	Elschesheim	66-1131
WOTZEL, Jos.	32	Bohemia	64-0687
Anna 18, Theresa 14			
WOZADLO, Johann	19	Doli	66-1031
Mary 17, Johanna 13			
WRANGEMANN, Ewald	28	Giamus	64-0840
WREDE, Aug.	21	Herstelle	64-0593
WREDE, Margarethe	34	Ehrenbreitst.	66-0576
Martin 8, Carl 5, Margarethe 6m			
WREDEN, Heinr.	21	Hannover	64-0432
WRENGER, Wilhelm	22	Wehren	64-0840
WRESE, P.A.	31	Aachen	66-0413
WREWERMANN, Henry	32	St. Louis	66-0704
Anna 30			
WROCKLAGE, Anna	17	Notrup	65-1024
Adelheid 15			
WUEBBELING, Wilh.	30	Osnabrueck	65-0189
WUEBBELKING, Frd.H	19	Aschmar	64-0138
WUEBBEN, Els.	32	Oldenburg	66-1203
Carl 2, Anna 9m			
WUEBBEN, Heinr.	29	Emden	66-0577
WUEBBER, Joh.	53	Cappeln	64-0665
Dorothea 47, Eduard 22, Marie 16			
Johann 19			
WUEBOKE, Marie	27	Buehren	66-0576
WUECHNER, Conr.	40	Gossmannsdorf	65-0007
Doroth. 29			
WUELBERN, Cathar.	18	Bremervoerde	66-0109
WUELFING, Caroline	35	Barmen	65-0007
WUELFING, Ernst	25	Elberfeld	64-0138
WUELFING, F.	24	Giebels	64-0782
WUELFING, Johann	60	Merscheide	65-0151
Robert 22, Reinhard 18, Bertha 26			
Ewald 7			
WUELKEN, Bernhard	34	Hagel/Old.	64-0920
WUELLMERS, Heinr.	32	New York	63-0168
WUELLNER, Friedr.	42	Guetersloh	63-1038
WUENPFHEIMER, Abr.	29	Basel	66-0734
WUENSCH, Carl Fr.	25	Nuertingen	64-0433
WUENSCH, Caroline	22	Nuerlelingen	66-1093
WUENSCH, Johs. B.	22	Wichershausen	64-0886
Caroline 18			
WUENSCHMANN, Otto	30	Hettstedt	63-1010
WUERFEL, Leonhard	35	Chicago	66-0221
Margarethe 24			
WUERSCHING, Marg.	29	Nuernberg	63-1178
Cath.			
WUERSTEN, Cath.	57	Wangen	64-1161
Wilhelm 17, Gottlieb 14, Friedrich 6m			
WUERSTER, Joh. Ph.	35	Grafenberg	66-1373
Anna Maria 30			
WUERTHS, August	25	Solingen	63-0752
WUERTTNER, Joh.	21	Schwemmingen	64-0687
WUERTZ, A.	18	Klemensbingen	66-0413
WUERTZ, Augusta	23	Koenigsbach	64-0433
WUERTZ, Heinrich	19	Bretten	66-0576
WUERZ, Caspar	50	Durmersheim	66-0704
WUERZBACH, Friedr.	30	Harzestade	66-1327
WUERZBURGER, Gers.	26	Rhina	66-0679
WUERZBURGER, Leop.	21	Bieringen	66-0734
WUERZER, Mathias	59	Prahenricth	63-0693
Barbara 30, Michael 8			
WUERZWEILER, Mayer	19	Duehren	64-0687
Wolf 17			
WUEST, Barbara	35	Wuestenfelde	66-0837
WUEST, Charles	22	Esslingen	63-0551
WUEST, Friedrich	57	Lich	63-0693
WUEST, Th.	35	Darmstadt	64-0687
WUESTE, Rudolph	23	Osnabrueck	66-1155
WUESTEFELD, Andres	29	Gieboldehsn.	66-0984
WUESTEFELD, August	19	Herstelle	64-0593
Cath. 24			
WUESTEFELD, Conr.	16	Herstelle	64-0593
WUESTEFELD, Herm.	26	Braunschweig	64-0992

NAME	AGE	RESIDENCE	YR-LIST
WUESTEFELD, Joseph	23	Herstelle	64-0840
WUESTENBECHER, H.	24	Lippe Detmold	66-0413
Char. 20			
WUESTHOFF, Gust.	37	Merscheid	63-1038
Emilie 25, Hulda 5, Ida 3			
WUESTHOFF, Lisette	45	Solingen	66-1203
WUESTHOFF, William	20	Remscheid	63-0168
WUESTMANN, J.N.	36	Ft. Wayne	64-0687
Fr. 31, Ernestine 11m			
WUKE, Wilhelm	20	Halle	66-1128
Hermann 58, Catharine 35, Friedrich 7			
Wilhelmine 3m			
WULF, Friedrich	22	Dissen	66-1128
Franz 14			
WULF, Henry	38	Leer	63-0551
Gertrud 40, Lewis 6, Friedrich 9m			
WULF, Joh. Heinr.	28	Alserwarp	66-0984
Maria 26, Anna 10m			
WULF, Minna	26	Lehe	66-1127
Anna 5m			
WULFEKAMMER, F.W.	25	West Cappeln	64-0331
WULFERT, Hermann	36	Weddel	66-0984
Anna 35, Anna 7, Hermann 2			
WULFERT, Johann	17	Helmbrecht	64-1053
WULFES, Minna	21	Kleinsolchsen	64-0904
WULFETANGE, Joh.	31	Hollage	64-1022
WULFF, Caroline	18	Brokum	63-1136
WULFF, D.	32	Oldenburg	63-1085
WULFF, Friedrich	30	Uthlede	63-0752
Meta 21			
WULFF, H.	21	Bremen	63-1003
WULFF, Johann	24	Bremen	66-0984
WULFFSTEIN, Wolff	17	Corbeke	65-1031
WULLNER, W.	21	Osnabrueck	66-0413
WULSTEN, Johanna	28	Bremen	64-0363
Maria 11m			
WULZE, Geo.	31	Altenhagen	63-0482
Elisabeth 21			
WUNDER, Kunigunde	30	Nuernberg	66-0837
WUNDERLICH, Albert	24	Berlin	65-0770
WUNDERLICH, C John	38	Boehmen	63-1218
Joseph 30			
WUNDERLICH, Carl	15	Wuertemberg	63-0398
WUNDERLICH, Christ	22	Baden	66-0734
WUNDERLICH, Georg	38	Bergmansreuth	67-0806
Anna 38, Johann 16, Hernrich 14, Adam 11			
Margaretha 8, Johannes 4			
WUNDERLICH, Johann	33	Wunsiedel	65-1030
WUNDERLICH, Louise	32	Bamberg	66-1127
Johanna 7			
WUNDERLICH, Martin	27	Asch	66-1155
WUNDERLING, Anna	17	Vegesack	64-1161
WUNDERMANN, Louis	30	Memphis	64-0023
WUNSCH, Christoph	33	Pr. Minden	66-1127
WUNSCHA, Barbara	25	Kleinschoppen	64-0363
WUNSCHE, Julius	19	Kl. Welke	65-1088
WUPPENHORST, G.H.	28	Delmenhorst	63-0482
WURL, Johann	24	Neuschoenwald	66-0679
WURM, James	25	Philadelphia	63-0482
WURM, Martin	59	Vilbel	66-0346
WURMTHALER, Maria	27	Gruberg	66-0734
WURST, Wenzel	20	Boehmen	63-0917
WURSTER, Christian	18	Spielberg	66-0147
WURSTER, Franz	27	Wernersberg	66-0679
WURSTER, Johann	17	Woermersberg	66-0147
WURZBERMUHLE, Cath	23	Boln	66-1327
WURZELBERGER, Carl	17	Wuertemberg	66-0984
WUSTER, Chrs.	21	Philadelphia	66-0221
WUSTKE, Anna	18	Dreisen	66-1327
WUSTRACH, Ludw.	57	Solden	64-0214
WYCHERS, Henrica	40	Leer	66-1093
Veronica 9, Lorenz 8, Margaretha 6			
Anton 4			
WYNECKEN, Friedr.	25	Hannover	63-1085
WYTLACIL, Jos.	34	Boehmen	64-0495
YAENNEN, Bernhard	17	Neu Lorup	65-1030
YAHR, Christoph	19	Brunslar	65-1030
YELLI, M.	33	Lissa	65-0402

NAME	AGE	RESIDENCE	YR-LIST
YERTIN, Joseph	45	Boehmen	63-0693
Maria 46, John 18, Georg 13, Maria 16			
Maria 58			
YOESS, Joachim	43	Preussen	63-0693
Henriette 25, Ludwig C. 3, Hulda 2			
YORKAUER, L.	25	Bayreuth	64-0639
YRAL, Franz	37	Bohemia	66-0469
Johanna 27, Mathias 8, Marie 7, Franz 5			
Alberta 3, Anna 6m			
ZABEL, Winne	22	Marienfliess	63-0990
ZABEL, Wm.	35	Magdeburg	64-0427
Franz 7			
ZABELICKY, Maria	24	Malin	64-0433
ZACHELMEYER, Paul	36	Lebach	64-0214
ZACHER, C.(m)	19	Halle	65-0189
ZACHGO, August	40	Leer	64-0023
ZACKER, Amalie	33		66-1203
Conrad 8			
ZAEGEL, Hugo	15	Gera	64-0023
ZAELTZ, Georg	22	Darmstadt	64-0840
ZAENKER, Carl G.	26	Berlin	65-0007
ZAHN, B.	53	Baden	63-0168
ZAHN, Clara	15	Keiler	65-0007
ZAHN, Conrad	34	Hitzkirch	64-0739
ZAHN, Georg	18	Cassel	66-0576
ZAHN, Helene	32	Philadelphia	63-1218
Helene 1			
ZAHN, Jacob	21	Hofheim	66-1093
ZAHN, Johann	22	Cassel	66-1031
ZAHN, Louise	10	Landau	65-1024
ZAHN, Sophie	23	Calro	65-0116
ZAHNER, Francisca	20	Cleveland	66-0734
ZAHRT, Maria	46	Lippspringe	65-1095
ZAJITZ, Barbara	20	Boehmen	64-0023
ZAKOTELLECKY, Ant.	5	Boehmen	64-0495
Vinz 7, Ant. 60			
ZANDER, Dorothea	42	Berlin	63-0822
Anna 12, Friedrich 2			
ZANFT, M.	37	Barbaga	66-0413
H. 31, Gottlob 4, Adolf 3, Rudolf 9m			
ZANG, Wilh. Peter	30	Aschaffenburg	65-0950
Catharina 28			
ZANGEL, Christ.	26	Schleiz	67-0795
ZANITZ, August	35	New York	63-0244
ZANNER, Joh.	30	Miesbach	64-1161
Johanna 6, Therese 5, Rosina 3			
Sebastian 4, Marie 6m			
ZARECK, Peter	22	Runowo	66-0083
ZAROW, Johann	32	Lebehuke	66-0984
Rosalia 22, Albert 7, Theodor 2			
Rosalie 52			
ZASCHE, Louis	27	Altenburg	66-1203
Caroline 21, Robert 19			
ZAUFALIK, Franz	21	Boehmen	64-0427
ZAWICKI, Agatha	26	Mollis	65-0243
ZAZIE, Anna	7	Bohemia	64-0782
ZDROWSKY, Julius	18	Neunburg	66-0083
ZEBINDEN, H.	30	Switz.	64-0170
Mrs. 28, child 10, child 8, child 2			
ZECH, Jos.	36	Prion	64-0593
Cath. 28, Jos. 4			
ZECH, Martin	28	Sulzschmid	66-0679
Mechthilde 25, Mathilde 1			
ZECHA, Anton	31	Boehmen	63-1010
Anna 28, Wenzel 9			
ZECHIEL, L.(m)	37		64-0331
Johanna 21			
ZECK, Heinrich	30	Eichen	66-1327
ZEDLITZ, v. Sigism	25	Neukirch	63-0752
ZEDLITZ, v. W.(m)	32	New York	64-0363
ZEEGLIN, W.F.	25	Damnitz	65-1030
ZEESE, C. Georg	67	Cassel	64-1053
ZEH, August	17	Butzbach	66-1327
ZEH, Benjamin	45	Unterstetten	66-0412
Christiane 46, Henrike Car. 16, Johann 14			
Hinrike 7, Hermann 6			
ZEH, Casper	18	Sonnenberg	66-1127
ZEH, Eduard	28	Saalfeld	64-0992

NAME	AGE	RESIDENCE	YR-LIST
Wilhelm 26			
ZEH, Friedr. Wm.	25	Frankfurt	66-0109
ZEH, Marie	16	Dielingen	65-1024
ZEHFUSS, Mertin	54	Pittsburg	64-0687
ZEHLEIN, Bab.	19	Fuerth	64-0938
ZEHLER, Maximilian	38	Bergheim	64-1053
ZEHNDER, Daniel	31	Oberbrucken	65-0189
ZEIDLER, Martin	22	Preussen	66-0221
ZEILER, Georg	48	Buffalo	63-0015
Josepha 31, George 11m			
ZEIMER, L.	13	Kl.Lohrwitz	64-0782
Betti 17			
ZEIMER, Lazarus	27	Prestiz	66-0576
ZEINER, F.	26	Alt Herbsdorf	66-0413
ZEINER, Isaac	51	Lockwitz	65-1024
Anna 40			
ZEINER, Johann	58	Oberpomsdorf	66-0083
ZEINTAK, Anton	34	Gr.Lousk	66-0650
Antonia 26, Joseph 5, Johann			
ZEISNER, Erdm.	42	Luetz	63-1136
Fogisea 34, Maria 9, Agnes 7, Adelheid 5			
Hermann 11m			
ZEISS, Cath.	17	Manburg	64-0495
ZEISSLER, Johann	21	Wigheim	64-1053
ZEITLER, Christian	24	Sellz	66-1131
ZEITTLES, Theodor	24	Koenigsberg	66-0679
ZEITZ, J. G.	28	Hamelburg	63-1010
ZELCH, Heinrich	28	Imhausen	66-1093
ZELK, Carl	22	Schwartau	66-1248
ZELKEN, Metehippen	60	Backband	66-0412
ZELL, Johanna	20	Heiligenfelde	63-1136
ZELL, Pauline	26	Grunzheim	65-0594
ZELL, Sophia	56	Preussen	63-1136
Christ. 18, Anna 15, Maria 9m, August 29			
ZELLE, Augusta	39	Zirk	64-0456
Carl 10, Martha 5, Maria 4			
ZELLER, Augustin	34	Wuertemberg	66-0578
Marie 34, Moritz 13, Waldburga 9			
Johannes 5, Franziska 3, Agnes 3m			
ZELLER, Franz	28	Lingenfeld	67-0600
ZELLER, Gustav	23	Ulm	65-1088
ZELLER, Harmann	16	Heilbronn	63-0822
ZELLER, Joh.	30	Susbach	63-0244
ZELLER, P.P.	28	Pissighafen	63-1003
ZELLER, Wm.	36	Defiance	64-0138
ZELLERMEYER, Ther.	48	Dillingen	64-1022
ZELT, Johann	22	Baden	66-0734
ZELTMANN, Jacob	26	New York	63-1178
ZELTNER, John	40	Cincinnati	64-0687
ZEMPEL, Friedrich	23	Friedrichshor	65-1095
Wilhelmine 18, Augusta 2m			
ZENDEL, Jacob	28	Witzenhausen	66-0704
ZENIER, Barbara	16	Praschewitz	66-1373
ZENKE, Heinrich	19	Bremen	66-0679
ZENKEL, Marie	18	Pansa	66-0704
ZENZEL, Wilhelm	19	Ehrbach	66-1327
ZEPF, Ignatz	28	Tittlingen	64-0331
Johanna 21			
ZEPF, L.(m)	32	Wurmlingen	64-0331
Johanna 21			
ZEPP, Wilhelm	23	Rittensheim	65-0151
ZEPPENFELD, Herman	16	Hannover	66-0221
ZEPPENFELD, Joh.	26	Bremen	66-0221
Rosa 20, Rosa 6			
ZERBEL, Joh.	63	Preussen	66-0469
Maria 51, Johann 22, Herrmann 13			
Richard 7			
ZERWECK, Philipp	50	Libenau	64-0886
ZESTERFLETH, Fr.	33	Elsfleth	65-1088
ZETSCHE, Michael	34	Koltel	66-1327
ZETTLER, Christine	25	Marburg	64-0639
ZETZMANN, Christ.	48	Maggenbrunn	64-0427
Elisa 28, Anna 7			
ZEUCH, Frdr.	18	Volkershausen	66-0221
ZEUCH, Heinr.	19	Volkertshsn.	64-0363
ZEUGHER, Crezencia	26	Zuerich	64-0023
ZEUGNER, Friedr.	29	Giebichnstein	64-1108
ZEUMANN, Jac.	18	Wiltenthan	64-0073

NAME	AGE	RESIDENCE	YR-LIST
ZEUNER, Gust.	23	New York	64-0432
ZEUS, Joh.	20	Ostzell	64-1108
Benedict 7			
ZIBARTH, Mart.	33	Kross	63-0350
Juliane 35, Bertha 9, Joseph 8			
Apollonia 7, Martin 6, Anton 2, Julie 9m			
ZIBULSKI, Maria	25	Gr. Mustadt	66-0576
ZICHTINGER, Friedr	27	Asch	64-0739
ZICK, H.	26	Coppel	65-0974
ZICKA, Josef	53	Lomitz	63-0053
Eva 50, Josef 16, Franz 12, Anna 24			
ZICKEL, Louise	27	Alt Breisach	66-0349
Bertha 6			
ZICKLER, Georg	19	Dippach	64-0495
ZICKMANTEL, F.	27	Dresden	65-0007
ZICKUHR, Chr. Aug.	35	Zuech	66-0469
ZICKWOLF, Cathrine	26	Baden	66-0469
ZICROTT, August	41	Bargenewo	66-0413
Carl 10			
ZIEBELL, August	19	Preussen	64-0363
ZIEBOLD, Anna M.	25	Ottaschwande	64-0593
ZIEGEL, Leonhard	24	Oestersheim	66-0704
ZIEGELMANN, Aug.	22	Ukerwala	65-1030
ZIEGELMEIER, Peter	26	Hannover	66-1093
ZIEGENBAIN, Aug.	33	Worpswede	63-0953
ZIEGENBAIN, Carl	24	Kuelte	66-0984
ZIEGENER, Marie	26	Altmarschen	66-0623
ZIEGFELD, Florenz	23	Chicago	64-0687
ZIEGLER, (m)	45	New Orleans	63-1038
wife 36, mother 66, Wilhelmine 12			
Virginia 10, Celestine 7, Marie 2			
Franz 4			
ZIEGLER, Anton	37	Duedelsheim	64-0886
Marie 38, Elise 7, Dorothea 4			
ZIEGLER, Anton	33	Tegerfeld	65-0865
ZIEGLER, Carl	23	Esslingen	66-1093
ZIEGLER, Christ.	46	Schorndorf	64-0840
ZIEGLER, Christian	17	Grafenberg	66-0147
ZIEGLER, Christian	19	Grafenberg	66-0147
ZIEGLER, Heinrich	43	Homberg	65-1140
Conrad 19, Georg 15			
ZIEGLER, Jacob	44	Markt Erlbach	64-0214
Cath. 40, Christine 9			
ZIEGLER, Joseph	26	Obereschenbch	63-1010
ZIEGLER, Kilian	24	Pittsburg	64-0073
ZIEGLER, Lotti	47	Bohemia	64-0782
Jeanette 7, Emilie 5, Bertha 2, Sophie 19			
ZIEGLER, Ludwig	24	Waldangelbach	64-0073
ZIEGLER, Rosine	25	Grefenberg	66-0221
ZIEGLER, Samuel	42	Eschenstrudt	65-0038
Anna Cath. 41, Heinrich 16			
Martha Elis 10, Anna M. 7, Georg 11m			
ZIEGLER, v. Kilian	25	Wenkheim	63-0953
ZIEKENDRATH, Conr.	25	Hersfeld	63-1010
ZIELFELD, Leonhard	26	Muenchen	66-0576
ZIER, Richard	24	Loebenstein	66-0734
ZIERAU, Friedr.	22	Dessau	65-0189
ZIERER, Wenzel	32	Neuenstein	66-1373
ZIERLE, Caroline	54	Roighaim	64-0886
Marie 21, Anna 14, Pauline 7			
ZIESENITZ, Wm. Chr	28	Gadenstedt	64-0427
ZIESK, Gustav	37	Berlin	66-0679
ZIESLER, Otto	23	Lebnitz	65-1088
ZILINKA, Barbara	65	Boehmen	64-0427
ZILLMANN, Heinrich	40	Unshausen	64-0433
ZIMKA, Paul	22	Kolberg	64-0992
ZIMMER, Barbara	21	Bonheim	66-0576
ZIMMER, Ernst	30	Espa	65-0974
Elise 26, Heinrich 3, baby 11m			
Friedrich 14, Catharine 7, baby 2m			
ZIMMER, Heinrich	50	Armsheim	66-0412
Catharine El 46, Caroline 20, Georg 17			
Carl 15, Elisabeth 9, Heinrich 5			
Magdalene 3			
ZIMMER, Jos.	17	Tittlingen	64-0331
ZIMMER, Ursula	48	Saal	63-0398
Eugenia 18, Martina 15			
ZIMMERER, Cath.	20	Tristlingen	64-1206

NAME	AGE	RESIDENCE	YR-LIST
Agatha 8m, Leander 23			
ZIMMERER, Joseph	38	America	63-0917
ZIMMERLEIN, John	60	Horb	64-0593
ZIMMERLING, Henr't	22	Zeckreck	67-0353
ZIMMERLING, Paulne	46	Berlin	66-1131
ZIMMERMANN, Aug.	47	Behlheim	65-1030
Cath. 44, Peter 13			
ZIMMERMANN, August	22	Sachsen-Mein.	66-0349
ZIMMERMANN, Barbar	56	Mannheim	63-0482
ZIMMERMANN, Barbra	20	Nordhalber	66-0623
ZIMMERMANN, C.	23	Bindsachsen	63-1003
ZIMMERMANN, C.	57	Schafffhausen	66-0413
Barbara 55, Conrad 10, Elise 21			
ZIMMERMANN, C.F.	47	Carlsfeld	64-0593
Sophie 32, Gustavus 11, Alexander 7			
Jul.Mar.(f) 6, H.Anna 5, Margaretha 3			
Milka 1			
ZIMMERMANN, Carl	47	Carlsfeld	66-0147
ZIMMERMANN, Carl	40	Bavaria	66-0679
Louise 40, Lina 15, Ernst 9, Emilie 7			
Carl 5			
ZIMMERMANN, Carl	24	Putzihoh	64-1206
Ernestine 20, Emilie 3m			
ZIMMERMANN, Carol.	21	Baehle	63-0350
ZIMMERMANN, Christ	30	Kurhessen	66-0346
Elise 26, Friedr. 3, Carl 9m			
ZIMMERMANN, Chrs.	24	Biedenkopf	66-0221
ZIMMERMANN, Eva	20	Selzen	66-0704
ZIMMERMANN, Focke	39	Ihrhove	65-0243
Gretje 38, Berend 7, Elske 5, Bertha 4			
Engeline 2			
ZIMMERMANN, Fr.	52	Boernecke	65-0007
ZIMMERMANN, Franz	18	Sandhausen	63-1069
ZIMMERMANN, H.	23	Weimar	65-0898
ZIMMERMANN, H.(m)	21	Thedinghausen	64-0495
ZIMMERMANN, Heinr.	18	Schotten	66-1373
ZIMMERMANN, Herman	25	Neustadt	66-1155
ZIMMERMANN, Jacob	17	Zornheim	66-0147
Josef 24			
ZIMMERMANN, Jacob	21	Sandhausen	64-0427
ZIMMERMANN, Johann	28	Katzendahl	67-0007
ZIMMERMANN, Jos.	25	Mundelfingen	63-0296
ZIMMERMANN, Joseph	34	New York	63-0006
ZIMMERMANN, Julius	18	Berlin	66-1373
Emilie 8			
ZIMMERMANN, Louise	25	Stozewo	64-0840
ZIMMERMANN, Marg.	49	Sachsen	66-0413
ZIMMERMANN, Marg.	18	Weimar	65-1189
ZIMMERMANN, Maria	11m	Langensalz	64-0456
ZIMMERMANN, Moses	17	Oberseemen	66-0984
ZIMMERMANN, Ph.	24	Ottweiler	63-1038
ZIMMERMANN, R.	33	Bremen	66-0413
Wilh. 37, Anna 11m			
ZIMMERMANN, Sybill	18	Wuerzburg	63-1038
Conrad 8			
ZIMMERMANN, Wilh.	46	Esslingen	66-0679
ZIMMERMANN, Wilh.	31	Richmond	66-1127
ZIMPELMANN, Marg.	18	Mutterstadt	65-0189
ZIMPRICH, Theobald	24	Maltitz	66-0576
ZINGEL, Leonora	19	Obereickingen	64-0073
ZINGEN, John	28	Euren	63-0990
ZINGHAUS, Maria	25	Biberach	66-0346
ZINK, Casper	24	Hofheim	67-0007
ZINK, Franciska	16	Straubing	66-0576
ZINKAND, Math.	29	Volke	66-0349
ZINKMANN, Valentin	30	Grewenau	66-0578
ZINN, Adam	19	Greberhagen	66-0349
ZINN, Hartmann	16	Willersdorf	66-0578
ZINNKANN, Wm.	31	Oberfleiden	64-1053
ZINSSER, Bertha	17	Alsfeld	66-0704
ZINTGRAF, Eva M.	36	Kattenordheim	63-1038
ZINZER, Jacob	29	Gladenbach	63-0822
ZIPFEL, Math.	38	Pfullendorf	63-0296
Cath. 36, Francis 3, Marg. 1			
ZIPPER, Emmanuel	20		66-1203
ZIRCHER, Friedr. C	58	Hanau	63-0821
ZIRKEL, John	23	Kleeburg	63-1218
ZIRKEL, Lisette	19	Rainrod	64-0593
ZISKA, Carl	48	Muehlhausen	65-0856
Anna 44, Emilie 11, Carl 9, J. 6			
Marie 13			
ZISKA, Franz	35	Muehlhausen	65-0856
Marie 37, Johann 15, Eleonore 13, Carl 11			
Marie 9, Philipp 6			
ZLABECK, Franz	49	Wodnien	67-0007
ZLECHAN, Christian	24	Uhra	66-0083
ZLECHAN, Georg F.	50	Uhra	66-0083
Catharine 50, Caroline 20, Catharine 17			
Golliche 15			
ZLEORNIK, Joseph	16	Purik	66-1373
ZOBEL, (f)	45	Ohio	63-1038
ZOCK, F.O.	33	Nienburg	66-0413
Catharina 33			
ZOECKERT, Jos.	35	Bohemia	64-0782
ZOELLNER, Regina	50	Reutlingen	64-0639
ZOLL, John	20	Riedlingen	66-0147
ZOLLER, Anton	38	Bregels	64-0427
Cath. 27, Alfred 3, Anton 6m			
ZOLLWEG, Eduard	32	Germany	66-0666
Henriette 27, Reinhard 2m			
ZOLPER, Phil.	25	Eistorf	64-0331
ZONTUER, Jacob	28	Duerenbuchey	66-1373
ZORN, Gustav	33	Breslau	65-1030
ZORN, Magdalena	30	Bernsfelden	66-1203
ZOSCH, Kunigunde	32	Kuetzgau	66-1373
ZOTTMANN, Johann	22	Horsens	67-0806
ZOYBAUM, Wilh.	38	Naumburg	66-0349
ZRIMKANN, Gottfr.	32	Hesse-Darmst.	64-0432
ZUBBER, Conrad	27	Baden	67-0795
ZUBER, August	24	Constadt	66-0109
ZUBERBIER, Anna	34	Coppenbruegge	66-0679
ZUBILLER, Char.	22	Coeln	64-1053
ZUCKER, Christine	30	Kleinaschenhm	64-1206
ZUCKERMANN, Minna	20	Eger	66-1031
Bertha 18			
ZUEHLKE, Joh.	36	Camin/Pr.	65-0038
Augusta 37, Julius 10, Eduard 7			
Friedrich 5, Johann 2, Wilhelmine 6m			
ZUELCH, Barthel	17	Kirchhosbach	67-0795
ZUELCH, Conrad	25	Deute	65-1031
Christine 22, Georg 13, Anna 1			
ZUERCHER, Albertin	36	Lahr	64-0593
Max 14, Lisette 13, Henry 12, Albertine 4			
Mr. 40, Mrs. 32			
ZUERCHER, Sophie	22	Ob.Schaffhsn.	66-1093
ZUERN, Joseph	34	Galimau	66-1093
ZUGSCHWERDT, Joach	40	Hoechst	66-1128
Catharine 39, Elise 19			
ZUHLE, Jac.	21	Roth	65-0402
ZULEGER, Emil	24	Berlin	66-1248
Maria 22			
ZUMPE, Franz	46	Habendorf	67-0599
Theresia 56, Franziska 12			
ZUMPFF, A.	24	Minden	65-1024
ZUND, John J.	27	Altstaedten	63-1085
ZUNFTMEISTER, Joh.	48	Constanz	66-0576
Carl 18			
ZUPKA, Johann	24	Lankowitz	66-0469
ZUR, Carl	49	Viezig	66-0650
Louise 51, Karl 17, Eduard 7			
ZURHEIDEN, Wilhelm	37	Borghorst	66-0623
ZURLAGE, Herman	14	Wehbergen	66-1093
Minna 18			
ZUSCHMITT, Joh.	57	Dizingen	64-1053
Friederike 15, Jacob 7, Gottlob 5			
ZWACH, Anna	38	Kuttenberg	65-0189
ZWACK, Albertine	20	Bohemia	64-0073
Barbara 30			
ZWEIFEL, Ad.	49	Warsaw	64-0782
ZWEIGDT, Adolf	26	Schoenlinde	66-0147
ZWICKE, Franz	40	Stein	65-0402
Francisca 26, Carl 7, Max 2			
ZWICKI, Elisabeth	54	Oberrieden	66-1203
Gustav 19, Emil 9			
ZWINGER, August	25	Pittsburg	64-0427
ZWINK, Ludwig	20	Steinheim	67-0007

NAME	AGE	RESIDENCE	YR-LIST
ZWONICK, Anna	31	Merkoletz	64-0170
Julie 9			

CPSIA information can be obtained at www.ICGtesting.com
261043BV00005B/6/P

9 780806 312255